INTERNATIONAL BUSINESS

Visit the *International Business, 6th edition* Companion Website at **www.pearsoned.co.uk/rugman** to find valuable **student** learning material including:

- Multiple choice questions to test understanding
- Extensive links to valuable resources on the web
- An online glossary to explain key terms
- Electronic 'flashcards' to check understanding of key terms and definitions during revision

INTERNATIONAL BUSINESS

SIXTH EDITION

Alan M. Rugman
Henley Business School, the University of Reading

Simon Collinson
Henley Business School, the University of Reading

PEARSON

Harlow, England • London • New York • Boston • San Francisco • Toronto • Sydney
Auckland • Singapore • Hong Kong • Tokyo • Seoul • Taipei • New Delhi
Cape Town • São Paulo • Mexico City • Madrid • Amsterdam • Munich • Paris • Milan

Pearson Education Limited
Edinburgh Gate
Harlow
Essex CM20 2JE
England

and Associated Companies throughout the world

Visit us on the World Wide Web at:
www.pearsoned.com/uk

First published by McGraw-Hill, Inc. 1995
Sixth edition 2012

ISBN 978-0-273-76097-9

British Library Cataloguing-in-Publication Data
A catalogue record for this book is available from the British Library.

Library of Congress Cataloging-in-Publication Data
Rugman, Alan M.
  International business / Alan M. Rugman, Simon Collinson. — 6th ed.
    p. cm.
  Includes bibliographical references and index.
  ISBN 978-0-273-76097-9
 1. International business enterprises—Management.   I. Collinson, Simon. II. Title.
  HD62.4.R843 2012
  658'.049—dc23

                                                        2012001440

10 9 8 7 6 5 4 3 2 1
16 15 14 13 12

Typeset in 10/12.5 pt Minion by 73
Printed and bound by Rotolito Lombarda, Italy.

CONTENTS IN BRIEF

CONTENTS IN DETAIL

Part One
THE WORLD OF INTERNATIONAL BUSINESS

Chapter 1
Regional and Global Strategy

Chapter 2
The Multinational Enterprise   36

Part Three

INTERNATIONAL BUSINESS STRATEGIES

Chapter 8
Multinational Strategy   243

Chapter 9
Organizing Strategy   272

Chapter 10
Corporate Strategy and National Competitiveness   300

Chapter 22
Corporate Ethics and the Natural
Environment   700

Supporting resources

Visit **www.pearsoned.co.uk/rugman** to find valuable online resources

Companion Website for students
■ Multiple choice questions to test understanding
■ Extensive links to valuable resources on the web
■ An online glossary to explain key terms
■ Electronic 'flashcards' to check understanding of key terms and definitions during revision

For instructors
■ An Instructor's Manual containing teaching notes and guidance on case studies
■ Powerpoint slides that can be downloaded and used for presentations
■ Testbank of over 2000 assessment questions

Also: The Companion Website provides the following features:
■ Search tool to help locate specific items of content
■ E-mail results and profile tools to send results of quizzes to instructors
■ Online help and support to assist with website usage and troubleshooting

For more information please contact your local Pearson Education sales representative or visit
www.pearsoned.co.uk/rugman

LIST OF ILLUSTRATIONS

Figures

Tables

Maps

PREFACE

In the Sixth Edition, in the strategy section of Part Three, there is a new chapter on "Innovation, Entrepreneurship and 'Born Global' Firms." Innovation is the lifeblood of any firm, large or small. By persistently creating new and better products and services, new production processes, management practices and business models, they can stay ahead of the competition. Multinational firms have an added competitive advantage. Small firms lack the scale and scope advantages of large multinationals but can still benefit from a diversity of options for sourcing inputs and accessing markets if they internationalize. However, they arguably face greater challenges and risks than large firms when they do expand abroad. Those that succeed against the odds provide lessons for all entrepreneurs and innovators. Five new cases feature in this chapter: "Facebook: Global and Local?", "Innovation Networks at IBM," "Spreadshirt: Open Innovation," "GE Healthcare: Product Innovation Driven by Local Needs in India," and "SetJam: the Mini Multinational."

The book is also reorganized into five parts, of which three parts focus on strategies. Part One introduces the world of international business. Part Two discusses the environment of international business. Part Three focuses on international business strategies. Part Four deals with functional area strategies. Part Five pays specific attention to regional strategies. The major changes are in Part Three which now include the new Chapter 11 "Innovation, Entrepreneurship and 'Born Global' Firms," and the former Chapter 15 "Corporate Strategy and National Competitiveness" which now becomes Chapter 10. This chapter discusses the integration and responsiveness framework of multinational business strategy as well as the diamond and double diamond approach to international competitiveness. This now provides a more logical development of the key frameworks in the text which are: the FSA/CSA framework in Chapter 2 and throughout Parts One and Two; integration and responsiveness in Chapter 10 and throughout Parts Three and Four; the diamond and double diamond in Chapter 10; and the five-partners flagship framework in Chapter 22.

In addition, all tables and figures in the text and cases have been updated. As listed in the Guide to the Case Studies, all the cases have been updated and several new cases have been added. About 75 of the 105 cases have been revised and/or updated. There are seven new case studies (five new cases for the new Chapter 11), one new case each for Chapters 12 and 22 respectively. At the end of each chapter the bibliographies have been substantially revised and updated.

The additional material in the book consists of the following:

- Chapter 1. The Active Learning Case "Coke goes worldwide with a local strategy" and the two The Real Cases "Big oil gets bigger" and "Wal Mart" have been greatly updated. Data on the two cases International Business Strategy in Action "Amazon. com" and "Tata" have also been updated.

- Chapter 2: The Active Learning Case "Disneyland in Europe" has been updated. Data on the cases "Starbucks," "Italian Family Firms," and "Sony" have been updated.

- Chapter 3. The regional automotive industry discussion has been substantially rewritten and updated. The Active Learning Case "Boeing versus Airbus" and the International Business Strategy in Action "Large and Cemex: concrete multinationals" have been extensively updated. Data on the cases "Panasonic and Philips" and "Toys 'Я' Us" in Europe and Japan have been updated.

- Chapter 4. The Active Learning Case "How risky is investment in Russia?" and the Real Case "Embraer versus Bombardier" have been substantially updated.

- Chapter 5. The International Business Strategy in Action cases, "McDonald's" and "Danone and Parmalat—Going international, staying local" have been updated as has the Real Case "Sport can be local and global: Manchester United."

- Chapter 6. The Active Learning Case "Trade of the Triad and China" and the International Business Strategy in Action case "Microsoft shows the world is not flat" have been updated. Data on the Active Learning Case "Trade of the triad and China" and the Real Case "Job losses and offshoring to China" have been updated and the cases have been revised.

■ Chapter 7. Data on the Active Learning case "Barclays Bank International Financial Dealings" and the International Business Strategy in Action case "AngloGold Ashanti" have been updated. The Real Case "HSBC" has been substantially revised and updated.

■ Chapter 8. The Active Learning case "Vodafone" and answers have been greatly revised. Data and facts on the two cases of International Business Strategy in Action "Arthur Andersen, Accenture and McKinsey" and "Fuji Xerox and Xerox" have been updated. Data on the Real Case "Mountain Equipment Co-op: a Small Business" and "Benetton" have been updated.

■ Chapter 9. The International Business Strategy in Action case "Sanofi-Aventis" has been greatly updated. Data and facts on the Active Learning Case "Procter & Gamble", the two Real Cases on "LVMH: organizing luxury products in the international arena" and "Command Alkon: A Small Business" have been updated.

■ Chapter 10 (old Chapter 15): New text and examples relating to the diamond, double-diamond, and integration/responsiveness frameworks to the earlier FSA–CSA matrix have been added. The Active Learning Case "Worldwide Operation and Local Strategies of ABB," the International Business Strategy in Action case "Nokia and Ericsson," and the Real Case "There is No Global Beer, only Local" have been substantially revised and updated. Data on the case "IBM" have been updated.

■ Chapter 11 (new chapter) This chapter has five new cases: The Active Learning Case is about the social network "Facebook: Global and Local?"; two International Business Strategy in Action cases "Innovation Network at IBM" and "Spreadshirt: Open Innovation"; and two Real Cases "GE Healthcare: Product Innovation Driven by Local Needs in India" and "SetJam: The Mini Multinational." The entire text of this chapter is new.

■ Chapter 12 (old Chapter 10). The International Business Strategy in Action case "Greening the Supply Chain" is replaced by the new case "The Dark Side of Outsourcing: Boeing's Problems with Its 787." The International Business Strategy in Action "Gap Inc.: A Successfully 'Hollow Corporation'" and the two Real Cases "Flextronics" and "Nike" have been greatly revised and updated.

■ Chapter 13 (old Chapter 11). The Active Learning Case "Volkswagen in the United States," the

International Business Strategy in Action case "IKEA in International Markets," and the Real Case "Bang & Olufsen" have been revised and updated.

■ Chapter 14 (old Chapter 12). The International Business Strategy in Action "P&O, Carnival, and Dubai Port World" and "German Management Gets Tough" (now retitled as "German Management and Unions") and the Real Case "Executive Search Firms" have been extensively revised and updated.

■ Chapter 15 (old Chapter 13). The Weighted Country Risk Assessment Model has been revised with a new approach to calibrating the country comparisons. The International Business Strategy in Action cases "Political Risk for De Beers" and "Dell goes to Brazil" have been updated. The text on "Transparency and Corruption" has been updated and revised. The Real Case on "Yukos and the Russian oligarchs" has been updated and the footnotes and references extensively revised.

■ Chapter 16 (old Chapter 14). The International Business Strategy in Action case "Tax Havens" has been revised and updated. Data and facts on the Active Learning Case "British Airways," the International Business Strategy in Action "Sovereign Wealth Funds," and the Real Case "Skandia" have been updated.

■ Chapter 17 (old Chapter 16). Material on the composition and challenges of the EU has been revised. The Real Case "Accord Budget Hotels" and the Active Learning Case "France Telecom" have been updated. The International Business Strategy in Action case on "Ford and Volvo" has been updated as have sections of the text on evaluating locations. A new table and accompanying material on the World Bank "Doing Business" country analysis tool have been added along with a new section on regional incentives. All of the remaining cases have been revised and updated.

■ Chapter 18 (old Chapter 17). The International Business Strategy in Action "Kirin Beer Goes International" and the two Real Cases "Renault and Nissan: No Pain, No Gain" and "Canon" have been greatly revised and updated.

■ Chapter 19 (old Chapter 18). Data on the International Business Strategy in Action "Bombardier" and Real Case "GlaxoSmithKline in the United States" have been updated.

■ Chapter 20 (old Chapter 19). The Active Learning Case "Acer Taiwan Goes International" has been updated. Data and facts on the International Business

Strategy in Action "Korean Chaebols: Hyundai and Samsung" and the two Real Cases "The Indian IT, Software and Services Industry" and "Bumrungrad International in Thailand" have been updated.

- Chapter 21 (old Chapter 20). The Active Learning Case "Oxford Instruments in China," two International Business Strategy in Action "Airbus in China" and "Haier Abroad," and the Real Case "Citigroup in China" have been updated. The text for this chapter has also been substantially updated with new materials.

- Chapter 22 (old Chapter 21). The Active Learning Case "The Environment, NGOs and MNEs" is totally rewritten with new materials. The Real Cases "Dell: B2C" focusing on B2C and "Maersk Group" focusing upon its B2B flagship relationship have been greatly updated and revised.

At Pearson we thank Editor Rufus Curnow for his insight and promotion of this book. Very helpful comments have been received from Dr. Elena Beleska-Spasova.

Quyen T.K. Nguyen has provided excellent research and exceptional dedication in the preparation of this book. She has updated all the tables, and helped update, rewrite, and revise the text for all chapters (except the new Chapter 11), 75 case studies and the bibliographies, and also contributed one new case for Chapter 22. She is the author of the Instructor's Manual.

Alan M. Rugman
Simon Collinson

ABOUT THE AUTHORS

Dr. Alan M. Rugman is Professor of International Business at the Henley Business School. He is Head of School, International Business and Strategy at the University of Reading, UK. Previously he was L. Leslie Waters Chair of International Business at the Kelley School of Business, Indiana University, from 2002 to 2009. He was Thames Water Fellow in Strategic Management at Templeton College, University of Oxford, from 1998 to 2001. He remains an Associate Fellow of Green Templeton College, University of Oxford. Previously, he was Professor of International Business at the University of Toronto, Dalhousie University, and the University of Winnipeg. He has also been a visiting professor at Columbia Business School, London Business School, Harvard University, UCLA, MIT, Warwick Business School, the University of Paris–La Sorbonne, University of Sydney, Saint Louis University, and University of Lyon.

Dr. Rugman has published over 250 articles dealing with the economic, managerial, and strategic aspects of multinational enterprises and with trade and investment policy. These have appeared in such leading refereed journals as: *Journal of International Business Studies, Management International Review, American Economic Review, Strategic Management Journal, Journal of Management Studies,* and *Journal of Business Ethics.*

His books include: *Inside the Multinationals* (Columbia University Press, 1981 and Palgrave, 2006); *International Business* (McGraw-Hill, 1985); *Environmental Regulations and Corporate Strategy* (Oxford University Press, 1999); *Multinationals as Flagship Firms* (Oxford University Press, 2000); *The End of Globalization* (Random House, 2000); *The Oxford Handbook of International Business* (Oxford University Press, 2001, 2009); *The Regional Multinationals* (Cambridge University Press, 2005); *Regional Aspects of Multinationality and Performance* (Elsevier, 2007); *Rugman Reviews International Business* (Palgrave Macmillan, 2009); and *Multinationals and Development* (Yale University Press, 2009).

As a leading authority in international business, Dr. Rugman served as President of the Academy of International Business from 2004 to 2006, was elected a Fellow of the Academy in 1991, and now is serving as Dean of the Fellows. He is also a Fellow of the Royal Society of Arts, elected 1998. He serves on the Editorial Board of *Journal of International Business Studies,* and several other journals in international business. He is the editor-in-chief of the *Multinational Business Review.*

In 2004 he received the Booz, Allen Hamilton Award as Eminent Scholar in International Management, Academy of Management. He was also honored at a special plenary session of the European International Business Association annual meetings, Slovenia, December 2004 for the 25th Anniversary of his 1979 book, *International Diversification and the Multinational Enterprise.* In 2011, he received the Simon Fraser University Outstanding Alumni Award for Academic Achievement.

Dr. Rugman earned his BA in economics from Leeds University in 1966, MSc in economic development from London University's School of Oriental and African Studies (SOAS) in 1967, and his PhD in economics from Simon Fraser University in 1974. He was elected to an MA (Oxon) in 1998.

He has been a consultant to major private sector companies, research institutes, and government agencies. These include Exxon/Imperial Oil, Kodak, Royal Bank of Canada, Northern Telecom, the United Nations (UNCTAD), NAFTA's Commission on Environmental Cooperation, and the Organization for Economic Cooperation and Development (OECD). Dr. Rugman served as an outside advisor on free trade, foreign investment, and international competitiveness to two Canadian Prime Ministers over the 1986–1993 period.

Dr. Simon Collinson is Professor of International Business and Innovation at the Henley Business School of the University of Reading in the UK. He is also Guangbiao Chair Professor, School of Management, Zhejiang University in China. Previously, he was Professor of International Business and Innovation, and Head of the Marketing and Strategic Management Group at Warwick Business School (WBS), the University of Warwick (UK). He also held the post of Deputy Dean at WBS. Dr. Collinson sits on the Council of the UK Economic and Social Research Council

(ESRC) and is a member of the Board of Directors at the Advanced Institute of Management (AIM), UK and the Council of the British Academy of Management (BAM). He has had visiting positions at the Australian Graduate School of Management (AGSM) in Sydney, the Kelley School of Business, Indiana University, and the John Dunning Centre of International Business, Henley Business School, University of Reading.

Dr. Collinson was formerly Lecturer and Senior Research Fellow at Edinburgh University Management School and the Assistant Director of the Japanese–European Technology Studies (JETS) Institute for seven years. During this period he was awarded a Royal Society Fellowship to study in Japan, hosted by the National Institute for Science and Technology Policy (NISTEP) in Tokyo.

His research interests include global innovation strategies, R&D, knowledge, and intellectual asset management in multinational firms; the competitiveness of international UK firms; national systems of innovation and emerging economies; high-technology entrepreneurship, small-firm networks, and regional development; Japan and China: local business practices and cross-cultural management, foreign direct investment, and economic change. Dr. Collinson has received research funding awards from the UK Economic and Social Research Council, the UK government's Department of Trade and Industry, Japan's Science and Technology Agency, the British Royal Society, and DGXII of the European Union. He has research, consulting, and executive teaching experience with firms such as British Aerospace, Corus Steel, Diageo, HSBC, ICI, GKN, Jones Lang LaSalle, Kodak (Japan), Lloyd's Register, Nippon Steel, Philips, Prudential, and Sony.

He has published a range of books and in refereed journals including *Journal of International Business Studies, Organization Studies, International Journal of Technology Management, European Management Journal, R&D Management, Organization Dynamics,* and *Technology Analysis and Strategic Management.*

Born in Tanzania in 1964, Dr. Collinson earned a Joint BA (Hons.) in geography and sociology at Leeds University and an MA in human geography at the University of Florida, Gainesville. He was awarded his DPhil from the Science Policy Research Unit (SPRU) at Sussex University in 1991.

GUIDE TO THE CASE STUDIES

CHAPTER	TYPE OF CASE	ORGANIZATION/INDUSTRY	COUNTRY/REGION	NEW & REV.	PAGE
Chapter 1 **Regional and** **Global Strategy**	■ Active Learning Case	Coke goes worldwide with a local strategy	US	✓	4
	■ International Business Strategy in Action	Amazon.com is not a global business	US	✓	16
	■ International Business Strategy in Action	Tata	Emerging Economies: India/EU:UK	✓	22
	■ Real Case	Big oil gets bigger	US/EU/Japan	✓	29
	■ Real Case	Wal-Mart	US	✓	30
Chapter 2 **The Multinational** **Enterprise**	■ Active Learning Case	Disneyland in Europe	US/EU: France	✓	37
	■ International Business Strategy in Action	Italian family firms	EU: Italy	✓	44
	■ International Business Strategy in Action	Nestlé	EU/Emerging Economies		48
	■ Real Case	Starbucks	US	✓	59
	■ Real Case	Sony	Japan	✓	60
Chapter 3 **The Triad and** **International** **Business**	■ Active Learning Case	Boeing versus Airbus	US/EU	✓	72
	■ International Business Strategy in Action	Aflac	Japan/US		77
	■ International Business Strategy in Action	Lafarge and Cemex: concrete multinationals	US/Emerging Economies	✓	79
	■ Real Case	Panasonic and Philips	Japan/EU	✓	95
	■ Real Case	Toys "Я" Us in Europe and Japan	US/EU/Japan	✓	96
Chapter 4 **International** **Politics**	■ Active Learning Case	How risky is foreign investment in Russia?	Emerging Economies	✓	104
	■ International Business Strategy in Action	Softwood lumber: not-so-free trade	US/Canada		109

CHAPTER	TYPE OF CASE	ORGANIZATION/INDUSTRY	COUNTRY/REGION	NEW & REV.	PAGE
	■ International Business Strategy in Action	Non-governmental organizations and political power	US/EU		116
	■ Real Case	How environmental regulations can be used as trade barriers	US/Emerging Economies		127
	■ Real Case	Embraer vs. Bombardier	Canada/Emerging Economies: Brazil	✓	128
Chapter 5 International Culture	■ Active Learning Case	Culture clash at Pharmacia and Upjohn	EU: Sweden and Italy/US		133
	■ International Business Strategy in Action	McDonald's	US	✓	138
	■ International Business Strategy in Action	Danone and Parmalat—going international, staying local	EU: France and Italy/US	✓	153
	■ Real Case	Do not throw your *meishi*!	EU: UK/Japan		158
	■ Real Case	Sport can be local *and* global: Manchester United	EU/US/Asia	✓	159
Chapter 6 International Trade	■ Active Learning Case	Trade of the triad and China	US/EU/Japan/ Emerging Economies: China	✓	165
	■ International Business Strategy in Action	Microsoft shows the world is not flat	US/EU	✓	173
	■ International Business Strategy in Action	The courier wars	US	✓	178
	■ Real Case	Job losses and offshoring to China	US/Emerging Economies: China	✓	188
	■ Real Case	Dumping on trade complaints	Canada/US		189
Chapter 7 International Financial Markets and Institutions	■ Active Learning Case	Barclays Bank international financial dealings	EU: UK	✓	200
	■ International Business Strategy in Action	Wall Street and world financial markets	US		212
	■ International Business Strategy in Action	AngloGold Ashanti	Emerging Economies: South Africa	✓	220
	■ Real Case	HSBC	EU: UK	✓	227
	■ Real Case	World financial crises	Emerging Economies		228

CHAPTER	TYPE OF CASE	ORGANIZATION/INDUSTRY	COUNTRY/REGION	NEW & REV.	PAGE
Chapter 8 **Multinational** **Strategy**	■ Active Learning Case	Vodafone and the triad telecom market	EU	✓	244
	■ International Business Strategy in Action	Arthur Andersen, Accenture, and McKinsey	US	✓	249
	■ International Business Strategy in Action	Fuji Xerox and Xerox	US/Japan	✓	259
	■ Real Case	Mountain Equipment Co-op: a small business	Canada		266
	■ Real Case	Benetton	EU: Italy	✓	267
Chapter 9 **Organizing** **Strategy**	■ Active Learning Case	Procter & Gamble	US	✓	273
	■ International Business Strategy in Action	Sanofi-Aventis	EU: France/ Germany	✓	277
	■ International Business Strategy in Action	Making matrix work	EU/US/Japan		284
	■ Real Case	LVMH: organizing luxury products in the international arena	EU: France	✓	295
	■ Real Case	Command Alkon: A small business	US	✓	296
Chapter 10 **Corporate** **Strategy and** **National** **Competitiveness**	■ Active Learning Case	Worldwide operations and local strategies of ABB	EU	✓	301
	■ International Business Strategy in Action	Nokia and Ericsson	EU	✓	310
	■ International Business Strategy in Action	Kodak	US		316
	■ Real Case	There is no global beer, only local	US/EU	✓	325
	■ Real Case	IBM	US/EU	✓	326
Chapter 11 **Innovation,** **Entrepreneurship** **and "Born Global"** **Firms**	■ Active Learning Case	Facebook: global and local?	US	✓	332
	■ International Business Strategy in Action	Innovation networks at IBM	US	✓	339
	■ International Business Strategy in Action	Spreadshirt: open innovation	EU	✓	346
	■ Real Case	GE Healthcare in India: locally driven innovation	US/Asia	✓	354

CHAPTER	TYPE OF CASE	ORGANIZATION/INDUSTRY	COUNTRY/REGION	NEW & REV.	PAGE
	■ Real Case	SetJam: the mini multinational	US/Europe	✓	355
Chapter 12 Production Strategy	■ Active Learning Case	The GE production process and Six Sigma	US	✓	364
	■ International Business Strategy in Action	Gap Inc.: a successful "Hollow Corporation"	EU/US	✓	372
	■ International Business Strategy in Action (NEW)	The dark side of outsourcing: Boeing's problems with its 787	US	✓	374
	■ Real Case	Flextronics	Emerging Economies: Singapore	✓	393
	■ Real Case	Nike	US	✓	395
Chapter 13 Marketing Strategy	■ Active Learning Case	Volkswagen in the United States	EU/US	✓	400
	■ International Business Strategy in Action	Kola Real Group	Emerging Economies: Mexico		408
	■ International Business Strategy in Action	IKEA in international markets	EU: Sweden	✓	411
	■ Real Case	Bang & Olufsen	EU: Denmark US	✓	423
	■ Real Case	Brazilian soap operas: a world market	Emerging Economies: Brazil		425
Chapter 14 Human Resource Management Strategy	■ Active Learning Case	The Coca-Cola Company thinks local	US		431
	■ International Business Strategy in Action	P&O, Carnival, and Dubai Port World	EU/US/Middle East	✓	439
	■ International Business Strategy in Action	German management and unions	EU: Germany	✓	446
	■ Real Case	Offshoring to India	US/Emerging Economies: India		456
	■ Real Case	Executive search firms	EU	✓	457
Chapter 15 Political Risk and Negotiation Strategy	■ Active Learning Case	Kodak in China: changing the rules of the game	US/Emerging Economies: China		463

CHAPTER	TYPE OF CASE	ORGANIZATION/INDUSTRY	COUNTRY/REGION	NEW & REV.	PAGE
	■ International Business Strategy in Action	Political risk for De Beers	Emerging Economies: South Africa	✓	479
	■ International Business Strategy in Action	Dell goes to Brazil	US/Emerging Economies: Brazil	✓	481
	■ Real Case	Yukos and the Russian oligarchs	Emerging Economies: Russia	✓	491
	■ Real Case	Problems with ports	Japan/Emerging Economies: Kenya		492
Chapter 16 International Financial Management	■ Active Learning Case	British Airways	EU: UK/US	✓	498
	■ International Business Strategy in Action	Tax havens	Emerging Economies	✓	508
	■ International Business Strategy in Action	Sovereign wealth funds	Middle East/US/EU	✓	511
	■ Real Case	Skandia	EU: Sweden	✓	529
	■ Real Case	Repsol's acquisition of YPF	EU: Spain/ Emerging Economies: Argentina		530
Chapter 17 European Union	■ Active Learning Case	France Telecom	EU: France	✓	538
	■ International Business Strategy in Action	Ford and Volvo	US/EU: Sweden	✓	547
	■ International Business Strategy in Action	Deutsche Bahn: more than a railway	EU: Germany US	✓	555
	■ Real Case	Accor budget hotels	EU: France	✓	563
	■ Real Case	Carrefour	EU: France	✓	565
Chapter 18 Japan	■ Active Learning Case	Doing business in Japan	Japan		570
	■ International Business Strategy in Action	Kirin Beer goes international	Japan	✓	582
	■ International Business Strategy in Action	Wal-Mart takes Seiyu	US/Japan		590
	■ Real Case	Renault and Nissan: no pain, no gain	Japan/EU: France	✓	596

CHAPTER	TYPE OF CASE	ORGANIZATION/INDUSTRY	COUNTRY/REGION	NEW & REV.	PAGE
	■ Real Case	Canon Group	Japan	✓	599
Chapter 19 North America	■ Active Learning Case	NAFTA	US/Emerging Economies: Mexico and Canada		606
	■ International Business Strategy in Action	Bombardier	Canada/ Emerging Economies: Brazil	✓	611
	■ International Business Strategy in Action	Mexico and NAFTA	US/Emerging Economies: Mexico		627
	■ Real Case	Jumex of Mexico	Emerging Economies: Mexico		632
	■ Real Case	GlaxoSmithKline in the United States	UK/US	✓	633
Chapter 20 Emerging Economies	■ Active Learning Case	Acer Taiwan goes international	Emerging Economies: Taiwan	✓	638
	■ International Business Strategy in Action	From Oserian to Tesco: the Kenyan cut flower industry	Emerging Economies: Kenya		650
	■ International Business Strategy in Action	Korean *chaebols*: Hyundai and Samsung	Emerging Economies: S. Korea	✓	658
	■ Real Case	The Indian IT, software, and services industry	Emerging Economies: India	✓	661
	■ Real Case	Bumrungrad International in Thailand	Emerging Economies: Thailand	✓	664
Chapter 21 China	■ Active Learning Case	Oxford Instruments in China	EU: UK/Emerging Economies China	✓	670
	■ International Business Strategy in Action	Airbus in China	EU/Emerging Economies: China	✓	677
	■ International Business Strategy in Action	Haier abroad	Emerging Economies: China	✓	689
	■ Real Case	Citigroup in China	US/Emerging Economies: China	✓	692
	■ Real Case	Nanjing Auto makes the MG	EU: UK/Emerging Economies: China		694

CHAPTER	TYPE OF CASE	ORGANIZATION/INDUSTRY	COUNTRY/REGION	NEW & REV.	PAGE
Chapter 22 Corporate Ethics and the Natural Environment	■ Active Learning Case (NEW)	The environment, NGOs, and MNEs	EU/US	✓	701
	■ International Business Strategy in Action	3M	US		704
	■ International Business Strategy in Action	Is The Body Shop an ethical business?	EU: UK		716
	■ Real Case	Dell: B2C	US/Emerging Economies: China	✓	721
	■ Real Case	Maersk Group	EU: Denmark/US/ Asia	✓	723

GUIDED TOUR

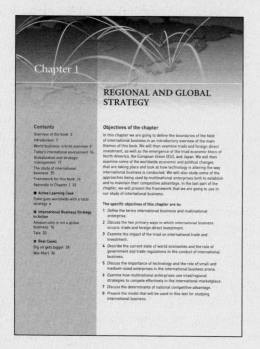

The opening page of each chapter indicates its key **Contents** and the **Objectives** that you should achieve by reading it.

An **Active Learning Case** runs through each chapter and illustrates the strategy and activity of multinational organisations.

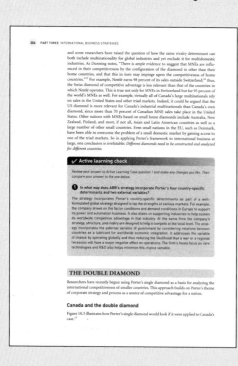

The **Active learning check** later in the chapter provides answers to the questions which support the Case.

International Business Strategy in Action draws on recent literature to highlight the role and application of strategic decisions in international business.

Real Cases are taken from recent newspaper and press sources, to illustrate day-to-day developments in business across the world.

At the end of each chapter, you will find a summary of **Key points** and **Key terms**, as well as **Review and discussion questions** which check your understanding and encourage class-room discussion of major issues.

Visit the companion website at **www.pearsoned.co.uk/rugman** and use the **Multiple choice questions** to test your understanding of key concepts, and electronic **Flashcards** to check your knowledge of key terms and definitions.

ACKNOWLEDGMENTS

We are grateful to the following for permission to reproduce copyright material:

Figures

Figure 3.3 from Toyota Motors: Revenue 2006–2009, Reproduced with permission from Toyota (GB) PLC; Figure 5.2 from *Geert Hofstede, Gert Jan Hofstede, Michael Minkov, "Cultures and Organizations, Software of the Mind", Third Revised Edition, McGrawHill 2010, ISBN 0-07-166418-1*, Copyright © Geert Hofstede; Figures 8.1, 8.3, 8.5 adapted from *COMPETITIVE ADVANTAGE: Creating and Sustaining Superior Performance*, Adapted with permission of Free Press, a Division of Simon & Schuster, Inc. (Michael E. Porter) Copyright © 1985, 1998 by Michael E. Porter. All rights reserved; Figure 9.11 adapted from *Comparative and Multinational Management* (Simcha Ronen) Copyright © 1986. John Wiley & Sons, Inc. Reproduced with permission of John Wiley & Sons, Inc.; Figures 10.1, 10.2 adapted from *THE COMPETITIVE ADVANTAGE OF NATIONS*, Adapted with permission of Free Press, a Division of Simon & Schuster, Inc. (Michael E. Porter) Copyright © 1990, 1998 by Michael E. Porter. All rights reserved; Figure 10.3 from *Fast Forward: Improving Canada's International Competitiveness*, Toronto: Kodak Canada (Alan M. Rugman and Joseph R. D'Cruz 1991) p. 35; Figure 10.7 from *Building and Managing the Transnational: the New Organizational Challenge in Competition in Global Industries*, the Harvard Business School Publishing Corporation (edited by M. E. Porter, Boston MA 1986) Copyright © the Harvard Business School Publishing Corporation, all rights reserved; Figure 14.1 from Who manages multinational enterprises, *Columbia Journal of World Business*, 33 (Lawrence G. Franko 1973), Copyright 1973, with permission from Elsevier Science; Figure 17.3 adapted from The Search for a Truly Pan-European Manufacturing System, *Journal of European Business*, 44 (Nigel Dunham and Robin Morgan 1991), Permission conveyed through Copyright Clearance Center; Figure 22.8 adapted from Maersk website, Business Areas http://www.maersk.com/AboutMaersk/Pages/BusinessAreas.aspx. With permission from Maersk

Tables

Tables 1A, 1B adapted from *Direction of Trade Statistics Yearbook*, Washington, DC: International Monetary Fund (2009), $799 for all seven IMF tables; Tables 1.a, 1.b adapted from *Direction of Trade Statistics Yearbook*, Washington, DC: International Monetary Fund (2009); Tables 1C, 1D adapted from *World Investment Report*, Washington, DC: International Monetary Fund (2009); Table 1.1 adapted from *Direction of Trade Statistics Yearbook*, Washington, DC: International Monetary Fund (2009) 2–5; Table 2.b adapted from *World Development Report database*, World Bank (2010); Table 3.6 adapted from *Annual Report, 2006–2009*, Reproduced with permission from Toyota (GB) PLC; Table 5.2 adapted from The importance of work goals: An international perspective, *Journal of International Business Studies*, Vol. 21, p. 81 (1990), Palgrave Macmillan. Reproduced with permission of Palgrave Macmillan; Table 6A adapted from Balance of payments: IMF presentation. Washington, DC: International Monetary Fund; Table 7.2 adapted from Chicago Mercantile Exchange, June 26, 2010, http://www.cmegroup.com/trading/fx/, Currency futures contract specifications at the Chicago Mercantile Exchange, CME Group; Table 8.1 adapted from Strategic planning for a global business, *Columbia Journal of World Business*, Summer (Chakravarthy, B.S. and Perimutter, H.V. 1985), Copyright © Elsevier Science & Technology Journals. With permission from Elsevier Science; Table 8.2 adapted from *PHATAK. INTERNATIONAL DIMENSIONS OF MANAGEMENT, 2E.* © 1989, South-Western, a part of Cengage Learning, Inc. Reproduced by permission. www.cengage.com/permissions; Table 1 on page 458 adapted from New insights into the internationalization of product services: Organizational strategies and spacial economies

for global headhunting firms, *Environment and Planning*, 40, pp. 210–234 (Faulconbridge J.R., Hall S.J.E. and Beaverstock J.V. 2008), Copyright © Pion Ltd, London (2008); Table 14.2 adapted from The culture assimilator: An approach to cross-cultural training, *Journal of Applied Psychology*, April, pp. 55, 97–98 (Fred E. Fielder, Terence Mitchell and Harry C. Triandis 1971), Copyright © 1971 by the American Psychological Association. Adapted with permission; Table 14.4 adapted from Competition and change: Mapping the Indiana HRM recipe against world-wide patterns, *Journal of World Business*, 32, p. 233 (Paul R. Sparrow and Pawan S. Budhwar 1997), Copyright © 1997 with permission from Elsevier Science; Table 15.4 adapted from The influence of culture on the process of business negotiations: An exploratory study, *Journal of International Business Studies*, p. 88 (John L. Graham 1985), Palgrave Macmillan. Reproduced with permission of Palgrave Macmillan; Table 17.3 adapted from *The World Competitiveness Report, 1989, 2008 and 2011*, IMD and World Economic Forum; Table 17.4 adapted from World Bank, Doing Business website: http://www.doingbusiness.org/rankings. June, 2011; Table 17.5 adapted from *Direction of Trade Statistics Yearbook, 2000 and 2009. Memorandum tables, EU*, Washington, DC: International Monetary Fund (2000) p. 70 (2000) and p. 41 (2009); Table 18.4 adapted from The Regional Nature of Japanese Multinational Business, *Journal of International Business Studies*, 39, pp. 215–230 (S. Collinson and A.M. Rugman), Palgrave Macmillan. Reproduced with permission of Palgrave Macmillan; Tables 19.1, 19.3 adapted from *Direction of Trade Statistics Yearbook, 2000 and 2009*, Washington, DC: International Monetary Fund; Table 19.2 adapted from *Direction of Trade Yearbook, 2000 and 2009*, Washington, DC: International Monetary Fund

Text

Active Learning Case Chapter 9 adapted from *The Regional Multinationals*, © Alan Rugman 2005, published by Cambridge University Press. Reproduced with permission.

Photographs

4 Getty Images: AFP; 22 Getty Images: AFP; 48 Corbis: Swim Ink 2, LLC; 59 Getty Images: News; 61 Getty Images: AFP; 79 Corbis: Raymond Gehman; 96 Getty Images: News; 104 Getty Images: Photodisc Green; 109 Getty Images: Alan kearney; 153 Alamy Images: Vario Images GmbH & Co KG; 159 Alamy Images: Len Grant Photography; 173 Getty Images: AFP / Jean-Christophe Verhaeagen / Stringer; 178 Getty Images: News; 220 Corbis: Reuters; 228 Corbis: Reuters; 244 Corbis: Reuters; 266 Getty Images: Taxi; 277 Corbis: Vincent Kessler / Reuters; 295 Corbis: Stephane Cardinale / People Avenue; 316 Getty Images: Ian Waldie; 326 Getty Images: Jung Yeon-Je; 372 Alamy Images: Niall McDiarmid; 393 Corbis: Thomas White / Reuters; 400 Corbis: Greg Smith; 411 Getty Images: Stephen Chernin; 424 Getty Images: Dennis Cox; 446 Corbis: Adam Wollfitt; 463 Alamy Images; 492 Getty Images: Peter Turner; 498 Getty Images: Ian Waldie; 508 Getty Images: Digital Vision; 511 Alamy Images: Travelstock44;de; 538 Getty Images: Pascal Le Segretain; 555 Rex Features: Action Press; 565 Getty Images: Omar Torres; 570 Getty Images: Junko Kimura; 582 Getty Images: John Chiasson; 606 Corbis: Bettman; 611 Corbis: Keith Dannemillar; 658 Corbis: Reuters; 664 Alamy Images: Blend Images; 670 tbc: Simon Collinson; 677 Getty Images: Chinafotopress; 689 Alamy Images: Lou Linwei; 716 Getty Images: Forrest Anderson; 722 Getty Images: Business Wire; 723 Alamy Images: Imagebroker.

Cover images: *Front:* Alamy Images

In some instances we have been unable to trace the owners of copyright material, and we would appreciate any information that would enable us to do so.

Part One

THE WORLD OF INTERNATIONAL BUSINESS

Chapter 1

REGIONAL AND GLOBAL STRATEGY

Contents

Objectives of the chapter

In this chapter we are going to define the boundaries of the field of international business in an introductory overview of the main themes of this book. We will then examine trade and foreign direct investment, as well as the emergence of the triad economic blocs of North America, the European Union (EU), and Japan. We will then examine some of the worldwide economic and political changes that are taking place and look at how technology is altering the way international business is conducted. We will also study some of the approaches being used by multinational enterprises both to establish and to maintain their competitive advantage. In the last part of the chapter, we will present the framework that we are going to use in our study of international business.

The specific objectives of this chapter are to:

1 *Define* the terms international business and multinational enterprise.

2 *Discuss* the two primary ways in which international business occurs: trade and foreign direct investment.

3 *Examine* the impact of the triad on international trade and investment.

4 *Describe* the current state of world economies and the role of government and trade regulations in the conduct of international business.

5 *Discuss* the importance of technology and the role of small and medium-sized enterprises in the international business arena.

6 *Examine* how multinational enterprises use triad/regional strategies to compete effectively in the international marketplace.

7 *Discuss* the determinants of national competitive advantage.

8 *Present* the model that will be used in this text for studying international business.

ACTIVE LEARNING CASE

Coke goes worldwide with a local strategy

Source: Getty Images/AFP

Coca-Cola is the largest-selling soft drink in the world, but sales vary by nation. For example, Americans consume almost 30 gallons (135 liters) of Coke annually, in contrast to Europeans who drink less than half this amount, and in some countries, such as France, Italy, and Portugal, the average is in the range of 10 gallons. In the 1990s, Coke took a number of steps to increase its European sales.

One of these was to replace local franchisors who had become too complacent with more active, market-driven sellers. In France, for example, Pernod, a Coca-Cola franchisee, was forced to sell some of its operations back to Coke which, in turn, appointed a new marketing manager for the country. In addition, Coke's price was lowered and advertising was sharply increased. As a result, per capita consumption in France went up.

In England, Beecham and Grand Metropolitan used to be Coke's national bottlers but that was turned over to Cadbury Schweppes, most famous for its Schweppes mixers. The latter immediately began a series of marketing programs that resulted in sales tripling within three years.

In Germany the pace has been even faster. Beginning in the early 1990s Coke identified Germany as one of its primary targets and began building a distribution network there to both package and sell Coke locally. Meanwhile, throughout the entire country the company has taken even bolder steps including the replacement of an inefficient bottling network and the institution of a new, well-financed marketing campaign. As a result, Germany became Coke's largest and most profitable market in Europe.

But all of this came at a price. For example, some government agencies and companies expressed concern about Coke's overriding emphasis on cost control and market growth and its willingness to push aside those who are unable to meet these goals. As a result, the European Union's Competition Department was asked to investigate possible anti-competitiveness tactics. Meanwhile, in the UK, the British Monopolies and Mergers Commission investigated Coke regarding its joint venture with Schweppes, and San Pellegrino, the mineral water company, filed a complaint with the Commission of the European Communities, contending that Coca-Cola abused its dominant position by giving discounts to Italian retailers who promised to stock only Coke.

Yet none of these actions stopped Coke's efforts to establish a strong foothold in Europe. As the European Union eliminated all internal tariffs, it became possible for a chain store with operations in France, Germany, Italy, and the Netherlands to buy soft drinks from the lowest-cost supplier on the continent and not have to worry about paying import duties for shipping them to the retail stores. Low cost and rapid delivery were going to be key strategic factors for success. Coke believes that its current European strategy puts it in an ideal competitive position against competitors.

Recent developments shed some doubt on whether the company will be as successful as it is forecasting. Worldwide market growth has been flat and there has been a move away from carbonated drinks. In Eastern Europe; it is the market for bottled water that is booming. Between 1998 and 2004, per capita consumption of bottled water in Eastern Europe doubled. Although Coca-Cola Water Division is one of four major players, it is not the market leader and smaller, local competitors account for a large portion of the market. Other efforts to develop innovative, non-carbonated products have not proven very successful. The company knows that its future growth is going to depend heavily on its ability to supplement its current product line with new offerings such as vitamin-enriched drinks, and perhaps coffee and tea offerings. Worst of all perhaps, a few years ago the company began centralizing control and encouraging consolidation among its bottling partners. Coke believed that by making all key operating decisions in Atlanta, it could drive up profitability. Unfortunately, at the same time that it was pushing for this centralized type of operation, regional markets began demanding that the company be more responsive to local needs. In short, Coke was going global while the market wanted it to go local.

Coke is now trying to turn things around. In particular, the firm is implementing three principles that are designed to make it more locally responsive. First, the company is instituting a strategy of "think local, act local" by putting increased decision making in the hands of local managers. Second, the firm is focusing itself as a pure marketing company and pushing its brands on a regional basis and local basis rather than on a worldwide basis. Third, Coke is now working to become a model citizen by reaching out to local communities and getting involved in civic and charitable activities.

Europe remains an important market for Coke, which derives about a quarter of its revenues from the region, about the same as the Asia–Pacific region. North America, though the dominant market, accounts for just under a third of Coke's revenues. Indeed, Coke now attracts both investors and consumers in Europe as it listed on the Paris NYSE Euronext from May 2011. Similar to many secondary listings, this move to Paris is more about raising awareness than cash. John Brock, chairman and chief executive, said the secondary listing "reflects our commitment to Europe and will provide convenient access" for European investors.

In the past, Coke succeeded as a multinational because of its understanding and appeal to global commonalities. Today, it is trying to hold its market share by better understanding and appealing to local differences.

Websites: www.coca-cola.com; www.cokecce.com; www.coca-colahbc.com; www.cadburyschweppes.com.

Sources: Alan Rugman and Richard Hodgetts, "The End of Global Strategy," *European Management Journal*, August 2001, p. 336; "Competition, Coolers, Drive East European Water Sales," *Food and Drink Europe*, February 2, 2004; John C. Gardner and Carl B. McGowan Jr., "A Note on the Regional Triad Model and the Soft Drink Industry," *Multinational Business Review*, Vol. 18, N 1 (2010); Adapted from Louise Lucas, "Coke Seeks Cultural Shift in Paris Listing," *Financial Times*, May 23, 2011.

1 Why did Coke engage in foreign direct investments in Europe?

2 How did Coke improve its factor conditions in Europe?

3 How is local rivalry helping to improve Coke's competitive advantage?

4 Is the Coca-Cola Company a multinational enterprise? Is it global? Why?

OVERVIEW OF THE BOOK

International business is a wonderful and exciting field of study. Today it can be said that all business is international business. The days are over when an understanding of domestic business alone was sufficient to prosper. In this book we will examine the basic data on business activities, operations, supply chains, strategies, structures, ethics, etc., and we will find that all of these have strong international elements. In other words, international business is not just the study of international trade, foreign direct investment, international joint ventures, cross-cultural management, international organizations, etc., although these topics will all be covered in the book. Today international business is much more than this: it is the study of the international aspects of business itself. Therefore, in this book, two parallel lines of thinking will be developed.

Country and firm factors

First, the book will help students to review and understand the classic components of an international business course. We will define and discuss country-level issues on international business. These will cover the importance and growth of international trade (imports and exports) and of foreign direct investment (FDI). We will define these terms and provide summary data on them later in this chapter. Next, we will discuss the nature and role of international institutions such as the World Bank, World Trade Organization, United Nations agencies, etc. We will define many of these terms later in this chapter and then explore them in greater detail in Chapter 4 which deals with the role of governments as they affect international business. We also discuss the relevance of the regional economies of the European Union, North American Free Trade Agreement (NAFTA), and the major economies in the Asia–Pacific. We refer to these as the broad "triad" regions, and again we will define these in more detail later in this chapter and, then discuss their importance in Chapter 3.

Second, the major focus of this book is upon the key actor on the stage of international business: the multinational enterprise (MNE). The MNE is defined later in this chapter, and, in Chapter 2, as a firm operating across national borders. The world's largest 500 MNEs dominate international business. It has been shown that they account for 90 percent of the world's stock of FDI and that they also undertake over half the world's trade.[1] In addition to these extremely large MNEs (with sales of $15 billion or more) there are thousands of smaller MNEs. There are also thousands of mainly small domestic firms. These small MNEs and small domestic firms are often parts of clusters (a type of network) affiliated with one or more of the world's large MNEs. The nature of these business clusters is analyzed in Chapter 22 of this book using the "flagship" framework of international business. Other forms of business organization besides the MNE are also studied. These include: international joint ventures, licensing agreements, and franchises. We explore the timing of foreign entry for these types of organizational forms starting in Chapter 2 and then in later parts of the book. We also report new research on the relationship between the degree of multinationality and the performance of MNEs and other types of organizations.

The preceding two paragraphs indicate that the book will have a focus upon country factors and firm factors. In Chapter 2 we develop a framework to integrate these two basic aspects of international business. We look into the advantages and disadvantages of the home-country effect. For example, when countries such as Canada or Sweden are endowed with bountiful natural resources, for example, trees, then this is likely to lead to the growth of pulp and paper and newsprint firms. Similarly, countries with oil deposits will generate energy firms. We call these country-specific advantages (CSAs). Of course some countries, for example, Japan, have no oil, so we can say that Japan has a country disadvantage in energy (a negative CSA). In a similar manner, using modern concepts about the strategic advantages of firms, we can use the concept of firm-specific advantages (FSAs). These are unique assets proprietary to the firm, sometimes called capabilities and/or core competencies in the resourced-based view of the firm.

International competitiveness and firm strategy

In order to examine the country effect in full detail, we will introduce issues in international competitiveness. We will examine the home-country "diamond" model popularized by Michael Porter.[2] This diamond framework is relevant for mainly large countries, but for smaller economies a double-diamond framework will be introduced in Chapter 10.

In a similar vein some of the complexities of international management strategy can be captured through use of an economic integration and national responsiveness framework. This integration responsiveness model of international management strategy is also introduced in Chapter 10 and is then used as a basis for the remaining sections of the book. We also discuss organizational structures which are used by MNEs and other types of businesses.

To summarize, building upon the distinction between country and firm factors in this book we adopt a strategic management focus. This serves to integrate and simplify the many topics relevant in the study of international business. To illustrate the relevance of the strategic management approach to international business we include over a hundred case studies in the book. There are five of these in each chapter. In addition, in the text itself we discuss many other examples of individual firm strategy and country-level institutions.

Globalization

International business is sometimes confused with globalization. We define international business as the study of country-level and firm-level factors, as outlined above. However, globalization needs to be more narrowly defined. In its extreme form, globalization means the existence of a perfectly integrated world economic system. In such a global system there would be perfect mobility of financial capital, goods, and people. There would be a global commonality whereby identical values and tastes would occur. Yet, such a situation of perfect integration (technically called homogenization) does not exist. In fact, the data in this book will demonstrate that there is not even a trend toward globalization; nor do most firms have a global strategy, defined as selling the same product at the same price around the world. Instead, there remain strong barriers to the integration of the world's goods markets and people tend to be highly immobile (only financial markets appear to be global). Government regulation, at the national and regional levels, serves to segment country and regional markets. As a result, international business needs to study the nature of regions and the importance of regional strategy.

Regionalization

This book on international business differs from all other textbooks in this area because of its focus on the reality of regionalization. Most of the world's business activity takes place across countries but within the broad triad regions of Europe, North America, and Asia–Pacific. Indeed, the core triad of the EU, NAFTA, and Japan account for the majority of world trade and FDI. Of the world's 500 largest firms, the vast majority are home-region based. There are only a handful of "global" firms operating at a significant level in all three broad regions of the triad. In fact the world's 500 largest firms average 77 percent of their sales (and assets) in their home region. (We discuss these data in Chapter 3.) This indicates that international business needs to be analyzed more carefully than is the tradition in international business textbooks. We are proud that this book offers students up-to-date data and new insights into the true nature of globalization and the reality of regional business activity. Again, these themes are illustrated in the dozens of cases reported throughout the book. It will be seen that the majority of the world's MNEs have a regional strategy rather than a global strategy.

INTRODUCTION

International business
The study of transactions taking place across national borders for the purpose of satisfying the needs of individuals and organizations

Multinational enterprise (MNE)
A company headquartered in one country but having operations in other countries

International business is the study of transactions taking place across national borders for the purpose of satisfying the needs of individuals and organizations. These economic transactions consist of trade, as in the case of exporting and importing, and foreign direct investment, as in the case of companies funding operations in other countries. Over half of all world trade and approximately 80 percent of all foreign direct investment is made by the 500 largest firms in the world. These companies, called **multinational enterprises (MNEs)**, are firms that are headquartered in one country but have operations in one or more other countries. Who are these firms? Some of them you know by name because you have used their products or seen their advertising. In order of annual revenue, here is a list of the largest 20 MNEs that each grossed more than $125 billion in 2009 (Fortune Global 500, 2010 ranking, data are for 2009):

1 Wal-Mart (US)
2 Royal Dutch/Shell Group (UK/Netherlands)
3 Exxon Mobil (US)
4 BP (UK)
5 Toyota Motor (Japan)
6 Japan Post Holdings (Japan)

7 Sinopec (P.R. China)	14 Total (France)
8 State Grid (P.R. China)	15 Bank of America Corp. (US)
9 AXA S.A (France)	16 Volkswagen (Germany)
10 China National Petroleum (P.R. China)	17 ConocoPhillips (US)
11 Chevron (US)	18 BNP Paribas (France)
12 ING Group (the Netherlands)	19 Assicurazioni Generali (Italy)
13 General Electric (US)	20 Allianz (Germany)

A close look at this list shows that 17 of these 20 companies come from one of three geographic regions: the United States, the EU, or Japan. We call this the core "triad." And of these 17 companies, 6 were from the United States, 9 from the EU, and 2 from Japan. It is noteworthy that 3 of the top 20 companies are from China. The list helps point up an important fact and one that we will continue to emphasize throughout the book: companies from one of these core three geographic regions account for most of the world's international business.

In the next section we will discuss the core triad in more detail. It is important that we include Japan in the core triad as in Asia there are 71 firms from Japan and 46 from China in the top 500. Overall there are 155 firms from Asia, 160 from the EU(15), and 152 from North America. So later, from Table 2.1, we can develop the concept of the "broad" triad of the EU, North America, and Asia. The implications of this statement will be explained in greater detail in this next section where a brief overview of the world of international business is provided. We then elaborate on the triad theme in Chapter 3.

WORLD BUSINESS: A BRIEF OVERVIEW

There are thousands of MNEs that collectively perform a wide range of operations and services.[3] However, if we were to examine what these companies are doing, we would discover that much of their activity could be classified into two major categories: (1) exports and imports and (2) foreign direct investment (FDI). International business operations are discussed in more detail in Chapter 2.

Exports and imports

International trade
The exchange of goods and services across international borders

Exports
Goods and services produced by a firm in one country and then sent to another country

Imports
Goods and services produced in one country and bought in by another country

International trade is the exchange of goods and services across international borders and is also known as exports and imports. **Exports** are goods and services produced by a firm in one country and then sent to another country. For example, many companies in China export clothing and other textile products to the United States. **Imports** are goods and services produced in one country and brought in by another country. Japan, for example, is a major importer of petroleum because it must rely on outside suppliers for all of its energy needs. For the UK, the City of London generates exports of financial services that are "invisibles" in the British balance of payments. (See the Appendix to Chapter 6 for further discussion of the balance of payments.)

In most cases people think of exports and imports as physical goods (clothes, oil, cars), but they also include services such as those provided by international airlines, cruise lines, reservation agencies, and hotels. Indeed, many international business experts now recognize that one of the major US exports is its entertainment and pop culture such as movies, television, and related offerings.

Table 1.1 World Trade, 2008

Country/region	Imports		Exports	
	Billions of US $	% of total	Billions of US $	% of total
North America	2,093.06	12.63	2,682.54	16.70
United States	1,338.51	8.07	2,036.77	12.68
Canada	458.60	2.76	394.86	2.45
Mexico	295.95	1.78	250.91	1.56
European Union (15)	5,801.39	35.00	6,169.56	38.42
Asia including Japan	4,931.92	29.76	4,245.34	26.43
Japan	830.66	5.01	684.06	4.26
Other Asia	4,101.26	24.74	3,561.28	22.17
All others	3,745.63	22.60	2,959.16	18.42
Total	16,572.00	100.00	16,056.60	100.00

Note: Data for European Union include intra-EU trade. Exports are calculated by including freight and insurance while imports do not include freight and insurance. As a result data might not be consistent with other data in this book.

Source: Adapted from International Monetary Fund, *Direction of Trade Statistics Yearbook, 2009* (Washington, DC: IMF, 2009), pp. 2–5.

Table 1.1 provides a breakdown of worldwide trade in a recent year. The data show that the EU is the world's single largest exporter, followed by Asia and North America. These data are for 2008, when there were 15 member countries in the EU (there are now 27). We call them the EU15. The EU is also the largest importer, followed by Asia and North America. If you were to investigate further, you would find that the majority of this export and import activity involves manufactured goods such as industrial machinery, computers, cars, televisions, Consumer electronics, and other electronic goods. However, as will be seen later, an increasing proportion of world trade is in services.

Information on exports and imports is important to the study of international business for a number of reasons. First, trade is the historical basis of international business and trade activities help us understand MNE practices and strategies. In 2008 the world's largest importers were the United States, China, and Germany (see the Appendix, Table 1A). The world's largest exporters were China, Germany, and the United States (see the Appendix, Table 1B). Note that the world's top importers are also the world's largest exporters but in a different order. Some of the major products that are traded by these countries include computers, farm machinery, machine tools, automobiles, and electronic goods.

Second, trade helps us better understand the impact of international business on world economies. For example, Japan imports all of its oil. So when the price of oil in the world market rises sharply, we can readily predict that the cost of manufacturing cars in Japan will rise and Japanese auto exports will decline. Conversely, if oil prices decline, we can predict that world imports of Japanese cars are likely to increase.

A third reason why exports and imports are important in the study of international business is that they are the main drivers of international trade (FDI is another driver, which we discuss below and then in detail in Chapter 3). When worldwide exports and imports begin to slow down, this is a very good sign that world economies are going into a slump.

The US trade ties to Canada and Mexico reflect the triad effect, as these three countries are members of the North American Free Trade Agreement (NAFTA). Indeed, more than 57 percent of the exports of the United States, Canada, and Mexico are intra-regional, that is, to each other.[4] A similar picture of regional trade concentrations appears in the EU, where over 67 percent of all the exports of the EU 15 member states are with each other.[5] Similarly, over 54 percent of Asian exports are to other Asian countries.[6] Table 1.2

Table 1.2 Intra-regional trade in the triad, 1980–2008

Year	Intra-regional exports (%)		
	EU	NAFTA	Asia
2008	67.6	57.0	54.2
2000	67.2	58.1	42.4
1980	53.5	33.6	27.3
Cumulative Average Annual Change			
1980–2008	0.26	0.70	0.90
2000–2008	0.01	−0.02	0.28

Note: Asia data were calculated using information for exports from Japan, China, India, Indonesia, South Korea, Malaysia, Singapore, Thailand, and Australia to the Asian region and the world. Data for EU are for intra-EU exports in 2000 and 2008 and intra-EEC Exports in 1980.

Source: Authors' calculations based on the IMF, *Direction of Trade Statistics Yearbook*, 2009 and 1985.

reports that the majority of exports of these triad areas now occurs within each region and that this intra-regional trade has increased significantly since 1980. The recent decrease in intra-regional trade in the Asian region is partly due to the emergence of China as a manufacturer for the US market.

Foreign direct investment

Foreign direct investment (FDI)
Equity funds invested in other nations

Foreign direct investment (FDI) is equity funds invested in other nations. It is different from portfolio (financial) investment in that FDI is undertaken by MNEs which exercise control of their foreign affiliates. Like exports and imports, FDI is a driver of international business and many companies use FDI to establish footholds in the world marketplace by setting up operations in foreign markets or by acquiring businesses there. Firms engage in FDI for a number of reasons: to increase sales and profits, to enter rapidly growing markets, to reduce costs, to gain a foothold in economic unions, to protect domestic markets, to protect foreign markets, and to acquire technological and managerial know-how. These will be discussed in more detail in Chapter 3.

When examined from an overall perspective, FDI data show that industrialized countries have invested very large amounts of money in other industrialized nations as well as smaller amounts in less developed countries (LDCs) such as those in Eastern Europe or newly industrialized countries (NICs) such as Korea and Singapore. However, most of the world's FDI is invested both by and within the three broad triad groups we identified earlier: NAFTA, EU 15, and Asia. The United States is an excellent example of a country that is a major target of investment as well as a major investor in other countries. Its high GDP per capita and consumer spending make it an attractive market for foreign multinationals. Conversely, US firms have specialized capabilities that can be exploited in other countries.

By 2008 the United States had become such a major investment target that foreign holdings were over $2.3 trillion. (See Table 1.3a on stocks of FDI in the United States.) The largest investors are the UK, Japan, the Netherlands, Canada, Germany, Switzerland, and France. Collectively these countries account for over two-thirds of the stock of all FDI in the United States. Note that the Chinese stock of FDI in the United States is still so small that it does not make the list. At the same time, as seen in Table 1.3b, US companies have substantial FDI in other countries which amounts to more than $3.2 trillion. The major areas for this FDI are the Netherlands, the UK, Canada, Bermuda, and Luxembourg. Note that the US FDI stock in China is now on this list, but still only 1.45 percent of the total. Using FDI flow data the amount of Chinese FDI in the United States is much higher, but

Table 1.3a Foreign direct investment in the United States, 2008 (by US$ size ranking)

Economy/region	Millions of US $	% of total
All economies/ all countries	2,278,892	100.00
Canada	221,870	9.74
Europe	1,622,911	71.21
United Kingdom	454,123	19.94
Netherlands	259,385	11.38
Germany	211,521	9.28
Switzerland	165,697	7.27
France	163,430	7.17
Luxembourg	113,248	4.97
Spain	38,662	1.70
Sweden	35,020	1.54
Ireland	34,094	1.50
Belgium	18,580	0.82
Italy	17,575	0.77
Finland	12,499	0.55
Norway	6,755	0.30
Denmark	4,992	0.22
Austria	2,406	0.11
Latin America and other Western hemisphere	49,233	2.16
UK Islands, Caribbean	21,604	0.95
Bermuda	10,750	0.47
Mexico	7,948	0.35
Africa	2,002	0.09
Middle East	14,676	0.64
Asia and Pacific	368,200	16.15
Japan	259,569	11.39
Australia	64,316	2.82
Korea, South	15,632	0.69
Singapore	12,718	0.56
Hong Kong SAR (P.R. China)	3,973	0.17
Taiwan (Taiwan Province of China)	3,900	0.17

Note: Data are on a historical-cost basis. Numbers might not add up due to rounding.

Sources: Authors' calculations and ranking by US$ size and US Department of Commerce, *Survey of Current Business*, July 2009. Table 1255. Foreign Direct Investment Position in the United States on a Historical-Cost Basis by Selected Country, and by Industry

this is not reflected in the stock FDI data as it is much newer than the US FDI in Europe and Japan, where this grows through retained earnings.

A close look at Tables 1.3a and Table 1.3b shows that the UK and Japan have larger FDI stocks in the United States than the United States has FDI stock in the UK and Japan. The United States has larger FDI stocks in Europe than Europe has FDI stocks in the United States. On the other hand, US businesses have more FDI in Latin America and the Western hemisphere relative to the Europeans or Japanese. US companies have put much more FDI into Australia than Australia has FDI in the United States.

These recent data reveal two important trends. First, the United States is a prime site for FDI by both Japan and countries in Western Europe. Second, US firms have invested most heavily in Canada, Europe, Latin America, and other Western hemisphere areas, and Asia–Pacific. These four areas account for over 97.8 percent of the stock of all US FDI. (For more on FDI see the Appendix, Tables 1C and 1D, at the end of this chapter. We also discuss FDI and the role of MNEs in more detail in Chapter 2.)

Table 1.3b Foreign direct investment by the United States, 2008 (by US$ size ranking)

Economy/region	Millions of US $	% of total
All economies/ all countries	3,162,021	100.00
Canada	227,298	7.18
Europe	1,809,876	57.23
Netherlands	442,926	14.00
UK	420,873	13.31
Luxembourg	163,167	5.16
Ireland	146,194	4.62
Switzerland	123,358	3.90
Germany	110,784	3.50
France	75,040	2.37
Spain	69,649	2.20
Belgium	65,054	2.06
Sweden	43,391	1.37
Italy	28,653	0.91
Austria	17,518	0.55
Poland	15,597	0.49
Latin America and other Western hemisphere	563,809	17.83
Bermuda	165,857	5.24
UK Islands, Caribbean	139,290	4.40
Mexico	95,618	3.02
Brazil	45,500	1.43
Africa	36,640	1.16
Middle East	32,488	1.02
Asia and Pacific	491,910	15.55
Singapore	106,529	3.37
Australia	88,549	2.80
Japan	79,235	2.51
Hong Kong SAR (P.R. China)	51,505	1.63
China	45,695	1.45
Korea, South	27,673	0.88

Note: Data are on a historical-cost basis. Numbers might not add up due to rounding.

Sources: Authors' calculations and ranking by US$ size and US Department of Commerce, *Survey of Current Business*, July 2009. Table 1260. U.S. Direct Investment Position Abroad on a Historical-Cost Basis by Selected Country

✔ Active learning check

Review your answer to Active Learning Case question 1 and make any changes you like. Then compare your answer to the one below.

1 **Why did Coke engage in foreign direct investments in Europe?**

Coke made these investments in order to improve its market position. This is being done in three ways. First, the construction of new bottling plants is helping the company produce a low-cost product. Second, marketing expenditures are helping the firm gain the product recognition needed for growth. Third, direct investments in facilities closer to the market are reducing delivery time and eliminating associated expenses.

The triad

Triad
The three major trading and investment blocs in the international arena: the United States, the EU, and Japan

As we noted above, companies in the United States, Western Europe, and Japan conduct most of the world's trade and FDI. Of these companies, those located in Western Europe mainly come from nations that are members of the EU. The core **triad** is a group of three major trading and investment blocs in the international arena: the United States, the EU, and Japan. Before looking more closely at the impact of the triad on international business, it is important to discuss the countries that are members of this group.

The first of these, the *United States*, has the largest economy in the world with a GDP of over $14.14 trillion (2009 estimate)![7] Sometimes when the United States is discussed as a member of the triad, Canada and Mexico are included. This is because these three countries implemented the **North American Free Trade Agreement (NAFTA)** in 1994, an international covenant that has resulted in the elimination of many trade and investment barriers between the three. We further discuss NAFTA in Chapter 19. In our discussions of the triad in the book, we will be talking only about the United States; if we intend to include Canada and Mexico we will indicate so by referring to them as members of NAFTA. The reason that our triad discussions will include only the United States is that the US economy is extremely large when compared to those of Canada and Mexico. As a result, if we were to talk about the 25 largest MNEs in NAFTA we would be discussing US firms only. Canadian or Mexican firms are not big enough to make this list of 25. Simply put, the US economy is so large that this one country constitutes an entire segment of the triad.

North American Free Trade Agreement (NAFTA)
A regional free trade agreement among Canada, the United States, and Mexico

The second segment of the triad is the *European Union*. This group of nations, whose history and current developments will be discussed in Chapters 3 and 17, was formed by six countries in the late 1950s. Today there are 27 members of the EU. This includes the EU15—Austria, Belgium, Denmark, Finland, Germany, Greece, France, Ireland, Italy, Luxembourg, the Netherlands, Portugal, Spain, Sweden, and the UK—an additional 8 East European countries that joined on May 1, 2004—Czech Republic, Estonia, Latvia, Lithuania, Hungary, Poland, Slovenia, and Slovakia—as well as Cyprus and Malta. Bulgaria and Romania became members of the EU in 2007 (see map, European Union timeline) while Turkey continues to negotiate its entry into the union. In this book, unless noted otherwise, data are for the EU15. These are the largest countries in the group, accounting for 90 percent of the GDP of the EU. Statistical information on the EU27 is not yet generally available. The collective GDP of the EU is greater than that of the United States or Japan, and a brief look at some of the economic data in this chapter helps show how important the EU is in the international arena. For example, in terms of imports and exports, as seen back in Table 1.1, the EU accounts for more than 35 percent of all imports and over 38.4 percent of all world exports. Again, over 60 percent is intra-EU trade. Quite clearly, the EU is a worldwide economic force.

The third group in the core triad is *Japan*, which like the other two members plays a major role in international business. This is made particularly clear by looking at areas such as importing, exporting, and FDI. As seen in the Appendix, Tables 1A and 1B, at the end of the chapter, Japan is the world's fourth largest importer and fourth largest exporter. At market prices it is the largest economy in Asia and it has by far the highest GDP per capita. Japan accounts for 5 percent of all the world's imports and 4.3 percent of all of the world's exports. Japan also accounts for 4.2 percent of all outward stocks of FDI. (See the Appendix, Table 1D.)

In examining the current state of world business, the core triad merits close attention. Every year companies from these three groups account for more trade and FDI than those of any other economic bloc. As a result, during the twenty-first century the triad will be of central importance in the study of international business. We will discuss the power of the core triad in greater detail in Chapter 3.

The European Union timeline
○ EU member

1951	1957	1973	1981	1986	1992	1995	2004	2007
Belgium, Germany, France, Italy, Luxembourg, and the Netherlands establish the European Coal and Steel Community (ECSC).	Treaty of Rome establishes the European Economic Community (EEC).	Denmark, Ireland, and the United Kingdom join the European Community.	Greece joins the European Community.	Spain and Portugal join the European Community.	Treaty of Maastricht establishes the European Union (EU).	Austria, Finland, and Sweden join the EU.	Czech Republic, Estonia, Cyprus, Latvia, Lithuania, Hungary, Malta, Poland, Slovenia, and Slovakia join the EU.	Bulgaria and Romania join the EU.

Although the triad dominates international business, as discussed in this book, over the past few years a number of emerging economies have become increasingly important for international business. In particular, Brazil, Russia, India, and China (BRIC) are growing players in international trade and FDI. These countries will be explored further in Chapters 20 and 21, which deal with non-triad economies. (Chapter 21 deals entirely with China.)

TODAY'S INTERNATIONAL ENVIRONMENT

Although the triad continues to dominate the international business arena, the international environment has been changing rapidly in recent years. Today the world economy is quite different from what it was just five years ago. Some of the reasons include an overall slowdown in the triad economies, the introduction of more local and international trade regulation, the impact of technology, and the rise of small and medium-sized multinationals. The following briefly examines each of these.

Economic developments are detailed by the **Organization for Economic Cooperation and Development (OECD)**, a Paris-based intergovernmental organization of the world's most economically advanced nations that provides its members with a forum for examining their economic problems and discussing solutions.

Organization for Economic Cooperation and Development (OECD)
A group of 30 relatively wealthy member countries that facilitates a forum for the discussion of economic, social, and governance issues across the world

International trade regulation

Another important international business trend has been the emergence of trade and investment liberalization. Firms in triad countries have prospered in more open markets. Yet, at the same time, triad rivalry has led to some setbacks in trade liberalization. For example, Japan and China have been threatened with trade sanctions by the United States unless they allow US firms to sell products and services in their countries. There are also trade conflicts between the EU and the United States over biotech foods and crops, steel, beef hormones, and export subsidies.[8] Many such trade disputes, however, are handled not by countries but by international organizations set up to regulate international commerce. The main one is the World Trade Organization.

The **World Trade Organization (WTO)** was established on January 1, 1995, and it is now the umbrella organization that governs the international trading system. It is the successor to the **General Agreement on Tariffs and Trade (GATT)**. The GATT was established in 1947. The purpose of the GATT was to liberalize trade and to negotiate trade concessions among member countries. Although the early years saw a great deal of progress in reducing tariffs, by the 1980s there was a trend toward protectionism by many countries. At the GATT's eighth round of negotiations in 1986 (called the Uruguay Round because this is where the group met), negotiations dragged on for years before culminating in a number of agreements including reductions on industrial goods and agricultural subsidies, the increased protection of intellectual property rights under the Agreement on Trade-Related Aspects of Intellectual Property Rights (TRIPS), the creation of the General Agreement on Trade in Services (GATS), and the creation of the WTO to implement the GATT agreement. Today the WTO is enforcing these agreements. Presently, the Doha Round of the WTO has opened the door for further trade negotiations.

World Trade Organization (WTO)
An international organization that deals with the rules of trade among member countries; one of its most important functions is to act as a dispute-settlement mechanism

General Agreement on Tariffs and Trade (GATT)
A major trade organization that has been established to negotiate trade concessions among member countries

When member nations have a dispute they can turn to the WTO to help resolve it. For example, the United States brought a case against the EU charging it with a discriminatory banana import policy and the WTO ruled in its favor. In another case the United States requested that Japan be instructed to reorganize its commercial economy so that Kodak could better compete in that market against Fuji, its major rival, but the WTO rejected the claim and ruled in Japan's favor. In recent years the United States, the EU, and Japan, in particular, have been using the WTO to help resolve trade disputes, and this bodes well for the future of the organization. The important thing to remember about the WTO is that it can enforce its decisions. Countries that refuse to comply can find themselves suffering severe consequences in the form of trade retaliation. Despite minor conflicts, international trade liberalization has arrived and this promises to help stimulate international business transactions.

Technology

Another major development that is changing the way MNEs do business is technology. Two areas, in particular, are having a major impact. One is communication technology that has advanced at such a rapid rate that all businesses now use computers and rely on the World Wide Web to both access and send information. In addition, thanks to cellular technology, individuals can now remain in constant contact with both their customers and their home office. Communication technology has advanced so much that the latest technology

INTERNATIONAL BUSINESS STRATEGY IN ACTION

Amazon.com is not a global business

There are thousands of "global" businesses on the internet. However, the best known of these may well be Amazon.com. Everyday, thousands of people go to the company's website to browse and purchase books. A novel that is reviewed by Sunday in *New York Times Book Review* is likely to get a minimum of 10,000 hits within the next week, as readers read the comments of others, and check for price and availability. For example, the *Times Book Review* gave a good review to *Nickel and Dimed*, a book which had to that date generated lukewarm sales and for which its publisher had little hope, thousands went to Amazon.com to place an order and within a few hours the current inventory was exhausted. The incident shows the impact of not only the *Times Book Review* but also Amazon.com. The first created the demand while the second facilitated the distribution.

Amazon.com was founded in 1995 by Jeff Bezos. In less than 10 years the company became one of the largest 1,000 US corporations according to Fortune. In 2009, sales were $24,509 million. On the other hand, Amazon.com has consistently lost money. In 2000, every dollar sales the company took in, it lost 51 cents. Losses continued through to 2003, when a small profit was first reported.

Amazon was initially created to change the way people buy books. The company wanted to offer buyers a virtual store where they could use their computer to place an order that would then be delivered to them by mail. Going to a bookstore was going to be a thing of the past. In addition to making it easy to buy books, Amazon's prices were lower than those at most bookstores – even when shipping costs were added in, it was often less expensive to shop online with Amazon than it was to visit the local bookstore.

From the beginning, Bezos's strategy was to grow as fast as possible. He began recruiting highly skilled staff to design the e-commerce end of the business, as well as less skilled workers to handle warehouse, distribution, and supply operations. Initially, all of the employees had a common vision regarding what the company wanted to do. However, in a few short years, this rapid growth resulted in both confusion and internal problems. Among other things, some of the personnel filed lawsuits against the company for better compensation. Continued losses and the dot.com crash of 2000 severely reduced the price of its stock.

Today the biggest problem for Amazon.com is that it is not a global company – it is a US firm. The Internet is really only a tool for business and, in Amazon's case, a way to sell products that are produced by others. While the company now sells more than just books, it continues to be a US company. One reason is because books tend to sell most heavily in the market where they are published. A college text published in North America, for example, will not sell very much in Europe or Japan. Quite simply, triad and geographic regions segment the market—and even within this grouping, it can be difficult to sell to other countries. For example, in 2009, Amazon generated 53.3 percent of its sales in North America and 47.7 percent internationally. But even in Canada, the firm continually confronts a number of problems doing business including how to address Canadian sales taxes and how to deal with the threat by Canadian publishers of having the state-run postal service refuse to deliver "foreign" books. In fact, these problems have created such a headache for Canadian buyers that many of them now order their online books from Canadian suppliers such as Chapters and Borders rather than from Amazon. And in Europe, where Amazon operates through foreign subsidiaries, such as Amazon.co.uk, Amazon.fr, and Amazon.de, the company offers a totally different stock of books from those marketed in North America, and it targets a smaller, more affluent group of customers in this niche. The same marketing strategy is used in Asia. On both of these continents, customers are finding that local book suppliers often do a better job of meeting their needs in terms of both the range of their offerings and the price of their products. In short, Amazon.com is finding that if it wants to be a global competitor it is going to have to formulate a strategy that helps it expand out of the US market and become much more competitive throughout the triad. At the present time, Amazon.com is only half of the way there.

Websites: www.amazon.com; www.amazon.co.uk; www.amazon.co.jp; www.amazon.fr; www.amazon.de.

Sources: Amazon.com, *Annual Report*, 2009; Alan M. Rugman, *The End of Globalization* (London: Random House, 2001; New York: Amacom, 2000; Toronto: McGraw-Hill Ryerson, 2001); Robert Spector, *Amazon.com Get Big Fast* (New York: HarperCollins, 2000; London: Random House, 2000); *Fortune*, April 16, 2000, p. F63; *Fortune*, the Fortune 500, May 3, 2010.

reports reveal that there now are more than 499 million mobile (cellular) phone users in the EU15 (2009), or 77 percent of the population. In some EU countries, mobile users account for 90 percent of the population![9] Over 55 percent of the US population has access to the Internet.[10] The case **International Business Strategy in Action: Amazon.com is not a global business** discusses the issues of fast growth of new service businesses.

The other major application of technology is for the production of goods and services. Modern factories can now produce goods in a shorter period of time and with fewer defects thanks to production process programs. One example is the introduction of "Six Sigma"— a statistical term that means 3.4 errors per million—that eliminates performance problems in the production process and encourages worker participation and innovation to create products that meet the needs and wants of consumers.[11] Since Motorola engineers introduced the concept into their production process in the 1980s, hundreds of MNEs, including GE, Coca-Cola, and Boeing, have adopted the process, reducing defects, lowering costs, and improving quality.[12] (See Chapter 12 for a discussion of Six Sigma and other production process programs.)

Small and medium-sized enterprises (SMEs)

SMEs or small-and-medium-sized enterprises (SMEs)
Defined by Governments using different criteria for policy purposes. SMEs are firms with less than 250 employees in Europe, but less than 500 in the United States. Indian manufacturing firms qualify as SMEs if they invest less than US$2 million in plant and equipment.

Whenever MNEs are discussed, it is common to hear about large firms. In fact, the best-known multinationals are companies that have become household words. In the auto industry everyone knows of Honda, General Motors, and Volkswagen. However, there are thousands of **small and medium-sized enterprises (SMEs)**, many of whom are suppliers to these MNEs.[13] Most of these companies have annual sales of less than $5 million, but thanks to innovation, technology, and a well-trained workforce, they are able to compete effectively and perform functions that multinationals cannot do as efficiently. For example, some SMEs are able to provide their customers with two-day deliveries. In this way, their customers can keep a minimum amount of inventory on hand because the suppliers will replenish the stock every other day. And since these SMEs are small operations that focus heavily on cost control and quality, they are critical to the success of their customers. The result is that SMEs are proving to be the backbone of many industries because of their efficiency and flexibility. In addition, a number of SMEs compete effectively against large companies in niche markets. In this book we will be studying a large number of international business concepts that are used not just by MNEs but also by SMEs. In particular, we discuss the strategies of some SMEs in cases like Command Alkon in Chapter 9 and Mountain Equipment Co-op in Chapter 8.

GLOBALIZATION AND STRATEGIC MANAGEMENT

At the end of each chapter in this book we use Real Cases to illustrate some of the ways MNEs use the ideas that have been presented. In this opening chapter we introduced the world of international business and showed the impact of the triad on international trade and investment. We also noted that the major world economies are beginning to slow down and this, of course, is putting increased pressure on MNEs to maintain growth and profitability. In this section we want to address three areas that are important in understanding how companies are coping with this international environment. First, we are going to look at some of the misconceptions that people have about MNEs and how they formulate their international strategies. Second, we are going to look at some of the criteria that are important to MNEs in achieving strategic competitive advantage. Third, we are going to examine some examples of MNEs that are using concepts that we have introduced in this chapter.

Regional triad strategies

There are a number of misconceptions that people have about the world of international business, and it is important to dispel these at the very start of this book. One is the belief that multinationals have far-flung operations and earn most of their revenues overseas.

Nestlé is often cited as an example. This company sells over 8,500 products in more than 100 countries and earns more than 65 percent of its revenues outside of Switzerland.[14] Although this is true, Nestlé is an exception to the rule. Most MNEs earn the bulk of their revenues either within their home country or by selling in nearby locales. In fact, recent research reports that:

> More than 85 percent of all automobiles sold in North America are built in North American factories owned by General Motors, Ford, Daimler, Chrysler, or European or Japanese MNEs; over 90 percent of the cars produced in the EU are sold there; and more than 93 percent of all cars registered in Japan are manufactured domestically.
>
> In the specialty chemicals sector over 90 percent of all paint is made and used regionally by triad based MNEs and the same is true for steel, heavy electrical equipment, energy, and transportation.
>
> In the services sector, which now employs approximately 70 percent of the work force in North America, Western Europe, and Japan, these activities are all essentially local or regional.[15]

To be successful, MNEs need to create strategies that are regional, not worldwide, in focus and they need to be responsive to local consumers as opposed to being global in nature and uniform throughout.

Another misunderstanding about MNEs is the belief that they are globally monolithic and excessively powerful in political terms. Actually, the latest research shows that, of the 500 largest MNEs, well over 400 are headquartered in North America, the EU, and in Japan/Asia. We discuss this further in Chapter 2, Table 2.1. In short, these firms are not spread out around the world but are clustered in the triad. This relatively even distribution across the three regions of the triad implies not a dominant MNE culture but the interaction of different cultures in the international business arena. Recent research has also shown that the vast majority of MNEs have not been able to spread their marketing operations evenly across the world but depend on their own regions of the triad for over half of their revenue.[16] These companies are engaged not in global competition but in triad/regional competition, and this rivalry is so strong that it has effectively eliminated the possibility of their either achieving sustainable long-term profits or building strong, enduring political advantage. In fact, it is now common to find MNEs joining forces with local firms which can help them in their efforts to penetrate local markets. In recent years the **strategic alliance**, a business relationship in which two or more companies work together to achieve a collective advantage, has become extremely popular with MNEs which now realize that they need to develop strategies with a regional or local focus if they hope to succeed.

Strategic alliance
A business relationship in which two or more companies work together to achieve a collective advantage

A third misunderstanding is the belief that MNEs develop homogeneous products for the world market and through their efficient production techniques are able to dominate local markets everywhere. In fact, multinationals have to adapt their products for the local market. For example, there is no worldwide, global car. Rather, there are regionally based auto factories that are supported by local and regional suppliers which provide steel, plastic, paint, seats, tires, radios, and other necessary inputs for producing cars for that geographic region. Additionally, the car designs that are popular in one area of the world are typically rejected by buyers in other geographic areas. The Toyota Camry that dominates the US auto market is a poor seller in Japan and fares even worse in Europe.[17] And the Volkswagen Golf, which does extremely well in Europe, has not made much of an impact in North America. Pharmaceutical firms, which manufacture medicines that are often referred to as "universal products," have to modify their goods to satisfy national and state regulations, thus making centralized production and worldwide distribution economically difficult.[18]

In this book we are going to use examples throughout of what is happening in the international environment and show how an understanding of international business concepts can be useful to companies in addressing these developments. In many cases you will find that things you believed to be true are not. There is a great deal of misinformation about the world of international business. One of these misperceptions is that MNEs are giant corporations that are world dominant. In fact, their success comes most heavily from formulating and implementing strategies on a regional and local basis.

Maintaining economic competitiveness

The United States is one of the most competitive nations in the world.[19] How do US companies manage to achieve and then maintain this international competitive advantage? Another way of asking this question is: why are some firms able to innovate consistently while others cannot? Michael Porter of Harvard University has provided one of the best answers to this question. After conducting a comprehensive study of 100 industries in 10 countries, Porter found that the success of nations in international competition is determined by four broad attributes that individually and interactively determine national competitive advantage: factor conditions, demand conditions, related and supporting industries, and the environment in which firms compete.[20] These four determinants are briefly discussed below. This "diamond" model of Porter can be applied not only to US firms but to firms from any country.

Factor conditions

Factor conditions
Land, labor, and capital

According to basic international trade theory, a nation will export those goods that make most use of the factor conditions with which it is relatively well endowed. These **factor conditions** include land, labor, and capital. As a result, if a country has a large, relatively uneducated workforce, it will seek to export goods that are highly labor intensive. On the other hand, if the workforce is highly educated, the country will seek to produce goods and services that tap the intellectual abilities of these people. However, there is more to international trade theory than merely capitalizing on these basic factors. To maintain a competitive position, a country must continually upgrade or adjust its factor conditions. For example, Denmark has two hospitals that specialize in studying and treating diabetes; Denmark also is a world leader in the export of insulin. By creating specialized factors and then working to upgrade them, the country has maintained its premier position in the health-care field. Similarly, the Netherlands, the world's leading exporter of flowers, has created research institutes in the cultivation, packaging, and shipping of flowers. As a result, no one has been able to dislodge that country's foothold in the international flower industry.

✔ Active learning check

Review your answer to Active Learning Case question 2 and make any changes you like. Then compare your answer to the one below.

② How did Coke improve its factor conditions in Europe?

Coke's factor conditions include land, labor, and capital. The company is using land and capital to build new bottling plants that are more efficient and better suited to meet market demand. It is working to improve the effectiveness of the labor force by getting the personnel to become more market oriented and to sell the product more vigorously throughout Europe.

Demand conditions

Porter states that a nation's competitive advantage is strengthened if there is strong local demand for its goods and services. This demand provides a number of benefits. First, it helps the seller understand what buyers want. Second, if changes become necessary, such as customer desires for a product that is smaller, lighter, or more fuel efficient, the local seller has early warning and can adjust or innovate for the market before more distant competitors can respond. In fact, the more sophisticated the local buyers, the greater the advantage to the local seller. For example, one reason that Japanese firms pioneered small, quiet air-conditioning units is that many Japanese live in small houses and apartments where loud noise can be a problem. Japanese firms also developed units that were powered by energy-saving rotary compressors because customers complained that the price of energy was very high and they wanted a more fuel-efficient unit. Similarly, Sweden, long concerned with helping the disabled, has spawned a competitive industry that focuses on the special needs of these people, and Denmark's environmental concern has resulted in Danish companies developing highly effective water-pollution control equipment and windmills. In the United States, consumers helped to develop a highly efficient fast-food industry, and as the desire for this cuisine spread worldwide, US franchisors like McDonald's and Pizza Hut have been able to tap international demand for their products.

Related and supporting industries

Porter's third major determinant of national competitive advantage is the presence of related and supporting industries that are internationally competitive. When suppliers are located near the producer, these firms often provide lower-cost inputs that are not available to the producer's distant competitors. In addition, suppliers typically know what is happening in the industry environment and are in a position to both forecast and react to these changes. By sharing this information with the producer, they help the producer maintain its competitive position. The Italian shoe industry is an excellent example. Shoe producers interact on a regular basis with leather manufacturers, exchanging information that is useful to each in remaining competitive. This interaction is mutually beneficial to both parties.[21]

Firm strategy, structure, and rivalry

Porter's fourth broad determinant of national advantage is the context in which the firms are created, organized, and managed, as well as the nature of domestic rivalry. No one managerial system is universally appropriate. Nations tend to do well in industries where the management practices favored by the national environment are suited to their industries' sources of competitive advantage. In Italy, for example, successful firms typically are small or medium sized; operate in fragmented industries such as lighting, furniture, footwear, and packaging machines; are managed like extended families; and employ a focus strategy geared toward meeting the needs of small market niches. Germany, in contrast, tends to have hierarchical organizations that emphasize technical or engineering content (optics, chemicals, complicated machinery) that demand precision manufacturing, a careful development process, after-sale service, and a highly disciplined management structure. In Japan, successful firms are often those that require unusual cooperation across functional lines and that demand management of complex assembly operations. Auto production, television manufacturing, and computer assembly are examples of such industries.

National goals are also important. Some countries want rapid results. Others tend to do best in industries where long-term development is valued more. In the United States, for example, investors like fast financial returns. So US firms are more likely to invest in new industries such as software and biotechnology where success can come quickly. In Germany and Switzerland, investments are held for long-term appreciation and are rarely traded. These countries are more likely to invest in mature industries where ongoing investment in research and development and new facilities are important but return on investment is only moderate.

Another area of importance is domestic rivalry. Researchers have found that vigorous domestic rivalry and competitive advantage are related. Nations with leading world positions often have a number of strong, local rivals. For example, in Switzerland, the pharmaceutical firms Roche and Novartis help the country to maintain its internationally competitive edge. In Germany, BASF and Bayer help the country to keep ahead in chemicals.

✔ Active learning check

Review your answer to Active Learning Case question 3 and make any changes you like. Then compare your answer to the one below.

 How is local rivalry helping to improve Coke's competitive advantage?

Coke faces strong competition in Europe. Europeans do not drink as much Coke as do Americans; beverages such as coffee and tea are more popular. As a result, Coke has had to modify its strategy to address this market. This includes the building of new bottling plants that can help drive down costs and make the company more price competitive, and new marketing campaigns that are designed to draw customers away from competing products. Coke is also working to develop non-carbonated drinks to address local tastes. Finally, competition from locals who better understand their market is forcing Coke to "think local, act local."

Porter's determinants as a system

As noted earlier, each of Porter's determinants of international competitiveness often depends on the others. For example, even if a country has sophisticated buyers that can provide a company with feedback about how to modify or improve its product (demand conditions), this information will not be useful if the firm lacks personnel with the skills to carry out these functions (factor conditions). Similarly, if suppliers can provide the company with low-cost inputs and fresh ideas for innovation (related and supporting industries) but the firm clearly and easily dominates the industry (firm strategy, structure, and rivalry) and does not feel a need to upgrade the quality of its products and services, it will eventually lose this competitive advantage.

Research shows that of Porter's determinants of competitiveness, domestic rivalry/ geographic clustering is particularly important. Domestic rivalry promotes improvements in the other three determinants and geographic concentration magnifies the interaction of the four separate influences.[22]

A firm's international abilities and competitiveness can also be described through a combination of firm-specific advantages (FSAs) and country-specific advantages (CSAs). This theoretical framework is developed in Chapter 2. The Porter country diamond framework, discussed in this section, is an excellent framework to capture the CSAs. In Chapter 2, we will start to discuss the FSAs of the MNE. The CSAs and FSAs can then be combined into the matrix of Chapter 2. This becomes the building block for the book. For example, the CSAs will be explored in more detail in Part Two of the book (Chapters 4, 5, 6, and 7), which deal respectively with political, cultural, trade, and financial issues. These are all issues affecting the environment of international business. Then, Part Three of the book looks into international business strategies. These includes MNE strategy, organizing strategy, corporate strategy and national responsiveness, and innovation, entrepreneurship and born global firms. Part Five provides insights of regional strategies. These includes European Union, Japan, North America, Emerging economies, China and corporate ethics and natural environment.

Multinationals in action

In each chapter of this book we are going to provide examples of how MNEs are using the ideas that we have been presenting. Usually we do this by highlighting a relevant case example, as in the box **International Business Strategy in Action: Tata**. In this first chapter we

INTERNATIONAL BUSINESS STRATEGY IN ACTION

Tata

One of India's largest multinational enterprises is Tata Group. In 2009, the total revenues for Tata Group are US $70.9 billion. The majority of its sales are still in Asia. Tata Group is one of the world's largest emerging economy MNEs. Its financial clout was shown when it purchased Corus in 2007, beating off a competing bid from a Brazilian company, Cia Siderurgica National.

Tata has about 100 different operating companies in all three regions of the triad, but still mainly in Asia. There are no data on its regional sales. Its major enterprises are: Tata Steel; Tata Consulting Services; Tata Motors; and Tata Tea. It employs over 250,000 people.

Its foreign holdings include the UK's largest steel company, Corus Group, which it bought in February 2007 for $12.2 billion. Its first foreign purchase was of the former stalwart of the British Empire, Tetley Tea, which it bought in 2000. Tata Group also own Eight O'Clock Coffee Co. of the United States which it bought in 2006 and Daewoo Commercial Vehicle Co. of South Korea which it bought in 2004. In September 2007 it was announced that Tata Motors Limited (part of the Tata Group) was going to buy up Jaguar and Land Rover from Ford Motor Company at a price of over $2 billion. Why has Tata become so successful?

Tata's history is tightly intertwined with the history of India. Jamsetji Nusserwanji Tata founded a trading company in 1868, when India was still under British control, and soon entered the textiles market. It then forayed into the hotels business with the construction, in Mumbai, of the Taj Mahal Palace and Tower, the first Indian-owned luxury hotel. The story surrounding this event is that the owner of Tata was not allowed into British hotels because he was Indian and so now the international hotel chain has become a symbol of national pride. Today, Tata's influence can be seen throughout the Indian economy. Near the hotel you can see a Tata Power Plant that generates about 80 percent of the power in India's largest city. The urban landscape is filled with Tata cars, buses, and trucks as well as billboards advertising everything from Tata Tea to Tata credit cards.

The recent growth of this vast conglomerate is the result of two important events, deregulation and the appointment of Ratan Tata as chairman of the company. In 1991, the Indian government began to dismantle many of the bureaucratic impediments that had constrained Indian businesses. The same year, Ratan Tata took control of his family's company and began to rationalize the group by divesting itself of hundreds of companies. He kept about a hundred companies in key sectors and began to implement

Source: Getty Images/AFP

a series of strategic plans, including internationalization. Since 2000, Tata has purchased Tetley Tea (of the UK), 30 percent of Glaceu (a US manufacturer of bottled water), and Eight O'Clock Coffee (a US firm), all these in the beverages sector alone. Foreign acquisitions have also been part of the strategic plan of Tata Steel and Tata Motors.

Over the past few years, the steel industry has been consolidating through acquisitions. One example of this is Mittal Steel's purchase of Arcelor in 2007. Run by an India-born UK entrepreneur, the new company had shown interest in setting up integrated iron and steel plants in India. Tata Steel is considered the lowest-cost producer in the world but it felt threatened by such industry-wide consolidation. Mittal–Arcelor production capacity is much higher than Tata Steel's and its entry into the Indian market could reduce its costs, thus eroding Tata Steel's competitive advantage. For years, Tata Steel has been growing its capacity through acquisitions. In 2004 it purchased Singapore's NatSteel and the following year Thailand's Millennium Steel. Its biggest acquisition, however, came at the heels of Mittal's acquisition of Arcelor. In 2007 Tata Steel beat a Brazilian company to purchase Corus, an Anglo-Dutch steel maker that was much larger than itself. The price was $12 billion, the largest outward foreign acquisition by an Indian firm. Together, the new company is the world's fifth-largest steel producer, though, notably, it is still smaller than Mittal–Arcelor.

In the automotive sector, Tata chose not to partner up with a foreign company to produce passenger cars. The company's strategy is to create a cheap, functional car for the large untapped markets of developing nations and use that as a stepping stone for markets in developed countries. In 1988, Tata Motors launched the Indica, and in 2005 the car was retailing at $7,000. Not cheap enough. The company then developed the Ace, a small car that turned profitable rather quickly, covering its developing costs within a year of its release. The car cannot be exported to developed countries because of safety and emission regulations. If all goes well Tata Motors will start production of a $3,000 car. However, it is not going at it alone. In 2004 it purchased Daewoo's Commercial Vehicles of South Korea and in 2008 it bought up Jaguar and Rover from Ford Motor for a price of about $2.3 billion. This will infuse the company with the knowledge, technology, and capacity to carve itself a new and more upmarket niche in the automobile world market.

Tata companies might have the highest profile, but they are hardly the only ambitious Indian companies expanding overseas. In the first three quarters for 2006, Indian companies made 115 foreign acquisitions for a total value of $7.4 billion. Almost as many as foreign companies have invested in Indian companies. Over the past few years, Wipro, an IT company, has purchased companies in Portugal, Finland, and California. Ranbaxy, a maker or generic drugs, purchased Etimed of Belgium and Munogen of Spain, the generics arm of GlaxoSmithKline. This foreign expansion is being driven by strong balance sheets due to a domestic boom in India, the availability of credit, and a capable and ambitious group of entrepreneurs with a new-found confidence.

In summary, with total group revenue of $70.9 billion and about 100 companies, the Tata Group is the largest publicly traded company in India. Highly diversified, the conglomerate produces steel, cars, tea, and chemicals, and provides a series of services, including hotels, consulting, and telecommunications. Most of its operations are in its home market of India, where it derives about two-thirds of its total revenues, but it has recently aggressively increased its international presence to access the triad markets of Europe and North America, in addition to its presence in Asia.

Sources: Adapted from *Wall Street Journal*, August 27, 2007, p. A6; BBC News; *Financial Times*, various pages; "Steel Logic," *The Economist*, October 6, 2006; "Circle the Wagons," *The Economist*, October 12, 2006; "What is next for Tata Group?" *Forbes.com*, October 31, 2005; Eric Ellis, "Tata Steels Itself for Change," April 21, 2002; www.thebostonchannel.com/automotive/16456794/detail.htm; Annual Reports of the company, www.tata.com.

have examined the roles of importing, exporting, and FDI in international business, as well as discussing some of the things that MNEs have to do in order to create sustainable competitive advantage. Here are an additional three examples of how multinationals are using some of these ideas in their operations.

Volkswagen

Volkswagen (VW) is well known in the auto market, although like most MNEs it does much better in its regional market (Europe, where it has 71.41 percent of its sales in 2009) than it does in other areas of the triad. North America, VW's second-largest market, accounts for just 10.83 percent of total sales. The company's VW and Audi brand groups collectively hold 18.2 percent of the West European new passenger car market and 4.8 percent of the US market. In the past decade VW's market share in both Europe and America has increased because the company has been doing a number of things well. One is the use of innovative design. The top-selling VW brands in the United States, for example, all have innovative features, such that dashboard instruments such as the speedometer and clock light up in red at night, while those items that the driver touches, such as the radio, are backlit in blue. Commenting on these design features, one auto researcher remarked, "It gives the vehicle some soul, which many of VW's competitors lack horribly."[23] A second factor accounting for VW's success is its commitment to using the most efficient technology in building its cars. Its Wolfsburg plant in Germany is one of the most innovative in the world. It has the largest state-of-the-art paint shop in Europe, which uses eco-friendly, water-based paints. A combination of human skill and automation allows VW to design each car to each customer's specifications. Yet VW is not counting on its present achievements in design and production processes to maintain its competitive advantage. It must continuously update these to keep at the top of its game.

Carrefour

Carrefour is the world's second-largest retailer (behind Wal-Mart) and the largest in terms of number of stores and geographic coverage. In 2009, Carrefour had 69 percent of its sales in Europe but it had almost 15,594 stores spread throughout 29 countries on four continents. What makes the company particularly successful is its ability to create a local strategy for each of its units. Carrefour has a knack for designing its stores to meet local tastes. At least 90 percent of the goods that it sells in a store cater to the local market because the company believes that each unit should reflect the image of that country.[24] "You have to adapt your food and other products to the local culture," notes the company's chairman and chief executive officer; and this is done in a wide variety of ways.[25] For example, in Catholic Poland, the latest Carrefour hypermarket has a special religion section featuring Bibles, candles, and primers for children who are preparing for their first communion. In China, where many shoppers are superstitious, the company takes care to ensure that vegetables are chopped vertically—not laterally—so as not to bring bad luck to shoppers. And to make sure that it does not stumble badly by getting into countries where it truly does not know how to do business effectively, the company never sets up operations until it has researched the local market for at least one year so that it familiarizes itself with the customs of doing business there. As a result, while Wal-Mart has had a wide variety of operating problems in markets such as China, Thailand, and Brazil, Carrefour's efforts in these countries have all worked out well.

Kawasaki and Suzuki

Competition in the international motorcycle marketplace today is greater than ever. Japan is a good example. In this market where Honda and Yamaha are the leaders and Kawasaki and Suzuki are the next largest competitors, the four firms have consistently led the world market with their technologically innovative sports bikes. The problem for all four, however, is that the high cost of R&D has resulted in very high prices for their bikes. And to make matters worse, international rivals such as Harley Davidson of the United States, Triumph of the UK, Ducati of Italy, and BMW of Germany have all been aggressively remodeling their own products, improving the quality and specifications of these machines, setting competitive prices, and stepping up their worldwide marketing efforts. To meet these challenges, Kawasaki and Suzuki have now created a strategic alliance.[26] This alliance, the first ever in the Japanese motorcycle industry, breaks the pattern of each company competing fiercely with the other three. In particular, the two firms are going to jointly develop new models and unify their parts procurement and production activities in order to cut costs. They also plan on developing and building off-road motorcycles and high-powered scooters. The alliance could not have come at a better time. Worldwide market demand for motorcycles is poor, and both companies have seen declining sales in all three of their market regions: Asia, Europe, and the United States. However, the biggest competition is in the large-bike market, and Kawasaki and Suzuki intend to bypass this niche and focus instead on small bikes and scooters. The two believe that, if they can produce quality products at a competitive price, they can make major inroads in China. In the past this market has proved very difficult for Japanese motorcycle makers because Chinese companies have been able to pirate copies of their machines and then produce them in their own factories, without fear of any government intervention to stop such practices.[27] Under WTO rules this is something that China will have to do in the future or run the risk of severe economic retaliation. The decision by Kawasaki and Suzuki to form a strategic alliance and focus on China may prove to be a very profitable strategic move.

✔ Active learning check

Review your answer to Active Learning Case question 4 and make any changes you like. Then compare your answer to the one below.

4 **Is the Coca-Cola Company a multinational enterprise? Is it global? Why?**

Coke indeed is an MNE. The firm conducts production and distribution activities in nations other than its home country. And in terms of strategy and management orientation, Coke does three things that illustrate its multinational nature. First, the company modifies its operations to meet local needs. The firm markets on a country-by-country basis. Second, Coke has international partners which help to run the operation and do not report directly to the company on day-to-day matters. Third, the multinational relies heavily on teamwork by all involved parties and, to a large degree, serves more as a coordinator and cheerleader for the product than as an on-site manager.

Coke is a global company. Together, the United States and Canada account for just a third of its revenues. European and Asian operations are just as important for the company. No one region absolutely dominates. Unlike MNEs that depend predominantly on their home market, Coke has a global view and a global strategy.

THE STUDY OF INTERNATIONAL BUSINESS

As you have seen from the material in this chapter, the world of international business is undergoing a number of major changes. Quite clearly, international business is both an interesting and a challenging area! In this book we are going to study what international business is all about and what MNEs are now doing in order to compete effectively. In this section we examine the current state of the field of international business and then discuss the approach that will be used in this book in studying this field.

From general to strategic emphasis

The field of modern international business began to develop in the 1950s. At this time there were not a great number of MNEs and most of them were American. World War II had ended less than a decade before and many nations, including Japan and the European countries, were more concerned with rebuilding than with overseas investing. Early international business textbooks were often written by US professors and offered a general, descriptive approach to the field. There were few international research studies to provide substantive information. International companies that served as teaching examples were often those with international divisions, rather than true MNEs. And professors teaching international business were frequently educated in areas such as economics or general business and relied on an interdisciplinary approach to address the varied needs of the course. (Table 1.4 provides additional comparisons.)

During the 1970s and 1980s the field of international business changed greatly. The economic growth of Europe and Japan, coupled with great strides by newly industrialized countries (NICs), resulted in more and more attention being focused on international business. Professors were now becoming much more research oriented and the number of PhD-granting institutions offering at least a minor in international business began to increase. Articles and books by Canadian, European, and Asian professors started to appear and US research sophistication significantly improved. International economics

Table 1.4 Comparative differences in the study of international business, 1950–2010

Topic	1950–1969	1970–1989	1990–2010
Focus of interest	General information	Functional areas of development	Strategic emphasis
Approach to studying international business	Descriptive	Analytical	Integrative
Method of explanation	Heavily historical	Functional	Multidisciplinary
Research emphasis	Interdisciplinary	More quantitative research methods and overseas travel	Quantitative research methods, overseas travel, and international assignment
Enterprise viewpoint	US enterprises	MNEs	Networks
Countries examined	Industrialized	Industrialized, NICs, and LDCs	Industrialized, NICs, and LDCs
Number of journals	Some	Many	Ever increasing
Journal emphasis	General international topics	Functional	Functional and strategic
Amount of joint research	Some	Much more	Ever increasing

and finance now became primary areas of interest and the general research approach of the 1950s and 1960s was supplanted by more rigorous quantitative and methodological designs. More and more research studies were conducted and the number of journals in the field rose sharply. In the latter part of the 1980s we also saw the beginning of efforts to bring together much of what was happening into a meaningful composite. How could we understand what was going on in the world of international business, when so much seemed to be occurring at the same time? It was becoming evident that many of the developments of the 1970s and 1980s were being studied in too micro a fashion and a more macro approach to the field was needed.

The 1990s saw the emergence of a strategic management focus for drawing together the field of international business. The descriptive ideas of the 1950s and 1960s and the analytical ideas of the 1970s and 1980s were now being combined into an integrative approach. Historical and quantitative research was now being incorporated into models for describing, explaining, and helping predict what was happening in the international business arena. The earlier interdisciplinary and functional approaches were being supplemented by a multidisciplinary approach that drew on information from a wide variety of disciplines that affected international business. New journals in the field were also taking a more strategic management view of developments. This theme of **strategic management**, managerial actions that include strategy formulation, strategy implementation, evaluation, and control, encompasses a wide range of activities, including environmental analysis of external and internal conditions and evaluation of organizational strengths and weaknesses. In this text strategic management will serve as the basis for our overall framework.

Strategic management
Managerial actions that include strategy formulation, strategy implementation, evaluation, and control and encompass a wide range of activities, including environmental analysis of external and internal conditions and evaluation of organizational strengths and weaknesses

FRAMEWORK FOR THIS BOOK

This book employs a strategic management approach to the study of international business. In each chapter we will first study international business concepts and then we will examine how MNEs integrate these concepts into their overall strategy.

There are five major parts in this text. Part One is an introduction and encompasses this chapter and Chapters 2 and 3. The focus of attention in this part of the book is on such areas as imports, exports, FDI, the nature of MNEs, and the role and importance of the triad. Part Two examines the environments of international business with particular attention on international politics, culture, trade, and finance. Part Three focuses on overall international business strategies with a new chapter on Entrepreneurship and Innovation (Chapter 11). Part Four focuses on functional area strategies with particular attention to production strategy, marketing strategy, human resource management strategy, political risk, negotiation strategies, and international financial management and accounting. Part Five looks at the ways in which the information presented thus far in the book is being used by organizations to do business internationally. In this part, specific attention is given to strategic alliances, the flagship framework, and ways of doing business in the EU, Asia, North America, and emerging economies, including China.

Figure 1.1 presents an illustration of the model that will be used throughout this book. The current chapter has set the stage for the study of international business. In Chapter 2 we will examine the key actor on this stage: the MNE.

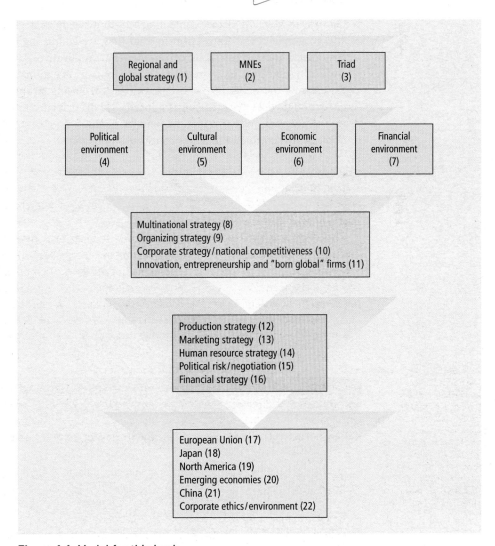

Figure 1.1 Model for this book

KEY POINTS

1 International business is the study of transactions taking place across national borders for the purpose of satisfying the needs of individuals and organizations. Two of the most common types of international business activity are export/import and foreign direct investment (FDI). In recent years both have been on the rise. Much of this is a result of large multinational enterprises (MNEs) that are headquartered in triad countries. In particular, triad members account for most of the worldwide trade and FDI. The majority of trade is intra-regional.

2 Small and medium-sized enterprises (SMEs) often function as the backbone of large MNEs, efficiently providing goods and services that are integrated into the production process of large MNEs. SMEs also compete with MNEs in niche markets.

3 Trade regulation has become an important issue in international business. Today the World Trade Organization is the major group responsible for governing the international trading system.

4 Changes taking place in both communication and production technologies are transforming the way in which MNEs do business.

5 One way in which MNEs are competing is by drawing up strategies that focus on regions and geographic areas, thus ensuring that they are addressing the needs of their local customers. Another way is by continuing to be innovative. A third is by maintaining competitive position by addressing the determinants of national competitive advantage: (a) creating the necessary factor conditions; (b) having strong local demand for the goods and services that are being produced; (c) having related and supporting industries that are internationally competitive; and (d) having a suitable strategy and structure and domestic rivalry that encourages continued innovation.

Key terms

- international business
- multinational enterprise (MNE)
- international trade
- exports
- imports
- foreign direct investment (FDI)
- triad
- North American Free Trade Agreement (NAFTA)
- Organization for Economic Cooperation and Development (OECD)
- World Trade Organization (WTO)
- General Agreement on Tariffs and Trade (GATT)
- small and medium-sized enterprises (SMEs)
- strategic alliance
- factor conditions
- strategic management

REVIEW AND DISCUSSION QUESTIONS

1 What is international business all about? In your answer be sure to include a definition of the term.

2 What are the two primary ways in which world trade is conducted?

3 What does international trade consist of?

4 What is the difference between international business and international trade?

5 Will foreign direct investment increase or decrease in the current decade? Why?

6 How important are the triad areas in promoting international commerce? Explain.

7 What role does the World Trade Organization play in the international business arena? Is the WTO helpful to international trade or is it a hindrance? Why?

8 Multinational enterprises do not formulate worldwide strategies, but rather regional strategies. What does this statement mean and how does it help us better understand international business?

9 How do the four determinants of national competitive advantage help explain how companies can maintain their economic competitiveness? Be complete in your answer.

10 What are two of the advantages associated with using strategic alliances?

REAL CASE

Big oil gets bigger

Between 1998 and 2009 there were a series of mergers in the oil industry that resulted in a handful of private companies emerging as dominant players. In the United States the largest of these was Exxon Mobil, the result of a 1999 merger. In 2009 this company had sales of $284.650 billion (see Table 1).

Table 1 Ranking of oil and gas MNEs, 2010

MNE	Country	Revenue (Millions of US $)
1 Royal Dutch Shell	UK/ the Netherlands	285,129
2 Exxon Mobil	United States	284,650
3 BP	UK	246,138
4 Sinopec	China	187,518
5 China National Petroleum	China	165,496
6 Chevron	United States	163,527
7 Total	France	155,887
8 ConocoPhillips	United States	139,515
9 ENI	Italy	117,235
10 Gazprom	Russia	94,472
11 Petrobras	Brazil	91,869
12 PDVSA	Venezuela	91,182
13 Pemex	Mexico	80,722
14 Statoil	Norway	74,000
15 Valero Energy	United States	70,035

Note: Revenues represent total revenues, including revenues from non-petroleum business.

Sources: Authors' calculations and research and Fortune, *The Fortune Global 500*, July 26, 2010 issue. Data are for 2009.

In Europe mergers and acquisitions had created two dominant firms. Royal Dutch/Shell Group is the largest with $285.129 billion in revenues, overtaking BP. In 2002, Royal Dutch/Shell purchased Pennzoil-Quaker State for $1.8 billion and consistently purchases stakes in other companies. Unlike most of its competitors, however, Royal Dutch has remained clear of any major mergers with competitors and has instead opted to rely on restructuring of its operations to remain competitive.

With $246.138 billion in revenues, the next largest European firm in the oil industry is BP. In 1998 Amoco merged with BP and subsequently the firm acquired a number of other companies, including Arco and Burmah Castrol. However, in 2010, BP had to conduct a massive divestment to raise funds of $30 billion by the end of 2011 to help meet the legal obligations for the environmental clean up arising from the explosion and fire accident on the Deep Horizon Rig in the Gulf of Mexico on April 20, 2010.

The fourth and fifth largest oil firms are Sinopec and China National Petroleum from China.

Texaco and Chevron merged in 2000 creating the world's sixth-largest oil firm. In 2001, Oklahoma-based Phillips Petroleum acquired Tosco, a major oil refiner. Soon after, Phillips merged into Conoco. Conoco Phillips is the world's eighth-largest oil firm, with revenues of $139.515 billion.

The seventh-largest firm in the industry is French-based Total, the result of a merger between Total Fina and Elf in 2000. Today the firm has revenues of $155.887 billion.

This pattern of increasing company size through acquisitions has also been occurring in Asia. In 1999 Nippon Oil bought Mitsubishi Oil, creating Japan's largest oil company. In 2005, Nippon Oil merged with Nippon Petroleum Gas. In 2006 Nippon Oil had revenues of $48.01 billion. In 2008, Nippon Oil conducted a management integration with Kyushu Oil.

Why are these oil companies merging? One of the main reasons is that the maturity of existing oil fields is forcing companies to search for new oil deposits in areas that are not easily accessible. Oil exploration in mountainous

▶

regions, the frigid Arctic, and ocean depths of more than a mile (1.6 km) requires extremely large capital outlays and entails a great deal of risk. In addition, these firms have to invest millions of dollars in research and development and sometimes end up spending years negotiating with governments for the right to drill for oil in the country (or in offshore waters that are controlled by them) and to build refineries and pipelines there. Only large companies with enormous financial resources are able to do this. State-owned oil MNEs are major competitors (see Table 2) and often hold a privileged position when accessing their own country's reserves. Moreover, if a company has a major oil strike, it has to be able to take advantage of economies of scale in order to bring the oil to market at competitive prices. Again, this development favors large firms. This is why experts in the energy business predict that there will be continual mergers and acquisitions in the industry as the large firms jockey for position and acquire smaller rivals and others in complementary businesses such as chemicals and oil-related products.

Websites: www.shell.com; www.exxon.com; www.bp.com; www.total.com; www.chevron.com; www.eni.it; www.repsol-ypf.com; www.marathon.com; www.conoco.com; www.sk.com; www.nmoc.co.jp; www.phillips66.com; www.saudiaramco.com; www.pdvsa.com; www.sinopec.com.cn; www.petrobras.com.br; www.statoil.com; www.iocl.com.

Sources: Adapted from annual reports; "The Fortune Global 500," *Forbes*, July 26, 2010; "In Praise of Big Oil," *The Economist*, October 19, 2000; "ChevronTexaco Merger Approved by US Regulator," BBC.co.uk, September 7, 2001;" BP To Sell $1.8bn Assets to Help Pay for Oil Spill Bill," BBC.co.uk, October 18, 2010.

Table 2 The largest state-owned oil MNEs, 2010

MNE	Country	Revenue (Millions of US $)
1 Sinopec	China	187,518
2 China National Petroleum	China	165,496
3 Petrobras	Brazil	91,869
4 PDVSA	Venezuela	91,182
5 Pemex	Mexico	80,722
6 Statoil	Norway	74,000
7 Petronas	Malaysia	62,577
8 Indian Oil	India	54,288

Sources: Authors' calculations and research and Fortune, *Fortune*, The Global 500, July 26, 2010 issue. Data are for 2009.

1 Are companies such as Exxon Mobil, BP Amoco, and Royal Dutch/Shell MNEs? What criteria do they meet that makes them MNEs?

2 How important is an understanding of governmental regulation to success in this industry?

3 In terms of Porter's determinants of national competitive advantage, which one of these four determinants is most important for these oil companies? Why?

REAL CASE

Wal-Mart

In 2001, Wal-Mart became the world's biggest company in terms of sales revenues, a title it has kept to date, a breath-taking achievement for the company that Sam Walton started in Arkansas as recently as 1962. Indeed, with revenues of $408.214 billion for the year ending in 2009, Wal-Mart is now ahead of General Motors and Exxon Mobil. The second-largest retailer, Carrefour with revenues of $121.452, is only about one-fourth the size of Wal-Mart.

Wal-Mart's success can be attributed to a scale strategy based on reduction of costs to steadily generate its "always low prices" formula and physical growth or market coverage. The United States offers the perfect landscape for Wal-Mart's expansion. Large, wealthy suburbs with vast, inexpensive land allow the firm to set up huge warehouse-style retail centers, reducing overall prices.

This is complemented by an entrepreneurial culture in which store managers have a lot of decision-making power. Wal-Mart pushes its suppliers to provide the best product they can at the lowest possible price, making its products of better quality than those of other discount stores.

Presently, Wal-Mart commands an 8 percent share of the retail sales in its home market and its growth shows no signs of slowing down any time soon. The firm's critics accuse it of exploiting its workers, destroying traditional retail stores, and eroding the manufacturing industry by importing from countries with low labor costs, among other things. Even those who sympathize with objectors, however, might not resist saving $100 for an appliance. The criticism can be argued both ways. Some traditional retail stores suffered as a result of Wal-Mart's expansion, but if Wal-Mart sets up shop in a run-down mall, neighboring stores benefit from the increased traffic. This might include dollar-stores, haircutting places, and sportswear outlets, among others. Wal-Mart's bicycle section falls short of offering all the equipment, not to mention the service, of a traditional bicycle store. A mother buying her daughter her first bicycle might go to Wal-Mart, but a young woman looking for quality, accessories, service, and a knowledgeable salesperson might instead visit her local bike store. The same can be said for most product sections within the store. Large competitors have either stopped competing with Wal-Mart or sought to beat it at its own game. Indeed, Wal-Mart may be responsible for a more consumer-oriented retail service sector in the United States.

One main criticism of Wal-Mart is its dependence on imports from low-cost countries such as China. In 2003, the firm purchased approximately $15 billion in Chinese products, a fraction of revenues perhaps, but a sizeable amount just above the total revenues of McDonald's for the same year. Here, Wal-Mart had done nothing more than take advantage of the opportunities, available to all US retailers, that arose from the liberalization of China.

Those things that have helped Wal-Mart grow might be the same things that eventually will halt its growth. Low-cost laborers have a higher turnover. The firm hires approximately 600,000 new employees a year, and if it wants to reduce the costs of searching for personnel and training them, it might find that increased salaries and benefits are its only alternative. The firm has been constantly lowering the prices of its products, but this too will come to a stop when it exploits all available opportunities in low-cost areas and as China begins to see its production costs increase in the face of development. Finally, the entrepreneurial nature of Wal-Mart's decentralized business structure has meant that the organization lacks a coordinated bureaucracy with the power to impose corporate rules on store managers. For that reason, the firm is now being plagued with lawsuits, including a class action suit by its female employees for gender discrimination.

For future long-term growth, Wal-Mart has looked beyond its borders. However, while it has done extremely well in Canada, Mexico, and the UK, it has had a rough time in other markets, including Germany, Japan and Korea.

Wal-Mart's international expansion began in 1992 when it entered into a joint venture with Cifra SA, a successful Mexican retailer, in which it held 50 percent interest in its partner's retail operations. In 1998, Wal-Mart acquired a controlling interest in Cifra and officially changed the company's name to Wal-Mart of Mexico in 2000. Wal-Mart entered Canada in 1994 when it acquired 122 Woolco stores. Since then, the firm has established itself successfully in the markets of its NAFTA partners. One reason for this success is that it can rely on suppliers for its US stores to deliver products for the Canadian and Mexican market.

In addition, the landscape, culture, and economic situation in Canada are much like in the United States.

The group entered Europe in the late 1990s, by purchasing the Wertkauf and Interspar supermarkets in Germany. Here, Wal-Mart ran into some trouble. Competitors in Europe had emulated the company's most successful strategies in cost reduction and supply-chain management, reducing Wal-Mart's relative competitive advantage. In Germany, local competitors offer very low prices, and Wal-Mart is not big enough to achieve the local economies of scale required to compete on price alone. There was also a different cost structure. Real estate development, when possible, was more costly and wages were also higher. The scale effect does not work in Europe. When the company must source 90 percent of its goods locally, which bargain or logistics savings can it cash in with so few stores? To top it all, Wal-Mart's US managers had problems adapting to the culture and did not speak German.

Wal-Mart entered the British market by acquiring ASDA and retained the name. ASDA had already adopted a focus on low prices and so it had exactly the type of consumer that Wal-Mart was looking for. Even though it has done relatively well in England, a low-cost strategy was secondary to developing long-term relationships with suppliers of well-known, quality-oriented, differentiated brands.

Wal-Mart launched its first store in South Korea in 1998, but in 2005, it ranked bottom of the nation's five discount store chains. Wal-Mart lost about 9.9 billion won in 2005 from its business in Korea, on sales of 750 billion won. In 2006, Wal-Mart pulled out of South Korea—selling its 16 Korean stores to the country's biggest discount chain. Shinsegae paid 825 billion won ($882 million) for Wal-Mart's South Korean operations.

Time, patient investment, and key expertise in each foreign market may help Wal-Mart to successfully expand its international operations to become a more international player. Until then, however, the firm remains extremely NAFTA focused.

Website: www.walmart.com

Sources: Adapted from www.walmart.com; Wal-Mart, *Annual Report 2002 and 2009*; *Fortune*, The Fortune Global 500, July 2002; Alan M. Rugman and Stephane Girod, "Retail Multinationals and Globalization: The Evidence Is Regional," *European Management Journal*, 21, no. 1 (2003), pp. 24–37; "How Big Can It Grow?" *The Economist*, April 15, 2004; 'Wal-Mart to Exit from South Korea," BBC.co.uk, May, 22, 2006; "Fortune Global 500," *Fortune*, July 26, 2010 issue.

1 Is Wal-Mart a multinational enterprise? Why?

2 Why is Wal-Mart making foreign direct investments in Europe?

3 Using the Porter model, what are the determinants of Wal-Mart's competitive advantage?

4 Is Wal-Mart's competitiveness in Europe dependent on the same determinants listed in question 3? Why?

ENDNOTES

1 Alan M. Rugman, *The End of Globalization* (London: Random House, 2000).

2 Michael E. Porter, "The Competitive Advantage of Nations," *Harvard Business Review*, March/April 1990, pp. 80–81.

3 United Nations, *World Investment Report 2007* (Geneva: UNCTAD, 2007) stated that there over 60,000 MNEs in the world. But most of them are small companies. The largest 500 MNEs account for over 80 percent of all the sales of the MNEs. We focus on the 500 MNEs in this book.

4 See Alan M. Rugman, *The End of Globalization* (London: Random House, 2000), Chapter 7, pp. 120–137. These data were for 1999 and have been updated for this book using the same sources.

5 Ibid. Chapter 7, pp. 120–129. These data were for 1999 and have been updated to 2009 for this book using the same sources.

6 Ibid. Chapter 7, pp. 120, 134–136. These data were for 1999 and have been updated to 2009 for this book using the same sources.

7 GDP is at purchasing power parity. CIA, *The World Factbook 2010*. www.cia.gov.

8 Nancy Dunne, "US Sends Top Official to Help Solve Trade Dispute," *FT.com*, November 27, 2001; United States Department of Agriculture, "U.S. and Cooperating Countries File WTO Case Against the EU Moratorium on Biotech Foods and Crops," *USDA News Release*, May 13, 2003; Jagdish Bhagwati, "The Unwinnable War," *FT.com*, January 29, 2002; "EU Hits Back Against US Steel Duties," *BBC News*, March 7, 2002; Andrew Walker, "EU Says Science Backs Its Beef Ban," *BBC News*, October 15, 2003.

9 EUROSTAT, Number of Mobile Phone Subscriptions (1000), http://epp.eurostat.ec.europa.eu "International Roaming," *Press Release*, July 26, 2004.

10 International Telecommunications Union, www.itu.int. The World in 2010: ICT Facts and Figures.

11 Richard M. Hodgetts, *Measures of Quality and High Performance* (New York: American Management Association, 1998).

12 Debby Arkell, "Better, Faster, Cheaper—But Most of All, Better," *Boeing Frontiers*, vol. 2, no. 3, July 2003.

13 Also see Paul Ellis and Anthony Pecotich, "Social Factors Influencing Export Initiation in Small and Medium-Sized Enterprises," *Journal of Marketing Research*, February 2001, pp. 119–130.

14 UNCTAD, *World Investment Report 2003* (New York: United Nations, 2003).

15 Alan Rugman and Richard Hodgetts, "The End of Global Strategy," *European Management Journal*, August 2001, pp. 333–343.

16 Alan M. Rugman, *The Regional Multinationals* (Cambridge: Cambridge University Press, 2005).

17 Dan Lienert, "The Best-Selling Cars," *Forbes*, August 2, 2004.

18 Rugman, op. cit. (2005).

19 IMD, World Competitiveness Yearbook, 2010.

20 The following section is based on Michael Porter, *The Competitive Advantage of Nations* (New York: Free Press, Macmillan, 1990), especially Chapters 3 and 4.

21 Michael E. Porter, "The Competitive Advantage of Nations," *Harvard Business Review*, March/April 1990, pp. 80–81.

22 Porter, ibid., p. 83.

23 Christine Tierney et al., "Volkswagen," *Business Week*, July 23, 2001, p. 64.

24 Sarah Ellison, "Carrefour and Ahold Find Shoppers Like to Think Local," *Wall Street Journal*, August 31, 2001, p. A5.

25 Richard Tomlinson, "Who's Afraid of Wal-Mart?" *Fortune*, June 26, 2000, p. 188.

26 David Ibison and Rpohit Jaggi, "Kawasaki Joins Suzuki in Search of an Easier Ride," *Financial Times*, August 30, 2001, p. 15.

27 "Kawasaki and Suzuki Join Forces," *BBC News*, August 29, 2001.

ADDITIONAL BIBLIOGRAPHY

Boddewyn, Jean J., Toyne, Brian and Martinez, Zaida L. "The Meanings of 'International Management'," *Management International Review*, vol. 44, no. 2 (Second Quarter 2004).

Collinson, Simon and Rugman, Alan, M. "Case Selection Biases in Management Research: Implications for International Business Studies," *European Journal of International Management*, vol. 4, no. 5 (2010).

Dicken, Peter. "*Global Shift*", 6th Edition (London: Sage, 2011).

Dunning, John H. "The Study of International Business: A Plea for a More Interdisciplinary Approach," *Journal of International Business Studies*, vol. 20, no. 3 (Fall 1989).

Forsgren, Mats and Yamin, Mo, "A Commentary on Adam Smith and International Business," *Multinational Business Review*, vol. 18, no. 1 (2010).

Fruin, W. Mark. "Bringing the World (Back) into International Business," *Journal of International Business Studies*, vol. 38, no. 2 (March 2007).

Ghemawat, Pankaj. "Distance Still Matters: The Hard Reality of Global Expansion," *Harvard Business Review*, vol. 79, no. 8 (September 2001).

Ghemawat, Pankaj. *Redefining Global Strategy: Crossing Borders in a World Where Differences Still Matter* (Harvard Business School: Harvard Business School Press, 2007).

Girod, Stéphane J.G. and Rugman, Alan M. "Regional Business Networks and the Multinational Retail Sector," *Long Range Planning*, vol. 38, no. 4 (August 2005).

Jones, Geoffrey and Khanna, Tarun. "Bringing History (Back) into International Business," *Journal of International Business Studies*, vol. 37, no. 4 (July 2006).

Morck, Randall and Yeung, Bernard. "History in Perspective: Comment on Jones and Khanna 'Bringing History (Back) into International Business'," *Journal of International Business Studies*, vol. 38, no. 2 (March 2007).

Porter, Michael E. *The Competitive Advantage of Nations* (New York: Free Press, Macmillan, 1990).

Rugman, Alan M. *Inside the Multinationals: The Economics of Internal Markets* (New York: Columbia University Press, 1981).

Rugman, Alan M. *Rugman Reviews International Business* (Basingstoke: Palgrave Macmillan, 2009).

Rugman, Alan M. "The International Financial Crisis and Multinational Enterprise Strategy," *Transnational Corporation*, forthcoming (2011).

Rugman, Alan M. and Girod, Stéphane. "Retail Multinationals and Globalization: The Evidence is Regional," *European Management Journal*, vol. 21, no. 1 (2003).

Rugman, Alan M. and Verbeke, Alain. "A New Perspective on the Regional and Global Strategies of Multinational Service Firms," *Management International Review*, vol. 48, no. 4 (2008).

Rugman, Alan M., Verbeke, Alain and Nguyen, Quyen T.K. (2011). "Fifty Years of International Business Theory and Beyond," *Management International Review*, vol. 51, no. 6 (November 2011).

Yip, George S. *Total Global Strategy 2* (Upper Saddle River, NJ: Prentice Hall, 2002).

APPENDIX TO CHAPTER 1

Table 1A The top 25 importers in the world, 2008

Rank	Country	Value of world imports (billions of US $)
1	United States	2,166.0
2	China, PR	1,526.3
3	Germany	1,204.8
4	Japan	761.8
5	France	706.7
6	UK	634.8
7	Netherlands	581.6
8	Italy	556.3
9	Belgium	470.2
10	Korea	435.2
11	Canada	408.2
12	Spain	403.0
13	Singapore	319.7
14	India	315.1
15	Mexico	308.6
16	Russia	266.9
17	Brazil	208.9
18	Poland	205.1
19	Turkey	201.9
20	United Arab Emirates	196.6
21	Australia	191.9
22	Austria	184.5
23	Switzerland	183.0
24	Thailand	178.5
25	Sweden	167.6

Note: China includes mainland China, Hong Kong, and Macao.

Source: Adapted from the individual country sections of the International Monetary Fund, *Direction of Trade Statistics Yearbook, 2009* (Washington, DC: IMF, September 2009).

Table 1B The top 25 exporters in the world, 2008

Rank	Country	Value of world exports (billions of US $)
1	China, PR	1,794.0
2	Germany	1,465.1
3	United States	1,300.0
4	Japan	783.1
5	France	606.6
6	Netherlands	638.6
7	UK	461.0
8	Italy	539.9
9	Belgium	477.1
10	Russia	459.7
11	Canada	456.5
12	Korea	426.7
13	Singapore	399.4
14	Saudi Arabia	303.9
15	Mexico	291.3
16	Spain	267.5
17	Brazil	202.5
18	Switzerland	200.0
19	Malaysia	199.5
20	India	198.2
21	Australia	185.6
22	United Arab Emirates	185.0
23	Sweden	184.0
24	Austria	181.7
25	Thailand	173.2

Note: China includes mainland China, Hong Kong, and Macao.

Source: Adapted from the individual country sections of the International Monetary Fund, *Direction of Trade Statistics Yearbook, 2009* (Washington, DC: IMF, September 2009).

Table 1C Inward stocks of world foreign direct investment, 2008 (by US$ size ranking)

Country/region	2000 (millions of US $)	% of total	2008 (millions of US $)	% of total
Developed countries	3,960,321	68.79	10,212,893	68.50
Europe	2,281,563	39.63	6,932,525	46.50
EU				
France	259,775	4.51	991,377	6.65
United Kingdom	438,631	7.62	982,877	6.59
Germany	271,611	4.72	700,471	4.70
Netherlands	243,733	4.23	644,598	4.32
Spain	156,348	2.72	634,788	4.26
Belgium	—	—	518,940	3.48
Italy	121,170	2.10	343,215	2.30
Sweden	93,995	1.63	253,502	1.70
Ireland	127,089	2.21	173,420	1.16
Poland	34,227	0.59	161,406	1.08
Denmark	45,916	0.80	150,492	1.01
Austria	31,165	0.54	139,340	0.93
Czech Republic	21,644	0.38	114,369	0.77
Portugal	32,043	0.56	99,820	0.67
Finland	24,273	0.42	87,860	0.59
Luxembourg	23,492	0.41	85,353	0.57
Hungary	22,870	0.40	63,671	0.43
Slovakia	4,746	0.08	45,933	0.31
Greece	14,113	0.25	36,703	0.25
Cyprus	2,910	0.05	20,706	0.14
Estonia	2,645	0.05	15,962	0.11
Slovenia	2,894	0.05	15,782	0.11
Lithuania	2,334	0.04	12,847	0.09
Latvia	2,084	0.04	11,447	0.08
Malta	2263	0.04	9,142	0.06
Belgium/Luxembourg	195,219	3.39	—	—
Other developed Europe	118,209	2.05	500,632	3.36
Switzerland	86,804	1.51	374,054	2.51
Norway	30,265	0.53	121,521	0.82
Others	1,140	0.02	5,057	0.03
North America	1,469,583	25.53	2,691,160	18.05
United States	1,256,867	21.83	2,278,892	15.29
Canada	212,716	3.69	412,268	2.77
Other developed countries	209,175	3.63	589,207	3.95
Australia	111,139	1.93	272,174	1.83
Japan	50,322	0.87	203,372	1.36
Others	47,714	0.83	113,661	0.76
Developing countries	1,736,167	30.16	4,275,982	28.68
Africa	154,244	2.68	510,511	3.42
Asia and Oceania	1,079,436	18.75	2,583,855	17.33
Latin America and the Caribbean	502,487	8.73	1,181,615	7.93
South East Europe and CIS	60,873	1.06	420,414	2.82
South-East Europe				
Total	5,757,360	100.00	14,909,289	100.00
Least developed countries	39,061	0.68	136,167	0.91

Note: Numbers might not add up due to rounding.

Source: Authors' calculations and ranking by US$ size and United Nations, *World Investment Report*, 2009, pp. 251–254.

Table 1D Outward stocks of world foreign direct investment, 2008 (by US$ size ranking)

Country/region	2000 (millions of US $)	% of total	2008 (millions of US $)	% of total
Developed countries	5,186,178	85.44	13,623,626	84.06
Europe	3,250,775	53.55	8,997,437	55.52
EU				
United Kingdom	897,845	14.79	1,510,593	9.32
Germany	541,861	8.92	1,450,910	8.95
France	445,091	7.33	1,396,997	8.62
Netherlands	305,461	5.03	843,737	5.20
Spain	129,194	2.12	601,849	3.71
Belgium	—	—	588,269	3.63
Italy	180,275	2.96	517,051	3.19
Sweden	123,256	2.03	319,310	1.97
Denmark	44,981	0.74	192,523	1.18
Ireland	27,925	0.46	159,363	0.98
Austria	24,821	0.40	152,562	0.94
Finland	52,109	0.85	114,526	0.71
Portugal	19,793	0.32	63,642	0.39
Luxembourg	7,927	0.13	62,664	0.38
Greece	6,094	0.10	32,441	0.20
Poland	1,018	0.01	21,814	0.13
Hungary	1,280	0.02	14,179	0.08
Cyprus	560	0.01	10,493	0.06
Czech Republic	738	0.01	9,913	0.06
Slovenia	768	0.01	8,650	0.05
Estonia	259	0.01	6,686	0.04
Lithuania	29	0.00	1,990	0.01
Slovakia	373	0.01	1,901	0.01
Malta	193	0.00	1,517	0.01
Latvia	24	0.00	1,066	0.01
Belgium/Luxembourg	179,773	2.96	—	—
Other developed Europe	266,850	4.39	910,633	5.61
Switzerland	232,161	3.82	724,687	4.47
Norway	34,026	0.56	171,164	1.05
Others	663	0.01	14,782	0.09
North America	1,553,886	25.59	3,682,420	22.72
United States	1,316,247	21.68	3,162,021	19.51
Canada	237,639	3.91	520,399	3.21
Other developed countries	381,518	6.28	943,768	5.82
Japan	278,442	4.58	68,033	4.19
Australia	85,385	1.40	194,721	1.20
Others	17,691	0.29	68,716	0.42
Developing countries	862,358	14.20	2,356,649	14.54
Africa	44,155	0.72	97,958	0.60
Asia and Oceania	613,815	10.11	1,697,259	10.47
Latin America and the Caribbean	204,388	3.36	561,432	3.46
South East Europe and CIS	21,345	0.35	225,387	1.39
South-East Europe				
Total	6,069,882	100.00	16,205,663	100.00
Least developed countries	3,172	0.05	10,284	0.06

Note: Numbers might not add up due to rounding.

Source: Authors' calculations and ranking by US$ size and United Nations, *World Investment Report,* 2009, pp. 251–254.

Chapter 2

THE MULTINATIONAL ENTERPRISE

Contents

Objectives of the chapter

Most of the best-known companies in the world are multinational enterprises, and many of their names are easily recognized because their products and services are so popular. This is true for US multinational enterprises, such as General Electric, Exxon Mobil, and Ford, but for others as well. Consider, for example, some of the largest industrial multinationals headquartered in the European Union: Unilever (UK/Netherlands), Fiat (Italy), Nokia (Finland), Volkswagen (Germany), Philips (Netherlands), and Peugeot (France); and in Japan: Sony, Fuji, and Toyota. There are also MNEs from non-triad areas such as Sinopec (China), Samsung (South Korea), Codelco (Chile), AngloGold (South Africa), and Bombardier (Canada). The primary objective of this chapter is to examine the nature and operations of multinational enterprises.

The specific objectives of this chapter are to:

1 *Describe* the characteristics of multinational enterprises.

2 *Explain* the internationalization process.

3 *Explain* why firms become multinational enterprises.

4 *Discuss* the strategic philosophy of these firms.

5 *Introduce* a country/firm framework for examining a firm's competitiveness.

6 *Study* some of the ways in which these firms use strategic management.

Disneyland in Europe

Between 1988 and 1990 three $150 million amusement parks opened in France. By 1991 two of them were bankrupt and the third was doing poorly. Despite this, the Walt Disney Company went ahead with a plan to open Europe's first Disneyland in 1992. Far from being concerned about the theme park doing well, Disney executives were worried that Euro Disneyland would be too small to handle the giant crowds. The $4.4 billion project was to be located on 5,000 acres in Seine-et-Marne, 20 miles (32 km) east of Paris. And the city seemed to be an excellent location; there were 17 million people within a two-hour drive of Euro Disneyland, 41 million within a four-hour drive, and 109 million within six hours of the park. This included people from seven countries: France, Switzerland, Germany, Luxembourg, the Netherlands, Belgium, and the UK.

Disney officials were optimistic about the project. Their US parks, Disneyland and Disneyworld, were extremely successful, and Tokyo Disneyland was so popular that on some days it could not accommodate the large number of visitors. Simply put, the company was making a great deal of money from its parks. However, the Tokyo park was franchised to others—and Disney management felt that it had given up too much profit with this arrangement. This would not be the case at Euro Disneyland. The company's share of the venture was to be 49 percent for which it would put up $160 million. Other investors put in $1.2 billion, the French government provided a low-interest $900 million loan, banks loaned the business $1.6 billion, and the remaining $400 million was to come from special partnerships formed to buy properties and to lease them back. For its investment and management of the operation, the Walt Disney Company was to receive 10 percent of Euro Disney's admission fees, 5 percent of food and merchandise revenues, and 49 percent of all profits.

The location of the amusement park was thoroughly researched. The number of people who could be attracted to various locations throughout Europe and the amount of money they were likely to spend during a visit to the park were carefully calculated. In the end, France and Spain had proved to offer the best locations. Both countries were well aware of the park's capability for creating jobs and stimulating their economy. As a result, each actively wooed the company. In addition to offering a central location in the heart of Europe, France was prepared to provide considerable financial incentives. Among other things, the French government promised to build a train line to connect the amusement park to the European train system.

Thus after carefully comparing the advantages offered by both countries, France was chosen as the site for the park.

At first things appeared to be off to a roaring start. Unfortunately, by the time the park was ready to open, a number of problems had developed, and some of these had a very dampening effect on early operations. One was the concern of some French people that Euro Disney was nothing more than a transplanting of Disneyland into Europe. In their view the park did not fit into the local culture, and some of the French press accused Disney of "cultural imperialism." Others objected to the fact that the French government, as promised in the contract, had expropriated the necessary land and sold it without profit to the Euro Disneyland development people. Signs reading "Don't gnaw away our national wealth" and "Disney go home" began appearing along roadways. These negative feelings may well have accounted for the fact that on opening day only 50,000 visitors showed up, in contrast to the 500,000 that were expected. Soon thereafter, operations at the park came under criticism from both visitors and employees. Many visitors were upset about the high prices. In the case of British tourists, for example, because of the franc exchange rate, it was cheaper for them to go to Florida than to Euro Disney. In the case of employees, many of them objected to the pay rates and the working conditions. They also raised concerns about a variety of company policies ranging from personal grooming to having to speak English in meetings, even if most people in attendance spoke French. Within the first month 3,000 employees quit. Some of the other operating problems were a result of Disney's previous experiences. In the United States, for example, liquor was not sold outside of the hotels or specific areas. The general park was kept alcohol free, including the restaurants, in order to maintain a family atmosphere. In Japan, this policy was accepted and worked very well. However, Europeans were used to having outings with alcoholic beverages. As a result of these types of problems, Euro Disney soon ran into financial problems.

In 1994, after three years of heavy losses, the operation was in such bad shape that some people were predicting that the park would close. However, a variety of developments saved the operation. For one thing, a major investor purchased 24.6 percent (reducing Disney's share to 39 percent) of the company, injecting $500 million of much needed cash. Additionally, Disney waived its royalty fees and worked out a new loan repayment plan with the banks, and new shares were issued. These measures allowed Euro Disney ▶

to buy time while it restructured its marketing and general policies to fit the European market.

In October 1994, Euro Disney officially changed its name to "Disneyland Paris." This made the park more French and permitted it to capitalize on the romanticism that the word "Paris" conveys. Most importantly, the new name allowed for a new beginning, disassociating the park from the failure of Euro Disney. This was accompanied with measures designed to remedy past failures. The park changed its most offensive labor rules, reduced prices, and began being more culturally conscious. Among other things, alcoholic beverages were now allowed to be served just about anywhere.

The company also began making the park more appealing to local visitors by giving it a "European" focus: 92 percent of the park's visitors are from eight nearby European countries. Disney Tomorrowland, with its dated images of the space age, was jettisoned entirely and replaced by a gleaming brass and wood complex called Discoveryland, which was based on themes of Jules Verne and Leonardo da Vinci. In Disneyland food services were designed to reflect the fable's country of origin: Pinocchio's facility served German food, Cinderella's had French offerings, and at Bella Notte's the cuisine was Italian. The company also shot a 360-degree movie about French culture and showed it in the "Visionarium" exhibit.

These changes were designed to draw more visitors, and they seemed to have worked. Disneyland Paris reported a slight profit in 1996, and the park continued to make a modest profit through to the early 2000s. In 2002 and 2003, the company was once again making losses, and new deals had to be worked out with creditors. This time, however, it wasn't insensitivity to local customs but a slump in the travel and tourism industry, strikes and stoppages in France, and an economic downturn in many of the surrounding markets.

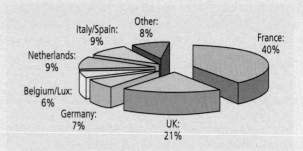

Geographic description of Disneyland Paris visitors, 2002

Source: Adapted from Euro Disney S.C.A., Annual Report, 2002.

Euro Disney has cut its annual losses by 28 percent, despite a fall in visitor numbers to Disneyland Paris. The company that runs the theme park said its net loss for the 12 months to 30 September, 2010 was €45.2m ($62m; £38m), down from €63m a year ago. Euro Disney said that while visitor numbers to Disneyland Paris fell 2.6 percent to 15 million, average spending per tourist rose 2.4 percent to €45.30. Annual revenues at the company were up 4 percent to €1.28bn. Euro Disney is 40 percent owned by Walt Disney, 10 percent by the Saudi royal family, and 50 percent by other shareholders. Philippe Gas, Euro Disney chief executive, said that despite a difficult economic context, Disneyland Paris remained Europe's most popular tourist destination.

Websites: www.disneyinternational.com; www.disneylandparis.com; www.disney.com.

Sources: Adapted from Euro Disney SCA, Annual Report, 2002; "Euro Disney Theme Park Cuts Loss, Shares Fall," Yahoo News: Reuters, April 22, 1998; Paulo Prada, "Euro Disney Does Nicely. So Why Are Investors Grumpy?" Wall Street Journal, September 6, 2000, p. A20; "Disneyland Paris Cuts Losses Despite Fewer Visitors," BBC Online, http://www.bbc.co.uk/news/business-11726261, November 10, 2010.

---

1 What are some of the characteristics of multinational enterprises that are displayed by the Walt Disney Company?

2 Why did Disney take an ownership position in the firm rather than simply licensing some other firm to build and operate the park and settling for a royalty on all sales?

3 In what way did Euro Disney reflect the strategic philosophy of Walt Disney as a multinational enterprise?

4 Did Disney management conduct an external environmental analysis before going forward with Euro Disney? Explain.

Multinational enterprise (MNE)
A company headquartered in one country but having operations in other countries

INTRODUCTION

A **multinational enterprise (MNE)** is a company that is headquartered in one country but has operations in one or more other countries. Sometimes it is difficult to know if a firm is an MNE because multinationals often downplay the fact that they are foreign held. For example, many people are unaware that Bayer, the drug company, is German owned; Nestlé, the chocolate manufacturer, is a Swiss company; NEC is Japanese; and Tata of Mumbai, India, now owns Jaguar, the British-based auto maker. Similarly, approximately 25 percent of banks in California are Japanese owned, but this is often not evident from their names. Simply put, many large MNEs have world holdings far beyond what is known to the casual observer. A closer look at these MNEs will reveal the impact they have on international business and the world economy.

THE NATURE OF MNEs

The United Nations has identified over 60,000 MNEs, but the largest 500 account for 80 percent of the world's foreign direct investment.[1] Table 2.1 shows the distribution of the world's largest 500 firms, most of which are MNEs. Of these, 370 are from the core "triad." There are 160 from the EU, 139 from the United States and 71 from Japan. The fact that nearly 80 percent of the world's largest 500 MNEs are from the core triad is highly significant. It means that the triad is the basic unit of analysis for MNE strategy. Also, about 80–85 percent of the world's top MNEs have been from the triad for the past 20–30 years.[2] Total annual sales of these 500 firms are in excess of $23 trillion.[3] These firms are engaged in a wide variety of operations including autos, chemicals, computers, consumer goods, financial services, industrial equipment, and oil and steel production.

The names of the largest triad-based MNEs, as well as those from non-triad countries, are listed in the Appendix, Tables 2A–2D. There are now 73 MNEs from the emerging economies of China, Korea, and India, as well as several others from similar economies. You should become familiar with at least some of these MNEs as we proceed through this book. We provide the websites for all the MNEs we discuss in the cases.

Table 2.1 The world's largest 500 multinational enterprises, 2010 ranking

Economy	Number of MNEs
EU 15	160
United States	139
Japan	71
China	46
Switzerland	15
Canada	11
South Korea	10
Australia	8
India	8
Taiwan (Taiwan Province of China)	8
Brazil	7
Russia	6
Mexico	2
Singapore	2
Malaysia	1
Norway	1
Poland	1
Saudi Arabia	1
Thailand	1
Turkey	1
Venezuela	1
Total	500

Note: Data are for 2009
Source: Authors' calculations and adapted from *Fortune*, "Fortune Global 500," July 26, 2010.

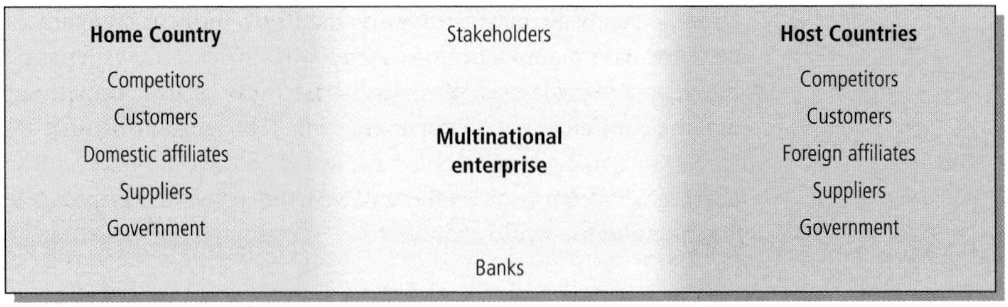

Home Country	Stakeholders	Host Countries
Competitors		Competitors
Customers		Customers
Domestic affiliates	**Multinational enterprise**	Foreign affiliates
Suppliers		Suppliers
Government		Government
	Banks	

Figure 2.1 The multinational enterprise and its environment

Characteristics of MNEs

One way of identifying the characteristics of MNEs is by looking at the environment in which they operate. Figure 2.1 shows some of the major forces in this environment. Notice that an MNE has two major areas of concern: the home country of its headquarters and the host countries in which it does business. Stakeholders are not included within these two areas of Figure 2.1 because they can come from anywhere in the world. For example, an investor in Switzerland can purchase stock in Sears Roebuck even though the company does not do business in Switzerland.

One characteristic of MNEs is that their affiliates must be responsive to a number of important environmental forces, including competitors, customers, suppliers, financial institutions, and government (again see Figure 2.1). In some cases the same forces are at work in both the home- and host-country environments. For example, many of Ford's competitors in the US market are the same as those in Europe: Toyota, BMW, Daimler, Honda, and Volkswagen, among others. Similarly, MNEs often use the same suppliers overseas that they employ domestically, and it is common to find home-country-based suppliers following their MNE customer to other geographic locales in order to provide the same types of services worldwide. In other cases, however, these same environmental factors can be very different on each of the markets in which the firm operates.

A second characteristic of an MNE is that it draws on a common pool of resources, including assets, patents, trademarks, information, and human resources. Because the affiliates are all part of the same company, they have access to assets that are often not available to outsiders. For example, both Ford and General Motors compete vigorously in Europe and many of the design and styling changes developed for their European cars have now been introduced in US models. The flow of information and technology between European and US affiliates has led to success in the worldwide market for many MNEs. Similarly, if an affiliate needs expansion funds, an MNE will often help out by working with the affiliate to raise the money. If a loan is needed, the affiliate is likely to find many financial institutions that are willing to provide the money because the MNE will back the loan.

A third characteristic of an MNE is that it links together the affiliates and business partners with a common strategic vision. Simply put, all of the firms with whom the MNE works fit into the company's overall plan of what it wants to do and how it intends to go about implementing this strategy. General Motors (GM) used to be a good example. The auto firm relied heavily on partnerships to help it grow.[4] GM realized that no auto maker has all of the resources for achieving leadership in every region of the world or in every product segment. As a result, the company formed a manufacturing partnership with Toyota to conduct research and development on fuel cell and gas–electric hybrid vehicles. GM also created an alliance with Fuji Heavy Industries and its Subaru brand that allowed GM to benefit from Fuji's strengths in small sport utility vehicles, continuously variable transmissions, and all-wheel-drive systems and, in turn, gave Fuji access to GM's vehicle platforms and other important manufacturing technologies. Today the company has been restructured following its bankruptcy in 2008/9 after the international financial crisis. Part of its failure was its diversification into financing whereby its credit division diverted it from its core business. And its Japanese competitors ended up making better cars—with better quality and lower prices. Today China and India are becoming big players in the car business.

✔ Active learning check

Review your answer to Active Learning Case question 1 and make any changes you like. Then compare your answer to the one below.

1 **What are some of the characteristics of multinational enterprises that are displayed by the Walt Disney Company?**

One of the characteristics of an MNE is that ties of common ownership link affiliated firms. In this case the Walt Disney Company holds a substantial interest in Disneyland Paris, in addition to its ownership of Disneyland and Disneyworld in the United States. A second characteristic is that the MNE draws on a common pool of resources. One way Euro Disney does this is through the use of trademarks and characters (Mickey Mouse, Goofy, Donald Duck) and the experience of the Disney team in setting up and running similar theme parks in the United States. A third characteristic is that MNEs have a common strategy for linking together the affiliates. The Walt Disney Company does this through its overall plan, such as the one it used for deciding where to set up Euro Disney and how to manage the park.

The internationalization process

Not all international business is done by MNEs. Indeed, setting up a wholly owned subsidiary is usually the last stage of doing business abroad, as is shown in Figure 2.2.

Figure 2.2 outlines the typical process by which a firm producing a standardized product will seek to involve itself in a foreign market.[5] This, however, is a generalization as firms ultimately make decisions depending on their particular circumstances. The process we illustrate here, however, is important because it is based on how the firm perceives risk and how it deals with it. In this **internationalization** process the firm regards foreign markets as risky due to the fact that, as these markets are unknown to it, the firm faces export

Internationalization
The process by which a company enters a foreign market

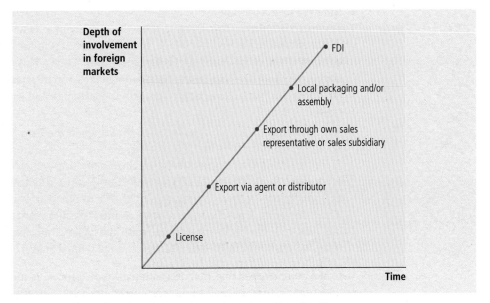

Figure 2.2 Entry into foreign markets: the internationalization process

marketing costs. To avoid such information costs and risk, its strategy is to go abroad at a slow and cautious pace, often using the services of specialists in international trade outside the firm. Over time, familiarity with the foreign environment will reduce the information costs and help to alleviate the perceived risk of foreign involvement. There is a "learning" effect as firms become familiar with a foreign market.[6]

Initially the firm may seek to avoid the risks of foreign involvement by arranging a joint venture or a license. A **license** is a contractual arrangement in which one firm, the **licensor**, provides access to some of its patents, trademarks, or technology to another firm, the **licensee**, in exchange for a fee or royalty. This fee often involves a fixed amount upon signing the contract and then a royalty of 2–5 percent on sales generated by the agreement. A typical licensing contract will run from five to seven years and be renewable at the option of either or both parties. This strategy is most suitable for a standardized product where there is no risk of dissipation of the firm's technological or managerial advantages. Otherwise, licensing will be reserved for a much later stage of entry. Indeed, when it is important for the firm to retain control over its firm-specific advantage in technology (as in internalization theory),[7] licensing will be the last stage of entry. The firms involved in the process of internationalization, on the other hand, typically are not concerned about losing their firm-specific advantages. Rather, they want to avoid exposure to an uncertain foreign environment. Abstracting from the licensing option (and the more complex problem of joint ventures), the major types of foreign entry for a firm are as follows:

1 The firm sees potential extra sales by *exporting* and uses a *local agent or distributor* to enter a particular market. Often the firm uses exporting as a "vent" for its surplus production and may have no long-run commitment to the international market. If it does well abroad, however, it may then set up its own local sales representative or marketing subsidiary, in the hope of securing a more stable stream of export sales.

2 As exports come to represent a larger share of sales, the firm may increase its capacity to serve the export market. It will set an office for its *sales representative* in a major market, or set up a *sales subsidiary*. This stage marks an important departure for the firm from simply viewing exports as a marginal contributor to sales volume or as a vent for surplus in times of excess capacity. At this stage the firm will often set up a separate *export department* to manage foreign sales and production for such markets and product design and the production process itself may be modified to tailor products for export markets.

3 After the firm has become more familiar with the local market, some of the uncertainty associated with foreign involvement has been overcome. Now the firm may begin to move on the foreign production side. Initially it may start to use host-country workers to engage in *local assembly and packaging* of its product lines. This is a crucial step, because the firm is now involved in the host-country factor market and must deal with such environmental variables as wage rates, cultural attitudes, and worker expectations in its new labor force.

4 The final stage of foreign involvement comes when the firm has generated sufficient knowledge about the host country to overcome its perceptions of risk. Because it is more familiar with the host-country environment, it may now consider a *foreign direct investment* (FDI) activity. In this it produces the entire product line in the host nation and sells its output there, or it may even be able to re-export back to the home country. These decisions depend on the relative country-specific costs; for example, if labor is inexpensive in the host nation (as in South-East Asia), more exporting takes place than if it is expensive (as in Western Europe and the United States).

It has become clear that the internationalization process is more complicated than it seems at first glance. Like all generalizations, this schematic path of export commitment

License
A contractual arrangement in which one firm (the licensor) provides access to some of its patents, trademarks, or technology to another firm in exchange for a fee or royalty

Licensor
A company that provides access to some of its patents, trademarks, or technology to another firm in exchange for a fee or royalty

Licensee
A firm given access to some of the patents, trademarks, or technology of another firm in exchange for a fee or royalty

relies on simplifications. In reality, the process of foreign entry is sufficiently complicated to depend on a careful weighing of many firm-specific and country-specific factors. A framework to model these firm-specific advantages (FSAs) and country-specific advantages (CSAs) is developed in the next section.

> ## ✔ Active learning check
>
> *Review your answer to Active Learning Case question 2 and make any changes you like. Then compare your answer to the one below.*
>
> **Why did Disney take an ownership position in the firm rather than simply licensing some other firm to build and operate the park and settling for a royalty on all sales?**
>
> Disney believed that the theme park was too lucrative a venture to settle for just a royalty on sales. The company felt that it would be giving up too much to simply "take the money and run" when by remaining and managing the operation it could garner a great deal more revenue. Moreover, not only is the revenue potential of the park extremely high, but Disney's initial investment of $160 million was extremely low given the amount of control it maintains and the fees and profits that would be generated should the park prove as highly attractive as company executives were forecasting. Disney also wanted to retain control over its brand name products and services in order to prevent imitation by substandard rivals, and this is best done with an ownership position.

Why firms become MNEs

Companies become MNEs for a number of reasons. One is to *diversify* themselves against the risks and uncertainties of the domestic business cycle. By setting up operations in another country, multinationals can often diminish the negative effects of economic swings in the home country. This is a form of international diversification, and it has been widely used by Japanese MNEs, for example, which have found that, while their home economy has been in an economic slump since the 1990s, their US operations have done quite well.

A second reason is to tap the growing world market for goods and services. For example, many MNEs have targeted the United States because of its large population and high per capita income. It is the world's single largest market in terms of gross domestic product. And since Americans have both a desire for new goods and services and the money to buy them, the United States can be an ideal market. MNEs are also targeting China. Although per capita gross domestic product is not very high, the country's large population and growing economy make it very attractive to multinationals. In 2001, China entered the World Trade Organization, and this acceptance of international rules made China more attractive for MNEs.

Firms also become MNEs in response to increased foreign competition and a desire to protect their home market share. Using a *follow the competitor* strategy, a growing number of MNEs now set up operations in the home countries of their major competitors. This approach serves a dual purpose: (1) it takes away business from their competitors by offering customers other choices; and (2) it lets competitors know that, if they attack the MNE's home market, they will face a similar response. This strategy of staking out global market shares is particularly important when MNEs want to communicate the conditions under which they will retaliate.

A fourth reason why companies become an MNE is to reduce costs. By setting up operations close to the foreign customer, these firms can eliminate transportation expenses,

INTERNATIONAL BUSINESS STRATEGY IN ACTION

Italian family firms

In Italy more than 90 percent of all small and medium-sized companies and some of the largest enterprises are family owned. In the fashion industry, for example, Versace, Missoni, and Benetton are family-held firms. In addition, Italian families own important manufacturers and hold operating control of some of the major banks and transportation companies in the country. For example, in 2009, the Fiat SpA Group's annual revenue is €50.102 billion and employs 190,014 people. It does this as a conglomerate consisting of 777 firms with holdings in agricultural and construction equipment, automobiles, aviation, commercial vehicles, communications, insurance services, metallurgical products, production systems, and publishing.

Another large family-owned Italian company is Pirelli &C SpA, which, in 2009, has had annual revenues of over €4.462 billion and employs about 29,570 people. Most of the firm's revenues (82 percent) are generated from its tire and cable businesses. Along with Benetton, Pirelli bought a controlling interest in Olivetti, the giant Italian computer and telecommunications corporation. Through Olimpia, Pirelli has an 18 percent stake in Telecom Italia SpA, a telecommunications, information, and communication technology company with annual revenues of €27.163 billion and a workforce of around 73,533 people in 2009. This acquisition has also brought both Benetton and Pirelli into the wireless telecommunications business.

These two examples, Fiat and Pirelli, are typical of the holdings and influence of large Italian families in the country. Through their vast holdings and political power, they have been able to maintain a tight rein on various sectors of the economy. In addition, these family firms are protected against foreign investment by a secretive banking system that is headed by the Milan Bank, Mediobanca. This bank has financed nearly all of the takeover deals in Italy during the last 35 years. The bank also holds board positions on many of the country's conglomerates.

On a macro basis, the Italian business system reflects the twin pressures of local family culture and the increasing demands of international business. Like their larger counterparts, small and medium-sized family businesses are now using their personal and business networks to create MNEs that are branching out into the EU, as well as putting together deals in both North America and Asia.

Websites: www.olivetti.com; www.versace.com; www.missoni.it; www.benetton.com; www.fiat.com; www.pirelli.com; www.montedison.it; www.mediobanca.it; www.telecomitalia.it.

Sources: Fred Kapner, "Pirelli Seeks Rumour Probe," *Financial Times*, September 11, 2000, p. 18; Paul Meller, "European Panel Approves Takeover of Montedison," *New York Times*, August 29, 2001, p. W1; Richard Owen, Clive Mathieson, and Caroline Merrell, *London Times*, August 4, 2001, p. 43; "Flattering to Deceive," *The Economist*, August 2, 2001; www._olivetti._com; Juliana Ratner, Krishna Guha, and Fred Kapner, "Small Stake Won Control of Telecom Italia," *Financial Times*, July 31, 2001; Pirelli, *Annual Report*, 2009; Fiat SpA, *Annual Report*, 2009.

avoid the overhead associated with having intermediaries handle the product, respond more accurately and rapidly to customer needs, and take advantage of local resources. This process, known as *internalization* of control within the MNE, can help to reduce overall costs.

A fifth reason is to overcome *protective* devices such as tariff and non-tariff barriers by serving a foreign market from within. The EU provides an excellent example. Firms outside the EU are subject to tariffs on goods exported to EU countries. Firms producing the goods within the EU, however, can transport them to any other country in the bloc without paying tariffs. The same is now occurring in North America, thanks to the North American Free Trade Agreement (NAFTA), which has eliminated tariffs among Canada, the United States, and Mexico.

A sixth reason for becoming an MNE is to take advantage of technological expertise by manufacturing goods directly (by FDI) rather than allowing others to do it under a license. Although the benefits of a licensing agreement are obvious, in recent years some MNEs have concluded that it is unwise to give another firm access to proprietary information such as patents, trademarks, or technological expertise, and they have allowed current licensing agreements to lapse. This has allowed them to reclaim their exclusive rights and then to manufacture and directly sell the products in overseas markets.

Firms become MNEs for the same reasons they engage in FDI. The next chapter will provide a more detailed examination of some of the reasons introduced in this chapter.

The strategic philosophy of MNEs

MNEs make decisions based on what is best for the overall company, even if this means transferring jobs to other countries and cutting back the local workforce. In the past decade IBM, ABB, and Sony, for example, have spent considerable sums of money to train and develop local managers to handle overseas operations because the companies are finding that these managers are often much more effective than those sent from the home country. MNEs also hire large numbers of non-managerial workers in overseas countries. For example, US-based Ford Motor has 66,000 employees in Europe and 15,000 employees in the Asia–Pacific region. European firm Siemens has 277,000 employees outside Germany.[8]

As a result there is a great deal of economic interaction in the international arena, giving business firms headquartered in one country a significant impact on the economies of other countries. This is true both when things are going well as well as when they are not. For example, with the recent slowdown of the world economy more and more MNEs are now trimming their workforces. Alcatel, the giant French telecommunications equipment maker, announced plans to cut 29 percent of its workforce and to reduce its factories to a dozen, using outsourcing to handle all other production needs.[9] Philips, the giant Dutch electronics firm, reacted to a severe slowdown in demand for mobile phones and semiconductors, and eliminated more than 7,000 jobs;[10] and Disney cut 4,000 positions, about 3 percent of its worldwide workforce.[11] These decisions were made to improve the situation of the company as a unit.

This same worldwide approach to operations can be seen in the way MNEs team up to get things done. One example is Embraer of Brazil, the fourth-largest aircraft manufacturer in the world. The company teamed up with 22 of its main suppliers, many of which are Japanese, to introduce a new family of aircraft. Suppliers became risk investors and by funding Embraer's plan secured future contracts from the company.[12] For more on Embraer, see the Real Case in Chapter 4. Another example is provided by the production of the V2500 engine by a consortium led by US Pratt & Whitney and British Rolls-Royce. Other partners are Japanese Aero Engines and Germany's MTU Aero Engines.[13] Simply put, MNEs make whatever agreements are in their best interests, even if this means bringing in firms from three or four different countries.

✔ Active learning check

Review your answer to Active Learning Case question 3 and make any changes you like. Then compare your answer to the one below.

3 **In what way did Euro Disney reflect the strategic philosophy of Walt Disney as a multinational enterprise?**

One way in which Euro Disney reflects the strategic philosophy of the company as an MNE is that Disney is willing to modify the park to meet the preferences of local visitors by catering to their markets. Euro Disney is not identical to Disneyland in California. The focus on European roots and culture is now an integral part of the park. In addition, notice how the company used an international approach to funding the project. The monies were not all raised in France. The government helped, but so did banks, private investors, and Disney itself. And when the operation ran into trouble, the company was willing to reconfigure its arrangement and give up some ownership and some revenue in order to get things back on an even keel.

Table 2.2 The international expansion of four MNEs

	Number of majority-owned foreign affiliates		
MNE	1970	1985	2000
Ford (US)	65	140	270
Unilever (EU)	94	146	244
Siemens (EU)	84	165	416
Marubeni (Japan)	16	44	170

Source: United Nations, *World Investment Report* 2001 (Geneva: United Nations Conference on Trade and Development, 2001).

Table 2.2 reports the geographical expansion between 1970 and 2000 of four of the world's largest MNEs, especially since 1985. The international scope of these MNEs is measured by the number of majority-owned foreign affiliates (subsidiaries) that they have. A similar picture emerges with later data.

STRATEGIC MANAGEMENT AND MNEs

As noted earlier, one of the characteristics of MNE affiliates is that they are linked by a strategic plan. As a result, units that are geographically dispersed and/or have diverse product offerings all work in accord with a strategic vision. The formulation and implementation of strategy will be discussed in detail in Chapter 8. Here we will look at the basic nature of the strategic management process and how select MNEs use strategic planning in managing their far-flung enterprises.

Strategic management of MNEs: an introduction

The strategic management process involves four major functions: strategy formulation, strategy implementation, evaluation, and the control of operations. These functions encompass a wide range of activities, beginning with an environmental analysis of external and internal conditions and an evaluation of organizational strengths and weaknesses. These activities serve as the basis for a well-formulated strategic plan, and by carefully implementing and controlling this plan, the MNE is able to compete effectively in the international arena. Figure 2.3 illustrates the five specific steps in this overall process.

Steps in the strategic management process

Basic mission
The reason that a firm is in existence

Strategic planning typically begins with a review of the company's **basic mission**, which is determined by answering the questions: What is the firm's business? What is its reason for existence? By answering these questions, the company clearly determines the direction in which it wants to go. Shell Oil, BP, and Chevron, for example, see themselves as being in

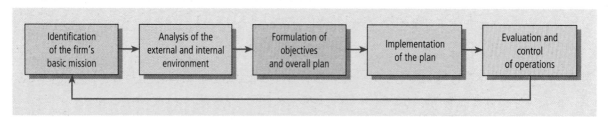

Figure 2.3 The strategic management process in action

the energy business, not in the oil business, and this focus helps to direct their long-range thinking. AT&T and France Telecom view themselves as being in the communications business, not in the telephone business. Coca-Cola and PepsiCo see themselves in the food business, not in the soft drink business. One of their strategic rivals is Nestlé.

In recent years a growing number of MNEs have revised their strategic plans because they realized that they had drifted too far away from their basic mission. Unilever, the giant Anglo-Dutch MNE, is a good example. After assessing its operations, the company concluded that it needed to adopt a "back to the core" strategy. As a result, it sold a wide range of peripheral operations, including transport, oil, milling, wallpaper, floor coverings, specialty chemicals, and turkey breeding. Today Unilever confines its business to consumer product goods: food, health and wellness products, personal care, and home care. The firm's strong research and development labs continue to develop new products in each of these areas, thus helping Unilever to remain competitive in worldwide markets.[14]

After determining its mission, an MNE will evaluate the external and internal environment. The goal of external environmental analysis is to identify opportunities and threats that will need to be addressed. Based on opportunity analysis, for example, a number of MNEs have been moving into the former East Germany. Adidas-Salomon now produces a large portion of its textiles in this part of Germany. Metro, a German retailer, now has a large presence in Hungary, Poland, the Czech Republic, and Russia.[15] These companies all see the region as having tremendous financial potential.

However, these expansion decisions were made only after the companies had analyzed the potential pitfalls, and there were many of them. One is that East Germans lived in a centrally planned bureaucracy for almost a half-century. Could they adapt to a free market economy? Would they be able to accept individual responsibility in a country where the state was no longer the major provider? Would they be able to upgrade their inefficient factories and improve the quality of output? Many MNEs believed that, with an influx of capital, the country's economy could be turned around. At the same time, their external environmental analysis showed that it would be necessary to increase worker productivity, improve the local infrastructure, and bring in qualified managers to run the operations until a local cadre could be developed.

The purpose of internal environmental analysis is to evaluate the company's financial and personnel strengths and weaknesses. Examining its financial picture will help the MNE decide what it can afford to do in terms of expansion and capital investment. Examining its financial picture will also help it to identify areas where cost cutting or divestment is in order. By making an evaluation of its personnel, an MNE will be able to determine how well its current workforce can meet the challenges of the future and what types of people will have to be hired or let go. In addition, the firm might like to include in its internal environmental analysis the reputation of its products, the structure of its organization, and its relationship with suppliers.

Internal and external analyses will also help the MNE to identify both long-range goals (typically two to five years) and short-range goals (less than two years). The plan is then broken down into major parts, and each affiliate and department will be assigned goals and responsibilities. This begins the implementation process. Progress is then periodically evaluated and changes are made in the plan. For example, an MNE might realize that it must stop offering a particular good or service because the market is no longer profitable or it might create a new product in order to take advantage of an emerging demand. Figure 2.3 describes the strategic management process. External and internal environmental assessments are discussed in more detail in Chapter 8.

The case **International Business Strategy in Action: Nestlé** provides an example of some aspects of the strategic management process.

INTERNATIONAL BUSINESS STRATEGY IN ACTION

Nestlé

With 230,000 employees, 6,000 brands, and factories spread around the world, Nestlé is the world's largest food company. Nescafé instant coffee, Perrier water, and KitKat chocolate are just some of the products that the company produces and markets around the world.

A significant portion of Nestlé's revenues derives from developing countries. In 2002, developing nations in Latin America, Africa, and the Middle East accounted for 33.7 percent of all sales. Nestlé's strategy in these nations consists of purchasing successful local brands, keeping their original names, and adding its own brand. In Peru, for instance, the company purchased ice cream and chocolate maker D'Onofrio, and continued to market its products under the D'Onofrio brand, capitalizing on the reputation of this brand while adding the Nestlé logo as a parent brand to all packaging. Not a bad analogy to the entire Nestlé business where a "think local" philosophy is meshed together at the multinational level.

Entering Third World countries can be risky and unrewarding. For one thing, there is a currency risk. During 1998–2002, Nestlé's volume sales in Brazil rose by 10 percent but because of the devaluation of Brazil's currency, revenues in Swiss francs fell by 30 percent. Products must be adapted to the local tastes. In China, red bean and sesame-flavored chocolate ice cream cubes are two of the more than 100 flavors of ice cream that Nestlé markets in China alone. Political risk, in terms of expropriation or war, is also higher in developing countries.

Dealings with Third World countries may also affect a company's reputation in its large industrialized markets. In 2002, Nestlé demanded that the Ethiopian government deliver $6 million for a company that was expropriated in 1975 under a communist regime. Non-governmental organizations (NGOs) and concerned citizens were outraged. At the time, Ethiopia was undergoing a famine that threatened as many as 11 million citizens with starvation. The Ethiopian government offered $1 million, but Nestlé rejected the offer. Oxfam decried the company's stance claiming that one of the richest companies in the world was trying to squeeze as much as it could from one of the poorest countries in the world. A spokesperson for the

Source: Corbis/Swim Ink 2, ILC

World Bank, which was brokering the deal, stated that the $1 million offer seemed reasonable and accused Nestlé of trying to get as much as it could. The backlash led Nestlé to accept $1.5 million in compensation and to donate the entire amount for famine relief in the country.

Website: www.nestle.com.

Sources: www.nestle.com; "Nestlé in Ethiopia Compensation Row," BBC.co.uk, December 18, 2002; "Selling to the Developing World," *Economist.com*, December 11, 2003.

✔ Active learning check

Review your answer to Active Learning Case question 4 and make any changes you like. Then compare your answer to the one below.

4 **Did Disney management conduct an external environmental analysis before going forward with Euro Disney? Explain.**

The company conducted a thorough external environmental analysis. First, the location of the European population was examined to identify how far people would have to travel to visit the park. Second, the company examined the cost of building the park and identified potential sources of funds. Third, the firm determined how the park was to be built and where it would find the necessary contractors. Fourth, the company made a forecast regarding the number of visitors to the park each year, how much they would spend, and what the firm's profit would be on the venture.

However, the company failed in its examination of the cultural preferences of Europeans and the relative competitiveness of its European operation against its North American operation. In particular, Disney failed to take into consideration the effect of exchange rates on the affordability of traveling to France as opposed to Florida to visit its amusement park.

A FRAMEWORK FOR GLOBAL STRATEGIES: THE FSA–CSA MATRIX

Much of the material in this book can be synthesized within a single analytical framework.[16] We develop this here to help summarize our key points. There are two basic building blocks in an international business course, as illustrated in Figure 2.4. First, there is a set of firm-specific factors that determine the competitive advantage of an organization. We call these **firm-specific advantages (FSAs)**. An FSA is defined as a unique capability proprietary to the organization. It may be built on product or process technology, marketing, or distributional skills. Second, there are country factors. These, of course, are unique to an international business course. They can lead to **country-specific advantages (CSAs)**. The CSAs can be based on natural resource endowments (minerals, energy, forests) or on the labor force and associated cultural factors.

Firm-specific advantages (FSAs)
Strengths or benefits specific to a firm and a result of contributions that can be made by its personnel, technology, and/or equipment

Country-specific advantages (CSAs)
Strengths or benefits specific to a country that result from its competitive environment, labor force, geographic location, government policies, industrial clusters, etc.

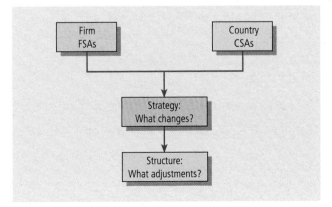

Figure 2.4 The basic components of international business

Managers of most MNEs use strategies that build on the interactions of CSAs and FSAs. They do this so that they can be positioned in a unique strategic space. The CSAs represent the natural factor endowments of a nation; they are based on the key variables in its aggregate production function. For example, CSAs can consist of the quantity, quality, and cost of the major factor endowment, namely resources.

Using Porter's terminology, the CSAs form the basis of the global platform from which the multinational firm derives a home-base "diamond" advantage in global competition.[17] Tariff and non-tariff barriers to trade and government regulation also influence CSAs. Building on these CSAs, the firm makes decisions about the efficient global configuration and coordination between segments of its value chain (operations, marketing, R&D, and logistics). The skill in making such decisions represents a strong, managerial FSA.

The FSAs possessed by a firm are based ultimately on its internalization of an asset, such as production knowledge, managerial or marketing capabilities, over which the firm has proprietary control. FSAs are thus related to the firm's ability to coordinate the use of the advantage in production, marketing, or the customization of services.

The FSA–CSA matrix

To help formulate the strategic options of the MNE, it is useful to identify the relative strengths and weaknesses of the CSAs and FSAs they possess. Figure 2.5, the FSA–CSA matrix, provides a useful framework for discussion of these issues. The "strength" or "weakness" of FSAs and CSAs is a relative notion, depending on the relevant market and the CSAs and FSAs of potential competitors. A strong FSA implies that, under identical CSAs, a firm has a potential competitive advantage over its rivals.

Quadrants (or cells) 1, 2, and 3 correspond broadly to the three generic strategies suggested: cost leadership, differentiation, and focus.[18] Quadrant 1 firms are generally resource based and/or mature, globally oriented firms producing a commodity-type product. Given their late stage in the product life cycle, production FSAs flowing from the possession of intangible skills are less important than the CSAs of location and energy

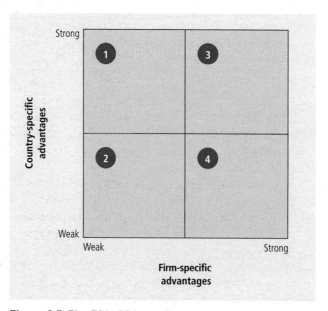

Figure 2.5 The FSA–CSA matrix

costs, which are the main sources of the firm's competitive advantage. Quadrant 2 firms represent inefficient, floundering firms with no consistent strategy, nor any intrinsic CSAs or FSAs. These firms are preparing to exit or to restructure. Quadrant 2 can also represent domestically based small and medium-sized firms with little global exposure. Quadrant 3 firms generally can choose to follow any of the generic strategies listed above because of the strength of both their CSAs and FSAs.

Firms in quadrant 4 are generally differentiated firms with strong FSAs in marketing and customization. These firms follow basically a differentiation strategy. In quadrant 4 the FSAs dominate, so in world markets the home-country CSAs are not essential in the long run. Thus these firms are following low-cost and price competition strategies.

In terms of business strategy, quadrants 3 and 2 are unambiguous in their implications. A quadrant 3 firm can benefit from strategies of both low cost and differentiation. Such a firm is constantly evaluating its production mix. As a product line matures and then declines, it eventually graduates to quadrant 2. However, by adopting new product lines, developing dynamic organizational capabilities, and maintaining an effective strategy, the firm can maintain its overall position in quadrant 3. In quadrant 2 there is no alternative but to restructure or to eventually leave the market.

Quadrants 4 and 1 are credible positions for different types of firms. For instance, a quadrant 4 firm that has strong FSAs in marketing (customization) can operate globally without reliance on its home-market CSA, or the CSAs of the host nation. For such a firm, quadrant 4 does not signal a CSA weakness; the CSA is not relevant. In contrast, quadrant 1 has mature multinationals or product lines determined more by CSAs than by FSAs. By improving potential FSAs in marketing or product innovation and increasing value added through vertical integration, the quadrant 1 firm can move to quadrant 3, where its profitability should be enhanced.

Although quadrants 1, 3, and 4 represent appropriate strategic positioning for some firms, there exists an asymmetry between quadrants 4 and 1. A quadrant 4 strategic choice may be a stable one for some firms; however, quadrant 1 firms should be able to aim for quadrant 3. The reason for this asymmetry is rooted in the fact that CSAs are for the most part exogenous to the firm, whereas FSAs are not. Even to the extent that CSAs can be influenced by government protection, there is always increased uncertainty associated with such strategies. For the firm in quadrant 4 already following an efficiency-based strategy there is no incentive, nor need, to move to quadrant 3.

It is useful to note the following two points. First, if the firm has a conglomerate structure it would be more useful to situate each division or product line individually, recognizing that different units of the diversified firm would use different generic strategies. Second, changes in the trading environment—such as the EU 1992 single-market measures, or the EU 1999 single currency, or the United States–Canada Free Trade Agreement and NAFTA—will affect the relative CSAs of the firms. To the extent that CSAs are improved, the firms will tend to move to quadrant 3, and, to the extent that the CSAs are hampered, the firm or some of its product lines may move to exit, as in quadrant 2.

For Dunning's related OLI theoretical framework see Appendix B to Chapter 2 (Table 2A).

Figure 2.5 can be reconciled with the OLI framework of Dunning (1981). In this eclectic paradigm Dunning has location factors (L), internalization factors (I), and ownership factors (O). The location variable (L) is entirely consistent with the vertical axis of Figure 2.5. The CSAs can be relabeled as location-specific advantages (LSAs) in order to better link to the eclectic paradigm. Indeed, given the finding that many MNEs operate largely within their home region of the triad, which implies that national borders are less important than triad borders, it would make sense to replace CSAs by LSAs. The logic of the axis remains entirely the same.

The horizontal axis shows the unique capabilities of the firm called FSAs. There is little value in distinguishing between the O and I aspects of FSAs. Clearly property rights (O) need to be established to overcome market imperfections, especially in the pricing and protection of knowledge, and it is clear that imperfect markets trigger internalization (I) by an institution such as the MNE. Thus O and I, in practice, are integrated features of FSA management within the MNE that cannot be decoupled in strategic decision making. While in principle the conceptual analysis of MNE evolution can indeed distinguish between O, L, and I, the more reductionist focus on FSAs and CSAs/LSAs alone provides an equally powerful theoretical tool, whereby any observation of internalization/de-internalization can be explained on the basis of the nature of FSAs and CSAs/LSAs and the interactions between these two sets of parameters.

IT'S REGIONAL, NOT FLAT

If MNEs are the key drivers of globalization and they operate regionally, why is it thought that globalization exists? For example, Thomas Friedman, the *New York Times* journalist, has sold over 3 million copies of his *The World is Flat*.[19] This is unfortunate since this book is based upon a faulty understanding of globalization, and it lacks any insight and balance into the underlying empirical context of world business. Basically, Friedman makes one point in his book, namely that today a large proportion of international business take place through offshoring. Indeed, much manufacturing and cost innovation take place in China with service sector activities, especially in information technology sectors, taking place in India. While both types of offshoring certainly exist (and are explained by factor cost arbitrage) it is apparent that Friedman vastly exaggerates the importance of offshoring in the IT-related area.

Friedman's book largely consists of interesting and well-written anecdotes referring to this particular sector. But it is incorrect to generalize the country effect (the CSA axis in Figure 2.5) and make it the sole explanation of globalization. Instead, the firm effects need to be analyzed across other sectors and the integration of firm and country effects needs to be brought together, as in quadrant 3 of Figure 2.5. It can be seen that Friedman's book is mainly about quadrant 1, and that he presents no evidence of the way FSAs can be developed such that CSAs in China and India are transformed into quadrant 3 firm-specific attributes.

This analysis counters the simplistic notions of writers such as Thomas Friedman. The world is not flat. International business suggests that there remain strong barriers as a business attempts to cross the boundaries of triad regions. It is pointless to assume globalization; instead, it is necessary to investigate the manner in which a firm's business model may need to be adapted such that its FSAs can overcome the liability of inter-regional foreignness.

MULTINATIONALS IN ACTION

The following five firms illustrate various topics examined in this chapter, including the internationalization process and the strategic management process.

Solectron

The Solectron Corporation, is a public subsidiary of Flextronics, Singapore, being acquired in 2007. It is headquartered in Milpitas, California, and is becoming very well known internationally in electronics manufacturing services (EMS), although the company's name does not appear on any of its products. This is because Solectron is an outsourcer that generates its revenues by producing goods for other companies.[20] Today Solectron runs a factory it bought from Sony and is able to provide the same type of electronic products to Sony at a lower cost than the giant Japanese firm could do itself. Like many electronic companies that design, manufacture, and sell their own products, Sony's return on investment has been shockingly low because of the large amount of capital that is tied up in its factories. In a typical year Sony's return on equity is around 5 percent. In contrast, Solectron is able to earn a return on equity in the range of 12 percent. By focusing exclusively on such things as customized electronics technology, state-of-the-art manufacturing, and supply-chain assistance, Solectron is able to achieve economies of scale that allow it to produce and deliver goods both quickly and inexpensively. As a result, its customer list is extensive. Large firms such as Cisco Systems, the giant Internet equipment company, rely on Solectron to handle a significant portion of their manufacturing needs. So too do smaller firms such as Handspring Inc., a California-based company that competes in the palm-size organizer market. In Handspring's case, the company realizes that its expertise is in designing and developing organizers as well as marketing them. As a result, it has turned over the production of these units to Solectron.

Today the cost of building new manufacturing plants is prohibitive for many firms. At the same time, the life cycle of products is becoming increasingly shorter. So if firms are going to reach their profit goals, they are going to have to find new ways to cut their expenses by outsourcing. (For more on contract manufacturing, see the Real Case: Flextronics, in Chapter 12.)

BMW

BMW is one of the world's best-known auto firms and for many years it has successfully produced and sold quality cars. As a result, the company has been able to capture and hold a solid share of the middle and upper-middle car market. In 2009, BMW has 56 percent of its sales in Europe and 25 percent in North America, where its cars and SUVs sell well in the upper end of the market. More recently, however, BMW has been turning its attention to the lower end of the market. One of its new objectives is to produce a small BMW and sell it at a premium price. This car line, which has been dubbed the 2 Series by the press, hit the market in 2004.[21]

Will BMW be successful in this venture? Some observers are quick to point out that small cars are a tempting but dangerous segment of the market. Profits are often elusive and competition is fierce. One of the big questions that is yet to be answered is how much of a premium buyers will be willing to pay for a small BMW. The company believes that there are customers who will pay a premium for value-added features and high performance. One of the features in the 2 Series will be rear-wheel drive, not the front-wheel drive that is common in most small cars. While front-wheel drive offers better fuel economy, BMW believes that rear-wheel drive will provide better handling and give the driver a better feel for the road. In addition, the company intends to give the 2 Series the same distinctive exterior look as its larger cars. As a result of these types of features, BMW feels that it will be able to attract buyers who are willing to pay a premium. In addition, the company is convinced that its name and reputation for quality will help it garner market share. In the past the firm has done exceptionally well and has consistently been one of the most profitable car makers in the world. However, this success has been in the upscale market. Making money in the small-car market while charging a premium price is going to be an interesting challenge for it.

Levi Strauss

Bruce Springsteen wore a pair of Levi's jeans on the cover of his *Born in the USA* album, and James Dean and Madonna also did their part in marketing the brand. Levi's success at infiltrating itself into US pop culture is such that it pops up in the memory of many baby boomers remembering their school years: The "cool" kids wore Levi's.

In the mid-nineteenth century denim was considered work wear, and Levi Strauss & Co. was a small dry goods store that sold functional items like clothing, linens, and bedding in California. Marketing of Levi's denim products borrowed from the American Western landscape featuring cowboys, fishermen, and mechanics, among others, at work in everything from their catalogues to the garment's tag. Durable, functional, and guaranteed were the pillars on which the firm built the reputation of its products.

By the start of the twentieth century, the firm had expanded its product line to include children's clothing. At the same time, the firm's marketing became more "artistic," taking on the cultural trends of the times and marking a significant shift in philosophy that would turn the brand into a US icon and make jeans a fashion statement.

Being a US tradition, however, has not been enough to spare the firm from the challenges facing the industry around the world. Over the past two decades the firm has underperformed as a result of increased competition and changing consumer trends around the world. Protecting the brand name it so painstakingly built might never have been such a difficult task.

Levi Strauss was one of the last firms to hold on to domestic manufacturing. After all, the value of the brand was closely tied to US manufacturing quality. As competitors flocked to Asia in the mid-1990s, the firm remained hopeful that its brand would survive the price competition. By 1999, the strategy shifted as Levi Strauss announced it would turn itself into a marketing firm and shed the manufacturing side of its supply chain. This, it argued, would allow the firm to have a more flexible price structure. By 2004, all US-based factories had been closed.[22]

Diesel, Guess, Buffalo, Silver, and Gap have also eroded the star power of Levi's jeans. Diesel jeans, for example, are considered a step above in terms of quality and design. While some competing brands might not be as durable as Levi's, they are less traditional in design, accommodating the ever-changing tastes of consumers who seasonally update their wardrobes.

In England, Levi Strauss went as far as suing Tesco, a major supermarket, for selling Levi's products at a discounted price. Levi Strauss argued that Tesco's actions devalued the brand by selling jeans next to household products, groceries, and produce. Tesco had purchased Levi's jeans in the gray market—from distributors whose products originated from Levi's, because it refused to sell jeans directly to Tesco or other supermarkets. A European Union law prohibits branded products purchased abroad from being sold in the EU market without the consent of the brand owner. The ruling forbade Tesco from purchasing products outside the EU for sale in the UK, but allowed it to continue purchasing jeans in other EU countries.[23]

Winning the lawsuit did little to solve the erosion of its market by competitors, and the company continued to make losses. Realizing the potential of using these "discount" marketing channels, Levi Strauss introduced a cheaper version of its jeans to be sold directly to supermarkets, including Tesco. Levi's "Signature" brand may solve the firm's problem of attracting as wide a customer base as possible while retaining the value of its original line of jeans.[24]

Levi Strauss is one of the few companies that pulled out of China during the mid-1990s because it felt that the government was guilty of pervasive human rights violations. The company stopped manufacturing jeans in China after it found evidence of child labor, forced labor, and a military presence at factories that were producing clothing for the firm. The company did not own any of these factories on the mainland; it relied on local subcontractors to perform the manufacturing. However, company guidelines prohibited the suppliers from using child labor, forced labor, or excessive work hours. So when Levi Strauss learned of these violations, it concluded that its association with the contractors would damage its reputation, and it began a phased withdrawal from China.

Now Levi Strauss is coming back into the marketplace and even has plans to start a direct-marketing operation on the mainland. The firm has promised to monitor its new Chinese factories carefully to ensure that they comply with human rights guidelines. At the same time, however, Levi Strauss is glad to be back because, like many other MNEs, the company believes that China is a marketplace of the future.[25] One senior executive in the company put it this way: "You're nowhere in Asia without being in China."

Canon

Canon is one of the world's leading camera and printer firms, but this has not always been true. For many years Canon followed the leaders and worked to improve its technology. However, in recent years the company has taken the lead against firms such as Leica in cameras and Xerox in photocopiers.[26] It is a "global" firm with 27.1 percent of its sales in North America, 41.0 percent in Asia, and 30.9 percent in Europe in 2009.[27]

Today Canon is in the top three in all of its major business lines, and its original product, cameras, now accounts for less than 10 percent of sales. However, the firm is the world leader in both single-lens reflexes and compacts, and earns almost one-third of its income from copiers. And to maintain its momentum, Canon has adopted a two-pronged strategy. First, it is seeking to maintain profits by cutting costs in its core business by making suppliers more efficient and by shifting work to factories in Taiwan, in order to reduce the high cost of building some of its products in Japan.

Second, Canon is moving into the digital age by cultivating alliances with companies that know the networking and computer world better than it does. For example, Canon has teamed with Hewlett-Packard, one of its major competitors, to build laser printers. The company is also looking into developing smart printers with personal-computer-like abilities, including electronic mail, and printers that produce high-quality photo prints on plain paper. Quite clearly, Canon believes that its future rests with the continued development of innovative products that draw on its core competencies in the optical field.

Zara

Zara is the world's fastest-growing fashion retailer. Its ultimate parent is Inditex S.A. Headquartered in north-western Spain, the company has expanded rapidly in recent years.[28] There are only a few Zara units in the United States, but the company's plans call for a rapid expansion there too.

There are two things that make Zara's implementation of its strategic plan so successful. One is that the company has created a lightning-speed production and distribution system. In an industry where competitors have their goods produced as much as five months in advance of delivery to stores, Zara's turnaround time is a mere three weeks. This means that the company can alter its designs and create new ones as the season moves along, thus allowing it to continually accommodate the changing tastes of its customers. Moreover, because Zara can change designs so quickly, none of its styles last more than four weeks. Coupled with this flexibility is a computerized inventory system that helps the firm minimize warehousing costs. Clothes are sorted in a single distribution center and then shipped out in preprogrammed lots directly to the stores. Twice a week each store receives deliveries that have been triggered by real-time inventory data that are collected through a network of computer handsets that feed information through the Internet into computers at headquarters. This system is so sophisticated and accurate that the company's inventory level is a mere 7 percent of annual revenues, sharply lower than the 13 percent of its main competitor.

The other factor that helps account for the firm's success in implementing its plan is the salespeople who act as grassroots market researchers. Each person has a wireless organizer that is used to enter trends, customer comments, and orders. As a result, if an item does not sell well, it can be off the shelf within weeks. Conversely, if it is successful, company designers can quickly learn this and turn out a new version in a myriad of colors in record time. As an example, when Zara store personnel sold pink dress shirts for men, they learned from the customers that they would have preferred purple. This information was conveyed to the company's in-house manufacturing team, which raced into action. Within two weeks Zara stores were selling purple shirts.

The company implements the same basic strategy worldwide. It does no advertising, and the products that it sells in Europe are similar to those in its stores in the United States. Inventory control is also given a strong emphasis with all US stores supplied by air from Spain. At the same time, however, Zara does try to create an image that fits local taste. For example, in one of its mid-Manhattan stores the company tore out the entire interior and put in marble-like floors and high-tech lights to create a stunning 10,000 ft^2 (900 m^2) emporium. Customers, most of whom are in their 20s, are attracted by the feeling of being in an upscale European boutique, even though the prices are sharply lower and are targeted to compete with those at Gap.[29]

Zara has been very effective in implementing its strategic plan as seen by the financial results. In an industry that has been seeing sluggish growth, Zara's sales have been rising by over 20 percent annually up to 2008, growing at 15.8 percent in 2009 in the context of economic slowdown. As a result the company is now increasing the number of stores in Europe, North America, and Asia, using the same basic approach for implementation that has proven successful thus far.

These examples of large MNEs sometimes give the misleading impression that MNEs are larger than some countries. This mistake is compounded by the simple listing of the sales of MNEs against the GDP of nations (see Table 2.3). In such a listing Wal-Mart appears 25th in the list and it is larger than Austria. Altogether there are 45 MNEs in the top 50. There are two problems with this.

First, even the sales of GM at $104.589 billion are tiny in comparison to the size of the US GDP at $14.14 trillion (2009 estimate). Similarly, the European MNEs are small compared to the EU size (which is not recognized in Table 2.3—as the individual 15 members are included—but was estimated at more than $26 trillion in 2009 (Eurostat). And the largest Japanese MNE, Toyota, at $204.106 billion is tiny compared to the GDP of Japan at $4,149 trillion.[30]

Second, the measures are biased against the countries. The GDP is a "value-added" concept. It considers the final sales of goods and services. To develop a comparable measure for MNEs requires that only their value added be calculated, not the total sales. If this is done, then the "size" of the MNEs is reduced by 70–80 percent. For example, in 2000, the value added of GM was only $46.2 billion, not the $176.6 billion reported as revenues.[31]

Table 2.3 The top 100 economies and MNEs, 2010 ranking

Rank	Country/company	Millions of US $	Rank	Country/company	Millions of US $
1	United States	14,502,626	51	AXA	175,257
2	Japan	4,830,313	52	Pakistan	172,855
3	China	4,815,821	53	Egypt, Arab Rep	172,023
4	Germany	3,484,689	54	China National Petroleum	165,496
5	France	2,754,606	55	Philippines	164,532
6	United Kingdom	2,567,480	56	Chevron	163,527
7	Italy	2,112,492	57	ING Group	163,204
8	Brazil	1,564,008	58	Chile	160,569
9	Spain	1,464,739	59	General Electric	156,779
10	Canada	1,422,977	60	Total	155,887
11	India	1,356,085	61	Algeria	154,202
12	Russian Federation	1,329,670	62	Bank of America Corp.	150,450
13	Korea, Republic	966,600	63	Volkswagen	146,205
14	Mexico	962,704	64	ConocoPhillips	139,515
15	Australia	957,529	65	BNP Paribas	130,708
16	Netherlands	815,769	66	Hungary	130,114
17	Turkey	653,096	67	Ukraine	128,848
18	Indonesia	513,356	68	Assicurazioni Generali	126,012
19	Belgium	488,826	69	Allianz	125,999
20	Poland	467,545	70	AT&T	123,018
21	Saudi Arabia	439,021	71	Carrefour	121,452
22	Sweden	455,197	72	Peru	121,435
23	Switzerland	431,136	73	Ford Motor	118,308
24	Norway	417,260	74	ENI	117,235
25	Wal Mart	408,214	75	Kuwait	116,984
26	Austria	391,822	76	New Zealand	114,518
27	Iran, Islamic Rep.	330,619	77	J.P. Morgan Chase & Co.	115,632
28	Denmark	325,847	78	Hewlett-Packard	114,552
29	Greece	323,055	79	E.ON	113,849
30	Argentina	306,040	80	Berkshire Hathaway	112,493
31	Venezuela, RB	289,443	81	GDF Suez	111,069
32	Royal Dutch Shell	285,129	82	Daimler	109,700
33	Exxon Mobil	284,650	83	Nippon Telegraph & Telephone	109,656
34	South Africa	284,499	84	Samsung Electronics	108,927
35	Thailand	254,690	85	Citigroup	108,785
36	BP	246,138	86	McKesson	108,702
37	Finland	243,850	87	Verizon Communications	107,808
38	Columbia	226,138	88	Kazakhstan	107,125
39	Hong Kong SAR, China	219,246	89	Crédit Agricole	106,538
40	Portugal	222,649	90	Banco Santander	106,345
41	Toyota Motor	204,106	91	General Motors	104,589
42	Japan Post Holdings	202,196	92	HSBC Holdings	103,736
43	Malaysia	198,650	93	Siemens	103,605
44	Ireland	197,206	94	American International Group	103,189
45	Sinopec	187,518	95	Lloyds Banking Group	102,967
46	Singapore	185,655	96	Cardinal Health	99,613
47	State Grid	184,496	97	Nestlé	99,114
48	Czech Republic	181,547	98	CVS Caremark	98,729
49	Romania	178,900	99	Wells Fargo	98,636
50	Nigeria	175,774	100	Hitachi	96,593

Notes: Country data represent gross national income (GNI) calculated using the World Bank Atlas method.

Sources: Adapted from World Bank, *World Development Report database*, July 1, 2010; *Fortune, The Global 500*, July 26, 2010 issue and individual company's annual report. Data are for 2009.

E-resources: http://data.worldbank.org/data-catalog, http://money.cnn.com/magazines/fortune/global500/2010/full_list/

KEY POINTS

1 A multinational enterprise is a company that is headquartered in one country but has operations in two or more countries. There is a series of characteristics that are common to multinational enterprises. These include (a) affiliated firms that are linked by ties of common ownership, (b) a common pool of resources, and (c) a strategic vision that guides all the affiliates.

2 Multinationals, especially large industrial enterprises, account for a large percentage of world sales and employment. MNEs, large or small, also engage in a wide variety of business activities ranging from manufacturing to retailing to consulting services.

3 The internationalization process is one of going abroad at incremental stages, on the premise that foreign markets are risky. Thus, a typical process is: license, export, sales office, and, finally, FDI.

4 Companies become MNEs for a number of reasons, including (a) a desire to protect themselves from the risks and uncertainties of the domestic business cycle, (b) a growing world market for their goods or services, (c) a response to increased foreign competition, (d) a desire to internalize in order to reduce costs, (e) a desire to overcome tariff barriers, and (f) the chance to take advantage of technological expertise by manufacturing goods directly rather than allowing others to do it under a license agreement.

5 MNEs do not see themselves as an extension of their domestic roots. They hire, fire, and transfer personnel to meet global needs, even if this means laying off home-country employees. They also combine their talents with those of other MNEs in creating, financing, and managing joint ventures.

6 Successful MNEs rely on the strategic management process, which has five major phases: (a) identification of the firm's basic mission, (b) external and internal environmental analysis, (c) formulation of objectives and overall plans, (d) implementation of these plans, and (e) evaluation and control of operations.

7 Managers of most MNEs use strategies that build on firm-specific advantages (FSAs) and country-specific advantages (CSAs). CSAs are natural factor endowments of a nation. FSAs are based on the firm's internalization of an asset.

8 The key concepts in this book can be brought together in the framework of the CSA–FSA matrix. The MNEs have FSAs that can be related to home and host CSAs.

Key terms

- multinational enterprise (MNE)
- internationalization
- license
- licensor
- licensee
- basic mission
- firm-specific advantages (FSAs)
- country-specific advantages (CSAs)

REVIEW AND DISCUSSION QUESTIONS

1 What is a multinational enterprise? Is it likely that the number of MNEs will increase during the next decade? Why?

2 What are the three common characteristics of an MNE? Identify and describe each.

3 Why do firms become multinational enterprises? Identify and discuss four reasons.

4 How are CSAs different than FSAs?

5 How successful are the large industrial MNEs? What accounts for this?

6 What are the five basic steps in the strategic management process? Identify and briefly describe each.

7 How has Zara used the strategic management process to help it become a successful multinational?

8 How has Levi Strauss used the strategic management process to help it improve its competitiveness?

REAL CASE

Starbucks

From its first location in Seattle's Pike Place Market in 1971, Starbucks has grown into one of the largest coffee chains with 16,635 locations in markets across the world in 2009. The company purchases and roasts high-quality coffee beans that are then brewed and retailed in trendy designer coffee shops that cater to a loyal following of young urban professionals who appreciate the distinct taste of Starbucks' coffee. In 2009 its sales were US $9.774 billion, about two-third the size needed to be in the top 500 world firms.

Source: Getty Images/News

The company's road to success began in 1985, when, after convincing the founders of Starbucks to test the coffee bar concept, the then director of retail operations, Howard Schultz, started his own coffee house to sell Starbucks coffee under the name Il Giornale. Within two years, Schultz purchased Starbucks and changed its company name to Starbucks Corporation. Since then, the company has expanded rapidly, opening stores in key markets and creating a "corporate coffee culture" in each of the urban areas in which it settled. Coffee bars are located in high-traffic areas and include large bookstores, suburban malls, universities, and high-traffic intra-urban communities.

Popularity has not come without a price for Starbucks. Coffee prices fell considerably in the late 1990s and led to the displacement of thousands of farmers. The main reason for a fall in the price of coffee was the oversupply that arose from improved production techniques and from a crop boom in the 1990s. Although Starbucks only purchases approximately 1 percent of the global supply of coffee, its high profile has made it a main target for protestors who accuse the coffee giant of not providing a fair price to coffee growers; this, despite Starbucks' policy of purchasing high-quality beans at premium market prices. To address the concerns of protestors, Starbucks introduced Fairtrade-endorsed coffee to its coffee houses. While the amount of Fairtrade coffee sold by the company is insignificant, at 1 percent of total sales, it is enough to portray the company as progressive and avert a consumer boycott.

The company directly operates 6,764 coffee houses in the United States in 2009. Unlike many coffee and fast-food chains, Starbucks does not franchise (license the right to operate one of its stores) to individuals in the United States. It does, however, negotiate licensing agreements with companies that have control over valuable retail space, such as an airport or hospital. In 2009, there were 4,364 Starbucks stores operating under licenses.

With coffee houses in 40 countries, today Starbucks has a global presence. In contrast to its domestic operations, the vast majority of Starbucks' international operations are through licenses. Indeed, of 5,507 international stores in 2009, 3,439 were licensed and in joint venture.

Starbucks might have operations in far-away countries like Australia, Oman, and China, but it is not global in its scope of operations. In 2009, 85.36 percent of its stores ▶

were located in its home region of North America, including operations in Canada, Mexico, and Puerto Rico. An even larger portion of Starbucks' revenues and operating income are home-region oriented. The United States alone accounts for 79.7 percent of revenues and 99 percent of operating income. International operations, including those that are directly owned and operated by Starbucks, require a higher degree of administrative support to be responsive to country-specific regulatory requirements. In addition, because these are mainly new markets, economies of scale in marketing and production have not yet materialized.

Website: www.starbucks.com.

Sources: Adapted from Starbucks, *Annual Report*, 2009; www.starbucks.com; Nicholas Stein, "Crisis in a Coffee Cup," *Fortune*, December 4, 2002; "Mug Shot," *The Economist*, September 19, 2002; Janet Williams, "Starbucks Takes on its Critics," BBC.co.uk, February 27, 2002.

1 Why does Starbucks rely on licenses for most of its international operations? Does the firm risk the dissipation of its managerial or technological advantages?

2 Can you argue that Starbucks is a global company regardless of the strong dominance of its home region in terms of sales and locations? Explain.

3 What accounts for the discrepancy between percentage of foreign locations and percentage of foreign net revenues?

4 What are some of the reasons why Starbucks chooses to retain operational control of its domestic operations?

REAL CASE

Sony

Very few companies can claim to be globally successful, but Sony, which brought us the Walkman and co-developed the CD and the DVD, has the numbers to prove it. In 2009, the company's $76.361 billion in revenues were evenly distributed across mainly three markets: Japan, the United States, and Europe.

Headquartered in Japan, Sony is best known for its high-quality consumer electronics, which account for 61 percent of total revenues, but the firm also produces games, music, and pictures. Consumers might not own a Sony electronic system, but the movie they watched last night or the CD they listen to while jogging may be the intellectual property of a Sony company. Sony's strategy boils down to producing electrical gadgets and controlling the content that goes through them much in the same way as its successful PlayStation 2 game console provides the hardware necessary for the firm to capture the games market.

In the 1980s, Sony's Betamax lost the VCR war to JVC's VHS. Both systems had been developed in the mid-1970s and initially Sony's Betamax was the clear winner. Indeed, all movies were originally released in Betamax format. General wisdom argues that Betamax lost the VCR war because it failed to license its software to rival manufacturers while Matsushita licensed to all. Today, the Betamax–VHS battle is often cited to argue the benefits of licensing new technology.

Yet, how could Sony have been so reckless as to ignore the benefits of licensing? The answer is that it did not. In 1974, a year before the Betamax release, Sony approached JVC and Matsushita seeking to reach an agreement on standards for the new product. In doing so, it freely disclosed Betamax's patented specification and technology to its rivals. The VHS format developed by JVC used very similar technology, but, because of its different size, was incompatible with Betamax. Matsushita was asked to choose between Sony's and JVC's product. Its decision came down to cost. It was cheaper to produce the VHS format because it had fewer components. With this, the players for the market were defined. The Betamax was to be manufactured by Toshiba, Sanyo Electric, NEC, Aiwa, and Pioneer. Matsushita, Hitachi, Mitsubishi Electric, Sharp, and Akai Electric manufactured JVC's VHS.

Perhaps more important than the size of the VCR disks of the two formats was that the VHS format allowed recording for two hours, twice that of Betamax. This would have allowed consumers to record an entire movie while away for the night. Sony was close to integrating technology into its format that would have increased the recording time to that of the VHS. If this was what tilted the balance, then all Sony would have needed is a bit of time. Potentially, at least, it could have bought itself some time if it owned the rights of the movies and refused to release them in

Source: Getty Images/AFP

cards are available across product lines in the industry and no other firm has Sony's reputation in the audio market, why, then, did Sony not come up with its own version? One argument is that the conglomerate must now weigh the benefits of developing a product in one division that may increase piracy of its music in another division.

If that is so, Sony is walking a fine line. Its electronics branch has ceased to produce stand-alone products and is instead integrating new products with others, which is likely to make piracy even easier than it is now. Soon, Sony hopes, your computer will be able to communicate with your television, stereo, and DVD player wirelessly, creating an integrated network of consumer electronics. And, if it all goes according to plan, Sony's media content will flow within these networks.

With PlayStation 2, Sony's dominance in the market for games was assured, at least in the short term, because it managed to capture most of the market and a games console creates a barrier to other game marketers because of lack of compatibility and intellectual property owned by the firm. Other forms of entertainment, however, are not as easily monopolized. Indeed, most new products, like the iPod, are based on technology that is standardized or can be adapted to work with that of competitors. If products do not do this, they might suffer the fate of the Betamax.

Websites: www.sony.com; www.sony.net.

Sources: www.sony.net; www.sony.com; Sony, *Annual Report*, 2009; Jack Schofield, "Why VHS Was Better Than Betamax," *Guardian*, January 25, 2003; *The Economist*, "The Complete Home Entertainer," *Economist.com*, February 27, 2003.

anything but Betamax format. And so it is that Sony's latest technological bets, the CD and DVD, have Sony Music Entertainment Inc. and Sony Pictures Entertainment to back them up.

In today's market, however, this type of vertical integration can hamper the ability of the consumer electronics division to develop the products that consumers want. Practically every major development in the consumer electronics industry in recent years has been developed by, or with the help of, Sony. Yet, very recently, Apple introduced the iPod, a very small and light device that can store up to 10,000 music files. The iPod is based on a small hard drive equipped with an audio function. Since similar memory

1 Is Sony a multinational enterprise?

2 If the vast majority of Sony's consumer electronics business is based and developed in Japan and the vast majority of Sony's music and movie business is based in the United States, does Sony make decisions that are best for the entire company regardless of location?

3 Why does Sony need to license its technology to competitors?

ENDNOTES

1 United Nations, *World Investment Report 2009* (Geneva: United Nations Conference on Trade and Development, 2009).

2 Alan M. Rugman, *The End of Globalization* (London: Random House, 2000), Chapter 7, especially p. 140.

3 *Fortune*, July 23, 2004.

4 Robyn Meredith, "In Policy Shift, G.M. Will Rely On Alliances," *New York Times*, January 18, 2000, pp. C1, C14.

5 This figure was first developed in Alan M. Rugman et al., *International Business: Firm and Environment* (New York: McGraw-Hill, 1985), pp. 89–93. It is based on the ideas in Alan M. Rugman, *Inside the Multinationals: The Economics of Internal Markets* (New York: Columbia Press, 1981).

6 Rugman (1981) n. 5 above.

7 Rugman (1981) n. 5 above.

8 Ford Motor, *Annual Report*, 2009 and Siemens, *Annual Report*, 2009.

9 Raphael Minder and Daniel Dombey, "Alcatel Cut Plans 'Stun' French," *Financial Times*, June 28, 2001, p. 21.

10 Suzanne Kapner, "Citing U.S. Slowdown, Philips Will Cut 7,000 Jobs," *New York Times*, April 18, 2001, p. W1.

11 Bill Carter, "Disney Is Cutting 4,000 Jobs Worldwide," *New York Times*, March 28, 2001, pp. C1, C13.

12 Andrew Carey, "Embraer: High Hopes for the Future," *CNN.com*, April 5, 2004.

13 Pratt & Whitney, "Japan Air System Awards Three-Year Maintenance Agreement To Pratt & Whitney Joint Venture," *Press Release*, September 29, 2003.

14 Unilever, *Annual Report*, 2003.

15 Michael Freedman, "Sturm und Drang," *Forbes.com*, July 26, 2004.

16 Alan M. Rugman, *Inside the Multinationals: The Economics of Internal Markets* (New York: Columbia University Press, 1981); Alan M. Rugman (ed.), *International Business in Canada: Strategies for Management* (Toronto: Prentice Hall Canada, 1989), Chapters 8, 13; Alan M. Rugman, *The Theory of Multinational Enterprises* (Cheltenham: Edward Elgar, 1996).

17 See Michael E. Porter, *The Competitive Advantage of Nations* (New York: Free Press, Macmillan, 1990).

18 See Michael E. Porter, *Techniques for Analyzing Industries and Competitors* (New York & London: Free Press, 1980).

19 Friedman, Thomas. *The World is Flat* (New York: Farrar, Straus & Giroux, 2005).

20 Peter Landers, "Why Some Sony Gear Is Made in Japan—By Another Company," *Wall Street Journal*, June 14, 2001, pp. A1, A10; Lucent Technologies, "Lucent Technologies closes agreement with Solectron for certain manufacturing assets in Massachusetts," *News Release,* May 31, 2002.

21 Scott Miller, "BMW Takes the High Road in Market for Small Cars," *Wall Street Journal*, August 3, 2000, p. A11 and BMW, *Annual Report*, 2009.

22 Malcom Mayhew, "Levi's fades as pop icon as last factory moves overseas," *Fort Worth Star-Telegram*, December 5, 2003.

23 BBC, "Tesco Defeated in Cheap Jeans Battle," *BBC News*, July 31, 2002.

24 BBC, "Levi Losses Trimmed as Sales Rise," *BBC News*, April 13, 2004.

25 Mark Landler, "Reversing Course, Levi Strauss Will Expand Its Output in China," *New York Times*, April 9, 1998, pp. 1, 5.

26 Edward W. Desmond, "Can Canon Keep Clicking?" *Fortune*, February 2, 1998, pp. 98–104.

27 Canon, *Annual Report*, 2009.

28 Richard Heller, "Galician Beauty," *Forbes*, May 28, 2001, p. 98.

29 William Echikson, "The Mark of Zara," *Business Week*, May 29, 2000, pp. 98, 100.

30 Alan M. Rugman, *The End of Globalization* (London: Random House, 2000), pp. 59–60.

31 Martin Wolf, "Countries Still Rule the World," *Financial Times*, February 6, 2002, p. 13.

ADDITIONAL BIBLIOGRAPHY

Beamish, Paul W. and Banks, John C. "Equity Joint Ventures and the Theory of the Multinational Enterprise," *Journal of International Business Studies*, vol. 18, no. 2 (Summer 1987).

Buckley, Peter J. and Casson, Mark C. "Models of the Multinational Enterprise," *Journal of International Business Studies*, vol. 29, no. 1 (First Quarter 1998).

Buckley, Peter J. and Casson, Mark C. "The Future of the Multinational Enterprise in Retrospect and in Prospect," *Journal of International Business Studies*, vol. 34, no. 2 (March 2003).

Buckley, Peter J. and Casson, Mark C. "The Internalization Theory of the Multinational Enterprise: A Review of the Progress of a Research Agenda After 30 Years," *Journal of International Business Studies,* vol. 40 (2009)

Collinson, Simon and Morgan, Glenn. *The Multinational Firm (Images of Business Strategy)* (Chichester, West Sussex, England; Hoboken, NJ: Wiley, 2009).

Chen, Shi-Fen S. "Extending Internalization Theory: A New Perspective on International Technology Transfer and Its Generalization," *Journal of International Business Studies*, vol. 36, no. 2 (March 2005).

Da Silva Lopes, Teresa. "The Entrepreneur, Ownership Advantages, and the Eclectic Paradigm," *Multinational Business Review*, vol. 18, no. 2 (Summer 2010).

Devinney, Timothy M. "Multinationals as Flagship Firms," *Academy of Management Review*, vol. 26, no. 3 (July 2001).

Dunning, John H. *International Production and the Multinational Enterprise* (London: Allen and Unwin, 1981).

Dunning, John H. "The Eclectic Paradigm of International Production: A Restatement and Some Possible Extensions," *Journal of International Business Studies*, vol. 19, no. 1 (Spring 1988).

Dunning, John H. *Global Capitalism at Bay?* (London: Routledge, 2001).

Dunning, John H. " Some Antecedents of Internalization Theory," *Journal of International Business Studies*, vol. 34, no. 2 (March 2003).

Eden, Lorraine and Li, Dai. "Rethinking the O in Dunning's OLI/ Eclectic Paradigm," *Multinational Business Review*, vol. 18, no. 2 (Summer 2010)

Henisz, Witold J. "The Power of the Buckley and Casson Thesis: The Ability to Manage Institutional Idiosyncrasies," *Journal of International Business Studies*, vol. 34, no. 2 (March 2003).

Hennart, Jean-François. "Can the New Forms of Investment Substitute for the Old Forms? A Transaction Cost Perspective," *Journal of International Business Studies*, vol. 20, no. 2 (Summer 1989).

Hennart, Jean-François. "Down with MNE-Centric Theories! Market Entry and Expansion as the Bundling of MNE and Local Assets," *Journal of International Business Studies*, vol. 40 (2009).

Johanson, Jan and Vahlne, Jan-Erik. "Commitment and Opportunity Development in the Internationalization Process: A Note on the Uppsala Internationalization Process Model," *Management International Review*, vol. 46, no. 2 (2006).

Johanson, Jan and Vahlne, Jan-Erik. "The Uppsala Internationalization Process Model Revisited: from Liability of Foreignness to Liability of Outsidership," *Journal of International Business Studies,* vol. 40 (2009).

Kogut, Bruce and Zander, Udo. "Knowledge of the Firm and the Evolutionary Theory of the Multinational Firm 10 years later," *Journal of International Business Studies*, vol. 34, no. 6 (November 2003).

Lundan, Sarianna M. "What are Ownership Advantages?" *Multinational Business Review*, vol. 18, no. 2 (Summer 2010).

Narula, Rajneesh. "Keeping the Eclectic Paradigm Simple," *Multinational Business Review*, vol. 18, no. 2 (Summer 2010).

Moore, Karl and Lewis, David. "The First Multinationals," *Management International Review*, vol. 38, no. 2 (Second Quarter 1998).

Rugman, Alan M. *The Theory of Multinational Enterprises* (Cheltenham: Edward Elgar, 1996).

Rugman, Alan M. "Reconciling Internalization Theory and the Eclectic Paradigm," *Multinational Business Review*, vol. 18, no. 2 (Summer 2010).

Rugman, Alan M. *The Regional Multinationals: MNEs and "Global" Strategic Management* (Cambridge, UK: Cambridge University Press, 2005).

Rugman, Alan M. and Collinson, Simon. "Relevance and Rigour in International Business Teaching: Using the CSA-FSA Matrix," *Journal of Teaching in International Business*, vol. 22, no. 1 (2011).

Rugman, Alan M. and Oh, Chang, Hoon. "Friedman's Follies: Insights on the Globalization/ Regionalization Debate," *Business and Politics*, vol. 10, no. 2 (August 2008).

Rugman, Alan M. and Verbeke, Alain. "A Note on the Transnational Solution and the Transaction Cost Theory of Multinational Strategic Management," *Journal of International Business Studies*, vol. 23, no. 4 (Fourth Quarter 1992).

Rugman, Alan M. and Verbeke, Alain. "Extending the Theory of the Multinational Enterprise: Internalization and Strategic Management Perspectives," *Journal of International Business Studies*, vol. 34, no. 2 (March 2003).

Rugman, Alan M. and Verbeke, Alain. "Liabilities of Regional Foreignness and the Use of Firm-Level versus Country-Level Data: A Response to Dunning *et al.* (2007)," *Journal of International Business Studies*, vol. 38, no. 1 (January 2007).

Rugman, Alan M. and Verbeke, Alain. "Internalization Theory and its Impact on the Field of International Business," in Jean Boddewyn, ed., *The Evolution of International Business Scholarship: AIB Fellows on the First 50 Years*, Research in Global Strategic Management, vol. 14 (Bingley, UK: Emerald, 2008).

Safarian, A. Edward. "Internalization and the MNE: A Note on the Spread of Ideas," *Journal of International Business Studies*, vol. 34, no. 2 (March 2003).

Tallman, S. "The Significance of Bruce Kogut's and Udo Zander's article, 'Knowledge of the Firm and the Evolutionary Theory of the Multinational Corporation'," *Journal of International Business Studies*, vol. 34, no. 6 (November 2003).

Verbeke, Alain. "The Evolutionary View of the MNE and the Future of Internalization Theory," *Journal of International Business Studies*, vol. 34, no. 6 (November 2003).

Verbeke, Alain and Yuan, Wenlong. "A Strategic Management Analysis of Ownership Advantages in the Eclectic Paradigm," *Multinational Business Review*, vol. 18, no. 2 (Summer 2010).

APPENDIX A TO CHAPTER 2

Table 2A The 25 largest US MNEs, 2010 ranking

Rank	Company	Revenues (millions of US $)	% intra-regional sales
1	Wal-Mart Stores	408,214	n.a
2	Exxon Mobil	284,650	36.82
3	Chevron	167,402	42.50
4	General Electric	156,783	54.20
5	Bank of America Corp.	150,450	82.80
6	ConocoPhillips	152,840	67.83
7	AT&T	123,018	n.a
8	Ford Motor	116,232	53.83
9	J.P. Morgan Chase & Co.	115,632	65.54
10	Hewlett-Packard	114,552	36.10
11	Berkshire Hathaway	112,493	76.08
12	Citigroup	108,785	31.80
13	McKesson	108,702	91.40
14	Verizon Communications	107,808	95.80
15	General Motors	104,589	n.a
16	American International Group	103,189	38.80
17	Cardinal Health	99,613	98.30
18	CVS Caremark	98,729	100.00
19	Wells Fargo	98,636	99.40
20	International Business Machines (IBM)	95,758	41.50
21	United Health Group	87,138	100.00
22	Procter & Gamble	76,694	39.50
23	Kroger	76,733	100.00
24	AmerisourceBergen	71,759	100.00
25	Costco Wholesale	71,422	92.80

Data are for 2009.

Source: Author's calculations and *Fortune*, The Global 500, July 26, 2010 and individual company's annual reports.

E-resources: http://money.cnn.com/magazines/fortune/global500/2010/countries/US.html

Table 2B The 25 largest European MNEs, 2010 ranking

Rank	Company	Country	Revenues (millions of US $)	% intra-regional sales
1	Royal Dutch Shell	Netherlands/ UK	285,129	37.20
2	BP	UK	246,138	43.00
3	AXA	France	175,257	60.62
4	ING Group	Netherlands	163,204	49.80
5	Total	France	155,887	70.50
6	Volkswagen	Germany	146,205	71.41
7	BNP Paribas	France	130,708	81.40
8	Assicurazioni Generali	Italy	126,012	n.a
9	Allianz	Germany	125,999	72.91
10	Carrefour	France	121,452	69.00
11	ENI	Italy	117,235	69.10
12	E.ON	Germany	113,849	97.34
13	GDF Suez	France	111,069	85.90
14	Daimler	Germany	109,700	46.20
15	Crédit Agricole	France	106,538	62.40
16	Banco Santander	Spain	106,345	59.09
17	HSBC Holdings	UK	103,736	32.66
18	Siemens	Germany	103,605	56.47
19	Lloyds Banking Group	UK	102,967	93.40
20	Nestlé	Switzerland	99,114	31.90
21	Dexia Group	Belgium	95,144	83.60
22	Électricité de France	France	92,204	86.10
23	Aviva	UK	92,140	83.70
24	Royal Bank of Scotland	UK	91,767	73.70
25	Metro	Germany	91,152	96.50

Data are for 2009.

Source: Authors' calculations and *Fortune*, The Global 500, July 26, 2010 and individual company's annual reports.

E-resources: http://money.cnn.com/magazines/fortune/global500/2010

Table 2C The 25 largest Japanese MNEs, 2010 ranking

Rank	Company	Revenues (millions of US $)	% intra-regional sales
1	Toyota Motor	204,106	51.43
2	Japan Post Holdings	202,196	n.a.
3	Nippon Telegraph & Telephone (NTT)	109,656	>90.00
4	Hitachi	96,593	82.50
5	Honda Motor	92,400	37.12
6	Nissan Motor	80,963	26.22
7	Panasonic	79,893	78.30
8	Sony	77,696	28.96
9	Nippon Life Insurance	72,051	n.a.
10	Toshiba	68,731	67.60
11	Dai-ichi Life Insurance	57,018	n.a.
12	Seven & I Holdings	54,701	70.48
13	Mitsubishi UFJ Financial Group	54,285	70.00
14	AEON	54,092	97.40
15	Tokyo Electric Power	54,026	90.00
16	JX Holdings	51,405	n.a.
17	Fujitsu	50,399	69.10
18	Mitsubishi	48,913	86.50
19	Meiji Yasuda Life Insurance	45,262	n.a.
20	Mitsui	44,120	92.60
21	Sumitomo Life Insurance	43,780	n.a.
22	NEC	38,591	90.14
23	Tokio Marine Holdings	38,458	84.40
24	Nippon Steel	37,563	75.90
25	KDDI	37,073	n.a.

Data are for 2009.

Source: Authors' calculations and *Fortune*, The Global 500, July 26, 2010 and individual company's annual reports.

E-resources: http://money.cnn.com/magazines/fortune/global500/2010

Table 2D The 25 largest MNEs from emerging economies, 2010 ranking

Rank	Company	Economy	Revenues (millions of US $)	% intra-regional sales
1	Sinopec (China Petroleum and Chemical Corporation)	China	187,518	98.00
2	State Grid	China	184,496	100.00
3	China National Petroleum	China	165,496	100.00
4	Samsung Electronics	Korea	108,927	49.70
5	Gazprom	Russia	94,472	100.00
6	Petrobras	Brazil	91,869	93.00
7	PDVSA	Venezuela	91,182	64.00
8	Pemex	Mexico	80,722	100.00
9	LG Electronics	Korea	78,892	45.50
10	China Mobile Communications	China	71,749	100.00
11	Hyundai Motor	Korea	71,678	62.91
12	Industrial & Commercial Bank of China	China	69,295	100.0
13	Lukoil	Russia	68,025	17.20
14	SK Holdings	Korea	64,396	94.97
15	Petronas	Malaysia	62,577	90.00
16	Hon Hai Precision Industry	Taiwan	59,324	98.0
17	China Construction Bank	China	58,361	98.60
18	Itaúsa-Investimentos Itaú	Brazil	57,859	99.00
19	China Life Insurance	China	57,019	100.00
20	Indian Oil	India	54,288	100.00
21	China Railway Construction	China	52,044	93.70
22	Banco Bradesco	Brazil	51,608	98.00
23	China Railway Group	China	50,704	100.00
24	Agricultural Bank of China	China	49,742	100.00
25	Bank of China	China	49,682	97.50

Data are for 2009.

Source: Authors' calculations and *Fortune*, The Global 500, July 26, 2010 and individual company's annual reports.

E-resources: http://money.cnn.com/magazines/fortune/global500/2010

APPENDIX B TO CHAPTER 2

In this chapter we developed the CSA–FSA framework for the study of international business. Here we examine a related approach to the study of the reasons behind the investments made by MNEs. The "eclectic" approach, first developed by John Dunning, provides a consolidation of the literature on FDI that draws on industrial organization theories, location theory, and market imperfections approaches.

Dunning's "eclectic" theory of MNEs

The eclectic theory specifies a set of three conditions that must be met if a firm is to engage in foreign operations: firm-specific advantages (FSAs), internalization advantages, and country-specific advantages (CSAs). (See Table 2E.)

Firm-specific (ownership-specific) advantages (FSAs)

The firm must possess net ownership advantages vis-à-vis firms of other nationalities in serving particular (and, in practice, mainly foreign) markets. These firm-specific

Table 2E Dunning's "eclectic" theory of international production

A Ownership-specific (firm-specific) advantages
Firm-specific knowledge advantages
Management, marketing, financial skills
Vertical integration
   Control of resources
   Control of markets
Risk diversification

B Internalization (by MNEs)
To enforce property rights and overcome other transaction costs
To reduce buyer uncertainty
To overcome government regulations

C Location-specific (country-specific) advantages
National production functions
Government controls and regulations
Political risk; cultural values

(or ownership) advantages largely take the form of the possession of intangible assets, which are, at least for a period of time, exclusive or specific to the firm possessing them.

Internalization advantages

A firm possessing an advantage can either use the advantage itself (internalize it) or sell or lease the advantage to other firms. This choice is usually explained in the context of transactions costs and internalization theory (Rugman 1981). There are costs involved in use of markets and in internal coordination and control. The FDI decision depends on which option presents the best net return (revenue minus cost), when the risks associated with each alternative are taken into account. According to internalization theory, both natural and unnatural market imperfections induce internalization by MNEs. The firm must consider not only government-imposed regulations, but also natural barriers and other transaction costs such as the creation of buyer uncertainty.

Assuming that a firm possesses unique ownership advantages, if it is to engage in FDI it must be more beneficial for it to internalize its FSA, for example, to secure property rights over its FSAs in knowledge, rather than to sell or lease them to foreign firms. This internalization is done through an extension of its own activities rather than by externalizing them through contacts at arm's-length prices (which, in any case, may not exist) with independent firms. The management of the firm must judge that alternatives to internalization such as licensing, management contracts, franchises, technical service agreements, turnkey projects, and subcontracts are either not feasible or the most profitable method of appropriating its FSAs.

Country-specific (location-specific) advantages (CSAs)

Assuming that the conditions stated in the two preceding sections are satisfied, if FDI is to take place it must be profitable for the enterprise to locate abroad, that is, to utilize these FSAs in conjunction with at least some factor inputs (including natural resources) outside its home country. Otherwise foreign markets would be served entirely by exports and home markets by domestic production. Therefore, the location-specific advantages of the MNE are important elements in its choice of modality for servicing foreign markets.

Relevance of the Dunning model

The net ownership, or firm-specific, advantages are required to offset the costs incurred by the MNE of operating at a distance from its home base. In the literature on the MNE, these costs are referred to, following Williamson (1975), as transaction costs. Transaction costs arise from the difficulties of communicating over large distances and of controlling many subsidiaries. Both factors come into play once production decisions are made across national boundaries. In contrast, these costs of operating internationally are not incurred by a local firm. The MNE must possess advantages that offset the disadvantages (additional costs) incurred in operating transnationally. If assets corresponding to those conferring the advantages to the MNE were available to local host-country firms, the MNE would not be able to compensate for the transaction costs of operating at a distance.

The use of the advantage in the host country is required if FDI is to take place. The cost of moving resources used in the host country must exceed the costs of controlling a subsidiary at a distance plus the costs of trade. Otherwise, the resource would be exported or moved to the home country, production would take place in the home country, and the foreign-country market would be served by exports.

Sources of FSAs

The range of advantages that can lead to FDI is large but can be summarized as follows:

1 Proprietary technology due to research and development activities.
2 Managerial, marketing, or other skills specific to the organizational function of the firm.
3 Product differentiation, trademarks, or brand names.
4 Large size, reflecting scale economies.
5 Large capital requirements for plants of the minimum efficient size.

Sources of internalization advantages

The conditions that favor internalization include:

1 The high costs of making and enforcing contracts.
2 Buyer uncertainty about the value of the technology being sold.
3 A need to control the use or resale of the product.
4 Advantages to using price discrimination or cross-subsidization.

Sources of CSAs

The location-specific advantages of the host country can include:

1 Natural resources.
2 Efficient and skilled, relatively low-cost labor force.
3 Trade barriers restricting imports.

The first and second of these CSAs can result in FDI that leads to exports as well as to production for the local market. The third CSA will be associated with production for the local market only.

Tariff and non-tariff barriers to trade, the country's competitive environment, and government regulations also influence CSAs. Building on these CSAs, the firm makes decisions about the efficient international configuration and coordination between segments of its value chain (operations, marketing, R&D, and logistics). The skill in making such organizational decisions represents a strong, managerial firm-specific asset in itself.

In a perfect market situation, free trade would be the most efficient means of servicing markets abroad; however, given the many barriers to trade presently affecting the market, MNEs are a necessary alternative. The ability of MNEs to create internal markets enables them to bypass the barriers to trade that governments often erect.

Managers and most MNEs use strategies that build on the interactions of CSAs and FSAs. They do this to position themselves in a unique strategic space. In Porter's terminology, the CSAs form the basis of the global platform from which the multinational firm derives a home-base "diamond" advantage of global competitiveness. The Porter "diamond" was discussed in Chapter 1 under "Maintaining economic competitiveness."

References

Rugman, Alan M. *Inside the Multinationals: The Economics of Internal Markets* (New York: Columbia University Press, 1981).

Williamson, Oliver E. *Markets and Hierarchies* (New York: Free Press, 1975).

Chapter 3

THE TRIAD AND INTERNATIONAL BUSINESS

Contents

Objectives of the chapter

As we noted in Chapter 1, a small number of economies account for a large portion of international investment and international trade. These triad economies—the United States, the EU15, and Japan—are referred to collectively as the core triad. In this chapter we are going to look more closely at the "broad" triad of North America, Europe, and Asia and examine the role and impact of these regions on international business activity. We will also consider their role in both trade and FDI, and look at examples of how each member of the triad pursues target markets in other triad countries. We will also examine some of the economic and political relationships that exist between triad members and how these can have an impact on the international business community. We will also link to future chapters, such as Chapters 8 and 9, dealing with strategy and structure, respectively. In this context, we develop reasons for the need for MNEs to develop regional/triad strategies rather than "global" strategies.

The specific objectives of this chapter are to:

1 *Describe* the major reasons for FDI.

2 *Explain* the role of triad-based MNEs in worldwide FDI and trade.

3 *Relate* select examples of inter-triad MNE business activity.

4 *Discuss* the economic interrelationships among triad members.

Boeing versus Airbus

In 1970 a European consortium consisting of Germany, France, and the UK (Spain later became a member) created Airbus Industrie. The objective of the consortium was to build commercial aircraft with Germany, the UK, and Spain taking on the job of constructing the aircraft and France assuming responsibility for assembling it. The logic of the arrangement was fairly straightforward. Given the growth of international travel, there would be a continual need for new commercial aircraft, and Airbus wanted to be a major player in this industry.

Until this time, when major air carriers such as American Airlines, Japan Airlines, and Lufthansa needed to replace aging aircraft or increase the size of their fleet, they turned to Boeing or McDonnell Douglas, the two giant US aircraft manufacturers. Cargo carriers such as FedEx and DHL also bought aircraft from them, and, as international air shipments continued to grow rapidly, the annual demand proved to be a boon for Boeing and McDonnell.

The initial challenge for Airbus was to capture some market share and thus establish a toehold in the industry. This, fortunately, was not a problem. The consortium had divided up the responsibility for building the aircraft among its members. In this way, each country was guaranteed some of the work and, in turn, could count on its respective government to provide financial assistance and contracts. In particular, the consortium would have to spend large amounts of money for research and development in order to build competitive, state-of-the-art craft, but by getting support from their respective governments a great deal of the initial risk would be eliminated. This, by the way, was the same approach that had been used in the United States and helped account for much of Boeing's and McDonnell's success in building large aircraft. For example, much of the funding to build the giant C-5A cargo plane was provided by the US military. Then, by using this same technology, it was possible for Boeing to build its giant passenger aircraft.

Realizing that the consortium would eventually be able to build competitive craft, Boeing and McDonnell lodged complaints with the US government claiming that Airbus was being subsidized by its governments, and Washington needed to take steps to protect the US commercial aircraft manufacturing industry. As the governments on both sides met to talk and discuss these issues, Airbus started building aircraft. It took quite a while, but by 1990 the consortium not only was becoming well established but had back orders for 1,100 aircraft and by 1997 this number had reached 2,300. In the process Airbus captured over 30 percent of the world market. One of the major reasons for its success was that it focused on building fuel-efficient craft at competitive prices. Its wide-body, medium-range models, the A300 and A310, for example, were very reliable and the orders started flowing in from a wide number of buyers including large US carriers such as American Airlines and Northwest. During the 1990s the battle in the aircraft market also saw Boeing and McDonnell Douglas merge their operations. McDonnell could not compete effectively in this new, highly competitive market, but when merged with Boeing it could provide the latter with a good chance to prevent Airbus from steamrolling the US aircraft manufacturing industry.

By 2001 Airbus was doing better than ever. Not only had it managed to catch up with Boeing and hold 50 percent of the overall market, but it was in the throes of making major decisions that could result in its becoming the dominant player in the industry. The company had decided to build a giant, double-decker superjumbo jet. Known as the A380, this aircraft is capable of carrying 555 passengers, and the first craft made its first commercial flight in 2007. A host of buyers signed firm orders with the company, including Qantas, which ordered 12 of the craft, Singapore Airlines, and Air France, which each placed orders for 10. In addition Singapore Airlines took an option for 15 more. The Singapore deal alone was worth over $8 billion to Airbus, showing how lucrative the market for a superjumbo jet could be. By 2010, other A380 users are Lufthansa and Emirates. However, the engine explosion on one of Qantas' A380 on November 4, 2010 sparked a safety review, in what was considered to be the most serious safety incident yet for the superjumbo in its three years of operation. The plane experienced midair explosion shortly after taking off. The pilots of the flight made a successful emergency landing in Singapore. The aircraft have undergone intensive work before they were resumed to fly three weeks later. The decision to restore A380 services followed an intensive Trent 900 engine inspection program carried out in close consultation with Rolls Royce and Airbus. Modifications have been made to the Rolls Royce engines used on 20 A380s by three airlines—Qantas, Lufthansa, and Singapore Airlines.

In response to Airbus's A380 aircraft, Boeing announced that it was going to build a smaller, faster, longer-range plane that would fly just below the speed of sound. Quite clearly the two competitors were moving in different directions.

Airbus was betting more than $12 billion that airlines will want a superjumbo jet that can carry a large number of passengers on long trips to a given region. Boeing was betting that there is a much larger demand for smaller, faster planes that can take people directly to their destination. In doing so, Boeing has ceded to Airbus a highly profitable jumbo market, wagering that the European group will not earn back its huge investment but rather end up stumbling badly. Boeing's decision to abandon the development of a larger plane (similar to what Airbus proposed) relied heavily on follow-on studies of the giant 747. The company's engineers concluded that, except in the case of a huge 800-passenger plane, a double-decker design had to be scaled back to a single decker to satisfy technical and safety standards. One reason, according to Boeing engineers, is because a double-decker arrangement is very inefficient. Another is that, in case of evacuation, a two-level aircraft can present major problems for those on board.

At this same time Airbus announced that its consortium arrangement was coming to an end and that the company would now be managed as a corporation. This move effectively ended Airbus's life as an organization that operated in the world of business and politics and one in which each partner held a veto, politically motivated committees made many of the important decisions, and when things did not go well state funds could be counted on to prop up the consortium. Now, with all of that behind it, Airbus worked to streamline its operations and, according to the business partners, shave off about $400 million in annual expenses.

Will Airbus continue to dominate the airways? Its initial challenge was to build the A380 superjumbo. If the demand for the huge craft does materialize, Boeing may find itself as a minor player in the industry. On the other hand, while in late 2001 Airbus recruited thousands of new workers to help with the project, it had trouble finding partners to help fund the venture. A number of European suppliers signed up but US and Japanese companies did not. For example, Airbus had offered Japanese manufacturers up to 8 percent of the work on the A380 in return for funding but had no takers. The company also wanted to get US firms to invest and thus defuse a potential political problem that could result in the US government making it difficult for Airbus to do business in the United States. When Airbus first got started, it relied heavily on governmental support. Now that it was very successful, it no longer needed this type of help. However, the US government was unlikely to sit by and let this company dominate the industry while Boeing might be forced to take a back seat. In a way, the situation is similar to that in 1970 when Airbus first got started—the main difference is that the two companies now seem to be in opposite positions.

The US and EU have been involved in a long dispute on subsidies for Boeing and Airbus. In 2004, the US lodged a complaint with the World Trade Organization (WTO). In 2010, the WTO ruled that the EU paid illegal subsidies to Airbus. EU governments were found to have unfairly financed Airbus through risk free loans, research and infrastructure funding. But the WTO did not uphold all of the US complaints. However, the EU rejected the US claim that state support had materially impacted the sector and challenged the WTO ruling. The EU said that support for Airbus was not found to have affected jobs and profits in the US aircraft industry. And Airbus said that the support system itself—based on loans repaid as planes are sold—had not been faulted.

Meanwhile, the EU has made a similar complaint over the US's alleged support of Boeing. However, the WTO's report into US government funding received by Boeing has been delayed.

Websites: www.boeing.com; www.airbus.com.

Sources: Adapted from Steven Greenhouse, "There's No Stopping Europe's Airbus Now," *New York Times*, June 23, 1991, Section 3, pp. 1, 6; Stuart F. Brown, "How to Build a Really, Really, Really Big Plane," *Fortune*, March 5, 2001, p. 152; Anne Marie Squeo, "Boeing Plans to Build Smaller, Faster Jet," *Wall Street Journal*, March 30, 2001, p. A3; Daniel Michaels, "Airbus Signs Up Partners to Help Build Jumbo Jet," *Wall Street Journal*, June 21, 2001, p. A14; Mark Odell and Victor Mallet, "Airbus Cuts Back 2003 Production Targets," *Financial Times*, August 8, 2001, p. 15; Daniel Michaels, Zach Coleman, and Guy Chazan, "Airbus Is in Talks with Beijing on Sale of Jets," *Wall Street Journal*, August 21, 2001, p. A12; "Qantas Resumes A380 Flights After Safety Scare," *BBC News*, www.bbc.co.uk, November 27, 2010; "EU Airbus Subsidies Illegal, says WTO," *BBC News*, news.bbc.co.uk, June 30, 2010; "EU Challenges WTO Ruling on Airbus Subsidies," *BBC News*, news.bbc.co.uk, July 21, 2010.

1 What are three reasons for the Europeans creating the Airbus consortium?

2 How will Airbus help the EU compete in the United States?

3 How will Airbus help the EU compete in Japan?

4 In what way did the Airbus consortium use a keiretsu approach to building the aircraft? Why do you think it opted for this approach?

INTRODUCTION

Triad
The three major trading and investment blocs in the international arena: the United States, the EU, and Japan

Over the past decade international business activity has increased dramatically, especially among the **triad** nations. As has already been noted in Chapter 1, foreign direct investment and trade are at an all-time high. At the same time, however, the most active economies in the international arena have remained the same: the United States, Japan, and the members of the EU15, especially Germany, France, the UK, and Italy. During the current decade, a growing number of other countries will become increasingly prominent on the international business stage. China is moving quickly to establish itself as a major player. Others that we will be hearing from increasingly will include Australia, Brazil, Canada, India, Mexico, the Netherlands, the Russian Federation, Singapore, South Korea, and China to name but 10. Yet despite the increase of international activity by these countries and others in emerging economies, MNEs from the triad will continue to account for most of the world's foreign direct investment and trade. For this reason, every student of international business should be familiar with the triad and be aware of its impact on world commerce.

In Chapter 1 we pointed out that two of the drivers of globalization are foreign direct investment and trade. In this chapter we want to look more closely at these drivers and the role that the triad plays in both. We begin by examining some of the main reasons for **foreign direct investment (FDI)** in a triad context.

Foreign direct investment (FDI)
Equity funds invested in other nations

Much FDI is intra-regional (see Table 3.1). It has also been growing faster within the EU15 region of the triad, rather than globally. It has, however, declined in North America as NAFTA has substituted freer trade for FDI. In Asia, there has been a recent increase in intra-regional FDI. Japan, the largest source of FDI in the region, has only 26.4 percent of its FDI in other Asian countries. The vast majority of Japanese FDI is in North America (33.6 percent) and Western Europe (36.5 percent).[1] (Table 3.1 on FDI is similar to Table 1.2 on trade.)

REASONS FOR FDI

FDI is the ownership and control of foreign assets. In practice, FDI usually involves the ownership, whole or partial, of a company in a foreign country. This is called a foreign subsidiary. This equity investment can take a variety of forms. One is through the purchase of an ongoing company. For example, Solectron, the world's largest contract electronics firm, bought C-Mac Industries of Canada in order to acquire C-Mac's expertise in assembling high-end telecommunications and networking systems.[2] Rather than building this business from scratch, Solectron bought its way into the industry through FDI. Later Flextronics, Singapore acquired Solectron in 2007. Another common example of FDI is to set up a new overseas operation as either a joint venture or a totally owned enterprise. For example, Panasonic, formerly known as Matsushita has positioned itself to become a major competitor in the European digital industry. It has entered into a joint venture with British Telecommunications plc for

Table 3.1 Fifteen years of intra-regional FDI in the triad, 1993–2008

Year	Intra-regional outward FDI (%)		
	EU15	NAFTA	Asia
2008	68.9	19.2	9.1
1993	58.0	24.0	8.6

Notes: EU intra-regional FDI is FDI stocks within Europe as a whole. NAFTA intra-regional FDI is US and Canada stocks within NAFTA. Asia intra-regional FDI is Japan, South Korea, Australia, and New Zealand stocks within Asia.

Source: Authors' calculations based on OECD, *International Direct Investment Statistics Yearbook*, 2009.

Portfolio investment

The purchase of financial securities in other firms for the purpose of realizing a financial gain when these marketable assets are sold

the purpose of developing multimedia wireless services and products.[3] It is important to remember that FDI is different from **portfolio investment**, which entails the purchase of financial securities (especially bonds) in other firms for the purpose of realizing a financial gain when these marketable assets are sold. The objective of FDI is to provide the investing company with the opportunity to actively manage and control a foreign firm's activities, whereas the objective of portfolio investment is to achieve growth in the value of its financial holdings.[4]

Businesses are interested in taking an ownership position or gaining control of foreign assets for a number of reasons. In Chapter 2 we briefly discussed six of these reasons. The following section elaborates on these reasons.

Increase sales and profits

Some of the largest and best-known multinationals earn millions of dollars each year through overseas sales. Table 3.2 shows the MNEs with the largest foreign assets in 2008 by

Table 3.2 The largest MNEs by size of their foreign subsidiaries, 2008

Ranking foreign assets	MNE	Region/country	Foreign assets (billions of US $)	Total assets (billions of US $)	Foreign assets as a % of total assets	Intra-regional sales as a % of total sales
1	General Electric	US	401.2	797.7	50.30	54.85
2	Royal Dutch/Shell	EU	222.3	282.4	78.73	40.32
3	Vodafone	EU	201.5	218.9	92.06	82.21
4	BP	EU	188.9	228.2	82.79	56.96
5	Toyota	Japan	169.5	296.2	57.24	42.64
6	ExxonMobil	US	161.2	228.0	70.71	37.27
7	Total	EU	141.4	164.6	85.90	70.22
8	E.ON AG	EU	141.1	218.5	64.59	97.76
9	Electricite de France	EU	133.6	278.7	47.96	95.97
10	ArcelorMittal*	EU	127.1	133.0	95.52	n.a
11	Volkswagen AG	EU	123.6	233.7	52.92	72.80
12	GDF Suez S.A	EU	119.3	232.7	51.30	83.17
13	Anheuser-Busch InBev NV	EU	106.2	113.2	93.88	35.20
14	Chevron	US	106.1	161.1	65.85	n.a
15	Siemens AG	EU	104.4	135.1	77.34	51.32
16	Ford Motor	US	102.5	222.9	46.01	48.70
17	Eni S.p.A	EU	95.8	162.2	59.05	73.38
18	Telefonica SA	EU	95.4	139.0	68.65	60.65
19	Deutsche Telekom AG	EU	95.0	171.3	55.44	74.93
20	Honda Motor	Japan	89.2	120.4	74.04	28.00
21	Daimler AG	EU	87.9	184.0	47.78	47.00
22	France Telecom	EU	81.3	132.6	61.36	79.35
23	Conocophillips	US	77.8	142.8	54.5	71.30
24	Iberdrola SA	EU	73.5	119.4	61.59	78.79
25	Hutchison Whampoa Limited	Hong Kong, China	70.7	87.7	80.65	38.33

Notes: The firms are ranked by the UN by size of foreign assets (foreign subsidiaries). EU foreign assets include the assets of MNEs in other member countries.

* Data are not available or company reports by business segments, not by geographic segments. Data are for 2008.

Sources: Authors' calculations of intra-regional sales percentage from individual company's annual reports; United Nations, *World Investment Report 2010*, Annex table 26. The world's top 100 non-financial TNCs, ranked by foreign assets, 2008.

the UN's World Investment Report ranking. In the EU, for example, companies in smaller economies need to look outside of their home borders. This helps to explain why 78.73 percent of Royal Dutch/Shell's assets and 82.79 percent of BP's assets are in foreign markets, including the markets of other EU members. General Electric has over 50 percent of its sales outside of the United States. Another 4.5 percent of GE's sales are in Canada and Mexico, yielding intra-regional sales at 54.85 per cent.

The same is true of revenues. In 2008, about 60 percent of Royal Dutch/Shell's sales originate outside its markets in the EU home region. Similarly 63 percent of BP's sales are from outside the EU.[5] Similarly, in North America, where Canada's economy is only 10 percent the size of that of the United States, Canadian companies like Thomson Reuters Corporation have 96.5 percent of their assets in foreign markets, most notably the United States whereas the assets in Canada only accounts for 3.5 percent in 2008.[6]

In regional terms, among firms with large foreign assets some continue to derive a considerable amount of revenues in their home region. For example, Vodafone and France Telecom derive 82.21 and 79.35 percent of total revenues, respectively, in the EU. Only 8 of the 25 firms with the highest assets abroad, as listed in Table 3.2, have over 50 percent of their sales in a region other than their own.

There are also thousands of smaller firms worldwide that earn the bulk of their revenue from international customers. For an example, see the case **International Business Strategy in Action: Aflac**. SMEs also find that with the growth of large multinationals there is often a need for local suppliers; if they do well, there is a good chance that the MNE will extend the contract and allow them to supply other worldwide locations. So they, too, are interested in FDI because it can help them increase their sales and profits.

Foreign markets often offer more lucrative opportunities than do domestic markets. This helps to explain why Coca-Cola and IBM now earn more sales revenue and profits overseas than they do in the United States and why PepsiCo has become Mexico's largest consumer products company. In Japan, it helps to explain why in 2009, 63 percent of Honda's and over 70 percent of Sony's revenues come from overseas sales (see Table 2C, Chapter 2).[7] It also helps account for the decision by Tesco plc, the British supermarket firm, to expand operations into Eastern Europe and Asia. And the same is true for Wal-Mart, which in recent years has expanded rapidly and now has stores on four continents and appears on the verge of becoming a major competitor in the EU thanks to its FDI in the UK.[8] However, for most firms, including some listed above, "foreign" means in its own region; for example, Wal-Mart has 94.5 percent in North America; Tesco has 93.6 percent in Europe.

Enter rapidly growing markets

Some international markets are growing much faster than others, and FDI provides MNEs with the chance to take advantage of these opportunities. A good example is China. Over the past few years the Chinese economy has grown at an annual rate of around 7–11 percent.[9] These data also suggest that, as the country continues to move toward a market-driven economy, MNEs are likely to find a huge demand for goods and services that cannot be satisfied by local firms alone. Simply put, China is a market where most multinationals want to have a presence despite the fact that there are many problems in doing business there, and few MNEs have been able to extract an adequate return on their investment.

China is not the only emerging market being targeted by multinationals. A growing number of companies are using FDI to gain a foothold in Eastern Europe by acquiring local firms or setting up joint ventures there. India has also become a large recipient of FDI, particularly in the technology sector (see the Real Case in Chapter 14).

INTERNATIONAL BUSINESS STRATEGY IN ACTION

Aflac

The insurance industry is dominated by many well-known names: Prudential, Aetna, Northwestern, etc. Prior to 2000, few people in North America had ever heard of Aflac Inc. of Columbus, Georgia. However, the company has been the most successful insurer in Japan, with annual revenues of $18.3 billion and profits well over $1.497 billion in 2009. Aflac is the world's leading seller of cancer insurance, which helps to pay the cost of treating the disease, and it holds 90 percent of the Japanese market for this coverage. The Japanese subsidary accounts for by 73.8 percent of Aflac's pretax earnings and insures one out of every four Japanese.

The firm began doing business in Japan in 1974. Initially Aflac approached big Japanese insurers as potential joint-venture partners; none of them was interested. Eventually the Ministry of Finance gave the company a license to sell insurance, primarily because no Japanese insurer was in the business so that there would be no competition for local firms.

A key to Aflac's rapid growth and profitability is its system of selling through corporate agencies. The firm has set up in-house subsidiaries in Japanese corporations to handle the sale of its insurance. These subsidiaries would be illegal distributors in the United States, but they are very common in Japan. As a result, Aflac eventually ended up with over 40,000 Japanese companies offering its policies to their employees. From Hitachi to Sony, Toyota to Nissan, and Mitsui to Mitsubishi, policyholders throughout the country pay premiums of approximately $21 a month through an automatic payroll deduction plan. Moreover, once they are signed up, few Japanese drop out. In contrast to the United States, where only 25 percent of health and accident insurance policyholders remain with the same company for a decade or more, in Japan 75 percent of Aflac policyholders have been with Aflac for 10 or more years.

Will Aflac be able to continue its success in the market? In many countries such as the United States, cancer insurance is declining in popularity because coverage is now provided by basic policies. In Japan, however, the first stage of cancer treatment can cost up to $50,000. Even though the Japanese government is expected to introduce national care insurance, it has made clear that it will not be able to cover the full cost. Furthermore, about four years ago the company began to diversify its product line. Today over 30 percent of all sales in Japan are for non-cancer-related insurance. As a result of the costs associated with cancer, Aflac's supplemental coverage remains very popular. The additional success of its new products makes Aflac find the Japanese market to be profitable.

Perhaps the biggest challenge to Aflac's Japanese market share is market deregulation. Aflac has functioned practically as a monopoly in Japan over the past 30 years. In 2001, the Japanese government allowed Nippon Life Insurance and Tokio Marine & Fire to compete in the supplementary insurance market. Aflac need not worry in the short term, since these companies' operating costs are four times its own. In the long run, however, other companies might want to wrestle this profitable market away from Aflac. The company is well aware of this and is expanding its reach by partnering with Dai-Ichi Mutual, Japan's second-largest insurance company, to distribute each other's policies. In addition, a joint venture with Communicationware Corporation has seen the development of aflacdirect.com, the first company to provide insurance solely on the Internet.

Aflac has also turned to its domestic market by launching an aggressive marketing campaign featuring a mascot. The Aflac duck, as it has become known, has appeared in a series of television ads screaming Aaaaflaack to oblivious characters. This has had its desired effect, and today 95 percent of Americans recognize the name Aflac.

Websites: www.aflac.com; www.aflac.co.jp.

Sources: Adapted from Steve Lohr, "Under the Wing of Japan, Inc., a Fledgling Enterprise Soared," *New York Times*, January 15, 1992, pp. A1, C5; *Forbes*, January 4, 1993, p. 167; *Fortune*, May 31, 1993, p. 218; www.reportgallery.com/aflac/japan.htm; www.oecd.org/publications/figures/money.html; Bethany McLean, "Duck and Coverage," *Fortune*, August 13, 2001; Aflac, *Annual Report*, 2009.

Reduce costs

An MNE can sometimes achieve substantially lower costs by going abroad than by producing at home (see the case **International Business Strategy in Action: Lafarge and Cemex: concrete multinationals**). If labor expenses are high and represent a significant portion of overall costs, an MNE may be well advised to look to other geographic areas where the goods can be produced at a much lower labor price. Surprisingly perhaps, in recent years some Canadian manufacturers have been moving operations across the border to take advantage of lower US labor unit costs.

A second important cost factor is materials. If materials are in short supply or must be conveyed a long distance, it may be less expensive to move production close to the source of supply than to import the materials.

A third critical cost factor is energy. If the domestic cost of energy for making the product is high, the company may be forced to set up operations overseas near sources of cheaper energy.

A fourth important factor is transportation costs. A highly price-competitive product in one country might have to retail at uncompetitive prices in another country once transportation costs are added. The case **International Business Strategy in Action: Lafarge and Cemex** illustrates this situation.

In recent years many firms have used all four of these reasons to justify moving assembly operations to other countries. For example, low-skill labor costs are much lower in Mexico than in the United States, Korea, Hong Kong, Taiwan, or Singapore, so Mexico has become a prime target for the manufacture of labor-intensive products. In fact, some US firms have even set up **twin factories**, or *maquiladoras*, which involve production operations on both sides of the border and the shipment of goods between the two countries. As a result, today US components are shipped into Mexico duty free, assembled by Mexican workers, and then re-exported to the United States or other foreign markets under favorable tariff provisions. We further discuss the *maquiladora* industry in Chapter 19.

Gain a foothold in economic blocs

As we have noted on a number of occasions thus far, there are three major international economic blocs. MNEs that acquire a company in one of these blocs or that enter into an alliance to do business in one of these economic strongholds can obtain a number of benefits including the right to sell their output without having to be burdened by import duties or other restrictions. In the case of NAFTA, for example, the United States–Canada Free Trade Agreement of 1989 was the initial step in fashioning a giant North American market. In January 1994 this agreement was expanded to include Mexico, and in 2005 the Free Trade Agreement of the Americas (FTAA). International MNEs wanting to do business in North America are finding that it is important to gain a foothold in this region through FDI. The same is true in the EU. In 2004, the membership of this bloc increased from 15 to 25 with the admission of Cyprus, the Czech Republic, Estonia, Hungary, Latvia, Lithuania, Malta, Poland, the Slovak Republic, and Slovenia. Bulgaria and Romania joined in 2007. Turkey has also requested to join the union. Meanwhile in Asia, while Japan continues to be the major economic power, we are likely to see the rise of an "Asian bloc" that includes countries such as Australia, China, India, Indonesia, Malaysia, the Philippines, South Korea, Taiwan, and Thailand. On February 27, 2009, ASEAN (Association of South East Asian Nations)–Australia–New Zealand Free Trade Area was signed and came into effect on January 1, 2010. The ASEAN plus four is a set of bilateral trade agreements/strategic partnerships between ASEAN and the four Asian countries of Japan, Korea, China and India. Through the use of intra-regional trade and FDI agreements, these countries are creating a bloc that provides a balance to NAFTA and the EU. During the next two decades, it is highly likely that the major economic powers and those in the next economic tier will cooperate to create these blocs in order to stimulate their respective economies and to provide a competitive stance for firms doing business under their umbrella. This means that in Europe we are likely to see most countries including the Russian Federation (but perhaps not Switzerland) becoming members of the EU, while in the Western hemisphere most countries of North and South America joining NAFTA through a more active FTAA.

Twin factories

(Also see *Maquiladoras*) Production operations set up on both sides of the US–Mexican border for the purpose of shipping goods between the two countries

Maquiladoras

(Also see *Twin factories*) Production operations set up on both sides of the US–Mexican border in a free trade zone for the purpose of shipping goods between the two countries

INTERNATIONAL BUSINESS STRATEGY IN ACTION

Lafarge and Cemex: concrete multinationals

Cement is extremely heavy and very costly to ship long distances. Producers must place cement plants near limestone deposits and/or a short distance from large urban areas so that materials can be shipped to their final destination. If the cement has to be shipped a long distance due to a lack of adequate resources, this is done by boat. For example, Canadian firms export cement to the United States by shipping it across the Great Lakes.

Originally, the need to be near natural resources as well as a given market created an industry of small local-ized cement companies. As sophisticated logistic systems allowed economies of scale to be achieved in this industry, firms began to merge with nearby rivals, eventually acquir-ing firms in foreign markets.

The largest of these is Lafarge, a French MNE that accounts for 10 percent of the world's cement capacity and has operations in 75 countries. The firm is the leader in the European market and depends on it for 50 percent of its revenues. In North America, the firm is the third-largest cement producer and derives 20 percent of its revenues in 2009. Yet, it is Asia where the company is now putting its focus. All but a few countries in this region still have significant building to do for their infrastructure to meet the needs of their populations and to catch up to industrial-ized countries.

Lafarge is already the market leader in both the Philippines and Malaysia, but it is in China where it sees the greatest opportunity. In China, where thousands of cement manufacturers with varying degrees of efficiency and technology are scattered throughout the country, Lafarge hopes to bring its state-of-the-art technology and experi-ence to make China one of the firm's major markets. China is presently the largest producer of cement, accounting for one-third of the world's production, and demand is expected to increase further as the country continues to modernize.

Cemex SA is Mexico's largest cement maker. It is also the third-largest cement maker in the world, and in recent years the company has been much more profit-able than its two larger competitors thanks to a series of well-executed strategies. These include an international expansion strategy that is very similar to Lafarge's: to look for markets with long-term economic growth potential, large and growing populations, and high pent-up demand from below-average construction. Cemex's efforts have paid off. Since 1985, when Lorenzo Zambrano took over as chief executive of his family business, the firm has become

Source: Corbis/Raymond Gehman

Mexico's top multinational with operations in 30 countries across five continents. In 2002, Cemex was the first firm from a developing country to enter the list of the world's top 100 transnational firms, according to the UN's *World Investment Report*. And, in Latin America, Cemex had the best-known construction brand in 2003.

The firm's international excursions began in 1992 with the acquisition of two Spanish cement companies. Soon after, Cemex acquired and fixed up smaller cement com-panies in Latin America and the Caribbean. Most recently it purchased Saraburi Cement of Thailand, a move designed to give it a base of operations in Asia. When Cemex initially embarked on this strategy, many bankers were concerned that the company would still be making most of its money in Mexico, and a devaluation of the peso would severely impact its international operations. In late 1994, when the Mexican government suddenly devalued its currency, Cemex was generating only 25 percent of its earnings from overseas operations, and the firm was highly lever-aged in dollars. However, instead of pulling back, Cemex convinced the bankers that the best strategy was to press forward and buy cement companies in Colombia and Venezuela. The decision was fortuitous. Venezuela soon devalued its own currency, but as its economy went into a tailspin Cemex sent in some of its own executives to straighten out the operation, reorganize the administrative and information system, and cut the workforce. By the end of the year Cemex had doubled the unit's annual cash flow to $200 million.

One distinct difference in Lafarge's and Cemex's strat-egies in developing countries is that Cemex is not entering the Chinese market, at least not yet. Although China has the characteristics that Cemex is looking for, in demographics,

▶

potential growth, and a lack of infrastructure, the country is riddled with price controls and a taxing system designed to drain profits. Whether losses in the present are warranted for future growth in China might not be relevant. Cemex is riddled with debt from all its acquisitions and might not be able to afford low levels of profits in China.

Cemex's expansion is not limited to developing markets. After its acquisition of Southdown for $2.6 billion in 2000, it became the largest cement producer in the United States. The move made sense after the United States imposed punitive antidumping tariffs on Mexican cement in 1990. Between August 2000 and July 2001, Cemex paid $29.5 million in duties which, in turn, were dispersed among US producers that claimed to be affected by the dumping.

Meanwhile in Mexico, in 2009, where the firm still generates 21 percent of its revenues, a stronger economy has resulted in higher sales and profits. As a result, Cemex is now paying down its debt and expanding operations in Europe and Asia where it is both buying and building

plants. In 2009, the company records annual revenue of $14.659 billion and EBIT (earnings before interest and tax) of $2.679 billion.

Lafarge's and Cemex's biggest assets are their financial strength, in terms of cash flow, technology, and expertise. They compete in an industry with a sea of small, often inefficient, players. At present, these firms are snatching market share from these smaller competitors across the developing world and competing with each other in the developed world.

Websites: www.lafargecorp.com; www.cement.bluecircle.co.uk; www.holnam.com; www.cemex.com.

Sources: Adapted from http://www.lafargecorp.com/lafarge2.nsf; www.cemnet.co.uk/news.htm; http://www.lafarge.com; http://www.cementindia.net/; "Bagged Cement," *The Economist*, July 17, 1999; "The Cemex Way," *The Economist*, June 14, 2000; "Mexico's Cemex Wins Bet on Acquisitions," *Wall Street Journal*, April 30, 1998, p. A14; Cemex, *Annual Report*, 2009; Lafarge, *Annual Report*, 2009; United Nations, *World Investment Report 2002*; "Google Voted Best Brand of 2003," BBC.co.uk, February 3, 2004; John Moody, "Mexican Cement Maker with a Worldview," *New York Times*, April 15, 2004.

The final result will be three "broad" triad regions, and any company that wants to do business worldwide will have to have a presence in all three blocs. Indeed, a "global" firm is best defined as one with at least 20 percent of its sales in each region of the triad. In 2001, only 9 of the largest 500 companies in the world fitted this description and the trend has been confirmed with 5-year data set 2001–2005.[10]

Protect domestic markets

Another reason for FDI is to protect one's domestic market. Many MNEs are now entering an international market in order to attack potential competitors and thus prevent them from expanding their operations overseas. These multinationals reason that a competitor is less likely to enter a foreign market when it is busy defending its home-market position. Similarly, sometimes an MNE will enter a foreign market in order to bring pressure on a company that has already challenged its own home market. For example, 10 days after Fuji began building its first manufacturing facility in the United States, Kodak announced its decision to open a manufacturing plant in Japan.

Sometimes the decision to go international also helps a firm to protect its position with current clients which are going international. For example, when Honda Motors set up operations in Indiana in 1989 through an Isuzu–Subaru plant in Lafayette, Nippondenso, a producer of automobile radiators and heaters, established a plant nearby. So did Mitsubishi Bank, the primary bank for Honda. In addition to the extra business it generates, this strategy helps to combat local competitors, such as Indiana manufacturers and banks, which might otherwise gain inroads and perhaps even threaten domestic business should they decide to set up operations in Japan.

Protect foreign markets

Sometimes MNEs will use FDI in order to protect their foreign markets. In the United States, for example, from 1981 to 1991 the total number of service stations had declined by over 50 percent. BP, which had a substantial presence in this market, realized that in order to protect its investment it would be necessary to make a substantial investment in order to upgrade its stations and increase its market share. The company refines and markets petroleum products and realized that if it could attract a growing number of customers to its service stations, it could profit handsomely by moving its products directly downstream to the final consumer. The company also merged with Amoco, thus assuring itself of a good North American refining and retail market share and, in the process, protecting its investment in this foreign market. Unfortunately BP inherited old refineries which had accidents, leading to legal hassles. Following the Gulf Oil spill accident of April 20, 2010, BP announced plans to sell assets, including those in the United States to raise funds of $30 billion to help pay compensation for the oil spill.

Acquire technological and managerial know-how

Still another reason for FDI is to acquire technological and managerial expertise. One way of doing this is to set up operations near those of leading competitors. This is why some US firms have moved some of their research and development facilities to Japan. With this strategy, they find it is easier to monitor the competition and to recruit scientists from local universities and competitive laboratories. Kodak is an excellent example.

The company made the decision to build an 180,000 ft^2 (17,000 m^2) research center in Japan, and it started cultivating leading scientists to help with recruiting. Kodak used all the same approaches that Japanese firms employ in the United States: financing research by university scientists and offering scholarships to outstanding young Japanese engineers, some of whom would later join Kodak. In addition, the company hired internationally known scientists to help attract experienced colleagues from leading Japanese companies and to recruit young graduates from host universities such as the Tokyo Institute of Technology. As a result, Japan is now the center of Kodak's worldwide research efforts in a number of high-technology areas.[11]

✔ Active learning check

Review your answer to Active Learning Case question 1 and make any changes you like. Then compare your answer to the one below.

1 **What are three reasons for the Europeans creating the Airbus consortium?**

One of the reasons for the Europeans creating the Airbus consortium was to enter a rapidly growing market. As can be seen from the data in the case, billions of dollars has been be spent on new aircraft from 2007 until now. Singapore Airlines alone was the first airline putting out over $8 billion for 25 A380 craft, and it is only one of a number of firms that have placed firm orders with Airbus. So there is a huge market for large craft, and the Europeans wanted to be in this lucrative market. A second reason for creating the consortium was to help build a stronger EU economy. Airbus provided thousands of jobs and billions of euros to the member countries, and, even with its new arrangement in which it is no longer managed by governments but rather by investors, the company is continuing to provide both jobs and revenues in Europe. A third reason that Airbus was created was to protect the domestic market by making it less reliant on foreign firms such as Boeing. Given that Airbus now holds 50 percent of the commercial aircraft market, this objective has clearly been attained.

FDI AND TRADE BY TRIAD MEMBERS

As seen thus far, there are many reasons why MNEs make FDI. In addition, much of this FDI, and trade as well, is made by the core triad members: the United States, the EU, and Japan. The following examines these findings in more depth.

The triad's domination of FDI and trade

Over the past decade the triad has accounted for an extremely large percentage of both FDI *and* world trade. For example, triad countries make billions of dollars of investments in one another. In 2008, total the United States' FDI was $1,809.876 billion in the EU and $79.235 billion in Japan. In turn the EU15 countries and Japan had total investments in the United States of $1,622.911 billion and $259.569 billion, respectively. EU15 FDI in Japan was $86.915 billion while Japanese FDI in the EU was $161.649 billion.[12] Quite clearly, triad countries are investing large sums of money in each other's operations.

In addition, as seen in Table 3.3a, the percentage of global FDI accounted for by the core triad countries in 2008 is 73.61 percent. Even though the amount of worldwide FDI has more than tripled over the past 10 years, the triad remained the engine of this growth. The EU15 now account for half of the world's FDI, partly because intra-regional FDI is included in this total.

Much the same picture holds for trade patterns in the triad as we saw for FDI; there are very strong two-way trade flows. The EU15 conduct a large amount of annual trade with Japan and the United States, and both Japan and the United States do a great deal of trading with both the EU15 and with each other. Table 3.3b reports the trade of the core triad and shows that in 2008 these three blocs accounted for 48.09 percent of all world imports and over 55.37 percent of all world exports. As a result of such trade (and FDI), it is clear that the core triad is the major economic force in the international arena.

Triad FDI clusters

The above data clearly show the importance of the triad in international business, but this impact extends well beyond the FDI and trade that take place among its members. Triad countries have also become major investors in poorer nations. For example, in 2008, US FDI in Latin America and other Western hemisphere was $563.809 billion.[13] Typically, recipients of FDI are part of an **FDI cluster**, which is a group of developing countries that are usually located in the same geographic region as the triad member and have some form of

FDI cluster
A group of developing countries usually located in the same geographic region as the triad member and having some form of economic link to this member

Table 3.3a Ten years of triad FDI

	1998		2008	
Country/regions	FDI stock (millions of US $)	% of total	FDI stock (millions of US $)	% of total
US	1,000,703	23.22	3,162,021	19.51
EU15*	1,955,783	45.39	8,086,804	49.90
Japan	270,035	6.26	680,331	4.19
Triad	3,226,521	74.88	11,929,156	73.61
All others	1,081,887	25.11	4,276,507	26.38
World	4,308,408	100.00	16,205,663	100.00

* EU15 numbers are in outward stocks of FDI by every EU15 member and thus include intra-EU15 FDI.

Sources: Authors' calculations; United Nations, *World Investment Report 1999*, pp. 495–500; United Nations, *World Investment Report 2009*, pp. 251–254.

E-resources: UNCTAD Statistics Online Database, Foreign Direct Investment, Major FDI Indicators, http://stats.unctad.org/FDI/

Table 3.3b Ten years of triad trade

Country/ regions	Exports				Imports			
	1999		2008		1999		2008	
	(billions of US $)	% of total	(billions of US $)	% of total	(billions of US $)	% of total	(billions of US $)	% of total
US	1,013.3	17.95	2,036.7	12.68	765.3	13.20	1,338.5	8.07
EU*	2,130.4	37.74	6,169.5	38.42	2,052.3	35.42	5,801.3	35.01
Japan	278.1	4.92	684.0	4.26	448.5	7.74	830.6	5.00
Triad	3,421.9	60.63	8,890.3	55.37	3,266.2	56.37	7,970.5	48.09
All others	2,221.8	39.36	7,165.6	44.62	2,527.3	43.62	8,601.4	51.90
World	5,643.8	100.00	16,056.0	100.00	5,793.6	100.00	16,572.0	100.00

* EU includes intra-EU FDI.

Note: Exports are calculated by including freight and insurance while imports do not include freight and insurance.

Sources: Authors' calculations and International Monetary Fund, *Direction of Trade Statistics Yearbook, 2000* (Washington, DC: IMF, 2000), pp. 2–5; International Monetary Fund, *Direction of Trade Statistics Yearbook, 2009* (Washington, DC: IMF, 2009), pp. 2–5.

economic link to it. For example, the United States tends to be a dominant investor in Latin America, and countries such as Mexico, Brazil, and Argentina are part of its FDI cluster. Similarly, Eastern Europe is a favorite investment target for the EU15 countries and helps account for the FDI made by Germany and France in the Czech Republic and the Russian Federation. The latter is part of the EU15 FDI cluster. And as might be expected, Japan's FDI cluster includes China, Singapore, and Thailand, countries where Japanese MNEs have invested large sums of money.

Not all developing countries, however, have been successful in attracting triad investment. One reason is because much of this investment has been used by multinationals to build regional networks, often starting near their home base and then working outward. For example, 69 percent of all FDI in Mexico comes from US firms and over 80 percent of all FDI in Estonia derives from the EU15 countries.[14] The UNCTAD has also found that in 2008, more than half of all investment into developing countries is going to three nations: Brazil, China, and India.[15] And much of this money comes from triad countries that are located in that part of the world. So Brazil and Mexico are recipients of much US FDI, and China and Singapore are favorite FDI targets for Japanese firms.

Such investment policies help reinforce our earlier comments about the triad's dominance of regional economic clusters. In the future, triad members may well continue to strengthen their FDI in specific regions, as in Europe, where the EU15 is a major force in economic development. At the same time, these types of investment strategies by triad members may restrict trade and investment opportunities for some developing countries. This is why it is so important for non-triad countries to be linked to the triad in some way. As will be explained later in the book, by gaining linkage to the triad, a country can benefit by tapping these enormous markets as a supplier to large MNEs or by selling directly to customers in these markets.

MULTINATIONALS IN ACTION: REGIONAL BUSINESS STRATEGY

During the first decades of this century, the triad will continue to dominate the international business scene. In particular, members will pursue market opportunities within their own triad as well as that of the other members. For example, retailing in the United States is dominated by Wal-Mart. However, the company is not content to simply sell in its home country so it has expanded within NAFTA (Canada and Mexico). It has also expanded into both Europe and Asia. In 2009, Wal-Mart reports, by segment data, that Wal-Mart US accounts for 64 percent, US Sam's Club 12 percent and International 25 percent.[16] In Europe, meanwhile, Tesco is expanding rapidly across Europe where it has 86.54 percent of its sales, and it is now pushing into Asia. As of September 2009, Carrefour, the French retail giant, has more than 13,687 stores throughout Europe (87.70 percent) out of 15,594 stores worldwide, where it has 69 percent of its sales and 1,228 stores in Latin America (8.87 percent of total stores), 679 stores in Asia (4.35 percent of total stores).[17] This intra-regional pattern of activity is common for triad firms. In fact, one of the best examples is provided by the automobile industry where auto makers are very much region based. For example, Ford Motors has 53.83 percent of its sales in North America.[18]

Thus, a more careful analysis of international business shows that "international" expansion does not necessarily mean "global" expansion. For example, Wal Mart has 76 percent sales (measured by absolute US$ sales figures by segments) in the United States alone (US Wal Mart and US Sam Club) and if Canada and Mexico is added, 94.5 percent of its total sales is in North America (see Chapter 1, Real Case: Wal-Mart). This means that the home region of the triad is still its locus for strategy. It does not have a "global" strategy. This even confuses other professors. For example, an entire chapter in a book on global strategy is directed to learning the "lessons from Wal-Mart's globalization."[19] Yet Wal-Mart is not really a global company. Indeed, in the United Nations *World Investment Report 2001* it is reported that Wal-Mart has one of the lowest scores of any of the 100 largest MNEs. On a transnational index Wal-Mart has a "network spread index" (a measure of actual to possible FDI—of which there were a possible 187 measures in 1999) of under 5 percent. Other low scores are for Woodbridge, Mitsubishi, Petróleos de Venezuela, Edison, and Nippon Oil. In contrast, many MNEs score over 30 percent, for example, Shell, Nestlé, Unilever, TotalFina, Aventis, and ABB.

As Figure 3.1 indicates, Wal-Mart is a regional but not a global business. As of 2009, the firm had 73 percent of its sales (as measured by stores) in its home region of NAFTA. Latin America accounted for 14 percent of sales and other regions for another 13 percent. The locus of its business model strategy and structure is regional (see Figure 3.1).

✔ Active learning check

Review your answer to Active Learning Case question 2 and make any changes you like. Then compare your answer to the one below.

2 How will Airbus help the EU compete in the United States?

Airbus will open up markets in the United States by offering alternative aircraft to those being produced by Boeing. These Airbus offerings are not only reliable but fuel efficient and, as noted in the case, are often provided at very competitive prices. As a result, Airbus has been able to tap a US market that had been previously closed to the EU because no European company could compete with Boeing and McDonnell Douglas. Now Airbus has been able to land contracts with US firms such as American Airlines, one of the largest carriers in the world. If the A380 proves successful, it will help Airbus compete ever more effectively in the United States.

The world's regional automotive industry

In 2001 there were 29 automotive firms in the world's largest 500 firms.[20] Now in 2009, there are still 29, and they average $56.257 billion in sales. Only one of these is a "global" firm, Mazda, defined as having at least 20 percent of sales in each of the three regions of the

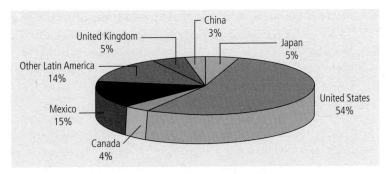

Figure 3.1 Wal-Mart's globalization: regional distribution of stores

Notes: Data are for 2009. US stores includes 56 stores in Puerto Rico.

Source: Wal Mart Stores, *Annual Reports*, 2009.

broad triad of the EU, North America, and Asia. Indeed 18 of the 29 auto and auto parts firms are home-region based, with an average of over 60 percent of their sales as intra-regional (see Table 3.4). There are a few special cases. There are 10 bi-regional firms, 7 auto makers and 3 parts makers, with over 20 percent of their sales in two parts of the triad and less than 50 percent in any region, including Toyota, Daimler, Honda, Nissan, Volvo, Tata Motors, and Magna. The weighted average of intra-regional sales in the automotive sector is 61.87 percent, quite close to the manufacturing sector's average of 65.6 percent. In 2001, the intra-regional sales in the automotive sector is 57.3 percent; in 2009, it is 61.87 percent, indicating an increasing trend. The auto makers were causalities of the worldwide economic downturn since 2008, they have to rely more on the intra-regional sales to survive.

The automotive sector is concentrated in the three triad regions of the United States (North America), Europe, and Japan (Asia). In each of these regions, domestic producers have a bigger share of the market than foreign producers. General Motors, Ford, Chrysler (a US company again for a short while after the merger with Daimler Benz collapsed in 2007, but it was subsequently sold to the Italian car maker Fiat in 2009) have well over half of the US market for motor vehicles. In 2000, the largest three domestic auto makers in the United States had 62.3 percent of the US market. Imports accounted for approximately 15 percent of the US market but do not include locally made Japanese brands. However, in 2008, US auto makers were in deep crisis. General Motors, along with Chrysler and Ford, was getting a bailout from the US government. General Motors, which used to be the biggest auto company in the US back in the 1950s, has been hit hard by the economic crisis and sought US federal protection from bankruptcy. General Motors has been restructured. With the bankruptcy and subsequent sale to Fiat, Chrysler is now known as Chrysler LLC. Among the big three auto makers, in 2009, Ford yielded profit for the first time after four consecutive years of making loss.[21]

In general, the European market is more fragmented than the North American market. According to European Automobile Manufacturers Association, in 2009, the top manufacturing groups in Europe was Volkswagen with 21.1 percent of the European market for passenger cars and light commercial vehicles. Peugeot SA and Ford followed with 12.9 percent and 10.3 percent of this market, respectively. The five largest European brands—Volkswagen, Fiat, Peugeot/ Citroen and Audi—accounted for 43 percent of the European market. Ford, the third-largest competitor in Europe, had 8.9 percent of the market. Japanese and South Korean firms accounted for approximately 12.3 percent and 4.1 percent, respectively.

The European car market declined by 1.6 percent in new passenger car registrations in 2009, compared to that of 2008. Car scrapping incentives, especially in Germany, France, and the United Kingdom prevented what would have otherwise been a dismal year for new car sales in Europe.

Table 3.4 The regional nature of the motor vehicles and parts industries, 2010 ranking

	500 rank	Company	Region	Revenues (millions of US $)	% intra-regional	North America % of total sales	Europe % of total sales	Asia–Pacific % of total sales
Global								
1	364	Mazda Motor	Asia Pacific	23,306	41.33	26.16	22.18	41.33
Bi-regional								
1	5	Toyota Motor	Asia Pacific	204,306	48.30	29.70	14.10	48.30
2	30	Daimler	Europe	109,700	46.19	20.99	46.19	15.75
3	51	Honda Motor	Asia Pacific	92,400	37.12	43.74	8.97	37.12
4	63	Nissan Motor	Asia Pacific	83,963	27.60	35.30	16.90	27.60
5	278	Volvo	Europe	28,551	45.58	18.42	45.58	20.73
6	280	Johnson Controls	North America	28,497	38.95	38.95	35.82	n.a.
7	289	Bridgestone	Asia Pacific	27,750	26.20	43.27	13.85	26.20
8	426	Michelin	Europe	20,581	45.60	33.73	45.60	n.a.
9	442	Tata Motors	Asia Pacific	19,501	40.80	10.90	26.70	40.80
10	488	Magna International	North America	17,367	46.96	46.96	48.81	n.a.
Home-region oriented								
1	16	Volkswagen	Europe	146,205	71.41	10.83	71.41	17.76
2	23	Ford Motor	North America	118,308	53.83	53.83	32.21	13.96
3	38	General Motors	North America	104,589	55.44	55.44	22.99	7.91
4	78	Hyundai Motor	Asia Pacific	71,678	62.58	22.24	15.17	62.58
5	82	BMW	Europe	70,444	56.09	24.53	56.09	19.38
6	85	Fiat	Europe	69,639	53.15	9.13	53.15	20.11
7	94	Peugeot	Europe	67,297	85.15	n.a.	85.15	8.16
8	129	Robert Bosch	Europe	53,060	63.27	18.37	63.27	18.37
9	154	Renault	Europe	46,858	83.48	7.65	83.48	7.10
10	182	Dongfeng Motor	Asia Pacific	39,402	100.00	n.a.	n.a.	100.00
11	223	Shanghai Automotive	Asia Pacific	33,629	100.00	n.a.	n.a.	100.00
12	232	Denso	Asia Pacific	32,060	68.80	17.69	13.50	68.80
13	258	China FAW Group	Asia Pacific	30,237	100.00	n.a.	n.a.	100.00
14	273	Koç Holding	Europe	28,845	100.00	n.a.	100.00	n.a.
15	287	Continental AG	Europe	27,932	63.37	17.65	63.37	13.91
16	308	Suzuki Motor	Asia Pacific	26,592	75.28	5.15	16.84	75.28
17	388	Aisin Seiki	Asia Pacific	22,127	73.30	10.66	6.53	73.30
18	490	MAN Group	Europe	17,320	61.67	n.a.	61.67	n.a.
Weighted average*				56,257	61.87			
Total				1,687,701				

*Weighted intra-regional sales average is weighted according to revenues.

Notes: Data are for 2009. The sales percent of North America, Europe, and Asia–Pacific might not be tied to 100 percent as the balance may represent percent sales in rest of the world (ROW).

Source: Authors' calculations and "Fortune Global 500," Fortune, July 26, 2010 and individual company's annual reports.

E-resources: http://money.cnn.com/magazines/fortune/global500/2010.

Although Volkswagen did well in Europe in 2009 by increasing both market share and number of cars sold, other German brands and manufacturers suffered with mostly double digit losses. Troubled Swedish car manufacturer Saab saw sales decline by 59.1 percent while Volvo lost 9.3 percent.

Manufacturers of cheaper car brands did generally better. The best performers in Europe in 2009 were Renault's budget Dacia brand (+29.2 percent) and Hyundai (+26.6 percent).

As a result of the ending of car scrapping incentives, 2010 was a very bad year for car sales in Europe. In October 2010, in the UK, new car sales were 8.9 percent lower, while France and Germany saw falls of 8.2 percent and 17.8 percent respectively compared to 2009. Spain saw the biggest fall, dropping 27.3 percent. Overall, registrations of new cars in Europe were 9.2 percent lower, with 1.26 million new vehicles registered.

The Japanese market is the most consolidated of all triad markets. In 2009, Toyota alone has 36.88 percent of the passenger car market, 18.29 percent of the truck market and 79.72 percent of the bus market. Honda, the second-largest Japanese auto maker, accounts for 11.82 percent of passenger car market. Together, Toyota, Honda, Renault–Nissan, and Suzuki, the four largest Japanese auto makers, have 71.26 percent of the Japanese passenger car market. Ford, which acquired domestic Mazda, accounts for 10.16 percent of the passenger car market. General Motors, the US leader and the world's largest car manufacturer, has a mere 0.4 percent of this market. VW, the European leader, has 1.2 percent. Imports are a mere 4.5 percent of the Japanese market and include imports by Japanese companies manufacturing abroad.[22]

Excluding Japan, Toyota is the market leader in two of the six largest countries in Asia–Pacific: Malaysia and Thailand. South Korea is dominated by Hyundai, which controls 72.9 percent of that market. In 2009, Maruti Suzuki India (MSI) was the leader in India, with 47.68 percent market share. In the comparable period 2008, MSI had a 53.13 percent share of the 440,069 units car market, with sales of 233,811 units. Indeed, only Australia and China have Western-based market leaders. In Australia, as at March 2009, Toyota is the top brand with sales with 26.49 percent of the market, followed by General Motors's brand Holden (Holden Commodore vehicle), which holds 14.64 percent of the market. Including Japan, the top six Asian auto makers control 69.5 percent of the Asian market. This includes Renault–Nissan (8.1 percent) and Ford–Mazda (4.4 percent), Japanese companies in which Western firms have a dominant share.[23]

Although the majority of the market in each of the three triad regions is controlled by home-region-oriented companies, foreign companies continue to play a major role in each region. For example, Ford holds 8.9 percent of the European market and is the third-largest competitor. A number of foreign companies attained a competitive position by acquiring the operations of a local producer, such as Tata Motors. Tata also acquired Daewoo Commercial Vehicle Co. of South Korea in 2004, and bought Jaguar and Land Rover from Ford Motor in 2007. Other companies developed their business through organic growth in foreign markets, such as Toyota and Honda in North America.

These findings counter a number of popular myths about the "archetypal global industry," many dating from the 1980s and early 1990s which saw the global expansion of Japanese firms in the industry. Common views included that a global car and a global car firm would soon evolve, that all production would shift to cheap labor regions leaving "hollow corporations" in the United States and Europe, and that sales by incumbents in the largest markets would be overtaken by more competitive foreign rivals. Yet such global car industry predictions have not come to pass for the key reason that the industry operates regionally, not globally.

The auto industry operates largely in "clusters" of localized activity within each major triad region.[24] There are networks of key suppliers, other suppliers, key distributors, other partners, and the original equipment manufacturers (OEMs) assemble cars from imports of literally thousands of suppliers, all location bound. This is why, of the 55 million vehicles produced each year, over 90 percent are sold where they are made.[25]

Auto firms are also strongly embedded in a range of other downstream activities and after-sales markets including financing (such as Ford Credit), insurance, maintenance and repairs (like Ford's Kwik-Fit operations), parts and accessories, and emergency rescue services (such as Ford's RESCU). These represent a substantial proportion of total revenues for the larger firms and are highly regionally specific.

Another persistent barrier to a global strategy or a global car is cultural barriers across regions. European consumers prefer performance cars with good engines while in the United States large comfortable cars are the norm. Even within NAFTA, while the United States and Canada prefer automatic transmissions, most cars in Mexico have manual transmissions. In terms of customer tastes, it is impossible to market the same car across regions, and usually all of the economies of scale for a model are achieved within each major region.

Another factor is fuel. Diesel continues to be popular in Europe but is being phased out in the United States because of its environmental implications. Rather than phase out the better milage fuel, European auto makers are seeking ways of making it a cleaner alternative.

Each regional market in which auto makers operate has its own set of environmental regulations. In the United States, auto makers must design vehicles to conform to the Environmental Protection Agency's (EPA's) regulations and the environmental regulations of individual states. Other regulations that relate to automotive design include noise control and fuel economy. The companies' industrial processes are also heavily regulated with laws relating to water discharges, air emissions, waste management, and environmental cleanup. European and Asia–Pacific markets have different environmental laws to which auto maker's operations must comply. For instance, the EU is making all car makers financially responsible for dismantling and recycling its own vehicles.

Finally, tariffs, ranging from 2.5 percent in the United States to 10 percent in some European countries to 100 percent in some developing countries, represent another significant barrier to globalization.

Each region has a particular regulatory and competitive environment in which the major world players compete for market share. Local competitors are more adept at meeting the demands of their regional markets because they possess know-how on consumer preferences, government regulations, and market trends. While foreign companies might hire local personnel, purchase local car manufacturers, and do extensive market research, companies headquartered in that region are more capable of responding to changing circumstances of their primary market. We now discuss three of the world's largest automotive firms in more detail.

General Motors

One of the world's largest manufacturers of automobiles is General Motors (GM) (although, by 2007, Toyota was overtaking it). In 2009, GM's revenues totaled $104.589 billion and GM accounted for nearly 15 percent of the world's market for trucks and automobiles. GM produces and manufactures vehicles in all three triad markets. Nonetheless, 47 percent of its sales originate in the United States, its home national market. Including Canada, Mexico, markets in North America, this number rises to 55.44 percent of total sales. On the production side, its network of North American factories—which exist partly as a result of NAFTA—accounts for 65.8 percent of production capacity. An international company, yes, but by no means a global company.

GM is primarily an automotive company, but it also operates communications services businesses and has a financing and insurance arm. Its automotive business is segmented geographically: GM North America, GM Europe, GM Latin America/Africa/Mid-East, and GM Asia–Pacific. Each of these regions has a set of brands it promotes. In North America, for example, these are Chevrolet, Pontiac, Saturn, etc. In Europe, GM's brands include Opel, Vauxhall, and Holden, among others. GM Daewoo is a brand marketed in South Korea and Vietnam.

GM is most successful in the North American market, where it holds 28 percent of the market, compared to 8.7 percent of the European market, and 3.4 percent of the Asia–Pacific market. In North America, GM has a competitive advantage in that it is already well situated in the market and has a loyal consumer base. In other regions, however, it faces competition from local auto makers that know their home regions very well. In Europe,

Table 3.5 General Motors, revenue 2006–2009 (US$ million)

	2009	2008	2007	2006
Revenue	104,589	148,979	179,984	192,604
% change	−29.79%	−17,23%	−6.55%	

Source: General Motors, *Annual Report*, 2006–2009; "Fortune Global 500," *Fortune*, issues of 2006–2009.

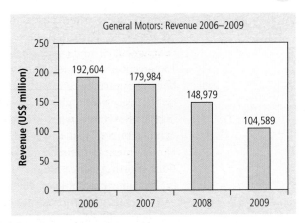

Figure 3.2 General Motors: revenue 2006–2009

Volkswagen, BMW, and Daimler build high-performance cars. In Asia, competitors build smaller, more fuel-efficient cars that cater to local preferences. GMs' primary market is North America, in particular the United States. It derives most of its revenue and most of its profits from its home-region operations. Its strategy must balance the benefit of investing in foreign regions to the benefits of investing in its home-region market. Foreign markets, though potentially profitable, do not offer the consolidated GM company sufficient incentive to switch the focus of its strategy. GM has plans to expand in China, but this is a country where rival MNEs are already active and where local Chinese producers are adept at appropriating the intellectual property of Western firms. In other words, China offers potentially high returns, but has great risks.

The world financial crisis and the US government's restructuring of GM had a dramatic effect on sales (see Table 3.5 and Figure 3.2).

In 2008, GM struggled to survive in the financial crisis. GM filed for bankruptcy, and a massive government bailout of $50 billion made it practically nationalized. On November 18, 2010, GM was reborn as a public company with initial public offer (IPO), although the US government is still a major shareholder. It began trading on the New York Stock Exchange and Toronto Stock Exchange after the biggest share sale in the US history. It is also a symbolic fresh start for one of America's biggest corporate failures.[26]

Toyota

In 2009, two regional markets accounted for 78 percent of Toyota's revenues: Asia (with Japan at 48.3 percent of revenues) and North America (at 29.70 percent of revenues); Europe was only at 14.1 percent of revenues and rest of the world 7.9 percent. So, it is a bi-region-focused company. In terms of units sold, the geographic distribution is similar: Asia and Oceania account for 46.2 percent of unit sales (Japan at 38 percent); North America for 30.8 percent; and Europe for 15 percent. Thus, in terms of revenue and units sold, Toyota is a bi-regional company. Market share shows a slightly different picture. Toyota holds approximately 40 percent of the Japanese market but only 10 percent of the North American market. Moreover, production is not as dispersed around the world; 75.9 percent of all Toyota cars are still produced in Japan. Only 14.9 percent are produced in North America. Other regions account for less than 10 percent of production.

Over 10 years, Toyota's intra-regional percentage of sales has decreased from 57.1 percent to 46.2 percent. One major reason for this is the Japanese market itself, where sales decreased from 48.4 percent of total revenues in 1993 to 38.3 percent in 2002. In contrast, North American, European, and non-triad sales have steadily increased in importance. In 1993, Toyota derived 25.4 percent of its sales from North America. This rose to 29.7 percent in 2009; EU restrictions on imports of Japanese cars were one reason why Toyota historically has been unable to be successful in the European market. European sales accounted for a mere 9.9 percent of total sales in 1993, but by 2009 Toyota almost doubled the number of units sold so that, in that year, the region accounted for approximately 15 percent of total sales. This is partly a result not only of more local production but also of Toyota learning to cater to the European market.

The Asian economies have been in a slump since the 1990s, and Europe has been growing slowly. This is why the North American market is very important for all Japanese manufacturers. Japanese car makers began to manufacture in the United States, the largest North American national market, in the 1980s to protect themselves from import restrictions. North America is Toyota's second-largest regional market in terms of revenues. It is also highly profitable. In 2002, one-fourth of Toyota's profits originated in this region.

Toyota manufactures locally over two-thirds of the cars it sells in the United States. The company's Canadian plant also serves this regional market, and a Mexican plant in Tijuana was expected to increase local production when it opened in 2005. Local responsiveness is important. Toyota introduced its luxury models to accommodate the aging and wealthier North American baby boomers in the 1990s. Today, the company is introducing cars to target the young American customer, the demographic echo of the baby boomers. Since 60 percent of US car buyers remain loyal to the brand of their first car, it is thus imperative to service this young market.

American consumers, for their part, have been responsive to the company's reputation for quality and in particular for the lower price at which Toyota's cars are sold. In fact, during economic downturns in which consumers seek more value for their money Toyota does better in the United States. The company's cars not only are less expensive, but also consume less gasoline than American cars. The resale value is also higher for Toyota cars. One major advantage for Toyota is that it has some of the best manufacturing facilities in the world, and it combines this with excellent relationships with its suppliers. The company is so efficient that, despite the lower price of its cars, it makes an average profit of $1,000 on each car sold compared to $330 for GM.

Toyota's European operations are money losers, but the company continues to try to access this market and increase its market share from its 3.8 percent level in 2002. To boost its image for performance in the region, the company began to compete in Formula One races. To protect itself from currency risk, Toyota will now produce a higher percentage of its cars within the region. That also means more local procurement. To this end, Porsche was asked to produce engines for its European models. Porsche already produces transmissions for the company.

Until recently, Toyota was one of the most efficient companies at outsourcing production to suppliers with whom it enjoys amicable long-term, sometimes *keiretsu*-style, relationships. If the auto industry is to become more like the electronics industry (as many believe may occur), vehicle brand owners (VBOs), such as Toyota, GM, and VW, will be the equivalent of original equipment manufacturers (OEMs) in the electronics industry, such as Nokia, IBM, and Microsoft, and will concentrate on designing, engineering, and marketing vehicles to be sold under their brand while others take care of manufacturing. Toyota is probably further along this outsourcing route than other triad auto makers.

In 2008, when General Motors stumbled towards bankruptcy, Toyota became the top car maker. Toyota sold 8.9 million, while GM sold 8.3 million vehicles. But the problem set in with pursuing the target of becoming the biggest. Since 2009, Toyota has been in the process of recalling millions of vehicles that are potentially prone to uncontrolled acceleration, following an accident, in which an off-duty traffic officer and three of his relatives had died in the United States. The accident accelerator got caught in the floor mat of the brand new Lexus, which was deemed a possible cause. Toyota said the wide-ranging vehicle check might spread from the United States and Europe to include the Middle East, Latin

Table 3.6 Toyota Motors: revenue 2006–2009 (US$ million)

	2009	2008	2007	2006
Revenue	204,306	229,997	204,782	185,893
% change	−11.17%	12.31%	10.16%	

Source: Toyota Motors, *Annual Report*, 2006–2009; "Global Fortune 500," *Fortune*, issues of 2006–2009.

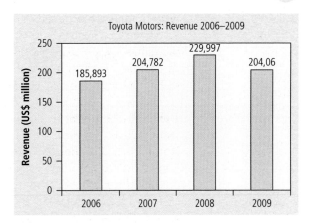

Figure 3.3 Toyota Motors: revenue 2006–2009

America, and Africa. Toyota estimated that the massive vehicle recall could cost it up to $2 billion in lost output and sales. In Spring 2009, it reported a $4.4 bn operating loss for the fiscal year to March. The accident was a blow to Toyota's reputation which is well known for its quality and "Toyota Way." The company was in crisis mode. Mr. Akio Yoyoda, President, said in Spring: "Toyota has become too big and distant from its customers." He criticized the executives for their "undisciplined pursuit of more" and for their arrogance, which he referred to as "hubris born of success."[27]

Toyota's sales changed as follows (see Table 3.6 and Figure 3.3).

Daimler AG

When German Daimler-Benz merged with US Chrysler, the aim of the German company was to secure a share in the large US economy-class car market. Synergies (for instance, in the area of purchasing), it argued, would reduce costs across all operations. At first glance, one can argue that the merger achieved its goal. In 2002, 58.7 percent of the company's revenues originated in North America, a trend that had remained relatively stable since 2000. These data define the firm as host-region oriented. The numbers can be deceiving, though; soon after the merger the Chrysler group was plagued by management defections and decreasing profits. In 2007, DaimlerChrysler sold Chrysler to a US private equity firm called Cerberus.

Two things help explain the troubles of this merger. The first is that these companies were producing very different products. Mercedes Benz, a Daimler-Benz brand, had a competitive edge in the luxury market. Chrysler produced popular cars for the US market. Although the expensive parts of Daimler's vehicles could be used for more affordable Chrysler cars and the cheaper Chrysler parts be used on Daimler vehicles, both these moves were likely to reduce the competitive advantage on each of the markets in which the original companies operated. Chrysler cars could have become less affordable while Daimler's brand might have lost its reputation for quality. In effect, while some parts can be shared and suppliers can manufacture different products for both vehicle brands at lower prices, the benefits from the merger were limited by the different product lines of each company.

The second, and perhaps most important, barrier to overcome was the cross-cultural differences between the German and US companies. From the beginning, Daimler's management dominated the merged company, which resulted in an outflow of key US personnel from management positions and the designer ranks. The Germans tended to be bureaucratic while US managers made decisions on the spot. Many US managers left, unable to deal with the imposed management style. Capable designers went to rivals GM and Ford. Over time, the company has improved its cultural management of the US operations, and this is improving the company's overall position in the motor vehicle market.

Table 3.7 Daimler AG, revenue 2006–2009
(US$ million)

	2009	2008	2007	2006
Revenue	109,762	144,028	139,014	124,579
% change	−23.79%	3.60%	11.58%	

Source: Daimler AG, *Annual Report*, 2006–2009; "Fortune Global 500," *Fortune*, issues of 2006–2009.

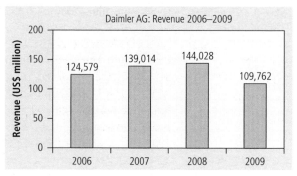

Figure 3.4 Daimler AG: revenue 2006–2009

In 2009, Daimler is a bi-region-based company where it derives 46.19 percent of its revenue from Europe and 20.99 per cent of its revenue from North America. Its sales changed as follows (see Table 3.7 and Figure 3.4).

A closer look back at the merged DaimlerChrysler organization shows, not a cohesive organization with a bi-regional market span, but two internal groups with individual global standings. The Mercedes Car Group, the non-commercial vehicle successor to the German part of the merger, derives 63 percent of its revenues from the European market. The Chrysler Group, on the other hand, continues to derive over 90 percent of its revenues from the North American market.

In terms of production, the Mercedes Group has eight production locations in Europe while the Chrysler Group has none. In the NAFTA region, the Chrysler Group has 38 production locations while the Mercedes Group has only one. This reflects two separate entities each trying to capitalize on knowledge of its home region, not a truly bi-regional or host-region-oriented company.

Like other big three US car makers, Chrysler also struggled to survive in the financial crisis. In 2009, Chrysler was saved with the US government's massive bailout program by a "narrow margin." It has subsequently been sold to the Italian car maker Fiat.[28]

✔ Active learning check

Review your answer to Active Learning Case question 3 and make any changes you like. Then compare your answer to the one below.

❸ How will Airbus help the EU compete in Japan?

Japanese airlines will continually need to replace and expand their current stock of aircraft. US aircraft manufacturers had previously satisfied this demand. However, thanks to Airbus the EU now has an industry that can offer Japan a competitive product. Moreover, until Japan creates its own worldwide competitive aircraft industry, Airbus will be able to continue to tap this market potential.

Mergers and acquisitions

Although all three triad groups have much intra-regional trade and FDI, this does not mean that trade or FDI between them has declined. As discussed above, they also have invested large amounts of money in each other. For example, in 2008, the EU countries had $1,622.911 billion of FDI in the United States and $86.915 billion in Japan. The United States imports $377 billion from the EU and $143.4 billion from Japan. So the three groups are closely linked in terms of both trade and FDI.[29]

Moreover, investors have poured billions of dollars into these economies, betting that they are going to profit handsomely from these investments. US investors, for example, spent more than $7 billion in the first five months of 1998 to purchase Asian proper-ties, most of them in Japan. Part of this development was a result of the weak Japanese economy. Many companies there had no capital for expansion and were facing declining demand for their goods and services. So they were willing to unload some of their assets as well as take on foreign partners who could provide funds and growth opportunities. At the same time, the impact of Japanese deregulation was beginning to take effect. For a long time both the United States and the EU have been encouraging Japan to reduce its protectionist policies and allow greater opportunities for foreign investors. In the early 1990s the government promised to open up its markets to more foreign goods and even agreed to buy more cars, auto parts, and computer equipment from outside vendors. As the local economy began to falter and the rules and regulations that used to stymie foreign investors began to be withdrawn, the result was a rush by foreign MNEs into this marketplace.

Similarly, EU firms are very interested in buying US firms and vice versa. Some of the largest acquisitions made by EU companies in the United States in recent years include the purchase of ARCO by BP Amoco of the UK for over $27 billion, France Telecom's acquisition of NTL for $5.5 billion, and Vivendi Universal's purchase of USA Networks for $10.3 billion. At the same time, US firms have been buying EU companies. Ford Motor put out $2.72 billion to acquire Land Rover from BMW and then Tata Motors, India bought Jaguar and Land Rover from Ford Motors for about $2.3 billion in 2008, and Cisco Systems paid $2.15 billion for Pirelli of Italy's fiber-optic operations.[30] So there is still a great deal of FDI being conducted between triad countries.

In addition to the high level of international business conducted across the triad, com-panies in the triad are constantly looking for new ideas from other regions that will make them more competitive. US and EU firms emulate successful Japanese business practices. In the United States, for example, the head of the Federal Reserve System has expressed the belief that US antitrust practices are out of date and that competitors should be allowed to acquire and merge with each other in order to protect themselves from world com-petition. This idea has long been popular in Japan where **keiretsus**, or business groups, which consist of a host of companies that are linked together through ownership and/or joint ventures, dominate the local environment and are able to use their combined wealth and connections to dominate world markets.[31] Many firms including Deere & Company, Ford, IBM, and Harley-Davidson, to name but four, are copying this form of cooperation. Simply put, what happens in one part of the triad often has an effect in other parts.

Keiretsus
Groupings of Japanese firms with long-term associations and cross-shareholdings

---

✔ Active learning check

Review your answer to Active Learning Case question 4 and make any changes you like. Then compare your answer to the one below.

4 **In what way did the Airbus consortium use a *keiretsu* approach to building the aircraft? Why do you think it opted for this approach?**

A *keiretsu* is a business group, which often consists of a host of companies that are linked together through ownership and/or joint ventures. In the case of Airbus, notice how Germany, the UK, and Spain built the aircraft and France assembled it. This is the same approach used by *keiretsus* that coordinate their operations in such a way that each provides products and services to the group at a very low price. Another reason that the consortium undoubtedly opted for this approach is that each participant benefits because of the money pumped into its economy for doing this work. Under the new organizational arrangement the governmental role in the *keiretsu* disappears but the basic operational approach will remain, and the company will still be a *keiretsu* type of organization.

KEY POINTS

1 Foreign direct investment (FDI) is the ownership and control of foreign assets. This usually means the ownership, whole or partial, of a company in a foreign country.

2 There are a number of reasons for FDI. These include increased sales and profits, a chance to enter rapidly growing markets, reduced costs, gaining a foothold in economic unions, protecting domestic markets, protecting foreign markets, and acquiring technological and managerial know-how.

3 While there is a great amount of FDI made every year, most of it (approximately 80 percent) occurs within or between triad countries. Much of the remaining FDI is in countries that are members of triad-based FDI clusters.

4 The triad nations dominate world trade and investments, and a great deal of this activity takes place both among and within triad countries. One of the major areas of triad trade is automobiles, which provides an excellent example of the economic interrelationships that exist among triad members.

Key terms

- triad
- foreign direct investment (FDI)
- investment
- portfolio investment
- twin factories
- *maquiladoras*
- FDI cluster
- *keiretsus*

REVIEW AND DISCUSSION QUESTIONS

1 What is FDI all about? Put it in your own words.

2 What are some of the reasons for FDI? Identify and describe four.

3 Why are MNEs interested in investing in Eastern Europe?

4 How much FDI does the EU and Japan have in the United States? What conclusions can you reach based on these data?

5 How much FDI does the United States and Japan have in the EU? What conclusions can you reach based on these data?

6 How dominant are the triad countries in terms of FDI and world trade? Explain.

7 What is an FDI cluster? Why are certain countries such as Mexico and Venezuela more likely to be in the US cluster than in the EU cluster?

8 Why does Toyota choose to manufacture in the United States?

9 Where is GM most successful? Why?

10 How active are US and EU firms in acquiring companies throughout the world? What accounts for this activity?

11 In what way can a *keiretsu* approach be of value to US and EU companies in becoming more competitive worldwide? Explain.

REAL CASE

Panasonic and Philips

In terms of triad-based competition, the 1980s saw the emergence of Japanese firms in the consumer electronics industry. One of the major companies is Panasonic, which was formerly known as Matsushita. The firm was initially successful with color TVs, but its best-known product has been the video cassette recorder (VCR), a field it dominates by using the VHS system instead of the Sony Betamax format VCR and others produced by European and US rivals. Paradoxically, the VCR was developed in California in 1956 by a US firm, Ampex, but the product development and distribution was captured by the clever global strategy of Matsushita/Panasonic.

To dominate world business in VCRs, by that time, Matsushita managed to make the VHS format the industry standard. The company achieved this not just by its own massive production and worldwide sales, but by licensing the VHS format to other MNEs such as Hitachi, Sharp, Mitsubishi, and even the major European-based rival, Philips. Other companies such as GE, RCA, and Zenith (which sold VCRs under their own brand names) were tied into the VHS format because of the production and process technology retained by Matsushita in its strong Japanese home base. The company's massive global economies of scale enabled it to cut VCR prices by 50 percent over its first five years.

In contrast, Philips was in desperate trouble by the 1980s. Built up in the interwar period of protectionism and strong government regulation, the company had developed a very highly decentralized organizational structure. Individual national country managers held the power in Philips, and they were slow to respond to the Japanese threat in the postwar period. As a result, Philips lacked economies of scale and its radios, TVs, and VCRs were too expensive compared to comparable Japanese products. Philips had more than 600 manufacturing plants across the world, all developing products for local markets. However, the challenge facing the firm was how to restructure its entire business away from locally responsive national organizations toward a more integrated and leaner manufacturer capable of reaping the necessary economies of scale through standard global production.

In essence, the Japanese changed the rules of the game in the consumer electronics business. Matsushita/Panasonic, as a centralized, high-quality, low-price, and innovative company, was able to beat the decentralized and nationally responsive European firm. One tactic used by European firms was to lobby their governments for protection in the form of antidumping actions and tougher customs inspection of Japanese products. But such "shelters" only bought some breathing room before MNEs such as Philips restructured and fitted their organizational capabilities to the required industry strategy.

Finally, the response of Matsushita/ Panasonic to more protection has been to switch overseas sales from export to foreign direct investment (FDI). With FDI the firm has been able to evade European trade barriers such as antidumping actions. For example, today it manufactures in a number of European countries including the UK, where it has a major plant in Cardiff, Wales. At the same time this means that Matsushita/Panasonic must make its foreign subsidiaries as effective as possible by encouraging local initiatives, and this strategy can conflict with its internationally centralized Japanese-based management culture. In short, the very government regulations that have made Philips too decentralized are now being reapplied half a century later to make Matsushita/Panasonic less global and more local.

Websites: www.mei.co.jp; www.panasonic.com; www.panasonic.co.jp; www.philips.com.

Sources: Adapted from Chris Bartlett and Sumantra Ghoshal, *Managing Across Borders*, 2nd ed. (Boston, MA: Harvard Business School Press, 1998); Matsushita, *Annual Report*, 2003; Panasonic, *Annual Report*, 2009; Philips, *Annual Report*, 2009; www.panasonic.com; www.philips.com.

1   What type of globalization strategy was followed by the Japanese firm Matsushita/Panasonic?

2   Why could the European firm Philips not compete well with its Japanese rival by the 1980s?

3   How can a government help its own firms against triad rivals?

REAL CASE

Toys "Я" Us in Europe and Japan

Toys "Я" Us opened its first international outlet in Canada in 1984, and then it moved to parts of Europe, Hong Kong, and Singapore, where the company's "discount formula" was as popular as in the United States. The international business model applied to new markets was the same as that used by the company in the United States: the stores resembled each other, and each store had a self-service supermarket format that offered a great variety of toys sold at low prices.

By 2009, 722 Toys "Я" Us stores were located outside the United States, of which Europe 287, Asia 255, Canada 69, Middle East 52, Australia 35 and Africa 24. Yet, entering a new market has not always been easy for the company. As this case shows, cultural differences and regulations can make establishing a foreign business model very difficult.

Source: Getty Images/News

Toys "Я" Us in Germany

Many multinationals like to set up operations in Europe, particularly in the largest economy, Germany. Despite its economic downturn in the 1990s, this country has a very strong economy, and it greatly influences what happens in the rest of the EU.

When Toys "Я" Us decided to enter the German market, it was greeted by a partial boycott and a public relations blitz that condemned the concept of a self-service toy supermarket as being alien and wrong. Even though the managing director of Toys "Я" Us was German, strong objections were directed against a US retailer wanting large-area sales space in Germany. The company soon learned that legal and cultural barriers could be effectively used to block foreign competition. When Toys "Я" Us applied for a construction permit in Cologne, the city fathers asked the local chamber of commerce and retailers' association how they felt about the application. The latter replied that a toy store belongs in the center of the city, not on the edge of town. Yet this is exactly where Toys "Я" Us needed to be located so that it could build a sprawling store and a parking lot that was the size of a football field. In addition, the German Toy Manufacturers Association questioned why a toy store would sell so many non-toy items.

The managing director for Toys "Я" Us refused to allow these early setbacks to thwart his efforts. He continued making the rounds of trade shows, negotiating for store sites, and presenting the company's plans to local officials; eventually he wore down the resistance. Even the competition began to realize that successful large toy stores could spark a boom in the toy market. Soon, competitors began copying some of the approaches used by Toys "Я"

Us, such as piling shelves at the back of the store with baby food and diapers. Parents who come in to get diapers or baby food seldom leave without buying a toy for the child.

The German experience has taught the management that despite cultural, legal, and technical barriers, a retail company can succeed in Europe if it is patient, maintains a strong consumer-oriented marketing focus, and is nationally responsive.

By 2009, Toys "Я" Us had 57 stores in Germany. It had another 287 outlets in Europe, including 75 in the UK, 39 in France, and 45 in Spain.

Toys "Я" Us in Japan

The Japanese toy market is one of the largest, making it an attractive market for Toys "Я" Us. Yet, when the firm decided to enter this market in 1991, it had some major hurdles to overcome. Despite the rapid growth it had experienced, Japan's toy industry remained highly fragmented and locally focused. Japanese reportedly preferred personal attention from the shop owner rather than low prices. In addition to customers' habits and personal loyalties, Japan's retail structure was also bolstered by a series of laws restricting the spread of larger retail stores.

At the time, a typical Japanese toy store was less than 3,200 ft^2 (300 m^2) in area. Nearly all retail shops were domestically owned and bought their toys from local wholesalers, usually for 75–80 percent of the manufacturer's "suggested price." Retailers then sold the toys for the suggested price, deviating from it only rarely. Fragmented wholesalers served these shops. These wholesalers sold their products through a complex distribution system that typically involved between three and five layers of intermediaries.

The Toys "Я" Us business model clashed with traditional business structures. Its self-serve format put more ▶

attention on lower prices, minimizing personal attention to each customer, and cutting out any intermediaries from the supply process. Japan not only presented great possibilities but also involved a high risk of failure, especially if the company didn't adapt its business model.

To overcome the problems of Japanese culture and history being incompatible with the Toys "Я" Us business model, Den Fujita, who had successfully run McDonald's Japan, was enlisted as a local partner. At the time, he was the only Japanese business leader who had succeeded in bringing foreign non-luxury retail business into the restrictive Japanese market. His experience, political influence, vision, and unique understanding of both Japanese and US cultures enhanced the probability of success of Toys "Я" Us in Japan.

With the help of Fujita, a powerful opinion leader who affects government policy making, and a younger generation that had started to realize that they were paying inflated prices for many consumer goods, many commercial restrictions were lifted, and Toys "Я" Us was able to implement a business model similar to that in the United States. As of 2009, Toys "Я" Us had 167 stores in Japan.

Websites: www.toysrus.co.uk; www.toysrus.fr; www.toysrus.de; www.toysrus.co.jp; www.toysrus.com; www.toysrusinc.com

Sources: Adapted from Ferdinand Protzman, "Greetings from Fortress Europe," *New York Times*, August 18, 1991, Section 3, pp. 1, 6; John Templeman et al., "Germany Fights Back," *Business Week*, May 31, 1993, pp. 48– 51; www.toysrus.com; Paul Klebnikov, "Trouble in Toyland," *Forbes*, June 1, 1998, pp. 56– 60; Michael Gestrin, Rory Knight, and Alan M. Rugman, *The Templeton Global Performance Index* (Templeton College, University of Oxford, 1998); Debora L. Spar, *Ruling the Waves* (New York: Harcourt, 2002).

1 What are the firm-specific advantages of Toys "Я" Us?

2 What specific cultural and political barriers to entry does it face?

3 Why was Toys "Я" Us more successful in Japan than in Germany?

ENDNOTES

1 Ministry of Finance, *Report on External Assets and Liabilities as of Year-End 2003*, May 21, 2004.

2 Scott Morrison, "Solectron Buys C-Mac for $2.7 Bn," *Financial Times*, August 10, 2001, p. 19.

3 David Pringle, "Matsushita Looks to Go Digital in Europe," *Wall Street Journal*, May 8, 2000, Section A, p. 39A.

4 For a discussion of an interesting combination of FDI and portfolio investment, see John Philips and Karen Woolfson, "Franco-German Banking Link-Up Ignores Sceptics," *The European*, April 12–14, 1991, p. 20.

5 United Nations, *World Investment Report 2010* (Geneva: United Nations Conference on Trade and Development, 2009) and individual company's annual reports.

6 United Nations, *World Investment Report 2003* (Geneva: United Nations Conference on Trade and Development, 2003); http://thomsonreuters.com/, Thomson Reuters, *Annual Report*, 2003 and 2008 (Thomson acquired Reuters in 2007).

7 Honda, *Annual Report*, 2009 and Sony, *Annual Report*, 2009.

8 Wal-Mart, *Annual Report*, 2009.

9 "China's economy reports 11.9% growth," *BBC News*, www.news.bbc.co.uk, April 15, 2010.

10 Alan M. Rugman, *The Regional Multinationals* (Cambridge: Cambridge University Press, 2005); Alan M. Rugman and Alain Verbeke, Appendix 6.1 Multinationals are Regional, Not Global, Chapter 6, Location, Competitiveness, and the Multinational Enterprise, in the *Oxford Handbook of International Business* (ed. Alan M. Rugman), 2nd Edition (Oxford, UK: Oxford University Press, 2009).

11 Susan Moffat, "Picking Japan's Research Brains," *Fortune*, March 25, 1991, p. 92.

12 US Bureau of Economic Analysis, *Survey of Current Business*, July 2009; Japan External Trade Organization (JETRO), Reports and Statistics, *Japan's Outward and Inward Foreign Direct Investment, FDI Stock (based on International Investment Position, net), Outward and Inward 1996–2009*. E-resource: http://www.jetro.go.jp/en/reports/statistics/.

13 US Bureau of Economic Analysis, *Survey of Current Business*, July 2009.

14 Michael Mortimore, *DI and TNC Activities in Latin America and the Caribbean*, Presentation at the UN's ECLAC, Ottawa, Canada, June 15, 2004 and Bank of Estonia.

15 United Nations, *World Investment Report 2009* (New York: United Nations Conference on Trade and Development, 2009).

16 Wal-Mart, *Annual Report*, 2009.

17 Richard Tomlinson, "Who's Afraid of Wal-Mart?" *Fortune*, June 26, 2000, pp. 186–196; Rugman, op. cit.; and Carrefour, *Annual Report*, 2009 and Carrefour, Q4 and *Full Year Sales*, 2009; www.carrefour.com.

18 General Motors, *Annual Report*, 2009.

19 Vijay Govindarajan and Anil K. Gupta, *The Quest for Global Dominance* (New York: Harcourt, 2001), pp. 52–53.

20 Rugman, op. cit. Data is updated with Fortune, *the Fortune Global 500*, July 26, 2010 issue. E-resource: http://money.cnn.com/magazines/fortune/global500/2010.

21 R. W. Morris, *Motor Vehicles 2000* (London: Random House, 2001); US Car Makers in Crisis, *BBC News*, www.bbc.ac.uk, November 19, 2008; Car Makers Suffer Around the World, *BBC News*, www.bbc.ac.uk, July 10, 2009; Ford, *Annual Report*, 2009; www.ford.com.

22 F. Henderson, *Capitalizing on Global Growth*, Presentation at 2003 Tokyo Analyst Conference, October 20, 2003; European

Automobile Manufacturers Association www.acea.be; Japan Automobile Manufacturers Association (JAMA) http://www.jama-english.jp/; "European Car Sales Sees 9.2% Fall," *BBC News*, www.bbc.co.uk, October 15, 2010.

23 Ibid. "Maruti's Market Share Still Below 50%," Business World, India, www.businessworld.in, August 9, 2010; Federal Chamber of Automotive Industries, *Australian and New Zealand March 2009 Sales Results: Australian Car Market in Freefall*, www.fcai.com.au, April 3, 2009.

24 Alan M. Rugman and Joseph D'Cruz, *Multinationals as Flagship Firms: Regional Business Networks* (Oxford: Oxford University Press, 2000).

25 McKinsey Quarterly, "How Far Can It Go?" *The McKinsey Quarterly*, Special Edition 4, pp. 27–30.

26 Adapted from Alan M. Rugman and Cecilia Brain, "Globalization and Regional International Production," in John Ravenhill (ed.) *Global Political Economy* (Oxford: Oxford University Press, 2004); "Fresh Start for General Motors," BBC *News*, www.bbc.co.uk, November 18, 2010.

27 Adapted from Rugman and Brain, op. cit. "Toyota Car Recall May Cost $2bn," www.bbc.co.uk, BBC News, February 2, 2010; "Toyota Reputation Could Be Tarnished for Years," *BBC News*, www.bbc.co.uk, February 4, 2010.

28 Rugman, op. cit. "Chrysler Saved by 'Narrow Margin,'" *BBC News*, www.bbc.co.uk, October 28, 2010.

29 US Bureau of Economic Analysis, *Survey of Current Business*, July 2009; Japan External Trade Organization (JETRO), Reports and Statistics, *Japan's Inward and Outward Direct Investment, 1996–2009*; IMF, *Direction of Trade Statistics Yearbook 2009*.

30 Marcus Walker and Anna Wilde Mathews, "As Euro Falls, US Firms Don't Pounce," *Wall Street Journal*, September 18, 2000, p. A28.

31 For a detailed discussion of *keiretsus*, see George Ming-Hong Lai, "Knowing Who You Are Doing Business with in Japan: A Managerial View of Keiretsu and Keiretsu Business Groups," *Journal of World Business*, vol. 34, no. 4 (1999), pp. 423–448.

ADDITIONAL BIBLIOGRAPHY

Agmon, T. "Who Gets What: The MNE, the National State and the Distributional Effects of Globalization," *Journal of International Business Studies*, vol. 34, no. 5 (September 2003).

Akhter, Syed H. and Beno, Colleen. "An Empirical Note on Regionalization and Globalization," *Multinational Business Review*, vol. 19, no. 1 (2011).

Almor, Tamar, Hashai, Niron and Hirsch, Seev. "The Product Cycle Revisited: Knowledge Intensity and Firm Internalization," *Management International Review*, vol. 46, no. 5 (2006).

Beugelsdijk, Sjoerd, Hennart, Jean-François, Slangen, Arjen, Smeets, Roger. "Why and How FID Stocks Are a Biased Measure of MNE Affiliate Activity," *Journal of International Business Studies*, vol. 41, no. 9 (2010).

Brouthers, Keith D. and Dikova, Desislava. "Acquisitions and Real Options: The Greenfield Alternative," *Journal of Management Studies*, vol. 47, no. 6 (September 2010).

Buckley, Peter J. "Cartography and International Business," *International Business Review*, vol. 13, no. 2 (April 2004).

Buckley, Peter J. and Ghauri, Pervez N. "Globalisation, Economic Geography and the Strategy of Multinational Enterprises," *Journal of International Business Studies*, vol. 35, no. 2 (March 2004).

Buckley, Peter J. and Strange, Roger. "The Governance of the Multinational Enterprise: Insights from Internalization Theory," *Journal of Management Studies*, vol. 48, no. 2 (2011).

Contractor, Farok J. "Contractual and Cooperative Forms of International Business: Towards a Unified Theory of Modal Choice," *Management International Review*, vol. 30, no. 1 (First Quarter 1990).

Collinson, Simon and Rugman, Alan M. "The Regional Character of Asian Multinational Enterprise," *Asia Pacific Journal of Management*, vol 24, no. 4 (2007).

Contractor, Farok J., Kundu, Sumit K. and Hsu, Chin-Chun. "A Three-Stage Theory of International Expansion: The Link between Multinationality and Performance in the Service Sector," *Journal of International Business Studies*, vol. 34, no. 1 (January 2003).

Datta, Deepak K., Liang, Xin, Musteen, Martina. "Strategic Orientation and the Choice of Foreign Market Entry Mode," *Management International Review*, vol. 49, no. 3 (2009).

Dhanaraj, Charles and Parkhe, Arvind. "Orchestrating Innovation Networks," *Academy of Management Review*, vol. 31, no. 3 (July 2006).

Dunning, John. *International Production and the Multinational Enterprise* (London: Allen and Unwin, 1981).

Dunning, John. "The Eclectic Paradigm of International Production: A Restatement and Some Possible Extensions," *Journal of International Business Studies*, vol. 19, no. 1 (Spring 1988).

Dunning, John. *Alliance Capitalism and Global Business* (London: Routledge, 1997).

Dunning, John. "Location and the Multinational Enterprise: A Neglected Factor?" *Journal of International Business Studies*, vol. 29, no. 1 (First Quarter 1998).

Dunning, John. "The Contribution of Edith Penrose to International Business Scholarship," *Management International Review*, vol. 43, no. 1 (First Quarter 2003).

Eckert, Stefan and Trautnitz, Georg. "A Commentary on Risk Reduction by Geographic Diversification," *Multinational Business Review*, vol. 18, no. 4 (2010)

Ghemawat, Pankaj. "Distance Still Matters: The Hard Reality of Global Expansion," *Harvard Business Review*, vol. 79, no. 8 (September 2001).

Ghemawat, Pankaj. "Semiglobalization and International Business Strategy," *Journal of International Business Studies*, vol. 34, no. 2 (March 2003).

Ghemawat, Pankaj. "Regional Strategies for Global Leadership," *Harvard Business Review*, vol. 83, no. 12 (December 2005).

Grosse, Robert. "Are the Largest Financial Institutions Really 'Global'?" *Management International Review*, vol. 45, no.1, Special issue (2005).

Hashai, Niron and Almor, Tamar. "Gradually Internationalizing 'Born Global' Firms: An Oxymoron?" *International Business Review*, vol. 13, no. 4 (August 2004).

Hejazi, Walid. "Reconsidering the Concentration of US MNE Activity: Is it Global, Regional or National?" *Management International Review*, vol. 47, no. 1 (2007).

Hennart, Jean-François (2009). "Down with MNE-centric theories! Market entry and expansion as the bundling of MNE and local assets," *Journal of International Business Studies*, vol. 40 (August 20, 2009).

Hutzschenreuter, Thomas, Voll, Johannes C. and Verbeke, Alain. "The Impact of Added Cultural Distance and Cultural Diversity on International Expansion Patterns: A Penrosean Perspective," *Journal of Management Studies*, vol. 48, no. 2 (March 2011).

Javalgi, Rajshekhar (Raj) G., Deligonul, Seyda, Ghosh, Amit K., Lambert Douglas M. and Cavusgil, S. Tamer. "Foreign Market Entry Mode Behavior as a Gateway to Further Entries: The NAFTA Experience," *International Business Review*, vol. 19, no. 3 (June 2010).

Oh, Chang Hoon. "Regional Sales of Multinationals in the World Cosmetics Industry," *European Management Journal*, vol. 24, nos. 2–3 (2006).

Makino, Shige and Tsang, Eric W. K. "Historical Ties and Foreign Direct Investment," *Journal of International Business Studies*, vol. 42 (2010).

Morschett, Dirk, Schramm-Klein, Hanna and Bernhard Swoboda, Berhard. "Entry Modes for Manufacturers' International After-Sales Service: Analysis of Transaction-specific, Firm-specific and Country-specific Determinants," *Management International Review*, vol. 48, no. 5 (2008).

Mirus, Rolf and Yeung, Bernard. "On the Mode of International Expansion: The Role of Agency Costs," *Multinational Business Review*, vol. 18, no. 4 (2010).

Nguyen, Quyen T. K. "The Empirical Literature on Multinational Enterprises, Subsidiaries and Performance," *Multinational Business Review*, vol. 19, no.1 (2011).

Peng, Mike W. "Identifying the Big Question in International Business Research," *Journal of International Business Studies*, vol. 35, no. 2 (March 2004).

Pitelis, Christos. "Edith Penrose and a Learning-Based Perspective on the MNE and OLI," *Management International Review*, vol. 47, no. 2 (2007).

Ramamurti, Ravi. "Developing Countries and MNEs: Extending and Enriching the Research Agenda," *Journal of International Business Studies*, vol. 35, no. 4 (July 2004).

Rugman, Alan M. "A New Theory of the Multinational Enterprise: Internationalization versus Internalization," *Columbia Journal of World Business*, vol. 15, no. 1 (Spring 1980).

Rugman, Alan M. (ed.) *New Theories of the Multinational Enterprise* (London: Croom Helm and New York: St Martin's Press, 1982).

Rugman, Alan M. "Regional Strategies for Service Sector Multinationals," *European Business Journal*, vol. 15, no. 1 (2003).

Rugman, Alan M. *The Regional Multinationals* (Cambridge: Cambridge University Press, 2005).

Rugman, Alan M. (ed.). *Regional Aspects of Multinationality and Performance* (Oxford: Elsevier, 2007).

Rugman, Alan M. and Boyd, Gavin (eds.). *European-American Trade and Financial Alliances* (Cheltenham: Edward Elgar, 2005).

Rugman, Alan M. and Collinson, Simon. "The Regional Nature of the World's Automotive Sector," *European Management Journal*, vol. 22, no. 5 (2004).

Rugman, Alan M. and Verbeke, Alain. "A Perspective on Regional and Global Strategies of Multinational Enterprises," *Journal of International Business Studies*, vol. 35, no. 1 (January 2004).

Rugman, Alan M. and Verbeke, Alain. "Towards a Theory of Regional Multinationals: A Transaction Cost Economics Approach," *Management International Review*, vol. 45, Special issue 1 (2005).

Rugman, Alan M., Verbeke, Alain and Nguyen, Quyen T. K. "Fifty Years of International Business Theory and Beyond," *Management International Review*, vol. 51, no. 6 (November 2011).

Sethi, Deepak, Guisinger, Stephan E., Phelan, Steven E. and Berg, David M. "Trends in Foreign Direct Investment Flows: A Theoretical and Empirical Analysis," *Journal of International Business Studies*, vol. 34, no. 4 (July 2003).

Shenkar, Oded. "One More Time: International Business in a Global Economy," *Journal of International Business Studies*, vol. 35, no. 2 (March 2004).

Slangen, Arjen and Hennart, Jean-François. "Greenfield or Acquisition Entry: A Review of the Empirical Foreign Establishment Mode Literature," *Journal of International Management*, vol. 13, no. 4 (December 2007).

Slangen, Arjen and Hennart, Jean-François. "Do Foreign Greenfields Outperform Foreign Acquisitions or Vice Versa? An Institutional Perspective," *Journal of Management Studies*, vol. 45, no. 7 (November 2008).

Tomassen, Sverre and Benito, Gabriel R. G. "The Costs of Governance in International Companies," *International Business Review*, vol. 18. No. 3 (June 2009).

Williamson, Oliver E. *Markets and Hierarchies* (New York: Free Press, 1975).

Yip, George S. *Total Global Strategy II: Updated for the Internet and Service Era* (Upper Saddle River, NJ: Prentice Hall, 2003).

Part Two

THE ENVIRONMENT OF INTERNATIONAL BUSINESS

Chapter 4

INTERNATIONAL POLITICS

Contents

Objectives of the chapter

Politics and economics are closely linked and often affect each other.
A good example is the economic changes that are sweeping Eastern
Europe and Asia today. As these countries embrace open markets,
their centrally planned economies are giving way to market-driven
economies. However, this latter development would have been
impossible had it not been preceded by the requisite political change
as reflected by more democratic governments. The purposes of this
chapter are to examine the linkage between political forces and
economic change and then to review some of the major forms of
economic integration that are being used to create regional trade
areas and common markets. In future chapters these topics will be
developed in more depth.

The specific objectives of this chapter are to:

1 *Compare* and *contrast* major political and economic systems and
note the linkage among them.

2 *Examine* the primary reasons for the current privatization
movement and the economic impact that this movement is having
on selected countries.

3 *Describe* the five major levels of economic integration and how
each works.

4 *Discuss* how MNEs are using strategic planning to benefit from
current worldwide economic integration efforts.

5 *Discuss* the impact of non-governmental organizations (NGOs) on
international business.

ACTIVE LEARNING CASE

How risky is foreign investment in Russia?

Making investments in any foreign country is a risky business. Each and every foreign country has a different set of legal, political, social, and economic institutions. Despite allegations that the world is flat, what we know is that there remains a large degree of variation in both country and regional institutional arrangements. Thus, no investor can afford to assume that doing business abroad is risk free. This logic applies to the current situation in Russia.

A number of problems continue to plague Russia. Natural resources account for 80 percent of the country's exports, including oil and natural gas, making the economy susceptible to world price fluctuations. The banking system is weak and, after the 1998 crisis, generally distrusted. In 2004, for instance, smaller banks faced a liquidity crisis as depositors, afraid for their savings, withdrew large sums of money. In addition, widespread corruption and government interference in the judiciary process stymies both domestic and foreign investment. A case in point is that of Yukos, one of Russia's largest oil companies, whose privatization was one of many corrupt undertakings in the transition to a market economy. The government sought to collect back taxes that are threatening to bankrupt the company. Yukos is charged with tax evasion, but critics claim the move was politically motivated and that the tools used to evade taxes were perfectly legal under Russian law when they were undertaken.

By 2010, the former Russian oil tycoon Mikhail Khodorkovsky of Yukos was already serving an eight-year jail term for fraud and tax evasion. In the verdict of the second trial on December 27, 2010, he and his business partner Platon Lebedev were found guilty of stealing billions of dollars from their own oil firm, Yukos, and laundering the proceeds between 1998 and 2003. They would have to stay in jail until 2017. Many critics believe the government wants the former tycoon kept behind the bars for as long as possible because he challenged the former president Vladimir Putin. As a result of this internal uncertainty foreign investors continue to reassess their opportunities in Russia.

It is being argued that such political events in Russia make it far too dangerous a place to do business. This is not an accurate assessment of the political and economic situation in Russia. The nationalization of key resource-based companies and the perceived inappropriate treatment of some foreign investors undoubtedly reflect an increase in Russian economic nationalism. However, this has not yet reached a significant level, nor is it likely to in the future.

The reason that Russian authorities will not engage in massive nationalization of foreign assets is that the Russian economy remains dependent on foreign investment. Russia has large supplies of energy resources, but it needs to sell these to foreign consumers. Russia's resources will lose value if they are restricted to Russian consumers. There is as yet no economic evidence that Russia is seeking to be a self-contained, protected, and isolated economy. Instead, it relies upon trade and foreign investment. However, at a time of increased concern over energy security, Moscow has more than once reminded the rest of the world of the power it yields as a major energy supplier. In 2006, it cut gas to Ukraine (a pro-Western government by that time) after a row between the countries, a move that also affected the supply of gas to Western Europe.

Today Russia is the 10th-largest economy in the world. It is attracting large amounts of foreign direct investment from members of the European Union, especially Germany and the UK. In July 2007 the British government expelled four Russian diplomats from London. British Foreign Secretary, David Miliband, stated that this action was taken because the government of

Source: Getty Images/Photodisc Green

former President Vladimir Putin refused to extradite the Russian national suspected of the murder of Alexander Litvinenko in London in November 2006. In response, the Russians expelled four diplomats. In late 2010, a British MP's Russia-born parliamentary aid was arrested over claims that she is a Russian spy. The latest allegations came after 10 Russian spy agents, including Anna Chapman who had dual Russian–UK citizenship, were expelled from the United States in July 2010. The Russian government is thought to have an "extensive shopping list of information" it is trying to acquire through covert means—on the aerospace industry, defense, and information technology, as well as in politics and diplomacy. Despite this reversion to Cold War diplomacy it is not anticipated that British investment in Russia will decrease. Nor is it expected that London will stop being a second home for many wealthy Russian businessmen. In short, the British/Russian political difficulties are unlikely to affect the growing economic relationships between the two countries.

In contrast to the British case, US political relations with Russia are more benign. The US government concluded a bilateral trade and investment agreement with Russia in November 2006. The United States is also helping Russia with its application to join the World Trade Organization. In general, US officials encourage US investment in Russia, and also welcome Russian investment in the United States. It is unlikely that the US government will take any action to offset its ongoing concerns about human rights violations in Russia or an increase in Russian economic nationalism.

This long-run analysis of why Russia will remain an integral part of the world economic system does not mean that specific investment projects can escape risk. Russia is still at an early stage of economic development. It is less than 20 years since the Berlin Wall crumbled and the former Soviet Union was opened to market forces. Russia has found it difficult to develop the appropriate market-based institutions to match its acceptance of worldwide capitalism.

Instead, Russia remains an autocratic regime, and foreign investors need to be careful in making commitments where the normal level and contractual arrangements available in the EU and North America do not yet fully exist. However, Russia is making progress on improving its institutional framework. In 2006 it hosted the annual meetings of the G8 leaders, and its businesses are becoming increasingly aware that they must conform to the market-based principles required by the WTO.

Today Russia is becoming increasingly integrated with the evolving EU (which now has 27 member states). Russia is also attracting investment from Japan and China. Investors need to adopt a long-term view and should not be thrown off by short-term political developments in Russia. Foreign investors should seek to build lasting personal relationships with Russia's leaders in business and economics.

Websites: www.ford.com; www.imf.org; www.worldbank.org; www.tetrapak.de; www.pepsico.com; www.mcdonalds.com; www.yukos.com; www.telia.se; www.sonera.fi; www.telecominvest.com.

Sources: Adapted from Alan Rugman, "Is it safe for Americans to Invest in Russia?" *Kansas City, Sunday Star*, October 7, 2007; "Cinderella's Witching Hour," *The Economist*, July 8, 2004; "Court 'Freezes' Key Yukos Assets," BBC.co.uk, April 19, 2005; Russia Country Profile, news.bbc.co.uk; "Prove my aid is Russian spy, says MP Mike Hancock," news.bbc.co.uk, December 5, 2010; "Russia postpones verdict on oil tycoon Khodorkovsky," news.bbc.co.uk, December 15, 2010; "Russian ex-tycoon Khodorkovsky appeals against jail term," news.bbc.co.uk, December 31, 2010.

1. What type of economic system now exists in Russia: market-driven, centrally determined, or mixed?

2. Would Russia benefit by gaining admission to one of the major economic unions such as the EU? Why?

3. Is Russia a good potential investment for Western business? Explain.

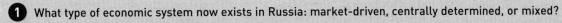

INTRODUCTION

Over the past two decades, many countries have seen a dramatic change in their political systems. In the Americas, both Chile and Nicaragua have returned to democracy. The former communist countries of Eastern Europe are building, in varying degrees, free market systems. In China, meanwhile, the central government is still communist, but the nation is no longer tightly managed by Beijing. Market-driven companies have blossomed in a growing number of geographic areas (most of them in the south-eastern region), lending credence to the contentions of those who hold that China will be a market-driven economy within a few decades. Whether or not this proves true, one thing is certain: political and economic changes are taking place everywhere, opening up new opportunities for MNEs.

In particular, the movement toward market-driven economies of countries that were once controlled by the former Soviet Union have affected international business. For example, Poland, Hungary, the Czech Republic, Latvia, Lithuania, and Estonia, to name but six, have all created market-driven economies. Years ago the former Soviet Union would not have permitted these satellite nations to abandon the command economy advocated by communist ideology and replace it with a free market system. Under Mikhail Gorbachev, however, the Soviet Union revised its political and economic thinking—and things have never been the same since.

Although this has proved to be good news for the satellite countries, Russia, as seen in this chapter's Active Learning Case, has not been as fortunate. As a result, until MNEs feel that the government is willing to take the steps necessary to ensure that promises are kept and they are able to repatriate their funds, they are going to proceed very cautiously with their investment plans. International politics is a primary concern for these firms. This explains why Cuba has found it so difficult to attract foreign capital.

China, on the other hand, realizing that it must walk a fine line between commitment to its current political philosophy and the need to attract outside investments, has been trying very hard to balance both of these concerns. At the turn of the century, former President Jiang Zemin noted that one of the country's primary economic objectives is to increase gross domestic product at an annual rate of 7 percent. During the interview, the president also said that capitalists should be welcomed into the Communist Party.[1] At the same time, China encouraged foreign capital investment in order to ensure that its economic engine continues to function efficiently—this implied a change in its political ideology. One development in this direction was a government announcement that the country could no longer ensure the survival of inefficient companies. Firms now have to be able to compete with MNEs or face the risk of going under. Workers, accustomed to job security, had to accept the fact that they could be laid off and be willing to be retrained in order to find employment in this new, competitive job market.[2] These reforms have come a long way. In 2005 the private economy accounted for nearly 40 percent of the gross product of Shanghai, China's largest urban center.[3]

These governmental decrees certainly represent a big change in the way things have been done in China for the past 50 years. The same is true worldwide. International politics and economic integration are altering the way international business is being conducted, and those nations that cannot keep up with these developments are going to find themselves falling farther and farther behind. In this chapter we will look at the major current economic and political systems and their impact on the world of international business. We will begin by examining political ideologies and economics.

Political ideologies and economics

Ideology
A set of integrated beliefs, theories, and doctrines that helps to direct the actions of a society

An **ideology** is a set of integrated beliefs, theories, and doctrines that helps direct the actions of a society. Political ideology is almost always intertwined with economic philosophy. For example, the political ideology of the United States is grounded in the Constitution, which guarantees the rights of private property and the freedom of choice. This has helped lay the foundation for US capitalism. A change in this fundamental ideology would alter the economic environment of the United States. The same is true, for example, for China and the former Soviet Union republics. Simply put, the political and economic ideologies of nations help to explain their national economic policies.

Democracy
A system of government in which the people, either directly or through their elected officials, decide what is to be done

Political systems

In the extreme, there are two types of political systems: democracy and totalitarianism. **Democracy** is a system of government in which the people, either directly or through their elected officials, decide what is to be done. Good examples of democratic governments include the United States, Canada, the UK, and Australia. Common features of democratic governments include (1) the right to express opinions freely, (2) election of representatives for limited terms of office, (3) an independent court system that protects individual property and rights, and (4) a relatively non-political bureaucracy and defense infrastructure that ensure the continued operation of the system.

Totalitarianism is a system of government in which one individual or political party maintains complete control and either refuses to recognize other parties or suppresses them. A number of types of totalitarianism currently exist. **Communism** is an economic system in which the government owns all property and makes all decisions regarding the production and distribution of goods and services. To date, all attempts at national communism have led to totalitarianism. The best example of communism is Cuba. Another form of totalitarianism is **theocratic totalitarianism**, in which a religious group exercises total power and represses or persecutes non-orthodox factions. Iran and some of the sheikdoms of the Middle East are good examples. A third form is **secular totalitarianism**, in which the military controls the government and makes decisions that it deems to be in the best interests of the country. Examples of this are communist North Korea and Chile under Pinochet. Political systems typically create the infrastructure within which the economic system functions; in order to change the economic system, there often needs to be a change in the way the country is governed.

Economic systems

The three basic economic systems are capitalism, socialism, and mixed. However, for the purposes of our analysis it is more helpful to classify these systems in terms of resource allocation (market-driven versus centrally determined) and property ownership (private versus public). In a **market-driven economy**, goods and services are allocated on the basis of demand and supply. If consumers express a preference for cellular telephones, more of these products will be offered for sale. If consumers refuse to buy dot-matrix printers, these goods will cease to be offered. The US and EU nations have market-driven economies. In a **centrally determined economy**, goods and services are allocated based on a plan formulated by a committee that decides what is to be offered. In these economies people are able to purchase only what the government determines should be sold. Cuba is the best example.

Market-driven economies are characterized by private ownership. Most of the assets of production are in the hands of privately owned companies that compete for market share by offering the best-quality goods and services at competitive prices. Centrally determined economies are characterized by public ownership. Most of the assets of production are in the hands of the state, and production quotas are set for each organization.

In examining economic systems, it is important to remember that, in a strict sense, most nations of the world have **mixed economies**, characterized by a combination of market-driven forces and centrally determined planning. Mixed economies include privately owned commercial entities as well as government-owned commercial entities. Governments in mixed economies typically own the utilities and infrastructural industries—railroads, airlines, shipping lines, and industries considered to be of economic and strategic importance—for instance, petroleum and copper. For example, the United States, a leading proponent of market-driven economic policies, provides health care and other social services to many of its citizens through government-regulated agencies, which gives it some aspects of central planning. Other democratic countries with mixed economies include the UK, Sweden, and Germany, all of which have even stronger social welfare systems than the United States.

Another example of the role of government in the economy is that of promoting business and ensuring that local firms gain or maintain dominance in certain market areas. The

---

Totalitarianism
A system of government in which one individual or party maintains complete control and either refuses to recognize other parties or suppresses them

Communism
A political system in which the government owns all property and makes all decisions regarding production and distribution of goods and services

Theocratic totalitarianism
A system of government in which a religious group exercises total power and represses or persecutes non-orthodox factions

Secular totalitarianism
A system of government in which the military controls everything and makes decisions that it deems to be in the best interests of the country

Market-driven economy
An economy in which goods and services are allocated on the basis of consumer demand

Centrally determined economy
An economy in which goods and services are allocated based on a plan formulated by a committee that decides what is to be offered

Mixed economies
Economic systems characterized by a combination of market- and centrally driven planning

US and EU governments continually pressure the Chinese to open their doors to foreign MNEs, and the Chinese government is very active in helping its local firms do business with the West.

As a result of such developments, there has been a blurring of the differences between market-driven and centrally determined economies. The biggest change has been the willingness of the latter to introduce free market concepts. Examples include Russia and other East European countries, which began introducing aspects of free enterprise such as allowing people to start their own businesses and to keep any profits that they make.[4] At the same time, however, many market-driven economies are increasingly adopting centrally determined ideas, such as using business–government cooperation to fend off external competitors, or the use of political force to limit the ability of overseas firms to do business in their country. In the United States, for example, the government is frequently being urged to play a more active role in monitoring foreign business practices. An instance of this can be seen in the box **International Business Strategy in Action: Softwood lumber: not-so-free trade**. On balance, however, we are now seeing a move from central planning to market-driven and mixed economies. The privatization movement that is taking place worldwide provides one prominent example.

Government control of assets

Privatization
The process of selling government assets to private buyers

Over the past decade or so, an increasing number of countries have begun moving toward **privatization**, the process of selling government assets to private buyers. To understand the reasons for, and the economic impact of, this process, it is helpful to examine both the potential benefits of government ownership and the advantages of moving to privatization.

Nationalization
A process by which the government takes control of business assets, sometimes with remuneration of the owners and other times without such remuneration

There are six common, and sometimes interdependent, reasons for countries to control business assets, a process known as **nationalization**. These include (1) promoting economic development, such as by coordinating the assets of many businesses into one overall master plan; (2) earning profits for the national treasury; (3) preventing companies from going bankrupt and closing their doors; (4) enhancing programs that are in the national interest; (5) increasing the political or economic control of those in power; and (6) ensuring goods and services to all citizens regardless of their economic status.[5]

The opposite situation, privatization, can take two forms. The most common form is **divestiture**, in which the government sells its assets. The other is **contract management**, in which the government transfers operating responsibility of an industry without transferring the legal title and ownership. The major trend today is toward divestiture.

Divestiture
(Also see *Privatization*)
A process by which a government or business sells assets

Contract management
A process by which an organization (such as the government) transfers operating responsibility of an industry without transferring the legal title and ownership

Some of the primary reasons for privatization are: (1) it is more efficient to have the goods and services provided by private business than by government-run companies; (2) a change in the political culture brings about a desire to sell these assets; (3) the company has been making money, and the government feels there is more to be gained by selling now than by holding on; (4) the purchase price can be used to reduce the national debt; (5) the company is losing money, and the government has to assume the losses out of the national treasury; (6) the company needs research and development funds in order to maintain a competitive stance and it is unwilling to make this investment; and (7) international funding agencies are making assistance to the country conditional on a reduction in the size of the government.[6]

Privatization in action

Many nations have privatization programs.[7] These include countries with moderate per capita gross domestic products, such as Argentina, Brazil, Chile, Mexico, and China, as well as economically advanced nations such as the United States, Japan, Germany, and the UK. All feel that their economies can be strengthened through privatization programs.

INTERNATIONAL BUSINESS STRATEGY IN ACTION

Softwood lumber: not-so-free trade

In 2003, both the North American Free Trade Agreement (NAFTA) and the World Trade Organization (WTO) ruled in favor of Canada on the issue of US tariffs on Canadian soft-wood lumber. The WTO ruling was non-binding, whereas NAFTA's ruling had to be addressed within 60 days. However, the agreement, reached in principle between the two countries, is far from free trade.

The rift between producers on each side of the border is 20 years old, and in 1996 it led to an agreement: the United States–Canada Softwood Lumber Agreement (SLA), in which Canada restricted exports to the United States to 14.7 billion board feet. At that time, Canadian producers claimed such a restriction cost them $480 million annu-ally and 11,000 jobs. When the agreement came to an end in 2001, US producers quickly lobbied their govern-ment to impose tariffs on Canadian producers. For its part, the Canadian government was hoping that the end of the SLA would lead to free trade. An investigation by the Department of Commerce determined that Canada's provincial governments were illegally subsidizing lumber production and imposed a tariff of 19.3 percent that was later increased to 27 percent.

At the core of the dispute are differences in the systems of production in both countries. In the United States, most harvested timber comes from private lands and is auc-tioned off to buyers. In Canada, provincial governments own the land and set cutting fees according to market conditions. US producers argue that government-set cut-ting fees are below market prices and thus constitute a 35 percent subsidy to the Canadian industry.

Softwood lumber is one of Canada's most successful exports to the United States. In fact, Canadian producers had held a 35 percent market share prior to the tariff, and exports to the United States had grown considerably in the 1990s, particularly as a result of the lower Canadian dollar. In addition, note the Canadian producers, the US claim ignores the extra expenses that Canadian firms have had to pay for road building, replanting, and environmental protection. As a result, the Canadians argue that the tariff is nothing more than protectionism.

The negative effects of the tariff are now being felt in both countries. The fact that US consumers are paying 10 percent more as a direct result has so upset some industry groups that an association of US homebuilders, consumers, and contractors lobbied Washington to remove the tariff. Within a month of the tariff's enactment, 10,000 industry workers had been laid off, a dozen mills were shuttered, and most of the plants were operating below capacity. By 2003, Canadian producers held about one-third of the US market.

Source: Getty Images/Alan Kearney

Favorable verdicts from WTO and NAFTA courts have resulted in almost no benefit to the Canadian industry. Both courts agreed that the Canadian system amounted to a sub-sidy to domestic producers; however, the WTO found that the subsidy was not enough to warrant retaliation from the United States, and NAFTA found that the tariffs that the United States imposed were excessive and miscalculated the subsidy by not taking into consideration market conditions in Canada. An agreement in principle in 2003 proposed the elimination of the 27 percent US tariff but reduced the amount Canadian producers can export to the United States without penalty. Canadian firms would only be able to capture 31.5 percent (down from 33 percent) of the US market and would have to pay $200 per each additional thousand board feet. The United States would return 52 percent of all tariffs collected since 2001, just over $800 million, but US companies would receive the remainder. Provinces that follow the US market system, such as New Brunswick and Nova Scotia, would benefit from more market access. Perhaps the most important section of this managed trade agreement is that it prevents Canada from further pursuing resolution through the WTO or NAFTA.

Websites: www.weyerhaeuser.com; www.dfait-maeci.gc.ca; www.wto.org.

Sources: Edward Alden, "Canada to Challenge United States Over Import Duties," *Financial Times*, August 21, 2001; Ian Jack, "US Hits Value-added Softwood," *Financial Post*, September 5, 2001; "Pettigrew Plans to Lobby Washington on Lumber," *The Toronto Star*, September 7, 2001; "Stump War," *The Economist*, August 30, 2001; "At Loggerheads," *The Economist*, May 22, 2001; Amina Ali, Sabrina Saccoccio and Justin Thomson, "Softwood Lumber Dispute," *CBC News Online*, March 2001 and updated on December 8, 2003; "Softwood Lumber Deal Caps Canadian Exports," *CBC TV News*, July 29, 2003.

In the case of Argentina, for example, the government has now ended the nation's phone monopoly and opened up the $10 billion market to outside investors. Previously the two telephone companies that monopolized all long-distance and local phone services had their territories firmly established, and neither could compete with the other. Now they can. Moreover, other telephone companies also have licenses to operate throughout the country. The Argentinean government believes that, as a result of privatization in this industry, competition will increase, phone rates will drop, and service will increase sharply.[8]

In the case of the UK, privatization and deregulation have proven to be a national boon. A few years ago British Telecommunications began downsizing its operations so as to increase its competitiveness and profitability. The firm slashed 100,000 jobs, and critics said that privatization and deregulation were hurting the economy. However, just the opposite occurred. Many of the workers who were laid off began finding jobs with small telecommunications firms that were springing up throughout the country. At the same time, there was an influx of large foreign competitors such as AT&T, the giant US telecommunications company, and AB L. M. Ericsson, the Swedish telecom-equipment maker, which hired thousands of people. As a result, between 1990 and 1999 the number of jobs in the UK's telecommunications industry increased, while prices decreased and service improved sharply.[9]

Another major group of nations turning to privatization is Russia and the East European countries. At the grassroots in Russia, a market economy has begun to evolve. Despite the lack of national or local laws to guide them, hundreds of small factories and service businesses are now privatizing themselves, and enterprises are pushing ahead with Russian-style versions of leveraged buyouts, employee stock ownership plans, and private spin-offs. Many are also taking their old, outmoded operations and modernizing them. A good example is the Vologda Textile Enterprise Company. By significantly reducing its workforce and rebuilding the looms, the firm has found that it can sell all of the textiles it produces to buyers in the EU.[10]

Privatization is not always a popular idea, and it is often part of election debates. Yet governments continue to assess the benefits of privatization against those of state ownership. Mexico and Japan provide two recent examples. Recently the Mexican government announced that it will privatize its two national airlines, Aeroméxico and Mexicana, on the hopes that it can provide cheaper service and compete with low-cost service from the United States.[11] Despite opposition from civil servants and some political parties, Japan Post is set for a slow privatization process that is to culminate in 2017.[12]

Government–business cooperation

The fact that governments are privatizing assets does not mean they are distancing themselves from business firms. Both Japan and the EU have seen a large amount of business–government cooperation that has been extremely beneficial to the business sector in these countries.

Ministry of International Trade and Industry (MITI)
A Japanese ministry charged with providing information about foreign markets and with encouraging investment in select industries and, in the process, helping to direct the economy

Japan and EU assistance

After World War II, the Japanese government began formulating plans for regenerating its economy. In this vein, it gave responsibility for implementing the country's trade and industrial policy to the **Ministry of International Trade and Industry (MITI)**. The initial focus of the ministry was to provide protection to Japanese companies and to assist in marketing the products of four major industries: electric power, steel, shipbuilding, and fertilizers. Incentives were created to encourage investment in these industries and to help firms export their products. In recent years, MITI's focus has been on targeting less energy-intensive industries for Japanese investment and growth. Prime examples include computers and chemicals, where MITI works cooperatively with Japanese businesses to help ensure success. The focus of MITI has changed from a proactive to a much more cooperative agency; its main role today is funding export markets for Japanese businesses.

Governments in the EU have also been very helpful in promoting businesses. One way has been to fund research consortia through research and development (R&D) support. One of the research programs that has been helped by EU governments is Research on Advanced Communications in Europe (RACE). Since the late 1980s, RACE has received billions of euros of government money to support its efforts in developing an integrated broadband telecommunications network. Another recipient of government largesse is the European Strategic Program for R&D in Information Technology (ESPRIT II). This consortium has engaged in hundreds of projects dealing with such high-tech areas as information technologies, microelectronics, and computer-integrated manufacturing. Perhaps the best-known R&D consortium is EUREKA, a pan-European group whose main objective is to create closer cooperation between private companies and research institutes in the field of advanced technologies for the purpose of exploiting commercial opportunities. The projects that are funded bring together companies throughout the EU and involve not only large firms but also small and medium-sized enterprises. Unlike many research consortia, however, EUREKA focuses on projects whose research is now ready to be applied.[13] (See the Active Learning Case: Boeing vs. Airbus in Chapter 3 for a closer look at government-established consortia.)

US competitiveness

The results of such governmental efforts have not been lost on Washington, which has long recognized the value of an industrial policy that provides benefits similar to those offered by MITI and EUREKA. As long ago as 1990, a special White House panel of experts from industry, academia, and the government released a list of 22 technologies that it deemed essential to US national defense and economic prosperity. Including composite materials, flexible computer-integrated manufacturing, and high-definition electronic displays, the list was intended to guide the Critical Technologies Institute, created by Congress in 1990 to conduct long-range strategic planning and to work closely with the private sector in developing important technologies.

Over the past two decades in particular, the US government has been active in supporting research consortia to help underwrite some of the costs associated with new technology development. A good example is Sematech, a consortium of 14 semiconductor manufacturing companies, which once received $100 million a year in subsidies from the US government to help shore up the chip-making equipment industry. By the mid-1990s these manufacturers were doing so well that Sematech's board voted to end federal funding, and the group is now funded entirely by private money.[14] Another consortium that has received government assistance is the National Center for Manufacturing Sciences, which has provided a host of important technology breakthroughs, including a method for hardening cutting tools by coating them with diamond film. A third has been the Microelectronics & Computer Technology Corporation, which has worked on advanced computing, software, and computer-aided design.

In the past, US administrations have supported research efforts that promoted industrial competitiveness and technological leadership. This often took one of two paths: (1) the funding of military research that could then be used to create commercially useful products; or (2) the direct funding of research efforts by US firms. The technology policy of the Bush administration is to continue the US focus on maintaining a strong, high-tech military and a world-class computer information industry.

Active learning check

Review your answer to Active Learning Case question 1 and make any changes you like. Then compare your answer to the one below.

1 **What type of economic system now exists in Russia: market-driven, centrally determined, or mixed?**

A mixed system currently exists. The country is moving away from a centrally determined economy, but there is a long way to go. As can be seen from the information in the case, the transition is causing a great deal of economic upheaval. This may even result in a regression toward some of the previously employed, centrally determined decision making. However, the country is not going to go back to the old way of doing things because it has too much committed to its current course of action. In particular, any further IMF loans or assistance from the United States, Japan, or the EU will depend on how well the country is holding the line and trying to make its market-driven economy work. So a mixed economic system will remain in place; in fact, this is really the only path the Russians can take in rescuing their economy.

ECONOMIC INTEGRATION

Economic integration
The establishment of transnational rules and regulations that enhance economic trade and cooperation among countries

Economic integration is the establishment of transnational rules and regulations that enhance economic trade and cooperation among countries. At one extreme, economic integration would result in one worldwide free trade market in which all nations had a common currency and could export anything they wanted to any other nation. At the other extreme would be a total lack of economic integration, in which nations were self-sufficient and did not trade with anyone. (The theory of these polar extremes will be discussed in Chapter 6.)

The concept of economic integration is attractive, but there are many implementation problems. In particular, it requires that the participants agree to surrender some of their national sovereignty, such as the authority to set tariffs and quotas. For example, if the United States and the EU agree to allow free trade of agricultural products, neither one can restrict the other's right to export these commodities. So although free trade may lead to lower prices, those who are unwilling to give up the right to control goods being imported into their country may well be opposed to it.

A number of regional economic efforts have been undertaken over the past 30 years to promote varying degrees of economic integration. The most successful has been the EU, although less developed countries (LDCs) have also made integration efforts.

Trade creation and trade diversion

Before examining economic integration in more depth, it is important to realize that the agreement of countries to integrate their economies will bring about a shift in business activity. This shift can result in trade creation as well as trade diversion.

Trade creation
A process in which members of an economic integration group begin to focus their efforts on those goods and services for which they have a comparative advantage and start trading more extensively with each other

Trade creation occurs when members of an economic integration group begin focusing their efforts on those goods and services for which they have a comparative advantage and start trading more extensively with each other. For example, the United States and Mexico have an agreement that allows cars to be assembled in Mexico and shipped to the United States. As a result, Mexico, a low-cost producer, supplies a large number of vehicles sold in the United States, and both countries prosper as a result.

Trade creation results in efficient, low-cost producers in member countries gaining market share from high-cost member producers, as well as generating increased exports. In fact, a growing number of US companies have moved some of their operations to Mexico or hired Mexican firms to be their suppliers because this is a more efficient approach than making the goods in the United States. And when efficient regional producers are able to offer lower-price and higher-quality output than their competitors, trade creation results.

Trade diversion occurs when members of an economic integration group decrease their trade with non-member countries in favor of trade with each other. One common reason is that the removal of trade barriers among member countries makes it less expensive to buy from companies within the group, and the continuation of trade barriers with non-member countries makes it more difficult for the latter to compete. Thus, trade diversion can lead to the loss of production and exports from more efficient non-member countries to less efficient member countries that are being protected by tariffs or other barriers. Quite obviously, the creation of economic integration groups is beneficial only if trade creation exceeds trade diversion. Otherwise, the economic union impedes international trade.

Trade diversion
Occurs when members of an economic integration group decrease their trade with non-member countries in favor of trade with each other

Levels of economic integration

There are five levels of economic integration, which extend from simple economic trade arrangements to full political integration characterized by a single government. The following examines each of these levels, beginning with the simplest.

Free trade area

A **free trade area** is an economic integration arrangement in which barriers to trade (such as tariffs) among member countries are removed. Under this arrangement, each participant will seek to gain by specializing in the production of those goods and services for which it has a comparative advantage and importing those goods and services for which it has a comparative disadvantage.

Free trade area
An economic integration arrangement in which barriers to trade (such as tariffs) among member countries are removed

One of the best-known free trade areas is the **North American Free Trade Agreement (NAFTA)**, which currently consists of Canada, the United States, and Mexico. The United States and Canada created this free trade area with the US–Canadian Free Trade Agreement of 1989, and the arrangement has now been expanded to include Mexico.[15] While trade diversion can occur under free trade arrangements, NAFTA has led to a great amount of trade creation. In fact, trade among the three members of NAFTA is nearly $1 trillion annually![16]

North America Free Trade Agreement (NAFTA)
A regional free trade agreement among Canada, the United States, and Mexico

Customs union

A **customs union** is a form of economic integration in which all tariffs between member countries are eliminated and a common trade policy toward non-member countries is established. This policy often results in a uniform external tariff structure. Under this arrangement, a country outside the union will face the same tariff on exports to any member country receiving the goods.

Under a customs union, member countries cede some of the control of their economic policies to the group at large. None of the regional integration groups in existence today has been formed for the purpose of creating a customs union; instead, many of them have sought greater integration in the form of a common market or economic union. However, because of the difficulty of attaining this high degree of integration, some countries have effectively settled for a customs union. The Andean Community, which will be discussed shortly, is an example.

Customs union
A form of economic integration in which all tariffs between member countries are eliminated and a common trade policy toward non-member countries is established

Common market

Common market
A form of economic integration characterized by the elimination of trade barriers among member nations, a common external trade policy, and mobility of factors of production among member countries

A **common market** is a form of economic integration characterized by (1) no barriers to trade among member nations, (2) a common external trade policy, and (3) mobility of factors of production among member countries. A common market allows reallocation of production resources, such as capital, labor, and technology, based on the theory of comparative advantage. Although this may be economically disadvantageous to industries or specific businesses in some member countries, in theory it should lead to the efficient delivery of goods and services to all member countries. The best example of a successful common market is the EU, although this group has now progressed beyond a common market and is now focusing on political and financial integration.

Economic union

Economic union
A form of economic integration characterized by free movement of goods, services, and factors of production among member countries and full integration of economic policies

An **economic union** is a deep form of economic integration and is characterized by free movement of goods, services, and factors of production among member countries and full integration of economic policies. An economic union (1) unifies monetary and fiscal policy among the member nations, including the same tax rates, and (2) has a common currency (or a permanently fixed exchange rate among currencies). Additionally, most of the national economic policies of the individual countries are ceded to the group at large. There are no true economic unions in the world, but the creation of a single currency, the euro, certainly moves the EU in this direction.

Political union

Political union
An economic union in which there is full economic integration, unification of economic policies, and a single government

A **political union** goes beyond full economic integration to encompass a single government. This occurs only when countries give up their individual national powers to be united and led by one government. One successful example is the United States, which combined independent states into a political union. The EU is now also on its way to becoming a political union. The European Parliament, for example, is directly elected by citizens of the EU countries, and its Council of Ministers, which is the decision-making body of the EU, is made up of government ministers from each EU country.

Economic integration: an overall perspective

Before concluding our discussion of levels of economic integration, four points merit consideration. First, a country does not need to pursue economic integration by starting with a free trade area and then working up to a common market or an economic union. For example, the UK was a member of a free trade area before deciding to leave and enter the EU. Simply stated, countries will choose the appropriate level of economic integration based on their political and economic needs.

Second, economic integration in the form of free trade typically results in a winning situation for all group members, since each member can specialize in those goods and services it makes most efficiently and rely on others in the group to provide the remainder. However, when a bloc of countries imposes a tariff on non-members, this often results in a win–lose situation. Those outside the bloc face tariffs, are thus less competitive with group member companies, and lose market share and revenue within the bloc. Among group members, however, increased competition often results in greater efficiency, lower prices, and increased exports to non-member markets.

Internal economies of scale
Efficiencies brought about by lower production costs and other savings within a firm

Third, and complementary to the above, bloc members often find that their businesses are able to achieve **internal economies of scale** brought about by lower production costs and other savings. So if a company in France was only moderately efficient when producing 1,000 units a week for the French market, it is now highly efficient producing 4,000 units a week for countries throughout the EU. The elimination of tariffs and trade barriers and the opening up of new geographic markets allow the company to increase production efficiency. In addition, since factors of production in a common market are allowed to flow freely across borders, the firm may also achieve **external economies of scale** brought about by access to low-cost capital, more highly skilled labor, and superior technology. In short, in-group companies can draw on resources in member countries to help increase efficiency.

External economies of scale
Efficiencies brought about by access to cheaper capital, highly skilled labor, and superior technology

Finally, in the short run, some bloc countries may suffer because other member countries are able to achieve greater efficiency and thus dominate certain industries and markets in the bloc. The adjustment period may last as long as a decade as these less efficient countries scramble to improve their technologies, retrain their workforces, and redirect their economies to markets in the bloc where they can gain and sustain an advantage vis-à-vis other members. In the long run, however, economic integration results in all bloc countries becoming much more efficient and competitive.

Despite the logic of free trade and economic integration, many **non-governmental organizations (NGOs)** criticize MNEs and international institutions. We now discuss these issues. See also the box **International Business Strategy in Action: Non-governmental organizations and political power.**

Non-governmental organizations (NGOs)
Private-sector groups that act to advance diverse social interests (See also *Civil society*)

Ethics, environment, MNEs, and the civil society

In December 1999, a coalition of NGOs and labor unions organized protests in Seattle that turned into riots, which hindered the launch of another round of the WTO. In July 2001, the violent riots in Genoa at the G7 Summit were another example of the work of some anti-globalization activists, mainly NGOs, attempting to prevent negotiations by world leaders.

Civil society
A group of individuals, organizations, and institutions that act outside the government and the market to advance a diverse set of interests

The **civil society** is a group of individuals, organizations, and institutions that act outside the government and the market to advance a diverse set of interests, including opposition to global business. Demonstrations against trade and investment agreements are mainly composed of environmentalists, anti-poverty campaigners, trade unionists, and anti-capitalists that are either part of an NGO or trade union, or simply individuals that share their views.[17] The lack of a common front across these organizations has meant that, while some protestors are chanting and throwing roses, others are throwing rocks and charging at the police. The more extremist groups would like to see an end to multinationals and international trade. More moderate demonstrators would like a transformation in the rules of trade with less developed nations, debt forgiveness, and better labor and environmental standards.[18] Protestors also have different agendas. Trade unionists from developed countries are concerned about the alleged loss of jobs due to globalization, whereas human rights NGOs are much more concerned with the situation of workers in less industrialized nations.

The success of the NGOs in criticizing businesses, especially multinational enterprises (MNEs), builds on less spectacular but consistent progress in influencing the environmental agenda of international organizations. The first notable success of environmental NGOs occurred in NAFTA in 1993 when the Clinton administration inserted two side agreements on environment and labor after the first Bush administration had successfully negotiated NAFTA over the 1990–1992 period.

The UNCED Rio Summit of 1992 reflected the agenda of environmental NGOs, leading to an agreement that sets commitments but which governments have been unable to deliver on. The Kyoto Summit in 1997 resulted in the standards for reduction of greenhouse gas emissions; again, however, important economies—most notably the United States—would not meet them because of the economic and political costs of doing so.

Non-governmental organizations and political power

When the topic of politics in the international business arena is discussed, one is likely to hear about such things as the impact of the government on international trade and the regulation of multinational enterprises (MNEs). In recent years another topic that has become more popular is the role of non-governmental organizations (NGOs) that have been gaining an increasing amount of political power.

An NGO is a non-profit organization run by volunteers with a specific mandate at a local, national, or international level. As such, NGOs take a number of different forms. Some are very large, such as the environmental group Greenpeace, the World Wildlife Fund (WWF), and Amnesty International, whereas others are smaller and less well known. NGOs' positions on international trade issues are as diverse as their mandates. For example, Oxfam, whose mandate is the long-term alleviation of poverty, suffering, and injustice, does not oppose trade itself. Indeed, it considers "fair trade" a means to achieve development in poorer countries and promotes other organizations that engage in this type of trade. The Institute for Leadership Development actively seeks to promote trade and the development of entrepreneurial skills in poorer countries. The US NGO Consumers for World Trade points out that protectionism is equivalent to a hidden tax and actively lobbies for free trade. Environmental and animal rights NGOs, on the other hand, lobby their governments and international bodies for trade rules that protect the natural environment. For example, in December 1997 at the Kyoto Summit, NGOs were instrumental in getting standards for the reduction of greenhouse gas emissions put into the agreement, even though the United States and other major economic powers refused to accept this standard because the technology was not available and the standard could not be met.

Protectionist or anti-trade, NGOs often grab the headlines. For example, the American Farm Bureau seeks to improve the financial well-being and quality of life for farmers and ranchers in the United States and opposes government policies to liberalize agricultural trade by reducing subsidies to US farmers. Yet other NGOs are more generally opposed to free trade and investment. In the 1997–1998 period, for example, NGOs were extremely effective in defeating the Multilateral Agreement on Investment (MAI). The MAI was designed to make it illegal for signatory states to discriminate against foreign investors and to liberalize rules governing foreign domestic investment among the members of the Organization for Economic Cooperation and Development. NGOs contributed to riots in Seattle in December 1999 and violent clashes with the police in Genoa in July 2001. The NGOs influenced the Clinton administration to add two side agreements to NAFTA: setting up an environmental body in Montreal and a labor standard body in Dallas. In a nutshell, these NGOs managed to work outside the NAFTA agreement to get provisions incorporated into the overall contract. In the process, they showed that NGOs were becoming an important force in the international political arena.

Notwithstanding the variety of views emanating from NGOs, a select group is portraying MNEs as big, bad, and ugly. But is it an accurate portrayal? Starbucks, for instance, has been heavily criticized for not selling Fairtrade coffee, yet it directly pays farmers a price higher than that received by farmers involved in fair trading. Being the best-known brand in North America was enough to make it the target of NGOs. In general, MNEs improve the well-being of workers across the world while manufacturing goods and providing services that improve the quality of life of consumers around the world. Given their rise in popularity over the last five years, NGOs are likely to be the focus of continuing interest by both international business analysts and local voters.

Websites: www.greenpeace.org; www.oxfam.org; www.fb.org; www.cwt.org; www.starbucks.com; www.oecd.org.

Sources: James Harding, "Activists Plan Ocean-borne Protests for WTO Meeting," *Financial Times*, September 11, 2001, p. 1; Edward M. Graham, *Fighting the Wrong Enemy: Antiglobal Activists and Multinational Enterprises* (Washington, DC: Institute for International Economics, 2000); Alan M. Rugman, *The End of Globalization* (London: Random House, 2000); Sylvia Ostry, "The Multilateral Trading System," in Alan M. Rugman and Thomas Brewer (eds.), *The Oxford Handbook of International Business* (Oxford: Oxford University Press, 2000), pp. 232–258; Robert Weissman, "Why We Protest," *Washington Post*, September 10, 2003.

These recent events portray the gulf between the environmental agendas of NGOs and the economic drivers of global business. How do we explain the existence of this gulf?[19] Basically, there is a traditional divide between the redistribution and equity concerns of NGOs and the economic and efficiency issues that drive business. Democratic governments in Western economies have incorporated these dual concerns in their political platforms, and, at least as part of a broader political package, voters have some say through the electoral process.

Complementary to the NGOs' perspective on international trade and investment is the intellectual failure of academic theory, in which the twin basic paradigms of economics and politics are found to develop explanations of today's global economy and the nature of foreign direct investment (FDI). In economics, the traditional efficiency-based neo-classical paradigm (with its associated theory of comparative advantages and the overall country gains from free trade) is unsuitable as an explanation of FDI. Despite the efforts by international business writers over the last 30 years to develop a modern theory of the MNE, most economists are unable to accept this explanation of the reasons for FDI. As a consequence, the GATT and WTO have developed institutional frameworks to deal with the "shallow" integration of tariff cuts, but have failed to deal with the "deep" integration of FDI.

Related to the out-of-date economics paradigm of free trade is the political science focus on the nation state. Despite minor modifications to nation state paradigms, such as to incorporate subnational units in decision making, there is a limited buy-in to the alternative international political economy (IPE) viewpoint. Indeed, there is another unfortunate parallel between economics and political science in that both sets of work on the role and power of the MNE have failed to change the out-of-date thinking of the majority of academics, despite the abundant evidence of the relevance of MNEs and the global economic and political systems of today. The NGOs have slipped into this vacuum with their view of MNEs as big, bad, and ugly. The NGO thinking is now more influential with governments in North America and Europe than is the work of serious academic scholars working on MNEs.[20]

The issue here is one of process. There is an "administrative heritage" of ideas. Today's media are poorly trained in economics, politics, and international business. Those few who have any training are usually victims of the out-of-date paradigms of traditional economics and political science, which cannot explain FDI and the MNEs. The MBAs of business schools, who are now exposed to the new thinking on MNEs, are in business rather than the media. The professional intermediaries, such as management consultants, focus on their business or government clients rather than the media, and their very skills of confidential advice and in-house retraining make them poor advocates compared to the NGOs. Finally, the civil service is basically useless in dealing publicly with anti-trade NGOs as bureaucrats attempt to support and influence ministers and other officials rather than entering into the public forum. This institutional failure of academics, consultants, and bureaucrats to prepare a credible case for initiatives such as the Multilateral Agreement on Investment (MAI) and be able to debate it publicly leaves the field open to NGOs.

During negotiations for the MAI, Canadian anti-globalization activists equated NAFTA's Chapter 11 provisions with investor protection mechanisms under MAI. Chapter 11 allows a company to sue national governments in trade matters that contravene NAFTA's principles. The provision had been used by Ethyl, a US company, to overturn a Canadian import ban on MMT, a gasoline additive that was deemed a health hazard. The Canadian Minister of the Environment could have averted litigation by banning the production of MMT as an environmental hazard, an internal matter subject to national law, but she ignored the advice of her bureaucrats and applied trade measures that came under the NAFTA. Several subsequent NAFTA Chapter 11 cases have been resolved on technical grounds with no loss of sovereignty to host nations in their environmental policies. The MAI had similar provisions to protect investors, which led to it being labeled a "NAFTA on steroids" by anti-globalization activists.

The late Edward Graham has exploded the myth that anti-global activists defeated the MAI.[21] Graham concludes that the draft MAI was a very weak document. In fact, the investment liberalization being negotiated in the MAI was so weak that the US business community stopped supporting it long before anti-global activists started to protest against it in Paris. There was also a lack of leadership by the US government, tepid support in the

EU, and eventually hostility to the MAI by the French government of Lionel Jospin, who was dependent on left-wing "green" support in his political coalition.

Perhaps what the MMT case really illustrates is the "dialogue of the deaf" taking place between trade experts and activists. The latter used the MMT case in a general assault on the MAI and on subsequent international trade and investment liberalization initiatives at the WTO and G7 Summits. Graham argues that, as a consequence, the environmental NGOs missed the boat. He states that trade negotiators were open and willing to incorporate environmental concerns into the MAI but that violent opposition to it has now closed the window for cooperation between NGOs and governments.

Any more Seattles and Genoas, with the attendant violence, however, will probably alienate the general public from the anti-capitalist agenda of the more extreme anti-global activists. This small and over-publicized section of the NGO movement, with its apparent opposition to reforming global governance mechanisms, continues to protest violently against MNEs. Eventually, the most serious NGOs, such as WWF and Oxfam, must disassociate themselves from these violent activists in order to push forward a more sensible cooperative reformist agenda for civil society.

The European Union (EU)

After World War II, Europe needed to be rebuilt and economic cooperation among these countries was paramount. One of the earliest and most successful cooperative endeavors was the 1952 creation of the **European Coal and Steel Community (ECSC)** for the purpose of creating a common market that would revitalize the efficiency and competitiveness of these industries. Six countries (Belgium, France, Italy, Luxembourg, the Netherlands, and West Germany) created the ECSC, and its success set the stage for the creation of what would eventually become the European Union.

Formation

The foundation of the European Union was laid in 1957 by the Treaty of Rome. The six nations that created the ECSC were the original founders of what was initially called the European Economic Community (EEC) and later the European Community (EC). By 1991 six other nations had joined the EC (the UK, Denmark, Greece, Ireland, Portugal, and Spain)—and in 1995 with the admission of Austria, Finland, and Sweden, the EC was renamed the **European Union**. In 2004, 10 new members joined the EU: Cyprus, Czech Republic, Estonia, Hungary, Latvia, Lithuania, Malta, Poland, Slovakia, and Slovenia. In 2007 Bulgaria and Romania joined. Today the EU is a major economic group, and a growing number of countries have applied for admission.[22] The main provisions of the founding treaty of 1957 were:

1 Formation of a free trade area among the members would be brought about by the gradual elimination of tariffs, quotas, and other trade barriers.

2 Barriers to the movement of labor, capital, and business enterprises would eventually be removed.

3 Common agricultural policies would be adopted.

4 An investment fund to channel capital from the more advanced regions of the bloc to the less advanced regions would be created.

5 A customs union characterized by a uniform tariff schedule applicable to imports from the rest of the world would be created.

Some of the countries that were not members of the initial EEC felt that the objectives of this group went beyond what they were willing to do, but they did feel that a free trade

European Coal and Steel Community (ECSC)
A community formed in 1952 by Belgium, France, Italy, Luxembourg, the Netherlands, and West Germany for the purpose of creating a common market that would revitalize the efficiency and competitiveness of the coal and steel industries in those countries

European Union (EU)
A treaty-based institutional framework that manages economic and political cooperation among its 27 member states: Austria, Belgium, Bulgaria, Cyprus, Czech Republic, Denmark, Estonia, France, Finland, Germany, Greece, Hungary, Ireland, Italy, Latvia, Lithuania, Luxembourg, Malta, the Netherlands, Poland, Portugal, Romania, Slovakia, Slovenia, Spain, Sweden, and the UK

European Free Trade Association (EFTA)
A free trade area currently consisting of Iceland, Liechtenstein, Norway, and Switzerland; past members included the UK (before it joined the EU). There are now 27 member states of the EU

Single European Act (SEA)
An Act passed by the EU that contains many measures to further integrate the member states, along economic and political dimensions, and that allows the Council of Ministers to pass most proposals by a majority vote, in contrast to the unanimous vote that was needed previously

European Council
Composed of the heads of state of each EU member country as well as the president of the European Commission. Meetings of the Council take place at least twice a year and their purpose is to resolve major policy issues and to set policy direction

Council of the European Union
The major policy decision-making body of the EU; it consists of one minister from each of the 27 member states and is one of four major institutions of the EU

agreement would be good for their own economies. As a result, these nations formed the **European Free Trade Association (EFTA)**, whose primary goal was to dismantle trade barriers among its members. Austria, Denmark, Norway, Portugal, Sweden, Switzerland, and the UK were the founding members. In time the distinctions between EFTA and the EC blurred, however, and some of the members (Austria, Denmark, Portugal, Sweden, and the UK) eventually joined the EC. Moreover, in 1992 EFTA signed a treaty that formally gives its members an economic association with the EU. Today EFTA members include Iceland, Liechtenstein, Norway, and Switzerland.

Growth and challenges

Over the years, the EU has made vigorous headway in pursuit of its objectives. For example, during the 1970s formal barriers to the free flow of labor and capital were gradually dismantled. The **Single European Act (SEA)**, which effectively prevents a country from vetoing any EU decision it deems to be in conflict with its vital interests, was enacted in the 1980s. In the past this veto power had often been used by EU members to protect their respective economic advantages, making it difficult for the group to make decisions.

Other major breakthroughs are occurring in the political and financial areas. With the EC 1992 measures, the EU has transformed itself into a political, economic, and monetary superpower that can speak with one powerful voice about everything from interest rates to defense. By moving in this direction, the EU political leaders negotiated and implemented a method for ratifying two new treaties that would extend the community's powers from their present largely economic role to foreign and security policy and monetary affairs and, eventually, to defense.[23] The EU's integration is now consolidating its financial and monetary system, which will facilitate the free flow of capital. Recently, a single European currency, the euro, was introduced to replace national currencies. Closely linked to this was the establishment of a central European bank that regulates the money supply and is thus able to stabilize interest rates throughout the EU. The effect of these actions may well be the creation of a "United States of Europe."

However, the EU still faces a number of problems. One is disagreement among the members regarding the relationship that should exist between the community and the rest of the world. A second problem is the protection that countries give to their own industries, which is in direct contrast to the spirit of EU rules. A related area is the community's agriculture policies, which provide subsidies and rebates to farmers and have resulted in charges of unfair trade practices. A third problem is the disagreement among the members regarding the amount of protection that poorer countries should be given before all trade barriers are dismantled. Even if all goals are not fully attained in the next decade, the EU is going to be an increasingly powerful economic force in the international arena. A close look at the community's organizational arrangement helps to explain why.

Organization

The major institutions managing the EU are: the European Council, the Council of the European Union, the European Commission, the European Parliament, the Court of Justice, and the Court of Auditors. (See Figure 4.1.) A brief description of each of these is set out below. (This predated the potential adoption of a quasi Constitution in late 2007, under which an EU president would be appointed.)

The **European Council** is composed of the heads of state of each EU member country as well as the president of the European Commission. The Council meets at least twice a year, and each head of state is typically accompanied to these meetings by a foreign minister. The purpose of the meetings is to resolve major policy issues and to set policy direction.

The **Council of the European Union** is the major policy decision-making body of the EU. Decisions are conducted by the relevant ministers from each country. If the environment is

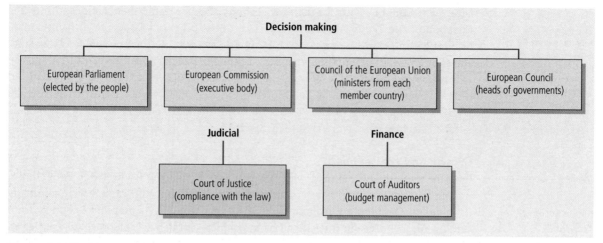

Figure 4.1 The European Union's institutions

on the agenda, the 27 environment ministers from each EU country will compose the council. This body is responsible for all final EU decisions, except for the budget.

European Commission
A 27-member group chosen by agreement of member governments of the EU; the Commission is the executive branch of the EU

The **European Commission** has 27 members who are chosen by agreement of the member governments. Each country presently has one member. After Bulgaria and Romania have joined the union, the number of members will be decreased, and a rotation will be introduced so that not all countries will have representation at a given time. The Commission, the executive branch of the EU, handles a great deal of the technical work associated with preparing decisions and regulations. The group is responsible for drafting legislation for proposal to the Council of the European Union, overseeing the implementation of EU policies, and carrying out studies on key policy issues.

European Parliament
A group of 785 representatives elected directly by voters in each member country of the EU; the Parliament serves as a watchdog on EU expenditures

The **European Parliament** currently has 785 members elected directly by the voters in each member country. The Parliament serves as a watchdog on EU expenditures in addition to evaluating other decisions of the Council. More recently, the power of the Parliament has been expanded; it now has the right to vote on the appointment of commissioners as well as to veto matters related to the EU budget and single-market legislation.

Court of Justice
A court that has one judge appointed from each EU member country; this court serves as the official interpreter of EU law

The **Court of Justice** has one judge appointed from each EU member country and serves as the official interpreter of EU law. In most cases this requires the judges to rule on the meaning or application of the Treaty of Rome, based on the actions of member countries, companies, and individuals. The Court of Justice has supremacy over national law, and as a result it is increasingly being used as a court of appeal over national decisions.

Court of Auditors
A court that has one judge appointed from each EU member country; this court monitors the financial aspects of the union

The **Court of Auditors** has one judge appointed from each EU member country and is responsible for ensuring that revenues and expenditures are implemented lawfully in accordance to the budget.

The future

The EU is a powerful economic union. Empirical studies show that the community has created much more trade than it has diverted from the rest of the world. Moreover, this market has a greater combined gross domestic product than either of the two other triad major markets: North America and industrialized Asia. At the same time it is likely that EU-generated projects will offer major competition to other worldwide industries. For example, Airbus, as seen in Chapter 3, is now a major force in the world aircraft manufacturing industry. Quite clearly, the EU promises tremendous economic gains for member countries.

Other examples of economic integration

While the EU is the most successful economic union, there are a host of others. The following briefly examines four of these.

Andean Community

Andean Community
An economic union consisting of Bolivia, Colombia, Ecuador, and Peru

The **Andean Community** is a customs union that was formed in 1969 with the signing of the Andean Pact by Bolivia, Chile, Colombia, Ecuador, and Peru. Venezuela was a member from 1973 to 2006, and Chile has withdrawn but remains an associate member country (www.comunidadandina.org). The union is also known as Comunidad Andina (CAN) or Andean Community (Ancom). The original objectives of the CAN countries were to integrate themselves economically, to reduce internal tariffs, to create a common external tariff, and to offer special concessions to the two smallest members, Bolivia and Ecuador. Initial restrictions that curtailed foreign investment led to Chile leaving the union. These restrictions have now been removed at the CAN level, but the legislation yields to individual national governments on the matter. Except for Peru, which is slowly removing its tariffs, the Andean Community is a customs union in which goods can travel free of duty among member states.

Mercosur

Mercosur
A free trade group that includes Argentina, Brazil, Uruguay, and Paraguay

Mercosur is a free trade group that was formed by Argentina and Brazil in 1988 to promote economic cooperation. Today the group has been expanded to include Paraguay and Uruguay, with Chile, Bolivia, and Peru as associate members. In 1995 the members agreed to a five-year program under which they hoped to perfect their free trade area and move toward a full customs union. However, things have not worked out very well in recent years. The group members have been unable to agree on a common agenda and each seems to be striking out in a different direction. For example, Argentina imposed tariffs on Brazilian televisions, shoes, and other goods; Brazil does not recognize Argentina's food-quality standards; and external tariffs are often double charged.[24] In 2004, Mercosur and the Andean Community agreed in principle to work toward a "South American Community of Nations" that will encompass 360 million people and a GDP of $1 trillion. First, however, these countries must resolve their differences.[25]

ASEAN

Association of South-East Asian Nations (ASEAN)
An economic union founded in 1967 that includes Brunei Darussalam, Cambodia, Indonesia, Laos, Malaysia, Myanmar, the Philippines, Singapore, Thailand, and Vietnam; this economic bloc focuses not on reducing trade barriers among members but, rather, on promoting exports to other nations

The **Association of South-East Asian Nations (ASEAN)** was founded in 1967 and now includes Brunei Darussalam, Cambodia, Indonesia, Laos, Malaysia, Myanmar, the Philippines, Singapore, Thailand, and Vietnam. This economic bloc is different from most others in that the primary emphasis is not on reducing trade barriers among the members, although this has been done with the agreement on the ASEAN Free Trade Area (AFTA), but rather on promoting exports to other countries. Members have been particularly successful in promoting exports to the Japanese market and to the EU. Until the late 1990s members of ASEAN experienced rapid economic growth, thanks in no small part to the efficiency and productivity of their members as well as to their impressive marketing skills.

FTAA

The Free Trade Area of the Americas (FTAA)
A free trade agreement of the Americas that has not yet been implemented

The **Free Trade Area of the Americas (FTAA)** was relaunched in Quebec City in April 2001. All the economies of North, Central, and South America, along with all Caribbean economies (except for Cuba), agreed in principle to start the FTAA in 2005. While the US Congress approved the CAFTA in July 2005, the larger FTAA is in limbo. One main problem is that Latin American countries are wary of entering the agreement if it does not involve the elimination of US agricultural subsidies. The US objective for the FTAA is to build on the framework of NAFTA, discussed in Chapters 6 and 19 in detail.

Active learning check

Review your answer to Active Learning Case question 2 and make any changes you like. Then compare your answer to the one below.

2 **Would Russia benefit by gaining admission to one of the major economic unions such as the EU? Why?**

Russia certainly would benefit by gaining admission to an economic union such as the EU. It could then take advantage of a wide variety of benefits, including free movement of goods and services across borders, trade creation, the possible development of internal economies brought about by the huge market that would then be available for Russian goods, and a strengthening of the nation's currency. Of course, admission to the EU or one of the other major economic unions is unlikely to occur, at least within the next few years, as the country is not stable. However, it would offer a very big boost to the nation's economy.

ECONOMIC INTEGRATION AND STRATEGIC MANAGEMENT

How can MNEs use strategic management planning to benefit from worldwide economic integration efforts? A number of steps are proving to be helpful, particularly the use of strategic alliances, acquisitions, and the localization of business operations.

Strategic alliances and acquisitions

One of the most common ways of benefiting from economic integration is by creating a strategic alliance, often in the form of a joint venture, with other firms that can provide important forms of assistance. The following examines the use of strategic alliances and acquisitions in the telecommunications and electronics industry and acquisitions in the brewery business.

Telecommunications and electronics

Over the past decade the telecommunications industry has been expanding in terms of both products and geographic coverage. This development represents the convergence of four distinct industries: telephone, mass media (print, broadcast, and cable), consumer electronics, and computers. The result has been a growing number of products and services such as cellular phones, personal computers, and televisions that are able to interact with each other in both receiving and transmitting information. In addition, the industry has become even more competitive and complex with the advent of wireless networks. In an effort to take advantage of these developments, a number of firms in the industry are relying on strategic alliances.[26]

Strategic alliance
A business relationship in which two or more companies work together to achieve a collective advantage

A **strategic alliance** is a business relationship in which two or more companies work together to achieve a collective advantage. These alliances can take a number of forms. In some cases companies jointly conduct research or combine their efforts to market a product. In other instances they will license a firm to produce and sell a particular product in a specific market region. In the telecommunications industry, strategic alliances have been very important because of the high investment and the need to attain market penetration. A good example is provided by Concert, which is a strategic alliance composed of AT&T and British Telecommunications. Concert provides voice and data telecom services to multinational corporations and individual users through a network of distributors. It is also interested in increasing its global market presence, as seen by its decision to buy a 30 percent stake in Japan Telecom.

Another example of a strategic alliance is provided by Lucent Technologies, which merged its consumer phone unit with that of Philips Electronics NV so that the two could produce a wide range of products, from corded and cordless telephones to answering machines to many types of digital cellular phones. This arrangement gave Philips's consumer phone business a strong boost while helping Lucent, which is very strong in network gear, high-tech chips, and software used in switches and phones, but which has been having trouble in the face of stiff competition from European suppliers.[27]

Yet another example is that of Microsoft and Sony, which teamed up to link personal computers and consumer electronics devices, thus moving closer together on technology standards for digital television and other consumer products. The two firms also endorsed a technology that can connect video cassette recorders, camcorders, personal computers, and other devices. Microsoft's objective in this alliance was to license the networking technology software from Sony to use with versions of an operating system that it was trying to standardize for non-personal computer (PC) products. The objective of the joint venture was to create a technology by which consumers could plug a camcorder easily into a PC or television set-top box for sending video mail over the Internet.[28]

Breweries

Not all strategic alliances and joint ventures involve giant multinationals. Many brewers have found, to their regret, that it is difficult to get customers to change brands. This is particularly true in countries such as Germany, the UK, and the Netherlands, where beer is popular. Customers are often fiercely loyal to local brands, and the only way of tapping into these markets is by purchasing the brewery. Major European brewers have long realized this and have not hesitated to buy operations in other countries. A good example is the purchase of La Cruz del Campo, Spain's largest brewery, by the UK's Guinness. However, the company has a long way to go before it will catch Heineken, which for years has been buying small brewers on the Continent, a strategy now being emulated by large US competitors.

Localization of business operations

MNEs cannot conduct business overseas in the same way they do at home. They have to target their offerings carefully to the needs of the regional and local customers. These efforts result in the localization of business operations and typically focus on four areas: products, profits, production, and management.[29]

Localization of products

The localization of products requires the development, manufacturing, and marketing of goods best suited to the needs of the local customer and marketplace. This typically requires the modification of products that have sold well in other geographic regions. For example, in North America buyers use motorcycles primarily for leisure and sports, so they look for high horsepower output and speed. In contrast, South-East Asians use motorcycles as a basic means of transportation, so they look for low cost and ease of maintenance; and in Australia, where shepherds use motorcycles to drive sheep, low-speed torque is more important than either high speed or ease of maintenance.[30]

MNEs commonly localize production by investing in research and development, so they can make the product that fits the specific needs of that market. This is sometimes more difficult than it appears, especially if the MNE has been successful with a product in the home market and is unwilling to change. A good example is provided by the Whirlpool

Corporation, which dominated the US market before going to Europe in the late 1980s. Believing that the giant $20 billion European appliance market with its dozens of marginally profitable companies was on the verge of consolidation, Whirlpool wanted to be one of the major players. So it bought a majority stake in a struggling appliance operation belonging to NV Philips, the Dutch electronics giant, and acquired the rest of the operation two years later for $1.1 billion. Whirlpool believed that the European market was highly regionalized because there were so many diverse consumer preferences. For example, the Swedish liked galvanized washers that could withstand salty air; the British washed their clothes more often than many others, so they wanted quieter washing machines; and so on. Stoves provided even greater examples of product diversity. However, Whirlpool believed that the market was ready for product consolidation, and therefore lent its support to a "world washer," a single machine that could be sold anywhere on the Continent. As product diversity was reduced, Whirlpool believed, the marginal producers would be driven from the market and its own share would climb. What the company found was that the European market was a lot more competitive than it realized. Sweden's AB Electrolux and Germany's Bosch–Siemens Hausgeraete GmbH proved to be excellent competitors. In particular, they revamped their factories and drove costs down sharply. They also began introducing new products that kept customers coming back. By thus appealing to local tastes, Electrolux and Bosch–Siemens managed to keep Whirlpool's profits to a minimum, while preventing it from gaining market share.[31]

Localization of profits

Localization of profits
The reinvestment of earnings in the local market

Localization of profits is the reinvestment of earnings in the local market. MNEs do this by taking their earnings and using them to expand operations, set up new plants and offices, hire more local people, and make the investment more self-sufficient. In the United States, for example, Honda started out with an initial investment of $250,000 and has gradually reinvested its US profits. Today the company has almost $2 billion in its motorcycle, auto, and engine manufacturing plants in Ohio. At the same time it has reinvested almost $200 million in Honda Canada, a manufacturing plant making Honda Civics.

Localization of production

Localization of production
The manufacturing of goods in the host market

Localization of production involves the manufacture of goods in the host market.[32] Many MNEs, upon entering a foreign market, handle this function by exporting from the home country. For a successful relationship, however, this is often only a short-run strategy and is eventually replaced by a local manufacturing base.[33] One strategy for localizing production is to increase the amount of local content in the product by making more and more of the subunits in the host country. The ultimate step, of course, is to produce the entire product locally. Honda, for example, decided back in the late 1980s to turn its Ohio auto manufacturing facility into a fully integrated, self-reliant entity. The plan involved a number of steps, including increasing the plant's production capacity so that it would be able to turn out 500,000 units annually and build them with at least 75 percent domestic content. In 2007 Honda started to build a parts plant in Greenburg, Indiana, employing workers within a one-hour drive of the plant. In the process, Honda localized its production.

The same is true for Toyota. The company increased the capacity of its Georgetown, Kentucky, and Princeton, Indiana, plants and its Ontario, Canada, facility. It also began production of its Lexus SUV in Canada. It increased the production capacity of its Burnaston, England, plant and increased auto production in its Thailand factory, while negotiating with the government to build an engine factory in Tianjin, China.[34]

Another way to localize production is to provide added value in operations by modifying the imported product and adapting it to local conditions and tastes. This approach is used when a product requires country-by-country (or regional) changes. Auto manufacturers, for example, take into account the terrain (unpaved roads require stronger underbody construction), the cost of gasoline (high costs often mean that the market wants smaller, more efficient cars), and which side of the road everyone drives on (right in the United States and Latin America; left in the UK and Asia).

The localization of production is often carried out in conjunction with a home-country partner which provides the plant and personnel, while the MNE is responsible for the initial product and the technology needed in assembling or modifying the goods. Sometimes, however, the MNE will own the entire operation and depend on local management to help run the organization.

Localization of management

There are a number of ways for MNEs to localize management. One is by encouraging home-office managers to learn the local culture and become part of the community. Research reveals that companies that staff their subsidiaries with older, mature senior managers from the home country who are fluent in the local language are often more highly productive than MNEs that staff operations with younger, less experienced managers.[35] A second way of localizing management is by delegating authority to host-country managers and developing and promoting these employees wherever possible. This strategy helps to create a bond between the host- and the home-country management. As one MNE spokesperson put it:

> we have become convinced that good communication between management and labor, as well as delegation of authority, elevate the employees' sense of participation in decision making. This, in turn, gives the employees a stronger sense of responsibility and motivation, which leads to improved productivity and maintenance of high-quality standards.[36]

✔ Active learning check

Review your answer to Active Learning Case question 3 and make any changes you like. Then compare your answer to the one below.

❸ Is Russia a good potential investment for Western business? Explain.

Arguments can be made on each side. Untapped natural resources and potential consumer demand could provide billions of dollars of annual sales for investing companies. On the other hand, the economy is in terrible shape, and it is likely to take years before Russia begins to provide an acceptable return on investment for many current projects. One of the major reasons for getting in now, of course, is to try to gain a strong foothold in the market and effectively block future competition. If this should happen, those coming later would find slim pickings. However, this potential benefit is unlikely to attract many investors. Most are likely to conclude that the best strategy is to proceed with caution and wait for the current uncertainty and turmoil to settle.

KEY POINTS

1 Political ideologies and economic systems are interwoven. Democracies tend to have market-driven economies; totalitarian governments tend to have centrally determined economies. However, few nations fit totally into one of these two paradigms. Most use a mixed economic model such as that of the United States, which is mainly a market-driven economy with some central planning, or China, which still relies on central planning but is moving to allow some degree of free enterprise.

2 Another current economic development is the trend toward privatization. Many countries are selling their state-owned enterprises. A variety of reasons can be cited for these actions. In most cases these are economic in nature, including (a) increased efficiency, (b) reduction in government outlays, and (c) generation of funds for the national treasury.

3 Economic integration is the establishment of transnational rules and regulations that permit economic trade and cooperation among countries. Effective integration brings about trade creation, although in some cases these efforts result in trade diversion. There are five levels of regional economic trade integration: free trade areas, customs unions, common markets, economic unions, and political unions. The most successful examples have been the EU and the NAFTA. Some NGOs criticize such trade and investment agreements.

4 NGOs are an important new actor on the stage of international business, and MNEs need to take account of the civil society in their strategies.

5 MNEs use a variety of strategies to benefit from integration efforts. One is strategic alliances and acquisitions with which they are able to scale the economic wall and gain an inside position in the economic alliance or free trade area. Another is through the localization of operations by focusing on products, profits, production, and management. MNEs typically use both of these strategic approaches.

Key terms

- ideology
- democracy
- totalitarianism
- communism
- theocratic totalitarianism
- secular totalitarianism
- market-driven economy
- centrally determined economy
- mixed economies
- privatization
- nationalization
- divestiture
- contract management
- Ministry of International Trade and Industry (MITI)
- economic integration
- trade creation
- trade diversion
- free trade area
- North American Free Trade Agreement (NAFTA)
- customs union
- common market
- economic union
- political union
- internal economies of scale
- external economies of scale
- non-governmental organizations (NGOs)
- civil society
- European Coal and Steel Community (ECSC)
- European Union (EU)
- European Free Trade Association (EFTA)
- Single European Act (SEA)
- European Council
- Council of the European Union
- European Commission
- European Parliament
- Court of Justice
- Court of Auditors
- Andean Community
- Mercosur
- Association of South-East Asian Nations (ASEAN)
- Free Trade Area of the Americas (FTAA)
- strategic alliance
- localization of profits
- localization of production

REVIEW AND DISCUSSION QUESTIONS

1 As political systems change, economic systems follow. What does this statement mean?

2 How does a centrally determined economy differ from a market-driven economy? Explain.

3 What are the benefits of privatization? Why will the trend toward privatization continue?

4 Why are government–business cooperative efforts beginning to increase? What benefits do they offer?

5 What is the purpose of research consortia? What is their future likely to be? Why?

6 How does trade creation differ from trade diversion? Compare and contrast the two.

7 There are five levels of economic integration. What is meant by this statement? Be complete in your answer.

8 How does the EU function? Identify and describe its organization and operation.

9 What is the purpose of the following economic alliances: the Andean Community, Mercosur, and ASEAN?

10 Some of the primary ways that MNEs use strategic planning to benefit from economic integration efforts is through strategic alliances and acquisitions. How do MNEs do this?

11 How do MNEs seek to localize their business operations? Describe three steps that they take.

REAL CASE

How environmental regulations can be used as trade barriers

With free trade areas evolving around the globe, many protected industries are now facing unwelcome competition. Free trade agreements generally include a principle of national treatment under which a country must treat all producers, domestic or foreign, equally. However, some seemingly neutral environmental regulations pose a greater burden on foreign producers than on their domestic competitors. Thus, they act as trade barriers under the disguise of environmental regulations.

For example, while environmental groups lobby for newsprint to contain a determined amount of recycled material and domestic producers of newsprint support the regulation, foreign newsprint companies, which have no recycling facilities in the host country, face a competitive disadvantage. This is what has been called a "Baptist–bootlegger" coalition. During the US prohibition era, Baptists were opposed to alcoholic consumption on moral grounds, while bootleggers actually benefited from prohibition by the sale of illegal alcoholic beverages. Today, environmental groups and domestic producers often form coalitions to promote their respective interests.

In the newsprint case, the foreign company would have two options if it were to continue to supply material from its home country. It could either open recycling plants in the host country and transport pulp from its own country to be processed there so as to meet the environmental regulations, or take the recycling material to its home country to be processed. Both alternatives would pose significant transportation costs to the foreign producer.

A similar case is presented by the Ontario Beer Can Tax. In the early 1990s the province of Ontario levied a tax of $0.10 on each aluminum beer can. The province argued that these cans were not environmentally friendly and that the tax was designed to encourage the use of refillable glass bottles. US producers of beer and aluminum cans contended that this was a protectionist move and that ▶

the Ontario government was singling out the competition with its beer industry since it had no similar tax for soft drinks and juice cans. Moreover, research studies found that aluminum cans and glass bottles both have the same effect on the environment, and that 80 percent of all the cans were being recycled. They also found that the larger, heavier glass required more energy to transport than did the lighter aluminum cans.

Sources: Adapted from Alan M. Rugman, John Kirton and Julie Soloway, *Environmental Regulations and Corporate Strategy: A NAFTA Perspective* (Oxford: Oxford University Press, 1999); M. Trebilcock and R. Howse, "Trade Policy and Domestic Health and Safety Standards," *The Regulation of International Trade*, 2nd ed. (London: Routledge, 1999); Julie Soloway, "Environmental Trade Barriers in NAFTA: The MMT Fuel Additives Controversy," *Minnesota Journal of Global Trade*, vol. 8, no. 1 (1998); David

Vogel and Alan M. Rugman, "Environmentally Related Trade Disputes between the United States and Canada," *The American Review of Canadian Studies*, Summer 1997, pp. 271–292.

---

1 How can a health and safety regulation become a trade barrier? Provide examples.

2 How can different environmental circumstances make one country's regulations inefficient in another country?

3 What are some reasons why the government might not be willing to make allowances for different countries?

REAL CASE

Embraer vs. Bombardier

Bombardier and Embraer compete in the mid-size aircraft market, the luxury jet market, and the military aircraft market. In 2004, both companies announced plans for bigger aircraft. In the United States, 61 percent of all flights take off with a higher number of passengers than either of their aircraft normally accommodated. Indeed, analysts believe that there has historically been a lack of flexibility from the two largest players, Boeing and Airbus, in supplying this category of aircraft.

In 1942 Joseph Armand Bombardier, a young Quebec mechanic turned industrialist, incorporated the world's first snowmobile manufacturer, L'Auto-Neige Bombardier. Although he had great plans for his innovative transportation inventions, he could never have foreseen the course his company would take in the next 50 years. For the year ended January 31, 2010, Bombardier is one of the world's top manufacturers of transportation products, including trains and aircraft, with yearly revenues of US $19.4 billion, with over 62,900 employees of 95 nationalities speaking 20 languages in more than 60 countries.

Bombardier's success is in no small part the responsibility of CEO Laurent Beaudoin, who over 30 years has followed a strategy of market entry and product improvement through acquisition, instead of relying strictly on R&D. This strategy has been exemplified by Bombardier's entry into the aerospace industry with the acquisition of Canadair in 1986.

In 1991, Bombardier took a risk on the undeveloped market of regional jets, which quickly paid off. Airlines could offer more short-haul flights at a more reasonable price at a time when airport hubs were overcrowded. Bombardier enjoyed a virtual monopoly on this airplane category until Embraer came along.

The beginnings of Embraer are very different. Founded in 1969 by a Brazilian military dictatorship, Embraer made its name building high-quality military and civilian aircraft. The airplanes were so expensive, however, that no one wanted to buy them, and for years the company lost millions in revenue. Then in 1994 it was privatized and given to Mauricio Botelho to turn around. He has. In 1995, the company launched a family of regional jets that were warmly received by US and European airlines. By 2009, Embraer had about half of the market; its sales reached $5.409 billion. But there was declining sales for Embraer by about 25 percent in 2009 compared to 2008.

Because direct subsidies by governments to domestic firms are illegal at the WTO, each company has attempted to obtain WTO approval on trade sanctions against its competitor in the late 1990s and early 2000s. Canada filed a complaint over Brazilian subsidies to Embraer. Brazil countered with its own complaint over Canadian subsidies to Bombardier. In total, there were four cases at the WTO:

1 WTO Dispute DS46: Brazil—Export Financing Programme for Aircraft (Complainant: Canada), 19 June, 1996.

2 WTO Dispute DS70: Canada—Measures Affecting the Export of Civilian Aircraft (Complainant: Brazil), 10 March, 1997.

3 WTO Dispute DS71: Canada—Measures Affecting the Export of Civilian Aircraft (Complainant: Brazil), 10 March 1997.

4 WTO Dispute DS222: Canada—Export Credits and Loan Guarantees for regional Aircraft (Complainant: Brazil), 22 January 2001.

Both countries were successful, and today they both have a green light to impose sanctions on each other. This is unlikely to happen, however, as it would strain bilateral relations between the two nations. Instead, both countries are seeking some form of a compromise.

Both companies argue that the other has an unfair advantage. Bombardier, argues Embraer, has access to top-of-the-line technology and low-interest loans from being located in an industrialized country. Embraer, argues Bombardier, has access to cheap labor and benefits from a weak currency. The initial WTO complaint was based on low-interest loans to Embraer customers by Proex, a Brazilian agency set up to promote exports. In addition to the price of an Embraer airplane being lower by about $3 million, its customers could save even more by getting one of these loans. Brazil's complaint cited subsidies from the Canadian government to three small airlines as an incentive to purchase Bombardier airplanes.

Now that the WTO has ruled against both countries, instead of applying punitive tariffs, Brazil and Canada are seeking to negotiate an agreement. Both have amended their subsidies. In a market with increased competition for regional flights, a trade war must be averted. At stake are negotiations for the Free Trade Area of the Americas (FTAA). Indeed, the airplane dispute highlights the difficulties facing countries from the developed North and the developing South.

There are several reasons why a trade war should be avoided. The regional jet sector is facing increasing competition pressure. Other companies are currently developing competitive products in the 40–100 seat category. These include the Commercial Aircraft Corporation of China Ltd. (COMAC), a state-owned company in which China Aviation Industry Corporation (formerly known as AVIC 1) holds an interest, Mitsubishi Heavy Industries Ltd. (MHI, Japan), and Sukhoi Company (JSC) (Sukhoi, Russia).

The financial crisis of 2008 continues to significantly affect the civil aerospace industry as a whole. Worsening economic conditions and restricted credit availability translate into a high level of order cancellations and deferrals of aircraft deliveries. This has caused most of the original equipment manufacturers (OEMs) to reduce their production rates and has reduced their profitability. As a result, the world airlines' net loss is forecasted to be $2.8 billion in 2010, compared to a net loss of $9.4 million in 2009. The limited availability of aircraft financing seen during 2009 also contributed to restraining airlines' ability to buy new aircraft in 2010. Given this climate and the planned production rate, Bombardier expects to deliver approximately 20 percent fewer commercial aircraft in 2011 than in 2010. Bombardier's sales fell for the year ended in January 30, 2010 by 2 percent compared to

that of 2009. Embraer also witnessed its sales decline by 25 percent in 2009 compared to the previous year's sales.

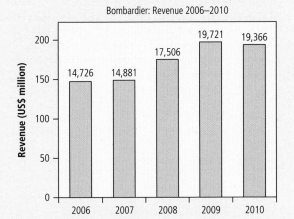

Bombardier: revenue 2006–2010

Source: Bombardier, *Annual Report*, 2006–2010

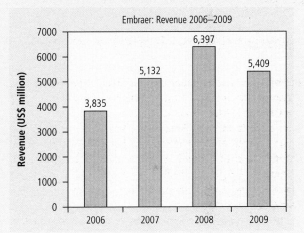

Embraer: revenue 2006–2009

Source: Embraer, *Annual Report*, 2006–2009

Websites: www.bombardier.com; www.embraer.com; www.boeing.com.

Sources: Rita Kolselka, "Let's Make a Deal," *Forbes*, April 27, 1992, pp. 62–63; Clyde H. Farnsworth, "Bombardier Snares DeHavilland," *New York Times*, January 26, 1992, p. 12; Jonathan Wheatly, "Embraer: The Sky's the Limit," *Business Week*, January 3, 2001; "Brazil's Embraer Hits the Stratosphere," *Business Week*, April 19, 2004; Bombardier, *Annual Report*, 2006–2010; Embraer, *Annual Report*, 2006–2009; "WTO Rules Against Canada Over Low Interest Loans for Bombardier Deal," *CBC News*, www.cbc.ca, October 19, 2001; "Embraer Commercial Aircraft Deliveries Drops 25% in 2009," *Air Transport Intelligence News*, www.flightglobal.com, January, 12, 2010.

1 How do factor conditions differ for Embraer and Bombardier?

2 How does the dispute reflect the difficulties in drafting the FTAA?

3 Why are governments involved in this trade dispute?

4 Why are Canada and Brazil hesitant to apply the punitive tariffs they were awarded?

ENDNOTES

1 Craig S. Smith, "Workers of the World, Invest!" *New York Times*, August 19, 2001, Section 3, p. 3.

2 For more on this, see Erik Eckholm, "Chinese President Is Optimistic About Relations with the US," *New York Times*, August 10, 2001, pp. A1, A8.

3 "Private economy yields 40% of gross product in Shanghai," *People's Daily Online*, March 9, 2005.

4 Paul Starobin and Olga Kravchenko, "Russia's Middle Class," *Business Week*, October 16, 2000, pp. 78–84.

5 R. Molz, "Privatization of Government Enterprise: The Challenge to Management," *Management International Review*, vol. 29, no. 4 (1989), pp. 29–30.

6 Ibid., pp. 32–33.

7 For excellent coverage of privatization, see Dennis J. Gayle and Jonathan N. Goodrich (eds.), *Privatization and Deregulation in Global Perspective* (New York: Quorum Books, 1990).

8 Clifford Krauss, "Argentina to Hasten End of Phone Monopoly," *New York Times*, March 11, 1998, Section C, p. 4.

9 Gautam Naik, "Telecom Deregulation in Britain Delivered a Nice Surprise: Jobs," *Wall Street Journal*, March 5, 1998, pp. A1, A6.

10 Michael Wines, "A Factory's Turnaround Reflects a Glimmer in Russia's Economy," *New York Times*, July 2, 2000, pp. A1, 8.

11 "Low-cost take off," *Economist.com*, March 23, 2005.

12 Mayumi Negishi, "Takenaka vows to get LDP members on board for Japan Post privatization," *Japan Times*, September 29, 2004.

13 For more on the current state of EUREKA, see Caroline Mothe and Bertrand Quelin, "Creating Competencies Through Collaboration: The Case of EUREKA R&D Consortia," *European Management Journal*, December 2000, pp. 590–604.

14 Alan Goldstein, "Sematech Members Facing Dues Increase; 30% Jump to Make up for Loss of Federal Funding," *Dallas Morning News*, July 27, 1996, p. 2F.

15 Larry Reibstein et al., "A Mexican Miracle?" *Newsweek*, May 20, 1991, pp. 42–45; Paul Magnusson et al., "The Mexico Pact: Worth the Price?" *Business Week*, May 27, 1991, pp. 32–35.

16 United States, BEA, *Survey of Current Business*, January and April 2005.

17 "Globalization, What on Earth Is it About?" BBC.co.uk, September 14, 2000.

18 "Who Are the Prague Protestors?" BBC.co.uk, September 26, 2000.

19 Alan M. Rugman, *The End of Globalization* (London: Random House, 2001).

20 Sylvia Ostry, "The Multilateral Trading System," in Alan M. Rugman and Thomas Brewer (eds.), *The Oxford Handbook of International Business* (Oxford: Oxford University Press, 2001), pp. 232–258.

21 Edward M. Graham, *Fighting the Wrong Enemy: Antiglobal Activists and Multinational Enterprises* (Washington, DC: Institute for International Economics, 2000).

22 Matthew Kaminski, "Europe's Leaders Set Date for EU Enlargement," *Wall Street Journal*, June 18, 2001, p. A15.

23 Philip Revzin, "EC Leaders Adopt 2-Year Plan to Forge Political, Monetary Unity in Europe," *Wall Street Journal*, December 17, 1990, p. A6.

24 "A Free-Trade Tug-of-War," *Economist.com*, December 9, 2004.

25 "Fraternity of 3,300 Metres," *Economist.com*, December 9, 2004.

26 Sylvia Chan-Olmsted and Mark Jamison, "Rivalry Through Alliances: Competitive Strategy in the Global Telecommunications Market," *European Management Journal*, June 2001, pp. 317–331.

27 John J. Keller, "Lucent, Philips to Produce Phones Jointly," *Wall Street Journal*, June 18, 1997, p. A3.

28 Don Clark and David Bank, "Microsoft, Sony to Cooperate on PCs, Devices," *Wall Street Journal*, April 8, 1998, p. B6.

29 Hideo Sugiura, "How Honda Localizes Its Global Strategy," *Sloan Management Review*, Fall 1990, pp. 77–82.

30 Ibid., p. 78.

31 Greg Steinmetz and Carl Quintanilla, "Whirlpool Expected Easy Going in Europe, and It Got a Big Shock," *Wall Street Journal*, April 10, 1998, pp. A1, A6.

32 Ferdinand Protzman, "Rewriting the Contract for Germany's Vaunted Workers," *New York Times*, February 13, 1994, Section F, p. 5.

33 "Pepsi Investing $350 Million in China Plants," *New York Times*, January 27, 1994, p. C3.

34 Brian Bremner et al., "Toyota's Crusade," *Business Week*, April 7, 1997, pp. 104–114.

35 See Robert O. Metzger and Ari Ginsberg, "Lessons from Japanese Global Acquisitions," *Journal of Business Strategy*, May/June 1989, p. 35.

36 Ibid., p. 79.

ADDITIONAL BIBLIOGRAPHY

Czinkota, Michael R., Knight, Gary, Liesch, Peter W. and Steen, John. "Terrorism and International Business: A Research Agenda," *Journal of International Business Studies*, vol. 41 (June/July 2010).

Dahan, Nicolas, Doh, Jonathan P., Oetzel, Jennifer and Yaziji, Michael. "Corporate-NGO Collaboration: Creating New Business Models for Developing Markets". *Long Range Planning*, vol. 43, no. 2 (2010).

Dunning, John H. (ed.). *Governments, Globalization and International Business* (Oxford: Oxford University Press, 1997).

Eden, Lorraine. "The Emerging North American Investment Regime," *Transnational Corporations*, vol. 5, no. 3 (December 1996).

Fratianni, Michele and Oh, Chang H. "Expanding RTAs, Trade Flows, and the Multinational Enterprise," *Journal of International Business Studies*, vol. 40 (September 2009).

Gomes-Casseres, Benjamin. "Competitive Advantage in Alliance Constellations," *Strategic Organization*, vol. 1, no. 3 (August 2003).

Graham, Edward M. *Fighting the Wrong Enemy: Antiglobal Activists and Multinational Enterprises* (Washington, DC: Institute for International Economics, September 2000).

Henisz, Witold, Mansfield, J., Edward, D. and Von Glinow, Mary Ann. "Conflict, Security, and Political Risk: International Business in Challenging Times," *Journal of International Business Studies*, vol. 41 (June/July 2010).

Hoffmann, Volker H., Trautmann, Thomas and Hamprecht, Jens. "Regulatory Uncertainty: A Reason to Postpone Investments? Not Necessarily," *Journal of Management Studies*, vol. 46, no. 7 (November 2009).

Howell, Llewellyn D. and Chaddick, Brad. "Models of Political Risk for Foreign Investment and Trade: An Assessment of Three Approaches," *Columbia Journal of World Business*, vol. 29, no. 3 (Fall 1994).

Jensen, Nathan M, Li, Quan and Rahman, Aminur. "Understanding Corruption and Firm Responses in Cross-National Firm-Level Surveys," *Journal of International Business Studies*, vol. 41 (2010).

Kobrin, Stephen J. "Sovereignty @ Bay: Globalization, Multinational Enterprises, and the International Political System," in Alan M. Rugman (ed.), *The Oxford Handbook of International Business*, 2nd ed. (Oxford: Oxford University Press, 2009).

Kolk, Ans. "Social and Sustainability Dimensions of Regionalization and (Semi)Globalization," *The Multinational Business Review*, vol. 18, no. 1 (2010).

Luo, Yadong. "Toward a Cooperative View of MNC-Host Government Relations: Building Blocks and Performance Implications," *Journal of International Business Studies*, vol. 32, no. 3 (Fall 2001).

Lee, Seung-Hyun, Oh, Kyeungrae, and Eden, Lorraine. "Why Do Firms Bribe?" *Management International Review*, vol. 50, no. 6 (December 1, 2010).

McCarthy, Daniel J., Puffer, Sheila M. and Naumov, Alexander I. "Russia's Retreat to Statization and the Implications for Business," *Journal of World Business*, vol. 35, no. 3 (Third Quarter 2000).

Muller, Alan and Kolk, Ans. "Extrinsic and Intrinsic Drivers of Corporate Social Performance: Evidence From Foreign and Domestic Firms in Mexico," *Journal of Management Studies*, vol. 47, no. 1 (2010).

Ostry, Sylvia. "The Multilateral Trading System," in Alan M. Rugman and Thomas Brewer (eds.), *The Oxford Handbook of International Business*, 1st ed. (Oxford: Oxford University Press, 2001).

Puffer, Sheila M. and McCarthy, Daniel J. "The Emergence of Corporate Governance in Russia," *Journal of World Business*, vol. 38, no. 4 (November 2003).

Puffer, Sheila M. and McCarthy, Daniel J. "Can Russia's State-Managed, Network Capitalism Be Competitive? Institutional Pull versus Institutional Push," *Journal of World Business*, vol. 42, no. 1 (March 2007).

Rugman, Alan M. (ed.). *Foreign Investment and NAFTA* (Columbia, SC: University of South Carolina Press, 1994).

Rugman, Alan M. "Towards an Investment Agenda for APEC," *Transnational Corporations*, August 1997.

Rugman, Alan M. (ed.). *North American Economic and Financial Integration* (Oxford: Elsevier, 2004).

Rugman, Alan M. and Gestrin, Michael. "The Strategic Response of Multinational Enterprises to NAFTA," *Columbia Journal of World Business*, vol. 28, no. 4 (Winter 1993).

Rugman, Alan M. and Verbeke, Alain. "Multinational Enterprise and National Economic Policy," in Peter J. Buckley and Mark Casson (eds.), *Multinational Enterprises in the World Economy: Essays in Honour of John Dunning* (Aldershot: Edward Elgar, 1992).

Rugman, Alan M. and Doh. Jonathan. *Multinationals and Development*. (New Haven, CT: Yale University Press, 2008).

Rugman, Alan M. and Verbeke, Alain. "Multinational Enterprises and Public Policy", in Alan M. Rugman (ed.), *The Oxford Handbook of International Business*, 2nd ed. (Oxford: Oxford University Press, 2009).

Safarian, A. E. *Multinational Enterprise and Public Policy* (Cheltenham: Edward Elgar, 1993).

Sen, Amartya. *Development as Freedom* (Oxford: Oxford University Press, 1999).

Spar, Debora L. *Ruling the Waves: Cycles of Discovery, Chaos and Wealth* (New York: Harcourt, 2001).

Spar, Debora L. "National Policies and Domestic Politics," in Alan M. Rugman (ed.), *The Oxford Handbook of International Business*, 2nd ed. (Oxford: Oxford University Press, 2009).

Trebilcock, Michael and Howse, Robert. The *Regulation of International Trade*, 3rd ed. (London: Routledge, 2005).

Weintraub, Sidney, Rugman, Alan M. and Boyd, Gavin (eds.). *Free Trade in the Americas* (Cheltenham: Edward Elgar, 2004).

Chapter 5

INTERNATIONAL CULTURE

Contents

Objectives of the chapter

Places and people differ. The Japanese tend to be very polite, the Australians characteristically blunt. Red means "danger" or "stop" to the British, but in Turkey it signifies death and in China, good fortune. In France getting into a *grande école* tends to guarantee good job prospects whereas in Saudi Arabia the wealth and status of your family is far more important.

Patterns of global diversity and the implications of these differences have been studied from a range of perspectives, by sociologists, psychologists, anthropologists, and political scientists. Here we are concerned with how cultural diversity and related differences in the behavior, norms, and expectations of particular groups of employees, managers, colleagues, or customers affect management decision making and corporate organizations. After an introduction to the kinds of business contexts in which cultural differences do matter, this chapter will describe some typologies of national cultural differences and discuss the implications of these for international managers.

The specific objectives of this chapter are to:

1 *Define* culture and explain the factors that underlie cultural differences.

2 *Show* where and why cultural differences matter to international managers.

3 *Explain* a number of frameworks that help identify important cultural differences.

4 *Examine* how firms can anticipate and cope with cultural differences.

ACTIVE LEARNING CASE

Culture clash at Pharmacia and Upjohn

Despite being part of the same advanced, industrialized world, Kalamazoo (Michigan, United States), Stockholm (Sweden), and Milan (Italy) are worlds apart in many important ways. Senior managers leading the merger between two pharmaceutical firms, Upjohn Company of the United States and Pharmacia AB of Sweden (with operations in Italy), came to realize how significant these differences were after the merger took place in 1995.

Swedes take off most of the month of July for their annual vacation, Italians take off most of August. Not knowing this, US executives scheduled meetings in the summer only to have to cancel many because their European counterparts were at the beach. As the more dominant US firm began to impose its way of doing things on the newly acquired European organizations, international relationships became increasingly strained.

Neither the Swedes nor the Italians were happy with impositions such as the drug and alcohol testing policy brought in by Upjohn, or the office smoking ban. These clashed with local ways of doing things and the more informal work environment that these cultures prefer. Although Upjohn later relaxed many of these work rules, allowing some local practices and preferences to prevail, ill-feeling and a degree of resistance had already developed among European colleagues.

The additional bureaucracy and the command-and-control style imposed by the Americans created more significant problems for the 34,000 employees and managers in Pharmacia and Upjohn Company. The Swedes were used to an open, team-based style of management where responsibilities are devolved; managers are trusted and not strictly monitored or closely managed. Swedish executives also tend to build up a consensus behind big decisions, "getting everyone in the same boat" (alla aer i baten) rather than handing orders down the hierarchy. As a traditional US multinational, however, Upjohn was more used to strong leadership and a centralized command-and-control structure. Its CEO, Dr. John Zabriskie, quickly created a strict reporting system, tight budget control, and frequent staffing updates, which clashed with the Swedish organization style. Swedish managers would leave meetings disgruntled, having been overruled by US executives keen to push their vision of the merged company.

The Swedes' own ways of doing things had already clashed with the Italian style of management, following the takeover of Farmitalia (part of Montedison) by Pharmacia in 1993. Italians are used to a distinctive division between workers (and their strong unions) and managers. Their steeper hierarchies contrast the more egalitarian Swedes. Italians also place a high value on families and will leave work to tend to sick relatives or help with childcare, which the Swedes frown upon. The addition of the Americans from Upjohn to this mix created further cultural confusion. Communication problems, beyond the obvious language differences, became a real barrier to honest dialogue. "You go there thinking you're going to streamline the place," said American Mark H. Corrigan, Pharmacia and Upjohn Vice President for Clinical Development, "and you leave just having added five pounds from some wonderful meals."

These differences, many of them small but important at the local level, quickly began to have an impact on the overall performance of the merged company. In the months and years following the merger unforeseen inefficiencies and added costs began to undermine the potential synergies of bringing together two such companies in the first place. At one level the problems amounted to things like canceled meetings, new organization demands (such as monthly report writing), and a general decline in staff morale. There were also unexpected difficulties integrating the IT systems across the various parts of the merged organization. These and other changes added an estimated $200 million to the predicted costs of the restructuring, taking the total cost to $800 million. Even more seriously, for a pharmaceutical company heavily reliant on its new drugs pipeline to survive, delayed product launches and the loss of key staff (including the head of R&D at Pharmacia) had a longer-term impact. "There was probably an underappreciation . . . of these cultural differences," says Art Atkinson, former Vice President for Clinical Research and Development.

Particular problems resulted from the restructuring of the firm's global R&D structure. Prior to the merger Upjohn owned well-known names such as Rogaine and Motrin and had annual sales of around $3.5 billion, but had a weak new product pipeline and slow sales growth compared to its larger competitors. Similar-sized Pharmacia had a more promising pipeline but weak distribution and sales in the US market, the world's largest. These amounted to a strong rationale for the merger. Together they could challenge the financial power and the larger R&D programs of their competitors. However, integrating and refocusing the various parts of the new R&D structure became a major problem. Rather than place the R&D headquarters in the United States, Sweden, or Milan, a decision was made to establish a new and neutral London-based center for the R&D function. This simply added a layer of management ▶

and a more complex matrix reporting structure, which further alienated key R&D personnel.

In 1997, after the stock price of the merged corporation had fallen significantly, CEO John Zabriskie resigned. Swede Jan Ekberg, the former head of Pharmacia, took over temporarily and began to rebuild aspects of the merged organization.

After acquiring a major part of Monsanto in 2000, Pharmacia and Upjohn became Pharmacia, which was then itself acquired by the US giant Pfizer in April 2003. This made Pfizer, according to its own Annual Report, the "number one pharmaceutical company in every region of the World."

All this proves is that going global is hard work. Not all of these problems could have been foreseen, but a real lack of awareness of cultural differences did lead to many of the organization difficulties and people problems with a real impact on the bottom line.

Websites: www.accenture.com/xdoc/en/ideas/outlook/1.2000/maa2.pdf; www.pfizer.com; www.pfizer.com/are/investors_reports/annual_2003/review/index.htm.

Sources: R. Frank and T. M. Burton, "Pharmacia & Upjohn Faces Culture Clash; Europeans Chafe Under US Rules," *Wall Street Journal*, February 4, 1997; R. J. Thomas, "Irreconcilable Differences," *Accenture Outlook*, vol. 1, 2000; and Pfizer, *Annual Report*, 2003.

1 What kinds of cultural differences matter when organizations from different countries merge?

2 How well do the characteristics described in the case match the respective, stereotypical national cultures of these countries?

3 What could senior managers have done before and after the merger to alleviate some of the problems that resulted from culture clash?

4 Explain why one organization might want to impose some of its ways of doing things on another, such as an acquired firm or subsidiary.

INTRODUCTION

The number of workers employed by foreign-owned companies has grown significantly over the past 20 years as a result of the expanding activities of foreign affiliates of MNEs around the world. For many people, both employers and employees, this has brought home the realities of globalization. An estimated 73 million people globally (including 24 million in China) now work for foreign companies, nearly three times the number in 1990. Companies such as Motorola, General Motors, British Petroleum, and General Electric are among the largest private-sector employers in economies such as Malaysia and Singapore.[1]

This growing multicultural workforce, part of the increasingly global patterns of exchange and interaction discussed earlier in this book, makes it more and more important to understand how people's preferences, beliefs, and values differ. Understanding international cultural differences allows us to be aware of and adapt to the differences that matter for managers.

WHAT IS CULTURE?

Socialization
The process of enculturation, or the adoption of the behavior patterns of the surrounding culture

Culture can be defined as "the sum total of the beliefs, rules, techniques, institutions, and artifacts that characterize human populations"[2] or "the collective programming of the mind."[3]

Sociologists generally talk about the **socialization** process, referring to the influence of parents, friends, education, and the interaction with other members of a particular society as the basis for one's culture. These influences result in learned patterns of behavior common to members of a given society.

Table 5.1 World population percentages in terms of home region, language, and religion

Home region	%	Language	%	Religion	%
Asia	58.4	Mandarin	14.4	Christianity, including:	33
Africa	12.4	Hindi	6.0	Catholics	20
Europe	9.5	English	5.6	Protestants	9
Latin America	8.4	Spanish	5.6	Orthodox	4
Former Soviet bloc	5.5	Bengali	3.4	Islam	22
North America	5.2	Russian	2.8	Hinduism	15
Australia and New Zealand	0.6	Portuguese	2.6	Non-religious	14
		Japanese	2.0	Buddhism	6
		German	1.6	Chinese traditional	4
		Korean	1.3	Primal–indigenous	3
		French	1.3	Other	3
		Other (approx. 200)	54.4		

Sources: www.census.gov; www.adherents.com.

As you can see, definitions of culture vary according to the focus of interest, the unit of analysis, and the disciplinary approach (psychology, anthropology, sociology, geography, etc.). This is significant in that studies of cultural differences adopt a specific definition and set of measurable criteria, which are always debatable. Research into culture and its impact in business and management studies is highly contentious and should not just be taken at face value, including the studies described below.

There is a strong consensus, however, that key elements of culture include language, religion, values, attitudes, customs, and norms of a group or society. Table 5.1 shows how the world's population is divided according to geography, language, and religion.

Language is perhaps the most important key to understanding culture in general and the specific values, beliefs, attitudes, and opinions of a particular individual or group. English is widely accepted as the language of business; many global institutions and companies have adopted English as their official language. For many firms, such as Toyota, NEC, Hitachi, and IBM Japan, English-speaking ability is a prerequisite for promotion.[4] However, any assumption that speaking the same language removes cultural differences is dangerous—it normally just hides them. Moreover, a reliance on English by British and American managers, and a lack of other language skills, can weaken their ability to empathize with and adapt to other cultures.

Religion, linked to both regional characteristics and language, also influences business culture through a set of shared core values. Protestants hold strong beliefs about the value of delayed gratification, saving, and investment. The sociologist Max Weber, writing in 1904, saw this Protestant work ethic as the "spirit of capitalism" during the Industrial Revolution.[5] Rather than spending, consuming, and enjoying life now, their religious beliefs prompted the Protestants to look to longer-term rewards (including those in the after-life). There are parallels with the Confucian and Shinto work ethics, which also view spiritual rewards as tied to hard work and commitment to the fruits of industry. Contrasting this, a more stoic attitude among some African populations partly explains their acceptance of the ways things are, because it is the "will of God" (*shauri ya Mungu*).

Corporate culture
The shared values, traditions, customs, philosophy, and policies of a corporation; also, the professional atmosphere that grows from this and affects behavior and performance

At the most general level culture can refer simply to the lifestyle and behavior of a given group of people, so **corporate culture** is a term used to characterize how the managers and employees of particular companies tend to behave. But the term is also used by human resource managers and senior management in their attempts to proactively shape the kind of behavior (innovative, open, dynamic, etc.) they hope to nurture in their organizations. Promoting a distinctive corporate culture is also expected to enhance the sense of community and shared identity that underpins effective organizations.

THE IMPORTANCE OF CULTURE IN DIFFERENT BUSINESS CONTEXTS

Cross-cultural management issues arise in a range of business contexts. *Within* individual firms, for example, managers from a foreign parent company need to understand that local employees from the host country may require different organization structures and HRM procedures. In cross-border mergers and acquisitions (M&As), realizing the expected synergies very often depends on establishing structures and procedures that encompass both cultures in a balanced way. Cross-border joint ventures, alliances, or buyer–supplier relationships *between* two or more firms also require a cultural compromise. Finally, for firms to sell successfully to foreign customers requires culturally sensitive adaptations to products, services, marketing, and advertising.

Figure 5.1 outlines, at the most general level, links between business contexts and particular characteristics of individuals or groups that are influenced by social and cultural norms of a particular region. At the face-to-face level in meetings the language and behavior of different peoples vary and their mutual understanding of each other's culture will influence the effectiveness and efficiency of communication between them. This influences how well multicultural workplaces operate at all levels, from strategy setting at the senior level to plant-floor operations.

Firms also tend to have different organizational and decision-making practices depending on where they have evolved and which cultures and subcultures they encompass. For firms to build successful alliances and partnerships, or for M&A activities to succeed at the company-to-company level, there needs to be an understanding of the organizational

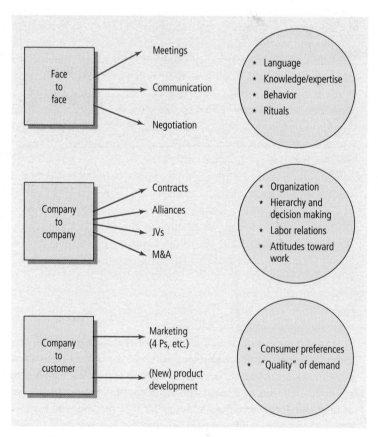

Figure 5.1 Cross-cultural business contexts

differences between them. This covers practically every element of corporate organizations from decision-making structures and systems and management–labor relationships to individual employees' attitudes toward their work and their employer.

Finally, culture influences the behavior and preferences of clients and customers. To sell successfully in a foreign market, a manager needs to adapt his or her product or service to meet the different needs of that particular group of customers. Any alteration in advertising, marketing, product or service features, after-sales support, technical back-up, documentation, etc., will be partly guided by cultural differences.

Failure to do this ends in the kinds of marketing mistakes and communication blunders that become marketing folklore. For example, Ford's low-cost truck was initially marketed as the Feira to Spanish-speaking people, but this means "ugly old woman" in Spanish. The Ford Comet, a high-end car, was sold as the Caliente in Mexico, which is local slang for "prostitute." Unsurprisingly neither model did well in these markets. This reinforces the above point about the importance of language, but also demonstrates how some of the largest and most experienced companies do not appear to do the most basic cultural due diligence (their homework!) when launching products and services in foreign markets. The chapter on marketing strategy in this book examines these kinds of issues more closely.

Ethnocentrism
The belief that one's own way of doing things is superior to that of others

Across all of the business contexts in Figure 5.1 ignorance of cultural differences represents a common stumbling block for international managers. **Ethnocentrism**, the belief that one's own way of doing things is superior to that of others, can also be a major barrier to good international management. The challenge lies in recognizing differences, combining the advantages that stem from different styles and approaches, adjusting and adapting to succeed with different people, in different partnerships, and in different markets.

✔ Active learning check

Review your answer to Active Learning Case question 1 and make any changes you like. Then compare your answer to the one below.

 What kinds of cultural differences matter when organizations from different countries merge?

The definition of culture itself gives some indicators of the kinds of differences that matter. Organizations from different countries will have developed different beliefs, values, and patterns of behavior based on their underlying national culture. A wide range of differences could be important, including attitudes toward work and workplace practices, management–labor relations, the decision-making hierarchy, and division of responsibilities. Cross-border M&A often also requires changes to the marketing and branding of products and services as sales are expanded into new markets. Differences in the language, values, and preferences of customers in different countries also need to be taken into account.

Culture has always been important

Cultural convergence
The growing similarity between national cultures, including the beliefs, values, aspirations, and the preferences of consumers, partly driven by global brands, media, and common global icons

Despite the various patterns and processes of globalization, cultural differences still remain important. Even with greater common access, via various media and the Internet, to the same brands, rock icons, and sports stars, differences remain. Terms like **cultural convergence** or, simply, Americanization (the homogenization of global consumer preferences through the ubiquity of McDonald's, Coca-Cola, and Ford) overstate the similarities between groups of people around the world. (See the case **International Business Strategy in Action: McDonald's.**)

INTERNATIONAL BUSINESS STRATEGY IN ACTION

McDonald's

When José Bové, a self-proclaimed leader of France's anti-globalization movement, was sentenced for vandalizing a McDonald's restaurant in 1999, he claimed to have the backing of the French people. That might have been an overstatement, but 40,000 French people were there to show their support. It was not only the French, however; in the 1990s McDonald's restaurants were vandalized in about 50 countries. At issue is the worldwide perception that McDonald's represents a particular friendly Ronald-McDonald type of US imperialism. Traditional lifestyles, critics say, are being eroded by McDonald's marketing practices, its value chain system, its fast-food concept, and the unhealthy food itself.

Yet, McDonald's bends over backwards to blend into local cultures. The company advertises itself to its critics as a global company owned and run by local people. Indeed, the franchise system makes it so that McDonald's Japan is run by the Japanese and Israel's McDonald's restaurants are run by Israelis. Local business owners choose their menu's offerings to fit their culture, find alternative suppliers, and create suitable marketing for their culture. An American in Saudi Arabia might seat single men with families at a McDonald's opening, but a Saudi Arabian owner would know that this is unacceptable and the restaurant will be designed to accommodate the culture.

In the land of José Bové, Asterix, a French comic-strip character who stands for individuality and ironically symbolizes local resistance to imperial forces, replaced the goofy Ronald McDonald in the company's marketing in the early 2000s. In 1999, French McDonald's went the extra mile to prove how local it was by printing advertisements making fun of US eating habits. In one ad, a large American cowboy complains that McDonald's France does not import American beef to "guarantee maximum hygienic conditions." French restaurants are more fashionably and more comfortably designed than North American ones to create an environment where customers may enjoy longer meals in accordance with French tradition. If they want, customers can order a beer from the menu.

In India, where local tastes are very different from those in the United States, the company crafted an entirely different menu that does not use beef or pork due to the mostly vegetarian population. The Indian Big Mac is made of lamb. In Israel, the locally owned McDonald's purchases over 80 percent of its ingredients from local producers, including 100 percent kosher hamburger meat, potatoes, lettuce, buns, and milkshake mix. There are no cheeseburgers in Israel's McDonald's because dairy products cannot be eaten together with meat.

On the other hand, McDonald's does bring its own culture to its foreign operations. In China, where children's birthdays are not traditionally celebrated, a successful McDonald's marketing strategy encouraged birthday parties at their establishments. Not a bad deal for children, but still a cultural effect from a foreign multinational. More mundane things, such as combo meals, are popularized through McDonald's expansion. By promoting its carbonated beverages in India, the firm is unsettling the country's tea culture. The company's presence creates a cultural exchange, not a one-sided cultural takeover.

Beyond reactionary behavior against McDonald's cultural "impositions," McDonald's has had to suffer simply for being born in the United States. Just hours after the United States began bombing Afghanistan in 2001 McDonald's restaurants were vandalized in cities in Pakistan and Indonesia and Muslim clerics asked for the boycott of US products.

For activists and cultural protectors, the most frustrating thing is that their calls go unheeded. Owners of McDonald's franchises continuously remind customers that they too are locals, that their employees are locals, and that their suppliers are mainly local. In Brazil, some anti-war protestors on their way home will stop at a McDonald's for a bite to eat.

Some of McDonald's major troubles, however, are in its most established markets in the United States, Canada, and the UK. Russian and Chinese go-getters might think that a meal in McDonald's puts them in a class above, but in its two major markets of North America and Europe, where the firm derives over two-thirds of all revenue, the food is considered unhealthy. Indeed, both Canada and the UK considered imposing a tax on fatty foods on the grounds that it was damaging to people's health and it costs the health-care system a substantial amount. The tax is unlikely to be imposed because of a strong backlash from poverty groups who argue that this tax would place an uneven burden on those who depend on cheap food for their everyday survival. In the United States, the firm is being sued over claims that it misled parents about the nutritional value of its products, leading their children to become obese and unhealthy. McDonald's in the UK reacted by eliminating supersized options from the menu. A set of healthier options has now been introduced in Europe and North America as the company fends off critics in some of its friendliest markets. The company has

▶

also embraced sustainability and extended its corporate social responsibility (CSR) activities and reporting in order to keep one step ahead of a wider set of critics. In 2011, McDonald's was among the Fortune's top 10 world's most admired companies.

What makes McDonald's such an admired, recognizable brand, even amid an enduring fast-food backlash? New items on the menu have helped: salads (with Newman's Own low fat dressing), wraps, oatmeal, and apple dippers. In addition, the chain constantly adds to its dollar menu, catering to those who have felt the recession's crunch.

McDonald's also operates a wide range of charity programs, including teacher awards and youth basketball games. And financially, the company is doing fine. In January 2011, the company announced that sales were up; since then the stock has continued to rise.

Sources: David Barboza, "When Golden Arches Are Too Red, White and Blue," *New York Times*, October 14, 2001; Tony Karon, "Adieu, Ronald McDonald," *Time.com*, January 24, 2002; Simon Romero, "War and Abuse Do Little to Harm US Brands," *New York Times*, May 9, 2004; McDonald's corporate website: http://www.aboutmcdonalds.com/mcd/csr/report.html, downloaded June 2011; "The World' Most Admired Companies", Forbes, http://money.cnn.com/magazines/fortune/mostadmired/2011/.

Cultures vary and these variations lead to real and significant differences in the ways that companies operate and people work. Moreover, *because* of globalization more and more firms are coming head to head with the added complexity of doing business globally, which stems from the huge amount of variety in the world that still exists (and arguably will always exist).

Before moving on to examine some typologies of global cultures, here is a word of warning. Much of this section will describe how various kinds of individual and group behavior can be linked to specific cultural groups and associate these cultural dispositions with different business styles and company structures. Acting on the basis of cultural stereotypes is highly sensitive and can be problematic. For example, at the simplest level a banker may be able to prove empirically that Pakistanis are more successful than Jamaicans at starting and running small businesses around the world. Using this insight as the basis for discriminating against Jamaicans wanting bank loans for business start-ups is not only unethical, but in most countries falls foul of race discrimination laws.

NATIONAL STEREOTYPES AND KEY DIMENSIONS OF CULTURE

Culture at two levels

There are traditionally two different approaches to looking at culture:

Psychic distance
A measure of the similarity or difference between two cultures; also commonly defined as the measurable distance between the home market and a foreign market resulting from the perception of cultural and business differences

- The psychic or psychological level, which focuses on the internalized norms, attitudes, and behavior of individuals from a particular culture (**psychic distance** is a measure of differences between groups).

- The institutional level, which looks at national (or group) culture *embodied* in institutions (government, education, and economic institutions as well as in business organizations).

In this chapter we will mainly discuss the first, culture as shared psychology, with a brief reference to national institutional differences at the end.

People who are born in, or grew up in, the same country tend to share similar cultural characteristics. Nordström and Valhne examined a sample of Swedish firms to understand the effects of psychic distance on market-entry strategies and costs.[6] They ranked 20 particular countries according to a range of national characteristics that contribute to psychic distance and found, as you might expect, that Denmark is closest to Sweden (1/20), the UK comes in at 6/20, Portugal at 15/20, Japan 16/20, Brazil 17/20 and Australia 20/20.

Nationality and culture tend to coincide, although nations encompass a wide variety of institutions, religions, beliefs, and patterns of behavior, and distinctive subcultures can always be found within individual countries. The only way to make sense of this wide diversity is to characterize distinct cultural groups through simplified national stereotypes.

Many studies have attempted to create these stereotypes by mapping and comparing the shared characteristics of managers and employees in different countries.[7] Researchers then examine the effects of key differences on business behavior, organization, structure, and ultimately the performance of companies from different countries. The following describes the milestone studies of this kind in the management field.

Hofstede's four dimensions of culture

Power distance
A cultural dimension that measures the degree to which less powerful members of organizations and institutions accept the fact that power is not distributed equally

Uncertainty avoidance
The extent to which people feel threatened by ambiguous situations and have created institutions and beliefs for minimizing or avoiding those uncertainties

Individualism
The tendency of people to look after themselves and their immediate family only

Geert Hofstede is a Dutch psychologist who conducted one of the earliest and best-known cultural studies in management, on IBM's operations in 70 countries around the world.[8] Getting answers to 32 statements from over 116,000 questionnaires, he mapped key cultural characteristics of these countries according to four value dimensions:

1. **Power distance** is the extent to which a culture accepts that power in organizations is distributed unequally. High power distance equates with steep organizational hierarchies, with more autocratic leadership and less employee participation in decision making (see Figure 5.2 for examples).

2. **Uncertainty avoidance** is the degree to which members of a society feel uncomfortable with risk and uncertainty. High uncertainty avoidance (Japan, Argentina, France) will be reflected in the high priority placed on rituals, routines, and procedures in organizations and society in general. Countries with low uncertainty avoidance (Denmark, UK, India, United States) tend to emphasize flexibility and informality rather than bureaucracy.

3. **Individualism** is the extent to which people are supposed to take care of themselves and be emotionally independent from others (see Figure 5.2 for examples).

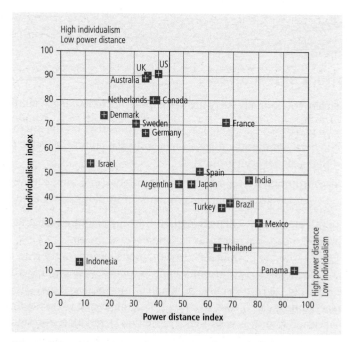

Figure 5.2 Hofstede's power distance against individualism for 20 countries

Source: Hofstede, G. (1983). The cultural relativity of organizational practices and theories, *Journal of International Business Studies*, Fall, p. 92. Copyright © Geert Hofstede.

Masculinity
The degree to which the dominant values of a society are success, money, and material things

4 **Masculinity** is the value attributed to achievement, assertiveness, and material success (Japan, Mexico, Germany, UK) as opposed to the stereotypical feminine values of relationships, modesty, caring, and the quality of life (Sweden, Netherlands, Denmark), according to Hofstede.

Figure 5.2 illustrates some of Hofstede's findings using two of the most useful dimensions, power distance against the degree of individualism/collectivism. It reflects some general stereotypes of the countries included, with clear grouping of Australia, the UK and the United States as highly individualistic and less hierarchical (small power distance) cultures against Mexico, Thailand, and Panama at the other extreme. We will elaborate on these definitions and their practical interpretation throughout this chapter.

Among his most important contributions, Hofstede provided strong evidence for the significance of national culture over professional role, gender, or race, as a determinant of variation in employees' attitudes, values, and behaviors, accounting for 50 percent of the differences his study observed. However, his studies have come in for significant criticism, despite widespread adoption of the four-dimensional framework. Three common criticisms are: (1) that the dimensions developed from data collected between 1968 and 1973 were relevant only for that particular period; (2) that corporate cultural and other influences from this one-organization (IBM) study created significant bias; (3) that the sole use of attitude-survey questionnaires was not a valid basis for the resulting values and dimensions his study concluded with.[9]

Although Hofstede has continued to write on culture, organizations, and management,[10] it is useful to look more deeply into the work of another well-known Dutch culture guru.

Trompenaars' seven dimensions of culture

Fons Trompenaars built on Hofstede's work by expanding the framework for stereotyping and comparing different national cultures and by focusing more on the management implications of cultural differences. Using initial research involving 15,000 employees in 50 countries, Trompenaars explored the "cultural extremes and the incomprehension that can arise when doing business across cultures," even when people are working for the same company.[11]

Trompenaars arrived at seven distinctive dimensions of culture and used the questionnaire responses in his study to map a wide variety of countries along a continuum from one extreme to the other within each dimension. The key to understanding this mapping approach is to identify where each country or culture is positioned *relative* to others on one or more of these dimensions.

Relative positioning gives insights into the kinds of conflicts, misunderstandings, and organizational and management problems that are likely to arise when individuals, groups, or firms from these countries interact in any of the ways described above.

Universalism
The uniform application of rules and procedures, regardless of situation, context, or individuals involved

Particularism
Judging a situation and adjusting rules and procedures according to the specific situation or individuals involved

1 **Universalism** *versus* **particularism**. In universalistic cultures rules and regulations are applied in all situations, regardless of particular conditions or circumstances. The example used by Trompenaars refers to a salesman who does not fulfill his monthly sales quota because he was looking after his sick son. Should he be penalized according to standard company regulations or should he be excused because of the particular circumstances?

According to Trompenaars' findings, Switzerland, Canada, and the United States are among the most universalist. Australia and the UK are also toward this end of the scale. Germany is closer to the center, as is France, but the latter sits on the particularist side of the scale. Korea, Russia, and China are the most particularist of countries. (Note that some of the countries studied by Hofstede, like the strongly particularist Yugoslavia, no longer exist.)

Collectivism
The tendency of people to belong to groups who look after each other in exchange for loyalty

Neutral
A preference for unemotional, objective analysis of a situation or a decision and for limited displays of emotions and feelings in the workplace

Emotional
An acceptance of emotion and subjectivity as the bases for some decision making and a preference for explicit displays of emotions and feelings in the workplace

Specific
A tendency to limit workplace relationships and obligations, including relative status and hierarchical position, to the workplace

Diffuse
A tendency for workplace relationships and obligations, including relative status and hierarchical position, to extend into social situations and activities outside of work

Achievement oriented
Where status is earned rather than a right; recruitment and promotion opportunities tend to be more dependent on performance, as in a meritocracy

Ascription oriented
Where status is more of a right than earned; recruitment and promotion opportunities tend to be more dependent on seniority, ethnicity, gender, religion, or birth

Sequential
Cultures that view time in a sequential or linear fashion; order comes from separating activities and commitments

Synchronic
Cultures that view events in parallel over time; order comes from coordinating multiple activities and commitments

2 *Individualism versus* **collectivism**. This dimension, clearly building on Hofstede, centers on whether individual rights and values are dominant or subordinate to those of the collective society.

The most individualist countries are Canada, the United States, Switzerland, and the UK. Among the most collectivist are Japan, Egypt, and India (and Nepal and Kuwait).

3 **Neutral** *versus* **emotional**. This reflects how much emotions are displayed in the workplace. More importantly it indicates whether emotional or subjective (rather than objective) forms of assessment are thought to be the basis for good decision making in organizations. Some organizations emphasize reports, data, and analytical decision making by managers, whereas others feel that opinions, intuition, and gut feelings are credible or valid criteria. Predictably the most emotional countries include Italy and France and the least emotional groups (in the workplace at least) are the Japanese, Germans, Swiss, Chinese, and Indonesians.

4 **Specific** *versus* **diffuse**. Do work relationships (such as the hierarchical relationship between a senior manager and a subordinate) exist just in the workplace (are they specific), or do they extend into the social context outside the workplace (diffuse)? Here a telling example is whether an employee is willing to help paint a senior manager's house over a weekend. Clearly Australian bosses are likely to get a characteristically blunt answer to this request! China, Japan, India, and Singapore display highly diffuse relationships, Australia and the Netherlands the most specific.

5 **Achievement** *versus* **ascription**. This dimension refers to one's status within organizations, contrasting those cultures where status, credibility, authority, and ultimately power tend to be based on merit (achieved) against those where class, gender, education, or age tend to be the defining characteristics (status is ascribed).

Countries where status tends to be ascribed include Egypt, Turkey, and Argentina (and slightly less so, Russia, Japan, and France), and those where it is achieved include Norway, Sweden, and predictably the United States, Australia, Canada, and the UK.

6 *Attitudes toward time.* **Sequential** (time as a sequence of events) versus **synchronic** (several events juggled at the same time) views of time tend to relate to punctuality for meetings and deadlines. Swedes and other northern European cultures tend to be punctual and plan according to specific timetables. Many southern European, Latin American, and Arabic cultures see punctuality and chronological precision as far less important. They also tend to naturally cope with a range of issues simultaneously, rather than one by one.

7 *Attitudes toward the environment.* This dimension reflects the emphasis a particular culture places on people's relationship with nature and the natural environment. On the one hand some cultures emphasize control and subjugation of environmental forces, whereas others emphasize the need to work with nature, in harmony with the environment. Clearly religious and philosophical differences around the world influence differences within this dimension.

Trompenaars' seven dimensions have been used in a variety of ways to gain insights into the kinds of problems that might arise in the contexts (face to face, company to company, and company to customer) outlined in Figure 5.1. In general they indicate the organizational characteristics we can expect from firms based in particular countries or dominated by certain nationalities. They are also used to measure changes in cultural values and behavior over time. Research shows that in both Japan and China, for example, achievement orientation is on the increase alongside some elements of individualism.[12]

The Japanese are moving away from a reliance on collectivism in the form of the state, large firms, and group associations and placing more value on personal responsibility and individual performance. In China there is a shift in companies toward performance-related rewards and individual initiative, built on the changing views of the growing urban elite. But there are also wider concerns regarding the social costs as well as the benefits of self-interest.

The GLOBE project's nine dimensions of culture

More recent research has built on the Hofstede and Trompenaars research. The Global Leadership and Organizational Behavior Effectiveness (GLOBE) project began in 1992 and continues today. It has involved 150 researchers collecting data on cultural values and management and leadership attributes from 18,000 managers across 62 countries in the telecommunications, food, and banking industries.[13] In the same way as Hofstede and Trompenaars before them, the researchers place countries along a standard 1 to 7 scale. The GLOBE project, however, ends up with nine key cultural dimensions:

1 *Assertiveness.* The United States, Austria, Germany, and Greece are high; Sweden, Japan, and New Zealand are low.

2 *Future orientation.* A propensity for planning, investing, delayed gratification: Singapore, Switzerland, and the Netherlands are high; Russia, Argentina, and Italy are low.

3 *Gender differentiation.* The degree to which gender role differences are maximized: South Korea, Egypt, India, and China are high; Hungary, Poland, and Denmark are low.

4 *Uncertainty avoidance.* A reliance on societal norms and procedures to improve predictability, a preference for order, structure, and formality: Sweden, Switzerland, and Germany are high; Russia, Bolivia, and Greece are low.

5 *Power distance.* Russia, Thailand, and Spain are high; Denmark, the Netherlands, and Israel are low.

6 *Institutional collectivism (individualism vs. collectivism).* Promoting active participation in social institutions: Sweden, South Korea, and Japan are high; Greece, Argentina, and Italy are low.

7 *In-group/family collectivism.* A pride in small-group membership, family, close friends, etc.: Iran, India, and China are high; Denmark, Sweden, and New Zealand are low.

8 *Performance orientation* (much like achievement orientation). Singapore, Hong Kong, and the United States are high; Russia, Argentina, and Italy are low.

Humane orientation
Cultures that emphasize helping others, charity, and people's wider social obligations

9 **Humane orientation**. An emphasis on fairness, altruism, and generosity: Ireland, Malaysia, and Egypt are high; Germany, Spain, France, Singapore, and Brazil are low.

As you can see, many of these dimensions match those of Hofstede and Trompenaars, and the overall GLOBE framework is very much an extension of their approach.

The GLOBE researchers have examined the HRM implications of these cultural differences for practicing managers and looked at ways to avoid the pitfalls of ignorance and insensitivity.[14] A similar long-running study by the CRANET network has focused on European cultural differences and reports similar findings.[15]

As with the other cultural mapping studies by Hofstede and Trompenaars, GLOBE has faced some critical appraisal, which helps us understand the strengths and weaknesses of its concluding framework. A recent set of debates has usefully raised some methodological issues associated with these kinds of studies, and provides interesting points of contention we should be aware of, rather than blindly accepting the above kind of research.[16]

Applying the national culture frameworks

Different styles of communication and interaction result from the cultural differences listed above. These can lead to workplace misunderstandings, poor interpersonal and intergroup relationships, inefficiency, and higher costs. Three examples provide some insights into how we can apply the above typologies.

US managers, according to all of the above studies, are highly assertive and performance oriented relative to managers from other parts of the world (they come around the mid-point on all the other dimensions). Their interaction style is characteristically direct and explicit. They tend to use facts, figures, and logic to link specific steps to measurable outcomes, and this is the main focus of workplace interaction. Greeks and Russians are less individualistic, less performance oriented, and show lower levels of uncertainty avoidance (are less driven by procedures) than the Americans. When Russian and Greek managers, employees, customers, suppliers, or public-sector officials interact with US counterparts, they may well find their approach too direct and results focused. For them communication is likely to be more about mutual learning and an exploration of relevant issues than an explicit agreement about specific expectations and end results. Similarly, the Swedes may find the US style too aggressive and unfriendly, working against the relationship-building process that for them is a major objective of workplace interaction.

The Koreans and Japanese have highly gender-differentiated societies with males tending to dominate decision making and leading most face-to-face communication. The agenda for discussion is likely set by males, and traditional language forms differ according to whether a man is addressing a woman or an older person talking to a younger person, and vice versa. Gender- (and age-)related roles, responsibilities, and behaviors are therefore deeply embedded in language and customs.[17] Poland and Denmark lie at the other end of the continuum on the gender-differentiation dimension. Perhaps even more than other Western managers, their lack of awareness of this cultural difference runs the risk of both embarrassing female employees and offending and alienating senior Japanese male managers. This kind of clash can make negotiations and interaction of all kinds between these groups that much more difficult.

Certain kinds of HRM techniques are inappropriate for organizations that show high power distance ratings. Companies and management consultancies in the UK, the United States, and northern European countries have developed fairly participative management systems to improve productivity, based on their characteristically low power distance and flat organizational hierarchies. Techniques such as 360-degree feedback systems for developing management–employee relationships are not likely to work, however, in Mexican, Panamanian, Thai, or Russian organizations, which have high power distance and steep hierarchies. Subordinates are uncomfortable being asked to evaluate senior managers, and managers would not see subordinates as qualified to comment on their performance. More than this, to employees in some countries this kind of consultation can give the impression that senior managers do not know what they are doing! The employees may lose faith in senior management's ability and leave!

None of the above examples means that international managers should (or ever could) entirely change their behavior to suit local values and practices. Like many of the challenges facing managers, cultural sensitivity and cross-cultural effectiveness come from striking a balance between one's own norms, values, and principles and those of the "foreigner." The lesson for multinational firms is that **ethnocentric** corporate cultures and completely standardized HR systems do not work. The key challenge is to adapt to get the best from local differences.

Ethnocentric
A belief in the superiority of one's own ethnic group; the dominance of the home-country culture in decision making, human resource management, and overall corporate culture in a multinational firm

✔ Active learning check

Review your answer to Active Learning Case question 2 and make any changes you like. Then compare your answer to the one below.

How well do the characteristics described in the case match the respective, stereotypical national cultures of these countries?

According to the above frameworks they match reasonably well. The US culture is characterized as individualistic, achievement/performance oriented, and assertive. Most of these traits clash with the "feminine" (in Hofstede's characterization) values of relationships, modesty, caring, and the quality of life emphasized by the Swedes. Hofstede finds US managers less hierarchical than most cultures, which is not indicated in the Pharmacia–Upjohn case. However, as Figure 5.2 shows, both countries have a low power distance and high individualism rating, relative to other countries, but the United States has slightly higher power distance (steeper management hierarchy) than Sweden. Sweden also has a relatively high uncertainty avoidance ranking, preferring order, structure, and formality, which does not stand out in the case study. Swedes are also high on institutional collectivism but low on family or small-group collectivism. The Italians are the opposite. Unlike the Americans, the Italians are not at all oriented toward achievement (Trompenaars) or performance (GLOBE). They are also more emotional than the Swedes and Americans according to Hofstede and have a relatively low future orientation (GLOBE).

"The way we do things here": the implications of cultural differences for organizations and managers

Mapping out a variety of national cultural typologies using the various dimensions of culture described above gives us some insights into the kinds of differences that exist among different groups of managers, employees, and organizations.

Two key questions about the role of the individual in a firm and the role of a firm in a society from Trompenaars' study give us a starting point to explore the management implications of cultural differences. The responses in Figure 5.3 reflect the degree of support for the particular proposition A or B for each of these questions.

Americans clearly display what has been termed (originally by the sociologist Max Weber) a mechanistic and functional view of the firm as an organization (A) and a shareholder-driven, profit-oriented view of this organization in society (although more than half the US vote in Figure 5.3 was for option B). The Japanese tend to have a more organic view of the firm, emphasizing the importance of social networks and the obligation of the firm to a wider constituency of stakeholders (although this is a characteristic of traditional Japan that has been strongly tested in the recent recessionary environment).

A wide range of factors within organizations are influenced directly or indirectly by the cultural predispositions of managers and employees. We know from the above studies and a wide range of other research that these factors include:

■ The general relationship between employees and the organization: their roles and responsibilities, obligations, and loyalties and the link this has with life outside the workplace.

■ Hierarchy, power and authority, and the accepted routes to attaining these, including factors that underpin status and credibility in different societies and organizations.

■ The role of formal rules and regulations versus the informal communication, personal networks, and hidden "rules of the game."

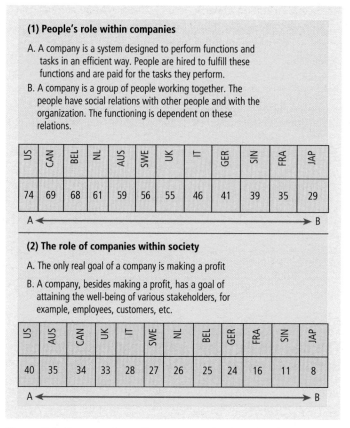

Figure 5.3 Excerpts from Trompenaars' cultural attitudes survey

Source: Hampden-Turner, C. and Trompenaars, F. *The Seven Cultures of Capitalism: Value Systems for Creating Wealth in the United States, Britain, Japan, Germany, France, Sweden and the Netherlands* (New York: Doubleday, 1993).

- The accepted basis for decision making, including rationale, scientific, mechanistic, and objective versus subjective, tacit, rule of thumb, etc.
- The degree to which employees act and are treated as individuals or groups and the role of interpersonal relationships.
- Motivation and rewards systems.
- Interaction and communication mechanisms.

Work attitudes and the appropriate management of work attitudes have a significant influence on productivity and innovativeness in a company. Managers and employees who are motivated by their core social values to work hard and continually strive to improve their company's products and services and the processes by which they are produced are clearly a source of competitive advantage. It is interesting to note how social norms may drive a strong work ethic despite individual dissatisfaction with workload or job responsibilities. This has been shown in several companies between US and Japanese factory workers where the Japanese are found to be more loyal and aligned with company objectives but far less satisfied individually.[18]

Table 5.2 compares interview responses from sample workforces in seven countries. The resulting ranking of what it is that employees value most from their jobs shows that "interesting work" is what tends to engage most people, beyond everything else.

Table 5.2 Average and intra-country ranking of work goals: a seven-nation comparison

Work goals	Belgium	UK	Germany	Israel	Japan	Netherlands	United States
Opportunity to learn	5.8[a]	5.55	4.97	5.83	6.26	5.38	6.16
	7[b]	8	9	5	7	9	5
Interpersonal relations	6.34	6.33	6.43	6.67	6.39	7.19	6.08
	5	4	4	2	6	3	7
Opportunity for promotion	4.49	4.27	4.48	5.29	3.33	3.31	5.08
	10	11	10	8	11	11	10
Convenient work hours	4.71	6.11	5.71	5.53	5.46	5.59	5.25
	9	5	6	7	8	8	9
Variety	5.96	5.62	5.71	4.89	5.05	6.86	6.10
	6	7	6	11	9	4	6
Interesting work	8.25	8.02	7.26	6.75	6.38	7.59	7.41
	1	1	3	1	2	2	1
Job security	6.80	7.12	7.57	5.22	6.71	5.68	6.30
	3	3	2	10	4	7	3
Match between the people and the work	5.77	5.63	6.09	5.61	7.83	6.17	6.19
	8	6	5	6	1	6	4
Pay	7.13	7.80	7.73	6.60	6.56	5.27	6.82
	2	2	1	3	5	5	2
Working conditions	4.19	4.87	4.39	5.28	4.18	5.03	4.84
	11	9	11	9	10	10	11
Autonomy	6.56	4.69	5.66	6.00	6.89	7.61	5.79
	4	10	8	4	3	1	8

[a] First row shows average rank on a scale of 1 to 10.

[b] Second row shows ranking of work goals within each country, with a rank of 1 being *most* important and 11 being *least* important.

Source: Adapted from Itzhak Harpaz, "The Importance of Work Goals: An International Perspective," *Journal of International Business Studies*, vol. 21, no. 1 (1990), p. 81.

CROSS-CULTURAL MANAGEMENT

Three key areas capture many of the factors covered by the above typologies and cultural stereotypes, where cultural differences can make a significant difference at the company-to-company and face-to-face levels. These are organization, leadership, and communication (see Figure 5.4).

Organization

Organization styles range from organic, informal, or people oriented to systematic or mechanistic, formal, or task oriented, in keeping with some common organizational dimensions described by sociologists throughout history (such as Max Weber and Emile Durkheim). Organizations that operate very much around personal relationships and social networks contrast those that are much more functional and logical. In fact different cultures and different firms display elements of both these characteristics, but the balance varies considerably and can create tensions when groups of people or firms from different ends of the spectrum interact or try to cooperate.

As an aid to predicting differences among individuals, groups, or firms, and understanding the significance of these variations, *relative* differences among countries, organizations, and groups of people are important, rather than any absolute scores. For example, family companies are characteristically directive, individual oriented but organic. Multinational firms are usually more autocratic and mechanistic. Consulting and professional services

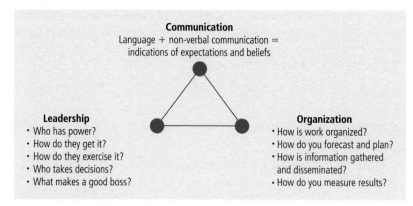

Figure 5.4 Management dimensions of culture

firms are often mechanistic and emphasize individual performance and rewards but may also be fairly team oriented. Entrepreneurial new ventures will usually be organic, unsystematic, and group oriented.

Leadership

Leadership styles range from individual oriented, directive, autocratic, top down, or authoritarian to group oriented, participative, democratic, bottom up, or egalitarian. Again, cultural groups and corporations often encompass both kinds of leadership but tend to reflect one dominant style.

Individual managers from cultures that score high on the power distance or assertiveness dimensions are likely to be viewed by those from other cultures as autocratic and directive but will tend to view others as indecisive and too compromising. They will not want to spend too much time discussing issues to achieve a consensus. If they also reflect an organic or informal (low uncertainty avoidance) culture, this will result in an instinctive or unsystematic decision-making and implementation style, and they might be viewed as an unpredictable autocrat. This contrasts the combination of high power distance and high uncertainty avoidance, which results in a more directive and mechanistic style. Such leaders prefer established formal routines and a command-and-control bureaucracy, while other managers are likely to see this as over-regulated and inflexible. The Pharmacia and Upjohn case demonstrates a range of these styles and the problems that result from the imposition of a new style of organization and leadership within a corporate merger.

Communication

Clearly, at the face-to-face level language differences can be the most prominent barrier to communication and therefore to cooperation and coordination. English speakers tend to have an advantage in many situations since English has emerged as the main language of business globally. However, this has led to complacency among some indigenous English speakers, notably the British and the North Americans. First, less effort is often made to learn other languages and their associated cultures, which normally limits a manager's understanding of foreign colleagues, workers, or customers. Second, the assumption is often made that once the language barrier is broken cultural differences are also removed, whereas these may remain, causing miscommunication and misinterpretation. As for much of this chapter on culture, preparation and awareness are the best starting points for minimizing differences that can create problems.

It is through efficient communication that two parties steer toward an understanding—a mutually agreed basis for doing business. The signs and signals on this route to an understanding are strongly influenced by culture. Different groups have different ways of displaying approval or of showing frustration in negotiations and different ideas of what constitutes a final agreement. The Japanese do not really have an equivalent word for the English "no" and indicate disapproval in a range of non-verbal ways. The Japanese word *hai* does mean "yes" but it often means "yes, I understand what you are saying" not "yes, I agree with what you are saying." Germans place a lot of emphasis on written communications and documented evidence rather than verbal interaction, compared to the Spanish and Italians to whom verbal interaction and agreement is recognized as binding in some contexts. The Americans prefer legal contracts and have armies of lawyers to make agreements highly specified. Other, more organic business cultures tend to work toward a relationship in which trust and understanding replace the need for legally binding contracts. Again, awareness through preparation and anticipation of differences is the best starting point for avoiding **culture clash**.

Culture clash
When two cultural groups (national or corporate) meet, interact, or work together and differences in their values, beliefs, rules of behavior, or styles of communication create misunderstandings, antagonism, or other problems

The corporate response

How have MNEs responded to the challenge of managing across cultural boundaries? What kinds of organization structures, HRM procedures, and corporate cultures have been developed to cope with the enormous differences among people and to unify this diversity toward a common purpose?

At a very general level good transnational firms develop an *awareness* and appreciation of cultural differences among their managers and employees. They also take steps to encourage *adaptation* of personal behavior or organizational practices, or products and services, to suit the changing mix of cultures within the firm, in subsidiaries and in key markets. Training programs, including a range of activities at the induction stage, when new recruits join a firm or existing personnel take up a role in a new country, are a standard way for firms to do these things. Job rotation, with a focus on developing international managers with personal experience in a variety of different countries, is also practiced by a number of firms. It is normally very difficult to assess such practices using any form of cost–benefit analysis. The costs are usually easily identifiable, but the benefits are very often intangible. For many experienced international companies, such as Shell or Nestlé, a long-term commitment to (and investment in) cultural awareness is simply accepted as a necessary part of being global.

Beyond awareness and adaptation, the best firms aim to *leverage* the diversity of cultures within their organizations and combine the best aspects of different ways of doing things. Corporate culture, a shared identity spanning culturally diverse groups of employees, provides a way to do this. Companies can usefully invest in their own socialization mechanisms, such as social events alongside regular meetings and conferences. Company magazines, intranets, and even in-house television channels for corporate communications can all support this process. These may not only improve cross-cultural awareness, but also promote shared values, symbols, and even language to help bind employees together.[19]

Here is a list of other useful strategies for managing cultural diversity distilled from a number of research studies:[20]

1 Recognize diversity. Identify and map the various national cultures and ethnic groups within the firm and use this to understand which elements of consistency and standardization can or should be promoted.

2 Build diversity issues into recruitment, HRM planning, strategy, location decisions, alliances, and partnerships. This helps avoid clashes and inefficiency and supports cultural awareness.

3 Identify where and to what degree local divisions should be encouraged or empowered to take the lead in expressing and managing diversity. Some degree of devolution of responsibility away from the center of the firm allows local divisions to identify aspects of diversity that are most important to them and their operations.

4 Encourage cross-border discussion and interaction as well as focused training. Include specific kinds/combinations of international experience for fast-track managers.

5 Aim for a cultural balance in particular areas of strategic and tactical decision making (such as brand changes for foreign markets). Ensure a (numerically) balanced pool of managers or appropriately diverse inputs into decision making.

6 Lead from the top. Aim to match the geographic diversity of the firm's businesses with a culturally mixed senior management group and board of directors (as in the case of Sony and Unilever).

✔ Active learning check

Review your answer to Active Learning Case question 3 and make any changes you like. Then compare your answer to the one below.

3 **What could senior managers have done before and after the merger to alleviate some of the problems that resulted from culture clash?**

A simple starting point would be to review the various frameworks (Hofstede, Trompenaars, and GLOBE, for example) to understand some generic differences between the national cultures involved in the merger and anticipate some of the likely problems. It would have also helped to examine the potential areas of organizational conflict with senior managers from each company and/or with managers with some experience of two or more of the countries and their ways of doing things. Some degree of cultural training or induction plus an investment in joint meetings and events to get to know each other could also have improved understanding and morale. However, the cost–benefit trade-off for these kinds of pre- and post-merger activity is difficult to precisely assess.

Multinational organization structures: imperialist or independent?

A key dilemma for international firms is the degree to which they promote or even impose a common, standardized corporate culture across the organization. Although this will create economies of scale and be more efficient in a number of respects, it will also stifle diversity and create clashes with local cultures and ways of doing things around the organization.

Firms respond to this dilemma in different ways, with different outcomes. At the simplest level we can map out a range of responses from what is termed *imperialist*, where a common culture is imposed wherever a company has a presence, to *federalist* or *independent* structures, where each national subsidiary bases its own culture on local norms and values. There are problems associated with either of these extremes and most firms try to steer a middle line, standardizing some elements across the whole organization to centralize and simplify some practices and unify employees, while allowing differentiation where necessary. This *transnational culture* allows for a compromise in work styles, values, and approaches, harnessing the strengths that lie in diversity.

Table 5.3 Organization types reflecting cultural predispositions

	Imperialist	Interventionist	Interactive	Independent
Organization	Ethnocentric	Ethnocentric	Geocentric	Polycentric
Structure	Steep hierarchy	Flat hierarchy	Network	Federation
Strategy	Dictated	Centrally decided	Jointly specified	Locally specified
Decision making	Centralized	Distributed	Shared	Devolved

Table 5.3 illustrates a range of organization types. In particular, it links elements of organization structure and design with cultural orientation, for example, in the relationship between headquarters and regional subsidiaries. It specifically extends the ethnocentric, **polycentric**, and **geocentric** typologies introduced by Perlmutter in the 1960s.[21]

Polycentric

Each subsidiary, division, or function reflects the culture of its host country; local managers' cultural predispositions and decision making dominate over those of home-country managers in a multinational firm

Geocentric

Neither home- nor host-country culture dominates decision making, human resource management, and overall corporate culture in a multinational firm

- *Ethnocentric* firms are where top management is dominated by home-country nationals, and procedures and management styles are transferred from the head office and imposed on regional subsidiaries in place of local ways of doing things.

- *Polycentric* firms tend to act like a federation of semi-autonomous organizations with financial controls or strict reporting structures holding them together. Subsidiaries are able to reflect the local cultural norms, and headquarters appreciates the need for different organization designs, procedural norms, rewards systems, etc., as long as profits flow to the center.

- *Geocentric* firms are seen as the ideal, collaborative, and meritocratic form of global organization. (Unilever is seen as an example based on the above statement.) An equal sharing of power and responsibility between headquarters and subsidiary; senior management promoted according to ability rather than nationality; subsidiaries that share worldwide objectives with managers focusing beyond national market interests.

In the geocentric organization the *benefits* of cultural diversity, such as knowledge of local customers and business practices, are harnessed for the good of the firm as a whole. The *costs* of diversity, such as language and communication problems, different values, and attitudes toward work, are minimized. Firms moving toward this more balanced, geocentric approach have to recognize diversity and its effects and identify which elements of consistency in regulations and values should be promoted, where and when. Local divisions must identify aspects of diversity that are most important to them and their operations and take the lead in expressing and managing these differences. Discussion, interaction, cross-divisional teamwork and job rotation, support, awareness, and understanding go alongside training programs, language courses, and cultural assimilation.

Unilever is an example of a firm that has closely examined the range of cultures it encompassed and made a deliberate attempt to use cultural differences as a strength rather than a weakness for fulfilling its strategic aims. As part of a high-profile internal campaign the company described itself as a *multi-local multinational*, and this was used to explicitly inform employees of its cultural tolerance. According to a statement from a Unilever board chairman, one of the firm's objectives was to "Unileverize our Indians and Indianize our Unileverians."[22]

Culture clash in cross-border M&A and joint ventures

The range of organization styles in Table 5.3 also reflects the range of ways multinational firms approach the management of joint ventures or of firms acquired through merger and acquisition (M&A). They can either impose their own style of management on these organizations or allow them the independence to reflect their own cultural norms and existing corporate cultures.[23]

Cultural differences often prove to be a significant post-merger barrier for managers looking to realize the synergies and added value of pooling the resources and capabilities of two companies from different parts of the world. The Pharmacia–Upjohn case above illustrates this clearly. Culture clash and its impact on the bottom line are often complex and difficult to predict. More often failure to anticipate culture clash results from the lack of awareness on the part of senior managers and deal makers driving the M&A strategy. Financial analyses that focus the due-diligence process of counting up assets and identifying cost-cutting benefits tend to miss any estimation of cultural and organizational synergy (or lack thereof). Anticipating such problems and preparing for the development of effective relationships between people from both sides of an M&A or an alliance is central to maximizing the rewards.

Daimler-Benz ran into these problems when it merged with Chrysler. A number of senior-level US managers either were asked to leave or left because they were unhappy about the style of management imposed by Daimler. Among these early leavers were members of the design team responsible for the PT Cruiser and other Chrysler successes of the late 1990s. Many went to arch-rival General Motors, which is not an unusual outcome. One study showed that on average 20 percent of a firm's top management will leave within one year of being acquired and 70 percent will go within five years.[24]

Cultural awareness and some degree of organizational adaptation can limit the number of key people who do leave following a cross-border M&A. Understanding how to predict and mitigate the negative effects of cultural differences should be on the agenda for all managers. Despite this, in some cases an ethnocentric, imperialist approach is precisely what is needed to drive a newly merged organization forward. When Carlos Ghosn led the partial takeover of Nissan by Renault, he imposed a very non-Japanese way of doing things on the firm. In terms of the firm within its broader economic and social context, breaking *keiretsu* ties and laying off employees were radical steps to take. Internally he instituted performance-related pay and promotion and cut through a range of traditional rituals around HRM, budget control, and decision making that were underpinned by the traditional Japanese culture of the company. These were the kinds of changes that needed to be made to reverse years of losses and indebtedness. It was also, arguably, impossible for the incumbent Japanese management to make such changes. (Chapter 18, on Japan, contains the full Nissan–Renault case.)

At the other end of the spectrum, reflecting again on Table 5.3, Tata Tea Limited, owner of 54 tea estates and the second-most popular tea brand in India, provides us with an example of a successful M&A which followed the "independent" approach vis-à-vis its newly acquired subsidiary. In March 2000 it bought one of the UK's top tea brands, Tetley Tea, some say on the basis of profits at Tata Consulting Services, the successful IT and software arm of the $9 billion Tata conglomerate. Coming more than 50 years after the end of 200 years of British colonial rule that had supported British ownership of tea estates in India, this shift of power is an appropriate symbol for the twenty-first century. But the takeover was barely noticed by the British public. In stark contrast to the imperialist approach of the British in India all those years ago, Tata took a hands-off approach, allowing the existing management, with its local knowledge and experience, to continue running Tetley. A federal structure with devolved decision making is supported by a polycentric organizational style.[25]

INTERNATIONAL BUSINESS STRATEGY IN ACTION

Danone and Parmalat—going international, staying local

The dairy industry, in the main, is a local industry. Most dairy products sold at local supermarkets come from processing plants within a 500 mile (800 km) radius. However, this does not mean that these firms are all small, local operations. On the contrary, there are a small number of very large MNEs in this industry that do business world-wide and target their dairy offerings to local demand. The best known of these is Nestlé, which began operations in 1904 when it opened evaporated milk factories in both Europe and the United States. Today the company is the largest dairy company in the world and has operations in 86 countries. There are a couple of other large competitors as well, although they do not compete on as broad a scale.

One of these is Danone, a French MNE with annual revenues of over €17 billion for 2010, which make it one of the world's 500 largest firms. The company's product line is not as broad as Nestlé, but it is just as big as the Swiss MNE in the dairy sector. Danone has operations in 120 countries and employs over 100,000 people. However, its primary base is Europe where it generates 56 percent from Europe, 14 percent from Asia and 30 percent from rest of the world.

Danone was originally a Spanish yogurt producer that merged with the French firm Gervais in 1967. Then in 1973 the company merged with BSN, a glass manufacturer, and adopted the packaging capability of the glass system to the food business. However, the glass business was dropped in the late 1970s, and since then Danone has focused on defining its place in the dairy industry and determining how it can better address the cultural demands of its local customers. With the decision to focus most heavily on Europe and to take advantage of the expanding EU, Danone set up centralized purchasing and research departments in order to obtain economies of scale in food distribution across that continent. At the same time the company looked to gain a greater presence in other markets, including North America, subsequently taking a 40 percent stake in Stonyfield Farm, an organic yogurt maker based in Londonderry, New Hampshire. Although Stonyfield continued to operate autonomously, the firm's strong customer relations program and its expertise in marketing fast-growing organic products provided Danone the opportunity to further increase its US market share to exploit the strengths of its new acquisition.

And to ensure that it continues to focus on its main business of dairy food, Danone has sold off its grocery business and withdrawn from brewing and packaging. Today the company's efforts are being directed most heavily toward

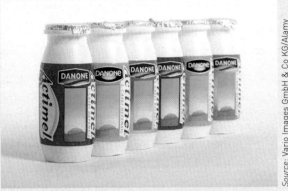

Source: Vario Images GmbH & Co KG/Alamy

the distribution of French-made dairy products. So in both Europe and its worldwide markets, Danone is working to answer the question: how can we develop and market French-made dairy products that meet the needs of the local market?

The other major global rival to Nestlé was the Italian MNE, Parmalat SpA. Like Danone, Parmalat marketed a wide variety of dairy products including milk, yogurt, desserts, butter, and cheese. Yet the company was best known for its development of ultra-high-temperature (UHT) pasteurized milk that allows milk to last up to six months without refrigeration. By specializing in the production and distribution of UHT milk across Europe, Parmalat was able to cut both production and distribution costs and to increase its profitability. At the same time, and unlike Danone, the company was more vigorous in its international expansion. In addition to moving into France and Germany in the 1970s, the company began expanding into North and South America soon thereafter. For the financial year ended December 31, 2010, Parmalat revenue was EUR4.3 billion. As a result, Parmalat earned 26 percent of its revenues in Europe, 47 percent in North, Central and South America, 17 percent from Australia and and 9 percent from Africa.

Like its two other competitors, Nestlé and Danone, Parmalat carefully targeted its products to the local market and sought to acquire local companies that had established markets. For example, Parmalat purchased Ault Dairies, one of Canada's largest operations, as well as Beatrice Foods, another major Canadian firm. Parmalat subsequently became that country's largest dairy firm. Parmalat also had its subsidiaries employ the company's food expertise to exploit their local markets. For example, drawing on its UHT technology, Parmalat's Australian subsidiary was able to export milk products throughout the Asian market, and the company's Argentinean subsidiary, which specialized in UHT milk products, was able to create export markets in Brazil and Venezuela. In addition, in catering to local tastes the company developed a wide variety of products such as a dessert called *dulce de leche*, which it exported to a large number of countries including the United States, the UK, Russia, Spain, Uruguay, and Venezuela.

Parmalat, however, tended to maintain locally known brands, rather than replacing them with its own. In the UK, for example, Parmalat owned the Loseley yogurt brand, which was well regarded as quite an upmarket brand. Similarly, consumers in Canada and Australia may be surprised to hear that their favorite brands, such as Beatrice or Pauls, were owned by Parmalat.

Danone and Parmalat are good examples of companies that sell products that are culturally influenced. In Danone's case, it has chosen to do so by staying primarily in Europe. Parmalat, on the other hand, has been much more active in the larger international arena. Both, however, have been successful because they have been able to blend their expertise with the needs of their specific markets.

In the case of Parmalat this success now appears to have come to an end. It reached sales of $9.4 billion in 2002 and managed acquired brands in 30 different countries. But in December 2003, with talk of fraud scandals in Italy, it was revealed that Parmalat had a reported $11 billion debt and $5 billion in cash missing. It has continued operating but it became a target for acquisition. but is much reduced in scale and global scope. It has sold off numerous national businesses and still faces ongoing litigation. In June 2011, the EC approved the take over of Parmalat by French rival Lactalis.

Websites: www.danone.com; www.parmalat.net; www.nestle.com.

Sources: Adrian Michaels, "Judge seeks Parmalat settlement," FT.com, December 6, 2006; "A Small Town's Big Cheeses," *The Economist*, May 29, 1997; Nikhil Deogun, "Danone Groupe Scoops Up 40% Stake in Stonyfield Farm," *Wall Street Journal*, October 4, 2001, p. B9; and Deborah Orr, "Who Gets Parmalat's Milk and Cookies?" *Forbes.com*, December 24, 2003, http://www.forbes.com/2003/12/24/cz_do_1223parmalat.html.; Paul Betts, "Danone could make Parmalat target of milk shake-up," *Financial Times*, May 27, 2009; http://www.ft.com/cms/; Danone, *Annual report*, 2010; Parmalat, *Annual report*, 2010; OneSource, Thomson Reuters, 2011.

 Active learning check

Review your answer to Active Learning Case question 4 and make any changes you like. Then compare your answer to the one below.

4 **Explain why one organization might want to impose some of its ways of doing things on another, such as an acquired firm or subsidiary.**

Standardizing ways of doing things across the overall organization, to a certain extent, can be more efficient. Differences can create difficulties in communication, teamwork, motivation, or coordination, and the impact on company performance can be significant. It is important to make the distinction between the values, beliefs, and norms, plus the associated work practices and management structures that stem from the dominant national culture (the imposition can then be described as ethnocentric) or from the corporate culture. In the latter case the firm will be aiming to derive the benefits of having a shared culture that bridges the national cultural differences across the overall organization.

Cultural differences between groups of people in the one firm, or between the employees of two firms engaged in a joint venture, are not necessarily a problem. However, when they do create difficulties in terms of communication, teamwork, motivation, or coordination, the impact on company performance can be significant, despite the fact that clear cause-and-effect relationships are often difficult to identify precisely. Rather than a single "best practice" for dealing with this, the examples above suggest that solutions are context specific.

CULTURE EMBODIED IN NATIONAL INSTITUTIONS

The second level at which we can analyze cultural differences and their effects is at the institutional level, where national cultural characteristics are *embodied* in institutions from government agencies and governance mechanisms to the education system, economic institutions, and business organizations.

Firms engaging in cross-border joint ventures or M&A need to take account of the national context in which the new partner or acquired firm is situated. Similarly, when marketing and selling products in a new national market, these broader differences matter. A country's distinctive political, legal, and institutional context partly reflects its dominant national culture. Education systems, labor laws, environmental regulations, capital markets, and the relationships between private-sector businesses and public-sector organizations will vary accordingly.[26]

Trompenaars uses his findings simply to divide various countries into subgroups reflecting shared characteristics stemming from common cultural influences (Figure 5.5).

- *Western pluralism* emphasizes individual competitiveness, commonly represented by separate ventures competing in price-defined markets for success. Survival of the fittest is the catchphrase, and companies tend to be run as meritocracies.

- *Command economies* are centrally planned hierarchies with less individualism and less individual incentive. Clearly, as global politics changes, countries are tending to move out of this category. For example, Poland is now an emerging capitalist country reflecting the characteristics of Western pluralism more than a command economy.

- *Organic ordering* refers to the family-centered hierarchies of Asia, southern Europe, and Latin America. Inter- and intra-organization interaction will be based around information sharing and collaborative competition.

- *Structured networks* reflect the more equal, structured relationships between companies and with public-sector organizations that exist in some countries.

France, with some comparisons with other Western economies and organizations, provides an example, giving a snapshot of some of the main characteristics that stem from the country's cultural distinctiveness.

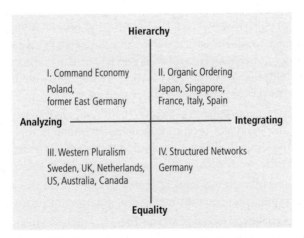

Figure 5.5 Shared characteristics stemming from common cultural influences

Source: Hampden-Turner, C. and Trompenaars, F. *The Seven Cultures of Capitalism: Value Systems for Creating Wealth in the United States, Britain, Japan, Germany, France, Sweden and the Netherlands* (New York: Doubleday, 1993).

France: cultural and social characteristics that create a national distinctiveness

National characteristics

- Central planning, national protectionism for domestic industry, and strong government intervention in the market (compared to other European economies) lie at the heart of the French system. Civil servants are intellectual and respected as in Japan (but not the UK) and well paid (unlike Japan).

- Communication tends to be vertical (up–across–down). Bypassing official channels is not common: uncertainty reduction tends to predominate.

- Hierarchy is important, bureaucracy respected. Clear hierarchy, divisionalization, and rules and regulations guide behavior. However, this exists alongside a respect for maverick gestures and individuals or groups that overcome the obstacles and beat the system.

- Government-to-business links are formal and informal, with the elitist groups from the *grande écoles* bridging public and private sectors at the senior level. Ascription dominates over achievement compared to the UK or the United States, again with parallels with Japan.

- Competition occurs at school age when success determines assignment to a particular *cadre* or *echelon* inside and outside the workplace (depending on the school attended as much as individual performance).

Mittelstand
About 3.4 million small and medium-sized firms defined as having less than €50 million turnover that make up the heart of the German economy

- France has a large number of family-owned and managed firms. It does not have the **Mittelstand** (small technical and engineering firms) that underpin the chemical and machine tool industries in Germany.

- Capital markets are competitive but are not as "short-termist" as in the UK and the United States, with an overwhelming emphasis on share values and dividends. France does not have the strong interfirm networks that exist in Germany and Japan (*keiretsu*), which include links between financial institutions (banks, institutional shareholders) and the companies they fund.

French organizations

Esprit de corps
The spirit of a group that makes the members want the group to succeed

- French companies also tend to be hierarchical, bureaucratic, and well structured, but there is a strong view of the company as a social entity (an **esprit de corps**) with an emphasis on obligation and loyalty rather than individual gain.

- Despite moves toward a more equal relationship, French managers continue to have a supervisory role over workers. German and Japanese managers, by comparison, tend to be more collegiate and cooperative across levels of the hierarchy, including mentoring arrangements between senior and junior managers.

- Hierarchical relationships are diffuse (in Trompenaars' terminology) rather than limited to the workplace (France ranks highest among European countries along this dimension). Companies have a responsibility toward the wider society, and managers, because of their professional status, have a role to play in society.

Gestion
The skill or practice of controlling, directing, or planning something, especially a commercial enterprise or activity

- Scientific management techniques, termed **gestion**, dominate, which parallels German zeal for quantification and measurement to guide performance improvement.

- There is a premium on technical and on-the-job training (similar to Germany and Japan). Marketing and accountancy skills are less valued than in the UK and the United States.

- A surprise to many observers is that one-fifth of the labor force is unionized. French labor law (*Code du Travail*) is comprehensive and enforced. Companies are relatively loyal to their employees compared to British or US firms, but there is not the strong social contract that exists in Japan.

KEY POINTS

1 Culture can be defined as "the sum total of the beliefs, rules, techniques, institutions, and artifacts that characterize human populations."

2 Cultural differences can have an important effect at the face-to-face or company-to-company levels and need to be taken into account in dealing with different groups of customers around the world.

3 Culture can be analyzed at two levels: the psychic distance between groups of people, and the differences in culture embodied in national institutions and socio-economic systems.

4 Hofstede, Trompenaars, and the GLOBE researchers have constructed useful frameworks for understanding broad differences between national cultures which underpin differences in the design of organizations and the behavior of managers and employees.

5 Differences in organization, leadership, and communication can be used to measure differences in groups and individuals and help managers anticipate when and why cultures may clash.

6 Company responses to the challenges of managing diversity range from the imperialist to the independent approaches.

7 Ethnocentric firms impose a common culture on all subsidiaries, polycentric firms allow subsidiaries to reflect local ways of doing things, and geocentric firms maintain a balance between center and subsidiary.

8 When in Japan, do not throw your *meishi*!

Key terms

- *grande école*
- culture
- socialization
- corporate culture
- ethnocentrism
- cultural convergence
- psychic distance
- power distance
- uncertainty avoidance
- individualism

- masculinity
- universalism
- particularism
- collectivism
- neutral
- emotional
- specific
- diffuse
- achievement oriented
- ascription oriented

- sequential
- synchronic
- humane orientation
- ethnocentric
- culture clash
- polycentric
- geocentric
- Mittelstand
- esprit de corps
- gestion

REVIEW AND DISCUSSION QUESTIONS

1 In your own words, what is meant by the term *culture*?

2 In what way do ethnocentrism and misconceptions about other cultures inhibit those doing business internationally?

3 Why is language so critical in understanding international culture? How can this problem be dealt with effectively?

4 Why are cultural differences an important factor when adapting products for new overseas markets?

5 Use Trompenaars' seven dimensions of culture to compare and contrast your own national stereotype to another.

6 Why are work attitudes of importance to MNEs? Cite and describe two examples.

7 What kinds of reward systems are likely to be effective in more individualistic and achievement-oriented cultures like the United States?

8 Explain how the GLOBE project has extended the dimensions of national culture beyond the work of Hofstede and Trompenaars.

9 In the Pharmacia–Upjohn merger how did employment practices and workplace regulations differ among the Americans, the Swedes, and the Italians, and what impact did these differences have on the operational efficiency of the merged company?

10 Show with examples how managers in multinational firms could improve their employees' awareness of the important differences among cultures.

11 What are the benefits and the problems for a polycentric MNE?

12 Why is an understanding of the institutional norms, regulations, and practices of other countries important for international firms? Give examples to illustrate your answer.

13 What does the French term *gestion* mean?

REAL CASE

Do not throw your *meishi*!

Some time ago the Competitiveness Division of the Department of Trade and Industry (DTI) in the British government commissioned research on British small and medium-sized enterprises (SMEs) that had managed to set up successful businesses in Japan, one of the toughest (though lucrative) global markets to break into for foreign firms (see Chapter 18). Numerous success stories from the study show how some firms managed to adapt to the differences in culture, society, and business practices that can act as barriers to foreign firms. But there are also numerous tales of the blunders that some managers made that undermined their efforts to establish themselves in Japan.

Meishi is Japanese for "business card," but has a deeper significance in Japan than elsewhere as a representation of the employee's allegiance to and respect for his or her company. The strong emphasis placed on loyalty and obligation between employees and their firms, lifetime employment based on a moral contract (rather than a price-based contract), and a manager's position as a member of a collective all have a strong influence on his (sometimes her) behavior when interacting with others. *Kaisha-in* literally means "company person," but it also denotes the individual as a representative of "our

company" in the sense of a shared group consciousness. The company name comes first, before the individual's name on the *meishi* and when making introductions. The exchange of *meishi* also establishes relative rank within the strict corporate and social hierarchy and therefore guides the correct behavior and even form of language used for interacting. Overall for the Japanese exchanging *meishi* is an important symbolic ritual.

A senior technology manager from Scotland on his first assignment to Japan was attempting to establish a strategic alliance with a local firm as a starting point for marketing and selling his firm's products locally. In his first meeting he faced six senior executives from the Japanese firm, ranged across a board room table traditionally in order of seniority. Almost the first act of the Scottish manager was to *throw* his newly printed *meishi* across the table to each of the Japanese executives in turn!

There is no way of knowing how significant this single act was in undermining this firm's market entry in Japan. It failed in its attempt to forge an alliance with this particular Japanese firm and with others, eventually leading it to abandon its attempts. What we can say for certain is that a small amount of preparation by this manager to build even a basic understanding of business etiquette in Japan would have improved this company's chances of building a successful business in Japan.

The overall study, including 30 detailed case studies of successful British firms in Japan, demonstrates very clearly that managers need to understand the cultural and social norms that underpin business practices in different countries if they are going to do business in those countries. The lesson applies to firms engaged in cross-border mergers and alliances, expanding into new markets through foreign direct investment activities, or even at the simple level, when hiring new recruits from overseas, outsourcing to foreign countries, or selling products and services abroad. Cultural awareness is critical to making business relationships work, at the face-to-face level or at the company-to-company level.

Sources: S. Collinson, *Small and Successful in Japan: A Study of 30 British Firms in the World's Most Competitive Market* (London: Avebury Press, Ashgate Publishing Group, 1996); C. Nakane, *Japanese Society* (Tokyo: Charles E. Tuttle, 1973).

1 Explain what kinds of broad cultural differences we are likely to find between the Japanese and the British.

2 What impression do you think the Scottish engineer made on the Japanese executives?

3 What steps could the Scottish firm have taken to avoid this kind of mistake?

4 How easy is it to do a simple cost–benefit analysis on investments into improved cultural awareness among employees?

REAL CASE

Sport can be local *and* global: Manchester United

For most sports there appears to be a natural connection with the cultures and communities of particular locations and even individual venues. Often history plays a strong role, even when sports are played internationally. St Andrews Links Course, Lord's Cricket Ground, and Wembley Stadium all have a particular symbolism to players and fans of golf, cricket, and football (soccer) in and beyond the UK.

These contrast with more "placeless" global sporting events, particularly the Olympic Games, which involve most nations of the World. Rather than creating a sense of common identity such events can reinforce national cultural identities through international competition.

Other sports remain local: Japanese Sumo Wrestling, Aussie Rules Football, and Hurling in Ireland, for example, where the connection with national culture, community and history are strongest. American football is played in several countries but only seriously in the United States. It is not only a huge commercial enterprise but, like basketball and baseball, strongly embedded in local communities through schools and colleges, as an important symbol of US cultural identity.

Some sports could be defined as regional, such as baseball which is predominantly based in North America, but also popular in Japan and played little elsewhere. A few sports are marked on a global basis, although not all parts of the triad are fully involved. Golf, tennis, and soccer

Source: Len Grant Photography/Alamy

have global television audiences and advertising revenues. Among these, soccer is recognized as the biggest, played by an estimated 240 million people with 1.5 million teams and 300,000 clubs worldwide. Many countries, from Brazil to Cameroon, Italy to South Korea, would claim the game as an important part of popular national culture. But soccer is not a major sport in North America, where it ranks well behind American football, baseball, hockey, and car racing.

Europe hosts some of the major soccer club brands, with 52 leagues and a combined income of over $13 billion.   ▶

Within this the English Premiership league is worth $3 billion. Perhaps the leading club in the Premiership is Manchester United. Not your average soccer club, but certainly one of the best illustrations in the sporting world of the evolving mix between local cultural heritage and international business.

Born in 1878, Manchester United long epitomized the connection between the local team and the local community. Its fan base was dominated for over a hundred years by local people, with Trafford Park and the Manchester Ship Canal, one of the world's first industrial centers, at its heart. The grassroots, blue-collar, working-man's passion and fierce loyalty remain at the cultural heart of the club today. Rather than symbolizing English culture it demonstrates the strength and persistence of the regional subculture of England's industrial north-west. This is reinforced by strong rivalry with other leading clubs such as Liverpool, Arsenal, and Chelsea. Now the brands of these teams are very multinational.

In the early 1990s, despite strong growth in international merchandising sales through Manchester United Merchandising, over 90 percent of revenues to the club still came from the domestic UK market. But a growing global fan club, the international spread of *Manchester United Magazine*, and the growing availability of televised games beyond the UK (particularly via Rupert Murdoch's global media networks) led to an export drive in the late 1990s and early 2000s. Countries with national teams but few big league teams, like Ireland, Scandinavia, and a range of Asian countries, where soccer is watched by millions on TV, became the club's best markets. By 2002 the global club membership had grown to 200 branches in 24 countries and with profits of over $25 million on turnover of over $100 million, it was considered the world's wealthiest club. MUTV, the club's own TV channel, and a large range of Internet sites fueled interest in the team. By 2003 Manchester United had attracted an estimated global fan base of 53 million.

Major sponsorship deals with Nike and later Vodafone (at $15 million per year) boosted its finances and its global brand footprint. The cross-border takeover by the US-based Glazer family in 2005 made the club even more international by any definition. Boosted by wins in the Premiership, the FA Cup and the European Champions League, the club's fan base had grown to an estimated 75 million worldwide. Significantly, 40 million of these were in Asia, compared to 23 million in Europe. Since then the actual number of global fans has been in dispute,

ranging from 'over 50 million' to 'over 300 million'. In 2006–2007 Manchester United generated revenues of $212 million, second only to Real Madrid's $236 million. Despite achieving revenues of $335 million in 2010, it has since been overtaken by Barcelona ($370 million) as well as Real Madrid (over $400 million). There are seven British clubs in the top twenty and four in the top ten, the others being Arsenal ($250 million), Chelsea ($230 million), and Liverpool ($205 million).

By this time the club had a range of regional sponsors, with PepsiCo, Anheuser-Busch InBev and Schick in North America, Ladbrokes in Europe, and Fuji Film and Air Asia in Asia. These were co-branding partners alongside global sponsors such as AIG, Vodafone, Nike, and Audi (and a few local partners like Dimension Data in South Africa). In some cases these have been the route to joint products and services, such as content services delivered by mobile phone to Manchester United fans through Vodafone. Pretax profits for the club are around $60 million and turnover, including merchandising and media partnerships, is over $250 million.

Despite the fact that, on average, over half the team comprises foreign players who play against the England national team in the World Cup, and despite the fact that the clubs fan base is (in terms of pure numbers) more Asian than English, the passion for the club is still as strong as ever around Manchester. Global sports teams like Manchester United are embedded in local folklore, passionately discussed in bars and clubs around the world, part of the cultural identity of communities, but at the same time they are multinational businesses with global brands and international strategies.

Sources: A. Rugman, *The End of Globalization* (London, Random House 2001); R. Bennet and J. Blythe, *International Marketing*, 3rd ed. (London: Kogan Page, 2002); W. Manzenreiter and J. Horne, *Football Goes East: Business, Culture and the People's Game in China, Japan and South Korea* (New York: Routledge, 2004); G. P. T. Finn and R. Giulianotti *Football Culture* (New York: Routledge, 2000); "Neo-imperialism at the point of a boot," *The Economist*, March 11, 2007, p. 56; http://www.manutd.com/; "Real top Man Utd in rich league," *BBC News*, February 14, 2008, http://news.bbc.co.uk/2/hi/business/7242490.stm; "Manchester United can break £100m barrier for commercial turnover," guardian.co.uk, Friday, May 13, 2011.

1 What makes a sport local, regional, or global?
2 What major drivers are responsible for the internationalization of Manchester United?
3 How important are Manchester United's strong local roots to its international success?

ENDNOTES

1 UNCTAD, *World Investment Report 2007*, United Nations, Geneva; http://www.unctad.org.

2 D. A. Ball and W. H. McCulloch, *International Business: The Challenge of Global Competition*, 7th ed. (Boston: Irwin McGraw-Hill, 1999), p. 258.

3 G. Hofstede, *Culture's Consequences: International Differences in Work Related Values* (Beverly Hills, CA: Sage, 1980).

4 K. Voigt, "Japanese Firms Want English Competency," *Wall Street Journal*, June 11, 2001, p. B7B.

5 M. Weber, *The Protestant Ethic and the Spirit of Capitalism*, 2nd Roxbury ed. (London: Roxbury, 1993).

6 K. A. Nordström and J.-E. Vahlne, "Is the Globe Shrinking? Psychic Distance and the Establishment of Swedish Sales Subsidiaries during the Last 100 Years," in M. Landeck, *International Trade – Regional and Global Issues* (Basingstoke: St. Martin's Press, 1994).

7 Many texts refer back to the work of Hall as one of the earliest authors in this field; E. T. Hall, "The Silent Language of International Business," *Harvard Business Review*, May–June, 1960, pp. 87–96.

8 G. Hofstede, "The Cultural Relativity of Organizational Practices and Theories," *Journal of International Business Studies*, Fall 1983, p. 92; G. Hofstede, *Cultures and Organizations; Software of the Mind: Intercultural Cooperation and Its Importance for Survival* (London: Harper Collins, 1983).

9 B. McSweeny, "Hofstede's model of national cultural differences and their consequences: a triumph of faith – a failure of analysis," *Human Relations*, vol. 55, no. 1 (2002), pp. 89–118, cites additional problems in a stronger critique of Hofstede's approach. Jowell, R. "How comparative is comparative research?" *American Behavioral Scientist*, vol. 42, no. 2 (1998), pp. 168–178, meanwhile suggests that Hofstede and other analysts' cross-national data are too concerned with "league tables of distributions showing merely 'gee whiz' national differences" rather than offering explanations and interpretations.

10 G. Hofstede, *Culture's Consequences: Comparing Values, Behaviors, Institutions and Organizations across Nations*, 2nd ed. (Thousand Oaks, CA: Sage, 2001); G. Hofstede et al., "What Goals Do Business Leaders Pursue? A Study in Fifteen Countries," *Journal of International Business Studies*, vol. 33, no. 4, (2002) pp. 785–804.

11 F. Trompenaars, *Riding the Waves of Culture: Understanding Cultural Diversity of Business* (London: Nicholas Brealey, 1993); F. Trompenaars and C. Hampden-Turner, *Riding the Waves of Culture: Understanding Cultural Diversity in Global Business* (London: Nicholas Brealey, 1998); Fons Trompenaars and Charles Hampden-Turner also run a consultancy specializing in advice and training on cross-cultural issues. The website for the firm has some useful resources for further research: http://www.7d-culture.nl/. A similar site, with a range of tools and techniques for understanding and managing differences in European cultures, is: http://www.johnmole.com.

12 C. C. Chen, "New Trends in Rewards Allocation Preferences: A Sino-US Comparison," *Academy of Management Journal*,

April 1995, p. 425; Y. Ono and B. Spindle, "Japan's Long Decline Makes One Thing Rise: Individualism," *Wall Street Journal*, December 29, 2000, pp. A1, 4.

13 M. Javidan and R. J. House, "Cultural Acumen for the Global Manager: Lessons from Project GLOBE," *Organizational Dynamics*, vol. 29, no. 4 (2001), pp. 289–305.

14 D. A. Light, "Cross-cultural Lessons in Leadership", *MIT Sloan Management Review*, Fall 2003, pp. 5–6.

15 This has involved 38 universities in annual surveys of around 7,000 organizations across Europe; C. J. Brewster and H. Harris (eds.), *International Human Resource Management: Contemporary Issues in Europe* (London: Routledge, 1999); C. Brewster, "HRM Practices in Multinational Enterprises," in M. J. Gannon and K. Newman, *Handbook of Cross-cultural Management* (Oxford: Blackwell, 2001); J. Van Ommeren et al., "The Cranet Survey 1999," UK Executive Report 1999, Cranfield Network on European Human Resource Management, Cranfield, Bedford.

16 P. C. Earley, "Leading cultural research in the future: a matter of paradigms and taste," *Journal of International Business Studies*, vol. 37, no. 6 (2006), pp. 922–931; G. Hofstede, "What did GLOBE really measure? Researchers' minds versus respondents' minds," *Journal of International Business Studies*, vol. 37, no. 6 (2006), pp. 882–896; P. B. Smith, "When elephants fight, the grass gets trampled: the GLOBE and Hofstede projects," *Journal of International Business Studies*, vol. 37, no. 6 (2006), pp. 915–921.

17 C. Nakane, *Japanese Society* (Tokyo: Charles E. Tuttle, 1973).

18 J. R. Lincoln, "Employee Work Attitudes and Management Practice in the United States and Japan: Evidence from a Large Comparative Survey," *California Management Review*, Fall 1989, p. 91.

19 There are many firms that offer advice and training services to help companies improve their cultural awareness and the ability of employees to adapt to cultural diversity. A useful starting point, however, is G. Wederspahn, "Do Your Employees Need Intercultural Services?" 2002, http://www.grovewell.com/pub-cultural-knowledge.html.

20 Financial Times, *Managing Global Business, Mastering Management Series* (London: Pearson, 2000); M. C. Gentile, *Managerial Excellence through Diversity: Text and Cases* (Chicago: Irwin, 1996); D. A. Thomas and R. J. Ely, "Making Differences Matter: A New Paradigm for Managing Diversity," *Harvard Business Review*, September–October 1996, pp. 79–90.

21 H. V. Perlmutter, "The Tortuous Evolution of the Multinational Enterprise," *Columbia Journal of World Business*, vol. 4, no. 1 (1969), pp. 9–18.

22 Perlmutter in Bartlett and Ghoshal, 2000, p. 77; C. A. Bartlett and S. Ghoshal, *Text, Cases and Readings in Cross-Border Management*, 3rd ed. (Boston: McGraw-Hill International Editions, 2000).

23 S. C. Collinson, "M&A as Imperialism?" in D. Angwin (ed.), *Images of M&A* (Oxford: Blackwell Publications, 2006).

24 J. P. Walsh, "Top Management Turnover Following Mergers and Acquisitions," *Strategic Management Journal*, vol. 9 (1988), pp. 173–183.

25 Collinson in Angwin, *Images of M&A*.
26 R. P. Appelbaum, W. Felstiner and V. Gessner (eds.), *Rules and Networks: The Legal Culture of Global Business Transactions* (Oxford: Hart Publishing, 2001); R. Whitley, *Competing Capitalisms: Institutions and Economies* (Cheltenham: Edward Elgar, 2002); R. Whitley, *The*

Multinational Firm: Organizing across Institutional and National Divides (Oxford: Oxford University Press, 2001); R. Whitley, *Divergent Capitalisms: The Social Structuring and Change of Business Systems* (Oxford: Oxford University Press, 1999).

ADDITIONAL BIBLIOGRAPHY

Ashkanasy, Neil M., Trevor-Roberts, Edwin and Earnshaw, Louise. "The Anglo Cluster: Legacy of the British Empire," *Journal of World Business*, vol. 37, no. 1 (2002).

Barr, Pamela S. and Glynn, Mary-Ann. "Cultural Variations in Strategic Issue Interpretation: Relating Cultural Uncertainty Avoidance to Controllability in Discriminating Threat and Opportunity," *Strategic Management Journal*, vol. 25, no. 1 (2004).

Berry, Heather, Guillén, Mauro F. and Nan Zhou, "An Institutional Approach to Cross-National Distance," *Journal of International Business Studies*, vol. 41, no. 9, 1460–1480 (2010).

Chevrier, Sylvie. "Cross-cultural Management in Multinational Project Groups," *Journal of World Business*, vol. 38, no. 2 (2003).

Collinson, Simon C. Small and Successful in Japan: A Study of 30 British Firms in the World's Most Competitive Market (London: Ashgate Press, 1996).

Collinson, Simon C. and Houlden, John. "Decision Making and Market Orientation in the Internationalization Process of Small and Medium-Sized Enterprises," *Management International Review*, vol. 45, no. 4 (Fourth Quarter 2005).

Collinson, Simon. C. and Pettigrew, Andrew. M., 'Comparative International Business Research Methods: Pitfalls and Practicalities,' Chapter 27 in Rugman (Ed.) *The Oxford Handbook of International Business*, 2nd ed. (Oxford: Oxford University Press, 2009).

Early, P. Christopher. "Leading Cultural Research in the Future: A Matter of Paradigms and Taste," *Journal of International Business Studies*, vol. 37, no. 6 (November 2006).

Fealy, Liz and Kompare, Dave. "When Worlds Collide: Culture Clash," *Journal of Business Strategy*, vol. 24, no. 4 (2003).

Friday, Ernest and Friday, Shawnta S. "Managing Diversity Using a Strategic Planned Change Approach," *Journal of Management Development*, vol. 22, no. 10 (2003).

Ghauri, Pervez. "Negotiating with the Chinese: A Sociocultural Analysis," *Journal of World Business*, vol. 36, no. 3 (Fall 2001).

Gratchev, Mikhail V. "Making the Most of Cultural Differences," *Harvard Business Review*, vol. 79, no. 9 (October 2001).

Hampden-Turner, Charles and Trompenaars, Fons. *The Seven Cultures of Capitalism: Value Systems for Creating Wealth in the United States, Britain, Japan, Germany, France, Sweden and the Netherlands* (New York: Doubleday, 1993).

Hofstede, Geert. "What Did GLOBE Really Measure? Researchers' Minds versus Respondents' Minds," *Journal of International Business Studies*, vol. 37, no. 6 (November 2006).

Holden, Nigel J. *Cross-Cultural Management: A Knowledge Management Perspective* (London: Prentice Hall, 2002).

Javidan, Mansour, House, Robert J., Dorfman, Peter J., Hanges, Paul J. and Sully de Luque, Mary. "Conceptualizing and Measuring Cultures and Their Consequences: A Comparative Review of GLOBE's and Hofstede's Approaches," *Journal of International Business Studies*, vol. 37, no. 6 (November 2006).

Kostova, Tatiana and Roth, Kendall. "Social Capital in Multinational Corporations & a Micro-Macro Model of its Formation," *Academy of Management Review*, vol. 28, no. 2 (2003).

Leung, Kwok, Bhagat, Rabi, Buchan, Nancy R., Erez, Miriam and Gibson, Cristina B. "Beyond National Culture and Culture-Centricism: A Reply to Gould and Grein (2009)," *Journal of International Business Studies*, vol. 42, no. 1, 177–181 (2011).

Li, Ji, Lam, Kevin and Qian, Gongming. "Does Culture Affect Behavior and Performance of Firms? The Case of Joint Ventures in China," *Journal of International Business Studies*, vol. 32, no. 1 (Spring 2001).

Maddox, Robert C. *Cross-cultural Problems in International Business: The Role of the Cultural Integration Function* (London: Quorum Books, 1993).

Marshall, R. Scott and Boush, David M. "Dynamic Decision Making: A Cross-cultural Comparison of US and Peruvian Export Managers," *Journal of International Business Studies*, vol. 32, no. 4 (2001).

McSweeny, Brendan. "Hofstede's Model of National Cultural Differences and Their Consequences: A Triumph of Faith—A Failure of Analysis," *Human Relations*, vol. 55, no. 1 (2002).

Mead, Richard and Andrews, Tim. G. *International Management: Cross-cultural Dimensions*, 4th ed. (Oxford: Wiley-Blackwell, 2009).

Mole, John. *Mind Your Manners: Managing Business Cultures in Europe* (London: Nicholas Brealey, 1996).

Morgan, Glenn, Kristensen, Per Hull and Whitley, Richard (eds.). *The Multinational Firm* (Oxford: Oxford University Press, 2001).

Muethel, Miriam, Hoegl, Martin and Parboteeah, K. Praveen. "National Business Ideology and Employees' Prosocial Values," *Journal of International Business Studies*, vol. 42, no. 2, 183–201 (2011).

Sam Han, Kang, Tony, Salter, Stephen and Yong Keun Yoo. "A Cross-Country Study on the Effects of National Culture on Earnings Management," *Journal of International Business Studies*, vol. 41, no. 1, 123–141 (2010).

Sarala, Riikka M. and Vaara, Eero. "Cultural Differences, Convergence, and Crossvergence as Explanations of Knowledge Transfer in International Acquisitions," *Journal of International Business Studies*, vol. 41, no. 8, 1365–1390 (2010).

Schneider, Susan C. and Barsoux, Jean-Louis. *Managing Across Cultures*, 2nd ed. (London: Prentice Hall, 2003).

Shenkar, Oded. "Cultural Distance Revisited: Towards a More Rigorous Conceptualisation and Measurement of Cultural Differences," *Journal of International Business Studies*, vol. 32, no. 3 (2001).

Simon, David G. and Lane, Peter J. "A Model of Cultural Differences and International Alliance Performance," *Journal of International Business Studies*, vol. 35, no. 4 (2004).

Sivakumar, K. and Nakata, Cheryl. "The Stampede Toward Hofstede's Framework: Avoiding the Sample Design Pit in Cross-cultural Research," *Journal of International Business Studies*, vol. 32, no. 3 (Fall 2001).

Smith, Peter B., Peterson Dr. Mark F. and Thomas, Dr. David C. *The Handbook of Cross-Cultural Management Research*. (California: Sage 2008).

Triandis, Harry C. "The Many Dimensions of Culture," *Academy of Management Executive*, vol. 18, no. 1 (2004).

Tung, Rosalie L and Verbeke, Alain. "Beyond Hofstede and GLOBE: Improving the Quality of Cross-Cultural Research," *Journal of International Business Studies*, vol. 11 (2010).

Venaik, Sunil and Brewer, Paul, "Avoiding uncertainty in Hofstede and GLOBE," *Journal of International Business Studies*, vol. 41, no. 8, 1294–1315 (2010).

Von Glinow, Mary-Ann, Shapiro, Debra L. and Brett, Jeanne M. "Can We Talk, and Should We? Managing Emotional Conflict in Multicultural Teams," *Academy of Management Review*, vol. 29, no. 4 (2004).

West, Joel and Graham, John L. "A Linguistic-Based Measure of Cultural Distance and Its Relationship to Managerial Values," *Management International Review*, vol. 44, no. 3 (Third Quarter 2004).

Chapter 6

INTERNATIONAL TRADE

Contents

Objectives of the chapter

An understanding of international trade is critical to the study of international business. The primary objective of this chapter is to examine key economic theories that help to explain why nations trade. In addition, the role and importance of a country's barriers to trade will be studied and discussion will focus on why most nations use trade barriers despite vigorous international efforts to eliminate them.

The specific objectives of this chapter are to:

1 *Define* the term *international trade* and discuss the role of mercantilism in modern international trade.

2 *Contrast* the theories of absolute advantage and comparative advantage.

3 *Relate* the importance of international product life cycle theory to the study of international economics.

4 *Explain* some of the most commonly used barriers to trade and other economic developments that affect international economics.

5 *Discuss* some of the reasons for the tensions between the theory of free trade and the widespread practice of national trade barriers.

ACTIVE LEARNING CASE

Trade of the triad and China

Over the last three decades, new entrants into the world export market have transformed the economies of industrialized countries and the types of products they export. At the beginning of this time period, the Japanese were a growing force in the international arena. They dominated the 1980s and were able to make substantial gains at the expense of such dominant exporters as the UK and the United States. Indeed, between 1980 and 1990, both these countries lost worldwide market share to the Japanese in such industries as automotive products, office machines, telecom equipment, machinery and transport equipment, chemicals, and textiles.

In the late 1980s, however, the world economy began to see major changes. Asia, South Korea, Singapore, Taiwan, Thailand, and China were growing much more competitive on the world stage. South Korea, for example, started expanding its automotive industry, while China's market share of office and telecom equipment rose from zero to about 1 percent of the market in 1990 to 4.5 percent by 2000; by 2009, it was 26 percent. Meanwhile, thanks to NAFTA—which decreased barriers to trade within North America—Mexico and Canada were increasing their market share of automotive products, machinery, and transport equipment. Such competition spurred the United States to radically restructure many of its industries; invest billions in new technology, plant, equipment, and information technology; and introduce improvement programs, such as Six Sigma, that allowed it to match the quality offerings of worldwide competitors. As a result, the US share of the world's export market in areas such as automotive products, machinery and transport equipment, chemicals, and textiles somewhat recovered. The big loser was Japan, which saw its export market share decline in most of these areas.

Today the biggest challenge to the export markets of industrialized countries is China. Between 2000 and 2009, China's share of the world's merchandise exports more than doubled—from 4.7 percent to 9.9 percent (see Table 1). This increase comes at the expense of exports by triad countries over the same period. By 2009, the core triad's share of world exports was 54.7 percent, with the EU accounting for over two-third of this (see Table 2). The United States and Japan were the hardest hit.

China's expansion is particularly evident in the clothing and textile markets. In 2009, the country holds 34 percent and 28.3 percent of each market, respectively (see the first table). More impressive, however, are China's improvements in exports of office and telecom equipment and of

Table 1 China's share of the world's market for exports of manufactures

Industry	2000	2009
All manufactures	4.7	9.9
Iron and steel	3.1	7.3
Chemicals	2.1	4.3
Machinery and transport equipment	3.1	n.a
Automotive products	0.3	n.a
Office and telecom equipment	4.5	26.2
Textiles	10.5	28.3
Clothing	18.3	34.0

Note: Manufactures are a subcategory within merchandise exports. These data include intra-regional EU exports.

Source: Authors' calculations based on data from World Trade Organization, *Statistics Database*, International Trade Statistics, 2010, Tables 1.6, 2.36, 2.38, 2.40, 2.62, 2.67.

Table 2 The triad's share of world merchandise exports

	1993	2003	2009	1993–2009
US	12.6	9.8	8.7	−31%
EU	45.4	45.9	41.2	−9%
Japan	9.9	6.4	4.8	−52%
Triad	67.9	62.1	54.7	−19%
Non-triad	32.1	37.9	45.3	41%

Note: Data are calculated using world trade minus intra-regional EU trade.

Source: Authors' calculations based on data from World Trade Organization, *Statistics Database*, International Trade Statistics, 2010, Table 1.6 – World merchandise exports by region and selected economy, 1948, 1953, 1963, 1973, 1983, 1993, 2003 and 2009.

machinery and transport equipment, both of which require significant technology know-how.

As can been seen in the tables, China's rise as a world exporter has decreased the share of the triad's share of world exports in manufactures. In response to China's increased competitiveness, triad countries are trying to balance the need to integrate this new player into the international business arena with the negative short-term effects to their economies.

Japan's attitude toward China took a turn from protectionism when it realized that this new trade partner could help it overcome some of the problems associated with its rigid economic system. Large amounts of inexpensive, low-skilled labor now allowed Japanese companies to outsource some of their manufacturing operations overseas, within its

▶

own region, while more skilled Japanese workers took care of the more specialized areas of the production process. In addition, China eased Japan's long dependence on the US economy for its industrial and consumer products.

While US and EU companies have also moved operations to Japan, the governments are reacting more aggressively to pressure from special interest groups that see China as a threat to US businesses and jobs. The United States, which runs a large trade deficit with China, has argued that the yuan is undervalued, creating an unfair advantage for Chinese producers. The United States is threatening to impose tariffs on Chinese products. A bill is set to go before the Senate that would call for retaliatory trade sanctions against countries such as China that intervene to weaken their currencies in order to boost export at the expense of its trading partners. China relaxed the yuan's fixed exchange rate against the dollar in June 2010, but since then it was allowed to appreciate by less than 3 percent. By November 2010, the exports to the United States were up to 29.5 percent compared to a year earlier. China export increased amid inflation fears. China's November 2010 inflation figure was set to hit a new 28-month high of 5.1 percent versus October's inflation figure of 4.4 percent and above the official inflation target of 3 percent.

Japan has joined this wagon and is pressuring China to move to a more flexible exchange rate. Yet, critics argue that no one truly knows the market value of the yuan and that a fall on its price after deregulation could only worsen matters. For its part, the EU has reacted by asking China to curtail exports of textiles into the union after exports of clothing increased by 534 percent in less than six months in 2005. By November 2010, the overall figure was a 33 percent rise in exports to Europe.

An increase in exports by any nation does not necessarily mean that other countries are losing out. In terms of trade alone, any new entrant to the world exports market, other things being equal, will decrease the share of world exports of all other countries. This, however, does not mean that other countries are exporting less. They could be exporting, in value terms, a significantly higher amount because a new trade partner also means a new market to which they can export. More specifically, however, trade creates losers and winners. Triad economies are being forced to specialize. While those with most to lose pressure their governments to impose trade barriers, those with most to win—high-skilled industries—are expanding to serve the Chinese market. Further, customers' real incomes increase when they can purchase the same products at lower prices.

The data on this case help to reinforce an important principle of international trade: specialize in those products in which you can achieve an advantage. Over time, of course, competitors may erode this advantage by developing even better offerings for the export market. In this case, it is important either to counterattack by improving your own offering to win back this market share, or to find other markets where the country's skills and resources will allow it to compete effectively. In light of the emergence of more and more industrial countries in Asia, the growing competitiveness of Latin America, and the emerging industries of Eastern Europe and the former Soviet Union, triad managers have their work cut out for them.

Sources: "Chinese Urged to Curb EU Exports," BBC.co.uk, May 12, 2005; "China's Yuan under Fresh Pressure," BBC.co.uk, May 6, 2005; "The HaloEffect," *The Economist*, September 30, 2004; "Chinese Export Jumps Unexpectedly Amid Inflation Fears," *BBC News*, news.bbc.co.uk, December 10, 2010; "US Ups China Pressure on Yuan," *BBC News*, news.bbc.co.uk, October 9, 2010; "China Stands Firm over Yuan Move," *BBC News*, news.bbc.ac.uk, October 8, 2010.

1 How does the process of the UK's finding market niches help illustrate the theory of comparative advantage?

2 How does an EU manager's desire to buy domestic products illustrate the importance of consumer taste in international markets?

3 In what way could the EU use trade barriers to protect its markets from foreign competitors? Who can be affected by these trade barriers?

INTRODUCTION

International trade
The branch of economics concerned with the exchange of goods and services with foreign countries

International trade is the branch of economics concerned with the exchange of goods and services with foreign countries. Although this is a complex subject, we will focus on two particular areas: international trade theory and barriers to trade.

Some international economic problems cannot be solved in the short run. Consider the US balance of trade deficit. US trade with Japan and China heavily affects its overall imbalance. Moreover, this trade deficit will not be reduced by political measures alone; it will require long-run economic measures that reduce imports and increase exports. Other nations are also learning this lesson—and not just those that have negative balances. After all, most countries seem to want a continual favorable trade balance, although this is impossible, since a nation with a deficit must be matched by a nation with a surplus.[1]

International trade has become an even more important topic now that so many countries have begun to move from state-run to market-driven economies.[2] Inflation and, in many cases, unemployment are severe problems for these nations. Fortunately, enhanced international trade is one way to address a weak macro economy.[3] International commitment to a free market will bring prosperity to the world economic system. Since the time of Adam Smith in 1790, economists have shown that free trade is efficient and leads to maximum economic welfare. In this chapter we will discuss the economic rationale for free trade and the political impediments to it.

INTERNATIONAL TRADE THEORY

To understand the topic of international trade, we must be able to answer the question: why do nations trade? One of the earliest and simplest answers to this question was provided by mercantilism, a theory that was quite popular in the eighteenth century, when gold was the only world currency. **Mercantilism** holds that a government can improve the economic well-being of the country by encouraging exports and stifling imports. The result is a positive balance of trade that leads to wealth (gold) flowing into the country.

Neo-mercantilism, like mercantilism, seeks to produce a positive balance of trade but without the reliance on precious metals. Most international trade experts believe that mercantilism is a simplistic and erroneous theory, although it has had followers. For example, under President Mitterrand in the late 1970s and early 1980s, France sought to revitalize its industrial base by nationalizing key industries and banks and subsidizing exports over imports. By the mid-1980s the French government realized that the strategy was not working and began denationalizing many of its holdings.[4] More recently, China has proven to be a strong adherent of mercantilism, as reflected by the fact that it tries to have a positive balance with all of its trading partners.

A more useful explanation of why nations trade is provided by trade theories that focus on specialization of effort. The theories of absolute and comparative advantage are good examples.

Theory of absolute advantage

The **theory of absolute advantage** holds that nations can increase their economic well-being by specializing in the production of goods they can produce more efficiently than anyone else. A simple example can illustrate this point. Assume that two nations, North and South, are both able to produce two goods, cloth and grain. Assume further that labor is the only scarce factor of production and thus the only cost.

Labor cost (hours) of production for one unit

	Cloth	Grain
North	10	20
South	20	10

Thus lower labor-hours per unit of production means lower production costs and higher productivity per labor-hour. As seen by the data in the table, North has an absolute advantage in the production of cloth since the cost requires only 10 labor-hours, compared to

Mercantilism
A trade theory which holds that a government can improve the economic well-being of the country by encouraging exports and stifling imports to accumulate wealth in the form of precious metals

Neo-mercantilism
A trade theory which holds that a government can improve the economic well-being of the country by encouraging exports and stifling imports

Theory of absolute advantage
A trade theory which holds that nations can increase their economic well-being by specializing in goods that they can produce more efficiently than anyone else

20 labor-hours in South. Similarly, South has an absolute advantage in the production of grain, which it produces at a cost of 10 labor-hours, compared to 20 labor-hours in North.

Both countries gain by trade. If they specialize and exchange cloth for grain at a relative price of 1:1, each country can employ its resources to produce a greater amount of goods. North can import one unit of grain in exchange for one unit of cloth, thereby paying only 10 labor-hours for one unit of grain. If North had produced the grain itself, it would have used 20 labor-hours per unit, so North gains 10 labor-hours from the trade. In the same way, South gains from trade when it imports one unit of cloth in exchange for one unit of grain. The effective cost to South for one unit of cloth is only the 10 labor-hours required to make its one unit of grain.

The theory of absolute advantage, as originally formulated, does not predict the exchange ratio between cloth and grain once trade is opened, nor does it resolve the division of the gains from trade between the two countries. Our example assumed an international price ratio of 1:1, but this ratio (P_{cloth} to P_{grain}) could lie between 2:1 (the pretrade price ratio in South) and 1:2 (the pretrade price ratio in North). To determine the relative price ratio under trade, we would have to know the total resources of each country (total labor-hours available per year), and the demand of each for both cloth and grain. In this way we could determine their relative gains from trade for each country.

Even this simple model of absolute advantage has several important implications for international trade. First, if a country has an absolute advantage in producing a product, it has the potential to gain from trade. Second, the more a country is able to specialize in the good it produces most efficiently, the greater its potential gains in national well-being. Third, the competitive market does not evenly distribute the gains from trade *within* one country. This last implication is illustrated by the following example.

Prior to trade, the grain farmers in North work 20 hours to produce one unit of grain that could be exchanged for two units of cloth. After trade, those who remain can exchange one unit of grain for only one unit of cloth. Thus, the remaining grain producers are worse off under trade. Cloth producers in North, however, work 10 hours, produce one unit of cloth, and exchange it for one unit of grain, whereas previously they received only half a unit of grain. They are better off. If grain producers in North switch to cloth production, then 20 hours of labor results in the production of two units of cloth, which they can exchange for two units of grain. Thus, international trade helps them. As long as North does not specialize completely in cloth, there will be gainers (cloth producers and grain producers who switched to cloth) and losers (those who continue as grain producers).

Because the nation as a whole benefits from trade, the gainers can compensate the losers and there will still be a surplus to be distributed in some way. If such compensation does not take place, however, the losers (continuing grain producers) would have an incentive to try to prevent the country from opening itself up to trade. Historically, this problem has continued to fuel opposition to a free trade policy that reduces barriers to trade. A good example is Japanese farmers who stand to lose their livelihood if the government opens up Japan to lower-priced agricultural imports.

A more complicated picture of the determinants and effects of trade emerges when one of the trading partners has an absolute advantage in the production of both goods. However, trade under these conditions still brings gains, as David Ricardo first demonstrated in his theory of comparative advantage.

Theory of comparative advantage
A trade theory which holds that nations should produce those goods for which they have the greatest relative advantage

Theory of comparative advantage

The **theory of comparative** advantage holds that nations should produce those goods for which they have the greatest relative advantage. In terms of the previous example of two countries, North and South, and two commodities, cloth and grain, Ricardo's model can be illustrated as follows:

Labor cost (hours) of production for one unit

	Cloth	Grain
North	50	100
South	200	200

In this example North has an absolute advantage in the production of *both* cloth and grain, so it would appear at first sight that trade would be unprofitable, or at least that incentives for exchange no longer exist. Yet trade is still advantageous to both nations, provided their *relative* costs of production differ.

Before trade, one unit of cloth in North costs (50/100) hours of grain, so one unit of cloth can be exchanged for half a unit of grain. The price of cloth is half the price of grain. In South, one unit of cloth costs (200/200) hours of grain, or one grain unit. The price of cloth equals the price of grain. If North can import more than half a unit of grain for one unit of cloth, it will gain from trade. Similarly, if South can import one unit of cloth for less than one unit of grain, it will also gain from trade. These relative price ratios set the boundaries for trade. Trade is profitable between price ratios (price of cloth to price of grain) of 0.5 and 1. For example, at an international price ratio of two-thirds, North gains. It can import one unit of grain in return for exporting one and a half units of cloth. Because it costs only 50 hours of labor to produce the unit of cloth, its effective cost under trade for one unit of imported grain is 75 labor-hours. Under pretrade conditions it costs North 100 labor-hours to produce one unit of grain. Similarly, South gains from trade by importing one unit of cloth in exchange for two-thirds of a unit of grain. Prior to trade, South spent 200 labor-hours producing the one unit of cloth. Through trade, its effective cost for one unit of cloth is $\frac{2}{3} \times 200$, or 133 labor-hours—cheaper than the domestic production cost of 200 labor-hours. Assuming free trade between the two nations, North will tend to specialize in the production of cloth, and South will tend to specialize in the production of grain.

This example illustrates a general principle. There are gains from trade whenever the relative price ratios of two goods differ under international exchange from what they would be under conditions of no trade. Such domestic conditions are often referred to as *autarky*, which is a government policy of being totally self-sufficient. Research shows that free trade is superior to autarky. In particular, free trade provides greater economic output and consumption to the trade partners jointly than they can achieve by working alone. By specializing in the production of certain goods, exporting those products for which they have a comparative advantage, and importing those for which they have a comparative disadvantage, the countries end up being better off.

The general conclusions of the theory of comparative advantage are the same as those for the theory of absolute advantage. In addition, the theory of comparative advantage demonstrates that countries jointly benefit from free trade (under the assumptions of the model) even if one has an absolute advantage in the production of *both* goods. Total world efficiency and consumption increase.

As with the theory of absolute advantage discussed previously, Ricardo's theory of comparative advantage does not answer the question of the distribution of gains between the two countries, nor the distribution of gains and losses between grain producers and cloth producers within each country. No country will lose under free trade, but in theory at least all the gains could accrue to one country and to only one group within that country.

Active learning check

Review your answer to Active Learning Case question 1 and make any changes you like. Then compare your answer to the one below.

1 **How does the process of the UK's finding market niches help illustrate the theory of comparative advantage?**

The theory of comparative advantage holds that nations should produce those goods for which they have the greatest relative advantage. The finding of market niches helps illustrate this theory because it shows that the UK is picking those areas in which it has a relative advantage over the competition and exploiting its strengths in those markets. Given the rise of competitiveness in all areas of worldwide exports, few nations have been able to maintain their market share for very long. So the UK will have to continue to use this approach in order to remain one of the world's major export nations.

Factor endowment theory
A trade theory which holds that nations will produce and export products that use large amounts of production factors that they have in abundance and will import products requiring a large amount of production factors that they lack

Heckscher–Ohlin theory
A trade theory that extends the concept of comparative advantage by bringing into consideration the endowment and cost of factors of production and helps to explain why nations with relatively large labor forces will concentrate on producing labor-intensive goods, whereas countries with relatively more capital than labor will specialize in capital-intensive goods

Leontief paradox
A finding by Wassily Leontief, a Nobel Prize-winning economist, which shows that the United States, surprisingly, exports relatively more labor-intensive goods and imports capital-intensive goods

International product life cycle (IPLC) theory
A theory of the stages of production of a product with new "know-how": it is first produced by the parent firm, then by its foreign subsidiaries, and finally anywhere in the world where costs are the lowest; it helps explain why a product that begins as a nation's export often ends up as an import

Factor endowment theory

In recent years more sophisticated theories have emerged that help clarify and extend our knowledge of international trade. The **factor endowment theory** holds that countries will produce and export products that use large amounts of production factors that they have in abundance, and they will import products requiring large amounts of production factors that they lack. This theory is also known as the **Heckscher–Ohlin theory** (after the two economists who first developed it). The theory is useful in extending the concept of comparative advantage by bringing into consideration the endowment and cost of production factors. The theory also helps explain why nations with relatively large labor forces, such as China, will concentrate on producing labor-intensive goods, whereas countries like the Netherlands, which has relatively more capital than labor, will specialize in capital-intensive goods.

However, the factor endowment theory has some weaknesses. One weakness is that some countries have minimum wage laws that result in high prices for relatively abundant labor. As a result, they may find it less expensive to import certain goods than to produce them internally. Another weakness is that countries like the United States export relatively more labor-intensive goods and import capital-intensive goods, an outcome that appears surprising. This result, discovered by Wassily Leontief, a Nobel Prize-winning economist, is known as the **Leontief paradox** and has been explained in terms of the quality of labor input rather than just labor-hours of work. The United States produces and exports technology-intensive products that require highly educated labor. The Leontief paradox not only shows one of the problems with factor endowment theory, but also helps us understand why no single theory can explain the role of economic factors in trade theory. Simply put, the subject is too complex to be explained with just one or two theories.

International product life cycle theory

Another theory that provides insights into international theory is Vernon's **international product life cycle (IPLC) theory**, which addresses the various stages of a good's life cycle. In particular, the theory helps explain why a product that begins as a nation's export often ends up becoming an import. The theory also focuses on market expansion and technological innovation, concepts that are relatively de-emphasized in comparative advantage theory.

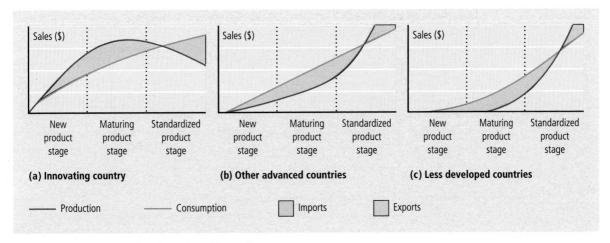

Figure 6.1 The international product life cycle

Source: Raymond Vernon and Louis T. Wells, Jr., *The Manager in the International Economy* (Englewood Cliffs, NJ: Prentice Hall, 1991), p. 85.

IPLC theory has two important tenets: (1) technology is a critical factor in creating and developing new products; and (2) market size and structure are important in determining trade patterns.

Product stages

The IPLC has three stages: new product, maturing product, and standardized product. A new product is one that is innovative or unique in some way (see Figure 6.1a). Initially, consumption is in the home country, price is inelastic, profits are high, and the company seeks to sell to those willing to pay a premium price. As production increases and outruns local consumption, exporting begins.

As the product enters the mature phase of its life cycle (see Figure 6.1b), an increasing percentage of sales is achieved through exporting. At the same time, competitors in other advanced countries will be working to develop substitute products so they can replace the initial good with one of their own. The introduction of these substitutes and the softening of demand for the original product will eventually result in the firm that developed the product now switching its strategy from production to market protection. Attention will also be focused on tapping markets in less developed countries.

As the product enters the standardized product stage (see Figure 6.1c), the technology becomes widely diffused and available. Production tends to shift to low-cost locations, including less developed countries and offshore locations. In many cases the product will end up being viewed as a generic, and price will be the sole determinant of demand.

Personal computers and the IPLC

In recent years a number of products have moved through the IPLC and are now in the standardized product stage. Personal computers (PCs) are a good example, despite their wide variety and the fact that some versions are in the new product and maturing product phases. For example, the early version of PCs that reached the market in the 1984 to 1991 period were in the standardized product stage by 1995 and sold primarily on the basis of price. Machines that entered the market in the 1996 to 1998 period were in the maturing stage by 1999. PCs with increased memory capability that were in the new product stage in 1999 quickly moved toward maturity, and by 2002 they were being replaced by even better machines with faster processors and more multimedia capabilities. Today, diskettes are standardized and rarely used while standard components include CD writers, DVD ROMs,

DSL and wireless Internet connectors, USB ports, advanced graphics and sound, flat LCD monitors, digital photography capabilities, etc.

Desktop computers have been replaced by laptop models that are lighter, faster, more sophisticated, and less expensive than their predecessors. In turn, these machines are being replaced by notebooks with advanced Pentium chips, long-term battery capability, and storage capable of holding billions of bytes complete with wireless equipment and serve as a complete communications center from which the international executive can communicate anywhere in the world. These machines will first be manufactured locally and then in foreign markets. This is largely because IBM (the inventor of the PC) computers became a commodity, and IBM's PC division was sold to the Chinese firm Lenovo in 2005. Lenovo has the benefit of low labor costs and it is better able to manufacture the laptops of today. Thus, computers will continue to move through an IPLC.

The IPLC theory is useful in helping to explain how new technologically innovative products fit into the world trade picture. However, because new innovative products are sometimes rapidly improved, it is important to remember that one or two versions of them may be in the standardized product stage while other versions are in the maturing stage and still others are in the new product phase.

Other important considerations

Many factors beyond those we have considered greatly influence international trade theory.[5] One is government regulation. Countries often limit or restrict trade with other countries for political reasons. For example, despite the benefits of international trade, the EU does not always see eye to eye with the United States on regulatory matters. As a result there are different government regulations affecting business in Europe, than in North America. For example, EU competition policy differs from US antitrust policy, see the box **International Business Strategy in Action: Microsoft shows the world is not flat**. Other important factors include monetary currency valuation and consumer tastes.

Monetary currency valuation

Monetary exchange rate
The price of one currency stated in terms of another currency

When examining why one country trades with another, we need to consider the **monetary exchange rate**, which is the price of one currency stated in terms of another currency. For example, from 1995 to 1998 the value of the Japanese yen declined significantly over the value of the US dollar. As a result, many Japanese businesses found their products becoming much more competitive in the US market. Thereafter, the Japanese government announced that because the yen was again getting too strong, it wanted to weaken its value, thus ensuring that Japanese businesses could maintain their international competitiveness. Another reason why monetary currency valuation is important is because a foreign firm doing business will report its revenues and profits in home-country currency. So if a British firm sold $10 million of machinery in Canada and the value of the Canadian dollar declined against the British pound, the UK company would report less revenue (in terms of British pounds) than if the Canadian dollar had remained stable or, better yet, increased in value against the pound. In mid-2005, the euro became so strong compared to the dollar that Volkswagen reported a 63 percent decline in pre tax profits.[6] In the next chapter we will discuss exchange rates in more detail.

Consumer tastes

International trade is not based solely on price; some people will pay more for a product even though they can buy something similar for less money. This willingness to pay more may be based on prestige, perceived quality, or a host of other physical and psychological reasons. Personal tastes dictate consumer decisions.

INTERNATIONAL BUSINESS STRATEGY IN ACTION

Microsoft shows the world is not flat

The dispute between Microsoft and the European Commission demonstrates that the world is not flat. Microsoft is a company that has ridden the wave of worldwide Internet access and software applications. Yet, it has run into a brick wall in Brussels. There the EU Directorate General for Competition and State Aid (DG Comp) has imposed large fines for breaking its competition rules.

In March 2004, the DG Comp ruled that Microsoft is abusing its dominant market position with its Windows operating system. Since then the DG Comp has been threatening to impose large daily fines because it says Microsoft is failing to comply with that ruling. On September 17, 2007, Microsoft lost an appeal to the European Court of First Instance ending a nine-year battle with the EU. It paid fines to the EU of $1.4 billion. In December 2007, the EU launched a new antitrust investigation against Microsoft after Norway's Opera complained about web browser. In January 2009, EU Commission accused Microsoft of illegally tying Internet Explorer to Windows. The Commission's concern was that the US computer giant may have broken competition rules by bundling its web browser with its dominant Windows operating system. Internet Explorer is used by more than half of global business users, with Mozila's Firefox at about 32 percent and Norway's Opera with 2 percent. In July 2009, Microsoft reached an agreement with EU antitrust regulators to allow European users a choice of web browsers. The accord ended 10 years of dispute between the two sides. Over that time, the EU imposed fines totalling €1.68 bn ($2.44bn, £1.5bn). The European Commission said Microsoft's legally binding agreement ended the dispute and averted a possible fine for the company.

This case illustrates that even the world's most successful Internet-based software company does not have unrestricted global market access for its products. Instead, the world is divided into a 'triad' with strong barriers for entry into the key regional markets of the EU, North America, and Asia–Pacific. Microsoft is simply the latest large MNE to misread the world marketplace. Today, business activity is organized mainly within each region of the triad, not globally. For US firms, going to a foreign triad market in Europe and Asia is fraught with peril.

The world's 500 largest firms, on average, sell 72 percent of their goods and services in their home region. Very few firms are truly global, defined as selling a significant percent of their products in each triad region. For example, the world's largest firm, Wal-Mart, has 94 percent of its

Source: Getty Images/AFP/Jean-Christoph Verhaegen/Stringer

sales in North America. Microsoft discloses the geographic dispersion of its sales by geographic segments: sales in the United States and sales outside the United States. Over five years' average (2006–2010), Microsoft generates 60 percent of its sales in the United States alone. If sales in Canada and Mexico are added on top of US sales, it is likely that a majority of its sales is in North America. Firms like Wal-Mart and Microsoft need to understand that a business model developed for North America will need to be adapted when going to Europe and Asia.

In the case of Microsoft the key difference is in the way that the EU regulatory system operates. In Europe competition policy can be used as a barrier to entry. EU antitrust regulations have traditionally proven stricter than American ones. An individual firm (in this case, Sun Microsystems and Opera) can signal an EU-wide investigation. In this process the deck is stacked against the foreign firm. In 2001 the US firm General Electric also made a similar mistake in its planned acquisition of Honeywell which was disallowed by the EU.

While the United States has somewhat similar antitrust provisions, the application of these is more business friendly than in Europe. US antitrust aims to help consumers, whereas EU law helps competitors. Microsoft was able to settle its antitrust case with the Bush administration, but it failed to do so with the EU. The regulatory climate in Europe is harsher than in North America. Multinational firms like Microsoft which assume free trade, worldwide market entry, and the other aspects of flat earth thinking are learning expensive lessons. In addition to

▶

differences in regulatory standards across the triad, there are major cultural, social, and political differences that deny globalization.

In terms of regulatory differences antitrust is but one of an array of market-entry barriers. Even worse are anti-dumping and countervailing duty laws which are used to keep out foreign rivals. The United States itself administers its antidumping and countervailing duty laws in favor of the home team. In 2006, on security grounds, the US Congress overturned the executive branch decision to allow Dubai Ports International to acquire the US ports owned by P&O, a British firm. The Europeans perceive that the US commitment to free trade is weak; this is stiffening their spine with regard to Microsoft. The end result is typical triad-based economic warfare, where market entry is denied by the local bureaucrats and politicians.

While the US system is transparent, the EU investigation of unfair trade law cases, as well as antitrust, can be opaque and self-serving. The EU bureaucrats have continued the case against Microsoft even after Sun Microsystems and other business rivals in Europe, like Novell and Real Networks, have settled their disputes. So now we can see the EU, as an institution, fighting a foreign multinational. Not exactly a flat world.

The lessons of the Microsoft case are the following. First, globalization is a myth; instead world business is conducted mainly on an intra-regional basis within each part of the triad. Second, it is unlikely that the regulatory standards across the triad will be harmonized; thus, multinationals must be prepared to adapt their business models when they enter foreign regions of the triad. Third, even

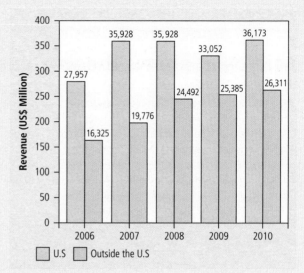

Microsoft: revenues by geographic segments 2006–2010

Source: Microsoft, *Annual Report*, 2006–2010

in high-tech areas such as software Internet applications, the technology itself does not guarantee the flat promise of worldwide market access. The world is not flat; rather, there are very strong regional fault lines.

Sources: Indiana University CIBER Director's Message, May 1, 2006; *Financial Times*, September 18, 2007; *Wall Street Journal*, September 18, 2007; *Financial Times*, January 15, 2008; "EU Fines Microsoft Record 1.4 Billion," *BBC News*, news.bbc.co.uk, February 27, 2008; "Microsoft Ends 10 Year Fight with Europe on Browser," *BBC News*, news.bbc.co.uk, December 16, 2009; Microsoft, *Annual Reports*, 2006–2010.

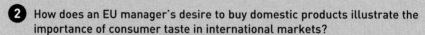

✔ Active learning check

Review your answer to Active Learning Case question 2 and make any changes you like. Then compare your answer to the one below.

2 **How does an EU manager's desire to buy domestic products illustrate the importance of consumer taste in international markets?**

This example shows that people often buy goods based on personal preference, rather than only on such characteristics as low price, high quality, or improved productivity. Of course, this "Buy EU" focus will often come into play only when all other factors are approximately equal. The manager is unlikely to turn down a China-made product that is 30 percent less expensive in favor of one that is made domestically. So there are limits to the effects of consumer taste on purchase decisions, though it is certainly one variable that has proven very important in international trade.

BARRIERS TO TRADE

Why do many countries produce goods and services that could be purchased more cheaply from others? One reason is trade barriers, which effectively raise the cost of these goods and make them more expensive to local buyers.

Reasons for trade barriers

One of the most common reasons for the creation of trade barriers is to encourage local production by making it more difficult for foreign firms to compete there. Another reason is to help local firms export and thus build worldwide market share by doing such things as providing them with subsidies in the form of tax breaks and low-interest loans. Other common reasons include:

1 Protect local jobs by shielding home-country business from foreign competition.
2 Encourage local production to replace imports.
3 Protect infant industries that are just getting started.
4 Reduce reliance on foreign suppliers.
5 Encourage local and foreign direct investment.
6 Reduce balance of payments problems.
7 Promote export activity.
8 Prevent foreign firms from *dumping* (selling goods below cost in order to achieve market share).
9 Promote political objectives such as refusing to trade with countries that practice apartheid or deny civil liberties to their citizens.

Commonly used barriers

A variety of trade barriers deter the free flow of international goods and services.[7] The following presents six of the most commonly used barriers.

Price-based barriers

Imported goods and services sometimes have a tariff added to their price. Quite often this is based on the value of the goods. For example, some tobacco products coming into the United States carry an ad valorem tariff (see below) of over 100 percent, thus more than doubling their cost to US consumers. Tariffs raise revenues for the government, discourage imports, and make local goods more attractive.

Quantity limits

Quota
A quantity limit on imported goods

Embargo
A quota set at zero, thus preventing the importation of those products that are involved

Quantity limits, often known as **quotas**, restrict the number of units that can be imported or the market share that is permitted. If the quota is set at zero, as in the case of Cuban cigars from Havana to the United States, it is called an **embargo**. If the annual quota is set at 1 million units, no more than this number can be imported during one year; once it is reached, all additional imports are turned back. In some cases a quota is established in terms of market share. For example, Canada allows foreign banks to hold no more than 16 percent of Canadian bank deposits, and the EU limits Japanese auto imports to 10 percent of the total market.

Table 6.1 Members of the Organization of the Petroleum Exporting Countries (OPEC), January 2007

Member country	Quotas (barrels per day)
Algeria	810
Indonesia	1,396
Iran	3,861
Iraq	na
Kuwait	2,105
Libya	1,398
Nigeria	2,164
Qatar	676
Saudi Arabia	8,561
United Arab Emirates	2,301
Venezuela	3,028
Total	26,300

Source: Adapted from www.opec.org.

International price fixing

Cartel
A group of firms that collectively agree to fix prices or quantities sold in an effort to control price

Sometimes a host of international firms will fix prices or quantities sold in an effort to control price. This is known as a **cartel**. A well-known example is OPEC (Organization of Petroleum Exporting Countries), which consists of Saudi Arabia, Kuwait, Iran, Iraq, and Venezuela, among others (see Table 6.1). By controlling the supply of oil it provides, OPEC seeks to control both price and profit. This practice is illegal in the United States and Europe,[8] but the basic idea of allowing competitors to cooperate for the purpose of meeting international competition is being endorsed more frequently in countries such as the United States.[9] For example, US computer firms have now created partnerships for joint research and development efforts.

Non-tariff barriers

Non-tariff barriers
Rules, regulations, and bureaucratic red tape that delay or preclude the purchase of foreign goods

Non-tariff barriers are rules, regulations, and bureaucratic red tape that delay or preclude the purchase of foreign goods. Examples include (1) slow processing of import permits, (2) the establishment of quality standards that exclude foreign producers, and (3) a "buy local" policy. These barriers limit imports and protect domestic sales.

Financial limits

Exchange controls
Controls that restrict the flow of currency

There are a number of different financial limits. One of the most common is **exchange controls**, which restrict the flow of currency. For example, a common exchange control is to limit the currency that can be taken out of the country; for example, travelers may take up to only $3,000 per person out of the country. Another example is the use of fixed exchange rates that are quite favorable to the country. For example, dollars may be exchanged for local currency on a 1:1 basis; without exchange controls, the rate would be 1:4. These cases are particularly evident where a black market exists for foreign currency that offers an exchange rate much different from the fixed rate.

Foreign investment controls

Foreign investment controls
Limits on foreign direct investment or the transfer or remittance of funds

Foreign investment controls are limits on foreign direct investment or the transfer or remittance of funds. These controls can take a number of different forms, including (1) requiring foreign investors to take a minority ownership position (49 percent or less), (2) limiting profit remittance (such as to 15 percent of accumulated capital per year), and (3) prohibiting royalty payments to parent companies, thus stopping the latter from taking out capital.

Such barriers can greatly restrict international trade and investment. However, it must be realized that they are created for what governments believe are very important reasons. A close look at one of these, tariffs, helps to make this clearer.

Tariffs

Tariff
A tax on goods shipped internationally

Import tariff
A tax levied on goods shipped into a country

Export tariff
A tax levied on goods sent out of a country

Transit tariff
A tax levied on goods passing through a country

Specific duty
A tariff based on the number of items being shipped into a country

Ad valorem duty
A tax which is based on a percentage of the value of imported goods

Compound duty
A tariff consisting of both a specific and an ad valorem duty

Dumping
The selling of imported goods at a price below cost or below that in the home country

A **tariff** is a tax on goods that are shipped internationally. The most common is the **import tariff**, which is levied on goods shipped into a country.[10] Less common is the **export tariff**, for goods sent out of the country, or a **transit tariff** for goods passing through the country. These taxes are levied on a number of bases. A **specific duty** is a tariff based on units, such as $1 for each item shipped into the country. So a manufacturer shipping in 1,000 pairs of shoes would pay a specific duty of $1,000. An **ad valorem duty** is a tariff based on a percentage of the value of the item, so a watch valued at $25 and carrying a 10 percent duty would have a tariff of $2.50. A **compound duty** is a tariff consisting of both a specific and an ad valorem duty, so a suit of clothes valued at $80 that carries a specific duty of $3 and an ad valorem duty of 5 percent would have a compound duty of $7.

Governments typically use tariffs to raise revenue and/or to protect local industry. At the same time, these taxes decrease demand for the respective product while raising the price to the buyer. This is illustrated in Figure 6.2, which shows how the quantity demanded declines from Q_1 to Q_2 when a tariff drives the price of a good from P_1 to P_2 (the world price plus the tariff). This price increase allows local producers to sell Q_3Q_2 and thus take market share away from foreign firms that were exporting Q_3Q_1 into the country. However, the figure shows this is done at the price of charging the consumer more money *and* reducing the number of buyers who purchase the product. At new price P_2, there are no longer any imports.

There are numerous reasons for using tariffs, such as to protect domestic industries or firms. The US government has used them to prevent foreign companies from selling goods at lower prices in the United States than back home. US auto makers have often accused their overseas rivals of using this tactic. In the case of Japanese car manufacturers, this was a particularly troublesome area when the value of the yen rose sharply in the early 1990s. As a result, argued the US car companies, imported parts and cars had to reflect the increased value of the yen or be subjected to tariffs.[11] Others have made similar arguments. Eastman Kodak, for example, asked the US Commerce Department to impose steep tariffs on the Fuji Photo Film Company. Kodak's argument was partially based on the rising yen. However, it also reflected a concern with **dumping**, which is the selling of imported goods at a price below cost or below that in the home country. In this case Kodak argued that Fuji sold color photographic paper for less than 20 cents a square foot in the United States, while charging almost 60 cents a square foot in Japan.[12] For an example of a protectionist tariff, see the box **International Business Strategy in Action: The courier wars**.

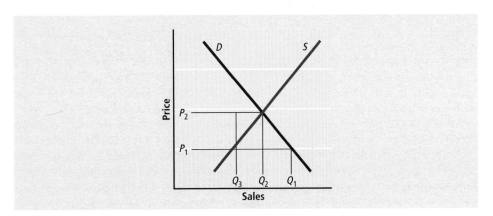

Figure 6.2 Impacts of a tariff

Source: Raymond Vernon and Louis T. Wells, Jr., *The Manager in the International Economy* (Englewood Cliffs, NJ: Prentice Hall, 1991), p. 85.

INTERNATIONAL BUSINESS STRATEGY IN ACTION

The courier wars

Local businesses have many reasons for encouraging their governments to erect barriers to trade. One of the most common is when an industry is not competitive on a worldwide basis and foreign competition could bring about the bankruptcy of local firms. The US steel industry is a good example. The efficiencies of both West European and Japanese steelmakers have brought new challenges to the US steel industry, which asked President George W. Bush to protect it from foreign imports.

Sometimes, however, local firms will seek protection from foreign competition even though they are profitable. Why? Because they don't want to give up any of their local market share—which will happen if more entrants are allowed into the industry. A good example is found in the courier wars now being fought in the United States. The three firms involved are FedEx, UPS, and DHL Express. The first two are US companies that collectively control 80 percent of the US market. The other is a German company that holds very little of the market. The total sales in 2009 of UPS are $45.297 billion; for FedEx, $34.734 billion; while for DHL Express there are no data except for its parent firm, Deutsche Post AG, at $64.253 billion.

FedEx operates out of Memphis, Tennessee, where it has a major distribution hub and a large number of aircraft to help meet its commitment of one-day delivery. UPS's airport hub is in Atlanta, Georgia, while DHL's hub is near Miami, Florida. All three firms do business in Europe, where they are also profitable. FedEx and UPS have been trying to prevent DHL from building an air fleet business in the United States to deliver packages and mail just like they do. Moreover, the two giant US firms have been receiving support from the Department of Transportation, which they have lobbied to prevent DHL from getting an air license.

One of the arguments made by FedEx and UPS is that although DHL Airways is 100 percent US owned, the parent company is controlled through an agreement by German owners with DHL's US subsidiary. This latter arrangement might seem a little strange, but a similar situation exists in Canada. The largest courier service in that country is Purolator, which is owned by the Canadian Post Office, a Crown monopoly. Yet despite this monopoly, both FedEx and UPS do quite well in Canada. US law, however, does not allow foreign entities to own more than 49 percent of the equity and 25 percent of the voting stock of a US air carrier.

Deutsche Post circumvented these regulations by selling a controlling stake of DHL Airways to an American

Source: Getty Images/News

with large stakes in DHL's international operations. Critics claimed that DHL Airways had entered into an agreement with Deutsche Post to be a captive vendor and that in practical terms Deutsche Post owned DHL. The Department of Transportation then forced DHL Airways to expand its contracts outside of DHL.

In 2003, DHL sought to expand its airline capacity by integrating Seattle-based Airborne's airline fleet. FedEx and UPS once again appealed to the Department of Transportation and to US politicians claiming that despite the new company being 100 percent owned by public shareholders, it would follow the same strategy that DHL Airways always did: working under an exclusive agreement with DHL.

In June 2003, DHL Airways Chairman and CEO were leading a US investor group in a buyout of the freight airline, whose largest customer was package-delivery company DHL Worldwide Express. DHL Airways moved to Miami from Chicago. They paid $57 million to buy the 95 percent of the airline which was owned by a subsidiary of Germany's Deutsche Post AG and two American private investors. The purchase put to rest a controversy about the company's ownership. The company changed its name to ASTAR Air Cargo.

The Dutch TNT (with worldwide sales of $17 billion) is emerging in 2007 as another foreign competitor with its US hub in Chicago.

In 2003, John Bartholdi, a Georgia Tech logistics professor, and his 60 students began the annual Great Package Race to determine which carrier is most efficient in delivering packages to worldwide locations. DHL Express is frequently the winner. In 2009, again, DHL Express was the winner—to be the first carrier to deliver the package from the US to the capital city of Mongolia, Ulan Bator.

Websites: www.fedex.com; www.dhl.com; www.ups.com; www.purolator.com, www.dhl-brandworld.com.

Sources: "A Tricky Business," *The Economist*, June 30, 2001, pp. 55–56; "Transportation Labor Urges US Government to Revoke DHL's Air Freight Forward License," *TTD News*, January 30, 2001; Gene G. Marcial, "DHL Could Help Airborne Take Off," *Business Week*, July 9, 2001; Brian O'Reilly, "They've Got Mail," *Fortune*, February 7, 2000; "A Package with Strings Attached," *Economist.com*, March 27, 2003; "Airborne Fires Back at UPS, FedEx 'Duopoly'," *Puget Sound Business Journal*, April 7, 2003; "DHL Buyout, Name Change," *South Florida CEO*, June 23, 2003; Great Package Race 2009 Wraps up – DHL First to Mongolia, While USPS Takes Opp, Alabama, Supply Chain Digest, www.scdigest.com, November 3, 2009.

Another reason for using tariffs is to raise government revenue. Import tariffs, for example, are a major source of revenue for less developed countries. A third reason is to reduce citizens' foreign expenditures in order to improve the country's balance of payments.

Tariffs continue to be one of the most commonly used barriers to trade, despite the fact that they often hurt low-income consumers and have a limited impact, if any, on upper-income purchasers. In recent years most industrialized countries have tried to reduce or eliminate the use of these trade barriers and to promote more free trade policies.[13] The United States is a good example. (The trade policies of the EU are discussed in Chapter 17 and those of Japan in Chapter 18.)

US trade policy

Despite being a highly protectionist nation in its early years, the United States has a policy today that generally strives to lower tariffs and trade barriers through the use of multilateral agreements. Since the protectionist disaster of the Depression years, the United States has sought to minimize the use of tariffs. It supported the General Agreement on Tariffs and Trade (GATT), and now it supports the 1994 World Trade Organization (WTO), which exists to liberalize trade and investment. Today US tariffs average only 2 to 3 percent advalorem to most countries of the world.[14]

The move away from tariffs does not mean US trade policy is completely open.[15] The US government employs a variety of approaches to promote or discourage international trade. For example, to encourage trade, there is the **North American Free Trade Agreement (NAFTA)**, which eliminates most trade restrictions (such as tariffs) among the United States, Canada, and Mexico and extends national treatment to foreign investment, and the **Caribbean Basin Initiative**, which eliminates tariffs on many imports from the Caribbean and Central American regions. Yet the **Trading-with-the-Enemy Act** disallows trade with countries judged to be enemies of the United States, including North Korea and Cuba. The US administration has the authority to prevent sales of goods to foreign governments when they are not deemed to be in the best interests of the United States. These goods can range from computers to chemicals to materials used for making nuclear weapons.[16]

The United States has also used negotiated agreements to limit the type or number of products entering the country. For example, a voluntary agreement with Japan restricts the number of cars imported to the United States. At the same time, exports are encouraged through legislation such as the **Foreign Sales Corporation Act**, which allows US exporters to establish overseas affiliates and not to pay taxes on the affiliates' income until the earnings are remitted to the parent company. The government also offers **trade adjustment assistance** to US businesses and individuals who are harmed by competition from imports. This aid takes such forms as loans for retooling and job counseling for those seeking alternative employment.

Caribbean Basin Initiative
A trade agreement that eliminates tariffs on many imports to the United States from the Caribbean and Central American regions

Foreign Sales Corporation Act
Legislation designed to allow US exporters to establish overseas affiliates and not pay taxes on the affiliates' income until the earnings are remitted to the parent company

Trade adjustment assistance
Assistance offered by the US government to US businesses and individuals harmed by competition from imports

✔ Active learning check

Review your answer to Active Learning Case question 3 and make any changes you like. Then compare your answer to the one below.

❸ In what way could the EU use trade barriers to protect its markets from foreign competitors? Who can be affected by these trade barriers?

The EU could take a number of steps to protect its markets from foreign competitors. Examples include establishing or increasing ad valorem tariffs, placing quantity limits on various imports, and limiting foreign direct investment. Of course, other countries could retaliate and take similar action against EU-produced goods, so the use of these trade barriers must be selective and should not be undertaken unless efforts at negotiated agreements prove fruitless.

NON-TARIFF BARRIERS TO TRADE

The economic effects of non-tariff barriers (NTBs) to trade are roughly similar to those of tariffs. They are inefficient distortions that reduce potential gains from trade. Table 6.2 lists a wide range of NTBs.

NTBs have gained prominence and importance in recent years as nations have begun resorting to them more frequently for protection. Sometimes they are not imposed by countries to interfere deliberately with trade.[17] Rather, they arise out of domestic policy and economic management. Examples include tax breaks to reduce regional income disparities or regulations designed to increase local purchasing or employment. These, in turn, result in a type of indirect export subsidy. Other NTBs are more blatant devices that restrict imports or foster exports.

Quotas

The most important NTBs are quotas that restrict imports to a particular level.[18] When a quota is imposed, domestic production generally increases and prices rise. As a result, the government usually ends up losing tariff revenues.

Table 6.2 Common non-tariff barriers to trade

Specific limitation	Customs administrative rules	Government participation	Import charges
Quotas (including voluntary)	Valuation systems	Procurement policies	Import deposits
Import licenses	Antidumping rules	Export subsidies and incentives	Supplementary duties
Supplementary incentives	Tariff classifications	Countervailing duties	Import credits
Minimum import limits	Documentation needed	Domestic assistance programs	Variable levies
Embargoes	Fees	Trade diverting	Border levies
Sectoral bilateral agreements	Disparities in quality and testing standards		
Orderly marketing agreements	Packaging, labeling, and marketing standards		

Historically, the GATT and WTO have prohibited import quotas except on agricultural products, as emergency measures, or when a country has short-run balance of payments problems. Countries have circumvented this regulation most notably for textiles, footwear, and automobiles by negotiating voluntary export restraint agreements that are useful in preventing retaliatory action by the importing country. In general, business would rather be protected by quotas than by tariffs. Under quotas, if future domestic demand is known, companies can determine their future production levels. Under tariffs, domestic producers must estimate the elasticity of the demand curve for imported products and the future movements in world prices, which is a more difficult challenge.

"Buy national" restrictions

"Buy national" regulations require governments to give preference to domestic producers, sometimes to the complete exclusion of foreign firms. In Europe, for example, many of the telephone, telegraph, electric utility, airline, and railroad industries are government owned and buy from national firms only, thus closing a large market to exporters. On the other hand, countries like the United States have a similarly wide range of inefficient "BuyAmerican" regulations at the national and state levels that discriminate against foreign suppliers. During the 1970s Tokyo Round of the GATT negotiations, a mild code to open up government contracts to foreign suppliers was negotiated. Only 28 governments have agreed to the WTO's Government Procurement Agreement and these must now publicize large procurement contracts to make public the winner's bid price or the basis for selecting the winning bid.

Customs valuation

Also during the GATT Tokyo Round, considerable progress was made in the area of customs valuation for the payment of duties. In the United States, there were nine valuation systems prior to the Tokyo Round. Value for duty is now generally based on the invoice cost, and the latitude of US customs to reclassify products has been reduced.

Technical barriers

Product and process standards for health, welfare, safety, quality, size, and measurements can create trade barriers by excluding products that do not meet them. Testing and certification procedures, such as testing only in the importing country and conducting on-site plant inspections, are cumbersome, time consuming, and expensive. The costs must be borne by the exporter prior to the foreign sale. National governments have the right and duty to protect their citizens by setting standards to prevent the sale of hazardous products. But such standards can also be used to impede trade. For example, at one point Japan excluded US-made baseball bats from the market because they did not meet the country's standard. No product produced outside Japan (even products made by foreign subsidiaries of Japanese MNEs) could bear the certification stamp of the Japanese Industrial Standard (JIS) or the Japanese Agricultural Standard (JAS), and selling in Japan without the JIS or JAS logo was difficult. Similarly, at one time the new regulations for automobile safety in the United States required that bumpers be above the height practical for imported subcompact cars, thus creating a technical barrier for these car manufacturers. Today the new code on technical barriers to trade requires consultation between trading partners before a standard that impedes trade is put in place. The code also requires that testing and certification procedures treat imports and domestic goods equally and that the importing country accept certification testing conducted in the exporting country.

Antidumping legislation, subsidies, and countervailing duties

The GATT and WTO allow importing countries to protect their producers from unfair competition, such as "dumping" goods at extremely low prices in an effort to gain market share and to drive out local competition. Importing countries are allowed to impose additional duties on products that have received export subsidies or are "dumped." Before the duties are imposed, however, the country must show that its domestic industry has suffered "material" injury from dumped or subsidized imports. Although products at these artificially low prices provide consumers in the importing country with a "good buy," such competition is thought to be unfair to domestic producers who object to dumping (and also to subsidized imports that can be offset by "countervailing" duties) if the domestic market of the exporting country is closed to them. A good example is the US auto industry, which claims that some Japanese cars are cheaper in the US market than at home, while Japan continues to impede exports of US cars into Japan.

The GATT and the WTO have developed a code on countervailing duties and anti-dumping duties that now expedites the process of determining whether exports have been dumped or subsidized and whether the domestic industry has been injured. This subject is exceedingly complex. Here are some examples (and answers):

> If the EU remits value-added taxes on exports by EU producers, is this a subsidy? (*No*)

> If Canada subsidizes production in a specific sector in one of its depressed regions for domestic purposes, are the exports of a subsidized firm subject to countervailing action? (*Yes*)

> If the British government subsidizes the British steel industry and its losses incurred by selling at home and abroad at prices below full cost, are its exports subject to antidumping or to countervailing duties? (*Maybe, sometimes*)

The problem is complex because of the difficulty in determining what material injury is and how it should be measured. This area is likely to be a point of contention for years to come.

Agricultural products

Trade in agricultural products is highly regulated by both quotas and fixed and variable tariffs. Domestic producers in most industrialized countries are often highly subsidized both directly and by artificially high domestic prices. Agricultural exports are often subsidized as well. And the EU flatly refused to discuss its Common Agricultural Policy (CAP) at the Tokyo Round. The CAP sets variable tariffs on imports to maintain high domestic prices by excluding or impeding imports. Major reforms in the CAP are now underway that will see continuing support for farmers but independently of production volumes. This is expected to improve the EU's negotiating position at the WTO. The United States is not without guilt in this area, however, since it also subsidizes the export of many agricultural products. The countries most affected by these subsidies are less developed countries with abundant and inexpensive labor and land and thus a competitive advantage in agricultural products. Agricultural subsidies have often stalled trade talks as these countries refused to further liberalize while developed countries continued to subsidize agriculture.

Export restraints

Over the vigorous objections of countries exporting natural resources, the GATT (and WTO) rounds have moved to tighten the conditions under which exports could be restrained. In general, world tariffs increase with the level of processing; for example, import duties increase as copper is processed from concentrate to blister, to refined copper, to copper wire and bars, to copper pots and pans. This tariff structure makes upgrading of natural resources in the producing country difficult. During the Tokyo Round, natural resource-producing countries were largely unsuccessful in their attempts to harmonize tariffs on a sectoral basis in order to increase their ability to upgrade prior to export. However, they did argue successfully for their right to restrict exports to induce further domestic processing.

OTHER ECONOMIC DEVELOPMENTS

In addition to the above, other economic developments warrant consideration. These include countertrade, trade in services, and free trade zones.

Countertrade

Countertrade
Barter trade in which the exporting firm receives payment in products from the importing country

Countertrade is essentially barter trade in which the exporting firm receives payment in terms of products from the importing country. Countertrade is important to the airline industry (for example, the purchase of Boeing 747s by British Airways if Boeing uses Rolls Royce engines) and in defense (for example, the purchase of US jet fighters by Canada if some of the parts are locally sourced in Canada). Barter sometimes takes the form of a buyback in which the exporter agrees to take products that are locally produced.

Countertrade tends to decrease the efficiency of world trade because it substitutes barter for the exchange of goods by the price system. For example, a US exporter of machinery to Indonesia may have to take payment in an "equivalent value" of palm oil or rattan. The exporting firm will then either have to sell these products, in which it has no expertise itself, or sell them through a broker or other firm. Some party to the trade—exporter, importer, or consumer—must bear these additional costs. Despite such obvious inefficiencies, countertrade appears likely to continue as an increasingly important factor in the international trade environment of the twenty-first century.

In one type of situation, however, countertrade may be beneficial. For example, if a US producer of textile machinery exports to China and agrees to take payment in the form of textile products, importers in the United States may perceive a lower risk of variability in product quality and delivery schedules (as a result of US technology and management), and the Chinese may perceive a lower risk of product failure in buying the machinery since the selling firm will not be "paid" unless the machinery performs to specifications.

Trade in services

International trade in services has received relatively little attention from governments or trade economists during trade negotiations. Reliable statistics are seldom collected. However, as high-income countries move toward a service economy, trade in services has grown and become a significant component of the current accounts of many countries.

In 2008, the United States exported goods worth $1.277 trillion and imported goods worth $2.117 trillion, which left a trade deficit of $840.251 billion on merchandise trade. In services it exported $550 billion and imported $405 billion for a trade surplus of $145 billion that partly offset its merchandise trade deficit. And, it had a surplus of $250 billion in the net income receipts from US FDI income (direct investment receipts/payments). Thus, the net deficit on these three accounts for the United States in 2008 was $706.068 billion. Details of the US goods, services, and FDI accounts appear in Table 6.3. (The balance of payments account will be explained in the Appendix of this chapter.)

Table 6.3 Overview of the US balance of current account, 2008

Items	Credits (1) (millions of US $)	Debits (2) (millions of US $)	Balance (1) – (2)
Trade of goods and services and income receipts	2,591,233	3,168,938	(577,705)
Trade of goods and services	1,826,596	2,522,532	(695,936)
Goods, balance of payments basis	1,276,994	2,117,245	(840,251)
Services	549,602	405,287	144,315
Transfers under U.S. military agency sales contracts	22,571	36,452	(13,881)
Travel	110,090	79,743	30,347
Passenger fares	31,623	32,597	(974)
Other transportation	58,945	72,143	(13,198)
Royalties and license fees	91,599	26,616	64,983
Other private services	233,529	153,267	80,262
US government miscellaneous services	1,245	4,469	(3,224)
Income receipts	764,637	646,406	118,231
FDI income	761,593	636,043	125,550
Direct investment receipts/payments	370,747	120,862	249,885
Other private receipts	385,940	349,871	36,069
US government receipts	4,906	165,310	(160,404)
Compensation of employees	3,044	10,364	(7,320)
Unilateral current transfers, net		128,363	(128,363)
Total	2,591,233	3,297,301	(706,068)

Source: Adapted from US Bureau of Economic Analysis, *Survey of Current Business*, June 2010, Table D.61 – International transactions; US Census Bureau, Table 1250, U.S. International Transactions by Type of Transactions.

E-resources: http://www.census.gov/compendia/statab/cats/foreign_commerce_aid/international_transactions.html.

The flow of services across/among countries is highly regulated. Internationally traded services such as banking, investment income, insurance, media, transportation, advertising, accounting, travel, and technology licensing are subject to a host of national and international regulations for economic, social, cultural, and political reasons. In 1995, the General Agreement on Trade in Services (GATS) came into effect. It covers all services except those provided by the government and those related to air traffic. Member countries are not forced to open all their service industries but can choose those areas for which they want to guarantee access to foreigners and, within a framework, how much access they want to provide. For example, a host nation might limit the scope of a foreign bank's operation through the use of licenses or by setting a maximum number of allowable branches. As of January 2000, more than 140 WTO members started negotiating to further liberalize services.

Whatever forum is used, negotiating reductions in service trade barriers will be difficult, complex, and lengthy. The barriers are often difficult to list, much less quantify for purposes of negotiation. And the issues are often highly charged and not subject to rational analysis. For example, Canada imposes Canadian content requirements on television, radio, and print media to foster a "national cultural identity," to protect its cultural heritage, and to protect the domestic arts, theater, and movie industries. A government that reduced these trade barriers or even agreed to negotiate them would be in trouble with the (protected) Canadian media, as well as with the general public.

Free trade zone

A designated area where importers can defer payment of customs duty while further processing of products takes place (same as a foreign trade zone)

Free trade zones

A **free trade zone** is a designated area where importers can defer payment of customs duty while products are processed further (same as a foreign trade zone). Thus, the free trade zone serves as an "offshore assembly plant," employing local workers and using local financing for a tax-exempt commercial activity. The economic activity takes place in a restricted area such as an industrial park, because the land is often being supplied at a subsidized rate by a local host government that is interested in the zone's potential employment benefits.

To be effective, free trade zones must be strategically located either at or near an international port, on major shipping routes, or with easy access to a major airport. Important factors in the location include the availability of utilities, banking and telecom services, and a commercial infrastructure.

More than 400 free trade zones exist in the world today, often encompassing entire cities, such as Hong Kong and Singapore. More than two-thirds are situated in developing countries, and most of their future growth is expected to occur there.

The advantages offered by free trade zones are numerous and mutually beneficial to all stakeholders. For private firms, the zones offer three major attractions. First, the firm pays the customs duty (tariff) only when the goods are ready to market. Second, manufacturing costs are lower because no taxes are levied. Third, while in the zone the manufacturer has the opportunity to repackage the goods, grade them, and check for spoilage. Secondary benefits to firms take the form of reduced insurance premiums (since these are based on duty-free values), reduced fines for improperly marked merchandise (since the good can be inspected in a zone prior to customers' scrutiny), and added protection against theft (resulting from security measures in the bonded warehouses).

At the state and local levels, advantages can be realized in terms of commercial services. On a more global level, free trade zones enable domestic importing companies to compete more readily with foreign producers or subsidiaries of MNEs, thereby increasing participation in world trade. Favorable effects are felt on the balance of payments because more economic activity occurs and net capital outflow is reduced. Finally, the business climate is improved due to reduced bureaucracy and resultant savings to business capital, currently inaccessible because of the delay in paying duties and tariffs. A free trade zone is a step toward free trade and can be an important signal by government to business that the economy is opening up. Opportunity replaces regulation, and growth of economic activity should result.

Before the establishment of more free trade zones becomes fully accepted and encouraged, governments must be convinced of their many economic benefits. Free trade zones are a vital necessity if nations are to remain competitive on an international scale. Not only will existing companies benefit from their use, but new industries will be attracted, keeping up the same benefits of world trade.

Maquiladora industry
A free trade zone that has sprung up along the US–Mexican border for the purpose of producing goods and then shipping them between the two countries

The ***maquiladora* industry** along the US–Mexican border is an excellent example of a free trade zone. The low wage rate in Mexico and the NAFTA of 1994 make the *maquiladora* region both accessible and important to labor-intensive firms in the United States and Canada. From only 12 *maquiladora* plants in 1965, approximately 3,000 existed in 2000. The *maquiladora* industry has been so successful that only oil earns Mexico more foreign currency today.

No Mexican taxes are paid on goods processed within the *maquiladoras*. Foreign companies doing such processing can benefit from lower wages and land costs than those in the United States as they increase the value added to their products. In return, Mexico attracts FDI into permanent plants, creates jobs, and collects taxes on any final products sold to the foreign firms, or within Mexico. Even though the United States has several hundred free trade zones of its own, many near seaports or airfields, these lack the low-wage workers of their Mexican counterparts.

Canada does not have free trade zones, but the federal government allows duty drawbacks, which arguably offer many of the same advantages. Unfortunately, these drawbacks, which are repayments of customs duties, apply retroactively and involve enough paperwork to discourage all but the largest or most dedicated organizations. As such, NAFTA and the lower-wage labor in Mexico have attracted Canadian firms producing labor-intensive products. Free trade zones exist in many other parts of the world than North America, and the advantages of these zones are enjoyed by businesses worldwide.[19]

KEY POINTS

1 International economics is the branch of economics concerned with the purchase and sale of foreign goods and services. This includes consideration of areas such as international trade, balance of payments, and barriers to trade.

2 A number of international trade theories help to explain why nations trade. These include the theory of absolute advantage, the theory of comparative advantage, the factor endowment theory, the Leontief paradox, and the international product life cycle theory. While no one theory offers a complete explanation of why nations trade, they collectively provide important insights into the area. Other key considerations that offer explanations for why nations trade include monetary currency valuation and consumer tastes.

3 There are a number of barriers to trade. Some of the most common include price-based barriers, quantity limits, international price fixing, non-tariff barriers, financial limits, and foreign investment controls.

4 Although tariffs are often introduced to maintain local jobs and assist infant industries, they are inefficient. This economic inefficiency results in higher prices of imported goods for the consumers. The redistribution of resources from more efficient industry further adds to the cost of a tariff. Such costs do not occur under free trade.

5 Non-tariff barriers (NTBs) provide similar economic inefficiencies to tariffs. Unlike tariffs, however, NTBs are not imposed by nations to interfere deliberately with trade; they arise out of domestic policy. There are several types of NTBs, including quotas, "Buy national" restrictions, technical barriers, and export restraints.

6 Countertrade is a form of barter trade in which the exporting firm receives payments in terms of products produced in the importing country. It is most pronounced in East–West trade, and although it may be beneficial to the trading partners, it increases the inefficiencies in the world trade system, which in turn raises costs and decreases trade volume.

7 Services are an important but somewhat misunderstood component of trade. Despite the trade of services in the billions of dollars among high-income countries, regulation has been outside the mandate of GATT. As services increase in importance, future discussion will take place concerning whether an international organization like GATT will carry the mandate to regulate this type of trade.

8 A free trade zone is a designated area where importers can defer payment of customs duty while further processing of products takes place. In essence, it is an offshore assembly plant. The majority of these areas exists in developing countries and handles approximately 20 percent of worldwide trade. Free trade zones are advantageous to all because they provide benefits such as increased employment and lower business costs.

Key terms

- international trade
- mercantilism
- neo-mercantilism
- theory of absolute advantage
- theory of comparative advantage
- factor endowment theory
- Heckscher–Ohlin theory
- Leontief paradox
- international product life cycle (IPLC) theory
- monetary exchange rate
- quota
- embargo
- cartel
- non-tariff barriers
- exchange controls

- foreign investment controls
- tariff
- import tariff
- export tariff
- transit tariff
- specific duty

- ad valorem duty
- compound duty
- dumping
- Caribbean Basin Initiative
- Foreign Sales Corporation Act

- trade adjustment assistance
- countertrade
- free trade zone
- *maquiladora* industry

REVIEW AND DISCUSSION QUESTIONS

1 Why is it difficult to solve international economic problems in the short run?

2 What is the supposed economic benefit of embracing mercantilism as an international trade theory? Are there many disadvantages to the use of this theory?

3 How is the theory of absolute advantage similar to that of comparative advantage? How is it different?

4 In what way does factor endowment theory help explain why nations trade? How does the Leontief paradox modify this theory?

5 If an innovating country develops a new technologically superior product, how long will it be before the country begins exporting the product? At what point will the country begin importing the product?

6 Of what value is the international product life cycle theory in helping to understand why nations trade?

7 How does each of the following trade barriers work: price-based barriers, quantity limits, international price fixing, non-tariff barriers, financial limits, and foreign investment controls?

8 What are some of the reasons for trade barriers? Identify and describe five.

9 How does the United States try to encourage exports? Identify and describe two ways.

10 Non-tariff barriers have become increasingly predominant in recent years. Describe a non-tariff barrier, and list four types, explaining how the United States does or could use such a device.

11 How does countertrade work? Is it an efficient economic concept?

12 What is a free trade zone? Is it an efficient economic concept?

13 What are two future problems and challenges that will have to be addressed by the international monetary system? Describe each.

14 What is meant by the term *balance of payments*?

15 What are the three major accounts in the balance of payments?

16 How would the following transactions be recorded in the IMF balance of payments?

   a IBM in New York has sold an $8 million mainframe computer to an insurance company in Singapore and has been paid with a check drawn on a Singapore bank.

   b A private investor in San Francisco has received dividends of $80,000 for stock she holds in a British firm.

   c The US government has provided $60 million of food and medical supplies for Kurdish refugees in Turkey.

   d The Walt Disney Company has invested $50 million in a theme park outside Paris, France.

Job losses and offshoring to China

It was not a difficult choice to make. Over the last 10 years, US imports of manufactured goods from China shot up. Cheap labor—Chinese labor is six times lower than Mexican labor—accounts for this. Continuing manufacturing operations in the United States and remaining price competitive is simply not feasible. When jobs are outsourced across national borders, e.g., from the United States to China, this is called offshoring.

Competition on quality, which can shelter domestic manufacturing from outsourcing to developing countries, was not an alternative because Chinese products for export are usually as good (although not in toys as Mattel found in 2007). When high labor intensity is tied to quality, the Chinese can outdo Western industrialized countries. Another factor is that the Chinese have a combination of highly skilled management and low-skilled labor, ensuring that production is efficient and that quality standards are met. This ability to produce high-quality goods is also what allows China to move from export manufacturing of Christmas decorations, toys, footwear, and clothing to household, consumer appliances, and, increasingly, the IT manufacturing sector.

National Presto, a US firm that makes high-quality pressure cookers and electric frying pans, had a difficult decision to make in the early 2000s. It could either offshore its production to China or see its market share continue to deteriorate. In 2002, the company closed plants in Mississippi and New Mexico, reducing its US workforce to less than half, and expanded its production in China. By 2003, all significant products marketed by the company were made in China.

Like many other US, European, and Japanese companies, National Presto uses an agent in Hong Kong to subcontract production to manufacturing plants in mainland China. Larger companies like Motorola, Philips, IBM, Toshiba, and GE have more control over their manufacturing plants in China. Kyocera of Japan, for example, invested $90 million in the early 2000s to construct a high-tech industrial park in Shilong Town of Dong guan City, Guangdong Province. Only 20 years ago Guangdong was dominated by paddy fields; today it is China's largest manufacturing cluster.

Proponents of free trade argue that political rhetoric against trade with China is meant to appease US fears of job losses. Yet, as seen in Table 1, 0.4 percent of all job losses in the United States in the third quarter of 2010 were the result of "out of country" relocation. While some

Table 1 Outsourcing and job losses in the United States, third quarter of 2010

Reasons for job losses	Separations	% of total
With separations reported, of which	3,074	1.64
Out of country relocation	737	0.40
Domestic relocation	2,337	1.26
Other	184,017	98.35
Total, private non-farm sector	187,091	100.0

Note: Data only cover layoffs in companies with at least 50 workers, who have filed for unemployment insurance, for at least 50 workers, and where unemployment lasted more than 30 days.

Source: US Bureau of Labor Statistics, "Extended Mass Layoffs, Third Quarter 2010," November 12, 2010. Table A, Selected measures of mass layoff activity; Table 10, Movement of work actions by type of separation where number of separations is known by employers, selected quarters, 2010.

argue that this percentage is undervalued because it does not take into consideration potential job gains that never materialized, others argue that given economic conditions there was no assurance that firms that created new jobs in China would have chosen to create these jobs in the United States if offshoring to China had not been a possibility.

China has become the world's largest manufacturer, ahead of the United States, Japan, and Germany. It has outpaced Japan to become the country having the largest trade surplus with the United States. US politicians and lobby groups blame Chinese protectionist practices for the growing trade deficit between the two nations, which in 2003 was estimated at $124 billion. In 2009, the deficit with China totalled $226.83 billion, still the largest imbalance with any nation, but down 15.4 percent from the all time record of $268.04 billion set in 2008. The deficit with China is expected to resume rising in 2010 as the US economy recovers, triggering rising orders for Chinese manufacturers of shoes, toys and other low cost items in high demand by American consumers.

Among the barriers the United States claims prevent a free flow of its goods to China are import barriers, unclear legal provisions applied in a discriminatory manner against US imports, and an undervalued yuan. The last one has generated the most controversy in the last few years. The Chinese yuan has been fixed at 8.28 to the dollar since 1994, a rate that critics argue to be up to 40 percent undervalued. China relaxed the yuan's fixed exchange rate against the dollar in June 2010, but since then it was allowed to appreciate by less than 3%. Yet economists do not all agree that the yuan is undervalued. Some fear that a sharp deterioration would hurt not only the Chinese economy but also those trading partners that are most heavily dependent on Chinese imports.

Sources: "Chinese Trade Reform 'Is Failing'," *BBC News*, April 1, 2004; "China Defiant on Currency Exchange," *BBC News*, September 2, 2003; Mary Hennock, "China: The World's Factory Floor," *BBC News*, November 11, 2002; www.worldbank.com; "Kyocera to Build High-Tech Industrial Park in Dongguan," *People's Daily*, September 13, 2000; "US Trade Deficit Surges to $40.18 Billion," *Associated Press*, www.msnbc.msn.com, October 2, 2010.

1 Does the theory of comparative advantage apply to China's trade with industrialized countries? How?

2 How does the factor endowment theory apply to China's trade with industrialized countries?

3 Are any of the countries mentioned operating in autarky?

4 How can distribution of gains from free trade cause much of the political debate regarding trade with China?

REAL CASE

Dumping on trade complaints

One of the biggest problems in international trade is the ability of domestic producers to lobby their home governments to erect barriers to trade. In the past, the textile, apparel, and shoe industries were able to obtain protection from cheaper imports through tariffs, quotas, and special measures. Now multilateral trade agreements under the GATT and WTO (and also regional and bilateral agreements such as NAFTA and the emerging Asian Pacific Economic Cooperation forum) outlaw such blatant instruments of protection. However, these agreements have been replaced by more subtle ones.

Prominent as a new type of protectionist device is the use of "unfair trade laws," especially antidumping (AD) and countervailing duty (CVD) actions. The economic logic of AD and CVD makes some sense. It is unfair for a foreign producer to "dump" a product in your country below its price in the home country, or below the cost of producing it. Similarly, subsidized foreign products should be offset by a CVD of equivalent effect. The problem, however, lies with the administration of the trade laws, which is subject to political lobbying.

A variety of studies have found that the bureaucrats who administer AD and CVD laws are subject to capture by the home industries, who then use AD and CVD cases as harassment tools against often economically efficient foreign rival producers. For example, Rugman and Anderson (1987) found that the US administration of AD and CVD was used in a biased manner against Canadian producers, especially in resource-based industries such as softwood lumber, fishing, and agriculture. Thus, in the Canadian–US Free Trade Agreement of 1989, and again in NAFTA, five-person binational panels of trade law experts were set up to review the decision of the US (and Canadian) trade law agencies.

In a subsequent study, Rugman and Anderson (1997) found that these binational panels were able to remand back (i.e. successfully challenge) the decision of the US agencies twice as often in cases involving Canada as in AD and CVD cases involving the rest of the world. In related work researchers have found that the EU is just as bad as the United States when it comes to taking questionable AD measures, especially against Asian countries. Indeed, one of the unresolved problems is how smaller countries can secure access to the protected markets of triad economies such as the United States and the EU. In Japan's case, there are similar arguments (including those from its triad rivals) that it has entry barriers in place preventing market access.

Website: www.wto.org.

Sources: Andrew D. M. Anderson, *Seeking Common Ground: Canada–US Trade Dispute Settlement Policies in the Nineties* (Boulder, CO: Westview Press, 1995); Alan M. Rugman, *Multinational Enterprises and Trade Policy* (Cheltenham: Edward Elgar, 1996); Alan M. Rugman and Andrew D. M. Anderson, *Administered Protection in America* (London and New York: Routledge, 1987); Alan M. Rugman and Andrew D. M. Anderson, "NAFTA and the Dispute Settlement Mechanisms," *The World Economy*, December 1997, pp. 935–950; Alan M. Rugman and Michael Gestrin, "EC Anti-Dumping Laws as a Barrier to Trade," *European Management Journal*, vol. 9, no. 4 (December 1991), pp. 475–482.

1 Why are AD and CVD measures brought and imposed?

2 What is the impact on a firm from a non-triad country if it faces an AD or CVD case in its major market?

3 What is the solution to the abusive use of AD and CVD measures by triad economies?

ENDNOTES

1 Asra Q. Nomani and Douglas Lavin, "US and Japan Nearing Accord in Trade Dispute," *Wall Street Journal*, March 10, 1994, p. A3; and Richard McGregor, "Beans are on the Beijing Menu as Bush Prepares to Talk Trade," *FT.com*, February 21, 2002.

2 Douglas Harbrecht et al., "Tough Talk," *Business Week*, February 20, 1994, pp. 26–28.

3 See, for example, Dana Weschler Linden, "Dreary Days in the Dismal Science," *Forbes*, January 21, 1991, pp. 68–71.

4 Also see Steven Greenhouse, "French Shift on State-Owned Sector," *New York Times*, April 8, 1991, p. C2.

5 For additional insights into trade theory, see Nicolas Schmitt, "New International Trade Theories and Europe 1991: Some Results Relevant for EFTA Countries," *Journal of Common Market Studies*, September 1990, pp. 53–74.

6 "Tested by the Mighty Euro," Economist.com, May 18, 2004.

7 See Richard W. Stevenson, "East Europe Says Barriers to Trade Hurt Its Economies," *New York Times*, January 25, 1993, pp. A1, C8.

8 Lucy Walker, "Sir Leon's Cartel Busters Take to the Road Again," *The European*, April 12–14, 1991, p. 25.

9 Edmund Faltermayer, "Is 'Made in the USA' Fading Away?" *Fortune*, September 24, 1990, p. 73.

10 Edward Alden and Robert Shrimsley, "EU Set to Retaliate if US Imposes Steel Tariffs," *Financial Times*, March 4, 2002.

11 See, for example, Doron P. Levin, "Honda to Hold Base Price on Accord Model," *New York Times*, September 2, 1993, p. C3.

12 Keith Bradsher, "Kodak Is Seeking Big Tariff on Fuji," *New York Times*, September 1, 1993, pp. A1, C2.

13 See, for example, Robert Cohen, "Grumbling over GATT," *New York Times*, July 3, 1993, p. 13.

14 Ed Gresser, "Tariffs Biggest US Tax on the Poor," *Reuters*, September 10, 2002.

15 See, for example, Chris Adams, "Ailing Steel Industry Launches a Battle Against Imports," *Wall Street Journal*, October 1, 1998, p. B4; and "Steel Vice," *Wall Street Journal*, October 1, 1998, p. A22.

16 As an example, see Clyde H. Farnsworth, "US Slows Computer for Brazil," *International Herald Tribune*, April 13–14, 1991, p. 5.

17 Claude Barfield, "Nerves of Steel," *Financial Times*, March 1, 2002.

18 Sometimes these are voluntary quotas, as seen in Andrew Pollack, "Japan Takes a Pre-emptive Step on Auto Exports," *New York Times*, January 9, 1993, pp. 17, 26.

19 Anthony DePalma, "Trade Pact Is Spurring Mexican Deals in the US," *New York Times*, March 17, 1994, pp. C1, 3.

ADDITIONAL BIBLIOGRAPHY

Anderson, Andrew D. M. *Seeking Common Ground: Canada–US Trade Disputes* (Boulder, CO: Westview Press, 1995).

Baggs, Jen and Brander, James A. "Trade Liberalization, Profitability, and Financial Leverage," *Journal of International Business Studies*, vol. 37, no. 2 (March 2006).

Baldauf, Artur. "Examining Determinants of Export Performance in Small Open Economies," *Journal of World Business*, vol. 35, no. 1 (Spring 2000).

Banalieva, Elitsa R. and Sarathy, Ravi. "The Impact of Regional Trade Agreements on the Global Orientation of Emerging Market Multinationals," *Management International Review*, vol. 50, no. 6 (2010), 797–826.

Barboza, Gustavo A. and Trejos, Sandra R. "Empirical Evidence on Trade Reform, Revealed Trade Openness, and Output Growth in Latin America. How Far Have We Come?" *Multinational Business Review*, vol. 16, no. 4 (2008).

Beleska-Spaova, Elena and Glaister, Keither W. "The Geography of British Exports: Country-Level Versus Firm-Level Evidence," *European Management Journal*, vol. 27 (2009).

Beleska-Spaova, Elena and Glaister, Keither W. "Geographic Orientation and Performance Evidence from British Exporters," *Management International Review*, vol. 50, no. 5 (2010).

Beleska-Spasova, Elena and Glaister, Keith W. "The Role of Firm-Specific Advantages in UK Export Initiation," *Multinational Business Review*, vol. 19, no. 2 (2011).

Bertrand, Olivier. "What Goes Around, Comes Around: Effects of Offshore Outsourcing on the Export Performance of Firms," *Journal of International Business Studies*, vol. 42 (2011).

Brewer, Thomas L. and Young, Stephen. *The Multinational Investment System and Multinational Enterprises* (Oxford: Oxford University Press, 2000).

Brewer, Thomas L. and Young, Stephen. "Multilateral Institutions and Policies: Their Implications for Multinational Business Strategy," in Alan M. Rugman (ed.), *The Oxford Handbook of International Business*, 2nd ed. (Oxford: Oxford University Press, 2009).

Buckley, Peter J. "Government Policy Responses to Strategic Rent Seeking Transnational Corporations," *Transnational Corporations*, vol. 5, no. 2 (August 1996).

Curran, Louise and Zignago, Soledad. "Intermediate Products and the Regionalization of Trade," *Multinational Business Review*, vol. 19, no. 1 (2011).

Deutsch, Klaus Gunter and Speyer, Bernhard (eds.). *The World Trade Organization Millennium Round* (London: Routledge, 2001).

Dunning, John H. and Mucchielli, Jean-Louis (eds.). *Multinational Firms: The Global-Local Dilemma* (London: Routledge, 2002).

Fratianni, Michele U. and Oh, Chang H. "Expanding RTAs, Trade Flows, and the Multinational Enterprise," *Journal of International Business Studies*, vol. 40 (2009).

Fratianni, Michele U., Marchionne, Francesco and Oh, Chang H. "A Commentary on the Gravity Equation in International Business Research," *Multinational Business Review*, vol. 19, no. 1 (2011).

Fung, Hung-Gay, Yau, Jot and Zhang, Gaiyan. "Reported Trade Figure Discrepancy, Regulatory Arbitrage, and Round-Tripping: Evidence from the China–Hong Kong Trade Data," *Journal of International Business Studies*, vol. 42 (2011).

Hennart, Jean-François. "Some Empirical Dimensions of Countertrade," *Journal of International Business Studies*, vol. 21, no. 2 (Second Quarter 1990).

Koka, Balaji R., Prescott, John E. and Madhavan, Ravindranath. "Contagion Influence on Trade and Investment Policy: A Network Perspective," *Journal of International Business Studies*, vol. 30, no. 1 (Spring 1999).

Liu, Runjuan, Feils, Dorothee J and Scholnick, Barry. "Why Are Different Services Outsourced to Different Countries?" *Journal of International Business Studies,* vol. 42 (May 2011).

Markusen, James R. "International Trade Theory and International Business," in Alan M. Rugman and Thomas L. Brewer (eds.), *The Oxford Handbook of International Business* (Oxford: Oxford University Press, 2001).

Ostry, Sylvia. *The Post-Cold War Trading System* (Chicago: University of Chicago Press, 1997).

Ramstetter, Eric D. "Export Performance and Foreign Affiliate Activity in Japan's Large Machinery Firms," *Transnational Corporations*, vol. 6, no. 3 (December 1997).

Robin, Donald P. and Sawyer, W. Charles. "The Ethics of Antidumping Petitions," *Journal of World Business*, vol. 33, no. 3 (Fall 1998).

Rugman, Alan M. *Multinational Enterprises and Trade Policy* (Cheltenham: Edward Elgar, 1996).

Rugman, Alan M. and Anderson, Andrew. *Administered Protection in America* (London: Croom Helm and New York: Methuen, 1987).

Rugman, Alan M. and Boyd, Gavin (eds.). *The World Trade Organization in the New Global Economy* (Cheltenham: Edward Elgar, 2001).

Rugman, Alan M. and Gestrin, Michael. "US Trade Laws as Barriers to Globalization," in Tamir Agmon and Richard Drobnick (eds.), *Small Firms in Global Competition* (New York: Oxford University Press, 1994).

Rugman, Alan M. and Verbeke, Alain. *Global Corporate Strategy and Trade Policy* (London and New York: Routledge, 1990).

Rugman, Alan M. and Verbeke, Alain. "Strategic Trade Policy Is Not Good Strategy," *Hitotsubashi Journal of Commerce and Management*, vol. 25, no. 1 (December 1990).

Rugman, Alan M. and Verbeke, Alain. "Location, Competitiveness, and the Multinational Enterprise," in Alan M. Rugman (ed), *The Oxford Handbook of International Business* (Oxford: Oxford University Press, 2009).

Sampson, Gary P. (ed.). *The Role of the World Trade Organization in Global Governance* (Tokyo, New York, Paris: United Nations University Press, 2001).

Zhang, Chun, Cavusgil, S. Tamer and Roath, Anthony, S. "Manufacturer Governance of Foreign Distributor Relationships: Do Relational Norms Enhance Competitiveness in the Export Market?" *Journal of International Business Studies*, vol. 34, no. 6 (November 2003).

APPENDIX TO CHAPTER 6: BALANCE OF PAYMENTS

How well do we keep track of the millions of transactions that take place annually among exporters and importers, international banks, and multinational companies? The bankers who tabulate the foreign exchange dealings of their own banks are only a part of the picture. How well can we account for the part of direct investment that occurs through overseas borrowing, yet affects the home country's international economic position? Even more simply, how well can we measure "international" transactions that are simply transfers of funds from the account of an importer to the account of a foreign exporter in the same bank?

The realistic answer to these questions is: not very well. National governments create elaborate accounts for the transactions between their residents and foreign residents, but it is often very difficult to obtain full and accurate information. Putting that problem aside for the moment, let us consider the methods that governments use to record each country's international transactions.

Balance of payments (BOP)
The value of all transactions between a country's residents and the rest of the world; the three broad BOP categories are the current account, capital account, and official reserves

The most widely used measure of international economic transactions for any country is the **balance of payments (BOP)**. This record attempts to measure the full value of the transactions between residents of one country and residents of the rest of the world for some time period, typically one year. The balance of payments is a flow concept, in that it records flows of goods, services, and claims between countries over a period of time, rather than a stock of accumulated funds or products. It is a value concept, in that all the items recorded receive a monetary value, denominated in the given country's currency at the time of those transactions. *The balance of payments thus is a record of the value of all the economic transactions between residents of one country and residents of all other countries during a given time period.*

Why do we worry about measuring these transactions? We do so because if a country records a substantial imbalance between inflows and outflows of goods and services for an extended period of time, some means of financing or adjusting away the imbalance must be found. For example, if the Eurozone countries record a persistent trade deficit with China for several years, there will be pressure either to devalue the euro relative to the Chinese currency, the renminbi, or for Chinese investors to place large and continuing investments into euro-denominated securities. This pressure presents both a political outcome (pressure on the Chinese government to revalue the renminbi) and an economic outcome (pressure on the euro to devalue and on European producers to lower their costs, perhaps by producing in China).

So, the importance of the balance of payments is not only macroeconomic, in the domain of government accountants, but also managerial, since an imbalance provides guidance to managers about expected government policies as well as about opportunities to take advantage of currency opportunities. Since the relatively open foreign exchange markets of many countries today leave the exchange rate substantially to supply and demand, the balance of payments is an indicator of exactly that supply and demand for a country's currency that will lead to changes in the exchange rate.

The supply and demand for a currency come from both trade flows (exports and imports) and capital flows (investments and borrowing). So, the balance of payments implications for exchange rates must include both sides of the story, the "real" flows and the financial flows.

Balance of payments accounting

There is no such thing as the balance of payments, since the accounts are organized in a double-entry bookkeeping system, and for every debit entry there is a credit entry of equal value. There are half a dozen BOP measures, which group some international transactions together and leave others in a second, "everything else" category. In each case the intent is to place the fundamental economic causes of transactions in the first group and leave the payments for them in the second group. In the actual accounts, the former transactions are listed "above the line," and the payments are left "below the line."

Current account

Current account
A BOP category that consists of merchandise trade, services, and gifts (unilateral transfers)

The **current account** consists of merchandise trade, services, and unilateral transfers. (See Table 6A, parts A and B.)

Merchandise trade is typically the first part of the current account. It receives more attention than any of the other accounts because this is where the imports and exports of goods are reported, and these are often the largest single component of all international transactions. In this account, sales of goods to foreigners (exports) are reported as credits because they are a source of funds or a claim against the purchasing country. Conversely, purchases of goods from overseas (imports) are recorded as debits because they use funds. This payment can be made by either reducing current claims on foreigners or increasing foreign liabilities.

Table 6A Balance of payments: IMF presentation

	Debits	Credits
I Current account		
A Goods, services, and income:		
1 Merchandise	Imports from foreign sources (acquisition of goods)	Exports to foreign destinations (provision of goods)
Trade balance		
2 Shipment and other transportation	Payments to foreigners for freight and insurance on international shipments; for ship repair, stores, and supplies; and international passenger fares	Receipts by residents from foreigners for services provided
3 Travel	Expenditures by residents (including internal transportation) when traveling in a foreign country	Receipts by residents for goods and services (including internal transportation) sold to foreign travelers in reporting country
4 Investment income	Profits of foreign direct investments in reporting country, including reinvested earnings; income paid to foreigners as interest, dividends, etc.	Profits of direct investments by residents in foreign countries, including reinvested earnings; income received by residents from abroad as interest, dividends, etc.
5 Other official	Foreign purchases by government not included elsewhere; personal expenditures of government civilian and military personnel stationed in foreign countries	Expenditures of foreign governments for goods and services, not included elsewhere; personal expenditures of foreign civilian and military personnel stationed in reporting country
6 Other private	Payments to foreigners for management fees, royalties, film rentals, construction, etc.	Receipts from foreigners for management fees, royalties, film rentals, construction, etc.
Goods, services, and income balance		
B Unilateral transfers:		
1 Private	Payments in cash and kind by residents to foreigners without a quid pro quo such as charitable gifts and gifts by migrants to their families	Receipts in cash and kind by residents from foreigners, individuals, or governments without a quid pro quo
2 Official	Transfers by government of reporting country for pensions, reparations, and grants for economic and military aid	Transfers received by government from foreigners in the form of goods, services, or cash as gifts or grants. Also tax receipts from non-residents
Current account balance		

Table 6A (continued)

	Debits	Credits
II Capital account		
C Capital, excluding reserves:		
1 Direct investment	(a) Increased investment in foreign enterprises controlled by residents, including reinvestment of earnings (b) Decreases in investment by residents in domestic enterprises controlled by foreigners	(a) Decreased investment in foreign enterprises controlled by residents (b) Increases in investment in domestic enterprises by foreigners
2 Portfolio investment	(a) Increases in investment by residents in foreign securities (b) Decreases in investment by foreigners in domestic securities such as bonds and corporate equities	(a) Decreases in investments by residents in foreign securities (b) Increases in investment by foreigners in domestic securities
3 Other long-term, official	(a) Loans to foreigners (b) Redemption or purchase from foreigners of government securities	(a) Foreign loan reductions (b) Sales to foreigners of government securities
4 Other long-term, private	(a) Long-term loans to foreigners by resident banks and private parties (b) Loan repayments by residents to foreign banks or private parties	(a) Long-term loans by foreigners to resident banks or private parties (b) Loan repayments by foreigners to residents
5 Other short-term, official	(a) Short-term loans to foreigners by central government (b) Purchase from foreigners of government securities, decrease in liabilities constituting reserves of foreign authorities	(a) Short-term loans to resident central government by foreigners. (b) Foreign sales of short-term resident government securities, increases in liabilities constituting reserves of foreign authorities
6 Other short-term, private	(a) Increases in short-term foreign assets held by residents (b) Decreases in domestic assets held by foreigners, such as bank deposits, currencies, debts to banks, and commercial claims	(a) Decreases in short-term foreign assets held by residents. Increase in foreign liabilities of residents (b) Increase in domestic short-term assets held by foreigners or decrease in short-term domestic liabilities to foreigners
III Reserves		
D Reserves:		
1 Monetary gold	Increases in holdings of gold, SDRs, foreign convertible currencies by monetary authorities; decreases in liabilities to IMF or increase in IMF assets position	Decreases in holdings of gold, SDRs, foreign convertible currencies by monetary authorities; increases in liabilities to IMF or decrease in IMF assets position
2 Special drawing rights (SDRs)		
3 IMF reserve position		
4 Foreign exchange assets		
E Net errors and omissions:	Net understatement of recorded debts or overstatement of recorded credits	Net understatement of recorded debts or overstatement of recorded credits
Balances:		
Balances on merchandise trade	A-1 credits minus A-1 debits	
Balance on goods, services, and income	A-1 through A-6 credits minus A-1 through A-6 debits	
Balance on current account	A and B credits minus A and B debits	

Merchandise trade transactions can affect a country's BOP in a number of ways. Assume that Nissan Motor of Japan has sold General Motors in the United States $600,000 worth of engines and these engines will be paid for from GM's account in a Detroit bank. In this case the imports are a debit to the current account (A-1) and a credit to the "other short-term, private" capital account (C-6b). Here is how the entry would be recorded:

		Debit	Credit
A-1	Merchandise imports	$600,000	
C-6b	Increase in domestic short-term assets held by foreigners		$600,000

The result of this purchase is that the United States has transferred currency to foreigners and thus reduced its ability to meet other claims.

Services

The services category includes many payments such as freight and insurance on international shipments (A-2); tourist travel (A-3); profits and income from overseas investment (A-4); personal expenditures by government, civilians, and military personnel overseas (A-5); and payments for management fees, royalties, film rental, and construction services (A-6). Purchases of these services are recorded as debits, while sales of these services are similar to exports and are recorded as credits. For example, extending the earlier example of Nissan and GM, assume that the US auto maker must pay $125,000 to Nissan to ship the engines to the United States. The transaction would be recorded this way:

		Debit	Credit
A-2	Shipment	$125,000	
C-6b	Other short-term private capital		$125,000

GM purchased a Japanese shipping service (a debit to the current account) and paid for this by increasing the domestic short-term assets held by foreigners (a credit to the capital account).

Unilateral transfers

Unilateral transfers are transactions that do not involve repayment or the performance of any service. Examples include the American Red Cross sending $10 million in food to refugees in Somalia; the United States paying military pensions to residents of the Philippines who served in the US Army during World War II; and British workers in Kuwait shipping money home to their families in London. Here is how the American Red Cross transaction would appear in the US BOP:

		Debit	Credit
B-1	Unilateral transfers, private	$10 million	
A-1	Merchandise exports		$10 million

Capital account

Capital account
A category of the BOP that consists of transactions that involve financial claims

Capital account items are transactions that involve claims in ownership. Direct investment (C-1) involves managerial participation in a foreign enterprise along with some account that involves degree of control. The United States classifies direct investments as those investments that give the investor more than 10 percent ownership. Portfolio investment (C-2) is investment designed to obtain income or capital gains. For example, if Exxon shipped $20 million of equipment to an overseas subsidiary the entry would be:

		Debit	Credit
C-1	Direct investment	$20 million	
A-1	Exports		$20 million

"Other long-term" capital accounts are differentiated based on whether they are government (C-3) or private (C-4) transactions. These transactions have a maturity of over one year and involve either loans or securities. For example, Citibank may have loaned the government of Poland $50 million. "Other short-term" capital accounts are also differentiated based on whether they are governmental (C-5) or private (C-6). Typical short-term government transactions are short-term loans in the securities of other governments. Private transactions often include trade bill acceptances or other short-term claims arising from the financing of trade and movements of money by investors to take advantage of interest differentials among countries.

Official reserves

Official reserves
Funds owned by national monetary authorities that are used for bringing BOP accounts into balance

Official reserves are used for bringing BOP accounts into balance. There are four major types of reserves available to monetary authorities in meeting BOP deficits (D1 through D4 in Table 6A). These reserves are analogous to the cash or near-cash assets of a private firm. Given that billions of dollars in transactions are reported in BOP statements, it should come as no surprise that the amount of recorded debits is never equal to the amount of credits. This is why there is an entry in the reserve account for net errors and omissions. If a country's reporting system is weak or there are a large number of clandestine transactions, this discrepancy can be quite large.

US BOP

The official presentation of the US BOP is somewhat different from the IMF format presented in Table 6A. Because the United States plays such a dominant role in the world economy, it is important to examine the US system. Table 6B presents US international transactions for two recent years.

A number of select entries in Table 6B help to highlight the US BOP. Lines 2 and 19 show that in 2008 exports of goods and services were $695.936 billion (line 73) less than imports. This trade deficit was smaller than 2006 when it stood at $763.267 billion, greater than that in 2002 when it stood at $421.7 billion, and 2003 when it was $496.5 billion, showing that the United States continues to have trade deficit problems.

To assess the trade situation accurately, however, we need to examine the data in more depth. This information is provided in Table 6C. The table shows that although US exports are strong in areas such as capital goods and industrial supplies and materials, the country also imports a large amount of these products. In addition, the United States is a net importer of foods, feeds, and beverages, automotive vehicles and parts, consumer goods, and petroleum and products.

In the early 1980s US trade deficits were offset by large amounts of income generated by direct investments abroad. Later in the decade massive international borrowing offset these deficits. More recently the situation has improved somewhat, and dollar devaluation has helped to generate stronger demand for US exports, thus partially reducing the growth rate

Table 6B US international transactions, 2008

Line	(Credits +; debits −)	2008 (in millions of US $)
	Current account	
1	Exports of goods and services and income receipts	2,591,233
2	Exports of goods and services	1,826,596
3	Goods, balance of payment basis	1,276,994
4	Services	549,602
5	Transfers under US military agency sales contracts	22,571
6	Travel	110,090
7	Passenger fares	31,623
8	Other transportation	58,945
9	Royalties and license fees	91,599
10	Other private services	233,529
11	US government miscellaneous services	1,245
12	Income receipts	764,637
13	Income receipts of US-owned assets abroad	761,593
14	Direct investment receipts	370,747
15	Other private receipts	385,940
16	US government receipts	4,906
17	Compensation of employees	3,044
18	Imports of goods and services and income payments	−3,168,938
19	Imports of goods and services	−2,522,532
20	Goods, balance of payment basis	−2,117,245
21	Services	−405,287
22	Direct defense expenditures	−36,452
23	Travel	−79,743
24	Passenger fares	−32,597
25	Other transportation	−72,143
26	Royalties and license fees	−26,616
27	Other private services	−153,267
28	US government miscellaneous services	−4,469
29	Income payments	−646,406
30	Income payments on foreign-owned assets in the US	−636,043
31	Direct investment payments	−120,862
32	Other private payments	−349,871
33	US government payments	−165,310
34	Compensation of employees	−10,364
35	Unilateral current transfers, net	−128,363
40	US-owned assets abroad, net (increase/financial outflow (−))	−106
55	Foreign-owned assets in the US, net (increase/financial inflow (+))	534,071
71	Balance on goods (lines 3 and 20)	−84,0252
72	Balance on services (lines 4 and 21)	144,316
73	Balance on goods and services (lines 2 and 19)	−695,936
74	Balance on income (lines 12 and 29)	118,231
75	Unilateral current transfers, net (line 35)	−128,363
76	Balance on current account (lines 1, 18, and 35 or lines 73, 74, and 75)	−706,068

Source: US Bureau of Economic Analysis, *Survey of Current Business*, Table D-61, June 2010,
US Census Bureau, *U.S. International Transactions by Type of Transaction*, Table 1250, June 2010.

E-resources: http://www.census.gov/compendia/statab/cats/foreign_commerce_aid/international_transactions.html.

of its annual trade deficit. However, more concerted action will be needed if the United States is to continue on this course. One way is to continue to increase US competitiveness in the international market. Another way is to get other countries to reduce their trade barriers and to make international markets more open.

Table 6C US merchandise trade, 2008

	2008 (millions of US $)
Exports	1,304,896
Foods, feeds, and beverages	108,349
Industrial supplies and materials	388,033
Capital goods, except automotive	457,655
Automotive vehicles, engines, and parts	121,451
Consumer goods, except automotive	161,292
Other	50,662
Adjustments	17,454
Imports	2,139,548
Foods, feeds, and beverages	88,997
Industrial supplies and materials	779,481
Capital goods, except automotive	453,743
Automotive vehicles, engines, and parts	231,242
Consumer goods, except automotive	481,643
Other	68,536
Adjustments	35,907
Memorandum	
Balance on goods	834,652

Source: US Bureau of Economic Analysis, *Survey of Current Business*, June 2010, Table D-60.

When a country suffers a persistent balance of trade deficit, the nation will also suffer from a depreciating currency and will find it difficult to borrow in the international capital market. In this case there are only two choices available. One is to borrow from the IMF and be willing to accept the restrictions that the IMF puts on the country, which are designed to introduce austerity and force the country back on to the right economic track. The other approach is for the country to change its fiscal policy (tariffs and taxes), resort to exchange and trade controls, or devalue its currency. To prevent having to undertake austerity steps, the United States will have to continue working very hard to control its trade deficit.

Chapter 7

INTERNATIONAL FINANCIAL MARKETS AND INSTITUTIONS

Contents

Objectives of the chapter

This chapter considers financial markets that allow firms to find sources and uses of funds outside their home countries and to deal in currencies other than the domestic one. It also considers the risks involved in operating in these markets and the tools available to deal with those risks. The main risk has to do with dealing in foreign currencies, so **exchange risk** and the functioning of the **foreign exchange** market are key elements of the discussion. For example, when a German firm borrows from a bank in dollars, because of the low interest rate, the firm faces a problem of exchange risk. The firm has to decide what to do in case the dollar rises in value relative to the euro and makes loan repayment more expensive.

The main goals of the chapter are to:

1 *Review* the basic characteristics of all the financial markets that may be available to a firm in international business.

2 *Examine* the foreign exchange market, its operation, and the main participants.

3 *Explain* the fundamental economic factors that determine the exchange rates in the absence of government intervention in the foreign exchange markets.

4 *Show* how firms can operate successfully in more than one currency without facing unacceptable levels of exchange risk.

5 *Give* insights into domestic money and capital markets that exist around the world.

6 *Describe* the functioning of the euromarkets, both short term and long term.

7 *Explain* how the international monetary system functions and how it relates to both private-sector firms and governments.

8 *Look* at a country's balance of payments and show what lessons can be drawn from it.

9 *Show* how firms can take advantage of the opportunities available in all of these markets.

ACTIVE LEARNING CASE

Barclays Bank international financial dealings

Barclays Bank, one of the largest banks in the world (measured by capital), had a worldwide spread of branches, representative offices, and other affiliates in the early 2000s. As at 2009, Barclays is the world's ninth largest banking and financial services group and the UK's second largest bank (Global Fortune 500, 2010 ranking). The bank was actively involved in businesses such as corporate finance for major firms around the world, retail banking in the UK and a few other countries in Europe, and in foreign exchange dealing in London, New York, Tokyo, and other financial capitals of the world. At the end of 2009 Barclays' business was divided among the currencies shown in Table 1. Growth in income and costs was constrained by foreign exchange translation movements. These are not necessarily major concerns for a multi-national bank, since Barclays has lengthy experience in using these currencies, and the bank regularly deals with foreign exchange risk. Still, some banks had encountered huge crises due to foreign exchange losses. For example, National Australia Bank lost US $360 million in 2003–2004 due to currency trading, and Allied Irish Banks lost more than US $770 million in 2002 from similar trading. Back in 1974 the entire world financial system was shaken by a pair of foreign exchange losses that caused two banks to fail

(Franklin National Bank in the United States and Bankhaus Herstatt in Germany) and the entire **eurocurrency** system to briefly come to a halt. (In 2008 the British government nationalized Northern Rock to prevent its failure, while banks in the United States also faced failure due to losses on the subprime mortgage market leading to the world financial crisis)

Barclays is heavily involved in financial activities in more than 30 countries worldwide. This is an overstatement of the firm's global activity. Instead, Barclays is a home region bank, with 60 percent of its revenues in Europe. A geographical analysis of revenues from external customers for continuing operations for the year ended December 31, 2009 shows that 44.06 percent of Barclays' revenues are in the UK, the bank's country of origin. Another 15.11 percent of the bank's business is in other European Union countries, about 19.06 percent in the United States, 10.24 percent in South Africa. This leaves 11.53 percent of Barclays' business in the remaining countries where it operates. With this exposure to risks in other countries, as Table 1 shows, Barclays has a large exposure in US dollars.

From another perspective, Barclays had an international financial exposure through its lending activities in various countries. Table 2 shows this distribution of activity.

Table 1 The Barclays Group's structural currency exposures as at December 31, 2009

Functional currency of the operation involved	Foreign currency net investment £m	Borrowings which hedge the investment £m	Derivatives which hedge the investment £m	Structural currency exposures pre economic hedges £m	Economic hedges £m	Remaining structural economic exposures £m
At 31/12/2009						
US dollar	16,677	3,205		13,472	6,056	7,416
Euro	6,772	3,418		3,354	2,902	452
South Africa Rand	4,055		1,542	2,513	189	2,324
Japanese Yen	4,436	3,484	940	12		12
Swiss Franc	2,840	2,734	92	14		14
Other	2,983		677	2,306		2,306
Total	37,763	12,841	3,251	21,671	9,147	12,524
At 31/12/2008						
US dollar	14,577	6,019		8,558	6,720	1,838
Euro	6,336	2,922		3,414	3,125	289
South Africa Rand	3,725		1,306	2,419	164	2,255
Japanese Yen	5,009	801	4,212	−4		−4
Swiss Franc	3,042	2,936	101	5		5
Other	2,940		880	2,060		2,060
Total	35,629	12,678	6,499	16,452	10,009	6,443

Table 2 Analysis of loans and advances to customers as at December 31, 2009

Credit risk concentrations by geographical sector (£m)	The Group		The Bank	
	2009	2008	2009	2008
United Kingdom	203,582	213,079	375,761	392,153
Other European Union	84,343	91,109	61,909	66,326
United States	58,355	75,826	47,520	59,971
Africa	47,495	44,373	3,654	2,987
Rest of world (ROW)	26,449	37,428	23,284	32,452
Total	420,224	461,815	512,128	553,889
Credit risk concentrations by maturity (£m)				
On demand	44,826	51,155	39,694	71,170
Not more than 3 months	68,876	87,624	226,426	216,131
Over three months but not more than six months	8,987	12,447	6,472	9,237
Over six months but not more than one year	17,848	21,976	10,977	15,692
Over one year but not more than three years	51,886	60,927	44,604	52,651
Over three years but not more than five years	38,357	44,982	35,637	38,584
Over five years but not more than ten years	63,180	57,409	57,177	55,631
Over ten years	126,264	125,295	91,141	94,793
Total	420,224	461,815	512,128	553,889

A key concern of Barclays is how to manage these overseas and foreign currency activities, especially with respect to the risk of currency losses. As an international bank, Barclays wants to operate in major financial centres, but as a prudently managed firm it doesn't want to take undue risk in foreign currencies or put significant amounts of assets in high-risk environments.

Website: www.barclays.com.

Source: Barclays, *Annual Report*, 2009.

1 What exchange risk does Barclays have as at December 31, 2009?

2 What should Barclays' expectation be about the value of the pound relative to the euro or the dollar?

3 How should Barclays deal with the risk involved in its foreign currency positions?

4 How can Barclays use the eurocurrency market in its international business, and will this help in dealing with the exchange rate problem?

Exchange risk
The risk of financial loss or gain due to an unexpected change in a currency's value

Foreign exchange
Foreign currency-denominated financial instruments, ranging from cash to bank deposits to other financial contracts payable or receivable in foreign currency

Eurocurrency
A bank deposit in any country that is denominated in a foreign currency. A yen-denominated bank deposit in Germany is a euro–yen deposit, a form of eurocurrency

INTRODUCTION

International financial markets are relevant to companies, whether or not they become directly involved in international business through exports, direct investment, and the like. Purchases of imported products or services may require payment in foreign exchange, thus involving exchange risk. A company may choose to invest in a foreign business or security, and face both different interest rates and different risks from those at home. Often companies find that borrowing funds abroad is less expensive than borrowing domestically, in the United States or in any other home country. The relatively unrestricted "euromarkets" generally offer better terms to borrowers (*and* lenders) than do domestic financial markets in any country. Likewise, in the 2000s, investors are discovering more and more opportunities to diversify their portfolios into holdings of foreign securities. This chapter explores the various foreign and international financial markets, including the foreign exchange market, and examines ways to utilize them for domestic and international business.

FOREIGN EXCHANGE MARKETS

Currencies, like any other products, services, or claims, can be traded for one another. The foreign exchange market is simply a mechanism through which transactions can be made between one country's currency and another's. Or, more broadly, a foreign exchange market is a market for the exchange of financial instruments denominated in different currencies. The most common location for foreign exchange transactions is a commercial bank, which agrees to "make a market" for the purchase and sale of currencies other than the local one. In the United States, hundreds of banks offer foreign exchange markets in dozens of cities. However, over 40 percent of all foreign exchange business is done through the 10 largest banks in New York.

Foreign exchange is not simply currency printed by a foreign country's central bank; rather, it includes such items as cash, checks (or drafts), wire transfers, telephone transfers, and even contracts to sell or buy currency in the future. Foreign exchange is really any financial instrument that carries out payment from one currency to another. The most common form of foreign exchange in transactions between companies is the draft (denominated in a foreign currency). The most common form of foreign exchange in transactions between banks is the telephone or Internet transfer, generally for transactions of $1 million or more. Far down the list of instruments, in terms of the value exchanged, is actual currency, which is often exchanged by tourists and other travelers.

Exchange rate
The value of one currency in terms of another; for example, US $1.2378 / €1

Since no currency is necessarily fixed in value relative to others, there must be some means of determining an acceptable price, or **exchange rate**. How many British pounds (£) should one dollar buy? How many Brazilian reals should be paid to buy a dollar? Since 1973, most of the industrialized countries have allowed their currency values to fluctuate more or less freely (depending on the time and the country), so that simple economics of supply and demand largely determines exchange rates. In graphic form, Figure 7.1 shows that the intersection of the supply curve and the demand curve for European euros (c) sets the price, or exchange rate, of euros in terms of dollars. Some of the participants in the foreign exchange market are listed below the graph; their specific activities are discussed in the following section.

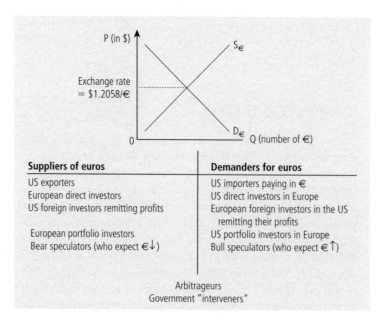

Figure 7.1 Foreign exchange market for euros in New York

The exchange rate of $1.2378 per euro is offered by one specific bank. This was the closing exchange rate quoted by Bankers Trust Company of New York for purchases of at least $1 million worth of euros on June 26, 2010. Another bank in New York may have quoted a slightly higher or slightly lower rate at the same time, and banks in San Francisco, London, or Tokyo probably quoted rates that differed even more. The rates quoted depend on each bank's interest in being involved in foreign exchange transactions and on the varying strategic positions and risks taken by the banks. Thus, the foreign exchange market among banks may be viewed as one large market or as many small markets with extensive (potential and actual) interrelations. Generally, the interbank market within any country is viewed as one market, and intercountry dealings are somewhat segmented by different rules and risks (though in the United States, the San Francisco market often offers quotations from various banks that differ noticeably from rate quotations in New York, due partly to the difference in time zones).

The differences in rate quotations may appear very small to an outsider. For example, Euros may be quoted at $1.23236 at Citibank in New York and at $1.23386 at Bank of America in San Francisco. This difference seems small, but for every 1 million euros sold, the buyer of dollars in San Francisco receives an extra $1,500. Since the transactions are generally rapid, for values of $5 million to $10 million such differences may add up to a substantial gain (or cost) to the participant in the foreign exchange market.[1]

The various foreign exchange transactions just mentioned involve large commercial banks and large amounts of money. Most of the companies that do international business also utilize foreign exchange markets, but far less frequently than banks and for transactions that involve less money. Consequently, these companies' access to foreign currencies differs from that of the banks. (Specifically, banks make the market and companies pay for the use of this service.) The next section describes the various participants in the US foreign exchange market.

Foreign exchange markets in the United States

Figure 7.2 presents an overview of the foreign exchange markets operating today in the United States. This section discusses each of these markets in some detail.

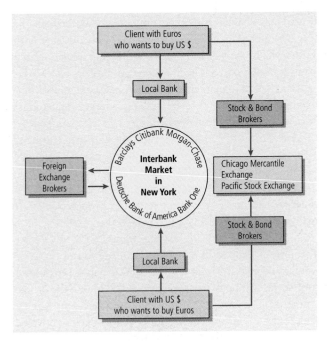

Figure 7.2 US foreign exchange markets

Source: Adapted from K. Alec Chrystal, *St. Louis Fed Review*, March 1984, Figure 1, p. 8.

The interbank market

Although the foreign exchange dealings of most managers involve a company buying from, or selling to, a bank, managers must understand the foreign exchange market among banks. This is because, as noted above, the vast majority of large-scale foreign exchange transactions are interbank, and these transactions tend to determine exchange rates, with which occasional market participants such as companies must deal.

Local and regional commercial banks may offer clients a foreign exchange service, which such banks provide on request by dealing through a larger bank, typically in a large city (such as New York, Los Angeles, or Chicago). If a local bank receives a request to buy Swiss francs (SF) for an importer in New Jersey, it will call its correspondent bank in New York (say, JP Morgan-Chase Bank) and arrange to buy the SF for, say, $0.6753/SF. Then the local bank will add on its service charge so that the importer pays $0.6853/SF. Thus, the local bank earns $0.01 per SF, or about 1.5 percent on the transaction.

Foreign exchange traders
Bankers who deal in foreign exchange, buying and selling foreign currencies on behalf of clients and/ or for the bank itself; typically they deal in foreign currency-denominated bank deposits

JP Morgan-Chase Bank, in turn, will either take the requested Swiss francs from its own holdings of that currency or enter the interbank market to buy them. Assuming that Chase does *not* have the SF on hand, one of its **foreign exchange traders** will call several other major banks (or brokerage houses, which are discussed below) and contract to buy Swiss francs from the lowest bidder.

The interbank market generally operates with large transactions only of about $1 million to $10 million exchanged for the equivalent foreign currency. On a typical day in 2010, the more than 45 members of the main association of commercial banks in foreign exchange dealings (called the Clearinghouse Interbank Payments System, or CHIPS) transacted roughly $2 trillion in currency trades.[2]

The brokers' market

Foreign exchange brokers
A company that provides specialized services to commercial banks in the interbank foreign exchange market, essentially functioning to unite interested buyers and sellers of foreign currency-denominated bank deposits; brokers intermediate about half of all wholesale foreign exchange transactions in New York and London

Another facet of large-scale foreign exchange dealing in the United States is the brokers' market. About six **foreign exchange brokers** make markets for foreign currencies in New York (as well as in London and elsewhere), creating trading in many currencies similar to that in the interbank market. In this case, the key differences are that the brokers seek to match buyers and sellers on any given transaction, without taking a position[3] themselves; they deal simultaneously with many banks (and other companies); and they offer both buy and sell positions to clients (where a bank may wish to operate on only one side of the market at any particular time). Also, the brokers deal "blind," offering rate quotations without naming the potential seller/buyer until a deal has been negotiated. Brokers play a large role in the total market, arranging about half of total interbank foreign exchange transaction in the early 2000s.

Before moving on to other foreign exchange markets, let us consider an example in which the spot market is used by a tourist planning a trip to Japan. This person wants to visit Tokyo to see a friend during the Christmas vacation and to do some sightseeing. She is taking $1,000 with her and has already purchased the round-trip airline ticket. Since dollars cannot be used for most purchases in Japan, she needs to buy Japanese yen. How should she do it?

Looking at the currency trading listing in Table 7.1, she sees that Bankers Trust is offering to sell large quantities of yen at the rate of 112 yen per dollar. At the "retail" level—that is, for small transactions such as this one—she can expect to receive fewer yen per dollar. Instead of carrying the cash with her, she wants to get traveler's checks. Upon calling the office of American Express in San Francisco, she found that yen-denominated traveler's checks were available but would cost her the exchange rate, plus a $5 service charge.

The tourist was willing to pay the extra cost to obtain the protection of traveler's checks, but one final problem arose. A friend who works in foreign exchange dealing at Wells Fargo Bank told her that the yen would probably decline in value relative to the dollar in the next few days. Since she would not leave for Tokyo for another week, she wondered whether it was worth waiting for the expected devaluation. The answer to this question is that no one knows! She can hope for a devaluation and delay purchase of the yen for

Table 7.1 Exchange rates in the inter-bank market, June 26, 2010

Foreign currency exchange rates (mid)	UK sterling (£)	Europe euro (€)	Japan yen (¥)
Spot rate—closing (foreign currency units per US dollar)	1.5072	1.2378	0.0112
Forward rate—closing			
1 month outright	1.4750	1.2200	0.0110
3 months outright	1.5000	1.2500	0.0109
12 months outright	1.5500	1.3000	0.0110

Source: Financial Times, June 26, 2010

Spot rate
The exchange rate offered on the same day as the request to buy or sell foreign currency; actual settlement (payment) may occur one or two days later

Forward rate
An exchange rate contracted today for some future date of actual currency exchange; banks offer forward rates to clients to buy or sell foreign currency in the future, guaranteeing the rate at the time of the agreement

a week, or ignore the potential gain or loss and buy the yen today. In such a short time period, it is probably better to ignore the few days' variability in the exchange rate—since it could be favorable or unfavorable—and just buy the yen at the most convenient time before departing for Tokyo. (One more point to confuse the matter: she could buy traveler's checks in US dollars and exchange them for yen in Japan when needed. Again, no one can be sure what the yen's value will be during her vacation time in Tokyo.)

Although this example does not offer a guaranteed way to make money from foreign exchange dealings, it does illustrate the kinds of problems that beset individuals and companies as they work with foreign currencies. Fortunately, there are some methods to help avoid the uncertainty involved in foreign exchange; they are discussed in the section below on "Protecting against exchange risk."

So far, our discussion has focused only on the *spot market*; that is, the market for immediate exchange of one currency for another. An additional, very large part of the US foreign exchange market is the set of instruments that allow contracting today for delivery of currency in the future. The main instruments of this type are forward contracts, foreign exchange futures contracts, and foreign currency options.

The forward foreign exchange market

The forward foreign exchange market at commercial banks in the United States offers banks, companies, and individuals the opportunity to contract *today* for a specific foreign exchange transaction in the *future*, at a fixed price (that is, exchange rate). Forward contracts are negotiated between the offering bank and the client as to size, maturity, and price. Referring to Table 7.1, we see that Bankers Trust was offering to sell British pounds for $1.5500/£ in 360 days on June 26, 2010 (for quantities of at least $1 million).

The rationale for forward contracts in currencies is analogous to that for futures contracts in commodities: the firm can lock in a price today to eliminate uncertainty about the value of a future receipt or a payment of foreign currency. A firm may undertake such a transaction because it has made a previous contract, for example, to pay €1 million to a supplier in three months for some needed inputs to its operations. If the firm wants to eliminate the risk that its payment in three months will change in dollar terms (that is, the €1 million may cost more dollars then), it can contract with a bank to buy €1 million three months forward, at a price established today. (From Table 7.1, we see that the price was $1.2500/EUR for a contract with Bankers Trust on June 26, 2010.) Thus, firms can use forward contracts to eliminate the risk of variability in future dollar costs or revenues due to exchange rate changes. This concept, called *hedging*, and other motives for using the forward market are discussed later.

Notice that in the above example, the forward contract used for hedging is not the same thing as an insurance contract. The forward contract does fix a minimum "loss" for the firm by setting the guaranteed price of exchange in the future. Even if the dollar devalues to $1.30 per € in three months, the forward contract holder is still able to buy €1 million for $1.3710/€. However, if the euro devalues over the next three months to, say, $1.2400/€, the forward contract holder will have an opportunity cost of the difference between the forward rate and the (eventual) future spot rate. Thus, the forward contract insures against potential losses *and* against potential gains in foreign currency value.

Forward markets exist in any currencies and for any maturities that banks are willing to offer. Most of the forward contracts used in the United States involve exchanges of US dollars for euros, Japanese yen, British pounds, Swiss francs, and Canadian dollars. Maturities tend to be six months or less, though single-year and multiyear forward contracts are sometimes available.

The futures market in currencies

A very similar type of instrument is available on several securities exchanges in the United States and abroad. The foreign exchange futures contract is an agreement to buy or sell a fixed amount of foreign currency for delivery at a fixed future date at a fixed dollar price. The main difference between futures and forward contracts in the United States is that futures contracts have fixed sizes (about $50,000 to $100,000, depending on the currency) and pre-established maturity dates. (All are 3-, 6-, 9-, or 12-month contracts maturing on the third Wednesday of March, June, September, or December.) Also, futures contracts are available for only a few currencies (Canadian dollars, euros, Swiss francs, British pounds, Japanese yen, Mexican pesos, Australian dollars, and a few others), and only if a buyer and a seller can be found at the time.

The futures market at the Chicago Mercantile Exchange is currently very thin (that is, few contracts are traded) except for the three-month contracts denominated in Canadian dollars, euros, Swiss francs, British pounds, and Japanese yen.

Futures contracts are more widely accessible to firms and individuals than forward contracts because of their smaller value and the margin requirements that enable brokers to obtain collateral from market participants. (However, the currently thin nature of this market does not allow participants the wide range of currencies and maturities that are available for large-scale transactions in the forward market.) The standard contracts available at the Chicago Mercantile Exchange (CME) are described in Table 7.2. Trading hours have been extended via the GLOBEX system, which permits worldwide access to CME contracts. In 2010, GLOBEX trading was available for about 19 hours per day around the world.

Foreign currency *options* are an additional instrument of the foreign exchange market in the United States; they offer participants the *right* to buy or sell foreign currency in the future rather than the obligation to do so. Foreign currency options are similar to foreign

Table 7.2 Currency futures contract specifications at the Chicago Mercantile Exchange

	British pound (£)	Eurozone euro (€)	Japanese yen (¥)
Trading Unit	£62,500	€125,000	¥12,500,000
Quotations	US $ per £	US $ per €	US $ per ¥
Minimum price fluctuation	0.0001	0.0001	0.000001
Value of 1 point	$6.25	$12.50	$12.50
Months traded	Six months in the March quarterly cycle (Mar, Jun, Sep, Dec) *GLOBEX (ETH): Sundays: 5:00 p.m. – 4:00 p.m. Central Time (CT) next day*		
Trading hours	*Monday – Friday: 5:00 p.m. – 4:00 p.m.* CT the next day, except on Friday – closes at 4:00 p.m. and reopens Sunday at 5:00 p.m. CT. CME ClearPort: Sunday – Friday 6:00 p.m. – 5:15 p.m. (5:00 p.m. – 4:15 p.m. Chicago Time/CT) with a 45–minute break each day beginning at 5:15 p.m. (4:15 p.m. CT) *OPEN OUTCRY (RTH): 7:20 a.m. – 2:00 p.m.*		
Last day hours	9:16 a.m. Central Time (CT) on the second business day immediately preceding the third Wednesday of the contract month (usually Monday).		

Source: Adapted from Chicago Mercantile Exchange, June 26, 2010.

E-resources: http://www.cmegroup.com/trading/fx/.

currency futures in the Unites States in that the contracts are for fixed quantities of currency to be exchanged at a fixed price in the future. The key difference is that the option may be *exercised*, that is, presented for currency exchange, at *any* time between its issuance and the maturity date, or not at all.[4]

Foreign exchange arbitrage involves simultaneous contracting in two or more foreign exchange markets to buy and sell foreign currency, profiting from exchange rate differences *without* incurring exchange rate risk. Foreign exchange arbitrage may be two-way, three-way, or intertemporal and is generally undertaken by large commercial banks that can exchange large quantities of money to exploit small rate differentials.

The simplest form of exchange arbitrage is two-way arbitrage, between any two currencies and between two places. Assume quotations for Swiss francs in the spot market on June 26, 2010, were:

At Bankers Trust in New York:	$0.91038/SF
At Bank of America in San Francisco:	$0.91158/SF
At Lloyds Bank in London:	$0.91398/SF

Arbitrageur

A person or firm that deals in foreign exchange, buying or selling foreign currency with simultaneous contracting to exchange back to the original currency; arbitrageurs thus do not undertake exchange risk

An **arbitrageur** can buy SF in New York and simultaneously sell them in London, making a profit of $0.0036/SF, or 0.37 percent per transaction. While the percentage gain is small, it translates to $3,600 for every SF 1 million traded, and it involves no exchange risk. By repeatedly arbitraging this price (exchange rate) differential, the arbitrageur will make a profit until the exchange rate differential drops below the transactions cost (that is, the telephone bill, plus the arbitrageur's salary, plus other relevant costs).

The same two-way arbitrage may also occur in the forward market or between forward and futures markets. From the quotations here, we see that profitable arbitrage opportunities exist between the New York forward market and the Chicago futures market, as well as between the New York and San Francisco forward markets:

At Bankers Trust in New York: ¥109.00/$ for delivery in 90 days.

At Bank of America in San Francisco: ¥109.90/$ for delivery in 90 days.

At the Chicago Mercantile Exchange: ¥107.38/$ for delivery on June 26, 2010.

An arbitrageur can buy yen in New York and sell them in San Francisco, both for exchange in 90 days, and earn ¥0.9/$, or 0.77 percent per transaction. Similarly, an arbitrageur can buy yen in Chicago and sell them in San Francisco, to make ¥1.62/$, or 1.4 percent per transaction. The difficulties with the latter transaction are that contracts may not be available for the desired amount or maturity date and transaction costs are higher for the inter-market exchanges. Nonetheless, both transactions may be feasible and profitable, even after costs are considered.[5]

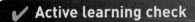

✔ Active learning check

Review your answer to Active Learning Case question 1 and make any changes you like. Then compare your answer to the one below.

❶ What exchange risk does Barclays have as at December 31, 2009?

Barclays has exchange risk on the various assets and liabilities that were on its books at year-end 2009. These include exposures of £6,056 million in US dollars and £2,902 million in euros, among others. From the second table in the case, it appears that these exposures may be from lending to corporations in the European Union and the United States (though this is not certain, since some other activities are missing from the table). These are net asset exposures, or long positions, since Barclays will receive future cash flows in these currencies, and their values may change in terms of British pounds.

DETERMINATION OF THE EXCHANGE RATE

Exchange rates are determined by the activities of the various actors described earlier. If one could calculate the supply and demand curves for each exchange market participant and anticipate government constraints on the exchange market, exchange rate determination would be fairly simple. The composite supply and demand for foreign exchange would be as depicted in Figure 7.1.

Lacking this information, the analyst can still rely on two fundamental economic relationships that underlie exchange rate determination. Note that this section considers only economic factors; government restrictions on the exchange market are ignored.

The two fundamental economic relationships are **purchasing power parity** and the **international Fisher effect**. The former posits that shifts in exchange rates will occur to offset different rates of inflation in pairs of countries, and the latter proposes that exchange rates will shift to offset interest rate differentials between countries.

Purchasing power parity

The theory of exchange rate determination that states that differences in prices of the same goods between countries will be eliminated by exchange rate changes

International Fisher effect

Theory of exchange rate determination that states that differences in nominal interest rates on similar-risk deposits will be eliminated by changes in the exchange rate

Purchasing power parity[6]

The purchasing power parity (PPP) theory is based on the law of one price and explains the long-run exchange rates. If two countries produce an identical product and transportation costs are extremely low, the price of the product should be the same in two countries. Under the law of one price, the price of the product is the same not only in two countries but also around the world. If a standard ton of polyurethane plastic costs $200 in the United States and €190 in Germany, PPP requires an exchange rate of $1.05/€. The same reasoning could be used for all products whose production processes are equivalent in two countries and that are traded between these countries. The exchange rate that comes closest to simultaneously satisfying all of these equilibrium conditions is the PPP rate—a rate that equates the internal purchasing power of the two currencies in both countries.

Assuming we begin from that exchange rate, what will happen if Germany' inflation is 5 percent and the US inflation is 10 percent in the following year? PPP requires that the exchange rate adjust to eliminate this differential. Specifically, it requires that:

$$\frac{1 + \text{Infl}_{US}}{1 + \text{Infl}_{Ger}} = \frac{XR_{t+1}}{XR_t}$$

where:

$\text{Infl} = $ inflation rate

$t = $ time period

This means that inflation in the United States relative to inflation in Germany should be the same as the future exchange rate compared to the spot exchange rate. The relationship can also be written in a form similar to the interest parity equation by rearranging terms:

$$(1 + \text{Infl}_{us}) = (1 + \text{Infl}_{Ger}) \frac{XR_{t+1}}{XR_t}$$

Purchasing power in each currency will be retained if:

$$XR_{t+1} = \frac{1.10}{1.05} (\$1.05/€) = \$1.10/€ \text{, or } €0.909/\$$$

International Fisher effect

The international Fisher effect (IFE) translates Irving Fisher's reasoning about domestic interest rates to the transnational level. Fisher showed that inflation-adjusted (that

Nominal interest rate
The actual rate of interest offered by a bank, typically given as an annual percentage rate

Real interest rate
The nominal interest rate adjusted for price changes. Domestically, this means adjusting for inflation; internationally, this means adjusting for exchange rate (currency price) changes

is, "real") interest rates tend to stay the same over time; as inflation rises or falls, so do **nominal** (unadjusted) **interest rates**, such that **real interest rates** remain unchanged. At the transnational level, nominal national interest rates are expected to differ only by the expected change in the national currency's price (that is, the exchange rate). The international Fisher effect thus concludes that interest differentials between national markets will be eliminated by adjustments in the exchange rate. In terms similar to PPP, we see that:

$$\frac{1 + i_{US}}{1 + i_{foreign}} = \frac{XR_{t+1}}{XR_t}, \text{ or } (1 + i_{US}) = (1 + i_{foreign})\frac{XR_{t+1}}{XR_t}$$

where i = the interest rate, usually on a eurocurrency deposit denominated in the given country's currency.

If the eurodollar deposit rate is 3 percent/year and the euro–euro rate is 6 percent/year, the euro will be expected to devalue in the coming year by:

$$\frac{1.06}{1.03} = 1.029, \text{ or } 2.9 \text{ percent}$$

Notice that the international Fisher effect *will* operate in a free market, because investors will receive a higher return in euros otherwise. As more and more investors put their money in euros, the spot price of the euro will rise. Similarly, as US investors return their euro earnings to dollars at the end of the period (year), this increased demand for dollars will cause the euro to devalue (in the future). Thus, dollar and euro earnings will tend to be equalized.

Combined equilibrium relationships

The future exchange rate, XR_{t+1}, will be partially determined by both of the above factors (PPP and IFE), which can be viewed in a general equilibrium context as shown in Figure 7.3. This figure also demonstrates the interest parity relationship, which provides another link between current and future currency values. Remember that these relationships are *equilibrium* economic conditions, which hold only approximately since substantial uncertainty exists about future conditions. Also, if a government intervenes to prohibit the market from determining exchange rates, the relationships may diverge substantially from the equilibrium conditions. Figure 7.3 shows the main economic influences that, along with government policies and other factors, combine to determine exchange rates. Note that the expected exchange rate is in the top box, and the determinants of that rate (interest difference and inflation difference) are presented as fractions, so that they show the precise relationship between the spot exchange rate, XRT, and the expected future rate, E[XRT].

A final caveat is in order. Despite the strong relationships among interest differentials, inflation differentials, and exchange rates, other important *economic* influences operate in international finance. Pure speculation can cause shifts in exchange rates, despite the fundamental economic conditions that have been described above. A country' balance of payments position may affect the exchange rate, even though that position also affects interest and inflation rates as well. Since the abandonment of the Bretton Woods system of fixed exchange rates, exchange rate determination has been extremely uncertain—perhaps similar to the determination of future values of stock exchange indexes.

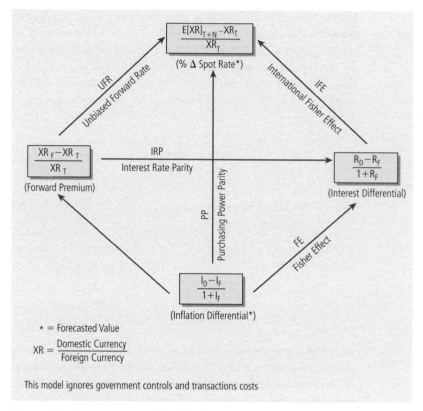

Figure 7.3 Exchange rate determination

Other factors determining exchange rates

PPP and IFEs explain overall exchange rate well, but other factors also determine exchange rates. In general factors affecting the demand and supply of domestic products over foreign products determine exchange rates because these factors affect the demand and supply of local and foreign currencies in exchange rate markets. First, changes in demand affect the exchange rate. For example, the changes in trade barriers, such as tariffs and quotas, can affect the exchange rate. If the United States raises the tariff rates over Chinese products due to antidumping or countervailing regulation, the demand for domestic products will be increased over Chinese products and the US dollar tends to appreciate. Second, the changes in supply will affect the exchange rate. For example, China becomes more productive than before. Chinese auto manufacturers recently developed their own models and produced them with great productivity, and the Chinese auto manufacturers can lower the price over foreign auto manufacturers. This affects the demand for Chinese automobiles, and the Chinese currency tends to appreciate. Third, national governments reserve foreign currencies and actively control foreign exchange rates to lower the price of exporting goods, to stabilize exchange rate volatility, and to protect the national economy from a currency crisis. According to the Central Intelligence Agency (CIA) and International Monetary Fund, China and Japan are the No.1 and No.2 country in terms of reserves of foreign exchange and gold. China's reserves for foreign exchanges and gold are $2.426 trillion (31 December 2009 est.) $1.953 trillion (31 December 2008 est.). Japan's reserves of foreign exchange and gold amounts of $1.024 trillion (31 December 2009 est.) and $1.011 trillion (31 December 2008 est.).

> ### ✔ Active learning check
>
> *Review your answer to Active Learning Case question 2 and make any changes you like. Then compare your answer to the one below.*
>
> **2** **What should Barclays' expectation be about the value of the pound relative to the euro or the dollar?**
>
> Barclays can forecast the value of the euro or the dollar based on PPP, the IFE, or a chartist method, in addition to simply using the forward exchange rate. Since Barclays' business includes currency trading, the bank probably should use one or more methods for the minute-by-minute activity in the foreign exchange market, and another method or methods for its longer-term concerns such as future maturities of loans and accounting reporting periods. In sum, Barclays should forecast using market-based tools such as IFE and PPP, as well as using additional methods such as technical forecasting or leading indicators for short periods of time such as hours or a few days.

PROTECTING AGAINST EXCHANGE RISK

Exchange risk is a very real concern for financial managers, whether or not their firms are directly involved in international business. The fact that the prices of imported products and services often vary with the exchange rate means that a local firm's costs may depend on the exchange rate. Similarly, if any of the firm's sales are exported, its earnings may vary as foreign sales change due to exchange rate changes. Even a purely domestic firm faces these problems, since suppliers and competitors that *are* doing international business will adjust to exchange rate changes, and this will affect the domestic firm.

From this perspective, exchange risk is *not* the risk that a local currency will decrease in value (devalue) relative to the home currency. *Exchange risk is the possibility that a firm will be unable to adjust its prices and costs to exactly offset exchange rate changes.* Thus, a US importer which faces 10 percent higher costs because of a dollar devaluation from €0.80/$ to €0.72/$ still has no exchange risk as long as the importer can raise its own prices by 10 percent without lowering total sales. (This result is the microeconomic version of PPP.) The problem may be viewed as one of "passing through" cost increases to the firm' customers via higher sales prices.

Similarly, the appropriate measure of exchange risk for financial instruments is the firm's possible loss or gain in purchasing power from exchange rate-adjusted interest rates. Investing in a US dollar account that pays 5 percent per year is better than investing in a Swiss franc account that pays 10 percent per year if, during the year, the franc devalues by 6 percent.

Alternatives to minimize exchange risk

Exchange risk exists whenever the firm's prices and costs cannot be exactly adjusted to offset changes in the exchange rate. Let us now consider a group of alternatives that will allow a firm to minimize (or at least reduce) its exchange risk. These alternatives fall into four categories:

1 Risk avoidance

2 Risk adaptation

3 Risk transfer

4 Diversification

INTERNATIONAL BUSINESS STRATEGY IN ACTION

Wall Street and world financial markets

International finance affects virtually every business. Companies with overseas operations, for example, are continually concerned with the rise and fall of the currencies in the countries where they operate. Indonesia is a good example as seen by the country's currency crisis of the late 1990s that sent shock waves through the Asian business market. As a result, thousands of firms went bankrupt, the country's currency lost 80 percent of its value, and the stock market plummeted by 60 percent. In the aftermath, Indonesia was hit with soaring unemployment and inflation led to riots that forced the resignation of the government. (See the Real Case "World Financial Crises" at the end of this chapter.)

Yet the international financial markets have never suffered anything like the initial effect from the terrorist attacks on the twin towers of New York City's World Trade Center (WTC) on September 11, 2001. In addition to totally demolishing the two buildings as well as several large surrounding structures, the terrorists killed nearly 3,000 people, many of them Wall Street employees, and rocked the major international financial markets from London to Tokyo. One of the hardest-hit groups was the insurers who had losses of more than $15 billion. In addition, while the important financial records of businesses in the WTC were located in safe havens such as central computer banks miles away from Ground Zero, the effect of the terrorist actions began to quickly surface.

This was reflected on Wall Street where the stock market began a sharp downturn. Within two weeks of the terrorist act, the New York Stock Exchange's (NYSE's) Dow Index had lost 14 percent of its value. Only during the Great Depression had the United States seen a downturn this sharp. And for the rest of the world, the financial shock was shared very quickly. The NYSE and other major international stock exchanges saw massive sell-offs as investors headed for the sidelines, and companies seeking to raise capital in the international market put their plans on hold. Simply put, as the US economy began to slow down and focus its investment efforts on rebuilding and regenerating its own hard-hit industries, there were going to be less funds available for other things. The international finance lesson is clear: today's money markets are linked very, very closely. And a catastrophe in one geographic area can have major implications in all of the others. New York City remains a financial hub of the business world, and the effects of the September 2001 crisis have passed. Yet the financial risks that international business firms must assume will not diminish because of the large interdependency that now exists between the major centers of worldwide commerce.

In 2007–2008 another international financial crisis occurred and until 2010, the world economy has not yet recovered. Following defaults by borrowers in the US subprime mortgage markets many banks found that their balance sheets were in a mess as their housing assets had been overvalued. Not only US banks suffered—in early 2008 the British bank, Northern Rock, was nationalized by Prime Minister Brown's government in order to stop its default. The US financial crisis became a worldwide problem for all financial institutions due to the close interconnections in the international money markets. International capital markets are highly integrated (indeed globalized), unlike goods markets (which are regional) and factor markets (where labor is localized).

Website: www.nyse.com.

Sources: *Financial Times*, September 12–30, 2001; October 1–13, 2001 and other supplemental news sources in 2007–2008.

Exchange risk avoidance
An exchange risk management technique through which the firm tries to avoid operating in more than one currency

Risk avoidance

Exchange risk avoidance is the strategy of trying to avoid foreign currency transactions. A purely domestic firm can try to make all of its purchases from local suppliers of locally produced goods and make all of its sales to local buyers in competition only with other domestic firms. Obviously, this strategy is impractical, if only because all firms are affected by goods priced in foreign currency—automobiles, chemicals, steel, and so on. Also, there are very few industries that do not use imported materials, export some of their output, or compete with imported products.

Risk adaptation

Exchange risk adaptation offers a more realistic alternative for protecting the firm against exchange risk. This strategy includes all methods of "hedging" against exchange rate changes. In the extreme, exchange risk calls for protecting all liabilities denominated in foreign currency with equal-value, equal-maturity assets denominated in that foreign currency. An illustration can best clarify this point.

Exchange risk adaptation
An exchange risk management technique through which a company adjusts its business activities to try to balance foreign currency assets and liabilities, and inflows and outflows

Assume a French firm has contracted to buy $100,000 of machinery from a foreign supplier for use in its manufacturing operations. The purchase is payable in six months in US dollars. To eliminate foreign exchange risk completely, the firm may do two things. First, it may raise its own prices to customers once the six months pass to equate euro devaluation to price increase. (Note that this does *not* involve a foreign currency hedge.) If this option is not available, which is often the case, the firm may look to its other option: obtain some equal-value *dollar asset* maturing in 180 days. This may be as simple as depositing funds in a dollar-denominated bank account for six months or as arcane as arranging a swap of the dollar liability for some other firm's euro liability. Fairly standard methods of hedging an exposed dollar liability include:

1 Obtaining a dollar-denominated financial asset (for example, a time deposit or a Certificate of Deposit (CD)) that matures when the liability comes due.

2 Finding a buyer for your firm's products and agreeing to receive payment in US dollars for the same value and time as the liability.

3 Finding a bank that will contract to buy euros from you and sell you dollars at a price fixed today for exchange when the liability comes due. (This is called a *forward contract*.)

4 Agreeing with another (for example, North American) firm to exchange your dollar liability for that firm's (that is, its French subsidiary's) euro liability.

5 Contracting for any other equal-value, equal-maturity dollar-denominated asset that will offset the exposed liability.

The firm's goal in choosing among these methods is to minimize the cost of protection against exchange rate risk.

Risk transfer

Exchange risk transfer
An exchange risk management technique through which the firm contracts with a third party to pass exchange risk on to that party, via such instruments as forward contracts, futures, and options

The third strategy for reducing exchange risk is **exchange risk transfer**. This strategy involves the use of an insurance contract or guarantee that transfers the exchange risk to the insurer or guarantor. In many countries, the central bank offers exchange risk guarantees to importers and exporters of some products according to the bank's policies. Technically, though perhaps not realistically, any firm or government agency could issue a guarantee covering exchange rate changes to a local importer, at a price that would presumably reflect the risk.

Diversification

Currency diversification
An exchange risk management technique through which the firm places activities or assets and liabilities into multiple currencies, thus reducing the impact of exchange rate change for any one of them

The final strategy for reducing exchange risk is **currency diversification**. Here a firm can reduce the risk of unexpected local currency devaluations by spreading its assets and liabilities across several currencies (for example, euros, Swiss francs, and pounds in addition to US dollars). This strategy simply means, "Don't put all of your eggs in one basket." Domestically, a firm should deal with several suppliers and a variety of customers to reduce risk through diversification. Internationally, a firm should hold assets (and liabilities) in several currencies to reduce the impact of unexpected exchange rate changes.

The strategy that is probably most useful to the majority of firms is risk adaptation, or hedging. A key point of this section is to recognize that other alternatives may be used in many instances when hedging would be more expensive or otherwise less desirable. Nonetheless, the central problem in exchange risk management is hedging, and corporate treasurers should always be on the lookout for new instruments and techniques.

✔ Active learning check

Review your answer to Active Learning Case question 3 and make any changes you like. Then compare your answer to the one below.

3 **How should Barclays deal with the risk involved in its foreign currency positions?**

As an international bank, Barclays is constantly becoming involved in foreign exchange transactions. The bank needs to have a policy for its traders and its other bankers as to how much exchange risk the bank is willing to tolerate before looking for protection. The bank presumably knows more than most people about what to expect in the foreign exchange market, and it is very likely that Barclays will choose to run exchange risk without hedging because of this knowledge. Still, the bank must limit its exposure, and the usual hedging techniques for banks are forward contracts and matching loans with deposits in the same currency.

FOREIGN MONEY AND CAPITAL MARKETS

In each country an MNE enters, it will be able to obtain some degree of access to local financial markets. The MNE will generally utilize such markets to perform necessary local financial transactions and often to hedge its local asset exposure through local borrowing (or its local liability exposure through local deposits or investments). But the MNE can also utilize local financial markets to obtain additional funding (or place additional funds) for its non-local activities. A Mexican firm, for example, may choose to borrow funds through its Houston affiliate to finance its local needs in Texas *and* finance some of its needs in Mexico.

Usually national financial markets are not fully accessible to foreign firms; they are largely reserved for domestic borrowers and lenders. In these cases, use of local financial markets must be supplemented by use of the financial markets in the country of the parent company or elsewhere. Typically, such problems arise in countries that impose exchange controls, which limit the MNE's ability to put needed funds in the affiliate.

MNEs and national money markets

The advantages MNEs obtain from entering national money markets as *borrowers* of funds stem from the portfolio effect of holding liabilities in more than one (fluctuating) currency and from the local risk hedging that occurs as the MNE moves to balance local assets such as plant and equipment with local liabilities, such as local-currency borrowing. Additional benefits may occur if the local government subsidizes such loans through interest rate reduction, through tax breaks, or otherwise; a policy of this kind may be offered to attract the MNE's investment. This may lower the whole MNE's cost of capital if the subsidy does not disappear and if the interest rate remains below the comparable home-currency rate during the borrowing period.

The advantages MNEs obtain from entering national money markets as *lenders* of funds stem from the portfolio effect of holding financial instruments in more than one currency. There may also be a gain from balancing local-currency assets and liabilities if an excess of local liabilities was held previously. In addition, local financial investments may be a necessary strategy when exchange controls or profit remittance limits exist; such investments offer the firm an outlet for retained earnings that yield interest. Sometimes an exchange control policy may make the local-currency interest rates higher than those available in other currencies (after adjusting for expected exchange rate changes). In these cases, higher-than-normal profits can be earned by investing funds in local instruments, although exchange controls may limit conversion of the profits into the home-country currency, or a government-imposed exchange rate change may wipe out the advantage.

MNEs and national capital markets

The advantages MNEs obtain from entering national capital markets as *borrowers* are similar to those obtained from entering national money markets. However, the opportunities are generally much more limited. Very few countries have substantially developed stock markets, and those that do usually restrict the issuance of shares by foreigners. A few exceptions exist, such as the United States, the UK, Germany, and France, but even they serve only the largest and most creditworthy MNEs. National bond markets, when they exist, are also very restrictive. Thus far, virtually all of the **foreign bond** issues have taken place in New York (called "Yankee bonds"), London, Switzerland, Germany, and Japan (called "Samurai bonds").

The **eurobond** market, which functions mostly outside the United States, is dominated by dollar issues, which constitute about 40 percent of that total. In all, dollar-denominated issues account for about 36 percent of the two types of international bonds.

The advantages MNEs obtain from entering national capital markets as *lenders* come mainly from diversification and from higher returns that may be protected by exchange controls, just as in the short-term market. Since the national capital markets are generally small, opportunities to use them are quite limited for foreign as well as domestic investors. Of course, since the main currencies of interest to MNEs and other international investors *are* those of the few large industrial countries, opportunities in those national capital markets do exist.

REGIONAL MONEY AND CAPITAL MARKETS

Until recently, the scope of financial markets and instruments was predominantly domestic or fully international, but not regional. In the past two decades, however, the European Union has designed both a regional monetary system (the **European Monetary Union**, or EMU) and a regional currency unit (the euro) for intergovernmental financial transactions in the European Union.

The eurocurrency market

A **eurodollar** is a dollar-denominated bank deposit located outside the United States. This simple statement defines the basic instrument called the eurodollar. (Eurodollars are *not* dollars in the pockets of people who live in Europe! They are deposit liabilities of banks.) The widely discussed eurocurrency market is simply a set of bank deposits located outside the countries whose currencies are used in the deposits. Since over half of the deposits are denominated in US dollars, it is reasonably accurate to call this the eurodollar market. Notice that the eurodollar market is not limited to Europe; very large eurodollar markets exist in Tokyo, Hong Kong, Bahrain, Panama, and other cities throughout the world. For this reason, the eurodollar market is sometimes called the *international money market.*

What is the significance of the international money market? Since the eurocurrency market rivals domestic financial markets as a funding source for corporate borrowing, it plays a key role in the capital investment decisions of many firms. In addition, since this market also rivals domestic financial markets as a deposit alternative, it absorbs large amounts of savings from lenders (that is, depositors) in many countries. In fact, the eurocurrency market complements the domestic financial markets, giving greater access to

Foreign bond
A bond issued by a foreign company in another country's financial market

Eurobond
A bond denominated in foreign currency issued in any country's financial market; most eurobonds are issued in London or in Luxembourg (for tax reasons)

European Monetary Union (EMU)
The agreement among, initially, 11 of the European Union countries to eliminate their currencies and create the euro; European Union countries do not necessarily have to join the EMU

Eurodollar
A dollar-denominated bank deposit outside the United States

borrowing and lending to financial market participants in each country where it is permitted to function. Overall, the eurocurrency market is now the world's single most important market for international financial intermediation.

This market is completely a creation of the regulatory structures placed by national governments on banking or, more precisely, on financial intermediation. If national governments allowed banks to function without reserve requirements, interest rate restrictions, capital controls, and taxes, the eurocurrency market would involve only the transnational deposits and loans made in each country's banking system. Instead, national governments heavily regulate national financial markets in efforts to achieve various monetary policy goals. Thus, the eurocurrency market provides a very important outlet for funds flows that circumvent many of the limitations placed on domestic financial markets. Many national governments have found the impact of the eurocurrency market on their firms and banks to be favorable, so they have allowed this market to operate.[7]

Since the eurocurrency market is a creation of the regulatory structure, it may be helpful to think about the key underpinnings of the system that allow eurodollars. Essentially three conditions must be met for a eurocurrency market to exist. First, some national government must allow foreign currency deposits to be made so that, for example, depositors in London can obtain dollar-denominated time deposits there. Second, the country whose currency is being used—in this example, the United States—must allow foreign entities to own and exchange deposits in that currency. Third, there must be some reason, such as low cost or ease of use, that prompts people to use this market rather than other financial markets, such as the domestic ones. The eurocurrency market has met these conditions for the past three decades, and its phenomenal growth testifies that the demand for such a market has been very large.

A wide range of countries allow foreign currency deposits to be held in their banking systems. Many of them impose restrictions (interest rate limits, capital controls, and so on) on these as well as on local-currency deposits, so that a free market does not exist. Other countries, including most of the developed countries and many of the newly industrializing countries, allow foreign currency deposits that are not subject to the regulations placed on domestic deposits. In such countries, participants find more favorable interest rates, greater availability of funds, and greater ease of moving funds internationally. These countries tend to be the euromarket centers.

Only a few currencies have become popular as eurocurrencies. Generally, these are the ones used widely in international trade—the US dollar, the euro, the British pound, and the Japanese yen. The governments of all the nations whose currencies are being used have consented (or, more accurately, have not objected) to allowing foreign banks, companies, and individuals to hold and use deposits denominated in those currencies. This may appear to be a trivial point, but any limitation on non-residents' use of dollar (or other eurocurrency) deposits would quickly eliminate that currency from the euromarket. The US government's temporary freeze on Iranian assets held in US banks in 1979 caused a tremendous crisis in the eurodollar market, because other participants saw the possibility of losing use of their eurodollars at the whim of the US government. The potential problem will continue to exist, but on the whole participants in the euromarket expect that full freedom to use the (dollar-denominated) deposits will continue indefinitely.

The third condition fundamental to the success of the euromarket is that it must possess advantages that will attract participants to the market. Those advantages include the ability to carry out dollar-denominated transactions outside the United States and the availability of favorable interest rates relative to rates in the domestic market. The first advantage clearly exists, because eurodollar account owners can sell their accounts to pay for other transactions, with no need to deal directly in the United States. The second advantage also exists, primarily because lack of regulation of the euromarket allows banks to reduce their costs and pass on the savings to clients in the form of lower loan rates and higher deposit rates. (The difference in lending rates to prime borrowers essentially disappeared during the 1980s.)

Eurocurrency interest rates

London interbank offered rate (LIBOR)
The interest rate on large-scale foreign currency-denominated deposits offered from one bank to another in London

The base interest rate paid on deposits among banks in the eurocurrency market is called **LIBOR**. (Outside London, which is the center of the entire euromarket, the base rate on deposits is generally slightly higher.) LIBOR is determined by the supply and demand for funds in the euromarket for each currency. Because participating banks could default (and, infrequently, do default) on their obligations, the rate paid for eurodollar deposits is always somewhat above the domestic Treasury bill rate. Also, because domestic banks must comply with Federal Reserve requirements, they offer slightly lower deposit rates than unregulated eurobanks. The history of the LIBOR rates is shown in Figure 7.4.

The lending rate has no name comparable to the prime rate, but it is determined as LIBOR plus some margin, or spread, charged to the borrower. Banks generally do not require compensating balances or other implicit charges in addition to the spread over LIBOR in the euromarket. This also helps reduce the cost of using the euromarket for borrowers. The total cost of borrowing in the euromarket for a prime US corporation historically was marginally below the domestic US prime rate. Because of competition among lenders in both markets, prime borrowers have been able to obtain the same rate in both markets since the early 1980s.

Interest rates on other eurocurrencies generally follow the same pattern, though when capital controls exist in a particular country (say, France), borrowing rates may be higher in the euromarket (which is not restricted) than in the domestic market. Figure 7.5 traces three-month eurocurrency deposit rates during the past two decades. Notice that the countries whose currencies have tended to decline relative to other currencies during this period (such as France and the UK) show generally higher eurocurrency deposit rates than the "strong-currency" countries (such as Germany and Japan).

Other market characteristics

Transactions in the eurodollar market generally involve $1 million or more, although in the past several years many deposits of $50,000 to $100,000 have been given at LIBOR, and loans of similar amounts have been offered at the analogous lending rates. The market is directly accessible to banks, which carry out about three-fourths of the total volume of transactions among themselves. Companies and individuals participate through their banks, generally at interest rates slightly less favorable than those offered among banks. (Investors may also participate in the euromarket indirectly by purchasing money market

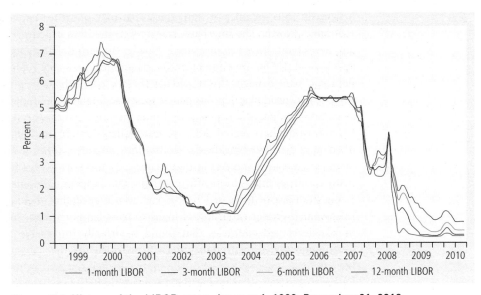

Figure 7.4 History of the LIBOR rates, January 1, 1999–December 31, 2010

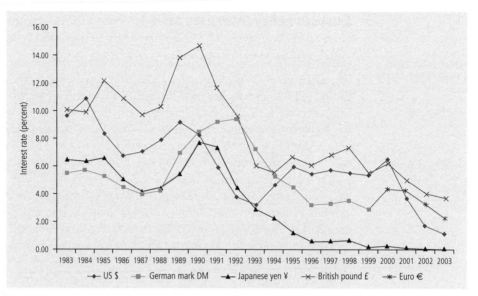

Figure 7.5 Three-month eurocurrency deposit rates (year-end)

funds in the United States, when the funds themselves place large portions of their pooled investments in eurodollar accounts.)

Criticisms of the euromarkets

Over the years, the eurodollar market has been criticized as contributing to worldwide inflation and creating major new risks in the international banking system. While neither claim has been proved (or disproved) conclusively, each is worth considering here.

Because the eurodollar market adds to the worldwide volume of dollar-denominated assets, it has been accused of increasing the global money supply beyond the control of the US authorities. This may be true to some extent, but a number of factors mitigate the total impact of eurodollars. First, eurodollars exist only as time deposits and certificates of deposit, never as demand deposits or cash. Hence, in the narrow definition of money that includes only cash and demand deposits, eurodollars do not even appear at all. Second, as already noted, about three-fourths of all eurodollars are interbank deposits rather than new credit to companies or individuals that may use it for capital investment and thus economic growth. The interbank transfers (sometimes called *pyramiding*) do not create any new credit, however measured. Finally, the eurodollar deposits used by companies and individuals for investment and consumption probably replace other (for example, domestic) bank deposits that would have been used for the same purposes anyhow. That is, because the eurodollar deposits pay interest rates higher than domestic deposits, they often substitute for domestic deposits, and thus they are used for the same purposes that those deposits would have served. All in all, eurodollars probably add slightly to the total volume of economic activity worldwide because they provide a form of financial intermediation between depositors (savers) in many countries and borrowers (investors or spenders) in many countries that is more efficient than that of individual domestic financial markets.

On the issue of increased risk, it has been argued that the eurocurrency market has led to much greater extension of loans to troubled borrowers, such as the governments of less developed countries that found it virtually impossible to repay in the 1980s. Unquestionably, the eurodollar market provided the mechanism through which these governments borrowed most of the money loaned to them in the 1970s. It is not clear, however, that any other financial markets would have fared any differently in the absence of eurodollars. Essentially, participation in the euromarket has opened one more type of business to international banks, and these banks must manage this business as prudently as they manage the other businesses in which they participate.

> ### ✔ Active learning check
>
> *Review your answer to Active Learning Case question 4 and make any changes you like. Then compare your answer to the one below.*
>
> **How can Barclays use the eurocurrency market in its international business, and will this help in dealing with the exchange rate problem?**
>
> Barclays can and does use the eurocurrency market for much of its international lending, since conditions in this market favor the large clients and banks with which Barclays deals extensively. Barclays can offer eurodeposits for various maturities in various currencies to its clients, and the bank can use this market to find offsetting exposures such as loans or investments in those same currencies and maturities.

Eurobonds and euroequities

Eurobonds are the long-term analogue of eurocurrencies. They are issued in countries of convenience and denominated in currencies other than the local one. With eurobonds, *taxation* of the interest income that investors receive is a key concern, so most of them are issued in tax jurisdictions that do not impose taxes on such interest payments (for example, Luxembourg). Eurobonds, like domestic US bonds, are issued by corporations and government agencies. They may be convertible into equity, and they may have fixed or floating interest rates.

Borrowers (namely, issuers of eurobonds) utilize this market for three main reasons. First, no regulatory agency establishes rules for disclosure by issuers, so substantial red tape is avoided; however, this generally limits participation to blue-chip corporations and governments. Second, the interest rates can be marginally lower than those on domestic issues, because investors can usually avoid taxes on their interest income. Third, the issuer gains access to potential investors in many countries simultaneously because the investment banks that place the issue offer it internationally. From time to time, eurobond issue is stimulated by additional reasons, such as domestic bond market restrictions that lead issuers to seek overseas funding. In 1964, for example, the United States established capital controls that made foreign bonds less attractive to US investors (the interest equalization tax was effectively a tax on interest received by US citizens from foreign bond investments) and limited lending by US parent companies to their foreign subsidiaries. As a result, both US and foreign issuers that were trying to place dollar-denominated bonds turned to the fledgling eurobond market for their funding.

For the investor, the eurobond market offers these advantages: (1) all issues are structured to allow exemption from interest withholding tax on the income earned; and (2) the terms of eurobond issues are more varied than those of domestic bond issues. For example, eurobonds usually have shorter maturities than domestic bonds (five to eight years) and often have floating-rate interest payments.

Euroequities

Euroequities have emerged in the past decade in the London Stock Exchange as another long-term euromarket, analogous to domestic stock markets. As the name implies, euroequities are shares of publicly traded stocks traded on an exchange outside the issuing firm's home country. They are bought and sold in shares denominated in the firm's home currency, so both company performance and exchange rate performance affect the returns on investments in euroequities.

In the United States, a market for such issues has operated for many years through an instrument called the American Depositary Receipt (ADR), which is essentially a claim on a share of stock in the foreign stock exchange intermediated by a securities broker who issues the ADR. Euroequities rival ADRs and offer the flexibility of being direct share issues by the non-local firms. The market exists primarily in London, and thus it encompasses non-British company shares. In fact, even the ADRs of British companies are now traded on the London Stock Exchange, so full global trading is possible through the exchange.

The London Stock Exchange euroequity market grew rapidly in the late 1980s. By 1989, 52 brokerage firms were making a market for euroequities issued by 707 firms. The monthly turnover during January 1989 was 278 million shares. The growing demand for these instruments (based on the firms available for investment and the tax-avoiding structure of the issues), as well as the growing supply (by firms that are blue chip and want to gain access to investors from many countries through the London Stock Exchange), make it likely that this market will increase in importance in global equities trading.

INTERNATIONAL BUSINESS STRATEGY IN ACTION

AngloGold Ashanti

When it comes to international finance, one of the primary concerns of MNEs is the ability to raise capital through new stock offerings and bank loans. For many years this was a major problem for the Anglo American Corporation of South Africa (AAC), which operated gold mines in that country. During South Africa's apartheid period, trade sanctions, controls on exchange currency, and protectionism all combined to isolate AAC from outside financial markets. Unable to do business in the international arena, AAC focused on expanding its domestic operations by acquiring holdings in a variety of industries including automobiles, newspapers, and vineyards.

As apartheid came to an end, however, there was a gradual liberalization of both trade and investment. And as its opportunity to move into the international arena began to increase, the firm put its gold mining activities into a new subsidiary, AngloGold, and began restructuring its operations. Non-core businesses were sold off and the company began focusing heavily on development of its gold and uranium mines. However, its profitability and performance were handicapped by the small size of the South African economy and the fact that the Johannesburg stock market was not very influential in the worldwide financial markets. In addition, the local currency, the rand, was weak and the company needed to tie its operations to a stronger currency.

In response, AngloGold determined that it needed to link itself to the triad and expand its mining operations

Source: Corbis/Reuters.

worldwide. As a result, in 1998 the company was listed on the New York Stock Exchange, and today it is also listed on the Ghana and Australian Stock Exchanges. The firm now has access to equity capital in the EU and North America, as well as Australia. In 2003 AngloGold merged with Ashanti Goldfields, so that the combined firm had mines in eight countries and a total market capitalization of about $3.5 billion in 2004. AngloGold Ashanti has 21 operations and a number of exploration programs in gold-producing regions of the world. As of December 31, 2009, AngloGold Ashanti's ore reserve totalled 71.4 million ounces. During the year ended December 31, 2009, the Company produced 4.6 million ounces of gold from its operations. AngloGold

Ashanti's main product is gold. Revenue is also derived from the sales of silver, uranium oxide and sulphuric acid. The Company sells its products on international markets. By the end of 2009, AngloGold Ashanti has a workforce of 62,895 and mining operations in North America, South America, Australia, and Africa. As a result of its recent expansion efforts, the company now accounts for 10 per-cent of the world' annual gold production, and it is able to raise money for expansion operations in a number of worldwide locations.

Websites: www.anglogold.com; www.nyse.com.

Sources: AngloGold, *Annual Report*, 2009 and company web page.

Sometimes an MNE will lend money in the international money market. For example, if Bank of America finds that it can get a higher interest rate in Singapore than in the United States, it may deposit some money there. Similarly, if General Motors finds that there are limitations on the amount of profit that it can transfer out of a country, the company may invest in local financial instruments and thus gain interest on funds that would otherwise sit idle.

THE IMF SYSTEM

International monetary system

The arrangement between national governments/ central banks that oversees the operation of official foreign exchange dealings between countries

International Monetary Fund (IMF)

The international organization founded at Bretton Woods, New Hampshire, in 1944 that includes most countries of the world and offers balance of payments support to countries in crisis along with financial advising to central banks

The last international financial market we will examine here may be viewed as either a very important framework for international financial dealings or a market that is generally irrelevant to private business managers. The **international monetary system** is a financial market in which only central banks and the **International Monetary Fund** (IMF, or "the Fund") operate, so private business plays no active role in it. On the other hand, rules for international financial dealings among countries are often set at the IMF, and substantial international loan decisions are made between governments and the IMF. Thus, the rules of the game in the other international financial markets are sometimes influenced by IMF activities.

The international monetary system oversees the exchange rate regime that prevails among the major developed countries, whose currencies are used for the vast majority of international payments. The IMF negotiates with governments of debtor nations (usually less developed countries) for loans directly from the Fund and for loan conditions that are used, subsequently, as a basis for lending by private banks to these same borrowers. In addition, the IMF serves as an intermediary for emergency loans between member govern-ments to cope with the capital flow or exchange rate crises that occur from time to time due to speculation in foreign exchange markets or other causes. All in all, the international monetary system plays an important role in determining the rules of the game for private companies and banks in some spheres of international business, so managers need to understand its functioning.

The IMF was designed in 1944 at a conference of the Allied nations held at Bretton Woods, New Hampshire. Its general purpose was to provide a multilateral framework for avoiding international financial crises by establishing rules for national exchange rate pol-icies and for adjustment to balance of payments disequilibria (discussed in the Appendix to Chapter 6). It was specifically intended to avoid the disastrous financial contraction that occurred during the 1930s. As originally negotiated, and as implemented in 1946 when the Articles of Agreement were signed by the initial 46 member countries, the IMF system required *fixed* exchange rates among member countries, with gold as the basis for currency valuation. The US dollar was initially fixed at a value of $35 per ounce of gold, and all other currencies were fixed at values expressed in both dollars and gold.

Fixed exchange rates were a fundamental base of the Bretton Woods system. Under the Articles of Agreement, each country was obligated to maintain its currency value at the initially set value (the "par" value), with a band of ±1 percent of flexibility around the par value. If a foreign central bank demanded to sell a country's currency back to the issuer, that country was required to pay the equivalent amount of gold, US dollars, or some other acceptable currency.

To join the IMF, a country was required to make a deposit of gold (25 percent), plus its own currency (75 percent), such that each member country's total deposit relative to the total of IMF deposits was roughly in proportion with its share of world trade. Then each member country received the right to borrow up to 200 percent of its initial deposit at the Fund, in any currency, to help pay for imbalances such as the one mentioned above. If a country borrowed more than its original deposit, the IMF would stipulate economic policies that the borrower had to follow to receive more financial support. (This imposition of policy demands by the IMF is called *conditionality*.)

While the IMF sought to provide assistance for nations facing balance of payments problems, its only resources were the contributions of its member countries: quotas based on each country's part in world trade, which initially constituted about $9 billion. This relatively small amount of liquidity was not sufficient to support the post-World War II economic recovery, or specifically the payments imbalances, of even the European countries.[8] Ultimately, the US Marshall Plan injected the needed funding into the international financial system, and specifically into Europe, during 1948–1952.

In fact, the IMF provided very little funding to its member countries in its early years. During the Suez crisis in 1956, it loaned $1.7 billion to the UK, France, and India. Later, during speculative runs on the British pound (that is, periods when **speculators** sold large quantities of pounds for other currencies in expectation of a devaluation of the pound) in 1961 and 1964, it extended loans to the UK. By the end of the 1960s, the IMF was regularly providing credit to member countries, though still not at the levels that many analysts believed necessary to stabilize the system. (The alternative view is that the IMF should not provide credit to the member countries at all; rather, these countries should be forced to adjust their economies to escape balance of payments problems.)

Speculator
A person or firm that takes a position in foreign exchange with no hedging or protection mechanism to try to gain from expected exchange rate changes

At the end of the 1960s, the US dollar began to be the object of speculative pressure. The problem was severe, since the dollar constituted the base for the entire system of value (through its formal link to gold at $35 per ounce). The United States was unable to devalue to stop the speculation, and later it was unwilling to continue selling its gold holdings to foreign central banks that wanted to redeem their dollars. In August 1971, President Nixon announced that the United States would no longer sell gold to foreign central banks in exchange for dollars. In December 1971, he announced a devaluation of the dollar to $38 per ounce of gold; in February 1972 it was devalued to $42 per ounce, and later that year the United States declared that it would not support the dollar value at any price in gold.

These events essentially destroyed the Bretton Woods system of fixed exchange rates. Many initiatives to repair the system were presented during the following two years, but the United States would no longer accept the responsibility of providing the dollar as a fixed base for other currencies. In subsequent months, the IMF system was changed de facto to a floating exchange rate system that allowed each country to leave the value of its currency free to change with market forces or to fix that value to some other currency. Since that time, the United States has allowed the dollar to float in value relative to all other currencies, with occasional efforts by the Fed (the Federal Reserve System) to influence the dollar's relationship to particular currencies, such as the former German mark and the Japanese yen.

Under the current IMF system, no limitations are set on each member country's decision either to fix its currency value relative to some other currency or to allow it to fluctuate as supply and demand dictate. (Note that it is impossible for one country to keep its currency fixed relative to all others if the others are not fixed relative to one another.) In 1976, an accord called the Jamaica Agreement altered the IMF charter to formally allow for floating exchange rates. Today, the exchange rate regimes used by each nation are substantially unrestricted, and government strategies to influence exchange rates are altered as desired.[9]

Special drawing right (SDR)
The currency of the IMF; accounts at the IMF are denominated in SDRs, and the IMF has issued about $204 billion of SDRs as currency since its inception in 1969

At about the same time that the link between the dollar and gold was broken, the IMF's members agreed to create a new currency that the Fund would issue when authorized to do so by a vote of the members. This currency, called the **special drawing right** (SDR), allows its holder to obtain (or draw) other currencies from the IMF (or from other members) when desired. SDRs have been created and issued on seven occasions to date. A total SDR of 21.4 billion existed in 2004; the total value was about $30 billion. In each instance, the SDRs were allocated to Fund members according to their quotas. This new "international money" has served to support a number of countries that encountered financial crises since 1971, allowing them to finance their imbalances, but it has not been a solution to imbalances in international financial flows. During the international debt crisis of the early 1980s, SDR use was wholly inadequate to deal with the more than $350 billion of dollar debt owed by Latin American countries to foreign lenders. Total IMF resources include member country quotas, which totaled over $300 billion at the end of 2004. With a general SDR allocation that took effect on August 28 and a special allocation on September 9, 2009, the amount of SDRs increased from SDR 21.4 billion to SDR 204 billion (equivalent to about $308 billion, converted using the rate of August 31, 2010). So the Fund actually has quite substantial lending power today.

During the late twentieth century, SDRs became fairly widely used as a currency of denomination for private-sector financial instruments such as bonds and long-term bank loans. Because the SDR has a value based on four currencies (see Figure 7.6), it is more stable as a borrowing or lending tool than any individual currency. As of 2006 an SDR consists of US dollars, euros, Japanese yen, and British pounds, and their relative contributions are 44, 34, 11, and 11 percent respectively.

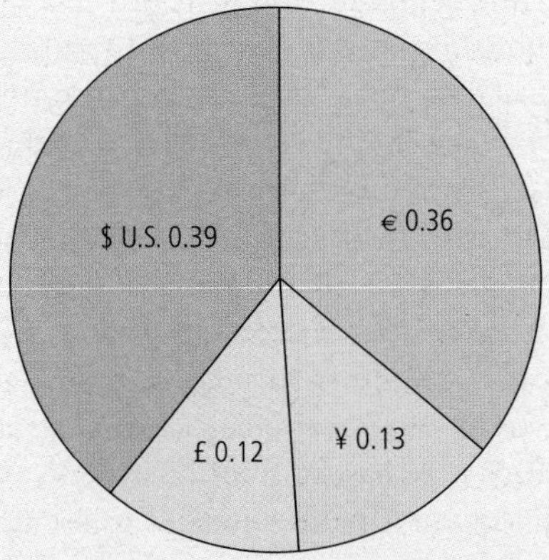

Distribution of value of the SDR, the basic monetary unit of the International Monetary Fund

For example, in dollars: $1 \text{ SDR} = \dfrac{\$(0.426)}{€} + \dfrac{\$(21)}{¥} + \dfrac{\$(0.0984)}{£} + \dfrac{(0.577)}{\$} = \$1.47$

Figure 7.6 Special drawing right (October 15, 2004)

When the dollar devalues relative to other widely traded currencies, so does the SDR—but only 39 percent of the SDR's value is affected negatively. The other 61 percent of the SDR's value is based on pounds, yen, and euros, and these currencies may rise or fall relative to the dollar in such a situation. Overall, the changes must net out over all currencies, and an instrument such as the SDR changes relatively little in value compared to any single currency. The SDR is really a "basket" of currencies whose value is generally more stable than that of any one of its components.

Just as the euro has gained wide acceptance as an instrument for denominating international financial transactions, so the SDR promises to maintain its acceptance as a risk-reducing instrument. (The SDR has the advantage of including the US dollar in the group of currencies that determine its value, whereas the euro is based only on European currencies.) At present private-sector investors and borrowers are using a much greater volume and value of euro-denominated instruments than SDR-denominated instruments.

Unresolved problems with the IMF system

The IMF system today differs dramatically from the model established at Bretton Woods in 1944. Flexible exchange rates have been substituted for fixed ones; gold has been greatly reduced as an international monetary asset,[10] and its link to the dollar has been severed; a new reserve currency, the SDR, has been created to increase world liquidity; and, perhaps most important, the US dollar is no longer the single base for the IMF system of value. These major changes have come in response to problems and crises that have occurred during the past 60 years—yet the IMF system itself survives. While few people would argue that the IMF has led directly to greater international financial stability over its history, at least the system has been flexible enough to accommodate the various crises that have threatened it.

Several problems that remain in the system deserve note. First, there has always been an uncomfortable tension between the countries that want to utilize the IMF simply as a bank for reducing the negative impacts of balance of payments difficulties and the countries that want to utilize it to subsidize economic development. The "link" between the IMF and development finance was originally delegated to the **World Bank** (the IMF' sister institution). Traditionally, the IMF has loaned funds only for short-term uses, sometimes extending to two or three years. Many borrowing countries, especially the less developed ones, have repeatedly called for greater use of IMF resources to finance development projects. While there are often no clear differences between financing payments imbalances and financing development projects that may later reduce those imbalances, the IMF has not substantially widened its scope. In the 1980s, under the cloud of multiple international loan renegotiations by Latin American countries, the Fund began to extend longer-term loans and to reconsider its strategy. The ultimate result of this crisis is, in the early 2000s, that the Fund retained its basic form, and the resources of the World Bank expanded to assist more heavily in economic development.

A second problem that continues to plague the Fund is the issue of exchange rate regimes. Even as the flexible rate system moves through its fourth decade, there are repeated calls for a return to fixed, or more tightly constrained, currency values. The great instability of international financial dealings during the period since the initial OPEC oil crisis of 1973–1974 has led some analysts to argue for a return to fixed rates. The decision of most European Union countries to set up a single currency, the euro, has placed a regional fixed exchange rate regime alongside of the floating rate system globally. The evidence during the entire twentieth century tends to suggest that no matter what exchange rate regime prevails, if international trade relations are unstable and payments imbalances are substantial, no exchange rate regime will be able to solve the problem. Thus, this problem most likely cannot be eliminated.

World Bank
The world's largest development bank, formed along with the IMF at Bretton Woods in 1944. Its original name was the International Bank for Reconstruction and Development (IBRD). The World Bank assists developing countries with loans and economic advising for economic development

On the whole, the international monetary system plays an important role in all international financial dealings by being the focal point for establishing rules on exchange rates, exchange controls, intergovernmental loans, and other official transactions. On a day-to-day basis, most international business people, especially in the triad countries, do not feel the international monetary system's impact.

MNEs AND INTERNATIONAL FINANCIAL MARKETS AND INSTITUTIONS

Whether or not a company or bank is involved in international trade, investment, or other international business, it is important that its managers understand some of the key aspects of international financial markets. The eurocurrency market may offer a low-cost borrowing opportunity, or the eurobond market may provide an outlet for selling new debt to a wider group of investors. The international monetary system establishes a framework within which governments set international financial policies that may affect many firms. The money and capital markets in foreign countries may offer opportunities to multinational firms that operate in those countries. The foreign exchange market determines the cost and availability of foreign currencies, used in business by many firms. Finally, all of these markets influence the functioning of the markets for real goods and services, the ultimate use for all financial claims.

KEY POINTS

1 Foreign exchange is any financial instrument that can be used to carry out payment from one currency to another. There are two major foreign exchange markets in the United States and the UK: interbank (including brokers) and futures/options (at stock and commodities exchanges). The most important participants in foreign exchange markets are banks—acting as traders, speculators, hedgers, and arbitrageurs. Exchange rates are determined by the activities of these five groups. The rates are also influenced by purchasing power parity, interest rates, and technical factors such as national economic statistics and seasonal demands.

2 There are a number of international finance strategies that can be of value to firms doing business overseas. Two of the most important are strategies for managing currency exchange rate risk and strategies for financing international operations.

3 The international monetary system is a market among central banks of the countries that belong to the International Monetary Fund (IMF). The IMF's objectives include the facilitation of balanced growth of international trade, promotion of exchange stability, and the making of financial resources available to the members of the Fund. In recent years the fixed monetary system created by the IMF members in 1944 has been replaced by a managed float system. Currently the IMF faces a number of major problems, including helping Third World countries to deal with their international debt crises and increasing international liquidity.

Key terms

- exchange risk
- foreign exchange
- eurocurrency
- exchange rate
- foreign exchange traders
- foreign exchange brokers
- spot rate

- forward rate
- arbitrageur
- purchasing power parity
- international Fisher effect
- nominal interest rate
- real interest rate
- exchange risk avoidance

- exchange risk adaptation
- exchange risk transfer
- currency diversification
- foreign bond
- eurobond
- European Monetary Union (EMU)
- eurodollar

- London interbank offered rate (LIBOR)
- international monetary system
- International Monetary Fund (IMF)
- speculator
- special drawing right (SDR)
- World Bank

REVIEW AND DISCUSSION QUESTIONS

1 If your firm had a subsidiary in Japan and about 100 million yen in exposed assets (that is, plant and equipment), how would you protect it against exchange risk?

2 If you managed the European operations of a large US-based MNE, in what market(s) would you seek long-term funding? Why?

3 Given that the euro area's inflation is about 3 percent per year at present, while US inflation is about 2 percent per year, what do you expect to happen to the euro/dollar exchange rate in the next few months? Why?

4 What is the difference between a eurobond and a domestic bond in the United States? Which one would you prefer to issue as a company manager? Which one would you prefer to buy as an investor? Why?

5 How can a firm such as Ajax Steel in Peoria, Illinois, utilize the eurodollar market to minimize its financing costs? This firm is a medium-size manufacturer with no foreign sales.

6 Assume that the interest rate on 12-month US dollar deposits in London is currently 2.6875 percent per year and the rate on British pound deposits there is 4.1875 percent per year. The spot exchange rate is US $1.93/£. What do you expect the exchange rate to be in one year?

7 If you were offered the opportunity to establish a deposit in London-denominated euros, would you choose that rather than a deposit in British pounds or dollars? Why or why not?

8 What are the important differences between the Bretton Woods fixed exchange rate system and the current IMF system? How do these differences affect the MNE manager?

9 How may the International Monetary Fund affect companies' activities in international business?

10 How would you hedge the value of your export sale of €10 million of computers to a French customer? You will be paid in 180 days in euros. On what basis would you choose among hedging methods?

REAL CASE

HSBC

What is the world's largest bank? Prior to the merger of Citicorp and Travelers in 1998, it was the Hong Kong and Shanghai Banking Corporation (HSBC). As at December 31, 2009, HSBC is the world's eighth largest banking and financial services group and the UK's No.1 largest banking group (Fortune Global 500, 2010 ranking). Formed in 1865 by a Scotsman in the then British Colony of Hong Kong, HSBC grew to over 10,000 bank offices in 76 countries by 2009. In the process it became the world's first truly global bank, offering a full range of financial services from retail to corporate banking to insurance and financial management. HSBC built this global business based on its strong Hong Kong base. The bank owns the Hong Kong Bank and most of the Hang Seng Bank, giving it over 40 percent of the market in the Hong Kong Special Administrative Region of China that was created on July 1, 1997.

Perhaps less well known is that HSBC is also the owner of the former Midland Bank chain in the UK, the Marine Midland and Republic New York Banks and Household Finance in the United States, and the Hong Kong Bank of Canada. It has also acquired large banks in Latin America including Banco Bamerindus in Brazil and Bital in Mexico. In all these cases HSBC greatly improved the efficiency of the underperforming local banks through better systems and processes. Over recent years, HSBC has implemented a rebranding strategy of all its subsidiaries under the HSBC title and logo "the world's local bank". This is meant to build HSBC into a global brand.

Today HSBC is well developed across the triad regions of Asia, Europe, and the Americas. It is a global bank in terms of assets, but not revenues. Its diversification strategy has helped to insulate it from the Asian financial crisis 1997–1998.

There is an old saying that the best test of a business is how well it does in a downturn. Again in the world financial crisis starting in 2007, HSBC looked pretty good. HSBC reported revenue of $142.069 billion and profits after tax of $5.728 billion for 2008. Although revenue was down 3 percent on a year earlier, but that looked very healthy compared to sickly peers such as Citigroup, UBS, and Royal Bank of Scotland (RBS). RBS required a British government bailout.

HSBC was thriving because of its strong presence in emerging markets including India, China, the Middle East, and Brazil to cushion the big losses it took in the US market due to subprime mortgage crisis. Since 2007, HSBC expanded into Japan, Korea, Vietnam, and India by launching new branches and services. Profits in some of HSBC's Middle East businesses, such as capital markets and private banking, were growing at a near 100 percent. HSBC reported revenue of $103.736 billion and profits after tax of $5.834 billion for 2009.

Significant events in 2009 included its decision to sell landmark buildings in New York, London and Paris to raise cash. HSBC agreed to sell its London base at Canary Wharf to the National Pension Service of Korea for $1.25 billion in cash and its New York headquarters to Israeli investment holding IDB Group for $330 million. HSBC sold its Paris building to private investors represented by French Properties Management for $573 million. HSBC would lease back these buildings. Importantly, HSBC announced in 2009 that it relocated the principal office of the Group Chief Executive to Hong Kong. This underscores HSBC commitments to emerging markets' businesses and reflects the historic shifts now taking place in the world economy. HSBC's corporate headquarters remain in the UK where it continues to benefit from being at the heart of the world's financial centers.

And its first-mover advantage as a truly global bank may prove hard to match by its competitors. There is constant pressure in banking to reduce costs through greater scale economies and improved information technology. HSBC is well positioned to continue as an industry leader because of its successful strategy.

In retrospect, one of the world's largest banks came from one of the world's smallest economies. And it did this despite the regulatory barriers to entry for foreign-owned firms in Europe and North America. As a result HSBC is an example of a bank using modern management systems and market forces to win out over old-fashioned protectionism in a highly regulated worldwide industry.

Perhaps the biggest influence of HSBC and its new efficient banking methods has been on British banking. A further restructuring occurred in British banking in November 1999 when one of the country's four major banks (Lloyds, Barclays, Natwest, and HSBC) was taken over by a much smaller bank. Natwest was acquired by the Royal Bank of Scotland, only one-third the asset size of Natwest, in a drawn-out and controversial takeover. Another bank, the Bank of Scotland, first bid for Natwest and the takeover efforts of both the Royal Bank of Scotland and the Bank of Scotland were defended by Natwest Chairman, Sir David Rowland, who was also President of Templeton College, University of Oxford. The takeover was successful because ▶

investors were critical of Natwest's old-style management and were supportive of the cost-cutting and new information technology methods of the Royal Bank of Scotland. After the acquisition, many Natwest branches were closed; bank buildings were turned into coffee bars, restaurants, and hotels; and a leaner, more efficient bank emerged to reclaim its place in British retail banking.

The Bank of Scotland and Halifax, the largest mortgage lender in the country, finalized a merger. This has fast-forwarded Halifax into mainstream banking and greatly increased the Bank of Scotland's scope of operations. Halifax then became a trading name of Bank of Scotland. The merger would also allow both banks to streamline their businesses and increase their market focus. These efforts toward restructuring operations and eliminating waste are not going unnoticed by rival banks. Barclays, for example, closed some of its branches in the early 2000s and introduced a wide array of tools and techniques that are designed to cut costs and increase operational efficiency. It realizes that, to be a successful international operation, it must not only have wide geographic coverage but also be able to offer efficient services. A takeover of Bank of Scotland by Lloyds TSB was approved by the Court of Session on January 12, 2009. On January 19, 2009, Bank of Scotland formally became part of Lloyds Banking Group.

In looking at these recent developments, it is clear that the steps taken by HSBC to modernize its own operations are proving to be a wake-up call for British banks as well.

Sources: www.hsbc.com; www.citigroup.com; www.bankofscotland.co.uk; www.royalbankscot.co.uk; www.natwest.co.uk; www.barclays.com; "HSBC: World's Strongest Bank," *Bloomberg Business Week*, www.businessweek.com, August 4, 2008; "HSBC to Sell New York Building for $330 Million," www.bloomberg.com, October 10, 2009; "HSBC to Sell Paris Building for $573 Million," in.reuters.com, December 21, 2009; HSBC, *Annual Report*, 2008–2009; Lloyds, *Annual Report*, 2009; "Fortune Global 500," *Fortune*, 2008, 2009, 2010 issues.

1 Since HSBC does business with the People's Republic of China and has substantial holdings of Chinese yuan (renminbi) on hand, what risk does this pose for the bank?

2 How could HSBC manage its currency exchange rate risk?

3 As the British retail banks are merged to achieve cost savings and economies, does this increase or decrease the barriers to entry for foreign banks wishing to do business in the EU?

REAL CASE

World financial crises

Throughout the 1990s, a series of financial crises rocked the world' economy. The first of these was the 1994 Mexico peso crisis. This was followed by the Asian crisis of 1997. Since then there have been the Russian crisis of 1998, the 1999 Brazilian financial crisis, the 2001 Argentine crisis, and the 2007 world financial crisis. The following examines the first two of these.

The Mexican peso crisis
In late 1994 Mexico suffered one of the worst financial crises in its history. In less than one month the Mexican peso devalued from 3.45 to the US dollar to 5.57 to the dollar, and by the end of 1995 it was trading at 6.5 to the dollar. This was accompanied by heavy inflation, unemployment, and a severe stock market crash. Some critics claimed that all of this was a result of NAFTA, but this was not so. The crisis was caused by the Mexican government itself, which had liberalized trade and financial flows but had not allowed the peso to float. Moreover, previous governments had kept the peso overvalued. As a result, in less than one

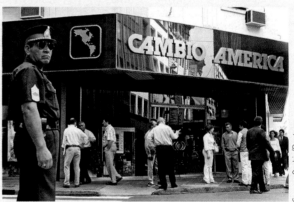

Source: Corbis/Reuters.

year Mexico's foreign reserves were depleted by 75 percent and the country's current account deficit was equal to 8 percent of GDP.

Other factors also contributed to the low price of the peso. For instance, as a result of the Zapatista armed rebellion of 1996 in Chiapas, in southern Mexico, both foreign and Mexican investors took tens of millions of dollars out of the country. These developments had far-reaching consequences throughout the region. For example, many investors in other Latin American countries, fearing a similar crash, withdrew their funds from these economies and deposited them in the United States for safe keeping.

One unexpected development of the Mexican peso crisis was the devaluation of the Canadian dollar, which was sideswiped by the Latin American currency crisis. Thanks to NAFTA, Canada and Mexico had become linked in the international currency markets. At the same time international investors began showing a preference for the US dollar against both the Mexican peso and the Canadian dollar.

Perhaps the most surprising thing about the peso crisis was how quickly the country bounded back. With the help of a $50 billion loan from the United States and other countries, a tough economic reform that saw cuts in government spending, and increases in deregulation and privatization, the Mexican economy began to revive. Hardly a year had passed when investors who were running from the region were quickly lured back by short-term interest rates of up to 40 percent. Additionally, the stock market crash had led to underpriced shares, and investors began buying these issues and driving the prices back up. Today the financial crisis of 1995 in Mexico is a thing of the past. The country' economy is healthy and investors are back.

The Asian financial crisis

In the early 1990s, the Asian economies of South Korea, Indonesia, Thailand, Malaysia, and Japan were being praised as economic miracles. In 1997, these countries faced one of the worst blows to their economies. The Asian crisis began in July 1997, when Thailand stopped pegging its currency to the US dollar. In two months the Thai bath had devaluated by nearly 40 percent. The effect was twofold. First, Asian exporters to Thailand faced decreased demand for their product. Second, there was the decrease of investor confidence in the region.

Individual countries in the region faced their own sets of problems. In Malaysia, it was excessive lending to the property sector. Once foreign investment was cut short, overlending, overinvestment, and overproduction led to a downward spiral in the economy. In South Korea, the *chaebols* (large manufacturing conglomerates) that dominated the economy had invested recklessly without regard to profit. In Indonesia, President Suharto's corruption and lack of accountability led investors to flee the country. In addition, the banking system that the government there had fostered was plagued with bad loans for many unreliable projects. These loans benefited and created wealth

for well-positioned individuals—in particular, members of the Suharto family—but they did nothing for the rest of the country.

Some financial observers believe that Western speculators were a major reason for the financial troubles in the region. The trend toward deregulation of the world capital markets and the free flow of capital, it was argued, contributed to the currency panic. Additionally, the relatively good health of these nations prior to 1997 made them attractive to foreign investors and lenders. Unfortunately, many of these loans were short term and were in foreign currency. So while the economy grew, the loans presented no problem. But when trouble looked likely the foreign lenders began calling in their loans. When this happened, the value of the local currencies plummeted and the loans payable in foreign currencies created a debt crisis.

It was initially believed that the Asian economic problem would be contained in that geographic region. However, by mid-1998 the crisis was having an effect on the world economy. The cross-border interconnections of global industries and the resulting interdependence pushed the problem to other regions. Among other things, the crisis led to decreases in the prices of many commodities including oil, metals, grain, pulp, and paper.

Industrial nations came to the aid of these Asian governments. The IMF negotiated billions of dollars in bailouts. Initially, the IMF wanted these governments to decrease their budget deficit and to maintain stable interest rates. By July 1998, however, the IMF was allowing increases in deficits and lower interest rates. This helped ease some of the problems, although there was still a great deal of disagreement regarding what else needed to be done. For example, some observers argued that the government needed to continue to deregulate the country's capital markets, while others blamed the economic disaster on this deregulation.

Sources: "Crisis-ridden Indonesia to Overhaul Ailing Banking Sector," *Boston Globe on Line*, January 27, 1998, www.boston.com/dailynews/; Richard Gwyn, "Asian Flu Shows No Sign of Letting Up," *Toronto Star*, July 10, 1998; "A Crisis of Dictatorship," *Washington Post*, January 11, 1998; Raffi Anderian, "Everybody Is Going Down," *Sunday Star*, July 12, 1998; "The Downward Spiral of the Asian Tigers," *BBC News*, January 8, 1998.

---

1 How does a decrease in the value of the Mexican peso affect foreign direct investment?

2 How is trade affected by currency devaluations as a result of a financial crisis?

3 How are customers in countries undergoing a financial crisis affected by the devaluation of the peso?

ENDNOTES

1 Exchange rate quotations come as two-digit numbers, bid/asked, with the preceding numbers assumed. A British pound quote of 50/70 on October 14, 2004, meant an actual price of:

$1.7950 bid to buy one British pound.

£1.7970 asked for selling one British pound.

The bank is offering (bidding) to buy pounds for 1.795 dollars per pound and also offering (asking) to sell pounds for 1.797 dollars per pound. Of course, the actual transaction will involve $1 million or more, to be exchanged at those prices.

Rates are typically quoted on the **Continental basis**, as units of foreign exchange per dollar, everywhere. US banks have traditionally used the **American basis**, quoting $US per unit of foreign exchange. Clearly, whether the quote is SF2.0/$ or $0.50/SF, the value is the same. The *Wall Street Journal* offers both types of quotations, as shown in Table 7.2.

Another means used to distinguish the two ways of presenting an exchange rate is to call a quotation of domestic currency/foreign exchange an **indirect quote**. Conversely, a quotation of units of foreign exchange/domestic currency is called a **direct quote**. This system has more general applicability to any pair of currencies, whereas the American/ Continental system relates only to rates involving the US dollar.

2 See http://www.chips.org.

3 "Taking a position" means purchasing an asset (or a liability) denominated in a foreign currency without simultaneously matching it with a liability (asset) of the same value and maturity in the same currency. Realistically, if any one government disallows the euromarkets, they can still function almost as effectively in other countries and currencies. At present, the US government has the most important role, since about 80 percent of eurodeposits are denominated in US dollars. If a US bank buys Swiss francs, it takes a position in Swiss francs. When the bank sells those Swiss francs to a client, it eliminates the position.

4 A **foreign currency option** is a contract offering the holder the right to buy (namely, a **call option**) or sell (namely, a **put option**) a fixed amount of foreign currency for a fixed price during a fixed time period. The buyer of a call option on British pounds obtains the right to buy £31,500 at a fixed dollar price (that is, the **exercise price**) at any time during the (typically) three-month life of the option. The seller of the same option faces a **contingent liability** in that the seller will have to deliver the British pounds at any time if the buyer chooses to exercise the option.

The market value (that is, the price on "premium" that the buyer must pay to purchase the option) of an option depends on its exercise price, the remaining time to its expiration, the exchange rate in the spot market, and expectations about the future exchange rate. An option may sell for a price near zero, for thousands of dollars, or for anywhere in between. Notice that the buyer of a call option on British pounds may pay a small price to obtain the option but does *not* have to exercise the option if the actual exchange rate moves favorably. Thus, an option is superior to a forward contract having the same maturity and exercise price because it need *not* be used, and the cost is just its purchase price. However, the price of the option is generally higher than the expected cost of the forward contract, so the user of the option pays for the flexibility of the instrument.

5 Yet another kind of foreign exchange arbitrage involves comparing interest rates on similar investments between two currencies. Interest arbitrage is the choice of investing, say, $1 million in a eurodollar bank deposit, versus investing the same money in pounds, depositing in a europound deposit, and contracting a forward contract to convert back to dollars. This comparison can be used for whatever currencies that may be available, and the investor benefits from taking the highest return available, with the exchange rates guaranteed through forward contracts (that is, with no exchange risk).

6 This entire discussion refers to *relative* purchasing power parity (PPP). The stronger, absolute version refers to parity in the values of factor inputs used in the production of products whose prices reflect relative factor productivities. Relative PPP considers only *changes* in the relative price levels between countries, not the initial (absolute) levels.

7 Realistically, if any one government disallows the euromarkets, they can still function almost as effectively in other countries and currencies. At present, the US government has the most important role, since about 80 percent of eurodeposits are denominated in US dollars.

8 See the Economic Cooperation Act of 1948 (Public Law 472, 80th Congress), US Code Congressional Service, 1948.

9 Exchange rate policies *are* constrained by the IMF if a country seeks to borrow more than its quota from the Fund. Also, a country does operate in violation of IMF rules if it imposes new exchange controls on current transactions without obtaining IMF approval; however, sanctions are seldom applied unless the country seeks to borrow as above.

10 Almost one-third of the world's monetary reserves were still being held in the form of gold at year-end 1991. See IMF *Survey*, November 8, 1993, p. 345.

ADDITIONAL BIBLIOGRAPHY

Agmon, Tamir. "Bringing Financial Economics into International Business Research: Taking Advantage of Paradigm Change," *Journal of International Business Studies*, vol. 37, no. 5 (September 2006).

Banalieva, Elitsa R. and Robertson Christopher J. "Performance, Diversity, and Multiplicity of Foreign Cross-Listing Portfolios," *International Business Review*, vol. 19, no. 6, (December 2010).

Beaulieu, Marie-Claude, Cosset, Jean-Claude and Essadam, Naceur. "The Impact of Political Risk on the Volatility of Stock Returns: The Case of Canada," *Journal of International Business Studies*, vol. 36, no. 6 (November 2005).

Berg, David M. and Guisinger, Stephen E. "Capital Flows, Capital Controls, and International Business Risk," in Alan M. Rugman and Thomas Brewer (eds.), *The Oxford Handbook of International Business* (Oxford: Oxford University Press, 2001).

Boulton, Thomas J, Smart, Scott B. and Zutter, Chad J. "IPO Underpricing and International Corporate Governance," *Journal of International Business Studies*, vol. 41 (2010).

Bowe, Michael, Filatotchev, Igor and Marshall, Andrew. "Integrating Contemporary Finance and International Business Research," *International Business Review*, vol. 19, no. 5 (October 2010).

Bowe, Michael "International Financial Management and Multinational Enterprises," in Alan M. Rugman (ed.), *Oxford Handbook of International Business*, 2nd ed. (Oxford: Oxford University Press, 2009).

Bowe, Michael and Saltvedt, Thina M. "Currency Invoicing Practices, Exchange Rate Volatility and Pricing-To-Market: Evidence from Product Level Data," *International Business Review*, vol. 13, no. 3 (June 2004).

Carrieri, Francesca and Majerbi, Basma. "The Pricing of Exchange Risk in Emerging Stock Markets," *Journal of International Business Studies*, vol. 37, no. 3 (May 2006).

Cheng, Louis T. W., Chan, Kam C. and Mak, Billy S. C. "Strategic Share Allocation and Underpricings of IPOs in Hong Kong," *International Management Review*, vol. 14, no. 1 (February 2005).

Connelly, Brian L., Hoskisson, Robert E., Tihanyi, Laszlo and Certo, S. Trevis. "Ownership as a Form of Corporate Governance," *Journal of Management Studies*, vol. 47, no. 8, (December 2010).

Covrig, Vincentiu Lau, Sie, Ting and Ng, Lilian. "Do Domestic and Foreign Fund Managers Have Similar Preferences for Stock Characteristics? A Cross-Country Analysis," *Journal of International Business Studies*, vol. 37, no. 3 (March 2007).

Cumming, Douglas– and Walz, Uwe. "Private Equity Returns and Disclosure Around the World," *Journal of International Business Studies*, vol. 41 (2010).

Bergh, Donald D. and Gibbons, Patrick. "The Stock Market Reaction to the Hiring of Management Consultants: A Signalling Theory Approach," *Journal of Management Studies*, vol. 48, no. 3 (May 2011).

Doidge, Craig, Carolyi, Andrew and Stulz, Rene M. "Why Do Foreign Firms Leave US Equity Market?", *Journal of Finance*, vol. 65, no. 4 (2010).

Eckert, Stefan, Dittfeld, Marcus, Muche, Thomas and Rässler, Susanne. "Does Multinationality Lead to Value Enhancement? An Empirical Examination of Publicly Listed Corporations from Germany," *International Business Review*, vol. 19, no. 6, (December 2010).

Eden, Lorraine and Rodriguez, Peter. "How Weak Are the Signals? International Price Indices and Multinational Enterprises," *Journal of International Business Studies*, vol. 35, no. 1 (January 2004).

Eiteman, David K., Stonehill, Arthur I. and Moffett, Michael H. *Multinational Business Finance*, 12th ed. (Boston, MA: Pearson Addison Wesley, 2009).

Faff, Robert W. and Marshall, Andrew. "International Evidence on the Determinants of Foreign Exchange Rate Exposure of Multinational Corporations," *Journal of International Business Studies*, vol. 36, no. 5 (September 2005).

Giddy, Ian and Dufey, Gunter. "Uses and Abuses of Currency Options," *Bank of America Journal of Applied Corporate Finance*, vol. 8 (1995).

Grosse, Robert. *The Future of Global Financial Services* (Oxford: Blackwell, 2004).

Hejazi, Walid and Pauly, Peter H. "Motivation for FDI and Domestic Capital Formation," *Journal of International Business Studies*, vol. 34, no. 3 (May 2003).

Hejazi, Walid and Santor, Eric. "Foreign Asset Risk Exposure, DOI, and Performance: An Analysis of Canadian Banks," *Journal of International Business Studies*, vol. 41 (2010).

Hearn, Bruce, Piesse, Jenifer and Strange, Roger. "Market Liquidity and Stock Size Premia in Emerging Financial Markets: The Implications for Foreign Investment," *International Business Review*, vol. 19, no. 5 (October 2010).

Hutson, Elaine and Stevenson, Simon. "Openness, Hedging Incentives and Foreign Exchange Exposure: A Firm-Level Multi-Country Study," *Journal of International Business Studies*, vol. 41 (2010).

Hutson, Elaine and O'Driscoll, Anthony. "Firm-Level Exchange Rate Exposure in the Eurozone," *International Business Review*, vol. 19, no. 5 (October 2010).

Ito, Kiyohiko and Rose, Elizabeth L. "The Implicit Return on Domestic and International Sales: An Empirical Analysis of US and Japanese Firms," *Journal of International Business Studies*, vol. 41 (2010).

Johnson, Robert and Soenen, Luc. "European Economic Integration and Stock Market Co-Movement with Germany," *Multinational Business Review*, vol. 17, no. 3 (2009).

Lessard, Donald R. "Finance and International Business," in B. Toyne and D. Nigh (eds.), *International Business: An Emerging Vision* (Columbia: University of South Carolina Press, 1997).

Leung, Kwok, Chahat, Rabi S., Buchan, Nancy R., Erez, Miriam and Gibson, Cristina B. "Culture and International Business: Recent Advances and Their Implications for Future Research," *Journal of International Business Studies*, vol. 36, no. 4 (July 2005).

Ling-yee, Li. "Effect of Export Financing Resources and Supply-Chain Skills on Export Competitive Advantages: Implications for Superior Export Performance," *Journal of World Business*, vol. 36, no. 3 (Fall 2001).

Lopez-Duerte, Cristina and Garcia-Canal, Esteban. "Stock Market Reaction to Foreign Direct Investments: Interaction between Entry Mode and FDI Attributes," *Management International Review*, vol. 47, no. 3 (2007).

Miller, Kent D. and Reuer, Jeffrey J. "Firm Strategy and Economic Exposure to Foreign Exchange Rate Movements," *Journal of International Business Studies*, vol. 29, no. 3 (Fall 1998).

Oxelheim, Lars and Randøy, Trond. "The Anglo-American Financial Influence on CEO Compensation in Non-Anglo-American Firms," *Journal of International Business Studies*, vol. 36, no. 4 (July 2005).

Radebaugh, Lee H., Gray, Sidney J. and Black, Ervin L. *International Accounting and Multinational Enterprises* 6th ed. (Hoboken, NJ: Wiley, 2006).

Remmers, Lee. "International Financial Management: 35 Years Later–What Has Changed?" *International Business Review*, vol. 13, no. 2 (April 2004), pp. 155–180.

Rugman, Alan M. *International Diversification and the Multinational Enterprise* (Lexington, MA: D.C. Heath, 1979).

Rugman, Alan M. "International Diversification and Multinational Banking," in Sarkis J. Khoury and Alo Gosh (eds.), *Recent Developments in International Banking and Finance* (Lexington, MA: D.C. Heath, 1987).

Rugman, Alan M. and Brain, Cecilia. "The Regional Nature of the World's Banking Sector," *The Multinational Business Review*, vol. 12, no. 3 (Winter 2004).

Rugman, Alan M. and Li, Jing (eds.). *Real Options and International Investment* (Cheltenham: Edward Elgar, 2005).

Purda, Lynnette D. "Risk Perception and the Financial System," *Journal of International Business Studies*, vol. 39 (2008).

Shapiro, Alan C. *Multinational Financial Management*, 9th ed. (New York: Wiley, 2009).

Strange, Susan. *Mad Money* (Manchester: Manchester University Press, 1998).

Strange, Roger, Filatotchev, Igor, Buck, Trevor and Wright, Mike. "Corporate Governance and International Business," *Management International Review*, vol. 49, no. 4 (2009).

Tang, Gordon Y. N. and Shum, Wai Cheong. "The Conditional Relationship between Beta And Returns: Recent Evidence from International Stock Markets," *International Business Review*, vol. 12, no. 1 (February 2003).

Tang, Gordon Y. N. and Shum, Wai Cheong. "The Relationships between Unsystematic Risk, Shrewdness and Stock Returns during Up and Down Markets," *International Business Review*, vol. 12, no. 5 (October 2003).

Tong, Tony W. and Reuer, Jeffrey J. "Real Options in Multinational Corporations: Organizational Challenges and Risk Implications," *Journal of International Business Studies*, vol. 38, no. 2 (March 2007).

APPENDIX TO CHAPTER 7: REGIONAL ASPECTS OF MULTINATIONALITY AND PERFORMANCE

In order to link Parts One and Two, this Appendix reports on recent research on the topic of multinationality and performance. A basic premise of international business is that foreign operations are profitable—otherwise, they would not take place! Thus it is hypothesized that the performance of the firm (usually an MNE) improves as its degree of foreign operations increases.

In Part One we have explored the reasons for MNEs and some ideas about why and how their degree of multinationality might increase across the home region, rather than globally. In Part Two we have examined country factors which (often indirectly) may affect firm performance. Thus, in this Appendix we bring these themes together by examining the regional aspects of multinationality and performance.

Introduction

Rugman (2005) has shown that the world's largest firms operate mainly on an intra-regional basis, in terms of both sales and assets. We relate traditional literature on multinationality and performance to the new metrics available, which includes new data on regional sales and on the return on foreign assets. Several recent papers examine regionalization and performance across industries, others over time and for various regions of the triad. This recent empirical work provides a very useful starting point in bringing the regional nature of MNEs into the literature on multinationality and performance.

In the field of international business one of the most basic issues is the relationship between multinationality and performance. Several hundred studies have examined the nature of this relationship, with somewhat inconclusive results. Here this literature is reviewed and extended and then related to the regional dimension of multinationality and performance. The regional aspects of multinational activity are explored in Rugman and Verbeke (2004) and Rugman (2005). The traditional empirical work on multinationality and performance can be extended by including this regional dimension.

Recent research on the S curve

Contractor (2007) presents a theoretical justification for the three-stage *S* curve, see Figure 7.7. The horizontal axis represents the degree of multinationality, here proxied by

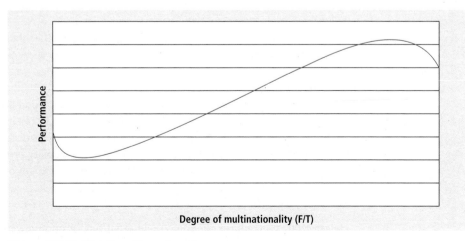

Figure 7.7 Multinationality and performance

the ratio of foreign (F) to total (T) sales, (F/T). The vertical axis represents a performance measure, here the return on total assets (ROTA). There is generally a positive relationship between these two variables. In an interesting twist Contractor argues that the middle stage is consistent with the observations on the regional nature of multinational activity. He also suggests that the final stage, where performance suffers due to excessive multinationality, is typically populated by relatively few firms. This fall-off in performance beyond a certain threshold of multinationality may correspond to an attempt by some companies to reach a "global" stage. While these propositions remain to be tested, Contractor provides strong new insights into the possible relationship between the regional dimension of multinationality activity and the emerging literature on the *S* curve. He also reviews seven generic reasons why studies of multinationality and performance yield different results, and he provides an agenda for research to further test the viability of the three-stage *S* curve concept.

Regional versus total sales

Oh and Rugman (2007) provide new data examining the trends of regional sales between 2001 and 2005. They start with the 2001 benchmark year used in the pathbreaking paper by Rugman and Verbeke (2004) as further developed in the databank reported in the book by Rugman (2005). They find a remarkable degree of stability over time where the ratio of regional to total sales averages 75.7 percent. They also provide data for the first time on the regional nature of assets of the world's largest 500 firms. This averages 76.7 percent again with less than a 1 percent variation over the five-year period.

Osegowitsch and Sammartino (2007) conduct an analysis by taking the set of 380 firms reported in Rugman and Verbeke (2004) and going back to 1991 to find trends in regionalization over the period 1991–2001. One problem is that this yields a greatly reduced sample of 159 firms biased towards US firms. Indeed, most of their results exclude the Asian firms completely, and represent only 90 North American firms and 36 from Europe. Osegowitsch and Sammartino (2007) find that there is a reduction in intra-regional sales for this small set of US and European firms from 84 percent to 76 percent. Over this period they also find that some firms increase their sales outside their home region. They also find that a somewhat larger percentage of firms can be classified as biregional in contrast to those found in the Rugman and Verbeke (2004) chapter. However, in contrast to their own conclusions their own data actually confirm the main two insights of Rugman and Verbeke (2004). First, the vast majority of firms remain home region oriented over the 1991–2001 period. Second, there are very few global firms. Their chapter is useful in provoking a debate about trends in regionalization and hopefully a more extensive dataset can be constructed to help reconcile their findings with those of Oh and Rugman (2007).

Goerzen and Asmussen (2007) use a set of Japanese MNEs to test the relationship between regional and global firms. They argue correctly that the performance of a firm is determined by its firm-specific advantages (FSAs). They show that regional firms build more upon location-bound FSAs, especially in the marketing area. In contrast, global firms have technological (R&D) FSAs, and these are presumed to be non-location bound. They find evidence that the FSAs of global firms are less location bound than the FSAs of regional firms. This work needs to be extended beyond the Japanese dataset in order to test the generalization of these findings. However, their theoretical logic is consistent with that of Rugman and Verbeke (2007), where it is argued that there is a liability of regional foreignness. In other words, the FSAs of MNEs are difficult to deploy and exploit outside the home region.

Gravity model

Hejazi (2007) introduces the logic of international economics and transaction costs to analyze the regional dimension of the activities of MNEs. He uses the well-known gravity model of international economics which has been used to analyze the importance of geography on the determination of international trade flows. He adapts the gravity model to measure foreign direct investment (FDI) instead of trade flows. The gravity model measures the country-level frictions affecting trade and can only be applied to FDI with some difficulty as FDI is partly a method to overcome such frictions. Thus the gravity model yields a new type of test of the activities of MNEs, although it is not a direct test of their strategies. Hejazi finds that there is a strong regional bias in the activities of MNEs from the EU, but he does not find this effect for North American MNEs, which is not surprising given the asymmetrical large size of the US market. (The size bias of the US market may also affect the results by Osegowitsch and Sammartino (2007).) While Hejazi does not test performance directly, his work offers new conceptual lenses on the nature of the regional dimension of multinationality. Such work using econometric techniques based on the gravity model needs to be taken up and related to the empirical literature on multinationality and performance.

Multinationality and performance

Bowen (2007) provides a theoretical critique of the extant empirical work in the multinationality and performance literature. He points out that basic statistical issues have not been resolved, including the issues of endogeneity and non-linearities in the tests. He argues that the multinationality and performance literature does not take into account the heterogeneous nature of firms, industries, or countries. He argues further that the multinationality and performance literature needs to be much better integrated into basic international business theory and that the various "modes of multinationality" (exporting, FDI, outsourcing) can affect measurement. Such variations in types of multinationality are consistent with the observations of Rugman (2005) on the regional nature of multinational activity. A related criticism of the lack of theoretical underpinnings in the multinationality and performance literature has been advanced by Verbeke, Li, and Goerzen (2009). It is clear that much more effort needs to be put into the development of appropriate theoretical frameworks to model the observed empirical relationship between multinationality and performance.

Bausch et al. (2007) conduct a meta-analysis of a large set of previously published studies in the literature on multinationality and performance. They confirm a positive relationship between multinationality and performance. They have a broad definition of multinationality and include the traditional type of merger and acquisition (leading to wholly owned subsidiaries through the process of FDI) along with the non-traditional type of alliance formation. This leads them to invent yet another term for multinationality, namely international business combinations. It is unusual to include alliances in this type of work since it is difficult to assess the impact of alliances on firm performance in a direct manner, as can be done with the merger and acquisition mode of multinationality. Some challenging ideas are presented in this paper which attempts to extend the field of study by adding the alliance as an additional unit of analysis. It is particularly important to extend these tests to fully address the regional significance of different types of international business combinations.

Fortanier et al. (2007) offer a cautionary tale for researchers on multinationality and performance. They find that the empirical results testing this relationship are strongly affected by moderating variables. In particular the so-called "strategic fit" affects performance in a significant and positive manner. Strategic fit moderates the basic aspects of multinationality and performance including the shape, size, and direction of the relationship. Strategic fit is based upon the integration and national responsiveness framework, which is also used by Li and Li (2007). Fortanier and her coauthors (2007) collect archival data on the chain of ownership of multiple subsidiaries that allow them to conduct more robust econometric analysis on aspects of integration and responsiveness. They have data for 336 of the world's largest 500 firms for the year 2002. These variables enter as moderators when testing the basic relationship between multinationality and performance. The results indicate a significant positive relationship between multinationality and return on sales, but this relationship is not a stable one since the strategic fit varies by firm. In other words, firms with an integration strategy perform well internationally in industries which are integrated. In contrast, in multidomestic industries only firms with a national responsiveness strategy do well internationally, so industry effects matter, as also found by Li and Li (2007). While the paper is interesting because it attempts to introduce organizational structure and strategy issues more explicitly into the literature on multinationality and performance, the regional dimension is not explored.

Kumar and Gaur (2007) examine the relationship between multinationality and performance within the context of 240 of India's MNEs, many of which are smaller firms than the world's largest 500 for which the regional effect has been tested. They find strong evidence of a positive J-shaped exponentially increasing relationship between the internationalization of Indian firms and their performance. They also find that India's outward FDI differs between developing and developed economies and between manufacturing and service sectors. A key contribution is that their data include relatively small and medium-sized firms, not just the world's largest 500 firms. This helps us better understand the country context in studies of multinationality and performance, as India has many small multinational firms. Usually size of firms is a moderating or control variable, but Kumar and Gaur link it to a country factor for India.

Nachum and Wymbs (2007) offer an interesting contrast to the literature as their geographic unit of analysis is the city. This is a subnational unit of analysis, and it can be contrasted with the triad regions developed in Rugman (2005). A very good reason is given for choosing cities—namely, that the data tested relate to the financial and professional service industries. These are clustered in the world's major cities. The authors analyze 673 MNEs in these service sectors that entered New York and London through mergers and acquisitions. They find an interaction between geographic location and the FSAs of these MNEs. It is a useful idea to apply the location decision for an industry and firm at the appropriate geographic level. These findings can be usefully contrasted with other papers where regions cross national borders, rather than being subnational.

Regional aspects of multinationality and performance

Li and Li (2007) provide an innovative test of the regional aspects of multinationality and performance. The authors use the well-known integration and responsiveness matrix to distinguish between a "global" industry, which has a high degree of economic integration, and a "multidomestic" industry, which is nationally responsive. They choose the computer and office equipment industry as an example of a global industry, and the soap, cleanser, and toilet goods industry as an example of a multidomestic industry. They find significant differences between the two industries in terms of international strategies, which lead to confirmation of the regional dimension in multinational operations. They also test the impact of FSAs in the two industries in terms of both R&D and marketing intensity. Their results indicate that FSAs are largely non-location bound in the global industry, but much home-region bound in the multidomestic industry. In addition, they show that internationalization pace has a direct positive impact on firm performance in the global industry but not in the multidomestic industry.

Rugman et al. (2007) introduce a new dependent variable called return on foreign assets (ROFA). They contrast it with the traditional variable, return on total assets (ROTA). They also introduce a regional variable representing regional sales. They test the explanatory power of the regional sales variable with linear, quadratic, and cubic fits. They find that the regional variable explains ROTA in terms of the cubic fit, but not ROFA. These data are focused upon a set of 27 UK multinationals of which 8 are in manufacturing and 19 are in service sectors; the regional variable represents sales in the EU. The results indicate that the 27 large UK MNEs experience strong intra-regional sales and that the regional sales variable is a significant variable affecting firm performance in a positive but non-linear manner allowing for standard control variables.

In a related chapter Sukpanich (2007) also includes an independent variable representing intra-regional sales, this time across MNEs in the triad regions of North America and the EU. She has data on 91 firms of which 67 are from North America and 24 from Europe. Of the 91 firms, 66 are in manufacturing and 25 in services. She uses the COMPUSTAT database to access data on the FSAs of MNEs. These FSAs include R&D and marketing variables. She finds a strong positive linear relationship between the measure of intra-regional sales and performance. Performance is higher for firms based in their home region. This result contrasts with that of Chen as discussed next.

Chen (2007) conducts a test of the multinationality and performance relationship across some service sector firms in an Asian context. He distinguishes between intra-regional sales and extra-regional sales for this set of service sector firms. He uses the same Osiris database as in Rugman et al. (2007). He does not find support for the hypothesis that intra-regional sales are a significant determinant of performance where performance is measured by return on total assets. Instead, he finds that extra-regional sales are significant, in contrast to Sukpanich (2007). To some extent this may support some findings by Osegowitsch and Sammartino (2007). Further research is required, but it is encouraging to see this focus on the Asian firms missing from Osegowitsch and Sammartino (2007).

Richter (2007) tests the importance of a regional sales variable across the UNCTAD set of the world's 100 largest firms as ranked by foreign assets. This is a somewhat unrepresentative sample as it consists of the world's most internationalized firms and is thus biased toward finding internationalization (and therefore regionalization). Richter uses the S curve and finds a significant cubic fit between performance and multinationality where the latter is measured by the UNCTAD transnationality index. When testing the foreign intra-regional sales variable, her results are ambiguous with either an S curve or inverted U curve being supported. However, as with other recent papers, she finds that this regional sales variable is a significant determinant of performance.

It would be useful to extend this type of research beyond the largest 100 firms (or the 500 largest in Rugman (2005)) to include many more MNEs that are small to medium sized. Indeed, it would be useful to test the regional dimension in the emerging literature on international entrepreneurship, some of which is focused upon the internationalization process of small and medium-sized firms. This will require some theoretical adjustments to the assumption that many of these firms are "born global." This literature seems to find relatively fast internationalization of small firms in the information technology and computer sector, but there has not been careful testing of the regional aspects of such internationalization, and other sectors need to be added. Furthermore, the normal metric used is a scope variable dealing with the opening of foreign subsidiaries, whereas a better metric is to use the ratio of foreign to total sales (in this case, regional to total sales).

While this work on international entrepreneurship remains to be undertaken, this recent empirical work provides a very useful starting point in bringing the regional nature of MNEs into the literature on multinationality and performance. There is uniformity in showing that the basic relationship between multinationality and performance is beset by issues of heterogeneity across countries, industries, and firms. Yet many of them also show that the regional nature of multinationality can be included in this work in a useful manner. Therefore, the regional dimension of strategy needs to be considered in future work analyzing the relationship between multinationality and performance.

References

Bausch, A., Fritz, T. and Bösecke, K. "Performance Effects of Internationalization Strategies: A Meta-analysis," in A. M. Rugman (ed.), *Regional Aspects of Multinationality and Performance* (Oxford: Elsevier, 2007).

Bowen, H. P. "The Empirics of Multinationality and Performance," in A. M. Rugman (ed.), *Regional Aspects of Multinationality and Performance* (Oxford: Elsevier, 2007).

Chen, S. "Testing Regional Effects in the International-Performance Relationship in Asia Service Firms," in A. M. Rugman (ed.), *Regional Aspects of Multinationality and Performance* (Oxford: Elsevier, 2007).

Contractor, F. J. "The Evolutionary or Multi-stage Theory of Internationalization and the Regionalization of Firms," in A. M. Rugman (ed.), *Regional Aspects of Multinationality and Performance* (Oxford: Elsevier, 2007).

Fortanier, F., Muller, A. and Tulder, R. van. "Internationalization and Performance: The Moderating Role of Strategic Fit," in A. M. Rugman (ed.), *Regional Aspects of Multinationality and Performance* (Oxford: Elsevier, 2007).

Goerzen, A. and Asmussen, C. G. "The Geographic Orientation of Multinational Enterprises and its Implications for Performance," in A. M. Rugman (ed.), *Regional Aspects of Multinationality and Performance* (Oxford: Elsevier, 2007).

Hejazi, W. "The Regional Nature of MNE Activities and the Gravity Model," in A. M. Rugman (ed.), *Regional Aspects of Multinationality and Performance* (Oxford: Elsevier, 2007).

Kumar, V. and Gaur, A. S. "Internationalization and Performance of Indian Firms," in A. M. Rugman (ed.), *Regional Aspects of Multinationality and Performance* (Oxford: Elsevier, 2007).

Li, L. and Li, D. "Testing the Global and Regional Strategies of Multinational Enterprises," in A. M. Rugman (ed.), *Regional Aspects of Multinationality and Performance* (Oxford: Elsevier, 2007).

Nachum, L. and Wymbs, C. "The Location and Performance of Foreign Affiliates in Global Cities," in A. M. Rugman (ed.), *Regional Aspects of Multinationality and Performance* (Oxford: Elsevier, 2007).

Oh, C.-H. and Rugman, A. M. "Multinationality and Regional Performance, 2001–2005," in A. M. Rugman (ed.), *Regional Aspects of Multinationality and Performance* (Oxford: Elsevier, 2007).

Osegowitsch, T. and Sammartino, A. "Exploring Trends in Regionalization," in A. M. Rugman (ed.), *Regional Aspects of Multinationality and Performance* (Oxford: Elsevier, 2007).

Richter, N. "Intra-regional Sales and the Internationalization and Performance Relationship," in A. M. Rugman (ed.), *Regional Aspects of Multinationality and Performance* (Oxford: Elsevier, 2007).

Rugman, A. M. *The Regional Multinationals: MNEs and 'Global' Strategic Management* (Cambridge: Cambridge University Press, 2005).

Rugman, Alan M. and Verbeke, Alain. "A Perspective on Regional and Global Strategies of Multinational Enterprises," *Journal of International Business Studies*, vol. 35, no. 1 (January 2004), pp. 3–18.

Rugman, A. M. and Verbeke, Alain "Liabilities of Regional Foreignness and the Use of Firm-level versus Country-level Data: A Response to Dunning *et al.* (2007)," *Journal of International Business Studies*, vol. 38, no. 1 (January 2007), pp. 200–205.

Rugman, A. M., Yip, G. S. and Kudina, A. "The Regional Dimension of UK Multinationals," in A. M. Rugman (ed.), *Regional Aspects of Multinationality and Performance* (Oxford: Elsevier, 2007).

Sukpanich, N. "Intra-regional Sales and Performance," in A. M. Rugman (ed.), *Regional Aspects of Multinationality and Performance* (Oxford: Elsevier, 2007).

Verbeke, A., Li, L. and Goerzen, A. "Towards More Effective Research on the Multinationality–Performance Relationship," *Management International Review*, vol. 49, no. 2 (2009), pp. 1–13.

Additional bibliography

Banalieva, E., Santoro, M. "Local, Regional, or Global? Geographic Orientation and Relative Financial Performance of Emerging Market Multinational Enterprises," *European Management* Journal, vol. 27, no. 5 (2009).

Beleska-Spasova, E. and Glaister, K. W. (2010). "Geographic Orientation and Performance," *Management International Review*, vol. 50, no. 5 (October 2010).

Chen, S. and Tan, H. "Region Effects in the Internationalization-Performance Relationship in Chinese Firms," *Journal of World Business* (2010). doi:10.1016/j.jwb.2010.10.022.

Oh, C. H. "The International Scale and Scope of European Multinationals," *European Management Journal*, vol. 27, no. 5 (2009).

Oh, C. H. "Value Creation and Home Region Internationalization of U.S. MNEs," *Multinational Business Review*, vol. 18, no. 4 (2010).

Qian, G., Khoury, T., Peng, M. W. and Qian, Z. "The Performance Implication of Intra- and Inter-regional Geographic Diversification," *Strategic Management Journal*, 31 (2010).

Rugman, A. M. and Oh, C. H. "Does the Regional Nature of Multinationals Affect the Multinationality and Performance Relationship?" *International Business Review*, vol. 19, no. 5 (2010).

Rugman, A. M. and Oh, C. H. "Methodological Issues in the Measurement of Multinationality of U.S. Firms," *Multinational Business Review* vol. 19, no. 3 (2011).

Rugman, A. M. and Oh, C. H. "Regional Integration and the International Strategies of Large European Firms," *International Business Review*, vol. 20 (2011), forthcoming.

Rugman, A. M. and Verbeke, A. "Internalization Theory and Its Impact on the Field of International Business," in J. J. Boddewyn (ed.) *International Business Scholarship: AIB Fellows on the First 50 Years and Beyond*, Research in Global Strategic Management, vol. 14 (Bradford: Emerald Group, 2008).

Rugman, A. M., Yip, G. S. and Kudina, A. "Testing the Link Between Multinationality and the Return on Foreign Assets," *Multinational Business Review*, vol. 17, no. 3 (2009).

Sullivan, Daniel. "Measuring the Degree of Internationalization of a Firm," *Journal of International Business Studies*, vol. 25, no. 2 (1994).

Verbeke, A. and Brugman, P. "Triple-Testing the Quality of Multinationality–Performance Research: An Internalization Theory Perspective," *International Business Review*, vol. 18, no. 3 (June 2009).

Verbeke, A., Li, L. and Goerzen, A. "Toward More Effective Research on the Multinationality–Performance Relationship," *Management International Review*, vol. 49, no. 5 (2009).

Part Three

INTERNATIONAL BUSINESS STRATEGIES

Chapter 8

MULTINATIONAL STRATEGY

Contents

Objectives of the chapter

Multinational enterprises are businesses that are headquartered in one country but have operations in other countries. In such a complex environment, it is particularly important for these MNEs to have well-formulated strategic plans. Large MNEs do this by conducting a thorough analysis of their environments and often developing detailed, comprehensive plans for coordinating worldwide activities. These plans set forth objectives for all major divisions and units and provide for systematic follow-up and evaluation. Smaller MNEs may use less sophisticated plans. However, all multinationals that conduct strategic planning go through a three-step process: formulation, implementation, and control.

The specific objectives of this chapter are to:

1 *Define* the term *strategic planning* and discuss the strategic orientations that affect this planning process.

2 *Explain* how strategy is formulated, giving particular emphasis to external and internal environmental assessment.

3 *Describe* how strategy is implemented, with particular attention to location, ownership decisions, and functional area implementation.

4 *Discuss* the ways in which MNEs control and evaluate their strategies.

ACTIVE LEARNING CASE

Vodafone and the triad telecom market

Vodafone had its beginnings in 1982, when the Racal Electronics Group Board successfully bid for a private-sector UK cellular license. The Racal Telecomms Division was established with 50 employees in the rural town of Newbury and launched the first cellular network on January 1, 1985. By the end of that year, Vodafone had 19,000 subscribers. For the year ended in March 30, 2010, London-based Vodafone was the world's second-largest mobile phone company measured by revenue of $70.8994 billion, of which 67 percent originated from Western Europe, and it had a workforce of 84,990 employees. (China Mobile Communications with revenue of $71.749 billion was the world's largest mobile phone company according to Fortune Global 500, 2010 ranking.) As of September 30, 2010, it had approximately 332 million mobile customers around the world. It operates network in over 30 countries and has partner network in over 40 countries. Let's review its growth.

Vodafone expanded globally through a carefully crafted "triad" strategy. From 1991 to 1998 its focus was on Europe, where it developed one of the basic ideas that it continues to use in most cases—acquire companies in association with partners and pay for it with equity. This strategy has given Vodafone access to new markets while providing it with partners that help deal with local regulatory environment agencies and provide assistance in addressing local market needs. For example, in the case of Libertel of the Netherlands, Vodafone purchased 70 percent of the company while Dutch ING, the local partner, held the rest. The company had interests in companies across most European markets with over 50 percent of the shares in many of these companies. As of September 30, 2010, Vodafone had 124 million customers in Europe. In geographic terms, 37 percent of Vodafone's subscribers and 64 percent of its turnover were in Western Europe.

To appease EU regulators during its acquisition spree in the 1990s, Vodafone had to divest itself of Orange, the UK's third-largest wireless operator. European acquisitions could not, therefore, be the company's only growth strategy. Rather, the best strategy was to go international, gain market share in all major economies, then link together all these firms into a worldwide network. This is precisely what it did.

In June 1999, Vodafone took a major step in implementing its worldwide strategy when it beat out Bell Atlantic for Airtouch Communications, a California-based firm. Creating Vodafone Airtouch (VA) gave the overall company

Source: Corbis/Reuters

a market capitalization of $154 billion and a total of 35 million wireless customers worldwide. Soon after the acquisition, VA entered into an agreement with Bell Atlantic (which was soon to merge with GTE) that gave it a 45 percent stake in a venture called Verizon Wireless. This decision had proved to be a very good one; prior to the merger of Cingular and AT&T Wireless in 2004, Verizon was the largest US mobile telephone operator. Indeed, Cingular snatched AT&T Wireless from Vodafone, which was seeking to further cement its presence in the United States through a controlling interest in the company.

By 2001 the US market had relatively low penetration levels compared to Europe and Japan. Yet it has the highest potential for growth across industrialized countries. As of September 30, 2010, Vodafone share in Verizon Mobile had 41.927 million subscribers compared to 38.9 million subscribers in 2001, a growth of 8 percent over 10 years.

Vodafone cemented its position in Japan in late 2001 by increasing its share of Japan Telecom to 69.7 percent. That decision completed the firm's "triad" strategy. By 2001, Vodafone had 10.4 million subscribers in Japan—7.8 percent of the company's total subscribers. Yet on March 17, 2006, Vodafone announced an agreement to sell all its interest in Vodafone Japan to Softbank for £8.9 billion, of which £6.8 billion was received in cash on closing of the deal. Vodafone Japan later changed its name to Softbank Mobile. In November 2010, Vodafone sold its remaining minority interest in its Japanese operations to current owner Softbank for £3.1 billion and exited Japan, as part of its new strategy, "offloading non core assets." Vodafone said it would focus on markets in Europe, India, and Africa.

To summarize, Vodafone was a major player in the EU with holdings in Omnitel, Mannesmann, and SFR. The company was a force in the US market through its minority holding in Verizon Wireless. And in Asia, where the largest market for mobile phones is in Japan, Vodafone held operating control of Japan Telecom and also owned J-Phone, a large mobile phone operator. However, Vodafone eventually divested its investment in Japan.

By 2010, Vodafone had carefully ventured into other markets. In Australia and New Zealand, it had wholly owned subsidiaries and about 6.024 million subscribers. This represented 50 percent growth if compared to 4 million subscribers in 2001. In non-industrialized countries, where the risk is higher, it held minority interests in most of its operations. Only in Egypt did it have more than 50 percent ownership. In South Africa, Kenya, and Fiji, it held between 35 and 40 percent. In China, the market with the largest potential growth, it held a mere 3.2 percent ownership of the venture in 2000. In such a huge market, however, that accounted for nearly 5 million subscribers. In September 2010, Vodafone sold its stake in China's biggest operator, China Mobile, for $6.5 billion for cash, and achieved a near doubling of Vodafone's original investment. Vodafone continues to cooperate with China's leading telecommunication companies in areas such as roaming, network roadmap development, multinational customers, and green technology.

On February 11, 2007, the Company agreed to acquire a controlling interest of 67 percent in Hutchison Essar Limited in India for US$11.1 billion. At the same time, it agreed to sell back 5.6 percent of its AirTel stake back to the Mittals. Vodafone would retain a 4.4 percent stake in Airtel. On September 21, 2007, Hutchison was rebranded to Vadafone in India. However, Vodafone has ongoing problems with the Indian tax authority who claimed that Vodafone owed value added tax (VAT) on the purchase in 2007 of the Indian telephone assets of the Hong Kong's Hutchison Whampoa. Vadafone decided not to set up provisions for this disputed £1.6bn tax bill in India in its financial statements. As at September 30, 2010, Vodafone had 115.553 million mobile customers in India.

Vodafone's strategy is to maximize its footprint with a common technology and offer the largest possible "roaming" wireless capability, which lends itself to overall lower costs. Perhaps surprisingly, this roaming technology was more prevalent in Europe than in the United States, mostly due to EU-wide cooperation between governmental regulatory authorities regarding common platforms.

Vodafone is not only relying on geographic diversification of acquisitions. Technology plays a major role in this industry, and Vodafone, like its competitors, purchased licenses to operate 3G technology. When the industry overestimated the pace at which the technology was developed, some providers stumbled badly, but this technology is now available in urban areas in Europe and Japan and is expanding quickly. Mobile telephones with video and picture technology are more established in the market, but it is data transfers that mobile service providers are counting on for increased profits. This new technology is expected to reduce overall costs and, competition permitting, might allow Vodafone to increase its revenue per subscriber.

The biggest challenge facing Vodafone will be that of coordinating all of its worldwide holdings so as to maximize shareholder value. In an effort to handle this problem, the company's head office has now abandoned the use of centralized control and opted for a decentralized type of operation. In the United States, for example, local partners and operating managers now make many of the major decisions regarding how to do business. The same is true in Europe. Vodafone is realizing that in order to manage all of these different units in worldwide markets where regulations and customer preferences are often quite different, the best approach is to create a strategic plan that recognizes and takes advantages of these differences.

Websites: www.vodafone.com; www.verizon.com; www.omnitelvodafone.it; www.mannesmann.de; www.nttdocomo.com; www.kddi.com.

Sources: "Vodafone Launches 3G in Europe," *BBC News*, May 4, 2004; Vodafone, *Annual Reports and Accounts*, 1999, 2000, 2004, 2009, 2010. News release, Vodafone Announces First Half 2010/2011 Results and Strategy Update, November 9, 2010. "*Fortune Global 500*," *Fortune*, July 26, 2010 issue, http://money.cnn.com/magazines/fortune/global500/2010; "Vodafone Pockets $6.5Bn in China Mobile Sales," *BBC News*, http://www.bbc.co.uk/news/business-11225509, September 8, 2010; "Vodafone Exits Japan and Raise Profit Forecast," BBC News, www.bbc.co.uk, November 9, 2010.

1 Given the competitiveness of the environment, how much opportunity exists for Vodafone in the international mobile phone market?

2 What type of generic strategy does Vodafone employ? Defend your answer.

3 What form of ownership arrangement is Vodafone using to gain world market share? Explain.

4 On what basis would a firm like Vodafone evaluate performance? Identify and describe two.

INTRODUCTION

In this chapter we provide an introduction to the key concepts of strategic management relevant to both MNEs and small and medium enterprises. We will review the rationale for strategic planning and the strategic orientation of firms (whether they are ethnocentric, polycentric, regiocentric, or geocentric). We will examine the process of strategy formulation and review the five forces of industry competitiveness. We then apply this thinking to analysis of a firm's value chain. We consider the basic generic strategies of firms. We apply these concepts to the implementation of strategy and discuss how this applies to different modes of entry, such as wholly owned subsidiaries, strategic alliances, and joint ventures. We will conclude with a section on the valuation of firm strategy and set the stage for discussion of relevant organization structures in Chapter 9.

Before becoming immersed in these details of strategic management, you should be aware of the linkages of strategy and structure to the previous work in this textbook discussing the theory of the MNE. In particular, the firm and country framework of Chapter 2 can be used to illustrate the special nature of strategic management as it applies to MNEs. In the FSA and CSA matrix of Chapter 2 it is useful to review cells 1 and 4 at this juncture.

Cell 1 is a situation with low FSAs but strong CSAs. In terms of strategic management the firm will build competitive advantages due to its home-country CSAs. For example, firms from Canada will build CSAs based upon natural resources. They will exploit CSAs in the forest products sector, in minerals, and in cheap hydroelectric power. Firms from China will develop CSAs in manufacturing based upon cheap labor. Firms from India will develop CSA in information technology based upon cheap skilled labor. Firms in the United States will develop economies of scale based upon the CSA of its huge domestic market: such CSAs (in terms of scale economies) can then be exploited abroad. The challenge for MNEs is to combine the CSAs with strong FSAs, a situation in cell 3 of the FSA–CSA matrix of Chapter 2. This chapter explores ways in which strategic management itself may be a type of FSA that can turn the CSAs of cell 1 into the combined country and firm advantages of cell 3.

In contrast, cell 4 of the FSA–CSA matrix is a situation of strong FSAs where these are independent of CSAs. This cell can best be described by the resource-based view (RBV) of strategy. The RBV is the basic theory of strategic management as explained in textbooks by Barney (2007), Grant (2008), Peng (2006), and Mintzberg et al. (1998). (These references are in the bibliography at the end of the chapter.) The core concept in the RBV is that a firm needs to develop a sustainable long-run competitive advantage, or capability. This is often called the core competence of the firm. In terms of international business the core competence is identical to the concept of an FSA as discussed in Chapter 2. In other words, the RBV is simply a more detailed examination of the nature, extent, and strength of FSAs. The weakness of the pure RBV is that it is confined to cell 4 of the FSA–CSA matrix. In other words, it has no international component since CSAs are not relevant to a firm's success in cell 4.

Obviously, cell 3 of the FSA–CSA matrix of Chapter 2 is a most intriguing one. This is where country and firm effects are combined. Such complementary assets lie at the heart of the modern theory of the MNE in particular and international business in general. Cell 3 is a situation requiring the integration of firm and country advantages in a sustainable and long-run manner. In terms of the RBV, cell 3 is a situation requiring dynamic capabilities. In terms of mode of entry theory, it is a situation where network analysis can be applied to explain the generation of FSAs by subsidiaries within the network of the MNE. Some cell 3 thinking can also be applied to analyze international joint ventures.

But before proceeding to this depth of analysis, it is first necessary to review the basic issues of strategic management (in this chapter) and organization structure (in the following chapter). We will return to aspects of the RBV and the nature of location-bound or non-location-bound FSAs in Chapter 10 when we introduce the concept of national responsiveness.

Strategic planning is the process of evaluating an enterprise's environment and internal strengths, identifying its basic mission and long- and short-range objectives, and implementing a plan of action for attaining these goals. MNEs rely heavily on this process because it provides them with both general direction and specific guidance in carrying out their activities. Without a strategic plan, these businesses would have great difficulty in planning, implementing, and evaluating operations. With strategic planning, however, research shows that many MNEs have been able to make adjustments in their approach to dealing with competitive situations and either redirect their efforts or exploit new areas of opportunity. For example, as a result of losing market share in Europe in recent years, General Motors cut its European capacity in an effort to stem further losses.[1] Meanwhile, Dell Computer expanded its international presence. In 2001 the company became the largest firm in the worldwide PC business, with a market share of 13 percent. On a different front, General Electric's strategy is to continue growing in spite of the European Commission's refusal to allow it to merge with Honeywell. GE Medical bought Data Critical, a maker of wireless and Internet systems for communicating health-care data; GE Industrial Systems acquired the Lentronics line of multiplexers from Nortel Networks; and GE Capital purchased Heller Financial, a company in the commercial financing, equipment leasing, and real estate finance business.[2] By carefully formulating their strategic plans, these MNEs are finding that they can better cope with the ever-changing challenge of worldwide competition.[3]

STRATEGIC ORIENTATIONS

Before examining the strategic planning process, we must realize that MNEs have strategic predispositions toward doing things in a particular way, which help determine the specific decisions the firm will implement. There are four such predispositions: ethnocentric, polycentric, regiocentric, and geocentric. Table 8.1 lists each predisposition and its characteristics.

An MNE with an **ethnocentric predisposition** will rely on the values and interests of the parent company in formulating and implementing the strategic plan. Primary emphasis will be given to profitability and the firm will try to run operations abroad the way they are run at home. Firms trying to sell the same product abroad that they sell at home use this predisposition most commonly.

An MNE with a **polycentric predisposition** will tailor its strategic plan to meet the needs of the local culture. If the firm is doing business in more than one culture, the overall plan will be adapted to reflect these individual needs. The basic mission of a polycentric MNE is to be accepted by the local culture and to blend into the country. Each subsidiary will decide which objectives to pursue, based on local needs. Profits will be put back into the country in the form of expansion and growth.

An MNE with a **regiocentric predisposition** will be interested in obtaining both profit and public acceptance (a combination of the ethnocentric and polycentric approaches) and will use a strategy that allows it to address both local and regional needs. The company will be less focused on a particular country than on a geographic region. For example, an MNE doing business in the EU will be interested in all the member nations.

Strategic planning
The process of evaluating the enterprise's environment and its internal strengths and then identifying long- and short-range activities

Ethnocentric predisposition
The tendency of a manager or multinational company to rely on the values and interests of the parent company in formulating and implementing the strategic plan

Polycentric predisposition
The tendency of a multinational to tailor its strategic plan to meet the needs of the local culture

Regiocentric predisposition
The tendency of a multinational to use a strategy that addresses both local and regional needs

Table 8.1 Typical strategic orientations of MNEs

MNE orientation	Ethnocentric	Polycentric	Regiocentric	Geocentric
Company's basic mission	Profitability	Public acceptance (legitimacy)	Both profitability and public acceptance	Both profitability and public acceptance
Type of governance	Top down	Bottom up (each local unit sets objectives)	Mutually negotiated between the region and its subsidiaries	Mutually negotiated at all levels of the organization
Strategy	Global integration	National responsiveness	Regional integration and national responsiveness	Global integration and national responsiveness
Structure	Hierarchical product divisions	Hierarchical area divisions with autonomous national units	Product and regional organization tied together through a matrix structure	A network of organizations (in some cases this includes stockholders and competitors)
Culture	Host country	Home country	Regional	Global
Technology	Mass production	Batch production	Flexible manufacturing	Flexible manufacturing
Marketing strategy	Product development is determined primarily by the needs of the home-country customers	Local product development based on local needs	Standardized within the region, but not across regions	Global products with local variations
Profit strategy	Profits are brought back to the home country	Profits are kept in the host country	Profits are redistributed within the region	Redistribution is done on a global basis
Human resource management practices	Overseas operations are managed by people from the home country	Local nationals are used in key management positions	Regional people are developed for key managerial positions anywhere in the region	The best people anywhere in the world are developed for key positions everywhere in the world

Source: Adapted from "Strategic Planning for a Global Business," *Columbia Journal of World Business*, Summer 1985. Copyright © Elsevier Science & Technology Journals. With permission from Elsevier Science.

Geocentric predisposition
The tendency of a multinational to construct its strategic plan with a global view of operations

An MNE with a **geocentric predisposition** will view operations on a global basis. The largest international corporations often use this approach. They produce global products with local variations and staff their offices with the best people they can find, regardless of country of origin. Multinationals, in the true meaning of the word, have a geocentric predisposition. However, it is possible for an MNE to have a polycentric or regiocentric predisposition if the company is moderately small or limits its operations to specific cultures or geographic regions.

The predisposition of an MNE will greatly influence its strategic planning process. For example, some MNEs are more interested in profit and/or growth than in developing a comprehensive corporate strategy that exploits their strengths.[4] Some are more interested in large-scale manufacturing that will allow them to compete on a price basis across the country or region, as opposed to developing a high degree of responsiveness to local demand and tailoring a product to these specific market niches.[5] Some prefer to sell in countries where the cultures are similar to their own so that the same basic marketing orientation can be used throughout the regions.[6] These orientations or predispositions greatly influence strategy.[7] For an example of strategic orientations, see the case **International Business Strategy in Action: Arthur Andersen, Accenture, and McKinsey.**

Arthur Andersen, Accenture, and McKinsey

During the 1990s, some of the fastest-growing global organizations were professional service firms that specialized in areas such as consulting, accounting, publishing, law, public relations, advertising, and so on. Today, more and more of these service firms are linking together their worldwide country offices in order to provide seamless service to their multinational clients. Arthur Andersen, Accenture, and McKinsey & Company, three major international consulting firms, provide good examples.

Founded in Chicago in 1913 to provide accounting services, Arthur Andersen had grown to over 85,000 employees in 84 countries by 2001. Until 1989, the firm's management and technology consulting group—Andersen Consulting Group—had complemented its audit and accounting services. However, in 1989, as part of a restructuring effort, Arthur Andersen and Andersen Consulting split and became two independent companies. The plan called for each to maintain its individual business and to cooperate under the umbrella of Andersen Worldwide. In 1997, however, Andersen Consulting sought arbitration claiming that Arthur Andersen had breached the agreement by expanding into business consulting in technology integration, strategic business planning, and business transformation. In 2000, the arbitrator ruled in favor of Andersen Consulting but also forced the consulting firm to drop the Andersen name. Today, under the name Accenture—a combination of "accent" and "future"—this company is a leader in global management and technology consulting with 204,000 employees in 200 cities in 53 countries and a revenue of $21.6 billion for the year ended August 31, 2010. Its five operating groups include communications & high tech, financial services, health & public service, products and resources. Arthur Andersen, on the other hand, ceased to exist after it was discovered that the company, which had been Enron's auditor since 1985, had been involved in the Enron scandal of 2001. When investigators discovered that Andersen had destroyed documents relating to the case, the reputation it had relied on was shattered and its clients departed.

In 1926, James O. McKinsey left his job as a University of Chicago accounting professor to found a company that would provide finance and budgeting services. Soon afterwards, however, McKinsey & Company came to be better known for providing advice on management and organizational issues. In the 1960s, as tariffs began to be lowered and US firms thought of ways to expand internationally, the McKinsey company provided consulting on how to expand, while expanding into Europe, Canada, and Australia itself. Today, the firm is the best-known management–consultancy

private firm in the world, with 16,500 employees in 99 offices in 56 countries and Forbes estimated its revenue of $6 billion for the year 2008. However, it has had mixed success at running its international operations. The German subsidiary is relatively independent, for example, while the French subsidiary is not. McKinsey's core strength is its brand name built on the in-house training and management of its highly skilled people, who have been recruited from top business schools. In 2001, the firm found itself with overcapacity and had to lay off some of its most recent employees. Nevertheless, by 2004, it was estimated that the firm was using only 50 to 60 percent of its capacity. When the IT bubble burst, McKinsey lost many of its clients. Other clients, not affected by IT, were reluctant to turn to consulting firms for advice due to the demise of one of McKinsey's largest competitors, Arthur Andersen. Enron was headed by the CEO, Jeff Skilling who was McKinsey's former partner in the energy and chemical consulting practices. Enron was one of McKinsey's biggest clients before it collapsed. And Mr. Skilling himself was sentenced to 24 years in federal prison as he was convicted of multiple federal felony charges relating to Enron's financial collapse in 2001.

In summary, consulting firms were originally designed to provide advice to managers on improving workplace efficiencies with the use of engineers and time and motion studies. But they soon began to realize that senior executives also needed advice on strategy and organization and began to offer it to their clients. The 1970s and 1980s saw the height of this type of consultancy service. In the 1990s, however, the rise of the IT sector meant that these firms themselves had to redefine their strategic focus. Today, consultancies offer accounting, legal, management, leadership training, strategic planning, operational analysis, and technology services, among others.

Consulting firms have often been deemed recession-proof because their services are needed regardless of what happens in the economy. For example, in good times, businesses need consulting assistance to help them deal with expansion, mergers, and acquisitions; in bad times, they need help in cutting back operations, trimming the workforce, and refocusing their strategy. The most recent worldwide economic slowdown, however, led to an unexpected and significant slowdown in consulting as well. In the 1990s, the market was growing by 20 percent annually; by 2001 this growth rate had shrunk to 3 percent. This slowdown has taken its toll. In the past, consulting firms focused their efforts on securing long-term relationships with large MNEs and other large organizations. And by drawing on ▶

their firm-specific advantages and reputation for quality, they were able to continually attract new clients. In the early 2000s, however, they have all begun to lay off junior staff, and recently hired MBAs are looking for innovative ways to get costs under control. Some critics have wondered aloud why they are having so many problems. If they are indeed experts at helping organizations solve the challenges associated with economic downturns, why do they not simply apply some of these solutions to their own current situation?

Websites: www.accenture.com; www.mckinsey.com.

Sources: Andersen Worldwide, *Annual Report*, 1996; C. A. Bartlett (1996), *McKinsey & Company: Managing Knowledge and Learning*, Harvard Business School Case No. 9-396-357; and http://www.mckinsey.com; http://www.mckinsey.com/about/feet_on_the_street.html; "The Real McKinsey," *Economist.com*, January 30, 2003; "McKinsey's Election Battle," *Economist.com*, February 27, 2003. Clayton Hirst, "The Might of the McKinsey Mob," *The Independent*, www.independent.co.uk, January 20, 2002; Robert Barnes, "Supreme Court to Review Ex-Enron CEO's Conviction," *The Washington Post*, www.washingtonpost.com, October 14, 2009.

STRATEGY FORMULATION

Strategy formulation
The process of evaluating the enterprise's environment and its internal strengths

Strategy formulation is the process of evaluating an enterprise's environment and internal strengths. This typically begins with consideration of the external arena, since the MNE will first be interested in opportunities that can be exploited. Attention is then directed to the internal environment and the resources the organization has available, or can develop, to take advantage of these opportunities.

External environmental assessment

The analysis of the external environment involves two activities: information gathering and information assessment. These steps help to answer two key questions: what is going on in the external environment; and how will these developments affect our company?[8] One of the most common ways to do this is through **competitive intelligence**, which is the use of systematic techniques for obtaining and analyzing public information about competitors. These data are particularly useful in keeping MNEs alert to likely moves by the competition.[9]

Competitive intelligence
The gathering of external information on competitors and the competitive environment as part of the decision-making process

Information gathering

Information gathering is a critical phase of international strategic planning. Unfortunately, not all firms recognize this early enough. In the case of Harley-Davidson, the large US-based motorcycle manufacturer, it was not until the Japanese began dominating the motorcycle market that Harley realized its problem. A systematic analysis of the competition revealed that the major reason for Japanese success in the US market was the high quality of their products, a result of extremely efficient manufacturing techniques. Today, Harley is competitive again. It achieved renewed success because it rethought its basic business, reformulated company strategy, vastly improved product quality, and rededicated itself to its core business: heavyweight motorcycles.

There are a number of ways that MNEs conduct an environmental scan and forecast the future. Four of the most common methods include: (1) asking industry experts to discuss industry trends and make projections about the future; (2) using historical industry trends to forecast future developments; (3) asking knowledgeable managers to write scenarios describing what they foresee for the industry over the next two to three years; and (4) using computers to simulate the industry environment and generate likely future developments. Of these, expert opinion is the most commonly used.[10] The Japanese and the South Koreans provide excellent examples. Mitsubishi has more than 700 employees in New York City, where its primary objective is to gather information on US competitors and markets. All large Japanese corporations operating in the United States employ similar strategies. The same is true for large South Korean trading firms, which require their branch managers to send back information on market developments. These data are then analyzed and used to help formulate future strategies for the firms.

Such information helps MNEs to identify competitor strengths and weaknesses and to target areas for attack. This approach is particularly important when a company is delivering a product or service for many market niches around the world that are too small to be individually profitable. In such situations the MNE has to identify a series of different niches and attempt to market successfully in each of these geographic areas.[11] The information is also critical to those firms that will be coming under attack.

Information assessment

Having gathered information on the competition and the industry, MNEs then evaluate the data. One of the most common approaches is to make an overall assessment based on the five forces that determine industry competitiveness: buyers, suppliers, potential new entrants to the industry, the availability of substitute goods and services, and rivalry among the competitors. Figure 8.1 shows the connections among these forces.[12]

Bargaining power of buyers

MNEs examine the power of their buyers in order to predict the likelihood of maintaining these customers. If the firm believes buyers may be moving their business to competitors, the MNE will want to formulate a strategy for countering this move. For example, the company may offer a lower price or increase the amount of service it provides.

Bargaining power of suppliers

An MNE looks at the power of the industry's suppliers to see if it can gain a competitive advantage here.[13] For example, if there are a number of suppliers in the industry, the MNE may attempt to play them off against one another in an effort to get a lower price. Or the company may move to eliminate any threat from the suppliers by acquiring one of them, thus guaranteeing itself a ready source of inputs.

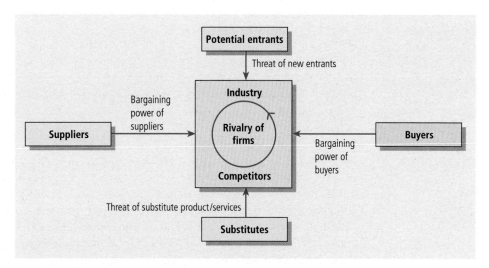

Figure 8.1 The five forces of industry competitiveness

Source: Adapted with the permission of The Free Press, an imprint of Simon & Schuster Adult Publishing Group, from *Competitive Advantage: Creating and Sustaining Superior Performance* by Michael E. Porter. Copyright © 1985, 1998 by Michael E. Porter. All rights reserved.

New entrants

The company will examine the likelihood of new firms entering the industry and will try to determine the impact they might have on the MNE. Two typical ways that international MNEs attempt to reduce the threat of new entrants are by (1) keeping costs low and consumer loyalty high, and (2) encouraging the government to limit foreign business activity through regulation such as duties, tariffs, quotas, and other protective measures.

Threat of substitutes

The MNE looks at the availability of substitute goods and services and tries to anticipate when such offerings will reach the market. There are a number of steps the company can take to offset this competitive force, including (1) lowering prices, (2) offering similar products, and (3) increasing services to the customer.

Rivalry

The MNE examines the rivalry that exists between itself and the competition and seeks to anticipate future changes in this arrangement. Common strategies for maintaining and/or increasing market strength include (1) offering new goods and services, (2) increasing productivity and thus reducing overall costs, (3) working to differentiate current goods and services from those of the competition, (4) increasing overall quality of goods and services, and (5) targeting specific niches with a well-designed market strategy.

As the MNE examines each of these five forces, it must decide the attractiveness and unattractiveness of each. This will help decide how and where to make strategic changes. Figure 8.2 shows the five-forces model applied to the semiconductor industry.

Notice in Figure 8.2 that at the time this analysis was conducted, the suppliers in the semiconductor industry were not very powerful, so they were an attractive force for the MNE. Buyers did not have many substitute products from which to choose (an

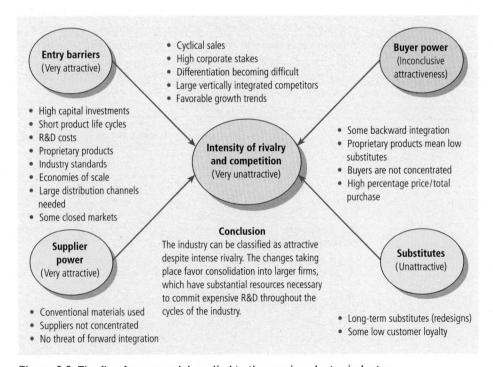

Figure 8.2 The five-forces model applied to the semiconductor industry

Source: Scott Beardsley and Kinji Sakagami, "Advanced Micro Devices: Poised for Chip Greatness," Unpublished student paper, Sloan School of Management, MIT, 1988. Reported in Arnoldo C. Hax and Nicolas S. Majluf, *The Strategy Concept and Process: A Pragmatic Approach* (Englewood Cliffs, NJ: Prentice Hall, 1991), p. 46.

attractive development), but there was some backward integration toward purchasing their own sources of supply (an unattractive development). Overall, the attractiveness of buyer power was regarded as inconclusive. The third force, entry barriers, was quite attractive because of the high costs of getting into the industry and the short product life cycles that existed there. It was very difficult for a company to enter this market. The fourth force, substitutes, was unattractive because new products were being developed continually and customer loyalty was somewhat low. The fifth and final force, industry rivalry, was also unattractive because of the high cost of doing business, the cyclical nature of sales, and the difficulty of differentiating one's products from those of the competition.

On an overall basis, however, the industry was classified as attractive. It also appeared that the industry would see consolidation of smaller firms into larger firms that would have greater resources to commit to research and development.

MNEs operating in the semiconductor industry would use this analysis to help them increase the attractiveness of those forces that currently are not highly attractive. For example, they could work to develop state-of-the-art semiconductors that might be substituted for the competition's products, and they would attempt to maintain a technological advantage so that the substitute force would not become a problem for them. In the process, they would likely better able to increase their power over the buyers since their products would be so high-tech that the customers could not do better by purchasing from a competitor. In summary, environmental assessment, such as that provided by an analysis of competitive forces, is used to determine MNE opportunities and threats and help identify strategies for improving market position and profitability.

 Active learning check

Review your answer to Active Learning Case question 1 and make any changes you like. Then compare your answer to the one below.

1 Given the competitiveness of the environment, how much opportunity exists for Vodafone in the international mobile phone market?

As seen from the case data, the international opportunities in this industry are great. One reason is because the market is going to continue growing and updating itself with new technology that may allow Vodafone to increase its revenue per subscriber and carve itself a larger portion of the market. The number of mobile phone users in the United States will increase sharply during this decade, and new technology will allow for expansion in all three triad markets. The key to success in this industry is to have a presence in all major markets, primarily the triad countries and others where the cost of mobile phones is within reach of the average person. China, for example, could be an important market because of its large population, but the market is highly competitive and favours local mobile companies. In 2010, Vadafone sold its 3.2 percent stake of investment to the joint venture partner—China Mobile. However, newly industrialized countries offer Vodafone more stability for its investment because the average GDP is much greater than that of China's and there is less political instability. Examples include Singapore, Malaysia, and Taiwan. Indeed, in 2003, Mobile signed a partner network with M1, one of the largest mobile companies in Singapore and a similar partner network agreement with Telekom Malaysia in 2006. In addition, Australia and New Zealand are important target markets. By focusing on these more affluent markets and offering both state-of-the-art products and competitive prices, Vodafone has a very good chance of outdistancing the competition. And Vodafone has expanded its operation in Australia through purchases of retail network, and deployment of latest mobile technology, etc.

Internal environmental assessment

The internal environmental assessment helps pinpoint MNE strengths and weaknesses. There are two specific areas that a multinational should examine in this assessment: (1) physical resources and personnel competencies; and (2) the way in which value chain analysis can be used to bring these resources together in the most synergistic and profitable manner.

Physical resources and personnel competencies

The physical resources are the assets that the MNE will use to carry out its strategic plan. Many of these are reported on the balance sheet as reflected by cash, inventory, machinery, and equipment accounts. However, this does not tell the whole story. The location and disposition of these resources is also important. For example, an MNE with manufacturing plants on three continents may be in a much better position to compete worldwide than a competitor whose plants are all located in one geographic area. Location can also affect cost. In the 1980s it was possible for Japanese steelmakers to sell their products in the United States at lower prices than their US competitors. During the 1990s US firms improved their steel-producing technology and erected small minimills that were highly efficient, thus offsetting the location advantage of their foreign competitors. By 2000, European steelmakers, in particular, had sharply increased their efficiency and, along with Japanese firms, were able to compete in the US market.[14] Between 1997 and 2003, 41 US steel firms went bankrupt, which led the industry to lobby the US government for protection from imports. In 2002, tariffs of 8–30 percent were imposed on imports from most countries to help the US industry restructure.[15] These were removed in 2003, after complaints by other countries to the WTO. Facing increased competition from China and other Asian economies, in 2007 EU Steel firms filed a complaint with the European Commission, seeking duties to be placed on goods imported from China, Taiwan, and South Korea. The European Confederation of Iron and Steel Industries (Eurofer) said the EU market had been "inundated" by imports. As a result EU prices had been undercut "by up to 25%" and threatened thousands of jobs. Steel from China to the EU was expected to double in 2007 from a year earlier, to 10 million tons.

Another important consideration is the degree of integration that exists within the operating units of the MNE. Large companies, in particular, tend to be divided into **strategic business units (SBUs)**. These are operating units with their own strategic space that produce and sell goods and services to a market segment and have a well-defined set of competitors.[16] SBUs are sometimes referred to as "businesses within the business." Mitsubishi, the giant Japanese conglomerate, has a host of SBUs that constitute its corporate network, including steelmaking, auto production, electronics, and banking. So when a Mitsubishi SBU that manufactures and sells consumer goods is looking for help with financing, it can turn to the banking SBU. If the bank finds that a customer needs a firm to produce a particular electronics product, it can refer the buyer to the electronics SBU.

In fact, some large MNEs use **vertical integration**, which is the ownership of all assets needed to produce the goods and services delivered to the customer. Many large Japanese manufacturing firms, in particular, have moved toward vertical integration by purchasing controlling interests in their suppliers.[17] The objective is to obtain control over the supply and thus ensure that the materials or goods are delivered as needed. Many US and European firms have shied away from this strategy because "captured suppliers" are often less cost effective than independents. For example, a number of years ago *Time* magazine owned the forests for producing the paper it needed. However, the company eventually sold this resource because it found that the cost of making the paper was higher than that charged by large paper manufacturers that specialized in this product. So vertical integration may reduce costs in some instances, but it can be an ineffective strategy in others.[18] A particular problem with vertical integration is defending oneself from competitors which

Virtual integration
A networking strategy based on cooperation within and across company boundaries

are less vertically integrated and are able to achieve cost efficiencies as a result. The latter rely heavily on outsourcers and employ **virtual integration**, which is the ownership of the core technologies and manufacturing capabilities needed to produce outputs coupled with dependence on outsourcers to provide all other needed inputs. Virtual integration allows an MNE to operate as if it were vertically integrated, but it does not require the company to own all the factors of production, as is the case with vertically integrated firms.

Personnel competencies are the abilities and talents of the people. An MNE should examine these because they reflect many of the company's strengths and weaknesses. For example, if an MNE has an outstanding R&D department, it may be able to develop high-quality, state-of-the-art products. However, if the company has no sales arm, it will sell the output to a firm that can handle the marketing and distribution. Conversely, if a company lacks a strong R&D department but has an international sales force, it may allow the competition to bring out new products and to rely on its own R&D people to reverse-engineer them—that is, to find out how they are built and develop technologies that can do the same thing—while relying on the sales force to build market share. This strategy has been used by many internationally based personal computer (PC) firms that have taken PC technology and used it to develop similar but far less expensive units that are now beginning to dominate the world market.

An understanding of what a company does well can help it decide whether the best strategy is to lead or to follow close behind and copy the leader. Not every MNE has the personnel competencies to be first in the field, and many are happy to follow because the investment risk is less and the opportunity for profit is often good.

Value chain analysis

Value chain
The way in which primary and support activities are combined in providing goods and services and increasing profit margins

A complementary approach to internal environment assessment is an examination of the firm's value chain.[19] A **value chain** is the way in which primary and support activities are combined to provide goods and services and increase profit margins. Figure 8.3 provides the general schema of a value chain. The primary activities in this chain include: (1) inbound logistics, such as receiving, storing, materials handling, and warehouse activities; (2) operations, in which inputs are put into final product form by performing activities such as machining, assembling, testing, and packaging; (3) outbound logistics, which involve distributing the finished product to the customer; (4) marketing and sales, which are used to encourage buyers to purchase the product; and (5) service for maintaining and enhancing the value of the product after the sale through activities such as repair, product adjustment,

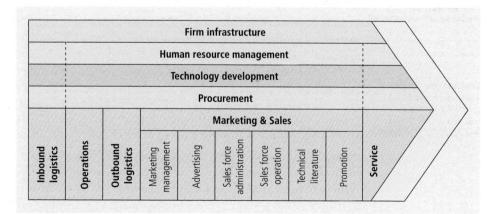

Figure 8.3 A basic value chain

Source: Adapted with the permission of The Free Press, an imprint of Simon & Schuster Adult Publishing Group, from *Competitive Advantage: Creating and Sustaining Superior Performance* by Michael E. Porter. Copyright © 1985, 1998 by Michael E. Porter. All rights reserved.

training, and parts supply. The support activities in the value chain consist of: (1) the firm's infrastructure, which is made up of the company's general management, planning, finance, accounting, legal, government affairs, and quality management areas; (2) human resource management, which is made up of the selection, placement, appraisal, promotion, training, and development of the firm's personnel; (3) technology in the form of knowledge, research and development, and procedures that can result in improved goods and services; and (4) procurement, which involves the purchasing of raw materials, supplies, and similar goods.

MNEs can use these primary and support activities to increase the value of the goods and services they provide. As such, they form a value chain. Any firm can apply this idea of a value chain. For example, Makita of Japan has become a leading competitor in power tools for professional users worldwide because it was the first to use new, less expensive materials for making tool parts and to produce in standardized models. As of March 31, 2010, the company had nine production bases, two located in each of Japan and China, and one each in the United States, Brazil, the United Kingdom, Germany, and Romania. It then sold worldwide. During the fiscal year ended March 31, 2010, approximately 77 percent of Makita's sales were outside of Japan, most of them made to professional users worldwide, including those engaged in timber and metal processing, carpentry, forestry, and concrete and masonry works. During fiscal 2010, Makita's primary products were power tools such as drills, rotary hammers, hammer drills, demolition hammers, grinders, and cordless impact drivers. Sales of these products accounted for more than 70 percent of Makita's total net sales.

Analysis of the value chain can also help a company determine the type of strategy that will be most effective. In all, there are three generic strategies: cost, differentiation, and focus.

Cost strategy

A strategy that relies on low price and is achieved through approaches such as vigorous pursuit of cost reductions and overhead control, avoidance of marginal customer accounts, and cost minimization in areas such as sales and advertising

Differentiation strategy

A strategy directed toward creating something that is perceived as being unique

Focus strategy

A strategy that concentrates on a particular buyer group and segments that niche based on product line or geographic market

Competitive scope

The breadth of a firm's target market within an industry

1 **Cost strategy** relies on such approaches as aggressive construction of efficient facilities, vigorous pursuit of cost reductions and overhead control, avoidance of marginal customer accounts, and cost minimization in areas like R&D, service, sales, and advertising.

2 **Differentiation strategy** is directed toward creating something that is perceived as being unique. Approaches to differentiation can take many forms, including the creation of design or brand image, improved technology or features, and increased customer service or dealer networks.

3 **Focus strategy** involves concentrating on a particular buyer group and segmenting that niche based on product line or geographic market. While low-cost and differentiation strategies are aimed at achieving objectives industrywide, a focus strategy is built around servicing a particular target market, and each functional policy is developed with this in mind.[20]

In addition, the firm will determine its **competitive scope**, which is the breadth of its target market within the industry. Figure 8.4 provides an example of these generic strategies as applied to the worldwide ship building industry.

The value chain can help an MNE create synergies within the organization's activities. For example, by combining the human resource talent of their salespeople with the expertise of their design and styling personnel, firms like PSA Peugeot-Citroën and Volkswagen have been able to increase their auto market share in Western Europe in recent years.[21] In particular, Peugeot and VW have been able to cut costs and offer a wide range of new models. Their overall success is found in their ability to manage the flow of new products, so that the offerings remain reasonably fresh without spending money on excessive investment in updates or redesign. Firms that cannot get this aspect of the product cycle correct have been falling behind in the European market, as seen by Ford, General Motors, and, most significantly, Renault.[22] Simply put, by analyzing the ways of combining their primary and support activities, some automotive MNEs have been able to create a strategy that allows them to draw heavily on their strengths while minimizing their weaknesses.[23]

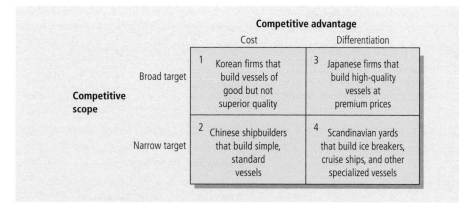

Figure 8.4 Generic strategies in worldwide shipbuilding

Source: Adapted with the permission of The Free Press, an imprint of Simon & Schuster Adult Publishing Group, from *Competitive Advantage: Creating and Sustaining Superior Performance* by Michael E. Porter. Copyright © 1985, 1998 by Michael E. Porter. All rights reserved.

✔ Active learning check

Review your answer to Active Learning Case question 2 and make any changes you like. Then compare your answer to the one below.

2 **What type of generic strategy does Vodafone employ? Defend your answer.**

Vodafone uses a focus strategy that is geared toward identifying market niches and meeting the needs of the mobile customers in these target groups. Notice that one of the guidelines it follows in most of its acquisitions is to be the major stakeholder (or at least hold a substantial ownership position) but also to have a partner which can help the company deal with the challenges in the local market. As the case notes, the company held over 50 percent of the shares in most of the European countries in which it operates, plus a large percentage of Verizon in the United States. Another generic strategy has been to pay for its acquisitions through equity, which saved it from the technology crash of the early 2000s. So the company targets selected markets in which there is little risk and provides innovative products at competitive prices in order to compete effectively.

Goal setting

External and internal environmental analyses provide an MNE with the information needed for setting goals. Some of these goals will be determined during the external analysis, as the company identifies opportunities it wants to exploit. Others will be finalized after the value chain analysis is complete. In either event, one of the outcomes of strategy formulation will be the identification of goals.[24]

There are two basic ways of examining the goals or objectives of international business operations. One is to review them on the basis of operating performance or functional area. Table 8.2 provides an illustration. Some of the major goals are related to profitability, marketing, production, finance, and human resources. A second way is to examine these goals by geographic area, or on an SBU basis. For example, the European group may have a profitability goal of 16 percent, the North American group's profitability goal may be 17 percent, and the Pacific Rim group may aim for 18 percent. Then there are accompanying functional goals for marketing, production, and finance. If the MNE has SBUs, each SBU in these geographic locales will have its own list of goals.

Table 8.2 Typical goals of an MNE

Profitability	Marketing	Production	Finance	Human resource management
Level of products	Total sales volume	Ratio of foreign to domestic production share	Financing of foreign affiliates—retained earnings or local borrowing	Development of managers with global orientation
Return on assets, investment, equity, sales	Market share—worldwide, region, country	Economies of scale via international production integration	Taxation—minimizing the burden globally	Management development of host-country nationals
Annual profit growth	Growth in sales volume	Quality and cost control	Optimum capital structure	
Annual earnings per share growth	Integration of country markets for marketing efficiency and effectiveness	Introduction of cost-efficient production methods	Foreign exchange management—minimizing losses from foreign fluctuations	

Source: Adapted from *International Dimensions of Management*, 2nd ed., by A. Phatak © 1989 South-Western, a part of Cengage. Reprinted by permission www.cengage.com/permissions/.

This approach uses what is called a "cascading effect"—like a cascade of water rippling down the side of a hill, it reaches the bottom by moving from one level to the next. The MNE starts out by setting a profitability goal for the overall enterprise. Each geographic area or business unit is then assigned a profitability goal that, if attained, will result in the MNE reaching its overall desired profitability. The same approach is used in other key areas such as marketing, production, and finance. Within each unit, these objectives are further subdivided so that every part of the organization understands its objectives and everyone is working toward the same overall goals.

STRATEGY IMPLEMENTATION

Strategy implementation
The process of attaining goals by using the organizational structure to execute the formulated strategy properly

Strategy implementation is the process of attaining goals by using the organization structure to execute the formulated strategy properly. There are many areas of focus in this process. Three of the most important are location, ownership decisions, and functional area implementation. The case **International Business Strategy in Action: Fuji Xerox and Xerox** illustrates how these considerations can be used in gaining market entry.[25]

Location

MNEs have greatly expanded their international presence over the past decade. Some of the areas in which they have begun to set up operations include China, the former Soviet Union, and Eastern Europe.

Location is important for a number of reasons. Local facilities often provide a cost advantage to the producer, particularly when the raw materials, parts, or labor needed to make the product can be inexpensively obtained close to the facility. Location is also important because residents may prefer locally produced goods. For example, many people in the United States like to "buy American." Some locations may also be attractive because the local government is encouraging investment through various means such as low tax rates, free land, subsidized energy and transportation rates, and low-interest loans while subjecting imported goods to tariffs, quotas, or other governmental restrictions, thereby making local manufacture more desirable. Finally, the MNE may already be doing so much

INTERNATIONAL BUSINESS STRATEGY IN ACTION

Fuji Xerox and Xerox

Fuji Xerox was created in 1962 as a 50/50 joint venture between UK-based Rank Xerox and Fujifilm Holdings Corporation. It is regarded as the most successful partnership between US and Japanese firms. The arrangement developed from a sales operation for Xerox products in Japan into a fully integrated organization with its own R&D and manufacturing. By 1990, Fuji Xerox revenues were $4 billion and the company had a world product mandate to supply the entire Xerox Group with the low-to-mid-range copiers that were the core of its business. Indeed, as Xerox's monopoly on large copiers began to dwindle in the 1970s, it was its Japanese partner, Fuji Xerox, that rode to the rescue with its new, high-quality smaller copiers.

In 1975, Xerox was forced by the US Federal Trade Commission to license its original core copier technology to rivals such as IBM, Kodak, Ricoh, and Canon. If it had not been for Fuji Xerox developing new copier technology, Xerox would have failed. The firm's early monopoly in the world copier business was eroded sharply by intense rivalry from Japanese competitors such as Canon and Ricoh as well as from Kodak and IBM. These rivals produced higher-quality, lower-priced, more technologically advanced, and more reliable copiers than Xerox.

When Fuji Xerox recognized the threat, its managers, acting autonomously, started R&D into new small copiers. The US head office was slow to take on board the technology and products of its Japanese partner. Loss of market share, however, especially to Canon, eventually led to ever-closer degrees of cooperation between Xerox and Fuji Xerox. In particular, the high quality standards of Fuji Xerox were spread throughout the Xerox Group, and its total quality management (TQM) techniques helped Xerox regain market. In this context, Xerox was helped by a partner that was the hotbed of TQM and copier innovation in the 1970s and 1980s.

One of the reasons for success in the collaboration between Xerox and Fuji Photo Films was that the latter acted as a silent partner in the 50/50 joint venture and allowed Fuji Xerox to develop its own management cadre, who became skilled in R&D and copier technology and in the manufacturing and marketing of small copiers. Fuji Xerox also transformed itself from a marketing subsidiary into a full-line business, thus ending up being more innovative and responsive to the market than Xerox itself.

In 2009, Fuji Xerox had revenues totalling US $11.080 billion with 40,646 employees. For its part, Xerox's revenues totalled $15.179 billion with 133,200 employees for the year ended December 31, 2009. For the year ended March 31, 2010 Fujifilm Holdings Corporation reported revenue of US $23.5 billion (Japanese Yen 2,181.7 billion) and 74,216 employees. Today, Fujifilm owns 75 percent of the company and Xerox owns the remaining 25 percent.

Websites: www.fujixerox.co.jp; www.xerox.com; www.fujifilm.com.

Sources: Adapted from Benjamin Gomes-Casseres and Krista McQuade, *Xerox and Fuji Xerox*, Harvard Business School Case 9-391-156; David T. Kearns and David A. Nadler, *Prophets in the Dark: How Xerox Reinvented Itself and Beat Back the Japanese* (New York: Macmillan, 1992); Benjamin Gomes-Casseres, "Group Versus Group: How Alliance Networks Compete," *Harvard Business Review*, July/August 1994, pp. 62–74; www.hoovers.com; FujiFilm Holdings Corporation, Annual Report, 2010; Xerox, Annual Report, 2009.

business in a country that the local government will insist that it set up local operations and begin producing more of its goods there. This is a major reason why Japanese auto manufacturers began to establish operations in the United States.

Although the benefits can be great, a number of drawbacks are associated with locating operations overseas. One is an unstable political climate that can leave an MNE vulnerable to low profits and bureaucratic red tape. In Russia, for example, the government has encouraged joint ventures, but because of political and economic uncertainty many business people currently regard such investments as high-risk ventures. A second drawback is the possibility of revolution or armed conflict. MNEs with operations in Kuwait lost just about all of their investment in the Gulf War, and MNEs with locales in Saudi Arabia and other Middle East countries affected by the Gulf War also withstood losses in the region. Most recently, businesses in areas targeted by international terrorists have been making plans to reduce their risks. In some cases firms are finding a way to "hedge their bets," as noted in the following example:

> Some . . . opt for locales where the cost of running a small enterprise is significantly lower than that of running a large one. In this way they spread their risk, setting up many small locations throughout the world rather than one or two large ones. Manufacturing firms are a good example. Some production firms feel that the economies of scale associated with a large-scale plant are more than offset by the potential problems that can result, should economic or political difficulties develop in the country. These firms' strategy is to spread the risk by opting for a series of small plants spread throughout a wide geographic region.[26]

Ownership

Ownership of international operations has become an important issue in recent years. Many Americans, for example, believe that the increase in foreign-owned businesses in the United States is weakening the economy. People in other countries have similar feelings about US businesses there. In truth, the real issue of ownership is whether or not the company is contributing to the overall economic good of the country where it is doing business. As one researcher noted, "because the US-owned corporation is coming to have no special relationship with Americans, it makes no sense for the United States to entrust its national competitiveness to it. The interests of American-owned corporations may or may not coincide with those of the American people."[27] Countries that want to remain economically strong must be able to attract international investors who will provide jobs that allow their workers to increase their skills and build products that are demanded on the world market. In accomplishing this objective, firms often engage in strategic alliances.

Strategic alliance

Strategic alliance or partnership
An agreement between two or more competitive multinational enterprises for the purpose of serving a global market

Sometimes companies prefer to invest in another country and maintain 100 percent ownership. This, however, is often very expensive and risky. Given that the MNE may not have much experience in that particular marketplace, local partners may be very helpful in dealing with all sorts of local barriers. As a result, it is becoming increasingly popular to find MNEs turning to the use of strategic partnerships. A **strategic alliance or partnership** is an agreement between two or more competitive MNEs for the purpose of cooperating in some manner in serving a global market.[28] The type of cooperation can be in marketing, research, or a more comprehensive manner. In recent years these partnerships have become increasingly popular,[29] although careful management of such agreements continues to be a critical area of concern.[30] An example of a strategic partnership is that of Matsushita Electric Industrial and Hitachi, Japan's two leading electronics manufacturers. These companies have jointly developed state-of-the-art technology in three areas: smart cards, home network systems, and recyclable and energy-efficient consumer electronics. In the past, both firms have developed their own products, but now they are turning to a strategic partnership to save money and shorten development time.[31] Another example of strategic partnerships is that between IBM and NTT. Under the terms of their agreement at the turn of the century, IBM provided outsourcing services to NTT, Japan's dominant telecommunications carrier. In turn, IBM was able to use NTT Comware staff in outsourcing and obtaining computer service contracts with other customers in Japan.[32]

International joint ventures

International joint venture (IJV)
An agreement between two or more partners to own and control an overseas business

An **international joint venture (IJV)** is an agreement between two or more partners to own and control an overseas business.[33] This is a special type of a strategic alliance that involves setting up a new business entity, generally involving management separate from that of the partners' own management teams. IJVs take a number of different forms[34] and offer myriad opportunities.[35] One of these reasons is government encouragement and legislation designed to make it attractive for foreign investors to bring in local partners. A second reason is the growing need for partners which know the local economy, the culture, and the political system and which can cut through red tape in getting things done—something IJVs often do very well.[36] Indeed, IJVs are often the result of two or more companies identifying the potential for "synergies," wherein each partner brings to the venture what the other partner needs but is lacking in. For example, an MNE might provide a local partner with technology know-how and an infusion of capital that, in turn, will allow the local firm to expand operations, raise market share, and begin exporting. An example is Toyota and PSA Peugeot-Citroën, which entered into an IJV to jointly develop and build a small, fuel-efficient car for the European market. The primary benefit for Toyota is the opportunity to expand its model line-up in Europe. The major advantage for Peugeot is that of gaining a new small car for its European product line while sharing the development costs with Toyota.[37]

Unfortunately, in many cases IJVs have not worked out well. Several studies found a failure rate of 30 percent for ventures in developed countries and 45–50 percent in less developed countries.[38] The major reason has been the desire by foreign MNEs to control local operation, which sometimes has resulted in poor decision making and/or conflicts with the local partners. In general, joint ventures are difficult to manage and are frequently unstable.[39] This issue of joint ventures and alliances is discussed further in Chapter 22 under the flagship firm analysis of business networks.

✔ Active learning check

Review your answer to Active Learning Case question 3 and make any changes you like. Then compare your answer to the one below.

③ What form of ownership arrangement is Vodafone using to gain world market share? Explain.

Vodafone uses two basic approaches. The most common is the international joint venture, which is seen by the company's decisions to acquire an ownership position in a local company but have a local partner hold the remainder of the ownership. An example is its minority stake in Verizon Wireless, which is now the largest US mobile telephone operator in America. In some cases, however, Vodafone opts for total ownership and purchases the entire company, usually when it believes it does not need a local partner. An example is Airtouch Communications, where Vodafone acquired the entire firm. In both cases, of course, the ownership arrangement is designed to help Vodafone continue to increase its market share in that geographic region.

Functional strategies

Functional strategies are used to coordinate operations and ensure that the plan is carried out properly.[40] The specific functions that are key to the success of the MNE will vary, but they typically fall into six major areas: marketing, manufacturing, finance, procurement, technology, and human resources. For purposes of analysis, they can be examined in terms of three major considerations: marketing, manufacturing, and finance.

Marketing

The marketing strategy is designed to identify consumer needs and formulate a plan of action for selling the desired goods and services to these customers.[41] Most marketing strategies are built around what is commonly known as the "four Ps" of marketing: product, price, promotion, and place. The company identifies the products that are in demand in the market niches it is pursuing. It apprises the manufacturing department of any modifications needed to meet local needs, and it determines the price at which the goods can be sold. Then the company devotes its attention to promoting the products and selling them in the local market.

Manufacturing

Designed to fit together with the marketing plan, the manufacturing strategy ensures that the right products are built and delivered in time for sale. Manufacturing also coordinates its strategy with the procurement and technology people to ensure that the desired materials are available and the products have the necessary state-of-the-art quality. If the MNE is producing goods in more than one country, it gives attention to coordinating activities where needed. For example, some firms manufacture goods in two or more countries, then assemble and sell them in other geographic regions. Japanese auto firms send car parts to the United States for assembly and then sell some of the assembled cars in Canada, Mexico, and South America. Whirlpool builds appliances worldwide with operations in Brazil, Canada, Mexico, the Netherlands, and seven other countries. Such production and assembly operations have to be coordinated carefully.[42]

Finance

Financial strategy often serves to both lead and lag the other functional strategies. In the lead position, finance limits the amounts of money that can be spent on marketing (new product development, advertising, promotion) and manufacturing (machinery, equipment, quality control) to ensure that the desired return on investment is achieved. In the lag position, the financial strategy is used to evaluate performance and provide insights into how future strategy should be changed.

Financial strategies used to be formulated and controlled out of the home office. In recent years, however, MNEs have learned that this approach can be cumbersome and, due to fluctuating currency prices, costly as well. Today's overseas units have more control over their finances than before, but they are guided by a carefully constructed budget that is in accord with the overall strategic plan. They are also held to account for financial performance in the form of return on investment, profit, capital budgeting, debt financing, and working capital management.

CONTROL AND EVALUATION

The strategy formulation and implementation processes are subject to control and evaluation. This process involves examining the MNE's performance to determine (1) how well the organization has done and (2) what actions should be taken in light of this performance. This process is tied directly to the overall strategy in that the objectives serve as the basis for comparison and evaluation.[43] Figure 8.5 illustrates how this process works.

If the comparison and evaluation show that the SBU or overseas operation is performing according to expectations, then things will continue as before. The objectives may be altered because of changes in the strategic plan, but otherwise nothing major is likely to be done. On the other hand, if there have been problems, the MNE will want to identify the causes and work to eliminate or minimize them.[44] Similarly, if the unit has performed extremely well and achieved more than forecasted, management may want to reset the objectives to a higher level because there is obviously greater market demand than was believed initially. In making these decisions, the company uses a variety of measures. Some are highly quantitative and depend on financial and productivity performance; others are more qualitative and judgmental in nature. The following discussion examines six of the most common methods of measurement used for control and evaluation purposes.

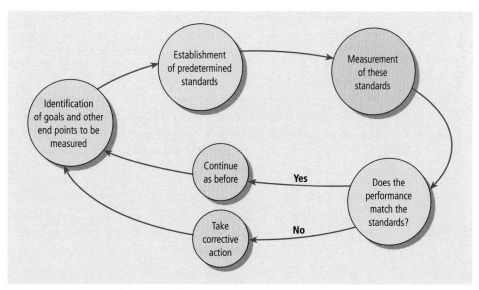

Figure 8.5 The control and evaluation process

Common methods of measurement

Return on investment (ROI)
A percentage determined by dividing net income before taxes by total assets

Specific measures will vary depending on the nature of the MNE and the goals it has established. However, **return on investment (ROI)**, which is measured by dividing net income before taxes by the costs of investment, is a major consideration in most cases. There are a number of reasons why ROI is so popular as a control and evaluation measure: (1) it is a single comprehensive result that is influenced by everything that happens in the business; (2) it measures how well the managers in every part of the world are using the investments at their command; and (3) it allows a comparison of results among units in the same country as well as on an intercountry basis. Of course, there are shortcomings as well: (1) if one unit is selling goods to another unit, the ROI of the former is being artificially inflated; (2) the ROI in a growing market will be higher than that in markets that are just getting off the ground or are maturing, so that a comparison of the ROI performance between units can be misleading; and (3) the ROI is a short-term measure of performance that, if relied on too heavily, will not help managers develop the necessary long-term time horizons. Despite these shortcomings, however, ROI remains a major measure of performance.

Another measure is sales growth and/or market share. Units are given sales targets that usually require greater sales this year than last year. If the firm has made an estimate of the total demand, a market share figure accompanies the sales target for two reasons: (1) the MNE wants to increase its sales; and (2) the firm at least wants to maintain, if not increase, market share. If the market is judged to be declining, sales targets are lowered but the MNE still tries to maintain market share.

A third performance area is costs. The MNE wants to achieve increased sales and market share at as low a cost as possible. It also wants to maintain close control of production costs. So expenses are monitored carefully. This is particularly important in declining markets, where the company will want to cut costs as sales decline. For example, if an MNE estimates that it has only three years of product life in the market, it is likely that much of the advertising and promotion expenses will be dropped as the company focuses attention on supplying an ever-decreasing number of customers. This strategy is often successful because the remaining customers are highly loyal and do not need promotional efforts to convince them to buy the product.

New product development is another area of performance measure. This area is extremely important for firms that rely on new offerings. A good example is Nintendo, the Japanese manufacturer of such well-known video games as Mario Brothers, which must continually introduce new product offerings in order to maintain market share and sales growth. MNEs in high-tech areas such as electronic goods and computers also fall into this category. In an environment where product improvement or innovation is critical to success, new product development is a key area for control and evaluation.

MNE/host-country relations is another performance area that must be evaluated. Overseas units have to work within the cultural and legal framework of the host country. Many attempt to do this by blending into the community, hiring local managers and employees, adapting their product to the demands of that market, reinvesting part (if not all) of their profits back into the country, and working to improve the area's economic conditions. As a result, they get on well in the country and there are no problems with the government or other local groups. One thing MNEs know from long experience is that poor host-country relations can seriously endanger profits and even result in a loss of invested capital.

Finally, management performance must be considered. In rating this criterion, the MNE considers two types of measures: quantitative and qualitative. In the quantitative area, in addition to those discussed above, other common considerations include return on invested capital and cash flow. In the qualitative area, in addition to host-country relations, consideration is given to relations with the home office, the leadership qualities of the unit's managers, how well the unit is building a management team, and how well the managers of the unit have implemented the assigned strategy.

These methods of measurement are used in arriving at an overall assessment of the unit's performance. Based on the results, the MNE can then set new goals and the international strategic planning process begins anew.

✔ Active learning check

Review your answer to Active Learning Case question 4 and make any changes you like. Then compare your answer to the one below.

4 **On what basis would a firm like Vodafone evaluate performance? Identify and describe two.**

Vodafone uses a number of bases on which to evaluate performance. One is market share. Note that the firm keeps track of how many subscribers it has by multiplying its ownership position in a venture by the venture's total subscription base. Another is overall worldwide market share. Finally, the firm evaluates its performance by its success in setting a footprint in all major markets.

KEY POINTS

1 Strategic planning is the process of determining an organization's basic mission and long-term objectives, then implementing a plan of action for attaining these goals. In carrying out their strategic plan, most MNEs tend toward one of four specific predispositions: ethnocentric, polycentric, regiocentric, and geocentric. Each was described in the chapter.

2 The international strategic planning process involves three major steps: strategy formulation, strategy implementation, and the control and evaluation of the process. Strategy formulation entails the evaluation of the enterprise's environment and the identification

of long-range and short-range objectives. The analysis of the external environment typically involves information gathering and assessment, wherein consideration is given to the five forces that determine industry competitiveness: buyers; suppliers; new entrants to the industry; the availability of substitute goods and services; and rivalry among the competitors. The analysis of the internal environment involves consideration of the firm's physical resources and personnel competencies and the way in which a value chain analysis can be used to bring these resources together in the most synergistic and profitable manner.

3 Strategy implementation is the process of attaining predetermined goals by properly executing the formulated strategy. Three of the most important areas of consideration are location, ownership decisions, and functional area implementation.

4 The control and evaluation process involves an examination of the MNE's performance to determine how well it has done and to decide what action now needs to be taken. Some of the most common measures include return on investment, sales growth, market share, costs, new product development, host-country relations, and overall management performance.

Key terms

- strategic planning
- ethnocentric predisposition
- polycentric predisposition
- regiocentric predisposition
- geocentric predisposition
- strategy formulation
- competitive intelligence
- strategic business units (SBUs)
- vertical integration
- virtual integration
- value chain
- cost strategy
- differentiation strategy
- focus strategy
- competitive scope
- strategy implementation
- strategic alliance or partnership
- international joint venture (IJV)
- return on investment (ROI)

REVIEW AND DISCUSSION QUESTIONS

1 Define the term *strategic planning*.

2 In what way can the following basic predispositions affect an MNE's strategic planning: ethnocentric, polycentric, regiocentric, geocentric?

3 How will an MNE carry out an external environmental assessment? Identify and describe the two major steps involved in this process.

4 Of what practical value is an understanding of the five-forces model presented in Figure 8.1? How would an MNE use this information in the strategic planning process?

5 In conducting an internal environmental assessment, why would an MNE want to identify its physical resources and personnel competencies?

6 What is a value chain? How can this chain be used in an internal environmental assessment?

7 What are the three generic strategies? When would an MNE use each? Support your answer with examples.

8 What are some typical MNE goals? Identify and briefly describe four major types.

9 One of the most important considerations when implementing a strategy is that of location. What does this statement mean?

10 When are MNEs likely to use an international joint venture? When would they opt for a strategic partnership? Defend your answer.

11 Functional strategies are used to coordinate operations and ensure that the plan is carried out properly. What are some of the most common types of functional strategies? Identify and describe three.

12 How do MNEs control and evaluate their operations? Describe the basic process. Then discuss some of the common methods of measurement.

REAL CASE

Mountain Equipment Co-op: a small business

Outside of Canada, few people have ever heard of the Mountain Equipment Co-op (MEC), but it is one of the most successful small businesses in the world. The company currently holds 65 percent of the Canadian market for outdoor equipment, far outdistancing all other competitive MNEs and retail brands in the country. In fact, MEC is so efficient that its products are priced lower than those of any North American competitor.

MEC was founded in 1969 when a group of six outdoor enthusiasts decided to get together and purchase expensive outdoor equipment. In August 1971 the organization was officially registered as a co-op and began operating under a member-elected board of directors that assumed responsibility for setting overall policy and overseeing management of all operations. Today MEC has 2.8 million members, operates stores in 14 cities across Canada, an international mail-order clientele and online shopping, and a worldwide network of suppliers. For a one-time $5 fee, members are able to enjoy a wide variety of benefits from an organization that focuses heavily on four primary objectives: keeping costs down, offering affordable goods, providing high-quality merchandise, and maintaining high ethical standards.

Regarding the first of these, MEC takes a number of steps to control costs and offer affordable products. One is to use the clout of its large membership as a basis for extracting the best possible prices from suppliers, thus being able to offer low-cost products. Another is to keep the number of staff to a minimum. Some of the ways it does this is through the use of self-service in all stores and the promotion of its international mail-order business, which can be handled by a small number of personnel. In addition, the co-op minimizes overall marketing expenses by relying

Source: Getty/Taxi

heavily on customer word-of-mouth and the mail-order network to help promote its products.

MEC also places a great deal of importance on the quality of goods. Its buyers and designers look not only for a low price from suppliers, but also for products that provide both functionality and durability. In addition, the co-op offers a lifetime guarantee on most of its products, regardless of whether it manufactured them, had them provided by an outsourcer, or purchased them from a large brand name company.

Co-op members are also assured that the company adheres to the highest ethical practices. MEC is an innovator in a number of areas ranging from human rights to the environment. Its stores are designed with the utmost attention to the environment, using as much natural light as possible, high-efficiency HVAC (heating, ventilation, and air-conditioning), low-consumption water fixtures, and recyclable materials. As an example, its Ottawa store uses only half the energy of a conventional building. In addition, as a member of the 1 percent for the Planet, the co-op gives 1 percent of gross sales each year to environmental and conservation groups. At the same time, its retail employees are among the best paid in the country and its buyers and inspectors are charged with ensuring that all factory workers in foreign countries receive a reasonable living wage and work under safe conditions.

MEC has undertaken many business initiatives to better serve its members, to secure long term financial sustainability and to promote its care about environment. For example, in 1997, MEC introduced its popular and free of charge online gear swap where members can recycle used outdoor gear.

Some suppliers, such as Sierra Designs, Salomon, Arc Tyrex, North Face, and Patagonia, see MEC as a threat and have refused to sell to it. In many cases, however, this strategy has proven to be counterproductive, resulting in MEC designing and manufacturing these products and then successfully competing with the traditional brands that were unwilling to sell to it. In addition, the co-op's increased involvement in manufacturing has enabled it to monitor its suppliers' operations more closely.

Over the past couple of decades, MEC's strategy has been more emergent than calculated. Yet it has proven to be a successful business venture that has brought together a large group of dedicated environmentalists and other customers who need products for outdoor activities. In the process, the co-op has created a "style" and "brand" presence that appeals to outdoor enthusiasts. In fact, MEC's outdoor gear has become so popular that even urbanites, highly unlikely to go trekking or camping in the outdoors, are now becoming members. As a result, annual revenues

are currently in the range of CAD$250 million and the company is continuing to expand operations across Canada.

MEC was able to flourish as a result of the huge margins enjoyed by its competitors. This allowed the co-op both to reduce prices and to maintain higher levels of environmental and labor practices than its competitors. Over the next few years, however, as competition grows and large outdoor retailers exert the same kind of pressure on suppliers that allowed it to sell at lower prices, MEC will have to switch its strategy to remain competitive. It has some advantages. For one, it has no shareholders and reinvests most of its surplus into the company. MEC still has to exploit to the fullest its community and environmental contributions. In the spirit of keeping advertising costs low, many members, not to mention potential members, have never heard of MEC's social policies or its charitable contributions.

Websites: www.mec.ca; www.sierra-designs.com; www.salomonsports.com; www.thenorthface.com; www.patagonia.com.

Sources: www.mec.ca; "Mountain Equipment Co-Op Live with Socially Responsible Retail," *PR Newswire*, May 22, 2001; "One of the Greenest Commercial Buildings in the World," *Sustainable Sport Sourceline*, July 2000; "Mountain Equipment Co-op to Stage Outdoors Skills Challenge in Celebration of its 2,000,000th Member," *Canada NewsWire*, June 16, 2004; Martin Mittelstaedt, "Mountain Equipment pulls water bottles off shelves," *globeandmail.com*, December 7, 2007.

1 How does the Mountain Equipment Co-op use value chain analysis to increase both its membership and its revenues?

2 What is the co-op's generic strategy? Describe it.

3 How does MEC measure its performance? What are two criteria it uses to evaluate how well it is doing?

REAL CASE

Benetton

Famous for its shocking advertisements, Benetton was founded in 1955 by Luciano, Giuliana, Gilberto, and Carlo Benetton. Initially the family sold colored sweaters door-to-door in Treviso, Italy. Over time, a regional network of family, friends, and agents set up a closely monitored set of distinctive retail outlets. Over a 15-year period, Benetton built up 300 affiliated but independently owned outlets in Italy and a factory with new methods to dye and condition wool. The company was not directly involved in the retail outlets, which received high-quality products at low

costs. Part of the manufacturing savings was realized by outsourcing to neighboring subcontractors. For the year ended December 31, 2009, Benetton had total revenue of US $2.849 billion (€ 2.049 billion) and a workforce of 90,000 employees.

Benetton has kept this loose network of independent production subcontractors and distribution agents but has now built up to a network of more than 6,000 retail stores in 120 countries around the world. Only a small fraction of these are flagship stores owned by the group. The great ▶

majority of its retail stores is operated by independent entrepreneurs. About 90 percent of production still takes place in Europe, mainly in the Northern Italian region around Treviso and the group produces over 150 million garments every year. And the company is still 69.35 percent owned by the Benetton family. Yet the wool it uses to produce its clothing line is now imported from foreign countries. The parent company raises sheep in 900,000 hectares of land in Argentina.

Benetton is one of those successful companies that succeeded partly because its production and design concept was built on a strong home base. It expanded the marketing end of its business through closely monitored (but not owned) independent stores, which were able to use the Benetton brand name and distinctive colors and were supported by clever international advertising.

Benetton does not advertise its clothes directly. Rather, its ads target a "lifestyle." The "United Colors of Benetton" ads were designed for a homogeneous global consumer interested in fast cars and a fast lifestyle. Benetton goes in for cutting-edge advertising that grabs public attention. This created an image of new-age awareness, as the company's advertising ads have featured AIDS, capital punishment, inter-racial relations, high art, and "attitude." The firm also sponsors a top Formula One team as well as teams in rugby, basketball, and volleyball, all of which contributes to the success of its brand name. Fabrica, Benetton's Communication Research Center just outside Treviso, is a mixture of philanthropy and advertising. The center sponsors 50 artists for a year and exhibits their work and publishes it in *Colors*, the company's art-focused magazine.

How well this plays out globally is uncertain. For example, Benetton had 700 retail stores in the United States in 1988, but only 150 by 1995. Is this because Benetton has too European an image to succeed in middle America? How can an Italian family firm understand the American lifestyle from its European bases? Indeed, 82 percent of its revenue was generated from its home region, Europe, of which 48 percent was derived from Italy, 34 percent from Europe (excluding Italy), Asia 14 percent, Americas only 3 percent and rest of the world 1 percent. The firm is now looking to expand into emerging markets where potential for growth among the growing middle class is greatest.

Website: http://www.benettongroup.com.

Sources: Adapted from: *Benetton SpA: Industrial Fashion (A)*, Harvard Business School Case No. 9-685-614; *Benetton (B)*, Harvard Business School Case No. 9-685-020; INSEAD-CEDEP Case No. 01/97-4520, 1996; David Stillit, "Benetton: Italy's Smart Operator," *Corporate Finance*, June 1993; "Benetton's Network," *Ivey Business Quarterly*, 1997; Benetton, *Annual Report*, 2009; Peter Crush, "CSR: Diversity Takes Central Stage," *PR Week*, April 18, 2005; "Benetton: IndíGenas Rechazan Oferta," *BBC.co.uk*, November 10, 2005; www.benetton.com.

1 Is Benetton a multinational enterprise?

2 What are the country-specific factors that have boosted Benetton's success?

3 What are Benetton's firm-specific advantages?

ENDNOTES

1 Tim Burt, "GM Outlines Plans to Cut European Capacity," *Financial Times*, September 27, 2001, p. 19; Jorn Madslien, "General Motors Gets Ready to Fix European Subsidiaries," *BBC News ONline*, March 3, 2011, http://www.bbc.co.uk/news/business-12625841.

2 Matt Murray, "Merger Machine: Can GE Keep Growing Through Deals?" *Wall Street Journal*, July 31, 2000, pp. C1, 2; "General Electric Debt Rating Cut," *BBC News*, March 12, 2009, http://news.bbc.co.uk/1/hi/business/7940191.stm.

3 Also see Roland Calori, Leif Melin, Tugrul Atamer and Peter Gustavsson, "Innovative International Strategies," *Journal of World Business*, vol. 35, no. 4 (Winter 2000), pp. 333–354; Kalevi Kyläheiko, Ari Jantunen, Kaisu Puumalainen, Sami Saarenketo and Anni Tuppura, "Innovation and Internationalization as Growth Strategies: The Role of Technological Capabilities and Appropriability," *International Business Review* (2010), doi:10.1016/j.ibusrev.2010.09.004.

4 M. A. Hitt, "The Meaning of Organizational Effectiveness: Multiple Domains and Constituencies," *Management*

International Review, vol. 28, no. 2 (Second Quarter 1988), p. 28.

5 David Lei, John W. Slocum, Jr. and Robert W. Slater, "Global Strategy and Reward Systems: The Key Roles of Management Development and Corporate Culture," *Organizational Dynamics*, August 1990, p. 29.

6 See David Norburn, Sue Birley, Mark Dunn and Adrian Payne, "A Four Nation Study of the Relationship Between Marketing Effectiveness, Corporate Culture, Corporate Values, and Market Orientation," *Journal of International Business Studies*, vol. 21, no. 3 (Fall 1990), pp. 451–468.

7 For a good example, see Keith Bradsher, "Effective Today, Chrysler and Daimler-Benz Are One," *New York Times*, November 12, 1998, p. C 4; and Tim Burt, "Daimler Chief to Speak on Strategy," *FT.com*, March 4, 2002.

8 For some specific applications of these ideas, see Michael M. Robert, "Managing Your Competitor's Strategy," *Journal of Business Strategy*, March/April 1990, pp. 24–28.

9 Sometimes, of course, competitive intelligence degenerates into corporate spying, as seen in Andrew Edgecliffe-

Johnson, "P&G Admits Spying on Unilever," *Financial Times*, August 31, 2001, p. 17; Rob Lemkin, "Dirty Little Secrets: Corporate Espionage," *BBC News*, 1 February 2008, http://news.bbc.co.uk/1/hi/business/7220063.stm; "US Spy for China Noshir Gowadia Jailed for 32 Years," *BBC News*, January 25, 2011, http://www.bbc.co.uk/news/world-asia-pacific-12272941.

10 J. E. Preble, P. A. Rau and A. Reichel, "The Environmental Scanning Practices of US Multinationals in the Late 1980s," *Management International Review*, vol. 28, no. 4 (Fourth Quarter 1988), p. 10.

11 For more on this, see R. C. Hoffman, "The General Management of Foreign Subsidiaries in the USA: An Exploratory Study," *Management International Review*, vol. 28, no. 2 (Second Quarter 1988), pp. 41–55.

12 For more on this, see Michael Porter, *The Competitive Advantage of Nations* (New York: Free Press, 1990), Chapter 2.

13 Andrew Pollack, "Nissan Plans to Buy More American Parts," *New York Times*, March 26, 1994, pp. 17, 26; "Vauxhall Boss Warns Over UK Car Making Future," *BBC News*, April 24, 2011, http://www.bbc.co.uk/news/business-13179589.

14 "A Tricky Business," *The Economist*, June 30, 2001, pp. 55–56.

15 "US steel tariffs," *Guardian*, November 11, 2003; "Steel Firms Oppose China Imports," *BBC News*, October 29, 2007, http://news.bbc.co.uk/1/hi/business/7068142.stm.

16 Arnoldo C. Hax and Nicolas S. Majluf, *The Strategy Concept and Process: A Pragmatic Approach* (Englewood Cliffs, NJ: Prentice Hall, 1991), p. 416.

17 Also see Julie Pitta, "Score One for Vertical Integration," *Forbes*, January 18, 1993, pp. 88–90.

18 For an excellent discussion of this topic, see Hax and Majluf, op. cit., Chapter 12.

19 C. K. Prahalad and Kenneth Lieberthal, "The End of Corporate Imperialism," *Harvard Business Review*, July/August 1998, pp. 69–79.

20 Hax and Majluf, op. cit., p. 83.

21 Uta Harnischfeger, "Audi Drives Out VW's Gloom," *FT.com*, March 1, 2002.

22 "The Art of Overtaking," *The Economist*, September 8, 2001, p. 68; "Car Shares Hit in Latest Market Sell Off," *BBC News*, 2 June 2011, http://www.bbc.co.uk/news/business-13627079.

23 For another good example, see Seth Lubove, "Make a Better Mousetrap," *Forbes*, February 1, 1993, pp. 56–57.

24 Leslie Kaufman, "Avon's New Face," *Newsweek*, November 16, 1998, pp. 59–60.

25 Also see W. Chan Kim and Peter Hwang, "Global Strategy and Multinationals' Entry Mode Choice," *Journal of International Business Studies*, vol. 23, no. 1 (Summer 1992), pp. 29–53.

26 Richard M. Hodgetts and Fred Luthans, *International Management*, 4th ed. (Burr Ridge, IL: McGraw/Irwin, 2000), p. 260.

27 Robert B. Reich, "Who Is Us?" *Harvard Business Review*, January/February 1990, p. 59.

28 Peter Lorange, Johan Roos and Peggy Simcic Bronn, "Building Successful Strategic Alliances," *Long Range Planning*, December 1992, pp. 10–17; Inkpen, Andrew C., "Strategic Alliances," in Alan M. Rugman (ed.), *The Oxford Handbook of International Business*, 2nd ed. (Oxford: Oxford University Press, 2009).

29 See Masaaki Kotabe, Hildy Teegen, Preet S. Aulakh, Maria Cecilia Coutinho de Arruda, Roberto J. Santillan-Salgado and Walter Greene, "Strategic Alliances in Emerging Latin America: A View from Brazilian, Chilean, and Mexican Companies," *Journal of World Business*, vol. 35, no. 2 (Summer 2000), pp. 114–132.

30 Mitchell Koza and Arie Lewin, "Managing Partnerships and Strategic Alliances: Raising the Odds of Success," *European Management Journal*, August 2000, pp. 146–151; Jorge Walter, Christoph Lechner, Franz W. Kellermanns, "Disentangling Alliance Management Processes: Decision Making, Politicality, and Alliance Performance," *Journal of Management Studies*, vol. 45, no. 3, May 2008, pp. 530–560.

31 Miki Tanikawa, "Electronics Giants Join Forces in Japan," *Wall Street Journal*, May 24, 2001, p. W1.

32 Robert A. Guth, "IBM Announces Deal with Japan's NTT," *Wall Street Journal*, November 1, 2000, p. 23.

33 Audrey Choi, "BMW's Chairman Plans Visit to Honda to Discuss Future of Jointly Held Rover," *Wall Street Journal*, February 18, 1994, p. A7.

34 Hemant Merchant, "Configurations of International Joint Ventures," *Management International Review*, vol. 40, no. 2 (Second Quarter 2000), pp. 107–140.

35 Hong Liu and Kelvin Pak, "How Important Is Marketing in China Today to Sino-foreign Joint Ventures?" *European Management Journal*, October 1999, pp. 546–554.

36 Gautam Naik, "AT&T, BT Form World-Wide Alliance," *Wall Street Journal*, July 27, 1998, p. A3.

37 John Tagliabue, "Toyota and Peugeot in Pact to Produce Car for Europe," *New York Times*, June 30, 2001, p. B2.

38 Stefan H. Robock and Kenneth Simmonds, *International Business and Multinational Enterprises*, 4th ed. (Homewood, IL: Irwin, 1989), p. 216.

39 See Sing Keow Hoon-Halbauer, "Managing Relationships Within Sino-Foreign Joint Ventures," *Journal of World Business*, vol. 34, no. 4 (Winter 1999), pp. 344–370.

40 See, for example, Caron H. St. John, Scott T. Young and Janis L. Miller, "Coordinating Manufacturing and Marketing in International Firms," *Journal of World Business*, vol. 34, no. 2 (Summer 1999), pp. 109–127.

41 Matt Marshall, "In Brazil, Coke Sells Foam as Well as Fizz," *Wall Street Journal*, July 28, 1997, p. A12.

42 Peter Marsh, "Pressing Ahead with Plastic," *FT.com*, March 4, 2002.

43 Jeffrey E. Garten, "Opening the Doors for Business in China," *Harvard Business Review*, May/June 1998, pp. 167–175.

44 Also see John Child and Yanni Yan, "Investment and Control in International Joint Ventures: The Case of China," *Journal of World Business*, vol. 34, no. 1 (Spring 1999), pp. 3–15; John Child, "China and International Business," in Alan M. Rugman (ed.), *The Oxford Handbook of International Business*, 2nd ed. (Oxford: Oxford University Press, 2009).

ADDITIONAL BIBLIOGRAPHY

Augier, Mie and Teece, David J. "Dynamic Capabilities and Multinational Enterprise: Penrosean Insights and Omissions," *Management International Review*, vol. 47, no. 2 (2007).

Asmussen, Christian G. "Local, Regional, or Global? Quantifying MNE Geographic Scope," *Journal of International Business Studies*, vol. 40 (September 2009). doi:10.1057/jibs.2008.85.

Banalieva, Elitsa R. and Athanassiou, Nicholas. "Regional and Global Alliance Network Structures of Triad Multinational Enterprises," *Multinational Business Review*, vol. 18, no. 1 (2010).

Barkeman, Harry G., Shenkar, Oded, Vermeulen, Freek and Bell, John H. J. "Working Abroad, Working with Others: How Firms Learn to Operate International Joint Ventures," *Academy of Management Journal*, vol. 40, no. 2 (April 1997).

Barney, Jay. *Gaining and Sustaining Competitive Advantage*, 3rd ed. (Upper Saddle River, NJ: Prentice Hall, 2007).

Buckley, Peter J. and Casson, Mark. "Edith Penrose's Theory of the Growth of the Firms and the Strategic Management of the Multinational Enterprise," *Management International Review*, vol. 47, no. 2 (2007).

Camuffo, Arnaldo. "Back to the Future: Benetton Transforms its Global Network," *Sloan Management Review*, vol. 43, no. 1 (Fall 2001).

Czechowicz, I. James, Choi, Frederick D. S. and Bavinish, Vinod B. *Assessing Foreign Subsidiary Performance: Systems and Practices of Leading Multinational Companies* (New York: Business International Corporation, 1982).

Dacin, M. Tina, Hitt, Michael A. and Levitas, Edward. "Selecting Partners for Successful International Alliances: Examination of US and Korean Firms," *Journal of World Business*, vol. 32, no. 1 (Spring 1997).

Davis, Peter S., Desai, Ashay B. and Francis, John D. "Mode of International Entry: An Isomorphism Perspective," *Journal of International Business Studies*, vol. 31, no. 2 (Summer 2000).

Demirbag, Mehmet, Tatoglu, Ekrem and Glaister, Keith W. "Institutional and Transaction Cost Influences on Partnership Structure of Foreign Affiliates," *Management International Review*, vol. 50, no. 6 (December 2010).

Domke-Damonte, Darla. "Interactive Effects of International Strategy and Throughput Technology on Entry Mode for Service Firms," *Management International Review*, vol. 40, no. 1 (First Quarter 2000).

Egelhoff, William G. "Great Strategy or Great Strategy Implementation—Two Ways of Competing in Global Markets," *Sloan Management Review*, vol. 34, no. 2 (Winter 1993).

Ghemawat, Pankaj. *Redefining Global Strategy: Crossing Borders in a World Where Differences Still Matter* (Boston, MA: Harvard University Press, 2007).

Govindarajan, Vijay and Gupta, Anil K. *The Quest for Global Dominance* (San Francisco: Jossey-Bass/Wiley, 2001).

Grant, Robert M. *Contemporary Strategy Analysis* (Oxford: Wiley-Blackwell, 2008).

Hamel, Gary and Prahalad, C. K. "Do You Really Have a Global Strategy?" *Harvard Business Review*, vol. 65, no. 4 (July/August 1985).

Hashai, Niron, Asmussen, Christian G., Benito, Gabriel R. G. and Petersen, Bent. "Technological Knowledge Intensity and Entry Mode Diversity," *Management International Review*, vol. 50, no. 6 (December, 2010).

Heracleous, L. and Collinson, Simon C. "HSBC's Strategy and Leadership," in K. Singh, N. Panagarkar and L. Heracleous *Business Strategy in Asia*, 3rd ed. (Singapore: Cengage, 2009).

Hult, G., Tomas, M., Ketchen, David J., Griffith, David A., Chabowski, Brian R., Hamman, Mary K., Dykes, Bernadine Johnson, Pollitte, Wesley A. and Cavusgil, S. Tamer. "An Assessment of the Measurement of Performance in International Business Research," *Journal of International Business Studies*, vol. 39 (September 2008). doi:10.1057/palgrave.jibs.8400398.

Jung, Jae C., Beamish, Paul W. and Goerzen, Anthony. "Dynamics of Experience, Environment and MNE Ownership Strategy," *Management International Review*, vol. 50, no. 3 (2010).

Kim, W. Chan and Mauborgne, Renée A. "Making Global Strategies Work," *Sloan Management Review*, vol. 34, no. 3 (Spring 1993).

Kim, W. Chan and Mauborgne, Renée A. "Effectively Conceiving and Executing Multinationals' World-wide Strategies," *Journal of International Business Studies*, vol. 24, no. 3 (Third Quarter 1993).

Merchant, Hemant. "Configurations of International Joint Ventures," *Management International Review*, vol. 40, no. 2 (Second Quarter 2000).

Merchant, Hemant. "Cooperative Strategy: Economic, Business, and Organizational Issues," *Academy of Management Review*, vol. 26, no. 2 (April 2001).

Meschi, Pierre-Xavier and Riccio, Edson Luiz. "Country Risk, National Cultural Differences Between Partners and Survival of International Joint Ventures in Brazil," *International Business Review*, vol. 17, no. 3 (June 2008).

Mintzberg, Henry, Ahlstrand, Bruce and Lampel, Joseph. *Strategy Safari* (New York: Free Press, 1998).

Mudambi, Susan M. and Tallman, Stephen. "Make, Buy or Ally? Theoretical Perspectives on Knowledge Process Outsourcing through Alliances," *Journal of Management Studies*, vol. 47, no. 8 (December 2010).

Parkhe, Arvind. "Understanding Trust in International Alliances," *Journal of World Business*, vol. 33, no. 3 (Fall 1998).

Peng, Mike W. *Global Strategy* (Mason, OH: Thomson, South-Western, 2006).

Porter, Michael E. "The Competitive Advantage of Nations," *Harvard Business Review*, vol. 68, no. 2 (March/April 1990).

Puck, Jonas F., Holtbrügge, Dirk and Mohr, Alexander T. "Beyond Entry Mode Choice: Explaining the Conversion of Joint Ventures into Wholly Owned Subsidiaries in the People's Republic of China," *Journal of International Business Studies*, vol. 40 (April 2009). doi:10.1057/jibs.2008.56.

Ricart, Joan Enric, Enright, Michael J. and Ghemawat, Pankaj. "New Frontiers in International Strategy," *Journal of International Business Strategy*, vol. 35, no. 3 (May 2004).

Roth, Kendall, Schweiger, David M. and Morrison, Allen J. "Global Strategy Implementation at the Business Unit Level: Operational Capabilities and Administrative Mechanisms," *Journal of International Business Studies*, vol. 24, no. 2 (Second Quarter 1993).

Rugman, Alan M. "Multinationals and Global Competitive Strategy," *International Studies of Management and Organization*, vol. 15, no. 2 (Summer 1985).

Rugman, Alan M. and Verbeke, Alain. *Analysis of Multinational Strategic Management: The Selected Scientific Papers of Alan M. Rugman and Alain Verbeke* (Cheltenham: Edward Elgar, 2005).

Rugman, Alan M. and Verbeke, Alain. "The Theory and Practice of Regional Strategy: A Response to Osegowitsch and Sammartino," *Journal of International Business Studies*, vol. 39, no. 2 (2008).

Rugman, Alan M. and Verbeke, Alain. "A Regional Solution to the Strategy and Structure of Multinationals," *European Management Journal*, vol. 26 (2008).

Tallman, Stephen B. and Yip, George S. "Strategy and the Multinational Enterprise," in Alan M. Rugman (ed.), *The Oxford Handbook of International Business*, 2nd ed. (Oxford: Oxford University Press, 2009).

Thakur, Manab and Das, T. K. "Managing the Growth-Share Matrix: A Four-Nation Study in Two Industries," *Management International Review*, vol. 31, no. 2 (Second Quarter 1991).

Verbeke, Alain. *International Business Strategy: Rethinking the Foundations of Global Corporate Success* (Cambridge: Cambridge University Press, 2009).

Vapola, Terhi Johanna, Paukku Markus and Gabrielsson Mika. "Portfolio Management of Strategic Alliances: An International Business Perspective," *International Business Review*, vol. 19, no. 3 (June 2010).

Verbeke, Alain and Yuan, Wenlong. "Entrepreneurship in Multinational Enterprises: A Penrosean Perspective," *Management International Review*, vol. 47, no. 2 (2007).

Chapter 9

ORGANIZING STRATEGY

Contents

Objectives of the chapter

The primary purpose of an organizing strategy is to help an enterprise implement its strategic plan. There are a number of basic organization structures from which to choose, although most MNEs tailor-make their design and sometimes use a combination of different structures. Another major area of organizing strategy is the organizational processes of decision making, communicating, and controlling. These processes are fundamental to the efficient operation of the structure, and management will need to decide how they should be carried out. This chapter examines the key elements of organizing strategy.

The specific objectives of this chapter are to:

1 *Examine* organization structures used by enterprises that are just beginning their international expansion.

2 *Describe* the international division and global structures that are used as firms increase their international presence.

3 *Analyze* the key structural variables that influence international organization designs.

4 *Review* the role of the organizational processes in ensuring that the structure is both effective and efficient.

Procter & Gamble

In 1837, William Procter, a candle maker, and his brother-in-law James Gamble, a soap maker, partnered to create a company that would manufacture and market soaps and candles from its base in Cincinnati, Ohio. When candles declined in popularity with the invention of the light bulb and production was eventually discontinued in the 1920s, soap became the basis from which the company built a successful product portfolio of cleaning products and eventually allowed Procter & Gamble to branch out into cosmetics, food, and pet products.

During P&G's first century, international expansion was an afterthought. In 1915, a Canadian plant was established, the first outside the United States. P&G's first overseas subsidiary was established with the purchase of Thomas Hedley & Sons Co., Ltd. in England in 1930. This coincided with the birth of P&G's brand management marketing system. Dedicated teams would work on marketing competing brands worldwide. In 1948, P&G established an overseas division to manage its growing international division, which at the time reached Asia, Europe, and Latin America. By 1963, as a result of European expansion, P&G established the European Technical Center in Belgium to serve common market subsidiaries. The Japanese market was entered in 1973 through the acquisition of the Nippon Sunhome Company, and in 1993 the Japan Headquarters and Technical Center opened in Rokko Island in Kobe City.

By 1995, sales outside the United States had reached more than 50 percent of total sales, and a new top management team, headed by John E. Pepper, changed the organization structure of the firm from US and International to four regional sectors: North America; Latin America; Asia; and Europe, the Middle East, and Africa. All regional sectors reported to the chief operating officer.

By 2004, P&G had the workings of a global company in terms of its structure. Three interactive parts, whose subsidiaries are strategically placed around the world to best achieve cost-effectiveness, marketing and production, and design quality, are the basis of this structure. First, there are seven Market Development Organizations (MDOs) responsible for marketing products in the following regions: North America; ASEAN, India, Australia; China; North-East Asia; Central and Eastern Europe, the Middle East, and Africa; and Western Europe and Latin America. Second, these MDOs collaborate with any one of five product-based Global Business Units (GBUs) responsible for R&D, design, and the manufacturing processes. Third, there are Global Business Services (GBSs) located mainly

in developing countries that provide accounting, human resource management, logistics, and system operations in a given region. Finally, a Corporate Functions (CF) segment oversees operations but delegates decision making to each structural unit.

In Figure 9.8 below, the MDOs are equivalent to marketing-based Area Profit Centers; the GBUs can be placed where the Business Profit Centers are. The GBSs, in turn, can take the place of Function Cost Centers. These three sectors interact with each other under the guidance of Corporate Functions.

This global three-axis matrix structure, however, has not resulted in an even distribution of sales across all three regions of the triad, or across P&G's seven-region segmentation. For the year ended June 30, 2010, P&G is ranked the 66th-largest company by sales (Fortune Global 500) with total revenue of US $78.937 billion. A closer analysis indicates that revenues in North America are 42 percent, Western Europe 21 percent, Central and Eastern Europe 13 percent, Latin America 9 percent, and Asia 15 percent. P&G reported that by market maturity, 34 percent and 66 percent of total sales are generated from developed and developing markets respectively.

The firm's most important firm-specific advantage (FSA) is its ability to market products in multiple regions. It does this through product adaptation, marketing, and packaging to the needs of customers in diverse regions and by creating successful brands. Indeed, the firm managed the top 23 brands that each generates more than billion dollars in annual sales. These 50 leadership brands account for 90 percent of P&G sales. Some of its most famous brands include Tide, Ariel, Pantene, and Crest.

P&G's strategy does not necessarily include developing global brands like Pringle's, its most globally diversified brand. Instead, the firm might choose locally trusted brands to channel new products to multiple regions. Blendax, a European brand, is now the portal through which P&G markets Whitestrips that are sold in North America under the Crest brand. Many successful brands were carefully picked up through acquisitions and then revamped with new marketing. Between 1980 and 2000, P&G acquired Cover Girl, Noxzema, Clarion, Oil of Olay, Blendax, Old Spice, Max Factor, and Pantene, among others. In other words, the firm finds regional brands to develop regionally.

Another firm-specific advantage is that P&G's portfolio of products allows the diffusion of R&D to different product ▶

lines in all regions. For example, a fabric detergent discovery may create improved versions of Tide and Cheer in North America, Ariel in Latin America, and Bold in Japan. It might also spill over to non-fabric cleaners such as Salvo. This, and the GBUs' ability to coordinate production across the world, translate into scale economies that are difficult to rival in the industry.

P&G has gone further than most companies in creating a global structure that incorporates non-industrialized countries. For example, in 2004, the GBS for the Americas was located in Costa Rica, while that in the Philippines provides services to the Asian region. Factories are located in Asia, Eastern Europe, and Latin America as well as in more developed countries. R&D, usually reserved for developed nations, has also seen its way to developing countries like China.

Website: www.pg.com.

Source: Alan Rugman, *The Regional Multinationals* (Cambridge: Cambridge University Press, 2005); P&G, *Annual Report*, 2010; *"Fortune Global 500," Fortune*, July 26, 2010 issue.

1. What type of organization structure does P&G have in place for its worldwide operations? Is this structure optimal?

2. Why was the international division replaced by the matrix structure?

3. Why does the company rely on decentralized decision making?

4. In controlling its operations, what are three areas that are paramount for the firm?

INTRODUCTION

This chapter on organization strategy is intimately related to the previous chapter on strategic management. Indeed, there is an unresolved debate about whether strategy follows structure or whether structure follows strategy. We do not need to resolve this debate, but simply to recognize the interconnections between strategy and structure. As shown in the introduction to the previous chapter, it is essential to link the issues of organization structure to the previous frameworks of international business. In particular, the FSA–CSA matrix of Chapter 2 is relevant.

In this chapter we will see that many firms operate in a centralized and hierarchical manner. These structures are suitable for firms pursuing strategies of economic integration, for example, where worldwide economies of scale are being obtained. As was shown in the previous chapter, a strategy of economic integration can occur in cell 1 of the FSA–CSA matrix. By the end of this chapter the student will realize that a centralized and hierarchical structure is usually followed by firms pursuing a cell 1 strategy of economic integration.

In contrast, firms which pursue marketing strategies and differentiate their products and or services by building strong brand names are best positioned in cell 4 of the FSA–CSA matrix. In cell 4, where FSAs are divorced from CSAs, the appropriate organization structure need not be one of hierarchy. A multinational firm may need to adapt its product or service to various foreign markets. This strategy of national responsiveness (discussed in Chapter 10) may require a decentralized organization structure, one where more autonomy is given to subsidiary managers.

Finally, in cell 3 of the FSA–CSA matrix it may be necessary to combine the advantages of both a centralized and decentralized organization structure. Somewhat paradoxically, this is often called a matrix structure. Such a matrix organization structure, where complementary assets need to be combined, is consistent with a strategy in cell 3 of the FSA–CSA matrix.

This chapter will now examine the various types of organization structures available to the senior management teams of multinational enterprises. We also examine how business networks can be managed. This thinking on strategy and structure is then applied to issues in production (Chapter 12); marketing (Chapter 13); human resource management (Chapter 14); political risk negotiations (Chapter 15); and international financial management (Chapter 16). This will then be applied as an example of regional strategy in the final set of chapters.

Organizations that have decided to expand internationally do so in a number of ways. Some simply ship their goods to a foreign market and have a third party handle sales activities. If a firm's international market is a large portion of total operations, however, the enterprise may play a more active role in the distribution and sale of its products, and this requires a more complex organization structure. Often, firms start off as exporters and then, as their foreign sales grow, develop more intricate structures that can handle their foreign operations.[1]

Major MNEs such as IBM, General Motors,[2] Mercedes, and Mitsubishi have sophisticated global structures that form the basis of their organizing strategies. Sometimes these firms will also have subsidiaries or affiliates that are integrated into the overall structure. For example, Mitsubishi has 28 core groups that are bound together by cross-ownership and other financial ties, interlocking directorates, long-term business relationships, and social and historical ties. Among these are Mitsubishi Bank, Mitsubishi Heavy Industries, Asahi Glass, Tokyo Marine and Fire Insurance, Nikon Corporation, and Kirin Brewery.[3] The Mitsubishi Group obviously needs a carefully designed global structure that allows it to integrate and coordinate the activities of these many businesses. Sometimes this undertaking involves more time and effort than the formulation of the strategic plan.

ORGANIZATION STRUCTURES

Multinational enterprises cannot implement their strategies without an effective structure.[4] The strategy sets out the plan of action, but the structure is critical in ensuring that the desired goals are met efficiently. A number of choices are available to an MNE when deciding on an organizational arrangement, and a number of factors can influence this choice. For example, firms that are just getting into the international arena are likely to choose a structure that differs from that of firms with established overseas operations. Conversely, companies that use their structures as worldwide sales organizations will have a different arrangement from those that locally manufacture and sell goods in various international markets. International structures will change in compliance with the strategic plan, and a structure that is proving to be unwieldy or inefficient will be scrapped in favor of one that better meets the needs of the company.[5] The following discussion examines some of the most common organizational arrangements used by MNEs.

Early organization structures

When a company first begins international operations, such activities are typically extensions of domestic operations. The firm's primary focus continues to be the local market; international involvement is of secondary importance. International transactions are conducted on a case-by-case basis, and there is no attempt to consolidate these operations into a separate department. Under this arrangement, international sales are viewed as supplements to the income earned from home-country operations.

As international operations increase, however, the MNE will take steps to address this growth structurally. One way is by having the marketing department handle international sales. All overseas operations are coordinated through this department; if sales warrant it, some of the salespeople will handle international transactions exclusively. In this way the

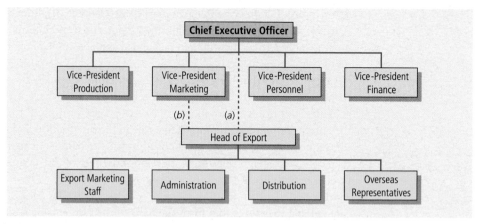

Figure 9.1 An export department structure

company develops marketing specialists who learn the specific needs and marketing techniques to employ in overseas selling.

An alternative arrangement is to create an export department. This department may report directly to the chief executive officer (CEO) (Figure 9.1, line (a)) or be a subdepartment within the marketing area (Figure 9.1, line (b)). If it operates independently of the marketing department (option (a)), it is either staffed by in-house marketing people whose primary focus is on the international market or operated by an outside export management company that is hired to provide the company with an international arm. Whichever approach is taken, MNEs planning to increase their international presence must ensure that the export department is a full-fledged marketing department and not just a sales organization.

Another possible arrangement is the use of overseas subsidiaries (see Figure 9.2). This is often a result of individual ventures in various geographic locales in which the head of the venture is given a great deal of autonomy and reports directly to the CEO. As long as the subsidiary shows sufficient profit, it is allowed to operate free from home-office interference.

As MNEs become more involved in foreign markets, the export department structure or subsidiary arrangement is generally discarded or supplemented because it cannot meet the organization's changing needs. As a result, the company will now look into joint ventures[6] and foreign direct investment, likely opting for an international division structure. To examine one company's international organization structure, see the case **International Business Strategy in Action: Sanofi-Aventis.**

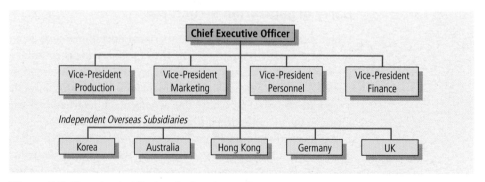

Figure 9.2 Use of subsidiaries during the early stages of internationalization

INTERNATIONAL BUSINESS STRATEGY IN ACTION

Sanofi-Aventis

The French firm Sanofi-Synthélabo acquired Aventis, its most important and much larger French rival, in 2004, creating the sixth-largest pharmaceutical company in the world, Sanofi-Aventis. The new company is the result of a succession of approximately 10 major mergers and acquisitions. Aventis itself was the product of a 1999 merger between French Rhône-Poulenc and Hoechst of Germany.

Sanofi-Aventis is a pharmaceutical group engaged in the research, development, manufacture and marketing of healthcare products. Its business includes two main activities: pharmaceuticals and human vaccines through Sanofi Pasteur. It is also present in animal health products through Merial Limited (Merial). In its pharmaceutical activity, it specializes in six therapeutic areas: diabetes, oncology, thrombosis and cardiovascular, central nervous system (CNS), and internal medicine. The global portfolio of Sanofi-Aventis also consists of a range of other pharmaceutical products in Consumer Health Care (CHC) and other prescription drugs, including generics. It offers vaccines in five areas: pediatric combination vaccines, influenza vaccines, adult and adolescent booster vaccines, meningitis vaccines, and travel and endemic vaccines.

In 2009, Sanofi-Aventis had revenues totaling $43.405 billion (see Table 1), and was in the process of deciding the organization structure that will best help it coordinate all of its worldwide operations. The company continues to be based in France, but most of its sales are to foreign markets. Europe, its home-region base, accounts for 41.1 percent of its sales. The United States alone accounts for 32.2 percent. The remaining 26.7 percent of sales originate in other

Source: Corbis/Vincent Kessler/Reuters

countries, most prominently Canada, Latin America, Asia, and the Middle East.

Mergers in the pharmaceutical industry are the result of increasing pressures to consolidate in order to achieve further economies of scale in R&D, marketing, and distribution. Aventis itself had managed to become one of the major competitors in its industry through mergers and acquisitions. Back in the mid-1980s Rhône-Poulenc was the 12th-largest chemical firm in the world, with 80 percent of sales being generated in Europe. In this environment it competed with a large number of firms, including US-based giants DuPont, Dow Chemical, and leading European chemical companies such as Hoechst, BASF, Ciba-Geigy, and ICI.

During this period, the chemical industry was being increasingly structured on a "triad" basis. As a result,

Table 1 World's 13 largest pharmaceutical companies, 2009

Rank	Companies	Country of origin	Revenue (millions of US$)	Profit (million US$)
1	Johnson & Johnson	United States	61,897	12,266
2	Pfizer	United States	50,009	8,635
3	Roche Group	Switzerland	47,109	7,169
4	Novartis	Switzerland	45,103	8,400
5	GlaxoSmithKline	United Kingdom	44,240	8,626
6	Sanofi-Aventis	France	43,405	7,318
7	Bayer	Germany	43,322	1,889
8	AstraZeneca	United Kingdom/Sweden	32,804	7,521
9	Abbott Laboratories	United States	30,765	5,746
10	Merck	Germany	27,428	12,901
11	Eli Lilly	United States	21,836	4,329
12	Bristol-Myers Squibb	United States	21,634	10,612
13	Boehringer Ingelheim	Germany	18,630	2,445

Source: Adapted from *"Fortune Global 500," Fortune,* 2010. Data are for 2009.

Rhône-Poulenc decided to consolidate its successful European base and move into the North American market. In the late 1980s the firm made 18 acquisitions in the United States, including Union Carbide Agrochemical Products and Stauffer Basic Chemicals. These acquisitions made the company the seventh-largest chemical manufacturer in the world, generating over 20 percent of its total sales in the US market.

Managing its US operations was not easy. The takeover of Union Carbide worked pretty well because the latter's pesticide products were complementary to those of Rhône-Poulenc's herbicides and fungicides and its corporate culture was similar. However, the Stauffer acquisition proved to be more difficult because there were overlapping product lines and the US managers at Stauffer had little international experience.

To improve the efficiency of its diverse US operations, Rhône-Poulenc adapted a highly decentralized organization structure, consolidating its US business operations into a US country group with headquarters at Princeton, New Jersey. The firm also established English as the official language of the company, even though its parent company was French. And as an intermediate step on the path toward true globalization, the firm's US regional headquarters served to create a strong US presence in the face of vigorous competition from rivals with both efficient production and effective staffing. Rhône-Poulenc's plan for the future was to create a "transnational" structure.

The new Sanofi-Aventis can take advantage of the steps already taken by Aventis and its predecessor, Rhône-Poulenc, to maintain a strong presence in the US market. However, that might not be enough. In 2007, rumors started to circulate that Sanofi-Aventis was considering purchasing Bristol-Myers Squibb, which presently has a distribution deal with Sanofi-Aventis. This deal would be a strong push toward becoming a strong competitor in the US market. However, as of 2010, Sanofi-Avenvis and Bristol-Myers Squibb are still two separate pharmaceutical companies.

Websites: http://en.sanofi-aventis.com; www.dupont.com; www.dow.com; www.hoechst.com; www.basf.com; www.ciba.com; www.novartis.com; www.ici.com.

Sources: D. Hunter, "Reshaping Rhône-Poulenc," *Chemical Week*, vol. 156, no. 23 (1995), p. 30; Alan M. Rugman, *The Regional Multinationals: MNEs and "Global" Strategic Management* (Cambridge: Cambridge University Press, 2005); Matthew Herper, "Why Bristol and Sanofi Shouldn't Merge," *Forbes*, February 2, 2007; "Fortune Global 500," *Fortune*, 2010; Onesource, Thomson Reuters, 2011.

The international division

International division structure
An organizational arrangement in which all international operations are centralized in one division

The **international division structure** centralizes all international operations (see Figure 9.3), an arrangement that offers a number of advantages. First, it reduces the CEO's burden of direct operation of overseas subsidiaries and domestic operations.[7] Second, it creates a management team that prioritizes overseas operations. All information, authority, and decision making related to foreign efforts is channeled to this division, so there is one central clearing point for international activities. This structure also helps the MNE to develop a cadre of internationally experienced managers.

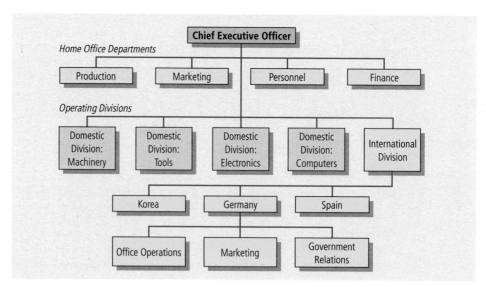

Figure 9.3 An international division structure

But the international division structure also has some significant drawbacks. One is that separating operations into two categories, domestic and international, can create rivalries between the two. Second, this arrangement puts pressure on the home office to think in global terms and to allocate resources on the basis of overall market opportunity. This can be extremely difficult for a management that has been domestically focused and makes the majority of its sales in the home market. Despite these drawbacks, the international division structure remains dominant among US MNEs.

Global organization structures

As MNEs generate more and more revenues from their overseas operations, their strategies become more global in focus and the structures used to implement them follow suit. European firms are a good example. Because their domestic markets are fairly small, these companies have traditionally had global structures. In all, there are six basic types: (1) global product, (2) global area, (3) global functional, (4) matrix, (5) mixed, and (6) transnational network.

Global product structure

Global product structure
An organizational arrangement in which domestic divisions are given worldwide responsibility for product groups

A **global product structure** is an arrangement in which domestic divisions are given world-wide responsibility for product groups. Figure 9.4 provides an example. In this arrangement, each product division sells its output throughout the world. As seen in the case of Product Division C, the European group operates in a host of countries. The same would be true for the other four geographic areas noted. In each case, the manager of the product division would have internal functional support for the entire product line. All production, marketing, personnel, and finance activities associated with Product C would be under the control of this individual. In recent years, Procter & Gamble has used this arrangement to market its wide assortment of products, from paper goods to beauty care, whereas Ford Motor Company has worked to establish a single automotive operation that relies on a global product structure.[8]

This arrangement employs a product division structure that relies on the "profit center" concept. Each product line is expected to generate a predetermined return on investment

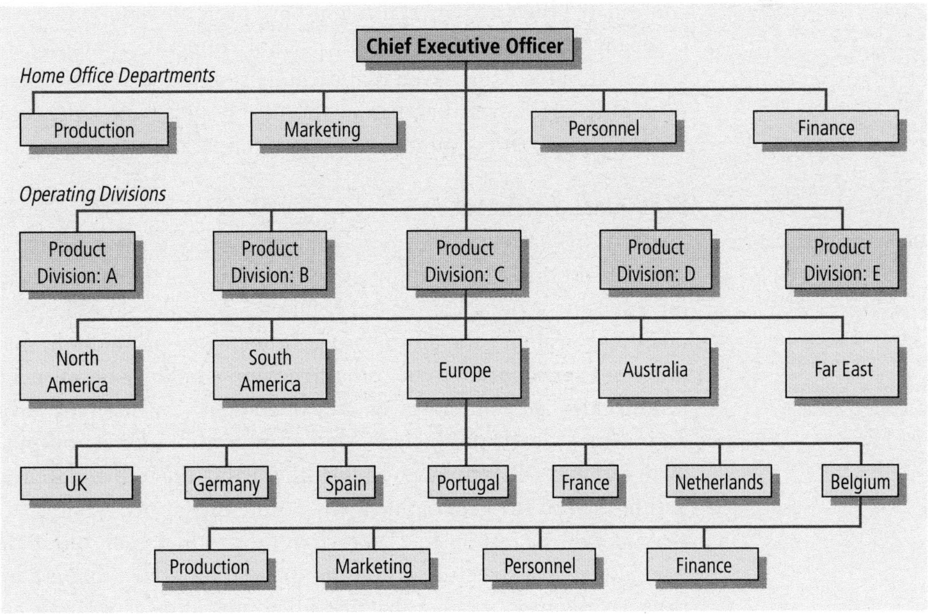

Figure 9.4 A global product structure

(ROI), and the performance of each line is measured on this profit basis. Each product line is also operated like an autonomous business, with the product division manager having a great deal of authority over how to run the operation. As long as the product line continues to generate the desired ROI, the division is usually allowed to operate unfettered by home-management controls. The only major exception is budgetary constraints that are imposed by central management.

A global product division structure has several benefits. If the firm produces a large number of diverse products, the structure allows each major product line to focus on the specific needs of its customers, which would be particularly difficult to achieve if the company were trying to sell all these products out of one centralized marketing department. The structure also helps develop a cadre of experienced, well-trained managers who understand a particular product line. And it helps the company match its marketing strategy to specific customer needs. For example, a product may be in the introduction stage in some areas of the world, and in the growth, maturity, or decline stage in others. These differing life cycles require close technological and marketing coordination between the home market and the foreign market, which can best be achieved by a product division approach. The product structure also helps the organization establish and maintain the necessary link between the product development people and the customer. By continually feeding back information from the field to the home office, product division personnel ensure that new product offerings meet consumer needs.

At the same time, there are drawbacks to the product division arrangement. One is the necessity of duplicating facilities and staff personnel within each division. A second is that products that sell well are often given primary attention while those that need special handling or promotion are often sidetracked, even though this may result in the long-run loss of profit. A third is that an effective product division requires managers who are knowledgeable about the worldwide demand for their products. Most managers know the local market but do not know a lot about international markets. So it takes time to develop the necessary managerial staff to run this type of structure. A fourth shortcoming is the difficulty of coordinating the activities of different product divisions. For example, the electronics division may decide to subcontract components to a plant in Germany, while the computer division is subcontracting work to a firm in France. If the two divisions had coordinated their activities, it might have been possible to have all the work done by one company at a lower price. Finally, lack of cooperation among the various product lines can result in lost sales, given that each division may have information that can be of value to another. However, because of the profit center concept, each product line operates independently, and communication and cooperation are downplayed, if not discouraged.

Global area structure

A **global area structure** is a polycentric (host country-oriented) structure in which primary operational responsibility is delegated to area managers, each of whom is responsible for a specific geographic region. Figure 9.5 provides an example. Every regional division takes responsibility for all functions in its area—production, marketing, personnel, and finance. There appears to be some structural similarity between a global area and a global product arrangement; however, they operate in very different ways. With a global product arrangement, each product division is responsible for its output throughout the world. With a global area structure, on the other hand, the individual product lines are subsumed within each of the geographic areas. So the manager in charge of Belgian operations, for example, will be responsible for each of the product lines sold in that region.

A global area structure is commonly used by MNEs that are in mature businesses and have narrow product lines that are differentiated by geographic area. Food products are a good example.[9]

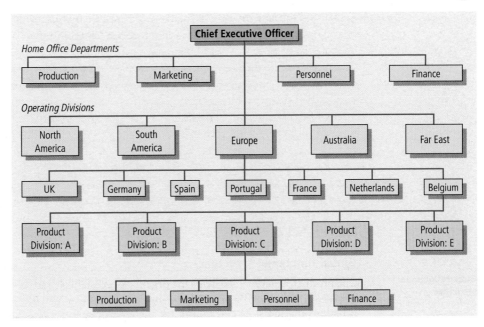

Figure 9.5 A global area structure

The global area structure provides division managers with the autonomy to make rapid decisions that depend on local tastes and regulations; because of this, the firm can become more "nationally responsive." Also, the company gains a wealth of experience in how to satisfy these local tastes, often building a strong competitive advantage in the process. The global area structure works well when economies of scale in production require a region-sized unit for basic production. For example, by setting up operations in the EU, a US company is able to achieve production cost advantages that would not otherwise be possible. Finally, the company can eliminate costly transportation associated with importing goods produced overseas.

If a product sells well in the United States, the company is likely to try to market it worldwide without making any modifications for local taste. Under the area structure the opposite viewpoint holds: the product must be adapted to local tastes. But this means that the usual product emphasis in a company must be subsumed to the company's geographic orientation and the authority of the area managers. Another shortcoming with this organization structure is the expense associated with duplicating facilities. Each division has its own functional areas and is responsible for both production and marketing. Because production efficiency is often based on the amount of output, small plants are usually less efficient than large ones. Companies using a global area division structure also find it difficult to coordinate geographically dispersed divisions into the overall strategic plan. Quite often international cooperation and synergy among divisions end up being sacrificed. Finally, companies that rely heavily on R&D to develop new products often find that the global area divisions do not readily accept these offerings. This is because each group is trying to cater to the specific needs of its current market, and new products often require modification to meet those needs. Research shows that division managers prefer to sell products that have already been accepted by the market and are reluctant to take on new, untried products. Unfortunately, because most products have fairly short life cycles, this attitude is potentially dangerous to the long-term success of the MNE. The home office must continually fight such "anti-new product" drift.

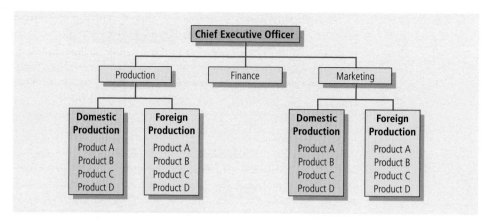

Figure 9.6 A global functional structure

Global functional structure

A **global functional structure** is one built around the basic tasks of the organization. For example, in manufacturing firms, production, marketing, and finance are the three primary functions that must be carried out for the enterprise to survive. Figure 9.6 shows such an arrangement. The head of the production department is responsible for all domestic and international manufacturing. Similarly, the head of marketing is responsible for the sales of all products here and abroad. This structure is most commonly used by MNEs with a narrow product line that has reached a stable plateau of global coverage and a level of demand that does not face major changes in a competitive attack.

The advantages of the global functional structure are allowing a small group of managers to maintain control over a wide-reaching organization, little duplication of facilities, and tight, centralized control. One disadvantage is difficulty in coordinating the production and marketing areas, since each operates independently of the other. This can be particularly troublesome if the MNE has multiple product lines. A second disadvantage is that responsibility for profits rests primarily with the CEO because there is little diffusion of operating authority far down the line.

Researchers have found that the global functional arrangement is most common among raw materials extractors with heavy capital investment. Energy firms also use it. However, this is not a structure that suits many other kinds of businesses.

Matrix structure

A **matrix structure** is an organizational arrangement that blends two organizational responsibilities such as functional and product structures or regional and product structures. The functional emphasis focuses on the activities to be performed, whereas the product emphasis focuses on the good that is being produced. This structure is characterized by a dual command system that emphasizes both inputs (functions) and outputs (products), thereby facilitating development of a globally oriented management attitude. Figure 9.7 illustrates a product–region matrix.

Regions / Products	Country A	Country B	Country C
Product 1			
Product 2			
Product 3			

Figure 9.7 Geographic matrix structure

Regional managers
In a geocentric matrix, managers charged with selling products in their geographic locale

Product managers
Managers responsible for coordinating the efforts of their people in such a way as to ensure the profitability of a particular business or product line

Resource managers
In a matrix structure, managers charged with providing people for operations

Business managers
Managers responsible for coordinating the efforts of people in a corporate organization; for example, in a matrix structure

There are three types of managers in this geocentric matrix structure: regional managers, product managers, and matrix managers. **Regional managers** are charged with business in their markets. Their operation budgets include selling any of the products made by the MNE, subject to the decision of each regional manager. Their focus is polycentric. **Product managers** are responsible for coordinating the efforts of their people in such a way as to ensure the profitability of a particular business or product line. Their attitude is ethnocentric. The matrix managers are responsible to *both* regional and product managers—they have two bosses.

With its three dimensions, the matrix design in Figure 9.8 is more complex than that in Figure 9.7. It illustrates how the matrix organizational arrangement can be used to coordinate and manage wide-reaching international operations. **Resource managers** are charged with providing the people for operations, whereas **business managers** are responsible for coordinating the efforts of these people to make profits for the product line. The resource managers are concerned with inputs, business managers with outputs. The bottom of Figure 9.8 shows functional specialists from such areas as marketing, manufacturing, and research. Individuals from each of these areas are assigned to each of the company's nine businesses. In turn, these nine profit centers operate in five different areas of the world, including the United States, Europe, and Asia. Each business is run by a business board (not shown in the figure) that reports to senior-level management.

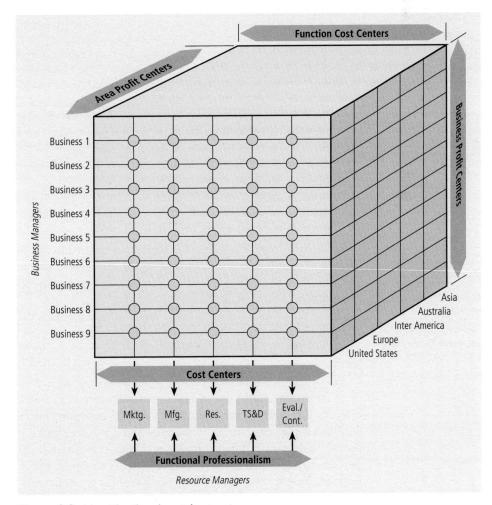

Figure 9.8 A multinational matrix structure
Source: Allan R. Janger, *Matrix Organizations of Complex Business* (New York: The Conference Board, 1979), p. 31.

Making matrix work

Many multinationals use matrix structures in their international operations. Some of these structures work out very well; some do not. Success can often be attributed to three important criteria: clarity, continuity, and consistency. If all three are achieved, the matrix tends to work well; if one or more are missing, the structural design is often ineffective.

Clarity refers to how well people understand what they are doing and why they are doing it. If the company's basic objectives are clear, if relationships in the structure are spelled out in direct, simple terms, and if the relevance of jobs is enunciated, there is a good chance that clarity will be achieved. A good example is NEC, the Japanese giant that decided to integrate computers and communication and to make this the focus of its business efforts. This message was clearly communicated to the personnel so that everyone in the organization understood what the company wanted to do. On the other hand, competitors like AT&T tried the same strategy but failed to clarify what they were doing. As a result, NEC has been more successful.

Continuity means that the company remains committed to the same core objectives and values. This provides a unifying theme and helps ensure that the personnel are committed. General Electric's Brazilian subsidiary is a good example of how a lack of continuity can hurt. In the 1960s the subsidiary built televisions. During the 1970s it was told to switch to large appliances. Then it was told to

focus on housewares. By this time the company's dominant franchise in Brazil's electrical products market had all but dissipated. In contrast, Unilever set up operations in Brazil and, despite volatile changes in the economy, continued to focus its efforts on the electrical products market. By the 1990s Unilever had a thriving market in that country.

Consistency relates to how well all parts of the organization are moving in accord with each other. This is often a reflection of how well managers of the various operating divisions are pursuing the same objectives. For example, Philips NV launched an international strategy for its video cassette recording system, the V2000. However, its US subsidiary did not support these efforts because it felt that Matsushita's VHS format and Sony's Beta system were too well established. Because of this, Philips was unable to build the efficiency and credibility it needed to challenge the Japanese dominance of the VCR business.

Matrix structures can be complex organizational arrangements. However, if the MNE is able to achieve clarity, continuity, and consistency, the matrix approach can be very effective.

Websites: www.nec.com; www.att.com; www.ge.com; www.unilever.com; www.sony.com; www.philips.com.

Sources: Christopher A. Bartlett and Sumantra Ghoshal, "Matrix Management: Not a Structure, a Frame of Mind," *Harvard Business Review*, July/August 1990, pp. 138–145; Courtland L. Bovee et al., *Management* (New York: McGraw-Hill, 1993), pp. 321–323; Richard M. Hodgetts and Fred Luthans, *International Management*, 4th ed. (Burr Ridge, IL: Irwin/McGraw, 2000), Chapter 7.

The matrix design in Figure 9.8 is sometimes referred to as a three-dimensional model because when it is drawn it has width, height, and depth. This multidimensional matrix addresses three major areas: function, product, and geography. So the structure is really a combination of some of the designs discussed earlier.

One of the major advantages of the multinational matrix is that it allows management to address more than one primary area of consideration. As Figure 9.8 shows, the company is able to focus on functional, product, and geographic considerations. MNEs that need to balance a product and a global location strategy can benefit from this type of structure.[10]

A drawback to the use of the matrix structure in international operations is the complexity of the design and the use of dual command, which can result in confusion about what everyone is responsible for doing and to whom one reports on various matters. A second drawback is the large number of meetings and discussions that often result from efforts to coordinate a variety of different groups, each with its own agenda. A third is that it often takes time for managers to learn to operate in a matrix structure, and if the enterprise has rapid turnover, there is always a significant portion of the personnel who do not fully understand how to function effectively in this environment. The case **International Business Strategy in Action: Making matrix work** describes how some of these problems can be handled.

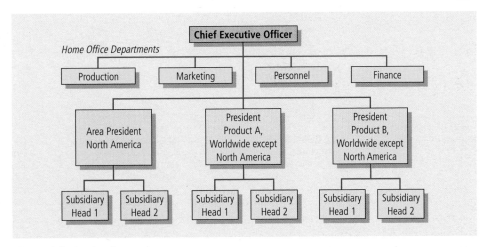

Figure 9.9 A mixed structure

Mixed structure

A **mixed structure** is a hybrid organization design that combines structural arrangements in a way that best meets an enterprise's individual needs. Figure 9.9 provides an illustration. While pedagogically it is important to look at the models illustrated above, in practice a pure function, product, or area structure hardly ever exists. Most firms have some sort of mixed structure. Different businesses with different patterns of global demand, supply, and competition demand different management structures. Some structures might be very close to those mentioned above, but there is always some adaptation to be able to meet the needs of each specific enterprise.

Transnational network structure

One of the newest forms of international organizational arrangements to emerge is the **transnational network structure**, which is designed to help MNEs take advantage of global economies of scale while also being responsive to local customer demands. This structural design combines elements of functional, product, and geographic designs, while relying on a network arrangement to link the various worldwide subsidiaries. At the center of the transnational network structure are nodes, which are units charged with coordinating product, functional, and geographic information. Different product group units and geographical area units have different structures depending on what is best for their particular operation. A good example of how the transnational network structure works is provided by Philips NV, which has operations in more than 60 countries and produces a diverse product line ranging from light bulbs to defense systems. In all, the company has six product divisions with a varying number of subsidiaries in each—and the focus of the latter varies considerably. Some specialize in manufacturing, others in sales; some are closely controlled by headquarters, others are highly autonomous.

The basic structural framework of the transnational network consists of three components: dispersed subunits, specialized operations, and interdependent relationships. *Dispersed subunits* are subsidiaries that are located anywhere in the world where they can benefit the organization. Some are designed to take advantage of low factor costs, whereas others are responsible for providing information on new technologies or consumer trends. *Specialized operations* are activities carried out by subunits that focus on particular product lines, research areas, and marketing areas, and are designed to tap specialized expertise or other resources in the company's worldwide subsidiaries. *Interdependent relationships* are used to share information and resources throughout the dispersed and specialized subunits.[11]

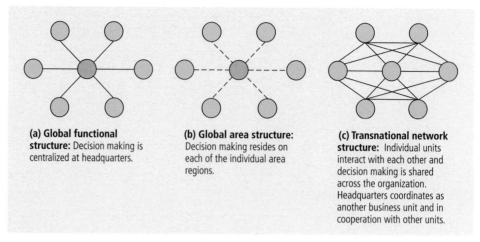

(a) Global functional structure: Decision making is centralized at headquarters.

(b) Global area structure: Decision making resides on each of the individual area regions.

(c) Transnational network structure: Individual units interact with each other and decision making is shared across the organization. Headquarters coordinates as another business unit and in cooperation with other units.

Figure 9.10 Transnational network structure

The transnational network structure is difficult to draw in the form of an organizational chart because it is complex and continually changing. Figure 9.10 gives a graphic scheme for the structure in comparison to the functional and area structures. The functional structure is one in which all decision making is made at headquarters, which coordinates all operations. The area, or geographic structure, is one in which each subunit acts independently from the others. That is, decision making is totally decentralized. The transnational network structure is a combination of both. Individual units interact with each other and decision making is shared across the organization. Headquarters is another business unit that coordinates the enterprise in coordination peripheral business units.

Let us now take a closer look at the transnational network structure. The peripheral circles represent the dispersed specialized subunits, each of which takes advantage of the different resources available in its environment to feed the organization. The connectors show the flows of components, know-how, labor, financial and marketing information, etc., among the different subunits. The central circle represents the headquarters, which helps to coordinate the interaction of the individual subunits using shared decision making.

✔ Active learning check

Review your answer to Active Learning Case question 1 and make any changes you like. Then compare your answer to the one below.

❶ What type of organization structure does P&G have in place for its worldwide operations? Is this structure optimal?

P&G follows a three-axis matrix structure in which the organizational responsibilities are divided among (a) regional marketing, (b) product-based R&D and manufacturing, and (c) regional logistics. These, in turn, are overseen by the Corporate Functions department. Because of the scale and international reach of its operations, a matrix structure allows high levels of national responsiveness in the marketing of P&G's branded products, economies of scale in R&D and production to be materialized through the Global Business Units, and economies of scale in logistics through the Global Business Services. Other types of organization structures would either constrain national responsiveness in marketing or undermine the company's capacity to achieve economies of scale at a regional level.

STRATEGIC MANAGEMENT AND ORGANIZING STRATEGY

Research has shown that effective organizations follow the adage "From strategy to structure."[12] They begin by formulating a strategy and only then design a structure that will efficiently implement this plan. In determining the best structure, three questions must be answered:

1 Can the company operate efficiently with domestic divisions or are international divisions also necessary?

2 On what basis should the organization be structured: product, area, function, mixed, or matrix?

3 How can the necessary coordination and cooperation be most effectively achieved?

These answers are usually determined through a careful analysis of five key variables.

Analysis of key structural variables

There are five key variables that MNEs examine in choosing from among alternative organization structures. In some cases one of these variables will outweigh the others, and the structure will be designed to accommodate this one. In most cases, however, there are three or four interacting variables that the structure must address.

First, the MNE will evaluate the relative importance of international operations at the time and project what the situation might be within three to five years. If the company is currently doing 5 percent of its business overseas and has an export department handling these sales, this organization structure may be adequate for now. However, if the MNE estimates that international sales will grow to 25 percent of total revenues in five years, the company will want to consider adopting an international division structure or one of the global arrangements. Unless the firm is prepared to make this transition, it may prove difficult to handle the anticipated rapid growth.

Second, the company will take into account its past history and experience in the international arena. If the firm has done very little business abroad, it is likely to choose a simple structure that is easy to understand and control. If the company has been doing business overseas for many years, it will probably have experienced managers who can work well in a more sophisticated structure, so it may choose a mixed design or a matrix.

A third area of consideration is the company's business and product strategy. If the company offers a small number of products and there is little need to adapt them to local tastes, a global functional structure may be the best choice. On the other hand, if the products must be tailored for local markets, a global product arrangement will usually be more effective. If the company is going to be doing business in a number of diverse geographic areas, a global area structure will typically be used. For example, to improve sales growth in Europe and Asia, Coca-Cola reinforced its global area organizational arrangement by putting new managers into positions overseeing operations in these regions.[13]

A fourth influencing variable is management's philosophy of operating. If the company wants to expand rapidly and is prepared to take risks, the firm will choose a structure that is quite different from that used by an MNE that wants to expand slowly and is conservative in its risk taking. Similarly, if the home office wants to keep a tight rein on operations, it will not use the same structure as a firm that gives local subsidiaries autonomy and encourages them to make decisions about how to keep the unit competitive at the local level.

French and German subsidiaries, for example, tend to be more centralized than US units. There are also differences in the way operations are controlled. For example, Japanese MNEs like to use face-to-face informal controls, whereas US multinationals prefer budgets, financial data, and other formalized tools.

A final key variable is the enterprise's ability to adjust to organizational changes. As MNE world sales increase, there are continual modifications in the structure. For example, when the company is small, the domestic divisions dominate. As the international side of operations grows, the managers of the domestic divisions have to cede some of their authority and influence. If they are unable or unwilling to do this, the structure is affected. Similarly, if international executives begin gaining greater authority and there is a need to revamp overseas operations, their willingness to adjust to organizational changes will affect the structure. In some cases MNEs have found that overseas managers, just like their domestic counterparts, build small empires and often are unwilling to give up this power.

The ultimate choice of organization structure rests with top management. However, this group seldom tries to force such a decision on those who will be directly affected. Instead, there is a give-and-take in which the needs of the enterprise and the personnel are considered.

In recent years the increase in mergers and acquisitions has had an important impact on MNE decision making. Deutsche Telekom's T-Mobile International provides a good example. By 2001 this company had an ownership position in a large number of mobile phone companies in a host of different countries, including Voice Stream (US), One2One (UK), BEN (Netherlands), max.mobil (Austria), and Radio Mobil (Czech Republic). In March 2011, Deutsche Telekom sold T-Mobile USA to rival AT&T for $39bn, creating the largest US wireless network. The deal sent Deutsche Telekom shares surging. The deal still needs approval from regulators. Coordinating the operations of these holdings requires a carefully designed structure coupled with the appropriate amount of decentralized authority.[14] The result can be a structure that is both efficient and humanistic. In carrying this out, companies will address the organizational processes that take place within the structure.

✔ Active learning check

Review your answer to Active Learning Case question 2 and make any changes you like. Then compare your answer to the one below.

② Why was the international division replaced by the matrix structure?

The international division is a fairly primitive type of organization structure of an MNE. It is used at an early stage of international expansion (by P&G in the 1940s and 1950). As P&G's sales in the international market increased beyond 20 percent or so, it turned to a more complex global organization structure, the three-axis global matrix, with which it could be nationally responsive and achieve economies of scale.

Coordination

The formal structure provides the skeletal framework within which the personnel operate. The structure is designed to answer the question: what is to be done? The organizational processes—decision making, communicating, and controlling—help make the structure

Table 9.1 Factors that encourage centralization or decentralization of decision making in multinational operations

Encourage centralization of decision making	Encourage decentralization of decision making
Large enterprise	Small enterprise
Large capital investment	Small capital investment
Relative importance of the unit to the MNE	Relative unimportance of the unit to the MNE
Highly competitive environment	Stable environment
Strong volume-to-unit-cost relationship	Weak volume-to-unit-cost relationship
High degree of technology	Moderate to low degree of technology
Low level of product diversification	High level of product diversification
Homogeneous product lines	Heterogeneous product lines
High interdependence between the units	Low interdependence between the units
Few highly competent managers in the host country	Many highly competent managers in the host country
High experience in international business	Low experience in international business
Small geographic distance between home office and subsidiary	Large geographic distance between home office and subsidiary

work efficiently. These processes help answer the questions: who should do what, and how will they do it? These processes help put the organization structure into action.

Decision making

Decision making

The process of choosing from among alternatives

Decision making is the process of choosing from among alternatives. In international operations one of the primary areas of consideration is where the ultimate decision-making authority will rest on important matters. If the home office holds this control, decision making is centralized; if the subsidiary can make many of these important decisions without having to consult the home office, decision making is decentralized. Table 9.1 provides some examples of factors that encourage both these types of decision making.[15]

Research shows that decision making in MNE subsidiaries tends to vary from country to country or culture to culture. For example, among British organizations there is a great deal of decentralized decision making. Many upper-level managers do not understand the technical nature of business operations, such as financial budgeting or cost control, so they delegate the authority for these matters to middle-level managers while they focus on strategic matters.

French and German subsidiaries tend to be fairly centralized in their decision-making approaches. French senior executives like to maintain control of operations and tend to delegate less authority than do their British counterparts. German managers are hierarchical in their approach and most important decisions are made at the top.

In Scandinavian countries like Norway, Sweden, and Denmark, operations are highly decentralized both in Scandinavian-based firms and abroad. The Scandinavians place a great deal of emphasis on the quality of work life, and they are more interested in the well-being of the worker than in maximizing profit.

Ringi

Decision making by consensus; this process is widely used in Japan

The Japanese use a combination of decentralization and centralization. They make heavy use of a decision-making process called **ringi**, or decision making by consensus.[16]

At the same time, top management maintains a great deal of authority over what will be discussed at lower levels. Thus, senior-level management exercises both decentralization and centralization.

US MNEs, perhaps surprisingly, tend to use fairly centralized decision making in managing their overseas operations. This is particularly true in areas such as marketing policies, financial matters, and decisions on production capacity. Ford Motor, for example, in 2001 reduced the number of managers reporting to the CEO in order to better control operations.[17] On the other hand, Wal-Mart has been very successful in Canada by using a decentralized approach to accommodate the local market.[18] Moreover, this is the current trend worldwide as MNEs work to increase economies of scale and attain higher operational efficiency. One way in which many are doing this is through outsourcing, thus simplifying their structures and delegating the authority for some operations to their suppliers.[19]

✔ Active learning check

Review your answer to Active Learning Case question 3 and make any changes you like. Then compare your answer to the one below.

③ Why does the company rely on decentralized decision making?

The primary reason why the firm relies so heavily on decentralized decision making is because the demands of the local areas are so great that it cannot make all important decisions from headquarters. This applies to the MDOs, which must market to different cultures with different languages and business environments. But it also applies to the GBSs catering directly to a given region, which must function in the relevant languages and understand regionally specific logistics environments. Decision making is also delegated to the GBUs, which specialize to provide the most efficiency and innovation in each product category and to dissipate R&D knowledge across product families.

Communication

Communication

The process of transferring meanings from sender to receiver

Communication is the process of transferring meanings from sender to receiver. However, the way of doing this often varies from one MNE to another. For example, US MNEs use direct communications with their subsidiaries and overseas units.[20] Directives are spelled out clearly and precisely. Meanwhile, Japanese MNEs prefer more indirect communications in which things are implied and it is up to the listener to determine what to do. The direct approach works well for Americans, whose culture encourages openness and specific communications. The indirect approach works well for the Japanese, whose culture encourages indirect and implied communications.[21] Ouchi, after conducting a series of interviews with Americans working for a Japanese bank in the United States, found that this problem can be particularly disconcerting because each side is unable to understand the other's approach, as illustrated by the following:

American managers:
We have a non-stop running battle with the president. We simply cannot get him to specify a performance target for us. We have all the necessary reports and numbers, but we can't get specific targets from him. He won't tell us how large a dollar increase in loan volume or what percent decrease in operating costs he expects us to achieve over the next month, quarter, or even year. How can we know whether we're performing well without specific targets to shoot for?

Japanese bank president:
If only I could get these Americans to understand our philosophy of banking. To understand what the business means to us—how we feel we should deal with our customers and our employees. What our relationship should be to the local communities we serve. How we should deal with our competitors, and what our role should be in the world at large. If they could get that under their skin, then they could figure out for themselves what an appropriate objective would be for any situation, no matter how unusual or new, and I would never have to tell them, never have to give them a target.[22]

These types of culturally based differences can greatly affect an MNE's ability to get things done.

Another communication-based problem is non-verbal messages. In international business these take two major forms: kinesics and proxemics. **Kinesics** deals with the conveying of information through the use of body movement and facial expression. For example, when verbally communicating with someone in the United States, it is good manners to look the other party in the eye. However, in many other cultures, such as the Arabic and Middle Eastern, this is not done, especially if one is talking to a member of the opposite sex. Such behavior would be considered rude and disrespectful.[23]

Proxemics deals with how people use physical space to convey messages. For example, in the United States, business people typically stand 2 to 3 feet (75 cm) away from those with whom they are communicating. However, in the Middle East and in many South American countries it is common to stand right next to the person. This often makes Americans feel very uncomfortable because this space is generally reserved only for family members and close friends. Business is not conducted at this distance. One group of authors summarized the problem this way:

> Americans often tend to be moving away in interpersonal communication with their Middle Eastern or Latin counterparts, while the latter are trying to physically close the gap. The American cannot understand why the other is standing so close; the latter cannot understand why the American is being so reserved and standing so far away; the result is a breakdown in communication.[24]

Another example of proxemics is office layout and protocol. In the United States, a large office connotes importance, as does a secretary who screens visitors and keeps away those whom the manager does not wish to see. In Japan, most managers do not have large offices; if they do, they spend little time in them since they are generally out talking to the employees and walking around the workplace. If the manager were to stay in the office all day, it would be viewed as a sign of distrust or anger at the work group. In Europe, many managers do not have walled-in offices. The bosses are out in the same large room as their people; there is no one to screen the brokers from the boss.

Every country has some unique communication patterns or behaviors.[25] These behaviors can be particularly troublesome to outsiders who are working locally and are unfamiliar with local approaches to communication. Figure 9.11 provides an interesting example in the form of epigrams that have been drawn from organization structures throughout the world.

Controlling

Controlling is the process of determining that everything goes according to plan and that performance is rewarded. It consists of three steps: (1) establishing standards; (2) comparing performance against standards; and (3) correcting deviations. Controlling is closely linked to communication since it is virtually impossible to evaluate performance and make changes without communicating information. Many of the same organizational problems discussed above also apply here.

One of the major differences between US and Japanese firms is the use of explicit versus implicit control. A major difference between US and European firms is that US MNEs tend to rely more heavily on reports and other performance-related data, whereas Europeans make heavy use of behavioral control. US multinationals compare results of a foreign unit to those of other foreign units, as well as with domestic units, in evaluating performance. European MNEs tend to be more flexible and to judge performance on an

Kinesics
A form of non-verbal communication that deals with conveying information through the use of body movement and facial expression

Proxemics
A form of non-verbal communication that deals with how people use physical space to convey messages

Controlling
The process of determining that everything goes according to plan

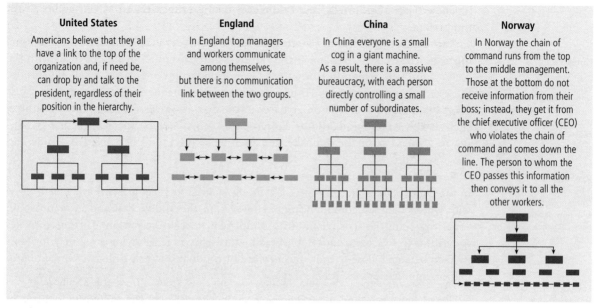

Figure 9.11 Organizational epigrams

An epigram is a terse, witty statement. The organizational epigrams are designed to poke fun at the way communication flows in international organizations. Each was created by an individual with experience in the respective country. The explanation accompanying the respective epigram explains the logic behind the drawing. These epigrams illustrate that communication flows throughout the world are less efficient than the enterprise would like. They also illustrate that each country has its own unique approach to conveying information.

Source: Adapted from Simcha Ronen, *Comparative and Multinational Management*. Copyright © 1986 John Wiley & Sons, Inc. Reproduced with permission of John Wiley & Sons, Inc.

individual basis rather than simply making a comparative judgment. Other differences include:

1 Control in US MNEs relies on precise planning and budgeting that is suitable for comparison purposes. Control in European MNEs takes into consideration a high level of company-wide understanding and agreement over what constitutes appropriate behavior and how such behavior supports the goals of the subsidiary and the parent company.

2 US multinationals do not encourage their managers to remain in overseas positions for a long period of time. As a result, they use large central staffs and centralized information gathering to carry out evaluations. European multinationals, on the other hand, encourage their managers to remain in overseas positions and rely heavily on these managers to provide input on how well the unit is doing.

3 Managers of US MNEs often report to a counterpart back in headquarters who, in turn, conveys information up the line. European multinationals have a more direct reporting channel so that the head of a foreign subsidiary reports to someone who is closer to the top of the structure.[26]

Another major difference is the way in which personnel are evaluated. In the United States and Europe, it is common to single out high performers and reward them. In Japan, however, credit is given to the entire group rather than just to one or two individuals. Singling people out for special attention is not regarded as complimentary. Rather, such attention would make individuals feel they were not regarded as team players, which would be insulting. Another important difference is the time period for personnel evaluations. Most US and European firms evaluate their people on an annual basis. However, in Japan the first major evaluation often does not occur until the employee has been with the firm for almost a decade.[27] These controlling differences greatly affect the way the structure is managed. As a result, running an overseas operation the same way as at home is often difficult.

✔ Active learning check

Review your answer to Active Learning Case question 4 and make any changes you like. Then compare your answer to the one below.

 In controlling its operations, what are three areas that are paramount for the firm?

There are a number of areas P&G needs to control. One of these is profit. The company must ensure that its divisions are profitable in each market in which it operates. A second area is cost control. Presently, P&G's matrix structure is designed to be nationally responsive and decrease costs through economies of scale. A third area is innovation. One of the firm's principal competitive advantages is its ability to improve its brands against the competition; as a result, it must weigh its advances in R&D against that of the competition. A fourth area of control is the brand awareness of consumers for P&G's brands.

KEY POINTS

1 When a company first enters the international arena, it is common to find that these efforts are mere extensions of domestic operations. The MNE will typically handle foreign sales directly through its own marketing department, an export department, or an overseas subsidiary that is the result of a joint venture. As international operations become more important, however, the firm is likely to centralize these operations by adopting an international division structure. This organizational arrangement remains quite popular with many MNEs.

2 As multinationals generate increased revenues from their overseas operations, they are likely to adopt a global organization structure. There are six basic types: global product, global area, global functional, mixed, matrix, and transnational network. Each type has specific advantages and disadvantages.

3 There are five key variables that MNEs examine in choosing from among alternative organization structures: (a) the relative importance of international operations, (b) past history and experience in the international arena, (c) the company's business and product strategy, (d) management philosophy, and (e) the firm's ability to adjust to organizational changes.

4 The formal structure provides the skeletal framework within which the personnel operate. The organization process of decision making, communicating, and controlling make the structure work efficiently. In the decision-making process, one of the key areas of consideration is the amount of centralization or decentralization that will be used by the home office. In communicating, culturally based differences will be of major importance, including non-verbal messages. In controlling, areas of concern include explicit and implicit control and the ways in which personnel will be evaluated.

Key terms

- international division structure
- global product structure
- global area structure
- global functional structure

- matrix structure
- regional managers
- product managers
- resource managers
- business managers
- transnational network structure

- mixed structure
- decision making
- *ringi*
- communication
- kinesics
- proxemics
- controlling

REVIEW AND DISCUSSION QUESTIONS

1 How does an export department structure function? Who handles the overseas sales?

2 If a company's initial international expansion is conducted through the use of subsidiaries, how closely does it control these subsidiaries? Why?

3 Why do MNEs use an international division structure? Are there any drawbacks to this organizational arrangement?

4 How does a global product structure work? Why would an MNE opt for this arrangement? What are two drawbacks to using this structure?

5 When would an MNE use a global area structure? When would the firm reject this structural arrangement in favor of a different structure?

6 How does a global functional structure work? When would it be a popular approach? When would it be of very little value in organizing international operations?

7 When would a company opt for a mixed structure? Why? Defend your answer.

8 How does a matrix structure work? When would an MNE opt for this organizational arrangement?

9 There are five key variables that MNEs examine in choosing from among alternative organization structures. What are these five? Identify and briefly describe each.

10 Why are some overseas operations highly decentralized while others are very centralized? What factors influence this arrangement?

11 Why are US international operations more centralized than those in Sweden? Why is the US model becoming more popular among MNEs?

12 In what way is implicit versus explicit communication important in understanding how home-office managements coordinate international activities?

13 What type of control techniques do US MNEs prefer? How does this preference differ from that of the Japanese? Compare and contrast the two.

REAL CASE

LVMH: organizing luxury products in the international arena

LVMH is the French-based, world-leading luxury goods group that was founded in 1987 with the merger of Louis Vuitton and Moët Hennessy. Christian Dior, Dom Pérignon, Givenchy, and Moët & Chandon are just a few of LVMH's world-famous luxury brand names. By 2010, revenues for the group totalled €20.320 billion—putting it among the top five marketers of luxury items (including wines). LVMH had 2,545 stores across the world and employed more than 83,542 people, 77 percent of whom work outside France. The company generates the bulk of its sales in foreign markets; only 13 percent of all revenues are earned in France. The United States is the company's single largest market comprising 23 percent of revenues. It is important to note that although France earns a small fraction of LVMH's revenues, Europe as a whole (including France) accounts for 34 percent. Japan accounts for 9 percent, while Asia (excluding Japan) accounts for 25 percent. The remaining 9 percent is generated mainly in the Pacific, Latin America, and Canada. With over 20 percent of sales in each broad region of the triad LVMH is a true global company.

LVMH's organizational arrangement is much more than that of a typical conglomerate. The whole organization focuses on shared costs and synergies, both backward and forward in its value chain. The five main lines of business are really strategic business units (SBUs) that are set up to market well-known, high-quality products while responding to local tastes and regulations. They are: (1) LVMH Fashion and Leather Goods; (2) Wines and Spirits; (3) Perfumes and Cosmetics; (4) Watches and Jewelry; and (5) Selective Retailing. By carefully overseeing major operations from the top while allowing the individual SBUs to make the decisions that directly affect their own local markets, LVMH employs a combination of "tight and loose" control to maximize its international presence. In the process, it has become the most global retail company.

The profit margin on luxury goods is very high, so control over production, distribution, and advertising is central to profitability. LVMH ensures that production standards in its manufacturing operations are the highest. It centralizes manufacturing by using a common laboratory for cosmetics research and integrates the operations for all the branch offices in each group to ensure maximum efficiency.

Marketing is a very important part of LVMH's strategy. The company spends 11 percent of all its revenues on

Source: Corbis/Stephane Cardinale/People Avenue

worldwide advertising and purchases media products in bulk to receive the best value for its money. The "Made in France" label is stressed to appeal to its home country's reputation for high-quality luxury products. The company sources only in France, Italy, and Switzerland.

The vision of a totally integrated group was and continues to be an important part of the global strategy that has positioned LVMH as an industry leader. The company walks a fine line between the exclusivity required of luxury goods and the size and scope of its operations. It might operate around the world, but its products are not accessible to all.

Websites: www.lvmh.com; www.vuitton.com; www.moet.com; www.dior.com; www.givenchy.com.

Sources: Adapted from www.lvmh.com; LVMH, *Annual Report*, 2010; Stéphane Girod and Alan M. Rugman, "Regional Business Networks and the Multinational Retail Sector," *Long Range Planning*, vol. 38, no. 4 (2005), pp. 335–357.

1 What type of organization structure does LVMH have?

2 What is the role of the SBUs in the organization structure of LVMH? What problems might arise if each SBU were run independently?

3 Compare the organization structure of LVMH to that of Procter & Gamble. Are there any similarities? How are these organizations different?

4 What are some of LVMH's FSAs that are listed in this case?

5 How would outsourcing to less developed countries affect LVMH?

REAL CASE

Command Alkon: a small business

Based in Birmingham, Alabama, in the United States, Command Alkon is the world leader in the design and supply of computer software for the construction business. With $79.2 million in revenues in 2010, Command Alkon is a small MNE but it has tremendous capabilities in technology standardization and is number one in its software in terms of market share, revenues, and distribution. Employing over 300 people, it has international offices in India, Colombia, France, the Netherlands, and the UK that market its products in each region through independent sales representatives. Roughly 20 percent of the company's business is now derived outside North America.

Command Alkon is the result of a merger in December 2000 of Command Data and Alkon, two construction material software and service firms. The merger was designed to pool their R&D resources to compete more effectively in the fast-changing computer software business. Individual products were already compatible and the merger eliminated duplication of effort. The company specialized in the construction business, which was largely ignored by booming software firms, so it was able to become the largest player in a niche market. At present, it competes only with two smaller, local competitors and the systems developed in-house by customers.

Command Alkon has a purely ethnocentric strategy and organization structure. All decisions are centralized and hierarchical micromanagement is the name of the game. The dominant culture is that of the US home office. There is no customization, no marketing department, no investment in local offices. It is not a "born global" firm; it is a US firm. Like most small businesses, Command Alkon is driven by its basic product or service, and it replicates its firm-specific advantage overseas.

One of the problems for small businesses is that the top management team is itself small. Often it comprises just the founder of the firm, his or her immediate family, and a few friends, so there is little managerial experience and a limited opportunity to develop international business skills, which leads to ethnocentric behavior. Indeed, most small business leaders do not have the internal resources to build an overseer business by foreign direct investment; instead, they are drawn to the export mode of foreign entry. Thus, they need an international division structure.

There are thousands of small and medium-sized businesses (SMEs) like Command Alkon. Their business strategy is not as complicated as that of MNEs; usually SMEs are in only one line of business. The international experience of SMEs is usually through licensing and/or exporting. Rarely do they engage in foreign direct investment or develop global organization structure because the cost of doing business in foreign markets is often too high. As they expand internationally, even in software, they do so regionally (in their home triad) rather than globally.

Websites: www.commandalkon.com; www.systechsystems.com.

Sources: www.commandalkon.com; Gilbert Nicholson, "Command Alkon Found Its Niche and Dug In," *Birmingham Business Journal*, November 2, 2001; Steven Lang, "The Merits of Specialization," *VARBusiness*, February 18, 2004; Thomson Reuters, *OneSource*, 2011.

1 Why does a small business like Command Alkon usually have little or no foreign direct investment? How does it go international?

2 What is the typical type of organization structure for a small business like Command Alkon?

3 Why are software businesses usually ethnocentric in their organization structure?

ENDNOTES

1 See, for example, Yigang Pan and Xiaolian Li, "Joint Venture Formation of Very Large Multinational Firms," *Journal of International Business Studies*, vol. 32, no. 1 (First Quarter 2000), pp. 179–189; and Tim G. Andrews and Nartnalin Chompusri, "Lessons in 'Cross-Vergence': Restructuring the Thai Subsidiary Corporation," *Journal of International Business Studies*, vol. 30, no. 3 (First Quarter 2000), pp. 77–93; and Namrata Malhotra and C. R. (Bob) Hinings, "An organizational model for understanding internationalization processes," *Journal of International Business Studies* (2010) 41, 330–349; doi:10.1057/jibs.2009.75.

2 Brad Mitchener, "GM Takes a Gamble on Eastern Europe," *Wall Street Journal*, June 23, 1997, p. A10.

3 William J. Holstein et al., "Mighty Mitsubishi Is on the Move," *Business Week*, September 24, 1990, p. 99; and Mure Dickie in Tokyo, "Japanese Yards Claim to Have Edge over Rivals," *The Financial Times Online*, February 7, 2011.

4 Robert L. Simison, "New Data Illustrate Reshaping of Auto Parts Business," *Wall Street Journal*, September 2, 1997, p. B4; and Lindsay Whipp in Tokyo, "Japan to Invest in Quake-Struck Auto-Parts Industry," *The Financial Times Online*, May 29, 2011.

5 A good example is offered by Peter Siddall, Keith Willey and Jorge Tavares, "Building a Transnational Organization for BP Oil," *Long Range Planning*, February 1992, pp. 37–45.

6 For some excellent examples, see Charles H. Ferguson, "Computers and the Coming of the US Keiretsu," *Harvard Business Review*, July/August 1990, pp. 55–70; and Benjamin Gomes-Casseres, "Joint Ventures in the Face of Global Competition," *Sloan Management Review*, vol. 30, no. 3 (Spring 1989), pp. 17–26.

7 Richard M. Hodgetts and Fred Luthans, *International Management*, 4th ed. (Burr Ridge, IL: McGraw/Irwin, 2000), p. 303.

8 Joann S. Lublin, "Place vs. Product: It's Tough to Choose a Management Model," *Wall Street Journal*, June 27, 2001, pp. A1, 4.

9 Hodgetts and Luthans, op. cit., p. 306.

10 Yves L. Doz, Christopher A. Bartlett and C. K. Prahalad, "Global Competitive Pressures and Host Country Demands," *California Management Review*, Spring 1981, p. 66.

11 See Sumantra Ghoshal and Christopher A. Bartlett, *Managing across Borders: The Transnational Solution* (London: Random House, 1998).

12 Alfred D. Chandler, Jr., *Strategy and Structure* (Garden City, NY: Anchor Books, Doubleday, 1966).

13 Betsy McKay, "Coke Reorganization Puts Three as Contenders for No. 2 Position," *Wall Street Journal*, July 31, 2001, p. B2; and Louise Lucas in London, "Coca-Cola Seeks Cultural Shift in Paris Listing," *The Financial Times Online*, May 23, 2011; and Jonathan Birchall in New York, "Coca-Cola Sees Broad Global Growth," *The Financial Times Online*, February 9, 2011.

14 William Boston, "Can Telekom Turn a David into a Goliath?" *Wall Street Journal*, June 1, 2001, pp. A11, 13; and Julia Caesar, "AT&T and T-Mobile Create Biggest US Firm in $39 bn Deal," *BBC News Online*, March 21, 2011.

15 Also see Rebecca Blumenstein, "GM Is Building Plants in Developing Nations to Woo New Markets," *Wall Street Journal*, August 4, 1997, pp. A1, 5; and Jorn Madslien, "Changed Landscape for Global Carmakers," *BBC News Online*, May 10, 2011.

16 Raghu Nath, *Comparative Management: A Regional View* (Cambridge, MA: Ballinger, 1988), p. 125.

17 Tim Burt and Nikki Tait, "Ford Refines Chain of Command in US," *Financial Times*, August 16, 2001, p. 13.

18 Bernard Simon, "Canada Warms to Wal-Mart," *New York Times*, September 1, 2001, pp. B1, 3.

19 See, for example, "Japan Inc. on the Treadmill," *The Economist*, June 9, 2001, pp. 63–64; and Rakesh B. Sambharya and Kunal Banerji, "The Effect of Keiretsu Affiliation and Resource Dependencies on Supplier Firm Performance in the Japanese Automobile Industry," *Management International Review*, vol. 46, no. 1 (2006).

20 Bruce T. Lamont, V. Sambamurthy, Kimberly M. Ellis and Paul G. Simmonds, "The Influence of Organizational Structure on the Information Received by Corporate Strategists of Multinational Enterprises," *Management International Review*, vol. 40, no. 3 (Third Quarter 2000), pp. 231–232.

21 For some excellent insights into how Japanese companies function, see Noboru Yoshimura and Philip Anderson, *Inside the Kaisha* (Boston, MA: Harvard Business School Press, 1997).

22 For an excellent contrast of American and Japanese communication problems, see William G. Ouchi, *Theory Z* (Reading, MA: Addison-Wesley, 1981), pp. 33–35.

23 Jane Whitney Gibson, Richard M. Hodgetts and Charles W. Blackwell, "Cultural Variations in Nonverbal Communication," in *Proceedings of the 55th Annual Convention of the Association for Business Communication*, 1990, p. 213.

24 Hodgetts and Luthans, op. cit., p. 212.

25 David E. Sanger, "Tokyo's Tips For New York," *New York Times Magazine*, February 6, 1994, pp. 28–29.

26 William G. Egelhoff, "Patterns of Control in US, UK, and European Multinational Corporations," *Journal of International Business Studies*, vol. 15, no. 2 (Fall 1984), pp. 81–82;

27 Ouchi, op. cit., p. 22.

ADDITIONAL BIBLIOGRAPHY

Ambos, Björn and Schlegelmilch, Bodo B. *The New Role of Regional Management* (Basingstoke: Palgrave Macmillan, 2010).

Ambos, Björn and Mahnke, Volker. "How Do MNC Headquarters Add Value?" *Management International Review*, vol. 50, no. 4 (August 2010).

Ambos, Tina C. and Birkinshaw, Julian. "Headquarters' Attention and Its Effect on Subsidiary Performance," *Management International Review*, vol. 50, no. 4 (August 2010).

Ambos, Tina C. and Ambos, Björn. "Organizational Capabilities and the Effectiveness of Knowledge Flows within Multinational Corporations," *Journal of International Management*, vol. 15, no. 1 (2009).

Andersson, Ulf and Forsgren, Mats. "In Search of Centre of Excellence: Network Embeddedness and Subsidiary Roles in Multinational Corporations," *Management International Review*, vol. 40, no. 4 (Fourth Quarter 2000).

Bartlett, Christopher A. and Ghoshal, Sumantra. *Managing Across Borders: The Transnational Solution* (Boston: Harvard Business School Press, 1989).

Bartlett, Christopher A. and Ghoshal, Sumantra. "Matrix Management: Not a Structure, a Frame of Mind," *Harvard Business Review*, vol. 68, no. 4 (July/August 1990).

Beamish, Paul W., Karavis, Lambros, Goerzen, Anthony and Lane, Christopher. "The Relationship between Organizational Structure and Export Performance," *Management International Review*, vol. 39, no. 1 (First Quarter 1999).

Beldona, Sam, Inkpen, Andrew C. and Phatak, Arvind. "Are Japanese Managers More Long-Term Oriented than United States Managers?" *Management International Review*, vol. 38, no. 3 (Third Quarter 1998).

Benito, Gabriel R. G., Grøgaard, Birgitte and Narula, Rajneesh. "Environmental Influences on MNE Subsidiary Roles: Economic Integration and the Nordic Countries," *Journal of International Business Studies*, vol. 34, no. 5 (September 2003).

Birkinshaw, Julian. *Entrepreneurship in the Global Firm* (London: Sage, 2000).

Bjorkman, Ingman, Barner-Rasmussen, Wilhelm and Li, Li. "Managing Knowledge Transfer in MNCs: The Impact of Headquarters Control Mechanisms," *Journal of International Business Studies*, vol. 35, no. 5 (September 2004).

Bouquet, Cyril, Morrison, Allen J. and Birkinshaw. Julian M. "International Attention and Multinational Enterprise Performance," *Journal of International Business Studies*, vol. 40, no. 1 (2009).

Buckley, Peter J. and Carter, Martin J. "A Formal Analysis of Knowledge Combination in Multinational Enterprises," *Journal of International Business Studies*, vol. 35, no. 5 (September 2004).

Buckley, Peter J. and Strange, Roger. "The Governance of the Multinational Enterprise: Insights from Internalization Theory," *Journal of Management Studies*, vol. 48, no. 2 (March 2011).

Ciabuschi, Francesco, Dellestrand, Henrik and Kappen, Philip. "Exploring the Effects of Vertical and Lateral Mechanisms in International Knowledge Transfer Projects," *Management International Review*, vol. 51, no 2 (April 2011).

Ciabuschi, Francesco, Martín, Oscar and Ståhl, Benjamin. "Headquarters' Influence on Knowledge Transfer Performance," *Management International Review*, vol. 50, no. 4 (August 2010).

Collinson, Simon and Morgan, Gareth. *Images of the Multinational Firm* (Oxford: Wiley-Blackwell, 2009).

De la Torre, José R., Esperança, José Paulo and Martínez, Jon I. "Organizational Responses to Regional Integration among MNEs in Latin America," *Management International Review*, vol. 51, no. 2 (April 2011).

Egelhoff, William G. "How the Parent Headquarters Adds Value to an MNC? " *Management International Review*, vol. 50, no. 4 (August 2010).

Foss, Nicolai J., Husted, Kenneth and Michailova, Snejina. "Governing Knowledge Sharing in Organizations: Levels of Analysis, Governance Mechanisms, and Research Directions," *Journal of Management Studies*, vol. 47, no. 3 (May 2010).

Foss, Nicolai Juul and Pedersen, Torben. "Organizing Knowledge Processes in the Multinational Corporation: An Introduction," *Journal of International Business Studies*, vol. 35, no. 5 (September 2004).

Ghoshal, Sumantra and Bartlett, Christopher A. "The Multinational Corporation as an Interorganizational Network," *Academy of Management Review*, vol. 15, no. 4 (October 1990).

Ghoshal, Sumantra and Bartlett, Christopher A. *The Individualized Corporation: A Fundamentally New Approach to Management* (New York: HarperBusiness, 1997).

Heracleous, Loizos. *Strategy and Organization* (Cambridge: Cambridge University Press, 2003).

Inkpen, Aandrew C. "Knowledge Transfer and International Joint Ventures: The Case of NUMMI and General Motors," *Strategic Management Journal*, 29 (2008).

Keupp, Marcus Matthias, Palmié, Maximilian and Gassmann, Oliver. "Achieving Subsidiary Integration in International Innovation by Managerial, 'Tools,'" *Management International Review*, vol. 51, no. 2 (April 2011).

Kogut, Bruce and Zander, Udo. "Knowledge of the Firm and the Evolutionary Theory of the Multinational Corporation," *Journal of International Business Studies*, vol. 24, no. 4 (Fourth Quarter 1993).

Kostova, Tatiana and Zaheer, Srilata. "Organizational Legitimacy Under Conditions of Complexity: The Case of the Multinational Enterprise," *Academy of Management Review*, vol. 24, no. 1 (October 1999).

Levy, Orly, Beechler, Schon, Taylor, Sully and Boyacigiller, Nakiye A. " What We Talk About When We Talk About 'Global Mindset': Managerial Cognition in Multinational Corporations," *Journal of International Business Studies*, vol. 38, no. 2 (March 2007).

Li, Guey-Huey, Yu, Chwo-Ming and Seetoo, Dah-Hsian. "Toward a Theory of Regional Organization," *Management International Review*, vol. 50, no. 1 (February 2010).

London, Ted and Hart, Stuart L. "Reinventing Strategies for Emerging Markets: Beyond the Transnational Model," *Journal of International Business Studies*, vol. 35, no. 5 (September 2004).

Martinez, Jon I. and Jarillo, J. Carlos. "The Evolution of Research on Coordinating Mechanisms in Multinational Corporations," *Journal of International Business Studies*, vol. 20, no. 3 (Fall 1989).

Meyer, Klaus E. "Contextualising Organisational Learning: Lyles and Salk in the Context of Their Research," *Journal of International Business Studies*, vol. 38, no. 1 (January 2007).

Minbaeva, Dana, Pedersen, Torben, Björkman, Ingmar, Fey, Carl F. and Park, Hyeon J. "MNC Knowledge Transfer, Subsidiary Absorptive Capacity, and HRM," *Journal of International Business Studies*, vol. 34, no. 6 (November 2003).

Mudambi, Ram and Navarra, Pietro. "Is Knowledge Power? Knowledge Flows, Subsidiary Power and Rent-Seeking Within MNCs," *Journal of International Business Studies*, vol. 35, no. 5 (September 2004).

Nachum, Lilach, "International Business in a World of Increasing Returns," *Management International Review*, vol. 43, no. 3 (Third Quarter 2003).

Parkhe, Arvind. "Interfirm Diversity, Organizational Learning, and Longevity in Global Strategic Alliances," *Journal of International Business Studies*, vol. 22, no. 4 (Fourth Quarter 1991).

Piekkari, Rebecca, Nell, Phillip C. and Ghauri, Pervez N. "Regional Management as a System," *Management International Review*, vol. 50, no. 4 (August 2010).

Roehl, Tom. "The Evolution of a Manufacturing System at Toyota," *Academy of Management Review*, vol. 25, no. 2 (April 2000).

Rosenzweig, Philip M. and Singh, Jitendra V. "Organizational Environments and the Multinational Enterprise," *Academy of Management Review*, vol. 16, no. 2 (April 1991).

Roth, Kendall. "International Configuration and Coordination Archetypes for Medium-Sized Firms in Global Industries," *Journal of International Business Studies*, vol. 23, no. 3 (Third Quarter 1992).

Rugman, Alan M. and Verbeke, Alain. "A Note on the Transnational Solution and the Transaction Cost Theory of Multinational Strategic Management," *Journal of International Business Studies*, vol. 23, no. 4 (Fall 1992).

Rugman, Alan M. and Verbeke, Alain. "Extending the Theory of the Multinational Enterprise: Internalization and Strategic Management Perspectives," *Journal of International Business Studies*, vol. 34, no. 2 (March 2003).

Rugman, Alan M. and Verbeke, Alain "A Regional Solution to the Strategy and Structure of Multinationals," *European Management Journal*, vol. 26 (2008).

Sinkovics, Rudolf R., Roath, Anthony S. and Cavusgil, S. Tamer. "International Integration and Coordination in MNEs," *Management International Review*, vol. 51, no. 2 (April 2011).

Spencer, Jennifer W. "Global Gatekeeping, Representation, and Network Structure: A Longitudinal Analysis of Regional and Global Knowledge-Diffusion Networks," *Journal of International Business Studies*, vol. 34, no. 5 (September 2003).

Sullivan, Daniel. "Organization in American MNCs: The Perspective of the European Regional Headquarters," *Management International Review*, vol. 32, no. 3 (Third Quarter 1992).

Tallman, Stephen and Chacar, Aya S. "Knowledge Accumulation and Dissemination in MNEs: A Practice-Based Framework," *Journal of Management Studies*, vol. 48, no. 2 (March 2011).

Tran, Yen, Mahnke, Volker and Ambos, Björn. "The Effect of Quantity, Quality and Timing of Headquarters-initiated Knowledge Flows on Subsidiary Performance," *Management International Review*, vol. 50, no. 4 (August 2010).

Wan, William P. and Hillman, Amy J. "One of these Things Is Not Like the Others: What Contributes to Dissimilarity among MNE Subsidiaries' Political Strategy?" *Management International Review*, vol. 46, no. 1 (2006).

Westney, Eleanor D. and Zaheer, Srilata. "The Multinational Enterprise as an Organization," in Alan M. Rugman (ed.), *The Oxford Handbook of International Business*, 2nd ed. (Oxford: Oxford University Press, 2009).

Westney, Eleanor. "Challenging the Transnational Model," *Socio-Economic Review*, vol. 12 (2008).

Wolf, Joachim and Egelhoff, William G. (2010). "Limitations of the Network Organization in MNCs," in J. Pla-Barber and J. Alegre (eds.), *Progress in International Business Research*, vol. 5 (Amsterdam: Emerald).

Wolf, Joachim and Egelhoff, William G. "Network or Matrix? How Information-Processing Theory Can Help MNCs Answer This Question," in A. Bøllingtoft, L. Donaldson, G. P. Huber, D. Døjbak Håkonsson, and C. C. Snow (eds.), *Collaborative Communities of Firms – Purpose, Process, and Design*. (Springer Science, Business Media B.V, 2011).

Verbeke, Alain. "International Acquisition Success: Social Community and Dominant Logic Dimensions," *Journal of International Business Studies*, vol. 41 (2010). doi:10.1057/jibs.2009.70.

Verbeke, Alain and Kenworthy, Thomas P. "Multidivisional versus Metanational Governance of the Multinational Enterprise," *Journal of International Business Studies*, vol. 39, no. 2 (2008).

Zahra, Shaker A. "The Dynamic Firm: The Role of Technology, Strategy, Organization, and Regions," *Academy of Management Review*, vol. 24, no. 4 (October 1999).

Chapter 10

CORPORATE STRATEGY AND NATIONAL COMPETITIVENESS

Contents

Objectives of the chapter

The primary objective of this chapter is to develop two frameworks for understanding how both nations and MNEs must fashion their strategies to achieve international competitiveness. In doing so, we give particular consideration to the regional economic integration of North America, although these frameworks are also relevant for other triad economies and also for emerging economy firms.

The specific objectives of this chapter are to:

1 *Examine* the determinants and external variables in Porter's "diamond" model of national competitiveness and critique and evaluate the model.

2 *Present* a "double-diamond" model that illustrates how firms in non-triad countries such as Canada are using their diamond to design corporate strategies for the North American market.

3 *Discuss* the benefits and effects of the North American Free Trade Agreement on both Mexico and Canada.

4 *Describe* how Mexico is using a double-diamond model to tap into the North American market.

5 *Define* the terms *economic integration* and *national responsiveness* and relate their importance to MNE strategies throughout the world.

ACTIVE LEARNING CASE

Worldwide operations and local strategies of ABB

Headquartered in Zurich, Switzerland, Asea Brown Boveri (ABB) is one of Europe's major industrial firms. Since the merger in 1987 that created it, ABB has been acquiring or taking minority positions in a large number of companies throughout the world. In recent years it has purchased Westinghouse's transmission and distribution operations and Combustion Engineering, the manufacturer of power generation and process automation equipment.

ABB Ltd (ABB) provides power and automation technologies for its utility and industrial customers. It focuses on power transmission, distribution, and power-plant automation and serves electric, gas, and water utilities, as well as industrial and commercial customers. ABB also delivers automation systems that measure, control, protect, and optimize plant applications across a range of industries. By 2009, the conglomerate, which employs over 116,000 people worldwide, had annual revenues of $31.797 billion; 41.18 percent of its revenues comes from Europe, 19.03 percent from the Americas, and 27.31 percent from Asia. The remainder, 12.48 percent, comes from Africa and the Middle East.

ABB operates on both local and global terms. On the one hand it attempts to maintain deep local roots wherever it operates so that it can modify both products and operations for that market. For example, managers are trained to adapt to cultural differences and to learn how to communicate effectively with local customers. At the same time the company works to be global and to make products that can be sold anywhere in the world because their technology and quality give them a worldwide appeal.

A good example of a business that demonstrates ABB's advantages is products and services. In 2009, the company generates $9.370 billion revenues in power products (29.47 percent), $7.897 billion in automation products (24.84 percent), $7.150 billion in process automation (22.49 percent), $6.356 billion in power systems (20 percent), and the balance in robotics. This is possible for four reasons: (1) ABB's research and development makes it a leader in power and automation technology, enabling it to develop and build products and services throughout the world; (2) its operations are structured to take advantage

of economies of scale and thus keep prices competitive; (3) it adapts to local environments and works closely with customers so that it is viewed as a national rather than a foreign company; and (4) it works closely with companies in other countries that are favored by their own government but need assistance in financing and producing equipment for that market. As a result, ABB is able to capitalize on its technological and manufacturing expertise and develop competitive advantages in both triad and non-triad markets.

In some cases ABB has gone so far as to take an ownership position in companies located in emerging economic markets. For example, the firm purchased 76 percent of Zamech, Poland's leading manufacturer of steam turbines, transmission gears, marine equipment, and metal castings. And it has bought into two other Polish firms that make a wide range of generating equipment and electric drives. ABB reorganized these firms into profit centers, transferring its own expertise to local operations, and developing worldwide quality standards and controls for production. In Mexico, ABB acquired FIP SA in 2001, an oil and gas production equipment company. In October 2009, ABB Ltd. acquired Sinai Engineering Corporation to enhance its presence and capabilities in Western Canada. In January 2011, the Company acquired Baldor Electric Company (the United States) at the value of $4.2 billion, including $1.1 billion of net debt. These acquisitions also need to be better incorporated into its structure.

ABB works hard to be a "good citizen" of every country in which it operates, while also maintaining its supranational status. As a result, the company is proving that it is possible to have worldwide operations and local strategies that work harmoniously.

Website: www.abb.com.

Sources: Adapted from William Taylor, "The Logic of Global Business: An Interview with ABB's Percy Barnevik," *Harvard Business Review*, March/April 1991, pp. 91–105; Carol Kennedy, "ABB: Model Merger for the New Europe," *Long Range Planning*, vol. 25, no. 5 (1992), pp. 10–17; Edward L. Andrews, "ABB Will Cut 10,000 Jobs and Switch Focus to Asia," *New York Times*, October 22, 1997, p. C2; Alan M. Rugman, *The Regional Multinationals* (Cambridge: Cambridge University Press, 2005); ABB, *Annual report*, 2009. Thomson Reuters, *Onesource*, 2011; "Fortune Global 500," *Fortune*, 2010.

1 In what way does ABB's strategy incorporate Porter's four country-specific determinants and two external variables?

2 Why did ABB buy Zamech? How can the company link Zamech to its overall strategic plan?

3 How does ABB address the issues of globalization and national responsiveness? In each case, cite an example.

INTRODUCTION

In this chapter two frameworks are developed. Again it is useful to relate these to the basic firm and country model first outlined in Chapter 2 of this textbook. In this chapter we will first review the single-diamond model of Michael Porter (1990). We will apply it to analyze the international competitiveness of large economies such as the United States, Japan, and Germany. We then introduce the double-diamond framework which is more suitable for somewhat smaller but open trading economies, such as Canada, New Zealand, Korea, Singapore, and, indeed, most countries in the world. Both the Porter single diamond and the double diamond deal with CSAs. There are rankings of countries based on the manner in which their CSAs are being utilized to improve their international competitiveness. Yet, in this work on international competitiveness, the manner in which CSAs are turned into FSAs is often not made explicit.

The second framework outlined in this chapter is the famous economic integration and national responsiveness matrix. The economic integration axis is largely explained by CSAs. The national responsiveness axis is a pure FSA. Indeed, only in international business can this type of FSA arise. The managers of a multinational enterprise (MNE) have a network of subsidiaries and national responsiveness is relevant when making decisions about the strategy and organizational structure of such firms. In contrast, purely domestic firms cannot experience FSAs in national responsiveness. Together, these two frameworks provide the students with the basic insights necessary to analyze the complex nature of the strategy and structure of multinational enterprises and other firms involved in international business.

Some MNEs rely on their home market to generate the research, development, design, or manufacturing needed to sell their goods in international markets. More and more, however, they are finding that they must focus on the markets where they are doing business as well as on strategies for tapping the resources of those markets and gaining sales entry. In short, multinationals can no longer rely exclusively on the competitive advantage they hold at home to provide them with a sustainable advantage overseas.

In addition, many small countries realize they must rely on export strategies to ensure the growth of their economies. Those that have been most successful with this strategy have managed to tap into markets within triad countries. Good examples are Canada and Mexico, both of which have found the United States to be a lucrative market for exports and imports. As a result, many successful business firms in these two countries have integrated themselves into the US economy, while creating what some international economists call a North American market. In the future many more MNEs are going to be following this pattern of linking into the economies of triad members.

The basic strategy that these MNEs are following can be tied directly to the Porter model presented in Chapter 1, although some significant modifications of this model are in order. We will first examine Porter's ideas in more detail and then show how these ideas are serving as the basis for developing corporate strategies and international competitiveness in Canada and Mexico.

THE SINGLE DIAMOND

In Chapter 1 we identified four determinants of national competitive advantage, as set forth by Porter (see Figure 10.1). We noted that these factors can be critical in helping a country build and maintain competitive advantage. We now return to Porter's "diamond" framework in more depth, examining how his findings apply specifically to triad countries and determining how the ideas can be modified and applied to nations that are not triad members.

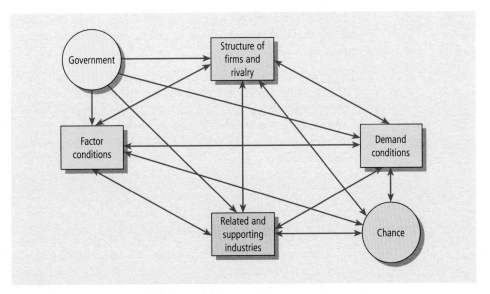

Figure 10.1 Porter's single-diamond framework

Determinants and external variables

Porter's "diamond" model is based on four country-specific determinants and two external variables. The determinants include:

1 *Factor conditions.* These include (a) the quantity, skills, and cost of the personnel; (b) the abundance, quality, accessibility, and cost of the nation's physical resources such as land, water, mineral deposits, timber, hydroelectric power sources, and fishing grounds; (c) the nation's stock of knowledge resources, including scientific, technical, and market knowledge that affect the quantity and quality of goods and services; (d) the amount and cost of capital resources that are available to finance industry; and (e) the type, quality, and user cost of the infrastructure, including the nation's transportation system, communications system, health-care system, and other factors that directly affect the quality of life in the country.

2 *Demand conditions.* These include (a) the composition of demand in the home market as reflected by the various market niches that exist, buyer sophistication, and how well the needs of buyers in the home market precede those of buyers in other markets; (b) the size and growth rate of the home demand; and (c) the ways in which domestic demand is internationalized and pulls a nation's products and services abroad.

3 *Related and supporting industries.* These include (a) the presence of internationally competitive supplier industries that create advantages in downstream industries through efficient, early, or rapid access to cost-effective inputs; and (b) internationally competitive related industries that can coordinate and share activities in the value chain when competing or those that involve complementary products.

4 *Firm strategy, structure, and rivalry.* These include (a) the ways in which firms are managed and choose to compete; (b) the goals that companies seek to attain as well as the motivations of their employees and managers; and (c) the amount of domestic rivalry and the creation and persistence of competitive advantage in the respective industry.

The four determinants of national advantage shape the competitive environment of industries. However, two other variables, chance and government, also play important roles:

1 *The role of chance.* Chance events can nullify the advantages of some competitors and bring about a shift in overall competitive position because of developments such as (a) new inventions, (b) political decisions by foreign governments, (c) wars, (d) significant shifts in world financial markets or exchange rates, (e) discontinuities in input costs such as oil shocks, (f) surges in world or regional demand, and (g) major technological breakthroughs.

2 *The role of government.* Government can influence all four of the major determinants through such actions as (a) subsidies, (b) education policies, (c) the regulation or deregulation of capital markets, (d) the establishment of local product standards and regulations, (e) the purchase of goods and services, (f) tax laws, and (g) antitrust regulation.[1]

Figure 10.1 provides an illustration of the complete system of these determinants and external variables. Each of the four determinants affects the others, and all in turn are affected by the role of chance and government.

Critique and evaluation of the model

In applying this model to international business strategy, we must first critique and evaluate Porter's paradigm and supporting arguments. First, the Porter model was constructed based on statistical analysis of aggregate data on export shares for 10 countries: Denmark, Italy, Japan, Singapore, South Korea, Sweden, Switzerland, the UK, the United States, and West Germany. In addition, historical case studies were provided for four industries: the German printing press industry, the US patient monitoring equipment industry, the Italian ceramic tile industry, and the Japanese robotics industry. In each case the country is either a member of the triad or an industrialized nation. Since most countries of the world do not have the same economic strength or affluence as those studied by Porter, it is highly unlikely that his model can be applied to them without modification.

Second, the government is of critical importance in influencing a home nation's competitive advantage. For example, it can use tariffs as a direct entry barrier to penalize foreign firms, and it can employ subsidies as an indirect vehicle for penalizing foreign-based firms. Government actions such as these, however well intentioned, can backfire and end up creating a "sheltered" domestic industry that is unable to compete in the worldwide market.[2]

Third, although chance is a critical influencing factor in international business strategy, it is extremely difficult to predict and guard against. In a similar vein, technological breakthroughs in computers and consumer electronics have resulted in rapid changes that, in many cases, were not predicted by market leaders.

Fourth, in the study of international business, the Porter model must be applied in terms of company-specific considerations and not in terms of national advantages. As Porter so well notes in his book, "Firms, not nations, compete in international markets."[3]

Fifth, in support of his model, Porter delineates four distinct stages of national competitive development: factor-driven, investment-driven, innovation-driven, and wealth-driven (see Figure 10.2). In the factor-driven stage, successful industries draw their advantage almost solely from the basic factors of production such as natural resources and the nation's large, inexpensive labor pool. Although successful internationally, the industries compete primarily on price. In the investment-driven stage, companies invest in modern,

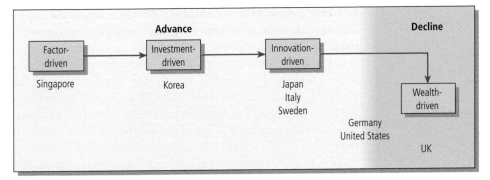

Figure 10.2 The four stages of national development and the historical position of select nations

efficient facilities and technology and work to improve these investments through modification and alteration. In the innovation-driven stage, firms work to create new technology and methods through internal innovation and with assistance from suppliers and firms in related industries. In the wealth-driven stage, firms begin to lose their competitive advantage, rivalry ebbs, and the motivation to invest declines. As seen in Figure 10.2, Porter believes that Singapore is in the factor-driven stage, Korea is investment driven, Japan is innovation driven, Germany and the United States are between the innovation and wealth-driven stages, and the UK is wealth driven. Because the stage of development greatly influences the country's competitive response, the placement of countries in Figure 10.2 is critical. So too is the logic that countries move from one stage to another, rather than spanning two or more stages, because there are likely to be industries or companies in all major economies that are operating at each stage.

Sixth, Porter contends that only outward FDI is valuable in creating competitive advantage, and inbound foreign investment is never the solution to a nation's competitive problems. Moreover, foreign subsidiaries are not recognized by Porter as sources of competitive advantage.[4] These statements are questionable and have already been rejected in this text. For example, scholars such as Safarian,[5] Rugman,[6] and Crookell[7] have all demonstrated that R&D undertaken by foreign-owned firms is not significantly different from that of Canadian-owned companies. Moreover, Rugman has found that the 20 largest US subsidiaries in Canada export virtually as much as they import (the rate of exports to sales is 25 percent, whereas that of imports to sales is 26 percent).[8]

Seventh, as seen in Figure 10.2, reliance on natural resources (the factor-driven stage) is viewed by Porter as insufficient to create worldwide competitive stature.[9] However, Canada, for one, has developed a number of successful megafirms that have turned the country's comparative advantage in natural resources into proprietary firm-specific advantages in resource processing and further refining—sources of sustainable advantage.[10] Moreover, case studies of the country's successful multinationals such as Alcan, Noranda, and Nova help illustrate the methods by which value added has been introduced by the managers of these resource-based companies.[11]

Eighth, the Porter model does not adequately address the role of MNEs. Researchers such as Dunning[12] have suggested including multinational activity as a third outside variable (in addition to chance and government). Certainly there is good reason to question whether MNE activity is covered in the "firm strategy, structure, and rivalry" determinant, and some researchers have raised the question of how the same rivalry determinant can both include multinationality for global industries and yet exclude it for multidomestic industries. As Dunning notes, "There is ample evidence to suggest that MNEs are influenced in their competitiveness by the configuration of the diamond in other than their home countries, and that this in turn may impinge upon the competitiveness of home countries."[13] For example, Nestlé earns 98 percent of its sales outside Switzerland;[14] thus, the Swiss diamond of competitive advantage is less relevant than that of the countries in which Nestlé operates. This is true not only for MNEs in Switzerland but for 95 percent of the world's MNEs as well. For example, virtually all of Canada's large multinationals rely on sales in the United States and other triad markets. Indeed, it could be argued that the US diamond is more relevant for Canada's industrial multinationals than Canada's own diamond, since more than 70 percent of Canadian MNE sales take place in the United States. Other nations with MNEs based on small home diamonds include Australia, New Zealand, Finland, and most, if not all, Asian and Latin American countries as well as a large number of other small countries. Even small nations in the EU, such as Denmark, have been able to overcome the problem of a small domestic market by gaining access to one of the triad markets. So in applying Porter's framework to international business at large, one conclusion is irrefutable: *Different diamonds need to be constructed and analyzed for different countries.*

✔ Active learning check

Review your answer to Active Learning Case question 1 and make any changes you like. Then compare your answer to the one below.

1 **In what way does ABB's strategy incorporate Porter's four country-specific determinants and two external variables?**

The strategy incorporates Porter's country-specific determinants as part of a well-formulated global strategy designed to tap the strengths of various markets. For example, the company draws on the factor conditions and demand conditions in Europe to support its power and automation business. It also draws on supporting industries to help sustain its worldwide competitive advantage in that industry. At the same time the company's strategy, structure, and rivalry are designed to help it compete at the local level. The strategy incorporates the external variable of government by considering relations between countries as a lubricant for worldwide economic integration. It addresses the variable of chance by operating globally and thus reducing the likelihood that a war or a regional recession will have a major negative effect on operations. The firm's heavy focus on core technologies and R&D also helps minimize this chance variable.

THE DOUBLE DIAMOND

Researchers have recently begun using Porter's single diamond as a basis for analyzing the international competitiveness of smaller countries. This approach builds on Porter's theme of corporate strategy and process as a source of competitive advantage for a nation.

Canada and the double diamond

Figure 10.3 illustrates how Porter's single diamond would look if it were applied to Canada's case.[15]

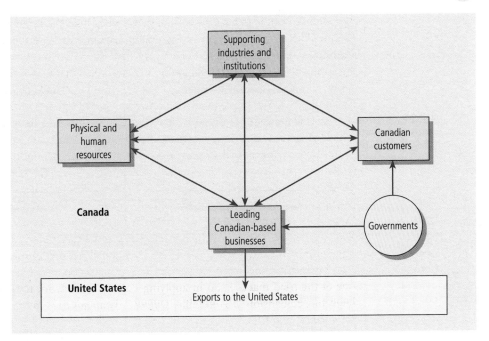

Figure 10.3 The single-diamond view

Source: Adapted from Alan M. Rugman and Joseph R. D'Cruz, *Fast Forward: Improving Canada's International Competitiveness* (Toronto: Kodak Canada, 1991), p. 35.

Two themes have recurred consistently in Canadian industrial policy: export promotion for natural resource industries and import substitution in the domestic arena. The Canadian market has always been seen as too small to support the development of economies of scale required in modern industry. Hence it has been the practice in Canada to provide the base for developing large-scale resource businesses that are designed to exploit the natural resources found in the country. Export strategies have emphasized commodity products that have been developed in isolation from major customers. In the past these strategies had been encouraged by US government policies that removed or eliminated tariffs on imports of commodities that are not produced extensively in the United States. The Canadian government's role had been to help leading Canadian-based businesses by establishing relatively low taxes on resource extraction and by subsidizing the costs of capital through grants, low-interest loans, and loan guarantees.

With respect to import substitution, the Canadian goal had been to use tariff and non-tariff measures to provide a protected environment for developing secondary industry. Under this arrangement the country's approach to business was largely focused inwardly, relying solely on the extent and quality of natural resources as the basis for the creation of wealth.

By the mid-1960s, however, it had become clear that a more international focus was needed. The 1967 Canada–United States Auto Pact demonstrated that significant economic benefits would result from the elimination of tariffs on trade between the two countries in autos and parts. This agreement eventually became the model for the United States–Canada Free Trade Agreement.[16] In the process Canadian plants gained economies of scale by producing for the North American market as a whole rather than for the Canadian market alone. For corporate strategy, the result of North American economic integration has been the development of a Canadian–US "double diamond," which shows that the two countries are integrated for strategy purposes into a single market (see Figure 10.4).

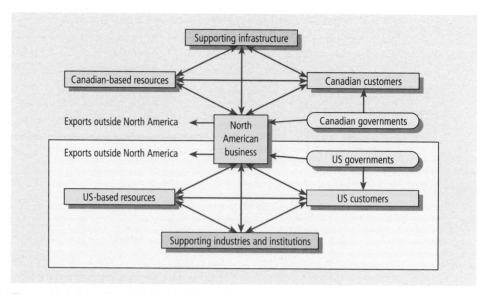

Figure 10.4 Canadian–US double diamond

Source: Adapted from Alan M. Rugman and Joseph R. D'Cruz, "The 'Double Diamond' Model of International Competitiveness: the Canadian Experience," *Management International Review*, vol. 33, Special Issue 2 (1993), p. 32.

Under this new arrangement, Canadian businesses are now in direct competition with firms operating in a diamond of their own in the United States.[17] To survive this rivalry with leading US firms, Canadian businesses have to develop competitive capabilities of a high order.[18] They can no longer rely on their country's home diamond and natural resource base. Innovation and cost competitiveness are equally important, and this requires strategies that are designed to access the US diamond. Now Canadian managers need a "double-diamond perspective" for their strategic decisions. The double diamond is, of course, relevant for other small, open economies such as Finland and Sweden. The case **International Business Strategy in Action: Nokia and Ericsson** provides an example.

The Free Trade Agreement has also created a series of unique pressures on the Canadian subsidiaries of US multinationals, many of which were created for the purpose of overcoming Canadian tariff barriers that were designed to encourage the development of local operations. These subsidiaries are now unnecessary, and many of them are currently in direct competition with their US-based parent. If they cannot compete successfully, future business will go south of the border.[19]

Meanwhile, major Canadian companies are working to develop competitive positions in the United States as well as worldwide.[20] A good example is Magna International, Canada's leading diversified automotive supplier headquartered in Aurora, Ontario, Canada. The company designs, develops and manufactures automotive systems, assemblies, modules and components, and engineers and assembles complete vehicles, primarily for sale to original equipment manufacturers (OEMs) of cars and light trucks in three geographic segments: North America, Europe and rest of world (primarily Asia, and South America). It is Canada's largest automobile part manufacturer and also one of the world's 500 largest companies. The firm has now established a significant manufacturing and product development presence in the United States. As at September 2010, the company had 245 manufacturing divisions and 80 product development, engineering, and sales centers in 25 countries. In 2009, Magna derives 18.6 percent of its total revenues from Canada, 21.6 percent from the United States, 6.7 percent from Mexico (North America 46.9 percent) western Europe 38.6 percent, the United Kingdom 4.3 percent, other European countries 5.6 percent (Europe 48.5 percent) and the remainder from rest of world.[21]

Bombardier Inc. provides another example. Beginning as a Canadian manufacturer of snow-going equipment, the company has now grown into a multinational firm with interests in aviation, transportation, and financial services. In the aviation/aerospace business, Bombardier has major operations in Canada and the United States, among other locations, and manufactures a line of business aircraft, commercial aircraft, including regional jets, turboprops and single-aisle mainline jets and amphibious aircraft. The company's transportation operations are located throughout North America and Europe and manufacture passenger trains, mass transit railcars, and engines. It also provides bogies, electric propulsion, control equipment and maintenance services, as well as complete rail transportation systems and rail control solutions.[22]

Other major Canadian firms are following suit, operating from a North American perspective in order to lay the groundwork for becoming globally competitive.[23] This involves viewing the United States and Canada as home-based markets and integrating the use of both "diamonds" for developing and implementing strategy. In particular, this requires:

1 Developing innovative new products and services that simultaneously meet the needs of the US and Canadian customer, recognizing that close relationships with demanding US customers should set the pace and style of product development.

2 Drawing on the support industries and infrastructure of both the US and Canadian diamonds, realizing that the US diamond is more likely to possess deeper and more efficient markets for such industries.

3 Making free and full use of the physical and human resources in both countries.[24]

Strategic clusters in the double diamond

The primary advantage of using the double diamond is that it forces business and government leaders to think about management strategy and public policy in a more productive way. Rather than viewing the domestic diamond as the unit of analysis, managers from smaller countries are encouraged to always be outward looking. Doing well in a double diamond is the first step toward global success.

Once a country has recognized the benefit of the double-diamond perspective, it should first identify successful and potentially viable clusters of industries within its borders and then examine their linkages and performances across the double diamond. A **strategic cluster** is a network of businesses and supporting activities located in a specific region, where the flagship firms compete globally and the supporting activities are home based, although some can be foreign owned. In addition, some of the critical business inputs and skills may come from outside the country, with their relevance and usefulness being determined by the membership of the strategic cluster. A successful strategic cluster will have one or more large MNEs at its center. Whether these are home or foreign owned is irrelevant so long as they are globally competitive. They are the flagship firms on which the strategic cluster depends. Ideally, they operate on a global basis and plan their competitive strategies within the framework of global competition. A vital component of the cluster is companies with related and supporting activities, including both private- and public-sector organizations. In addition, there are think tanks, research groups, and educational institutions. Some parts of this network can even be based outside the country, but the linkages across the border and the leadership role of the nation's flagships result in world-class competitive multinationals.[25]

Currently Canada has several strategic clusters. One is the auto assembly and auto parts industry in south-western Ontario, led by the Big Three US auto multinationals with their related and affiliated suppliers and distributors. There are linkages to various high-tech firms and research groups that span the border, as does the auto assembly industry itself. Other strategic clusters are based in banking and financial services in Toronto, advanced

Strategic cluster
A network of businesses and supporting activities located in a specific region, where flagship firms compete globally and supporting activities are home based

Nokia and Ericsson

Based in one of the world's smallest countries, the largest producer of mobile phones is Finland's Nokia. Founded in 1865, Nokia was a major manufacturer of paper products before it transformed itself into a high-tech producer of electronic products, especially cellular phones, starting in the 1970s. By 2009, Nokia was the largest company in Finland and also among the world's largest 500 companies with sales of US $56.966 billion. Production facilities span 13 countries, and R&D is performed in 13 locations worldwide. It generates sales in 130 countries and employs some 132,427 people. In 2009, Nokia derived 36 percent of its total sales from Europe, 38 percent from Asia–Pacific, including China, the Middle East and Africa 14 percent, Latin America 7 percent, and North America 5 percent. However, Nokia's 2009 sales dropped 23 percent compared to 2008 sales as industry watchers comment that Nokia has been falling behind its competitors (for example, Apple) for some years. In February 2011, Nokia announced a strategic alliance whereby it plans to abandon its Symbian smartphone operating system in favour of Microsoft's Windows Phone 7, in order to challenge the growing popularity of phones powered by Google's Android operating software and the Apple iPhone. The Apple's iPhone (driven by Apple's proprietary iOS) has captured the top of the smartphone market while devices powered by Android—free, open source software— are now available from a number of manufacturers. In fact, there are now more smartphones powered by Android than iPhones in the hands of users. The iPhone benefits from a "cool" and desirable image and a huge store of proved applications, while Android phones are cheaper and have an impressive user interface. RIM's BlackBerry e-mail devices, which enjoyed a very short "cycle of dominance," may also have missed the leading position. Taiwanese smartphone maker HTC is the world's third-biggest mobile phone maker by market value. Samsung (Korea) is one of leading players in the fast growing smartphone and tablet PC market.

From the beginning, Nokia has pursued foreign sales. In 2009, Nokia derives less than 1 percent of its total sales from Finland, and 99 percent are foreign sales. This internationalization strategy is necessary because Finland has only 3 million people and only a small share of its sales originates in its home base. So Nokia became the mobile phone leader in Scandinavia, despite competition from Ericsson of Sweden. From there it progressed to becoming the leader in the UK and then the rest of Europe, and formed strategic alliances with US distributors such as Radio Shack and US telecom companies like AT&T. The firm has also developed special phones for Chinese and Japanese users. Nokia spends a large amount on R&D, which allows it to continuously introduce new handset models. For instance it introduced handsets with MP3 technology that allows a mobile phone to also be a portable music player. Nokia has a joint venture with the German electronic and electrical engineering Siemens AG to form Nokia Siemens Networks.

L. M. Ericsson employs more than 82,493 people and has sales of US $26.997 billion in the 140 countries in which it operates. In 1997, Ericsson was the world's largest producer of digital mobile phones. In 2009, 1.98 percent of its sales are from Sweden, 19.61 percent in Western Europe, 24.57 percent in Central and Eastern Europe, Middle East and Africa, 31.86 percent in Asia Pacific (including China and India), 12.28 percent in North America, and 9.70 percent in South America. Unlike Nokia, which started as a paper and rubber producer, Ericsson has always been in telecommunications, beginning in 1876 as a telephone manufacturer. It has always been innovative; today, one in four employees works in R&D. In other areas of business it has developed telephone switches in which it competes with firms such as Siemens Nokia Networks, France's Alcatel Lucent and Japan's NEC. Ericsson was well positioned to benefit from the telecom deregulation of the 1980s and 1990s. This has created new demand, especially for new equipment like mobile phones in areas with few local monopoly producers.

Ericsson has formed alliances with Intel, Hewlett-Packard, and Texas Instruments. These firms act as key suppliers of components and products that Ericsson uses for voice and data transmission. The company's relative weakness, compared to Nokia and Motorola, is its brand name. Ericsson has strong production technology but needs to improve on its marketing side.

Companies like Ericsson and Nokia will benefit from the alliance between AT&T and British Telecom (BT), and that between Sprint, France Telecom, and Deutsche Telekom. Such big alliances help set standardized services to which mobile phone producers can respond efficiently. In the future, mobile phones will become even smaller, but the two producers from small countries, Nokia of Finland and Ericsson of Sweden, will become even bigger.

Websites: www.nokia.com; www.ericsson.com; www.motorola.com; www.nortelnetworks.com; www.alcatel.fr; www.att.com; www.compaq.com; www.hp.com; www.intel.com; www.ti.com.

Sources: Richard Hylton, Nick Moore and Roger Honour, "Making Money in the Tech Market," *Fortune*, May 13, 1996; Erick Schonfeld, "Hold the Phone: Motorola Is Going Nowhere Fast," *Fortune*, March 30, 1998; Caroline Daniel, "World's Most Respected Companies," *FT.com*, December 17, 2001; Nokia, *Annual Report*, 2009; Ericsson, *Annual Report*, 2009; Alan Cane, "Perspectives: Longevity Can Be a Tricky Stunt to Pull Off," *Financial Times*, March 16, 2011, "HTC Phone Sales Beat Expectations," *BBC News Online*, July 6, 2010; "HTC Profits Double as Smartphone Demands Grows," *BBC News Online*, June 6, 2011.

manufacturing and telecommunications in Toronto, forest products in western and eastern Canada, energy in Alberta, and the fisheries in Atlantic Canada. Some are led by flagship Canadian-owned multinationals such as Bombardier, Magna International, Research in Motion (RIM best known as the developer of the Blackberry smart phone); others are led by, or include, foreign-owned firms such as IBM Canada and DuPont Canada.[26]

Many Canadian clusters are resource based. The challenge for managers in these clusters is to continue to add value and eliminate the commodity nature of Canada's resource industries. One way to do this is to develop a global marketing strategy that builds on the Canadian–US double diamond instead of remaining as the extractor or harvester of resources. To implement such a global strategy requires a large investment in people who will bring strong marketing skills and develop a global intelligence network to identify the different tastes and preferences of customers. This network provides a role for smaller knowledge-intensive marketing research and consulting firms to participate in the resource-based cluster. There is also the potential for collaborative ventures.

The IMD World Competitiveness Scoreboard ranks Canada as one of the most competitive countries in the world. Yet, in contrast with the United States, Canada does not fare so well. According to the IMD, the United States is the world's most competitive nation.[27] A study of productivity (GDP per hours worked) by Statistics Canada shows Canada trailing the United States by about 6 percent. That is, for each hour of work, Canadians produce 94.2 percent, in dollar terms, of their US counterparts.[28]

Further research is required to investigate Canadian strategic clusters and their competitive advantages in comparison to rival clusters in North America and around the world. This will require two types of work. First, the intrafirm competition of clusters in North America needs new data that do not ignore the nature of foreign ownership and whether US and Canadian FDI by sector is inbound or outbound. Instead, direct investment in North America must be regarded as "domestic" and be contrasted with "external" direct investment from Japan[29] and the European Union.[30] Similarly, trade flows between Canada and the United States must be thought of as intrafirm when they occur between components of a cluster or even between and among clusters.

This approach is so radical that many existing concepts must be rethought. For example, the level and extent of subsidies available to clusters located in the United States (for example, in the Great Lakes region) must be related to those paid by provinces in Canada (such as Ontario). Yet there is little or no published work on state or provincial subsidies; even the work on federal subsidies in either country is extremely thin.

Finally, the real sources of Canadian competitive advantage are to be discovered not only by statistical analysis but also by interviews of managers and officials—that is, by fieldwork in the strategic clusters. Such "hands-on" research is exceptionally time consuming and expensive. However, to make the task feasible a number of important strategic clusters can be selected for analysis, self-audits can be made, conferences can be held, and so on. The future success of these efforts will depend heavily on leadership by Canadian business leaders and government officials.

Mexico and the double diamond

We can also adapt the Porter diamond model to analyze company strategies and international competitiveness in Mexico. The basic concepts in this framework are the same as those discussed in the Canadian diamond.

Linking to the US diamond

Mexico's linkage to the US diamond is somewhat different from Canada's. One reason is the fact that there are few home-based MNEs that have the capital to invest in the United

Table 10.1 FDI positions by Canada, the United States, and Mexico, 2000–2009

Year	Canada's FDI in:		US FDI in:		Mexico's FDI in:	
	US	Mexico	Canada	Mexico	US	Canada
2000	118,616.8	2,571.1	132,472.0	39,352.0	7,462	94.7
2001	118,347.2	2,066.4	152,601.0	39,352.0	7,336	104.8
2002	126,614.9	2,026.6	166,473.0	56,303.0	7,829	115.2
2003	131,474.8	2,366.3	187,953.0	56,851.0	9,022	165.6
2004	163,083.5	2,143.5	214,931.0	63,384.0	7,592	238.5
2005	183,543.7	2,698.0	231,836.0	73,687.0	3,595	276.2
2006	192,231.6	4,425.2	205,134.0	82,965.0	5,310	199.1
2007	229,180.2	4,908.4	250,642.0	91,046.0	7,688	265.2
2008	243,111.6	3,491.0	239,170.0	89,610.0	9,444	268.2
2009	249,714.3	4,635.5	259,792.0	97,897.0	11,361	256.1

Note: Data are in millions of US $.

Source: OECD, Foreign Direct Investment Statistics, FDI Positions by Partner Country, OECD.StatExtracts Online, http://
stats.oecd.org/ (for data of Canada's FDI in the United States and Mexico; the United States' FDI in Canada and Mexico);
US Department of Commerce, Survey of Current Business, Table "Historical-Cost Foreign Direct Investment Position in
the United States and Income Without Current-Cost Adjustment, by Country of Foreign-Parent-Group Member and of the
Ultimate Beneficial Owner, 2002–2009" (for Mexico's FDI in the United States); UNCTAD, country profile www.unctad.org;
Canada Department of Foreign Affairs and International Trade (DFAIT), "Foreign Direct Investment (Stocks) in Canada,
CANSIM Table 376-0051" (for Mexico's FDI in Canada), http://www.international.gc.ca/economist-economiste/statistics-
statistiques/investments-investissements.aspx?lang=eng; Bank of Canada, http://www.bank-banque-canada.ca/en/rates/
exchform.html.

States or Canada.[31] (Review Chapter 3 for information on how and why FDI is used by MNEs.) In fact, as seen in Table 10.1, during the period 2000–2009 Mexico's FDI in the United States increased by $3,899 million and $161.4 million in Canada. In contrast, by 2000 Canada had just $2,571.1 million invested in Mexico, whereas the United States had $39,352 million there. More important by 2009, US FDI in Canada reached $259,792 million, and Canada's FDI in the United States was also equivalently high at $249.714 million. Overall, in 10 years 2000–2009, Canada's FDI in the United States increased more than double (increase by 2.11 times) while the United States' FDI in Canada also went up 1.96 times. Thus, Mexico's strategy with its North American neighbors relies more heavily on trade than on FDI for outward market access, while using inward FDI to help promote internal development.

As seen in Figure 10.5, in 2008 US exports to Mexico were $151.53 billion and import from Mexico were $218.08 billion, while Mexico's exports to the United States were $233.52 billion and imports from the United States $151.33 billion. Canada's exports to Mexico were $5.49 billion and imports from Mexico $16.73 billion, while Mexico's exports to Canada were $7.10 and import from Canada of $9.44 billion. Mexico is the second-largest trading partner of the United States, and although it has a negative trade balance with the world, it runs a positive balance with the United States. In fact, in recent years the latter has accounted for 80.15 percent of Mexico's exports and 49.03 percent of its imports. So Mexico is closely linked with the US economy, and its economic growth will depend heavily on participation in this North American market.[32] Figure 10.6 illustrates this idea with the US–Mexican double diamond.

Mexico is linking itself to the US diamond in a number of ways. One is by serving as a customer for outside goods. For example, Caterpillar supplies heavy equipment for road building in Mexico; Coca-Cola holds about half of the market for soft drinks in Mexico; and US soybeans dominate the Mexican oilseed market.[33]

At the same time, Mexican businesses and foreign subsidiaries based in Mexico are working to expand their links to the US market. Between 1993 and 2002, exports to the US market increased from $46 billion to almost $106 billion. Much of this output is in the

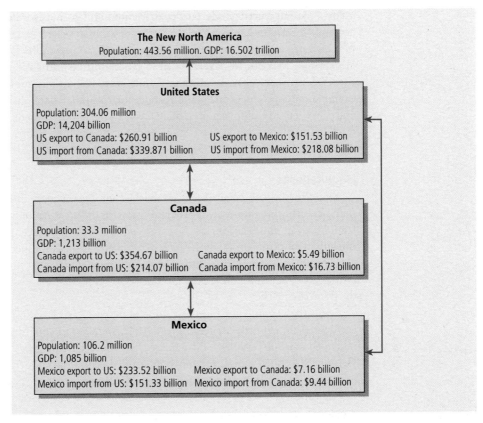

Figure 10.5 The shape of North America

Note: Population data, GDP and trade data are for 2008.

Sources: World Bank, 2010 http://data.worldbank.org/indicator; World Trade Organization, International Trade Statistics 2009, http://www.wto.org/english/res_e/statis_e/statis_e.htm; IMF, Direction of Trade Statistics Yearbook, 2009.

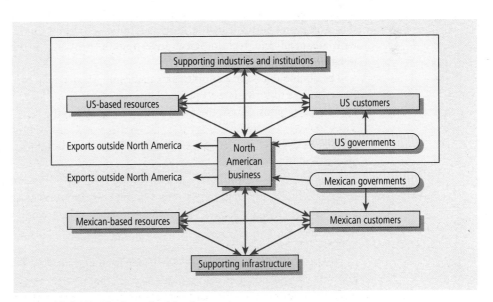

Figure 10.6 US–Mexican double diamond

Source: Richard M. Hodgetts, "Porter's Diamond Framework in a Mexican Context," *Management International Review*, vol. 33, Special Issue 2 (1993), p. 48.

form of manufactured goods, particularly automobiles. In fact, auto production in Mexico accounts for more than 450,000 workers and generates close to 1.5 million vehicles, most of which are targeted for the US market.[34] Ford, for example, is investing $1 billion in Hermosillo, Mexico, to develop a next generation of mid-sized vehicles.[35] At the same time, US firms are also investing in a wide array of non-automotive projects.[36] IBM, for example, now produces magnetic readers for computer hard-disk drives in Guadalajara and flies them to California on a daily basis. In the entertainment industry, Mexican productions have found an eager US audience with films like *Amores Perros* and *Y Tu Mamá También*.[37]

Maquiladoras

In 1965 the Mexican government established the *maquiladora* industry to attract foreign manufacturing operations. Imported products for the *maquiladoras'* production are exempt from Mexican duties as long as they are used for exports. In recent years certain items not directly involved in production, such as transportation equipment and computers, have also been made exempt from duties. Moreover, *maquiladoras* are no longer restricted to the border zone, and some have been permitted to settle inland and sell finished products on the domestic market.

Today the *maquiladora* industry is one of the country's largest sources of hard-currency earnings from exports, after oil. From 12 *maquiladora* plants in 1965, the number had increased to 2,900 by 2004.[38] Principally US owned, these businesses are widely considered to have established a basis for more intensified economic cooperation anticipated under an FTA.[39] At the same time, their growth is creating friction because many Americans feel that the low wage rates in Mexico are causing firms to transfer work there and lay off employees back home.

What will the future hold regarding Mexico and North America? The most likely developments will be continued investment by US and Canadian firms and the establishment of worldwide competition there. Mexico was manufacturing and shipping many more products back north as well as exporting to more countries than it did before NAFTA. Canada is still trying to create and nurture Canadian-owned MNEs that will compete worldwide. Mexico hopes to build these businesses internally with financial and technological investments, primarily from its North American neighbors.[40]

The double-diamond examples of Canada and Mexico help explain how MNEs can use Porter's ideas to formulate strategies. However, these firms also need to address the issue of national responsiveness, the focus of the discussion in the next section.

✔ Active learning check

Review your answer to Active Learning Case question 2 and make any changes you like. Then compare your answer to the one below.

2 **Why did ABB buy Zamech? How can the company link Zamech to its overall strategic plan?**

ABB bought Zamech for a number of reasons. Zamech provides a springboard to the East European market, which is likely to grow dramatically during the coming decade. ABB links Zamech to its overall strategic plan by using the same approach that US firms are employing with Mexico. ABB has purchased an equity position and is helping to set up a manufacturing operation that can provide goods for the local market as well as for other markets in both Eastern and Western Europe.

INTEGRATION AND RESPONSIVENESS

A major trend that has affected the thinking of corporate MNE strategists over the last decade or so is that of balancing a concern for economic integration with national responsiveness. Somewhat unfortunately, economic integration has been known as "globalization" in the literature in this field. **Globalization** can be defined as the production and distribution of products and services of a homogeneous type and quality on a worldwide basis.[41] To a large extent, MNEs have homogenized tastes and helped to spread international consumerism. For example, throughout North America, the wealthier nations of Europe, and Japan there has been a growing acceptance of standardized consumer electronic goods, automobiles, computers, calculators, and similar products. However, the goal of efficient economic performance through a universal globalization strategy has left MNEs open to the charge that they are overlooking the need to address national concerns.

National responsiveness is the ability of MNEs to understand different consumer tastes in segmented regional markets and to respond to the different national standards and regulations imposed by autonomous governments and agencies. Throughout the coming years, multinationals will continually have to deal with the twin goals of economic integration and national responsiveness.[42] See the case **International Business Strategy in Action: Kodak.**

Globalization
The production and distribution of products and services of a homogeneous type and quality on a worldwide basis

National responsiveness
The ability of MNEs to understand different consumer tastes in segmented regional markets and to respond to different national standards and regulations imposed by autonomous governments and agencies

Integration versus national responsiveness

To reconcile the twin issues of integration and national responsiveness, transnational MNEs can analyze them conceptually through the use of Figure 10.7, which has been adapted from Bartlett[43] and Bartlett and Ghoshal. The vertical axis measures the need for globalization, frequently called "economic integration." Movement up the axis results in a greater degree of economic integration, which generates economies of scale as a firm moves into worldwide markets, selling a single product or service. These economies are captured as a result of centralizing specific activities in the value-added chain. They also occur by reaping the benefits of increased coordination and control of geographically dispersed activities.

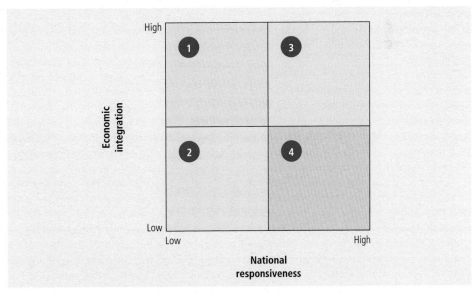

Figure 10.7 Integration and national responsiveness

Source: Reprinted by permission of Harvard Business School Press. Adapted from C. A. Bartlett, "Building and Managing the Transnational: the New Organizational Challenge," in *Competition in Global Industries*, edited by M. E. Porter, Boston, MA, 1986. Copyright © 1986 by the Harvard Business School Publishing Corporation; all rights reserved; and *Managing Across Borders: The Transnational Solution*, 2nd ed. by C. A. Bartlett and S. Ghoshal, Boston, MA, 1998. Copyright © 1998 by Harvard Business School Publishing Corporation; all rights reserved.

INTERNATIONAL BUSINESS STRATEGY IN ACTION

Kodak

"You press the button, and we do the rest," was Eastman Kodak's slogan when it introduced the Kodak Brownie in 1900. The user-friendly camera put photography within reach of the average person. Today, Kodak is recycling the slogan to promote its easy-to-use digital photography cameras. But this time, Kodak no longer has a sustainable technology-based firm-specific advantage in the market. Its old FSAs in development and film have been overtaken by the digital age. Its brand name, a surviving FSA, might just give it an edge against its competitors in the digital photography market. Indeed, Kodak filed for bankruptcy protection in January 2012.

Kodak pioneered digital cameras in 1976, but unlike Kodak's early innovations, which mostly went unchallenged, digital photography is turning out to be a battle ground for competitors, including electronics and computer manufacturers like HP and Sony that have access to digital technology. In addition a number of upstarts have jumped into the market, including Ezonics and Vivitar, with lower-quality bargain cameras.

Slowly, but surely, digital photography has become the most popular form of recording images. Consumer reaction to this new technology is yet to define the revenue generation model for producers. Traditionally, photographic companies derived revenues from selling cameras, but most importantly, from selling film and developing and printing photographs. Today, the digital camera user has a number of alternative printing methods, if he or she wants to print at all.

Consumers might choose to use one of two external printing options: take their memory card to an Internet kiosk to have prints developed, or send their picture files over the Internet to be printed and mailed back to them. Kodak's retail network might give it a competitive advantage if consumers can be convinced to drop by and use full-service or self-serve printing machines at their locations. If, however, consumers choose to do everything from home, sending photographs to a virtual kiosk that would then mail prints, upstarts might gain a hold in the better part of the market.

Kodak's brand name, however, is likely to provide a significant advantage even on the Internet. If customers want to develop photos, they might just try www.kodak. com. That is, if Windows will allow it. Kodak's collaboration with Microsoft became confrontational when Microsoft developed its own photo software that popped up automatically when a camera chip was connected. The Windows

Source: Getty Images/Ian Waldie

software directed users to photo developers who paid fees to Microsoft. For Kodak, the consequences could be devastating. The company needs to be able to enter the Web-based printing market to make up for losing profits in its traditional film business. To add insult to injury Microsoft teamed up with Kodak's archrival Fuji, listing it as one of the photo-developing service providers. Kodak complained to antitrust regulators.

Another consumer alternative is to print photographs at home using a regular color printer or a more specialized photograph printer available at many computer and office supplies stores. As similar things happen in the photographic industry, it would likely take revenues from traditional photographic companies to manufacturers of printer-friendly photographic paper, ink, cartridges, and toner. Will there be a spot left for Kodak to contribute in this market? The company certainly hopes so and has teamed up with computer companies such as HP and Lexmark to position itself should the market go this way. Yet, even this type of revenue generation is at risk since the European Commission began to investigate whether printer companies were illegally forcing consumers to purchase their ink, toners, and cartridges.

Perhaps the bleakest prediction for this industry is the near extinction of printing and developing revenue. Research shows that most people never print their digital photographs. Why would consumers print their photographs if they can store them in a computer, save them on disks, and share them with family and friends around the world at no cost or at a negligible cost? It is likely that only a select few photographs will ever make it to paper.

Other types of revenue generation include the manufacturing and selling of cameras, digital camera software and compatible computer software, and photographic printing machines. Kodak has entered all of these markets, but whether it can be successful in all of them for the long run is still being decided.

Outside the digital wars, Kodak is consistently challenged by competitors in many other of its business lines. In 1997, Kodak and Fuji participated in a price war on traditional film that threatened to make film into a commodity. In the mid-1990s, Kodak pushed forth a case in the WTO claiming Japan's trade regulations did not allow it to enter the Japanese market. This, it claimed, allowed Fuji to reduce profit margins in the US market, effectively dumping products. The WTO dismissed all charges.

Kodak's traditional competitive advantages are being challenged by innovations that have increased the number of competitors and changed the rules of the game. Its brand name in photography now competes with other well-known brand names in the electronics industry for a market and revenue stream that is yet to be defined.

Websites: www.kodak.com; www.fujifilm.com; www.microsoft.com; www.ezonics.com; www.vivitar.com.

Sources: Adapted from Alan M. Rugman, *The Regional Multinationals* (Cambridge: Cambridge University Press, 2005); www.kodak.com; Kodak, *Annual Report*, 2003; "Eastman Kodak files for bankruptcy protection," *BBC Business Online*, 19 January 2012, www.bbc.co.uk.

The horizontal axis measures the need for corporations to be nationally responsive. Companies must address local tastes and government regulations, which may result in a geographic dispersion of activities or a decentralization of coordination and control for individual firms.

On the basis of the two axes in Figure 10.7, four situations can be distinguished. Quadrants 1 and 4 are the simplest cases. In quadrant 1, the need for integration is high and the need for awareness of sovereignty is low. This focus on economies of scale leads to competitive strategies that are based on price competition. In such an environment, mergers and acquisitions often occur.

The opposite situation is represented by quadrant 4, where the need for national responsiveness is high but the integration concern is low. In this case companies adopt products to satisfy the high demands of sovereignty and to ignore economies of scale because integration is not very important.

Quadrants 2 and 3 also reflect opposing situations. Quadrant 2 incorporates those cases where the need for both integration and national responsiveness is low. Both the potential to obtain economies of scale and the benefits of being sensitive to sovereignty are of little value. Typical strategies in quadrant 2 are characterized by increased international standardization of products and services. This can lead to lower needs for centralized quality control and centralized strategic decision making, while simultaneously eliminating requirements to adapt activities to individual countries.

In quadrant 3 the needs for integration and national responsiveness are both high. There is a strong need for integration in production, along with higher requirements for regional adaptations in marketing. Quadrant 3 is the most challenging and the one in which many successful "transnational" MNEs operate. Using this framework, we can analyze the impact of various exogenous policy shocks and trends on different industries, firms, banks, and other private-sector institutions.

The Lexus and the Olive Tree

This economic integration and national responsiveness matrix can also be applied to analyze the influential book by Thomas Friedman on the Lexus and the Olive Tree.[44] Friedman uses the Lexus as a symbol for economic integration. In contrast, the Olive Tree is a symbol for the historical, political, religious, and social aspects which present obstacles to economic integration. Therefore, the logic of the Lexus view of globalization would fit on the vertical axis of Figure 10.7 whereas the Olive Tree would be assigned to the horizontal axis representing the need for national responsiveness. Friedman himself discusses the extreme cases of the Lexus in quadrant 1 and the Olive Tree in quadrant 4. However, based on our analysis of Figure 10.7 it is apparent that quadrant 3 represents another interesting case where both globalization and national responsiveness are equally important. The other point is that Figure 10.7 is a strategy diagram to be put into operation by managers of MNEs (or other firms). Therefore, it is the interpretation of the Lexus and the Olive Tree axes which is important for strategic management. A potential for strategy in quadrant 3 would require that an MNE is able to organize itself to cope with both axes.

In his later work Friedman argues that the Olive Tree is no longer relevant and that only globalization matters. In his book *The World is Flat*[45] Friedman shows that there are three types of globalization, the latest version of which is driven by the Internet and individual use of personal computers such that business can be done globally. Friedman calls this type of globalization 3.0. It has replaced globalization 2.0 which was led by MNEs and was organized at firm level rather than at individual level. In turn, this replaced globalization 1.0 which existed from 1492 to 1800 in which labor costs and natural resources were drivers of international trade and finance and the world was organized at country level.

Balancing the trade-offs

MNEs in every industry apply the ideas in Figure 10.7, but they do so in a variety of ways. The following are select examples from three different industries: entertainment, personal computers, and automobiles.

Entertainment

One of the most successful entertainment firms in the world is the Walt Disney Company. Its Disneyland Paris operation in France is a good example of how integration and national responsiveness are balanced. The park offers many of the same features (integration) found in Disney's Orlando (Florida), Anaheim (California), and Tokyo operations, including amusement rides and cartoon characters such as Mickey Mouse, Goofy, and Donald Duck. The company has recently expanded its European facilities along the lines of its MGM studios near Orlando.[46] Stressing uniformity among the geographically scattered parks, this integration focus is supplemented by national responsiveness that is designed to appeal to European visitors. English and French are the official languages of the park, and multilingual guides are conversant in Dutch, German, Spanish, and Italian. A second example of national responsiveness is found in the international emphasis the company has given its Disney characters: Pinocchio is Italian, Cinderella is French, Peter Pan is British. At its movie theater in the park, Disney shows a European history film offering (in the United States, the film is a travelogue of America).

Another example of integration/national responsiveness is offered by Sega Enterprises, best known for its Sonic the Hedgehog video game character. Using computer simulation technology like that used to train airline pilots, Sega is developing small theme parks that will provide the same thrills as a roller coaster or a trip through space. By building a series of different amusement simulators, Sega intends to offer a wide array of "rides" without having to bear the expense of physically building the facilities. The idea is captured in the term *virtual reality*, which means that participants experience the effects of a situation without literally being there.[47] "Scramble Training," a Sega simulator that is part video and part movie, provides an example. This interactive game allows eight players to enter a small space capsule and take their position as pilot trainees. The captain appears on a screen in front of the simulator and gives orders to the players, who in turn launch the capsule and swerve through space, firing missiles and competing for points. When the captain is wounded, the controls are turned over to the player with the best score, who then steers the capsule in for a landing. Sega intends to develop a host of different interactive simulators that will allow it to compete with amusement parks such as Disney. (In fact, Sega's concept is often referred to as "Disney in a Box.") The simulators are uniform in design and construction, allowing the company to employ an integration emphasis. However, the types of games will vary from country to country (national responsiveness), depending on the entertainment interests of the local populace. For example, Sega has found that Americans are very sports oriented, so there is likely to be an opportunity for players to participate in a World Series baseball simulation. In Europe, this game would have little attraction, but many players there would like to participate in the World Cup soccer finals, so the company can modify its product characteristics to meet the needs of the customer.[48]

Personal computers

Most personal computer (PC) makers compete on the bases of technology and price. They offer state-of-the-art machines and try to hold down their costs by outsourcing components and improving assembly efficiency. This strategy is particularly important in markets such as Japan, where less than 25 percent of the population in the early 1990s owned PCs, and where local demands, such as the need to write in *kanji*, had discouraged foreign competition.

In 2001, however, US firms have been making major headway in this market, thanks to their ability to exploit both integration and national responsiveness.[49] For example, Compaq and Dell have entered this market with low-priced units that were the same as those sold elsewhere (integration) but offered sharply lower prices (national responsiveness). As a result, both firms have been able to garner market share. IBM has employed a similar strategy in addition to addressing the desire of local customers to write in *kanji*. The company has now perfected a bilingual version of Microsoft's DOS, the standard operating system that controls approximately 80 percent of the world's PCs. This version allows these machines to prepare or search documents with Japanese characters, the Western alphabet, or both. Apple is also having very good success in Japan, thanks to its willingness to adapt to local needs. For example, the company has a Japanese management team that has helped to surmount local barriers to "buying foreign." It has also cultivated a strong network of dealers and worked to develop an image as an innovator, both of which are critical in the Japanese market. As a result of this careful balance of integration and national responsiveness, Apple and IBM alone account for almost 16 percent of the Japanese PC market in 2001. With the merger of HP and Compaq, and IBM divestment by selling its PC business to Lenovo (China) in 2004, HP and Dell are active in the Japanese PC market. According to Mintel Market Navigator, HP is the fourth largest laptop PC provider in Japan with a market share of 7.3 percent whereas Dell had a modest market share of 2.7 percent by the middle of 2011.[50]

Other US firms are also using a carefully formulated integration/national responsiveness strategy to gain market share. Microsoft has written a special version of Windows—one of the most popular PC software programs of all time—for the Japanese market. Until 1993, only 440,000 copies of the program had been sold, but when the company unveiled its newer version, more than 65,000 copies were snatched up in two days.[51]

Automobiles

Every car manufacturer uses economic integration by producing autos that can be made and marketed around the world. In a few cases, the Volkswagen Beetle being the best example, a car will not need to be modified for the local market.[52] Usually, however, an integration strategy is complemented by national responsiveness in the form of design, engineering, and manufacturing changes. Ford's Mondeo provides a good example. Developed for the world market, this car has uniform worldwide engineering standards with almost every specification expressed in the metric system. The company also has created uniform stand-ards for raw materials, design, procurement, and manufacture of individual parts. Identical production tools are used at both European and US locations so that economies of scale can be maximized. At the same time, Ford has taken national responsiveness into consideration. European buyers prefer manual transmissions, whereas US buyers like automatic drive. Europeans demand cars that handle well, but this is not a priority issue with American customers. On the other hand, Americans want air-conditioned cars, and many Europeans do not. The overall cost of developing the Mondeo was $6 billion. However, initial sales in Europe were brisk and Ford believed it could maintain this momentum in the US market. It also believed it could create additional car models from the Mondeo program and thus develop a series of new offerings. If this is true, the integration and national responsiveness strategies used for the Mondeo will help smooth the way for future auto sales and help the company to recoup this enormous investment.[53]

Honda offers another example of integration and national responsiveness strategies. The firm now builds a variety of different car sizes from one production platform by bend-ing and stretching the autos to fit the demands of the market. As a result, Honda is able to build cars in the United States that are longer and roomier, while offering smaller, more compact models of the same car in Japan. The company is now using this same approach to build sports utility vehicles for the world market.[54]

General Motors offers yet another example of integration and national responsiveness strategies. Like Ford, GM often develops cars for the European market, then introduces them into the United States. As a result, the cars are frequently identical in styling and design but have different features to accommodate local tastes. The Celta, a subcom-pact offering in Brazil, has fewer features and 50 percent fewer parts than competitive models. In collaboration with its suppliers, GM created a modular assembly plant with just-in-time supplier delivery. Efficiency costs of such an integration strategy allowed for an inexpensive subcompact for developing markets, where price and reliability are most important.[55] When the auto is made in another developing market, it will be possible to build and assemble each unit quickly because the process will have been perfected in Brazil. This integration focus is complemented by national responsiveness. In Brazil, marketing of the Celta stresses security locks and anti-theft devices, whereas in safer developing countries, the car's suspension system and handling on tough roads will receive more emphasis.

Competitiveness in the triad

From the viewpoint of MNEs, one of the most important business decisions regards the trade-off between integration and national responsiveness. Successful MNEs know they can no longer afford to ignore the latter and concentrate solely on globalization through economic integration.

In the United States

The United States experiences considerable decentralization in economic decision mak-ing. It is a country in which subnational units continue to increase in importance. This issue should not be confused with pluralism. A variety of political opinions and parties is a strength of democracy. The problem arises when the institutional structure of the nation and its businesses cannot operate in an efficient manner, relative to global competitors.

The US Constitution was designed to allow Congress to be a broker for regional and special interests. On occasion, Congress works with the Executive branch to formulate and implement a coordinated economic policy and even a social policy. Examples of social reform and government economic activity in the Kennedy–Johnson years can be contrasted with a return to more market-based principles and a somewhat reduced role for government in the Reagan years.

However, in many areas affecting the private sector today, the overwhelming characteristic of doing business in the United States is the responsiveness of governments to special interest groups and lobbies. The more decentralized the level of government, the more responsive will be the regulatory activity to the lobbyist. On occasion businesses themselves can be lobbyists, but there are many other groups, such as environmentalists and social activists, who seem to be growing in power. Examples of conflicts in business lobbying occur in the areas of administration of US trade remedy laws and in the current US debate about the possible regulation of inward foreign direct investment (FDI).

Rugman and Anderson,[56] as well as others, have demonstrated that the current administration of US countervailing duty (CVD) and antidumping (AD) laws is highly responsive to domestic producer interests and biased against foreign firms. US corporations use CVD and AD as a competitive strategy to erect entry barriers against rival firms.[57] Between 1980 and 2003, US businesses filed 1,510 AD and CVD cases against foreign competitors with the US International Trade Commission; 37 percent of these cases, or 559, were found to be justified after the commission investigated the complaints. Table 10.2 lists a number of selected products that were slapped with import tariffs.

Approximately 5 percent of all cases between 1980 and 2003 went against Canada.[58] Thus, even when the US government was pursuing negotiations for free trade with Canada, individual US corporations were still using the CVD and AD laws to help restrict Canadian imports. This is a clear example of US national interests being offset by selective producer interests. There were more than 22 CVD and AD cases against Canada in the 1990s.[59] More of the same is in store in the future, although Canadian concerns about the administration of CVD and AD laws have been somewhat answered by the establishment of binational panels under the terms of the FTA and then NAFTA.

Another area of concern is inward FDI, which some congressional leaders now wish to restrict, and some Americans seem concerned with the growing amount of Japanese FDI. Some members of Congress have urged more screening of such FDI, and there is a strong "Japan-bashing" stance in US trade policy. Yet at the same time, state officials have been actively seeking Japanese FDI because they want the jobs and the tax base. This potential clash between Washington "beltway" thinking (anti-Japanese) and state-level activity (pro-Japanese) parallels Canada's experience with the regulation of FDI.

The United States seems destined in the next 10 years to repeat many of the mistakes made in Canada over the last 30 years. In 1974 the Trudeau government introduced the Foreign Investment Review Agency (FIRA), which was designed to screen FDI on economic criteria to assess whether there was a net benefit to Canada. Between 1974 and 1985,

Table 10.2 AD and CVD orders by product category, as of July 20, 2007

Product category	No. of orders
Iron and steel products	134
Chemicals and pharmaceuticals	42
Miscellaneous manufactured products	32
Agricultural, forest, and processed food products	29
Minerals and metals	25
Plastics, rubber, stone, and glass products	4
Electronics and communication products	1
Machinery and electronic/scientific equipment	1
Transpiration products	1
Textiles and apparel	1

Source: Authors' calculations based on USITC data from www.usitc.gov.

FIRA responded to Ottawa's political winds, at times rejecting as much as 30 percent of applications but at other times (especially 1982 to 1985) approving virtually everything.[60] The administrators at FIRA and the responsible ministers made political decisions just as the US International Trade Commission and the US Commerce Department do today in US trade law cases.

In 1985, FIRA was abolished and a new agency, Investment Canada, was created with the mandate to attract FDI rather than scare it away.[61] This change in thinking about FDI came with a change in government, after the Progressive Conservatives were elected in 1984 with a mandate of job creation. Throughout the lifetime of FIRA, most provinces, especially those in Atlantic Canada, wanted FDI for jobs and taxes. The clash between the provinces that favored FDI and the central Canadian economic nationalists led to the federal government giving up many of its powers to regulate FDI by buying into the agenda of the provinces, especially their overwhelming priority about jobs. Perhaps this is some evidence of the triumph of decentralized economic power. But a paradox emerges. In Canada, the economic nationalists who have used central government power are in retreat, whereas it appears that in the United States economic nationalism is just beginning to take off. If Japan bashing continues, then the US proponents of restrictions on FDI will have the same unhappy experience with FIRA as did Canada. Private-sector US corporate strategists will, therefore, need to respond to a large dose of economic nationalism and its associated protectionist inefficiencies.

In Eastern Europe

Another example of the use of sovereignty and the destruction of centralized economic power and values was the 1989 revolution in Central Europe and the collapse of the Soviet Union in 1991. The rejection of totalitarian communist regimes by the people of countries such as Romania, Belarus, and Russia has many implications for business. The key point is that these countries are very poor, with inefficient economic and financial systems. Their economic development will probably be through FDI rather than through joint ventures. Popular wisdom to the contrary, joint ventures between poor nations and wealthy corporations rarely work. The preferable mode of international business is FDI because Western firms can then control their proprietary advantages and not risk dissipation through joint ventures.[62] Studies on joint ventures in developing countries have found a great deal of instability and failure.[63] Multinationals prefer FDI and countries such as India and Mexico, which once greatly restricted FDI, experienced inefficient economic development and eventually had to lift such regulations. This experience is relevant for Eastern Europe.

Doing business in Eastern Europe for the next 5–10 years will be dominated by the need for economic efficiency. The globalization concept will overwhelm concerns about adapting products for sovereignty. It is in the EU nations that national responsiveness will be important for corporations. In the wealthy triad powers, adapting to sovereignty matters; in the developing world and in Eastern Europe, economic efficiency is what matters.

In Japan

A key explanation for the success of Japanese MNEs is that they benefit from a highly centralized home-market economy. This has permitted Japan to use levers of industrial and strategic trade policies that could not be implemented successfully in the other areas of the triad.

Centralized government policy is critical to implementing effective corporate strategy.[64] The Japanese cultural, religious, social, and political system is much more centralized in nature than other triad blocs, enabling the country's MNEs to follow globalization strategies. Thus, for example, after the two OPEC oil crises of the 1970s, Japanese industry was rapidly transformed out of shipbuilding, heavy engineering, and other energy-intensive manufacturing and into computer-based manufacturing, consumer electronics, and high value-added services, including banking and finance. The government and the MNEs worked together to implement a new industrial strategy in an effective and efficient manner.

Such radical restructuring through industrial policy is unlikely to work in North America and Europe because of the decentralized nature of economic power. Attempts by the United States or Canada to implement a new industrial policy are likely to fail. Whatever government incentives and subsidies are made available will be appropriated by industries seeking shelter from competitors in the triad. To erect entry barriers against foreign competitors, companies will use the decentralized nature of the economic system. This has already occurred in the United States, with companies seeking protection from competitors through the use of CVD and AD laws. US steel, forest products, fish, and semiconductor industries, among others, have been using short-term legal remedies instead of investing in the development of sustainable, proprietary, firm-specific advantages.

What are the implications for corporate strategy of these asymmetrical developments in the triad? Japanese MNEs will continue to pursue an integration/globalization strategy, but they may face difficulties when they need to operate in the decentralized environments of North America and Europe, since marketing-type skills will become more important than production skills. Over the last decade, MNEs from Europe and North America have often abused the nature of their home-country decentralized systems, and sovereignty has hindered efficient corporate development. However, MNEs from North America and Europe have a potential competitive advantage over Japanese MNEs if they can learn from their past mistakes. Awareness of sovereignty can make the former companies better equipped in the future to be more nationally responsive than their Japanese counterparts. Indeed, Japanese MNEs may become locked into a "globalization-only" strategy, just as the world begins to demand much more corporate responsiveness to sovereignty.

✔ Active learning check

Review your answer to Active Learning Case question 3 and make any changes you like. Then compare your answer to the one below.

3 **How does ABB address the issues of globalization and national responsiveness? In each case, cite an example.**

ABB addresses the issue of globalization by producing state-of-the-art products for worldwide markets. It may be necessary to make modifications to address local geographic and climatic conditions, of course, but the basic technology and manufacturing techniques are similar. At the same time, ABB addresses national responsiveness by trying to be a local firm that is interested in the needs of that market. As a result, the company balances globalization and sovereignty—a feat that most MNEs do not accomplish very well.

KEY POINTS

1 Porter's single-diamond model is based on four country-specific determinants and two external variables (chance and government). This model is extremely useful in examining strategies among triad and other economically developed countries. However, when applying the model to smaller, open, trading economies, a modification is in order.

2 Canada's economic success will depend on its ability to view itself as part of the North American market and to integrate itself into this overall market. This requires the use of a "double-diamond" model for corporate strategy, resulting in Canadian firms developing competitive capabilities that allow them to compete successfully with US firms in the United States. This is being done by (a) developing innovative products and services that simultaneously meet the needs of the US and Canadian customer, (b) drawing on the support industries and infrastructure of both the US and Canadian diamonds, and (c) making free and full use of the physical and human resources in both countries.

3 Mexico's economic success also depends on its ability to integrate itself into the North American market. However, this strategy is different from that of the Canadians because Mexico does not have the FDI to invest in the US market. Much of its linkage is a result of low labor costs that allow the country to produce inexpensive goods and export them into the United States. The North American Free Trade Agreement worked out with the United States and Canada in 1993 will determine part of Mexico's future economic success.

4 A major trend that has affected the thinking of corporate MNE strategists over the past 10 years is balancing a concern for economic integration and globalization with that of national responsiveness. Many MNEs have focused on integration without giving sufficient attention to the sovereignty issue. However, there will have to be a reversal of this trend and MNEs will have to become much more interested in national responsiveness if they hope to succeed in overseas markets.

Key terms

● strategic cluster   ● globalization   ● national responsiveness

REVIEW AND DISCUSSION QUESTIONS

1 Porter's Diamond is based on four country-specific determinants and two external variables. What does this statement mean? Put it in your own words.

2 Porter notes, "Firms, not individual nations, compete in international markets." How does this statement help explain some of the major challenges facing MNEs?

3 Using Figure 10.2 as your point of reference, how does the current national development of the United States differ from that of Korea? How does the UK's differ from that of Singapore?

4 Why does Porter's Diamond need to be modified in explaining the international competitiveness of countries such as Canada and Mexico?

5 How does the double diamond, as illustrated in Figure 10.4, help explain international competitiveness in Canada?

6 How can Canadian firms view the United States and Canada as home-based markets and integrate the use of both diamonds for developing and implementing strategy? Be complete in your answer.

7 Of what value are strategic clusters in the double diamond? Explain.

8 How does the double diamond in Figure 10.6 help explain Mexico's international business strategy?

9 How important are the *maquiladoras* to the growth of the Mexican economy? In what way do these businesses link Mexico with the Canadian–US double diamond?

10 In what way are economic integration/globalization and national responsiveness important to MNE strategies?

11 In the entertainment industry, which is more important, integration or national responsiveness?

12 Based on current developments in the PC market in Japan, which is more important for US MNEs, integration or national responsiveness? Why?

13 Which is more important for US auto makers doing business in Europe, integration or national responsiveness? Why?

REAL CASE

There is no global beer, only local

Beer is a good example of an industry that is local, not global. Indeed, beer is stubbornly local. Because beer is bulky and too expensive to export, it is brewed domestically; foreign producers will license their brand name products to local producers to gain a local market presence. In addition, imports of alcoholic beverages are traditionally heavily taxed. Rival domestic producers usually tie up local distribution channels. Governments also protect domestic breweries, such as in Germany, where the Reinheitsgebot purity rules have protected indigenous beer for over 400 years.

In Canada, domestic brewers were exempted from the national treatment provision of the United States–Canada Free Trade Agreement of 1989 (and later from NAFTA in 1993). The reason is that, initially, each Canadian company needed to have a brewery in each province, resulting in rather small and inefficient breweries in the low-population Atlantic provinces. In light of such inefficiency and import protection, Labatt was taken over by the Belgian brewery, InBev, Molson has merged with Coors.

The local, fragmented nature of the brewing industry can be offset by acquisitions. The half-dozen leading world brewers are constantly attempting to increase their market share in both developed and developing countries. Belgium's InBev has made huge gains in the world market, buying up such companies as Bass Brewers of the UK, Becks of Germany, Labatt in Canada, Anheuser-Busch in the United States, and others. South African Breweries (SAB) merged with Miller. The new company, SABMiller, is now the world's number two brewer. Table 1 lists the world's largest brewers.

There are a few premium "designer" beers (high-end beers that have been developed into global brands), but they are usually produced under license. This has led to cross-licensing and distribution arrangements as well as to mergers and acquisitions. Today there is some consolidation in this segment to a few large brewers such as Heineken, InBev. But the premium lager segment is

a minority of the total world beer market, which still has mainly local beer.

Anheuser-Busch (in St. Louis, the United States) used to be the world's largest beer company and sold 90 percent of its Budweiser brand in the United States, a local beer. On July 13, 2008, Belgian brewing company InBev completed the acquisition of Anheuser-Busch for US $52 billion dollar in equity, creating the world's largest beer company, Anheuser-Busch InBev. It has a portfolio of well over 200 beer brands. These include global flagship brands Budweiser, Stella Artois and Beck's; multi-country brands, such as Leffe and Hoegaarden; and many local champions, such as Bud Light, Skol, Brahma, Quilmes, Michelob, Harbin, Sedrin, Klinskoye, Sibirskaya Korona, Chernigivske and Jupiler. In 2009, its total sales were US $36.758 billion, of which 45.79 percent was generated in North America, 22.61 percent in Latin America—North, 5.61 percent in Latin America—South, 12.75 percent in Western Europe, 7.37 percent in Central and Eastern Europe, and 5.87 percent in Asia–Pacific. The Belgian brewery has aggressively gone the farthest in expanding from its EU base into North America since the 1990s. It purchased Canada's largest brewer, Labatt, in 1993. The Company also produces and distributes soft drinks, particularly in Latin America.

In 2009, the Dutch brewery company Heineken generates a revenue of US $20.490, of which 52.89 percent of its sales is within Western Europe, another 21.65 percent from Central and Eastern Europe, only 10.48 percent from the Americas, 12.29 percent from the Middle East and Africa, and the remainder, 2.69 percent, from Asia–Pacific.

According to the UK-based researcher Plato Logic World Beer Report 2009, the world's four biggest brewers Anheuser-Busch InBev, London listed SABMiller, Heineken, and Denmark's Carlsberg accounted for over half of the world beer market. In fifth place was China's Tsing Tao Brewery, in sixth place was the North America Molson-Coors Brewing Co., while Mexico's Grupo Modelo, China's

▶

Table 1 Largest worldwide brewers

Name	Country	Volume (million hectoliters)
Anheuser-Busch InBev	Belgium	350
SABMiller	UK	< 250
Heineken	Netherlands	> 200
Carlsberg	Denmark	125
Tsingtao	China	> 50
Molson Coors	Canada/US	50
Modelo	Mexico	50
Yanjing	China	< 50
Kirin	Japan	< 50
Asahi	Japan	< 50
Total (of above)		< 50

Source: "Top Four Brewers Make Up Half of the World Beer Market," *Reuters News*, February 8, 2010; "Top World Brewer and Brand Sales – 2009," *Plato Logic Limited*, 2010.

Beijing Yanjing Brewery Co. Ltd., and Japanese brewers Kirin Holding Company Limited and Asahi Breweries Limited made up the rest of the top 10. These are "global" companies with local beer.

Websites: www.molsoncoors.com; www.heineken.com; www.ab-inbev.com; www.sabmiller.com; www.carlsberg.com; www.asahi.com; www.kirin.com.

Sources: *Reuters News*, February 8, 2010; Anheuser-Busch InBev, *Annual report*, 2008, 2009; Heineken, *Annual reportt*, 2009; "Top World Brewer and Brand Sales – 2009," *Plato Logic Limited*, 2010; "Top Four Brewers Make Up Half of the World Beer Market," *Reuters News*, February 8, 2010; Thomson Reuters, *Onesource*, 2011.

1 Is the production and distribution of beer nationally responsive?

2 If beer is mainly local, why are there mergers and acquisitions of beer companies?

3 In the integration/responsiveness matrix, where would you position the world's largest brand-name beer companies and why?

REAL CASE

IBM

In 1911, four recording and processing equipment manufacturers in the United States merged to form the Computer-Tabulating-Recording Company (C-T-R). The new company merged its Canadian operations in 1917 under the name of International Business Machines Company. This name was adopted by all the company's operations in 1924; today, most people simply recognize it as IBM.

A pioneer of the personal computer (PC), IBM is also well known for leading the way to globalization. However, the computer industry is at a mature stage of manufacturing. Eventually in 2004, IBM got out of personal computers altogether, selling the business to China's Lenovo as PC becomes commoditized.

Today, its operations span more than 200 countries with a total 309,499 employees worldwide and its research laboratories are located in nine countries across the triad. Indeed, according to Rugman 2005, IBM is the largest of only nine "global" companies in the *Fortune* 500. In 2009, IBM's revenue was US $95.758 billion and it derived 42.04 percent of all its revenue from the Americas, compared to 31.93 percent from Europe, the Middle East, and Africa and 23.22 percent from Asia–Pacific. The remaining 2.80 percent of its revenue comes from its uncategorized global operations.

Source: Getty Images/AFP/Jung Yeon-Je

Production is also spread around the world. Product lines are clustered in regions that offer plentiful labor or specialized technology, depending on the nature of the product. ThinkPads used to be manufactured in Shenzhen, China, desktops in Guadalajara, Mexico. This reliance on developing countries allows IBM to take advantage of low labor costs while placing it inside some of the fastest-growing markets in the world.

IBM was an international company at its conception. C-T-R had brought together the international operations of all its predecessors. In the decades following its establishment, the company aggressively pursued expansion across the world. In Latin America, an office opened in Brazil in 1917. Within the next 20 years, IBM secured contracts with governments and corporations in Argentina, Mexico, Ecuador, Chile, Cuba, Uruguay, and Peru. In Asia, the company opened its first office in Bombay, India, in 1920. The Philippine market was entered in 1925, followed the next year by the first IBM equipment being installed in Osaka, Japan, for the Nippon Mutual Life Insurance Company. In China, the first IBM machines were installed at the Peking Union Medical College in 1934.

IBM's entry into the European market started when a branch of the International Time Recording Company, an IBM forerunner, opened in France in 1914. It was only in 1919 that a consolidated IBM was introduced in Europe. In the 1920s and 1930s, IBM manufacturing facilities sprang up in Germany, France, England, and Italy.

Although IBM's organizational segments are product based, a company sales and distribution segment has a geographic focus as well as a specialized and global industry focus. Small and medium business contracts are dealt with through a global sales and distribution segment. Its foreign subsidiaries share technology, logistics, business principles, and a common source of manufacturing, but have the power to implement local strategies. In other words, they can choose their product lines and marketing strategy to respond to the needs of the local environment, including regulations, customer tastes, income levels, and the competitive environment.

In terms of production, IBM's highest commitment to globalizing production is its growing reliance on electronic manufacturing service providers. More than two-thirds of the company's Intel-based products are manufactured in worldwide factories by contract manufacturers, including Sanmina-SCI and Solectron. (See the Flextronics Case Study, Chapter 12.)

IBM is one of only a few companies that have successfully penetrated foreign regional markets in terms of revenues and production. A main reason is that the computer, office, and electronics industry in which IBM operates is one of the most global, with average intra-regional sales of 56.2 percent. Electronics are easy to transport and are standardized across all world regions. Seven of the nine global firms are from this industry. This extra-regionality is the result of standardized components that can be transported cheaply across the world, allowing for a global supply chain.

In terms of assets, however, IBM is highly intra-regional; 62.9 percent are in the United States. There are a number of reasons for this: (1) foreign production facilities are often owned by contract manufacturers; (2) the cost of land and equipment is higher in the United States than in many of the developing countries in which the company manufactures; and (3) the United States remains the most important market for IBM. Indeed, although IBM has over 20 percent of its sales in each triad market, the Americas continue to account for the largest portion. It is difficult to argue that this is merely the result of a home-region advantage. The United States is, after all, the largest triad economy and the largest market for technology products.

Sources: www.ibm.com; IBM, *Annual Report*, 2009; Alan M. Rugman, *The Regional Multinationals* (Cambridge: Cambridge University Press, 2005); "IBM Outsourcing to Solectron, Sanmina-SCI," *Internet News*, January 7, 2003; "Fortune Global 500," *Fortunes*, 2010.

1 Is IBM a multinational enterprise? Is it global?

2 How does contract manufacturing fit into IBM's strategy?

3 Using the integration and national responsive matrix, in what quadrant does IBM's strategy fall?

ENDNOTES

1 For a detailed discussion of these variables and determinants, see Michael E. Porter, *The Competitive Advantage of Nations* (New York: Free Press, 1990), pp. 69–130.

2 Alan M. Rugman and Alain Verbeke, *Global Corporate Strategy and Trade Policy* (London and New York: Routledge, 1990).

3 Michael E. Porter, *The Competitive Advantage of Nations* (New York: Free Press, 1990), p. 33.

4 Ibid., p. 671.

5 A. E. Safarian, *Foreign Ownership of Canadian Industry* (Toronto: McGraw-Hill, 1968).

6 Alan M. Rugman, *Multinationals in Canada: Theory, Performance and Economic Impact* (Boston, MA: Martinus Nijhoff, 1980).

7 Harold Crookell, *Canadian–American Trade and Investment Under the Free Trade Agreement* (Westport, CT: Quorum Books, 1990).

8 Alan M. Rugman, *Multinationals and Canada–United States Free Trade* (Columbia, SC: University of South Carolina Press, 1990).

9 See Alan M. Rugman, "Strategies for National Competitiveness," *Long Range Planning*, vol. 20, no. 3 (1987), pp. 92–97.

10 Alan M. Rugman and John McIlveen, *Megafirms: Strategies for Canada's Multinationals* (Toronto: Methuen/Nelson, 1985).

11 Ibid.

12 John H. Dunning, "Dunning on Porter." Paper presented at the Annual Meeting of the Academy of International Business, Toronto, October 1990, and published in John H. Dunning, *The Globalization of Business* (London and New York: Routledge, 1993); and John H. Dunning, "Internationalizing Porter's Diamond," *Management International Review*, vol. 33, Special Issue 2 (1993), pp. 7–16.

13 Ibid., 1990, p. 11.

14 United Nations, *World Investment Report* (New York: United Nations, 2000); and see also Nestle, *Annual Reports*, 2006–2010.

15 Alan M. Rugman and Joseph R. D'Cruz, *Fast Forward: Improving Canada's International Competitiveness* (Toronto: Kodak Canada, 1991); and Alan M. Rugman and Joseph R. D'Cruz, "The 'Double Diamond' Model of International Competitiveness: The Canadian Experience," *Management International Review*, vol. 33, Special Issue 2 (1993), pp. 17–40.

16 For another view of the FTA, see John N. Turner, "There Is More to Trade Than Trade: An Analysis of the US/Canada Trade Agreement 1988," *California Management Review*, Winter 1991, pp. 109–119.

17 Alan M. Rugman, "The Free Trade Agreement and the Global Economy," *Business Quarterly*, Summer 1988, pp. 13–20.

18 Alan M. Rugman and Alain Verbeke, "Strategic Responses to Free Trade," *Hitotsubashi Journal of Commerce and Management*, December 1988, pp. 69–79; and Alan M. Rugman and Alain Verbeke, "Foreign Subsidiaries and Multinational Strategic Management: An Extension and Correction of Porter's Single Diamond Framework," *Management International Review*, vol. 33, Special Issue 2 (1993), pp. 71–84.

19 See, for example, Joseph R. D'Cruz and James Fleck, *Yankee Canadians in the Global Economy* (London, Ontario: National Centre for Management Research and Development, 1987); and Alan M. Rugman and Joseph D'Cruz, *New Visions for Canadian Business: Strategies for Competing in the Global Economy* (Toronto: Kodak Canada, 1990).

20 See Doug Struck, "Canada Looks for Spot in the Big Picture," *Washington Post*, December 29, 2004.

21 www.magna.com; Magna, *Annual report*, 2009; Global Fortune 500, *Forbes*, 2010.

22 www.bombardier.com; Bombardier, *Annual report, 2010*; Global Fortune 500, *Forbes*, 2010.

23 Doug Struck, "Canada Looks for Spot in the Big Picture," *Washington Post*, December 29, 2004.

24 Also, see Alan M. Rugman and Alain Verbeke, "Multinational Corporate Strategy and the Canada–US Free Trade Agreement," *Management International Review*, vol. 30, no. 3 (Third Quarter 1990), pp. 253–266; and Alan M. Rugman and Alain Verbeke, "How to Operationalize Porter's Diamond of International Competitiveness," *International Executive*, vol. 35, no. 4 (July/August 1993), pp. 283–299.

25 For more details of this business network approach, see Joseph R. D'Cruz and Alan M. Rugman, *New Compacts of Canadian Competitiveness* (Toronto: Kodak Canada, 1992); Joseph R. D'Cruz and Alan M. Rugman, "Business Networks for International Competitiveness," *Business Quarterly*, vol. 56, no. 4 (Spring 1992), pp. 101–107; and Joseph R. D'Cruz and Alan M. Rugman, "Developing International Competitiveness: The Five Partners Model," *Business Quarterly*, vol. 58, no. 2 (Winter 1993), pp. 60–72.

26 D'Cruz and Rugman, *New Compacts of Canadian Competitiveness*, op. cit. pp. 29–36; and see also The Forbes, *The Global Fortune 500*, 2009–2011 issues, http://money.cnn.com/magazines/fortune/fortune500/

27 IMD, *World Competitiveness Yearbook*, 2009.

28 John R. Baldwin, Jean-Pierre Maynard and Fanny Wong, "The Output Gap Between Canada and the United States: The Role of Productivity (1994–2002)," *Statistics Canada Analytical Papers*, January 2005.

29 Alan M. Rugman, *Japanese Direct Investment in Canada* (Ottawa: Canada–Japan Trade Council, 1990).

30 See Alan M. Rugman and F. Bill Mohri, "Trade and Investment Among Canada and the Triad," Working paper, University of Toronto, July 1991; and Alan M. Rugman (ed.), *Foreign Investment and NAFTA* (Columbia, SC: University of South Carolina Press, 1994).

31 Alan M. Rugman and Alain Verbeke, "Foreign Direct Investment in North America: Current Patterns and Future Relationships in Canada, the United States, and Mexico," Ontario Centre for International Business, Research program working paper, no. 57, November 1991, p. 4, published in Khosrow Fatemi and Dominick Salvatore (eds.), *North American Free Trade Agreement* (London: Pergamon Press, 1994).

32 IMF, *Direction of Trade Statistics Yearbook*, 2000 and 2009.

33 Ben Juarez and Gabriel Hernandez, "Mexico's Market a Winning Bet for U.S. Soybeans," *FAS Online*, December 2000.

34 "Why Mexico Scares the UAW," *Business Week*, August 3, 1998, p. 37; and "U.S. Slowdown Adds to Mexican Auto Industry's Woes," *Forbes.com*, April 19, 2001 and www.amia.com.mx.

35 Jamie Butters, "Mexico Wins Production of Ford Futura," *Detroit Free Press*, October 7, 2003.

36 Joel Millman, "High-Tech Jobs Transfer to Mexico with Surprising Speed," *Wall Street Journal*, April 9, 1999, p. A18.

37 "The Mexicans Are Coming!" *The Economist*, October 3, 2002.

38 Rugman and Verbeke, "Foreign Direct Investment in North America," op. cit., p. 12; and Geri Smith, "Made in the Maquilas Again," *Business Week*, August 16, 2004.

39 United States International Trade Commission, *The Likely Impact on the United States of a Free Trade Agreement with Mexico*, USITC Publication 2353, February 1991, pp. 1–5.

40 Also, see *Lloyd Economic Report* (Guadalajara, Mexico), March 1994.

41 For a discussion of various definitions of globalization, see Chapter 1 of Alan M. Rugman, *The End of Globalization* (London: Random House, 2000 and New York: McGraw Hill/Amacom, 2001).

42 See Alan M. Rugman and Karl Moore, "How Global Is Globalisation?" *FT Mastering Management Online*, November 2001.

43 Christopher A. Bartlett, "Building and Managing the Transnational: The New Organizational Challenge," in M. E. Porter (ed.), *Competition in Global Industries* (Boston, MA: Harvard Business School Press, 1986), pp. 367–401; and Christopher A. Bartlett and Sumantra Ghoshal, *Managing Across Borders: The Transnational Solution* (Boston, MA: Harvard Business School Press, 1989).

44 Thomas L. Friedman, *The Lexus and the Olive Tree* (London: HarperCollins, 2000).

45 Thomas L. Friedman, *The World Is Flat* (New York: Farrar, Straus and Giroux, 2005).

46 "Disney's Euro Problem," *Miami Herald*, July 9, 1993, p. C3.

47 Andrew Pollack, "Sega Takes Aim at Disney's World," *New York Times*, Section 3, July 4, 1993, pp. 1, 6.

48 For more on Sega, see Irene M. Kunii, "Sega: 'We're Going to Blow Them Out of the Water'," *Business Week*, December 7, 1998, p. 108; and Dave Lee, "Twenty years of Sonic the Hedgehog," *BBC News Online*, June 23, 2011.

49 Brenton R. Schlender, "US PCs Invade Japan," *Fortune*, July 12, 1993, pp. 68–73.

50 See also "PC Market Has Ups and Downs," *Asia Times*, December 5, 2001; Apple, *Guide to Japan for Macintosh Developers*, 2000 Edition; and Mintel Global Navigator (Market research database), http://gmn.mintel.com/query/10056853/shares/single, 2011.

51 Schlender, op. cit., p. 73.

52 Gabriella Stern, "VW's US Comeback Rides on Restyled Beetle," *Wall Street Journal*, May 6, 1997, pp. B1–2.

53 Alex Taylor III, "Ford's $6 Billion Baby," *Fortune*, June 28, 1993, pp. 76–81.

54 Keith Naughton et al., "Can Honda Build a World Car?" *Business Week*, September 8, 1997, pp. 100–108.

55 "GM do Brasil Launches de Chevrolet Celta," *Automotive Intelligence News*, September 5, 2000.

56 Alan M. Rugman and Andrew Anderson, *Administered Protection in America* (London and New York: Routledge, 1987).

57 Rugman and Verbeke, *Global Corporate Strategy and Trade Policy*, op. cit.

58 United States International Trade Commission, "Import Injury Investigations Statistics," November 2004.

59 International Trade Administration, *Antidumping and Countervailing Duty Cases Initiated Since January 01, 1980 Current Through January 01, 2000*, January 2000.

60 Rugman, *Multinationals in Canada*, op. cit.

61 Alan M. Rugman and Leonard Waverman, "Foreign Ownership and Corporate Strategy," in Leonard Waverman (ed.), *Corporate Globalization Through Mergers and Acquisitions* (Calgary: University of Calgary Press, 1991), pp. 59–87.

62 Alan M. Rugman, *Inside the Multinationals: The Economics of Internal Markets* (London: Croom Helm and New York: Columbia University Press, 1981).

63 Paul W. Beamish, *Multinational Joint Ventures in Developing Countries* (London and New York: Routledge, 1989).

64 Rugman and Verbeke, *Global Corporate Strategy and Trade Policy*, op. cit.

ADDITIONAL BIBLIOGRAPHY

Arregle, Jean-Luc., Beamish, Paul W. and Hébert, Louis. "The Regional Dimension of MNEs' Foreign Subsidiary Localization," *Journal of International Business Studies*, vol. 40 (January 2009). doi:10.1057/jibs.2008.67.

Bartlett, Christopher and Ghoshal, Sumantra. *Transnational Management* (Boston, MA: Irwin, 1992).

Bartlett, Christopher and Ghoshal, Sumantra. *Managing Across Borders: The Transnational Solution*, 2nd ed. (Boston, MA: Harvard Business School Press, 1998).

Benito, Gabriel R. G., Lunnan, Randi and Tomassen, Sverre. "Distant Encounters of the Third Kind: Multinational Companies Locating Divisional Headquarters Abroad," *Journal of Management Studies*, vol. 48, no. 2 (March 2011).

Birkinshaw, Julian and Pedersen, Torben. "Strategy and Management in MNE Subsidiaries," in Alan M. Rugman (ed), *The Oxford Handbook of International Business* (Oxford: Oxford University Press, 2009).

Birkinshaw, Julian and Hood, Neil. "Characteristics of Foreign Subsidiaries in Industry Clusters," *Journal of International Business Studies*, vol. 31, no. 1 (First Quarter 2000).

Boyd, Gavin (ed.). *The Struggle for World Markets: Competition and Cooperation between NAFTA and the EU* (Cheltenham: Edward Elgar, 1998).

Collinson, Simon C., Sullivan-Taylor, Bridgette and Wilson, David C. "Extending the Integration-Responsiveness Framework: Delivering a Global Service Strategy at British Airways," *Strategic Innovators Journal*, vol. 3, no. 3 (2010).

Cho, Dong-Sung and Moon, Hwy-Chang. *From Adam Smith to Michael Porter: Evolution of Competitiveness Theory* (Singapore and River's Edge, NJ: World Scientific, 2000).

Cho, Dong-Sung, Moon, Hwy-Chang Moon and Kim, Min-Young, "Does One Size Fit All? A Dual Double Diamond Approach to Country-Specific Advantages," *Asian Business & Management*, vol. 8, no. 1 (2009).

Davies, Howard and Ellis, Paul. "Porter's *Competitive Advantage Of Nations*: Time For The Final Judgement?" *Journal of Management Studies*, vol. 37, no. 8 (December 2000).

Devinney, Timothy M., Midgley, David F. and Venaik, Sunil. "The Optimal Performance of the Global Firm: Formalizing and Extending the Integration Responsiveness Framework," *Organization Science*, vol. 11, no. 6 (November–December 2000).

Dickson, Peter R. and Czinkota, Michael R. "How the United States Can Be Number One Again: Resurrecting the Industrial Policy Debate," *Columbia Journal of World Business*, vol. 31, no. 3 (Fall 1996).

Dunning, John H. "Internationalizing Porter's Diamond," *Management International Review*, vol. 33, no. 2 (Second Quarter 1993).

Dunning, John H. "The Geographical Sources of Competitiveness of Firms: Some Results of a New Survey," *Transnational Corporations*, vol. 5, no. 3 (December 1996).

Enright, Michael J." The Location of Activities of Manufacturing Multinationals in the Asia-Pacific," *Journal of International Business Studies*, vol. 40 (June/July 2009). doi:10.1057/jibs.2009.2.

Grant, Robert M. "Porter's 'Competitive Advantage of Nations': An Assessment," *Strategic Management Journal*, vol. 12, no. 7 (October 1991).

Harzing, Anne-Wil. "An Empirical Analysis and Extension of the Bartlett and Ghoshal Typology of Multinational Companies," *Journal of International Business Studies*, vol. 31, no. 1 (First Quarter 2000).

Hutzschenreuter, Thomas and Gröne, Florian. "Product and Geographic Scope Changes of Multinational Enterprises in Response to International Competition," *Journal of*

International Business Studies, vol. 40 (September 2009). doi:10.1057/jibs.2009.4.

Kotler, Philip. *The Marketing of Nations* (New York: Free Press, 1997).

Leong, Siew Meng and Tan, Chin Tiong. "Managing Across Borders: An Empirical Test of the Bartlett and Ghoshal (1989) Organizational Typology," *Journal of International Business Studies*, vol. 24, no. 3 (Third Quarter 1993).

Martinez, Jon I. and Jarillo, J. Carlos. "Coordination Demands of International Strategies," *Journal of International Business Studies*, vol. 22, no. 3 (Third Quarter 1991).

Meyer, Klaus E., Mudambi, Ram and Narula, Rajneesh. "Multinational Enterprises and Local Contexts: The Opportunities and Challenges of Multiple Embeddedness," *Journal of Management Studies*, vol. 48, no. 2 (March 2011).

Moon, Hwy-Chang, Rugman, Alan M. and Verbeke, Alain, "A Generalized Double Diamond Approach to the Global Competitiveness of Korea and Singapore," *International Business Review*, vol. 7, no. 2 (April 1998).

Moon, Hwy-Chang, Geddis, Lorna and Jin Uk Kim. "A Fresh Look at an Old Debate on Globalization versus Localization,"*Journal of Organization and Management Development* vol. 2, no. 1 (2009).

Narula, Rajneesh. "Technology, International Business and Porter's 'Diamond': Synthesizing a Dynamic Competitive Development Model," *Management International Review*, vol. 33, no. 2 (Second Quarter 1993).

Ostry, Sylvia. "Government and Corporations in a Shrinking World: Trade and Innovation Policies in the United States, Europe & Japan," *Columbia Journal of World Business*, vol. 25, nos. 1–2 (Spring/Summer 1990).

Prahalad, C.K. and Doz, Yves L. *The Multinational Mission: Balancing Local Demands and Global Vision* (New York: Free Press, 1987).

Porter, Michael E. "The Competitive Advantage of Nations," *Harvard Business Review*, vol. 68, no. 2 (March/April 1990).

Porter, Michael E. *On Competition*, updated and expanded ed. (Boston, MA: Harvard Business School Press, 2008).

Roth, Kendall. "International Configuration and Coordination Archetypes for Medium-Sized Firms in Global Industries," *Journal of International Business Studies*, vol. 23, no. 3 (Third Quarter 1992).

Roth, Kendall and Morrison, Allen J. "An Empirical Analysis of the Integration–Responsiveness Framework in Global Industries," *Journal of International Business Studies*, vol. 21, no. 4 (Fourth Quarter 1990).

Rugman, Alan M. "Diamond in the Rough," *Business Quarterly*, vol. 55, no. 3 (Winter 1991).

Rugman, Alan M. "Porter Takes the Wrong Turn," *Business Quarterly*, vol. 56, no. 3 (Winter 1992).

Rugman, Alan M. and D'Cruz, Joseph. "The Double Diamond Model of International Competitiveness: The Canadian Experience," *Management International Review*, vol. 33, no. 2 (Second Quarter 1993).

Rugman, Alan M. and D'Cruz, Joseph. *Multinationals as Flagship Firms: Regional Business Networks* (New York: Oxford University Press, 2000).

Rugman, Alan M. and Oh, Chang Hoon. "Multinationality and Regional Performance, 2000–2005," in Alan M. Rugman (ed.), *Regional Aspects of Multinationality and Performance* (Oxford: Elsevier, 2007).

Rugman, Alan M. and Oh, Chang Hoon "The International Competitiveness of Asian Firms," *Journal of Strategy and Management*, vol. 1, no. 1 (2008).

Rugman, Alan M. and Verbeke, Alain. *Beyond the Three Generics*, Research in Global Strategic Management, vol. 4 (Greenwich, CT: JAI Press, 1993).

Rugman, Alan M. and Verbeke, Alain. "Foreign Subsidiaries and Multinational Strategic Management: An Extension and Correction of Porter's Single Diamond Framework," *Management International Review*, vol. 33, no. 2 (Second Quarter 1993).

Rugman, Alan M. and Verbeke, Alain. "How to Operationalize Porter's Diamond of Competitive Advantage," *International Executive*, vol. 35, no. 4 (July/August 1993).

Rugman, Alan M. and Verbeke, Alain. *Analysis of Multinational Strategic Management: The Selected Scientific Papers of Alan M. Rugman and Alain Verbeke* (Cheltenham: Edward Elgar, 2005).

Rugman, Alan M. and Verbeke, Alain. "A Regional Solution to the Strategy and Structure of Multinationals," *European Management Journal*, vol. 26 (2008).

Rugman, Alan M., Oh, Chang Hoon and Lim, Dominic "The Regional and Global Competitiveness of Multinational Firms," *Journal of the Academy of Marketing Science*, DOI 10.1007/s11747-011-0270-5 (2011).

Rugman, Alan M., Verbeke, Alain and Yuan, Wenlong. "Reconceptualizing Barlett and Ghoshall's Classification of National Subsidiary Roles in the Multinational Enterprises," *Journal of Management Studies*, vol. 48, no. 2 (2011).

Rugman, Alan M. and Waverman, Leonard. "Foreign Ownership and Corporate Strategy," in Leonard Waverman (ed.), *Corporate Globalization through Mergers and Acquisitions* (Calgary: University of Calgary Press, 1991).

Vahlne, Jan-Erik, Ivarsson Inge and Johanson, Jan. "The Tortuous Road to Globalization for Volvo's Heavy Truck Business: Extending the Scope of the Uppsala Model," *International Business Review*, vol. 20, no. 1 (February 2011).

Venaik, Sunil, Midgley, David F. and Devinney, Timothy M. "A New Perspective on the Integration Responsiveness Pressures Confronting Multinational Firms," *Management International Review*, vol. 44, Special no. 1 (2004).

Yip, George S., Rugman, Alan M. and Kudina, Alina. "International Success of British Companies," *Long Range Planning*, vol. 39, no. 2 (June 2006).

Yu, Jisun and Zaheer, Srilata. "Building a Process Model of Local Adaptation of Practices: A Study of Six Sigma Implementation in Korean and US Firms," *Journal of International Business Studies*, vol. 41 (April 2010). doi:10.1057/jibs.2009.82.

Chapter 11

INNOVATION, ENTREPRENEURSHIP, AND "BORN GLOBAL" FIRMS

Contents

Objectives of the chapter

Innovation is the lifeblood of any firm, large or small. By persistently creating new and better products and services, new production processes, management practices, and business models, they can stay ahead of the competition. Multinational firms have an added competitive advantage. By continually recombining resources, assets, and capabilities from different locations to meet the changing needs of clients and customers in different markets around the world, multinational firms have the scale, scope, and diversity of options to out-innovate local rivals.

Small firms lack these scale and scope advantages but can still benefit from a diversity of options for sourcing inputs and accessing markets, if they internationalize. They arguably face greater challenges and risks than large firms when they do expand abroad. Those that succeed against the odds provide lessons for all entrepreneurs and innovators.

By connecting the above themes in this chapter, our specific objectives are to:

1 *Understand* the international dimensions of innovation, for large and small firms. What innovation advantages can firms gain from being international, in theory and practice?

2 *Examine* how companies in various industries can organize different kinds of innovation activity in different locations, to derive particular benefits.

3 *Analyze* small-and-medium-sized enterprises (SMEs), with a particular focus on why and how they internationalize, the practical challenges they face, and the kinds of theories that help explain why they venture beyond their own national borders.

4 *Explain*, using concepts such as dynamic capabilities, born global and born regional, entrepreneurial life cycles, networks, and industry clusters, what differentiates success from failure for international and innovative small firms.

ACTIVE LEARNING CASE

Facebook: global and local?

For a firm recently valued at $50 billion yet with just over 2,000 employees and only 14 offices in countries outside of the United States, Facebook cannot be classed as one of the big multinationals. But it has grown to earn estimated revenues of over $2 billion annually and host over 600 million active users from virtually no income or users in 2006 when it opened up its membership to the world.

It is also amongst a growing breed of business enterprises which have captured the imagination of many observers, partly because they appear to offer a quick route to personal riches. The founder, Mark Zuckerberg, was said to be the youngest billionaire in history and replaced Bill Gates as the role model for budding entrepreneurs globally. Facebook was created by Zuckerberg at Harvard, in 2004, and its genesis (involving computer hacking, lawsuits, and now famously broken friendships) became the subject of an Oscar-winning film, *The Social Network*, in 2010.

Like other online enterprises, its phenomenal growth is based primarily on the way it can connect customers globally. It offers a platform for individuals and groups to interact and share experiences, particularly through sharing pictures, news, and friends. Users can also communicate with each other through Chat, personal messages, Wall posts, Pokes, or Status Updates.

Some argue that online social media networks like Facebook, Twitter, or YouTube are a new form of trust-based social engagement which marketers can benefit from. They can do this by building "relationships" with customers rather than streaming generic advertising messages at them. In this way customers can also become co-creators of products and services, as user feedback is built directly into the innovation process. These are important issues for Facebook as its revenues come primarily from advertising, but it still only earns about the same per year that Google earns each month. This has put pressure on the firm to gradually open up its online environment to commercial interests to try to leverage the size of the network for additional revenue.

Other business-related uses of Facebook include recruitment, although professional networks such as LinkedIn are better suited to this, and as a mechanism for firms to access outside expertise and knowledge as inputs into their own innovation and marketing challenges.

Over 70 percent of the platform's users are outside of the United States and it is seen to be the top social network platform across a number of country markets

Table 1 The 10 largest countries in terms of Facebook users

1	United States	152,189,880
2	Indonesia	35,174,940
3	United Kingdom	28,940,400
4	Turkey	26,428,300
5	Philippines	22,849,340
6	India	22,057,280
7	Mexico	21,892,020
8	France	21,040,560
9	Italy	18,438,760
10	Canada	17,381,700

Source: http://www.checkfacebook.com/ (accessed March 2011)

including: the United States, the UK, Canada, Australia, the Philippines, Indonesia, Malaysia, Singapore, New Zealand, Hong Kong, and Vietnam. Table 1 shows the top 10 countries in terms of users.

Other platforms dominate in other markets, including Mixi.jp in Japan, Google-owned Orkut in India, RenRen in China, Vkontakte in Russia, CyWorld in South Korea, and Yahoo!'s Wretch.cc in Taiwan. Globally some of the largest competitors to Facebook include Twitter, Myspace and Gmail (Google), Habbo, and Tencent QQ. The latter, Chinese network is said to have the most users of all, around 700 million. But Facebook has made some inroads into these markets recently, in its drive to become the leading global social networking site. Orkut, for example, is losing ground to Facebook in terms of registered users in India. Vkontakte and RenRen, however, appear to be benefitting from a number of location-specific advantages in their respective countries. These include specialized local language characters (Russian Cylliric and Simplified Chinese), investment in local content, and (particularly in the case of RenRen) a degree of government-supported protectionism.

Since 2009 Facebook has expanded internationally in a more traditional sense, through foreign direct investment, establishing its international HQ in Dublin, Ireland and offices in Hamburg, Hong Kong, Hyderabad, London, Madrid, Milan, Paris, Selangor, Singapore, Stockholm, Sydney, Tokyo, and Toronto.

The Dublin-based hub provides advertisers and users with service and support in their native languages across the region. According to the director of online operations in

Dublin (recruited from Google to establish this subsidiary), the aim is to "meet user needs in a localized and speedier way across Europe." In 2010 staff levels were increased to over 200 across the advertising sales, account management, and platform operations divisions, as the regional hub's role was extended.

In addition to the global nature of its user base, the firm benefits from a large and very international network of entrepreneurs and developers, from more than 190 countries, who build with Facebook Platform. One of the software programs most widely used by third-party developers is the translation tool, for localizing Facebook globally. So, both its "supplier-inputs," in terms of the knowledge and expertise that develop its online services, and its "customer-outputs," in terms of the services themselves, are more global than

the firm's distribution of assets, sales, or employees would suggest.

Sources: Billington, C. and Davidson, R. (2010) "Using knowledge brokering to improve business processes," *McKinsey Quarterly*, 2010, issue 2, pp.110–111; Bonfils, M. "Why Facebook is Wiping Out Orkut in India & Brazil," April 13, 2011, http://searchenginewatch.com/3642183; Carlson, N. "Goldman to Clients: Facebook Has 600 Million Users," *Business Insider* (2011), http://www.msnbc.msn.com/id/40929239/ns/technology_and_science-tech_and_gadgets/; Facebook factsheet (2011), http://www.facebook.com/press/info.php?statistics; Kiss, J. "Facebook Ireland Chief: Tax Breaks, 100 New Staff and a 'Reputation for Driving Revenue'" Guardian online, (2010), http://www.guardian.co.uk/technology/pda/2010/dec/07/facebook-dublin-colm-long; Parent, M. Plangger, K., and Bal, A. "The New WTP: Willingness to Participate," *Business Horizons*, vol. 54, no. 3, (May 2011) pp. 219–229; Smith, W. P. and Kidder, D. L. "You've Been tagged! (Then again, maybe not): Employers and Facebook," *Business Horizons*, vol. 53, no. 5, (September 2010), pp. 491–499; Womack, B. (2010-12-16). "Facebook 2010 Sales Said Likely to Reach $2 Billion, More Than Estimated," Bloomberg (December 16, 2010), retrieved January 5, 2011.

1 What limits Facebook's ability to become the dominant platform in every country market and how might this change in the future?

2 How has Facebook engaged in foreign direct investment (FDI) and why does it need to?

3 Explain how Facebook sources inputs globally. What advantages does this provide?

INTRODUCTION

Innovation

The renewal and enlargement of the range of products and services and the associated markets; the establishment of new methods of production, supply and distribution; the introduction of changes in management, work organization, and the working conditions and skills of the workforce

In this chapter we examine the connected themes of innovation, entrepreneurship, small international firms, and "born global" firms. **Innovation** can simply be thought of as "the successful exploitation or commercialization of new ideas." But an expanded and more useful definition is: "the renewal and enlargement of the range of products and services and the associated markets; the establishment of new methods of production, supply and distribution; the introduction of changes in management, work organization, and the working conditions and skills of the workforce."[1]

All firms, regardless of their size, have to innovate to survive. Where firms locate innovation-related activities is of growing interest to managers, policymakers, and international business researchers. Moreover, the ways in which multinational firms link and integrate inputs (specialist knowledge, capabilities, and ideas as well as assets and other resources) from various locations and connect these with market opportunities elsewhere is an increasingly important part of the "performance puzzle." The management of innovation and the location of innovation activities not only differentiate firms in terms of their performance, but have a significant impact on foreign direct investment flows and patterns of regional employment and development.

Entrepreneurship and innovation go hand-in-hand. Entrepreneurs, whether they are working in small or large firms, as owner-managers or employees, are distinctive because they have the capability and motivation to pursue innovative commercial opportunities that are riskier and more radical than normal. They identify such opportunities and assemble the resources and capabilities needed to create value.

"Born global" is a term used to describe a firm that is, from its beginnings, immediately or very quickly reliant on a global presence to survive and succeed. Leveraging particular firm-specific advantages (FSAs), such as new technologies, unique products or services, or a valuable capability derived from one or more locations, such firms serve customers locally or globally. We could say that the very existence of born global firms is due to their position as international entrepreneurial "brokers," exploiting commercial opportunities that arise from bridging resource inputs and market niches in different global locations. However, the precise, defining characteristics of born global firms are the subject of some debate in international business studies, as we discuss below.

INTERNATIONAL DIMENSIONS OF INNOVATION

A major defining feature of multinational enterprises (MNEs) is that they manage business operations across a range of country contexts, each of which represents a different set of opportunities for innovation, in two specific ways. First, a distinctive set of market opportunities, which offer the potential for an MNE to sell customized products and services to particular groups of customers across a variety of market locations. Second, country locations offer a unique set of resources, or inputs into the innovation process, including scientific and technological assets and capabilities, or expertise and knowledge in R&D, engineering, or design, at a particular price. By continually linking innovation input opportunities and output opportunities, multinational enterprises, regardless of their size, are to a greater or lesser extent entrepreneurial.

National contexts vary in terms of their economic, social, cultural, political, and institutional characteristics and this variety underpins both of these kinds of innovation opportunity. These factors influence the kinds of resources and capabilities that are available in a particular location and the kinds of customers and markets that develop there. Studies also show how different forms of competitive advantage at the national, industry, and firm levels stem from the particular characteristics of the **national innovation system (NIS)**.[2] The quality of local scientific, technological, design-related, and creative expertise, combined with institutional relationships between enterprises, universities, and government research organizations, underpins this competitiveness. These are one form of country-specific advantage (CSA) that supports the development of firm-specific advantages (FSAs). Firms that evolve in regions with high-quality capabilities and institutions benefit from this by gaining competitive advantages that help them expand internationally. These location endowments also make such locations attractive to other firms engaged in FDI.

These issues have long been of concern for policymakers in OECD countries, where almost all R&D activity used to be located. However, as discussed in Chapter 20, emerging economies are growing in importance as a source of innovation and as a preferred location for R&D investment.

As more firms become more international the networks and processes for innovating also become more global. The section in Chapter 12 on "Research, Development and Innovation," introduces process innovation and product/service innovation as two key forms of innovation managed by firms. It also examines how global R&D networks help companies tap into local sources of scientific and technological expertise and integrate these to develop new or improved products, services, and processes.

Figure 11.1 outlines some of the main drivers for internationalization in relation to innovation in MNEs. The two main forms of internationalization, "market-seeking" and "resource-seeking," are referred to elsewhere in this book. Very often they go hand-in-hand, because local specialists, whether engineers, plant managers, distribution specialists, or customer-relationship managers, are usually the best-equipped to customize processes, products, and services to local conditions. Local assets and knowledge need to be leveraged to develop or adapt products and services for local customers.

National Innovation Systems (NIS)
Characterized by the quality of local scientific, technological, design-related, and creative expertise, combined with institutional relationships between enterprises, universities, and government research organizations. Regional variations in these components partly account for firm-level differences in innovation-related capabilities and competitiveness

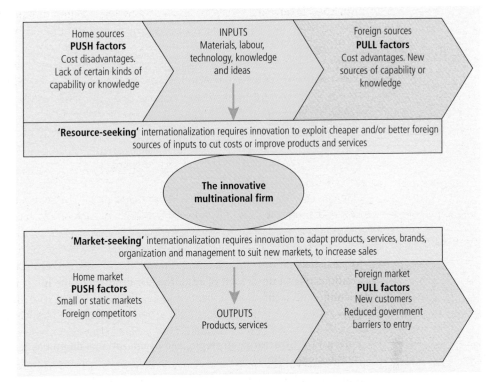

Figure 11.1 Internationalization drivers for the innovative multinational firm

THE LOCATION OF INNOVATION ACTIVITIES IN THE MNE

As discussed elsewhere in this book, multinational enterprises have to cope with the competing pressures of integration and responsiveness. That is, to derive benefits such as economies of scale from the integration and standardization of their operations globally while at the same time customizing and adapting in response to local customers and contexts.

As shown in Figure 11.2, adapted from the groundbreaking work of Christopher Bartlett and Sumantra Ghoshal, we can also feature innovation in this balancing act. In theory, some innovation activities should be centralized and/or standardized and some should be de-centralized and/or customized (or "localized"). We find this is also the case in practice, as described below.[3]

A second framework, developed by Nohria and Ghoshal, extends this logic by describing several archetypal MNE structures for managing different kinds of innovation.[4] Figure 11.3 shows this basic typology, differentiating between three generic forms of innovation activity: sensing, responding and implementing. The framework shows how it may be appropriate either to separate or to combine these three activities, depending on industry conditions and the product or service in question.

In some industries, such as semiconductors, heavy engineering, or pharmaceuticals, innovation is predominantly technology-driven, rather than market-driven. This is normally because the needs of customers are clear cut (faster processors, stronger bridges, or a cure for cancer) but difficult to achieve. Moreover, there are strong economies of scale in centralization of R&D and innovation efforts to achieve scientific or technological breakthroughs ahead of competitors. Sensing opportunities for innovation, like new drug compounds to cure known diseases or faster semiconductor chip designs, and responding to these by allocating capital investment and putting together dedicated project teams,

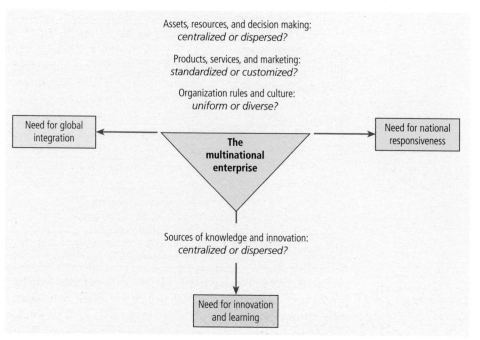

Figure 11.2 Structural, strategic, and organizational dilemmas for the innovative multinational firm

Source: Adapted from Bartlett and Ghoshal (2002).

Innovation processes	Location where different tasks are carried out		
	Sensing	Responding	Implementing
Center-for-global	At the center (possibly with input from a subsidiary)	Always at the center	In many units worldwide
Local-for-local	In a particular national unit	In the same national unit	In the same national unit
Local-for-global	In a particular national unit	In the same national unit, possibly with help from the center	In the national unit initially, then many units worldwide
Global-for-global	In many units, including the center, plus many subsidiaries	In many units, including the center, plus many subsidiaries	In many units worldwide

Figure 11.3 Global MNE structures for managing innovation

Source: Adapted from Nohria and Ghoshal (1997).

will tend to happen at one location. This specialist unit or "center of excellence" may also implement the innovation by developing and launching the product for sale around the world. This is referred to as "**center-for-global**" in the framework, in cases where the new technology or product is developed centrally but can be used at the local level. Nohria and

Ghoshal use the example of telecoms switching systems, which have clear-cut technology development drivers and obvious economies of scale in R&D, making it appropriate for firms to focus resources and efforts in central R&D units. These create fairly standard components which can be used in telecoms networks around the world.

For market-seeking internationalization it may be appropriate for the local subsidiaries of a firm to sense the opportunity or need for product or service changes to suit local preferences. Headquarters may then allocate to these subsidiaries the discretionary decision-making powers and the resources and capabilities to respond to these opportunities and implement changes to existing products or services, for the local market. These are labeled "**local-for-local**" innovations, where new or customized products and services are entirely developed by local subsidiaries because they suit the specific characteristics of the local market or country conditions.

"**Local-for-global**" is where a locally developed product or service turns out to fit other markets beyond the location of the subsidiary responsible for creating it. Nohria and Ghoshal describe how Unilever gave its Indian subsidiary the remit for developing a new kind of clothes detergent to improve sales across the country. Because many people in India washed clothes by hand in rivers, a local team designed a soap bar with the same detergent properties as soap powders (which had the inconvenient tendency to drift downstream and wash someone else's clothes!). This became a big-selling brand in India and then proved popular in developing countries in other parts of the world for the same reasons.

The fourth typology, "**global-for-global**," is seen as the "ideal" organization structure for "transnational" corporations (as opposed to multinational corporations). Here firms pool inputs, including resources, knowledge, and capabilities, in response to changing technological and market opportunities globally. By effectively coordinating their many subsidiaries around the world, transnational companies can leverage the advantages of their size (scale advantages) and diversity (scope advantages), integrating specialist assets and expertise in response to their changing competitive environments. Nohria and Ghoshal also call this ideal organizational form the "differentiated network," building on previous studies of multinational networks.[5]

Center-for-global, local-for-local, local-for-global and global-for-global
Structural archetypes for the location of three innovation-related activities; sensing, responding, and implementing. These result from the need for some innovation activities to be centralized and/or standardized and others to be de-centralized and/or customized (or "localized").

The innovative MNE as a differentiated network

MNEs, large and small, have to both adapt to local conditions and optimize their scale and scope advantages by standardizing products, services, brands, and organizational practices as much as possible. Hence, they face the dilemma of having to be both "global" and "local" at the same time. But one of the major natural competitive advantages of MNEs results from their ability to combine (and continually recombine) various inputs (particularly knowledge and expertise) into the innovation process, from different locations, to serve different customer needs across a variety of markets. Their ability to exploit this advantage depends to a significant degree on how they are structured to manage networks which connect these locations and incentivize specialists to connect across these networks to add value.[6]

Differentiated networks require strong integrative and dynamic capabilities to operate effectively. Not only must they integrate disparate resources and knowledge from the various parts of the firm, but they must also continually develop and recombine these assets in response to the complex and changing range of external innovation opportunities. In theory this is straightforward, in practice there are many organizational barriers and constraints to resource and knowledge-sharing. Moreover, which opportunities should be targeted and which areas of resource-allocation or knowledge-development should be prioritized is continually contested.

Firms that do develop more effective ways of integrating specialist knowledge for innovation tend to have a degree of "slack" in their configuration of assets, resources, and expertise. Clayton Christensen notes this in his analysis of how firms become locked into certain sets of markets, resources, and capabilities by focusing on cost-cutting and efficiency. Over time they lose the flexibility to explore and experiment and innovate their way on to a new "S-curve."[7] Firms that operate as dynamic networks also balance the division of decision–making responsibility for innovation between headquarters (the centre) and subsidiaries (the periphery) and develop organizational mechanisms, such as project structures, incentives, communication channels, IT systems, roles, and responsibilities for connecting specialist sources of knowledge around the firm and leveraging these to serve clients and customers.

Research has shown how and why firms differ in their "integrative" innovation capabilities. Sony, for example, in comparison with counterparts like Panasonic (formerly known as Matsushita) and Philips, has a strong set of organization coordination mechanisms, communication practices, and employee incentives for connecting market opportunities with technological potential in its consumer electronics division.[8] This involves combining software and hardware specialists to create new functionalities in multimedia products and linking them effectively with consumers to develop some expertise in what drives patterns of adoption and use. Rather than relying on the marketing function to produce data and analysis on customers, Sony tends to encourage engineers and technologists to observe or work with customers directly to understand what kinds of innovation add value for them.

Ambidexterity

The ability of a firm "to be aligned and efficient in its management of today's business demands while simultaneously being adaptive to changes in the environment"

Compared to other Japanese firms Sony is fairly unusual in its so-called "**ambidexterity**." That is, its ability "to be aligned and efficient in its management of today's business demands while simultaneously being adaptive to changes in the environment."[9] Sony is continually coming up with new technology platforms (CDs, DVDs, minidisks, and so on) and new products based around these platforms. But it also invests in improving current product lines, with new models and new features, and it strives to make them cheaper through economies of scale and continuous improvement in manufacturing. Many Japanese firms are renowned for their incremental process and product innovation capabilities, but are weaker in terms of their radical or R&D-driven innovation. Moreover, they tend to be more locked into domestic market R&D and innovation networks, compared to counterparts from the United States or Europe.[10]

The original studies leading to the concept of the differentiated network focused predominantly on manufacturing firms, but as innovation in multinational networks has become more widely analyzed, knowledge-based services and other business sectors have also been examined.[11]

✔ Active learning check

Review your answer to Active Learning Case question 1 and make any changes you like. Then compare your answer to the one below.

❶ What limits Facebook's ability to become the dominant platform in every country market and how might this change in the future?

The Facebook platform has the advantage of massive positive network externalities. That is, as more people use the platform, the greater the value to other users. However, it is still subject to the same local market constraints, such as government regulations and protection, local suppliers and network infrastructure, culture, and language that limit the global spread of any standard product or service. Its origins, structure, in-built culture, and current (Western-dominated) membership give it a "liability of foreignness" that local versions do not have. There are a number of ways this might change in the future. The least likely is a standardization (or "Americanization"?) of local cultural preferences, removing one major barrier to global dominance. There is in fact evidence of a rejection of a uniform set of global values and beliefs and a resurgence of local cultures. The alternative future may lie in the adaptation of Facebook itself into a more diversified range of locally shaped platforms, interfaces, and membership groups. By balancing the global and the local, Facebook may evolve into a true transnational corporation. However, advertisers, who drive revenues and therefore have a strong influence over the strategic direction taken by the firm, will be more interested in some markets than others.

In the next section we will explore the world of small and international firms, starting with an introduction to SMEs (small-and-medium-sized enterprises) and returning to the topic of innovation later in the chapter.

INTERNATIONAL BUSINESS STRATEGY IN ACTION

Innovation networks at IBM

Between the summer of 2010 and early 2011 an IBM computer named "Watson" challenged and eventually beat other (human) contestants on the US game-show "Jeopardy!" It was seen to be a step-change in computing intelligence and a demonstration of the excellence of IBM's global R&D network. The computer, named after an IBM research lab and two of the firm's original founders, Thomas J. Watson Sr. and his son Thomas J. Watson Jr., can understand natural language and find answers to real questions across a wide range of subject areas. Built by linking 90 servers using IBM's "DeepQA architecture," it is the result of years of work by the company's leading researchers and is now being deployed as a support tool in healthcare, finance, and customer services.

IBM has long been a dominant global force in science and technology development. In 2010 the company was awarded more US patents (5,896) than any other company, for the 18th consecutive year. Over 70 percent of these were for software and services. The firm invests around $6 billion in R&D annually, resulting in intellectual property (IP) income of about $1 billion each year as well as a stream of new technologies, products, and services.

In 2008 the incoming director of R&D at IBM, John Kelly, embarked on a restructuring program in response to both the development of new R&D competitors, such as Microsoft and Google, and new opportunities in emerging economies. This took the lead from CEO Sam Palmisano who had a clear view of what a "globally integrated enterprise" should look and act like: "a new kind of enterprise which is best understood as global rather than multinational." Kelly visited the eight IBM research labs around the world, including China, India, and Israel, to gain insights from the firm's global workforce of 3,200 researchers. On the basis of this, he decided to further internationalize the company's R&D structure and consolidate the fragmented allocation of resources into larger-scale, leading projects. Both of these strategies have been seen by insiders as signaling a shift from the traditional US-based R&D centers to new initiatives in emerging economies. The firm has since added a 10th R&D lab, in Brazil, to its worldwide portfolio and is planning another lab in Australia (see table 1).

Global alliances and collaboration are also a central part of the strategy. Kelly uses the term "**collaboratories**" to denote "agile, in-market research" activities which connect with universities and science and technology institutes in different countries, rather than investing in large-scale brick-and-mortar laboratories. Significantly, this also means conducting research closest to the problem. For example, instead of tackling transportation issues in the United States, where the infrastructure is in line with growth, he suggests that IBM will focus on a country, city, and area where road traffic is a primary problem, such as Mumbai.

IBM has developed a number of unique networking mechanisms for connecting researchers and employees for innovation. It holds a "smart camp" and uses Facebook to host discussions between its in-house researchers and other experts around the world. "Jams" or "jamming" are another unusual way the firm promotes technology-based creativity. These are online brainstorming sessions for huge numbers of people to share ideas and discuss key challenges which can be commercial or related to social or environmental issues. In 2006 the "Innovation Jam" connected over 150,000 people from 104 countries and 67 companies. Ten new IBM businesses were launched as a result, with seed investment totaling $100 million. An Innovation Jam in 2008 demonstrated how powerful "crowd-sourcing" for new ideas could be. Since then IBM has coordinated online Jams on governance, technology, and security. In 2011 the Prince of Wales in the UK kicked-off "Start Jam" focusing on sustainable business practices.

Some of the IBM's global networking efforts are clearly, at least in part, public relations exercises. But it has obviously developed a sophisticated range of networks and organization mechanisms to connect and leverage the huge range of in-house R&D expertise it has invested in and simultaneously tap into external sources of knowledge and capabilities for innovation.

Sources: Business Week, 'Setting IBM's R&D Agenda', April 2008; a video of John Kelly, Director of Research at IBM, is available at: http://www.businessweek.com/innovate/content/apr2008/id20080416_955900.htm; Samuel J. Palmisano, The Globally Integrated Enterprise, Foreign Affairs, May/June 2006; http://www.facebook.com/ibmwatson; http://www.ibm.com/developerworks/community; http://www.research.ibm.com/worldwide/index.shtml; http://www.youtube.com/watch?v=cU-AhmQ363I&feature=relmfu; http://www-03.ibm.com/press/us/en/pressrelease/32757.wss; https://www.collaborationjam.com/.

▶

Table 1 IBM's Research Labs

Where?	Established when?	Doing what?
Almaden, San Jose, CA, USA	1955	Computer science, database, user interface, web software, storage systems software & technology, physical sciences, materials science, nanotechnology, life sciences, services research
Zurich, Rüeschlikon, Switzerland	1956	Nanoscience and technology, semiconductor technology, storage systems, advanced server technology, systems design, IT security and privacy, business optimization, mobile enablement, services research; industry solutions lab
Watson, NY and MA, USA	1961	Computer science, database, data mining, business intelligence, user interface, storage systems software, materials science, nanotechnology, life sciences, services research, mathematics, semiconductor technology
Haifa, Israel	1972	Storage and business continuity systems, verification technologies, multimedia, active management, information retrieval, programming environments, optimization technologies, and life sciences
Tokyo, Yamato, Japan	1982	Analytics and optimization, software engineering, middleware, system software, security and compliance, electronic and optical packaging technology, engineering and technology services, text mining and speech technology, and accessibility center
Beijing, China	1995	Business integration and transformation, information and knowledge management, future embedded systems and devices, resilient and pervasive infrastructure, and user interactions
Austin, TX, USA	1995	High performance/low power VLSI design and tools, system-level power analysis, and new system architectures
Delhi and Bangalore, India	1998	Speech technologies, pervasive computing, e-governance, information management, e-commerce, life sciences, distributed computing, software engineering
São Paulo and Rio de Janeiro, Brazil	2010	Smarter natural resource management, smarter devices, smarter human systems, service systems and underlying technologies including analytics and optimization, distributed systems, mobile technologies, semiconductor packaging, and high performance computing.
Melbourne, Australia	2011	Smarter natural resource management related to resource discovery, production, supply chain and operations. Smarter natural disaster management including real-time event (stream) processing, weather modelling, traffic management and mobility analytics.

Source: adapted from http://www.research.ibm.com/worldwide/index.shtml.

Collaboratories
"Agile, in-market research activities which connect with Universities and science and technology institutes in different countries." While the term is used by IBM, the approach is used by many R&D-intensive firms

INTERNATIONAL SMALL-AND-MEDIUM-SIZED ENTERPRISES (SMEs)

Studying small international firms provides a useful contrast to large multinational firms, which are the focus of much of this book. Comparisons particularly reveal the importance of scale and scope as sources of certain kinds of competitive advantages for international-ization, as outlined by Alfred Chandler.[12] Small firms have neither the manpower nor the financial resources to spread their options geographically or make many mistakes when they take the first steps into new markets. This means that they have to be particularly entrepreneurial, innovative, and adaptive when expanding abroad.[13]

In the sections that follow we focus on some of the defining characteristics of small and international firms and examine some of the challenges they face in relation to their inter-national expansion. After a brief overview of small firms outlining their general economic importance, we will examine how and why they extend their businesses outside their home markets. We will also discuss various theories of international new ventures and how both dynamic and innovation-related capabilities are key elements for their survival. Finally, some of the practical challenges for internationalizing SMEs are described.

What are small firms?

Each country tends to have a different legal definition of "small," sometimes depending on the industry in question. The Small Business Administration in the United States generally specifies a small business as having fewer than 500 employees for manufacturing businesses and less than $7 million in annual revenues for most non-manufacturing businesses. This contrasts the European Union definition where a small firm generally has less than 50 employees, a micro-enterprise has less than 10 employees, and a medium-sized firm has less than 250. See Table 11.1 for some selected comparisons.

In the United States, small businesses account for around half the GDP and more than half the employment. In the EU the term **small-and-medium-sized enterprise (SME)** is commonly used and these account for 99 percent of all firms, 65 percent of jobs, and about 58 percent of turnover, compared to 69 percent of jobs and 53 percent of output in Japan. In India the Micro and Small Enterprises (MSEs) sector accounts for about 39 percent of manufacturing output and employs an estimated 31 million people in 12.8 million enterprises. While small firms in India have achieved higher growth rates in recent years, relative to larger firms they also have a labor intensity that is almost four times higher than large enterprises.

Within studies of SMEs in general there is some evidence that they are more innovative than their larger counterparts. According to the US Small Business Administration (US-SBA), firms of less than 500 employees in the United States represent 99.7 percent of all employer firms and employ just over half of all private-sector employees. Although the US-SBA has adopted a more inclusive definition of an SME (less than 500 employees) than many other countries, this set of firms does stand out for their innovativeness. They have created 64 percent of net new jobs in the United States in the past 15 years and hire 40 percent of high-tech workers such as scientists, engineers, and computer programmers. Moreover, they produce 13 times more patents per employee than large patenting firms and these patents are twice as likely as large firm patents to be among the 1 percent most cited.[14]

SMEs or small-and-medium-sized enterprises (SMEs)
Defined by governments using different criteria for policy purposes. SMEs are firms with less than 250 employees in Europe, but less than 500 in the United States. Indian manufacturing firms qualify as SMEs if they invest less than US$2 million in plant and equipment

Table 11.1 Various definitions of small-and-medium-sized enterprises (SMEs)

| Enterprise category | European Union | | United States | Japan | | India | |
	Employees	Turnover	Employees	Manufacturing enterprises: employees	Retail/ service enterprises: employees	Service enterprises: investment in equipment	Manufacturing enterprises: investment in plant and equipment
Medium-sized	< 250	≤ €50 mill (US$70 mill)	< 500	< 300	< 50	Rs.5 crore (US$1 million)	Rs.10 crore (US$2 million)
Small	< 50	≤ €10 mill (US$14 mill)	< 100	< 300	< 50	Rs.2 crore (US$40,000)	Rs.5 crore (US$1 million)
Micro/small offices	< 10	≤ €2 mill (US$2.8 mill)	< 10	< 300	< 50	Rs.10 lakh (US$20,000)	Rs.25 lakh (US$50,000)

Sources: Annual Report, 2008–09. Ministry of Micro, *Small and Medium Enterprises, India*, www.msme.gov.in; Shambhu Ghatak, 2009. *Micro, Small and Medium Enterprises (MSMEs) in India: An Appraisal*, http://www.esocialsciences.com/data/eSSResearchPapers/eSSWPArticle20091126151144.pdf; EU Enterprise and Industry directorate, SME definition: http://ec.europa.eu/enterprise/policies/sme/facts-figures-analysis/sme-definition/index_en.htm; USAID, 2007, *Booklet of Standardized Small and Medium Enterprises Definition–2007*, the United States Agency for International Development, http://pdf.usaid.gov/pdf_docs/PNADM845.pdf.

The international activities of SMEs

How international are small firms? The data show that, in general, a relatively small number of SMEs sell products and services outside their domestic market, compared to the total number of active SMEs. When we consider another key measure of internationalization, foreign direct investment (FDI), again SMEs are less prominent than large multinational firms as sources of FDI. This makes sense when we think that the majority of small firms in most countries are likely to be family-owned shops or hairdressers, restaurants, and local tradesmen such as plumbers, painters, or carpenters.

In the European Union just a quarter of all SMEs export or have exported at some point during the past three years. Moreover, their international activities are mostly geared toward other countries inside the internal European market and only about 13 percent of EU SMEs are active in markets outside the EU. However, SMEs are responsible for a larger proportion of total exports from some countries than we might expect. In India, SMEs account for an estimated 40 percent of total exports. In the United States just over 97 percent of all identified exporters are SMEs and these firms produce 30 percent of the known export value.

Table 11.2 shows how international SMEs can be engaged in trade and/or FDI to access inputs or to sell outputs from abroad. If they stick to trading via imports (for inputs such as resources, materials, or expertise) and exports (for their outputs, i.e., products or services) then they are relying solely on international market transactions to underpin their relative position in the industry value chain. As discussed elsewhere in this book, by engaging in FDI a firm "internalizes" a particular input or output activity based outside its home region. In this way it becomes a multinational firm.[15] So, for example, a small retailer might import products from abroad to sell locally, or export products to sell internationally. Only when this firm establishes its own shops abroad, to sell directly to customers, thereby internalizing the overseas sales function, do we refer to it as a multinational firm. Similarly, if it were to acquire a key supplier based abroad, thereby internalizing the overseas supply function (and engaging in vertical integration along the value chain), we would refer to it as a multinational firm.

Given that firms have the option to import or export and engage in FDI instead of one or both of these forms of trading, we can map out four modes of international operation (1a and 1b plus 2a and 2b in Table 11.2). The five case examples show how firms can develop a portfolio that includes one, several, or all of these modes of operation.

The examples are all taken from the UK International Track 100, a ranking of rapidly internationalizing firms compiled by the *Sunday Times* newspaper on the basis of CAGR (compound annual growth rate). International sales have to exceed £1 million ($1.6 million) and be at least 10 percent of total sales (http://www.fasttrack.co.uk). The majority of firms in this list are small or medium-sized, with less than 300 employees. Thirty one percent are small firms, with less than 50 employees. So all of these firms have internationalized very rapidly, but they are in very different businesses and have adopted very different modes of international operation.

Intamarque was established by the twin Shortt brothers in 2006 in Cheltenham. The firm assembles, packages, and distributes customized selections of consumer products globally. It employs just 10 staff and yet achieved international export sales of $18.5 million (just over 50 percent of total sales) in 2010, up from less than $2 million in 2008. This average annual growth rate of 207 percent was partly driven by the popularity of many British-branded products in Asia and the Middle East. (http://www.intamarque.com/)

SMS Electronics was born from a local management buy-out of Siemens Manufacturing Services in Nottingham in 2002. It is a precision design and contract manufacturing

Table 11.2 Types of international SMEs by trade and FDI up and down the value chain

Different types of international SMEs	(1) International *inputs*: Foreign sourcing of materials or expertise . . .		(2) International *outputs*: Foreign sales of products or services . . .	
Internalization; foreign ownership?	(1a) Yes. Input-oriented FDI	(1b) No. Sourcing via markets	(2a) Yes. Output-oriented FDI	(2b) No. Selling via markets
For example?	Foreign greenfield production facilities, procurement offices, R&D JVs	*Imports* from foreign suppliers, outsourcing contractors or online service providers	Part or fully-owned foreign distribution, retail outlets, after-sales service providers	*Exports* direct to foreign customers or via distributors, or online service delivery
Company examples:				
Intamarque	None	None	None	Exports to wholesalers and retailers
SMS Electronics	None	Small volume of materials imports	None	Exports direct to manufacturers
Forward Internet Group	None	Offshore software developers	None	Online commissions from Ebay and internet sales firms globally
Wilton Group	Limited input of expertise from Brazil-based offices	None	Sales and technical services offices in Brazil	Exports to clients
Ultimate Products	Offices in Belgium and Hong Kong for sourcing new products	Imports wide range of products for UK clients	Offices in Belgium and Hong Kong for selling products	Exports wide range of products for foreign clients

firm with 131 employees which has had a particular boost from the growing market for video-conferencing technologies. Exports grew by 418 percent per year from 2008, when foreign sales accounted for just 3 percent of total sales, to reach $30 million in 2010. In 2011 60 percent of the firm's sales were in mainland Europe. (http://www.smselectronics.co.uk/)

Forward Internet Group, started in 2004 as an online marketing agency, now focuses on the use of its "Invisible Hand" technology which notifies Internet users of cheaper prices elsewhere on other websites and gets commissions for sales that result from this switching behavior. Ebay is a client. International sales grew from $4.8 million per year in 2007 to $73 million in 2009, when the firm had less than 50 employees. By 2011 it had grown to over 150 employees. It used offshore software developers between 2005 and 2007 and has an estimated 1.3 million US users. (http://www.forward.co.uk/)

The *Wilton Group* has 227 staff providing a range of services, including project management and engineering, to customers in the oil-and-gas industry. Its international sales grew by 187 percent per year from 2008 to reach $8.5 million (out of total sales of $61 million) in 2010, with its technical personnel working on projects with firms like BP across Europe, Africa and the Far East. More recently it has opened offices in Brazil to support the growing oil drilling business in the country. (http://www.wilton-group.co.uk/)

Ultimate Products is a home-ware designer, sourcer, importer and exporter, and the largest "hard goods" importer in the UK. With 231 employees it delivers over 6,000 different products to retailers such as Tesco in the UK, Carrefour in France, and Wal-Mart in the United States. The firm's international sales grew by 73 percent per year from 2008 to reach $36.5 million in 2010. It relies on traveling sourcing and sales managers but has also opened offices in Belgium and a showroom in Hong Kong. (http://www.ultimate-products.co.uk/)

Active learning check

Review your answer to Active Learning Case question 2 and make any changes you like. Then compare your answer to the one below.

2 **How has Facebook engaged in foreign direct investment (FDI) and why does it need to?**

Facebook has only recently "physically" internationalized through FDI in Dublin, Ireland (its international HQ), Hamburg, Hong Kong, Hyderabad, London, Madrid, Milan, Paris, Selangor, Singapore, Stockholm, Sydney, Tokyo, and Toronto. These local offices predominantly deal with local or regional sales and technical support. They have to work closely with advertisers, which can mean joint platform and software development as well as service agreements and account management. Without a local presence the firm would not achieve the same level of advertising sales and would not be able to provide a quick, customized local support service for advertisers or users. Staff at these offices are leading moves toward some degree of localization of the platform.

INTERNATIONAL BUSINESS THEORY AND INTERNATIONAL NEW VENTURES

Alongside the rapid growth of small, young, and international firms, driven by the same factors that underlie general globalization processes, there has been a growth of academic research in the field of international entrepreneurship. McDougall and Oviatt produced some of the most influential early studies on the topic and defined international entrepreneurship as the "discovery, enactment, evaluation, and exploitation of opportunities—across national borders—to create future goods and services" by small and young ventures called **"born global" firms**. Born global firms are also referred to as international new ventures (INVs) in the international entrepreneurship literature. They can be defined as "business organizations that, *from inception*, seek to derive significant competitive advantage from the use of resources and the sale of outputs in multiple countries."[16]

Born global firms
"Business organizations that, from inception, seek to derive significant competitive advantage from the use of resources and the sale of outputs in multiple countries"

A number of ongoing debates have developed around the concept and the empirical reality of the born global firm. Three key areas of dispute are: (1) the applicable definition of global, specifically is a firm born global (or global at all) if it simply exports and imports products and services and has no FDI (which is a common definition of an MNE)? (2) Are born global firms really global in terms of their cross-border trade and/or FDI, or are they regional? (3) How quickly does a small firm need to develop a global presence to be called a born global firm? That is, what does "from inception" mean in the above-mentioned definition?

Some studies define "new" in this context as less than six years old and it was this aspect of INVs that was most at odds with established theories of internationalization. The accepted wisdom was that the internationalization process, particularly when it underpinned the sustained, long-term multinational operations of a firm, was slow and step-wise. Firms were seen to accumulate knowledge and experience of unfamiliar and risky foreign markets before committing their scarce resources and capabilities to an internationalization strategy. Studies at Uppsala University by Johanson and Vahlne, among others, famously argued that domestic firms decide to become multinational enterprises (MNEs) by expanding into foreign-country markets only after developing their home-country market successfully. Moreover, the process of internationalization conventionally began with entry into nearby countries first, only followed by further expansion into more remote countries once the firm had developed experience of operating beyond its domestic market. Low-commitment entry modes, including joint-ventures and alliances, rather than M&A or wholly owned greenfield investments, were seen as necessary stages in the learning process, to reduce risk and uncertainty.[17] As many small firms do rapidly internationalize, without going through the gradual, step-wise process depicted by the Uppsala model, this presents a challenge for international business theory.

Another debate has focused on the scope of internationalization by small firms. Based on the broad concept of the triad regions (i.e., North America, European Union, and Asia–Pacific), Rugman and Verbeke introduced a regional aspect to the Uppsala school's step-wise and incremental internationalization process of multinational enterprises. They put forward evidence of a clear limit to the geographic market coverage where multinational enterprises can extract over a majority of their sales revenue from foreign business operations. Utilizing the sales segment data across the triad by *Fortune Global 500* multinational enterprises, they showed that 320 out of the 380 companies have achieved over 80 percent of their sales revenue from their home region of the triad on average. They argued that the world's largest multinational enterprises do not operate globally and evenly across the triad, but tend to be clustered in the nearby countries of their home region of the triad.[18]

This same argument therefore applies to international new ventures. In fact, because they are subject to the multiple liabilities of smallness, newness, and foreignness, they are expected to show stronger home-region orientation than large-sized and already-established multinational enterprises. Given their limited resources, small firms can be expected to reduce risk by selecting nearby countries in their home region as the final destination of their internationalization strategy from inception. As a result, international new ventures are likely to be born regionally, not globally, within their home region of the triad when going abroad into foreign markets.

Other theoretical perspectives in the management field can be found to support the assertion that international new ventures are more likely to be born regional, not global. The resource-based view (RBV) of firms proposes that, since international new ventures face a liability of foreignness by operating in unfamiliar and risky foreign markets, they should possess unique and distinctive resources and capabilities in order to overcome and counteract the liability effectively.[19] The hard-to-replicate resources and capabilities internalized within firm boundaries are referred to as firm-specific advantages (FSAs), and they can be best exploited in similar institutional contexts within intra-regions than across inter-regions, because they are usually location-bound.

Transaction cost economics (TCE) also argues that international new ventures face a substantial level of transaction costs in both information search and monitoring processes when launching international operations across different foreign countries. We would normally expect transactions costs to be lower within the INV's home region of the triad due to spatial proximity, cultural and institutional similarities, psychical closeness, and, as a result, ease of transportation and communication. According to the organizational learning perspective, small and young ventures may be able to acquire hard-to-codify and tacit information about local customers' preferences and/or local business practices more easily within nearby countries in their home region than across different regions, because learning commonly takes place efficiently and effectively under culturally related and proximate external environments. As a result, we would expect **born regional** INVs to adapt their products and services more easily to meet the specific needs of local customers in the same home region.[20]

Despite a substantial increase in research on international new ventures as born global firms, most empirical studies in the international entrepreneurship literature are based on

born regional
Firms tend to locate their overseas businesses in their home region of the triad to escape the liability of inter-regional foreignness

INTERNATIONAL BUSINESS STRATEGY IN ACTION

Spreadshirt: open innovation

In March 2001 a student in Leipzig (Germany) called Lukasz Gadowski developed an online company for designing and selling t-shirts. He was joined by Matthias Spiess, who financed the initial phase of the start-up and by January 2002, 100 online affiliate ventures or "partner shops" had joined from around the world. Despite the enterprise being judged an "unrealistic business model" at the Cologne Business Plan Competition, 500,000 shops had joined by mid-2008 and the "Spreadshirt" company had made history.

The company's goal is to be "THE creative apparel platform, inspiring people to create, buy or sell individualized fashion." It has an unusual business model, with customers playing the roles of buyers, sellers, and designers. They can buy customized t-shirts, hoodies, jackets, bags, or accessories directly from the online store. Whether they are individuals or corporate customers they can also sell via the Spreadshirt online platform by setting up a shop. Firms like CNN, Holiday Inn, Nissan, and the Sun newspaper in the UK have done this to sell their own branded designs. But individual entrepreneurs anywhere in the world can also offer customized clothing through their own Spreadshirt shop website, while Spreadshirt takes care of inventory management, manufacturing, logistics, payments, and other aspects of customer service for their partner shops. This allows designers to sell their own designs without the investment required to establish their own full-service companies. However, providing the capability for individuals to design one-off shirts without the need to set up a shop now makes up 40 percent of Spreadshirt's business.

Spreadshirt also runs "laFraise," Europe's largest t-shirt design competition whereby each week designers from all over the world put forward their latest creations and the Spreadshirt community votes for the best. Winners get prizes as well as having their designs printed and sold globally. This is "crowd sourcing," effectively outsourcing the complex decision regarding which, out of hundreds of design options, a company should print and try to sell. By manufacturing a limited set of designs a producer benefits from significant economies of scale and higher profits, but this requires a process for selecting the most popular designs. Rather than trying to asses this through market research, Spreadshirt and its "designer-seller-customers" use crowd sourcing.

Spreadshirt's primary activities take place via a range of online networks. It is both global and local in a way that firms with business models based on fixed assets can never be. As partner shops join and leave, the firm's international portfolio of "resources" and its online profile in country markets change. But it does also have a physical presence of branch offices in France, Britain, the United States, Spain, Ireland, Italy, Poland, and the Netherlands, to support its head office in Germany.

Despite being the European market leader in its field, Spreadshirt has a limited number of employees (300) and outsources the "physical" aspects of its business on behalf of customers. Manufacturing, logistics, and supply chain management and even elements of its marketing are done via contracts with other firms. The firm has half-a-million partner shops and millions of customers worldwide. Revenues grew from €12.2 million in 2006 up to 15.3 million (+25.7 percent) in 2007 and an estimated €21 million in 2009, although accurate figures are not available after 2007 (Krisch, 2009).

Websites: http://eu.techcrunch.com/2010/, http://www.spreadshirt.com/, http://www.spreadshirt.co.uk/

Source: Krisch, J. "Spreadshirt Swaps CFO; Makes 21 Million Euro Revenue," optaros.com blog (August 18, 2009), http://www.optaros.com/blogs/spreadshirt-swaps-cfo-makes-21-million-euro-revenue.

case studies and/or convenience surveys with a small-sized sample of firms. A recent study with a large-sized sample of 2,236 firms contains empirical evidence that Korean INVs achieve over 90 percent of their export sales from Asia–Pacific, the home region of Korean firms. The same study also shows that born regional INVs perform better than others as they become more internationalized.[21]

Although additional empirical research is yet to be needed to achieve a solid conclusion on this issue, both current theoretical foundations and recent empirical evidence for small and young ventures' internationalization process in the international business literature raise the following critical discussion point: international new ventures are actually born regional, not global, with a major focus on their home region of the triad. In other words, when small and young ventures decide to go abroad in foreign markets beyond their domestic countries, they tend to locate their overseas businesses in their home region of the triad to escape the liability of inter-regional foreignness. Born global firms as identified in other studies may well be statistical outliers, i.e., the exception, rather than the rule.[22]

DYNAMIC CAPABILITIES AND SMALL FIRMS

Dynamic capability
The firm's ability to integrate, build, and reconfigure internal and external competences to address rapidly changing environments

Dynamic capability is "the firm's ability to integrate, build, and reconfigure internal and external competences to address rapidly changing environments." The dynamic capabilities approach has also been seen as a useful conceptual and analytical framework for understanding small, adaptable firms. Because of their relative lack of financial and human resources and the often-cited need to respond quickly to temporary opportunities, such as new-technology waves or consumer fads, dynamic capabilities and organizational agility are seen to be more important to the survival and success of such firms.[23]

While it may not be particularly representative of small firms in general, the popular stereotype of a successful, fast-growing, high-tech start-up does seem to match what we might expect from a firm with the most dynamic of capabilities. They are the focus of attention partly because they are seen as the ideal-type of wealth-creating organization (see the Active Learning Case on Facebook at the start of this chapter), but also because they are seen to hold lessons for other kinds of firms, large and small, looking to improve their responsiveness and innovativeness.

Research suggests that dynamic capabilities relate to the processes by which, and the success with which, small firms learn to grow and adapt to changing threats and opportunities in their surrounding competitive environment. This includes a heightened ability to sense external changes that present new threats or opportunities and the strategic and organizational flexibility to adapt to these. Dynamic capability theories refer to "search and selection" capabilities alongside "configuration and deployment" capabilities. Together these enable firms to orchestrate co-specialized assets, including outside knowledge and expertise, in a continuous way to maintain alignment with this changing environment. This way they are quicker at creating, extending, and modifying resources and assets to maintain competitive advantages, relative to firms with less dynamic capabilities.[24]

There are obvious parallels with Darwinian evolutionary theory and indeed dynamic capabilities approaches draw extensively from concepts such as "requisite variety," "selection and retention," and "evolutionary fitness" and from the work of evolutionary economists, such as Joseph Schumpeter. Schumpeter coined the term "creative destruction" to refer to the process by which superior new ways of doing things continually usurp old ways in an inevitable cycle of renewal. Schumpeter identified innovation as the critical dimension of economic change, contrary to the popular theories of the day, and placed the entrepreneur at the centre of his view of economic systems.[25]

Life cycles, networks, and clusters

Studies of dynamic capabilities in firms of all sizes refer to the concept of capability life cycles. These depict how firms need to periodically renew their capabilities as they expand and evolve, either through internal upgrading and/or via acquisitions, joint-ventures, and other kinds of external alliances. Failure to renew increases the dangers of other, newer, or faster firms developing capabilities that underpin superior competitive advantages.[26]

Life-cycle models are commonly used to depict the growth profiles of SMEs.[27] Whether "born global" or as a local start-up, small firms follow a rocky road to maturity. Lack of investment capital is a key limitation, preventing many small firms from moving between stages of growth, for example by diversifying their product portfolio, expanding into new markets, adding production capacity to achieve economies of scale, or investing in R&D. Lack of specialist expertise, particularly for high-tech start-ups, is also a major limitation. Because of these and other constraints on survival and growth, the ability of the individual entrepreneur to utilize personal networks to access sources of finance, materials, others' expertise, and knowledge about market opportunities is of paramount importance. Creating, developing, and leveraging networks to steer the small firm through these obstacles to growth is the core dynamic capability of the entrepreneur.

Industry clusters or agglomeration economies
Geographic concentrations of interconnected businesses, including suppliers, specialist contractors, and associated institutions

For some time researchers and policymakers have emphasized the importance of local networks or **clusters** as the lifeblood of new business growth. Popularized by studies by Annalee Saxenian and others on Silicon Valley in California, the roots of these analyses lie further back in research on "agglomeration economies" by economic geographers. A unifying theme is the need for a critical mass of entrepreneurs, venture capitalists, and particular kinds of specialists plus a risk-embracing culture of trial-and-error. The ingredients create a dynamic mix underpinning a self-reinforcing local growth cycle. A thousand flowers bloom and some survive.[28]

High-tech and low-tech clusters, or geographic concentrations of related businesses, exist all over the world, from Boston, Route 128 (biotech), Austin, Texas (computing), and Raleigh-Durham, North Carolina (life sciences) in the United States; Cambridge (biotech) and the M4 corridor (ICT) in the UK; Aachen (lasers, ceramics, IT) in Germany; Prado (textiles and fashion) in North Italy; Rajcot (diesel engines) and Ludhiana (woollen knitwear and knitting machines) in India; São Paulo (ethanol and biofuel technology) in Brazil. In China, huge but specialized production clusters have developed more recently, predominantly in the east, including for example: Zhili in Zhejiang province (children's clothes), Datang (socks–6 billion pairs each year!), and Dali in the Nanhai district (aluminum products).

Industry clusters research show that, up to a point and for certain kinds of businesses, small firms are the product of their immediate environment. They rely on local resources, capabilities, and connections and the success of the entrepreneur depends on his or her ability to orchestrate these via local networks in a dynamic way, responding to the shifting threats and opportunities in that same environment. Face-to-face interaction for building trust, as well as for communicating, coordinating, and negotiating, remains important, despite the rise of e-business. This, alongside the efficiency of co-locating specialist industry suppliers and contractors, underpins the importance of geographic proximity.

However, most clusters have relied on access to international markets for some time, often through exports, sometimes through FDI. Silicon Valley evolved by selling information and communication products to the rest of the world and the people of Datang, China do not buy the 6 billion pairs of socks they make each year! The input-side is largely locally bound, while the output-side is global.

But many of these co-location drivers apply to businesses built around physical production, distribution, and sales networks. A growing volume of economic activity is based on buying and selling knowledge and expertise, from media content and software products to financial, legal, and consultancy services. While trust and relationship-building are still critical ingredients, new generations of entrepreneurs develop these online, thereby exploiting the advantages of being able to leverage the cheapest and the best inputs from multiple locations around the world to serve global markets. We have many examples, including case studies on Facebook and Spreadshirt in this chapter, of how small start-ups can quickly extend their reach globally by connecting and continually reconnecting local capability endowments via dynamic international networks. This flexible, connective capability is perhaps *the* critical dynamic capability for large and small multinational firms.

✔ **Active learning check**

Review your answer to Active Learning Case question 3 and make any changes you like. Then compare your answer to the one below.

③ Explain how Facebook sources inputs globally. What advantages does this provide?

Facebook benefits from the inputs of a wide range of entrepreneurs and developers from over 190 countries around the world who add features and customize the platform and content for different groups of users. Third-party developers particularly use Facebook's translation software to create local versions of content in their own countries. They can launch products and services associated with the Facebook platform and Facebook benefits by the resulting snowball effect of new products and services extending the use of their network and bringing more users to their websites. But this form of "open innovation" also enables Facebook to benefit from the ideas, drive, creativity, and initiative of a large global network of programmers and content developers, rather than relying on in-house R&D investment to develop their business. External developers also provide a better interactive connection to local user needs than the firm is able to maintain on its own, even by investing in its offices abroad.

THE PRACTICAL CHALLENGES FOR INTERNATIONALIZING SMEs

Elsewhere in this book we discuss the competitive strengths of large multinational firms, some of which stem from what Alfred Chandler, an emeritus professor at Harvard Business School, described as scale and scope advantages. Scale provides financial power and various economies of scale across the functions of the firm. This is combined with scope, which refers to the breadth and diversity of assets and capabilities which provide large firms with a portfolio of geographic and innovation-related options, enhancing their ability to attain superior profits.[29]

SMEs face significant limitations compared to large firms, across both these dimensions, making internationalization strategies riskier. They do not have the financial muscle to "buy" their way into new markets, or spend on customizing products and brands for local customers. They also lack the range of specialists to draw on to shape and implement market-entry strategies, such as legal experts or managers with experience of local cultures. As described below, these limitations mean that small firms often need to be that much more entrepreneurial and innovative and/or take risky short-cuts, to expand across national borders. It also means that some elements of established theories of internationalization fail to adequately explain the patterns and processes of small firm internationalization.[30]

How do SME managers know which markets to enter?

Mathews and Zander propose three milestones of international entrepreneurial processes: (1) the discovery of new opportunities; (2) the deployment of resources in the exploitation of these opportunities; and (3) engagement with competitors.[31]

The first major challenge for any firm looking to expand internationally is to decide which market location offers the best cost–benefit opportunity. Larger firms can invest in the due-diligence process underlying this decision. Managers can employ in-house resources and expertise and/or external specialists to help identify the most promising country markets in which to expand. As described in Chapter 15, this can entail a complex analysis comparing the relative risks and rewards of different country markets.

Decision-makers in both small and large firms also rely on their personal experience and existing international network relationships, both informal and formal, to assess the potential of different markets. This includes knowledge gained from existing buyers and suppliers and alliance partners, even when these are import and export contractors.[32] But there is evidence that shows that these personal experiences and relationships are much more important to the decision-making process in small firms. Studies show how small firms, and particularly the smallest, owner-managed enterprises, tend to decide which markets to enter on the basis of fairly subjective evidence. This includes the views and opinions of personal contacts abroad and the experience and personal characteristics of small firm owners themselves.[33] A senior manager might spot a market opportunity during a family holiday abroad and this chance experience can be a strong influence on a small firm's market expansion strategy.

Mental maps

"Cognitive representations of the nature and attributes of the spatial environment" and show how "psychic distance" operates in practice for SME managers

A study by Collinson and Holden used **mental maps** to capture the perceptions of decision-makers in a sample of British SMEs of the relative risks and rewards of foreign markets. Mental maps are defined as "cognitive representations of the nature and attributes of the spatial environment." They represent images of spatial environments developed by individuals based on their collated influences and experiences and information available to them. Figure 11.4 shows the mental map for all of the firms in the study, with darker shading denoting more attractive foreign markets.[34]

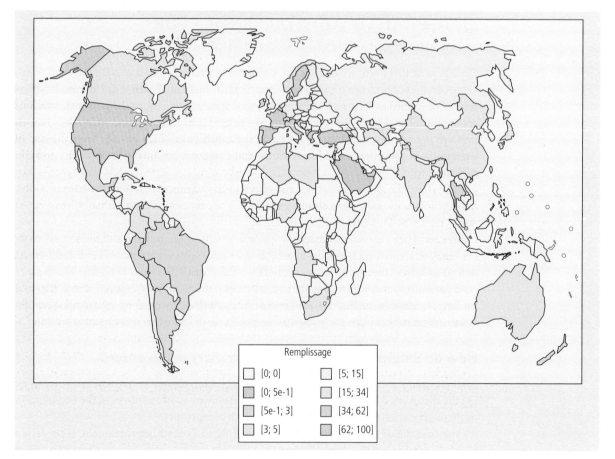

Figure 11.4 Risk vs. reward: country market attractiveness for SME managers

Source: Collinson and Holden (2005).

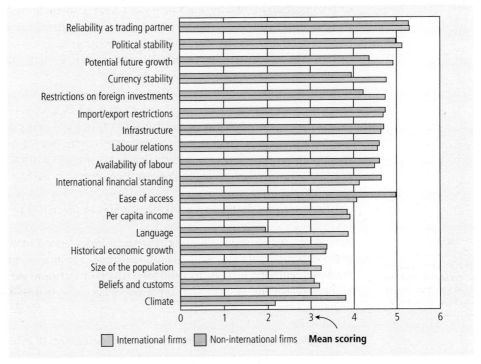

Figure 11.5 Foreign market selection criteria for international and non-international SMEs

Source: Collinson and Holden (2005).

The map shows that mainland Europe and the United States represent the most attractive markets, given their size and familiarity to these British respondents. Much of Africa and parts of the Middle East, Southeast Asia and central Europe are either less well known or seen to be high-risk areas. Collinson and Holden concluded that the mental maps of decision-makers do reflect their individual and group perceptions of opportunity and risk and subsequent geographical bias. They vividly illustrate how "psychic distance"—the perceived degree of cultural, social and psychological differences between a home country and a foreign country—operates in practice. These perceptions do form the basis of internationalization decisions.

The study also compared the views of managers in small firms that had internationalized, and therefore had experience of international location selection and market-entry, with non-internationalized firms. Figure 11.5 compares their responses.

It shows how factors such as language, future potential growth, currency stability, and foreign investment restrictions are rated higher as influences on the country selection decision for firms that have experience of internationalization. Managers in non-international firms are more concerned about the international financial standing of the target market, general ease of access, and climate. The relative ratings of language and climate show a complete contrast. Managers who have direct experience of working across language barriers know how this creates far more additional complexity, uncertainty, and risk than differences in the weather!

Modes of entry and adaptation for success in foreign markets

There is a general consensus across the entrepreneurship literature that more innovative small firms engage in exporting because they are producing superior products relative to local competitors. Similarly, small firms that expand internationally through FDI are likely to be more innovative than their counterparts because they have successfully adapted not just products and services but their management practices to other cultural and institutional contexts. In this way, innovation and internationalization are complementary activities.[35]

In terms of modes of market-entry, studies suggest that firms tend to opt for higher commitment and higher-risk entry modes (such as M&A or greenfield investments) with increasing firm size. SMEs are often assumed to opt for low equity and cooperative strategies because they have less access to financial assets or the level of human resources needed to support these higher-commitment modes of entry. This also means that they have to quickly reach a level of profitability when they enter new markets because of their limited ability to raise investment capital.[36]

Clearly the specific challenges vary depending on the nature of the target country market and the individual firm. One in-depth study of British SMEs in Japan confirmed the general conclusion above, showing that small firms tended to enter into joint-ventures and collaborative alliances with Japanese enterprises in order to gain local knowledge and credibility with *keiretsu* networks and to share the investment risks. The study also showed how market barriers faced by all firms proved to be more challenging for small firms. These included:

- The high costs of start-up and operation, including costs of living and working in Japan, the high tax burden, labor and property costs.

- Local recruitment difficulties, partly stemming from traditional lifetime employment and lack of status for Japanese working in small foreign enterprises.

- Complex employment legislation and very different HRM practices, including the culturally embedded obligations of employers in Japan adding to the more generic barriers of language and culture.

- Market restrictions, including barriers associated with trading associations, "*dango*" and *keiretsu* structures, sometimes supported by government standards and trading legislation. The "tied" system of distribution in Japan, bound by strong face-to-face ties as well as cross-shareholding or financing arrangements between sellers and buyers at each level, proved to be a particular problem. These add to the costs and difficulties of getting products introduced into the market and distributed across different regional markets.

- Government-related complications such as local and national standards, accounting and taxation regulations are not "user-friendly" for non-Japanese and governance processes can be ambiguous.

- Demanding customers and intense rivalry, which have been the drivers of Japanese innovative capabilities in the past, place huge pressures on foreign entrants to adapt marketing, product and service quality and features, and after-sales support to meet the expectations of consumers and corporate customers.[37]

Small survivors are the SME success stories in large, complex markets like Japan. Their success is evidence of their dynamic capability to adapt and their ability to continually innovate. Lessons for other firms are relevant because these SMEs have proven their ability to adapt products and services as well as their own processes and management practices to the economic, institutional, and cultural contexts of foreign markets. Moreover, they have not only adapted to fit into these competitive environments but to succeed against local competitors. Their "fitness" is of a Darwinian kind.

KEY POINTS

1 The ability to continually recombine resources, assets, and capabilities from different locations to meet the changing needs of customers in different markets around the world gives multinational firms, large and small, firm-specific innovation advantages. However, their lack of scale and scope advantages means that small firms face greater risks when expanding abroad. They need to develop more entrepreneurial and dynamic capabilities to succeed.

2 Firms centralize or de-centralize various innovation activities (sensing, responding to, and implementing) globally depending on the trade-offs between standardization and economies of scale and the need for national responsiveness. The center-for-global, local-for-local, local-for-global, and global-for-global typology and the concept of differentiated networks for innovation capture this key trade-off.

3 Definitions of SMEs vary around the world; in Europe these are firms with less than 250 employees, in the United States it includes firms below 500 employees. A small proportion engage in international trade and relatively few engage in FDI. International SMEs manage various combinations of market mechanisms (imports and exports) and internalization (input and output-oriented FDI) to benefit from location endowments worldwide.

4 Born global firms depend from "birth" on a global presence for their survival. A key debate is whether firms count as born global if they simply trade, rather than engage in FDI. There is also strong evidence to suggest that most are born regional, not global, particularly because they are subject to the multiple liabilities of smallness, newness, and foreignness.

5 Dynamic capability is: "the firm's ability to integrate, build, and reconfigure internal and external competences to address rapidly changing environments." The dynamic capabilities approach is useful for understanding international new ventures because their survival through the entrepreneurial life cycle depends on the continuous renewal of assets, knowledge, and global networks.

6 Industry clusters evolve from the efficiencies of co-locating specialist industry suppliers and contractors. But part of their evolution is also due to the continuing value of face-to-face interaction for building trust, co-specialization networks, and entrepreneurial cultures. As knowledge-based products and services grow in economic importance relative to physical products, virtual network hubs or nodes will grow in importance relative to location-bound clusters.

7 Because SMEs lack the resources to invest in rigorous market analysis, personal experience plays a greater role in market-entry decision making. Mental maps show how risk-perception influences market selection and internationalization strategies.

8 SMEs need to be more entrepreneurial, innovative, and adaptable to successfully break into foreign markets, given they lack the resources, scale, and scope advantages of larger firms. Tough and expensive country markets like Japan present greater risks and demand even greater levels of innovation and adaptability.

Key terms

- Innovation
- National Innovation Systems (NIS)
- Center-for-global, local-for-local, local-for-global, and global-for-global innovation
- Ambidexterity
- Collaboratories

- Small-and-medium-sized enterprises (SMEs)
- Born global firms
- Born regional firms
- Dynamic capability
- Industry clusters or "agglomeration economies"
- Mental maps

REVIEW AND DISCUSSION QUESTIONS

1 What is innovation? What innovation advantages do all multinational firms have? What disadvantages to SMEs have relative to large multinational enterprises for innovation?

2 As a form of country-specific advantage (CSA), how might a strong national system of innovation (NSI) support the development of innovation-related firm-specific advantages (FSAs) for an internationalizing firm?

3 List some examples of innovation FSAs for market-seeking internationalization and for resource-seeking internationalization.

4 Give an example of "local-for-global" innovation (from one of the case studies in this chapter if you can find it . . .).

5 Why do national governments need specific criteria for defining an SME? Why might different governments use different definitions?

6 Explain, with an example, why an international new venture or SME might combine trading activity (imports and exports) with FDI to maintain an international business.

7 What are the key debates around the definition of the born global firm and why do these make a difference in terms of our measurement and understanding of them?

8 Why are dynamic capabilities particularly important for small and internationalizing firms?

9 Why might the importance of physical co-location in industrial clusters diminish relative to online networks or virtual hubs of specialists?

10 How do mental maps help us better understand market selection decision-making in small firms?

REAL CASE

GE Healthcare in India: locally driven innovation

GE's Mac 400 is an ultra-portable electrocardiogram (ECG) which is made in India and has sold well locally, partly because it costs one-third of the price of an equivalent imported product. It is also light-weight, battery-operated, and easily serviced, making it ideal for India's rural areas where patients are far from specialist hospitals and power outages are common. The reason that the Mac 400 is so well suited to India is because it was conceptualized, designed, and sourced, as well as manufactured, in India, all following local customer requirements.

GE employs over 13,000 people in India and exports over $1 billion in products and services. One of its major business divisions, GE Healthcare, has invested in local joint ventures and manufacturing plants since the beginning of the 1990s, to reduce costs and increase local sales. But it is only much more recently that it has devolved some of the responsibility, capability, and resources to the local subsidiaries to pursue locally appropriate innovation.

The John F Welch Technology Center (JFWTC) in Bangalore was established in 2000 and is GE's first and largest multidisciplinary Research and Product Development Center outside of the United States. It collaborates with GE's four other R&D facilities that form the GE Global Research team (in New York, Munich, Shanghai, and Rio de Janeiro) to conduct R&D for all of GE's businesses worldwide. With over 4,000 employees and over 1,000 patents to its credit, it has hosted a range of technology development projects from train engines and aviation turbo fans to baby warmers in the healthcare field.

These investments, together with the organizational and cultural changes underpinning the devolution of power and resources to the local management in India, are beginning to pay dividends. Although India accounts for less than 2 percent of GE Healthcare's US$17 billion in revenue, this is set to rise dramatically as India's economic growth translates into increased buying power and better healthcare provision. At the same time GE's India-based R&D efforts are creating products that are being sold globally. Two thousand of the 7,500 Mac 400's that GE Healthcare has sold have been bought by Indian customers; the rest have been bought by customers in other country markets.

The drivers that underpin the focus of healthcare product innovation in India, including accessibility, quality, and low cost, apply to other developing and emerging markets. So new products designed and developed in India are likely to sell well in these markets. This has been termed "low-cost" (or "frugal") innovation and "innovation for the

bottom-of-the-pyramid" (Prahalad, 2006). By allowing local management to drive innovation, GE is able to target this rapidly growing market segment globally.

Success in one market segment can, however, create challenges elsewhere. The fact is that products like the Mac 400 have the potential to significantly undercut more expensive (and profitable) products sold in more advanced markets like Europe and the United States. This leaves GE with a potential problem of its own making: new products from its emerging economy subsidiaries may increasingly 'cannibalize' the firm's existing products in its more advanced markets.

Sources: Govindarajan, V. "On: Innovation, Strategy, Global business. 10 Tips for Creating Distinct-but-Linked Innovation Groups," Harvard Business Review blogs, (2010), at: http://blogs.hbr.org/govindarajan/2010/08/10-tips-for-creating-distinct-.html; Mahajan-Bansal, N. and Goyal, M. "Finger On The Pulse, At Last," Forbes India, Forbes.com (2009) at: http://www.forbes.com/2009/12/09/forbes-india-ge-healthcare-jeff-immelt-john-flannery.html; Prahalad C.K. (2006) *The Fortune at the Bottom of the Pyramid: Eradicating Poverty Through Profits* (Wharton School Publishing); "Reverse Innovation: GE Makes India a Lab for Global Markets" Published May 20, 2010 in India Knowledge@Wharton, at: http://knowledge.wharton.upenn.edu/india/article.cfm?articleid=4476; http://www.ge.com/in/company/factsheet_in.html; GE Innovation timeline at: http://www.ge.com/innovation/timeline/index.html.

1 In what ways is GE's Mac 400 ECG the result of 'local-for-local' innovation?

2 Why would GE establish R&D facilities in India?

3 What indications are there that the Mac 400 ECG has become an example of 'local-for-global' innovation?

4 How can multinational firms destroy their own profits by engaging in low-cost or 'bottom-of-the-pyramid' innovation?

REAL CASE

SetJam: the mini multinational

SetJam was founded in June 2009 and, like the vast majority of high-tech start-ups (but unlike the success stories we tend to hear about), it remains small and highly innovative but not exceptionally profitable.

SetJam works like a Google search engine for online video content, such as movies and TV shows. It allows users to search the web and create a directory of TV programs, both free and paid content, to view at any time. Its founder, Ryan Janssen, promotes the venture by describing how an organization of fewer than 15 people managed to build a "better search engine than Google for less than

$50,000." Like Google, however, the firm hopes to make money by taking customers where they want to go online faster and more efficiently than anyone else. On the back of the rise of broadband-enabled TV the central idea is to make online TV quick and simple for customers, filtering out the massive volume of user-generated content on the net and providing just regular programs for viewers to watch whenever they have time.

SetJam is headquartered in New York City's "Silicon Alley," an area associated with high-tech start-ups including Foursquare, Hot Potato, Six Apart, Flickr, Trust Art, and ▶

Vimeo, and named to echo the larger and better-known Silicon Valley in California. But in contrast to its Californian counterpart, this New York high-tech cluster has evolved around the media, publishing, luxury goods, and fashion industries. Start-up firms develop software for consumer-oriented services and social media websites, rather than for enterprises or electronics products. Many of the largest firms in these industries are headquartered in New York, so start-ups in the Silicon Alley cluster thrive on connections with client firms and the availability of experienced media and fashion industry employees to co-develop their platforms.

SetJam's client and investor connections are developed and maintained by CEO Ryan Janssen together with a project manager and the rest of a small team in the firm's New York office. The rest of SetJam's employees, consisting of six full-time developers and three quality assurance specialists, are all based 4,300 miles away in Warsaw, Poland. The six-hour time difference, the language barrier, and the complexities of dealing with a different set of employment regulations all beg the question: Why split the company in this way? The answer lies in human capital; the cost and availability of experienced software programmers and developers in Warsaw, relative to New York.

Human capital, rather than fixed assets, and not just the cost but the availability of highly educated people, with particular kinds of expertise, is a key driver for location decisions even in the smallest of firms. Poland has the youngest population in Europe and 45 percent of 20–24-year-olds are in higher education, compared to 34 percent in the United States. Eighty percent of students speak English (33 percent speak two foreign languages) and the country also has an excellent ICT (information and communication technologies) education and training infrastructure. These location attractions have prompted many of the large multinationals to establish R&D centres in Poland, including ABB, Fujitsu, GlaxoSmithKline, IBM, Intel, Motorola, Oracle, and Siemens. But they also make it an ideal location for offshore software engineering, an industry in which global spending is expected to grow tenfold over the next 10 years to an estimated $150 billion. With labor costs that are not far off those of India, Poland is set to benefit from this growth.

For SetJam, new technology is not just the focus of its business model; it underpins the way the company copes with its divided structure, enabling innovative ways of remote recruitment and team-working. Janssen found the first programmers through a process involving emails, Skype talks and an evaluation of their "online presence," including blogs and open source contributions. He also viewed their profiles and work experience on specialist collaborative software development hosting sites, such as Github and Django People. The latter is a global network of over 7,600 software developers from over 140 countries working on a variety of contract projects and represents a worldwide pool of "pay-as-you-go" expertise.

Digital bridges connect the two parts of the firm. "Campfire," a team collaboration platform with a real-time chat facility, and "Lighthouse," a project planning and workflow tracking system, are used to communicate and coordinate development projects. Skype video is also permanently on, providing a constant window between New York and Warsaw and creating a social interface as well as a business portal. Janssen is happy with the level of unity created across this small but ambitious organization by these online connections, despite quips by the Warsaw-based team that they, at development HQ, have outsourced the CEO role to the United States.

Sources: Krysztofiak-Szopa, J. "Polish programmers are joining U.S. startups – but staying in Poland," *Techcrunch* (November 7, 2010); Wortham, J. "New York Isn't Silicon Valley. That's Why They Like It," (March 6, 2010), *The New York Times*; Viteri, A. "Why RightSource to Poland? Quality, Stability, and Peace of Mind," Neubloc, http://www.neubloc.com/news.asp?nid=4.

E-references: http://www.setjam.com, http://djangopeople.net/, https://github.com/, http://campfirenow.com/

1 In what ways are SetJam's product or service particularly innovative?

2 How might SetJam's organization structure be seen as innovative? What specialist capabilities does the firm gain from each its two global locations?

3 Is there evidence that SetJam has particularly strong dynamic capabilities?

4 What are the benefits of sourcing specialist expertise online, as an input into the firm? What factors underpin the continuing importance of physically co-located specialists or businesses for SetJam?

ENDNOTES

1 Although slightly dated this definition is still one of the best. European Commission, "Green Paper on Innovation," *Bulletin of the European Union, Supplement 5/95* (Brussels, The European Commission, 1995).

2 C. Freeman, "The National System of Innovation in Historical Perspective," *Cambridge Journal of Economics*, no. 19 (1995), pp. 5–24; B-A. Lundvall, *National Systems of Innovation: Toward a Theory of Innovation and Interactive*

Learning (London: Anthem Press, 2010); R. Nelson (ed.), *National Innovation Systems: A Comparative Analysis* (Oxford: Oxford University Press, 1993).

3 C. Bartlett and S. Ghoshal, *Managing across Borders: The Transnational Solution* (Boston, MA: Harvard Business School Press, 2002).

4 N. Nohria and S. Ghoshal. *The Differentiated Network: Organizing MNCs for Value Creation* (San Francisco: Jossey-Bass, 1997).

5 In addition to Nohria and Ghoshal (1997 op cit.), a range of related readings on this topic can be found in C. Bartlett, S. Ghoshal and J. Birkinshaw, *Transnational Management: Text, Cases, and Readings in Cross-Border Management* (London: McGraw Hill, 2004).

6 M. Adenfelt and K. Lagerström, "The Development and Sharing of Knowledge by Centres of Excellence and Transnational Teams: A Conceptual Framework," *Management International Review*, vol. 48, no. 3 (2008) pp. 319–338.

7 C. M. Christensen, *The Innovator's Dilemma: When New Technologies Cause Great Firms to Fail* (Boston, MA: Harvard Business School Press, 1997).

8 S. C. Collinson, "Organising for Multimedia Product Development: Sony and Philips Compared," *Communications and Strategies*, vol. 19 (1995) pp. 47–77.

9 S. Raisch and J. M. Birkinshaw, "Organizational Ambidexterity: Antecedents, Outcomes, and Moderators," *Journal of Management*, vol. 34, no. 3 (2008) pp. 375–409.

10 S. C. Collinson and A. M. Rugman, "The Regional Nature of Japanese Multinational Business," *Journal of International Business Studies*, vol. 39, no. 2 (2008) pp. 215–230. S. C. Collinson and D. C. Wilson, "Inertia in Japanese Organizations: Knowledge Management Routines and Failure to Innovate," *Organization Studies*, vol. 27, no. 9 (2005) pp. 1359–1387.

11 See, for example, M. L. Mors, "Innovation in a Global Consulting Firm: When the Problem Is Too Much Diversity," *Strategic Management Journal*, vol. 31, no. 8 (2010) pp. 841–887.

12 A. D. Chandler, *Scale and Scope* (Cambridge, MA: The Belknap Press of Harvard University, 1990). See also Bartlett and Ghoshal (2002) op cit.

13 G. A. Knight and D. Kim, "International Business Competence and the Contemporary Firm," *Journal of International Business Studies*, vol. 40, no. 2 (2009), pp. 255–273; G. A. Knight, "Entrepreneurship and Strategy in the International SME," *Journal of International Management*, vol. 7 (2001), pp. 155–171; S. C. Collinson, *Small and Successful in Japan: A Study of 30 British Firms in the World's Most Competitive Market* (London: Avebury Press, 1996).

14 US Small Business Administration at: http://www.sba.gov/advocacy/7495/8420.

15 This distinction lies at the heart of Oliver Williamson's "transaction cost economics" (TCE) (Williamson, 1975) between market and hierarchy. The latter refers to the situation where transactions are internalized within the firm ("hierarchy") because this incurs lower transactions costs compared to the market. In a similar vein, but with a different approach, Edith Penrose (1959) asked "why do firms do what they do?" I.e. what determines the boundaries of the firm? She explored why firms left some business activities to the market and encompassed others internally. This is of central interest in international business theory, but only when the internalization involves incorporating overseas assets or business activities into the firm, rather than relying on (import-export) markets. By taking this step firms become multinationals.

16 P. P. McDougall and B. M. Oviatt, "Defining International Entrepreneurship and Modeling the Speed of Internationalization," *Entrepreneurship Theory and Practice*, vol. 29 (2005), pp. 537–553; P. P. McDougall and B. M. Oviatt, "International Entrepreneurship: The Intersection of Two Research Paths," *Academy of Management Journal*, vol. 43, no. 5 (2000), pp. 902–906; B. M. Oviatt and P. P. McDougall, "Toward a Theory of International New Ventures," *Journal of International Business Studies*, vol. 25 (1994), pp. 45–64.

17 J. Johanson and J.-E. Vahlne, "The Internationalization Process of the Firm: A Model of Knowledge Development and Increasing Foreign Market Commitments," *Journal of International Business Studies*, vol. 8, no. 1 (1977), pp. 23–32.

18 A. M. Rugman and A. Verbeke, "A Note on the Transnational Solution and the Transaction Cost Theory of Multinational Strategic Management," *Journal of International Business Studies*, vol. 23, no. 4 (1992), pp. 761–771; A. M. Rugman and A. Verbeke, "A Perspective on Regional and Global Strategies of Multinational Enterprises," *Journal of International Business Studies*, vol. 35, no. 1 (2004) pp. 3–18; A. M. Rugman, *The Regional Multinationals* (Cambridge: Cambridge University Press, 2005); A. M. Rugman and A. Verbeke, "Liabilities of Regional Foreignness and the Use of Firm-Level Versus Country-Level Data: A Response to Dunning et al.," *Journal of International Business Studies*, vol. 38, no. 1 (2007), pp. 200–205.

19 B. Wernerfelt, "The Resource-Based View of the Firm," *Strategic Management Journal*, vol. 5, no. 2 (1984), pp. 171–180; J. B. Barney, "Is the Resource-Based Theory a Useful Perspective for Strategic Management Research? Yes," *Academy of Management Review*, vol. 26, no. 1 (2001), pp. 41–56.

20 Rugman and Verbeke (1992, op cit.). See also: D. J. Teece, "Transactions Cost Economics and the Multinational Enterprise: An Assessment,' *Journal of Economic Behaviour and Organization*, vol. 7 (1986), pp. 21–45.

21 I. H. Lee, "The M Curve: The Performance of Born Regional Firms from Korea," *Multinational Business Review*, vol. 18, no. 4 (2010), pp. 1–22.

22 T. Fan and P. Phan, "International New Ventures: Revisiting the Influences Behind the 'Born-Global' Firm," *Journal of International Business Studies*, vol. 38, no. 7 (2007), pp. 1113–1131; L. E. Lopez, S. K. Kundu and L. Ciravegna, "Born Global or Born Regional? Evidence from an Exploratory Study in the Costa Rican Software Industry," *Journal of International Business Studies*, vol. 40, no. 7 (2009), pp. 1228–1238.

23 See some of the original work on dynamic capabilities: D. Teece, G. Pisano and A. Shuen, "Dynamic Capabilities and Strategic Management," *Strategic Management Journal*, vol. 18, no. 7 (1997), pp. 509–533; K. Eisenhardt and

J. Martin, "Dynamic Capabilities: What Are They?" *Strategic Management Journal*, vol. 21 (2000), pp. 1105–1122. Also see: S. A. Zahra, H. J. Sapienza and P. Davidsson, "Entrepreneurship and Dynamic Capabilities: A Review, Model and Research Agenda," *Journal of Management Studies*, vol. 43, no. 4 (2006), pp. 917–955.

24 C. E. Helfat et al., *Dynamic Capabilities: Understanding Strategic Change in Organisations* (Oxford: Wiley-Blackwell 2007) is the best overview of the dynamic capabilities field, from a theory perspective. A good set of papers also appears in: M. Easterby-Smith, M. A. Lyles and M. A. Peteraf, "Dynamic Capabilities: Current Debates and Future Directions," *British Journal of Management*, vol. 20, no.1 (2009), pp. S1–S8. Some studies explicitly focus on dynamic capabilities in small firms, such as: E. Døving and P. Gooderham, "Dynamic Capabilities as Antecedents of the Scope of Related Diversification: The Case of Small Firm Accountancy Practices," *Strategic Management Journal*, vol. 29, no. 8 (2008) pp. 841–857.

25 J. A. Schumpeter, *Capitalism, Socialism and Democracy* (New York: Harper, 1942).

26 Research on capability life cycles, such as: C. E. Helfat and M. A. Peteraf, "The Dynamic Resource-Based View: Capability Lifecycles," *Strategic Management Journal*, vol. 24 (2003) pp. 997–1010, has obvious parallels with research on S-curves. S-curves show how firms can become over-dependent on and "locked" into an over-reliance on certain kinds of products, assets, and capabilities, such that when markets or technologies change they are unable to reinvent themselves and go into decline. See, amongst other work: C. Christensen, *The Innovator's Dilemma* (Boston, MA: Harvard Business School Press, 1997).

27 For a review of lifecycle theory see: J. Levie and B. Lichtenstein, "A Terminal Assessment of Stages Theory: Introducing a Dynamic States Approach to Entrepreneurship," *Entrepreneurship Theory and Practice*, vol. 34, no. 2 (2010), pp. 317–350.

28 Alfred Marshall is seen as the earliest scholar to focus on the importance of agglomeration economies; A. Marshall, *Principles of Economics* (London: Macmillan and Co., 1920, 8th ed.). Annalee Saxenian's books: A. Saxenian, *The New Argonauts Regional Advantage in a Global Economy* (Boston, MA: Harvard University Press, 2007) and A. Saxenian, *Regional Advantage: Culture and Competition in Silicon Valley*

and Route 128 (Boston, MA: Harvard University Press, 1996) popularized the concept of high-tech clusters. Michael Porter also strongly influenced regional policymakers; M. Porter, "Location, Competition, and Economic Development: Local Clusters in a Global Economy," *Economic Development Quarterly*, vol. 14, no. 1 (2000) pp. 15–34. P. Dicken, *Global Shift: Mapping the Changing Contours of the World Economy* (London: Sage, 2010, 6th ed.) provides by far the best overview of economic geography, including modern-day clusters, available.

29 A. D. Chandler (1990, op cit.)

30 For a summary, which particularly focuses on the reliance of small firms on intangible capabilities for successful internationalization, see: G. A. Knight and D. Kim, "International business competence and the contemporary firm," *Journal of International Business Studies*, vol. 40, no. 2 (2009), pp. 255–273. Also: O. Burgel, G. Murray, A. Fier and G. Licht, *The Rapid Internationalization of High Tech Young firms in Germany and the United Kingdom, A Summary Report for the Anglo-German Foundation for the Study of the Industrial Society* (2000).

31 J. A. Mathews and I. Zander "The International Entrepreneurial Dynamics of Accelerated Internationalisation," *Journal of International Business Studies*, vol. 38, no. 3 (2007) pp. 387–403.

32 J. W. Liu and P. W. Beamish, "The internationalization and performance of SMEs," *Strategic Management Journal*, vol. 22 (2001) pp. 565–586.

33 S. McGaughey, D. Welch and L. Welch, "Managerial Influences and SME Internationalization," in I. Bjorkman and M. Forsgren (eds.), *The Nature of the International Firm* (Copenhagen: Handelshojskolens Forlag, 1997), pp. 165–188.

34 S. C. Collinson and J. Holden, "Decision-Making and Market Orientation in the Internationalization Process of Small-and-Medium Enterprises," *Management International Review*, vol. 45, no. 4 (2005), pp. 413–436.

35 B. Cassiman and E. Golovko, "Innovation and Internationalization through Exports," *Journal of International Business Studies*, vol. 42, no. 1 (2011), pp. 56–75.

36 K. D. Brouthers and G. Nakos, "SME Entry Mode Choice and Performance: A Transaction Cost Perspective," *Entrepreneurship Theory and Practice*, vol. 28, no. 3 (2004), pp. 229–247.

37 S. C. Collinson (1996, op cit.).

ADDITIONAL BIBLIOGRAPHY

Acs, Zoltan J. and Audretsch, David B. (eds.) *Handbook of Entrepreneurship Research* (New York: Springer, 2nd ed. 2010).

Adenfelt, Maria and Lagerström, Katarina. "The Development and Sharing of Knowledge by Centres of Excellence and Transnational Teams: A Conceptual Framework," *Management International Review*, vol. 48, no. 3 (2008), pp. 319–338.

Almor, Tamar. "Dancing as fast as they can: Israeli high-tech firms and the Great Recession of 2008," *Thunderbird International Business Review*, vol. 53, no. 2 (2011), pp. 195–208.

Bell, Jim, Crick, David and Young, Stephen. "Small firm internationalization and business strategy," *International Small Business Journal*, vol. 22, no. 1 (2004).

Bessant, John and Tidd, Joe. *Innovation and Entrepreneurship* (London: John Wiley & Sons, 2nd ed., 2011).

Blundel, Richard and Lockett, Nigel. *Exploring Entrepreneurship: Practices and Perspectives* (Oxford: OUP, 2011).

Burns, Paul. *Entrepreneurship and Small Business: Start-up, Growth and Maturity* (Basingstoke: Palgrave Macmillan, 3rd ed., 2010).

Calcagnini, Giorgio and Favaretto, Ilario. *The Economics of Small Businesses: An International Perspective* (Physica-Verlag HD, 1st ed., 2011).

Cassiman, Bruno and Golovko, Elena. "Innovation and internationalization through exports," *Journal of International Business Studies*, vol. 42, no. 1 (2011) pp. 56–75.

Capelleras, Joan-Lluis, Mole, Kevin F., Greene, Francis J. and Storey, David J. "Do More Heavily Regulated Economies Have Poorer Performing New Ventures? Evidence from Britain and Spain," *Journal of International Business Studies*, vol. 39, no. 4 (2008) pp. 688–704.

Chesbrough, Henry, Vanhaverbeke, Wim and West, Joel. *Open Innovation: Researching a New Paradigm* (Oxford: Oxford University Press, 2008).

Coviello, Nicole E. "The Network Dynamics of International New Ventures," *Journal of International Business Studies*, vol. 37, no. 5 (2006) pp. 713–731.

Delios, Andrew and Beamish, Paul W. "Regional and Global Strategies of Japanese Firms," *Journal of International Business Studies,* vol. 45 (2005).

Dodgson, Mark and Gann, David, M. *Innovation: A Very Short Introduction*, Very Short Introductions (Oxford: Oxford University Press, 2010).

Dodgson, Mark, Gann, David, M. and Salter, Ammon. *The Management of Technological Innovation: Strategy and Practice* (Oxford: Oxford University Press, 2nd ed., 2008).

Drucker, Peter F. *Innovation and Entrepreneurship* (Oxford: Butterworth-Heinemann, 2007).

Fabian, Frances, Molina, Henry and Labianca, Giuseppe. "Understanding Decisions to Internationalize by Small and Medium-sized Firms Located in an Emerging Market," *Management International Review*, vol. 49, no. 5 (2009) pp. 537–563.

Fagerberg, Jan, Mowery, David C. and Nelson, Richard R. *The Oxford Handbook of Innovation* (Oxford: Oxford University Press, 2006).

Gabrielsson, Mika, Kirpalani, Manek, Dimitratos, Pavlos, Solberg, Carl, A. and Zucchella, Antonella. "Born Globals: Propositions to Help Advance the Theory," *International Business Review*, vol. 17, No. 4 (2008), pp. 385–401.

Ghemawat, Pankaj. "Semiglobalization and International Business Strategy," *Journal of International Business Studies*, vol. 34, no. 2 (2003).

HBR, *Harvard Business Review on Succeeding as an Entrepreneur* (Boston, MA: Harvard Business School Press, 2011).

Javalgi, Rajshekhar G. and Todd, Patricia R. "Entrepreneurial Orientation, Management Commitment, and Human Capital: The Internationalization of SMEs in India," *Journal of Business Research*, vol. 64, no. 9 (2011) pp.1004–1010.

Jones, Oswald and Tilley, Fiona (eds.). *Competitive Advantage in SMEs: Organising for Innovation and Change* (London: John Wiley & Sons, 2003).

Jones, Marian V. and Coviello, Nicolle E. "Internationalisation: Conceptualising an Entrepreneurial Process of Behaviour in Time," *Journal of International Business Studies*, vol. 36 (2005) pp. 284–303.

Jones, Marian V., Dimitratos, P., Fletcher, M. and Young, S. (eds.) *Internationalization, Entrepreneurship and the Smaller Firm: Evidence from Around the World* (London: Edward Elgar, 2009).

Knight, Gary A. and Cavusgil, S. Tamar. "Innovation Organizational Capabilities and the Born-Global Firm," *Journal of International Business Studies*, vol. 35, no. 2 (2004), pp. 124–141.

Lee, In Hyeock. "The M Curve: The Performance of Born Regional Firms from Korea," *Multinational Business Review*, vol. 18, no. 4 (2010).

Lianxi Zhou, Wei-ping Wu and Xueming Luo. "Internationalization and the Performance of Born-Global SMEs: The Mediating Role of Social Networks," *Journal of International Business Studies*, vol. 38, no. 4 (2007) pp. 673–690.

Meyer, Marc H. and Crane, Frederick G. *Entrepreneurship: An Innovator's Guide to Startups and Corporate Ventures* (London: Sage, 2011).

Morgan-Thomas, Anna and Jones, Marian V. "Post Entry Internationalisation Dynamics: Differences between SMEs in the Development Speed of their International Sales," *International Small Business Journal*, vol. 27, no. 1 (2009).

Ohmae, Kenichi. *Triad Power: The Coming Shape of Global Competition* (New York: The Free Press, 1985).

Penrose, Edith. *The Theory of the Growth of the Firm* (New York: Wiley, 1959).

Prahalad, C. K. and, Krishnan, M. S. *The New Age of Innovation: Driving Co-created Value Through Global Networks* (New York: McGraw-Hill Professional, 2008).

Roza, Marja, Van den Bosch, Frans A. J. and Volberda, Henk W. "Offshoring Strategy: Motives, Functions, Locations, and Governance Modes of Small, Medium-Sized and Large Firms," *International Business Review*, vol. 20, no. 3 (2011) pp. 314–323.

Rugman, A. M. and Almodovar, P. "The Born Global Illusion and the Regional Nature of International Business," in R. Ramamurti and N. Hashai (eds.), *Research in Global Strategic Management, Volume 15, The Future of Foreign Direct Investment and the Multinational Enterprise* (Bingley: Emerald, 2011), pp. 265–283.

Shih, Tsui-Yii and Wickramasekera, Rumintha. "Export Decisions within Taiwanese Electrical and Electronic SMEs: The Role of Management Characteristics and Attitudes," *Asia-Pacific Journal of Management*, vol. 28, no. 2 (2011) pp. 353–377.

Spence, Martine, Orser, Barbara and Riding, Allan. "A Comparative Study of International and Domestic New Ventures," *Management International Review*, vol. 51, no. 1 (2011) pp. 3–21.

Storey, David J. and Greene, Francis. *Small Business and Entrepreneurship* (London: Financial Times/Prentice Hall, 2010).

Tidd, Joe and Bessant, John. *Managing Innovation: Integrating Technological, Market and Organizational Change* (London: John Wiley & Sons, 2009).

Williamson, O. E. *Markets and Hierarchies: Analysis and Antitrust Implications: A Study in the Economics of Internal Organizations.* (New York: Free Press, 1975).

Wright, Mike, Westhead, Paul and Ucbasaran, Deniz. "Internationalization of Small and Medium-Sized

Enterprises (SMEs) and International Entrepreneurship: A Critique and Policy Implication," *Regional Studies*, vol. 41, no. 7 (2007).

Zahra, Shaker A. and George, Gerry. "International Entrepreneurship: The Current Status of the Field and Future Research Agenda," in M. Hitt, D. Ireland, D. Sexton, and M. Camp (eds), *Entrepreneurship: Creating an Integrated Mindset* (Oxford: Blackwell, 2002) pp. 255–88.

WWW RESOURCES

http://www.entrepreneur.com/
http://ec.europa.eu/enterprise/policies/sme/index_en.htm
http://www.fasttrack.co.uk
http://www.fsb.org.uk/
http://www.msme.gov.in

http://www.oecd.org/home
http://www.sba.gov/
http://www.ukti.gov.uk/investintheuk/
globalentrepreneursprogramme.html
http://www.usaid.gov/

Part Four

FUNCTIONAL AREA STRATEGIES

Chapter 12

PRODUCTION STRATEGY

Contents

Objectives of the chapter

Production strategy is critical to effective international operations.
Most goods and services have very limited lives, so MNEs must
continually provide new offerings, which can be accomplished
only through a well-formulated production strategy. This chapter
examines how MNEs carry out this process. In doing so, we will
focus on the entire range of production strategies from research and
development to manufacturing, shipment, and the final international
destination. We will look at the most current approaches, including
speed-to-market, concurrent engineering, and continuous cost
reduction.

The specific objectives of this chapter are to:

1 *Examine* the role of research, development, and innovation in
production strategy.

2 *Relate* some of the most critical steps in generating goods and
services, including global sourcing, costing techniques, quality
maintenance, effective materials handling, inventory control, and
the proper emphasis on service.

3 *Describe* the nature and importance of international logistics in
production strategy.

4 *Review* some of the major production strategies being used by
MNEs, including strategic alliances and acquisitions.

ACTIVE LEARNING CASE

The GE production process and Six Sigma

General Electric is a multibillion-dollar multinational corporation whose products range from 65 cent light bulbs to billion-dollar power plants. Based on revenues, assets, profits, and market value, the company was listed by *Fortune* magazine as number 13 in the world in 2010. One reason for GE's annual revenue of $156,779 million is its ability to manage a diverse multi product-line operation, handling such products as major appliances, lighting, medical diagnostic imaging equipment, motors, and commercial and military aircraft engines and engineering materials. GE also provides a range of services, including those related to electricity provision, media (GE owns NBC in the United States), and multimedia programming and distribution. Much of the company's success can be attributed to the production-related concepts it has employed over the last two decades. During the 1980s, work-out, process mapping, and best practices were GE's applied concepts.

Work-out is a training program designed to empower employees to implement their problem-solving ideas. A group of 40 to 100 people, picked by management from all ranks and functional areas, attend a three-day meeting. The first day consists of a manager leading the group in roughing out an agenda addressing areas in which productivity can be increased. Then the manager leaves and for the next l\ days the group breaks into teams to tackle the agenda. On the last afternoon the manager returns and one by one the team members make their proposals for improved productivity. The manager can make only three responses: agree, disagree, or ask for more information; in the last case, an individual manager must empower a team to get the information by an agreed-upon date. These work-out sessions have proved extremely successful. In one case, a group of workers convinced management to allow their factory to bid against an outside vendor for the right to build new protective shields for grinding machines. As a result, the GE group completed the job for $16,000 versus $96,000 for the vendor.

The second method, *process mapping*, is to create a flowchart that shows all the steps, no matter how small, involved in making or doing something. The map is analyzed for ways to eliminate steps and save time and money. One work group was able to reorganize production, cut manufacturing time in half, and reduce inventory by $4 million.

The third method, *best practices*, consists of finding companies that do things better than GE does and emulating them. GE personnel try to answer the question: what is the

secret of this other company's success? Quite often the answer includes such things as getting products to market faster than anyone else, treating suppliers like partners, or having superior inventory management. As a result of best practices, GE is now keeping executives in their jobs for longer periods of time rather than rotating them quickly through new jobs; the best practices process revealed that frequent changes create problems in new product introductions. The company also learned how to use continuous improvement processes more effectively to bring a new product into the market ahead of the competition and then work on introducing new technologies. In the past the firm would try to perfect all technologies first and then introduce the final product version.

In the 1990s, the dominant production concept was Six Sigma, a name that originates from a statistical method for deriving near-perfect quality, equal to 3.4 defects per million operations. The Six Sigma process allows GE to measure how many "defects" there are in a given process and then systematically work to eliminate them to approximate "zero defects." Six Sigma recognizes three elements: the customer, the process, and the employee. The customer is the key to defining quality. GE uses the term "Delighting Customers" to generate a mentality whereby customer expectations of performance, reliability, competitive price, on-time delivery, service, clear and correct transaction processing, and other customer needs become a key factor in all processes. The second element, the process, promotes "Outside-In Thinking Quality." GE must understand the transaction life cycle from the customer's point of view and identify significant value and improvement from that same perspective. Under the banner "Leadership Commitment People," the third element of Six Sigma, the employee, requires that all personnel use their talents and energies to satisfy customers. All employees are trained in Six Sigma, including statistical tools, strategy, and techniques of Six Sigma quality. At the core of the process is a workforce mentality on customer quality expectations, defect reduction, process capability, variation (the customer reacts to the variance rather than the average results), stability of operations, and designing processes to meet customer expectations.

GE's advantage over failing conglomerates is its ability to transfer knowledge over the whole company. This can be attributed to former CEO Jack Welch, who oversaw GE's transformation from a mainly manufacturing firm to a service-oriented, knowledge-based company. He defined

GE's culture by creating a workforce that can identify opportunities and implement changes.

Despite GE's firm-specific advantages (FSAs) in production, its competitive edge has not been transferred equally to other parts of the world, especially not other triad nations that have significant domestic competitors. While GE used to be a home-region company with 64 percent of its sales in the Americas, now the company is more diversified. GE now derives 46.20 percent of its revenues from the US alone. Once its revenues from Canadian and Latin American operations are added on top of the US sales, the number rises to nearly 54.30 percent. Europe, its largest foreign regional market, accounts for only 23.50 percent of revenues, whereas countries in the Pacific Basin account for 13.20 percent. The remaining 7 percent are accounted for by other regions (2.6 percent) and non-segmented US exports to other countries (6.4 percent).

In October 2000, GE, as the world's largest producer of jet engines, and Honeywell, a manufacturer of aircraft electronics, agreed to a $42 billion merger. The two US-based companies secured antitrust authorities' approval in the United States and Canada, but the deal came to a halt because of the European Union. This was the first time the EU had blocked a merger between two US companies. The European competition commissioner claimed that such a merger would have closed the market to competitors and asked GE to divest itself of GE Capital Aviation Services by selling it to one of its main rivals. GE offered to sell the company privately, but the EU countered that a friendly transaction might not result in true divestiture. US politicians, frustrated by the European stand, threatened to retaliate if the EU did not approve the merger. Republican Senator Phil Gramm went as far as to accuse the EU of enacting policies to protect its companies. The EU rejected US government intervention in the matter and the merger did not materialize.

Website: www.ge.com.

Sources: "The World's Super Fifty," *Forbes*, July 27, 1998, p. 118; www.ge.com; General Electric, *10KSEC Filing*, 2002; "EU Rejects Latest GE Offers," *BBC. co.uk*, June 29, 2001; "EU Blocks GE/Honeywell Deal," BBC.co.uk, July 3, 2001; "US Senators Lash Out at EU Over GE Deal," BBC.co.uk, June 15, 2001; "Fortune Global 500," *Fortune*, 2010, at http://money.cnn.com/magazines/fortune/global500/2010/; GE, *Annual Report*, 2009.

1 How did GE use work-out to increase speed-to-market?

2 How has GE used Six Sigma to reduce cost and improve quality in consumer goods? In each case, give an example.

3 In what way could best practices help GE develop more effective international strategies? Explain.

INTRODUCTION

Production management has been responsible for many new goods and services. Examples are as varied as Palm's handhelds, Apple's iPod, Honda's hybrid cars, HP's digital cameras, eBay's Internet auctions, and five-star hotel operations at the Ritz-Carlton. The nature of production management in the MNE is similar in many respects to that in domestic firms. Both are concerned with the efficient use of labor and capital. Both are also interested in investing in research and development (R&D) and in organizing operations to generate successful new product lines and increase production and service efficiency.

Like domestic firms, MNEs need to organize their production management so they can minimize operating costs through the use of logistics and inventory control. Canon, for example, relocates production to China only if labor accounts for over 5 percent of production costs.[1] Acer, the successful upstart from Taiwan, makes sure that computer parts with short product life cycles are shipped by air, and those with long product life cycles are shipped by sea (see Active Learning Case in Chapter 20). However, pressures from host-country governments or special interest groups can affect a multinational's decision making in these areas. For example, host governments often criticize resource-based MNEs for their backward, forward, and horizontal integration. **Backward integration**, which is the ownership of equity assets used earlier in the production cycle (such as an auto firm acquiring a steel company), is criticized for doing little for employment or development

Backward integration
The ownership of equity assets used earlier in the production cycle, such as an auto firm that acquires a steel company

Forward integration
The purchase of assets or facilities that move the company closer to the customer, such as a computer manufacturer that acquires a retail chain that specializes in computer products

Horizontal integration
The purchase of firms in the same line of business, such as a computer chip firm that acquires a competitor

in the host nation. **Forward integration**, which is the purchase of assets or facilities that move the company closer to the customer (such as a computer manufacturer that acquires a retail chain that specializes in computer sales), is criticized on the basis that MNEs use the strategy to homogenize consumer tastes to the detriment of national identities. **Horizontal integration**, which is the acquisition of firms in the same line of business (such as a computer chip manufacturer that buys a competitor), is attacked for introducing similar product lines on a worldwide basis and undercutting the existence of local firms, most of which lack the economies of scale that can be achieved by MNEs.[2]

There are similar challenges in the industrial relations area, where MNEs must take into account different labor practices and wage rates. For example, multinationals are often under pressure from host governments to use local sourcing for their supplies, hire local workers, train home-country managers and supervisors, and help improve the production environment in the host nation. These decisions can sometimes result in higher production costs, although most international auto firms, for example, use local suppliers and workers to offset this problem.

The financing of operations is another production-related challenge. The choice between local and international borrowing and the use of internally generated funds to minimize the cost of capital is complicated by foreign exchange risk, international tax laws, and government controls on capital (see Chapter 16). Additionally, MNEs need to know where they are on their production cost curves in each country, as well as globally, so as to exploit any cost advantages with an appropriate organization structure. For example, as Toyota's worldwide market share began to stabilize, the firm found it needed to become increasingly more efficient.[3]

The above examples illustrate some of the common production-related problems facing international firms. However, experienced MNEs have learned how to deal with these challenges. In doing so, they employ a wide gamut of production strategies that address research, development, innovation, global sourcing, costing techniques, and inventory control.[4] The following sections examine each of these production strategies.

RESEARCH, DEVELOPMENT, AND INNOVATION

Production strategies do *not* begin with manufacturing. In the past many MNEs focused most heavily on this aspect of operations, failing to realize that an effective production strategy begins with new product development. This conclusion gains in importance when one considers that many of today's best-selling products and services were unavailable a short while ago. Examples include laptops, cellular phones, satellite navigation devices, DVD players, broadband DSL lines, and specialized discount stores that cater to selective product lines such as home-related goods or office supplies. Many other products and services have been greatly improved over the last decade or so. Examples include antidepressant medication, automobiles, facsimile machines, hazardous waste treatment services, home-delivery food services, medical diagnostic equipment, pacemakers, personal computers, photocopiers, telephones, and televisions. MNEs have come to realize that if they are not developing new goods and services, they must be improving their current offerings. In either case the focus is on R&D and innovation.

Innovation can be broadly divided into product/service development and process development. The former refers to activities that support the creation of new products and services that customers want, or improvements to existing products/services that make more customers want them instead of those of rival firms. The latter refers to innovation activities that improve the way products/services are produced, making them quicker, cheaper, or better quality. Continuous innovation lies at the heart of sustained competitive advantage, and managing it effectively has a strong international business component.

Most large firms are involved in all of these activities. Sony, for example, is continually coming up with new technology platforms (CDs, DVDs, minidisks, and so on) and new products based around these platforms. But it also invests in improving current product lines, with new models and new features, and it strives to make them cheaper through economies of scale and continuous improvement in manufacturing.

For us, concerned with the international strategy and organization of innovation and R&D, there are several key issues. The first is the question of how far products, services, and the processes that create them should be standardized across all locations, as opposed to customizing these to suit local markets. This lies at the heart of the "integration-responsiveness" theme that runs through this book. Despite the highly standardized nature of their products, even firms like McDonald's and Coca-Cola customize these for particular markets. Like all firms they have to manage a natural tension between country market managers who would like more customization to suit their local customer needs and head-office managers in the marketing, operations, human resource management, R&D, and strategy departments which would prefer to standardize across all markets.

A related issue is: where should firms locate different innovation-related activities? The answer to this depends on the industry and often the product or service in question. It is worth examining this by looking at the factors that influence the organization of R&D around the firm.

MNEs tend to operate several types of R&D networks, as shown on Figure 12.1. There is an innovation hierarchy from basic, long-term, or blue-sky R&D, which is often based around finding scientific breakthroughs, to applied, near-market, or demand-led innovation:

- Blue-sky or basic R&D centers are often linked to universities or government research institutes to tap into highly specialized expertise, wherever it is in the world.

- Technical design and development centers focus on more practical, near-market R&D and may be separate or co-located with regional headquarters or major business units.

- Applied technical development and customization departments, often situated within manufacturing centers, will focus on incremental improvements to production processes or minor adaptations to products to suit local markets.

Home country-based central R&D often sets the overall R&D strategy across a firm, but funding and other resources may partly come from country market managers who will

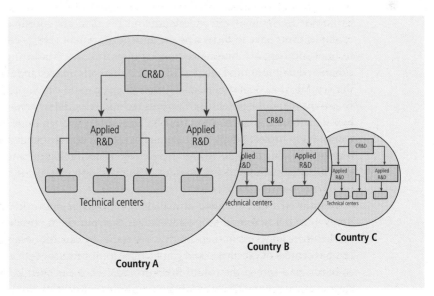

Figure 12.1 Global R&D: markets and hierarchies

push for more applied R&D activities to adapt products and services for their markets. For a large MNE, a few key locations may have R&D units, the firm's main markets may all have one or more applied R&D centers, and production locations will have technical centers. The complexity of managing strategy and implementation up and down the innovation hierarchy and across the different country locations should not be underestimated.

In terms of both product and process development, MNEs need to prioritize country locations according to both (1) local market requirements in terms of adaptation, design and development, and engineering support and (2) local technological resources, expertise, contract companies, universities, and so on, often called the "national system of innovation."

Hewlett-Packard (HP) is a good example of these kinds of structures. It has six basic R&D centers in Palo Alto, California; Cambridge, Massachusetts; Bristol, England; Grenoble, France; Haifa, Israel; and Tokyo, Japan. These explore a wide range of technologies more or less linked to its product range. Its Advanced Studies Research Labs include a subgroup doing information theory research, linking the Mathematical Science Group based in Bristol with experts at the US universities at Stanford and Berkeley. Grenoble specializes in business PC design and development and Israel in image and document processing, among other areas.

These centers of research excellence are linked to HP's global product divisions, mainly headquartered in the United States, and its national subsidiaries around the world, which encompass most of its 85,500 employees.

The Palo Alto center pioneered HP's thermal ink-jet technology, for example. Its Consumer Products group headquartered in San Diego, California, designed, developed, and led the manufacturing of a range of imaging products using this technology. The firm's subsidiary in Singapore customizes the design and produces thermal inkjet printers for the Japanese and Asian markets.

The R&D structure of the firm evolved a step further when the Singaporean subsidiary took the lead from San Diego for the design, development, and manufacturing of a new range of portable inkjet printers. It had built up a range of specialist capabilities, through learning from other parts of the internal network and through local Asian technical partnerships and subcontractors that made it the best place to lead innovation efforts in this area for the firm as a whole.[5]

The above organization structures are important because they affect how well firms leverage their R&D efforts for competitive advantage. The efficiency with which specialist knowledge inputs from experts around the firm are coordinated is paramount. For example, firms have to focus new product development (NPD) efforts at the point where technological opportunities meet market opportunities. Marketing departments and subsidiaries, distributors and retailers in country markets understand customer needs, whereas the central R&D department and technical design and development centers around the firm understand the potential of various technologies. These areas of specialist knowledge have to combine efficiently to direct NPD, and this is often done within cross-functional teams. NPD project teams are continually created and disbanded in manufacturing and service firms in response to the ever-changing technological and market opportunities they are faced with, and the strength of internal and external networks determines how well firms manage this process.[6]

Large MNEs that are good at managing knowledge networks are in a better position to leverage the scale and scope advantages that put them ahead of smaller or domestic market firms in terms of their innovativeness. They can afford large (scale) and specialist (scope) centers of excellence and can manage joint ventures with other big players to pool resources and spread the risk of R&D projects. They can then link these R&D centers to their markets around the world, prioritizing areas of development on which to focus their efforts to reap the most rewards in terms of sales of new and improved products.

Global innovation management and knowledge management are seen to be increasingly important to the long-run performance of all firms. Nohria and Ghoshal use the terms *distributed innovation* and *differentiated networks* to characterize how firms should learn globally and exploit this learning globally to improve production processes and products in all markets.[7] Other studies also emphasize the internal processes, within multinational structures, that constrain or facilitate this kind of global capability.[8]

Speed-to-market

One of the major manufacturing challenges facing MNEs is the speed with which they develop and get new products to market.[9] In recent years, many firms have found that a "speed-to-market" strategy can be extremely profitable. Table 12.1 provides some data to support this statement. Notice that a company that enters the market one month ahead of the competition can increase annual gross profits by $150,000 on a product that generates $25 million and $600,000 on a product that generates $100 million. Simply put, by carefully designing the product and getting it out of the door fast, the company can dramatically increase profitability.

MNEs have taken a number of steps to ensure early delivery of their products. For example, Cisco Systems has outsourced the production of routers and switches to Flextronics, a contract electronics manufacturer. Flextronics receives an electronic order from Cisco, manufactures the product under the Cisco brand, and then delivers it directly to the customers.[10] BMW has combined engineering, development, and production planning in bringing new cars to market in record time.[11]

Time-to-market accelerators
Factors that help reduce bottlenecks and errors and ensure product quality and performance

The strategic emphasis is on increasing speed by developing **time-to-market accelerators**, which are factors that help reduce bottlenecks and errors and ensure product quality and performance. These accelerators vary from firm to firm, but they all produce the same results. For example, in 2000, Pirelli, the Italian tire maker, unveiled its **modular integrated robotized system (MIRB)**, which enables the entire production system to be robotized. Small and flexible, MIRB allows smaller batches to be produced in different locations, potentially locating them next to Pirelli's industrial customers.[12]

Modular integrated robotized system (MIRB)
A software-based production process that relies entirely on robots

In the past, many MNEs placed the bulk of their production attention on the manufacturing side of the operation. However, recent research shows that the best way to reduce defective products and speed delivery is by placing the greatest attention on product design and planning of operations. This is accomplished through what is known as **concurrent engineering**, which involves design, engineering, and manufacturing people working together to create and build the product. Concurrent engineering is useful for two reasons.

Concurrent engineering
The process of having design, engineering, and manufacturing people working together to create a product, in contrast to working in a sequential manner

Table 12.1 The cost of arriving late to market (and still be on budget)

If the company is late to market by:					
6 months	**5 months**	**4 months**	**3 months**	**2 months**	**1 month**
Gross potential profit is reduced by:					
233%	225%	218%	212%	27%	23%
If time-to-market is improved profit will go up by:					
11.9%	9.3%	7.3%	5.7%	4.3%	3.1%
For revenues of $25 million, annual gross profit will increase by:					
$400,000	$350,000	$300,000	$250,000	$200,000	$150,000
For revenues of $100 million, annual gross profit will increase by:					
$1,600,000	$1,400,000	$1,200,000	$1,000,000	$800,000	$600,000

Source: Academy of Management Executive, "The New Competitors: They Think in Terms of 'Speed-to-Market'," by Joseph T. Vesey. Copyright © 1991 The Academy of Management (NY).

First, if the product is carefully designed, fewer changes are needed later on and the good can be brought to market swiftly. Second, the costs associated with changes increase as the product gets closer to completion; that is, it is almost twice as expensive to correct a problem during production than during product design.

Once a product or service has been planned out, the MNE's attention turns to production. This strategy is focused very heavily on minimizing costs and increasing quality and productivity.

✔ Active learning check

Review your answer to Active Learning Case question 1 and make any changes you like. Then compare your answer to the one below.

1 **How did GE use work-out to increase speed-to-market?**

The primary way GE used work-out to increase speed-to-market was by looking for ways to eliminate production bottlenecks and streamline operations. The strategy of work-out asked the participants: how can we change the operation to get more done in less time? The workers who were familiar with the operations often had a wealth of information to share, and this was sometimes the first time anyone had asked them for their opinions. They were delighted to offer suggestions and recommendations. As a result, the company produced more products in less time than ever before.

GENERATION OF GOODS AND SERVICES

Most people think of the production process as one in which physical goods are produced. However, the process can also be used in generating services, and the two are quite often interlinked.[13] For example, GM manufactures cars but also offers auto maintenance and repair services[14] whereas Boeing both builds and services aircraft. In other cases, services are primary, such as the Hilton Corporation offering hotel accommodations, Hertz and Avis leasing cars, and CNN providing international news coverage.

Sometimes goods and/or services are provided directly by the MNE; other times the MNE has an arrangement with outside firms or suppliers (some of them being direct competitors) to assist in this process. For example, other firms make some of the HP printers, but HP has its name put on the units and assumes responsibility for marketing them.[15] Service organizations follow a similar strategy. Some airlines purchase their in-flight food from companies like Marriott, and some rely on aircraft maintenance firms such as Ryder to service their craft. Many motels subcontract their food service to companies that specialize in this area, including fast-food franchisors such as McDonald's and Burger King. So there is often a mix of product/service strategies at work when generating goods and services. The following discussion examines some of the most important functions that are carried out in this process. The production of goods is emphasized most heavily because some of the areas under discussion do not lend themselves to services—although one that does is global sourcing, a primary area of consideration in production strategy.

Global sourcing

Global sourcing
The use of suppliers anywhere in the world, chosen on the basis of their efficiency

Sometimes MNEs produce all the goods and services they need. However, they often use **global sourcing** by calling upon those suppliers which can provide the needed output more efficiently regardless of where they are geographically located.[16]

Global sourcing has become important for a number of reasons. The most obvious one is cost. If GM wants to be price competitive in the European Union, one strategy is to build and ship cars from Detroit to Europe at a price equal to, or less than, that charged by EU competitors. Because this is not possible, GM uses overseas suppliers and assembly plants to build much of what it sells in Europe. In deciding who will provide these parts and supplies, the company uses global sourcing, as do other MNEs.

Not all global sourcing is provided by outside suppliers. Some MNEs own their own source of supply or hold an equity position in a supplier. This relationship does not guarantee that the supplier will get the MNE's business on every bid. However, if the supplier is unable to match the cost or quality performance of competitive suppliers, the MNE will eventually terminate the relationship. So there is a great deal of pressure on the supplier to develop and maintain state-of-the-art production facilities. Additionally, because the supplier works closely with the MNE, the company knows how its multinational client likes things done and is able to operate smoothly with the MNE's design and production people.

In recent years some giant MNEs have taken equity positions in a number of different suppliers. Japanese multinationals are an excellent example. These firms often have a network of parts suppliers, subcontractors, and capital equipment suppliers they can call on.

> At the same time these suppliers often provide goods and services to other firms. This helps them to maintain their competitive edge by forcing them to innovate, adapt, and remain cost effective. If these suppliers are in similar or complementary industries, as in the case of NEC's suppliers, then technological innovations or revolutionary changes in manufacturing processes will be quickly accepted or copied by others. So the close proximity of the suppliers coupled with their business relationships helps to ensure that they attain and hold positions as world-class suppliers, and this advantage carries over to the customers, who gain both innovative ideas and high-quality, low-cost supplies.[17]

A good example is the leather footwear industry in Italy. Manufacturers regularly interact with leather suppliers, designers, and producers of other leather goods. As a result, the manufacturers are extremely knowledgeable about industry technology, production techniques, fashion trends, and supply sources.

These advantages also help explain why many US suppliers are going international. By setting up operations near world-class competitors, these suppliers find it easier to monitor developments, remain alert to changes in technology and production processes, and maintain state-of-the-art facilities.[18] In fact, when manufacturers expand operations to another country, it is common to find their major suppliers setting up operations nearby in order to continue serving the manufacturers. The other reason is to prevent local competitors from capturing some of this business, which often happens when the supplier attempts to compete from the home country.

The global clothing industry provides a good example of these trends. The production of clothing sits within a broader value chain, which includes textiles and fibers for a range of both household and industrial goods. Upstream, the textile industry relies on access to sources of natural fibers, a "natural" factor endowment in Porter's Diamond of Advantage, compared to the "acquired" factor endowments associated with the chemicals industry for the production of artificial fibers. Clearly, each has favored different countries at different stages of the industry's development. Downstream, distribution and retailing and, in particular, branding and marketing have remained predominantly within the major markets of industrially advanced countries (and under their ownership). The case **International Business Strategy in Action: Gap Inc.** illustrates these patterns.

The clothing industry itself can be subdivided into three activities: design, preparation, and production. The last two have remained relatively labor intensive, which is why most preparation and production are done in cheap-labor locations. China's share of world exports in clothing grew from 4 percent in 1980 to over 18 percent in 2000, and it is now the

INTERNATIONAL BUSINESS STRATEGY IN ACTION

Gap Inc.: a successful "Hollow Corporation"

In 1999, after 28 years, founders Don and Doris Fisher still owned 24 percent of Gap Inc. and still played a leading role in managing the operations of this $2 billion clothing firm. By 2010 Gap's revenue had grown to $14,197 million and the Fisher family was still very much involved. As with other high-street clothing firms, its competitive advantage stemmed from linking cheap manufacturing in contract production facilities in around 45 countries, with design and fashion expertise and huge distribution and sales chains in the United States and Europe.

Just 1 percent of its own employees have any production-related role: 600 quality control employees in eight shipment processing facilities in North America, Europe, and Asia. Gap is essentially a distribution, retailing, sales, and, particularly, marketing firm—a specialty retailer operating 3,095 stores selling casual apparel, personal care products, and accessories. Its brands include Gap, GapKids, BabyGap, Banana Republic, Old Navy, Althleta, and Piperlime. Gap measures its own success on its sales and its expansion rate, in terms of new stores, so in part it is also a real estate business. These provide an indication of its ongoing performance, its multinationality at any point in time, and its international expansion or retrenchment overtime. In the late 1990s it was opening over 100 stores per year. More recently its overall growth and its international expansion have slowed (see Table 1). For example, due to losses, Forth & Towne brand stores were closed by the end of June 2007. In the past 3 years, the number of stores decreased from 3,167 store locations in 2007 to 3,095 stores in 2010 (a decrease of 71 stores, or 2.3 percent). Despite Gap being a well-known brand in Europe, it is heavily reliant on its North American sales (87.8 percent), with only 10 percent of its stores situated in Europe and Asia, where it generates 12.2 percent sales. Gap's product development offices are based in New York City, where product managers, designers, and graphic artists monitor (and create) customer trends in its main consumer markets.

Source: Niall McDiarmind/Alamy.

Table 1 Gap Inc. number of store locations, by region, 2010

GAP North America	1,152
GAP Europe	178
GAP Asia	120
Old Navy North America	1,039
Banana Republic North America	576
Banana Republic Asia	27
Banana Republic Europe	3
Total	3,095

Source: GAP, *Annual report,* 2010

The Sourcing and Logistics Group, together with buying agents around the globe, draw up production schedules and place orders with the approved third-party clothes plants located around the world. Like other mid-range department stores, such as Neiman-Marcus or Macy's in the United States, Marks & Spencer in the UK or Karstadt in Germany, Gap's higher-quality, higher-priced garments are sourced from countries like South Korea, Taiwan, Hong Kong, Singapore, Turkey, Brazil, Mexico, and parts of India and China. In terms of the global clothing value chain, these garments sit "below" fashion designer clothing from Armani, Donna Karan, Boss, or Gucci, which is manufactured in small, high-quality batches in Italy and high-capability locations in South-East Asia. But they sit "above" the discount chains like Wal-Mart and Kmart in the United States, Asda and Matalan in the UK, and Carrefour in France which source in bulk from lower-cost and lower-quality locations such as Malaysia, Indonesia, Vietnam, China, India, Mexico, Chile, Hungary, Kenya, and Pakistan. The value hierarchy in clothing is mirrored by a global hierarchy of locations, ordered by virtue of their cost base and local endowments that underpin quality, and speed of delivery, from related infrastructure to relevant expertise.

Each Gap brand has its own marketing team based in the San Francisco Bay area, which creates advertising posters, in-store design and graphics, and magazine and TV commercials. Distribution centers receive goods from overseas production plants, check the quality, sort the goods and redistribute them to retail outlets in each of the country markets, the United States, Canada, Japan, the UK, and the Netherlands. The subcontracting arrangement with overseas manufacturers sometimes involves financial and technical support but mainly relies on imposing strict quality and cost limitations which independent suppliers must adhere to in order to maintain their contracts.

There are clear similarities in this strategy with Nike (see Real Case: Nike, below). Nike, however, has closer ties with its first-tier suppliers often including some equity-share, technology transfer, management, and design training. Nike is also well known for its poor record on ethical labor practices, through well-publicized studies of its South-East Asian "sweatshops." These triggered damaging reprisals from shareholders and customers, sending out a warning sign to many consumer goods manufacturers which relied on a strong brand that exploitation of cheap labor can sometimes be highly unprofitable.

Websites: http://www.gap.com; http://www.gapinc.com.

Sources: P. Dicken, *Global Shift: Mapping the Changing Contours of the World Economoy*, 6th ed. (London: Sage, 2011); OECD, "A New World Map in Textiles and Clothing: Adjusting to Change," Paris (210 pp.), at http://www.oecd.org/; GAP, *Annual report*, 2010.

world's dominant exporter. Over 2 million Chinese are employed in the sector. By contrast the United States has the biggest trade deficit in clothing ($48 billion in 2004). Scotland and Italy, two dominant forces in textiles and clothing at one time, for example, have shifted upmarket to specialize in design and high-quality/fashion items. Employment has fallen drastically in these countries as a result and the patterns of trade have also reversed.

When MNEs turn to global sourcing, there is typically a hierarchical order of consideration. The company gives first preference to internal sources, such as having subassemblies produced by the manufacturing department or the subsidiary that specializes in this work. However, if a review of outside sources reveals a sufficient cost/quality difference that would justify buying from an external supplier, this is what the company will do. In fact, sometimes an MNE will not attempt to make a particular part or product because it lacks the expertise to do so efficiently. The firm will simply solicit bids from outside suppliers and award the contract based on predetermined specifications (price, quality, delivery time, etc.). Over time the MNE will learn which suppliers are best at providing certain goods and services and will turn to them immediately. When this process is completed, attention will then focus on the actual manufacture of the goods.

Recently, environmentalists have reviewed the global supply chains of MNEs. They argue that all suppliers to an MNE should follow environmentally sensitive policies—in other words, be "green." Some firms face high risks due to dependence on global outsourcing. Outsourcing to suppliers may open up opportunities for competitors. Similarly, outsourcing production to different suppliers may prevent the development of new insights, innovations, and solutions which typically require cross-functional teamwork. Finally, outsourcing may risk key knowledge leakage. The case **International Business Strategy in Action, The dark side of outsourcing: Boeing's problems with its 787** examines this issue.

Manufacturing of goods

MNEs face a variety of concerns in manufacturing goods and services. Primary among these are cost, quality, and efficient production systems.

Cost

Multinationals seek to control their costs by increasing the efficiency of their production processes. Often this means using new, improved technology such as state-of-the-art machinery and equipment. Although these purchases can be expensive, they may be the best way to raise productivity and lower costs, thus maintaining competitive advantage. A good example is provided by the automobile industry in Brazil, which is the heart of the South American automobile market. The country is host to 13 auto makers, including DaimlerChrysler, Volkswagen, and Ford, which are investing over $20 billion to update Brazilian plants to modular manufacturing. **Modular manufacturing** allows suppliers of parts to take on some of the assembly. Dana Corporation, which has set up shop near a Chrysler factory in the city of Curitiba, is now responsible for the assembly of the Dakota's

Modular manufacturing
A manufacturing process that consists of modules that can be easily adapted to fit changing demand

INTERNATIONAL BUSINESS STRATEGY IN ACTION

The dark side of outsourcing: Boeing's problems with its 787

In general, offshoring (which is outsourcing across national borders) is potentially beneficial when a firm needs to economize on costs, especially labour costs in manufacturing, assembly, or in routine service delivery. However, offshoring can prove to be a disaster for a firm when proprietary technology, engineering skills, managerial capabilities in systems integration, and other aspects of firm specific advantages, are put at risk of dissipation by engaging with independent contractors, especially those embedded in foreign cultures and environments.

Such was the case with the Being 787. This "Dreamliner" advanced airplane suffered from over three years of delays when dozens of foreign component manufacturers failed to deliver quality components on time. Boeing itself had to reintegrate many of the outsourced components back into its basic assembly systems in order to re-establish quality control and timely delivery. These costs of delay of delivery of the 787 Dreamliner amount to between $10 million and $18 billion.

Why did such a sophisticated world leading company such as Boeing make such a basic mistake in throwing away decades of internal, integrated, processed based R&D and engineering skills by adopting a misguided outsourcing strategy? The failed outsourcing strategy, started in 2003, led to the termination of its champion, Boeing Chairman, Harry Stonecipher, in 2005.

It appears that the top management team at Boeing used outsourcing as a technique to improve its Return on Net Assets (RONA). This ratio can obviously be improved if in-company assets (in the form of factories and employees directly owned by Boeing) are reduced and outsourced to independent contractors. Unfortunately, the unsatisfactory nature of some of the outsourced production of components for the Boeing 787 led to a fall in revenues and thus a poor RONA. It also resulted in the loss of vital in-house engineering knowhow, a hollowing out of Boeing, and the loss of reputation and brand equity due to the first major failure in the history of Boeing's products.

It has been alleged that this catastrophic, strategic mistake in turning to outsourcing was due to the experience of McDonell Douglas. This St. Louis, Missouri-based aerospace company was acquired by Boeing. McDonnel Douglas had been very successful in supplying military aircraft to the US Department of Defence. Once a contract to supply military hardware was obtained, McDonnel Douglas was able to obtain full payment for its development costs. Once Boeing made the strategic decision to outsource, it did not anticipate that it would have to bear the cost of any risks involved. In order to improve RONA. Boeing forgot that such strategic errors in outsourcing would come back to haunt its revenues and stock price, which were no longer guaranteed by the US government. All in all, outsourcing is the wrong strategy for technologically intensive producers.

Sources: Pilita Clark in Seattle, "Boeing Suspends Dreamliner Parts Shipments," Financial Times, April 28, 2010; Pilita Clark in Seattle, "Boeing Pushes Back Dreamliner Delivery," Financial Times, January 18, 2011; Hal Weitzman in Chicago, "Dreamliner Delays to Hit Boeing Profits," Financial Times, January 26, 2011; The Seattle Times, "A Prescient Warning to Boeing on 787 Trouble," February 6, 2011, Section D.

basic skeleton, which represents approximately 30 percent of the total cost of production. Once this skeleton reaches Chrysler, it is mounted with an engine and a body. Entire assembly lines had to be rebuilt to accommodate this process. Volkswagen, Ford, and General Motors are also developing similar assembly plants to test their efficiency for future implementation to their other factories.[19]

A second approach is to tap low-cost labor sources. A good example is the *maquiladora* industry (as discussed in Chapter 10) that has sprung up in Mexico just across the US border. Hundreds of US plants have been established in this area. Examples include TRW Inc., which has a factory where workers assemble seat belts, and Mattel, which has a plant where workers turn out Barbie-doll houses and Disney teething rings.[20] Labor costs in these facilities are less than 20 percent of those of similar workers in the United States. Also, because this is a free trade zone, US duties are levied on the imports only to the extent of the value added in Mexico, so low wage rates in Mexico help keep down the import duty.

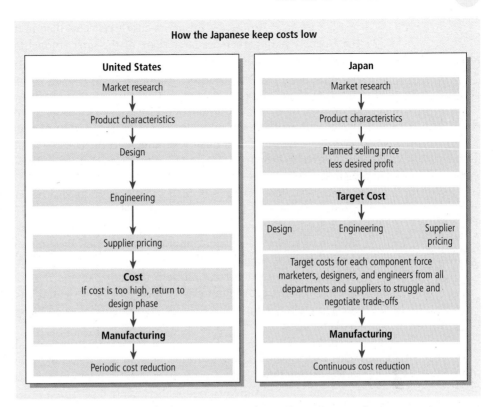

How the Japanese keep costs low

United States
- Market research
- Product characteristics
- Design
- Engineering
- Supplier pricing
- **Cost** — If cost is too high, return to design phase
- **Manufacturing**
- Periodic cost reduction

Japan
- Market research
- Product characteristics
- Planned selling price less desired profit
- **Target Cost**
- Design — Engineering — Supplier pricing
- Target costs for each component force marketers, designers, and engineers from all departments and suppliers to struggle and negotiate trade-offs
- **Manufacturing**
- Continuous cost reduction

Figure 12.2 Cost reduction approaches: the United States versus Japan

Source: Ford S. Worthy, "Japan's Smart Secret Weapon," *Fortune*, August 12, 1991, p. 73.

A third approach is the development of new methods used to cut costs.[21] For example, in the United States, it is typical for a firm to calculate selling price after a new product is developed. If the price is judged to be too high, the product is sent back to the drawing board to be reworked, or the company accepts a smaller profit on the product. A different system has been introduced in Japan, where firms begin by determining the target cost of the product *before* going into design, engineering, and supplier pricing, and the latter groups then work to bring the product in at the desired price. This unique cost management system has helped Japanese firms cut costs for some time (Figure 12.2).[22]

A fourth method that is gaining popularity with MNEs is that of costing products not on an individual basis but as part of a portfolio of related goods. Instead of evaluating the expenses of developing one new soft drink, for example, a company looks at the costs and revenues associated with the entire line of beverages. Coca-Cola of Japan provides an example. Every year it introduces more than 1,000 new soft drinks, fruit drinks, and cold coffees into the Japanese market. Ninety percent of them fail, but this does not stop Coke from introducing approximately one new product a month. From a cost accounting standpoint this is not a profitable strategy. However, as one Coke executive in Japan puts it, "We know that some of these products will survive only a month or two, but our competitors have them, so we have to have them."[23] As a result, Japan is Coke's most profitable market and the company sells a variety of non-carbonated drinks to complement its main brand.[24]

Quality

For well over a decade, quality has been one of the major criteria for business success.[25] As the president of an international consulting firm puts it, "Products are expected to be

Kaizen
A Japanese term that means continuous improvement

nearly perfect."[26] Nowhere is this more clearly reflected than in the auto industry, where the Japanese have garnered a large share of the international market by using what is called **kaizen**, or continuous improvement.[27] A good example is Toyota Motors, which has continually worked to reduce costs and improve quality. One way Toyota has achieved this goal is partly through large R&D expenditures. Another is through meticulous design, engineering, and production processes that ensure a proper fit of all parts and overall durability of the unit.[28] In recent years US auto manufacturers have also succeeded in improving their quality, gaining market share as a result. European car makers today are also heavily focused on quality, aware that the Japanese are a major threat to their markets.[29]

Other excellent examples of MNEs that have succeeded because of a strong focus on quality include such lesser-known firms as Stanley Works, the WD-40 Co., and A. T. Cross. Stanley Works manufactures tape measures in Asia, then has the accuracy of samples checked by sophisticated laser computers back in New Britain, Connecticut, before selling them worldwide. Stanley has also developed a host of other high-quality products, from double-toothed saws that cut on both the upstroke and the downstroke for the Asian market, to hammers without claws for carpenters in Central Europe (who prefer to use pliers to pull out bent nails), to levels shaped like elongated trapezoids, which the French market prefers.

The WD-40 Co. of San Diego manufactures WD-40, a water-displacing lubricant that fights rust, cleans heel marks from linoleum and walls, and provides a variety of other services around the house. Car mechanics use it to loosen sticky valves and remove moisture from balky carburetors; odd jobbers apply it to frozen locks and screws. Today the blue-and-yellow spray can is found in stores throughout the world, where it enjoys fanatical customer loyalty. WD-40 is a best-seller in the UK and is rapidly gaining market share throughout Europe and Asia.[30]

A. T. Cross of Providence, Rhode Island, has been manufacturing mechanical pens and pencils for almost 150 years. The units are assembled by hand and "every one of the company's hourly employees is a quality control expert who is responsible for checking the tolerances of the engraved grooves to within one ten-thousandth of an inch and for detecting nearly microscopic scratches or the slightest clotting of ink on a pen ball."[31] A. T. Cross's product quality is so high that, despite a lifetime guarantee, less than 2 percent of its products are ever returned for repair. Today these pens and pencils are one of the most popular US-made gifts in Japan.[32]

Production systems

Production system
A group of related activities designed to create value

A **production system** is a group of related activities designed to create value. In the generation of goods and services this system includes location, layout, and material handling.

Location

Location is important because of its impact on production and distribution costs. Many MNEs have found that governments (national and local) are willing to provide tax breaks or other financial incentives to encourage them to set up operations. Accompanying considerations include the availability and cost of labor, raw materials, water, and energy as well as the development of the country's transportation and communication systems. As noted earlier, many suppliers set up operations near their major customers. So Ford has built up an integrated production network in Western Europe (see the map on the Ford Fiesta production network). Ford suppliers are part of this production network so as to maintain their business relationship. Location is also important to service enterprises because they usually require face-to-face contact with their customers. Hotels and airlines are typical examples. Personal service firms such as those of accountants, lawyers, and management consultants also fall into this category.[33]

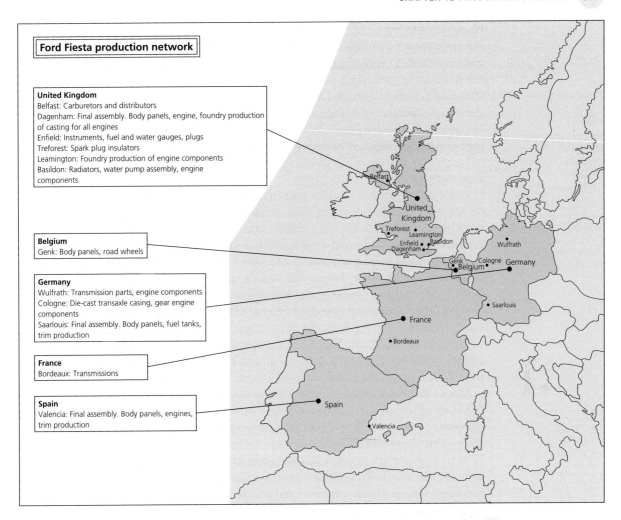

Ford Fiesta production network

United Kingdom
Belfast: Carburetors and distributors
Dagenham: Final assembly. Body panels, engine, foundry production of casting for all engines
Enfield: Instruments, fuel and water gauges, plugs
Treforest: Spark plug insulators
Leamington: Foundry production of engine components
Basildon: Radiators, water pump assembly, engine components

Belgium
Genk: Body panels, road wheels

Germany
Wulfrath: Transmission parts, engine components
Cologne: Die-cast transaxle casing, gear engine components
Saarlouis: Final assembly. Body panels, fuel tanks, trim production

France
Bordeaux: Transmissions

Spain
Valencia: Final assembly. Body panels, engines, trim production

Layout

Plant layout is important because of its impact on efficiency. For example, most auto producers use an assembly line layout in which the workers remain at their station and, as the cars move past them, perform the necessary functions such as installing radios, air-conditioners, interior trim, and so on. In the case of Volvo, the employees work in small teams to build an entire car and the plant is laid out to accommodate this work flow.[34] In other manufacturing settings, however, worldwide competitive firms tend to use U-shaped-cell flow lines, which are more efficient. Schonberger, an internationally known manufacturing expert, has noted that U-shaped production designs enable one person to tend several workstations and increase the speed at which materials can be delivered and defective parts can be reworked.[35] Finally, Maytag has chosen to combine different layouts to cater to each production line in just one factory. A traditional long conveyer belt assembly line makes its standardized models. A second area makes more sophisticated models in smaller production cells instead of a long line. The third area makes the most sophisticated machines. In this setting, workers are craftworkers putting together a substantial part of the machine.[36]

Layout varies widely in service organizations, although it appears to be universal in use. Most hotels, regardless of the country, have the check-in and check-out areas in the same place as such support groups as the bellhops, concierge, and cashier. In fast-food units, the food preparation area is situated so that the personnel can quickly serve both in-unit and drive-through customers. In movie theaters, the concession area is located in the lobby and the projection room at the back of the theater.

Material handling
The careful planning of when, where, and how much inventory will be available to ensure maximum production efficiency

Process mapping
A flowchart of every step that goes into producing a product

Just-in-time inventory (JIT)
The delivery of parts and supplies just as they are needed

Demand-Flow™ Technology (DFT)
A production process that is flexible to demand changes

Material handling

Material handling involves the careful planning of when, where, and how much inventory will be available to ensure maximum production efficiency. Part of this is resolved through careful inventory control processes. Part of it is handled when the production layout is determined. For example, General Electric uses **process mapping**, a flowchart that shows every small step in producing a product. As a result, the company is able to study every part of an operation and determine those that are redundant or that can be streamlined. Consequently, the company has been able to reduce work time on some jobs by as much as 50 percent.[37]

Inventory control

Inventory control has received a great deal of attention in recent years because a well-designed inventory strategy can have dramatic effects on the bottom line.[38] One of the most popular concepts has been **just-in-time inventory (JIT** for short), which is based on delivering parts and supplies just as they are needed. If this concept were carried to the extreme, it would mean that manufacturers would not need to store materials because suppliers would be delivering them just in time for shipment to the factory floor.

JIT is an important concept that has been adopted by MNEs throughout the world. However, the degree of use varies based on the product and the company's production strategy. For example, the Big Three US auto makers use JIT to keep inventory to a minimum. In Japan, firms like Toyota have taken the concept even further and apply it the same way airlines handle reservations: supply is matched directly to demand. Dealers order directly from the factory, which means that customers can get their built-to-order car in 7 to 10 days.

One of the major problems with JIT is that its success rests heavily on the quality and reliability of the suppliers. In Japan, where MNEs often have an equity position in these companies, suppliers will go out of their way to meet partners' demands. However, in the United States and Europe, most suppliers are independent businesses that work under a contract relationship, so the bonds are often not as strong between the two parties. This helps explain why Toyota, which buys US-made parts for cars made in the United States, also keeps Japanese-made parts on hand as insurance against defective US materials.[39]

A second problem with JIT is that, although it works well in managing delivery of parts to the assembly line, few firms have been able to apply the concept to the entire production process. Most firms still manufacture and ship their output to dealers to sell, in contrast to Toyota's approach of matching supply and demand before producing.

One of the most important things to remember about JIT is that it needs strong support from the workers and the suppliers. Everyone must be operating in unison. If the workers are slow, there will be excess inventory on hand; if the supplier is late, the workers will be sitting by idly.

Demand-Flow™ Technology (DFT) is a production process that allows for flexible changes in the middle stages of production. Typically used to produce standardized assembly products, such as computers, DFT permits quick reactions to changes in demand and technology. A surge of demand for Pentium IV computers, for instance, would immediately shift inputs from other computers to be combined with Pentium IV chips to respond to demand. This virtually eliminates inventories.[40] Intermec, a company that makes bar code scanners, mobile computers, and related products, reduced inventory by 50 percent after implementing DFT. It was also able to consolidate five different printer lines into one flexible mixed-model line, decreasing the amount of required manufacturing floor space by 20 percent.[41]

Developing a strong service orientation

As noted earlier, many products have a service element associated with them. Sometimes this element is more important than the product itself. For example, many people will not

Product-dominated businesses	Equally balanced	Service-dominated businesses
Farm produce (corn, wheat, etc.)	Aircraft manufacturing	Advertising agency
Home construction	Fast-food unit	Theater production
Auto production	TV network	Teaching

Figure 12.3 Product- and service-dominated businesses

purchase a car or home appliance unless it can be serviced easily. Service is also important when choosing a bank, insurance agent, lawyer, or doctor. Many of the ideas we have discussed in this section, including sourcing, cost, and quality, are also key factors in shopping for services. In addressing this area, MNEs will do two things: (1) consider whether their strategy needs to be oriented toward a product, a service, or a combination of the two; and (2) determine the ideal degree of service to provide.

Determining the product/service balance

Some outputs lend themselves to a strong production orientation, whereas others require much more attention to service. Figure 12.3 offers an illustration. Designed more as a point of reference than as a factual source that addresses every firm in the respective industry, the figure nonetheless shows that some MNEs need to have a strong product-dominated focus whereas others benefit most from a service orientation. A good example is offered by aircraft manufacturers that must be concerned with both ends of the continuum. Olympus and Pentax, both manufacturers of flexible endoscopic equipment, provide another example. To develop their brand names in Latin America, these companies offer medical professionals the surgical training necessary to use their equipment. Because after-sales service is also an important consideration for prospective buyers, including hospitals, all major endoscope manufacturers have service stations in the region.

On the other hand, some manufactured products require far less service than they used to need. A good example is photocopiers. Manufacturers of these machines have improved product quality so substantially that many units are now sold on the basis of price. Service is no longer a major factor because everyone's product is of such high quality.

Knowing whether to sell on the basis of product or service (or a combination of the two) is critical to the success of many MNEs. A mistake at this point can result in emphasis on the wrong sales factors.

Providing the right amount of service

Once the MNE has determined the proper balance of product and service domination, it evaluates the specific type of service warranted. This is particularly important because many MNEs find that the strategy used in their own country does not work overseas. A good example is the Japanese approach to retail services.[42] The amount of personal service provided in Japan would surprise many Westerners. For example, auto dealers typically provide pick-up and delivery for repair service customers and make new car sales calls to customers' homes. In department stores, it is common to find executives and sales clerks alike lined up to bow to the first customers in the store. Japanese banks often help their customers sell or buy homes, find distributors for merchandise, and provide them with tax advice.

Although these services help Japanese companies maintain customer satisfaction, research has found that they are of little value to doing business in other countries. For example, Japanese banks in the United States have discovered that US customers want only a limited amount of quality service; they prefer quantity and efficiency in the form of a variety of different services offered at low prices. As a result, Japanese banks here offer the same types of services as do other US banks. Would they be more successful if they changed this strategy and tried to emulate the approach used back home? Given the nature of the US market, they believe this would be a mistake. The lesson is clear: when competing in terms of service, one must match the competition but not exceed it unless the customer is willing to pay for this service. In the United States, the banking customer is not willing.[43]

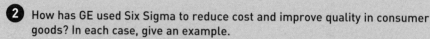

✔ Active learning check

Review your answer to Active Learning Case question 2 and make any changes you like. Then compare your answer to the one below.

2 How has GE used Six Sigma to reduce cost and improve quality in consumer goods? In each case, give an example.

Six Sigma allows GE to use process mapping to reduce cost by identifying those activities that can be eliminated or combined in the production process. For example, can an individual who is performing one assembly line task take on other tasks and thus reduce the number of people needed to produce the product? Can inventory be ordered and delivered in smaller amounts, thus making greater use of just-in-time? Consideration of these types of questions can help reduce cost. In improving product quality, the work group can examine how well all parts of the product fit together, examine the durability of the unit, and look for additional ways of testing the product to ensure that it measures up to quality standards.

INTERNATIONAL LOGISTICS

International logistics
The designing and managing of a system to control the flow of materials and products throughout the organization

International logistics is the designing and managing of a system to control the flow of materials and products throughout the firm. This includes the inflow of materials, movement through the production process, and outflow to the wholesale/retail firm or final consumer. International logistics is an important area of strategic consideration because these expenses can account for 10 percent of the total costs.[44] The material management aspect of international logistics has already been addressed. The following discussion examines three other key topics: transportation, packaging, and storage.

Transportation

Container ships
Vessels used to carry standardized containers that can be simply loaded onto a carrier and then unloaded at their destination without any repackaging of the contents of the containers

Unconventional cargo vessels
Vessels used for shipping oversized and unusual cargoes

Roll-on-roll-off (RORO) vessels
Ocean-going ferries that can carry wheeled cargo such as automobiles, trailers, and trucks that drive onto built-in ramps and roll off at the point of debarkation

In examining international logistics, we focus on the primary modes of transportation: ocean and air. The others—rail, pipeline, and motor carrier—are of importance in some regions (such as the European Union), but they are not as commonly used in moving goods from an MNE's plant to their final destination. Moreover, their use is highly dependent on the infrastructure of the country—that is, the extensiveness and quality of the nation's road system and rail network. In many non-triad countries the infrastructure is poor and the MNE's use of them is greatly limited.

Ocean shipping

International firms can choose from a fairly wide variety of ocean carriers. The three most common carriers are conventional container ships, cargo vessels, and roll-on-roll-off (RORO) vessels. **Container ships** are used to carry standardized containers that can be simply loaded onto the carrier and then unloaded at their destination, without any repackaging of the contents of the containers. **Unconventional cargo vessels** are used for shipping oversized and unusual cargoes. **Roll-on-roll-off (RORO) vessels** are ocean-going ferries that can carry wheeled cargo such as automobiles, trucks, semi-trailer trucks, trailers, or railroad cars that drive onto built-in ramps and roll off at the point of debarkation. A carrier similar to the RORO is the **lighter aboard ship (LASH) vessel**, which consists of barges that are stored on the ship and lowered at the point of destination. These individual barges can then operate on inland waterways.

Lighter aboard ship (LASH) vessels
Barges stored on a ship and lowered at the point of destination

One of the major problems in planning an ocean shipping strategy is the limitations caused by the lack of ports and port services. In developing countries, for example, seaports sometimes lack the equipment necessary to load or unload container cargo, thus limiting the country's ability to export and import. In recent years a number of Third World countries have been working to improve their ports so they can become more active in the international trade arena.

Air shipping

Most countries have airports that can accommodate air freight. The problem with this mode of transportation is its high cost. Thus, although international air freight has grown dramatically over the last 30 years, it still accounts for less than 1 percent of the total volume of international shipments. It is used in trade more commonly among industrialized nations than any others, and it is usually restricted to high-value items that must reach their destination quickly.

Several developments have occurred over the past couple of decades that have helped increase the use of air shipments. These include more efficient ground facilities, larger aircraft, and better marketing of these services to shippers. In particular, the development by aircraft manufacturers of jumbo cargo jet planes and combination passenger and cargo aircraft has helped immensely.

Choice criteria

In deciding the best transportation mode to use, MNEs tend to focus on four important criteria: time, predictability, cost, and non-economic factors.

Time

The period between departure and arrival of a carrier can vary significantly between an ocean freighter and an aircraft. So one of the questions a firm must answer is: how quickly is delivery needed? A number of factors can influence the answer. One is the perishability of the product. Exotic flowers from South America are flown to the United States because they would not survive a sea voyage. A second factor is how soon the goods are needed to replenish current stocks. Autos from Japan are brought into the United States by ship because the length of the trip does not hurt the supply of cars on hand at local dealerships.

In businesses where speed is critical, companies are now coordinating their worldwide supply chains in order to reduce the amount of time needed to get the goods through the production cycle and to the customer. Victor Fung, CEO of Li & Fung, Hong Kong's largest export trading company and an innovator in the development of supply-chain management, has provided an example of how this is being done:

> Say we get an order from a European retailer to produce 10,000 garments. It's not a simple matter of our Korean office sourcing Korean products or our Indonesian office sourcing Indonesian products. For this customer we might decide to buy yarn from a Korean producer but have it woven and dyed in Taiwan. So we pick the yarn and ship it to Taiwan. The Japanese have the best zippers and buttons, but they manufacture them mostly in China. Okay, so we go to YKK, a big Japanese zipper manufacturer, and we order the right zippers from their Chinese plants. Then we determine that, because of quotas and labor conditions, the best place to make the garments is Thailand. So we ship everything there. And because the customer needs quick delivery, we may divide the order across five factories in Thailand. Effectively, we are customizing the value chain to best meet the customer's needs. Five weeks after we have received the order, 10,000 garments arrive on the shelves in Europe, all looking like they came from one factory, with colors, for example, perfectly matched.[45]

Predictability

Although both air and water transportation are basically reliable, they are subject to the vagaries of nature. Bad weather can close an airport; inadequate seaport facilities can slow the loading and unloading of cargo. Because of the great difference in delivery time between the two modes, the choice is often obvious. If a company needs to have a package delivered tomorrow, it will come by air; if the firm wants to clear merchandise out of the warehouse today but the international customer does not need it for 90 days, it will be sent by water. However, certain carriers are more reliable than others, and the MNE will use its experience in determining which companies to choose for delivery. Reliability is particularly important for air shipments, where a difference of one day could significantly influence the salability of the product.

Cost

The expense associated with shipping is a major consideration when choosing an international transportation mode. Because air freight is significantly more costly than shipment by water, the cost must be economically justifiable. Typically, an MNE will use air shipments only when time is critical and/or the product has high value. For example, if the company has purchased expensive watches in Zurich for its specialty outlets in New York and San Francisco, the watches will be flown to the retailers. Similarly, if a London-based MNE has bought a US-made supercomputer for the home office and wants it installed immediately, the unit will be flown over from the United States. On the other hand, if the merchandise is bulky or the cost of air freight is a significant portion of the value of the product, it will be sent by water. Autos are exported by ship, as are bulk commodities and resources such as oil and coal.

Non-economic factors

Sometimes non-economic factors influence the choice of transportation mode. For example, in the United States all government cargo must use national flag carriers when available, so there is seldom a question of how to send these goods. Similarly, other governments own or subsidize their carriers, and there is pressure on MNEs to use these transportation modes when doing business with those countries. Such political considerations must be taken into account when formulating the transportation strategy.

Packaging

Packaging is important in ensuring that a product is shipped in a safe container and arrives undamaged. When goods are transported a long distance or to areas with climates different from the one where they are manufactured, the container can prevent spoilage or leakage. Chemicals, for example, must be carefully sealed in containers that can withstand impact and will not crack open if tipped over or dropped. Machines, such as personal computers, must have interior packing that prevents damage during transit.

Packaging is also important because of its direct effect on cost. If units must be shipped in odd-shaped containers, fewer of them can be loaded into the hold of the transport than if they are shipped in square or rectangular containers and can be loaded atop and alongside each other. The weight of the packing material is also important, especially when goods are being shipped by air and costs are based on both distance and weight.

Intermodal containers
Large metal boxes that fit on trucks, railroad trains, and aircraft and help reduce handling costs and theft losses by placing the merchandise in a tightly sealed, easy-to-move unit

Packaging is also important in reducing loading and unloading costs and minimizing theft and pilferage. In recent years many shippers have begun using **intermodal containers**, which are large metal boxes that fit on trucks, railroad trains, and aircraft and help cut handling costs and theft losses by placing the merchandise in an easy-to-move unit that is tightly sealed.

As more goods are shipped internationally, packaging will continue to be a focal point of attention. Such considerations can help an MNE maximize shipping space and minimize transportation costs.

Storage

In some cases, goods that are shipped internationally have to be stored before being moved to their final destinations. In the United States, public storage is widely available. In other countries, including Japan, warehousing facilities are in short supply. Additionally, the configuration of many warehouses is different from that in the United States. Ceilings are often lower and there is little automation for handling such common chores as loading and unloading packages or stacking containers on top of each other. In such cases, the MNE must decide whether to invest in warehouse facilities or ship goods only when needed, thus eliminating the warehouse function.

Foreign trade zones
Areas where foreign goods may be held and processed and then re-exported without incurring customs duties (same as a free trade zone)

As discussed in Chapter 6, some countries have **foreign trade zones**, which are areas where foreign goods may be held and processed and then re-exported without incurring customs duties (same as a free trade zone). These zones are usually found at major ports of entry (including international air terminals). Their effective use can help an MNE: (1) temporarily store its goods while breaking a large shipment into smaller ones to be shipped to other locales; (2) combine small shipments into larger ones and then reship them; (3) process the goods and perform a host of value-added activities before repackaging them for the market; and (4) give those goods that will remain in the local market a "made in" status so that they can be sold as locally produced products.

An effective storage strategy can be particularly helpful in carrying out the final stages of an MNE's production plan. The strategy can also help minimize overall product cost, reduce delivery time, and increase customer satisfaction.[46]

DIFFERENT KINDS OF GLOBAL PRODUCTION SYSTEMS

Location is a key factor in deciding the global structure of firms' production systems. But it needs to be considered alongside other factors which vary considerably by industry.

Companies tend to focus on the functions and innovation activities where they have the major advantage and often outsource activities, or parts of the value chain where they add less value. This determines the "boundaries" of the firm, what activities are internalized, and what are externalized or left to other firms to provide on a contract basis. Figure 12.4 shows a number of example industries and firms that have very different global production systems, determined by the functions and activities that add the most value.

Production system / Where is the value added?	Internalized (within the firm's hierarchy)	Mixed	Externalized (to other firms in the market)
R&D/technology	Example: semiconductors (Intel)		Example: telecoms (Ericsson)
Manufacturing		Example: autos (Toyota)	
Marketing			Example: clothing (Gap)

Figure 12.4 Global production systems: where is the value added?
Source: Adapted from UNCTAD, *World Investment Report 2002.*

Although Intel does a lot of marketing, its main competitive advantage lies in the continual development of new semiconductors, the heart of PCs and other IT and electronic devices. Product and process development are internalized and highly centralized because this suits the type of technology and product that the firm focuses on. It alone accounts for around 25 percent of all R&D investment in the semiconductor industry. Much of its high-value manufacturing, particularly wafer production and fabrication, is done in the United States, where 75 percent of its manufacturing workforce is based. Other production sites are in Israel and Ireland. Much of its labor-intensive assembly and testing takes place in Malaysia, the Philippines, China, and Costa Rica, but is owned by Intel (internalized).

Ericsson also keeps much of its research, design, and development activities within the firm but not so long ago decided to let other firms make many of the components that make up its telecom systems. In 2001 Flextronics, a $14.5 billion Singaporean firm, took over much of Ericsson's manufacturing and supply-chain activities in Brazil, Malaysia, Sweden, and the UK. It externalized these activities because it decided they were not part of its core competencies, and it could safely contract other firms to supply these components. (See Real Case: Flextronics at the end of this chapter.)

Gap Inc. and other clothing firms have externalized the manufacturing function for many years now. Their focus is clothing design, marketing, branding, and real estate management. There are enough producers in cheap labor locations (such as China, which exports more garments than any other country by far) for Gap to use the market to contract out this activity to the cheapest and/or best. Intermediaries in this industry, like Flextronics in telecoms, include Mast Industries, which works with 400 factories in 37 countries, and Li & Fung, a $5 billion Hong Kong company that connects around 700 US and European brand owners with a network of 7,500 suppliers (1.5 million workers) around the world (of which 2,000 are active at anyone time).

Toyota lies in the middle of these two extremes. Because manufacturing, and particularly maintaining continuous improvement in manufacturing, is so central to its competitive advantage, Toyota is partly vertically integrated down the supply chain. New product development (new car models and features) and process development (improving price and quality) are closely linked and involve good relationships with (and/or ownership of some) component suppliers. It cannot externalize car production because it is the source of many of its core competitive advantages.

Finally, for diversified or multiproduct firms, configuring the right kind of global production system can get complicated. Philips, for example, makes semiconductors, like Intel, but also has large consumer electronics and consumer products divisions. It has to manage both technology-driven and market-driven innovation and production activities.

STRATEGIC MANAGEMENT AND PRODUCTION STRATEGY

MNEs are currently focusing on a number of areas in improving their production strategies. Three that are getting particular attention include (1) technology and design, (2) continuous improvement of operations, and (3) the use of strategic alliances and acquisitions.

Technology and production design

MNEs are now spending more money on R&D than they have in the past. For example, Aventis, Eli Lilly, AstraZeneca, and Pfizer spend over 15 percent of their revenues on R&D, which provides the backroom for the introduction of new pharmaceutical products.[47] Yet, R&D is not only developing new products, but also helping firms find alternative parts as well as production techniques.

A second current trend is the use of concurrent engineering, which was discussed earlier in the chapter. Many MNEs are now realizing that a team approach to product development, which combines the talents of research, design, and manufacturing people as well as customers and clients, results in a more successful product. Ford Motors is an excellent example. Ford put together a group called Team Taurus to develop its Taurus and Sable automobile lines. Team members were drawn from designing, engineering, and production and were brought together with customers. Collectively the group discussed how to build the new cars and replaced the sequential approach to manufacturing autos (first design the cars, then produce them, then market them) with a concurrent approach that involved addressing the design, production, and marketing issues all at the same time. The result of this strategy was a Taurus that captured a significant market niche and helped Ford close the gap between itself and the competition.[48]

Empowerment
The process of giving employees increased control over their work

Coupled with these strategies are innovative human resource development programs that are designed around the concept of **empowerment**, which involves giving employees greater control over their work. This strategy is particularly effective because it creates a feeling of pride and ownership in the job and makes employees feel they are important assets. The use of empowerment is not limited to the research and design areas; it is important in all phases of production, beginning with product creation. Additionally, if things go smoothly at this early stage of the production cycle, there are likely to be fewer problems later on.

Continuous improvement

Due to the success of Japanese MNEs, *kaizen* (continuous improvement) has been emulated by MNEs worldwide. No matter what the good or service is, every day the company tries to do the job better. Some consultants have referred to this strategy as "rapid inch-up,"[49] which certainly captures the essence of the concept. US firms in particular have benefited from this idea. A good example can be found in the automotive industry. In the 1980s and 1990s, Toyota and Honda were able to offset the rising value of the yen with cost saving in their factories, thus allowing them to hold the price line on many of their new cars. These innovations were exported to US plants. By the early 2000s, however, US firms had successfully fought back by imitating and improving Japanese production techniques. In 2004, four of the five most efficient auto plants in the United States were owned by GM.[50]

A large number of firms helped account for these results. One is Xerox, internationally known for its photocopiers. At the beginning of the 1980s the company was losing market share to overseas competitors. However, the firm then began implementing a production strategy for dramatically improving quality and reducing cost. Today Xerox is again a world leader in copiers.

Another example is TPG, which services Ford's Toronto factory by arranging for 800 deliveries a day from 300 parts makers. The parts arrive at 12 different stages of production within 10 minutes of scheduled time to decrease the amount of parts inventory in the plant.[51]

As discussed in an earlier section, JIT is a related concept that the MNEs are using to achieve continuous improvement. In the past JIT was used almost exclusively for managing inventory, but now the concept is being employed in other ways. For example, Toyota's use of JIT helps it assemble a car in 13 labor-hours, compared to 19 to 22 labor-hours for Honda, Nissan, and Ford.

Alliances and acquisitions

Another current strategic production trend is the development of alliances and acquisitions. Many MNEs are finding they cannot compete effectively without entering into joint ventures or other alliances with MNEs that can complement their production strategy. For example, Compaq is well known for its personal computers, but many of the components in these machines are purchased from outside suppliers or are developed by these firms under an alliance agreement. When Compaq needed a hard disk drive for its first laptops, it financed Conner Peripherals, a Silicon Valley start-up with a disk drive already underway, rather than develop the machine inhouse. More recently, Compaq has ventured into the market for powerful desktop workstations used primarily by scientists and engineers. Instead of going head-to-head with market leaders such as Sun Microsystems and HP, the company assembled a dozen hardware and software firms, including these two computer giants, and put together an alliance aimed at defining a new technical standard for highspeed desktop computing. The objective of the alliance is to develop a standard that will suit any workstation, thus allowing customers the freedom to buy the latest, fastest machine without fear of being tied to any single manufacturer.

Compaq's approach is not unique; the Japanese *keiretsu* system has been using it for years.[52] In fact, some researchers claim that industry alliances account for more of the success of Japanese firms than does JIT or any other manufacturing technique. Working in unison with each other, *keiretsu* companies have been able to wield a great deal of power. Many have monthly meetings in which they exchange information and ideas. Table 12.2 provides a brief overview of two of the country's major *keiretsu* members. Looking closely

Table 12.2 The Mitsubishi and Mitsui *keiretsu* in Japan

	Mitsubishi	Mitsui
Financial services and insurance	BOT Lease	Mitsui & Co. Financial Services Ltd.
	ACOM The Bank of Tokyo-Mitsubishi	Mitsui & Co. Financial Services (Asia) Ltd.
	BOT Lease Defined Contribution Plan Consulting of Japan	Mitsui & Co. Financial Services (Europe) B.V.
		Mitsui & Co. Financial Services (U.S.A.) Inc.
	JACCS JALCARD	Mitsui Bussan Trade Services Ltd.
	Jibun Bank kabu.com Securities	Mitsui Bussan Credit Consulting Co., Ltd.
	MDAM Asset Management Mitsubishi Auto Leasing	Mitsui & Co. Energy Risk
	Mitsubishi Corporation Capital Mitsubishi Corporation Futures	Mitsui & Co. Precious Metals, Inc.
		Mitsui Bussan Precious Metals (Hong Kong) Limited
	Mitsubishi Electric Credit Mitsubishi UFJ Asset Management	Mitsui Bussan Commodities Ltd.
	Mitsubishi UFJ Capital The Mitsubishi UFJ Factors	MVC Corporation.
	Mitsubishi UFJ Financial Group	Mitsui & Co. Venture Partners, Inc.
	Mitsubishi UFJ Lease & Finance	Mitsui & Co., Principal Investments Ltd.
	Mitsubishi UFJ Merrill Lynch PB Securities	Mitsui & Co., Logistics Partners Ltd.
	Mitsubishi UFJ Morgan Stanley Securities	Mitsui & Co, Realty Management Ltd.
	Mitsubishi UFJ NICOS	Japan Alternative Investment Co., Ltd.
	Mitsubishi UFJ Securities Holdings	JA Mitsui Leasing, Ltd.
	Mitsubishi UFJ Trust and Banking	
	MMC Diamond Finance	
	NBL Tokyo Credit Services	
	Union Bank of California N.A.	
	Meiji Yasuda General Insurance	Mitsui Bussan Insurance Co., Ltd.
	Meiji Yasuda Life Insurance	Mitsui Direct General Insurance Company, Limited
	Mitsubishi Corporation Insurance	
	Mitsubishi Estate Home	
	MST Insurance Service	
	Nippon Oil Trading	
	Shunjusha Tokio Marine & Nichido Fire Insurance	
	The Tokio Marine Life Insurance	

(continued)

Table 12.2 (continued)

	Mitsubishi	Mitsui
Computers, electronics, and electrical equipment	DIA Instruments CHORYO CONTROL SYSTEM CHORYO DESIGNING MC Medical Meiryo Technica Meldas System Engineering Mitsubishi Electric Business Systems Mitsubishi Cable Industries Mitsubishi Electric Mitsubishi Electric Building Techno-Service Mitsubishi Electric Business Systems Mitsubishi Electric Consumer Products (Thailand) Mitsubishi Electric Engineering Mitsubishi Electric Home Appliance Mitsubishi Electric Lighting Mitsubishi Electric Micro-Computer Application Software Mitsubishi Electric OSRAM Mitsubishi Electric Plant Engineering Mitsubishi Electric System & Service Mitsubishi Precision Ryoden Kasei Ryoden Koki Engineering	
Information, communication, and IT	Bewith CHORYO DESIGNING Choryo Software Hiroshima Dia System Infosec Isuzu IT Frontier JAPAN SPACE IMAGING M.H.I. Digital System Material Business Support MCC Meldas System Engineering Mitsubishi C&C Research Association Mitsubishi Electric Control Software Mitsubishi Electric Information Network Mitsubishi Electric Information Systems Mitsubishi Electric Micro-Computer Application Software Mitsubishi Electric System & Service Mitsubishi Kagaku Media Mitsubishi Shoji & Sun MITSUBISHI SPACE SOFTWARE Mitsubishi UFJ Information Technology Mitsubishi UFJ Research and Consulting MTEC Nagoya Nikon Systems Ryoin Ryoka Systems Ryoyu Systems T-GAIA Tokio Marine & Nichido Systems	Grand Marche Co., Ltd. J-SCube Inc. Kids Station Inc. Mitsui Knowledge Industry Co., Ltd. Mitsui Bussan Secure Directions, Inc. Mitsui Electronics Inc. MITSUI & CO. VIXIA INC. Moshi Moshi Hotline, Inc. Nihon Unisys, Ltd. QVC JAPAN INC. ShopNet Co., Ltd. T-GAIA Corporation VIXIA INC. World Hi-Vision Channel, Inc.
Motor vehicles	Mitsubishi Motors Mitsubishi Automotive Engineering Mitsubishi Fuso Truck & Bus Mitsubishi Corporation Technos Mitsubishi Heavy Industries	Car Sharing Japan Co., Ltd. MITSUI BUSSAN AUTOMOTIVE INC. Mitsui Automotriz S.A. Mitsiam Motors Co., Ltd. MITSUI BUSSAN MACHINE TEC Co., Ltd.

(continued)

Table 12.2 (continued)

	Mitsubishi	Mitsui
	MITSUBISHI HEAVY INDUSTRIES TRANSPORTATION EQUIPMENT ENGINEERING & SERVICE Mitsubishi Nagasaki Machinery Mfg. RYOJYU COLDCHAIN	P.T. Bussan Auto Finance Penske Automotive Group, Inc. PT Yamaha Indonesia Motor Manufacturing Toyota Canada Inc. Toyota Chile S.A.
Food, beverages, feeds, and retail	ART COFFEE Coca-Cola Central Japan Dai-Nippon Meiji Sugar Kentucky Fried Chicken Japan Kirin Beverage Kirin Brewery Kirin Holdings KIRIN MC DANONE WATERS Koiwai Dairy Products KOIWAI FARM KOIWAI FARM PRODUCTS MARUICHI MC Beverage & Foods MC FOODS Mercian Mitsubishi Shoji Foodtech Mitsubishi-Kagaku Foods Nagano Tomato NITTO FUJI FLOUR MILLING Ryoshoku SAN-ESU SANYO FOODS TOSHO	Corner Stone Research & Development, Inc. Kadoya Sesame Mills Incorporated MCM Foods B.V. Mikuni Coca-Cola Bottling Co., Ltd. Mitsui Foods Co., Ltd. Mitsui Norin Co., Ltd. Mitsui Sugar Co., Ltd. Multigrain AG Novus International, Inc. PRI Foods Co., LTD. San-ei Sucrochemical Co., Ltd. Toho Bussan Kaisha, Ltd. Vendor Service Co., Ltd. United Grain Corp. Wilsey Foods, Inc.
Construction	Daiya Building Service DAIYAPR HIGASHI CHUGOKU RYOJU ESTATE Hiroshima Ryoju Kousan Kakoki Plant & Environment Engineering Kanmon Dock Service Kinki Ryoju Estate The Kodensha KOIWAI FARM Mitsubishi Cable Industries Mitsubishi Chemical Engineering Mitsubishi Chemical Functional Products Mitsubishi Electric Building Techno-Service Mitsubishi Estate Mitsubishi Estate Home MITSUBISHI HEAVY INDUSTRIES BRIDGE & STEEL STRUCTURES ENGINEERING Mitsubishi Jisho Sekkei Mitsubishi Materials Techno Mitsubishi Rayon Engineering Nagoya Ryoju Estate P.S. Mitsubishi Construction Ryoju Estate Ryoken Kiso Seibu Construction	Mitsui Bussan Construction Materials Co.
Metals, mining, and non ferrous metal	Isuzu Metal One Kyushu Steel Center Metal One Corporation Metal One RYOWA Metal One Speciality Steel	Coil Center Co., Ltd. Champions Pipe & Supply, Inc. Mitsui & Co. Steel Ltd. MITSUI BUSSAN KOZAI HANBAI CO., LTD. MBK Steel Products West Co., Ltd. Mitsui Bussan Construction Materials Co., Ltd.

(continued)

Table 12.2 (continued)

	Mitsubishi	Mitsui
	Metal One Steel Products	MITSUI BUSSAN STEEL TRADE CO., LTD.
	Metal One Steel Service	Nippon Steel Trading Co., Ltd.
	Mitsubishi Corporation Technos	Regency Steel Asia Pte Ltd.
	Mitsubishi Nagasaki Machinery Mfg.	Siam Yamato Steel Co., Ltd.
	MOBY Suzuyasu	Shanghai Bao-Mit Steel Distribution Co., Ltd.
	Hosokura Metal Mining	Steel Technologies Inc.
	Mitsubishi Corporation Exploration	Coral Bay Nickel Corporation.
	Ryoko Lime Industry	Japan Collahuasi Resources B.V.
	Hosokura Metal Mining	Inner Mongolia Erdos Electric Power &
	Japan New Metals	Metallurgical Co., Ltd
	Mitsubishi Aluminum	Mitsui Iron Ore Development Pty. Ltd.
	Mitsubishi Cable America	Mitsui-Itochu Iron Pty. Ltd.
	Mitsubishi Cable Industries	Mitsui Raw Materials Development
	Mitsubishi Corporation Unimetals	Pty. Limited .
	Mitsubishi Materials	MITSUI BUSSAN METALS CO., LTD.
	Mitsubishi Nuclear Fuel	NIPPON AMAZON ALUMINIUM CO., LTD.
	Mitsubishi Materials Natural Resources Dev.	SUMIC Nickel Netherlands B.V.
	Mitsubishi Shindoh	Valepar S.A.
	Onahama Smelting and Refining	
	Sus-Tech	
Real estate	Chitose Kosan	Bussan Community Company
	HIGASHI CHUGOKU RYOJU ESTATE	Bussan Real Estate Co., Ltd.
	Hiroshima Ryoju Kousan	Mbk Real Estate Europe Limited
	IMS	Sumisho & Mitsuibussan Kenzai Co., Ltd.
	Izumi Parktown Service	
	Kinki Ryoju Estate	
	Marunouchi Yorozu	
	Mitsubishi Electric Life Service	
	Mitsubishi Estate Building Management	
	Mitsubishi Estate	
	Mitsubishi Estate Home	
	Mitsubishi Jisho Property Management	
	Mitsubishi Jisho Retail Property Mgmt.	
	Mitsubishi Jisho Towa Community	
	Mitsubishi Real Estate Services	
	Mitsubishi UFJ Real Estate Services	
	Nagoya Ryoju Estate	
	Ryoju Estate	
	Sotsu Corporation	
	Tamachi Building	
	Yokohama Sky Building	
Resources and energy	Astomos Energy Corporation	BHP Mitsui Coal Pty. Ltd.
	Marunouchi Heat Supply	Japan Australia LNG (MIMI) Pty. Ltd.
	MHI Nuclear Engineering	Kokusai Oil & Chemical Co., Ltd.
	Mitsubishi Chemical Functional Products	Kyokuto Petroleum Industries, Ltd.
	Mitsubishi Gas Chemical Company	MitEnergy Upstream LLC
	Mitsubishi Heavy Industries	Mitsui Coal Holdings Pty. Ltd.
	Mitsubishi Materials	Mitsui E&P Australia Pty Limited
	Mitsubishi Nuclear Fuel	Mitsui E&P Middle East B.V.
	Nippon Oil	Mitsui Gas Development Qatar B.V.
	Nippon Petroleum Refining	Mitsui Marubeni Liquefied Gas Co., Ltd.
	Nuclear Development	Mitsui LNG Nederland B.V.
		Mitsui Oil Co., Ltd.

(continued)

Table 12.2 (continued)

	Mitsubishi	Mitsui
		Mitsui Oil Exploration Co., Ltd.
		Mitsui Sakhalin Holdings B.V.
		Mittwell Energy Resources Pty., Ltd.
		Tensho Electric Industries Co., Ltd.
		United Petroleum Development Co., Ltd.
		Westport Petroleum, Inc.
Chemicals	Asahi Glass Kibikasei	Advanced Composites, Inc.
	Kyowa Hakko Kirin Mitsubishi Chemical	DAIICHI TANKER CO., LTD.
	Mitsubishi Chemical America	Daito Chemical Industries, Ltd.
	Mitsubishi Chemical Analytech	Japan-Arabia Methanol Company Ltd.
	Mitsubishi Chemical Holdings	Hi-Bis GmbH.
	Mitsubishi Chemical Medience	Honshu Chemical Industry Co., Ltd.
	Mitsubishi Engineering-Plastics	Mitsui AgriScience International SA/NV
	Mitsubishi Gas Chemical	Mitsui Bussan Agro Business Co., Ltd.
	Mitsubishi Kagaku Media	Mitsui Bussan Chemicals Co., Ltd.
	Mitsubishi Plastics	Mitsui Bussan Plastics Trade Co., Ltd.
	Mitsubishi Gas Chemical Company	P.T. STANDARD TOYO POLYMER.
	Mitsubishi Pharma	P.T. Kaltim Pasifik Amoniak
	Mitsubishi Rayon	Sanko Gosei Ltd.
	Mitsubishi Rayon America	Shark Bay Salt Pty Ltd.
	Mitsubishi Shoji Agri-Service	Soda Aromatic Co., Ltd.
	Mitsubishi Shoji Chemical	Tensho Electric Industries Co., Ltd.
	Mitsubishi Shoji Plastics	
	Mitsubishi Tanabe Pharma	
	MKV DREAM Nippon Polypenco	
	RYOBI TECHNO Ryoden Kasei	
	Ryouei Tokyo Shokai	
Marine and aerospace		Orient Marine Co., Ltd.
		Mitsui Bussan Aerospace Co., Ltd.
Warehousing and transport	DAIYA LOGISTICS	Intercontinental Terminals Company LLC
	Isuzu	TRI-NET (JAPAN) INC.
	Metal One SSS West Japan	TRI-NET LOGISTICS (ASIA) PTE. LTD.
	MHI AEROSPACE LOGITEM	
	Mitsubishi Chemical Logistics	
	Mitsubishi Corporation LT	
	Mitsubishi Electric Logistics	
	Mitsubishi Logistics	
	Nippon Yusen Kabushiki Kaisha Ryowa Logitem	
Pulp and paper	DIA HOZAI	
	DIAMIC	
	Mitsubishi Paper Mills	
	Mitsubishi Paper Sales	
	PICTORICO	
	Tokyo Shokai	
Consumer service		AIM Services Co., Ltd.
		ALCANTARA S.P.A.
		Burberry International K.K.
		BUSSAN REAL ESTATE CO., LTD.
		HANAE MORI Associates Co., Ltd
		HOUSE DEPOT PARTNERS CO., LTD.
		Mitsui Bussan Inter-fashion Ltd.
		MITSUI BUSSAN PACKAGING CO., LTD

(continued)

Table 12.2 (continued)

Mitsubishi	Mitsui
	MITSUI BUSSAN TECHNO PRODUCTS CO., LTD.
	Mitsui Bussan Woodchip Oceania Pty. Ltd.
	Storage Plus Corp.
	Sumisho & Mitsui Bussan Kenzai Co., Ltd.
	SOGO MEDICAL CO., LTD.
Infrastructure project business unit	Atlatec Holdings, S.A. de C.V.
	AES JORDAN HOLDCO, LTD.
	Compañía de Generación Valladolid S. de R.L. de C.V.
	IPM Eagle LLP.
	IPM (UK) Power Holdings Limited.
	MBK Project Holdings Ltd.
	Mitsui & Co. Plant Systems, Ltd.
	Mitsui Power Ventures Limited.
	MIT POWER CANADA LP INC.
	Mitsui Rail Capital Holdings, Inc.
	MRCE Group.
	Mitsui Rail Capital Participações Ltda.
	MITSUI GAS E ENERGIA DO BRASIL LTDA.
	P.T. Paiton Energy.
	Toyo Engineering Corporation.

Sources: The individual websites of each business group (www.mitsubishi.com and www.mitsui.co.jp).

at the table, we see that it illustrates how valuable cooperation among the members can be. The idea has not been lost on US firms, among others, which are now beginning to put together their own *"mini-keiretsus."* For example, Eastman Kodak has acquired a number of distributors in Japan and has taken small stakes in some 50 suppliers and customers, and IBM is investing venture capital in a host of small European computer-related firms. Motorola has not taken equity positions, but it uses a *keiretsu* approach by developing extremely close ties with suppliers.

 Active learning check

Review your answer to Active Learning Case question 3 and make any changes you like. Then compare your answer to the one below.

3 In what way could best practices help GE develop more effective international strategies? Explain.

Best practices could help GE develop more effective international strategies by encouraging it to identify those MNEs that are most successful and then discover how they accomplish that feat. Do these firms manage to develop more new products than do their competitors? Or are they best at getting their new goods into the marketplace quickly? Do they produce the highest-quality goods? Or are they lowest-cost producers? What accounts for their ability to achieve such an excellent performance? By asking and answering these questions, GE can gain insights into how it needs to change its own production processes in order to emulate those MNEs successfully.

KEY POINTS

1 Many of today's goods and services will be replaced in the future with faster, more efficient, and cheaper substitutes. For this reason, MNEs need to continually research, develop, and bring new offerings to the marketplace. One way this is being done is through the use of time-to-market accelerators. A good example is concurrent engineering.

2 The generation of goods and services entails a number of specific functions. One is obtaining materials or supplies. Many MNEs have found that global sourcing is the best strategy because it helps keep down costs while providing a number of other benefits, including ensuring an ongoing source of supply and helping the company penetrate overseas markets.

3 In the production of goods and services, MNEs focus on a number of key factors, including cost, quality, and well-designed production systems. While these three factors are often interrelated, each merits specific attention. Multinationals have also developed very effective inventory control systems that help minimize carrying costs and increase productivity. Attention is also focused on gaining the proper balance between production and service domination. Figure 12.3 illustrates this point.

4 International logistics is the designing and managing of a system to control the flow of materials and products throughout the firm. In addition to inventory control, this involves transportation, packaging, and storing.

5 MNEs are currently focusing on a number of areas in improving their production strategies. Three approaches that have been receiving particular attention include (a) technology and design, (b) continuous improvement of operations, and (c) the use of strategic alliances and acquisitions. These approaches are helping multinationals meet new product and service challenges while keeping costs down and quality up.

Key terms

- backward integration
- forward integration
- horizontal integration
- time-to-market accelerators
- modular integrated robotized system (MIRB)
- concurrent engineering
- global sourcing
- modular manufacturing
- *kaizen*
- production system
- material handling
- process mapping
- just-in-time inventory (JIT)
- Demand-Flow™ Technology (DFT)
- international logistics
- container ships
- unconventional cargo vessels
- roll-on-roll-off (RORO) vessels
- lighter aboard ship (LASH) vessels
- intermodal containers
- foreign trade zones
- empowerment

REVIEW AND DISCUSSION QUESTIONS

1 Why are MNEs so interested in new product development? Why do they not simply focus on improving their current offerings?

2 Why is speed-to-market such an important production strategy? Explain.

3 What are time-to-market accelerators? In what way is concurrent engineering one of these accelerators?

4 Why do many MNEs use global sourcing? Why do they not produce all the parts and materials in-house? Be complete in your answer.

5 Why are world-class suppliers often located next to world-class manufacturers? What forms of synergy often exist between the two groups?

6 How do MNEs try to cut production costs? Identify and describe three steps.

7 In what way is the continuous reduction cost method used by Japanese manufacturers different from the periodic cost reduction method employed by many US firms? Compare and contrast the two.

8 Some MNEs use a production strategy that involves costing a portfolio of related goods rather than just costing each individually. What is the logic behind this strategy?

9 How does kaizen help bring about increased quality? Is this approach limited to Japanese firms or are other MNEs using it as well?

10 What types of issues does an MNE confront when it seeks to improve its production system? Identify and describe three.

11 How does JIT help an MNE control its inventory? Give two examples.

12 How is employee training an important factor in implementing JIT and DFT production processes?

13 Why would an MNE want to determine the degree to which its primary business was product dominated and service dominated? Explain.

14 Why are MNEs concerned with international logistics? How does this help the companies increase their competitiveness?

15 In recent years MNEs have been focusing on a number of areas in improving their production strategies. What are two of these? Identify and describe each.

REAL CASE

Flextronics

You wouldn't think that company rivals such as Sony and Philips, or Ericsson, Alcatel, and Motorola, would choose to share the same factories to build competing products, but that is just what has been happening since the emergence of electronic manufacturing service providers (EMSPs). Contract manufacturing has become a sweeping trend in electronics manufacturing. Companies unknown to the public, such as Flextronics, Sanmina-SCI, Celestica, and Jabil, among others, now make such well-known products as IBM PCs, the Microsoft Xbox video console, Web TV set-top boxes for Philips and Sony, and portable phones for Ericsson, Alcatel, and Motorola. In 2006, EMSP industry revenues were estimated at over $200 billion. In 2007 two of the largest EMSP companies, Flextronics and Solectron, combined when Flextronics, with revenues of $18.854 billion, acquired Solectron, with revenues of $10.561 billion.

Flextronics, the largest EMSP, is one of the *Fortune* Global 500 companies, but most end-customers who use its

Source: Corbis/Thomas White/Reuters

products have never heard of it. Incorporated in Singapore in 1990, Flextronics is a provider of vertically integrated advanced design and electronics manufacturing services (EMS) to original equipment manufacturers (OEMs). It ▶

provides these services to various markets, which include infrastructure, mobile communication devices, computing, consumer digital devices, industrial, semiconductor capital equipment, clean technology, aerospace and defense, and white goods, automotive and marine, and medical devices. As of March 31, 2010, Flextronics total manufacturing capacity was approximately 26.6 million square feet. The company helps customers design, build, ship, and service electronics products through a network of facilities in 30 countries across four continents. Though officially headquartered in Singapore, the company has strong ties to the US market and most of its customers are US companies. Flextronics are listed on NASDAQ (the United States) and the Frankfurt Stock Exchange (Germany).

Over the years Flextronics has expanded by purchasing smaller EMSP contractors and factories from its customers. In 2001, Flextronics purchased half of Xerox's office equipment-making operations for $220 million. The deal came with a five-year outsourcing contract for Flextronics to manufacture Xerox products. Currently its 10 largest customers, including Sony-Ericsson, Motorola, and Hewlett-Packard, account for about 64 percent of net sales from continuing operations.

In 2010, Flextronics total revenue was US $24,110.7 million. It generated 48 percent of its sales from Asia, 31 percent from the Americas and 20 percent from Europe. According to Rugman (2005), Flextronics is among nine "global" MNEs which derived 20 percent sales or more from each of the triad regions of North America, Europe and Asia.

Because of lower transportation costs as a percentage of total value, electronics can be transported by air, whereas cars are always transported by sea. This is one main reason why contract manufacturing has been so successful in the electronics industry, where parts might travel the world over before the product is finished.

Prior to the merger with Solectron, Flextronics had six industrial parks in low-cost regions near each large triad market. In Asia, two industrial parks in China, one in Malaysia and one in India and a network of regional manufacturing facilities supply printers, cell phones, telephone switching boards, and PDAs, among other products. In the Americas, products from its two industrial parks (one in Mexico, one in Brazil) and its network of manufacturing facilities include automotive, telecommunications, networking equipment, and hardware products, among others. In Eastern Europe, Poland and Hungary host two industrial parks and one in Ukraine that are also supported by nearby manufacturing facilities and that produce telecommunications infrastructure, electronics for auto-motives, printers, and disposable cameras, among others.

The choice of location for production facilities is determined by the quality of the labor force, the cost of producing in the country, and the proximity to a triad market. Mexico, for example, is the low-cost region in the North American market. Brazil has the best industrial capabilities among countries in South America and strong ties to large international firms from Europe and North America. China has abundant labor, high expected economic growth, and proximity to the large Japanese market where international firms like Canon, NEC, and Sony are headquartered. Eastern Europe is the low-cost production area for West European markets. It is no surprise that the Flextronics industrial park in Poland is located near a university from which it can acquire skilled labor.

EMSPs do much more than provide cost-effective manufacturing. They help in the design of products to make them easier to manufacture; they also provide logistics services, such as material procurement, inventory management, vendor management, packaging and distribution, and automation of key components of the supply chain through advanced IT. In addition, they offer after-market services such as repair and warranty services.

Today's electronic manufacturers have come a long way from the cheap labor-based contractors that used to dominate the industry. Robotic automation is now a significant part of the production process and is handled mostly by specialists. It is their manufacturing expertise that makes for lower costs, but EMSPs provide many more advantages to OEMs. They decrease the risk of manufacturing because OEMs no longer need to make large investments in a new factory to create a new product that might or might not be successful. EMSPs can also purchase inputs at lower prices because they are making cell phones not only for Alcatel, but also for Motorola and Ericsson, increasing their purchasing power.

Contract manufacturing accounts for less than one-fourth of electronic manufacturing; however, there are reasons to believe that EMSP companies will dominate the industry in the future. This process will redefine the role of OEMs in the electronics industry to one of design and marketing.

Sources: Karyn McCormack, "Flextronics Adds a Key Part," *Business Week*, June 4, 2007; "Let the Bad Times Roll," The *Economist*, April 5, 2001; Jonathan Sprague, "Invasion of the Factory Snatchers," *Fortune*, August 15, 2002; Flextronics, *Annual Report*, 2010; www.flextronics.com; Alan M. Rugman, *The Regional Multinationals* (Cambridge: Cambridge University Press, 2005).

1 Keeping in mind that Flextronics does not sell to end-customers, how does that change your interpretation of the regional sales data presented in this case?

2 What effect does the emergence of EMSPs have for new entrants into the electronics industry?

3 Why should OEMs be concerned about using EMSPs?

REAL CASE

Nike

One of the rules of international production strategy is: manufacture the highest-quality product and the world is likely to beat a path to your door. A number of firms help illustrate this rule. One is Nike, the sports shoe producer. Making a wide variety of high-quality shoes, Nike catalogues more than 800 models for use in approximately 25 sports. In 1999 it had 35 percent of the world's market for training shoes (and 45 percent in the United States). In 2010 its sales were $19,014 million. In an effort to keep ahead of the competition, Nike updates each shoe at least every six months. Most of these ideas are generated by Nike's R&D center in Beaverton, near Portland, Oregon, where physiologists and mechanical engineers study the stresses on an athlete's feet and collaborate with stylists on new shoe ideas.

The aim of the takeover of Umbro on March 3, 2008 was to extend these scale advantages.

Although Nike sells its products in over 140 countries and produces in more than 33 countries, it is really a triad MNE. In 2010, over 89 percent of its sales are in the triad markets of the United States, Europe, and Asia and 11 percent from emerging markets. Nike is still strong in its home market. In 2010 and 2009, sales in the United States including US sales of other businesses accounted for approximately 42 percent of total revenues, compared to 43 percent in 2008. For the fiscal years 2010 and 2009, other businesses primarily comprised of Cole Haan, Converse, Hurley, NIKE Golf, and Umbro. In 2008, the other businesses primarily consisted of Cole Haan, Converse, Exeter (whose primary business was the Starter brand business which was sold on December 17, 2007), Hurley, NIKE Bauer Hockey (which was sold on April 17, 2008), NIKE Golf, and Umbro. In 2010 and 2009, non-US sales (including non-US sales of other businesses) accounted for 58 and 57 percent of total sales, respectively.

Nike's high-quality production is matched by superb marketing skills. The world might be beating a path to Nike's door, but the company makes sure the world knows where it is. It spends 11 percent of its revenue on marketing, and its "swoosh" brand is recognized the world over. The company continues to use sports stars to endorse its products. Besides American stars like Tiger Woods and Andre Agassi, it has used European soccer players and cricket players in India, and has gone to China for the 2008 Olympic Games in Beijing. The idea is: if you can make the "cool" guys wear your products, the rest will follow.

Perhaps the only thing Nike does not like to be remembered for is the bad publicity around its labor practices in Asia. Nike has outsourced all of its production to low-wage areas. In 2010, virtually all of Nike footwear is produced by contract factories in Vietnam, China, Indonesia, Thailand, and India which accounted approximately 37 percent, 34 percent, 23 percent, 2 percent, and 1 percent of total NIKE brand footwear, respectively. Nike also had manufacturing agreements with independent factories in Argentina, Brazil, Mexico, and India to manufacture footwear for sales within those countries. In addition, all its apparel is produced in 33 host countries by independent contract manufacturers. Most of the apparel production occurred in China, Thailand, Indonesia, Malaysia, Vietnam, Sri Lanka, Turkey, Cambodia, El Salvador, Mexico, and Taiwan. And NGOs have criticized the poor working conditions in some of its Asian factories, from Pakistani children stitching Nike's soccer balls to Vietnamese working in unsafe conditions. NGOs in the Western world started campaigns to boycott Nike, and demonstrators protested in front of Nike's stores. Allegations of long working hours, bad ventilation, and physical abuse of a mostly young female workforce have tarnished Nike's reputation.

Nike's industry dominance was a main reason for its being severely targeted. Many of its competitors were found to have the same labor practices, but were not subjected to the same level of criticism. More recently Nike has acknowledged its corporate responsibility to improve working conditions in its own factories and help influence its suppliers.

Websites: www.nike.com.

Sources: Sydney H. Schanberg, "On the Playgrounds of America, Every Kid's Goal Is to Score: In Pakistan, Where Children Stitch Soccer Balls for Six Cents an Hour, the Goal Is to Survive," *Life*, June 1996; Harry Dunphy, "Nike to Improve Conditions," *Associated Press*, May 12, 1998; Tom Braithwaite, "Nike Moves Closer to Deal for Umbro," *Financial Times*, December 21, 2007; Nike, Annual report, 2009; www.nike.com; Nike, *Annual report*, 2010.

1 What is the key to Nike's production strategy? Explain.

2 What are the advantages of frequent design changes in Nike's sneakers?

3 Why was it important for Nike to clean up its labor practices in Asia? What more should the company do?

ENDNOTES

1 "(Still) Made in Japan," *The Economist,* April 7, 2004.

2 Also see Emily Thornton, "Mazda Learns To Like Those Intruders," *Business Week,* September 14, 1998, p. 172.

3 Alex Taylor III, "How Toyota Copes with Hard Times," *Fortune,* January 25, 1993, pp. 78–81; and Joah Muller and Katie Kerwin, "Detroit Is Cruising for Quality," *Business Week,* September 3, 2001.

4 For a good example of these challenges, see Ferdinand Protzman, "Daimler's Quest Collides with Slump," *New York Times,* August 3, 1993, pp. C1, C5.

5 C. W. L. Hill, *International Business: Competing in the Global Marketplace,* 3rd ed. (New York: McGraw-Hill, 2000); and http://www.hp.com.

6 Simon C. Collinson, "Knowledge Management Capabilities in R&D: A UK–Japan Company Comparison," *R&D Management,* vol. 31, no. 3 (2001), pp. 335–347.

7 Nohria, N. and Ghoshal, S. *The Differentiated Network: Organizing Multinational Corporations for Value Creation* (San Francisco: Jossey-Bass, 1997).

8 T. W. Malnight, "Emerging Structural Patterns within Multinational Corporations: Toward Process-based Structures," *Academy of Management Journal,* vol. 44, no. 6 (2001); and Hansen, M. T. and B. Løvås, "How Do Multinational Companies Leverage Technological Competencies? Moving from Single to Interdependent Explanations," *Strategic Management Journal,* vol. 25, no. 8/9 (2004).

9 See Don Clark, "Intel to Ship Its Next-Generation Chip in 1995, Boosts Outlay for Production," *Wall Street Journal,* January 28, 1994, p. B5.

10 Gene Bylinsky, "Heroes of US Manufacturing," *Fortune,* March 20, 2000.

11 Also see C. K. Prahalad and Kenneth Lieberthal, "The End of Corporate Imperialism," *Harvard Business Review,* July/August 1998, pp. 69–79.

12 Joseph T. Vesey, "The New Competitors: They Think in Terms of 'Speed- to-Market'," *Academy of Management Executive,* May 1991, pp. 23–33; and "Re-inventing the Wheel," *The Economist,* April 20, 2000.

13 Saul Hansell, "Is This the Factory of the Future?" *New York Times,* July 26, 1998, Section 3, pp. 1, 12.

14 Rebecca Blumenstein, "GM Is Building Plants in Developing Nations to Woo New Markets," *Wall Street Journal,* August 4, 1997, pp. A1, 5.

15 Gene Bylinsky, "Heroes of US Manufacturing," *Fortune,* March 20, 2000.

16 Larry Holyoke, William Spindle and Neil Gross, "Doing the Unthinkable," *Business Week,* January 10, 1994, pp. 52–53; and Andrew Pollack, "Nissan Plans to Buy More American Parts," *New York Times,* March 26, 1994, pp. 17, 26.

17 Michael E. Porter, *The Competitive Advantage of Nations* (New York: Free Press, 1990), p. 103.

18 For more on this, see Earl Landesman, "Ultimatum for US Auto Suppliers: Go Global or Go Under," *Journal of European Business,* May/June 1991, pp. 39–45.

19 "The Modular T," *The Economist,* September 3, 1998; and David Welch, "Why Detroit is Going to Pieces," *Business Week,* September 3, 2001.

20 Larry Reibstein et al., "A Mexican Miracle?" *Newsweek,* May 20, 1991, p. 42.

21 Ernest Beck, "Why Foreign Distillers Find It So Hard to Sell Vodka to the Russians," *Wall Street Journal,* January 15, 1998, pp. A1, 8.

22 Ford S. Worthy, "Japan's Smart Secret Weapon," *Fortune,* August 12, 1991, pp. 72–75.

23 Ibid., p. 75.

24 Suh-kyung Yoon, "Working Up a Thirst to Quench Asia," *Far Eastern Economic Review,* February 1, 2001.

25 See Louis Kraar, "Korea Goes for Quality," *Fortune,* April 13, 1994, pp. 153–159; and Gale Eisenstodt, "Sullivan's Travels," *Forbes,* March 28, 1994, pp. 75–76.

26 Erick Calonius, "Smart Moves by Quality Champs," *Fortune,* Spring/Summer 1991, p. 24.

27 See, for example, Christopher Palmeri, "A Process That Never Ends," *Forbes,* December 21, 1992, pp. 52–54.

28 "The Car Company in Front," *Economist.com,* January 27, 2005.

29 Richard A. Melcher and Stewart Toy, "On Guard, Europe," *Business Week,* December 14, 1992, pp. 54–55.

30 Louis S. Richman, "What America Makes Best," *Fortune,* Spring/Summer 1991, p. 80.

31 Ibid., p. 81.

32 Michael Shari and Pete Engardio, "The Sweet Sound of Success," *Business Week,* September 8, 1997, p. 56.

33 See Michael E. McGrath and J. Gordon Stewart, "Professional Service Firms in Europe Move Toward Integrated European Practices," *Journal of European Business,* May/June 1991, pp. 26–30.

34 Steven Prokesch, "Edges Fray on Volvo's Brave New Humanistic World," *New York Times,* July 7, 1991, p. F5.

35 Richard J. Schonberger, *Building a Chain of Customers* (New York: Free Press, 1990), pp. 50–51.

36 "A Long March," *Economist.com,* July 12, 2001.

37 Thomas A. Stewart, "GE Keeps Those Ideas Coming," *Fortune,* August 12, 1991, p. 48.

38 Lucinda Harper, "Trucks Keep Inventories Rolling Past Warehouses to Production Line," *Wall Street Journal,* February 7, 1994, p. B3.

39 Alex Taylor III, "Why Toyota Keeps Getting Better and Better and Better," *Fortune,* November 19, 1990, p. 79.

40 Gene Bylinsky, "Heroes of U.S. Manufacturing," *Fortune,* March 20, 2000.

41 "Intermec Recognized for Its Use of Demand Flow™ Technology," *Intermec News Release,* May 21, 1997.

42 David A. Aaker, "How Will the Japanese Compete in Retail Services?" *California Management Review,* Fall 1990, pp. 54–67.

43 For still other examples of service-related problems in Japan, see Jon Woronoff, *The Japanese Management Mystique: The Reality Behind the Myth* (Chicago: Probus, 1992), pp. 120–124.

44 "A Moving Story," *Economist.com,* December 5, 2002.

45 Joan Magretta, "Fast, Global, and Entrepreneurial: Supply Chain Management, Hong Kong Style: An Interview with Victor Fung," *Harvard Business Review,* September/October 1998, pp. 105–106.

46 See, for example, Hellene S. Runtagh, "GE Tracks Transportation and Distribution Opportunities in the EC," *Journal of European Business*, September/October 1990, pp. 22–25.

47 See Alan M. Rugman and Cecilia Brain, "Regional Strategies of Multinational Pharmaceutical Firms," *Management International Review*, vol. 44, no. 3 (2004), pp. 7–25.

48 Vesey op. cit.

49 Ibid.

50 "Fighting Back," *The Economist*, September 2, 2004.

51 "A Moving Story," *Economist.com*, December 5, 2002.

52 See "Breaking Japan's *Keiretsu*," *The Economist*, March 20, 2003.

ADDITIONAL BIBLIOGRAPHY

Adler, Paul S. and Cole, Robert E. "Designed for Learning: A Tale of Two Auto Plants," *Sloan Management Review*, vol. 34, no. 3 (Spring 1993).

Ambos, Björn and Schlegelmilch, Bodo B. "The Use of International R&D Teams: An Empirical Investigation of Selected Contingency Factors," *Journal of World Business*, vol. 39, no. 1 (February 2004).

Bellak, Christian and Cantwell, John. "Revaluing the Capital Stock of International Production," *International Business Review*, vol. 13, no. 1 (February 2004).

Bhappu, Anita D. "The Japanese Family: An Institutional Logic for Japanese Corporate Networks and Japanese Management," *Academy of Management Review*, vol. 25, no. 2 (April 2000).

Brouthers, Lance Eliot, Werner, Steve and Matulich, Erika. "The Influence of Triad Nations' Environments on Price–Quality Product Strategies and MNC Performance," *Journal of International Business Studies*, vol. 31, no. 1 (Spring 2000).

Cantwell, John. "Innovation and Information Technology in the MNE," in Alan M. Rugman and Thomas Brewer (eds.), *The Oxford Handbook of International Business* (Oxford: Oxford University Press, 2001).

Collins, R. and Schmenner, R. "Taking Manufacturing Advantage of Europe's Single Market," *European Management Journal*, vol. 13, no. 3 (May/June 1995).

Collinson, Simon C. "Organising Knowledge to Manage R&D: A UK-Japan Company Comparison," *R&D Management*, vol. 31, no. 3 (2001).

Contractor, Farok J., Kumar, Vikas, Kundu, Sumit, and Pedersen, Torben. *Global Outsourcing and Offshoring: An Integrated Approach to Theory and Corporate Strategy* (Cambridge: Cambridge University Press, November 2010).

Contractor, Farok J., Kumar, Vikas, Kundu, Sumit K. and Pedersen, Torben. "Reconceptualizing the Firm in a World of Outsourcing and Offshoring: The Organizational and Geographical Relocation of High-Value Company Functions," *Journal of Management Studies*, vol. 47, no. 8 (December 2010).

Cusumano, Michael A. "Manufacturing Innovation: Lessons from the Japanese Auto Industry," *Sloan Management Review*, vol. 30, no. 1 (Fall 1988).

Douglas, Susan P. and Wind, Yoram. "The Myth of Globalization," *Columbia Journal of World Business*, vol. 22, no. 4 (Winter 1987).

DuBois, Frank L., Toyne, Brian and Oliff, Michael D. "International Manufacturing Strategies of US Multinationals: A Conceptual Framework Based on a Four-Industry Study," *Journal of International Business Studies*, vol. 24, no. 2 (Second Quarter 1993).

Dyer, Jeffrey H. and Chu, Wujin. "The Determinants of Trust in Supplier–Automaker Relationships in the US, Japan, and Korea," *Journal of International Business Studies*, vol. 42, 10–27 (January 2011). doi:10.1057/jibs.2010.34.

Flaherty, M. Therese. "Global Sourcing Strategy: R&D, Manufacturing, and Marketing Interfaces," *Journal of International Business Studies*, vol. 24, no. 1 (First Quarter 1993).

Frost, Tony S. and Zhou, Changhui. "R&D Co-Practice and 'Reverse'; Knowledge Integration in Multinational Firms," *Journal of International Business Studies*, vol. 36, no. 6 (November 2005).

Griffith, David A. and Myers, Matthew B. "The Performance Implications of Strategic Fit of Relational Norm Governance Strategies in Global Supply Chain Relationships," *Journal of International Business Studies*, vol. 36, no. 3 (2005).

Hagedoorn, John, Cloodt, Danielle and Kanenburg, Hans van. "Intellectual Property Rights and the Governance of International R&D Partnerships," *Journal of International Business Studies*, vol. 36, no. 2 (2005).

Hansen, Morten T. and Løvås, Bjorn. "How Do Multinational Companies Leverage Technological Competencies? Moving from Single to Interdependent Explanations," *Strategic Management Journal*, vol. 25, nos. 8/9 (2004).

Hodgetts, Richard. *Measures of Quality and High Performance: Simple Tools and Lessons from America's Most Successful Firms* (New York: Amacom, 1998).

Jensen, Ørberg Peter D. and Pedersen, Torben. "The Economic Geography of Offshoring: The Fit Between Activities and Local Context," *Journal of Management Studies*, vol. 48, no. 2 (March 2011)

Kotabe, Masaaki. "The Relationship Between Offshore Sourcing and Innovativeness of US Multinational Firms: An Empirical Investigation," *Journal of International Business Studies*, vol. 21, no. 4 (Fourth Quarter 1990).

Kotabe, Masaaki and Murray, Janet Y. "Linking Product and Process Innovations and Modes of International Sourcing in Global Competition: A Case of Foreign Multinational Firms," *Journal of International Business Studies*, vol. 21, no. 3 (Third Quarter 1990).

Kotabe, Masaaki and Omura, Glenn S. "Sourcing Strategies of European and Japanese Multinationals: A Comparison," *Journal of International Business Studies*, vol. 20, no. 1 (Spring 1989).

Levy, David L. "Lean Production in an International Supply Chain," *Sloan Management Review*, vol. 38, no. 2 (Winter 1997).

Louise, Curran and Soledad, Zignago. "How Regional is the Supply Chain in the Enlarged EU?" *Multinational Business Review*, vol. 18, no. 1 (2010).

Malnight, Thomas W. "Emerging Structural Patterns within Multinational Corporations: Toward Process-based Structures," *Academy of Management Journal*, vol. 44, no. 6 (2001).

Nieto, María and Rodríguez, Jesús Alici. "Offshoring of R&D: Looking Abroad to Improve Innovation Performance," *Journal of International Business Studies*, vol. 42 (April 2011). doi:10.1057/jibs.2010.59.

Nohria, Nitin and Ghoshal, Sumantra. *The Differentiated Network: Organizing Multinational Corporations for Value Creation* (San Francisco: Jossey-Bass, 1997).

Ojah, Kalu and Monplaisir, Leslie. "Investors' Valuation of Global Product Design and Development," *Journal of International Business Studies*, vol. 34, no. 5 (September 2003).

Patel, Pari and Pavitt, Keith. "Large Firms in the Production of the World's Technology: An Important Case of 'Non-Globalization'," *Journal of International Business Studies*, vol. 22, no. 1 (First Quarter 1991).

Quinn, James Brian and Hilmer, Frederick G. "Strategic Outsourcing," *Sloan Management Review*, vol. 35, no. 4 (Summer 1994).

Reddy, Prasada. "New Trends in Globalization of Corporate R&D and Implications for Innovation Capability in Host Countries: A Survey from India," *World Development*, vol. 25, no. 11 (November 1997).

Rehder, Robert R. "Building Cars as if People Mattered: The Japanese Lean System vs. Volvo's Uddevalla System," *Columbia Journal of World Business*, vol. 27, no. 2 (Summer 1992).

Rondinelli, Dennis and Berry, Michael, "Multimodal Transportation, Logistics, and the Environment: Managing Interactions in a Global Economy," *European Management Journal*, vol. 18, no. 4 (August 2000).

Rugman, Alan M. and Bennett, Jocelyn. "Technology Transfer and World Product Mandating," *Columbia Journal of World Business*, vol. 17, no. 4 (Winter 1982).

Rugman, Alan M. and Brain, Cecilia. "Regional Strategies of Multinational Pharmaceutical Firms," *Management International Review*, vol. 44, Special Issue 3 (2004).

Rugman, Alan M. and Verbeke, Alain. "Subsidiary-specific Advantages in Multinational Enterprises," *Strategic Management Journal*, vol. 22, no. 3 (March 2001).

Rugman, Alan M., Jing, Li and Oh, Chang Hoon. "Are Supply Chain Global or Regional?" *International Marketing Review*, vol 26, no. 4/5 (2009).

Serapio, Manuel G., Jr. "Macro-Micro Analyses of Japanese Direct R&D Investments in the US Automotive and Electronics Industries," *Management International Review*, vol. 33, no. 3 (Third Quarter 1993).

Sobek, Durward K. II, Ward, Allen C. and Liker, Jeffrey K. "Toyota's Principles of Set-Based Concurrent Engineering," *Sloan Management Review*, vol. 40, no. 2 (Winter 1999).

Swamidass, Paul M. and Kotabe, Masaaki. "Component Sourcing Strategies of Multinationals: An Empirical Study of European and Japanese Multinationals," *Journal of International Business Studies*, vol. 24, no. 1 (First Quarter 1993).

Vandermerwe, Sandra. "Increasing Returns: Competing for Customers in the Global Market," *Journal of World Business*, vol. 32, no. 4 (Winter 1997).

Yip, George S. "Global Strategy. In a World of Nations?" *Sloan Management Review*, vol. 31, no. 1 (Fall 1989).

Chapter 13

MARKETING STRATEGY

Contents

Objectives of the chapter

Every multinational has a marketing strategy designed to help
identify opportunities and take advantage of them. This plan of action
typically involves consideration of four primary areas: the product or
service to be sold, the way in which the output will be promoted, the
pricing of the good or service, and the distribution strategy to be used
in getting the output to the customer. The primary purpose of this
chapter is to examine the fundamentals of international marketing
strategy. We will look at five major topics: market assessment,
product strategy, promotion strategy, price strategy, and place
strategy. We will consider such critical marketing areas as product
screening, modification of goods and services in order to adapt
to local needs, modified product life cycles, advertising, personal
selling, and ways in which MNEs tailor-make their distribution
systems.

The specific objectives of this chapter are to:

1 *Examine* the process used to conduct an international market
assessment of goods and services.

2 *Study* the criteria that affect an MNE's decision to alter a good or
service in order to adapt it to local market tastes.

3 *Describe* some of the ways in which MNEs use advertising
and personal selling techniques to promote their products in
worldwide markets.

4 *Review* some of the major factors that influence international
pricing and distribution strategies.

Volkswagen in the United States

During the 1960s, Volkswagen AG, the "people's car" in German and "VW" to everyone else, held more market share in the United States than all other auto imports combined. In the 1970s, despite growing foreign competition, VW sales reached 300,000 units annually. This included the early version of the famous VW Golf, branded the Rabbit in the US market (and the Caribe in Latin America), under the audacious advertising slogan: "Why Detroit's engineers are secretly praising Volkswagen's Rabbit." However, the 1980s and early 1990s were not good for the company: annual sales in the US market were down to 150,000 units. The Rabbit in particular developed a bad reputation for its build quality, in contrast to the marketing PR. In less than 10 years, market share had dropped from 3 percent to 0.5 percent, and VW had become a minor competitor in the North American part of the triad. Part of the problem had been that VW's American cars were competing head on with US brands that produced the traditional mid-sized car. VW could produce great cars in this range, but could not achieve the cost advantage of Japanese competitors.

In the early 2000s, however, VW made a great comeback in the United States, particularly on the back of sales of the New Beetle, which was introduced in March 1998. The car is distinct not only because it appeals to the nostalgia of the Old Beetle, but also because of its slick European design. The New Beetle was the third-largest VW seller, after the Jetta and the Passat. In addition to brisk first-year sales, the Beetle was selected as the 1999 North American Car of the Year by an independent jury of 48 journalists who cover the auto industry for daily newspapers, magazines, television, radio, and the Internet. In 2002, VW delivered over 420,000 vehicles to the US market and accounted for approximately 10.1 percent of the passenger car import market. Including imports and domestic production, VW held about 6.6 percent of the US passenger car market. But a period of success was brought to an end by the rising costs of producing cars in Europe relative to the declining US dollar. By 2005 VW was losing money on each car it exported to the United States, leaving it with $1.1 billion of losses from its US operations. Its North American sales stood at 224,195, rising to 235,140 in 2006, but with continued weak profitability. This is despite a return to marketing the VW Golf under the Rabbit name once again.

In its home region of Europe, where VW is the market leader, nearly 20 percent of all new cars sold are from the Volkswagen Group. In 2009, during the economic downturn, Volkswagen's revenue was €105.187 billion and it delivered a total of over 6.3 million vehicles to

Source: Corbis/Greg Smith

customers worldwide, a slight increase in sales by 0.6 percent year-on-year compared to the reporting period 2008. European region accounts for 71.49 percent of VW's total revenue, of which Germany alone accounts for 28.4 percent and the rest of Europe 43.1 percent. North America as a whole accounts for only 10.83 percent, and the rest of world (Asia–Pacific and South America) accounts for 17.76 percent. The year 2010 witnessed an impressive growth 15.4 percent in the number of vehicle sales of 7.3 million units. VW achieved revenue of €126.875 billion, significantly exceeding the 2009 year figure and representing an increase of 20.6 percent, greater than that of the market as a whole, thanks to its strategies with model range updated and rationally expanded. For example, in the year 2010, the VW passenger car brand updated its outstanding range by launching a new generation of numerous models, including the Passat and the Touran. In addition, vehicles designed for specific markets were presented. Therefore, the brand's operating profit increased significantly.

Despite its resurgence in the United States, VW is still facing many problems: as at February 16, 2008, 20.26 percent of VW's shares are still held by the government of Lower Saxony, which prevents VW from cutting labor costs in Germany. As a result, VW is stuck paying $1,700 more to make a car in Germany than if it were manufacturing it in Eastern Europe or Portugal, limiting its ability to compete on price. This had not been a major problem when VW's reputation for quality allowed it to charge a premium, but since Mercedes-Benz and BMW started to compete in VW's market segment, the company's edge on quality diminished.

VW's problems are not new. A decade earlier the company had to reinvent itself to become competitive without reducing its labor costs. At the time, its strategy consisted of brand acquisition and manufacturing improvements. In about a decade VW purchased the Skoda, SEAT, Audi, Bentley, Scania (on February 20, 2009, the VW acquired Scania AB), Lamborghini, and Bugatti brands and set out to create synergies in their manufacturing processes. In the early 1990s, VW was making 30 different models using 16 floor plants. This was subsequently slimmed down to 4 floor plants, making 54 models, with significant savings. This means that many of its cars, whether sold under the Skoda, Audi, or VW brand, share many parts. It is each brand's reputation and design that now carry the car. Under the hood, a Skoda is very similar to a VW but the company has ensured a different market by letting Czech engineers design the Skoda. This brand-based strategy has paid off, increasing VW's market share around the world. Yet, as critics point out, the company's return on capital is lower than that of its competitors, and its brands might eventually erode each other's market share. VW continues to bargain with its union and with its major shareholder to curb labor costs in Germany or to be allowed to close plants there. However, the compromises continue to put it at a disadvantage with competitors. In addition, consumers might not take long to realize that a Skoda, which is promoted as part of the VW family, is cheaper but equivalent to a VW. Its upmarket brands, such as the Lamborghini and Bentley, might also suffer from a perception that many of their parts are comparable to that of VW's other brands.

Websites: www.vw.com; www.gm.com; www.ford.com; www.daimlerchrysler.com.

Sources: Alan M. Rugman, *The Regional Multinationals* (Cambridge: Cambridge University Press, 2005); Bernard Avishai, "A European Platform for Global Competition," *Harvard Business Review*, July/August 1991, pp. 103–113; www.vw.com; Christine Tierney, Andrea Zammert, Joann Muller and Katie Kerwin, "Volkswagen," *Business Week*, July 23, 2001; "Problems with the People's Car," *The Economist*, March 14, 2002; David Kiley, *Getting the Bugs Out: The Rise, Fall and Comeback of Volkswagen in America* (New York: Wiley, 2001); "Higher Wages or More Job Security," *The Economist*, September 16, 2004; Michael Frank, "2005 Volkswagen Touareg V-10," *Forbes.com*, June 21, 2005; Gail Edmondson, "Volkswagen Still on Shaky Ground," *Business Week*, August 22, 2006; Kristina Spiller, "VW Looks to Triple Market Share in US," *Financial Times*, January 8, 2007; Volkswagen, *Annual Report*, 2009 and 2010.

1. How would VW use market assessment to evaluate sales potential for its cars in the United States?

2. Does VW need to modify its cars for the US market? Why or why not?

3. Would the nature of VW's products allow the company to use an identical promotional message worldwide, or would the company have to develop a country-by-country promotion strategy?

4. How would currency fluctuations affect VW's profit in the US market?

5. What type of distribution system would be most effective for VW in the United States?

INTRODUCTION

International marketing
The process of identifying the goods and services that customers outside the home country want and then providing them at the right price and place

International marketing is the process of identifying the goods and services that customers outside the home country want and then providing them at the right price and location.[1] In the international marketplace, this process is similar to that carried out at home, but with some important modifications that can adapt marketing efforts to the needs of the specific country or geographic locale.[2] For example, some MNEs are able to use the same strategy abroad as they have at home. This is particularly true in promotions where messages can carry a universal theme. Some writing implement firms advertise their pens and pencils as "the finest writing instruments in the world," a message that transcends national boundaries and can be used anywhere. Many fast-food franchises apply the same ideas because they have found that people everywhere have the same basic reasons for coming there to eat. In most cases, however, a company must tailor-make its strategy so that it appeals directly to the local customer.

These changes fall into five major areas: market assessment, product decisions, promotion strategies, pricing decisions, and place or distribution strategies. The latter four areas—product, promotion, price, and place—are often referred to as the four Ps of marketing,[3] and they constitute the heart of international marketing efforts.

INTERNATIONAL MARKET ASSESSMENT

International market assessment
An evaluation of the goods and services that the multinational can sell in the global marketplace

International marketing strategy starts with **international market assessment**, an evaluation of the goods and services that the MNE can sell in the global marketplace. This assessment typically involves a series of analyses aimed at pinpointing specific offerings and geographic targets. The first step is called the initial screening.

Initial screening: basic need and potential

Initial screening
The process of determining the basic need and potential of the multinational's goods and services in foreign markets

Initial screening is the process of determining the basic need and potential of the MNE's goods and services in foreign markets. This screening answers the question: who might be interested in buying our output? International auto manufacturers list the EU countries, North America, and Japan as potential buyers. Boeing targets the countries that will be rebuilding their air fleets in the next few decades. Kellogg's, General Mills, and Nestlé are interested in the United States and the European Union as well as any developing nations that offer potential new markets.

One way to carry out initial screening is by examining the current import policies of other countries and identifying the goods and services being purchased from abroad. A second way is by determining local production. A third is to examine the demographic changes taking place in the country that will create new, emerging markets. These cursory efforts help an MNE to target potential markets. Following the initial screening, the company begins to narrow its selection.

Second screening: financial and economic conditions

Secondary screening is used to reduce the list of market prospects by eliminating those that fail to meet financial and economic considerations. Financial considerations include inflation rates, interest rates, expected returns on investment, the buying habits of customers, and the availability of credit. These factors are important in determining whether markets that passed the initial, general screening are also financially feasible.

Market indicators
Indicators used for measuring the relative market strengths of various geographic areas

Market size
An economic screening consideration used in international marketing; it is the relative size of each market as a percentage of the total world market

Market intensity
The richness of a market or the degree of purchasing power in one country as compared to others

Market growth
The annual increase in sales in a particular market

Economic considerations relate to a variety of market demand influences, including market indicators. **Market indicators** are used for measuring the relative market strengths of various geographic areas, and focus on three important areas: market size, market intensity, and market growth. **Market size** is the relative size of each market as a percentage of the total world market. For example, industrialized countries account for a sizable part of the market for cellular telephones, and a few nations such as the United States and Japan account for the largest percentage of this total. Nevertheless, non-industrialized countries with large populations also have a significant market size. In fact, China, the world's largest country in terms of population, is also the world's largest mobile phone market in terms of subscribers.[4] **Market intensity** is the "richness" of the market, or the degree of purchasing power in one country compared to others. For example, the United States and Canada are extremely rich markets for automobiles, telephones, and computers, so MNEs selling these products tend to highlight these two countries. **Market growth** is the annual increase in sales. For example, the market for cell phones and laptop computers in the United States will continue to grow in the years ahead, whereas the market for autos will grow much more slowly. However, given the large purchasing power in the US economy, MNEs selling these products will continue to target the United States. In recent years, other economies, such as South Korea, have become increasingly rich in terms of purchasing power, so they too are now target markets for high-tech products. Infrastructure and economic development can also influence market growth. For example, consumers in developing countries who have not yet been able to acquire a fixed line might choose instead to purchase a portable phone.

Trend analysis
The estimation of future demand by either extrapolating the growth over the last three to five years and assuming that this trend will continue or by using some form of average growth rate over the recent past

Estimation by analogy
A method of forecasting market demand or market growth based on information generated in other countries, such as determining the number of refrigerators sold in the United States as a percentage of new housing starts and using this statistic in planning for the manufacture of these products in other world markets

Regression analysis
A mathematical approach to forecasting that attempts to test the explanatory power of a set of independent variables

Cluster analysis
A marketing approach to forecasting customer demand that involves grouping data based on market area, customer, or similar variables

Quite often these data are analyzed through the use of quantitative techniques. Sometimes these approaches are fairly simple. **Trend analysis**, for example, is the estimation of future demand either by extrapolating the growth over the last three to five years and assuming that this trend will continue or by using some form of average growth rate over the recent past. A similar approach is **estimation by analogy**, through which forecasters predict market demand or growth based on information generated in other countries. For example, if the number of refrigerators sold in the United States is 2.5 times the number of new housing starts, a US MNE that is planning to manufacture these products in the European Union will estimate demand based on the same formula. A more sophisticated approach is the use of **regression analysis**, a mathematical approach to forecasting that attempts to test the explanatory power of a set of independent variables. In the case of selling refrigerators in the European Union, for example, these would include economic growth, per capita income, and the number of births, in addition to other variables such as new housing starts. Another sophisticated approach is **cluster analysis**, a marketing approach that involves grouping data on the basis of market area, customer, and so on, based on similar variables, so that a marketing strategy can be formulated for each group. For example, US MNEs providing services in such areas as insurance, legal, financial, and management consulting know that their approaches must often vary from country to country.

Third screening: political and legal forces

The third level of screening involves taking a look at political and legal forces. A primary consideration is entry barriers in the form of import restrictions or limits on local owner-ship of business operations. Analysis of these barriers often results in identifying loopholes around the various restrictions or data that indicate barriers are far less extensive than initially believed.[5] For example, some MNEs have been able to sidestep legal restrictions by forming joint ventures with local firms. Production restrictions or limitations on profit remittance that restrict operating flexibility must also be considered. Government stabil-ity is an important factor in starting a successful operation; however, it is often difficult to predict. Despite the eagerness of investors to flock to the Russian market in the early 1990s, auto makers were hesitant to invest in Russia because of its uncertain political and economic environment. It was only in 1998 that Fiat made a commitment to the Russian market.[6] Another consideration is the protection offered for patents, trademarks, and copy-rights. In some countries, such as China and Taiwan, pirating has been fairly common, resulting in markets being flooded with counterfeit or look-alike products.

Fourth screening: socio-cultural forces

The fourth level of screening typically involves the consideration of socio-cultural forces such as language, work habits, customs, religion, and values. As noted earlier, culture greatly affects the way people live, and MNEs need to examine how well their operations will fit into each particular culture. For example, although Japanese auto manufacturers have set up assembly plants in the United States, those operations are not identical to the ones in Japan because of the work habits and customs of Americans. In the United States, the work pace is less frantic and most people are unwilling to work the typical 5½-day week which is so common in Japan. Moreover, US managers are accustomed to going home to their fami-lies after work, whereas Japanese managers often go out for dinner and drinks and discuss business until late in the evening. MNEs will examine these socio-cultural differences in determining where to locate operations.

Another study by an advertising firm shows that Muslims in the United States are among the richest and well educated of the US population. Their buying patterns are heavily influenced by Islamic law. The religious beliefs and cultural norms of this subgroup of the US population particularly influence their buyer preferences in the consumer markets of food, finance, and packaged goods.[7]

Fifth screening: competitive environment

The fifth level of screening is typically focused on competitive forces. If three or four locations are equally attractive, an MNE will often make a final choice based on the degree of competition that exists in each locale. In some cases companies do not want to enter markets where there is strong competition. However, they will often decide to enter a competitive market because they believe the potential benefits far outweigh the drawbacks. By going head-to-head with the competition, the company can force itself to become more efficient and effective and thus improve its own competitiveness. The MNE can take market share away from competitors and put them on the defensive, forcing them to commit more resources to defending the market under attack and thereby reducing their ability to retaliate effectively. Of course, these conditions do not always hold true, but they help illustrate why MNEs consider entering markets that are dominated by competitors.

Final selection

Before making a final selection, MNEs usually enhance their information by visiting the sites and talking to trade representatives or local officials. Such field trips are very common and can do a great deal to supplement currently available information. Sometimes these trips take the form of a trade mission: a visit sponsored by commercial officers in a country's local embassy and designed to bring together executives from MNEs that are interested in examining the benefits of doing business in the particular country.

Based on the outcome of the screenings and the supplemental data, the MNE chooses which goods and services to offer overseas. The marketing strategy employed in this process revolves around what are commonly called the four Ps of marketing: product, promotion, price, and place.

 Active learning check

Review your answer to Active Learning Case question 1 and make any changes you like. Then compare your answer to the one below.

1 **How would VW use market assessment to evaluate sales potential for its cars in the United States?**

There are several steps VW could take. One is to look at the number of cars being imported into the country, as well as the number being built locally; this would provide important information regarding current product supply. Another would be to find out the number of auto registrations and how fast it is growing annually; this would be useful in predicting new sales potential. A third would be to examine the trend of new car sales over the last couple of years and forecast overall industry sales for the next two to three years. A fourth would be to compare the strengths offered by VW cars to those offered by the competition and evaluate how the company can position its offering for maximum market penetration.

PRODUCT STRATEGIES

Product strategies vary depending on the specifics of the product itself and the characteristics of the target market segment. Some products can be manufactured and sold successfully both in the United States and abroad by using the same strategies. Other products must be modified or adapted and sold according to a specially designed strategy. Figure 13.1 shows a range of possibilities. Products and services located on the left side of the continuum require little modification; those on the right must be modified to fit the market. To some degree this range of options parallels the more general international business manager's challenge to strike an appropriate balance between being "global or local", to standardize or customize, to integrate across all dimensions of the business or respond to local differences.

Little or no modification

Industrial goods and technical services are good examples of products that need little or no modification. A bulldozer, a laptop, and a photocopying machine serve the same purposes and are used the same way in the United States as they are in France or in China.[8] Alterations would be minor and would include such things as adapting the machine to the appropriate electric voltage or changing the language used for its instructions and labels. The same is true for many types of services. For example, international engineering and construction firms find that their product strategies are similar worldwide. People interested in having a dam or power plant constructed use the same basic concepts and have similar needs throughout the world. In fact, experience is the greatest selling point in convincing clients to hire an MNE in engineering or construction. Foreign design and construction firms that proved themselves in the Burj Al Arab Hotel project in Dubai, for example, were invited to participate in the unprecedented Palm Jumeirah artificial island project.

Companies with a strong international brand image have also been able to succeed without a differentiation strategy. For example, the world-famous Scotch Chivas Regal is sold in many countries and is identical in each one. Schweppes (tonic water) and Perrier are internationally known and are also identical worldwide.

Moderate to high modification

A number of factors can compel an MNE to use moderate to high product modification. These include economics, culture, local laws, and product life cycle.

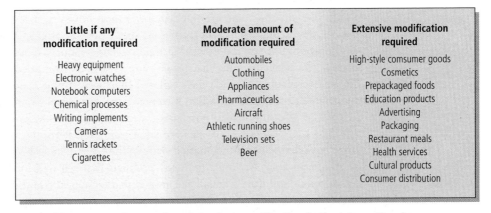

Little if any modification required	Moderate amount of modification required	Extensive modification required
Heavy equipment	Automobiles	High-style comsumer goods
Electronic watches	Clothing	Cosmetics
Notebook computers	Appliances	Prepackaged foods
Chemical processes	Pharmaceuticals	Education products
Writing implements	Aircraft	Advertising
Cameras	Athletic running shoes	Packaging
Tennis rackets	Television sets	Restaurant meals
Cigarettes	Beer	Health services
		Cultural products
		Consumer distribution

Figure 13.1 Selected examples of product modification in the international arena

Economics

There are many examples of how economic considerations affect the decision to modify a product. For example, chewing gum packages often contain 10 to 20 sticks in the United States. But in many other countries, weak customer purchasing power necessitates packaging the gum with only five sticks. Countries vary in terms of the use of cars versus public transport and in terms of average house sizes (therefore storage space), so buying patterns also vary accordingly and firms must customize product size and packaging to suit local preferences.

Economics is also important when the cost of a product is either too high or too low to make it attractive in another country. For example, cash registers are electronic in economically advanced countries; virtually no one uses hand-cranked machines. However, in many other countries they are too expensive and sophisticated for most retail stores and small establishments, so MNEs like National Cash Register continue to manufacture the hand-cranked versions. On the other hand, inexpensive calculators are widely used throughout the world, and many stores use handheld calculators to total customer purchases (although in some places calculations may be cross-checked for accuracy with an abacus).

Similarly, in economically advanced countries products are likely to have frills or extras, whereas only the basic model is offered in poorer countries. For example, bicycles in the United States are used for exercise and recreation and have a number of special features that make bicycle riding particularly enjoyable, whereas in many other countries they are a primary source of transportation. US bikes are built for comfort and ease of handling; elsewhere they are built for economy and ease of maintenance. As a result, manufacturers need to modify the product to fit customer needs.

Culture

A product must sometimes be adapted to different ways of doing things. Consider washing machines. The French prefer washers that load from the top, the British like front-loading units, the Germans prefer high-speed machines that take out most of the moisture in the spin-dry process, and the Italians like slower spin speeds because they prefer to hang-dry laundry in the sun. So manufacturers which sell washing machines in the European Union must produce a variety of different units.

Food is an item that often must be modified or sold differently. In fast-food franchises like McDonald's, portions of the menu are similar throughout the world while other items are designed to cater specifically to local tastes. Coffee in South American units tends to be a much stronger blend than that sold in North America. In certain parts of Europe and Asia, the food is more highly seasoned in keeping with local tastes. For products that are not modified, the marketing focus is different because of the way the item is used. Schweppes, for example, is typically served as a mixer in the United States and UK, where drinks like gin and tonic are popular. In France, however, it is drunk without alcohol. Clearly, marketing approaches differ in these two situations. The marketing message is also important when selling hard liquors. The products remain the same, but many places have social customs that frown on excessive consumption. In these cases, MNEs such as Seagram of Canada have tailored their advertising messages along the lines of moderate drinking and the use of mixers to reduce the alcoholic content per serving.

Culture also influences purchasing decisions on the basis of style or aesthetics. Cosmetics and other beauty aids are good examples. Perfumes that sell well in Europe often have difficulty gaining market share in the United States because they do not appeal to American women. Similarly, many products that sell well in the United States, such as shampoos and deodorants, have limited market appeal elsewhere. People may not use these products, or they may find it hard to differentiate a product from local offerings. For example, Gillette has found it is difficult to develop a distinctive edge in selling toiletries because many people feel these products are all basically the same.

Convenience and comfort are other culturally driven factors that help explain the need for product modification. Early Japanese autos in the United States were designed to attack other foreign imports, specifically the VW Beetle. Researchers found that the two biggest complaints with the Beetle were the small amount of room in the back seat and the heater, which took too long to warm up the car. Aware that Americans wanted an economical car with these additional features, Japanese imports offered greater leg room for back seat passengers and a heater that was superior to the VW offering. Within a few years these imports had began to erode VW's market share. Foreign manufacturers also identified a group that wanted several convenience and comfort features. The result has been the emergence of luxury Japanese and German cars that now compete extremely well with US models in the upper end of the market.

Other culturally based reasons for product modifications include color and language. In the United States, the color black is worn for mourning, whereas in other countries white is for mourning and thus is not used for consumer goods. Similarly, most American shampoos are light colored, whereas in some Oriental countries consumers prefer dark-colored shampoo. Language can be an important point of modification because a product may need to carry instructions about contents or use. In locations where two or more languages are spoken, such as Canada and Switzerland, this information is provided in all appropriate languages. Language is also important in conveying the right image for the product. Quite often it is difficult to replicate the message because the saying or slogan has no meaning in another language.

Local laws

Local laws can require product modification in order to meet environmental and safety requirements. For example, US emission-control laws have required Japanese and European car importers to make significant model changes before their autos can be sold in the United States. Food and pharmaceutical regulations require packaging and labeling that are often quite different from those in the home country. In Saudi Arabia, the label of any product containing animal fat or meat must clearly state the kind of animal used and the fact that no swine products are included. Brand name protection can also require product modification. Ford found that in Mexico it had to rename its Ford Falcon because this brand name was registered to another firm. The same thing happened to Ford in the case of the Mustang in Germany.

Product life cycle

Another reason for modifying a product is to cope with its limited product life cycle (PLC). Although Ford was extremely profitable in Europe during the 1980s, those earnings had disappeared by the early 1990s because Ford did not develop new, competitive products.[9] Contrast this to Coca-Cola of Japan, which introduces an average of one new soft drink per month and has the competition scurrying to keep up. Yet Kola Real has been particularly effective in offsetting the technology and marketing of Coca-Cola to bring its own products to market in Mexico. The case **International Business Strategy in Action: Kola Real Group** describes the company's approach.

One of the most effective strategies has been to shorten the PLC by offering new goods and services before the demand for the old ones has dropped significantly. Figure 13.2 provides a graphic illustration. Note that there are two types of PLCs: (1) the standard PLC, which covers an extended time continuum, often four to five years, and (2) a short life cycle that lasts a much shorter time. Many companies are discovering that by shortening the PLC and offering new product adaptations they are able to capture and retain a large market share. This is typically done by offering a new product, then modifying it, and bringing out a new version before the competition can effectively combat the first offering. For example, Intel first offered a Pentium processor. This was followed by the introduction of the Pentium II, Pentium III, and Pentium IV processor, all of which were faster

INTERNATIONAL BUSINESS STRATEGY IN ACTION

Kola Real Group

You may have heard of the cola wars in the 1980s and early 1990s, but you probably have not heard of the current Mexico cola war. Mexico is the world's second-largest market for non-alcoholic drinks and an important market for the world's largest cola brands. Coca-Cola derives 11 percent of its world sales from this market, and in 2000 it held about 70 percent of the market for carbonated drinks. Pepsi had 15 percent of the market, with the remaining 15 percent dispersed among smaller competitors. Mexico was, by all accounts, a saturated market. But since 2002, when upstart Kola Real entered the market, the competitive environment has gotten tougher for the big players. Today, Coca-Cola is constantly monitoring the marketing schemes of Kola Real to prevent further erosion of its market share.

Kola Real was founded in 1988 by the Añaños family in the capital city of the province of Ayacucho, Peru. At the time, the founders were rural immigrants running from the violence brought about by the emergence of the Shining Path guerrillas in the countryside. Once in the city, they realized that the demand for carbonated drinks was not being met by either Coca-Cola or Pepsi, which routinely discontinued deliveries because their trucks were often robbed by the guerrillas or common criminals. So Jorge Añaños, an agricultural engineer, developed a formula for a new drink. The family borrowed $30,000 and started producing it. In the early 1990s the rest of the family joined the firm to market the drink and opened a series of plants in the provinces. It was only in 1997 that the firm entered Lima, the largest market in Peru. Today, the firm has a 20 percent market share in its domestic market.

Kola Real's first international excursion was to Venezuela in 1999. At the time, plastic containers accounted for only 3 percent of the carbonated market. Kola Real saw an opportunity in this because the cost of plastic bottles is lower than for glass. More recently the firm controlled 17 percent of the Venezuelan market. In 2001, it entered the Ecuador market because of its proximity to the northern part of Peru; it managed to hold 12 percent of that market.

Kola Real was lured to the Mexican market because of its size and its high per capita consumption of carbonated beverages. It established its first plant in 2002, choosing Puebla because it is well linked to the rest of the country, the cost of land is reasonable, there is an excellent source of water, and it is not too far from Mexico City. Only two years later, the firm had captured 4 percent of the market. A new plant opened in the northern part of Mexico in 2005 and is expected to contribute to the company's goal

of reaching a 10 percent market share by 2009. Cielo, its bottled water, is presently the market leader.

A number of factors have contributed to Kola Real's success. One is that it has chosen the poorest part of the population as its market segment. When the firm started operations in Ayacucho, the city was filled with poor rural immigrants. Both the guerrillas and the Peruvian military had all but destroyed the province's economy. And this was the province that had given birth to the insurgents. There was a heightened displeasure with social injustice. Kola Real responded by providing a much cheaper product under the banner "The drink at the just price." By doing this, it not only appealed to its customers but assured them that its slogan did not use the words *cheap* or *inexpensive*, which would have undermined the quality of the product. This slogan and the accompanying low price were then exported across the nation and into the three other Latin American markets, where they were welcomed by the same lower-income population segments.

Another reason is that the firm's expenses are very austere, allowing it to offer the lowest prices in the market and still enjoy a substantial profit. Whenever possible, the firm has maintained its own distribution system. Administrative costs are kept to a minimum. Although its plants use top-of-the-line technology for production, the administrative offices are very modestly furnished. Finally, the firm relies on word of mouth to market its products.

Analysts argue that large competitors are often unable or unwilling to respond to the poorest segments of society in Latin America, relying instead on large-scale distribution to establishments servicing the middle and upper classes. Before Kola Real entered the Mexican market, the same bottle of Coca-Cola that cost $1.00 in the United States cost $1.40 in Mexico—despite the lower per capita income. Although Kola Real may be found at Carrefour stores across Mexico, the firm relies heavily on its sales force to push the product in small establishments, which account for 80 percent of the Mexican market and serve the chosen market segment. Kola Real argues that by providing more personalized and fitted service to these points of sale it has increased the size of the market, not stolen a big chunk of the large players' market.

Coca-Cola is not sitting idly by. When Kola Real introduced the 2.6 liter "Big Cola" at a price of $0.75 to market to poor large families, Coca-Cola followed suit and introduced its own 2.5 liter bottle. However, it sells it for almost twice as much at $1.30. To counter Kola Real growing expansion, Coca-Cola began to offer discounts and incentives to many of its clients. This led to a warning from the Mexican bureau that regulates competition. Meanwhile, Kola Real recently introduced the 3.1 liter Mega Big Cola in Mexico. In the future, it is likely to introduce a larger variety of carbonated drinks.

There have always been no-frills carbonated drinks in Latin America. They have been able to succeed despite being inefficient because of the large difference between production costs and the price charged by the market leaders.

Kola Real's international success was possible because it manufactured and marketed its products efficiently.

Websites: www.cocacola-femsa.com.mx; www.coca-cola.com; www.pepsico.com; www.carrefour.com.mx.

Sources: Mario Vargas Llosa, "Los Añaños," *Caretas*, November 20, 2003; David Suarez, "Grupo Real se expande con éxito en cuatro paises," businessperu.com. pe, February 2004; "Cola Down Mexico Way," *The Economist*, October 9, 2003; Christopher J. Robertson, Anthony van der Hoek and Rhonda Kallman, "Case Study: Kola Real's low-cost international expansion strategy," *Thunderbird International Business Review*, vol. 50, no. 1 (2007), pp. 59–74.

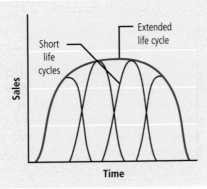

Figure 13.2 Product life cycles: two different approaches

than their predecessors. As processors get faster, they consume more energy and generate more heat, so for the meantime, until these issues are resolved, Intel cannot produce faster processors. As a result, more task-specific chips have been introduced.[10] The Centrino processor now caters to wireless users and the Desktrino caters to desktop users. The video game platform market provides another example of strategic continuous innovation. Nintendo and Sony constantly introduce new products and games to capture the market, always leaving the competition scurrying to keep up.[11] As long as a firm can continue such an adaptation strategy, it can outmode the old product (and those of competitors as well) and maintain market position. At some point the competition may gain the advantage by offering a product that revolutionizes the field, but as long as a product improvement strategy remains viable, the firm will continue to be the product leader. This strategy is being implemented by MNEs throughout the world.

✔ Active learning check

Review your answer to Active Learning Case question 2 and make any changes you like. Then compare your answer to the one below.

2 Does VW need to modify its cars for the US market? Why or why not?

Based on the case data, it appears that VW needs to make some changes in styling and engineering. The company is convinced that Americans will buy cars that offer German engineering and quality, but in the past it has made the mistake of producing cars that look "too American." Because of this, many people bought cars from Ford, GM, and Chrysler because there were no distinctive qualities that VW could use in attracting these buyers. By modifying its cars and giving them European styling and German engineering, VW can lead from strength and exploit its market advantage.

PROMOTION

Promotion is the process of stimulating demand for a company's goods and services.[12] MNEs promote their goods and services through advertising and personal selling. The specific approach used, however, will be determined by the nature of the product.

Nature of the product

In promoting a product, a company can use a variety of approaches. The choice is heavily influenced by whether the firm believes the same message can be used worldwide or needs to be adapted, and whether the product will remain the same or need to be modified. Here are four variations on this theme:

- *Identical product and identical message.* This approach is used when the MNE intends to sell the same product worldwide and believes that an identical promotional appeal can be used in all markets. A. T. Cross, for example, uses this strategy because writing instruments do not need to be adapted to local markets.

- *Identical product but different message.* This strategy is used when the product satisfies a different need in various markets. For example, in the United States many car companies tout the luxury and convenience of their products, whereas in other countries the same cars are promoted on the basis of their fuel efficiency or ability to meet basic transportation needs.

- *Modified product but same message.* This strategy is used when the market requires a different version of the product but the needs of the consumer are the same. For example, whether washing machines load from the top or the front, they provide the same function and meet the same customer needs. Similarly, in many countries the seasoning of foods differs from that of foods sold in the United States. So although the product is changed, the promotion message remains the same because the buyer's needs are the same.

- *Modified product and modified message.* When the product use and buying habits of customers are different from those in the MNE's home market, both the product and promotion message will be modified. For example, breakfast cereal companies such as Kellogg's and General Mills are developing new versions of their popular American cereals for sale in the European market. Many Europeans do not eat cereal for breakfast, however, so the promotion campaign is geared toward changing eating habits rather than getting consumers to switch product loyalty.

Advertising

Advertising is a non-personal form of promotion in which a firm attempts to persuade consumers to a particular point of view. In many cases MNEs use the same advertising message worldwide; again, because many products fill similar worldwide needs, a company can use a universal message and reduce advertising costs at the same time. However, there are times when the advertising must be adapted to the local market.[13] Two of the most common reasons are that (1) the way in which the product is used differs from that in the home country, and (2) the advertising message does not make sense if translated directly. An example of the latter is the Nike commercials that encourage the viewer to "Just do it," or Budweiser commercials that ask, "Why ask why?" These ads make sense to American viewers, but they are too culturally grounded to be used in many other countries, and would leave the viewer confused as to what the advertiser was saying. As a result, advertisers are very careful to tie their messages to buyer needs and wants. On the other hand, there are many advertisements that have been only moderately modified or carried in their entirety because they *do* make sense in other cultures. For example, Nike's ads featuring such internationally known sports stars as Tiger Woods and David Beckham transcend national boundaries, especially after the media exposure they have received. The case **International Business Strategy in Action: IKEA in international markets** provides some examples of how this is being done.

INTERNATIONAL BUSINESS STRATEGY IN ACTION

IKEA in international markets

From its founding as a small, private Swedish furniture retailer in 1943, IKEA has grown to become a multinational business with 127,000 employees and annual sales of €23.1 billion in 2010. As of August 2010, there are IKEA stores in more than 38 countries, with 280 stores in 26 countries belonging to the IKEA Group.

The parent company of the IKEA Group of companies INGKA Holding BV (the Netherlands) is owned by the Stichting INGKA Foundation in the Netherlands. The Stichting INGKA Foundation in the Netherlands was founded in 1982 by the IKEA founder, Mr. Ingvar Kamprad to create an ownership structure and an organization that stand for independence and taking a long term approach. It has two purposes: to reinvest in the IKEA group and to fund charity through the Stichting Foundation. The company is headquartered in Delft, the Netherlands.

In 2010, for the first time, IKEA published some information about its financial data to dismiss the "secretive" image. With the published date, it is clear that IKEA is a home region based private multinational in terms of sales, purchases and employees. For the year 2010, IKEA generated 79 percent of its total sales from Europe, 15 percent from North America and 6 percent from Asia and Australia. In addition, IKEA purchases 62 percent of goods for sales from Europe, 34 percent from Asia and 4 percent from North America. Furthermore, IKEA had 103,500 employees in Europe, 15,500 employees in North America and 8,000 employees in Asia and Australia.

With its international expansion strategy, today, Muscovites and Londoners can buy towels produced in Turkey at one of the retailer's warehouse stores.

This internationalization process is all the more remarkable in that IKEA has remained true to the basic philosophy of its founder, Ingvar Kamprad, throughout its global expansion. Kamprad redesigned the furniture industry by introducing knock-down kits that customers could take away from the store and assemble themselves, enabling the company to stock larger quantities of furniture in its warehouses. Costs were lowered because these kits were easier to transport, took up less space in IKEA's large warehouse stores, and there was no need for assembly or delivery. In turn, customers could have their furniture immediately and could transport it in their own cars, saving on delivery costs. IKEA did a lot more than just provide convenient, easy-to-transport products, however. First, the products are carefully designed and more stylish than bargain do-it-yourself competitors. Second, IKEA changed furniture shopping from its traditional frosty "showroom" mentality to a more "fun" place with children's playpens, nurseries, and cafés in the stores. Indeed, a trip to an IKEA store is entertainment for the entire family. IKEA also built on the fast-growing informal suburban culture by providing abundant parking.

IKEA's relaxed, informal, yet efficient image was extended to Oslo and Denmark in the 1960s. It entered Switzerland in 1973, Munich in 1974. By 1980, IKEA had opened an additional 10 stores across Germany and followed this with an expansion through Western Europe that culminated with its entry into the UK in 1987. In 1990, it entered the East European market with a store in Hungary; shortly after it entered Poland, the Czech Republic, and Slovakia. In 2000, it opened its first store in Moscow.

Expansion into other parts of the triad has been slower. In Asia and Oceania, IKEA opened its first store in Australia in 1975 and in Singapore in 1978. But its next expansion was in 1988, when it entered Hong Kong. Taiwan, Malaysia, and mainland China were added in the 1990s. In North America, IKEA opened a store in 1976 in Canada and used its Canadian operations to expand into

Source: Getty/Stephen Chernin

the United States in 1985. The company also has operations in the Middle East.

IKEA also brought innovation to the logistics of furniture production by setting up groups of key suppliers to produce components at low cost. It has more than 2,000 suppliers in 50 countries around the world. These subcontractors, in turn, make money by getting large-volume orders for standardized components from IKEA.

The company also has kept tight control over product design and quality to maintain its brand name and the distinctive identity of its furniture. It was able to expand rapidly because it did not have to establish expensive manufacturing facilities around Europe, but rather retained centralized control over the subcontractors.

IKEA's marketing strategy has been to build on the Swedish home-base stereotype of clean and efficient service. All furniture is well designed, modern, functional, durable, of high quality, and price competitive. Its image and brand name are well established and have survived numerous imitators. As a result, IKEA has been able to move from its Scandinavian base to being a strong regional player in Europe, and is now competing successfully in the global arena. The firm increasingly relies on a Web-based interface with customers, with different websites for different countries to reflect local tastes. As with many consumer products firms, this is evolving from being just a marketing and sales tool into a market-research tool. The 3D kitchen designer, for example, allows customers to design their own kitchens online using appliances and furniture from IKEA. IKEA can then use these designs to understand changing customer preferences.

Overall, IKEA is a successful multinational business because it has introduced a highly differentiated product into a traditional industry and has built a globally recognized brand name for high-quality, inexpensive, and attractive furniture. It has also combined the generic strategies of differentiation, low cost, and niching and has outsourced both production and delivery components of the value chain.

Website: www.ikea.com

Sources: Christopher A. Bartlett and Ashish Nanda, *Ingvar Kamprad and IKEA*, Harvard Business School Case No. 9-390-132; Joseph R. D'Cruz and Alan M. Rugman, "Developing International Competitiveness: The Five Partners Model," *Business Quarterly*, vol. 58, no. 2 (Winter 1993), pp. 60–72; James Schofield, "IKEA Wows the Russians," *BBC News*, February 22, 2002; Patric Jackson, "IKEA's Enormous Niche Market," *BBC News*, August 1, 2003; www.ikea.com; www.hoovers.com; Louise Armitstead, "Ikea Reveals Profits For First Time to Dispel 'Secretive' Image," *The Telegraph*, October 1, 2010; IKEA Welcome Inside 2010 Update http://www.ikea.com/ms/en_GB/pdf/yearly_summary/Welcome_inside_2010_update.pdf.

As in the United States, MNEs use several media to carry their advertising messages. The three most popular are television, radio, and newspapers. Some of the major differences between the approach used in the United States and that used in other countries include government regulation of media advertising and the fact that many stations do not carry advertising, although in recent years this has been changing. In particular, the use of television advertising has been increasing in Europe, whereas in other areas of the world, such as South America and the Middle East, newspapers remain the major medium for promotion efforts. However, there are restrictions on what can be presented. Examples include: (1) some countries prohibit **comparative advertising**, in which firms compare their products with those of the competition; (2) some countries do not allow certain products to be advertised because they want to discourage their use (such as alcoholic beverages and cigarettes) or because they want to protect national industries from MNE competition; and (3) some countries (such as Islamic nations) censor the use of any messages considered erotic.

Comparative advertising
The comparing of similar products for the purpose of persuading customers to buy a particular one

Personal selling

Personal selling
A direct form of promotion used to persuade customers to a particular point of view

Personal selling is a direct form of promotion used to persuade customers to a particular point of view. Some goods, such as industrial products or those that require explanation or description, rely heavily on personal selling. Avon, the cosmetics company, has been very successful with this approach even in countries where people are unaccustomed to buying cosmetics from a door-to-door salesperson. In Mexico, for example, Avon managed to gain acceptance by first introducing the idea of personal selling through a massive advertising campaign so that housewives became aware that the Avon salesperson was not a common door-to-door vendor but a professional trained to help clients look beautiful.

Personal selling is also widely used in marketing products such as pharmaceuticals and sophisticated electronic equipment. For example, Pfizer and Upjohn use salespeople to call on doctors and other individuals who are in a position to recommend their products, and General Electric and salespeople use the same approach in selling overseas that they use in the United States.

Because many international markets are so large, some MNEs have also turned to telemarketing. This approach has been very successful in the United States, and the overseas subsidiaries of such US firms as IBM and Ford have been using telemarketing to generate new sales. European firms such as Peugeot have been adopting this approach as well.

MNEs have also focused attention on recruiting salespeople on an international basis. In some countries this work is not highly regarded, so MNEs have given these people managerial titles that command importance, such as territory manager or zone manager. Recruiting local talent is extremely important because these people are often better able to sell to local customers. If the product requires special training to sell, MNEs often bring new salespeople to the home office for training, introduce them to those who are manufacturing the products, and create a feeling of teamwork among the field staff and personnel so that the salespeople are energized to go back into the field and sell.

✔ Active learning check

Review your answer to Active Learning Case question 3 and make any changes you like. Then compare your answer to the one below.

③ Would the nature of VW's products allow the company to use an identical promotional message worldwide, or would the company have to develop a country-by-country promotion strategy?

This answer will depend on where VW is selling its product. In less developed countries, the message would be geared toward economy and efficiency. In more developed countries, the message would focus on styling, handling, engineering, and non-economic factors as well. So VW would need to develop a series of different messages to address the wide number of market niches. No one message would appeal to everyone in the same way.

PRICING

The pricing of goods and services in the international marketplace is often influenced by factors present in home-market pricing. These factors include government controls, market diversity, currency fluctuations, and price escalation forces.

Government controls

Every nation has government regulations that influence pricing practices. Some countries dictate minimum and maximum prices that can be charged to customers. Minimum prices can help protect local companies from more efficient international competitors because of a floor on price that can help ensure a profit for national firms. For example, if the minimum price for a particular type of personal computer is $1,000 and local companies can produce and sell the product for $700, they will make $300 a unit. Foreign competitors may be able to produce and sell the product for $500 and make a $500 profit per unit, but the minimum price laws prevent them from driving out local competition. Without this law, overseas competitors might price the unit at $600 and then raise the price dramatically after local competitors went out of business.

Dumping
The selling of imported goods at a price below cost or below that in the home country

Governments also prohibit **dumping**, or the selling of imported goods at a price below cost or below the cost in the home country. The General Agreement on Tariffs and Trade (GATT) and WTO specifically prohibit this practice, which is designed to help MNEs drive out the local competition, establish a monopoly, and subsequently raise prices at will. A number of US firms have been influential in getting the US government to bring dumping charges against Japanese competitors.

Market diversity

Consumer tastes and demands vary widely in the international marketplace, resulting in MNEs having to price some of their products differently. For example, companies have found that they can charge more for goods sold overseas because of the demand. In the United States, there is a greater demand for light turkey meat than for dark turkey meat. The latter is typically sold at a lower price and is often purchased by animal food producers. However, the plump dark meat of turkey thighs has a strong market in Europe. As a result, firms like the Shenandoah Valley Poultry Company export thousands of metric tons of dark turkey meat to Europe each year.

A second factor influencing market diversity is the perceived quality of the product. For example, in the United States, German auto makers such as Mercedes found that some Americans were willing to pay a premium for German cars. In contrast, the Japanese are not willing to pay a premium for German autos, so Mercedes' pricing structure in Japan is different. More recently, Japanese luxury autos have proved to be strong competitors for Mercedes in the US market.

Another factor is the tax laws and attitudes about carrying debt. In the United States, some interest payments are tax deductible and most people have no aversion to assuming at least some debt. In many other countries, interest payments are not tax deductible and people are unaccustomed to carrying debt. In Japan, for example, little use is made of consumer credit. In pricing products, MNEs will adjust the local strategy to accommodate the impact of the tax laws and the consumer's willingness to assume debt.

Currency fluctuations

As noted in Chapter 7, when selling products overseas, MNEs often end up assuming the risks associated with currency fluctuations. This risk is particularly important when the companies have a return on investment target because this objective can become unattainable if the local currency is devalued. For example, if it costs Mercedes $40,000 to manufacture and ship a particular model to the United States, and the company sells the car to its dealer for $50,000, Mercedes is making a 25 percent profit on the sale ($10,000/$40,000). However, if the dollar decreases in value by 10 percent against the euro, then the company's profit percentage will decline and the firm will have to choose between the following options: (1) increase the price of the car to the dealer to make up the loss of dollar value; (2) absorb the loss and leave the price the same; or (3) absorb part of the loss and raise the price to the dealer to make up the difference. The value of the US dollar did fall, from a high of 0.85 euros in 2005 to a low of 0.66 by the end of 2007. During this period Mercedes was forced to absorb some of the losses because price increases would have resulted in sharply lowered demand for the cars and even less overall profit for the company. In 2007 and 2008, just as happened in the late 1980s, US firms found that their products were becoming much more attractive to European buyers, thanks to the lower value of the dollar and the accompanying rise in purchasing power of buyers on the Continent.

Table 13.1 The effect of MNE pricing on final consumer costs

MNE price	Price charged by each intermediary				
	1	2	3	4	5
$10	$12.00	$14.40	$17.28	$20.74	$24.88
$13	$15.60	$18.72	$22.46	$26.96	$32.35

Ultimate effect of a $3 increase in MNE price: $32.35 − $24.88 = $7.47 or 30 percent.

Price escalation forces

A problem similar to that discussed above is price escalation forces that drive up the cost of imported goods. In the case of Mercedes, for example, if the cost of the car rose from $30,000 to $33,000, the company would want to pass this along to the dealer. In the case of MNEs that sell through a marketing channel with a series of intermediaries, the effect of a price escalation can be even greater because everyone in the channel adds a percentage increase. For example, if an MNE exports and sells a consumer good for $10 to a large wholesaler and there are five additional intermediaries in the channel, each of whom marks up the good by 20 percent, as seen in Table 13.1, the final price to the consumer is $24.88. If the MNE's cost rises from $10 to $13, the final price to the consumer is now $32.35, a 30 percent increase. So price increases by the MNE can dramatically affect what the customer pays, and as long as the company continues to export rather than manufacture locally, price will be a key marketing consideration because of its effect on consumer demand. In this example it is likely that customer demand would drop substantially unless there were no effective substitutes for the product.

✔ Active learning check

Review your answer to Active Learning Case question 4 and make any changes you like. Then compare your answer to the one below.

4 **How would currency fluctuations affect VW's profit in the US market?**

Currency fluctuations would affect VW's profit in the US market according to the value of the euro in relation to the dollar. If the value of the euro were to decline, VW's profit per car sold in the United States would rise because these dollars would buy more euros. Conversely, if the value of the euro increased, profit per car would decrease because these dollars would buy fewer euros.

PLACE

The importance of international logistics was discussed in Chapter 12. The focus of attention here will be on the distribution differences among countries and conditions with which MNEs must be familiar. **Distribution** is the course that goods take between production and the final consumer. This course often differs on a country-by-country basis, and MNEs will spend a considerable amount of time in examining the different systems in place, the criteria to use in choosing distributors and channels, and how to employ distribution segmentation.[14]

Distribution
The course that goods take between production and the final consumer

Different distribution systems

It is often difficult to standardize a distribution system and use the same approach in every country because there are many individual differences to be considered. For example, countries such as Finland feature a predominance of general line retailers that carry a wide assortment of merchandise. In contrast, the wholesale and retail structure in Italy is characterized by a wide array of stores, many of which specialize or carry limited lines of merchandise. So in distributing goods in these two countries, MNEs need to employ different strategies.

Consumer spending habits can also negate attempts to standardize distribution. In the United States, many intermediaries are geared to handling credit sales, whereas in Japan most consumer purchases are on a cash basis. In both Germany and the United States, mail-order buying has increased dramatically in recent years, whereas in Portugal and Spain the market is quite small. So the route that the goods take to the consumer will vary.

The location where consumers are used to buying will also influence distribution. In economically developed countries where supermarkets have become commonplace, customers purchase a wide variety of food and other products under one roof. In most countries, however, purchases are made in smaller stores, and distribution requires the MNE or the local sales manager to deal with a large number of retailers, each of which is selling a small amount of merchandise. In recent years, some wholesalers and retailers have been expanding their operations to other countries. Wal-Mart, the giant US retailer, has expanded into Mexico and Europe; in 1999 it bought the British supermarket chain Asda. However, most intermediaries operate exclusively within one country—another factor helping to explain why it is still difficult to standardize distribution on an international basis.

Choosing the best distribution system

MNEs use a number of criteria in creating the most efficient distribution system. One is to get the best possible distributors to carry their products. A key factor in evaluating potential distributors is the financial strength of the wholesaler or retailer, because the multinational wants to know that the distributor will be able to survive in the long run. MNEs that sell goods requiring periodic maintenance and servicing will be interested in businesses that can keep sufficient inventory on hand. This is particularly important when selling products such as autos, computers, and electronic equipment. A second factor is how well connected the distributor is in terms of knowing the right people and providing assistance in handling governmental red tape. This is a key consideration for Coca-Cola when choosing overseas distributors. A third factor is the number and types of product lines the distributor carries currently so that the multinational can identify intermediaries who are most likely to give its goods a strong marketing push.

In many cases, distributors have competitive products or feel that they do not need to add any new product lines. If the multinational wants to tap into this distribution system, it will have to formulate an incentive program that is designed to convince the distributor to carry its products. Some of the ways in which this is done include (1) helping to pay for local promotion campaigns of the product, (2) providing generous sales incentives, (3) conducting marketing research to identify customer niches and sales forecasts to help the distributor decide how much inventory to carry,[15] and (4) ensuring that unsold or outmoded merchandise can be returned for a full refund.

Depending on the nature of the market and the competition, the multinational may give exclusive geographic distribution to one local seller or arrange to have a number of sellers jointly selling the product. For example, auto manufacturers often have more than one dealer in a major metropolis but are willing to give exclusive geographic distribution rights to dealers in rural areas. This is in contrast to food products that can be sold in a wide variety of outlets and for which exclusivity is unnecessary. In these cases the multinational will try to get a variety of distributors to carry the product.

✔ Active learning check

Review your answer to Active Learning Case question 5 and make any changes you like. Then compare your answer to the one below.

⑤ What type of distribution system would be most effective for VW in the United States?

VW would use the same type of distribution system as that employed by other car manufacturers (that is, auto dealerships). The big challenge would be to open new dealerships and thus increase market coverage. The market in the United States is fairly well blanketed with dealerships, but the company could look for successful dealers who would be willing to carry the VW line as well as their current offerings. Another approach is to build VWs in the United States and thus reduce the distance the product has to be transported along the distribution system. This not only reduces cost but also helps ensure faster delivery.

STRATEGIC MANAGEMENT AND MARKETING STRATEGY

Marketing strategies play a key role in helping MNEs formulate an overall plan of action. Many approaches are directly related to the major areas that have been examined in this chapter, including ongoing market assessment, the use of effective pricing, internet marketing, and "open innovation." Table 13.2 illustrates the worldwide market penetration of several MNEs to be discussed in this section.

Ongoing market assessment

One of the major areas that MNEs are continuing to pay attention to is data collection and analysis for the purpose of developing and updating market assessments. In some cases this causes multinationals to change their market approach, whereas in other cases it supports maintaining a current strategy.

Clarins

The French cosmetics firm Clarins SA is a good example of a firm that is continuing to refine its market strategy based on market assessment data. For more than two decades the company has been gathering feedback from customers on what they like and do not like about the firm's cosmetics. From these surveys the company has learned that women want makeup that is long lasting, easy to choose, and easy to apply. This information has been invaluable in helping Clarins increase market share in an industry where competition is fierce. In fact, the company's growth rate in France has been more than twice the industry average, and Clarins is now achieving similar results in the US market. It is particularly interesting that this growth has been achieved despite the cost of Clarins' products. For example, one of its facial hydrating formulas sells for over $50. Aware of what up-scale customers are willing to buy, Clarins has been very successful in using market assessment information to develop and market high-quality skincare products. One marketing consultant has referred to Clarins as a "Body Shop for rich people"; certainly this target market has paid off well for the company.

Table 13.2 International market penetration: location of subsidiaries, holdings, and joint ventures

General Motors (US)		Clarins (French)	Daewoo (Korean)	Mitsubishi Electric (Japanese)	Royal Dutch/Shell Group (Dutch/British)	
North America						
Canada		Canada	Canada	Canada	Canada	
Mexico		Mexico	Mexico	Mexico	Mexico	
US		US	US	US	US	
Western Europe						
Austria	Italy	Austria	France	Austria	Austria	Italy
Belgium	Luxembourg	Belgium	Germany	Belgium	Belgium	Luxembourg
Denmark	Netherlands	France	Greece	Denmark	Denmark	Netherlands
Finland	Norway	Germany	Ireland	Finland	Faroe Islands	Norway
France	Portugal	Italy	Italy	France	Finland	Portugal
Germany	Spain	Netherlands	Netherlands	Germany	France	Spain
Greece	Sweden	Portugal	Portugal	Greece	Germany	Sweden
Iceland	Switzerland	Spain	Spain	Ireland	Gibraltar	Switzerland
Ireland	Turkey	Switzerland	Sweden	Iceland	Greece	Turkey
	UK	UK	UK	Italy	Iceland	UK
				Luxembourg	Ireland	
				Netherlands		
				Norway		
				Portugal		
				Spain		
				Sweden		
				Switzerland		
				Turkey		
				UK		
Central and Eastern Europe						
Bulgaria	Malta	Russia	Croatia	Bulgaria	Bulgaria	Poland
Croatia	Montenegro		Czech Rep.	Croatia	Croatia	Romania
Cyprus	Poland		Hungary	Czech Rep.	Czech Rep.	Russia
Czech Rep.	Romania		Poland	Estonia	Estonia	Serbia
Estonia	Russian Fed.		Romania	Hungary	Hungary	Slovakia
Hungary	Serbia		Russia	Kazakhstan	Latvia	Slovenia
Latvia	Slovakia		Ukraine	Latvia	Lithuania	
Lithuania	Slovenia		Uzbekistan	Lithuania	Montenegro	
Macedonia				Montenegro		
				Poland		
				Romania		
				Russia		
				Serbia		
				Slovakia		
				Slovenia		
				Ukraine		
				Uzbekistan		
Asia and Oceania						
Australia		Hong Kong	Australia	Australia	Australia	Indonesia
China		Japan	Azerbaijan	Azerbaijan	Azerbaijan	Japan
Hong Kong		Malaysia	Bangladesh	China	Brunei	Kazakhstan
India		Singapore	China	Hong Kong	Cambodia	Malaysia
Indonesia		South Korea	Hong Kong	India	China	New Zealand
Japan		Taiwan	India	Indonesia	Fiji	Pakistan
Malaysia			Indonesia	Japan	Guam	Philippines
New Zealand			Japan	South Korea	India	Singapore

(continued)

General Motors (US)		Clarins (French)	Daewoo (Korean)	Mitsubishi Electric (Japanese)	Royal Dutch/Shell Group (Dutch/British)	
Philippines			Malaysia	Malaysia		South Korea
Singapore			Myanmar	New Zealand		Sri Lanka
South Korea			Philippines	Pakistan		Taiwan
Taiwan			Singapore	Philippines		Thailand
Thailand			South Korea	Singapore		Vietnam
Vietnam			Taiwan	Taiwan		
			Thailand	Thailand		
			Vietnam	Vietnam		
South America, Central America, and the Caribbean						
Argentina			Argentina	Argentina	Argentina	Guatemala
Brazil			Brazil	Brazil	Barbados	Honduras
Chile			Chile	Chile	Bolivia	Nicaragua
Colombia			Colombia	Colombia	Brazil	Panama
Ecuador			Panama	Panama	Chile	Peru
Uruguay			Peru	Peru	Colombia	Puerto Rico
Venezuela			Venezuela	Venezuela	Costa Rica	Surinam
					Dominican Rep.	Trinidad &
					Ecuador	Tobago
					El Salvador	Venezuela
					French Antilles	
					and Guiana	
Middle East						
Bahrain	Oman	UAE	Iran	Kuwait	Iran	Syria
Israel	Qatar		Iraq	Saudi Arabia	Jordan	UAE
Jordan	Saudi Arabia		Israel	UAE	Kuwait	Yemen
Kuwait	Syria		Jordan	Lebanon	Oman	
Lebanon	United Arab		Libyan Arab		Qatar	
	Emirates (UAE)		Jamahiriya		Saudi Arabia	
			Saudi Arabia			
			UAE			
Africa						
Egypt			Algeria	Egypt	Algeria	Libya
South Africa			Angola	South Africa	Angola	Madagascar
			Egypt		Benin	Mali
			Kenya		Botswana	Mauritius
			Morocco		Burkina Faso	Morocco
			Nigeria		Cameroon	Mozambique
			South Africa		Cape Verde	Namibia
			Tunisia		Congo	Nigeria
					Côte d'Ivoire	Senegal
					Djibouti	South Africa
					Egypt	Sudan
					Ethiopia	Swaziland
					Gabon	Tanzania
					Gambia	Togo
					Ghana	
					Guinea	
					Kenya	
					La Ric	
					Leso	

Sources: Adapted from www.gm.com; www.shell.com; www.mitsubishi.com; www.clarins-financials.com; www.daewoo. available as of June 2010.

Shell Oil

Shell Oil is an MNE whose market assessment has showed the importance of not making significant changes in product or delivery systems.[16] In recent years, Shell has limited its product diversification to tightly linked and synergistic energy and chemical businesses. The company has learned that it is most profitable when staying close to what it knows best. Today Shell works to balance its upstream (exploration and production), downstream (refining and marketing), and related chemical (industrial, agricultural, and petrochemical) businesses. It is also developing a strong network of service stations around the world and has learned that its ability to assess situations and react quickly is an important element in its marketing strategy.

Shell is also famous as both an active user and a developer of scenario planning.[17] These were historically used to examine energy futures, in terms of supply and demand, as well as exploration opportunities and relative risks. But they have expanded to encompass a range of socio-political, economic, and environmental trends and the likelihood and impact of specific disruptive events. Shell is now used by many firms as a benchmark firm for tools and practices to help "future-proof" strategies.

Effective pricing

Some MNEs use a high-price strategy and skim the cream off the top of the market. Others employ a low-price strategy designed to penetrate and capture a larger share of the middle and lower parts of the market. Depending on the nature of the market, both strategies can be successful.

Bang & Olufsen

Bang & Olufsen is a Danish electronics company that manufactures stereo components, televisions, and video equipment.[18] The firm targets the upper end of the market, selling to style-conscious consumers who are unlikely to flinch at paying $4,000 for an audio system, $4,100 for a 28-inch color television with matching video recorder, or $5,600 for a 28-inch video system. One of the primary reasons customers buy from Bang & Olufsen is that the products are well engineered and designed. Televisions are sleek, thin, and modern looking; stereo consoles are trim, polished, and futuristic in design. But, rather than developing a stereotypical image as a provider of "boys' toys," the firm focuses heavily on women's design preferences as more than half of all buying decisions are made by women (and they exert a strong influence on the other half).[19] While many customers prefer to buy less stylish-looking products at one-third the price, Bang & Olufsen continues to have a steady stream of consumers who are willing to pay top dollar. Because of this, the company's worldwide sales are now over $800 million. See more about Bang & Olufsen in the Real Case below.

Wal-Mart and Cifra Inc.

In 1997, Wal-Mart acquired a controlling interest in Cifra Inc. of Mexico, the country's biggest retailer.[20] Established in 1957, Cifra was selling a wide variety of products by the 1990s, from powdered milk and canned chili to Korean television sets and video cassette recorders. Wal-Mart's acquisition fueled expansion throughout Mexico. Today, Wal-Mart has 545 stores there including department stores, warehouse retailers, clothing stores, and restaurants. One of Wal-Mart Cifra's biggest selling points is low prices. The company pushes what is called a "bodega concept": fast-moving, non-perishable goods that are sold in bulk in poor neighborhoods. By keeping gross margins in the range of 10–12 percent and net profits at 3–5 percent, the bodegas are able to average over $1 million per store each month. These sales are more than twice those of similar Kmart and Wal-Mart stores in the United States.

Internet marketing and "open innovation"

The Internet is becoming a central tool, not just for marketing but for market research and innovation, for many multinational firms. Because consumers, and industry buyers, increasingly use the Internet to assess the portfolio of products and services offered by a company, websites have become critically important for marketing purposes. They provide a window into the quality, credibility, achievements, and ethics of a firm, all of which underpin its corporate brand. Moreover, this now happens across a global platform that reaches more people in more countries than traditional marketing media such as radio or TV.[21]

Some large multinationals have been highly adaptive in keeping pace with the development of more sophisticated online platforms. Many have developed quite subtle positions in Facebook and MySpace, for example, using these to promote specific products, but also convey a particular kind of image by interacting with young, early adopters on these kinds of user networks.[22] This kind of online branding and marketing has evolved into a science of its own, partly because marketers have found online platforms play by different rules and often encourage a more liberal, unregulated environment than found in the 'real' world. British advertisers, including Vodafone, Virgin Media, and insurance firm Prudential, withdrew adverts from Facebook when they found themselves next to the ultra right-wing British National Party (BNP) which was also promoting itself on the site.[23]

Open innovation

Interactive, collaborative networks of product or service providers and customers or users which help firms innovate more efficiently

As shown by the IKEA example above, firms have moved beyond using websites as one-way channels to present information and images to customers; now they are interactive portals for developing a better understanding of, and relationship with, product and service "users." **Open innovation** is the term used to describe interactive, collaborative networks of product or service providers and customers. They allow users of products and services to help shape their development, and enable companies to design, develop, and distribute them more efficiently, by building in user preferences.[24] The Internet has proved to be ideal for developing open innovation platforms.

Shell, above, provides a good example. It has established Shell "GameChanger"[25] as an online venturing network to gather radically new ideas for innovations in the "energy and mobility" industry. For the best ideas it can provide funds and contacts for would-be entrepreneurs and has a stage-gate process for assessing proof of concept into development. The firm is effectively using the Internet to externalize part of its high-risk, blue-sky innovation activity.

Spreadshirt.com (www.spreadshirt.com/) provides another good example. Rather than designing T-shirts and other clothing, by second-guessing changing customer preferences, Spreadshirt invites customers to design their own online which can then be produced by the firm. This is similar to Dell's value chain business model, whereby customers can piece together a preferred desktop PC before ordering it. Spreadshirt's production is outsourced abroad, so its main activity is to connect consumers with production processes. But, through the flow of design ideas coming from a global network of potential customers, it is able to: (1) achieve economies of scale by focusing on the standard clothing designs that attract the most customers; (2) assess changing customer markets, and changing market segments, as they evolve over time; and (3) innovate more efficiently by focusing resources on the best new product development opportunities.

It is important to understand the significance of these kinds of online activities as tools and techniques for helping solve some of the major dilemmas facing all multinational managers. Key questions faced by market analysts are: how much do we need to customize our products or services for particular market segments (geographic, demographic, cultural, etc.) to maximize market share and profitability? What kinds of product, service, design, marketing, branding features can we standardize to optimize profitability? How are the preferences of different customer groups changing over time and where should we focus our innovation efforts? Open innovation and interactive Internet networks, like the ones described above, can harness the direct input of (often unsuspecting) customers and users from all around the world to help solve these dilemmas.

KEY POINTS

1 Marketing strategy begins with an international market assessment: the evaluation of the goods and services the MNE can sell in the global marketplace. There are a number of steps in this process, including an initial screening that is designed to determine the basic need potential of the company's goods and services, followed by additional screenings that culminate in a final selection of those outputs that the company will market internationally.

2 Product strategies will vary depending on the specific good and the customer. Some products need little or no modification, and others require extensive changes. Some of the factors that influence the amount of modification include economics, culture, local laws, and the product life cycle.

3 There are a number of ways in which MNEs promote their products, although the final decision is often influenced by the nature of the product. The two major approaches used in promotion are advertising and personal selling. Many multinationals try to use the same message worldwide because it is easier and more economical. However, this is not always possible because some messages either have no meaning in other languages or lack the impact of those in other markets. Similarly, while personal selling is used in some markets, in other markets the customer is unaccustomed to this promotion approach and non-personal approaches must be used, or the customer must be educated to accept this new form.

4 Pricing in international markets is influenced by a number of factors, including government controls, market diversity, currency fluctuations, and price escalation forces.

5 Place strategy involves consideration of distribution, or the course goods will take between production and final consumer. This course often differs on a country-by-country basis, and MNEs will spend a considerable amount of time in examining the different systems in place, the criteria to use in choosing distributors and channels, and how distribution segmentation can be accomplished.

6 MNEs are using a variety of marketing strategies when formulating their strategic plans. Three of the most important strategies are ongoing market assessment, effective pricing internet marketing, and 'open innovation'.

7 The Internet has become an essential part of any firm's marketing and market analysis toolkit. It is also ideal for developing open innovation platforms to connect better with users and customers.

Key terms

- international marketing
- international market assessment
- initial screening
- market indicators
- market size
- market intensity
- market growth
- trend analysis
- estimation by analogy
- regression analysis
- cluster analysis
- promotion
- advertising
- comparative advertising
- personal selling
- dumping
- distribution
- open innovation

REVIEW AND DISCUSSION QUESTIONS

1 How does initial screening help an MNE evaluate those goods and services that might be sold in the international market? What are some ways in which this screening is carried out?

2 After an MNE has completed an initial screening of its goods and services, what other steps can it take in further refining the choice of those products to sell internationally? Briefly describe the remainder of the process.

3 Why can some goods and services be sold internationally without having to undergo much, if any, modification? Explain.

4 What factors influence the need for moderate to high modification of goods and services that have sold well in the home country and will now be marketed overseas? Identify and describe three of the most influential factors.

5 When should an MNE use the same promotion strategy overseas that it uses at home? When should it modify the approach?

6 Many MNEs find that their advertising messages can be used in overseas markets without much, if any, modification. Why is this so?

7 Why do MNEs sometimes have to modify their personal selling strategies when marketing their goods in international markets?

8 What kinds of factors influence the pricing of goods and services in the international marketplace? Identify and describe three.

9 Why do many MNEs find that they cannot use the same distribution strategy overseas that they have used at home?

10 In choosing the best distribution system, what types of criteria do MNEs use? Identify and discuss three.

11 In what ways are multinationals using the following concepts to help them gain greater international market share: ongoing market assessment, effective pricing, internet marketing and 'open innovation'? In each case, offer an example.

12 Explain how open innovation networks using the Internet can help firms decide on whether to customize or standardize product features.

REAL CASE

Bang & Olufsen

Introduction

Headquartered in Denmark and dating back to 1925, Bang & Olufsen has evolved into the Rolls-Royce of the audio and visual industry. Producing luxury televisions, audio systems, loudspeakers, and telephones, B&O claims to be in the unique position of having no direct competitors. From a total of 1,400 stores in 60 countries, B&O sells select high-end, luxury niche products at high prices. The customer is typically male, over 35, and affluent, but B&O

has also identified three other customer groups including the young and educated, the design fanatic, and the "gray gold" couples whose children have left the nest.

However, on the backdrop of economic downturn, the company experienced sharp decline in sales and incurred significant losses. In fiscal year 2009/2010, the result was (Danish Krone) DKK2,762 million in sales ($453 million) compared to DKK 4,225 million sales in 2005/2006, reflecting a sale decline of 34.62 percent. The company ▶

derived only 3.2% of its sales from foreign markets. Its revenue was 0.58 percent of Sony's 2009 revenue of $77,696 million. A restructuring plan included 300 layoffs in Denmark on October 21, 2008, and the abandonment of development of new mobile phones, MP3 players and stand-alone systems like DVD2 and HDR2. In 2009/2010 also witnessed the decline in the B1 Shops. At the end of May 2010, there were a total of 703 B1 Shops across the world against 758 shops at the end of 2008/2009 financial year. The company will focus on its traditional strengths: high quality audio and video products as well as sound systems for the automotive industry.

The B&O's marketing strategy 4Ps are as follows.

Source: Getty Images

Product strategies

B&O's approach to product development differs substantially from industry norms. Essentially, it is believed that consumers often are unaware of what they want. Instead, ideas are generated based on a deep understanding of how consumers live. Consumer research, corporate ethnographers, and creative teams are replaced with the visions of a handful of contract designers who enjoy unprecedented decision-making power. All of the designers can veto anything failing to meet their visionary standards and, in the past, product design clearly took precedence over engineering capability. The popular BeoSound 9000 CD player was conceived without consulting the B&O engineers who needed two years to produce the technology making the design possible. That particular piece was designed by David Lewis, knighted by the Queen of Denmark for his work, while three of his B&O products are featured in the Museum of Modern Art's permanent collection in New York. Unlike those produced by Sony and Samsung, new B&O products come few and far between. In fiscal year 2010, only 7 new models were released; instead products tend to follow differing life cycles. Many are kept on the market for up to a decade even without lowering prices. For example, the BeoLab 8000 speakers, first introduced in 1992 at a price of $3,000 a pair, are now selling well at $4,500. The BeoSound 9000 introduced in 1996 continues to demand a price of $4,750. Cutting-edge technology coupled with legendary design make this possible. In addition, each B&O product is part of an interconnected system, allowing B&O to offer living room solutions that are centrally controlled. Although proven successful in the past, relying on only a handful of designers can prove a risky proposition. Key designers are growing older, and finding replacements can be troublesome.

Promotion

Demand for B&O products is stimulated in a variety of ways; however, the general message of pristine quality and design is central. Through an estimated $50 million

(£25 million) global media planning and buying account, B&O promotes through varying advertising vehicles and also engages in advertiser-funded programming. As such, B&O products have appeared in *The Apprentice* as well as films such as *Thunderbirds* and *Charlie's Angels*. Most of B&O's selling take place in the retail stores located in major cities across the globe. Here, well-to-do customers can experience the powerful products first hand, frequently in private sessions catered to their needs. Lately B&O has engaged in symbiotic relationships with premium European car makers, supplying customized audio systems. The German car maker Audi was the first to offer the B&O sound system to its audience. The $6,155 option was expected to entice 100 Audi buyers in the first year. Instead, 15 percent of A8 Audi buyers opted for the alternative, resulting in the system being installed in almost 4,000 cars. This success led to valuable promotional exposure and one additional agreement with British car maker Aston Martin. Although 10 other European auto makers have expressed interest in cooperation, B&O chooses its partners carefully so as to protect the premium image. The agreement with Aston Martin was a result of the recognition of a similar culture and heritage rooted in passion, performance, design, and craftwork. B&O's other B2B offerings also provide substantial exposure, stimulating consumer demand. Later in 2007, B&O secured an agreement with the luxury Grand Lisboa hotel located in Macau, China. At this hotel alone, an estimated 50,000 tourists annually will be exposed to B&O TV and speaker systems.

Place

B&O products have been described as art in the living room. They need space and air to be fully appreciated, which means that they must be presented to the public quite differently than lower-priced alternatives. Worldwide, B&O relies primarily on company-owned stores and private retailers featuring premium products. In recent years, these locations have relied more heavily on customer databases to gain a better understanding of the individual customer. So far, B&O has resisted temptations of both the growing Internet market and powerful big-box retailers, and instead continued to open company retail locations worldwide. Although selling premium solutions, B&O serves customers in both developed and developing economies worldwide. In fact, the two best-selling B&O retail locations are located in Moscow where there exists a small set of extremely rich oligarchs. The emerging economies in Asia with otherwise low average incomes have also proven to be financially attractive due to the new millionaires and high-end luxury enterprises catering to world travelers. From the regional head office in Singapore, B&O is represented in 10 countries in the Asia–Pacific Region and its products are available from over 40 stores.

Price

Along with all other aspects of B&O communication with the public, selected retail prices match the general message of exclusivity. For example, retailing for $13,250.00, the 40-inch BeoVision 7 HDTV commands a premium price over other TV alternatives. The company targets a very limited segment (niche) of the world population, and can command these prices due to documented premium quality and sustainability of its products. The substantial profit margin has the advantage of shielding the company against unfortunate economic conditions. In late 2007, the US dollar depreciated substantially against the world's premier currencies. If prices are left unchanged, this translates directly into lower profits for foreign companies operating in the United States and exchanging dollars into home

currency. In the case of B&O, a substantial part of sourced components originates from the United States, which meant that production costs decreased accordingly.

Conclusion

In the coming years, B&O hopes to grow its market share by focusing on its niche. In doing so, the company must carefully consider what action to take and what message product, place, promotion, and price should send to make its goal a reality.

Websites: www.beoworld.org; www.bang-olufsen.com.

Sources: "COO Discusses Bang & Olufsen's Opportunity to Benefit from Improving Market Conditions," *twist.com*, March 3, 2004; "Bang & Olufsen Joins Forces with Aston Martin for Creative Partnership," *Wireless News*, December 16, 2007; Tony Lewin, "Top Marques Turn to Branded Audio," *Automotive News Europe*, October 1, 2007; "Danish B&O Eyes More Automotive Partnership Deals in 2008," *Danish News Digest*, December 11, 2007; Gwendolyn Bounds, "A Way to Fight Big Rivals: Play Up Style, Service," *The Capital (Annapolis)*, April 1, 2007; Leo Jakobson, "Divine Designs," *Incentive*, September 12, 2007; Christopher Lim, "Bang & Olufsen Hot on Customization," *Business Times Singapore*, September 22, 2007; "Denmark: B&O Will Double Its Size," *Esmerk Danish News*, September 26, 2007; Adeline Paul Raj, "Bang & Olufsen to Jazz Up Image," *Business Times*, November 29, 2007; Ian Darby, "Bang & Olufsen Reviews £50m Global Media," *Campaign*, April 14, 2006; Jay Greene, "Where Designers Rule," *Business Week*, November 5, 2007; Bang & Olufsen, *Annual Report*, 2009/2010.

1   Why does Audi use B&O equipment in its high-end cars?

2   How does B&O combine actions on product, place, promotion, and price?

3   How can B&O double its market share by expanding on its successful niche in the future?

REAL CASE

Brazilian soap operas: a world market

I let myself get hooked on Brazilian soap operas. But those are so wild and over-the-top, the whole country stops to watch them. They're nothing like American soaps.

Paula Sharp, US writer

When *Roque Santeiro* aired in Brazil after 10 years of censorship, São Paulo, a city comparable to New York, suddenly came to a halt. The 8.00 pm soap opera has become a ritual in many households; people leave anything they are doing to glue themselves to the TV. Not surprisingly, leading TV stations compete heavily for this market. Indeed, soap operas are the

main source of income for Brazilian TV stations, including TV Globo, Sistema Brasileiro de Televisão (SBT), and Manchete.

Fierce competition has helped Brazilian soap operas become among the very best in the world. *Roque Santeiro* revolutionized editing and launched its scriptwriter as an icon in Brazil. Period-set costumes were used for *Escrava Isaura*. And in *Torre de Babel*, the shopping mall in which most of the action takes place was built for $1.1 million, only to be blown to pieces as the plot developed.

Brazilian soap operas differ from their American counterparts by their running time and the structure of their ▶

plot. While American soap operas can run for 10 years or more, Brazilian soap operas run an average of eight months and tend to have a very specific storyline and plot structure.

With a population of 172 million, Portuguese-speaking Brazil is one of the biggest markets for soap operas in the world. It is also one of the biggest producing countries, at nearly 20 soaps per year, as well as a leading exporter. Soap operas from Brazil are dubbed into foreign languages and exported to 128 countries around the world, including the United States, China, Italy, and Spanish-speaking Latin America. In Cuba, the communist government even rescheduled its electric energy rationing to allow citizens to tune into *Escrava Isaura*. Since its Brazilian premiere in 1977, *Escrava Isaura*, the story of a white slave on a Brazilian plantation, has been aired in nearly 80 countries.

Why are Brazilian soaps so successful? One reason is that audiences in other non-triad nations can identify with what is portrayed as Brazilian reality. Since their beginning in the 1960s, Brazilian soap operas have often dealt with such controversial issues as religion, the role of the state, class differences, abortion, sexuality, and racism. These issues were portrayed with due consideration to Brazil's predominantly conservative and religious audience. Soap operas have become not only entertainment but also a means for social dialogue in Brazil. The audience shares the plot lines with friends and co-workers and discusses the moral dilemmas that are brought up in the story. TV stations have also tended to borrow from the proven success of stories in other media. The literary works of Mario Benedetti, Mario Vargas Llosa, Jorge Amado, João Guimaraes Rosa, the classics of Greek and Roman literature, and folk stories have all inspired soap operas. These universal themes help Brazil export its soap operas around the world. Whenever the story is an original, as it often is, it has more in common with a novel (not surprisingly the name for soap operas in Brazil is *telenovelas*) than with the scattered plot line of an American soap.

TV Globo

In terms of audience, the fourth-largest private TV network in the world is Brazil's TV Globo, which held 54 percent of the Brazilian viewership in 2003 and over 77 percent of the TV advertising market. TV Globo is part of the Globo Group, which also controls the country's number one radio station, the second-largest magazine group, and the cable TV company Globo Cabo.

TV Globo had its beginning in 1965 with the inauguration of Channel 4 in Rio de Janeiro. Soon after, the company purchased TV Paulista to broadcast in São Paolo, Brazil's biggest city. To enter the Belo Horizonte market, the company acquired J. B. Amaral Group in 1968, then expanded in 1971 to Recife by purchasing the Vitor Costa Group.

By 2003, a combination of acquisitions and broadcasting licenses had made TV Globo the largest network in Brazil, with 115 TV stations reaching 99.98 percent of Brazil's population.

It was in 1966 that TV Globo produced its first two soap operas. At first they were relatively low budget, but by 2000 production costs reached over $100,000 per one-hour episode, a sizable expense for a Brazilian production. Because a 30-second ad during the 8 pm soap opera costs approximately $102,000, soaps constitute the largest source of income for TV Globo. The firm has its own recording studios with a staff of 1,500 scriptwriters, and its soaps are the most successful in the market, capturing upwards of 60 percent of the audience.

At less than 10 percent of total sales, foreign sales are a tiny but growing portion of revenues for producers. A one-hour soap opera episode can be priced anywhere between $300 in Cuba and $40,000 in Italy. The number of TV sets per capita, the purchasing power of the country, and the amount that the stations can earn on advertising determine prices to foreign TV stations. In collaboration with Telelatino, the US-based broadcaster, TV Globo is planning to enter the US market with a $10 billion, 150-episode soap opera called *At All Costs*. The target group is the large Latin American market. TV Globo will use its proven storylines and reshoot them with an all-Spanish-speaking cast from different Latin American countries.

TV Globo faces competition on various fronts. In the domestic market, SBT and Manchete produce their own soaps to compete with those of TV Globo. Although TV Globo remains by far the most successful, other domestic networks have been able to erode the 80 percent audience the network enjoyed in the late 1970s. TV Globo's response was to support its own star system, invest in a scriptwriting school in São Paolo, and create stories that are more responsive to TV audiences. The station is very protective of its directors, scriptwriters, and actors, often keeping them sitting idle under salary rather than allowing them to go to the competition. Audience panels and rating information are used to change plots of soaps that do not reach desired ratings.

TV Globo also faces competition from established soap opera industries in other Latin American countries, including Mexico, Argentina, Venezuela, and Colombia. Although these productions have a limited share of the Brazilian market, TV Globo competes with them in their own markets and in non-Latin American markets. These competitors have traditionally made lower-quality soaps. Over the last few years, however, improvements in casting, scriptwriting, and directing have begun to increase their notoriety in international markets.

During Ramadan, mosques in Côte d'Ivoire changed the prayer time schedule to allow the faithful to see the last episode of the Mexican soap *Marimar*. This soap was also an international hit in Indonesia and the Philippines, where the female lead actress was received with all the honors of royalty.

Another source of competition comes from importing nations, such as Spain, Italy, Portugal, Greece, and China. Local storylines are being created that are likely to erode TV Globo's market share. Growing competition from foreign companies is forcing TV Globo to find innovative ways of capitalizing a market. For example, it recently partnered with a Chinese company to develop a soap about a Chinese man who falls in love with a Brazilian woman and goes to Brazil to court her. This guarantees access to the Chinese market.

Thirty-five years of experience in the soap opera market have given Brazil and TV Globo a competitive advantage against new entrants. As production develops in these countries, however, Brazil must adapt to increasing competition to continue its lead. There are a number of ways in which to do this, including specializing in some types of soaps, partnering with foreign producers, and moving into other areas of entertainment. In fact, the soap opera business has left Brazil with excellent producers, scriptwriters, directors, camera operators, editors, and actors who can be used to create anything from commercials, drama series, and sitcoms to theater and films. This last has already begun to occur. In 1999, a long-acclaimed Brazilian soap opera actress, Fernanda Montegro, was nominated for a best actress Oscar for her part in *Central Station*, a movie that was also nominated for best foreign film.

Websites: http://redeglobo1.globo.com/home; www.sbt.com.br.

Sources: Daniel Mato, "Telenovelas: Transnacionalización de la industria y transformación del género," in N. Garcia Canclini (ed.), *Industrias culturales e integración latinoamericana* (Mexico: Grijalbo, 1999); Nora Mazziotti, *La industria de la telenovela* (Buenos Aires: Paidós, 1996); "Home-grown Films First for Brazil," *BBC.co.uk*, May 8, 2001; "Brazil Media Giant Winks at Wall Street," *Sunday Times*, November 12, 2000; David Templeton, "Soap Box," *Sonoma Country Independent*, October 4, 2000; Alex Bellos, "Obituary: Roberto Marinho," *Guardian*, August 8, 2003; Andrei Khalip, "Brazil Cues Pan-Latin Lovers For US-Bound Soaps," *Entertainment Design*, June 28, 2002.

1 How is language an issue when marketing Brazilian entertainment to other countries?

2 What competitive advantages does Brazil have in the development of a film industry? What types of barriers does this industry face in international markets?

3 In what way can foreign capital prove to be a key strategy for TV Globo and the Globo Group?

ENDNOTES

1 See, for example, Graham Hooley, John Saunders, Nigel F. Piercy and Brigitte Nicoulaud, *Marketing Strategy and Competitive Positioning*, 4th ed. (Harlow: Prentice Hall, 2008).

2 Nanda K. Viswanathan and Peter R. Dickson, "The Fundamentals of Standardizing Global Marketing Strategy," *International Marketing Review*, vol. 24, no. 1 (2007), pp. 46–63.

3 Philip Kotler and Gary Armstrong, *Principles of Marketing*, 12th ed. (Harlow, Prentice Hall, 2007).

4 "China Goes Mobile Crazy," *BBC.co.uk*, August 15, 2001.

5 See, for example, Joseph A. McKinney, "Degree of Access to the Japanese Market: 1979 to 1986," *Columbia Journal of World Business*, Summer 1989, pp. 53–59.

6 "Turin Meets Detroit—in the Volga," *The Economist*, May 5, 1998.

7 "Food, Fashion and Faith," *The Economist*, August 4, 2007.

8 Also see Daniel McGinn and Adam Rogers, "Operation Supercar," *Newsweek*, November 23, 1998, pp. 48–53.

9 Richard A. Melcher and John Templeman, "Ford of Europe is Going in for Emergency Repairs," *Business Week*, June 17, 1991, p. 48; and Daniel Howes, "Ford's Blue Oval Takes on Added Luster in Europe with Thursfield," *Detnews.com*, December 4, 2001.

10 "Intel's Right-hand Turn," *Economist.com*, May 12, 2005.

11 "Hand-to-Hand Combat," *Economist.com*, December 16, 2004.

12 See Graham Hooley et al., op. cit.

13 In a *Wall Street Journal* interview Martin Sorrell, CEO of the advertising conglomerate WPP, argues that standardized advertising is practically impossible; Erin White and Jeffrey A. Trachtenberg, "One Size Doesn't Fit All," *Wall Street Journal—Eastern Edition*, October 1, 2003, pp. B1–2.

14 Joan Magretta, "Fast, Global, and Entrepreneurial Supply Chain Management, Hong Kong Style," *Harvard Business Review*, September/October 1998, pp. 103–114.

15 See, for example, Robert T. Green and Ajay K. Kohli, "Export Market Identification: The Role of Economic Size and Socioeconomic Development," *Management International Review*, vol. 31, no. 1 (First Quarter 1991), pp. 37–50.

16 Keetie E. Sluyterman, *Dutch Enterprise in the Twentieth Century* (London: Routledge, 2005).

17 For a wealth of resources see www.shell.com/scenarios.

18 Andrew Tellijohn, "Bang & Olufsen Will Bring High-End Audio to Galleria," *The Business Journal*, November 15, 2002.

19 Andrew Davidson, "Bang & Olufsen's Mr Cool," *The Sunday Times*, January 6, 2008.

20 Matthew Schifrin, "Partner or Perish," *Forbes.com*, May 21, 2000.

21 Richard Gay, Alan Charlesworth and Rita Esen, *Online Marketing: A Customer-led Approach* (Oxford: Oxford University Press, 2007).

22 "Word of Mouse," *The Economist*, November 10, 2007, pp. 77–78.

23 Carlos Grande, "Facebook Loses More Ads in BNP Row," *Financial Times*, August 3, 2007.

24 Henry William Chesbrough, *Open Innovation: The New Imperative for Creating and Profiting from Technology* (Boston, MA: Harvard Business School Press, 2003).

25 See http://www.shell.com/home/content/gamechanger-en.

ADDITIONAL BIBLIOGRAPHY

Alexander, Nicholas, Rhodes, Mark and Myers, Hayley. "International Market Selection: Measuring Actions Instead of Intentions," *Journal of Services Marketing*, vol. 21, no. 6 (2007).

Andersson, Ulf, Johanson, Jan and Vahine, Jan-Erik. "Organic Acquisitions in the Internationalization Process," *Management International Review*, vol. 37, Special Issue (1997).

Aspelund, Arild, Madsen, Tage Koed and Moen, Øystein. "A Review of the Foundation, International Marketing Strategies, and Performance of International New Ventures," *European Journal of Marketing*, vol. 41, nos. 11/12 (2007).

Auger, Pat, Devinney, Timothy M., Louviere, Jordan J. and Burke, Paul F. "The Importance of Social Product Attributes in Consumer Purchasing Decisions: A Multi-Country Comparative Study," *International Business Review*, vol. 19, no. 2 (April 2010).

Blois, Keith. *The Oxford Textbook of Marketing* (Oxford: Oxford University Press, 2000).

Dirk M. Boehe. "Captive Offshoring of New Product Development in Brazil," *Management International Review*, vol. 50, no. 6 (2010).

Broderick, Amanda J., Greenley, Gordon E. and Mueller, Rene Dentiste. "The Behavioural Homogeneity Evaluation Framework: Multi-Level Evaluations of Consumer Involvement in International Segmentation," *Journal of International Business Studies*, vol. 38, no. 5. (September 2007).

Capon, Noel, Berthon, Pierre, Hulbert, James M. and Pitt, Leyland F. "Brand Custodianship: A New Primer for Senior Managers," *European Management Journal*, vol. 19, no. 3 (May 2001).

Ching, Ha Lau and Ellis, Paul. "Does Relationship Marketing Exist in Cyberspace?" *Management International Review*, vol. 46, no. 5 (2006).

Czinkota, Michael R. and Ronkainen, Ilkka A. "A Forecast of Globalization, International Business and Trade: Report from a Delphi Study," *Journal of World Business*, vol. 40, no. 2 (May 2005).

Paul D. Ellis. "Is Market Orientation Affected by the Size and Diversity of Customer Networks?," *Management International Review*, vol. 50, no. 3 (2010).

Fahy, John, Hooley, Graham, Cox, Tony, Beracs, Jozsef, Fonfara, Krysztof and Snoj, Boris. "The Development and Impact of Marketing Capabilities in Central Europe," *Journal of International Business Studies*, vol. 31, no. 1 (Spring 2000).

Gabrielsson, P. and Gabrielsson, M. "Globalizing Internationals: Business Portfolio and Marketing Strategies in the ICT Field," *International Business Review*, vol. 13, no. 6 (December 2004).

Gabrielsson, Peter, Gabrielsson, Mika and Gabrielsson, Hannele. "International Advertising Campaigns in Fast-moving Consumer Goods Companies Originating from a SMOPEC Country," *International Business Review*, vol. 17, no. 6, (December 2008).

Hewett, Kelly, Roth, Martin S. and Roth, Kendall "Conditions Influencing Headquarters and Foreign Subsidiary Roles in Marketing Activities and Their Effects on Performance," *Journal of International Business Studies*, vol. 34, no. 6 (November 2003).

Hoang, Peter B. "A Causal Study of Relationships between Firm Characteristics, International Marketing Strategies, and Export Performance," *Management International Review*, vol. 38, Special Issue (1998).

Jain, Subhash C. *Handbook of Research in International Marketing* (Cheltenham: Edward Elgar, 2003).

Jiménez, Nadia Huitzilin and San Martín, Sonia. "The role of country-of-origin, ethnocentrism and animosity in promoting consumer trust. The moderating role of familiarity," *International Business Review*, vol. 19, no. 1 (February 2010).

Kanso, Ali M. and Nelson, Richard Alan. "Multinational Corporations and the Challenge of Global Advertising," *International Marketing Review*, vol. 24, no. 5 (2007).

Kaynak, Erdener. "A Cross Regional Comparison of Export Performance of Firms in Two Canadian Regions," *Management International Review*, vol. 32, no. 2 (Second Quarter 1992).

Kotabe, Masaaki, "Contemporary Research Trends in International Marketing: The 1990s," in Alan M. Rugman and Thomas Brewer (eds.), *Oxford Handbook of International Business* (Oxford: Oxford University Press, 2001).

Landry, John T. "Differentiate or Die: Survival in Our Age of Killer Competition," *Harvard Business Review*, vol. 78, no. 3 (May/June 2000).

Lim, Lewis K. S., Acito, Frank and Rusetski, Alexander. "Development of Archetypes of International Market Strategy," *Journal of International Business Studies*, vol. 37, no. 4 (July 2006).

Manolopoulos, Dimitris, Papanastassiou, Marina and Pearce, Robert. "Technology Sourcing in Multinational Enterprises and the Roles of Subsidiaries: An Empirical Investigation," *International Business Review*, vol. 14, no. 3 (June 2005).

Michael, Steven C. "Determinants of the Rate of Franchising among Nations," *Management International Review*, vol. 43, no. 3 (Third Quarter 2003).

Mitchell, Will, Shaver, J. Myles and Yeung, Bernard. "Performance Following Changes of International Presence in Domestic and Transition Industries," *Journal of International Business Studies*, vol. 24, no. 4 (Fourth Quarter 1993).

Nachum, Lilach. "The Impact of Home Countries on the Competitiveness of Advertising TNCS," *Management International Review*, vol. 41, no. 1 (Spring 2001).

Norburn, David, Birley, Sue, Dunn, Mark and Payne, Adrian. "A Four-Nation Study of the Relationship between Marketing Effectiveness, Corporate Culture, Corporate Values, and Market Orientation," *Journal of International Business Studies*, vol. 21, no. 3 (Third Quarter 1990).

Almodovar, Paloma and Rugman, Alan M. "The Regionalization and Performance of Standardizing versus Customizing Firms," Henley Business School, University of Reading, Dunning Centre for International Business Discussion Paper Series, mimeo (2011).

Papu, Ravi, Quester, Pascale G. and Cooksey, Ray W. "Country Image and Consumer-Based Brand Equity: Multi-Level Evaluations of Consumer Involvement in International Segmentation," *Journal of International Business Studies*, vol. 38, no. 5 (September 2007).

Powers, Thomas L. and Loyka, Jeffrey J. "Market, Industry, and Company Influences on Global Product Standardization," *International Marketing Review*, vol. 24, no. 6 (2007).

Rubera, Gaia, Ordanini, Andrea and Griffith, David A. "Incorporating Cultural Values for Understanding the Influence of Perceived Product Creativity on Intention to Buy: An Examination in Italy and the US," *Journal of International Business Studies* (2011) vol. 42, 459–476. doi:10.1057/jibs.2011.3.

Reynolds, Nina L., Simintiras, Antonis C. and Diamantopolous, Adamantios. "Theoretical Justification of Sampling Choices in International Marketing Research: Key Issues and Guidelines for Researchers," *Journal of International Business Studies*, vol. 34, no. 1 (January 2003).

Rugman, Alan M. "The Myth of Global Strategy," *International Marketing Review*, vol. 18, no. 6 (2001).

Roth, Katharina Petra Zeugner / Diamantopoulos, Adamantios / Montesinos M Ángeles. "Home Country Image, Country Brand Equity and Consumers' Product Preferences: An Empirical Study," *Management International Review*, vol. 48, no. 5 (2008).

Rugman, Alan M., Oh, Chang H. and Lim, Dominic S.K. "The Regional and Global Competitiveness of Multinational Firms," *Journal of the Academy of Marketing Science*, (2011). doi:10.1007/s11747-011-0270-5.

Rugman, Alan M. and Verbeke, Alain. "Trade Policy and Global Corporate Strategy," *Journal of Global Marketing*, vol. 2, no. 3 (Spring 1989).

Samiee, Saeed. "Brand Origin Recognition Accuracy: Its Antecedents and Consumers' Cognitive Limitations," *Journal of International Business Studies*, vol. 36, no. 4 (July 2005).

Samiee, Saeed and Walters, Peter G. P. "Relationship Marketing in an International Context: A Literature Review," *International Business Review*, vol. 12, no. 2 (April 2003).

Schlegelmilch, Bodo B. and Chini, Tina Claudia. "Knowledge Transfer between Marketing Functions in Multinational Companies: A Conceptual Model," *International Business Review*, vol. 12, no. 2 (April 2003).

Schmid, Stefan and Kotulla, Thomas. "50 Years of Research on International Standardization and Adaptation—From a Systematic Literature Analysis to a Theoretical Framework," *International Business Review*, vol. 20, no. 5 (October 2011).

Sharma, Piyush. "Country of Origin Effects in Developed and Emerging Markets: Exploring the Contrasting Roles of Materialism and Value Consciousness," *Journal of International Business Studies*, vol. 42, no. 2 (February/March 2011).

Singh, Jagdip, Lentz, Patrick, and Nijssen, Edwin J. "First- and Second-Order Effects of Consumers' Institutional Logics on Firm Consumer Relationships: A Cross Market Comparative Analysis, *Journal of International Business Studies*, vol. 42, no. 2 (February/March 2011).

Solberg, Carl Arthur and Durrieu, François. "Access to Networks and Commitment to Internationalisation as Precursors to Marketing Strategies in International Markets," *Management International Review*, vol. 46, no. 1 (2006).

Srinivasan, Narasimham, Jain, Subhash C. and Sikand, Kiranjit. "An Experimental Study of Two Dimensions of Country-of-Origin (Manufacturing Country and Branding Country) Using Intrinsic and Extrinsic Cues," *International Business Review*, vol. 13, no. 1 (February 2004).

Steenkamp, Jan-Benedict E. M., Batra, Rajeev and Alden, Dana L. "How Perceived Brand Globalness Creates Brand Value," *Journal of International Business Studies*, vol. 38, no. 1 (January 2003).

Taylor, Charles R. and Okazaki, Shintaro. "Who Standardizes Advertising More Frequently, and Why Do They Do So? A Comparison of U.S. and Japanese Subsidiaries' Advertising Practices in the European Union," *Journal of International Marketing*, vol. 14, no. 1 (2006).

Theodosiou, Marios and Leonidou, Leonidas. "Standardization versus Adaptation of International Marketing Strategy: An Integrative Assessment of the Empirical Research," *International Business Review*, vol. 12, no. 2 (April 2003).

Townsend, Janell D., Yeniyurt, Sengun, Deligonul, Z. Seyda, and Cavusgil, S. Tamer. "Exploring the Marketing Program Antecedents of Performance in a Global Company," *Journal of International Marketing*, vol. 12, no. 4 (2004).

Veale, Roberta and Quester, Pascale. "Do Consumer Expectations Match Experience? Predicting the Influence of Price and Country of Origin on Perceptions of Product Quality," *International Business Review*, vol. 18, no. 2, (April 2009).

Walters, Peter G. P. and Zhu, Mingxia. "International Marketing in Chinese Enterprises: Some Evidence from the PRC," *Management International Review*, vol. 35, no. 3 (Third Quarter 1995).

Yang, Deli and Fryxell, Gerald E. "Brand Positioning and Anti-counterfeiting Effectiveness," *Management International Review*, vol. 49, no. 6 (2009).

Chapter 14

HUMAN RESOURCE MANAGEMENT STRATEGY

Contents

Objectives of the chapter

Human resource management strategy provides an MNE with the opportunity to truly outdistance its competition. For example, if HP develops a laser printer that is smaller, lighter, and less expensive than competitive models, other firms in the industry will attempt to reverse-engineer this product to see how they can develop their own version. However, when a multinational has personnel who are carefully selected, well trained, and properly compensated, it has a pool of talent that the competition may be unable to beat. Products and brands may, to some extent, be imitable; knowledge and capabilities, and the processes that combine and leverage them for competitive advantage, tend not to be. For this reason, human resource management (HRM) is a critical element of international management strategy. This chapter considers the ways in which multinationals prepare their people to take on the challenges of international business. We focus specifically on such critical areas as selection, training, managerial development, compensation, and labor relations.

The specific objectives of this chapter are to:

1 *Define* the term *international human resource management* and discuss human resource strategies in overseas operations.

2 *Describe* the screening and selection criteria often used in choosing people for overseas assignments.

3 *Relate* some of the most common types of training and development that are offered to personnel who are going overseas.

4 *Discuss* the common elements of an international compensation package.

5 *Explain* some of the typical labor relations practices used in the international arena.

6 *Describe* some of the human resource management strategies that are currently receiving a great deal of attention from MNEs.

ACTIVE LEARNING CASE

The Coca-Cola Company thinks local

The Coca-Cola Company has been operating internationally for most of its 120-year history, since it first started operations in Canada in 1906. Today the company operates in 200 countries and employs 139,600 people as at 2010. Its human resource management (HRM) strategy helps explain a great deal of its success. It now follows a strategy of "national responsiveness" by adapting to local market conditions. For example, it transferred more than 300 professional and managerial staff from one country to another under its leadership development program, and the number of international transferees is increasing annually. One senior-level HRM manager explained Coca-Cola's strategy by noting:

> We recently concluded that our talent base needs to be multilingual and multicultural. . . . To use a sports analogy, you want to be sure that you have a lot of capable and competent *bench strength*, ready to assume broader responsibilities as they present themselves.

In preparing for the future, Coca-Cola includes a human resource recruitment forecast in its annual and long-term business strategies. It also has selection standards on which management can focus when recruiting and hiring. For example, the company likes applicants who are fluent in more than one language because they can be transferred to other geographic areas where their fluency will help them to be part of Coca-Cola's operation.

The firm also has a recruitment program that helps it identify candidates at the college level. Rather than just seeking students abroad, Coca-Cola looks for foreign students who are studying in the United States at domestic universities. The students are recruited in the United States and then provided with a year's training before they go back to their home country. Coca-Cola also has an internship program for foreign students who are interested in working for the company during school breaks, either in the United States or back home. These interns are put into groups and assigned a project that requires them to make a presentation to the operations personnel, including a discussion of what worked and what did not. The interns are then evaluated individually and management decides their future potential with the company.

Coca-Cola believes these approaches are extremely useful in helping to find talent on a global basis. Not only is the company able to develop internal sources, but its intern program provides a large number of additional individuals who would otherwise end up with other companies. Coca-Cola earns a greater portion of its income and profit overseas than it does in the United States. Its HRM strategy helps explain how, despite the success of its policies, Coca-Cola found itself facing a series of problems as it entered the millennium. During the 1980s the firm expanded its global reach and began to centralize control and encourage consolidation among all bottling partners. In the 1990s, however, the world began to change. Many national and local leaders began seeking sovereignty over their political, economic, and cultural futures. As a result, the very forces that were making the world more connected and homogeneous were also triggering a powerful desire for local autonomy and the preservation of unique cultural identity. Simply put, the world was demanding more nimbleness, responsiveness, and sensitivity from MNEs, while Coca-Cola was centralizing decision making, standardizing operating practices, and insulating itself from this changing environment. It was going global when it should have been going local.

Today, Coca-Cola is beginning to turn things around. Under its most internationally experienced CEO ever, Neville Isdell, it is focusing on marketing-led growth. In particular, it has begun implementing three principles designed to make it more locally responsive. First, it is instituting a strategy of "Think local, act local" by putting more decision making in the hands of local managers. Second, it is focusing itself as a pure marketing company that pushes its brands on a regional and local basis. Third, it is working to become a model citizen by reaching out to the local communities and getting involved in civic and charitable activities. In the past, Coca-Cola succeeded because it understood and appealed to global commonalities; in the future it hopes to succeed by better understanding and appealing to local differences.

Websites: www.cocacola.com; www.cokecce.com.

Sources: "The veteran," *The Economist*, June 2, 2007; Coca Cola, *Annual Report*, 2010; OneSource, *Thomson Reuters*, 2011.

▶

1. Does the Coca-Cola Company have a local perspective regarding the role of human resource management?

2. On what basis does Coca-Cola choose people for international assignments? Identify and describe two.

3. What type of training does Coca-Cola provide to its interns? Of what value is this training?

4. How useful is it for Coca-Cola's managers to be fluent in more than one language? Why?

INTRODUCTION

International human resource management (IHRM)

The process of selecting, training, developing, and compensating personnel in overseas positions

Home-country nationals

Citizens of the country where the multinational resides

Expatriates

Individuals who reside abroad but are citizens of the multinational's parent country; they are citizens of the home, not the host, country

Host-country nationals

Local people hired by a multinational

Third-country nationals

Citizens of countries other than the one in which the multinational is headquartered or the one in which they are assigned to work by the multinational

International human resource management (IHRM) is the process of selecting, training, developing, and compensating personnel in overseas positions. This chapter will examine each of these activities. Before doing so, however, it is important to clarify the general nature of this overall process, which begins with selecting and hiring.

There are three basic sources of personnel talent that MNEs can tap for positions.[1] One is **home-country nationals**, who reside abroad but are citizens of the multinational's parent country. These individuals are typically called **expatriates**. An example is a US manager assigned to head an R&D department in Tokyo for IBM Japan. A second is **host-country nationals**, who are local people hired by the MNE. An example is a British manager working for Ford Motor Company in London. The last is **third-country nationals**, who are citizens of countries other than the one in which the MNE is headquartered or the one in which it has assigned them to work. An example is a French manager working for Sony in the United States.

Staffing patterns may vary depending on the length of time the MNE has been operating. Many MNEs will initially rely on home-country managers to staff their overseas units, gradually putting more host-country nationals into management positions as the firm gains experience. Another approach is to use home-country nationals in less developed countries and employ host-country nationals in more developed regions, a pattern that is fairly prevalent among US and European MNEs.[2] A third pattern is to put a new operation under the supervision of a home-country manager but turn it over to a host-country manager once it is up and running. Figure 14.1 provides an illustration of the types of managers, by nationality mix, required over the stages of internationalization. When an MNE is exporting into a foreign market, host-country nationals will handle everything. As the firm begins initial manufacture in that country, the use of expatriate managers and third-country nationals begins to increase. As the company moves through the ensuing stages of internationalization, the nationality mix of the managers in the overseas unit continues to change to meet the shifting demands of the environment.

In some cases staffing decisions are handled uniformly. For example, most Japanese MNEs rely on home-country managers to staff senior-level positions. Similarly, some European MNEs assign home-country managers to overseas units for their entire careers. US MNEs typically view overseas assignments as temporary, so it is more common to find many of these expatriates working under the supervision of host-country managers.

The size of the compensation package also plays an important role in personnel selection and placement. As the cost of sending people overseas has increased, there has been a trend toward using host-country or third-country nationals who know the local language and customs. For example, many US multinationals have hired English or Scottish managers for the top positions at subsidiaries in former British colonies such as Jamaica, India, the West Indies, and Kenya.[3]

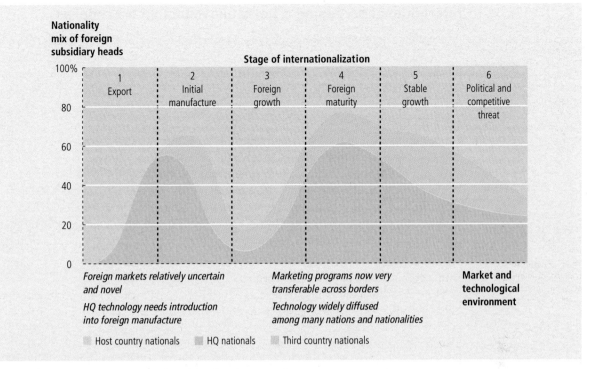

Figure 14.1 The management of multinational enterprises

Source: Reprinted from *Columbia Journal of World Business*, Summer 1973, Lawrence G. Franko, "Who Manages Multinational Enterprises?" p. 33, Copyright 1973, with permission from Elsevier Science.

The above factors influence IHRM strategies and help MNEs integrate an international perspective into their human resource policies and practices.[4]

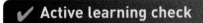

✔ **Active learning check**

Review your answer to Active Learning Case question 1 and make any changes you like. Then compare your answer to the one below.

1 Does the Coca-Cola Company have a local perspective regarding the role of human resource management?

The company certainly does have a local perspective regarding the HRM role. Coca-Cola is interested in recruiting people from anywhere in the world, training and developing them, and sending them to assignments around the globe. It does not confine itself to recruiting, training, developing, or promoting people from any one particular region or country. Both Americans and non-Americans have equal opportunities in the company, further reinforcing this international perspective.

SELECTION AND REPATRIATION

Two of the major HRM challenges facing MNEs are those of selecting qualified people for overseas assignments and, in the case of home-country nationals, effectively repatriating them into the workforce upon their return. Each presents a significant challenge.

International screening criteria and selection procedures

International screening criteria are those factors used to identify the individuals regarded as most suitable for overseas assignment. Some MNEs use an extensive list, whereas others rely on only a handful of factors. A number of screening criteria are commonly used in determining who to send overseas. These criteria focus on both individual and family considerations.

Adaptability

One criterion is an individual's ability to adapt to cultural change.[5] Research shows that many managers are initially pleased to learn they are being sent overseas. However, within a few months many of them begin to suffer from culture shock brought on by the large number of changes to which they are subjected. This often results in a decline in job satisfaction. However, as they continue their overseas assignment, satisfaction goes back up. Torbiorn, for example, reports that by the end of the first year most managers are through the cultural change phase and are beginning to adjust to their new conditions. Among those who stay overseas for two or more years, Torbiorn has found that satisfaction reaches new heights and continues rising.[6] Researchers have also found that men tend to adjust slightly faster than women, and that people over the age of 35 have somewhat higher levels of satisfaction after the first year.

In determining how well an individual will adapt to cultural change, MNEs examine a number of characteristics, including (1) work experiences with cultures other than one's own, (2) previous overseas travel, (3) knowledge of foreign languages (fluency is not generally necessary), (4) the ability to solve problems within different frameworks and from different perspectives, and (5) overall sensitivity to the environment.[7]

Self-reliance

Managers who are posted to overseas assignments must be self-reliant and independent because they often have to make on-the-spot decisions without consulting the home office. In determining self-reliance, MNEs evaluate the amount of field experience the individual has had, as well as experience in special projects and task forces—assignments that often require and nurture self-reliance. Consideration is also given to hobbies or avocations that require a high degree of personal independence.

Age, experience, and education

MNEs often find that young managers are eager for international assignments and want to learn more about other cultures. On the other hand, older managers have more experience and maturity to bring to the assignment. To balance the strengths of the two groups, many firms send both young and seasoned personnel to the same overseas post so that each can learn from the other.

Some MNEs believe that a college degree, preferably a graduate degree, is important for international managers. However, there is no universal agreement on this point. Multinationals that sell highly technical products tend to prefer people with science degrees. Others hold that a good education helps develop logical thinking, creative ideas, and a broad perspective of the world, so they prefer individuals with a liberal arts education.

Health and family status

Expatriates must have good physical and emotional health. Those with physical problems that will limit their activities are screened from consideration. So are those judged less likely to withstand culture shock.

Multinationals also take into account a person's family situation. An unhappy family life will hurt employee productivity. One survey of US multinationals found that the primary reason for expatriate failure was the inability of the manager's spouse to adjust to a different physical or cultural environment. For this reason, some firms interview both the spouse *and* the manager before deciding whether to approve the assignment.[8]

The increasing number of dual-career families in Western countries creates a further challenge for MNEs. Equally career-minded spouses might find their careers interrupted during their spouses' overseas assignments. In fact, a study of 332 repatriates and spouses found most dissatisfaction with MNEs resulted from lack of employment support for the trailing spouse.[9]

Motivation and leadership

Another selection criterion is the individual's desire to work abroad and potential commitment to the new job. Many people who are unhappy with their position at home will consider an overseas assignment, but this is not sufficient motivation. Motivational factors include a desire for adventure, a pioneering spirit, a desire to increase one's chances for promotion, and the opportunity to improve one's economic status.[10]

Additionally, one group of researchers recently examined the factors associated with employee willingness to work overseas and concluded the following:

- Unmarried employees are more willing than any other group to accept expat assignments.

- Married couples without children at home or those with non-teenage children are probably the most willing to move.

- Prior international experience seems associated with willingness to work as an expatriate.

- Individuals most committed to their professional careers and to their employing organizations are prone to be more willing to work as expatriates.

- Careers and attitudes of spouses will likely have a significant impact on employee willingness to move overseas.

Employee and spouse perceptions of organizational support for expats are also critical to employee willingness to work overseas.[11]

Applicants are also evaluated on the basis of their leadership potential, since most expatriates end up supervising others. Although this is a difficult factor to assess, a number of characteristics are commonly sought when making this evaluation, including maturity, emotional stability, the ability to communicate well, independence, initiative, and creativity. These characteristics are good indications of leadership potential.

Selection procedures

The most common selection procedure is the interview. A general consensus is that extensive interviews of candidates and their spouses by senior executives still ultimately provide the best method of selection. For example, 52 percent of the US MNEs that Tung surveyed conducted interviews with both the manager and the spouse, whereas 47 percent conducted interviews with the candidate alone. In the case of technically oriented positions, these percentages were 40 and 59 percent. Other MNEs follow a similar pattern. Based on her research, Tung has concluded that multinationals are becoming increasingly cognizant of the importance of interviewing in effective performance abroad.[12]

Some companies also use tests to help in making the final choice of who will perform well in overseas assignments. However, this approach has not gained a great deal of support because it is expensive and many MNEs feel that tests do not improve the selection process. As a result, the candidate's domestic record and evaluations from superiors and peers, along with the interview, tend to be relied on most heavily.

Repatriation of expats

Repatriation
The process of returning home at the end of an overseas assignment

Repatriation is the process of returning home at the end of an overseas assignment. Managers are repatriated for a number of reasons. The most common one is that the pre-determined time assignment is completed. For expatriates, an overseas assignment usually lasts two to three years, although some companies are now encouraging their people to consider making the international arena a lifetime career choice. Another reason is the desire to have their children educated in the home country. The expatriate may be unhappy overseas and the company may feel there is more to be gained by bringing the person back than in trying to persuade the individual to stay on. Finally, as in any position, if a manager has performed poorly, the MNE may decide to put someone else in the position.

Readjusting

Although many expatriates look forward to returning, some find it difficult to adjust. A number of reasons can be cited. One is that the home-office job lacks the high degree of authority and responsibility the expat had in the overseas job. Another is that the expat feels the company does not value international experience and the time spent overseas seems to have been wasted in terms of career progress.[13] A third reason is a change in the standard of living. While overseas, many expats have generous living allowances and benefits that they cannot match back home. An accompanying problem is the change in cultural lifestyle. For example, a person who is transferred from a cosmopolitan city such as Vienna to a small town in Middle America may find it necessary to make major adjustments, ranging from social activities to the pace of life in general. Additionally, it is common to find that those who sold their house before leaving and have been overseas from three to five years are stunned by the high price of a replacement home. Not only have they lost a great deal of equity by selling, but they must also come up with a substantial down payment and much larger monthly mortgage payments. Some companies do not have plans for handling returning managers. If these individuals are assigned jobs at random, they can find their career progress jeopardized.

Recent research shows that the longer people remain overseas, the more problems they are likely to have being reabsorbed into the operations back home. In addition to the factors considered above, several factors make repatriation of such people after longer periods difficult: (1) they may no longer be familiar to people at headquarters; (2) their old jobs may have been eliminated or drastically changed; or (3) technological advances at headquarters may have rendered their existing skills and knowledge obsolete.

In many cases, it takes from 6 to 12 months before a returning manager is operating at full effectiveness. Adler reports that many expatriates have moderate to low effectiveness for the first 60 to 90 days, but they become more effective month after month as they readjust to life back home.[14]

Adjustment strategies

Transition strategies
Strategies designed to help smooth the move from foreign to domestic assignments

Repatriation agreement
An agreement that spells out how long a person will be posted overseas and sets forth the type of job that will be given to the person upon returning

In recent years, MNEs have begun to address adjustment problems faced by returning expatriates. Some have now developed **transition strategies** that are designed to help smooth the move from foreign to domestic assignments.

One of these strategies is the **repatriation agreement**, which spells out how long a person will be posted overseas and sets forth the type of job the person will be given upon returning. The agreement typically does not spell out a particular position or salary, but it does promise a job that is at least equal in authority and compensation to the one the person held overseas. Such an agreement relieves a great deal of the anxiety expatriates encounter because it assures them that the MNE is not going to forget them while they are gone and that there will be a place for them when they return.

A second strategy is to rent or maintain the expatriate's home during the overseas tour. Both Union Carbide and the Aluminum Company of America have such arrangements. These plans help reduce the financial burden managers face when they go on a three-year or four-year tour.

A third strategy is to assign a senior executive as a sponsor for every manager posted abroad. This ensures that there is someone looking after each expatriate and ensuring that his or her performance, compensation, and career path are on track. When the expatriate is scheduled to return home, the sponsor begins working internally to ensure a suitable position. Companies such as IBM and Union Carbide use this form of the mentoring process, which is proving to be very effective.

A fourth strategy is to maintain ongoing communications with expatriate managers, ensuring that they are aware of what is happening in the home office. If they are scheduled to be home on leave for any extended period of time, the company works them into projects at headquarters. In this way they can maintain their visibility at headquarters and increase the likelihood that they are viewed as regular members of the management staff rather than as outsiders.

These strategies that help MNEs maintain a proactive approach in dealing with expatriate concern are becoming more widespread. The best-managed multinational firms tend to have (1) mentor programs consisting of one-on-one pairing of an expatriate with a member of the home-office senior management staff, (2) a separate organization unit with primary responsibility for the specific needs of expatriates, and/or (3) maintenance of constant contacts between the home office and the expatriate.[15]

✔ Active learning check

Review your answer to Active Learning Case question 2 and make any changes you like. Then compare your answer to the one below.

 On what basis does Coca-Cola choose people for international assignments? Identify and describe two.

One of the bases on which Coca-Cola chooses people is the ability to speak at least two languages fluently. A second is familiarity with at least two cultures. Both are viewed as critical for success in international assignments.

TRAINING AND DEVELOPMENT

Training
The process of altering employee behavior and attitudes in a way that increases the probability of goal attainment

Managerial development
The process by which managers obtain the necessary skills, experiences, and attitudes that they need to become or remain successful leaders

Training is the process of altering employee behaviors and attitudes in a way that increases the probability of goal attainment. **Managerial development** is the process by which managers obtain the necessary skills, experiences, and attitudes they need to become or remain successful leaders. Training programs are designed to provide those who are going overseas with information and experience related to local customs, cultures, and work habits, thus helping them interact and work more effectively with local employees.[16] Development is typically used to help managers improve their leadership skills, stay up to date on the latest management developments, increase their overall effectiveness, and maintain high job satisfaction.[17]

Types of training

MNEs use several types of training and development programs.[18] These can be grouped into two general categories: standardized and tailor-made.

Standardized training programs
Generic programs that can be used with managers anywhere in the world

Standardized training programs are generic and can be used with managers anywhere in the world. Examples include programs for improving quantitative analysis or technical skills that can be used universally. Research reveals that many behaviorally oriented concepts can also be handled with a standardized program (although follow-up programs must be tailor-made to meet specific country needs). Examples include programs designed to acquaint participants with the fundamentals of communicating with, motivating, or leading people. Another form of standardized training presently offered by large MNEs addresses cultural differences on a global scale. For instance, with operations in 200 countries, managers of Colgate-Palmolive are often exposed to more than one foreign culture. To address this, the company has offered cultural diversity training to its managers.[19]

Tailor-made training programs
Programs designed to meet the specific needs of the participants, typically including a large amount of culturally based input

Tailor-made training programs are designed to meet the specific needs of participants and typically include a large amount of culturally based input. These programs are more commonly developed by large MNEs and by multinationals that need a working knowledge of the local country's beliefs, norms, attitudes, and work values. Quite often the input for the programs is provided by managers who are currently working in the country (or have recently worked there) and by local managers and personnel who are citizens of that country. In most cases this training is provided to expatriates before they leave for their assignment, but in some cases it is provided on site.

Research shows that the following six types of programs are most popular:

1 Environmental briefings used to provide information about such things as geography, climate, housing, and schools.

2 Cultural orientation designed to familiarize the participants with cultural institutions and value systems of the host country.

3 Cultural assimilators using programmed learning approaches designed to provide the participants with intercultural encounters.

4 Language training.

5 Sensitivity training designed to develop attitudinal flexibility.

6 Field experience, which sends the participant to the country of assignment to undergo some of the emotional stress of living and working with people from a different culture.[20]

Typically, MNEs use a combination of the above programs, tailoring the package to fit their specific needs. A good example is provided by Underwriters Laboratories Inc., which uses a two-day, in-house program to train those personnel who will be dealing extensively with Japanese clients in the United States. The program is designed around a series of mini-lectures that cover a wide range of topics, from how to handle introductions to the proper way of exchanging gifts. It employs a variety of training techniques, including lectures, case studies, role-playing, language practice, and a short test on cultural terminology. The two-day training wraps up with a 90-minute question-and-answer period during which participants are given the opportunity to gain additional insights into how to develop effective client relationships.

Some firms extend their training focus to include families. In addition to providing language training, firms such as General Electric Medical Systems (GEMS) Group, a Milwaukee-based firm with expatriates in France, Japan, and Singapore, match up the family that is going overseas with another family that has been assigned to this country or geographic region. The latter family will then share many of the problems it faced during the overseas assignment and relate some of the ways these situations were resolved. It is also common to find MNEs offering cultural training to all family members, not just to the manager. This helps create a support group that will work together to deal with problems that arise during the overseas assignment. The case **International Business Strategy in Action: P&O, Carnival, and Dubai Port World** details how an MNE's IHRM training is tightly related to its global expansion.

INTERNATIONAL BUSINESS STRATEGY IN ACTION

P&O, Carnival, and Dubai Port World

Few people know that the "Princess" cruise ships, which were the "love boats" of TV fame, were at the time owned by British P&O Princess Cruises plc. The Peninsular and Orient Steam Navigation Company, known as P&O, was the sea transportation backbone of the old British Empire. In the nineteenth century it won British government contracts to deliver mail (post) to the Spanish peninsula and (via Africa and the Indian subcontinent) to Australia and the Far East. In the past P&O's ships have been commandeered by the British government in wartime to serve as transport vessels. In the Falklands War of 1982, the large flagship *Canberra* played a central role in the British war effort.

In January 2000, P&O Princess Cruises was spun off from P&O. Since then it has been known as P&O Princess Cruises International Ltd. It was then taken over by Carnival plc in August 2002. Carnival became the ultimate parent of P&O Princess Cruises. Carnival's stock is dually listed on the New York Stock Exchange under symbol CCL and on the London Stock Exchange under symbol POC. Headquartered in Miami, Carnival operates 100 ships whereas P&O Princess Cruises still maintains its head office in London.

Today, Carnival, including P&O Princess Cruises, is the largest cruise company in the world with revenues of US $15,782.9 million, net income $8,665.1 million and total assets of $1,417,089.8 million in 2009. In June 2011, P&O Princess Cruises owner Carnival has ordered a new 141,000 tonne cruise liner which it says will be the largest built specifically for the British market. The liner, costing €559m ($807m; £489m) and scheduled to enter service in March 2015, will be built by Italian shipbuilder Fincantieri. The as-yet unnamed ship will be able to carry a maximum of 4,372 passengers. Rival Royal Caribbean claims to have the world's biggest cruise ship, *Allure of the Seas*, weighing 225,282 tonnes. The 16-deck *Allure* can carry 5,400 guests and went into service in late 2010.

With an older population of North American and European "baby boomers," the growth of cruises has been

Source: Dennis Cox/Alamy

striking. Occupancy is usually at 100 percent capacity. The industry is also now trying to attract a younger demographic. Carnival now owns 12 brands. It is the leading cruise operator along the North American West Coast to Alaska, an area that P&O Princess Cruises had dominated. To enter the continental Europe market, P&O Princess Cruises purchased a majority stake in Germany's AIDA in 1999 and the remaining stake in 2000. It also purchased Germany's Seetours, a competing cruise line with 40 years of experience, and merged it with AIDA. Since then, AIDA has become the best-known cruise line in Germany. These brands are now incorporated under the Carnival name.

Prior to the merger with Carnival, P&O Group faced an interesting strategic challenge of integrating diverse businesses, from trucks to boat shows, from ports management to luxury cruise ship excursions. In particular, it needed to link its port management business and its very capital-intensive cargo ships, which require good information technology and operational efficiency, with its cruise ships, which are in the leisure and entertainment business. Molding an engineering and technical culture with the marketing, sales, and service activities of the cruise ships is an interesting managerial challenge that the P&O Group tackled by providing extensive management training

The world's largest cruise companies, 2009

Cruise company	Revenue (millions of US$)
Carnival Plc.	15,782.9
Royal Caribbean Cruises Ltd.	5,889.8
Genting Hong Kong (formerly known as Star Cruises Limited, a public subsidiary of Genting Berhard, Malaysia)	3,768.0

Sources: Individual Companies' Annual Reports, 2009; OneSource, *Thomson Reuters*, 2011.

programs. For example, in the late 1990s, it developed a series of senior management programs at Templeton College, Oxford University, which both improved business efficiency and moved managers into new areas of customer service, such as environmental and regulatory issues. As a result, P&O Group was a successful and growing business with a global mindset among its managers.

In 2006, the port business of P&O was purchased by Dubai Port World Limited (DP World) for $6.8 billion. Strategically located in the Persian Gulf, DP World is a world-class port operator by the 1990s with ports in the Middle East, India, and Europe. The company is an arm's-length commercial enterprise of the UAE government and it is run by an international management team that includes US citizens. Nonetheless, the deal brought a lot of criticism from within the United States because of concerns over national security. Congress intervened to review the deal, although both P&O and DP World were foreign-owned firms, and so there was really no legal basis for rejection of the DP World ownership. President Bush, whose administration had already reviewed the merger with DP World and approved it, threatened to veto any congressional action against the deal. The opposition came as a surprise to DP World since ports in the United States are but a small fraction of P&O's business. Yet, within a month of DP World taking over P&O, it sold all of its US port management assets to AIG Global Investment Group, a US firm.

Today DP World, together with its subsidiaries, operates in the business of international marine terminal operations and development, logistics, and related services. In 2010, it operates 50 marine terminals in 28 countries worldwide to a gross capacity of 67 million TEU (twenty-foot equivalent unit) and has a further nine projects under development and major extensions. It provides logistics, infrastructure development and consultancy services. Its logistics services include general and bulk cargo handling, roll on, roll off vessels handling, and passenger terminals handling. It has other subsidiaries located in different countries such as P&O in the United Kingdom, DP World FZE in the United Arab Emirates, and DP World Maritime Cooperative U.A. in the Netherlands, among others. For the fiscal year ended 31 December 2010, DP World's total revenue increased 9 percent to $3.078 billion compared to the previous year. DP World started trading on the London Stock Exchange alongside the existing Nasdaq Dubai listing in June 2011.

Websites: www.poprincesscruises.com; www.carnival.com; www.dpworld.com.

Sources: P&O, *Annual Reports*; www.poprincesscruises.com; "Dubai Mulls over £6bn P&O Float less than a Year after Takeover," *Independent*, December 13, 2007; Ben White, "Uproar Surprised Dubai Firm," *Washingtonpost.com*. February 24, 2006; "Bush Says It Will Veto Any Bill to Stop UAE Port Deal," *Foxnews.com*. February 22, 2006; "P&O owner Carnival orders 'largest UK cruise ship'", *BBC News Online*, June 1, 2011, http://www.bbc.co.uk/news/business-13612329; OneSource, *Thomson Reuters*, 2011; Dubai Port World, *Annual Report*, 2010.

✔ Active learning check

Review your answer to Active Learning Case question 3 and make any changes you like. Then compare your answer to the one below.

3 **What type of training does Coca-Cola provide to its interns? Of what value is this training?**

The company puts interns into groups and assigns projects that require them to investigate or study certain areas of operations. The interns are then evaluated on the outcome. This training is useful in helping the firm identify those individuals who offer the most promise for the company.

COMPENSATION

In recent years compensation has become a primary area of IHRM attention.[21] On the one hand, multinationals want to hire the most competent people. On the other hand, they want to control costs and increase profits. Sometimes these two objectives are not compatible; it can be expensive to relocate an executive overseas. A close look at the breakdown of international compensation packages helps to make this clear.

Common elements in an international compensation package

A typical international compensation package includes base salary, benefits, and allowances. In addition, most packages address the issue of tax protection and/or tax equalization. The following examines these four elements.

Base salary

Base salary is the amount of cash compensation an individual receives in the home country. This salary is typically the benchmark against which bonuses and benefits are calculated. Survey research reveals that the salaries of expatriates are tied to their home country, so a German manager working for a US MNE and assigned to Spain will have a base salary tied to the salary structure in Germany.[22] This salary is usually paid in the home currency, local currency, or a combination of the two.

Salary has become an issue when foreign firms have merged or acquired companies in other countries where salaries are significantly higher. For example, when Chrysler and Daimler-Benz merged, the Chairman and CEO of Chrysler had a salary of $1.6 million, whereas his Daimler-Benz counterpart was earning $1.1 million.[23] Moreover, international differences in salaries also create difficulties, as discussed below.

Benefits

Benefits often make up a large portion of the compensation package. There are also a number of difficult issues that typically must be resolved, including how to handle medical coverage, what to do about social security, and how to handle the retirement package. Some of the specific issues that receive a great deal of attention are:

1 Whether or not to maintain expatriates in home-country programs, particularly if the company does not receive a tax deduction for it.

2 Whether companies have the option of enrolling expatriates in host-country benefit programs and/or making up any difference in coverage.

3 Whether host-country legislation on termination affects benefit entitlements.

4 Whether expatriates should receive home-country or host-country social security benefits.

5 Whether benefits should be maintained on a home-country or host-country basis, who is responsible for the cost, whether other benefits should be used to offset any shortfall in coverage, and whether home-country benefit programs should be exported to local nationals in foreign countries.

Most US MNEs include their expatriate managers in the company's benefit program and the cost is no more than it would be back home. In cases in which a foreign government also requires contribution to a social security program, the company picks up this expense for the employee. Fortunately, in recent years a number of international agreements have been signed that eliminate requirements for dual coverage.

MNEs also provide vacations and special leave to expatriates. This often includes company-paid air fare back home for the manager and family on an annual basis, as well as emergency leave and expense payments in case of death or illness in the family.

Allowances

Cost-of-living allowance
A payment to compensate for differences in expenditures between the home country and the foreign location

Allowances are another major portion of some expatriate compensation packages. One of the most common is the **cost-of-living allowance**, which is a payment to compensate for differences in expenditures between the home country and the foreign location. Designed to provide employees with the same standard of living they enjoyed in the home country, this allowance can cover a wide variety of areas, including relocation, housing, education, and hardship.

Relocation expenses usually include moving, shipping, and storage charges associated with personal goods that the expatriate is taking overseas. Related expenses can include perquisites such as cars and club memberships, which are commonly provided to senior-level managers.

Housing allowances cover a wide gamut. Some firms provide managers with a residence while overseas and pay all expenses associated with running the house. Other firms provide a predetermined amount of money each month, and the managers can make the housing choice personally. Some MNEs also help individuals sell their houses back home or rent them until their return. The company usually pays expenses associated with these activities. Other MNEs such as General Motors encourage their people to retain ownership of their homes by paying all rental management fees and reimbursing the employees for up to six months' rent if the house remains unoccupied.

Education allowances for an expatriate's children are an integral part of most compensation packages. These expenses cover such things as tuition, enrollment fees, books, supplies, transportation, room, board, and school uniforms. In some cases attendance at post-secondary schools is also provided.

Hardship allowance
A special payment made to individuals posted to geographic areas regarded as less desirable

A **hardship allowance** is a special payment made to individuals who are posted to areas regarded as less desirable. For example, individuals posted to Eastern Europe, China, and some Middle East countries typically receive a hardship premium as an inducement to accept the assignment. These payments can be in the form of a lump sum ($10,000 to $25,000) or a percentage (15 to 50 percent) of the individual's base compensation.

Taxation

MNEs provide tax protection and/or tax equalization for expatriates. For example, a US manager sent abroad can end up with two tax bills: one for income earned overseas and the other for US taxes on these monies. Section 911 of the US Internal Revenue System code permits a deduction of up to $70,000 on foreign-earned income. For some executives, however, some US taxes might still be due. In handling these situations, most MNEs have a tax equalization program under which they withhold an amount equal to the home-country tax obligation of the manager and then pay all taxes in the host country. With tax protection, the employee pays up to the amount of taxes equal to those he or she would pay based on compensation in the home country. In this case, the employee is entitled to any difference if total taxes are less in the foreign country than in the home country. Other MNE tax considerations involve state and local tax payments and tax return preparation.

The most common approach is for the MNE to determine the base salary and other extras (bonuses etc.) the manager would make while living in the home country. The taxes on this income are then computed and compared to the total due on the expatriate's income, and the multinational pays any taxes over and above the amount that would have been due in the home country.

Compensation trends and comparisons

In terms of compensation, the MNE's objective is to ensure that expatriates do not have to pay any additional expenses as a result of living abroad. Figure 14.2 illustrates this idea. The income taxes, housing, goods and services, and reserve from the home country are protected so that the individual's out-of-pocket expenses remain the same. As we see from the figure, the overall package can be substantial. This is why there is a trend toward not sending expatriates to overseas positions unless there is a need for their specific services. In fact, the costs have become so prohibitive that firms like Dow Jones & Company, owner of the *Wall Street Journal*, long ago radically revised its formula for paying allowances for housing, goods, and services.[24] In addition, MNEs are increasingly replacing permanent relocation and long-term assignments with as-needed short trips that typically last less than a year.[25]

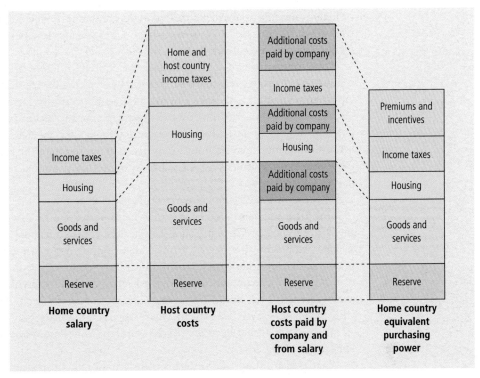

Figure 14.2 Cost of expatriate managers

Source: C. Reynolds, "Compensation of Overseas Personnel," in J. J. Famularo (ed.), *Handbook of Human Resource Administration*, 2nd ed. (New York: McGraw-Hill, 1986), p. 51.

Another trend is the creation of special incentive systems designed to keep expatriates motivated. In the process, a growing number of MNEs are now dropping bonuses or premiums for overseas assignments and replacing them with lump-sum premiums. This approach has a number of benefits. One is that expatriates realize they will be given this payment just once—when they move to the international locale. So the payment tends to retain its value as an incentive. A second is that the costs to the company are less because there is only one payment and no future financial commitment.

The specific incentive program used will vary. Researchers have found that some of the factors that influence the type and amount of incentive include whether the person is moving within or between continents and where the person is being stationed. Table 14.1 provides some of the latest survey information related to these incentive practices.

Table 14.1 Employer incentive practices around the world

Type of premium	Asia (%)	Europe (%)	North America (%)	Total (%)
Respondents paying for moves within continents				
Ongoing	62	46	29	42
Lump sum	21	20	25	23
None	16	27	42	32
Respondents paying for moves between continents				
Ongoing	63	54	39	49
Lump sum	24	18	30	26
None	13	21	27	22

Source: Geoffrey W. Latta, "Expatriate Incentives: Beyond Tradition," *HRfocus*, March 1998, p. S4. © *HRfocus*, March 1998. 212/244-0360. http://www.ioma.com.

Finally, it is important to realize that many companies are beginning to phase out incentive premiums. Instead, they are focusing on creating a cadre of expats who are motivated by non-financial incentives.

More companies are starting to take an entirely different approach, paying *no* premiums to expatriates regardless of where they send them. According to this philosophy, an assignment itself is its own reward. It is an opportunity for an employee to achieve personal and career growth. In some organizations, succession planning for senior-level positions requires international experience. Others view expatriate assignments as a step toward achieving globalization. Companies that subscribe to the philosophy of paying no premiums only consider cost-of-living issues, not motivational rewards, when designing pay packages.

When we step back and compare salaries across countries we get an insight into some of the difficulties maintaining parity or equality across groups of managers doing basically the same job but in different places. The starkest contrasts appear when we compare CEO salaries around the world. The United States stands out in terms of the average remuneration for CEOs compared to any other industrialized nation. For example, a group of non-US advanced countries (including Japan, most of Western Europe, and Canada) averaged only 33 percent of US foreign CEO pay. Over the 1988–2003 period, US foreign CEO pay increased by 196 percent, whereas the set of non-US countries only increased by 129 percent.[26] This has been the source of a significant amount of criticism in the United States and beyond.[27]

What is also interesting in terms of international compensation comparisons is the gap between CEO pay levels and workers' salaries around the world. For a similar sample of advanced nations the gap ranges from 10 percent, in Japan at one extreme, to 45 percent in the United States at the other. Moreover, according to this source this is an underestimation of the gap in most of these countries because certain areas of compensation are not included in the figures.[28] The variation across national systems seems to be symbolic of broader socio-economic and cultural differences between these countries.[29] Differences in corporate governance systems, the role of financial incentives, and, more fundamentally, differences in the role of corporations in society are reflected in these data.

LABOR RELATIONS

One of the major challenges facing MNEs is that of orienting their strategy to meet the varying demands of organized labor around the world (see Figure 14.3). National differences in economic, political, and legal systems create a variety of labor relations systems, and the strategy that is effective in one country or region can be of little value in another country.

In managing labor relations, most MNEs use a combination of centralization and decentralization, with some decisions being made at headquarters and others being handled by managers on site.[30] Researchers have found that US MNEs tend to exercise more centralized control than European MNEs such as the British ones. A number of factors have been cited to explain this development: (1) US companies tend to rely heavily on formal management controls and a close reporting system is needed to support this process; (2) European companies tend to deal with labor unions at an industry level, whereas US MNEs deal at the company level; and (3) for many US firms the domestic market represents the bulk of their sales (a situation that is not true for many European MNEs) and the overseas market is managed as an extension of domestic operations.[31]

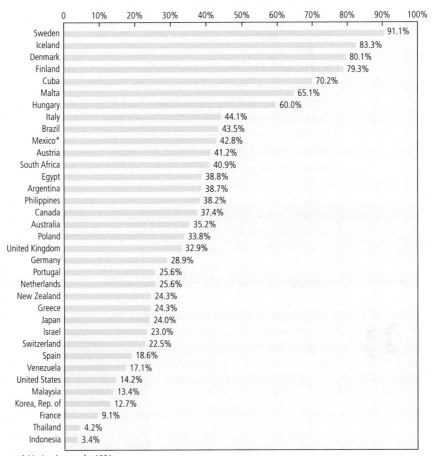

* Mexico data are for 1991.

Figure 14.3 Labor unions worldwide, 1995 (percentage of labor force that is unionized)

Source: International Labor Organization, *World Labour Report*, November 1997.

Labor relations practices

Labor relations practices vary widely. In some countries the economy is strong and unions are able to make major demands; in other countries the economy is weak and the unions' ability to bargain is diminished. Similarly, some countries have strong pro-management governments whereas others are heavily union oriented. A third factor is the willingness of unions to strike or walk out as opposed to continuing to talk with management in the hope of resolving differences. Germany and Japan provide some interesting contrasts.[32]

Germany

Labor unions traditionally have been strong in Germany. Although a minority of the labor force is organized, unions set the pay scale for about 90 percent of the country's workers, with wages determined by job classifications. Union membership is voluntary, but there is only one union in each major industry. This union negotiates a contract with the employers' federation for the industry, and the contract covers all major issues, including wages and terms of employment. If there is a disagreement over the interpretation or enforcement of the contract, the impasse is typically resolved between the company and the worker with the participation of a union representative or work council. If this procedure is unsuccessful, the matter can then be referred to a German labor court for final settlement.

Despite their power, unions have a much more cooperative relationship with management than do their counterparts in the United States. One reason is that workers serve on the board of directors and can ensure that the rank and file are treated fairly.

Strikes tend to occur after the contract has run out and a new one has yet to be ratified by the workers. As in the United States, several agreements may be in force in a particular company, and they do not have the same termination dates. So one group of workers may be striking or working without a contract while another is working under contract. On occasion, and in violation of the law, there may be strikes in the middle of a contract period, but this is rare and union and management typically have a good working relationship. However, whether this will continue in the future is difficult to say; the case **International Business Strategy in Action: German management and unions** examines this issue.

INTERNATIONAL BUSINESS STRATEGY IN ACTION

German management and unions

During the 1970s and 1980s, German manufacturing workers made substantial gains at the bargaining table. However, these successes are now coming back to haunt both them and their unions. In 1990, the average hourly manufacturing cost in the United States was $15 while Germany's was $22. Between 1985 and 1990, manufacturing cost in US dollars in Germany increased by 130 percent due to the strength of German currency and a 28 percent increase in labor costs in German currency. By 2003, average hourly manufacturing cost in Germany was at the $29.91 level, mainly as a result of the rising euro. This is much higher than in the rest of Western Europe. In Italy it is $18, in the UK $20, and in Portugal it is a mere $6.23. In the Czech Republic, labor costs in manufacturing are only $4.71 per hour. Across the Atlantic, US hourly manufacturing costs average $21.97.

Source: Corbis/Adam Woolfitt

In 1999, Volkswagen was prevented from laying off some 30,000 excess German workers by tough unions and labor laws. Job security and high wages are not the only labor disadvantages for German firms, which provide shorter labor-hour weeks, six weeks of paid vacation, and a very generous sick leave plan that promotes absenteeism. As a result, German products were having trouble finding international markets. In response, employers began looking for ways to turn things around.

In particular, companies began demanding wage concessions and started working to eliminate jobs. IBM's German subsidiary, which had almost 25,000 employees, divided itself into five companies, leaving only the 6,000 workers in the production unit working under a union contract. The remainder of the employees were not covered by the collective agreement, allowing the company to increase their work week to 40 hours. Other companies

began implementing similar strategies, convinced that labor leaders would make concessions in order to ensure the long-run survival of the business. In particular, managers pointed to the fact that international competition was threatening German jobs and, unless productivity could be increased, there was a good chance that more and more local firms would go out of business. These strategies, and a decrease in the exchange rate, have led to real wage decreases and a restructuring of the labor market over the last few years.

A growing number of companies are now winning concessions from their unions. One is CED Informationstechnik GmbH, a small firm that assembles personal computers. The firm's union contract allows it to cut back the workforce when orders are weak. And since CED focuses on delivery of computers within 24 hours of receiving an order, it has no need to build inventory. Thus, the workforce size is tied directly to the amount of orders on hand, allowing CED to operate with a basic crew of only 200 people. In turn, another group of approximately 40 workers has contracts guaranteeing them at least 1,000 hours of work annually, so these people can count on approximately 20 hours a week on average—although this is all tied to work orders. The remaining 300 employees at CED work as needed and can find after a month or two of large orders that things dry up and they have no work for the next couple of months. It is a chance they have to take.

An 8.5 percent and 18.5 percent unemployment rate in West and East Germany, respectively, and the relocation of operations outside Germany by both domestic and foreign companies have increased the pressure on unions to accept less favorable contracts. While all of this is a big change from the days when the unions used to dictate terms, it is one that is accepted by both the workers and the CED's worker council. This attitude is reflective of a growing number of unions. In 1999, when Wacker-Chemie workers were in danger of losing their jobs because the company was losing millions of dollars, the union proactively allowed the adjustment of wages and an adjustment in workers' hours. As a result, jobs were saved and Wacker-Chemie was allowed to get back on its feet. Thanks to compromise on the part of its union, management in the chemical sector can, upon consultation with workers, decrease wages by up to 10 percent per year, eliminate Christmas bonuses, and adjust the hours of work. In 2000, workers at Philipp Holzmann, a construction firm undergoing problems, bargained a wage decrease with the condition that workers will share the company's future gains. This new-found flexibility offers the promise of making German industry more competitive than it has been in a long time.

Indeed, during the economic crisis, Germany export rose 18.5 percent in 2010. In March 2011, German exports totaled €98.3bn ($142bn; £87bn), almost 16 percent higher than the same month in 2010. This figure was the highest monthly total since data started to be compiled in 1950. One difference was that Germany has embraced reforms. At the same, German companies made changes — but without the big bang of deregulation. The country embraced labor market reforms, but in a measured way. It is now easier to hire and fire. Companies have also taken advantage of the pool of workers in the east of the country (after the full opening of the German labour market on May 1, 2011). Volkswagen and BMW, for example, have found it easy to move production to lower cost eastern sites around Leipzig. Unions now recognize that the quid pro quo for government help in the recession is some restraint on pay. BMW is hiring another 2,000 workers; BASF, the world's biggest chemical company, reported a 40 percent jump in earnings; Siemens, Europe's biggest engineering company, said profits would nearly double in 2011. Bosch has post-recession sales at a record of €47bn.

Websites: www.vw.com; www.volkswagen.de; www.ibm.com; www.wacker.de.

Sources: Michael Calabrese, "Should Europe Adopt the American Economic Model?" *IntellectualCapital.com*, August 6, 1998; United States, Bureau of Labor Statistics, "It's Those People All Over Again," *The Economist*, August 12, 2004; Stephen Evans, "The secret to Germany's export success," *BBC News*, May 9, 2011; Stephen Evans "German exports rise to all-time high," *BBC News*, May 9, 2011; "German exports rose 18.5% in 2010," *BBC News*, February 9, 2011.

Japan

In Japan, union–management relationships are extremely cooperative. Social custom dictates non-confrontational behavior. So although labor agreements are often general and vague, disputes over interpretations tend to be settled amicably. Sometimes it is necessary to bring in third-party mediators or arbitrators, but there are no prolonged, acrimonious disputes that end up in a plant being closed down because the two sides cannot work together. Typically, a strike is used merely to embarrass the management and seldom lasts longer than one week. Although it is possible to resort to legal action in resolving strikes, this is typically frowned upon by both labor and management, and both sides try to stay away from using this means of bringing about solutions to their problems.

Japanese unions are most active during the spring and at the end of the year, the two periods during which bonuses are negotiated. However, these activities do not usually end up in a union–management conflict. If there is a strike, it is more likely at a time when a Japanese union is negotiating with management during industry-wide negotiations. Even here, the objective is to show that the workers are supportive of the union and not to indicate a grievance or complaint with management. In overall terms, Japanese workers tend to subordinate their interests and identities to those of the group. This cultural value helps account for a great deal of the harmony that exists between labor and management.[33]

Industrial democracy

Industrial democracy
The legally mandated right of employees to participate in significant management decisions

Unlike the United States, many countries have **industrial democracy**, which is the legally mandated right of employees to participate in significant management decisions. This authority extends into areas such as wages, bonuses, profit sharing, work rules, dismissals, and plant expansions and closings. Industrial democracy can take a number of different forms.

Forms of industrial democracy

At present there are a number of forms of industrial democracy. In some countries one form may be more prevalent than others, and it is common to find some of these forms existing simultaneously. The following describes three of the most popular forms.

Codetermination

Codetermination
A legal system that requires workers and their managers to discuss major strategic decisions before companies implement the decisions

Codetermination is a legal system that requires workers and their managers to discuss major strategic decisions before companies implement them. It has brought about worker participation on boards of directors and is quite popular in Europe, where Austria, Denmark, the Netherlands, and Sweden have legally mandated codetermination. In many cases the workers hold one-third of the seats on the board, although it is 50 percent in private German companies with 2,000 or more employees. On the negative side, some researchers report that many workers are unimpressed with codetermination and feel that it does not provide sufficient worker input to major decisions.

Work councils

Work councils
Groups that consist of both worker and manager representatives and are charged with dealing with matters such as improving company performance, working conditions, and job security

Work councils are groups that consist of both worker and manager representatives and are charged with dealing with such matters as improving company performance, working conditions, and job security. In some firms these councils are worker or union run, whereas in others a management representative chairs the group. The councils are a result of either national legislation or collective bargaining at the company–union level, and they exist throughout Europe. However, their power varies. In Germany, the Netherlands, and Italy, work councils are more powerful than they are in the UK, France, and Scandinavia.

Shop floor participation

Shop floor participation takes many forms, including job enrichment programs, quality circles, and various other versions of participative management. These approaches give workers an opportunity to make their voices heard and play a role in identifying and resolving problems. Shop floor participation is widely used in Scandinavian countries and has spread to other European nations and the United States over the last two decades.

Industrial democracy in action

Industrial democracy can be found in different forms throughout the United States, Europe, and Asia. The following discussion examines three examples.[34]

Germany

Industrial democracy and codetermination are both very strong in Germany, especially in the steel and auto industries. Private firms with 2,000 or more employees (in the steel industry it is 1,000 employees) must have supervisory boards (similar to a board of directors in the United States) composed of workers as well as managers. There must also be a management board responsible for daily operations to which company employees elect members.

Researchers have found that codetermination works well in Germany. Some critics have argued that too many people are involved in the decision-making process, which slows things down, resulting in inefficiencies. However, Scholl reports that a study he conducted of both managers and work councils found no such problems.[35]

Denmark

Industrial democracy in Denmark gives workers the right to participate in management on both a direct and an indirect basis. The direct form maintains that employees are members of semi-autonomous work groups that provide ideas on how to enhance productivity and quality and schedule work. In the indirect form, shop stewards on the floor represent fellow workers on the board of directors, and on cooperation committees that consist of both management and worker representatives. Industrial democracy works exceptionally well in Denmark, where researchers have found that cooperation committees contribute substantially to openness, coordination of effort, and a feeling of importance on the part of workers.[36]

Japan

Japan's use of industrial democracy concepts is not tied to political philosophy as in Europe; rather, it is oriented more to Japanese culture and the belief in group harmony. Moreover, Japanese industrial democracy is not as extensive as that in the West. Japanese workers are encouraged to identify and to solve job-related problems associated with quality and the flow of work. Management in turn is particularly receptive to worker ideas that will produce bottom-line results. This process is carried out in a paternalistic setting in which the company looks after the employees and the latter respond appropriately.

Unions play virtually no role in promoting industrial democracy or participative management because they are weak and, in many cases, only ceremonial. One group of researchers put it this way:

> In truth, most workers think of themselves as company employees who are simply associated with the union. Moreover, it is not uncommon to find a union strike in a company with two or three work shifts and no loss of work output. This is because, when the strikers are done picketing or marching, they then go to work and the group coming out of the factory takes up the strike activity. In a factory with three shifts, a line employee will work a full shift, picket for a while, go home to eat and sleep, and then return to the factory for her or his shift.[37]

As a result, Japanese MNEs face the greatest challenge from industrial democracy because they are least accustomed to using the idea. On the other hand, as Japanese firms continue to expand into Europe and the United States, there will likely be a growing use of authority-sharing concepts such as codetermination, work councils, and other approaches that are becoming so common in Western firms.

STRATEGIC MANAGEMENT AND IHRM STRATEGIES

A number of HRM strategies are currently receiving attention from MNEs.[38] There are too many to address here, but four that do warrant consideration are language training, cultural adaptation, competitive compensation, and specially designed HRM programs.

Language training

English is the primary language of international business. However, training in the host-country language can be particularly useful because it allows managers to interact more effectively with their local colleagues and workers and communicate more directly with suppliers and customers. Another advantage is that the training allows the manager to monitor the competition more effectively. For example, in recent years a growing number of US MNEs have set up operations in Japan, including DuPont, Eastman Kodak,

Hewlett-Packard, IBM, Procter & Gamble, and Rockwell International. Many of these MNEs' expatriate managers and R&D personnel have been given language training, which has paid off handsomely. For example, when Rockwell International entered into negotiations with a Japanese firm over royalties on a patent it holds on advanced semiconductor processing technology, the Japanese company said it had no intention of using Rockwell's patent. However, the company negotiators were able to show the Japanese an article from a Japanese newspaper in which their company had boasted about using the new technology. As a result, Rockwell now receives royalties on the use of this technology by the Japanese company.[39] In fact, thanks to language training, Rockwell was able to discover a host of patent infringements on the same technology by other Japanese firms.

Language training is useful in recruiting local talent and developing good relations with local organizations. IBM Japan, for example, hires 30 percent of its research scientists from Japanese universities or companies. Other US firms follow a similar pattern, offering large salaries ($150,000 and up) to attract senior Japanese scientists who can help create new high-tech products. Language training also comes in handy in developing and sustaining relationships with universities and government agencies. In fact, Dow Chemical has created a team for just this purpose.

Another benefit of language training is the ability to monitor competition. MNEs often locate near their major competitors because new developments by these firms are most likely to be reported in local newspapers and other sources. It is often possible to learn more about what a competitor is doing through local news media than one could ever find out from an investigation conducted by MNE headquarters. Many foreign MNEs have personnel who are fluent in English, peruse the *Wall Street Journal, New York Times,* and US industry publications on a daily basis, then compile a thick folder on the strategies of their US competitors.

Language training is also useful in helping to learn about a country's culture and to interact socially with the people. Research reports that most US expatriate managers give little importance to the value of a second language. In contrast, executives from South America, Europe, and Japan place a high priority on speaking more than one language. Fortunately, universities in the United States are now stepping in to help. For example, the Massachusetts Institute of Technology and other institutions of higher learning now offer courses in how to read technical Japanese and understand the Japanese research culture; this educational focus is likely to expand to other countries in the future. For the moment, however, language training continues to be a weak link in the development of an effective IHRM strategy for many MNEs.

✔ Active learning check

Review your answer to Active Learning Case question 4 and make any changes you like. Then compare your answer to the one below.

 How useful is it for Coca-Cola's managers to be fluent in more than one language? Why?

Coca-Cola's managers must be fluent in other languages because the company believes this allows them to operate effectively in at least two different cultures. This permits the company to transfer managers from one geographic region to another and to know that the managers will be able to become acculturated within a minimum time period. Moreover, because there are common languages in many regions of the world, a manager who is fluent, say, in English and Spanish could be transferred to countries throughout North America, South America, Europe, Africa, and Australia. Thus, bilingualism provides the company with a cadre of managers who can literally span the globe.

Cultural adaptation

Closely tied to language training is the need for managers to understand the culture of the country to which they are assigned. The importance of culture was discussed in Chapter 5, where it was noted that major differences exist between cultural clusters. In preparing managers for overseas positions, MNEs are now using three basic approaches. The simplest and least expensive is to design a program that provides cultural orientation by familiarizing individuals with the country's cultural institutions and value systems. This is often done through a formal training program and/or meetings with company personnel who have just returned from a posting in that country. The second is to provide individuals with language training and, if time and money permit, allow them to visit the country. Some MNEs tie this approach to a manager's assignment by setting aside the first couple of weeks on site for orientation and acculturation. A third approach that is fairly expensive but has received high marks for its value is the use of cultural assimilators.

Cultural assimilators

Cultural assimilator
A programmed learning technique designed to expose members of one culture to some of the basic concepts, attitudes, role perceptions, customs, and values of another culture

A **cultural assimilator** is a programmed learning technique designed to expose members of one culture to some of the basic concepts, attitudes, role perceptions, customs, and values of another. Cultural assimilators are developed for pairs of cultures, such as familiarizing managers from the United States with the culture in Germany. Of course, an assimilator can be developed for expatriates who are assigned to any culture in the world, and the approach almost always takes the same format: the person being trained is asked to read a short episode of a cultural encounter and then choose an interpretation of what has happened and why. If the response is correct, the individual goes on to the next episode. If not, he or she is asked to reread the episode and then make another choice. Table 14.2 provides an illustration.

Cultural assimilators use critical incidents as the basis for training. These incidents are typically ones in which (1) the expatriate will be interacting with a host nation, (2) the situation may be misinterpreted or mishandled if the expatriate is not properly trained, and (3) the event is relevant to the expatriate's task or mission requirements.[40] The incidents are provided by expatriates who have served in this particular country, as well as by members of the host nation. Once they are written, they are tested on people who have had experience in the country in order to ensure that the responses are realistic and that one choice is indeed preferable to the others. Typically, 150 to 200 incidents are developed and the list is pruned to 75 to 100 incidents, which are eventually included in the assimilator booklet.

Assimilators can be expensive to create. The typical cost for developing one is approximately $50,000. However, for MNEs that are continually sending people to a particular overseas location, the cost can be spread over many trainees and the assimilator can remain intact for a number of years. A $50,000 assimilator that is used with 500 people over a five-year period costs the company only $100 per person, and the cost of revising the program is often quite small, so over the long run the assimilators can be very cost effective.

Competitive compensation

MNEs are also beginning to evaluate more carefully the cost of sending people overseas as well as to review the expense of maintaining executive talent in the international arena. The first of these concerns focuses on all expatriates. The second addresses top-level managers only.

Compensation costs vary widely because goods and services in some countries are sharply higher (or lower) than in others. For example, food, clothes, and entertainment in the United States are fairly inexpensive compared to Japan, Hong Kong, Taiwan, or the

Table 14.2 A cultural assimilator situation

Sharon Hatfield, a schoolteacher in Athens, was amazed at the questions that were asked of her by Greeks whom she considered to be only casual acquaintances. When she entered or left her apartment, people would ask her where she was going or where she had been. If she stopped to talk, she was asked questions like, "How much do you make a month?" She thought the Greeks were very rude.

Page X-2

Why did the Greeks ask Sharon such "personal" questions?

1 The casual acquaintances were acting like friends do in Greece, although Sharon did not realize it.

Go to page X-3

2 The Greeks asked Sharon the questions in order to determine whether she belonged to the Greek Orthodox Church.

Go to page X-4

3 The Greeks were unhappy about the way in which she lived and they were trying to get Sharon to change her habits.

Go to page X-5

4 In Greece such questions are perfectly proper when asked of women, but improper when asked of men.

Go to page X-6

Page X-3

You selected 1: The casual acquaintances were acting like friends do in Greece, although Sharon did not realize it.

Correct. It is not improper for in-group members to ask these questions of one another. Furthermore, these questions reflect the fact that friendships (even "casual" ones) tend to be more intimate in Greece than in the United States. As a result, friends are generally free to ask questions that would seem too personal in the United States.

Go to page X-1

Page X-4

You selected 2: The Greeks asked Sharon the questions in order to determine whether she belonged to the Greek Orthodox Church.

No. This is not why the Greeks asked Sharon such questions. Remember, whether or not some information is "personal" depends on the culture. In this case the Greeks did not consider these questions too "personal." Why? Try again.

Go to page X-1

Page X-5

You selected 3: The Greeks were unhappy about the way in which she lived and they were trying to get Sharon to change her habits.

No. There was no information given to lead you to believe that the Greeks were unhappy with Sharon's way of living. The episode states that the Greeks were acquaintances of Sharon.

Go to page X-1

Page X-6

You selected 4: In Greece such questions are perfectly proper when asked of women, but improper when asked of men.

No. Such questions are indeed proper under certain situations. However, sex has nothing to do with it. When are these questions proper? Try to apply what you have learned about proper behavior between friends in Greece. Was Sharon regarded as a friend by these Greeks?

Note: Page X-1 returns the reader to the start of the exercise.

Go to page X-1

Source: Adapted from Fred E. Fiedler, Terence Mitchell and Harry C. Triandis (1971), "The Culture Assimilator: An Approach to Cross-Cultural Training," *Journal of Applied Psychology*, April 1971, 55, 97–98. Copyright © 1971 by the American Psychological Association. Adapted with permission.

UK (see Table 14.3). In particular, the cost-of-living allowance for managers in Europe and Japan adds significantly to the MNE's overhead. For this reason, major MNEs, from General Motors to IBM to TRW, are looking for ways to recruit and develop local talent to staff operations and thus reduce their reliance on expatriates.

The other major area of compensation that is receiving increased attention is that of hiring and retaining top management talent. Research shows that the cost of hiring senior-level managers is extremely high, and in most cases these individuals received a substantial salary raise when they moved into their new position. Moreover, as the demand for talented executives rises, the salaries of international managers will continue to rise. This is one reason why many MNEs are now hiring people for specific locations and leaving them

Table 14.3 Cost of living in select cities (New York = 100), 2009

Location	Cost	Location	Cost
Oslo	88.1	Rome	69.4
Zurich	84.7	Toronto	63.0
Compenhagen	81.8	Seoul	50.9
Geneva	85.5	Sao Paulo	48.9
Tokyo	85.3	Shanghai	48.9
Dubai	78.4	Bangkok	41.0
Paris	76.6	Buenos Aires	37.0
Hong Kong	75.2	Lima	35.6
Singapore	70.7	Mexico	34.3
London	69.9	Dehli	28.0

Source: Adapted from UBS, *Price and Earnings,* 2009.

E-resources: http://www.ubs.com/1/e/wealthmanagement/wealth_management_
research/prices_earnings.html

in place for extended periods of time. This strategy is less costly than continually moving managers from one geographic location to another.

HRM strategy will become an increasingly important part of the overall MNE strategic plan. Rising compensation costs are one of the major reasons for this trend.

Specially designed HRM programs

Another emerging trend is specially designed HRM programs. In recent years a growing number of MNEs have begun to realize that HRM practices have to be tailor-made. This has been clearly illustrated by Sparrow and Budhwar, who compared data from 13 different countries on the basis of HRM factors. Five of these factors included the following:

1 Structural empowerment characterized by flat organization designs, wide spans of control, the use of flexible cross-functional teams, and the rewarding of individuals for productivity gains.

2 Accelerated resource development characterized by the early identification of high-potential employees, the establishment of both multiple and parallel career paths, the rewarding of personnel for enhancing their skills and knowledge, and the offering of continuous training and development education.

3 Employee welfare emphasis characterized by firms offering personal family assistance, encouraging and regarding external volunteer activities, and promoting a culture that emphasizes equality in the workplace.

4 An efficiency emphasis in which employees are encouraged to monitor their own work and continually improve their performance.

5 An emphasis on long-term results such as innovation and creativity rather than just weekly and monthly short-term productivity.[41]

When Sparrow and Budhwar used these HRM approaches on a comparative country-by-country basis, they found worldwide differences in HRM practices. Table 14.4 shows the comparative results, after each of the 13 countries was categorized as being either high or low on the respective factors.

These findings reveal that countries are unique in their approach to HRM. What works well in the United States may have limited value in France. In fact, a close analysis of Table 14.4 shows that none of the 13 countries had the same profile, each was different. This was even true in the case of Anglophone nations such as the United States, Canada, Australia, and the UK, where differences in employee welfare emphasis, accelerated resource development, long efficiency orientation, and long-term vision resulted in unique HRM

Table 14.4 HRM practices in select countries

	Structural empowerment		Accelerated resource development		Employee welfare emphasis		Efficiency emphasis		Long-termism	
	High	Low	High	Low	High	Low	High	Low	High	Low
United States	X			X	X		X			X
Canada	X			X	X			X		X
United Kingdom	X			X		X		X		X
Italy		X		X		X		X		X
Japan		X		X	X		X		X	
India		X		X	X			X	X	
Australia	X		X			X	X		X	
Brazil	X		X		X			X	X	
Mexico	X		X		X			X		X
Argentina		X	X		X			X		X
Germany		X	X			X		X	X	
Korea		X	X			X	X		X	
France		X	X			X	X			X

Source: Adapted from *Journal of World Business*, Vol. 32, No. 3, 1997, Paul R. Sparrow and Pawan S. Budhwar, "Competition and Change: Mapping the Indiana HRM Recipe Against World-Wide Patterns," p. 233, Copyright © 1997 with permission from Elsevier Science.

profiles for each. Similarly, Japan and Korea differed on two of the factors, as did Germany and France; India, which many people might feel would be more similar to an Anglophone culture than to an Asian one, differed on two of the factors with both the United States and the UK, three of the factors with Canada, and all four factors with Australia.

These findings point to the fact that MNEs in the future will have to focus increasingly on HRM programs designed to meet the needs of local personnel. A good example is provided in Eastern Europe, where international managers are discovering that in order to effectively recruit college graduates their firms must provide training programs that give these new employees opportunities to work with a variety of tasks and help them specialize in their particular fields of interest. At the same time, the MNEs are discovering that these recruits are looking for companies that offer a good social working environment. A survey of more than 1,000 business and engineering students from Poland, the Czech Republic, and Hungary found that almost two-thirds of the respondents said they wanted their boss to be receptive to their ideas, 37 percent were looking for managers who had strong industry experience, and 34 percent wanted a boss who was a good rational decision maker. These findings indicate that multinational HRM is now becoming much more of a two-way street: both employees and managers need to adjust continually to emerging demands.[42]

KEY POINTS

1 International human resource management (IHRM) is the process of selecting, training, developing, and compensating personnel in overseas positions. IHRM strategies involve consideration of staffing, selecting, training, compensating, and labor relations in the international environment.

2 A number of screening criteria are used in choosing people for international assignments. These include adaptability, self-reliance, age, experience, education, health, family status, motivation, and leadership. The most common selection procedure is the interview, although some firms also use testing. In recent years MNEs have also begun formulating repatriation strategies for integrating returning managers back into the workplace at home.

3 Training and development programs are another key part of IHRM strategies. There are a wide variety of these programs, ranging from environmental briefings to language training.

4 There are a number of common parts in a typical international compensation package, including base salary, benefits, allowances, and tax protection and/or equalization. In essence, the package's objective is to ensure that the expatriate does not have to pay any additional expenses as a result of living abroad.

5 Labor relations practices vary widely in the international arena. For example, union–management relations and industrial democracy approaches are different throughout Europe, and these differ dramatically from those in Japan.

6 A number of HRM strategies are currently receiving a great deal of attention from MNEs. Three of these are language training, cultural adaptation, and competitive compensation.

Key terms

- international human resource management (IHRM)
- home-country nationals
- expatriates
- host-country nationals
- third-country nationals
- international screening criteria
- repatriation
- transition strategies
- repatriation agreement
- training
- managerial development
- standardized training programs
- tailor-made training programs
- cost-of-living allowance
- hardship allowance
- industrial democracy
- codetermination
- work councils
- cultural assimilator

REVIEW AND DISCUSSION QUESTIONS

1 Many US MNEs are accused of not focusing their efforts sufficiently on internationalization. How can they develop an international perspective among their managers? Offer three suggestions.

2 What are some of the most common screening criteria for individuals being chosen for international assignments? Identify and discuss four of them.

3 Why do MNEs tend to prefer interviews to testing when selecting people for international assignments?

4 In what way is repatriation proving to be a major problem for MNEs? How can they deal with this issue? Offer two substantive recommendations.

5 What are some of the most common forms of training and development offered to people going international or already operating abroad? Identify and describe three of them.

6 What are the most important parts of an international compensation package? Identify and describe three of them.

7 Why do some compensation packages have a hardship allowance?

8 In terms of compensation, why do many MNEs prefer to use a local manager rather than bring in an expatriate?

9 What are some of the primary differences in labor relations practices between Germany and Japan? Identify and discuss two of them.

10 How does industrial democracy work? Compare and contrast its use in Denmark, Germany, and Japan.

11 How are MNEs attempting to improve the language training given to their personnel being posted overseas?

12 How would an MNE use a cultural assimilator to prepare people for overseas assignments?

13 What are some of the latest trends in competitive compensation in the international arena? Identify and describe two of them.

REAL CASE

Offshoring to India

When outsourcing crosses national borders it is called off-shoring, but over the last few years, British trade unions and US politicians have been campaigning to stop offshoring—at a time when a growing number of firms, including Lloyds TSB, HSBC, Abbey, IBM, and JP Morgan, are using India's service professionals. In the mid-2000s, India's high-tech sector was growing at 30 percent per year and the volume of outsourcing contracts at 50 percent per year. IT sector exports were $12 billion in 2004 and rose to $32 billion by 2007.

The growth of the Indian IT sector is surprising because it lacked the domestic factors typically associated with the development of a competitive industry. First, local demand for software was non-existent. Second, related and sup-porting industries such as telecoms or computing were highly underdeveloped. Third, the national communication infrastructure was among the worst in the world. Fourth, despite India's relatively higher level of education in relation to other countries, it was nowhere near the level of the triad countries. Finally, financial capital was in short supply.

Clearly, some general conditions help account for the time of the growth period, not least the global shortage of soft-ware programming skills relative to demand. The imbalance between supply and demand pushed up the price of software skills, globally increasing the cheap labor advantage held by Indian firms. This, coupled with strong English language skills, made Indian programmers good substitutes for more expensive Western programmers. Software engineers tech-nically trained in the United States and Europe had devel-oped customer links to the major customer firms (banks,

telecoms, IT companies, and so on) in the West and then returned to India to establish their own ventures. New tech-nologies enabled Indian firms to service the needs of over-seas customers via satellite and the Internet. Transportation costs are insignificant and the geographic time difference can be an asset, allowing Indian firms to work through the "Western night." Finally, the Indian government had identi-fied software as an area of potential growth in the 1970s and supported it through the 1990s, when the industry began to explode. Another important factor has been the willingness of computer firms, such as Computer Associates, to invest in the Indian market.

In the United States, fears of job losses are forcing poli-ticians to take a stand. A US government regulation now pro-hibits the offshoring of government services. This, however, has little effect on India's industry, which has traditionally relied on private contracts. Supporters of outsourcing argue that it is beneficial to customers who can now pay less for services and that the rise in wealth in India would increase bilateral trade, creating opportunities for US firms. Indeed, a recent study by McKinsey estimates that for every dol-lar of US outsourcing, 78 cents are value created in the United States and only 22 cents are retained by the foreign country. The British government is taking a different stand than the US government and it is offshoring to India the IT systems for the National Health Service. It is no longer just IT jobs. Offshoring of accountant services, medical services, research, and data entry to India is also growing.

Offshoring does not always run smoothly. In the case of call centers, despite employee training in different English accents, customers have complained of problems communicating. In addition, the cultures might clash. On the other hand, many argue that Indian workers are more professional and better educated than their Western counterparts. The industry might be attracting a disproportionate number of bright minds in India because of the relatively higher standard of living enjoyed by those in the industry.

Today, Indian IT firms like Tata Consultancy Services, Infosys Technology, Wipro Technologies, and Satyam Computer Services are diversifying their portfolios and increasingly relying on e-commerce and other Internet-related businesses to cushion themselves against changes in the outsourcing market. Four factors drive this diversification: political risk from protectionists, rising wages, the rising value of the rupee, and growing competition from other nations such as China and Russia.

Websites: www.ca.com; www.wipro.com; www.infosys.com; www.tata.com; www.satyam.com.

Sources: Zuhair Ahmed, "India Dismisses Outsourcing Fears," *BBC News*, February 9, 2004; "US Outsourcing Is 'Accelerating'," *BBC News*, June 17, 2004; Kaushik Basu, "Outsourcing: Long-term Gains for All," *BBC News*, March 29, 2004; "NASSCOM-McKinsey Report 2005: Extending India's leadership in the global IT and BPO industries," http://www.nasscom.in/Nasscom/templates/NormalPage.aspx?id=2599; http://www.nasscom.in/.

1 Porter's well-known 1990 study on the competitive advantage of nations describes factors that have promoted high rates of innovation in certain industries in certain countries. These are summarized as the Porter Diamond framework showing how factor conditions, related and supporting industries, demand conditions, and the strategy, structure, and rivalry of other local firms can force continual improvements in productivity and new product development. How does the development of Indian IT fit into this framework?

2 What are the threats and opportunities for Western software firms arising from this shift in the competitive landscape? How are they strategically responding to these?

3 What factors must a firm considering outsourcing take into account?

REAL CASE

Executive search firms

Commonly known as headhunters, executive search firms (ESFs) are a specialized branch of management consulting that work directly with clients, usually MNEs, to identify, evaluate, and recruit senior executives. Most *Fortune* 1,000 companies use ESFs to fill positions ranging from entry-level to CEO and board member. Worldwide ESFs are an $18 billion industry. Their fees are a percentage of the salary (including equity) the chosen candidate will receive in the first year of employment, which creates the right incentives for bargaining for high salaries by their executives. The largest firms are shown in Table 1. These firms are highly competitive, particularly in North America and Europe. There are also many small local boutique firms, but these often work with the major international chains for MNE recruiting.

After several years of dot.com-driven prosperity, the slowdown of the world economy hit the ESFs hard. Between 1998 and 2000, the industry had enjoyed a boom with annual growth of over 20 percent. In the United States, growth was even higher at 31 percent in 2000. By the first few years of the new century, however, the crash of the IT industry and the US recession reduced the number of executive spots and put a freeze on new hiring for many positions. Between 2000 and 2003, almost all ESFs were reporting losses and many headhunters were looking for work themselves. By 2004, things had started to turn around for ESFs, especially in financial services, real estate, security, and construction, which once again began to hire. Since then business has picked up once again: 2006 saw a 9 percent increase in searches and a 13 percent increase in revenues for ESFs.

To offset the strong dependence on the business cycle, ESFs are increasingly diversifying. Korn/Ferry and Heidrick & Struggles now offer strategic management assessments and executive development services. A third of Egon Zehnder International's revenues come from non-search work. The company has become a consultant for private investors who want to evaluate a firm's quality of management. Like its competitors, it has entered the human resource development business by providing mid-sized MNEs with an assessment team. It now has 283 consultants serving client needs from 58 offices worldwide. Diversification has allowed these companies to reduce reliance on executive searches as a line of business; ▶

Table 1 The largest executive search firms in the world—2006

No Name	N America	Other America	Europe	SE Asia	Other	Total
1 AIMS	7	11	53	11	6	88
2 IESF	6	24	28	27	1	86
3 InterSearch	12	9	45	11	8	85
4 The Amrop Hever Group	10	11	42	16	3	82
5 Boyden	16	6	30	19	2	73
6= Korn/Ferry	22	8	24	15	3	72
6= EESN	0	0	70	1	1	72
7 Egon Zehnder International	13	6	28	11	3	61
8 Heidrick & Struggles	18	7	22	11	1	59
9 TRANSEARCH International	10	5	32	9	2	58
10 IIC Partners	12	6	25	14	0	57
11 Stanton Chase International	14	9	20	9	2	54
12= The Taplow Group	12	7	27	7	0	53
12= Ray & Berndtson	9	4	33	5	2	53
13= EMA Partners	7	10	24	6	3	50
13= Spencer Stuart	18	4	19	8	1	50
14 INAC	0	3	33	6	2	44
15 IMD International	2	0	28	12	0	42
16= DHR International	33	1	3	3	0	40
16= AEA International	0	1	31	7	1	40
17 IRC Recruitment	3	0	34	1	0	38
18 World Search Group	11	2	15	6	2	36
19 Russell Reynolds Associates	12	2	13	8	0	35
20 CFR Consulting Group	0	0	31	1	0	32

Source: Search-Consult Magazine "The Largest Search Firms in the World 2006," AIMS International Issue 28, 2006.

branching into consulting, however, is unlikely to provide much respite for ESFs since consulting firms face similar challenges.

Alongside some degree of diversification ESFs have significantly internationalized in recent years (as shown in Table 2), following the relocation of clients and the growth of executive search services outside the Triad regions.

Korn Ferry, for example, has 500 consultants in 80 offices in 39 countries and has expanded its presence in China and India considerably over the past few years. Research by Faulconbridge et al. (2007) has shown how the industry has evolved through several stages: organic growth after the 1960s, M&A from the late 1970s, and the development of a variety of alliance networks more recently. This expansion path has given rise to several distinctive organizational forms: the wholly owned multinational, such as Heidrick & Struggles International, Spencer Stuart, and Egon Zehnder International; the networked transnational, such as the Globe Search Group; and hybrid organizations, such as Korn Ferry, which adopt either, depending on the market context or client needs.

But analysis of the figures in Executive Grapevine in 2010, an annual report on headhunting, suggests that some parts of the industry face pressure from business networking websites such as LinkedIn, which completed

Table 2 Leading 15 global executive search firms: office change by region, 1992–2004 (ranked by worldwide revenue)

Region	1992	2004	Absolute Change	% change
Europe	247	306	+59	+24
North America	115	144	+29	+25
South America	29	66	+37	+128
Asia and Pacific	68	122	+54	+79
Middle East and East	2	15	+13	+650
Totals	461	676	+215	+47

Source: Faulconbridge et al., *Environment and Planning A* 40 (1) 210–234, 2008 Copyright © Pion Limited, London (2008).

a successful initial public offering in May, 2011. More significant is the way that companies are using business networking websites to negotiate better rates for external searches. The report indicates that employers no longer need headhunters to put names on a shortlist. They need them to do the selling, to persuade people to move. At the top levels people are still not used to social networks. They tend to be older and once they step outside certain sectors, like technology, the social networks have not really had an impact. Headhunters themselves are divided over the impact of business networking websites. Some believe it can be useful in executive searches. Historically, it might have taken 10 days or so to find a particular person who had disappeared off the radar. Now it takes you 20 seconds. Some do not believe it will replace executive search firms any time soon. Even so, some practitioners believe that the continued growth of networking websites may force headhunters out of the market at the lower end of their current business model, because they will make it hard for search firms to raise fee levels even when general market conditions improve. This would leave the headhunters even more heavily exposed to the fortunes of the high earners in the financial sector, for example in the UK than they are already.

Websites: www.kornferry.com; www.heidrick.com; www.spencerstuart.com; www.russreyn.com; www.zehnder.com; www.hhgroup.com; www.rayberndtson.com; www.onrec.com/newsstories/; www.amrophever.com.

Sources: James R. Faulconbridge, Sarah J. E. Hall and Jonathan V. Beaverstock, "New Insights into the Internationalization of Producer Services: Organizational Strategies and Spatial Economies for Global Headhunting Firms," *Environment and Planning A*, vol. 40, no. 1 (2008), pp. 210– 234; www.kornferry.com; Kathy Showalter, "Headhunting Firm Benefits from Stable Relationships," *Columbus Business First*, September 19, 2003; Alison Smith and Gill Plimmer, "Headhunters track down fee increases," *Financial Times*, July 10, 2011.

1 When staffing the needs of the foreign subsidiary of a German company, what pool of candidates can the ESF choose from? Why would an international ESF be more capable of performing this task than the MNE's internal human resources department?

2 How would compensation negotiations differ for home-, host-, and third-country candidates?

3 What types of factors would the ESF use to identify a potential candidate for an overseas assignment?

ENDNOTES

1 Chris Brewster, Paul Sparrow and Guy Vernon, *International Human Resource Management*, 2nd ed. (London: Chartered Institute of Personnel and Development, 2007).

2 Rosalie L. Tung, "Selection and Training Procedures of US, European, and Japanese Multinationals," *California Management Review*, vol. 25, no. 1 (Fall 1982), p. 59.

3 Richard M. Hodgetts and Fred Luthans, *International Management*, 4th ed. (Homewood, IL: Irwin/McGraw, 2000), p. 430.

4 Anne-Wil K. Harzing and Joris Van Ruysseveldt (eds.), *International Human Resource Management: Managing People Across Borders*, 2nd ed. (London: Sage, 2003).

5 Rosalie L. Tung and Edwin L. Miller, "Managing in the Twenty-first Century: The Need for Global Orientation," *Management International Review*, vol. 30, no. 1 (First Quarter 1990), pp. 5–18.

6 Ingemar Torbiorn, *Living Abroad* (New York: Wiley, 1982), p. 98.

7 Hodgetts and Luthans, op. cit., p. 434.

8 Bernd Kupka and Virginia Cathro, "Desperate Housewives–Social and Professional Isolation of German Expatriated Spouses," *International Journal of Human Resource Management*, vol. 18, no. 6 (2007), pp. 951–968.

9 Michael Harvey, "Dual Career Expatriates: Expectations, Adjustments and Satisfaction with International Relocation," *Journal of International Business Studies*, vol. 28, no. 3 (Winter 1997). See also Hung-Wen Lee, "Factors that Influence Expatriate Failure: An Interview Study," *International Journal of Management*, vol. 24, no. 3 (2007), pp. 403–413.

10 Torbiorn, op. cit., pp. 156–161.

11 Patricia C. Borstorff, Stanley G. Harris, Hubert S. Field and William F. Giles, "Who'll Go? A Review of Factors Associated with Employee Willingness to Work Overseas," *Human Resource Planning*, vol. 20, no. 3 (1997), p. 38.

12 Tung, op. cit., p. 64.

13 Helene Mayerhofer, Linley C. Hartmann and Anne Herbert, "Career Management Issues for Flexpatriate International Staff," *Thunderbird International Business Review*, vol. 46, no. 6 (2004), pp. 647–666.

14 Nancy J. Adler and Susan Bartholomew, "Academic and Professional Communities of Discourse: Generating Knowledge on Transnational Human Resource Management," *Journal of International Business Studies*, vol. 23, no. 3 (Third Quarter 1992), pp. 551–569.

15 Brewster et al., op. cit.

16 See, for example, J. Bernard Keys and Robert M. Fulmer, *Executive Development and Organizational Learning for Global Business* (New York: International Business Press, 1998), pp. 1–9.

17 Jie Shen, "International Training and Management Development: Theory and Reality," *Journal of Management Development*, vol. 24, no. 7 (2005), pp. 656–666.

18 Paul R. Sparrow, "Globalization of HR at Function Level: Four UK-based Case Studies of the International Recruitment and Selection Process," *International Journal of Human Resource Management*, vol. 18, no. 5 (2007), pp. 845–867; Steven H. Rhinesmith, "An Agenda for Globalization," *Training and Development Journal*, February 1991, pp. 22–29.

19 "Company Culture in the Global Village," *Philips' What's Up Archive*, July 12, 1999; see also Leandra Celaya and Jonathan S. Swift, "Pre-departure Cultural Training: US Managers in Mexico," *Cross Cultural Management*, vol. 13, no. 3 (2006), pp. 230–243.

20 Tung, op. cit., p. 65.

21 Brewster et al., op. cit.

22 Peter J. Dowling and Randall S. Schuler, *International Dimensions of Human Resource Management* (Boston, MA: PWS-Kent Publishing, 1990), p. 121. Also see Marion Festing, Judith Eidems and Susanne Royer, "Strategic Issues

and Local Constraints in Transnational Compensation Strategies: An Analysis of Cultural, Institutional and Political Influences," *European Management Journal*, vol. 25, no. 2 (2007), pp. 118–131.

23 Greg Steinmetz and Gregory L. White, "Chrysler Pay Draws Fire Overseas," *Wall Street Journal*, May 26, 1998, p. B1.

24 Alex S. Jones, "Dow Jones Plans to Tighten Foreign Policy for Workers," *New York Times*, September 9, 1991, p. C6.

25 "Nasty, Brutish and Short," *The Economist*, December 14, 2000.

26 John Alexander Burton and Christian E. Weller, "Supersize This: How CEO Pay Took Off While America's Middle Class Struggled" Washington, DC: (Center for American Progress, May 2005).

27 Eduardo Porter, "More Than Ever, It Pays to Be the Top Executive," *New York Times*, May 25, 2007; http://www. nytimes.com/2007/05/25/business/25execs.html.

28 Burton and Weller, op. cit.

29 Marion Festing, Judith Eidems and Susanne Royer, "Strategic Issues and Local Constraints in Transnational Compensation Strategies: An Analysis of Cultural, Institutional and Political Influences," *European Management Journal*, vol. 25, no. 2 (2007), pp. 118–131.

30 See, for example, Laurie Hays, "IBM's Finance Chief, Ax in Hand, Scours Empires for Costs to Cut," *Wall Street Journal*, January 26, 1994, pp. A1, A6.

31 C. K. Prahalad and Y. L. Doz, The Multinational Mission: Balancing Logical Demands and Global Vision (New York: Free Press, 1987).

32 Howard F. Gospel and Andrew Pendleton, *Corporate Governance and Labour Management* (Oxford: Oxford University Press, 2005).

33 Mari Sako, *Shifting Boundaries of the Firm: Japanese Company–Japanese Labour* (Oxford: Oxford University Press, 2006).

34 For a European country comparison of labor involvement in industrial decision making, see Mark Fenton-O'Creevy, "Survey—Mastering People Management," *Ft.com*, November 26, 2001.

35 Wolfgang Scholl, "Codetermination and the Ability of Firms to Act in the Federal Republic of Germany," *International Studies of Management & Organization*, Summer 1987, pp. 27–37.

36 Reinhard Lund, "Industrial Democracy in Denmark," *International Studies of Management & Organization*, Summer 1987, pp. 27–37.

37 Hodgetts and Luthans, op. cit., p. 504.

38 Günter K. Stahl and Ingmar Björkman, *Handbook of Research in International Human Resource Management* (Cheltenham: Edward Elgar, 2006).

39 Susan Moffat, "Picking Japan's Research Brains," *Fortune*, March 25, 1991, p. 94.

40 Fred E. Fiedler, Terence Mitchell and Harry C. Triandis, "The Culture Assimilator: An Approach to Cross-Cultural Training," *Journal of Applied Psychology*, April 1971, p. 95.

41 Paul R. Sparrow and Pawan S. Budhwar, "Competition and Change: Mapping the Indian HRM Recipe Against World-Wide Patterns," *Journal of World Business*, vol. 32, no. 3 (Fall 1997), p. 231.

42 Bodil Jones, "What Future European Recruits Want," *Management Review*, January 1998, p. 6.

ADDITIONAL BIBLIOGRAPHY

Adler, Nancy J. and Bartholomew, Susan. "Academic and Professional Communities of Discourse: Generating Knowledge on Transnational Human Resource Management," *Journal of International Business Studies*, vol. 23, no. 3 (Third Quarter 1992).

Athanassiou, Nicholas A. and Roth, Kendall. "International Experience Heterogeneity Effects on Top Management Team Advice Networks: A Hierarchical Analysis," *Management International Review*, vol. 46, no. 6 (2006).

Bhanugopan, Ramudu and Fish, Alan, "Replacing Expatriates with Local Managers: An Exploratory Investigation into Obstacles to Localization in a Developing Country," *Human Resource Development International*, vol. 10, no. 4 (December 2007).

Bolino, Mark C. "Expatriate Assignments and Intra-Organizational Career Success: Implications for Individuals and Organizations," *Journal of International Business Studies*, vol. 38, no. 5 (September 2007).

Boyacigiller, Nakiye. "The Role of Expatriates in the Management of Interdependence, Complexity and Risk in Multinational Corporations," *Journal of International Business Studies*, vol. 21, no. 3 (Third Quarter 1990).

Boyacigiller, Nakiye A., Goodman, Richard A. and Phillips, Margaret E. *Crossing Cultures: Insights from Master Teachers* (New York: Routledge, 2003).

Briscoe, Dennis R. and Schuller, Randall S. *International Human Resource Management* (London: Routledge, 2004).

Caprar, Dan V. "Foreign Locals: A Cautionary Tale on the Culture of MNC Local Employees," *Journal of International Business Studies*, vol. 42. doi:10.1057/jibs.2011.9 (2011).

Carr, Stuart C., Inkson, Kerr and Thorn, Kaye. "From Global Careers to Talent Flow: Reinterpreting 'Brain Drain'," *Journal of World Business*, vol. 40, no. 4 (November 2005).

Chen, Stephen, Geluykens, Ronald and Choi, Chong Ju. "The Importance of Language in Global Teams: A Linguistic Perspective," *Management International Review*, vol. 46, no. 6 (2006).

Chiang, Flora F. T. And Birch, Thomas A. "Appraising Performance across Borders: An Empirical Examination of the Purposes and Practices of Performance Appraisal in a Multi-Country Context," *Journal of Management Studies*, vol. 47, no. 7 (November 2010).

Collings, David G., Scullion, Hugh and Morley, Michael J. "Changing Patterns of Global Staffing in the Multinational Enterprise: Challenges to the Conventional Expatriate Assignment and Emerging Alternatives," *Journal of World Business*, vol. 42, no. 2 (June 2007).

De Cieri, Helen and Dowling, Peter J. "Strategic International Human Resource Management: An Asia–Pacific Perspective," *Management International Review*, vol. 37, Special Issue (1997).

Fang, Yulin, Jiang, Guo-Liang, Frank, Makino, Shige and Beamish, Paul W. "Multinational Firm Knowledge, Use of Expatriates, and Foreign Subsidiary Performance," *Journal of Management Studies*, vol. 47, no. 1 (January 2010).

Fey, Carl F, Morgulis-Yakushev, Sergey, Park, Hyeon Jeong and Björkman, Ingmar. "Opening the Black Box of the Relationship Between HRM Practices and Firm Performance: A Comparison of MNE Subsidiaries in the USA, Finland, and Russia," *Journal of International Business Studies*, vol. 40 (May 2009). doi:10.1057/jibs.2008.83.

Gammelgaard, Jens, McDonald, Frank, Tüselmann, Heinz, Dörrenbächer, Christoph and Stephan, Andreas. "Subsidiary Role and Skilled Labour Effects in Small Developed Countries," *Management International Review*, vol. 49, no. 1 (2009).

Geringer, J. Michael and Frayne, Colette A. "Human Resource Management and International Joint Venture Control: A Parent Company Perspective," *Management International Review*, vol. 30, Special Issue 1 (1990).

Goerzen, Anthony and Beamish, Paul W. "The Penrose Effect: 'Excess' Expatriates in Multinational Enterprises," *Management International Review*, vol. 4, no. 2 (2007).

Holtbrügge, Dirk and Mohr, Alex T. "Subsidiary Interdependencies and International Human Resource Management Practices in German MNCs," *Management International Review*, vol. 51, no. 1 (2011).

Jun, Sunkyu, Gentry, James W. and Hyun, Yong J. "Cultural Adaptation of Business Expatriates in the Host Marketplace," *Journal of International Business Studies*, vol. 32, no. 2 (June 2001).

Kirkman, Bradley L., Lowe, Kevin B. and Gibson, Cristina B. "A Quarter Century of Culture's Consequences: A Review of Empirical Research Incorporating Hofstede's Cultural Values Framework," *Journal of International Business Studies*, vol. 37, no. 3 (March 2006).

Law, Kenneth S., Tse, David K. and Zhou, Nan. "Does Human Resource Management Matter in a Transitional Economy? China as an Example," *Journal of International Business Studies*, vol. 34, no. 3 (May 2003).

Lawler, John J, Chen, Shyh-jer, Wu, Pei-Chuan, Bae, Johngseok and Bing Bai, Bing. "High-Performance Work systems in Foreign Subsidiaries of American Multinationals: An Institutional Model," *Journal of International Business Studies*, vol. 42, 202–220 (14 October 2010). doi:10.1057/jibs.2010.42.

Loess, Kurt H. and Yavas, Ugur. "Human Resource Collaboration Issues in International Joint Ventures: A Study of US-Japanese Auto Supply IJVs," *Management International Review*, vol. 43, no. 3 (Third Quarter 2003).

Maloney, Mary M. and Zellmer-Brun, Mary. "Building Bridges, Windows and Cultures: Mediating Mechanisms between Team Heterogeneity and Performance in Global Terms," *Management International Review*, vol. 46, no. 6 (2006).

Mezias, John M. and Scandura, Terri A. "A Needs-Driven Approach to Expatriate Adjustment and Career Development: A Multiple Mentoring Perspective," *Journal of International Business Studies*, vol. 36, no. 5 (September 2005).

Milliman, John, Von Glinow, Mary Ann and Nathan, Maria. "Organizational Life Cycles and Strategic International Human Resource Management in Multinational Companies: Implications for Congruence Theory," *Academy of Management Review*, vol. 16, no. 2 (April 1991).

Morris, Shad S. and Snell, Scott A. "Intellectual Capital Configurations and Organizational Capability: An Empirical Examination of Human Resource Subunits in the Multinational Enterprise," *Journal of International Business*

Studies, vol. 42, (August 2011), pp. 805–827. doi:10.1057/jibs.2011.14.

Nielsen, Sabina. "Top Management Team Internationalization and Firm Performance," *Management International Review*, vol. 50, no. 2 (2010).

Punnett, Betty Jane, Greenidge, Dion and Ramsey, Jase. "Job Attitudes and Absenteeism: A Study in the English Speaking Caribbean," *Journal of World Business*, vol. 42, no. 2 (June 2007).

Reiche, B. Sebastian, Kraimer, Maria L. and Harzing, Anne-Wil. "Why Do International Assignees Stay? An Organizational Embeddedness Perspective," *Journal of International Business Studies* 42, (May 2011), pp. 521–544. doi:10.1057/jibs.2011.5

Robson, Matthew J., Paparoidamis, Nicholas and Ginoglu, Dimitrios. "Top Management Staffing in International Strategic Alliances: A Conceptual Explanation of Decision Perspective and Objective Formation," *International Business Review*, vol. 12, no. 2 (April 2003).

Roth, Kendall and O'Donnell, Sharon. "Foreign Subsidiary Compensation Strategy: An Agency Theory Perspective," *Academy of Management Journal*, vol. 39, no. 3 (June 1996).

Schuler, Randall S. *Managing Human Resources in Cross-Border Alliances* (London: Routledge, 2004).

Shaffer, Margaret A. "Dimensions, Determinants, and Differences in the Expatriate Adjustment Process," *Journal of International Business Studies*, vol. 30, no. 3 (September 1999).

Shay, Jeffrey P. and Baack, Sally A. "Expatriate Assignment, Adjustment and Effectiveness: An Empirical Examination of the Big Picture," *Journal of International Business Studies*, vol. 35, no. 3 (May 2004).

Shenkar, Oded and Zeira, Yoram. "Human Resources Management in International Joint Ventures: Directions for Research," *Academy of Management Review*, vol. 12, no. 3 (July 1987).

Taylor, Sully, "Creating Social Capital in MNCs: The International Human Resource Management Challenge," *Human Resource Management Journal*, vol. 17, no. 4 (2007).

Taylor, Sully, Beechler, Schon and Napier, Nancy. "Toward an Integrative Model of Strategic International Human Resource Management," *Academy of Management Review*, vol. 21, no. 4 (October 1996).

Thomas, David C., Lazarova, Mila B. and Inkson, Kerr. "Global Careers: New Phenomenon or New Perspectives?" *Journal of World Business*, vol. 40, no. 4 (November 2005).

Tung, Rosalie L. "American Expatriates Abroad: From Neophytes to Cosmopolitans," *Journal of World Business*, vol. 33, no. 2 (Summer 1998).

Tung, Rosalie L. and Miller, Edwin L. "Managing in the Twenty-First Century: The Need for Global Orientation," *Management International Review*, vol. 30, no. 1 (First Quarter 1990).

Welch, Denice E. "Globalisation of Staff Movements: Beyond Cultural Adjustment," *Management International Review*, vol. 43, no. 2 (Second Quarter 2003).

Zellmer-Bruhn, Mary and Gibson, Cristina, "Multinational Organization Context: Implications for Team Learning and Performance," *Academy of Management Journal*, vol. 49, no. 3 (June 2006).

Yamazaki, Yoshitaka. "Expatriate Adaptation," *Management International Review*, vol. 50, no. 1 (2010).

Chapter 15

POLITICAL RISK AND NEGOTIATION STRATEGY

Contents

Objectives of the chapter

For international managers different countries represent different business contexts with new sources of opportunity and risk. Political change, whether gradual or sudden, can be a source of both, and tends to be a particularly important factor in emerging and developing countries. Changes in institutions, governance systems, and business-related legislation are frequent in such countries and can radically change the local "rules of the game." An important management priority is to fully assess the risks as well as the potential rewards before and after investing in these kinds of new markets. Major political changes in China and India in the early 1990s, for example, opened up these economies for foreign investors. They had always been attractive markets, but were made accessible by government-led liberalization. However, the high level of control still held by these governments over their economies, combined with the continued uncertainty regarding political change, results in a high level of political risk for investors.

Beyond these major political shifts, smaller changes in any government's policies toward foreign investors—from taxes and tariffs to profit repatriation to local input content to employment legislation to corporate governance practices—can tilt the balance between profit and loss.

This chapter examines political risk in the context of overall country risk assessment. We look at how multinational enterprises (MNEs) try to forecast this risk, how they can understand governments' policy agendas, and how they can use negotiating tactics to minimize their political risk.

The specific objectives of this chapter are to:

1 *Examine* the nature of political risk.

2 *Understand* how to apply some of the tools and resources that companies can use to measure and forecast political risk.

3 *Discuss* some of the ways that firms manage risk.

4 *Review* typical strategies and tactics used in negotiating agreements.

ACTIVE LEARNING CASE

Kodak in China: changing the rules of the game

Fewer than one Chinese household in ten owns a camera today. And that camera exposes about four rolls of film each year. If only half the people in China shot a single 36-exposure roll of film a year—a fraction of usage rates in other countries—that would swell the number of worldwide "clicks" by 25%. Each second, 500 more photos would be taken. That's the equivalent of adding another U.S. or Japan to the world photographic market. China offers more potential for photography than any other market in the world.

George Fisher (Kodak CEO), May 23, 1998

(Kodak press release at: http://www.kodak.com/US/en/corp/pressReleases/pr19980323-01.shtml)

Source: Alamy

In 1997 Kodak faced growing competition in its domestic US market and was struggling with the impending technological and market shift toward digital imaging, away from its traditional stronghold in film-based products. It was also losing a long-running battle with regulatory authorities in Japan, challenging what it saw as anti-competitive practices that protected its key rival Fuji's hold on its own domestic market. At this time it had a limited presence of 600 people in the fastest-growing market, China, importing, distributing, and selling film worth $250 million. It was competing head-to-head with Fuji and local manufacturers, but falling behind; Fuji had the greater market share.

The options open to foreign investors in China then were far more restrictive than they are today. Outside-in M&As or even majority foreign-owned joint ventures were not allowed under highly protective government regulations. Kodak needed more than a change of strategy; it needed a change in the local "rules of the game." Kodak's overall aims were for exclusive rights to produce and sell locally (shut out rivals); to establish distribution, retailing, and marketing operations to tap into the growing consumer market in China; to establish production facilities for China and the South-East Asian region; and to use a combination of M&A and joint ventures to tap into local film business knowledge and resources.

Surprisingly, it achieved all of these objectives. Under the direction of CEO George Fisher, who had led Motorola's developments in China, the firm engineered what is now considered to be a very successful series of M&As and joint ventures. These resulted in an investment of $1.2 billion and a massive expansion in local production, sales, and marketing operations.

The key was an agreement with the Chinese government orchestrated from the very top, between Fisher and Prime Minister Zhu Rongji. This gave Kodak exclusive rights to the local market by placing a moratorium on other foreign investment in the industry (blocking Fuji and Agfa) and forcing all but one of the existing Chinese competitors to close or be acquired. Kodak was allowed to purchase majority control of three local film companies in Xiamen, Shantou, and Wuxi. Two of these had supplier relationships with Fuji, which were severed, leaving Fuji to rely on a Hong Kong company, China–Hong Kong Photo Products Holdings, to distribute its products on the mainland. Three other failing local film companies were forced to close.

The two companies formed under Chinese company law, Kodak (China) and Kodak (Wuxi) in Figure 15.1, are Kodak-controlled Chinese companies. The government agreement allowed Kodak a greater proportion of ownership and more management control than any other foreign company had ever been granted in China up to that point. It gained a 70 percent share in Kodak (Wuxi), which manufactures and sells chemical products for photographic processing, and an 80 percent share of Kodak (China), which manufactures film and paper. The corporate structure adopted (a limited-liability shares company) represented a radical departure from traditional equity joint-venture structures allowed previously by the Chinese authorities. This was helped by a key change in the mid-1990s whereby some foreign companies were allowed to establish foreign investor shareholding corporations (FISCs) for the first time.

▶

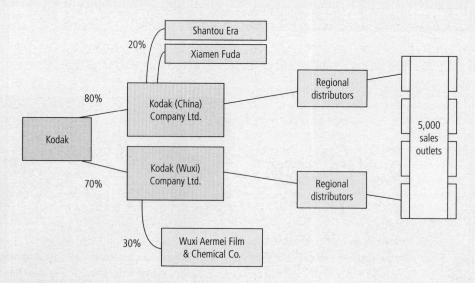

Figure 15.1 Kodak's structure in China

Kodak introduced a new system of management control, topped by a Kodak-controlled board of directors. Shantou Era and Xiamen Fuda were limited to the appointment of one director each to Kodak (China) Company's 10-person board. Key objectives were to introduce best-in-class management practices and processes, invest in local training programs, create a performance-based culture, and establish core Kodak values with local characteristics.

The overall investment has paid off for Kodak. It now controls most of the indigenous Chinese photo film industry and has a market share of around 60 percent, from 40 percent in 1998. The only remaining local competitor is the aptly named Lucky Film Corporation, which has about 20 percent of the market and with which Kodak signed a $100 million 20-year cooperative agreement in 2003 (selling its stake in 2008). In the same year China became Kodak's largest market in the world for cameras when it sold over 1 million. It has continued to invest in manufacturing operations in China while also pursuing its global digital strategy in the growing domestic market.

Although the relationship between Fisher and Zhu Rongji set the all-important tone for the negotiations, the so-called Grand Plan was a massive initiative stretching over several years. It involved seven state-owned enterprises, six provincial governments, ten city governments, five ministries and commissions, local tax authorities, and several banks and trust companies. All of this was under the umbrella of the Central Coordinating Committee designated by the Chinese government. The critical key, though, was Zhu Rongji's broader, long-term ambitions for the liberalization of the Chinese economy and his immensely powerful position at the pinnacle of a steep, complex government hierarchy.

Foreign funds and employment were major attractions for the Chinese side. Shantou Era Photo Materials and Xiamen Fuda Photographic Materials (with 2,000 employees) were in debt to the tune of $843 million prior to the takeover. According to the *People's Daily* newspaper (August 1999), the tax paid by the Xiamen joint cooperative venture after it went into operation last year alone surpassed the total taxes paid by the old factory over the previous 14 years. Kodak also donated funds to community initiatives including the Shanghai Children's Medical Center in Pudong and Project Hope School under China Youth Development Fund and established scholarship programs with five top universities in China. These benefits came alongside the direct and indirect employment created by the new ventures and the inflows of technology and expertise from Kodak. In retrospect we can now see that Kodak's expertise and technology were quickly becoming redundant. Despite its initial success in China, Kodak failed to adapt to the new realities of digital photography and in January 2012 it filed for bankruptcy in the US courts.

Sources: S. Collinson, "M&A as Imperialism?" in D. Angwin (ed.), *Images of M&A* (Oxford: Wiley-Blackwell, 2007); P. Nolan, *Transforming China: Globalization, Transition and Development* (London: Anthem, 2004); P. Nolan, *China and the Global Economy: National Champions, Industrial Policy and the Big Business Revolution* (Houndsmill: Palgrave, 2001); W. R. Vanhonacker et al., *Kodak in China (B): A Billion for a Billion*, Case Clearing House (ECCH), http://www.ecch.cranfield.ac.uk/; W. J. Holstein, "All the Film in China," *US News Online, Business and Technology*, July 6, 1998, at http://www.usnews.com/usnews/issue/980706/6koda.htm; Kodak Company website at http://www.kodak.com/; H. D. Petit, *Kodak in China: Growth and Localization*, speech by Henri D. Petit, Chairman and President, Greater Asia Region, Eastman Kodak Company, http://www.kodak.com/; *China Daily*, October 24, 2003, www.chinadaily.com.cn; supporting material from authors' interviews with Ira Wolf, Vice President of Kodak, Japan, in May 1997.

1 Why was the timing right for Kodak's market (re-)entry into China?

2 What kinds of political risk did Kodak face and how did it attempt to mitigate these risks?

3 What did both sides, Kodak and the Chinese government, gain from the deal?

4 What are the lessons for other firms looking to enter emerging markets like China?

INTRODUCTION

A range of strategy frameworks in this book—such as the strategy matrix, Porter's value chain, competitor analysis, or Porter's five forces—help managers understand their competitive environment and identify their firm's unique competitive advantages. Country risk analysis can build on these approaches by providing insights into the country-level factors that will affect the leveraging of these advantages in a particular country, and help managers balance potential risks against rewards. **Country risk analysis** examines the chances of non-market events (political, social, and economic) causing financial, strategic, or personnel losses to a firm following FDI in a specific country market. Rather than looking at market, industry, or group of competitors, country risk analysis tries to predict macroeconomic and political sources of change that might undermine a firm's position in a local market.[1] This kind of analysis is used to compare country markets before making investment decisions. Decision makers supplement strategic information about market size, market growth, presence of local suppliers, support industries, and the strengths of local competitors with, for example, estimates of current and future socio-economic and political risks that are country specific. In this chapter we will particularly examine political risk, but first we will examine a well-known, general framework for analyzing and comparing country conditions: PEST analysis.

Country risk analysis
Examines the chances of non-market events (political, social, and economic) causing financial, strategic, or personnel losses to a firm following FDI in a specific country market

Generic PEST analysis

One of the simplest, most general, and multidisciplinary frameworks for understanding change at the broadest level is the **PEST framework** (Figure 15.2). This is used to map out particular competitive environments or investment *contexts* for firms at the regional or national level, compare country conditions, and build future scenarios to understand short-term and long-term threats and opportunities. Influential factors are divided into political, economic, social or socio-cultural, and technological (PEST), which in combination create particular opportunities and threats for firms. PEST can be extended to PESTLE by adding legal factors, reflecting national legislative institutions and policies, and environmental factors, including local policies on waste and pollution. It can be used specifically to assess new investment environments as an input into global expansion and market-entry strategies.

PEST framework
Examines the political, economic, socio-cultural, and technological conditions in particular country markets

Clearly, there are strong interactions between the categories of factors. Political developments have a strong influence over economic change, particularly in emerging markets like China. Similarly, economic, social, and technological factors are interdependent. However, the PEST breakdown makes the task of analyzing a complex range of influences more manageable.

On the face of it, this kind of framework may look too general and simple to guide management strategy. The general PEST overview shown above, however, is just a starting point to organize more focused analyses. Rigor can be added and accuracy improved in two ways:

1 *Add depth.* To fully understand the nature of the changes taking place within each of the categories, further tools and techniques are needed:

- Political scientists and analysts conduct formal risk assessments on political change within regions or countries. Formal rankings are published to guide investors along

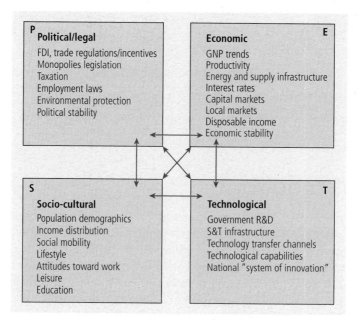

Figure 15.2 PEST framework for country analysis

the same lines as insurance assessors (see related discussions later in this chapter). Such analyses also map out the key political constituencies, central and regional agencies, key ministers and bureaucrats, as well as changing forms of legislation in different countries as an input into MNE strategy and implementation (for example, aiding the development of personal contacts and networks in target countries).

■ Economic analyses cover everything from national-level to industry-sector or market-specific trends. Companies compiling return on investment (ROI) projections need to know something about productivity levels that can be expected in would-be plants, encompassing data on employees, technologies, support industries, local utilities, and so on. Any investment that relies on some element of local financing will need data on local interest rate trends, lending conditions, and the general stability of domestic capital markets, for example.

■ Social trends analyses are relevant for firms looking to market new products and services in new countries. Mapping patterns of disposable income, customer preferences, and regional differences in these requires a combination of quantitative and qualitative analyses. Statistical overviews covering demographics, buying patterns, and market research need to be complemented with insights into socio-cultural norms and changing patterns of expectations if advertising messages are to be pitched correctly.

2 *Add foresight.* Arguably the most difficult challenge facing any decision maker is to predict the future. The complexity that results from the variety of factors managers need to consider when making international business decisions adds immeasurably to this uncertainty. Accurate scenario building is central to the strategic planning and future success of any firm and can be done using the PEST framework as a starting point. Rather than creating grandiose visions of the future, managers need to extrapolate accurately and objectively from the past and current trends across all the PEST dimensions to map out the likelihood of different futures and the implications of these for particular global strategies.

✔ Active learning check

Review your answer to Active Learning Case question 1 and make any changes you like. Then compare your answer to the one below.

1 **Why was the timing right for Kodak's market (re-)entry into China?**

Kodak's success in China was partly due to the timing of its initiative. Political factors favored the unusual agreement struck with the Chinese government, adding to the economic, social, and strategic factors that led to its success. A PEST framework helps identify these factors.

Political trends in the mid- to late 1990s included a strong move toward liberalization in China with specific concessions for firms making large capital investments, employing local labor, and transferring particular technologies. This was associated with government-driven privatization and industry deregulation. Specifically for Kodak, the ownership regulations and the introduction of the FISC status was critical. External relations changed dramatically with a move toward WTO entry and the reciprocal moves by other dominant economies, notably the United States with Clinton's state visit in August 1998. China was seen to be politically stable with little chance of retrenchment to a central command-and-control economy.

Economic trends pointed to a strong economy growing moderate to fast (around 8 percent GNP growth per year); large flows of inward FDI, including particularly large investments from US MNEs (GM, GE, Motorola, Coca-Cola); and strong growth of disposable income in the domestic market. On the downside, growing unemployment from denationalized industries was a destabilizing influence, and there were additional uncertainties about local capital markets, which were highly unsophisticated.

Socio-cultural change in China was also dramatic, including growing income levels and growing expectations, changing consumer tastes and preferences, coupled with the rise in unemployment and reduction in state-sponsored social welfare. Capitalist entrepreneurship was on the rise, creating distinct social tensions between old and new.

Technological strengths had long existed in China, founded on a good education system and a relatively advanced science and technology infrastructure. The country had some specific weak points and gaps in its industrial capabilities that government policy makers were keen to fill through alliances with Western firms and governments, again providing opportunities for particular MNEs.

POLITICAL RISK

Risk

Danger   +   Opportunity

This is the Chinese character for "risk." The first symbol is for "danger," the second symbol is for "opportunity." Risk is seen as danger and opportunity combined.

Political risk
The probability that political forces will negatively affect a multinational's profit or impede the attainment of other critical business objectives

Political risk is the probability that political forces will negatively affect a firm's profit or impede the attainment of other critical business objectives. The study of political risk addresses changes in the environment that are difficult to anticipate. Common examples include the election of a government that is committed to nationalization of major industries or one that insists on reducing foreign participation in business ventures.

Most people believe that political risk is confined to Third World countries or to those with unstable governments. However, the shifting policies of triad region governments illustrate that political risk is also an issue for firms doing business in highly industrialized nations. Governments routinely protect key industries for reasons of national security, self-sufficiency, or national culture. Examples include US restrictions on foreign investment in the banking, defense, and commercial airline industries; Japanese protection of its rice producers; and France's limitations on foreign involvement in its film and media businesses. The EU and US governments have long supported their regional champions in the aerospace industry, partly for security reasons, partly to protect local firms. Airbus spent $11 billion on building the A380 double-decker jumbo jet, one-third of which came from European taxpayers. This exacerbated the trade battles in this industry, refereed by the WTO.[2]

Much of this political sparring is predictable. It is unanticipated change stemming from complexity and uncertainty that creates more dangerous kinds of risk. However, these examples indicate the pervasiveness of political risk. Given the large number of international markets in which MNEs operate, political risk is going to remain an area of concern. In dealing with this issue, effective negotiating can help to reduce and contain problem areas. This will be explained later in the chapter.

Deregulation and political risk

Overall there has been a general trend toward liberalization, deregulation, and the opening up of national borders over the past 15 to 20 years, and this has been a major driver of globalization. Table 15.1 shows the growing number of regulatory changes that have been favorable to FDI. In particular, the progressive liberalization of countries with large domestic markets and extensive privatization or denationalization programs underway, such as China, Brazil, and India, has significantly changed the global economy. Huge opportunities exist for MNEs in these countries, and they have responded by investing to establish themselves in these new markets.

FDI inflows into these countries, particularly China, have grown immensely. India recorded inflows of only $237 million in 1990, then increased to $2,151 million in 1995. The inflows jumped to $6,598 million in 2000 following the politically led liberalization process. By 2008, the figure was at $41,554 million. In 2008, FDI into developing countries rose to $620,733 million compared to $36,897 million in 1990, representing an increase of 1,682 times. It accounted for an estimated 36.57 percent of global FDI inflows, compared to 18 percent in 2000.[3] Since then China in particular has risen to be a leading recipient of FDI each year. In 2008, the FDI inflows to China was $108,312 million (see chapter 20 Emerging economies).

For these giant emerging markets major political shifts led to the start of the process of integrating with the global economy and the opening up of their borders to foreign investors. Continuous, small, but significant changes to their policies and legislation regarding FDI and the activities of MNEs mean that ongoing assessments of political risk in these countries is of paramount importance to investors. The governments of these countries, together with their massive, complex civil service bureaucracies, maintain a strong level of control over their economies, and the direction and pace of change remains unpredictable.

Table 15.1 Changes in national regulations on FDI, 1992–2008

Item	1992	1993	1994	1995	1996	1997	1998	1999	2000	2001	2002	2003	2004	2005	2006	2007	2008
Number of countries that introduced changes	43	56	49	63	66	76	60	65	70	71	72	82	103	93	93	58	55
Number of regulatory changes of which:	77	100	110	112	114	150	145	139	150	207	246	242	270	205	184	98	110
More favorable to FDI	77	99	108	106	98	134	136	130	147	193	234	218	234	164	147	74	85
Less favorable to FDI	0	1	2	6	16	16	9	9	3	14	12	24	36	41	37	24	25

Source: UNCTAD, *World Investment Report 2009*, p. 31 (Geneva: UNCTAD, 2009).

E-resources: http://www.unctad.org/en/docs/wir2009_en.pdf.

The nature of political risk

We can examine political risk at two different levels, as seen in Figure 15.3.[4] Legal/governmental risks are potentially harmful to foreign businesses but are the product of, or permissible within, the existing political, economic, and legislative system. Non-legal or extra-governmental risks lie outside this system and are a violation of existing laws. Macro-level risks affect all foreign firms evenly, and micro-level risks harm individual or specific groups of firms.

Macro political risk

Macro political risk
A risk that affects all foreign enterprises in the same way

Expropriation
The governmental seizure of private businesses coupled with little, if any, compensation to their owners

Indigenization laws
Laws which require that nationals hold a majority interest in all enterprises

A **macro political risk** is one that affects all foreign enterprises in the same general way. **Expropriation**, the governmental seizure of private businesses coupled with little, if any, compensation to the owners, is an example of a macro political risk. Communist governments in Eastern Europe and China expropriated private firms following World War II. Fidel Castro did the same in Cuba from 1958 to 1959. In more recent years governments in Angola, Chile, Ethiopia, Peru, and Zimbabwe have expropriated private enterprises. In some cases this stems from **indigenization laws**, which require that nationals hold a majority interest in all enterprises. The privatization of a range of state-owned industries in Russia marked a turning point in that country's history. However, the corruption and racketeering that led to politically connected individuals building massive fortunes from, for example, the oil and aluminum industries may have triggered another turning point (see **Real Case: Yukos and the Russian oligarchs** in this chapter). The government has threatened to re-nationalize key industries.[5]

Macro political risk can also be the result of political boycotts. During the war in Iraq, following 9/11 in the United States, American consumers boycotted French imports and avoided holidaying in France because the French were unsupportive of the military invasion of Iraq.[6] In all these cases both large and small businesses feel the impact of the political decision.

Micro political risk

Micro political risk
A risk that affects selected sectors of the economy or specific foreign businesses

A **micro political risk** is one that affects selected sectors of the economy or specific foreign businesses. These risks are typically a result of government action in the form of industry regulation, taxes on specific types of business activity, and local content laws.

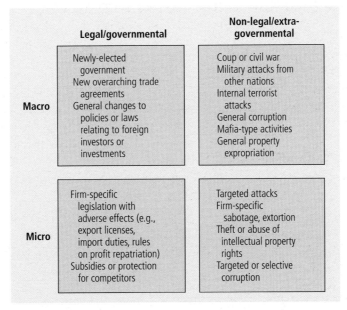

Figure 15.3 **Types and levels of political risk**

A number of factors help to determine the degree of micro political risk. One is the dominance of foreign firms or the growing competitiveness of their products in an industry. For example, small and medium-sized makers of precision tools for the electronics industry in the United States joined forces to lobby for higher tariffs on imports that compete with their products, including those made by large US firms offshore. Prompted by the growing trade deficit and job losses in manufacturing, they have used the National Association of Manufacturers to push the government to defy WTO regulations and protect their particular businesses by increasing specific tariffs.[7]

The end of the global textile quota system in January 2005 drastically changed the competitive environment for countries like Kenya and Pakistan. Under this system the United States and the European Union restricted textile imports according to their country of origin. This had the effect of partly protecting these countries from direct competition with countries like India and China, because they had a guaranteed volume of exports to the big markets. Up to 60 percent of Pakistan's annual export income came from the textile sector, which employed more than half of the country's industrial workforce, so this change has had a significant impact on its economy.[8]

This last example shows that some political risks are predictable and can be partly planned for. Others are not and tend to have a more significant effect. The changing priorities of governments, often swayed by powerful interest groups, are an important source of this kind of risk. As discussed below, governments have specific economic, social, and often military agendas, and changes in these will result in adjustments to the various levers that control trade and the activities of foreign investors.

Sources of political risk

There are a number of sources of political risk. Table 15.2 presents some important sources and their effects.

So a variety of motivations help to explain political risk. The MNE's challenge is to identify these motivations and then to decide how to manage them.

Table 15.2 Political risk: sources, agents, and effects

Sources of political risk	Groups that can generate political risk	Effects of political risk
Political philosophies that are changing or are in competition with each other	Current government and its various departments and agencies	Expropriation of assets (with or without compensation)
Changing economic conditions	Opposition groups in the government that are not in power but have political clout	Indigenization laws
Social unrest	Organized interest groups such as teachers, students, workers, retired persons, etc.	Restriction of operating freedom concerning, e.g., hiring policies and product manufacturing
Armed conflict or terrorism	Terrorist or anarchist groups operating in the country	Cancellation or revision of contracts
Rising nationalism	International organizations such as the World Bank or the United Nations	Damage to property and/or personnel from terrorism, riots, etc.
Impending or recent political independence	Foreign governments that have entered into international alliances with the country or that are supporting opposition to the government	Loss of financial freedom such as the ability to repatriate profits
Vested interests of local business groups	—	Increased taxes and other financial penalties
Competing religious groups	—	—
Newly created international alliances	—	—

COUNTRY ANALYSIS AND POLITICAL RISK ASSESSMENT

As described above, the PEST framework provides a simple way of mapping the pros and cons of foreign investment opportunities in particular countries for MNEs. There are many other analytical tools and techniques to measure the cost–benefit or risk–reward ratio for a specific investment proposition. These range from scenario planning, Delphi exercises, and multivariant risk analyses to simple observation. The degree to which companies actually use these techniques before investing abroad varies a great deal.

Small firms, especially owner-managed firms, often move from simple exporting to engage in FDI on the basis of the owner, CEO, or senior manager seeing an opportunity when on holiday in a foreign country! Little or no rigorous risk analysis or comparison of opportunities between countries is conducted, partly because it takes time and is expensive, but often because managers are unaware of the need for analysis and/or ignorant of the tools, techniques, and information resources that can help them make these decisions.[9] Most firms, however, will conduct some level of analysis to capture the likely costs and benefits and probable risks relating to a particular overseas investment.

There are many sources of information on the PEST conditions in different country markets for use in comparative risk analysis. Country risk rating services are provided by a range of agencies that produce general reports and may conduct specific analyses on behalf of client companies. Such agencies include the Bank of America World Information Services, the Business Environment Risk Intelligence (BERI) SA, the Control Risks Information Services (CRIS), the Economist Intelligence Unit (EIU), Standard and Poor's Ratings Group, the Political Risk Services (ICRG), and Moody's Investor Services.

BERI political risk services, for example, began in 1966 using 15 variables, such as bureaucratic delays, monetary inflation, and political stability, to "isolate to the degree possible the political process affecting business." It contained a weighting to emphasize certain criteria (such as political stability) over others in terms of their significance and impact. The sum of the weights was 25 and each of the 15 factors was then scored at four times its weight, so the highest possible points and lowest risk was 100. A global panel of experts (although US-based experts dominated) then assessed the score for each variable in a Delphi-style validation to help rank 40 to 50 countries according to the resulting consensus. Scores between 70 and 56 were defined as moderate risk, denoting overall stability despite the varied risk of complications that might affect day-to-day operations for businesses. Any country with a rating under 56 was considered unstable.

The FORCE Country Reports from BERI also provide a qualitative analysis of socio-political, economic, and financial forecasts. They include scenario analyses and so-called political, operations, and remittance/repatriation risk indices and profit opportunity recommendations (POR). The BERI risk measurement components include several categories of information, such as political factionalization, linguistic/ethnic/religious tension, coercive measures to maintain regime, prevalence of corruption, radical left strength, dependence on major external power, and so on.[10]

Online risk information resources

An increasing number of country rating and indexing schemes are available online. One of the best is the World Bank and IMF site (http://rru.worldbank.org/DoingBusiness/), which is a useful resource for off-the-shelf reports, such as *Doing Business* in country X this year. But it also allows users to create customized reports using an online database of indicators across 145 countries. This is linked to specialized topic areas covering practical guidelines for investing and managing in different countries, including Starting a

Business, Hiring and Firing Workers, Enforcing Contracts, Getting Credit, and Licensing and Inspections. The World Bank's Multilateral Investment Guarantee Agency (MIGA) is also a good source (http://miga.org) as are the following sites: http://www.countryrisk.com/; http://www.economist.com/countries; and http://www.worldbank.org/data/countrydata/countrydata.html.

One of the most widely used and well-respected sources of information is the Economist Intelligence Unit (EIU) (www.eiu.com). Alongside fairly general information it has a host of interactive services, most of which are for subscribers only. Its Risk Services site (http://www.eiuresources.com/ras/default.htm) provides free snapshots of risk ratings and currently shows Iraq, Zimbabwe, and Myanmar as the riskiest propositions globally and Singapore, Spain, and Hong Kong at the top of its list. The EIU site also describes some of the indicators and the methodology underlying its Country Risk Service.

The Fraser Institute, with its very overt political view, compiles the Index of Economic Freedom (http://www.fraserinstitute.ca and http://www.freetheworld.com/). This compares 23 components across seven areas (economic structures, monetary policy, etc.) to measure the degree to which host-country institutional arrangements and policies intervene in or influence the operation of the economy. It also attempts to assess how predictable these arrangements and policies are and therefore how important they are as a source of market uncertainty.

PricewaterhouseCoopers (PwC) compiles an opacity index, which is closer to the kinds of analyses that examine non-legal activities by governments that might influence or intervene in business (http://www.opacity-index.com). This measures the impact of business, economic, legal, and ethical opacity on the cost of capital around the world.

Finally, as an indication of the importance of these kinds of analyses, the World Economic Forum (WEF) has developed a Public Institutions Index as an input for its overall annual global competitiveness ranking (http://www.weforum.org/). This index comprises a Contracts and Law subindex (covering judicial independence, property rights, organized crime, favoritism in government decision making) and a Corruption subindex (including irregular payments for imports and exports, tax collection, and public utilities). The Public Institutions Index for Africa, for example, rates Botswana top and Chad bottom of a list of 21 African countries. This ranking is one factor influencing the overall attractiveness and competitiveness of each country.

Quantifying risk vulnerability

As shown by the above risk ratings services, all risk is relative. Measuring risk therefore involves comparing options, one investment proposition against another. This means combining investment appraisal and country appraisal techniques. There are factors that may be more important for one kind of investment than another. So a production plant will have different requirements than a distribution or marketing operation, or an offshore IT service office, for example. Therefore different risk criteria are more or less relevant at the country level. Table 15.3 shows the **Weighted Country Risk Assessment Model** for combining both.

Weighted Country Risk Assessment Model
Combines an investment project appraisal with country risk analysis

Two different country cases (A and B) are compared using 30 different criteria; 15 are political in nature and 15 are economic, although many of the latter are also directly or indirectly influenced by the governments. The Risk column gives a rating (1 is low risk; 5 is high) comparing Country A and Country B on this criterion and can represent either a direct comparison (for example, high or low current disposable income levels) or a risk measure—the potential for change that would harm the investment proposed (for example, the likelihood that disposable income levels will fall significantly in the future). So, for example, Country A is rated as more politically stable than B and has a lower likelihood of internal conflicts, more predictable policies, a more stable tax and tariff regime, and fewer

Table 15.3 The Weighted Country Risk Assessment Model

		Selected criteria	Country A Risk (5 = High)	Country A Importance (5 = High)	Country A Combined score (/ 25)	Country B Risk (5 = High)	Country B Importance (5 = High)	Country B Combined score (/25)
Political environment	1	Stability of the local political system	2	4	8	4	4	16
	2	Likelihood of internal conflict	1	4	4	4	4	16
	3	External threats to stability	3	3	9	3	3	9
	4	Harmful Government intervention in the economic system	1	4	4	4	4	16
	5	Reliability of the country as a trading partner	3	4	12	3	4	12
	6	Policy continuity/predictability	2	5	10	4	5	20
	7	Stability of tax and tariff regime	1	4	4	3	4	12
	8	Effectiveness of public administration	2	3	6	3	3	9
	9	Prevalence of corruption	1	3	3	5	3	15
	10	Bureaucratic delays	1	4	4	5	4	20
	11	Enforceability of contracts	2	4	8	4	4	16
	12	Corporate governance and ethics legislation	3	2	6	4	2	8
	13	Labour unions and labour relations	3	5	15	3	5	15
	14	Linguistic/ethnic/religious tensions	2	1	2	3	1	3
	15	Social stability	2	2	4	3	2	6
International economic environment	16	Import restrictions	4	4	16	4	4	16
	17	Export restrictions	3	5	15	3	5	15
	18	Attitudes towards foreign investors	2	3	6	3	3	9
	19	Respect for intellectual property rights (patents, brands)	2	4	8	5	4	20
	20	Restrictions on monetary transfers	3	5	15	3	5	15
	21	Revaluation of the currency during the last 5 years	3	2	6	4	2	8
	22	Balance of payments situation	2	2	4	2	2	4
Domestic economic environment	23	Per capita income	3	1	3	3	1	3
	24	Economic growth over the last 5 years	2	1	2	4	1	4
	25	Potential growth over the next 3 years	2	1	2	2	1	2
	26	Inflation over the past 2 years	3	3	9	4	3	12
	27	Accessibility of domestic capital markets to outsiders	2	4	8	2	4	8
	28	Availability of high-quality local labor force	2	5	10	2	5	10
	29	Availability of energy resources	2	4	8	2	4	8
	30	Infrastructure; transportation and communication systems	3	4	12	3	4	12
		TOTALS	67	100	223	101	100	339

Sources: The approach and the items in the table draw from prior risk assessment models and studies, including D. W. Conklin, "Analyzing and Managing Country Risks," *Ivey Business Journal*, vol. 66, no. 3 (January/February 2002), pp. 36–42; S. T. Cavusgil, "Measuring the Potential of Emerging Markets: An Indexing Approach," *Business Horizons*, vol. 40, no. 1 (1997); A. I. J. Dyck, *Country Analysis* (Boston, MA: Harvard Business School Press, 1997); E. Dichtl and H. G. Köglmayr, "Country Risk Ratings," *Management International Review*, vol. 26, no. 4 (1986), pp. 4–12. This latest version of the framework benefited from the advice and feedback of Dr. Derek Condon, Senior Teaching Fellow, Warwick Business School.

(less likelihood of) bureaucratic delays. Economically the two countries are a little more similar, although Country A, for example, clearly rates higher in terms of upholding intellectual property rights, so there is less risk of breaches of copyright, patents, or brands. They have fairly similar domestic economic environments in terms of the listed criteria, with Country A having experienced better growth in the past five years, but expecting the same growth prospects as B for the next three years. This relative country rating across the three categories is summarized by the totals at the foot of the table: 67 for Country A and 101 for Country B.

The Importance column rates each of the same 30 criteria in terms of relevance to the kind of investment proposed. This example has been designed to reflect an overseas investment for a production facility, mainly for exports. Criteria such as export restrictions, the availability of high-quality labor, the stability of taxes and tariffs, policy continuity, bureaucratic delays, and enforceability of contracts, for example, are considered important (rating 5 or 4). Economic growth and per capita income, for example, are considered less important. These would be important if we were considering a sales and distribution operation for consumer products, for example. As this illustration shows a country comparison, not a comparison of different types of investment, the Importance columns for Country A and Country B are identical. If we were to compare types of investment, we would change the ranking of the various criteria (between 1 and 5), but the total for this column would still need to add to 100, otherwise the weighting method would not work. In this case we would simply be changing the *relative* importance of different risk factors to suit a different type of investment proposition.

The combined score weights each country criteria according to respective importance to the type of investment under consideration, and the combined totals provide an overall comparison of the two countries. The higher the final score the riskier the combination of investment and location. Country A, with 223 out of a possible 500 appears to be a better option for this kind of investment than Country B with 339.

Table 15.3 presents a fairly basic example. The list of criteria can be changed and extended to far more than 30 and sub-criteria (for example, different kinds of bureaucratic delays under item 10) can be added. The balance among political, economic, social, technological, or legal criteria can also be altered according to the investment proposition and/or the countries to be considered. We could also use a different Likert scale, such as from 1 to 10 rather than 1 to 5. The model can be extended to compare more than two country cases. For any extension of the model it is important to remember that the ratings are *relative*. For example, the above-mentioned BERI political risk ratings show Zimbabwe as riskier than Peru. We might give the former 5 for some of the political criteria in the Risk column and the latter a comparative 2 or 3. If we were to add Sweden to the comparison, the rating in the Risk column would need to reflect the change, perhaps by giving Zimbabwe and Peru 5 in some categories and Sweden 1. So the rating scores are not absolute. They depend on the country comparison being made.

Note that this model only provides a summary framework for estimating relative country risk. In practice it will only reflect the intelligence that goes into the relative risk ratings. A thorough and rigorous analysis of all the factors that underlie even the limited number of 30 criteria in Table 15.3, in terms of both current and future investment conditions is not easy. In some cases quantitative data are available, including from some of the agencies and sources listed above. For other criteria, such as political stability or the likely impact of corruption, there is no such thing as perfect information, and assumptions, estimates, and some subjective guesswork are always necessary. However, the better the expertise, information, and experience that can be leveraged to make such assessments, whether from inside or outside the firm, the more accurate the relative final scores are going to be.

What the model also helps decision makers do is identify the kinds of risks they may be able to reduce, adapt to, prepare for, or guard against prior to or following an investment. Knowing which sources of risk you can influence, and which you cannot, puts you in a better position to manage a market-entry strategy. Negotiating with government agencies, customs officials, or local unions; establishing alliances with local recruitment agencies or banks; or generally developing networks of local contacts and advisors can all help monitor and alleviate some of these risks and are essential.

In practice, a common problem is for managers to fail to consider the full range of country risks that might affect an investment or to make uninformed assumptions in their appraisal. A project team responsible for capital budgeting in an accounting or finance department of a firm may not know a great deal about different country conditions. Project investment models and financial scenarios may be transferred with a range of built-in assumptions that can hide additional costs or risks from the appraisal. For example, differences in labor rates are a key driver for the movement of manufacturing plants and for offshoring. Many companies build in the reduced labor cost, which makes savings and resulting profits look impressive, but assume similar levels of productivity and transactions costs for the new overseas operation. The additional costs and risks may become more obvious over time, with experience, and profit can quickly turn to loss. This has happened to some of the large numbers of companies that have outsourced parts of their IT and back-office operations to India, for example.[11] So how can we build country risk analysis into our financial planning tools?

Accounting for country risk

International managers can incorporate elements of the above kinds of risk analysis into financial appraisal models when considering FDI. A five-year ROI (Return on Investment) or ROA (Return on Assets) model should take account of a range of risks as an input into financial estimates of costs and revenue. This enables a more realistic comparison between countries as locations for various kinds of investment. Although never perfect, because we have incomplete information about the past and present, and it is impossible to accurately forecast the future, this can still help decision makers build better estimations. They can develop a better understanding about the likely impact of certain events or changes on specific investment propositions; they can compare investment propositions across different country contexts; and they can revise estimates for investment returns on the basis of this kind of analysis.

Companies that try to incorporate risk estimation in financial appraisals tend to build on standard financial models at the project level. The most common work on the basis of net present value (NPV), ROI, or internal rate of return (IRR) calculations, and these can incorporate country risks in a number of ways. A common approach is to increase the hurdle rate for ROI at the pre-project consideration stage, which will deselect the riskiest propositions. The hurdle rate is the set rate of financial return over a period of time that covers both project costs and the cost of the capital needed for the investment. Companies or business units will often have a set rate of return below which they will not invest. A simple rule of thumb would be to increase the rate of return in line with the additional risks associated with locating the investment in a particular country, compared to another.

Also common is to adjust the cash flows of the project to reflect the potential impact of a particular event on the value of the project. So, for example, if policy changes that will lead to an increase in tax rates, import duties, or labor costs are likely, this risk needs to be built into the long-run calculation of the break-even point of an investment. There is a probability that costs will rise and net revenues will decline so this can be built into a five- or six-year forecast for an investment. The term **adjusted present value** (APV) is sometimes used to denote an NPV that takes into account the riskiness of the project's expected future cash flows.

Adjusted present value (APV)
An NPV that takes into account sources of country risk that might impact a project's expected future cash flows

More sophisticated techniques for accounting for country risk have been developed. Some firms attempt to place specific probabilities on certain events taking place and calculate the direct cost implications for the project. This approach works well as an extension of the above country risk assessment model, but again relies on accurate information and intelligence to derive realistic probabilities. If political analysts estimate that there is, say, a 20 percent chance that the government of a particular developing country will change in the next three years resulting in a radical change in policies toward foreign investors, this risk can be reflected in a higher hurdle rate for the APV and an alternative location for the investment might look more promising. This kind of approach is often termed *sensitivity analysis* and can be combined with formal *scenario analyses*. More sophisticated real-options analyses might attempt to calculate relative costs and benefits of, for example, closing a facility, moving it to another country, scaling down operations, or continuing in the face of a significant economic or political shock.

✔ Active learning check

Review your answer to Active Learning Case question 2 and make any changes you like. Then compare your answer to the one below.

2 **What kinds of political risk did Kodak face and how did it attempt to mitigate these risks?**

There were a range of uncertainties facing Kodak, from the macro to the micro, stemming from the ways that government agencies intervened both legally and illegally in the operations of foreign firms in China. From the start it was clear that top-level negotiations were going to be required to secure the kind of joint-venture arrangements needed both to establish a significant production operation and to exclude rival Fuji from the same access. George Fisher's direct connections with the most senior political figure of the time, Zhu Rongji, could have been the key that unlocked doors all the way down the central and regional bureaucracies. This well-publicized, high-level support also helped mitigate against discrimination and corruption at the lower levels, since the deal had the backing (and the attention) of senior officials in Beijing (and the United States). Kodak still had to make a range of payments and gestures of good citizenship to appease the powerful local constituencies in the places where it invested. In the years following the investment, various changes in policy and in the networks of power undoubtedly meant that at various levels Kodak has had to continue "smoothing the way" just like any other firm in China. Beyond these more predictable risks, there were, and always will be, highly uncertain and uncontrollable kinds of risks, such as widespread social unrest or large-scale political upheaval, which even powerful firms such as Kodak can do little to influence.

These techniques not only alert managers to relative sources of risk when comparing investment propositions, but also can help develop strategies to reduce risk. In the case of the developing country where the change of political party is likely to adversely affect foreign investors, this may lead to political lobbying by foreign firms with investments at risk. It also leads, unfortunately, to MNEs actively intervening in unethical ways in the national politics of smaller nations to secure their interests.

NEGOTIATION STRATEGIES

There are two key steps in developing effective negotiating strategies. First, MNE managers need to evaluate their own position and that of the other group(s) in order to determine how the interests of both can fit together. Second, they need to understand the "modus operandi" of the other groups: who has the power to make what kinds of decisions and what negotiating style are they likely to adopt?

Earlier in this chapter we discussed how widespread deregulation and liberalization were opening up emerging markets, like China and India, to foreign investors. Central and regional government agencies still maintain a strong control over these economies and the rules of engagement for foreign investors, so it is imperative that MNE managers understand: (1) their political, economic, and social policy objectives; (2) their levers of power, the mechanisms by which they can influence the costs and benefits of doing business (taxes, tariffs, quotas, regulations on capital transfers, local input requirements, etc.); (3) the structures, networks, and institutional agencies through which they operate (who has the power to influence what?); and (4) their negotiation style and tactics. These represent the why's and how's of government intervention in market forces, and firms have to adapt to these to improve their chances of investment success.

Figure 15.4 depicts the interplay among: (1) the elements that attract multinational firms to a particular region, which have been discussed throughout this text (central column); (2) the strategic aims of MNEs; and (3) some general policy aims of governments.

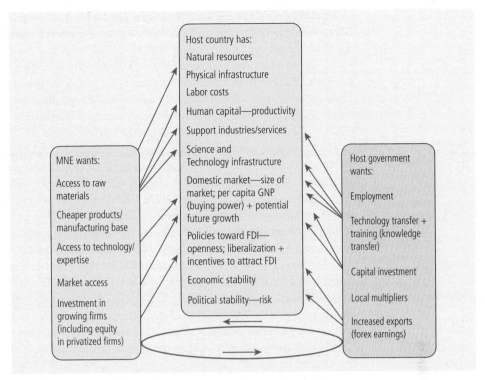

Figure 15.4 FDI drivers: the strategic objectives of MNEs, host-country attractiveness, and host-government requirements

MNE objectives may or may not fit with government aims and this will affect the investment decision.

Taking this a step further, the most effective negotiation strategies are those that incorporate (1) the relevant risk criteria in Table 15.3 that can be influenced through negotiation, (2) the evolving government policy priorities, and (3) the appropriate government agencies, local organizations, and key individuals who should be approached. This helps reduce the risk or increase the potential rewards from cross-border investments. If energy resources are important for a large-scale manufacturing facility, can local authorities guarantee energy supplies at a particular cost over a particular period in return for the plant being located in their region? If labor costs are an important factor, can these be fixed for a period of time through negotiations with local trade unions?

Negotiations between MNEs and national governments or local organizations are a two-way bargaining process where each party has something the other wants. We can identify power resources or bargaining chips held by MNEs looking to invest globally on the one hand and by the governments of host countries on the other. Governments look for inflows of capital and technology, for large local employers, and for access, via MNEs, to overseas markets to boost exports and foreign exchange reserves. To get these they leverage their attractiveness, which may consist of large or growing domestic markets, natural resources, cheap or productive labor, and economic and political stability to which they may add specific incentives, such as tax breaks or higher levels of foreign ownership or profit repatriation than normally allowed.

The bargaining strength of both firms and governments is limited by the degree of competition. If other MNEs offering similar levels of capital investment, employment, or technology exist, the negotiating position of one MNE is weakened. If other regions offer cheaper labor, more economic or political stability, or better incentives to foreign investors, the negotiating position of the government is weakened.

The bargaining strengths for an MNE may come from its technology, products, services, managerial expertise, and capital. For example, when General Motors sets up a new operation in Mexico, the company invests capital, uses modern technology to build the autos, and employs managerial expertise in getting the operation off and running. When the Hilton Corporation builds a new hotel in Germany, it invests capital, employs managerial expertise, and offers a variety of world-class hospitality services to the guests. MNEs also hire local personnel, stimulate the economy, and in industries such as manufacturing, textiles, and mining help to generate exports for the country.

The bargaining strengths of the country will include such factors as large consumer markets, economic and political stability, sources of capital, tax breaks, and an appropriate labor force. The United States, for example, offers all these strengths to MNEs. As a result, the bargaining position of foreign MNEs vis-à-vis the US government is diminished. This is in comparison to the situation faced by companies looking to set up operations in less developed countries where the latter have a weak bargaining position because of their small consumer market, political instability, and/or financial strength.

Other parties involved in a negotiation will also have specific strengths. For example, in many cases a local partner knows the market and has conducted business there for years. This makes the partner valuable to the MNE. Other contributions of local partners can include capital, a well-trained workforce, factories or retail outlets for moving the goods to the customer, and government contractors who can help to eliminate red tape.

Other parties to the transaction can include stockholders or other interest groups that monitor the company's operations. During the 1980s many MNEs stopped doing business in South Africa because of pressure from these investor groups (see the case **International Business Strategy in Action: Political risk for De Beers**). Companies involved in manufacturing war material, producing chemicals, and building nuclear energy plants have also come under investor and social pressure. MNEs may also encounter complaints from partners in other joint ventures who feel that this latest investment will negatively affect their current venture.[12]

The membership of the WTO and various trading blocs around the world, particularly the EU and NAFTA, directly affect the degree to which national governments *can* intervene in trade and FDI. Governments in emerging markets and developing countries have more direct influence over the running of the economy and the rules and regulations governing trade and investment. However, once they have joined the WTO (as China did in 2001) their use of legislation governing foreign equity participation, profit repatriation, cross-border M&A, and local content rules, as well as tax and investment incentives, becomes more restricted. At this stage, though, and in the foreseeable future for such countries, a higher level of direct control over the economy and foreign relations represents a significant influence over the ever-changing opportunities and risks for investors.

Finally, individual politicians and civil servants in less developed countries are able to use their own influence more effectively to block or to facilitate a particular MNE investment. This is partly due to the higher level of government control over the economy and individual businesses, but also because of the relative lack of legal or institutional recourse to challenge government actions. Couple this with the fact that salaries for government officials and bureaucrats in poorer countries tend to be very low and you get an insight into why corruption is so much more prevalent in developing countries, as discussed in the following section.

Behavioral characteristics of the participants in negotiations

When it comes to the actual process of cross-border negotiations there is a range of cultural, behavioral, and tactical differences between groups that international managers need to understand if they are to negotiate effectively.

Political risk for De Beers

With an estimated $7 billion in 2011, Nicky Oppenheimer is one of the richest people in Africa, the world's poorest continent. His family still owns nearly half of De Beers and a sizable piece of Anglo American, another mining giant with interests in gold, platinum, construction, and forestry. De Beers is 45 percent owned by the mining company Anglo American, while South Africa's Oppenheimer family owns 40 percent. The government in Botswana owns the remaining 15 percent.

The De Beers name is synonymous with diamonds. Established in 1888 in Johannesburg, South Africa, it is the largest mining company in the world. It recently reported earnings of $483 million. But De Beers once controlled (not directly mined) about 80 percent of the world supply of rough stones. The De Beers Groups Diamond Trading Company (DTC), formerly the Central Selling Organization (CSO), maintained a cartel for limiting supply and driving up prices. Competitors have reduced this share by challenging its single-channel distribution system and by developing other sources of diamonds outside of its control. In Canada, Australia, and Russia rival mining firms like BHP Billiton, Rio Tinto, and Alrosa have found huge deposits of lucrative stones and developed new technologies to mine them efficiently. As recently as 1998 De Beers' share was down to around 65 percent, and today production from its own mines gives it just a 45 percent share. Add to this its contract to sell Russian stones and its overall market share is around 55 percent, in a global market for rough diamonds worth about $8 billion.

In 2009, De Beers announced plans to raise up to $1bn (£607m) from investors. The rights issue was designed to help reduce the company's debts, which currently totaled $3.5bn. The move came at the end of a bad year for De Beers, which saw first-half profits fall by 99 percent as a result of a collapse in the price of diamonds. Falling demand for diamonds forced De Beers mines in South Africa, Botswana, and Canada to take production holidays earlier in 2009.

De Beers faces a range of political risks. It is under threat from anti-globalization and ethical business groups for its involvement in civil wars in Sierra Leone, Angola, and Congo. It is also facing potentially damaging political and governance changes in South Africa, including calls to re-nationalize and/or place into "black hands" a range of natural resource-based industries including mineral mining. More worrying for the Oppenheimers is a legal campaign by activists who want reparations from firms that worked in apartheid South Africa. This is not currently being supported by South Africa's government, but this may change. De Beers has some leverage since its operations have resulted in lucrative and stable tax revenues for the South African government, as well as for Botswana, Namibia, and Tanzania.

It has also built more stable relationships with some governments through joint ventures and cross-shareholdings. Debswana, for example, is jointly owned (50–50) by De Beers and the Botswana government. It supports local supplier development and training programs, as well as boosting the country's diamond exports (which account for four-fifths of total exports). The Botswana government currently owns 15 percent of De Beers.

The firm has been trying to cope with other sources of political risk, hindering its expansion into the end-consumer markets of the triad for some time. De Beers was banned from directly entering the US market because of an antitrust legal ruling that sees it as a monopoly. Under the CSO, the group's market dominance had allowed it to manipulate market prices by accumulating inventory. De Beers is allowed to operate in the EU, but has faced anti-competition action, particularly in relation to its Russian and East European operations. A major watershed occurred in 2004 as De Beers finally pleaded guilty to charges of price fixing of industrial diamonds in an Ohio court and agreed to pay a $10 million fine, thereby ending a 60-year-long lock-out of the US market. De Beers is now working directly in the largest diamond market, the United States. This might help it further leverage its recent partnership with luxury products firm LVMH to sell De Beers-brand diamonds.

Websites: www.billionaires.forbes.com/topic/Nicky_Oppenheimer; www.debeersgroup.com; www.lvmh.com; www.adiamondisforever.com.

Sources: UNCTAD, *World Investment Report 2007: Transnational corporations, the extractive industries and development* (Geneva: UNCTAD, 2007), http://unctad. org; "The Cartel Isn't for Ever," *The Economist*, July 17, 2004; T. Buck and N. Innocenti, "De Beers Offer Set to End EU Probe," *Financial Times*, December 21, 2004; "South Africa's Cuban Missile," *The Economist*, August 9, 2003; R. Smith, "Diamond's Are Not Forever," BBC.com, July 26, 2001; "De Beer's Worst Friend," *The Economist*, August 20, 1998; "De Beers sells diamond mine for $210m," *BBC News*, January 21, 2011, http://www.bbc.co.uk/news; "De Beers plans $1bn rights issue to cut debt," *BBC News*, December 1, 2009, http://news.bbc.co.uk.

Cultural differences

Although the objective of the negotiation process may be universal (strike as good a deal as possible), the way in which the process is carried out will be greatly influenced by the cultural values and norms of the participants. Many of the following observations build on Chapter 5, which examines cultural differences between people from different countries around the world.

> ## ✔ Active learning check
>
> *Review your answer to Active Learning Case question 3 and make any changes you like. Then compare your answer to the one below.*
>
> **❸** **What did both sides, Kodak and the Chinese government, gain from the deal?**
>
> Many of the clues to answering this question lie in the answers to question 1 and question 2. The timing of Kodak's investment suited the Chinese government in a number of ways. Zhu Rongji was leading a massive process of liberalization and deregulation across the economy as part of the shift toward a free market system. In the time leading up to Kodak's entry, 300,000 firms were privatized, resulting in an increase in unemployment and some degree of social unrest. The Chinese government needed foreign firms to provide employment and new sources of income through capital investment. The government's economic development plans also highlighted the need for technology transfer and training to improve China's capacity to create technologically sophisticated, higher-value manufactured products. Finally, the failure of many local firms, many of them recently privatized, had pushed local and some national banks into debt. Foreign capital was needed to maintain the pace of investment.
>
> Kodak offered all of this. In return it wanted and gained exclusive access to produce locally, avoiding the tariff barriers; experienced local managers and engineers from the film-manufacturing sector, as well as low-cost employees; land, facilities, and infrastructure; and help with the complicated local rules and regulations, permissions, and licenses required to establish any operation in China. As a result, Kodak's market share has grown impressively since its investment and China continues to thrive (to date).

Commenting on the difference between Arab and US negotiators, one group of researchers noted:

> [Arabs] treat deadlines as only general guidelines for wrapping up negotiations. They tend to open negotiations with an extreme initial position. However, the Arabs believe strongly in making concessions, they do so throughout the bargaining process, and they almost always reciprocate an opponent's concessions. They also seek to build a long-term relationship with their bargaining partners. For these reasons, Americans typically find it easier to negotiate with Arabs than with representatives from many other regions of the world.

One of the major differences is the amount of authority that the negotiator has to approve an agreement. In some societies, such as the United States and UK, negotiators are given authority to make deals or at least to express agreement on the basic arrangement that is being negotiated. This approach works well when doing business with many Western firms, as well as with Chinese negotiators. However, it is often of limited value when dealing with people from other cultures. In fact, the other parties may not have the authority to give the go-ahead on anything. For example, Japanese and Russian negotiators are often lower-level personnel who are not authorized to approve agreements. This can be frustrating to Americans who feel that they are wasting their time. The lack of face-to-face interaction with those who will be making the final decision can be unsettling. On the other hand, many foreign negotiators use this ploy because they have learned that it often leads to greater concessions from US business people, who become anxious to sign a deal and thus are more flexible on terms. These are some of the issues that Dell's decision makers needed to consider when they approached potential business partners in Latin America (see **International Business Strategy in Action: Dell goes to Brazil**).

INTERNATIONAL BUSINESS STRATEGY IN ACTION

Dell goes to Brazil

In the late 1990s Dell examined the opportunities and risks of investing in Latin America. It was looking to replicate not just its direct sales activities but the whole of its "build to order" (BTO) model to serve the Latin American market.

At that time, Dell was growing faster than most other *Fortune* Global 500 firms and was rated as the number one performing stock in the Standard and Poor's 500 for that decade. It was selling PCs globally, manufacturing in Xiamen, China, Penang, Malaysia, and Limerick, Ireland, as well as in the United States. However, despite its 20 percent share of the US market, in the large and growing Latin American market it trailed behind Compaq (22 percent share and 36 percent growth rate), IBM, HP, and several others. Dell ranked ninth and had barely 1.2 percent of the market.

One of the reasons for this was that Latin American consumers did not adopt the Internet as fast as US consumers making it difficult for Dell to implement the direct marketing strategy that had worked so well in other markets. Instead, consumers ordered Dell computers via a toll-free number and the company shipped the product from its manufacturing facilities in Texas.

Dell sought to turn this around by changing its Latin American strategy. The major aims were to establish market leadership by taking advantage of the rise in Internet penetration in Latin America to increase sales from 80,000 units to 800,000 units in five years and to manufacture locally to avoid excessive import duties (an estimated 30 percent) and transport and logistics costs. Not only did prospective market growth look healthy, with demand for PCs rising, but the growing use of the Internet and increasing propensity for Latin Americans to buy online suited Dell's model. Brazil was seen as the best place to locate Dell's Latin American activities. It represented the largest country market in its own right, with one-fifth of the population in the middle or upper middle-class income bracket and the recent appearance of free ISPs to encourage use of the Internet. For investing in production it had a central location, educated labor force, and government incentives for high-technology FDI. Moreover, PCs produced in Brazil could be exported without tariff to other Mercosur countries, which include Argentina, Uruguay, and Paraguay.

Chile was considered as an alternative. But by comparison it had a more expensive (though on average better educated) labor force, fewer local suppliers, a higher level of local competition (relative to the size of the domestic market),

similar government incentives to invest but a higher degree of political instability and a smaller local market.

But there were also risks, many of them macro-level risks shared with any other MNE looking to invest in Brazil. These included political instability regarding FDI regulations, tariff barriers, labor regulations, and economic instability regarding inflation and possible currency devaluation. Further uncertainties would affect Dell more directly. Shipping and distribution infrastructure was weak and there were also some reasonably strong, local, low-cost PC producers that may have reacted strongly to new entrants (IBM and HP already operated at that time in Brazil). It was also difficult to assess the skill and capabilities of the local workforce not only for manufacturing, but also for sales and after-sales service, which were key elements of Dell's direct model.

In 1999 Dell opened an assembly plant in Eldorado do Sul, Brazil. In retrospect we know that both the global economic and competitive macro environment and the country-level environment in Brazil went through some turbulent changes after 1998 that would have been very difficult to predict, regardless of which of the country risk analysis techniques Dell had applied. The removal of many non-tariff import barriers in Brazil worked against the investment decision. However, market analysis shows that local competitors have done very well, regardless of Dell's investment. In 2000 Latin America's top five—Compaq, Dell, HP, IBM, and Acer—all lost market share. The firms not in the top five saw market share increase from 50 to 59 percent, and local firms, such as Itautec and Metron from Brazil and Mexico's Alaska, performed even better. Other events, such as the 1999 currency (real) devaluation, high interest rates, the energy crisis, and the knock-on effects of the Argentinean financial crisis in 2001, followed by a general economic slowdown, all added complexity and further uncertainty after the investment had been made. By 2006, however, things looked well, the company was expanding into Hortolandia, São Paulo, by building a state-of-the-art plant. This has since enabled Dell to capture a better percentage of the growing market for IT hardware and software.

Globally Dell's revenues have maintained remarkable growth, reaching $61 billion in 2011. Of this, 52 percent is generated from the United States and 48 percent from foreign countries. In terms of assets, 73 percent of total companies assets are in the United States and 27 percent in foreign countries. The growth was particularly strong

▶

in the BRIC countries—Brazil, Russia, India, and China—where revenues increased by 21 percent. They now represent almost one dollar in every seven Dell makes. Growth in Europe and the Americas lagged behind at 3 percent.

This is particularly important in light of future forecasts which show that emerging markets overall (including these key Latin American countries) will be responsible for two-thirds of the growth in the industry in the coming years. Dell needs to work out a better way of getting a bigger piece of this particular pie.

Website: http://www.dell.com.

Sources: K. Kraemer and J. Dedrick, *Dell Computer: Organization of a Global Production Network* (Irvine, CA: Center for Research on Information Technology and Organizations (CRITO), 2002), http://www.crito.uci.edu/GIT/publications/pdf/dell.pdf; S. Yates, "Sizing the Emerging-Nation PC Market," *Forrester Market Analysis*, 2004, http://www.forrester.com/Research/Document/Excerpt/0,7211,34889,00.html; Gartner Research, "Gartner Says Strong Notebook Sales Helped Drive Latin American PC Market to an 8 Percent Increase in 2003," 2004, http://www4.gartner.com/press_releases/pr25feb2004b.html; Dell, *Annual Report*, 2011; "Dell Opens Exemplary Plant in Hortolandia," *Dell.com*, May 14, 2007; "Dell Shares Rise 12% After Profits Almost Treble," *BBC News*, February 16, 2011, http://www.bbc.co.uk/news.

Another cultural difference in negotiating style is the objective of the negotiators. As the typologies in chapter 5 show, American, German, and British managers, for example, tend to be very practical and to focus on short-term results. Negotiators from the Far East tend to move more slowly, like to get to know the other party, and have a more long-run focus. Gift giving, social custom, and certain rituals can play an important part in negotiations and are part of the initial process of developing trust and mutual respect.[13]

Language is also a key factor. When negotiators do not speak the same language and must use interpreters, there are more chances for a misinterpretation or misunderstanding to occur. This problem also exists in written communications. Schermerhorn, for example, has found that, when documents are translated from one language to another and then translated back to check for accuracy, there are interpretation problems.[14] The original translation appears to convey the desired information, but, when another person is called in to translate the document back into the original language, some parts of it are different from that intended initially.

A related cultural problem is the use of written documents. In some countries a written document is used as a basis for establishing what is to be done. As a result, the document is detailed and factual. In Germany it will be precise and technical, in the United States it will be legalistic. In other countries, however, a written document is viewed as the basis for a general agreement and the parties then negotiate the implementation as they go along. Chinese and other Far East negotiators often view detailed contracts as a sign of distrust and believe a more open-ended agreement should be used.

Acceptance zones

Acceptance zone
An area within which a party is willing to negotiate

Each party to a negotiation will have an **acceptance zone** or an area within which it is willing to negotiate. For example, if Anheuser-Busch InBev, Begium (InBev acquired Anheuser-Busch in 2008) wants to buy a brewery in Düsseldorf, Germany, the Begium MNE will determine three prices: the highest price it is willing to pay, the price it would like to pay, and the offer at which it will begin the bargaining. For purposes of illustration, assume that Anheuser-Busch InBev, Begium is willing to pay up to €25 million for the company but hopes to make the acquisition for €23 million and intends to start the negotiation at €20 million.

Will Anheuser-Busch InBev be successful? This depends on the acceptance zone of the Düsseldorf brewer. If the company will not sell for less than €27.5 million, there will be no deal because the buyer's maximum offer is less than the seller's minimum acceptance. However, assume that the German firm will not sell for less than €21 million, would like to get €24 million, and intends to start the negotiation at €28 million. In this case the two sides should be able to strike a deal since they have overlapping zones of acceptance, as illustrated in Figure 15.5.

Notice from Figure 15.5 that, when the acceptance zones of the two parties overlap, there is common ground for negotiating. Additionally, keep in mind that, if the zones do

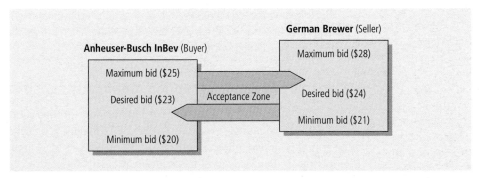

Figure 15.5 Zones of acceptance in the negotiating process (in millions of US $)

not overlap, negotiations will not always end in a stalemate. After listening to each other the parties may agree to change their respective bids and offers, adjust the acceptance zones, and end up with common negotiating ground.

In the case of Figure 15.5 the two parties would eventually negotiate within a range of $21 million (the least amount the seller will take) and $25 million (the most the buyer will pay). It is not possible to say what the final price will be because this will depend on how willing each side is to concede ground to the other. However, whatever the final price, the seller is going to get at least the desired minimum and the buyer will not pay more than the established maximum.

Bargaining tactics

Negotiators use a range of bargaining tactics, including promises, threats, rewards, commitments, and the use of self-disclosure, in their drive for a better deal. Some of these are also linked to different cultural characteristics, as shown in Table 15.4. Keeping silent is a standard Japanese practice when negotiating with each other as well as with foreigners. Table 15.4 shows that each group of Japanese, American, and Brazilian negotiators has a series of behaviors that make it different from the other two. For example, the Japanese like to make recommendations, the Americans make wide use of promises, and the Brazilians rely heavily on self-disclosure.[15]

Table 15.4 Twelve examples of the differences in verbal behaviors among Japanese, American, and Brazilian negotiators

Behavior (description)	Number of times behavior was used in a 30-minute negotiating session by members of each group		
	Japanese	American	Brazilian
1 Making promises	7	8	3
2 Making threats	4	4	2
3 Making recommendations	7	4	5
4 Giving warnings	2	1	1
5 Offering rewards	1	2	2
6 Making commitments	15	13	8
7 Asking questions	20	20	22
8 Giving commands	8	6	14
9 Revealing personal information about oneself	34	36	39
10 Making a first offer	61.5	57.3	75.2
11 Granting initial concessions	6.5	7.1	9.4
12 Using the word "no"	5.7	9.0	83.4

Source: Adapted from John L. Graham (1985) "The Influence of Culture on the Process of Business Negotiations: An Exploratory Study," *Journal of International Business Studies*, Spring, p. 88, Palgrave Macmillan. Reproduced with permission of Palgrave Macmillan.

These behaviors and tactics are often used in international negotiations. Effective negotiators learn how to use them and how to counteract their use by the opposition. Some examples are provided in the next section.

Transparency and corruption: politically sensitive political risk

One of the most difficult aspects of foreign business for international managers is how to cope with corruption. A very large number of firms engage in bribery of various kinds, but the ethical issues are not straightforward. In many cases they argue that to opt out would simply mean they lose out to less ethically minded competitors. In other cases it is genuinely difficult to know whether such practices are simply the accepted local rules of the game. In the UK an extra payment to rail companies buys you a better seat on the train in a less crowded compartment. This is called "First Class." In India an extra payment may get you onto a train that is already overbooked (or that you are told is overbooked). The only difference is that the payment will go straight into the ticket collector's pocket, rather than the railway company. However, in many places it is accepted that workers in national industries or officials in government agencies will top up their incomes by offering these kinds of "discretionary services."

There are very different levels of corruption, from the small scale to the very large scale. Our Indian ticket collector may make a few extra rupees each month from small-scale bribes. One estimate suggests that Mohamed Suharto, President of Indonesia from 1967 to 1998, built a personal fortune of between $15 and $35 billion through embezzlement, in a country with an average GDP per capita (an indication of average annual salaries) of $695.[16]

Governments, particularly those in previously centrally planned economies, are directly responsible for a large volume of purchasing. The volume of government expenditure on public procurement in China jumped from $0.4 billion in 1998 to $18.7 billion in 2003, as its economy and the need for large-scale infrastructure projects grew. By 2011 Chinese officials' overseas trips, the procurement and maintenance of government cars and the fees for official receptions alone cost an estimated $132 billion a year. The country attracted a great deal of international attention for the 2008 Olympic Games in Beijing and Expo 2010 in Shanghai. Government-funded events such as these pushed the government to limit corrupt practices through policies such as the Public Procurement Act. But such activities are not confined to emerging and developing countries. Bid rigging is widespread in Japan, particularly in the construction industry. The 2003 Act Concerning Elimination and Prevention of Involvement in Bid Rigging was an attempt by the Japanese government to curb such practices, which involve collusion among powerful *keiretsu*, industry bodies, and government agencies. The amount lost due to bribery in government procurement globally is thought to be at least $400 billion.

The Berlin-based organization Transparency International (TI) produces a number of reports each year, of which the best known is the Corruption Perceptions Index (CPI). The CPI has promoted research into, and more open discussion of, the causes and consequences of corruption. **Corruption** is defined by TI as "the misuse of public power for private benefit," and each year TI has evolved the methodology to improve consensus and acceptance of the metrics that underlie the country rankings.

Corruption
The misuse of public power for private benefit

The extent of corruption is a measure of the *frequency* and *value* of corrupt payments and the resulting obstacle imposed on businesses. A composite index from different polls and surveys from independent institutions, including the World Economic Forum, the World Business Environment Survey of the World Bank, the Institute of Management Development (in Lausanne), PricewaterhouseCoopers, the Economist Intelligence Unit, and Gallup International on behalf of Transparency International, are used in the CPI. The 2010 survey shows Denmark, New Zealand, and Singapore as the least corrupt economies,

Germany 15th, Japan 17th, the UK 20th, United States 22nd, France 25th, Spain 30th, Italy 67th, Brazil 69th, China 78th, India 87th, Russia 154th, and the most corrupt countries as Iraq 175th, Myanmar 176th, and Somalia 178th.

Another report is the *Bribe Payers Index* (BPI), which measures the "propensity of companies from 30 leading exporting countries to bribe abroad." It is based on the responses of more than 11,000 business people across 125 countries, polled in the World Economic Forum's Executive Survey. Although multinational firms from advanced countries usually rank high in the index, they still regularly pay bribes. Companies from emerging economies, including the BRIC countries, tend to rank amongst the worst. Despite high-profile campaigns to reduce the amount of local corruption in these countries, their firms actively bribe when abroad.

Other reports by TI examine other elements of corruption, including the most prominent offenders in specific countries, usefully comparing, for example, the judiciary, customs, police, local administrators, registry and permit officials, tax officials, and traffic police in various countries. Case studies and intra- or inter-regional comparisons also make up much of TI's analysis.[17]

Transparency
The *clarity* and *consistency* of policies and legislation applied in the governance of businesses

The global corruption report by TI shows a clear correlation between corruption and income. Poorer countries (like Bangladesh) tend to have the highest incidence of corruption. In low-income, developing, and emerging markets, transparency is also more of a problem. **Transparency** reflects the *clarity* and *consistency* of policies and legislation applied in the governance of businesses and is strongly associated with corruption. There is considerable debate about the relative levels of corruption and transparency prevalent in developing and advanced countries. The latter do tend to have more governance checks and balances and arguably more freedom of the press and leeway for interest groups to reveal and oppose corrupt practices and transparency problems.

There is, however, a socio-cultural dimension to such issues, and in some countries certain established, recognized, and accepted business practices are considered to be the "local rules of the game" that should simply be respected and adapted to, rather than criticized as non-Western. Again, China provides a useful illustration. One of the key obligations for China as it joins a growing range of international organizations (such as the WTO) and legal treaties is to improve its transparency. In the past, import duties have been found to vary between 10 and 20 percent for the same product because customs officers across the country do not have a standard definition or system for categorizing product types. This has not just led to MNE managers and local importers having to engage in extended discussions with local officials regarding product categorization, but significantly increased the incentive and opportunity for bribery.

Government clean-up campaigns in China have focused on the standardization of rules governing both domestic and foreign businesses. The licensing procedures for both have tended to be unregulated and very much at the discretion of local officials who are said frequently to abuse the yearly check-up system (*Nianjin*) to earn additional fees before approving licenses. However, foreign firms without the necessary *guanxi* (informal, reciprocal obligation networks) connections are subject to these and other additional charges. The more bizarre include the "spiritual civilization fee" and a "wall-cleaning fee" that can run into thousands of US dollars.

STRATEGIC MANAGEMENT AND POLITICAL RISK

MNEs take many steps to ensure that their strategies do not go awry because of unexpected developments. One of the most beneficial steps is the use of integrative and protective/defensive techniques.

Use of integrative and protective/defensive techniques

Integrative techniques
Strategies designed to help
a multinational become a
part of the host country's
infrastructure

There are a variety of stratagems that MNEs employ in reducing risk. Some are collectively known as **integrative techniques**, which are designed to help the MNE become a part of the host country's infrastructure.[18] The objective of an integrative technique is to help the company blend into the environment and to become less noticeable as a "foreign" firm. One of the simplest ways is to use a name that is not identified with an overseas company and, if an acquisition is made, keep the old name in place. For example, Bridgestone is a Japanese tire company, but no one would know this based on the name of the company. Additionally, Bridgestone owns Firestone Tire & Rubber, but few Americans are aware of this fact. Similarly, Hoechst of Germany owns the Celanese Company, and most people do not know this. Nor do many people realize that almost 25 percent of the banks in California are Japanese owned; their names provide no clues to their real owners. This tactic deflects public attention and concern that US assets are being swallowed up by overseas investors.

Another common integrative technique is to develop good relations with the host government and other political groups and to produce as much of the product as possible locally. In turn the MNE will hire and promote local personnel and use them to run a large portion of the operations. This strategy endears the company to the government and, if any action is taken against foreign firms, these firms are likely to be spared.

**Protective and
defensive techniques**
Strategies designed to
discourage a host country
from interfering in
multinational operations

Protective and defensive techniques are strategies that are designed to discourage a host country from interfering in multinational operations. In contrast to integrative techniques, protective and defensive measures are aimed at fostering *non-integration* of the MNE into the local environment. A good example is conducting research and development (R&D) at other geographic locales and importing this knowledge as needed. Should the government suddenly decide to seize the firm's facilities, the company's R&D base would not be threatened.

Another protective and defensive technique is to limit the role of the local personnel to those operations that are not vital to the running of the facility. So if the government decides to take over the operation, the host-country personnel will not be able to handle things efficiently. Those with the requisite knowledge and training are overseas personnel who are sent on site by the multinational.

A third technique is to raise as much capital as possible from the host country and local banks. When this happens, the government is reluctant to interfere in operations because this may threaten its own investment and that of the home-country banks. In a manner of speaking, this strategy co-opts the government and brings it onto the MNE's team. Any strike against the multinational is a blow against the host country.

A fourth technique is to diversify production among a number of countries. In this way, if the government seizes the MNE's facilities, only one area of production is disrupted. The company can then reallocate production and get back on stream in short order.

Combination strategies

MNEs often use a combination of integration and protective/defensive techniques to reduce and manage their political risk. Figure 15.6 provides an example of how companies can do this. In the case of the low-technology manufacturing firm (#1 in Figure 15.6), the only way to employ a protective/defensive strategy is to raise capital locally. As a result, this firm will work to integrate itself into the country and to act very much like a local firm.

An international air carrier (#2 in Figure 15.6) will use an integrative strategy by setting up local operations and by hiring people to staff the facilities, to maintain the aircraft, and to handle arrivals and departures. The airline will also help to generate money for the country by bringing in tourists and business people. At the same time the company will

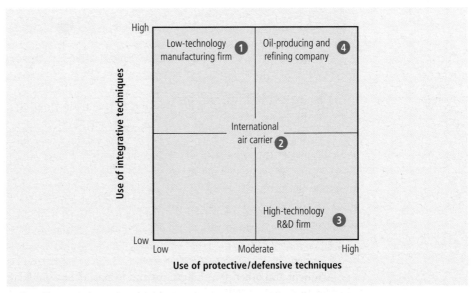

Figure 15.6 Select examples of the use of integrative and protective/defensive techniques

seldom have more than a small percentage of its aircraft in this locale on any one day. Additionally, the pilots will often come from other countries and be highly skilled individuals, and the top management team will be operating out of headquarters in the home country. So while the air carrier will take some steps to accommodate the country, it will also be well positioned should the country decide to seize its aircraft or to increase taxes or airport fees. Moreover, aside from facilities at the airport, the company will usually have no other fixed assets except for the aircraft. Therefore any crackdown on the airline might result in retaliatory action by other airlines, which would refuse to fly into the country. Such action could seriously hamper the country's economic growth. Consequently, a strategy that provides for the intermediate use of both integrative and protective/defensive techniques often works extremely well.

A high-technology R&D firm (#3 in Figure 15.6) will not put much emphasis on integrative techniques because it does not want to become integrated into the local economy. The firm may be situated where it is because the company finds that it is easier to recruit top talent to live in that region. Or other competitors may be headquartered there, and the company finds that it is easier to keep tabs on these firms by situating nearby. So while the company may hire local people to staff basic operations, personnel from other countries who live locally will handle all the R&D and other sophisticated functions. If the firm should hire local people for some of these R&D positions, the company will work to keep them loyal to the firm and not to the country. Thus if there is an attempt to seize the firm's R&D facilities, the loss will be minimized.

In the case of an oil-producing and refining company (#4 in Figure 15.6), the firm is likely to make strong use of both integrative and protective/defensive techniques. The company will need to get on well with the government since it is tapping the country's natural resources. There is likely to be a great deal of hiring of local personnel for routine jobs. The firm will also work hard to generate as much revenue as possible since the government is unlikely to interfere with the operations of a revenue-producing firm. At the same time the MNE will maintain control of the more sophisticated jobs so that these cannot be carried out by anyone else. If the company were to be taken over, local workers would be unlikely to know how to operate the machinery and equipment efficiently.

✔ Active learning check

Review your answer to Active Learning Case question 4 and make any changes you like. Then compare your answer to the one below.

④ What are the lessons for other firms looking to enter emerging markets like China?

A simple lesson from the Kodak case is that understanding political risk and its underlying sources can significantly increase your chances of making a successful investment in an uncertain emerging market. Kodak took the time and made the effort to understand what the risks were and how it could change some of the local rules of the game to its advantage. Kodak's success stemmed from the way it matched its power resources with the needs of the different levels of Chinese government, from senior politicians in Beijing to the more junior officials who regulated business activities at the local level. It developed an understanding of the problems facing the Chinese administration and engineered its negotiations approach to highlight how the investment could help solve some of these problems. Following this, Kodak's senior managers showed huge commitment to their investment, enduring several years of complex discussions with six provincial governments, ten city governments, five ministries and commissions, local tax authorities, and several banks and trust companies. They also had the foresight (or were co-opted) to fund a number of community projects, which earned them local support for the project and perhaps the brand. But do not forget that Kodak had the local government connections, the financial muscle, and a degree of political support from the US government to achieve all of this. The majority of international firms do not, and this can make the task of successfully investing in somewhere like China even harder and far riskier.

Identifying sources of potential risk and assessing the possible impact on foreign investments of all kinds is difficult to do. Emerging and developing countries generally represent riskier markets, as well as potentially more rewarding markets for MNEs. Their rapid rate of growth, strongly interventionist policies, less mature government institutions, and evolving governance systems all create additional uncertainties for foreign investors. These add to the existing complexities of trying to cope with different economic, social, and cultural ways of doing things. International managers looking to invest in these countries need to develop an in-depth understanding of the ever-changing official, formal rules and regulations governing different kinds of investment. In addition to the country risk analysis techniques introduced here, there is no substitute for direct experience. Only by visiting and learning about the geographic, socio-cultural, economic, and political context in which business takes place can managers develop a qualitative, tacit understanding about the official, formal and the unofficial, informal local rules of the game.

KEY POINTS

1 Country risk analysis examines the chances of non-market events (political, social, and economic) causing financial, strategic, or personnel losses to a firm following FDI in a specific country market.

2 A PEST analysis provides a starting point for examining and comparing political, economic, socio-cultural, and technological conditions in countries that present investment opportunities. Add depth and foresight to make PEST a little more rigorous.

3 Political risk is the probability that political forces will negatively affect an MNE's profit or impede the attainment of other critical business objectives. This risk can be examined in terms of macro and micro factors. A macro political risk is one that affects

foreign enterprises in the same general way. A micro political risk is one that affects selected sectors of the economy or specific foreign businesses.

4 General trends toward liberalization and deregulation have opened up a range of emerging markets to FDI, but governments maintain a strong level of control over the economy and the activities of foreign firms. Their ever-changing policies are a source of both new opportunities and risk.

5 There are a number of sources of political risk. Among others, these include the political philosophy of the government in power, changing economic conditions, rising nationalism, social unrest, terrorism, the vested interests of local business groups, and newly created international alliances.

6 There are numerous sources of information on political risk and global rankings of various kinds showing how countries compare. Online resources provide a quick and convenient way of starting a country risk analysis.

7 When assessing risk vulnerability at the project level quantitative and qualitative information need to be combined in an analysis of both the investment proposition and the country conditions. The Weighted Country Risk Assessment Model can provide a framework for this. Information gaps and uncertainty will always remain but the process can improve FDI decision making.

8 Country risk analyses can be incorporated into financial forecasts to produce revised NPV, ROI, or IRR calculations. The adjusted present value (APV) takes into account country risk estimates.

9 Understanding the policy objectives, policy tools, institutional structures and networks, and negotiating tactics of government agencies will help foreign managers negotiate better local conditions for FDI.

10 Power resources are the bargaining chips used by companies and governments in investment negotiations.

11 Corruption is defined by Transparency International as "the misuse of public power for private benefit." It can be difficult to distinguish between corrupt practices and local rules of the game that stem from differences in local market structures and business cultures.

12 There are three key steps in developing effective negotiating strategies. First, the MNE will evaluate its own position and that of the other parties to the negotiation. Second, the firm will examine the behavioral characteristics of the other parties in order to better understand their style of negotiation. Third, the MNE will use this information to hammer out an agreement that is acceptable to both sides. Identifying the acceptance zone of the other party is an important step.

13 MNEs tend to use a combination of integrative and protective/defensive techniques in minimizing political risk.

Key terms

- country risk analysis
- PEST framework
- political risk
- macro political risk
- expropriation
- indigenization laws

- micro political risk
- Weighted Country Risk Assessment Model
- adjusted present value (APV)
- acceptance zone

- corruption
- transparency
- integrative techniques
- protective and defensive techniques

REVIEW AND DISCUSSION QUESTIONS

1 How can a country risk analysis help an international manager making decisions about which countries to invest in?

2 How can we make a simple PEST analysis more robust, accurate, and useful?

3 What is meant by the term *political risk*? Is there political risk in every country of the world? Explain.

4 Show, with an example, how the process of deregulation and liberalization is opening up opportunities for foreign investment in emerging markets.

5 How does macro political risk differ from micro political risk? Compare and contrast the two.

6 What are some factors that help to determine the degree of micro political risk? Identify and describe three of them.

7 What resources are available online for comparing political risk in two or more countries? Give two examples and say how their measures and rankings differ.

8 What difficulties would a manager face compiling an accurate Weighted Risk Assessment Model for two emerging market countries?

9 What is an adjusted present value calculation? Give examples of the kinds of country risks that could be incorporated into an APV calculated for a manufacturing investment in a less developed country.

10 When predicting political risk, why will an MNE be interested in examining the economic development agenda and policies of the government?

11 Choose a well-known MNE and describe the kinds of power resources or bargaining chips it could use in FDI negotiations with a country government.

12 Why does corruption tend to be more prevalent in poorer countries?

13 Describe one method for comparing the levels of corruption to be expected in two different countries.

14 Why is improving transparency important for investors and for local populations in less developed countries?

15 Why will an MNE be interested in the behavioral characteristics of the participants in a negotiation? How can such information help to improve its negotiating position?

16 In a negotiation, why would an MNE be interested in the acceptance zone of the other party?

17 What are some bargaining tactics that are used in international negotiating? Identify and describe three of them.

18 How do MNEs use integrative techniques in order to reduce their political risk? Describe an example.

19 How do MNEs use protective/defensive techniques in order to reduce their political risk? Describe an example.

Yukos and the Russian oligarchs

Russia has been making overtures toward a free market economy for a considerable time. During the early 1990s investment from the West was seen as a way to improve the economy. However, significant changes needed to take place to reduce political risk in Russia. Initially, five steps were recommended by outside experts: (1) change the relationship between the national government and the republics in order to set up a federal political system in which central powers are limited; (2) eliminate or slash most state subsidies, including defence spending, and create a uniform sales tax and personal and corporate income tax system; (3) establish a commercial banking system, boost interest rates, and create an independent bank that will halt current inflationary practices; (4) break up state monopolies and industrial cartels; and (5) free the price of most goods immediately and gradually add to this list those changes that must be phased in more slowly: energy, public transportation, housing, and basic consumer goods such as milk, bread, and meat.

By 1997, the private sector accounted for more than half of Russia's output. Some 18,000 industrial firms had been privatized and over 1 million new businesses were created. The old Russia, its ideology and institutions, appeared to have gone. Despite currency and interest rate problems in the late 1990s, by 2001, for the first time since the end of communism, Russia had a balanced budget, a trade surplus, reserves, and a growing economy. Inward foreign direct investment (FDI) also surged, growing 10-fold between 2000 and 2009, with a peak of almost $80 billion in 2008. It jumped again in 2011, with high investments by firms like BP and Pepsi.

But foreign investors in Russia have learned to be cautious. Government bureaucracy, endemic corruption and periodic interference in the economy by political leaders, including a habit of re-nationalizing assets in particular industries, have proved to be enduring characteristics of the country. The practice of giving preferential treatment for oligarchs, the powerful individuals that span the political and business worlds also continues. This biased system, where the state uses an administrative mechanism, rather than a market one, to distribute assets, property, and commercial opportunities to powerful individuals in return for their political support, was favored by Yeltsin. President Vladimir Putin came to power promising to end it but has a tendency to slide back into these old ways.

The turbulent history of Yukos, Russia's largest oil company provides an interesting example. It was privatized in the 1990s along with a number of government-owned utilities and natural resource companies. These included Sibneft, the oil company in which the flamboyant Roman Abramovich had the major shareholding, and the source of the wealth with which he bought the English soccer club Chelsea. Other well-connected individuals made fortunes from the sell-offs, which were generally well below market prices. Some channeled surplus funds offshore, including the head of Yukos, Mikhail Khodorkovsky. A US investor, Kenneth Dart, who had unwisely bought stakes in Yukos's production subsidiaries, lost many millions of dollars as Mr. Khodorkovsky stripped their assets and siphoned money into offshore accounts.

Putin appeared to be both trying to stem the flows of capital from these previously state-owned enterprises and to transfer power to his own favored oligarchs. As Mr. Khodorkovsky's political ambitions grew he was sent to jail on flimsy charges of tax evasion in 2000. The Russian state subsequently seized a large stake in Yukos, its Yuganskneftegaz subsidiary, which represented 60 percent of its oil production capacity, apparently to pay some of Yukos's unpaid taxes. It then sold this for $9.35 billion, well below market value, to the Baikal Finance Group in December 2004. It then emerged that the Rosneft, a state-owned oil company headed by Igor Sechin, a close confidant of Mr. Putin, had bought Baikal for an undisclosed sum. So the state had taken back Khodorkovsky's prime asset by the back door. A close advisor to Putin, Andrei Illarionov, said at the time that this constituted "expropriation of private property" and should take the prize for the "swindle of the year." He has since lost his job.

Around this time Putin also directed the Russian government to limit foreign firms' involvement in a range of industries for "strategic" reasons. In early 2005 the Ministry of Natural Resources stated that foreign groups and Russian companies with more than 49 percent foreign ownership would be banned from participating in tenders to exploit oil and metal deposits. Officials argued, for example, that Siemens, the German industrial giant, should be barred from buying a stake in Power Machines Engineering Company, on national security grounds. It just so happens that a company controlled by one of Russia's most powerful and Putin-friendly oligarchs, Oleg Deripaska, expressed a strong interest at the same time.

Illarionov's verdict was that Russia had shifted, regrettably, to "an interventionist model of economic development, with extremely incompetent intervention in economic life by state officials." While the Kremlin still argues for entry into ▶

the World Trade Organization and Russia's integration into the global economy, in practice it has been raising barriers.

Sources: Kuznetsov, Alexey "Inward FDI in Russia and its policy context," Vale Columbia Centre on Sustainable International Investment (2010), http://www.vcc.columbia.edu/files/vale/documents/Profiles_Russia_IFDI_Final_November_30_2010.pdf; "The Outspoken Silenced," *The Economist*, January 8, 2005; "Method and Madness: Yukos, Putin and the Oligarchs," *The Economist*, January 1, 2005; "And the Owner Is?" *The Economist*, November 8, 2003; R. Norton and K.-L. Hubert, "The Good News About Russia," *Fortune*, April 14, 1997, p. 32; S. H. Hanke, "Is the Rouble Next?" *Forbes*, March 9, 1998, p. 64; D. Yergin and T. Gustafson, "Don't Write Off Russia—Yet," *Fortune*, September 28, 1998, pp. 99–102; D. F. Cavallo, "The Immensity of Russia's Problems," *Forbes*, August 24, 1998, p. 263.

1 What political risks do MNEs face in Russia? Identify and describe three of them.

2 What strengths would a foreign oil or energy firm bring to the country? What Russian needs would it help to meet?

3 How could this firm employ integrative or protective/defensive techniques in the country? Identify and describe one approach that could be used for each.

REAL CASE

Problems with ports

Ports are important. Despite the shift to services and intangibles, trade in physical goods has continued to grow significantly. Today, over 7 billion tons of seaborne trade flows through the world's ports each year. Ports are also the location of some of the commonest types of political risk, from organized, government-connected cartels to petty corruption. Here we briefly compare and contrast the problems of two port systems in two countries separated by huge economic, political, and cultural differences as well as thousands of miles: Japan and Kenya.

Japan's ports have long been slower and more expensive than any other in the Asia region. At the end of the 1990s, when the problem was at its worst, it took three to four days to clear customs and immigration in a Japanese port and cost $36,000 to $40,000 to unload a vessel, compared to one day in most other ports and $11,000 in Singapore and $16,000 in the United States. Partly as a result of this lack of competitiveness Kobe, for example, was the third-largest port in the world in 1978, in terms of container volume handled, and by 2002 it had fallen to number 27, below not just Hong Kong, Singapore, and Pusan, but even Rotterdam and Antwerp. By 2009 it was 42nd in the world. A key reason for these problems lies in the near-monopoly power of the Japan Harbor Transportation Association (JHTA). At its height the JHTA was a cartel of 2,000 member organizations encompassing the waterfront services (stevedoring, cargo handling, and transfer documentation) across 130 ports in Japan. It was run by Chairman Takashima, the so-called king of the waterfront, eight vice chairmen, and 85 directors from the various port companies. The JHTA was (and continues to be) responsible for two kinds of anti-competitive practices.

Source: Getty Images/Pete Turner

First, the system of prior consultations between shipping companies and the labor unions of cargo-handling companies takes place via JHTA. Foreign firms cannot select which firm handles their cargo on the basis of quality or cost; JHTA chooses for them. It also controls schedule changes, changes in berths and route calls, centrally regulating and slowing down the entire process. There is no formal documentation, application, or appeals procedure; the system operates through informal lobbying. Second, licensing requirements for technical operators and stevedoring firms act as barriers to foreign firms (and to non-cartel Japanese firms) entering the market. Foreign firms cannot perform stevedoring or port services for themselves or appoint third parties without the consent of JHTA.

The JHTA connects both government departments and *yakuza* (mafia-like groups in Japan) in ways that non-Japanese cannot easily understand. A US Embassy study found that 110 ex-officials from the Ministry of Transport had moved to senior management positions in waterfront companies over the previous decade. This is *amakudari* (literally, "descent from heaven"), a system of second-ment or "semi-retirement" for bureaucrats common in Japan. The *yakuza* have also long had strong interests in stevedoring firms and exert an influence over all the constituencies.

Foreign pressure grew on Japan to change the anti-competitive ports practices through the 1990s. The European Commission took Japan to the World Trade Organization and US firms lobbied via their Chamber of Commerce in Tokyo. Finally in April 1997 the US Federal Maritime Committee imposed port sanctions on Japanese ships entering the United States in retaliation for restrictive practices in Japanese ports. A penalty of $100,000 per US port entry by a Japanese ship from abroad was imposed. Japanese port workers subsequently went on strike and Takashima personally (sidestepping the Japanese gov-ernment entirely) threatened the US administration with counter-penalties! By November the situation was diffused and US Secretary of State Madeleine Albright signed an agreement with the Japanese authorities with a package of solutions.

A sure sign of the power of cartels and the difficulties of unwinding the complex relationships between the govern-ment and the private sector in Japan (and many countries) is the fact that Japanese ports are still as costly, slow, and uncompetitive as they were in the 1990s. In January 2005 the Japanese government again promised to take meas-ures to reduce the cost of using its main ports by 30 to 40 percent to "arrest a dramatic drop in competitiveness." However, the anti-competitive networks described above still persist as a symbol of the socio-political nature of this sector in Japan.

Kenya's main port of Mombasa is a world away from Kobe or Japan. Different problems concern port users including, according to one study, security and theft; bureaucratic forwarding and clearing procedures (cost increases due to procedural delays); customs and excise harassment (leading to corruption, otherwise further delays); obsolete, poorly maintained port handling and lifting equipment (leading to further delays); high tariffs for poor service; and just plain corruption, in that order.

As with many other service operations either currently or previously owned or regulated by government agen-cies in less developed countries, what they do, how they do it, and how much it costs is highly dependent on gov-ernment influence. Many of Africa's problems are seen to stem from a generic "culture of corruption." Many forms of corruption exist in Kenya including petty cor-ruption (to obtain a small service or get it done faster), corruption by harassment (where the private sector is

harassed into bribing), political corruption (soliciting bribes for favors), and grand-scale corruption (evading tax on a grand scale or fixing government tenders worth hundreds of millions of dollars). Political interference in Kenya's ports takes a number of forms. Particularly important are:

1 Political appointments to key management functions, resulting in unqualified and sometimes corrupt personnel in critical power positions.

2 Political undercurrents in labor recruitment; tribal affiliations and ruling political party affinity lead to biases in the recruitment of low-wage labor as well as more senior posts.

3 Regular interference in tender allocations; for government-related tenders, kickbacks (bribes) are necessary to win contracts.

4 Well-connected port users have an advantage and can queue-jump or get better services or security protection, creating frustration for other port users.

Beyond these kinds of problems, small-scale corrup-tion is rife. Port users may need to bribe petty officials to release goods or pay security guards protection money to avoid theft (which they can often be responsible for). The uncertainty for foreign managers unfamiliar with these local rules of the game is increased by the constant change in key officials and their political affiliations. Moreover, bribing the wrong person not only is a waste of money, but also can create big problems for anyone caught "playing the game" during sporadic government crack-downs.

Website: http://www.iaphworldports.org/trade/main-trade.htm.

Sources: Mariko Sanchanta, "Japanese Government to Cut Main Port Costs by Up to 40%," *Financial Times*, January 7, 2005, p. 3; Michiyo Nakamoto, "Port City Seeks to Nurture New Enterprises," *Financial Times*, April 27, 2004, p. 3; Parit Shah, "A Strategy for the Port of Mombasa," Unpublished MBA dissertation, Warwick Business School, Coventry, 2004; US Embassy in Tokyo, *Third Report to the Leaders on the US–Japan Regulatory Reform and Competition Policy Initiative*, June 8, 2004, http://tokyo.usembassy.gov/e/p/tp-20040609-01.html; Lucy Kilalo, "10 Charged with Stealing at Port," *The Daily Nation*, March 12, 2003; A. Mutunba-lule, "Bogus Clearing Agents Have Nowhere to Hide," Maritime Report, *The Daily Nation*, March 20, 2000; authors' interview with Richard Neal, Head of John Swire and Sons (Japan) Ltd., March 17, 1997.

1 What are the main differences in the barriers and risks faced by foreign firms in the Japanese port system compared to Kenya's Mombasa?

2 Why is it difficult for foreign firms to challenge these unfair practices in either Kenya or Japan?

3 How could a manager looking to use these ports minimize the risk and uncertainty created by local ways of doing things?

ENDNOTES

1 Witold J. Henisz, Edward D. Mansfield, and Mary Ann Von Glinow, "Conflict, security, and political risk: International business in challenging times," *Journal of International Business Studies*, vol. 41, No. 5 (2010), pp. 759–764; S. Sakarya, M. Eckman and K. H. Hyllegard, "Market Selection for International Expansion. Assessing Opportunities in Emerging Markets," *International Marketing Review*, vol. 24, no. 2 (2007), pp. 208–238; S. Bridgewater, "Assessing Market Attractiveness," in S. Bridgewater and C. E. Egan (eds.), *International Marketing Relationships* (Basingstoke: Palgrave, 2002); W. J. Henisz, *Politics and International Investment: Measuring Risk and Protecting Profits* (Cheltenham: Edward Elgar, 2002); K. D. Miller, "A Framework for Integrated Risk Management," *Journal of International Business* (Summer 1992), pp. 311–331; D. Kern, "The Evaluation of Country Risk and Economic Potential," *Long Range Planning*, vol. 18, no. 3 (1985), pp. 17–25; and M. Perlitz, "Country Portfolio Analysis—Assessing Country Risk and Opportunity," *Long Range Planning*, vol. 18, no. 4 (1985), pp. 11–26.

2 D. O'Connell, "Dogfight," *The Sunday Times*, September 19, 2004.

3 Adapted from United Nations, *World Investment Report*, 2006 and 2009, key data downloads at http://www.unctad.org (Geneva: United Nations Conference on Trade and Development).

4 This framework partly comes from C. R. Kennedy, Jr., *Managing the International Business Environment: Cases in Political and Country Risk* (Englewood Cliffs, NJ: Prentice Hall International, 1991).

5 A. Ostrovsky, "Economics Minister Hits at Putin Policy," *Financial Times*, January 12, 2005.

6 D. Brewster and A. Hill, "US Opts for Homegrown Products," *Financial Times*, April 1, 2003.

7 E. Alden, "Small Manufacturers Drive Trade Protectionism Up the US Agenda," *Financial Times*, February 1, 2005.

8 F. Bokhari, "Pakistan Weaves into a New Era," *Financial Times*, January 12, 2005; H. K. Nordas, "The Global Textile and Clothing Industry Post the Agreement on Textiles and Clothing," *World Trade Organization*, 2004, http://www.wto.org/english/res_e/booksp_e/discussion_papers5_e.pf.

9 S. C. Collinson and J. Holden, "Decision-Making and Market Orientation in the Internationalization Process of Small and Medium-Sized Enterprises," *Management International Review* (MIR), vol. 45 (2005) pp. 413–436.

10 The Business Environment Risk Information (BERI) model contains a variable that it calls "Mentality" in its formula for national risk assessment. The idea behind inclusion of this concept is that there can be a national attitude, a mentality that would be resistant or corrosive to foreign investment and prevent efficient and productive investment and business operations. Details about the criteria and methodology used by BERI are available at http://www.beri.com/.

11 Oshri, Ilan, Julia Kotlarsky and Leslie P. Willcocks (eds.) *The Handbook of Global Outsourcing and Offshoring* (Basingstoke: Palgrave, October 2009).

12 The bargaining environment can be captured by the structure of a complex, interrelated network. The bargaining power of individual constituencies is related to their basis of power, network position, bargaining outcome preferences, and motivation to influence bargaining (James Nebus and Carlos Rufin, "Extending the bargaining power model: Explaining bargaining outcomes among nations, MNEs, and NGOs," *Journal of International Business Studies*, vol. 41, no. 6 (2010), pp. 996–1015.)

13 Nancy J. Adler, *International Dimensions of Organizational Behavior*, 2nd ed. (Boston, MA: PWS-Kent Publishing, 1991), p. 197. Fons Trompenaars and Charles HampdenTurner, *Managing People Across Cultures*, Culture for Business Series (London: Capstone, 2004).

14 John R. Schermerhorn, Jr., "Language Effects in Cross-Cultural Management Research: An Empirical Study and a Word of Caution," *National Academy of Management Proceedings*, 1987, pp. 102–105; S. C. Collinson and A. M. Pettigrew (2009) "Comparative International Business Research methods: pitfalls and practicalities," Chapter 27 in A. M. Rugman (ed.), *The Oxford Handbook of International Business*, 2nd ed. (Oxford: Oxford University Press.)

15 For additional insights into negotiating, see Carl Rodrigues, *International Management: A Cultural Approach* (Thousand Oaks, CA: Sage, 2008)

16 Transparency International, *Global Corruption Report 2010*, http://www.globalcorruptionreport.org/.

17 See http://www.globalcorruptionreport.org/ and http://www.transparency.org/index.html.

18 For a good example of how Japan does this, see Andrew Pollack, "Japan Takes a Pre-emptive Step on Auto Exports," *New York Times*, January 9, 1993, pp. 17, 26; and Richard W. Stevenson, "Japanese Cars Get British Accents," *New York Times*, February 25, 1992, pp. C1, C14.

ADDITIONAL BIBLIOGRAPHY

Alessandri, Todd M., Ford, David N., Lander, Diane M., Leggio, Karyl B. and Taylor, Marilyn. "Managing Risk and Uncertainty in Complex Capital Projects," *Quarterly Review of Economics & Finance*, vol. 44, no. 5 (December 2004).

Aulakh, Preet S. and Mudambi, Ram. "Financial Resource Flow in Multinational Enterprises: The Role of External Capital Markets," *Management International Review*, vol. 45, no. 3 (2005).

Barclay, L. A. *Foreign Direct Investment in Emerging Economies: Corporate Strategies and Investment Behaviour in the Caribbean* (London and New York: Routledge, 2000).

Chatterjee, Sayan et al. "Integrating Behavioural and Economic Concepts of Risk into Strategic Management: The Twain Shall Meet," *Long Range Planning*, vol. 36, no. 1 (2003).

Chen, Charles J. P., Yuan Ding, Kim and Chansog, Francis. "High-Level Politically Connected firms, Corruption, and

Analyst Forecast Accuracy Around the World," *Journal of International Business Studies*, vol. 41, no. 9 (December 2010).

Chi, Tailan. "Business Strategies in Transition Economies," *Academy of Management Review*, vol. 26, no. 2 (April 2001).

Click, Reid W. "Financial and Political Risks in US Direct Foreign Investment," *Journal of International Business Studies*, vol. 36, no. 5 (September 2005).

Coeurderoy, Régis and Murray, Gordon. "Regulatory Environments and the Location Decision: Evidence From the Early Foreign Market Entries of New-Technology-Based Firms," *Journal of International Business Studies*, vol. 39, no. 4 (June 2008).

Desbordes, Rodolphe. "The Sensitivity of U.S. Multinational Enterprises to Political and Macroeconomic Uncertainty: A Sectoral Analysis," *International Business Review*, vol. 16, no. 6 (2007).

Di Gregorio, Dante. "Re-Thinking Country Risk: Insights from Entrepreneurship Theory," *International Business Review*, vol. 14, no. 2 (2005).

Feinberg, Susan E. and Gupta, Anil K. "Country Risk and Network Linkages within Multinationals," *Academy of Management Conference Proceedings* (New Orleans, 2004).

Filatotchev, Igor, Strange, Roger, Piesse, Jenifer and Yung-Chih Lien. "FDI by Firms From Newly Industrialised Economies in Emerging Markets: Corporate Governance, Entry Mode and Location," *Journal of International Business Studies*, vol. 38, no. 4 (July 2007).

Gaba, Vibha, Pan, Yigang and Ungson, Gerardo R. "Timing of Entry in International Market: An Empirical Study of US *Fortune 500* Firms in China," *Journal of International Business Studies*, vol. 33, no. 1 (2002).

Goerzen, Anthony, Sapp, Stephen and Delios, Andrew. "Investor Response to Environmental Risk in Foreign Direct Investment," *Management International Review*, vol. 50, no. 6 (Dec 2010).

Grosse, Robert. "Restrictive Business Practices in International Service Industries: Examples from Latin America," *Transnational Corporations*, vol. 6, no. 2 (August 1997).

Henisz, Witold J. *Politics and International Investment: Measuring Risk and Protecting Profits* (Cheltenham: Edward Elgar, 2002).

Henisz, Witold and Delios, Andrew. "Uncertainty, Imitation and Plant Location: Japanese Multinational Corporations, 1990–1996," *Administrative Science Quarterly*, vol. 46, no. 3 (2001).

Henisz, Witold J. and Zelner, Bennet A. "Legitimacy, Interest Group Pressures and Change in Emergent Institutions: The Case of Foreign Investors and Host Country Governments," *Academy of Management Review*, vol. 30, no. 2 (2005).

Hillman, Amy and Keim, Gerald. "International Variation in the Business–Government Interface: Institutional and Organizational Considerations," *Academy of Management Review*, vol. 20, no. 1 (January 1995).

Hoti, Suhejla and McAleer, Michael "An Empirical Assessment of Country Risk Ratings and Associated Models," *Journal of Economic Surveys*, vol. 18, no. 4 (2004).

Inkpen, Andrew C. and Beamish, Paul W. "Knowledge, Bargaining Power, and the Instability of International Joint Ventures," *Academy of Management Review*, vol. 22, no. 1 (January 1997).

Jimenez, Alfredo. *Three Essays on the Proactive Use of Political Risk: The Case of the Internationalization Strategy of Spanish Multinational Companies* (LAP Lambert Academic Publishing, 2011).

Keating, Robert J. and Abramson, Neil R. "A New Framework in the Quest for Cultural Understanding Using Australia, Thailand and Japan as an Example," *International Journal of Business Studies*, vol. 17, no. 1 (June 2009).

Keillor, Bruce D. and Hult, G. Tomas M. "Predictors of Firm-Level Political Behavior in the Global Business Environment: An Investigation of Specific Activities Employed by US Firms," *International Business Review*, vol. 13, no. 3 (June 2004).

Kobrin, Stephen. "When Does Political Instability Result in Increased Investment Risk?" *Columbia Journal of World Business*, vol. 13, no. 3 (1978).

Kumar, Rajesh, Rangan, U. Srinivasa and Rufin, Carlos. "Negotiating Complexity and Legitimacy in Independent Power Project Development," *Journal of World Business*, vol. 40, no. 3 (August 2005).

Makhija, Mona V. and Stewart, Alice C. "The Effect of National Context on Perceptions of Risk: A Comparison of Planned versus Free-Market Managers," *Journal of International Business Studies*, vol. 33, no. 4 (2002).

Mudambi, Ram and Navarra, Pietro. "Political Tradition, Political Risk and Foreign Direct Investment in Italy," *Management International Review*, vol. 43, no. 3 (2003).

Peng, Mike W. "Controlling the Foreign Agent: Case Studies of Government–MNE Interaction in a Transition Economy," *Management International Review*, vol. 40, no. 2 (Summer 2000).

Peng, Mike W., Wang, Denis Y. L. and Jiang, Y. "An Institution-Based View of International Business Strategy: A Focus on Emerging Economies," *Journal of International Business Studies*, vol. 39, no. 5 (July/August 2008).

Ramamurti, Ravi. "Reassessing Risk in Developing Countries," *Long Range Planning*, vol. 36, no. 4 (August 2003).

Ramamurti, Ravi and Hashai, Niron (eds.). *The Future of Foreign Direct Investment and the Multinational Enterprise: 15*, (Research in Global Strategic Management series (Emerald Group Publishing Limited, 2011).

Reuer, Jeffrey J., Shenkar, Oded and Ragozzino, Roberto. "Mitigating Risk in International Mergers and Acquisitions: The Role of Contingent Payouts," *Journal of International Business Studies*, vol. 35, no. 1 (2004).

Rothaermel, Frank T., Kotha, Suresh and Steensman, H. Kevin. "International Market Entry by U.S. Internet Firms: An Empirical Analysis of Country Risk, National Culture, and Market Size," *Journal of Management*, vol. 32, no. 1 (2006).

Sauvant, Karl, *Yearbook on International Investment Law & Policy 2009–2010* (New York: Oxford University Press, 2010).

Shi, Xinping. "Antecedents of International Business Negotiations in the China Context," *Management International Review*, vol. 41, no. 2 (Summer 2001).

Stasavage, D. "Private Investment and Political Institutions," *Economics and Politics*, vol. 14, no. 1 (2002).

Strange, Roger, Filatotehev, Igor, Yung-chih Lien and Piesse, Jenifer. "Insider Control and the FDI Location Decision," *Management International Review*, vol. 49, no. 4 (Aug 2009).

Tahir, Rizwan and Larimo, Jorman. "Understanding the Location Strategies of the European Firms in Asian Countries," *Journal of American Academy of Business*, vol. 1, no. 2 (2004).

Yiu, D. and Makino, S. "The Choice Between Joint Venture and Wholly Owned Subsidiary: An Institutional Perspective," *Organization Science*, vol. 13, no. 5 (2002).

WWW RESOURCES

http://www.tdctrade.com
http://www.wto.org
http://www.worldbank.org/wbi/governance/govdata2001.htm
http://www.worldbank.org/data/countrydata/countrydata.html
http://rru.worldbank.org/DoingBusiness/
http://miga.org
http://www.countryrisk.com/

http://www.economist.com/countries
http://www.eiu.com
http://transparency.org
http://www.globalcorruptionreport.org/
http://www.opacity.index.com
http://www.fraserinstitute.ca
http://www.freetheworld.com/

Chapter 16

INTERNATIONAL
FINANCIAL MANAGEMENT

Contents

Objectives of the chapter

This chapter discusses the opportunities and problems that face multinational enterprises (MNEs) because they operate in a multicurrency, segmented-market world.

The specific objectives of this chapter are to:

1 *Compare* and *contrast* how polycentric, ethnocentric, and geocentric solutions are used in determining the financial planning and controlling authority that is given to subsidiaries.

2 *Study* some of the most common techniques that are used in managing global cash flows, including funds positioning and multilateral netting.

3 *Examine* foreign exchange risk strategies that are used to protect the multinational against transaction, translation, and economic exchange risks.

4 *Explain* how capital budgeting is carried out in a multinational firm.

5 *Describe* how international financing opportunities for an MNE differ from those available to a domestic firm.

6 *Provide* examples of international financial strategies currently being used by multinationals.

ACTIVE LEARNING CASE

British Airways

By the early 2000s there were only four major airlines in the United States: American, Continental, Delta, and United. All faced financial difficulties due to rising oil prices and other costs. Other US airlines were smaller carriers (for example, Southwest) and were also facing significant financial problems. Throughout the 1990s, British Airways (BA) had been seeking to merge with a US airline to create a giant transatlantic alliance. In mid-1992, BA announced it was entering an arrangement with USAir (the former name of US Airways) that would have allowed passengers to travel throughout Europe and the United States by relying on just one carrier: BA/USAir. The alliance would have coordinated ticket pricing, catering, advertising, and the network of flights and connections. The major US airlines asked the US government to block this arrangement because it gave too much of the US market to a foreign company. After failed negotiations with the US and British governments, BA decided instead to hold a 24.6 percent minority of the voting shares in USAir. The US restricts foreign ownership of voting shares in an airline to 25 percent.

In 1997, BA announced it would sell its share of USAir and instead seek an alliance with American Airlines (AA). The proposed alliance would have allowed BA and AA to code-share, coordinate routes and schedules, and integrate frequent flyer programs. Rival US airlines denounced the move, claiming it would reduce competition and allow the alliance a large share of the transatlantic traffic. To allow the alliance to continue, EU antitrust authorities demanded the alliance give up 267 weekly slots in London's Heathrow, or 10 percent of their total. BA/AA refused to do this, claiming it would hamper their competitiveness. The two airlines' cooperative efforts were thus reduced to their mutual participation in the One World international alliance.

A very interesting financial issue arises in this context: if BA were permitted to go all the way to merge with or acquire American, how would it finance the acquisition? This step would most likely cost more than US $10 billion to BA. The funding probably could be accomplished partially by the issuance of new shares in BA to existing shareholders of AA—but a significant amount of the funding would need to be raised in international markets. This issue was moot for the moment, until opposition to further links between these two airlines could be removed.

Four years after their initial proposal, BA/AA once again tried to win antitrust immunity. In 2001 the two airlines approached regulators, claiming that a new set of

Source: Getty Images/Ian Waldie

factors had emerged to support their case. These factors included the continued expansion of Open Skies agreements between the United States and many European nations that had increased competition; the emergence of international alliances that provide global networks; the relative decrease in Heathrow's European dominance as airports in Frankfurt, Amsterdam, and Paris increased traffic; and the development of similar alliances among competitors.

US competitors, Delta, Continental, and Northwest, once again asked the US Department of Transportation to hold a judicial hearing, arguing that most of the concerns were the same as in 1996 and that the case must be evaluated by an independent arbiter. Ironically, two of the three companies opposing the deal have similar deals of their own with other European carriers. The Delta–Air France and KLM–Northwest alliances are very similar to what BA/AA proposed. Why then all the fuss over another alliance? Back in 2004, BA is the largest European airline with $14.8 billion in revenues and serves 550 destinations in 94 countries. AA is the second-largest airline in the United States with $18.7 billion in revenues in 2004 and serves 250 destinations in 40 countries. The alliance would create a dominant company with control over transatlantic flights. BA and AA each have 263 and 273 US–Europe flights respectively and, between them, they control 38 percent of Heathrow's slots.

In Europe, the UK's Office of Fair Trading and the European Commission's Competition Directorate examined the proposal. The loudest opposition by a competitor came from the UK's Virgin Atlantic. News of the proposal resurrected Virgin's No Way BA/AA campaign. Virgin contended that BA/AA would hold 60 percent of all Heathrow–US services and fly 50 percent of all passengers traveling between the United States and the UK. Together, BA/AA flew 9 million passengers between the UK and the United States in 2001; the next biggest carrier flew 3.5 million. Virgin claimed that this dominance would effectively eliminate smaller airlines from the transatlantic market.

At the center of the proposal was BA's access to the US market and US carriers' access to London's Heathrow. Presently, BA flies to 25 US airports but it cannot pick up passengers in one US city to fly them to another US city. If the deal with AA had gone through, BA/AA would have had total access to the US and EU markets. US carriers had the opposite problem. Only two US airlines, American and United, had access to Heathrow Airport. For years the US and British governments have been negotiating an Open Skies agreement without much progress. The proposed alliance added momentum to Open Skies. The British government had indicated that it would be willing to negotiate an Open Skies agreement if the BA/AA was granted antitrust immunity.

In 2002, the US government approved the merger of BA and AA on condition that the merged company surrender over 200 slots in Heathrow Airport. Both airlines announced that they would not merge due to the excessive strategic cost imposed by regulators. The "final" result of the discussions and negotiations by 2005 was to leave BA and AA in the One World alliance, with code sharing, and with occasional expansion of routes to additional pairs of US–UK cities—but not a merger of the two airlines, and not the full access that they requested which would have virtually monopolized the UK–US air traffic. (Open Skies came into effect in April 2008 but with no BA/AA alliance.).

For the year ended in March 31, 2009, BA reported $15.168 billion in revenues and had a workforce of 44,987 employees. AA's revenue was $19.917 billion, 14 percent and 16 percent lower, respectively, compared to a year earlier.

Websites: www.aa.com; www.british-airways.com; www.usairways.com; www.oneworldalliance.com; www.delta.com; www.nwa.com; www.airfrance.com; www.continental.com; www.klm.com.

Sources: Agis Salpukas, "The Big Foreign Push to Buy into US Airlines," *New York Times*, October 11, 1992; Adam Bryant, "British Air Halts Move into USAir," *New York Times*, March 8, 1994; "Predators in the Air," *The Economist*, June 8, 2000; Peter Spiegel, "US Rivals Call for Hearing on Deal by BA and American," *Financial Times*, November 20, 2001; "Branson Slams BA/AA Alliance," *Virgin Atlantic News Release*, November 12, 2001; "Let Fly," *The Economist*, March 8, 2001; British Airways Plc, *Annual Report*, 2008 and 2009; AMR Corporation (American Airlines), *Annual Report*, 2008 and 2009.

1 Is the BA/AA alliance going to use a polycentric, ethnocentric, or geocentric solution to handling operations?

2 If the two carriers were to complete a merger and the US dollar then weakens against the British pound as it did in 2004–2005, how will this affect the financial statements of the company?

3 If BA believed that the British pound was going to appreciate in relation to the euro, how is it likely to deal with receivables and payables?

4 Assuming that BA might choose to acquire all or part of American, United, or Delta Airlines in the United States, how could BA finance the major capital budgeting need in international markets, and what are some of the important considerations in choosing among alternative financing sources?

INTRODUCTION

Any firm with affiliates in at least two countries (even with a simple sales office abroad) needs to deal with differences in the financial environments of those countries—differences in their tax systems, their currency systems, and numerous other areas. Can you imagine trying to keep the books of a company such as Johnson & Johnson, which is required to maintain financial records according to the different accounting standards in the dozens of countries where it operates, plus records for use in internal control? Beyond the chores of record keeping, the firm operating at this level obtains opportunities to transfer funds (and products) between countries, utilize financial markets in each country to serve its global needs, and diversify its risks internationally. Increasing numbers of MNEs, such as Ford and

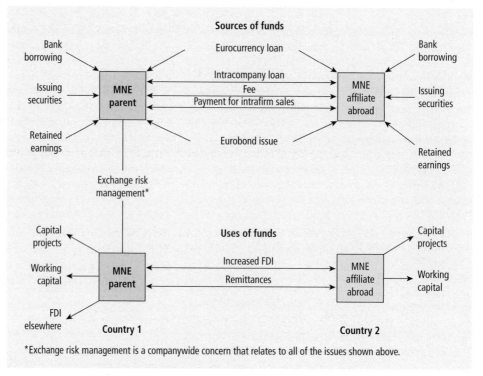

Figure 16.1 Financial management in the MNE

General Electric, are building internal financial institutions so that they can take advantage of these opportunities around the world. This chapter explores the opportunities and problems of firms in such an environment.

National financial markets and the euromarkets were discussed in Chapter 7; here the emphasis is on using these markets to optimize the financial position of the multinational firm. The issue of transaction exchange risk was treated in Chapter 7; this chapter considers such risk in the context of a firm that does repeated international business and maintains long-term assets abroad. Finally, we consider the full set of financial issues in a firm whose subsidiaries in different countries compete for use of the available financial resources. This chapter treats the topic of multinational financial management as a whole.

The chapter is structured to cover major issues in corporate finance as they apply to the international context. Basic financial management can be divided into two broad headings: (1) choice and management of *sources* of funds; and (2) choice and management of *uses* of funds. At the international level, exchange risk management must be added. Figure 16.1 depicts the topics that constitute the substance of the chapter. Overall financial management requires *control* over each type of decision depicted in the figure, especially since financial managers in each affiliate may make decisions that affect the total corporation's financial position.

In the next section, we explore aspects of the parent–subsidiary financial relationship within the MNE. Then the discussion turns to the issue of managing cash flows in the MNE. Next, we consider a more comprehensive presentation of exchange risk management than that given in Chapter 7. After that, we look at the two sides of financial management in the context of the MNE: namely, use of available funds (particularly for capital budgeting) and financing for the firm's short- and long-term needs. A section on control of the financial activities in an MNE follows. And finally, some strategic considerations for the firm in international finance are presented.

DETERMINING PARENT–SUBSIDIARY RELATIONSHIPS

Because finance is such an important area of operations, it is critically important that parent companies firmly establish the relationships that will exist regarding financial planning and control authority. On the one hand, each branch or subsidiary should be responsible for its own planning and control system. On the other hand, there must be some central control in order to coordinate overall operations and to ensure both efficiency and profitability. In addressing this challenge, MNEs tend to opt for one of three managerial solutions: polycentric, ethnocentric, or geocentric, just as these choices are used in other strategic areas.

Polycentric solution

Polycentric solution
A decentralized decision-making framework in which financial decisions are largely allocated to foreign affiliates, and financial evaluation of affiliates is done in comparison to other firms in that context

A **polycentric solution** is to treat the MNE as a holding company and to decentralize decision making to the subsidiary levels. In this arrangement financial statements are prepared according to generally accepted accounting principles in both the overseas subsidiary's and the parent's home country, and the subsidiary's performance is evaluated against that of similar domestic and foreign concerns.

The advantages of the polycentric approach are those commonly obtained with decentralization. Decisions are made on the spot by those most informed about market conditions, and international subsidiaries tend to be more flexible, motivated, efficient, and competitive. On the other hand, this solution reduces the authority of the home office, and senior corporate management often dislikes this dilution of its authority. Additionally, an MNE may find that a polycentric approach results in competition between different international subsidiaries and lowers overall profits for the company.

Ethnocentric solution

Ethnocentric solution
A centralized decision-making framework in which financial decisions and control for foreign affiliates are largely integrated into home-office management

The **ethnocentric solution** is to treat all foreign operations as if they were extensions of domestic operations. In this case each unit is integrated into the planning and control system of the parent company.

Working capital
Short-term financial instruments such as bank deposits and marketable securities that can be optimized by the MNE on a global basis

The advantage of this system is that management is able to coordinate overall operations carefully. This usually results in centralization of the finance function so that cash not needed for day-to-day operations can be invested in marketable securities or transferred to other subsidiaries or branches that need **working capital**. The primary drawback of this solution is that it can cause problems for the individual subsidiary, which may feel that it needs more cash than is left on hand or that it is hindered in its efforts to expand because the parent company is siphoning off necessary resources.

Geocentric solution

Geocentric solution
A decision-making framework in which financial decisions and evaluation related to foreign affiliates are integrated for the firm on a global basis

The **geocentric solution** is to handle financial planning and controlling decisions on a global basis. These decisions are typically influenced by two factors. One is the nature and location of the subsidiary. For example, British investment in North America has predominantly been via holding companies, the polycentric approach, since the quality of local management largely rewards decentralization. Conversely, investment in developing countries has typically been more centralized, with the parent company maintaining close control of financial expenditures. The second influencing factor is the gains that can be achieved by coordinating all units in a carefully synchronized way. When an MNE's overseas units face a myriad of tax rates, financial systems, and competitive environments, it is often more efficient to centralize most of the financial control decisions because this is the best way to ensure that profit and efficiency are maximized. For example, if two subsidiaries are equally able to sell a particular product to a major customer, with centralized financial planning the parent company could ensure that the sale would be made by the unit located in the country with the lowest corporate income tax rate. Additional examples of the ways in which financial operations could be directed by using a geocentric solution are seen in the management of global cash flows.

✔ Active learning check

Review your answer to Active Learning Case question 1 and make any changes you like. Then compare your answer to the one below.

❶ Is the BA/AA alliance going to use a polycentric, ethnocentric, or geocentric solution for handling operations?

The alliance is going to use a geocentric solution to handle operations. This is clear from the way in which the two air carriers are beginning to merge their operations so that they are both working in harmony. An alliance of equals, BA/AA can capitalize on their individual regional/triad strengths.

MANAGING GLOBAL CASH FLOWS

One of the key areas of international financial management is the careful handling of global cash flows. There are a number of ways in which this is done. Three of the most important ones include the prudent use of internal funds flows, the use of funds positioning, and the use of **multilateral netting**. The following sections examine each of these three.

Internal funds flows

Multilateral netting
Payment of net amounts due only between affiliates of an MNE that have multiple transactions among the group, which can be partially netted out among them, so then only the net funds need to be transferred

When an MNE wants to expand operations or fund activities, one of the simplest ways of obtaining the needed monies is by getting them from internal sources such as working capital, which is the difference between current assets and current liabilities. For example, if General Electric's German subsidiary wants to hire more employees, it may be able to pay for this payroll increase out of the funds it generates from ongoing operations. Another way of raising money internally is by borrowing from a local bank or from the parent company. For example, an MNE's Chilean subsidiary will get a loan from the parent company or the German subsidiary and then repay the money with interest out of operations. A third way is by having the parent company increase its equity capital investment in the subsidiary. In turn the subsidiary could pay the parent dividends on the investment. These examples are illustrated in Figure 16.2 and help to show that there are many ways for multinational firms to generate internal cash for operations.

Which method is most likely to be used? The answer will depend on a number of factors, including government regulations regarding intercompany lending. For example, when tax rates are high for a profitable subsidiary, it is common to find those units willing to lend money at low rates of interest to other subsidiaries in the MNE that need funds to expand into growth markets. The logic behind this strategy is quite simple: the highly profitable unit does not need to charge a high interest rate because much of this interest earning will be lost to the high local taxes. Conversely, the subsidiary that is borrowing the money needs low interest rates so as to conserve its cash for expansion purposes.

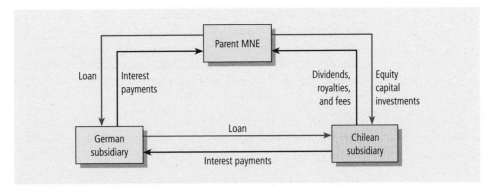

Figure 16.2 Common examples of internal sources and flows of funds

By shifting the money around in this fashion, the MNE is able to support expansion efforts, to minimize taxes, and to increase the sales potential of the subsidiaries. In an effort to prevent multinationals from taking advantage of such tax loopholes, in recent years some governments have changed their tax laws and established a minimum rate that can be charged on these intercompany loans.

Another area of concern is government limits on a parent company's ability to charge subsidiaries a licensing or royalty fee for the use of technology or to assess a management fee that covers the subsidiary's fair share of corporate overhead. When there are no government restrictions in these areas, the MNE has greater freedom in drawing funds from subsidiary operations, thus providing the parent with a pool of money that can be used for other worldwide operations. The ways in which this is done are commonly referred to as funds positioning techniques.

Funds positioning techniques

**Funds positioning
techniques**
Mechanisms such
as transfer pricing,
intercompany loans, and
timing of payments that are
used to move funds from
one affiliate to another in a
multinational firm

Funds positioning techniques are strategies that are used to move monies from one multinational operation to another. While there are a variety of approaches, three of the most common are transfer pricing, use of tax havens, and fronting loans.

Transfer pricing

Transfer price
The price used for an
intracompany payment for
shipment of products or
services from one affiliate
to another in an MNE;
these prices can be used to
reduce taxes, move funds to
desired locations, and so on

A **transfer price** is an internal price that is set by a company in intrafirm trade such as the price at which the Chilean subsidiary will purchase electric motors from the German subsidiary. An initial conclusion would be that the German firm will sell the motors at the same price as it would to any outside purchaser. A second conclusion is that the Chilean subsidiary will receive a discount because it is an intrafirm transaction and the parent will not allow its subsidiaries to profit at the expense of each other. However, both of these conclusions are incorrect when a transfer pricing strategy is employed. The final price will be determined by local regulations and will be set at a level that allows the MNE to achieve certain desired goals such as to increase profit, to reduce costs, and/or to move money among the subsidiaries.

Arm's-length price
The price that exists or
would exist on a sale of a
given product or service
between two unrelated
companies—as contrasted
with an intracompany
transfer price

A good example is provided by a multinational that has a subsidiary located in Country A, which has a low corporate income tax and is selling goods to a subsidiary located in Country B, which has a high corporate income tax. If the transfer price is set carefully, it is possible to reallocate taxable income away from the highly taxed subsidiary to the subsidiary with the low tax rate. Table 16.1 provides an example by contrasting arm's-length pricing with transfer pricing. An **arm's-length price** is the price a buyer will pay for merchandise in a market under conditions of perfect competition. As seen in the table, it cost the subsidiary in Country A $8,000 for the goods it is selling to the subsidiary in Country B.

Table 16.1 Shifting profits by transfer pricing

	Arm's-length price		Transfer price	
	Country A	Country B	Country A	Country B
Sales	$10,000 exports	$12,000	$12,000 exports	$12,000
Costs of sales	8,000	10,000	8,000	12,000
Profit	2,000	2,000	4,000	Nil
Tax rate (A: 40%, B: 50%)	800	1,000	1,600	Nil
Net profit	1,200	1,000	2,400	Nil

Under an arm's-length price the seller is adding $2,000 for profit and selling the goods for $10,000. In turn the second subsidiary is selling these goods for $12,000. Thus both subsidiaries are making a profit of $2,000. As also seen in the table, the tax rate in Country A is 40 percent, whereas in Country B it is 50 percent. So the first subsidiary will have a net profit of $1,200, whereas the second subsidiary will net $1,000.

Under a transfer price arrangement, however, the objective is to maximize profits in the-low-tax rate country and to minimize them in the high-tax-rate country. In this case, as seen in Table 16.1, the first subsidiary sells the goods for $12,000, and after paying 40 percent tax on the $4,000 profit, it ends up with a net profit of $2,400. The second subsidiary sells the goods for $12,000 and makes no profit. However, thanks to the transfer pricing strategy, the multinational's overall profit is greater than it was with arm's-length pricing ($2,400 versus $2,200).

Note that taxes are not the only considerations. Import tariffs also influence the decision to use transfer pricing. If the importing country has high tariffs, the firm needs to consider whether a high or low transfer price will maximize after-tax, after-tariff profits.

One of the obvious benefits of transfer pricing is that it allows the multinational to reduce taxes. A second benefit is that the strategy lets the firm concentrate cash in specific locales such as with the first subsidiary, or to move funds away from a country facing significant exchange rate risk, or to reduce payment of import tariffs. One of the problems with transfer pricing is that the financial statements do not accurately reflect subsidiary performance because the profit margins are manipulated. A second problem is that the strategy may not encourage efficient performance by the seller in a low-tax jurisdiction, whose primary objective is to unload merchandise on the other subsidiary at a profit as high as can be justified.

In recent years countries have been rewriting their tax codes to prevent arbitrary transfer pricing. In the United States, for example, the Internal Revenue Service (IRS) now asks multinationals to apply for an advanced determination ruling before establishing a transfer pricing policy. After the firm submits the request, the IRS will determine whether or not the policy is appropriate. The objective of the tax agency is to ensure that MNEs charge their overseas subsidiaries the same price for components and products as they charge independent third parties, thus effectively eliminating price manipulation for tax purposes. Because a large part (about one-third) of international trade in the early twenty-first century is intrafirm, transfer prices are a necessary aspect of much of international business.

Use of tax havens

Tax havens
Jurisdictions that offer the MNE a lower tax rate (or no tax) than in other places, so that MNEs can locate some of their business activities there and thus reduce overall tax payments

A second funds positioning technique is the use of **tax havens**, which are low-tax countries that are hospitable to business (see accompanying map). This strategy is typically used in conjunction with transfer pricing and involves a subsidiary selling its output at a very low cost to a subsidiary in a tax haven, which in turn sells the merchandise at a very high price to a third subsidiary.[1] Table 16.2 provides an example, which is similar to that in Table 16.1, except that the sales are now routed through a subsidiary located in a tax haven, Country B,

Table 16.2 Transfer pricing through tax havens

	Country A subsidiary	Country B subsidiary (tax haven)	Country C subsidiary
Sales	$8,000 exports	$12,000 exports	$12,000
Costs of sales	8,000	8,000	12,000
Profit	—	—	—
Tax rate (A: 40%, B: 0%, C: 50%)	—	—	—
Net profit	0	4,000	0

where no tax is paid at all. The result of the example in the table is a net profit of $4,000. This is greater than that illustrated in Table 16.1, where a simple case of transfer pricing was employed. For more on the matter of tax havens, see the case **International Business Strategy in Action: Tax havens.**

Fronting loans

Fronting loan

A third-party loan in which an MNE home office deposits funds with a financial institution, which then lends to the MNE's affiliate in a country where the MNE faces political risk or currency transfer restrictions

A **fronting loan** is a funds positioning strategy that involves having a third party manage the loan. For example, if a US multinational decided to set up operations in China, the MNE might be concerned with the political risk that accompanies such a decision. Is it possible that the government might expropriate the subsidiary's assets, including all the cash on hand? In an effort to protect its investments, the parent company could deposit funds with a major international bank that has strong ties to China and is on good terms with the government. In turn the subsidiary would apply for a loan with this bank and the multinational company's deposit would be given to the subsidiary in the form of a loan. It is highly unlikely that the Chinese government would expropriate the subsidiary and endanger the loan or its relationship with the international bank. Thus the MNE has successfully positioned its funds.

Funds positioning strategies are important in moving money around a multinational, as well as in helping the MNE to cope with political and legal roadblocks that stand in the way of such action. However, an internally operated netting process that controls the flow of funds and ensures that bills are paid promptly always complements these strategies. This process is often collectively referred to as multilateral netting.

Multilateral netting

When subsidiaries do business with each other, each may owe money to the others and in turn be owed money by them. Figure 16.3 provides an example of four subsidiaries that have both amounts due and amounts payable from each of the others. Over time, of course,

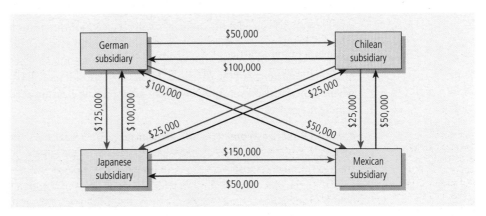

Figure 16.3 Multilateral dollar flows between subsidiaries

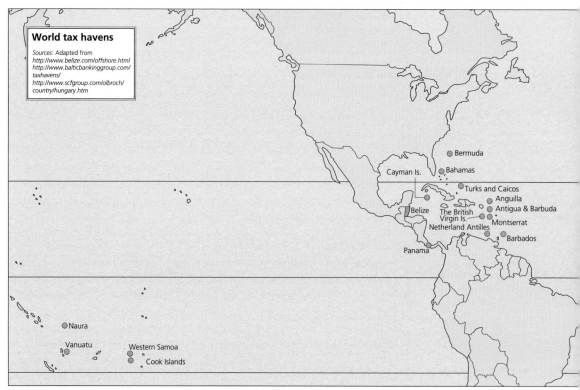

Note: No jurisdiction is currently listed as an uncooperative tax haven by the OECD's Committee on Fiscal Affairs according to the progress report as at January 4, 2011.

Sources: "A Progress Report on the Jurisdictions Surveyed by OECD Global Forum in Implementing the Internationally Agreed Tax Standards, progress made as at January 4, 2011" (Original Progress Report April 2, 2009), *OECD*, www.oecd.org

Clearing account
A centralized cash management bank account in which one MNE affiliate reviews payment needs among various MNE affiliates and arranges to make payments of net funds due from each affilate to others through the clearing account

these obligations will be resolved by the individual subsidiaries. In an effort to make the process more efficient, however, many multinationals have now set up **clearing accounts** in a certain location and assigned the manager at this location the authority to make the transfers that are necessary to pay intracompany subsidiary obligations. This process of multilateral netting, which involves a determination of the net amount of money owed to subsidiaries through multilateral transactions, begins with a computation of the amounts owed to each. Table 16.3, which has been constructed based on the information in Figure 16.3, shows these net positions. Based on this information, those that owe money are required to transfer it to a centralized clearing account (see Figure 16.4), whereas those that are owed money are paid from this central account.

The clearing account manager is responsible for seeing that this process occurs quickly and correctly. Typically, this manager will receive monthly transaction information from all the subsidiaries and will use these data to determine the net position of each unit. The manager will then see that the necessary transfers are made. These transfers usually take place in the currency of the payer, so the German subsidiary will pay its obligation in euros, whereas the Mexican subsidiary will pay in pesos. The clearing account manager's staff will handle the process.

Table 16.3 Net cash positions of subsidiaries

Subsidiary	Total receivables	Total payables	Net positions
German	$300,000	$225,000	$75,000
Chilean	125,000	150,000	225,000
Japanese	200,000	275,000	275,000
Mexican	225,000	200,000	25,000

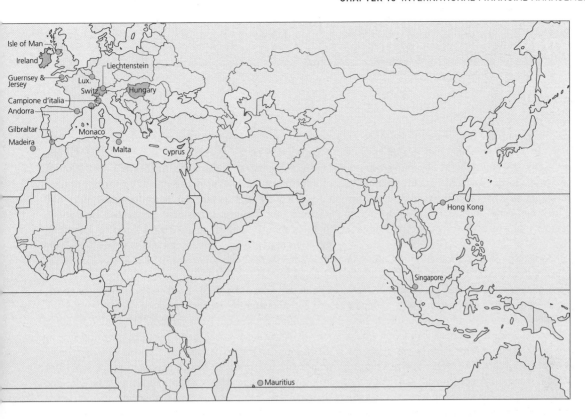

There are a number of reasons that multilateral netting has become popular. One advantage is that it helps the parent company to ensure that financial interactions between the units are quickly brought to completion. If bills are allowed to be outstanding for months at a time, it can result in the other units not wanting to do business with slow-paying subsidiaries. Netting helps to reduce the likelihood of such problems. A second advantage is that those units that are owed money have faster access to their funds. A third advantage is that the parent company knows which subsidiaries are amassing large amounts of cash and can tap these sources if necessary to support activities in other locales. A fourth advantage is that the cost of converting foreign exchange is minimized because the central clearing account manager can convert large amounts at the same time.

There are also some problems associated with multilateral netting. One is that many governments place controls on these operations by allowing them only for trade

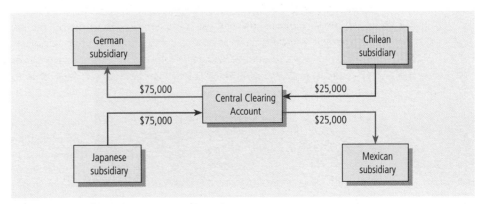

Figure 16.4 Centralized netting process in action

INTERNATIONAL BUSINESS STRATEGY IN ACTION

Tax havens

What do Switzerland, the Bahamas, Monaco, and Andorra have in common? By some definition, they are all considered to be tax havens. In general, a tax haven is a country or a jurisdiction that allows individuals or corporations to set up a subsidiary and to avoid paying taxes in their country of residence, thus depriving their home governments of some tax revenues that are used to provide government services.

One of the underlying problems that led to the creation of tax havens in the first place is that there is no single international tax standard. Individual governments have different tax policies, so MNEs have an incentive to deploy their overall financial assets around their worldwide network of subsidiaries in order to minimize taxation. It would not be possible for MNEs to do this if there were a common unitary world tax system. The MNEs are reacting to the lack of a global standard in government tax policy, yet governments then blame them for using legal tax havens to reduce overall taxes paid.

Each tax haven jurisdiction has its own sets of laws on taxation and transparency. Tax havens are also sometimes accused by governments and NGOs such as Oxfam as being a means for money laundering and of hiding the proceeds of criminal activity, including political corruption, illicit arms dealing, and drug trafficking. In fact, these are serious concerns, and each of the tax haven jurisdictions has taken significant steps in recent years to reduce the possibility of being used for these purposes.

The OECD lists a number of factors used to identify a tax haven. Among these, a tax haven is a country or jurisdiction that: (1) imposes no or nominal taxes and is used by foreigners to escape taxes in their own countries (this includes "ring-fencing" jurisdictions that reserve preferential treatment to foreigners, thus shielding the country from tax avoidance by its own residents); (2) has laws or administrative practices that prevent the exchange of information with other governments on taxpayers benefiting from low taxation; (3) lacks transparency; and (4) does not require substantial productive operations in the country, suggesting policies geared to attracting income only on a preferential tax basis. Of all these factors, only the first one is necessary for the identification of a tax haven.

In recent years, the OECD has been pressuring countries and jurisdictions to reverse what it calls harmful tax competition and lack of transparency. The United Nations, for different reasons, has been trying to curb the use of tax havens for money laundering. The EU has also challenged the use of unfair tax competition by US exporters in the World Trade Organization and won. Under US law, US exporters could set up a sales operation in an offshore tax haven and avoid paying taxes on the proceeds of this business. The British and French governments have also each targeted their own tax haven jurisdictions, the British challenging the Channel Islands and Isle of Man offshore tax havens.

Reluctantly, many of these countries have reacted to OECD pressures and reformed their policies. The Channel Islands and the Cayman Islands both have anti-money-laundering legislation. Under pressure from the French government, Monaco also signed an agreement to prevent money laundering, increase transparency, and remove some tax concessions.

Yet the total eradication of tax havens will not come without confrontation. For one, tax havens and their financial institutions depend heavily on these deposits. The Bahamas, which considers itself a major international financial hub, can foresee a tremendous loss of income, especially if other countries, including Switzerland and Luxembourg, are not ready to implement the same policies. The Bahamas has argued that the OECD is using a two-tier system, cooperatively designing legislation with its member countries and then imposing this regime on smaller, less developed, non-member countries.

Switzerland, for its part, is willing to work out a tax reimbursement

Source: Getty Images/Digital Vision

scheme with the EU and the United States, but is not willing to increase its transparency. Though this might address the tax concerns of OECD nations, it does little to prevent criminal activity or to address the tax concerns of poorer countries, which are estimated to lose over $50 billion a year from tax evasion.

Another group opposing these reforms are MNEs that use tax havens. In the UK, at least one company threatened to move its operations if the government continued its attempts to prevent the use of tax havens. Despite this type of opposition, the OECD continues to pressure for reform.

In a report issued in 2000, the OECD identified a number of jurisdictions as tax havens according to criteria it had established. Between 2000 and April 2002, 31 jurisdictions made formal commitments to implement the OECD's standards of transparency and exchange of information. Seven jurisdictions (Andorra, the Principality of Liechtenstein, Liberia, the Principality of Monaco, the Republic of the Marshall Islands, the Republic of Nauru and the Republic of Vanuatu) did not make commitments to transparency and exchange of information at that time and were identified in April 2002 by the OECD's Committee on Fiscal Affairs as uncooperative tax havens. All of these jurisdictions have subsequently made commitments and were removed from the list of uncooperative tax havens. Nauru and Vanuatu made their commitments in 2003 and Liberia and the Marshall Islands in 2007. In May 2009, the Committee on Fiscal Affairs decided to remove all three remaining jurisdictions (Andorra, the Principality of Liechtenstein, and the Principality of Monaco) from the list of uncooperative tax havens in the light of their commitments to implement the OECD standards of transparency and effective exchange of information and the timetable they set for the implementation. As a result, no jurisdiction is currently listed as an uncooperative tax haven by the Committee on Fiscal Affairs according to the progress report as at January 4, 2011.

Websites: www.oecd.org; www.oxfam.org.

Sources: OECD, *Harmful Tax Competition*, 1998; "Offshore Financial Centers Hit at OECD Tax Competition," *Financial Times*, November 21, 2001; Oxfam, *Oxfam Policy Papers—Tax Havens*, June 2000; "A Progress Report on the Jurisdictions Surveyed by OECD Global Forum in Implementing the Internationally Agreed tax Standards, Progress made as at January 4, 2011" (Original Progress Report April 2, 2009), *OECD*, www.oecd.org.

transactions. So the MNE's ability to use netting for moving funds can be limited. A second problem is that in other cases governments have required that payment for imports be delayed until these goods clear customs, thus slowing down the netting process by as much as 60 to 90 days. A third is that of getting local subsidiary managers to cooperate and keep the central clearing account manager fully apprised of all transactions affecting this process. Sometimes there is a reluctance to cooperate on the part of those managers whose cash outflows are substantially larger than their inflows. Under a netting process they can no longer delay payments for three or four months while working to reverse the flow and to pay their bills out of current earnings.

Multilateral netting can help an MNE to ensure that intersubsidiary accounts are balanced, and the process is extremely useful in assisting the parent company in managing global cash flows. However, there is an inherent problem in this process that requires special attention and which netting cannot resolve: foreign exchange risk as typified by the fluctuating value of international currencies. This risk is particularly important when MNEs do business with buyers who are paying in weak currencies. In dealing with this dilemma, MNEs often formulate a foreign exchange risk management strategy.

Managing cash

Hedge
A strategy to protect the firm against risk, in this case against exchange rate risk

Consider a multinational firm such as Nestlé (based in Switzerland) whose network of affiliates extends around the world. Each affiliate has its own customers and suppliers, as well as financial ties to the rest of the company. Viewing the company as a single unit for purposes of cash management can yield far better results than would be obtained if each affiliate managed its cash independently. For example, much less foreign exchange protection is generally needed if all of the affiliates are evaluated together than if each affiliate **hedges** its own position. The French subsidiary may have a large amount of accounts payable in euros that can be hedged simply by consolidating the German affiliate's excess cash which is also in euros. Similarly, the Canadian subsidiary may possess a large amount of Canadian dollar assets that can be hedged by having the US company contract some liabilities (for example, by purchasing equipment or taking out loans) denominated in Canadian dollars. The whole company may coordinate its borrowing efforts through the British subsidiary, which uses the London eurocurrency market.

Centralized cash management offers five kinds of potential gains to the MNE:

1   By pooling the cash holdings of affiliates where possible, the MNE can hold a smaller total amount of cash, thus reducing its financing needs.

2   By centralizing cash management, it can have one group of people specialize in the performance of this task, thus achieving better decisions and economies of scale.

3   By reducing the amount of cash in any one affiliate, it can reduce country risks as well as financial costs.

4   As noted previously, it can net out intracompany accounts when there are multiple payables and receivables among affiliates, thus reducing the amount of money actually transferred among affiliates.

5   Its central cash management group can ensure that cash management decisions aim at corporate goals rather than the goals of individual affiliates when these might conflict.

The first kind of gain results simply from better use of the cash held by the firm. If each affiliate holds enough cash to meet its transactions needs, precautionary needs, and speculative needs (following the Keynesian categories of money demand), far more cash is likely to be held than is needed *companywide*. A domestic company centralizes the cash management function at one location (usually the home office), and an MNE can do the same. The key difference between the two is that the MNE is often restricted in its ability to shift funds among affiliates internationally; thus, less centralization is possible at the MNE level. Any reduction in cash holdings, however, enables the firm to reduce its financing needs, thus lowering costs.

The second kind of gain relates to the development of management skills. By centralizing the cash management function, even if funds are left in the affiliates for the most part, the firm can utilize the skills of a specialized group of cash managers. Gains from this group's decision making should include economies of scale in borrowing, since the group can borrow to meet the entire company's needs and then distribute funds to affiliates as required. Also, the group should develop detailed knowledge of financial opportunities worldwide, thus enabling the firm to borrow at lower cost or lower risk than firms lacking such expertise.

If the MNE reduces its total assets through centralized cash management, it also reduces both its exchange risk and its country risk in that fewer assets are at risk worldwide. The country risk does not change, but the exposure of the company to that risk decreases. Country risk may also be hedged or transferred by the decision makers in the cash management group, who have greater access to protection tools than do managers in any one affiliate.

The fourth kind of benefit, from multilateral netting of accounts, is primarily cost savings from the reduced need to transfer funds between affiliates.

The fifth kind of gain from centralized cash management relates to business strategy. Placing the cash management function in one location, either at the home office or at a location closely monitored by the home office, makes better control possible. In this way, the firm can ensure that cash management decisions are made to meet global corporate needs rather than to improve an affiliate's position, possibly at the expense of the rest of the company. This is especially true with respect to hedging, which should be decided at the corporate level, since virtually every affiliate is likely to have assets or liabilities in another currency that are partially or totally hedged by balance sheet items of other subsidiaries.

While centralized cash management offers obvious and potentially very large benefits, it also presents some problems. Most importantly, if freedom to manage cash is taken away from the affiliate manager, some of the affiliate's ability to improve its performance is also removed. The evaluation of each affiliate must recognize this point. (This idea is discussed further in the section on controls.)

Another problem with internationally centralized cash management arises when national rules restrict financial transfers into or out of some countries. Virtually all less developed countries and many developed ones limit funds outflows through exchange controls or taxation. Some countries specifically disallow international netting of payments. Because of such restrictions, international cash management today requires a great deal of knowledge about national financial constraints and often requires a decentralized strategy of funds transfers due to these constraints.

The whole idea of international funds transfer and management is a major opportunity for firms that have operations in multiple countries. Not only can transfer pricing, multilateral netting, and so on be used to move funds as needed in the firm, but other policies such as dividend remittances, payment of royalties and fees, and intracompany loans are among the many alternatives that can be used to optimize the firm's overall financial situation.

INTERNATIONAL BUSINESS STRATEGY IN ACTION

Sovereign wealth funds

In terms of international financial management a recent development illustrates the tensions between the workings of financial markets and the sovereignty of nations. Mainly due to its large and persistent balance of trade deficit, the United States has long been a destination for inward financial flows. Basically, the US trade deficit has to be balanced by a surplus on its capital (monetary) accounts. Another way of saying this is that as Americans consume more in imports than they export, leading to a trade deficit, it is necessary to sell US financial assets to foreigners. The end result of these financial capital inflows is that foreigners own more American assets.

For many years foreigners bought US Treasury bonds and other financial assets. However, as the value of the US dollar decreased in 2007 and 2008 the yields on US financial investments also started to fall. Financial assets denominated in US dollars became less valuable compared to assets in other currencies such as the euro. Even the Canadian dollar was worth more than a US dollar in late 2007.

The result of the falling US dollar was that foreigners switched from financial investments into the US stock market. Equity ownership of US firms became a substitute for US bonds for foreigners. Many US firms welcomed such foreign investment, even as it diluted American ownership of their companies. For example, some US financial institutions, such as Citigroup, Merrill Lynch, and Morgan Stanley, were bailed out by foreign private equity funds in early 2008. However, this has raised issues of sovereignty as the richest private equity funds are owned by governments from the Middle East and China. They are called sovereign wealth funds.

Source: Travelstock44.de/Alamy

For example, one of the world's richest sovereign wealth funds is owned by the government of Dubai. Previously (as reported in the case in Chapter 14 on P&O, Carnival, and Dubai Port World) the takeover of some US ports by Dubai Ports was criticized by Senator Hillary Clinton and many of her colleagues in the US Congress. As a result of the controversy President Bush was forced to reopen the process by which Dubai Ports had been allowed to take over the US ports previously owned by P&O. While Senator ▶

Table 1 Largest sovereign wealth funds by assets under management

Country	Fund name	Launch year	Billions of US $	Origin
UAE (Abu Dhabi)	Abu Dhabi Investment Authority (ADIA)	1976	627.0	Oil
Norway	Government Pension Fund – Global	1990	512.0	Oil
Saudi Arabia	SAMA Foreign Holdings	n.a	439.1	Oil
China	SAFE Investment Company	1997	437.1 (est.)	Non commodity
China	China Investment Corporation	2007	332.4	Non commodity
China, Hong Kong	Hong Kong Monetary Authority Investment Portfolio	1993	259.3	Non commodity
Singapore	Government of Singapore Investment Corporation (GIC)	1981	247.5	Non commodity
Kuwait	Kuwait Investment Authority	1953	202.8	Non commodity
China	China National Social Security Fund	2000	146.5	Non commodity
Russia	National Welfare Fund	2008	142.5 (est.)	Non commodity
Singapore	Temasek Holdings	1974	133.0	Non commodity
Qatar	Qatar Investment Authority	2005	85.0	Oil
Libya	Libya Investment Authority	2006	70.0	Oil
Australia	Australian Future Fund	2004	67.2	Non commodity
Algeria	Revenue Regulation Fund	2000	56.7	Oil

Source: *Sovereign Wealth Fund Institute* (updated November, 2010), http://www.swfinstitute.org/fund-rankings/.

Clinton argued that US ports should not be foreign owned, she seemed to have forgotten that these ports were already foreign owned since P&O is a British company. What she and her congressional colleagues really objected to was that Dubai Ports was a Middle Eastern government-owned financial company against which discriminatory measures should be used.

Ultimately the US government can discriminate against foreign investors on the grounds of national security. In the case of US ports there is some logic to such discrimination, especially in a post-9/11 world. However, it is difficult to apply this logic of national security to many of the protectionist arguments raised by labor groups and others opposed to foreign investment. The confusion arises because the large state-run private equity funds of the Middle East and China are seen as instruments of their governments. They are not seen as purely financial investment houses, although they operate in world financial markets in the same way as the banks and financial institutions of Western economies.

The control of strategic entities in the United States will continue to be controversial. The Dubai Ports case sparked discussion of whether any of the 360 US ports should be allowed to be operated by foreign entities. Three out of five terminals in New York and New Jersey, and 80 percent of the Port of Los Angeles, are now being operated by foreign firms. At the time of the controversy, only about 5 percent of the approximately 26,000 containers arriving daily at the US coasts were inspected by the US government, leaving the responsibility of screening the rest to companies that own and operate the ports. One of these companies is Denmark-based Maersk Group, vertically integrating into port management from its core business of vessel operation. In operating terminals in 12 different ports across the United States the company plays a part in US national security efforts.

This issue is also relevant in Europe, where European firms such as Swiss bank UBS received funds from the Singapore Investment Corporation (GIC). The British bank, Barclays, received investments from Temasek of Singapore.

The world's largest sovereign wealth funds are reported in Table 1. The largest sovereign wealth fund is the Abu Dhabi Investment Authority (ADIA) founded in 1976, while Singapore's Temasek was set up in 1974. The China Investment Corporation, a much newer fund, invested $3 billion in US buyout firm Blackstone.

It is not clear how the issue of sovereign equity funds will be resolved. At a macroeconomic level it is necessary for world financial and trade imbalances to be reconciled. As long as the United States has a large trade deficit there will need to be inward flows of foreign investment. If a large proportion of these inward flows are from private equity funds, then there is little that the United States can do to scare them away.

Sources: *Financial Times*, January 24, 2008; Mimi Hall, Bill Nichols and Sue Kirchhoff, "Security Issues Goes Beyond Ports Flap," www.usatoday.com, February 23, 2006; Jessica Holzer, "Dubai's Olive Branch," www.forbes.com, October 3, 2006; David Shuster, "Who Owns the United States Ports?" www.msnbc.msn.com, February 22, 2006; www.maersk.com; *Sovereign Wealth Fund Institute* (updated November, 2010), http://www.swfinstitute.org/fund-rankings/.

EXCHANGE RISK MANAGEMENT

We have discussed exchange risk primarily in relation to *transactions* denominated in foreign currency. In addition, exchange risk exists in the translation of financial statements and, in principle, for future, so-far unspecified activities of the firm. Three kinds of exchange risk should be differentiated: (1) transaction risk; (2) translation risk; and (3) economic risk. Each kind of risk is important to the MNE, and each leads to somewhat different conclusions for hedging strategies.

Transaction risk

Transaction risk
The risk of financial loss or gain to an MNE due to unanticipated exchange rate changes affecting future cash flows from transactions that are denominated in foreign exchange

When a specific contracted asset or liability is denominated in a foreign currency, it is subject to **transaction risk**, or the risk of an unexpected change in its home-currency value during the time to maturity. Accounts payable and receivable, loans, and bank deposits denominated in foreign currencies are examples of items that are subject to such exchange risk. Each foreign currency transaction can be hedged (or not) with some offsetting transaction in the same currency and with the same maturity. This topic was discussed in Chapter 7, and a new example is presented at the end of this section.

Translation risk

Translation risk
The risk of losses or gains on the MNE's balance sheet, due to unhedged exchange rate changes during an accounting period

Translation risk, or accounting risk, is the risk of value changes in foreign currency assets and liabilities on the balance sheet, whether or not the transactions occur during the accounting period. For example, the plant and equipment of foreign subsidiaries is subject to valuation change even if no purchase or sale of such items takes place during the accounting period. Because balance sheet information is reported in most countries to securities regulators and in published financial statements, valuation changes in the foreign operations of multinational firms become public knowledge. Loss in the value of foreign currency assets, regardless of its impact on company earnings, may negatively affect investors' perceptions of a firm. To avoid the appearance of weakness due to the devaluation of foreign assets, firms often try to hedge their balance sheets through financial contracts (such as forward contracts or money market hedges).

Consolidation
The translation of foreign affiliate accounts and addition to home-country accounts for the purpose of reporting the complete (global) condition of a company; consolidation of foreign affiliate accounts that are denominated in other currencies necessarily produces translation risk

A good example of this exposure for a US MNE is when the currency of a local country weakens in relation to the dollar. For example, if the Chilean peso declined by 10 percent against the dollar, the value of the Chilean subsidiary's peso account at the local bank would also decline when translated into dollars in the **consolidation** process. If the company had the equivalent of $100,000 (US) on deposit, this account would now be worth $90,000 in translation and consolidation. Of course, this decline would not affect the number of pesos on deposit, and the local purchasing power of these pesos, at least in the short run, would remain the same. However, the decline would negatively affect the subsidiary's ability to purchase imports from countries with strong currencies since it would now take more pesos than before to buy these goods.

Balance sheet hedging
The use of financial instruments denominated in foreign currency to eliminate exchange rate (translation) risk from the balance sheet of a company

Conclusions as to the desirability of **balance sheet hedging** are ambiguous. On the one hand, since investor decisions may be based on valuation changes in foreign currency assets, the firm should hedge to avoid investor preoccupation with such changes. On the other hand, since the valuation of foreign currency assets may not affect the economic viability of the project, it would be a waste of effort for the firm to deal with such changes.

Economic risk

Economic risk
The risk of financial loss or gain to an MNE due to the effects of unanticipated exchange rate changes on future cash flows that are denominated in foreign currencies

Economic risk is the risk of unexpected changes in future cash flows from foreign operations (and from activities denominated in foreign currencies, wherever they occur). Such risk is most important to the firm, since future cash flows are the basis for the firm's value. Unfortunately for the manager, it is not possible to know with certainty the full set of future cash flows that will occur. Thus, a hedging strategy cannot be perfectly matched with such cash flows. To deal with economic risk, the firm may choose to follow a generalized strategy of hedging transactions when they are contracted and trying to balance foreign currency assets and liabilities as they appear on the balance sheet. Or the firm may choose not to hedge at all, on the assumption that future currency fluctuation will be approximately offset by price changes in each country (that is, purchasing power parity will approximately hold). Despite the inherent difficulty of predicting future foreign exchange exposures, ultimately the firm should be concerned about economic (foreign exchange) risk as the key variable in exchange risk management.

Consider the economic risk involved with a subsidiary's assets. If the value of the local currency strengthens, the sale of inventory will generate larger dollar profits. However, would it be wiser to lower the price, to take less profit per item, but to generate more demand? Similarly, would it be wise now to sell fixed assets such as buildings or factories and then to lease them back from the purchaser? Some US firms in Tokyo found that by the early 1990s the land and buildings that they had bought years before were now worth hundreds of times their original purchase price. Believing that the local real estate market was as high as it was going to go and feeling that it would be more advisable to sell the properties and rent them back, these firms sold their office buildings and made tremendous profits. The ensuing decline of Tokyo real estate prices showed that these firms had made very wise (lucky) decisions.[2]

Another example of economic exposure is the risk that companies take when selling to a country with a weakening currency. In this case many MNEs have sought to increase their own production efficiency, lower their costs, and continue to generate acceptable profit. Firms such as Honda, Nissan, and BMW have complemented this strategy by setting up operations in the United States, their largest international market.[3] In the process the firms have reduced their economic exposure.

In fact, all three kinds of foreign exchange risk play important parts in the management of an international firm. No single hedging strategy can cover them all, so the MNE manager must devise plans for dealing with each. Fortunately, both transaction and economic risk deal with future cash flows; thus, the management of these two kinds of risk can be combined fairly readily. For example, the firm can hedge all occasional exports denominated in foreign currencies and seek local-currency financing for the entire production of its foreign affiliates. Then, if it does not employ balance sheet hedging (as suggested earlier), it can follow a consistent and simple hedging strategy. Judging from the immense volume of material dealing with corporate foreign exchange management strategies, it is safe to say that MNEs generally do *not* follow such simple strategies. Instead, they combine some hedging with some speculation in an effort to maximize their results from foreign exchange dealings. Table 16.4 lists a range of exchange risk hedging techniques that can be used to deal with one or more of these exchange risk categories.

Table 16.4 Exchange risk hedging techniques*

To hedge an exposed liability	To hedge an exposed asset
Buy foreign exchange in the forward market	Sell foreign exchange in the forward market
Buy foreign exchange in the futures market	Sell foreign exchange in the futures market
Buy foreign exchange call options	Buy foreign exchange put options
Invest/deposit in a foreign exchange instrument	Borrow in a foreign exchange instrument
Incur accounts receivable in foreign exchange	Incur accounts payable in foreign exchange
Swap liabilities with another firm	Swap assets with another firm
Obtain any other foreign exchange asset	Obtain any other foreign exchange liability

* These techniques assume no expectation about the direction of exchange rate change. If devaluation is expected, then creation of a net liability position is attractive, and vice versa for expected revaluation. In each instance, the hedge must produce an equal-value asset (liability) in the same currency with equal maturity to offset the exposed liability (asset).

Active learning check

Review your answer to Active Learning Case question 2 and make any changes you like. Then compare your answer to the one below.

2 **If the two carriers were to complete their merger and the US dollar then weakens against the British pound, as it did in 2004–2005, how will this affect the financial statements of the company?**

This will depend on whether the two carriers continue to issue separate financial statements. If they do, AA's financials will be affected only by the amount of sterling that it has on hand. Otherwise there will be no effect, since changes in the pound do not affect the cost to AA of doing business in the United States. In the case of BA the accounts payable that are due in dollars will negatively affect the airline's financials. If the two carriers combine their statements into one, the overall effect will be a result of how these transactions net out. This would be determined based on the rules in FASB (Financial Accounting Standards Board) Statement No. 52.

An example of exchange risk management

Consider the situation faced by a US-based firm such as American Express Company (AMEX) when its subsidiary in the UK reports the purchase of £5 million of office equipment (mainly furniture and computer terminals) for the subsidiary's tourist service offices throughout that country. This equipment is to be paid for in 180 days in British pounds. The strategies for dealing with exchange risk in this transaction depend on the whole firm's position in British pounds. The problem can be analyzed as follows.

First, if American Express already has an existing asset exposure in the UK due to its subsidiary's ongoing activities, that position may partially or wholly cover the new transaction. In other words, if American Express(UK) has a balance sheet that shows net sterling (pound) assets, typically because foreign subsidiaries have some dollar liabilities, the new account payable may partially offset that asset exposure.

Second, the same results may occur even if the British subsidiary has been operated to cover ongoing exchange risk in the UK. In the event that American Express has placed funds in euro–British pound deposits in one of its other subsidiaries (for example, in France or Germany), the new account payable may offset the existing exposure. *Note that the exposure is still not covered unless the maturity of the existing asset matches the six-month maturity of the new liability.*

Third, American Express can look for some financial hedging technique to avoid the exchange risk. For example, some new asset such as a bank deposit or short-term security could be purchased with a maturity of 180 days and a value of £5 million. Or a forward contract could be arranged with a bank to sell dollars and buy pounds in 180 days. Through the London International Financial Futures Exchange (LIFFE) or through one of the US futures exchanges, American Express could arrange a futures contract or **currency option** contract to hedge the account payable. The alternatives are numerous, but the basic goal is to find some British pound asset that matures in 180 days, worth £5 million, to hedge the new liability that calls for a cash outflow of £5 million in 180 days.

The following table lists relevant financial information if American Express were making this hedging decision on January 13, 2011:

Currency option is a derivative financial instrument where the owner has the right but not the obligation to exchange money denominated in one currency into another currency at a pre-agreed exchange rate on a specified date. The right to buy is the call option and the right to sell is the put option. It allows the company to take advantage of favorable movements in exchange rates. Options are the only form of hedging that does this.

Spot exchange rate	US$1.57680/£1
180-day forward exchange rate	US$1.57350/£1
180-day LIBOR rate in pounds is 1.06375%	2.1275%/year
180-day LIBOR rate in dollars is 0.45681%	0.91362%/year
6-month sterling call option (to buy) strike price:	
The options cost US $875 per contract at the CME, with £31,250 per contract	US $1.5840/£1
For this option, the premium is US $0.0072/£	
6-month sterling futures contract rate:	
The futures contracts have £62,500 per contract	US $1.5800/£1
Ignore commissions and other transaction costs for these instruments	

Sources: Financial Times, http://markets.ft.com/markets/currencies.asp; *The Wall Street Journal,* http://online.wsj.com/mdc/public/page/2_3020-moneyrate.html; http://www.global-rates.com/interest-rates/libor/libor.aspx.

American Express can use this information to evaluate various financial hedges for the sterling account payable.

First, the firm can use a simple forward contract to hedge the exposure. A forward exchange contract to buy British pounds would cost about US $7.8675 million in six months, as follows:

$$£5,000,000 \times US\$1.57350/£ = US\$7,867,500$$

This forward exchange contract completely hedges the account payable, because it will result in receipt from the bank of £5 million in 180 days, which will be used to pay the supplier of office equipment.

A second alternative is called "money market hedging." The first step is to place funds now into a pound-denominated investment that matures in six months. The choice shown above is a eurosterling account that pays 2.1275 percent per year for the six-month period. The dollar value of pounds for American Express to buy today can be calculated by discounting the future pounds that are needed to a present value of pounds that must be deposited today to achieve that sum in six months. The calculations are as follows:

$$£5,000,000/(1.043003) = £4,793,850.17$$

This first step shows that the interest earned in the eurosterling deposit for 180 days will be 1.06375 percent (that is, 2.1275%/2) and that £4,793,850.17 must be deposited today to reach the value needed to pay the account payable. Next, the dollars that must be used today to buy these pounds is:

$$£4,793,850.17 \times US\$1.57680/£1 = US\$7,558,942.95$$

The hedging cost is lower for this alternative, since the funds must be paid *now* rather than in 180 days. To compare the two choices, they must be placed in the same time period. This requires discounting the forward contract value using the relevant discount rate, which would be a deposit interest rate in dollars for the same time period:

$$US\$7,867,500/(1.018421) = US\$7,725,194.28$$

The discount amount (1.018421) is the implicit return to depositing funds in a eurodollar account (comparable to the europound deposit) for six months at 0.91362 percent per year. This results in a lower cost of hedging in the money market hedging (US$166,251.79).

A third alternative is to use a futures contract hedge in the LIFFE or the Chicago Mercantile Exchange (CME). Using the CME's quotes, we see that American Express could buy future pounds for US $1.5800 per pound in contracts worth £62,500 per contract. Multiple contracts could be bought, so that with 80 contracts the company could obtain the needed £5 million. However, since the exchange rate is worse than the forward rate (that is, it costs more dollars to buy the pounds), American Express will not consider a futures hedge.[4]

Each of these financial hedges can protect American Express against foreign exchange risk. The company will want to choose the least costly hedge in this case, namely the forward market hedge. In other situations, one or another of these three alternatives will be the most beneficial to the firm. Beyond these choices, American Express should consider the possibility of structuring its business such that it could use British pound assets (for example, accounts receivable, investments, etc.) to hedge liabilities such as this purchase of equipment.

Developing forecasting and reporting systems

The management of foreign exchange risk can be both complex and cumbersome. A multinational with 20 subsidiaries can present a formidable challenge to the parent company because so many foreign exchange risk decisions need to be made and monitored. However, there are a number of steps that MNEs typically take in creating the necessary system for managing these decisions. They may:

1 Decide the types and degrees of economic exposure that the company is willing to accept.

2 Develop the necessary expertise (in-house personnel and/or outside economists or consultants) for monitoring exchange rates and for forecasting those rates that are applicable to the identified exposures.

3 Construct a reporting system that allows the firm to identify exposed accounts, to measure this exposure, and to feed back information on what the firm is doing and the status of these decisions.

4 Include all MNE units in this reporting system so that each better understands the risks it is assuming and is aware of the actions that must be taken to deal with these risks.

5 Keep senior-level management fully apprised of what is going on in each area of responsibility so that every regional or divisional manager is able periodically to revise the exposure risk and to make those strategy changes that will help more effectively to manage the process.

As firms begin to implement these five steps, they are better able to deal with the management of foreign exchange risk.

✔ Active learning check

Review your answer to Active Learning Case question 3 and make any changes you like. Then compare your answer to the one below.

3 If BA believed that the British pound was going to appreciate in relation to the euro, how is it likely to deal with receivables and payables?

If BA believed that the pound was going to get stronger against the euro, and if it were owed euros, the firm would try to collect them immediately before their value declined. At the same time BA would delay payment of those obligations that were fixed in euros, for it would be getting more euros per pound after the appreciation, thus making it easier to pay those bills. The firm would lead collections and lag payables.

CAPITAL BUDGETING IN THE MNE

Capital project evaluation follows many of the same principles in an international firm as in a domestic firm, though additional variables and risks must be considered. Specifically, foreign projects must be evaluated for exchange risk, country risk, different financing costs, and any problems associated with the transfer of products, services, or funds due to government controls in any of the relevant countries. To see how these factors appear in the analysis, consider the following example of a food processing plant to be constructed by a US-based company in Shapironia (a fictitious country).

The company has developed the following pro forma income statement for the proposed investment project:

Proposed Shapironia Processing Plant Pro Forma Income Statement, Typical Year (in local currency)

Sales	10,000,000
Cost of goods sold:	
Local materials	1,000,000
Imported materials	2,000,000
Labor	3,000,000
Overhead expenses	600,000
Interest on loan from parent firm	400,000
Net income before tax	3,000,000
Local tax: 50%	1,500,000
Net income after tax	1,500,000

Assuming the investment made by the parent firm is 4 million in local currency, the project appears to have a simple return on capital of about 38 percent per year (1,500,000/4,000,000). As long as the firm's cost of capital is less than 38 percent, the project is worth undertaking.[5] The normal, domestic concerns apply to this project evaluation; that is, the estimate is only as good as the forecasts of costs and sales. In addition, this foreign project faces potentially important considerations such as exchange risk, currency inconvertibility and other country risks, and preferential local borrowing opportunities. Chapter 15 provides more detailed discussion of this problem of country risk evaluation and management.

Exchange risk will affect the US dollar value of the profits earned, potentially raising or lowering them substantially. For example, if the local-currency value rises by 10 percent in relation to the dollar, net income after tax will rise (in dollar terms) by 10 percent, other things equal. However, if imported materials come from the United States, that cost (in local currency) will fall. Similarly, if the loan is made in dollars, interest cost (in local-currency terms) will fall. Sales, if any are exported from Shapironia, may decrease due to the exchange rate change.[6] In sum, a rise in the value of the local currency relative to the US dollar will tend to cause an increase in dollar profits from the affiliate, and such profits will tend to fall if the local currency devalues relative to the dollar.

Country risk (defined in Chapter 15) is another concern in the attempt to evaluate this project properly. If the host government decides to restrict profit remittances, then, no matter how profitable the project, the MNE will not be able to utilize its earnings elsewhere in the firm or to distribute them to shareholders. This problem is known as **currency inconvertibility**, regardless of whether the cause is a political decision or simply an economic reality. If discontent with the Shapironia government leads to strikes or violent confrontation between the government and opposition groups, the plant may be

Currency inconvertibility
The inability of a firm to transfer profit from a subsidiary in a host country to other areas of the organization or to shareholders because of host-government restrictions on profit remittances

damaged or its production curtailed. Not all country risk is negative; if the government chooses to reduce corporate taxes to stimulate greater investment, the project may generate greater profitability than that shown above. In sum, country risks need to be considered when the full set of the project's financial implications is being judged.

Borrowing costs may differ in Shapironia and the United States. Thus, if the firm uses its **weighted-average cost of capital** in capital budgeting decisions, this project should be adjusted to account for any locally subsidized borrowing opportunity that exists. Many countries (and states or provinces within countries) offer low-interest loans to corporate investors to attract production facilities and jobs. If this is true in Shapironia and if the firm chooses to borrow some funds locally, the subsidized capital cost should be reflected in the capital budget. The project as shown uses an intracompany loan whose interest may be charged at the parent's actual cost of funds or marked up (or down) to achieve greater (or lesser) transfer of funds to the parent.

Finally, recall that the capital budget measures the project's *incremental impact* on the whole firm. Thus, if there are export sales from the parent to this new affiliate, those new sales must be counted in the evaluation. If the project replaces sales that were formerly exported to Shapironia, those lost sales must be counted. Any other intracompany impacts should also be measured in the project evaluation. This means the project should be judged in comparison to other alternatives available to the firm serving the Shapironia market. If exports from the United States offer a greater incremental profitability than the proposed plant, exports should be chosen. In summary, the incremental gains to the firm from the proposed project should be compared to the potential gains from other international business alternatives that may be available.

In contrast to domestic projects, one additional key question must be answered: who should conduct the analysis, the parent or the foreign subsidiary? Typically, the initial analysis is done at the subsidiary or branch level and then passed up to the head office for modification and/or approval. For example, two subsidiaries may both want to build a new tire plant and sell to the same market. Without coordination, they would compete against each other and the expected profits would not materialize. So the parent corporation will make a decision that benefits the entire organization. In this latter role the parent may have to turn down a positive NPV project from one subsidiary in favor of a higher NPV project from another subsidiary. The same process applies in reverse to plant closures: the shutdown will be at the plant with the largest negative NPV. Similarly, factories or holdings that do not generate sufficient profit may be sold.

Use of NPV

The parent company will review expenditure proposals because it has the necessary overall information to make these decisions. Moreover, such expenditure decisions will often be different from those of the subsidiary because the latter may use faulty valuation techniques or fail to address adequately the impact of political risk. In explaining why these differences occur, we must first review the basic NPV criterion. This criterion separates the financing and operating parts of the problem by discounting operating cash flows by a weighted-average cost of capital that embodies the financing decision. The NPV equation is:

$$\text{NPV} = \sum_{t=0}^{T} \frac{I_t + C_t}{(1 + K_A)} \tag{16.1}$$

where:

$$K_A = k_e \frac{S}{V} + k_d(1-t_x)\frac{D}{V} \tag{16.2}$$

Weighted-average cost of capital (WACC)
The firm's cost of obtaining funds from the various sources available. Each source of funds is weighted (multiplied) by the percentage of total capital it provides. Thus, the WACC is W_1 (cost of using retained earnings) + W_2 (cost of bank borrowing) + W_3 (cost of other source of funds), where each cost is stated as an annual percentage rate and each W is the percentage of total capital from that source

The definitions of the terms are:

I_t = investment cash outlays in year t

C_t = cash inflows in year t

T = terminal date or end of project

K_A = weighted-average cost of capital

k_e = cost of equity capital

k_d = cost of debt financing

t_x = tax rate

D/V, S/V = debt and equity ratios, respectively

NPV = incremental net present value for the project.

In examining what determines the NPV, we must realize that disagreement between parent and subsidiary can arise because of the discount rate K_A, investment cost, and annual cash flows. Political risk can also affect all values. For example, the risk of foreign currency controls can cause some of the future cash flows to be largely ignored by the parent. From the parent's perspective, if funds can no longer be remitted, their value is substantially reduced since they are not available for dividend payments or for reinvestment elsewhere. Conversely, once foreign exchange controls are in place, the parent will often treat blocked funds as being less valuable. From the parent's perspective, the cost of future investments in the country, financed by these blocked funds, is reduced. In both cases the subsidiary is not directly concerned with the problem of foreign exchange controls, and it will discount all cash flows that are incremental from its own perspective.

Similarly, country risk may cause the parent to increase the discount rate or required return to reflect that risk. However, if the subsidiary does not agree with that perception, it will not increase the discount rate, so its calculation of the present value of the cash inflows and NPV will be higher. Moreover, if foreign exchange controls are enforced, the local capital markets can be isolated from the international capital market. From the subsidiary's perspective, the result may be lower local real interest rates, which make local investment opportunities seem attractive. However, the parent, looking at global opportunities, may decide that it will make more sense to draw capital out of the country for reinvestment elsewhere.

Another reason that parent and local NPVs may differ is faulty application of the NPV framework. The most common errors are in incorrectly choosing t_x and K_A. The tax rate t_x is relevant in two places, the incremental tax that results from the incremental profits and the incremental tax shield that results from debt financing. Here, the errors usually come from a failure to determine the incremental tax rate. From the subsidiary's perspective the tax rate is the extra tax that it pays locally. However, the parent must also consider any incremental tax that it will pay once dividends are remitted.

In determining the discount rate K_A, several problems emerge. First, it is common that discount rates differ by several percentage points. The reason is obvious: inflation differs across different countries, and thus the inflationary premium built into the discount rate will differ. What the firm can never do is to use a discount rate from one country to evaluate cash flows denominated in another currency. The correct procedure is to calculate the real discount rate and then to "gross it up" for the inflationary expectations of the relevant country.

Additionally, debt ratios differ across subsidiaries, and the weights in Equation 14.2 may alter the cost of capital. This will inevitably occur if the multinational maximizes the use of debt financing in a country with subsidized borrowing rates. However, the debt ratio of that country is then not appropriate for determining the cost of capital since the excess debt can be carried only because that subsidiary is part of a multinational. Similarly, it is a mistake to use the local real cost of debt to determine the cost of capital. In both these examples, if the MNE uses local debt norms and local debt costs, it is negating the advantage of being a multinational. That advantage is the ability to raise debt internally where it is the cheapest. As a result, in a country with a high debt cost the firm may have very little debt, whereas in a country with subsidized interest costs it may have a large amount of debt. In both cases there is no effect on the overall cost of funds to the multinational. Hence local debt norms and interest costs will be ignored unless local regulations restrict the use of debt funds to projects within that country. In this instance, if the firm accepts a local project, it can also raise more subsidized foreign debt. If the money cannot be removed from the country by transfer pricing or whatever, then its cost is relevant in Equation 16.2.

Institutional features

Thus far the focus has been on the technical question of how to evaluate capital expenditures. However, a very important institutional factor that warrants attention is the impact of government policies such as subsidies and controls.

Foreign investment review agency
A government agency that reviews applications for foreign direct investment projects and approves or disapproves the projects, according to standards established by the government

Government intervention can affect the profitability of a project or its financing. For example, in considering foreign investments, countries such as Australia and Canada have **foreign investment review agencies**, which review these investments to ensure that they benefit the local economy. As a result, foreign investment is often contingent on factors such as local employment quotas, local sourcing of components, the transfer of technology, and a degree of local ownership. This intervention can obviously complicate capital expenditure analysis. Frequently the result is to forecast specific, quantitative outcomes. For example, if technology is locally licensed, what is the possible impact of its being leaked to different countries? If the MNE has to train local middle management and to sell shares locally, how does this affect the probability of forcible divestiture at some future date? In many cases the result of local content regulations is to expropriate all the advantages possessed by the multinational. One of the particular problems here is local ownership requirements. The parent's viewpoint is dominant on the assumption that the objective of the firm is to maximize its market value, which is owned by shareholders in the home country. However, once joint ventures and significant minority shareholdings are traded locally, this solution breaks down. The problem now becomes whose market value should be maximized. The result is that while minority ownership reduces the political risk of expropriation, it restricts the multinational's freedom of action. It is, therefore, not surprising that, where political risk is lowered, minority shareholders get bought out. For example, Ford acquired its British minority shareholdings in 1961, and Shell bought out its minority US shareholdings in 1984.

However, government regulation is not all bad. Outside North America the interventionist approach of most governments creates unique opportunities for the MNE. For example, most countries provide concessionary financing that is contingent on the use of certain local resources. The British Export Credits Guarantee Department (ECGD) has some of the lowest-cost money for export financing as long as the borrower uses British equipment. By structuring an investment to use British equipment, a multinational might be able to borrow $10 million at 3 percent interest instead of at a market rate of, say, 9 percent. In effect, this subsidized loan represents a gift by the British taxpayers. This value has to be factored into the analysis. The inclusion of subsidies also occurs in domestic capital expenditure analysis, for example, with the proliferation of small-business financing programs. However, in an international project, rather than being unusual, it is rare not to determine the value or cost of a particular government program. Recently government regulation of MNEs has been falling, leading to more cross-listings on the world stock exchange.

INTERNATIONAL FINANCING IN THE MNE

The home office of an MNE should have available to it funding from the domestic money and capital markets, as well as from international money and capital markets. The funding sources available to a *foreign affiliate* of an MNE include debt and equity from the parent and local financing in the host country. Table 16.5 presents a view of these sources that expands on the view presented in Figure 16.1 and on the discussion in Chapter 7. The sources of credit to the MNE are divided between short- and long-term loans and between direct and intermediated provision of funds through a bank or some other financial institution.

Notice that in addition to the funding that was discussed earlier in the intrafirm context, numerous sources of external funding are available to the MNE. These sources include funding from domestic money and capital markets in each country where the firm operates, as well as funding from the euromarkets in money centers such as London, New York, and Tokyo. A large firm from Norway, for example, could seek financing in the US market through international bank loans, through bond issue, or even through issuing stock shares or American Depositary Receipts.[7]

Financial structure

Debt–equity ratio
The value of a firm's total debt divided by the value of its total equity; a higher ratio implies greater leverage, and potentially greater risk

Financial structure in an MNE is complicated by the fact that the "normal" **debt–equity ratio** differs from industry to industry and from country to country. For example, the average debt–equity ratio in large Japanese companies is about 2.75 to 1. In the United States, this ratio is generally far less than 1, averaging about 0.6 for non-financial industries as a whole. As a rule, the total financial structure of an MNE follows the standards of the home-country financial market, since shares are usually traded there. On the other hand, a US company's affiliate in Japan may be able to operate successfully with far higher leverage than that of the parent, given local conditions in Japan. Thus, the financial structures of foreign affiliates may differ from that of the overall firm or that of the parent in particular. The only limitation is that the financial structure of the affiliate must not cause the financial structure of the entire firm to deviate from acceptable standards in the home country.

Table 16.5 International sources of credit (including markets and intrafirm transfers)

Borrowing	Domestic inside the firm	Domestic market	Foreign inside the firm	Foreign market	Euromarket
Direct, short term	Intrafirm loans, transfer pricing, royalties, fees, service charges	Commercial paper, other promissory notes, commercial credit	International intrafirm loans, international transfer pricing, dividends, royalties, fees	Commercial credit	Eurocommercial paper
Intermediated, short term	Short-term bank loans, discounted receivables	International back-to-back loans	Short-term bank loans, discounted receivables	Euro short-term loans	
Direct, long term	Intrafirm loans, investment in affiliates	Stock issue, bond issue	International intrafirm long-term loans, FDI	Stock issue, bond issue, ADR issue	Eurobonds, euroequity
Intermediated, long term		Long-term bank loans	International back-to-back loans	Long-term bank loans	Euro long-term loans

Direct means borrowing from owners of wealth (e.g., investors); *intermediated* means borrowing from a financial intermediary (e.g., a bank). International back-to-back loan means a loan in which two companies in different countries borrow offsetting amounts from one another in each other's currency.

The entire MNE may choose to meet its external financing needs by borrowing through an affiliate in a low-interest country if such funding is available and if exchange rate protection still leaves financing costs lower than those in other currencies. As already noted, since the MNE is evaluated by investors in the home country, its overall debt–equity structure must satisfy the financial community in that country. However, if the firm sells shares of an affiliate in the host country's financial market, the debt–equity position of the affiliate is an important issue.

For a wholly owned foreign subsidiary that does not sell shares in the host country, the debt–equity ratio should be determined by overall corporate needs. If funding is available at low cost (adjusted for expected exchange rate changes), local borrowing is appropriate. If a substantial amount of assets is exposed locally, local borrowing provides a hedge to both exchange and country risks. If the local currency is expected to devalue substantially, then, even if local interest rates are high, it may make sense to borrow locally, assuming the expected postdevaluation interest costs would be lower than the home-country costs.

Local equity financing may be forced on the firm if the host government demands partial local ownership of foreign enterprises. This situation exists today in many less developed countries and in most of the formerly communist countries. In this case, the affiliate's debt–equity ratio may be skewed toward equity, especially if the parent seeks to avoid sending funds into that country. That is, financing for the affiliate would come from the local partner's equity investment plus retained earnings, and other funding would be sought only after these sources were used up.

In countries with restrictions on funds transfers, such as profit and royalty remittances, equity financing would again be sensible—using those funds that cannot be taken out of the country. That is, if funds are blocked from transfer abroad, the MNE must reinvest them locally; investing the funds in the existing operation (that is, profit reinvestment) may offer a greater benefit than placing them in local financial instruments such as bank deposits or government securities. This strategy is widely used by multinationals, though most would prefer the freedom to take their funds out of the host country.

Finally, notice that *if* the MNE is able to lower its total borrowing costs by utilizing foreign sources of funds, it has gained an advantage relative to domestic firms that limit themselves to domestic financial markets in any country. If the MNE has a lower weighted-average cost of capital for any given capital budget, it will undertake more projects than the purely domestic firm (or will be more profitable in the same projects).

 Active learning check

Review your answer to Active Learning Case question 4 and make any changes you like. Then compare your answer to the one below.

4 Assuming that BA might choose to acquire all or part of American, United, or Delta Airlines in the United States, how could BA finance the major capital budgeting need in international markets, and what are some of the important considerations in choosing among alternative financing sources?

BA can use the eurocurrency markets in London to minimize its short-term borrowing costs, and it can also issue commercial paper in New York or London to obtain working capital. For longer-term borrowing BA could issue shares in the United States or in another money center such as Frankfurt or Tokyo, as well as issuing bonds in a low-tax jurisdiction such as Luxembourg. The choices depend on interest rates, exchange rates, and currencies in which BA will have cash flows in the future.

CONTROL: IDENTIFYING OBJECTIVES, EVALUATING AFFILIATE PERFORMANCE, AND MAKING PERFORMANCE CONSISTENT WITH GOALS

Control

The fundamental function of management that involves developing profit plans for the firm and its divisions and then deciding what to do when actual operating results differ from those planned

Control is the fundamental function of management that involves developing profit plans for the firm and its divisions and then deciding what to do when actual operating results differ from those planned. For a foreign investment project, the financial control process generally begins with putting together a set of pro forma financial statements (income statement, balance sheet, cash flow report). Then detailed budgets are developed for individual divisions, allocating the full capital budget to the specific purposes for which it will be used. During the time period after the creation of these plans, the firm's management observes the results and notes any deviations from the budget. Usually, of course, actual results differ from budgeted ones. Finally, the firm develops and implements a management plan for dealing with the deviations. The process is cyclical—as each planning period ends, another begins—and new budgets and managerial contingencies may be developed.

In the multinational firm, the potential for substantial home-office control over affiliates exists because major capital budgeting usually requires more resources than those available in an affiliate, and home-office assistance is needed to carry out capital projects. In addition, financial reporting to the parent company provides an informational basis for controls, which may or may not be exercised, depending on the extent of the firm's decentralization. Finally, because the people assigned to manage foreign affiliates are usually well known to the home-office managers, an informal, personal contact ties affiliates to the home office. All of this means that the home office has the potential to impose heavy controls on the activities of foreign affiliates.

The process described so far is substantially equivalent to the one used to evaluate and control domestic divisions in a firm. But foreign affiliates face a wide range of additional factors that may affect their performance, and these factors should be considered when setting the goals and judging the performance of affiliates. How should the managers of foreign affiliates be evaluated for their financial performance? If they are evaluated in local-currency terms, the home office must worry about hedging foreign currency exposures and about remitting or reinvesting profits. If they are evaluated in home-currency terms, affiliate managers must deal with exchange risk and remittance policy. If they are limited in their financial dealings due to centralized cash and foreign exchange management policies but are evaluated in home-currency terms, it must be recognized that their options are limited. On another issue, if transfer prices are set to move funds to the home office, foreign profitability will look lower than it would if these prices were set to keep more funds in the affiliates. Correct evaluation of the performance of affiliate managers must take into account the constraints imposed on the affiliates.

Most managers and outside analysts agree that foreign affiliates must be evaluated in home-currency terms, since home-currency investors judge the firm as a whole. Therefore, the firm must create an evaluation scheme that produces home-currency performance measures, adjusted to account for the limitations placed on the affiliate by the home office.

STRATEGIC INTERNATIONAL FINANCE

There are a number of ways that MNEs apply the international financial concepts that have been discussed in this chapter. One way is by employing a geocentric approach that helps to coordinate subsidiary operations and ensures that there is a uniform, harmonious strategy. This approach is particularly evident in the way that some multinationals are now closing local operations in favor of overseas production and are using joint ventures and other partnership arrangements to reduce their financial risk.[8] Another approach is the manner in which financial management analysis is used in choosing sites for overseas operations. This is particularly true for foreign firms with strong currencies.

Establishing overseas operations

Because the United States is a major market for many international firms, foreign MNEs have been particularly concerned about the value of the US dollar. For example, when Ford Motor acquired Volvo's automotive business, the Swedish firm insisted on receiving the purchase price in kronor. In 2009, when GM and Chrysler filed for bankruptcy and were bailed out by US taxpayers, Ford had to sell its luxury division, which included Jaguar, Land Rover and Volvo cars.[9] This concern has also resulted in foreign firms setting up operations in the United States in order to offset the competitive impact associated with having a currency that is very strong vis-à-vis the US dollar. For example, BMW built an auto production facility in South Carolina because it found it was 20 percent less costly to produce cars in South Carolina than to bring them in from Germany.[10] Other companies have made acquisitions in the US market in order to protect their overall profitability. For example, BASF has acquired a Mobil plastic unit for $330 million; Benckiser purchased Coty, the fragrance maker, from Pfizer for $440 million; Siemens spent $1.2 billion to purchase ROLM, a manufacturer of telecommunications equipment, from IBM; and Daimler-Benz bought Chrysler for almost $40 billion. However, the buyout failed to produce the trans-Atlantic automotive powerhouse dealmakers had hoped for, and DaimlerChrysler announced on May 14, 2007 that it would sell Chrysler to Cerberus Capital Management of New York, a private equity firm that specializes in restructuring troubled companies. On October 4, 2007 a DaimlerChrysler Extraordinary Shareholders' Meeting approved the renaming of the company. From October 5, 2007, the company has been titled Daimler AG. The US company adopted the name Chrysler LLC when the sale completed on August 3, 2007.[11]

At the same time US firms are continuing to move abroad, especially since many Asian currencies are at a low ebb and purchase prices have fallen. General Motors, for example, is now producing light trucks in China, has 16 ventures there related to producing auto components, and has opened a Buick plant in Shanghai. As of the end of 1998 the company was assembling close to 500,000 cars annually, most of which were small sedans or subcompacts.[12] At the same time Atlantic Richfield and Phillips China have invested in ventures for drilling for methane gas, IBM is expanding its investment there in the computer business, Telluride International Energy is building a power plant, and Lucent Technologies has earmarked millions of dollars to expand its Internet backbone in the country.[13] All of these moves to overseas operations give the multinational firm a reduced currency risk by diversifying the company's cash flows into additional currencies.

European and US firms are not alone in their efforts to establish overseas operations. Pacific-based MNEs are also realizing the benefits of going local, and this group is not limited to auto makers. South Korean firms such as LG Group and Samsung are now using direct investment and joint ventures to help open markets in Europe and the United States. High labor costs, runaway interest rates, and low-cost competition are battering these firms at home, and local content laws have been holding down market acceptance abroad. In an effort to circumvent these problems, LG is using alliances to widen its market share, as seen by its collaboration with Gepi of Germany and Iberna of Italy to produce refrigerators for the European market. LG designs the units in its Ireland facility, Gepi supplies the components, and Iberna assembles the finished products. Samsung has purchased Werk für Fernsehelektronik, a former East German picture tube maker, and is spending $120 million to upgrade the plant, which will be capable of turning out 1.2 million television sets annually. The company also bought an even larger German television maker, RFT, and moved its Portuguese and Spanish color television plants to England and its video cassette recorder plant from England to Spain in order to lower operational costs, to improve quality, and to increase employment. Again, the issue of concern here is that these firms are achieving a financial goal along with their strategic choices to go abroad; they are reducing exchange rate risk by diversifying their cash flows into different currencies.

Reducing financial risk

Although some of the above strategies are useful in reducing risk, there are other tactics that are also particularly useful, including mergers, acquisitions, joint ventures for new, high-risk projects, partnering with established MNEs in order to gain international market share, and cutting operating costs through new plant design.

Alliances

In recent years an increasing number of MNEs have been joining together to share the costs of high-tech projects. This sharing involves not only research and development expenses, but also the costs of manufacturing and selling the finished products.

One example is provided by Microsoft, which has entered into an alliance with Sony to link personal computers and consumer electronics devices, thus moving closer together on technology standards for digital television and other consumer products. The two firms have endorsed a technology that can connect video cassette recorders, camcorders, personal computers, and other devices.[14] Another example is GM and Isuzu, which are now extending their alliance in advanced vehicle technologies such as electric vehicles and fuel cells.[15] A third example is Kita Kyushu Coca-Cola Bottling and Sam Coca-Cola Bottling, two major bottlers in south-west Japan which have agreed to merge their operations and thus combine a somewhat fragmented distribution system into a smoother, seamless approach that should boost profitability.[16] A fourth example is Citigroup, which acquired a 15 percent equity in Taiwan's Fubon Group. This alliance will serve as a springboard for future expansion in the Asian region.[17]

Cost cutting

Other key financial strategies include cutting costs and investing in new plant and equipment, resulting in higher productivity and lower expenses. Still another strategy is the re-negotiation of labor contract agreements in high-cost areas of the world. While one strategy that is increasingly popular calls for moving production overseas to lower-cost locations, another response to this problem of high costs is to look for ways to reduce them in the existing operations.

Investment in new plant and equipment to achieve efficiencies is critical to the success of MNEs today just as it has been in the past. This is particularly true in Japan, where auto manufacturers are finding it increasingly difficult to hire new people. Worse yet, the turn-over rate in some factories runs as high as 50 percent annually. In explaining the reason for this turnover, many workers refer to the three Ks: *kiken* (dangerous), *kitsui* (difficult), and *kitanai* (dirty). Young people, in particular, prefer the slower-paced world of office work where people wear suits and ties, take leisurely lunch hours, and are not exhausted at the end of a long day.

In an effort to deal with this problem, Nissan Motors has built a new factory that promises to be far less stressful on the workers than anything yet. Company officials refer to it as a "dream factory" and claim that it is designed to reduce many of the pitfalls of past manufacturing plants. The latter, for example, are characterized by the traditional conveyor belt from which cars are suspended. When the car reaches the workers, the employees scramble to install parts and to complete their tasks as quickly as possible. This typically involves squatting on the floor, stretching across the seat or the hood, ducking under the car, or reaching across the top of the vehicle to install or tighten something. If the workers are unable to keep up with the line, the conveyer belt must be stopped until they finish because all cars advance in lockstep. In contrast, Nissan's new plant has done away with the conveyer belt. All cars are now placed on motor-driven dollies. These dollies can be raised or lowered so that the workers do not have to stretch or squat. Additionally, even if it takes longer than usual to complete a particular task, this creates no problem for the factory. The workers can simply scoot the dolly up to the next station as soon as they are finished.

Another difference between the Nissan plant and more conventional ones is that the work area is brightly lit with natural sunlight filtering in through skylights, compared to the poorly lit work environments in other plants. Additionally, the factory is air-conditioned and the temperature is kept at 77°F (25°C), in contrast to other auto plants where there is no air-conditioning. Another welcome feature is the use of robots to perform the dirtiest and most difficult jobs, painting and welding. And to reduce worker exhaustion, robots carry out a large percentage of the actual assembly. A huge robot arm, for example, grabs seats from an overhead rack and swings them into the car with a flick of its mechanical wrist. Then a small robot arm bolts the seat to the floor. Nissan contends that this new plant will not only cut down on worker absenteeism and turnover, but also be 30 percent more efficient than those of the competition.

Other Japanese manufacturers are also heavily focused on cost cutting, but through the use of overseas production. For example, Honda and Toyota operations in the United States have been simultaneously reducing costs while increasing quality. The result is that car prices for many of their models have remained the same or dropped slightly in recent years, while the number of features has increased. This "more value for your money" concept has been influential in helping both auto makers to increase their US market share and profitability.[18] Ford has been following a similar approach through a vigorous outsourcing program and by seeking to cut $1 billion from its costs, thus boosting its return on investment from the North American market and, hopefully, helping drive up stock price as well.[19] Simply put, cost cutting is a critical part of financial investment strategies.

KEY POINTS

1 International financial management encompasses a number of critical areas, including the management of global cash flows, foreign exchange risk management, capital expenditure analysis, and international financing. In carrying out these financial activities, MNEs can use three approaches or solutions: polycentric, ethnocentric, or geocentric.

2 There are three main areas of consideration in managing global cash flows. One is the movement of cash so that each subsidiary has the working capital needed to conduct operations. A second area is the use of funds positioning techniques that can help to reduce taxes and to deal with political and legal roadblocks that impede cash flows. A third is multilateral netting, which ensures that transactions between the subsidiaries are paid in a timely manner.

3 Foreign exchange risk management encompasses a variety of financial strategies that are designed to limit the multinational's exposure to exchange rate fluctuations. In particular, the MNE will want to reduce translation, transaction, and economic exposure. One of the most common ways of doing this is through hedging. Examples include the

purchase of forward exchange contracts and the balancing of foreign currency assets with foreign currency liabilities.

4 A third major strategic financial issue is capital expenditure analysis. This entails computation and deliberation of such matters as the weighted cost of capital and the degree of political risk that is being assumed. Some of the methods of dealing with these issues were discussed with attention given to the fact that the final decision on capital expenditures is often affected by subjective considerations as well as by objective evaluations.

5 At present MNEs are taking a number of important international financial steps. Some of the primary ones include designing global foreign exchange management programs, establishing international cash management centers, and creating coordinated international borrowing programs for affiliates.

Key terms

- polycentric solution
- ethnocentric solution
- working capital
- geocentric solution
- multilateral netting
- funds positioning techniques
- transfer price
- arm's-length price

- tax havens
- fronting loan
- clearing account
- hedge
- transaction risk
- translation risk
- consolidation
- balance sheet hedging
- economic risk

- currency option
- currency inconvertibility
- weighted-average cost of capital (WACC)
- foreign investment review agency
- debt–equity ratio
- control

REVIEW AND DISCUSSION QUESTIONS

1 In determining parent–subsidiary relationships, how does a polycentric solution differ from an ethnocentric or geocentric solution? Compare and contrast all three.

2 What is meant by the term *working capital*, and what are two of the most common ways that parent companies can provide this capital to their subsidiaries? What are two ways in which the parent can obtain funds from the subsidiaries?

3 How can an MNE shift profits through the use of transfer pricing? Provide an example.

4 Of what value is multilateral netting in helping MNEs to manage cash flows? Give an example.

5 If a foreign country is facing high inflation, what are three financial strategies that the local multinational unit might employ? Identify and describe each.

6 Why are MNEs interested in translation and consolidation of financial statements? Of what practical value is this activity to the company?

7 Under what conditions will an MNE face translation exposure? What financial strategy might the organization use to minimize this exposure?

8 When might an MNE face transaction exposure? What is a financial strategy that the firm could use to minimize this risk?

9 What is meant by the term *economic exposure*? What is a financial strategy that an MNE could use to minimize this risk?

10 When would a multinational use a lead strategy to hedge a risk? When would a multinational use a lag strategy for this purpose? In each case, give an example. A lead strategy is a choice by an MNE to make intracompany payments (for example, from an affiliate to the home office) earlier than in an arm's-length situation, to move funds out of the country of the affiliate more rapidly. A lag strategy is a choice by an MNE to make intracompany payments (for example, from an affiliate to the home office) later than in an arm's-length situation, to hold funds longer in the affiliate country.

11 When might an MNE use a forward exchange contract (a contract with a bank to buy or sell foreign exchange at a future date, with the exchange rate and value fixed today)? When might the firm decide to forgo this strategy and leave a particular foreign currency transaction unhedged?

12 What role does net present value (NPV) play in the review of capital expenditure proposals? Give an example.

13 How can country risk affect the computation of NPV? Will the risk result in the MNE wanting a higher or a lower NPV? Explain.

14 Why do parent and local subsidiaries sometimes differ in their calculation of NPV for a particular project or expenditure? How can this difference be resolved?

15 What are some of the financing alternatives available to MNEs that are not available to domestic firms? Give an example.

REAL CASE

Skandia

Information technology has transformed the financial services and insurance business into a universal product. Instead of large numbers of white-collar clerical workers toiling in large local banking and insurance halls (like Bob Cratchit in Dickens's *A Christmas Carol*) today such services can be provided on the Internet by smaller, more entrepreneurial groups and even from a home office. This is part of the new global knowledge-based economy.

Skandia is a Stockholm-based insurance and financial service company, founded some 150 years ago. In 2000, the Skandia Group had revenues of 21.7 million krona (US $2.30 million), six times the 1995 figure, and operations in 20 countries. In 1900 Skandia became the first non-British insurance company to enter the US market, but it incurred losses in the San Francisco earthquake of 1906 and in World War I, to the extent that its international business was largely dormant and confined to reinsurance (business accepted for another company to diversify risk).

In 1986, the Assurance and Financial Services Division (AFS) of Skandia, headed by CEO Jan Carendi, made a big push in the United States. Over the next 12 years it grew by 45 percent per year. By 1998 the AFS Unit had sales of $3.5 billion with fewer than 2,000 employees. It sold a unit-linked variable life insurance product to independent insurance brokers. The product can be sold on the Internet. Basically, Skandia purchased mutual funds from other companies but included its own insurance package with them. Skandia was one of the first insurance companies to use such a self-directed unit trust (or mutual fund) that allowed customers to regard life insurance as being like a retirement savings plan.

To derive an ongoing competitive advantage in knowledge management, Jan Carendi transformed the AFS Division of Skandia from a traditional bricks and mortar insurance company into a "clicks and mortar" virtual organization. He was one of the first to appoint a director of intellectual capital, retraining managers to be more flexible, innovative, and responsive to the consumers. While acting as a change agent, Carendi traveled some 200 days a year to pull together a new "federal" model of internal management structure. One aspect of this was a group of independent fund managers; another was a new software package to manage the complex administrative structure.

▶

By the 1980s Skandia consisted of four divisions:

1 An actuarial function, designing insurance products based on risk assessments.
2 A sales and marketing group that sold directly to consumers.
3 An investment management group that invested premiums.
4 An administrative group that managed the customer, accounting, and regulatory paperwork.

Many of the traditional insurance functions were outsourced by Carendi. The fund management and also the sales and distribution functions were outsourced. Both of these required local knowledge of regulations for mutual funds and of personal networks for sales and distribution. Instead, AFS focused on internationally mobile knowledge capabilities, using high tech and the Internet.

An overdependence on the US market, from which 60 percent of all Skandia's revenues originate, led to a slower year in 2001. When the high-tech stocks plummeted in 2001 after the dot.com bust, Skandia's customers stopped buying. In July 2001, sales of variable annuities in the United States were halved to $2.5 billion, down from $5.7 in the previous year. Diversification into the more stable markets of Germany, Japan, and Spain over the subsequent years may help to recover the company's profitability. Meanwhile, Skandia's actuaries were busy creating new, more cautious products to be ready when US investors are ready to buy again. In 2003, Prudential Financial purchased American Skandia. In 2005 South African/British financial services group Old Mutual Plc launched a $6.5bn (£3.6bn) bid to acquire majority control of Skandia, which was met with resistance from some of Skandia's shareholders and directors. On February 3, 2006, Old Mutual completed its acquisition of Skandia, which was subsequently delisted from the Stockholm and London stock exchanges.

The lesson is that reliance on Internet-based business on a global scale is just as risky as the old-fashioned, centuries-earlier business cycles. In those times there were speculative stock market crashes, such as the South Seas Bubble (in 1720). In modern times, we have seen a similar dot.com/high-tech bubble burst in 2001, with profound repercussions, even in the stodgy world of insurance.

Sources: Christopher A. Bartlett, *Skandia AFS*, Harvard Business School, Case No. 9-396-412, 1996; "Skandia: Client Focus Brings Spectacular Rewards," *Financial Times*, June 23, 2000; Skandia, *Annual Report*, 2000; "Old Mutual Gets Backing for Hostile Takeover of Skandia," *The Independent*, www.independent .co.uk, December 21, 2005.

1 Why has insurance changed from local salespeople to an Internet-provided "universal" product?
2 Why was Swedish-based Skandia so successful in the US market?
3 Was CEO Jan Carendi "Swedish" or "global" in his management style?

REAL CASE

Repsol's acquisition of YPF

In 1993 the Argentine government sold controlling ownership in the national oil company, YPF (Yacimientos Petroliferos Fiscales), through an initial public offering on the Argentine stock market and through an American Depositary Receipt (ADR) issue on the New York Stock Exchange, as well as a Global Depositary Receipt (GDR) issue on the London Stock Exchange. This was the largest privatization in Latin America at that time, bringing the Argentine government about US $3 billion in the initial issue of about half of YPF's total shares.

The initial privatization was carried out in July 1993, when YPF was sold in this initial public offering to literally thousands of investors in the open market. The government hired and installed a team of managers who took YPF through a huge and painful restructuring of its business and then the public sale of the company. Once YPF began to operate in the private sector as a listed company, the government continued to sell its remaining shares over time. The privatization itself was not an example of foreign direct investment, since foreign investors only purchased small percentages of YPF shares or depositary receipts. However, in 1998, the Spanish oil company Repsol decided to purchase control of YPF, and did so by buying 14.99 percent of YPF shares from the government's remaining 20 percent stake at that time. Repsol was able to obtain controlling interest in YPF in 1999 for a price of US $2.01 billion.

In mid-1999 Repsol raised its stake in YPF to 97.5 percent, by making a tender offer for all the ADRs in New York and GDRs in London, along with shares in the Buenos Aires

Stock Exchange that it did not already own. The total cost of this tender was US $13.1 billion. These share acquisitions were financed by Repsol borrowing in Spain and in the euromarkets, in addition to internal funding.

The net result of these purchases made Repsol the owner of almost 98 percent of total outstanding YPF shares, with only small shareholdings outstanding to investors who failed to participate in the tender offer in 1999. The total foreign direct investment replaced portfolio investment by those investors who had purchased ADRs or GDRs back in 1993, accounting for about 40 percent of total YPF shares. These investors probably did not reinvest their funds in Argentina once they sold their depositary receipts to Repsol, so no new investment went into Argentina at that time. Of course, the original portfolio investment in the ADRs or GDRs was an international investment, bringing new funds into Argentina to pay for the depositary receipts. Those flows were recorded in 1993, and did not appear subsequently in the 1999 FDI process. That is, the investors in New York and London who had originally purchased shares of YPF in the ADR and GDR offerings there chose to sell those shares to Repsol, thus receiving Repsol's cash, but not (necessarily) sending any funds to Argentina. All that happened was a change of foreign owners of those shares—but the new foreign owner was a direct investor rather than a portfolio, passive investor. This accounted for approximately US $10 billion of the total direct investment by Repsol, and thus for no new money coming into the country. The shares that were purchased from shareholders in the Buenos Aires Stock Exchange (about US $3 billion of the total) did likely bring new funds into Argentina, assuming that the sellers kept the funds in the country.

The purchase of the government's shareholdings in 1998 *did* imply direct financial transfers from abroad to Argentina, as Repsol paid the government for those shares and financed the purchase with funds from abroad. This US $2.01 billion thus *was* a transfer of funds to Argentina, different from the bulk of the investment. And as noted above, Repsol obtained the funds primarily through taking out bank loans in the eurocurrency market, denominating the loans in dollars, since YPF's earnings were mostly in dollars.

Websites: www.repsolypf.com/home00.asp.

Sources: UBS Warburg, "Repsol YPF," *Global Equity Research*, January 2002; Carmen Llorente, "Repsol el Cambio Tras la Compra de YPF," *El Mundo*, January 24, 1999; "Spanish Businesses in Argentina," *The Economist*, January 3, 2002; Robert Grosse and Juan Yañes, "Carrying Out a Successful Privatization: The YPF Case," *Academy of Management Executive*, May 1998, pp. 51–63.

1 Did Repsol make a good decision in acquiring YPF in 1998–1999?

2 What is the difference between foreign direct investment and foreign portfolio investment? Is this a relevant issue in the case?

3 What are American Depositary Receipts? Were they a useful tool for YPF in selling shares to the public?

ENDNOTES

1 For more on tax havens, see "Gimme Shelter," *The Economist*, January 7, 2000; Nicholas Shaxson and John Christensen, "Time to Black-List the Tax Haven Whitewash," *The Financial Times Online*, April 4, 2011; Alice Ross, "Treasure Islands," *The Financial Times Online*, January 17, 2011.

2 Also, see Neil Weinberg, "Rent Shokku," *Forbes*, June 7, 1993, p. 108; and

3 For more on Honda, see Alex Taylor III, "How Toyota Copes with Hard Times," *Fortune*, January 25, 1993, pp. 78–81.

4 The option contract can also be used to hedge this transaction. American Express could buy 160 call options as listed in the example, for a total premium of US $125,000. For this price, American Express would receive the right to buy pounds at the strike price of US $1.5800 per pound, a worse price than the forward and futures contracts. (Actually, options for lower strike prices are available at much higher premiums.) The option does not look attractive unless American Express wants to speculate that the pound will go down in value even below the forward contract price. If this happens, by not exercising the options, American Express could simply buy pounds in the spot market in 180 days and benefit from the lower price. The option is generally useful if the firm wants to speculate or if the original commercial contract may not be fulfilled so that the pounds may not be needed after all.

5 A full set of the measures used in capital budgeting appears in basic finance texts, such as Richard A. Brealey and Stewart C. Myers, *Principles of Corporate Finance*, 9th ed. (Boston, MA: McGraw-Hill, 2010).

6 However, if the local-currency price goes up due to the currency revaluation and demand is price inelastic, the total revenue received may go up even if the quantity sold declines.

7 ADRs (American Depositary Receipts) are a derivative instrument based on shares of stock in a company. The issuing company typically sells a large quantity of shares in a block to an investment bank, which in turn holds those shares in its own treasury. The investment bank then issues ADRs whose value is based completely on the original shares, converted into US dollars, in the US market. See, for example, http://daytrading.about.com/cs/educationtraining/a/adrs.htm.

8 See Brian Coleman and Thomas R. King, "Euro Disney Rescue Package Wins Approval," *Wall Street Journal*, March 15, 1994, p. A3; "Disneyland Paris Cuts Losses Despite Fewer Visitors," *BBC News*, November 10, 2010; and Scheherazade Daneshkhu in Paris, "Euro Disney Signs Expansion Deal," *The Financial Times Online*, September 14, 2010.

9 "Ford to Pay $6.47 Billion in Volvo Deal," *Wall Street Journal*, January 29, 1999, Section A, pp. 3, 6; Jorn Madslien, "Changed Landscape for Global Carmakers," *BBC News Online*, May 10, 2011.

10 Also, see John Templeman and James B. Treece, "BMW's Comeback," *Business Week*, February 14, 1994, pp. 42–44; "BMW to Invest £500m in UK Factories," *BBC News Online*, June 9, 2011.

11 Keith Bradsher, "Industry's Giants Are Carving Up the World Market," *New York Times*, May 8, 1998, pp. C1, 4; and Robyn Meredith, "A Joining of Opposites Could Help Customers," *New York Times*, May 8, 1998, p. C4; and www.daimler.com; "DaimlerChrysler Board Approves Chrysler Sales," *Dow Jones*, May 16, 2007.

12 Seth Faison, "GM Opens Buick Plant in Shanghai," *New York Times*, December 18, 1998, pp. C1, 19; and Juliana Liu,

"Shanghai Auto Show: Global Car Makers Rev up in China," *BBC News Online*, April 20, 2011.

13 "Opening the Door a Crack," *New York Times*, June 30, 1998, p. A10.

14 Don Clark and David Bank, "Microsoft, Sony to Cooperate On PCs, Devices," *Wall Street Journal*, April 8, 1998, p. B6.

15 Lisa Schuchman and Joseph B. White, "Global Consolidations in Autos Heat Up," *Wall Street Journal*, December 21, 1998, p. A2.

16 Nikhil Deogun, "Coca-Cola to Put Together the Merger of Two Bottlers in Japan to Lift Sales," *Wall Street Journal*, January 14, 1999, p. A4.

17 "Citigroup and Taiwan's Fubon Group Announce a Powerful Strategic Partnership," Citigroup Press Release, May 6, 2000.

18 Valerie Reitman, "Honda Sees Performance and Profits from New Accord," *Wall Street Journal*, August 27, 1997, p. B4.

19 Fara Warner and Joseph B. White, "Ford Plans to Reduce Costs by Another $1 Billion," *Wall Street Journal*, January 8, 1999, p. A3; and see also "Fat Pharm: Mechanics of Cost Cutting," *The Financial Times Online*, June 15, 2011.

ADDITIONAL BIBLIOGRAPHY

Agmon, Tamir and Lessard, Donald R. "Investor Recognition of Corporate International Diversification", *The Journal of Finance*, vol. 22, no. 4 (1977).

Bates, Thomas W., Kahle, Katheleen M. and Stulz, Rene M. "Why Do US Firms Hold So Much More Cash Than They Used to?" *The Journal of Finance*, vol. 64, no. 5 (October 2009).

Bartram, Soehnke M., Brown, Gregory W. and Minton, Bernadette A. "Resolving the Exposure Puzzle: the Many Facets of Exchange Rate Exposure," *Journal of Financial Economics*, vol. 95, no. 2 (2010).

Christopher, Stephen E. "Hysteresis and the Value of the US Multinational Corporation," *The Journal of Business*, vol. 70, no. 3 (1997).

Clark, Terry, Kotabe, Masaaki and Rajaratnam, Dan. "Exchange Rate Pass-Through and International Pricing Strategy: A Conceptual Framework and Research Propositions," *Journal of International Business Studies*, vol. 30, no. 2 (Summer 1999).

Denis, David J., Denis, Diane K. and Yost, Keven. "Global Diversification, Industrial Diversification, and Firm Value," *Journal of Finance*, vol. 57, no. 5 (2002).

Di Gregorio, Dante. "Re-Thinking Country Risk: Insights from Entrepreneurship Theory," *International Business Review*, vol. 14 (2005).

Dos Santos, Marcelo B., Errunza, Vihang R. and Miller, Darius P. "Does Corporate International Diversification Destroy Value: Evidence from Cross-Border Mergers and Acquisitions," *Journal of Banking and Finance*, vol. 32, no. 12 (2008).

Eckert, Stefan and Trautnitz, Georg. "A Commentary on Risk Reduction by Geographic Diversification," *Multinational Business Review*, vol. 18, no. 1 (2010).

Eden, Lorraine. "Taxes, Transfer Pricing, and the Multinational Enterprise," in Alan M. Rugman (ed.), *The Oxford Handbook of International Business* (Oxford: Oxford University Press, 2009).

Eden, Lorraine, Juarez Valdez, Luis F. and Li, Dan. "Talk Softly but Carry a Big Stick: Transfer Pricing Penalties and the Market Valuation of Japanese Multinationals in the United States," *Journal of International Business Studies*, vol. 36, no. 4 (July 2005).

Egehoff, William G., Gorman, Liam and McCormick, Stephen. "How FDI Characteristics Influence Subsidiary Trade Patterns: The Case of Ireland," *Management International Review*, vol. 40, no. 3 (Fall 2000).

Errunza, Vihang, and Senbet, Lemma W. "The Effects of International Operations on the Market Value of the Firm: Theory and Evidence," *The Journal of Finance*, vol. 36, no. 2 (1981).

Errunza, Vihang, and Senbet, Lemma W. "International Corporate Diversification, Market Valuation, and Size Adjusted Evidence, " *The Journal of Finance*, vol. 39, no. 3 (1984).

Errunza, Vihang. "Emerging Markets in Global Finance," in B. Toyne and D. Nigh (eds.), *International Business: An Emerging Vision* (Columbia: University of South Carolina Press, 1997).

European Commission. *Company Taxation in the Internal Market* (Brussels, October 2001).

Gande, Amar, Schenzler, Christoph and Senbet, Lemma W. "Valuation Effects of Global Diversification," *Journal of International Business Studies*, vol. 40 (2009). doi:10.1057/jibs.2009.59.

Gao, Ting. "Exchange Rate Movements and the Profitability of US Multinationals," *Journal of International Money and Finance*, vol. 19 (2000).

Geringer, J. Michael , Beamish, Paul W. and daCosta, Richard C. "Diversification Strategy and Internationalization: Implications for MNE Performance," *Strategic Management Journal*, vol. 10. No. 2 (1989).

Grosse, Robert, with Shannon Mudd and John Mathis. "Dealing with Financial Crises in Emerging Markets," *Thunderbird International Business Review*, vol. 44, no. 3 (2002).

Grosse, Robert, *The Future of Global Financial Services* (Oxford: Blackwell, 2004).

Gubbi, Sathyajit R., Aulakh, Preet S., Sougata, R., Sarkar, M. B. and Chittoor, Raveendra. "Do International Acquisitions by Emerging-Economy Firms Create Shareholder Value? The Case of Indian Firms." *Journal of International Business Studies*, vol. 41 (2010). doi:10.1057/jibs.2009.47.

Hermes, Niels, Smid, Peter and Yao Lu. "Capital Budgeting Practices: A Comparative Study of the Netherlands and China," *International Business Review*, vol. 16, no. 5 (October 2007).

Jacquillat, Bertrand and Solnik, Bruno. "Multinationals are Poor Tools for Diversification," *Journal of Portfolio Management*, vol. 4 (1978).

Kogut, Bruce and Kulatilaka, Nalin. "Operating Flexibility, Global Manufacturing and the Option Value of a Multinational Network," *Management Science*, vol. 40 (1994).

LaPorta, Rafael, Lopez-de-Silanes, Florencio, Shleifer, Andrei and Vishny, Robert. "Legal Determinants of External Finance," *Journal of Finance*, vol. 52 (1997).

Lee, Seung-Hyun and Makhija, Mona. "The Effect of Domestic Uncertainty on the Real Options Value of International Investments," *Journal of International Business Studies*, vol. 40, no. 3 (2009).

Markides, Constantinos C. and Ittner, Christopher D. "Shareholder Benefits from Corporate International Diversification: Evidence from US International Acquisitions," *Journal of International Business Studies*, vol. 25, no. 2 (1994).

Markides, Constantinos C. and Oyon, Daniel. "International Acquisition: Do They Create Value for Shareholders?" *European Management Journal*, vol. 16, no. 2 (April 1998).

Mishra, Chandra. S. and Gobeli, David H. "Managerial Incentives, Internalization and Market Valuation of Multinational Firms," *Journal of International Business Studies*, vol. 29, no. 3 (1998).

Morck, Randall and Yeung, Bernard. "Why Investors Value Multinationality?" *The Journal of Business*, vol. 29, no. 3 (1998).

Oxelheim, Lars, Stonehill, Arthur, Ranødy, Trond, Vikkula, Kaisa, Dullum, Kare and Modén, Karl-Markus. *Corporate Strategies to Internationalise the Cost of Capital* (Copenhagen: Copenhagen Business School Press, 1998).

Qi, Yaxuan, Roth, Lukas and Wald, John K. "How Legal Environments Affect the Use of Bond Covenants," *Journal of International Business Studies* vol. 42 (2011). doi:10.1057/jibs.2010.52.

Randøy, Trond, Oxelheim, Lars and Stonehill, Arthur. "Corporate Financial Strategies for Global Competitiveness," *European Management Journal*, vol. 19, no. 6 (December 2001).

Rangan, Subramanian. "Do Multinationals Operate Flexibly? Theory and Evidence," *Journal of International Business Studies*, vol. 29, no. 2 (1998).

Reuer, Jeffrey J., Shenkar, Oded and Ragozzino, Roberto. "Mitigating Risk in International Mergers and Acquisitions: The Role of Contingent Payouts," *Journal of International Business Studies*, vol. 35, no. 1 (January 2004).

Rugman, Alan M. *International Diversification and the Multinational Enterprise* (Lexington, MA: D.C. Heath, 1979).

Rugman, Alan M. "Implications of the Theory of Internalization for Corporate International Finance," *California Management Review*, vol. 23, no. 2 (Winter 1980).

Rugman, Alan M. "Twenty-Five Years of 'International Diversification and the Multinational Enterprise'," in Alain Verbeke (ed.), *Internalization, International Diversification and the Multinational Enterprise – Essays in Honour of Alan M. Rugman* (London: Elsevier, 2005).

Rugman, Alan M. and Eden, Lorraine. *Multinationals and Transfer Pricing* (London: Croom Helm and New York: St. Martin's Press, 1985).

Rugman, Alan M. and Jing, Li. "Real Options and the Theory of Foreign Direct Investment," *International Business Review*, vol. 16, no. 6 (December 2007).

Rugman, Alan M. and Oh, Chang Hoon. "Regional Multinational Enterprises and the International Financial Crisis," in J. Berrill, E. Houston and R. Sinkovics (eds.) *Firm-level Internationalization, Regionalism and Globalization* (Basingstoke: Palgrave, 2011).

Rugman, Alan M. and Verbeke, Alain. "Strategic Capital Budgeting Decisions and the Theory of Internalization," *Managerial Finance*, vol. 16, no. 2 (1990).

Solnik, Bruno. "Why Not Diversify Internationally Rather Than Domestically?" *Financial Analysts Journal*, vol. 30, no. 4 (1974).

Sundaram, Anant. "Management of Exchange Rate Exposure by the Multinational Corporation," in D. Logue and J. Seward (eds.), *Handbook of Modern Finance* (New York: Warren Gorham Lamont, 2004).

Wallace, Wanda. "The Value Relevance of Accounting: The Rest of the Story," *European Management Journal*, vol. 18, no. 6 (December 2000).

Part Five

REGIONAL STRATEGIES

Chapter 17

EUROPEAN UNION

Contents

The EU environment 539

Conducting a strategic analysis 546

Strategy issues 549

■ **Active Learning Case**

France Telecom 538

■ **International Business Strategy in Action**

Ford and Volvo 547

Deutsche Bahn: more than a railway 555

■ **Real Cases**

Accor budget hotels 563

Carrefour 565

Objectives of the chapter

The European Union (EU) is one of the world's triad markets. It is the home of one-third of the world's largest 500 firms. Also, many foreign MNEs from Asia and North America are now doing business in the EU or are targeting the area in their expansion plans. This chapter examines the EU environment and reviews some of the major strategy considerations that must be addressed by companies doing business in this economic bloc.

The specific objectives of this chapter are to:

1 *Describe* the Single European Market and the competitive status of the EU in relation to other triad members.

2 *Discuss* how firms carry out an overall strategic analysis of the EU market in terms of competitive intelligence and evaluation of location.

3 *Relate* some of the major strategy issues that must be considered when doing business in the EU, including exporting, strategic alliances and acquisitions, manufacturing considerations, marketing approaches, and management considerations.

ACTIVE LEARNING CASE

France Telecom

A good example of an organization that has become very strong in its home part of the triad is France Telecom, which has built up a major presence in the EU first through strategic alliances and through acquisitions of competitors. It can now use its strong EU home base as a staging ground to enter the North American and Asian markets, as was discussed in the earlier case on Vodafone (in Chapter 8).

France Telecom SA is a leading telecommunication operator in Europe. It offers services covering fixed and mobile communications, data transmission, the Internet and multimedia, and other value-added services for individuals, businesses and other telecommunications and operators. It operates in three segments: the Personal Communication Services (PCS), the Home Communication Services (HCS) and the Enterprise Communication Service (ECS). The PCS segment consists of the mobile telecommunication services in Central and Eastern Europe, Africa, the Middle East, the Carribean and Asia; the HCS segment includes the fixed-line telecommunication activities (fixed-line telephony, Internet services, operator services), as well as the distribution and support functions provided to the other segments of the France Telecom group, and the ECS segment provides communication solutions to large and small businesses worldwide. The company operates a number of subsidiaries, notably under the brand name Orange. It serves over 216 million customers in five continents, two-thirds of which come under its corporate brand 'Orange'. With €45.5 billion (US$60.262 billion) in revenues in 2010 and 163,813 employees (half outside France) the firm is one of Europe's largest telecommunication companies.

Up to 1988, France Telecom was a department in the Ministry of Posts and Telecommunications. It began a process of privatization in 1998, under Lionel Jospin's government, but the French government still owns part of the firm. This causes periodic clashes with EU competition commissioners, including an allegation that the firm was paid the equivalent of over $1 billion in unlawful subsidies in 2004.

France Telecom has come a long way since 1995, when 75 percent of its revenues were from fixed-line operations and foreign sales accounted for only 2 percent of revenues. Today, France accounts for 49 percent of revenues and most of this comes from mobile and Internet services. Revenue from Spain and Poland accounts for 17 percent, the rest of the world 17 percent, international carriers and shared services 2 percent and enterprise 15 percent.

Source: Getty Images/Pascal Le Segratain

The rise of France Telecom in the European market and its expansion into wireless and Internet are the result of a combination of R&D expenditures, alliances, and strategies. France Telecom R&D is one of the largest research centers in Europe, employing over 5,000 people and holding over 10,000 patents worldwide. R&D efforts strive to facilitate human interaction through telecommunications. France Telecom has also teamed up with other companies to complement its research efforts. It is working with Ericsson to provide integrated operator services for the home. An agreement with Motorola will seek to develop "seamless mobility" services for businesses. Meanwhile, it is collaborating with Nokia to provide mobile access to home multimedia content. These types of partnerships are also used to improve the process through which services are provided. For example, France Telecom and Alcatel are working on developing a new-generation network architecture to unify fixed, wireless, and Internet media.

R&D has helped France Telecom secure a place in the European market. However, the fractured nature of the European market made strategic alliances a necessary element in France Telecom's international strategy. The EU's 27 members lack not only a common language but also a common regulatory system. Each country awards its own mobile licenses, forcing new entrants to make alliances with license holders. In addition, the previous fixed-line companies continue to own much of the local telecom infrastructure, increasing the benefits of partnering up.

In 1995, France Telecom joined Telekom and Sprint to form the Global One alliance, which was expected to serve as a springboard into the US market while protecting France Telecom's home market from competition by Telekom. In 1999, Sprint was purchased by MCI World, effectively voiding the alliance. In the same year, Deutsche Telekom also rescinded its obligations when it sought a merger with Telecom Italia. As a result, France Telecom redesigned its international strategy and began to compete directly with Deutsche Telekom in the German market by purchasing 17 percent of E-plus, the country's third-largest mobile phone operator. This marked a turning point for France Telecom's international strategy. The company now favors acquisitions over alliances.

In January 2000, France Telecom purchased the Global One alliance from its partners, an event that marked the beginning of a purchasing spree. Later that year, it bought Orange (UK) from Vodafone. Orange had a presence in 20 countries around the world, including 13 in Europe. France Telecom combined its own mobile business with that of Orange to create Europe's second-largest mobile phone company. This acquisition was also a strategic move into the UK market. The firm's biggest competitor, Deutsche Telekom, had already purchased One2One in the UK. With 12.2 million active customers, Orange was the largest mobile operator in the UK, catapulting France Telecom into the big leagues.

France Telecom also purchased Equant NV and Freeserve in 2000. Equant NV was combined with Global One under the name Equant. The new company is a corporate service provider in 220 countries and has 3,700 large business customers. Freeserve, the UK's largest Internet service provider, was purchased by Wanadoo, France Telecom's Internet subsidiary in 2004, and from 2006 has been known as Orange Home UK plc.

Like other telecommunications firms, France Telecom experienced a sharp decrease in share value in the early 2000's as a knock-on effect of the the dot.com bust; the cost of buying 3G mobile licenses in the UK, Germany, France, and Italy, among others; accumulated debt from the firm's acquisitions and the lack of a strong market that would allow it to raise funds through the sale of equity. Despite this, and heavy competition from new entrants, France Telecom has been able to turn things around. Its share value has improved considerably and it remains a major European competitor. More recently its expansion has increased with purchases of One GmbH, the third-largest mobile operator in Austria, and 51 percent of Telkom Kenya in 2007. In 2009 it partly merged the UK operations of Orange and T-Mobile through agreements with Deutsche Telecom. It also won the rights to be the exclusive distributor of the Apple iPhone in France. It is now strategically prepared to take advantage of future profits from 3G mobiles, the deregulation of telecommunications and increased competition in local markets, economies of scale on ISP, and the growing integration of the EU market.

Websites: www.orange.com/en_EN/group/; www.francetelecom.com; www.sprint.com; www.equant.com; www.mci.com; www.one2one.co.uk; www.orange.co.uk; www.freeserve.com; www.wanadoo.fr; www.bt.com.

Sources: "T-Mobile and Orange in UK merger," *BBC News*, www.bbc.co.uk, September 8, 2009; "France Telecom: Battling Debt," *BBC.co.uk*, April 19, 2001; "French Giant Targets Alliance," *BBC.co.uk*, October 12, 1999; "France Telecom Clinches Orange Deal," *BBC.co.uk*, May 30, 2000; "France Telecom Takes Over Equant," *BBC.co.uk*, November 20, 2000; Richard Tomlinson, "5 Moves to Win the Telecom Game," *Fortune*, January 7, 2002; France Telecom, *Annual Report*, 2010; Associated Press, "France Telecom Shares Decline as Government Moves to Cut its Stake," *International Herald Tribune*, June 25, 2007; OneSource, *Thomson Reuters*, 2011; France Telecom, *Annual Report*, 2010.

1 Describe the stages in which France Telecom has built up a successful strategic base in the EU. What barriers to integration had to be overcome in the EU before France Telecom could buy up rival companies?

2 To what extent is the triad strategy of France Telecom the same as that of Vodafone (in Chapter 8)? Are there any differences?

3 In what ways will integration and localization be important issues for conducting mergers in the EU?

4 In what ways will both pricing and positioning be important for companies like France Telecom doing business in the EU?

THE EU ENVIRONMENT

The EU currently consists of 27 countries. This includes the pre-2004 EU15, 10 other European countries that joined in 2004, and Bulgaria and Romania which joined in 2007. The EU15 are closely linked both economically and politically and this group is more loosely linked to the 12 new members. In terms of monetary policy, 12 of the pre-2004 EU15 share a common currency, the euro, and constitute the eurozone. Today, the EU27

Table 17.1 Economic profile of the big three (in US dollars)

	US	Japan	EU15	EU27
The economy				
GDP (2008)	14.093 trillion	4.910 trillion	14.460 trillion	17.533 trillion
Real GDP growth rate (2008)	0.4%	−0.7%	0.5%	0.7%
Inflation (2008)	3.8%	1.4%	3.3%	3.7%
R&D expenditure as % of GDP (2008)	2.7%	3.4%	2.0%	1.9%
Workforce				
Population (2008)	304 million	127 million	322 million	497 million
Labour productivity per hour, indexed EU15=100 (2005)	118.4	77.8	100.0	86.9
Labour cost per hour in manufacturing (2007)	24.59	19.75	31.93	n.a.
Unemployment rate (2008)	5.8%	4.0%	7.0%	7.1%
Merchandise trade (US $ billions)				
Trade balance (2008)	(840.0) billion	57.2 billion	(229.0) billion	(342.0) billion
Exports (2008)	1.277 trillion	746.5 billion	3.820 trillion	3.416 trillion
Imports (2008)	2.117 trillion	708.3 billion	4.049 trillion	3.758 trillion
Public sector				
Government expenditure as % of GDP (2008)	35.31%	37.5%	47.2%	46.8%
Government debt as % of GDP (2008)	63.4%	172.1%	69.7%	61.6%
Consumers				
Broadband penetration rate (2008) (%)	24.0%	23.6%	24.3%	21.7%

Notes: Data for EU includes intra-EU trade. Exports are calculated by including freight and insurance while imports do not include freight and insurance. As a result data might not be consistent with other data in this book. Where EU27 data were not available, data are for the EU25.

Sources: Authors' calculations and Eurostat, *Structural Indicators*; CIA, *World Fact book*, 2010; US Bureau of Labor Statistics; US Census Bureau; Foreign Trade Statistics.

has a population of almost 500 million and generates an estimated 26 percent share of the world's nominal GDP (US $17.533 trillion). Doing business in this bloc offers huge opportunities, and many MNEs are interested in tapping this giant potential (see Table 17.1).

Emergence of a Single European Market

The origins of the EU go back to the formation of the European Economic Community (EEC) in the late 1950s, at which time there were six founding members: France, West Germany, Italy, Belgium, the Netherlands, and Luxembourg. By the late 1990s, the EU had grown to include Austria, Finland, the UK, Ireland, Denmark, Greece, Spain, Sweden, and Portugal. In 2004, an additional 10 countries were added: Poland, the Czech Republic, Hungary, Slovenia, Estonia, Latvia, Lithuania, Cyprus, Malta, and the Slovak Republic. Then in 2007 Bulgaria and Romania joined. (See the map of the EU in Chapter 1.) Over the last 40 years rapid economic growth has led to a high degree of political and social integration.

The objectives of the EU are:

1 Elimination of customs duties among member states.

2 Elimination of obstacles to the free flow of import and/or export of goods and services among member states.

3 Establishment of common customs duties and unified industrial/commercial policies regarding countries outside the community.

4 Free movement of people and capital within the bloc.

5 Acceptance of common agricultural policies, transport policies, technical standards, health and safety regulations, and educational degrees.

6 Common measures for consumer protection.

7 Common laws to maintain competition throughout the community and to fight monopolies or illegal cartels.

8 Regional funds to encourage the economic development of certain countries/regions.

9 Greater monetary and fiscal coordination among member states and certain common monetary/fiscal policies.[1]

In December 1985, EU leaders adopted a White Paper that contained 279 proposals aimed at achieving a single unified European market by December 31, 1992. Less than two years later the **Single European Act (SEA)** was passed.[2] A key part of the SEA was the EU **Council of Ministers**, one of the four major institutions of the EU. For each field of discussion, the EU Council of Ministers consists of one minister from each of the member states and is responsible for making major policy decisions for the union. The Council could now pass most proposals with a majority vote, in contrast to the unanimous vote needed previously. This opened the door for much faster progress toward both political and economic integration among member countries. Twelve of the EU15 countries have now adopted a single European currency, the euro, and have committed to a social charter, complete harmonization of social and economic policies, a common defense policy, and related measures that increase the power of the EU bureaucracy in Brussels. The Treaty of Lisbon, which came into force in 2009, was the last amendment to the constitutional basis of the EU. It provided for a greater role for the European Parliament and more ways for national governments and individual citizens to be involved in EU policy making.

Will the EU eventually bring about a **Single European Market (SEM)** in which the above stated goals are achieved? This will depend on the extent of progress in the area of free movement of goods and the practice of government procurement. It will also depend on whether the new member countries, and any others that join in the future, can be harmoniously integrated.

Free movement of goods

There have been no customs duties between most EU members since March 1, 1986. Most technical, safety, and other standards and regulations for trade have now been standardized throughout the EU. However, free movement of goods has been hampered by fragmented local markets. This fragmentation has been created by exploiting language differences between countries and by setting artificially high prices for goods. With the growth of discount stores, mail-order houses, cross-border buying deals, and e-commerce these differences are gradually being eliminated.

The EU has also created a single currency, the euro,[3] which some believe is beginning to challenge the US dollar's dominance of international trade and finance. In January 2002, the euro officially replaced individual countries' currencies in 12 member states. This had extended to 15 countries in the 'eurozone' by 2007, by which time it had the highest combined value of cash in circulation in the world, surpassing the US dollar. But some key countries, notably the UK, have not joined the single currency community and full financial integration across Europe has proved complex.[4] But the process of financial integration has helped generate new opportunities for both EU businesses as well as for foreign MNEs doing business there.[5]

Practice of government procurement

EU government procurements account for 17 percent of the union's GDP. In the past it has been common to find governments awarding contracts to national firms. However, with the emergence of the SEM and the Government Procurement Agreement (GPA), this is diminishing. The result will be greater efficiency, lower cost, and an economically stronger common market. On the other hand, it is important to realize that, in implementing this strategy, many companies are likely to find themselves losing business to competitors in

Single European Act (SEA)
An Act passed by the EU that contains many measures to further integrate the member states, along economic and political dimensions, and that allows the Council of Ministers to pass most proposals by a majority vote, in contrast to the unanimous vote needed previously

Council of Ministers
The major policy decision-making body of the EU and one of its major institutions, consisting of one minister from each of the member states

Single European Market (SEM)
A market consisting of all members of the EU, bound together by a single currency, a special charter, complete harmonization of social and economic policies, and a common defense policy

other EU countries that can provide higher quality and service and lower cost. This development will also probably be somewhat slow in coming because of the possible negative impact of the economic growth of individual countries and the desire to favor national firms when awarding government contracts. In 2004, a British government-commissioned study denounced the difficulties faced by British firms when competing for procurement contracts in other EU nations. Only 10 percent of all government contracts in the EU are awarded to foreign firms, compared to 20 percent in the private sector. It is not that the rules of government procurement are faulty but that governments evade them to favor domestic firms. For example, all contracts above a certain value must be publicly advertised but at least one government circumvented this rule by splitting the job into two smaller contracts.

Meanwhile, the EU continues to try to improve cross-border access to government procurement contracts. It has sought to standardize the procurement process to overcome language barriers. For example, the European Commission proposed a common vocabulary to be used in all public procurement notices that would standardize the procurement process and increase competition.

Enlargement of the EU

The ascension of additional members into the EU since 2004 has changed the panorama of the union and raised questions about the feasibility of a truly integrated region, economically and politically. With the exception of the war on Iraq, the EU15 had been able to maintain a relatively common front in regards to foreign policy. The EU's largest members disagreed on whether or not to support a US invasion of Iraq. France and Germany opposed the war while the UK strongly supported it.[6] Despite this, the union has been able to present a unified stance on a number of other international matters, including aid to poorer nations and other wars. The inclusion of new, mostly Central European nations, into the union has added a new factor that further complicates reaching a consensus. Most of the new members are pro-American politically and aspire to their economic system, including low corporate taxation. This contrasts with the policies of Germany and France, two founding members that rely heavily on government involvement and often disagree with US foreign policy. The UK is more aligned with their views, but it stands as a less involved member in the EU when contrasted with France and Germany. Another topic of disagreement is Russia. Both Germany and France have good relations with Russia, whereas the new members see it with distrust. A common foreign policy is now less likely to emerge.[7]

In addition, these new countries have not been fully integrated into the union. The prospect of a flood of cheap labor into the EU15 nations created a negative reaction from EU15 citizens. These new members, therefore, remain outside the Schengen zone of passport-free travel for at least a couple of years and cannot work in most EU15 countries for at least another six years. Indeed, only the UK, Ireland, and Sweden have opened their borders to workers from new member nations. The newer members have also been excluded from receiving the full amount of farm subsidies available to EU15 members. This is partly due to the expense of subsidizing farmers but also because the lower cost of producing in the new member countries would destabilize the EU15 member's agricultural industry. In addition, the EU, the United States, and Japan are under increasing pressure from less developed countries to eliminate farm subsidies altogether. Offering full subsidies to the 12 new members would only exacerbate the situation if the EU decided to phase out agricultural subsidies. Nonetheless, new members are finding the EU15 a welcoming market for their agricultural products, which are still competitive because of the lower costs of producing in their countries. Future enlargement is likely to follow the same or even more restrictive rights for new members.

Further enlargement also threatens to increase the differences among member countries, stymieing political and economic integration. In particular, the possibility that Turkey might join the union has created a lot of tension within the EU. Turkey's mainly Islamic population is relatively large, and the country has a relatively younger population that could have an impact on the political future of the aging EU. Many nationalist groups within the EU are against Turkey joining the union and, indeed, see any further enlargement as a dilution of their power within the union.[8] It is difficult to predict whether the EU27 has the potential to be as integrated politically and economically as did the EU15. For the time being, however, there is internal disagreement about further integration.

✔ Active learning check

Review your answer to Active Learning Case question 1 and make any changes you like. Then compare your answer to the one below.

1 **Describe the stages by which France Telecom has built up a successful strategic base in the EU. What barriers to integration had to be overcome in the EU before France Telecom could buy up rival companies?**

As a state-owned monopoly, France Telecom originally had a strong presence in its own market but relied heavily on fixed-line operations and had no significant international presence. Faced with deregulation, France Telecom sought to compete regionally but understood that to do so it had to have competitive products and access to international markets. Investment in R&D allowed the company to expand its product line while strategic alliances were sought to protect its market and expand into others. The Global One alliance with Telekom provided a period of competitive shelter from one of its major EU competitors. By the time this alliance was dissolved in 1999, France Telecom had the capacity to compete alone against major EU telecommunication companies and had begun to acquire companies to solidify its product line and enter new EU markets.

For France Telecom to be able to purchase rival firms, deregulation of telecommunications markets of individual countries in the EU had to occur. In addition, France Telecom acquisitions must overcome antitrust legislation in the EU.

The competitive status of the EU

The eventual emergence of an integrated EU will help greater Europe compete more effectively with the other triad members. However, several EU countries are currently at a competitive disadvantage in some areas.

Productivity

High wages, salaries, and fringe benefits put some EU firms at a disadvantage in competing with their US and Japanese counterparts. Labor laws in all EU countries make it extremely difficult to fire employees once they have been employed for a year. US companies have much greater freedom and flexibility in hiring and firing their workers on short notice. This means that employees must remain productive to retain their jobs and that companies can adjust more readily to changes in demand for their product or service. Japanese firms tend to treat their workers as a fixed cost and so find the practice of firing to be unnecessary; employees are grateful to their employers and are willing to work hard to upgrade their skills and increase the company's economic performance.

With some success, EUfirms are working to raise their productivity and match that of their major triad competitors. As shown in Table 17.2, in 2007, hourly compensation costs for production workers in manufacturing were higher in the main EU economies of France, Germany, the Netherlands, and the UK than in the United States. But costs were much lower in the newer EU countries and slightly lower in Japan. Over the last few years,

Table 17.2 Hourly compensation costs in manufacturing

Country/region	1996	2007
EU15 of which		
France	18.99	28.57
Germany	29.58	37.66
Italy	17.10	28.23
Netherlands	31.81	34.07
Portugal	5.33	8.27
Spain	13.33	20.98
UK	14.12	29.73
New EU members		
Czech Rep.	3.10	8.20
Hungary	2.73	7.91
United States	17.74	24.59
Japan	20.44	19.75

Source: US Bureau of Labour Statistics, November 10, 2009.

cooperation between EU workers and companies to protect jobs has decreased hourly salaries. (Also, see the case **International Business Strategy in Action: German management and unions** in Chapter 14.)

Investment spending

Investment spending in EU countries has traditionally lagged behind. Part of this can be explained by rapid increases in wages and benefits during the 1980s that were not offset by increases in productivity. As a result, EU firms found themselves without the capital to invest and had to resort to borrowing. Demands for loans resulted in higher interest rates, which also put a strain on investors. More recently, EU economies have been doing much better, stabilizing government spending. Despite this, most European countries continue to perform below the US level in terms of overall productivity. (See Figure 17.1.)

Education

Another area in which EU countries have failed to maintain a competitive edge is education. While all three triad groups spend approximately 5 percent of GDP on education, the

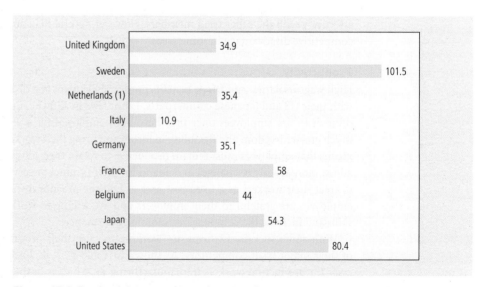

Figure 17.1 Productivity: percentage increase in output per hour, 1992–2008

Source: US Department of Labor, Bureau of Labor Statistics, February 2009.

approaches are different. In Europe, most vocational training is provided at the high school level, whereas in the United States and Japan it comes later. Moreover, in the United States a higher percentage of the population attends college than in Europe or Japan. The European university curriculum is more theoretical than in either the United States or Japan. European educational institutions are also more rigid and less able to adapt to the changing needs of business, and there is less interaction between European educational institutions and industry. Some believe that as a result, many European students receive training that is inappropriate for the employment needs of European business and industry. This in part explains the high unemployment rates in the age group under 25 in many regions of Europe. The major challenge for European countries will be to modify their education systems and make them more flexible, more practical, and better able to adapt to the changing demands of industry.

Overall evaluation

In overall terms, the EU has traditionally lagged behind its triad competitors, although recent downturns in the US economy contrast with sustained growth in some EU countries, including many in the south. As Table 17.3 shows, in 1989 all the EU15 countries ranked in the top 22 most competitive economies in the world. By 2008 there are 10 in this category and by 2011 just 8 as newly emerging economies from Asia and elsewhere join the top ranks. The world is becoming a more competitive place, and some EU countries are finding it hard to keep up.

What changes are likely to occur in the future? One is an increase in acquisitions and mergers among EU firms and between them and companies from outside the bloc. A second change is the emergence of new technologies that will be developed in EU laboratories. A third is additional free trade agreements and other economic arrangements among European countries that are designed to make the EU a stronger, more competitive market.[9]

Table 17.3 The world's most competitive economies

Rank	1989	2008	2011
1	Japan	United States	Hong Kong SAR (P.R. China)
2	Switzerland	Switzerland	United States
3	United States	Denmark	Singapore
4	Canada	Sweden	Sweden
5	Germany	Germany	Switzerland
6	Finland	Finland	Taiwan (Taiwan Province of China)
7	Netherlands	Singapore	Canada
8	Sweden	Japan	Qatar
9	Norway	United Kingdom	Australia
10	Australia	Netherlands	Germany
11	United Kingdom	Korea	Luxembourg
12	Denmark	Hong Kong SAR (P.R. China)	Denmark
13	France	Canada	Norway
14	Belgium/Luxembourg	Taiwan (Taiwan Province of China)	Netherlands
15	Austria	Austria	Finland
16	Ireland	Norway	Malaysia
17	New Zealand	Israel	Israel
18	Spain	France	Austria
19	Italy	Australia	China
20	Turkey	Belgium	United Kingdom
21	Portugal	Malaysia	New Zealand
22	Greece	Ireland	Korea

Source: Adapted from IMD and World Economic Forum, *The World Competitiveness Report*, 1989, 2008 and 2011.

Active learning check

Review your answer to Active Learning Case question 2 and make any changes you like. Then compare your answer with the one below.

2 **To what extent is the triad strategy of France Telecom the same as that of Vodafone (in Chapter 8)? Are there any differences?**

Both Vodafone and France Telecom have a stronger presence in the European market than in any other triad market. Acquisitions have been a major part of both their strategies to gain technology and market share in their own triad region and in other triad markets. One difference is Vodafone's continued reliance on alliances, such as its joint venture with Bell Atlantic, whereas France Telecom no longer seeks alliances but equity in competitors. Another difference is that the extent of Vodafone's international expansion is much larger than France Telecom's.

CONDUCTING A STRATEGIC ANALYSIS

As we have seen, the EU is likely to be a very competitive market in the future. In preparing to do business in the EU, foreign MNEs must first conduct an overall strategic analysis, focusing on the competitive nature of the industry being targeted. Assuming that the enterprise intends to set up operations by FDI or alternative investments rather than merely export to the market, the analysis must also evaluate location. This section examines both of these activities.

Using competitive intelligence

Competition in the EU has grown over the last few years. Some of the specific strategies employed have included careful market segmentation, increased R&D, and the use of mergers, acquisitions, and alliances to help build market share and improve competitive strength. For example, GM centralized the management of its European operations to save costs and better control regional operations some time ago.[10] Apple monitors prices in Europe and as a result charged about $100 more for a basic iPad in London, England, than in the United States, when it launched the product in Europe in 2010.[11] Competitor intelligence has been an essential part of these developments. This approach employs two complementary paths: external information gathering and internal infrastructural analysis.

External information gathering

The information that is critical for competitor analysis is typically located in a variety of sources. For example, in the UK, Denmark, and Ireland, centralized government-controlled company registration offices provide financial information on registered firms. Other useful sources of competitive information include the Department of Trade and Industry (DTI), trade associations, business information services, and regional and local publications. In France, a great deal of registration information is commonly found in local courthouses. This is also the case in Germany and Italy, where companies must register with the local civil courts in the region where they are headquartered. In these countries, chambers of commerce are also excellent sources of information because they work much more closely with business firms than do their counterparts in the United States. Central databases created by the EU Commission can be used to keep abreast of changes in national legislation, thus keeping companies aware of new laws and regulations. An understanding of the legal, technical, and cultural barriers often used to keep foreign competition at bay can be particularly important in an environmental analysis. The case **International Business Strategy in Action: Ford and Volvo** illustrates this point.

INTERNATIONAL BUSINESS STRATEGY IN ACTION

Ford and Volvo

Before it bought into Mazda and took over the four European auto manufacturers that made up its Premier Brands Group (PAG), Ford had already developed a relatively strong presence in Europe. In contrast to GM's mode of inter-nationalization through M&A, Ford had expanded organically through the development of local sales, distribution, and manufacturing activities around the world. In Europe, it began with a plant in Manchester, England, in 1911 before moving to the Dagenham site near London in 1932. At its peak, three-quarters of Ford's overseas production was located in Europe, with plants in Germany, Spain, the UK, and Belgium. Even then, however, including Brazil, around 50 percent of total production took place in the Americas, primarily in the United States, Mexico, and Canada. Table 1 shows the range of brands that came under the Ford group in 2002.

This distribution reflected the regional sales mix of the Ford core brand, listed in the table, with 62 percent of sales in North America, 29 percent in Europe, and a weak 5 percent showing in the Asia–Pacific region. This represents

Table 1 Ford and its brands, 2002

AUTOMOTIVE CORE BRANDS			
Primary brands	Ford	Lincoln	Mercury	Mazda
Dealers	13,000	1,561	2,141	6,131
Markets	137	38	15	145
Competitors	DaimlerChrysler, Fiat, GM, Honda, Nissan, Toyota, VW, Hyundai/Kia	DaimlerChrysler, GM, Honda, Nissan, Toyota, BMW	DaimlerChrysler, GM, Honda, Nissan, Toyota, VW	Toyota, Nissan, Honda, Mitsubishi, GM, DaimlerChrysler, VW
Vehicle retail sales . . . % of total	5,457,445	159,651	274,875	964,800
Sales mix	74%	2%	4%	13%
	62% N. America	98% N. America	98% N. America	39% Asia–Pacific
	29% Europe	2% Rest of world	2% Rest of world	36% N. America
	5% Asia–Pacific			20% Europe
	3% S. America			5% Rest of world
	1% Rest of world			
PREMIER AUTOMOTIVE GROUP (PAG)			
Primary brands	Aston Martin	Jaguar	Volvo	Land Rover
Dealers	100	787	2,500	1,808
Markets	25	66	100	142
Competitors	Lamborghini, Ferrari, Porsche	DaimlerChrysler (Mercedes), BMW, Toyota (Lexus), Porsche	BMW, Mercedes Benz, Audi, Lexus	Toyota, Nissan, GM, DaimlerChrysler, BMW
Vehicle retail sales . . . % of total	1,551	130,330	406,695	174.593
Sales mix	0%	2%	5%	2%
	30% N. America	50% N. America	60% Europe	61% Europe
	30% Europe	41% Europe	30% N. America	25% N. America
	30% UK	7% Asia–Pacific	10% Rest of world	14% Rest of world
	10% Rest of world	2% Rest of world		

Source: Corporate Annual Reports.

▶

the period when Ford maximized its European investments. The Premier Automotive Group (PAG) was created through a series of alliances and takeovers driven partly by the considerable drop in Ford's market share in Europe from 1994 to 1999, from almost 12 percent to just over 9 percent. A broad range of restructurings were initiated by then CEO Jacques Nasser, who stepped in to refocus on the central Ford brand operations and marketing. In 1999, Ford bought Volvo for $6.45 billion, the largest of the PAG companies, adding to Jaguar (bought in 1989), Aston Martin, and Land Rover. Since then it has sold all three. The dismantling of the PAG began in 2006, with Aston Martin sold to a UK group of investors in 2007, Jaguar and Land Rover sold to Tata Motors for $2.3 billion in 2008 and in 2010, Ford sold Volvo to the Chinese carmaker Geely for $1.8 billion.

At its peak, the overall Ford Group, combining the core brands group and the European-centered PAG, appeared to be one of the more global of the largest auto firms. It was, however, still heavily regional and primarily US oriented. The relative lack of integration among the group companies, particularly Volvo, further underlined its regional structure.

First produced in Gothenburg, Sweden, Volvos were initially designed to survive the rough roads and winter cold of Sweden. This emphasis on durability was eventually transformed into the concern for passenger safety upon which the company's reputation was built. Before the takeover, Volvo had made 70 percent of its cars in Sweden but had 90 percent of its sales abroad. The firm had developed as a high-quality niche manufacturer of safe vehicles, competing against rivals such as Saab, BMW, Audi, and Mercedes. It had its own unique culture and way of developing cars and conducting business.

Ford bought Volvo in 1999 for $6.45 billion and sold over ten years later for $1.8 billion. The need to clearly differentiate and segment individual brands was one major factor underlying the structural separation and cultural distinctiveness of the group companies in Ford. Whilst senior management at its Detroit HQ knew this it is safe to say that they underestimated the challenging complexities of managing a diverse group of brands spread across a different continent.

Websites: www.volvo.com and www.ford.com.

Sources: Economist, "Ford sells Volvo to Geely: Devolving Volvo," *The Economist*, March 28, 2010, http://www.economist.com/node/15804598?story_id=E1_TVRDQVJR; John Reed and Joe Leahy, "Ford and Tata Finalise $2.3bn Deal," *Financial Times*, March 26 2008; Alan M. Rugman and Simon C. Collinson, "The Regional Nature of the World's Automotive Industry," *European Management Journal*, vol. 22, no. 5 (2004), pp. 471–482; Ford, *Annual Reports*, 2003 and 2007; Alex Taylor III, "Volvo and Saab," *Fortune*, July 21, 1997; Christine Tierney, "Will Volvo Become Just Another Ford?," *BW Online*, December 10, 2001; and Christopher Brown-Humes, "Volvo Exceeds Earnings Forecasts," *FT.com*, February 11, 2002.

Coordinated infrastructure
An infrastructure used when there is a high degree of similarity among national markets and business units share resources in an effort to help each other raise overall sales

Market coordination infrastructure
An infrastructure used by firms that compete in similar national markets but do little resource sharing among their businesses

Resource-sharing infrastructure
An infrastructure used by firms that compete in dissimilar national markets but share resources such as R&D efforts and manufacturing information

Autonomous infrastructure
An infrastructure used by multinationals that compete in dissimilar national markets and do not share resources

Internal infrastructural analysis

The second step MNEs take is to analyze how to manage their infrastructure. Prescott and Gibbons have described four types of infrastructures that can be used to compete effectively: coordinated, market coordination, resource point sharing, and autonomous.[12] The choice of infrastructure is determined by the similarity of national markets among the MNE's businesses and the extent of resource sharing across businesses.

The **coordinated infrastructure** is used when there is a high degree of similarity among national markets and business units share resources in an effort to help each other raise overall sales. Computer firms often use this approach. Firms that compete in similar national markets but do little resource sharing among their businesses use a **market coordination infrastructure**. This approach is employed by companies that set up each operation as a separate, independent business, and sometimes by small firms that are geographically dispersed. Firms that compete in dissimilar national markets but share resources such as R&D efforts and manufacturing information use a **resource-sharing infrastructure**. Auto manufacturers use this approach. An **autonomous infrastructure** is used by MNEs that compete in dissimilar national markets and do not share resources. Highly diversified MNEs use this approach.

Evaluating locations

The European Union is the largest market in the world, but despite the overarching institutions of the EU and the principle of the 'single market', the ease of market access for foreign firms varies by industry and country location. The most important location factors tend to be: (1) access to customers, (2) quality of labor, (3) expansion prospects, (4) level of wage costs, (5) attractive environment, (6) access to suppliers, (7) non-financial regional assistance, (8) absence of restrictions for expansion, (9) infrastructure, (10) level of rents, and (11) public transportation.

Another factor often mentioned is the ease with which a company that is not doing well can withdraw. This includes laying off workers, selling facilities, and other factors involved in exiting a market.

Gathering location data and understanding negotiating terms can take a considerable amount of time, but the results often justify the investment. A great deal of useful and accessible data for market-entry evaluation is now online. The World Bank's Doing Business website provides an interactive analysis comparing countries around the world in terms of the relative ease and costs of opening, operating and closing businesses. Table 17.4 shows how a selected set of European and other (USA and Japan) countries compare according to some key evaluation criteria.

Regional incentives

Investment incentives take a number of forms, including grants, low-interest loans, reduced land prices, and training support for personnel. For example, both Poland and Slovakia offered incentives to the South Korean auto maker Kia to lure investment for a new manufacturing plant. The Czech Republic attracted a large amount of automotive FDI in the mid-2000's and began to supplement manufacturing investment with FDI in services and R&D. In 2008 one the country's first biotechnology clusters began to develop near Prague with 20 foreign companies initiating investments.[13] CzechInvest, the country's investment-promotion agency, and other Government departments use tax incentives and cheap loans to attract such investments. These extend the existing advantages of cheap land and labour (relative to Western Europe) as well as access to the growing markets of East and Central Europe.

Typically, incentives are higher when (1) the region is economically depressed, (2) many jobs are being created, (3) the company is making a large investment, and/or (4) the investment is likely to attract other investors. Before agreeing to any contract, however, it is important that the deal be "locked in" and that any repayment of subsidies be made clear up front.

STRATEGY ISSUES

We now focus on a number of strategic issues that need to be considered when doing business in the EU, including (1) an overall strategic analysis, (2) the feasibility of exporting, (3) the value of strategic acquisitions and alliances, (4) marketing considerations, (5) manufacturing approaches, and (6) management considerations. This section briefly examines each issue.

Overall strategic analysis for the EU

National responsiveness
The ability of MNEs to understand different consumer tastes in segmented regional markets and to respond to different national standards and regulations imposed by autonomous governments and agencies

In formulating a strategy for doing business in the EU, we should look at both the process of globalization through economic integration and the need for a firm's **national responsiveness**.[14] This is done on the matrix in Figure 17.2. The horizontal axis represents political sovereignty and the need for a firm to be nationally responsive. We call this the "national responsiveness" axis. As a political axis, it takes into account both consumer tastes and government regulations. The vertical axis, or "integration" axis, represents globalization through economic integration. This includes the need to develop economies of scale, use a value-added strategy, and reap the benefits of greater coordination and control of geographically dispersed activities.

Table 17.4 Comparison of location factors

Economy	Ease of doing business rank	Starting a business	Dealing with construction permits	Registering property	Getting credit	Protecting investors	Paying taxes	Trading across borders	Enforcing contracts	Closing a business
United Kingdom	2	6	3	8	1	6	5	9	15	6
United States	3	4	8	5	3	2	15	10	7	12
Denmark	4	8	2	10	6	11	3	1	19	4
Norway	6	13	23	2	19	9	7	5	3	3
Ireland	7	5	12	22	6	2	1	11	20	8
Finland	9	12	18	9	15	15	16	2	10	5
Sweden	10	16	6	7	25	11	11	3	21	15
Iceland	11	10	10	4	15	18	10	28	2	14
Japan	13	25	15	19	6	7	26	12	12	1
Germany	14	24	4	20	6	21	23	8	5	22
Belgium	15	11	13	30	19	7	17	21	13	7
France	16	7	5	27	19	18	14	14	6	26
Switzerland	17	23	11	6	6	30	5	20	17	25
Netherlands	19	21	27	16	19	24	9	7	18	9
Portugal	20	17	28	11	26	13	19	15	16	18
Austria	21	27	20	12	6	28	24	13	8	17
Slovak Republic	22	19	19	3	6	24	28	30	25	21
Slovenia	23	9	21	25	29	9	21	24	24	23
Luxembourg	24	22	14	26	29	26	4	18	1	27
Hungary	25	14	25	15	15	26	25	27	14	29
Spain	26	29	16	18	19	21	18	23	21	16
Czech Republic	27	28	24	17	19	21	29	26	27	20
Poland	28	26	30	23	6	13	27	22	26	30
Italy	29	19	26	24	26	15	29	25	30	19
Greece	30	30	17	29	26	29	20	29	28	28

Source: Adapted from the World Bank, Doing Business website: http://www.doingbusiness.org/rankings. June 2011.

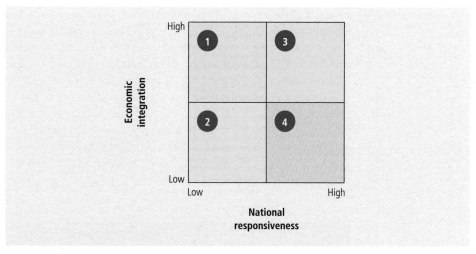

Figure 17.2 Business strategies for the EU

Source: Adapted from C. A. Bartlett, "Building and Managing the Transnational: the New Organizational Challenge," in *Competition in Global Industries*, edited by M. E. Porter, Boston, MA, 1986. Copyright © 1986 by the Harvard Business School Publishing Corporation; all rights reserved; and *Managing Across Borders: The Transnational Solution*, 2nd ed. by C. A. Bartlett and S. Ghoshal, Boston, MA, 1998. Copyright © 1998 by Harvard Business School Publishing Corporation; all rights reserved.

Quadrants 1 and 4 in Figure 17.2 present relatively simple strategy situations. Quadrant 1 requires a strategy in which the MNE does not need to be concerned with national responsiveness. The company is in a market driven by high integration and its strategy must be on achieving price competitiveness. Firms operating in this quadrant are often centralized in structure and thus can use mergers and acquisitions to benefit from high economic integration. Companies selling microcomputers frequently operate in quadrant 1.

In quadrant 4, economic integration is less important than national responsiveness, so the MNE must focus on adapting products to satisfy the specific demands of each country. In this case, integration is minimized in favor of a decentralized strategy of national responsiveness designed to appeal to select niches and target groups. Companies selling food products and designer clothes use this approach.

In quadrant 2, there is low integration and low national responsiveness. The potential of obtaining economies of scale and benefits of national or regional responsiveness are both small. MNEs operating in this quadrant are vulnerable to triad competitors. There is no advantage in centralized quality control or economies of scale and no ability to adapt activities to individual countries. MNEs selling inexpensive toys that are undifferentiated fall into this quadrant.

MNEs in quadrant 3 use a strategy of high integration and high national responsiveness characterized by strong price competitiveness and select target positioning. This is the most challenging quadrant to implement; the firm's organization structure is complex, but it is the one in which many successful triad-based adaptive multinationals operate. Auto companies fall into this quadrant.

A close look at events in the EU reveals that Brussels' administrators designed a strategy to help European firms move into quadrant 1. The plan is designed to create a natural entry barrier to outside firms and help ensure the success of local competitors. A survey of the top management of Europe's 300 largest corporations has confirmed this tendency toward integration. The survey found that European managers anticipate greater integration due to such developments as strategic partnerships, mergers, and takeovers as well as increasing economies of scale.[15] As a result, the managers expect the development of more efficient modern industries. The survey also found that European managers were confident that economic integration was a viable strategy for them but would be detrimental to non-European MNEs. Only 9 percent of the managers believed US firms would gain ground in Europe, whereas 42 percent said US firms would lose competitive strength.

Exporting firms operate in quadrant 4. As outsiders in the EU, US firms will find it increasingly difficult to export to Europe and compete on economies of scale in the face of integration by rival EU firms. Not only will costs be higher for exporters, but locally based competitors will have more access to competitive information. As a result, today many exporting firms will be switching from exporting to FDI in order to meet the new nature of competition in Europe.

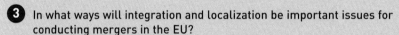

✔ Active learning check

Review your answer to Active Learning Case question 3 and make any changes you like. Then compare your answer to the one below.

3 **In what ways will integration and localization be important issues for conducting mergers in the EU?**

Companies successfully operating in different EU countries will seek mergers to achieve some economies of scale in R&D, design, sourcing, and distribution, among others. Nevertheless, the benefits of economies of scale have to be weighed against the need to tailor-make products for customers in different markets. Integration will therefore occur only in some sectors of the merged company.

Exporting

Those firms that continue to export to the EU will have to address a number of legal/financial matters. The following sections examine some of the most important issues. (See Table 17.5.)

Customs duties and taxes

Goods manufactured outside the EU are subject to customs duties at the point of entry. These duties are determined by an EU-wide tariff system that establishes common rates regardless of entry point. Most duties are based on the value of the good ad valorem, which in turn depends on the stage of assembly or completion of the end product.

Product standards

Products exported to the EU must meet standards and technical regulations. Many of these are common throughout the bloc, but when they are not the product must meet the standards of the country to which it is exported. In many cases, products made in outside countries must be modified in order to gain EU entry.[16]

Conducting export operations

In recent years, many US exporters of both goods and services have consolidated their operations with those of European companies, helping them to surmount EU barriers. For example, US accounting firms typically operate through local partnerships. Other examples are management consulting firms with international operations that help address the needs of local clients and law firms with overseas offices.

Table 17.5 Direction of EU trade

Country/region	Exports to				Imports from			
	1999		2008		1999		2008	
	(billions of US $)	% of total	(billions of US $)	% of total	(billions of US $)	% of total	(billions of US $)	% of total
EU15	1,371.80	62.65	3,978.24	67.89	1,268.80	59.50	3,851.81	63.00
Austria	48.07	2.19	144.41	2.46	34.67	1.62	122.42	2.00
Belgium	110.80	5.06	308.87	5.27	107.88	5.05	339.99	5.56
Denmark	29.68	1.35	77.60	1.32	26.08	1.22	74.09	1.21
Finland	21.39	0.97	57.30	0.97	22.33	1.04	57.63	0.94
France	213.09	9.73	507.00	8.65	181.15	8.49	385.53	6.30
Germany	282.76	12.91	771.22	13.16	295.81	13.87	896.25	14.65
Greece	19.24	0.87	53.17	0.90	5.47	0.25	16.39	0.26
Ireland	26.78	1.22	64.37	1.09	40.78	1.91	85.21	1.39
Italy	129.82	5.92	322.23	5.49	119.26	5.59	301.23	4.92
Luxembourg	8.03	0.36	24.53	0.41	5.09	0.23	25.55	0.41
Netherlands	117.61	5.37	289.67	4.94	141.18	6.62	462.12	7.55
Portugal	32.01	1.46	64.71	1.10	19.08	0.89	37.79	0.61
Spain	104.74	4.78	258.30	4.40	74.92	3.51	190.65	3.11
Sweden	46.23	2.11	119.15	2.03	47.86	2.24	116.58	1.90
United Kingdom	181.93	8.30	375.96	6.41	147.21	6.90	274.93	4.49
Other Western Europe	92.45	4.22	213.83	3.64	89.60	4.20	264.52	4.32
Iceland	1.44	0.06	3.35	0.05	1.44	0.06	3.98	0.06
Norway	24.99	1.14	64.50	1.10	31.13	1.46	141.06	2.30
Switzerland	66.00	3.01	145.98	2.49	57.02	2.67	119.48	1.95
Developing Europe	159.40	7.27	801.80	13.68	140.10	6.57	814.10	13.31
Total Europe	1,623.65	74.15	4,993.87	85.22	1,498.51	70.28	4,930.43	80.64
Non-European	565.95	25.84	865.43	14.77	633.58	29.71	1,183.27	19.35
United States	193.49	8.83	367.75	6.27	174.73	8.19	275.04	4.49
Japan	37.58	1.71	62.42	1.06	79.36	3.72	110.82	1.81
Total	2189.60	100	5859.30	100	2132.10	100	6113.70	100

Notes: EU data for 1999 is EU15, data for 2008 is EU27. Exports and imports from and to the EU are intra-EU trade.

Source: Adapted from IMF, *Direction of Trade Statistics Yearbook*, 2000 and 2009. Memorandum tables, EU, page 70 (2000) and page 41 (2009).

Those MNEs that do choose to export to the EU must carefully select their agents and distributors. Five steps are critical to this process:

1 Examine the legal and business considerations involved in appointing foreign intermediaries and establish criteria that reflect the particular geographic market.

2 Assemble a list of potential candidates by using the various directories and consulting with other sources of information.

3 Qualify such candidates by applying certain criteria and conducting a preliminary interview.

4 Visit the proposed intermediary to obtain additional information about its resources and facilities, to get a proper feeling for the intermediary's compatibility with the organization, and to check the objectives of the agent or distributor.

5 After selecting an agent or distributor, (a) negotiate an agreement that is fair and mutually beneficial, (b) comply in good faith with the terms of the agreement, (c) continue communication between the parties, and (d) make occasional adjustments in the relationship in response to changing circumstances.

Many small and intermediate MNEs will continue to export to the EU because it is too expensive for them to use any other route. Large MNEs, on the other hand, are turning more and more to strategic acquisitions and alliances.

Strategic acquisitions and alliances

Two of the most popular ways of gaining a foothold in the EU are strategic acquisitions and alliances. (See the case **International Business Strategy in Action: Deutsche Bahn: more than a railway.**) A *Harvard Business Review* study analyzed 49 strategic alliances and concluded that the chances of success are improved if the parties keep five guidelines in mind: (1) acquisitions work better than alliances when developing core businesses; (2) alliances are effective when firms want to gain entry into new geographic markets or businesses that are tangential to the core business; (3) alliances between strong and weak companies typically do not work well; (4) alliances that last are characterized by an ability to move beyond the initially established expectations and objectives; and (5) alliances are more likely to be successful when both sides hold an equal amount of financial ownership. In addition, more than three-quarters of the alliances studied ended with one of the parties acquiring full control.[17]

Making strategic alliances work

It is more common to find MNEs using strategic alliances than using acquisitions. One definition suggests that these are a cooperative arrangement between two or more companies in which:

- a common strategy is developed in unison and a win-win attitude is adopted by all parties;
- the relationship is reciprocal, with each partner prepared to share specific strengths with the other, thus lending power to the enterprise;
- a pooling of resources, investment and risks occurs for mutual gain.

Several important steps are involved in making these arrangements work. One is that each partner must complement the other.[18] If one company is strong in R&D and the other's strengths are in manufacturing and marketing, the alliance may be ideal. On the other hand, if both are strong in R&D and weak in manufacturing and marketing, there is no synergy and the two may end up trying to steal secrets from each other and competing rather than cooperating. Second, the goals of the two groups must be carefully spelled out. Once the partners have agreed on the primary criteria such as new product development, increased market share, and return on investment, they can then decide how to commit their resources. These goals provide a basis for overall direction.

Building working relationships across the two firms is essential for resolving problems and issues that come up. Communication, networking, and interpersonal relationships are extremely useful in ensuring that the spirit of the alliance is kept alive. Mutual understanding, trust and compromise are important to sustaining alliances over long periods of time, This needs to be underpinned by a reciprocal respect and understanding of the cultural differences between firms from different parts of the EU and elsewhere. (See Chapter 5 in this textbook on "International Culture" and the "Active Learning Case" on "Culture Clash at Pharmacia and Upjohn").

Marketing considerations

As the EU develops toward a true economic union, internal barriers to entry and mobility barriers within the bloc should disappear. This will create both challenges and opportunities. In particular, competition is likely to increase as it becomes easier for competitors to invade each other's territories. There is also a complex trade-off between integration and expansion, particularly as the latter encompasses a wider range of economies, institutions, and cultures, which works against some forms of standardization and harmonization.[19] As a result, marketing strategies in the future will have to reflect concern for both pricing and positioning.[20]

INTERNATIONAL BUSINESS STRATEGY IN ACTION

Deutsche Bahn: more than a railway

Deutsche Bahn is one of the world's largest passenger, freight, and logistics companies. It has a huge passenger railway station in the center of Berlin and has its executive training center in a Potsdam train museum. Deutsche Bahn Aktiengesellschaft (DB) was founded in 1994, and by 2001 its sales were US $14 billion. During the 2010 financial year, DB Group posted revenues of about €34.4 billion, and an EBIT of a good €1.9 billion after adjustments for special items. It was ranked 177 on the Global Fortune 500 list.

With its head office in Berlin, DB is well known to the 2.5 billion passengers who use its extensive Europe-wide train and bus network, served by about 290,000 employees, of which about 189,000 are located in Germany. DB also operates the subway (metro) system in Berlin and Hamburg, as well as many urban bus routes. Indeed, DB manages the densest and most complex rail network in the world and it is the European leader in rail freight and land transportation beating SNCF, Tenitalia, RCA, and DHL. The rail side of its operation accounts for over 50 percent of total turnover.

Despite attempts to harmonize the rail industry across the EU, there remain many obstacles to European expansion, including the differences in fuels and safety regulations and also language barriers. As a result, rather than expanding across its borders, though there have been some exceptional success stories on that front like the Paris–Frankfurt line, DB's CEO Martmut Mehdorn has sought to expand within its country by attracting the potential consumer who does not yet take advantage of the train system. The strategy has been to think outside the box and

look at how the train experience can become easier for passengers, businesses, and governments. For example, DB offers a car share program, a rent a car program, and even a bike rental program to its passengers. A state government, on the other hand, might turn to DB to organize its entire transportation system including rail, subway, rapid transit, and/or buses.

But DB is much more than a railway company. Outside of rail, which is a base for all its other operations, DB has expanded into air and sea transportation. It is this diversification, according to Mehdorn, that allowed the company to finally turn a profit in 2004, 11 years after the government changed the ownership and management structure of the company. Overall, DB logistics, with its five business units, (Rail Freight, Intermodal, Land Transport, Air/Ocean Freight, and Contract Logistics/SCM), is ranked second in the world behind DHL. Including its freight part of its rail business, logistics accounts for 57 percent of the group's revenues (most of the rest is from its passenger business, which, together with air freight, is organized under the Schenker business name). In global air freight the DB Schenker division ranks just behind DHL and ahead of UPS. Schenker is number three in global ocean freight behind DHL and Kuhne & Nagel.

DB is a home-region, not a global, company even though it operates in over 130 countries. Most of its employees work in Europe where it has the great majority of its sales (the geographic sales of the group, by region, are not reported). Virtually all of its passenger business is in Europe, and most of its logistic business, and this was further extended by its acquisition of UK-based transport firm Arriva in 2010. The firm has, however, some investments in North America because its Schenker division acquired the US logistics firm BAX in 2006 for $1.1 billion. In addition to its business in the United States, DB is also involved in China where it participates in an international consortia building a new rail and road transport system. It has an 8 percent stake in the consortium which is led by a Chinese state-owned firm, CRCTC. With the expansion of the EU into Eastern Europe, DB is well positioned to further develop its markets in Europe.

In summary, since the German government decided to distance itself from the

Source: Rex Features/Action Press

management of Deutsche Bahn in 1994, the company has turned itself from a subsidized railway system to a self-financing "mobility provider" that has now diversified into logistics, buses, sea freight, cars, and even bicycles. While, as of 2007, all of the company's shares were still owned by the government, a process of privatisation has taken place since then. Both management and the government see the benefits of going public at a time when the company is well on the way to being much more than a railway.

Sources: "Transport operator Arriva falls to Deutsche Bahn," *Guardian*, April 22, 2010, http://www.guardian.co.uk/business/marketforceslive/2010/apr/22/arriva-deutsche-bahn-takeover "Germany Agrees to Partly Privatize Railway System," *DW-World.de*, November 9, 2006; "Firms Seek Finance to Bid for Saudi Project," *Gulf News*, October 5, 2007; Deutsche Bahn, *Annual Report* 2006–2010; Hoover's Online; www.db.de.

Pricing

The European Commission has estimated that the price of goods and services throughout the EU will decline. Five specific developments will make this work: (1) decreasing costs of doing business, now that internal barriers and restrictions have been removed; (2) the opening up of public procurement contracts to broader competition; (3) foreign investment that will increase production capacity; (4) more rigorous enforcement of competition policy; and (5) general intensified competition brought about by economic reforms.

Price will become an even more important marketing factor to the extent that EU customers develop similar tastes and are willing to accept globally standardized products. As this happens, MNEs will be able to sell the same product throughout the bloc without having to make modifications for local tastes. Unfortunately, whereas some goods can be marketed with this strategy, many will require careful positioning for select target groups.[21]

Positioning

Some global products such as Coca-Cola, Pepsi, and Marlboro cigarettes have universal appeal, but these are more the exception than the rule. For example, in the UK Renault cars are viewed as good economy cars, but in Spain they are perceived as luxury automobiles. Similarly, in the UK and the Netherlands, toothpaste is viewed as a hygiene product and sells much better than in Spain and Greece, where it is marketed as a cosmetic.

As a result, the marketing motto "Plan globally, act locally" will continue to be a useful dictum. A good example is provided by the EU cellular communications market, which offers tremendous opportunities but is also extremely competitive because there are so many submarkets throughout the community. As a result, the mobile communications market will likely end up being divided among a host of major competitors, each of which will position itself for a particular local or regional target group.

✔ Active learning check

Review your answer to Active Learning Case question 4 and make any changes you like. Then compare your answer to the one below.

 In what ways will both pricing and positioning be important for companies like France Telecom doing business in the EU?

Companies like France Telecom must be prepared to take full advantage of the economies from EU integration. Costs must decrease in order to increase market share in the more competitive EU market. At the same time, companies must have access to the markets of the EU and market their products according to both customer expectation and profit maximization.

Direct marketing

Another strategy likely to receive a great deal of attention is direct marketing. Most EU firms tailor their products to narrow markets and direct mail is only now gaining attention. Unlike the United States, where businesses have been using telemarketing and other non-traditional channels for well over a decade, this is a new approach for European consumers, and MNEs will have to surmount a number of challenges if they hope to direct-market their products, such as: (1) consumers speak different languages, so a universal message or strategy will not work throughout the bloc; (2) inclusion of direct-response telephone numbers in television spots is forbidden by the privacy laws of some member states such as Germany; and (3) information about potential clients is fragmented and not easily obtainable. In addition, a high credit card fraud rate has slowed down the growth potential of e-commerce. Nevertheless, direct marketing is likely to play a major role in MNE efforts to create a pan-European marketing strategy.

One study proposes that the overall convergence associated with European market integration will lead firms to emphasize three advertising strategies: creating a uniform brand image, appealing to cross-market segments, and increasing cost performance in advertising.[22]

Manufacturing considerations

As individual country regulations are eliminated and EU members continue to standardize rules and regulations, it will be possible to produce uniform goods for the entire market. This will not come about immediately because of the time needed to change such things as electric systems so that toasters, television sets, and other home appliances can all be manufactured with the same type of plug. However, MNEs will eventually be able to produce many products with standard parts that work in all EU countries. At the same time, manufacturers will continue producing goods that appeal to local market tastes. For example, appliance makers now manufacture self-cleaning ovens for the French because of their tradition of high-temperature cooking. However, they typically leave out this option for the German market, where food is generally cooked at lower temperatures. Some major manufacturing considerations that warrant attention by those doing business in the EU include reducing costs, building factory networks, and entering into R&D alliances.

Reducing costs

There are now over 500 million consumers in Europe and their expenditure represents over half of the EU's GDP. One manufacturing benefit of producing for this size of market is the ability to reduce cost per unit through the use of standardized components and large production runs. Economies of scale are possible, with the cost of components kept to a minimum and large production runs allowing companies to spread fixed costs over more units. This means the cost per item can be sharply reduced. Moreover, economies of scale can be achieved even when production has to be tailored to local conditions. This is accomplished through the use of **delayed differentiation**, in which all products are manufactured in the same way for all countries or regions as late as possible in the assembly process. In these final stages, differentiation is then used to introduce particular features or special components.

MNEs also use outsourcing and just-in-time inventory systems to lower the cost of carrying parts and supplies. By tailoring deliveries and shipments to the production schedule, factories are able to minimize their investment in materials and work-in-process. This system is also used by large retailers such as Marks & Spencer of the United Kingdom, which employs its electronic network system to keep track of inventory at each store in England, as well as on the continent, and to replenish its outlets as needed.

Another way in which costs are being controlled is by redesigning production processes, thus scrapping old, inefficient techniques in favor of more streamlined methods. This

Delayed differentiation
A strategy in which all products are manufactured in the same way for all countries or regions as late as possible in the assembly process, at which time differentiation is used to introduce particular features or special components

includes careful study of competitive firms in order to identify and copy their successful approaches to cost control. It also entails the elimination of red tape and the use of well-trained, highly motivated work teams.

Factory networks

MNEs in Europe have developedsophisticated networks of factories that both produce components and finished goods and provide distribution and after-sales services. For example, the Philips television factory in Bruges, Belgium, uses tubes that are supplied from a factory in Germany, transistors from France, plastics produced in Italy, and electronic components that come from another factory in Belgium.

These factory networks are also integrated with computer software packages that can operate in multiple European countries without the need for modification. Figure 17.3 provides an illustration. The software packages allow companies to make supply, production, and distribution decisions while satisfying the requirements of the different legal entities in the countries where they operate. Some specific functions they help companies to perform include forecasting, logistics planning, inventory planning, production planning, and central updating of bills of materials. The software provides each factory manager with the specific information needed and does so in the manager's own language. As a result, MNEs are able to coordinate multiple activities and thereby develop an effective pan-European manufacturing system.

R&D alliances

Another emerging manufacturing strategy is participation in cooperative R&D programs. In the EU this is taking two complementary paths. First, many companies are teaming up to share R&D expenses. Siemens and Philips have used this approach to develop computer chips, and IBM has a number of agreements with European firms for developing advanced computer technology.

Second, many firms are trying to get some of these costs funded by participating in European cooperative R&D programs. The EU provides European industry with funding for

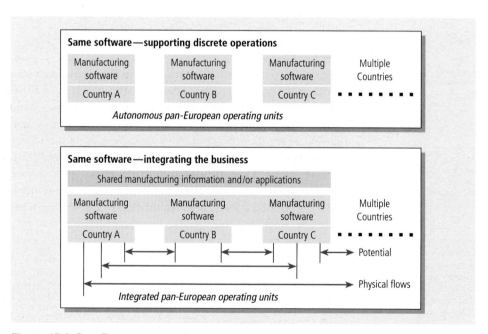

Figure 17.3 Pan-European manufacturing systems

Source: Adapted from Nigel Dunham and Robin Morgan, "The Search for a Truly Pan-European Manufacturing System," *Journal of European Business*, September/October 1991, p. 44. Permission conveyed through Copyright Clearance Center.

research in such areas as information technology, biotechnology, and energy. The objective of the program is to stimulate cross-border cooperation and make Europe more productive and competitive in the world market. One of the best-known programs is the **European Research Cooperation Agency** (Eureka, for short), which was launched in 1985 and emphasizes projects in the fields of energy, medicine, biotechnology, communications, information technology, transport, new materials, robotics, production automation, lasers, and the environment.[23] This program has helped develop a European standard for high-definition television (HDTV) and has funded semiconductor research. A central aim is to meet the European objective of raising investment in R&D. EU funding for large-scale projects and coordination across member states also drives economies of scale in R&D, to allow countries to compete in science and technology development with the USA, Japan and China. Firms that are interested in participating in these cooperative programs typically do so by carrying out six steps:

European Research Cooperation Agency
A research and development alliance that emphasizes projects in the fields of energy, medicine, biotechnology, communications, information technology, transport, new materials, robotics, production automation, lasers, and the environment

1 Find out if the company is eligible for EU-funded programs.

2 Carefully study the EU rules regarding rights of ownership and dissemination of results.

3 Carefully choose the best location for a European R&D center.

4 Determine those competitors and major customers that are already participating in the program.

5 Gather recommendations from the firm's EU and local management.

6 Put together the company's application for funding.

Management considerations

As more firms enter the EU, there is growing concern over their ability to manage Europeans effectively. Many firms enter the market with preconceived ideas about how to interact with their European partners or employees. Some, for example, believe that management styles that have been effective in their country will also work well in Europe. However, as the Japanese have discovered in the United States, effective management approaches must be tailor-made to meet the needs of the local situation. The primary focus must be on adjusting to cultural differences.

Adjusting to cultural differences

There are a number of differences between US and European workers. For example, Europeans are more accustomed to participating in decision making. They have a long history of worker participation programs and of holding seats on the board of directors.

Another difference is employee motivation. Researchers have found that quality of work life is extremely important in Scandinavian countries, whereas opportunities for individual achievement are of particular importance in the UK. French workers are interested in individual achievement but place strong emphasis on security. German workers place a high value on both advancement and earnings.[24] Clearly, no universal list of motivators can be applied throughout the EU. These facts illustrate the importance of MNEs having a global perspective as well as having managers who are focused on the country-specific needs of the area in which they are working.

Barriers to EU market access

Throughout this book, we have explored the need for access to triad markets. Although the EU has become the world's largest market, some EU-based MNEs and governments have sought to restrict access to this area. The overall trend during the postwar period has been toward an increasingly liberalized trade environment, but international managers nonetheless must know how to deal with, or at least anticipate, the use of administrative barriers in foreign markets.

Table 17.6 EU antidumping cases investigated by sector, 2002–2009

Product	2002	2003	2004	2005	2006	2007	2008	2009
Chemical and allied	5	3	8	3	13	2	2	9
Textiles and allied	2	2	4	1	2	0	0	3
Wood and paper	0	1	0	0	0	0	0	0
Electronics	3	2	0	7	5	0	0	1
Other mechanical engineering	4	0	2	2	2	0	0	0
Iron and steel	5	0	13	4	0	6	6	4
Others, metal	0	0	0	0	9	0	0	1
Other	4	0	2	9	5	1	1	3
All products listed	23	8	29	26	36	9	20	21
of which antidumping	20	7	29	24	35	9	18	15
of which antisubsidy	3	1	0	2	1	0	2	6

Note: Data for the year 2008 was not aligned between the investigations by country and investigations by product in the annex B, page 8 of the EU Commission, Trade, Anti-Subsidy, Safeguards Statistics Covering the first five months of 2010 (May 2010).

Source: European Commission, Trade; *Anti subsidy, safeguards statistics covering the first five months of 2010*, May 2010, Annex B, page 8
E-resources: http://trade.ec.europa.eu/doclib/docs/2010/january/tradoc_145673.pdf.

Countervailing duty (CVD)
Import tariff intended to protect domestic producers from harmful subsidization by foreign governments

Antidumping duty (AD)
Import tariff intended to protect domestic producers from foreign products sold at less than their cost of production or at lower prices than in their home market

The two most common trade law entry barriers are **countervailing duty (CVD)** laws and **antidumping duty (AD)** laws. (These were discussed earlier in Chapters 6 and 10.) While the United States uses CVD as an entry barrier (it had 90 percent of the world's CVD cases in the 1980s), the EU uses AD. Both CVD and AD are import tariffs intended to protect domestic producers from harmful dumping and subsidization by foreign governments. However, it has been demonstrated in several studies that these laws have been "captured" and used by weak firms seeking shelter from strong competition by rival MNEs in the triad.[25]

Table 17.6 shows both the high number of AD cases that were launched and the tendency toward sectoral concentration in the use of AD by EU firms during the period from 2002 to 2009. Many AD cases were brought in the chemical, electronics, iron and steel, and other "mature" sectors that have weak firm-specific advantages (FSAs).

The use of these trade law instruments to provide shelter is by no means unique to the EU, as the earlier discussion of AD and CVD in Chapter 10 showed.[26] However, from Table 17.6 it is clear that non-EU firms in the chemical, electronics, and iron and steel sectors should probably anticipate some resistance if they plan to begin exporting to the EU market with a view to competing with domestic producers.

Figure 17.4 shows the rationale for the use of AD and CVD laws by particular firms. As with all free market economies, the EU economy has, at any given point in time, a significant number of firms in difficulty due to the pressure of global competition. These firms are barely able to compete with their more efficient global rivals and find themselves on the verge of exit from the industry. If the main reason for this is international competition, and domestic administrative instruments are in place that would allow such a firm to continue operating by limiting foreign competition, the company is likely to use these instruments. Such a situation is a rare instance when it is logical for a firm to spend time and money on an activity that is not productive from a competitiveness standpoint. By using AD or CVD laws, the uncompetitive firm is able to remain in operation not by improving its firm-specific advantages but by artificially raising the price at which foreign competitors must sell in the domestic market.

The abusive use of AD and CVD is a particular problem for non-triad members and for MNEs from other parts of the triad because the administration of these trade laws is discretionary and subject to political pressures. Moreover, there is now strong evidence that the administration of these trade laws is biased in favor of domestic plaintiffs and against foreign

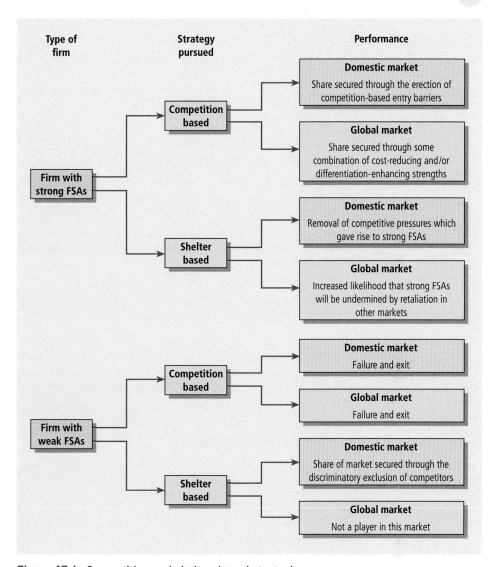

Figure 17.4 Competition and shelter-based strategies

firms.[27] The technical test of "material injury" due to the subsidies or dumped exports is routinely abused by the responsible administrative agencies in both the EU and the United States.[28] This is an extremely serious problem for global business and serves to reinforce the existence of the triad at the expense of a liberalized world trade and investment system.

KEY POINTS

1 The overall objective of the EU is to create a market in which there are no economic barriers to trade between the member countries. When this is achieved, the EU will be the largest economic bloc in the world. However, there are two areas in particular in which additional progress must be made: free movement of goods and the practice of government procurement. In addition, many new entrants into the EU (and a few of the original members) have yet to be integrated in terms of adopting the euro and are not yet allowed free movement of labor and passport-free travel. They also threaten the possibility of a unified regional foreign policy.

2 The current competitive status of the EU lags that of the United States and Japan in a number of areas, including productivity, investment spending, and education. Greater economic strides will be needed if the region is to compete effectively with its triad counterparts.

3 In preparing to do business in the EU, MNEs should focus on the competitive nature of the targeted industry and the evaluation of location. Competitive intelligence gathering involves external information gathering and internal infrastructural analysis. Location evaluation entails the consideration of such factors as regional incentives, operating costs, and distance from major markets.

4 Many aspects of strategy need to be considered when doing business in the EU, including (a) an overall analysis of the environment, (b) the feasibility of exporting, (c) the value of strategic alliances and acquisitions, (d) marketing considerations, (e) manufacturing approaches, and (f) management considerations. Managers need to weigh the choices of economic integration and/or national responsiveness very carefully.

5 The EU has a large internal market. Firms located in the EU can use non-tariff barriers to entry to keep out rival firms, namely, trade remedy legislation such as countervailing duty (CVD) laws and antidumping (AD) laws. Recent research has found that the use of both CVD and AD is a "shelter" strategy designed to protect uncompetitive domestic firms. However, the more successful EU firms concentrate on the development of sustainable firm-specific advantages rather than on the use of CVD and AD laws.

Key terms

- Single European Act (SEA)
- Council of Ministers
- Single European Market (SEM)
- coordinated infrastructure
- market coordination infrastructure
- resource-sharing infrastructure
- autonomous infrastructure
- national responsiveness
- delayed differentiation
- European Research Cooperation Agency
- countervailing duty (CVD)
- antidumping duty (AD)

REVIEW AND DISCUSSION QUESTIONS

1 What are the ultimate objectives of the EU? Identify and describe them.

2 Will the EU bring about the single European Market? What type of changes will have to take place for this to happen? Identify and describe three of them.

3 What is the competitive status of the main EU economies in terms of labor productivity and investment spending? Based on your answer, what is your overall evaluation of this status?

4 How can firms doing business in the EU use competitive intelligence? Identify and describe two major steps that can be used in this process.

5 What types of regional incentives do countries offer MNEs willing to set up operations in their locales? Identify and describe two of them.

6 In addition to regional incentives, what other evaluation criteria should MNEs employ when deciding where in the EU to establish operations? Identify and describe three of them.

7 In formulating a strategy for doing business in the EU, there are two primary areas of initial consideration: national responsiveness and economic integration. What does this statement mean? Be sure to include a discussion of Figure 17.2 in your answer.

8 What do companies that want to export to the EU need to know about doing business there? Discuss five facts or strategies that would be of value to them.

9 In gaining a foothold in the EU, when is it most effective to opt for an acquisition over an alliance? When is a strategic alliance a better choice? In each case, provide an example.

10 Why will marketing strategies in the EU have to reflect a concern for pricing? A concern for positioning? Give an example of when each would be the most important consideration.

11 What is the likely future of direct marketing in the EU? Defend your answer.

12 What are three major manufacturing considerations for companies doing business in the EU? Identify and describe each.

13 How important is it for EU managers to have a global perspective?

14 How can trade laws be used by EU firms to keep out global competitors?

15 What evidence is there that EU firms use antidumping laws?

16 The EU accepted 10 new members into the union in 2004 and another 2 in 2007. Are these members fully integrated? What problems might we envisage from new members in the future?

17 How are new entrants into the union likely to affect employment in the EU?

REAL CASE

Accor budget hotels

The largest manager of budget-priced hotels in the world is the French company Accor. In 2010 it owned over 4,200 hotels in 90 countries under the brands Sofitel, Pullman, Novotel, Mercure, Suitehotel, All Seasons, Ibis, Etap Hotel, Formule 1, and Motel 6 and its related activities, Thalassa sea & spa and Lenotre, which provide an offer ranging from luxury to budget class. About half of these are in the budget class of hotels. In 2010, with a workforce of 143,939 employees, Accor generated revenues of US$ 7.877 billion (€5.9 billion), of which 34 percent was generated in France, 39 percent in Europe (excluding France), 10 percent in North America, 5 percent in Latin America, 11 percent in rest of world. Accor is a home region firm with focus on Europe where its total sales is 73 percent (France and rest of Europe together). The Accor Group has developed international capabilities in being a major service provider to the tourist, business travel, and food business sectors. It is developing an international brand name for the group's

activities in these areas and uses B2B and B2C Internet services extensively for the purposes of promotion and managing partnerships. There are 860,000 restaurant managers, supermarket suppliers, and other affiliated workers using its B2B services, along with another 300,000 customers/small-business people using B2C.

The company began operations in 1967 and rapidly expanded its Novotel hotels across France. The acquisition of another hotel chain in 1974, Courtepailles, established Accor as a major player in the French market. During the next two years the company moved to develop a market presence in the two- and three-star hotel market segment, opening an Ibis two-star hotel in Bordeaux and acquiring the three-star Mercure hotel chain.

The first significant expansion outside France was the 1973 opening of Novotel in Warsaw, Poland. In 1976, Accor opened its first hotel in Brazil and over the next year began to rapidly develop in Latin America. In 1979, Accor ▶

entered the US market with hotels in Minneapolis and New York; in 1984 a large Novotel was erected in Broadway. To enter the affordable US hotel market, the Motel 6 chain was purchased in 1990. By acquiring Sofitel in 1980 the company entered the African market and strengthened its position in Europe. In 1986, Accor began development in Asia, including China and Thailand. In preparation for the 2008 Olympic games, Accor entered a joint venture with the Beijing Tourism Group to manage 50 hotels.

Accor is also in the travel business. In France it owns Carlson Wagonlit Travel and Frantour. Acquiring international travel companies has allowed Accor to complement its international hotel expansion plans. The acquisition of Africatours in 1984 allowed Accor to control the stream of tourism in the region. In 1987, Africatours acquired Asia Tours and America Tours. In 2000, Accor purchased a 38.5 percent stake in Go Voyages, an e-travel planner that targets the European traveler. Growing expertise in the hospitality business has also allowed the company to diversify into other areas, including restaurants and casinos. The table below shows the global spread of Accor hotels by region and brand.

A report by Datamonitor (www.datamonitor.com) outlines the Accor Group's main strengths and weakness in 2008. Strengths include: a wide range of product and service offerings, an improving financial position, and a strong focus on customer service. Weaknesses include: underperforming assets, an overdependence on hotels (65 percent of revenues), and a geographic concentration in Europe (68 percent of revenues). The recovering European hotel industry, current expansion in China and India, and the recovering business travel market are all opportunities for the group. These are offset by the growing range of competitors, particularly in the low-cost travel and leisure segments.

Accor Hotel portfolio by brand and region (2010)

Brand	France Hotel	France Rooms	Rest of Europe Hotel	Rest of Europe Rooms	North America Hotel	North America Rooms	Latin America Caribbean Hotel	Latin America Caribbean Rooms	Africa Middle East Hotel	Africa Middle East Rooms	Asia Pacific Hotel	Asia Pacific Rooms	Total Hotel	Total Rooms
Sofitel	12	1 597	21	4 871	9	2 893	9	1 623	21	5 068	44	13 548	116	29 600
Pullman	13	3 384	12	2 824	—	—	1	188	4	874	17	5 747	47	13 017
Novotel	123	16 257	140	26 640	7	1 956	18	2 980	22	4 359	82	19 567	392	71 759
Mercure	251	23 509	238	32 398	—	—	77	9 982	33	5 188	112	16 515	711	87 592
Adagio	24	3 302	6	648	—	—	—	—	—	—	—	—	30	3 950
Suitehotel	19	2 144	6	931	—	—	—	—	2	292	—	—	27	3 367
Coralia Club	—	—	—	—	—	—	1	385	3	677	—	—	4	1 062
Autres Marques	3	152	18	2 991	—	—	—	—	1	112	15	2 557	37	5 812
Upper and midscale	445	50 345	441	71 303	16	4 849	106	15 158	86	16 570	270	57 934	1 364	216 159
All Seasons	44	3 350	8	539	—	—	—	—	—	—	34	3 909	86	7 798
Ibis	380	33 549	318	40 504	—	—	64	9 489	34	5 610	83	15 630	879	104 782
Etap Hotel	294	22 677	118	12 030	—	—	—	—	—	—	—	—	412	34 707
Formule 1	261	19 434	31	2 216	—	—	11	3 125	24	1 696	24	2 348	351	28 819
Economy	979	79 010	475	55 289			75	12 614	58	7 306	141	21 887	1 728	176 106
Motel 6	—	—	—	—	1 010	99 569	—	—	—	—	—	—	1 010	99 569
Studio 6	—	—	—	—	61	6 783	—	—	—	—	—	-	61	6 783
Economy US					1 071	106 352							1 071	106 352
Total	1 424	129 355	916	126 592	1 087	111 201	181	27 772	144	23 876	411	79 821	4 163	498 617

Websites: www.accorhotels.com; www.accor.com; www.fourseasons.com; www.sixcontinents.com.
Sources: www.accorhotels.com; Raphael Minder, "Accor May Have to Rethink Casino Offer," *FT.com*, January 3, 2002; Raphael Minder, "Accor to Acquire Casino Group for E258m," *FT.com*, December 17, 2001; "Casinos on Threshold of Recomposition," *La Tribune*, January 3, 2002; "Accor Agrees Chinese JV to Manage Around 50 Hotels by 2008," *AFX Europe*, December 12, 2001; Anaïs Jouvancy, "European E-Travel Takes Off," *Le Monde Interactif*, November 8, 2000; Accor SA, *Annual report*, 2010; OneSource, *Thomson Reuters*, 2011

1 Why did Accor concentrate on the French and European markets before expanding into other regions?

2 How are acquisitions an important part of Accor's expansion strategy?

3 What are the advantages of increasingly relying on the Internet for B2B and B2C?

Carrefour

Saturated markets, growing economies in Asia and Eastern Europe, and improving transportation systems are all factors driving large retailers to expand abroad, with mixed success. Tesco has moved into China and the United States, Carrefour has pulled out of some East European countries in order to focus on expansion in China, and Wal-Mart is pushing for growth in a range of new markets. French retail giant Carrefour ("crossroads" in French) is the number one retailer in Europe and number two in the world. In 2009, Carrefour had 69 percent of its sales in Europe but it had almost 15,594 stores spread throughout 29 countries on four continents with revenues of $121.452 billion (€85.360 billion). In 2010, Carrefour SA's total revenue increased 5 percent to €91.51 billion.

Source: Getty Images/AFP/Omar Torres

Carrefour SA is a France-based company that is primarily engaged in retail distribution. It operates a network of hypermarkets, supermarkets, hard discount stores, convenience stores and cash-and-carry outlets, and offers e-commerce services. The company's hypermarkets, Carrefour and Atacadao, offer a range of food and non-food products. Carrefour SA's supermarket chains include, among others, Champion and Norte brands, which primarily offer food, clothing and household goods. The company's hard discount stores include Dia, Ed and Minipreco, and offer products at discount prices. Its convenience stores, such as Shopi and 8 a Huit, offer a range of convenience products and services. Carrefour SA's cash-and-carry stores, Promocash, Gross and Docks Market, offer wholesale products for businesses. As of December 31, 2009, the company was 10.69 percent owned by Blue Capital.

Anyone observing Carrefour over the last three decades must concede that international expansion is a key part of its strategic plan. Despite this, in 2008, 47 percent of its sales were in France alone and 81 percent in Europe. The 19 percent of sales outside the region were evenly divided across Asia and Latin America. By 2010, 42 percent of its sales were in France and 75 percent in Europe, 17 percent in Latin American and 8 percent in Asia. Carrefour is under pressure in its home market France as rivals keep prices low to gain market share.

In 1996, the French government introduced the "Raffarin law" to restrict the expansion of hypermarkets, with the aim of keeping the French countryside from turning into large warehouse-style retail structures. This in turn would protect the French way of life, in which local food farmers supply small local shops. For Carrefour, this meant that growth of its hypermarket business could come only from acquisitions in its local market or from expanding into foreign markets. Its success at following this strategy has varied considerably because of different competitive environments and cultural differences across regions.

In the United States, Carrefour opened three hypermarkets in Pennsylvania and closed them as a result of local competition. In its home region of Europe, however, Carrefour is the number one retailer in Spain, Portugal, and Greece, and the second largest in Italy.

Carrefour was the first Western hypermarket company to expand into the Asian market in the mid-1990s. By 2001 it was the third-largest retailer in China and had operations in Thailand and Japan. The company bet that Asian customers would be willing to move from their traditional outdoor markets to purchase at air-conditioned and "all under one roof" hypermarkets. These hypermarkets rely on local suppliers that could offer products at the same price level as those that supplied the local competition and cater to the tastes of locals. For their part, local suppliers are all too ready to enter contracts with Carrefour, which promises to put their products on shelves across the Asian region. Moreover, where local contacts are not readily available or insufficient, Carrefour's competitive advantage comes from centralized purchasing and other logistics.

Because products are offered in a comfortable environment at competitive prices, the local competition is nothing to worry about. In fact, Carrefour is more concerned about competition from other Western retailers such as Wal-Mart and Tesco. Both Tesco and Carrefour raced to open the first hypermarket in the Thai market and basically tied. Both their hypermarkets faced each other in a busy Bangkok street. If they want to survive in the long haul, however, Western companies should always be wary of potential local or regional competitors. In Hong Kong, ▶

where Jardine Matheson and Li Ka-shing dominate the market, Carrefour was forced to close operations. The group now sees strong potential for further international growth in the large national markets of China, Brazil, Indonesia, Poland, and Turkey.

But the benefits of international expansion are not completely clear. Carrefour and other large retailers have tended to enjoy higher operating margins in their domestic markets. They have also struggled to leverage scale economies on a global basis because in order to cater to local tastes, hypermarkets must purchase from local producers. Indeed, in November 2010, Carrefour announced the signing of an agreement with Big C, a subsidiary of Groupe Casino (France), for the divestment of its operations in Thailand for an enterprise value of €868 million. Carrefour plans to sell 19 stores in Malaysia and 2 in Singapore. Carrefour shut down its Xian outlet in China's Shaanxi Province in July 2010.

On the other hand, Carrefour SA announced the opening of its first Cash & Carry Store in India in December 2010. With a sales area of 5,200 m², this store located east of New Delhi in the Shahadra neighborhood will offer more than 10,000 stock-keeping units in food and non-food to professional businesses, institutions, restaurants, and local retailers. Carrefour opened three supermarkets by end of 2010 and two hypermarkets in 2011 in Romania. The supermarkets were opened in the capital Bucharest, in the southern town of Targoviste and in the northwestern town

of Cluj. The hypermarkets slated for a 2011 launch were located in Bucharest and in northern town of Botosani. Carrefour SA currently has 23 hypermarkets and 29 supermarkets in Romania.

In 2011, shares in Carrefour have fallen 6 percent after Europe's biggest retailer issued a warning that profits in its core French market were set to fall, as it is facing fierce competition from rivals in France.

Sources: www.carrefour.com; "Wal-Mart, Tesco and Carrefour Do Battle in the East: International Retailers Find Mixed Fortunes in Their Expansion Strategies," *Strategic Direction*, vol. 24, no. 2 (2008), pp. 5–7; Peter Child, "Lessons from a Global Retailer: An Interview with the President of Carrefour China," *McKinsey Quarterly*, Special Edition, 2006, pp. 70–81; Carrefour, *Annual Report*, 2008–2010; "French Fusion," *The Economist*, September 2, 1999; "A Hypermarket," *The Economist*, April 5, 2001; OneSource, *Thomson Reuters*, 2011; "Carrefour Shares Falll After Profit Warning," *BBC News*, June 17, 2011, http://www.bbc.co.uk/news/business-13805057.

1 How can Carrefour compete with local retailers in North America?

2 How can Carrefour compete with local retailers in Asia?

3 What strategy does Carrefour need to succeed in Europe?

4 What is Carrefour's basic strategy and structure?

5 Should Carrefour and other large retailers even attempt to expand internationally?

ENDNOTES

1 Spyros G. Makridakis and Michelle Bainbridge, "Evolution of the Single Market," in Spyros G. Makridakis (ed.), *Single Market Europe: Opportunities and Challenges for Business* (San Francisco: Jossey-Bass, 1991), p. 9.

2 Also see Trevor Merriden, "How 'Single' is the Single Market?" *Management Review*, March 1998, pp. 27–31.

3 Edmund L. Andrews, "11 Countries Tie Europe Together in One Currency," *New York Times*, January 1, 1999, pp. A1, 8.

4 John Grahl and Paul Teague, "Problems of Financial Integration in the EU," *Journal of European Public Policy*, vol. 12, no. 6 (2005), pp. 1005–1021.

5 Michael Hickins, "US Business Blinks at the Euro," *Management Review*, April 1998, pp. 33–37.

6 "EU Allies Unite Against Iraq War," *BBC.co.uk*, January 22, 2003.

7 Adriaan J. Schout, and Andrew J. Jordan, "From Cohesion to Territorial Policy Integration: Exploring the Governance Challenges in the European Union." *European Planning Studies*, vol. 15, no. 6 (2007), pp. 835–851.

8 "Rebels with a cause," *The Economist*, August 3, 2008; "The Shape of Things to Come," *The Economist*, June 23, 2005.

9 Clemets Fuest and Bernd Huber. "Can Regional Policy in a Federation Improve Economic Efficiency?" *Journal of Public Economics*, vol. 90, no. 3 (2006), pp. 499–511.

10 "GM Creates Europe-wide Management," *BBC.co.uk*, June 18, 2004.

11 Richard Wray (2010) "Apple reveals UK iPad prices," *The Guardian*, guardian.co.uk, May 7, 2010.

12 John E. Prescott and Patrick T. Gibbons, "Europe '92 Provides New Impetus for Competitive Intelligence," *Journal of Business Strategy*, November/December 1991, pp. 20–26.

13 The economist, "Czech Republic: Investment Regulations," Economist Intelligence Unit, January 11, 2011; http://www.eiu.com.

14 Robert Pearce and Julia Manea, "MNEs' Strategies in Central and Eastern Europe: Key Elements of Subsidiary Behaviour," *Management International Review (MIR)*, vol. 46, no. 2 (2006), pp. 235–255; Alan M. Rugman and Alain Verbeke, "Europe 1992 and Competitive Strategies for North American Firms," *Business Horizons*, November/December 1991, pp. 76–81.

15 Ibid., p. 78.

16 For more specifics on standards, see www.eurunion.org/eu/.

17 Joel Bleeke and David Ernst, "The Way to Win in Cross-Border Alliances," *Harvard Business Review*, vol. 69, no. 6 (1991), pp. 127–128. See also: *Harvard Business Review on Strategic Alliances* (2003; Harvard Business School Press).

18 Reshma H. Shah and Vanitha Swaminathan, "Factors Influencing Partner Selection in Strategic Alliances: The Moderating Role of Alliance Context," *Strategic Management Journal*, vol. 29, no. 5 (2008), pp. 471–494; "Strategic alliance: Alliances are often said to be like marriages," *The Economist* (10 Nov 2009); http://www.economist.com/node/14301470.

19 Stanley Paliwoda, "The Marketing Challenges Within the Enlarged Single European Market," *European Journal of Marketing*, vol. 41, nos. 3/4 (2007), pp. 233–244.

20 Urša Golob and Kiement Podnar, "Competitive Advantage in the Marketing of Products Within the Enlarged European Union," *European Journal of Marketing*, vol. 41, nos. 3/4 (2007), pp. 245–256.

21 Graham Hooley, Brigitte Nicoulaud and Nigel F. Piercy, *Marketing Strategy and Competitive Positioning*, 5th edition. (Harlow: Financial Times/Prentice Hall, 2011).

22 Shintaro Okazaki, Charles R. Taylor and Jonathan P. Doh, "Market Convergence and Advertising Standardization in the European Union," *Journal of World Business*, vol. 42, no. 4 (2007), pp. 384–400.

23 See http://www.eurekanetwork.org/.

24 For more on the cultural differences across Europe, and their consequences, go to Chapter 5.

25 The theory of shelter has been developed in Alan M. Rugman and Alain Verbeke, *Global Competitive Strategy and Trade Policy* (London: Routledge, 1990). A study on the use of EC trade law measures as a shelter strategy is that by Alan M. Rugman and Michael Gestrin, "EC Anti-Dumping Laws as a Barrier to Trade," *European Management Journal*, vol. 9, no. 4 (1991), pp. 475–482. Related data and analysis of EC trade law cases are reported in Patrick A. Messerlin, "Anti-Dumping Regulations or Procartel Law? The EC Chemical Case," *World Economy*, vol. 13, no. 4 (1990), pp. 465–492.

26 For an application of the concept of shelter by the use of US trade laws, see Alan M. Rugman and Michael Gestrin, "US Trade Laws as Barriers to Globalization," *World Economy*, vol. 14, no. 3 (1991), pp. 335–352. For earlier data and studies of US trade law cases used as a barrier to entry against rival Canadian firms, see Alan M. Rugman and Andrew D. M. Anderson, *Administered Protection in America* (London and New York: Routledge, 1987).

27 For an overall discussion of triad power and the use of trade laws as barriers to entry, see Francis G. Snyder, *Regional and Global Regulation of International Trade* (London: Hart Publishing, 2002); David Coen, Wyn Grant and Graham Wilson, *The Oxford Handbook of Business and Government*, Oxford Handbooks in Business and Management (Oxford: Oxford University Press, 2010). Also: Chris Turner and Jacqueline Martin, *Key Facts EU Law*, 3rd ed. (London: Hodder Education, 2011)

28 For evidence of the abuse of US trade law procedures, see Richard Boltuck and Robert Litan (eds.), *Down in the Dumps: Administration of the Unfair Trade Laws* (Washington, DC: Brookings Institution, 1991). For recent legal and economic research on this issue, see Michael J. Trebilcock and Robert C. York (eds.), *Fair Exchange: Reforming Trade Remedy Laws* (Toronto: C.D. Howe Institute and McGraw-Hill Ryerson, 1990).

ADDITIONAL BIBLIOGRAPHY

Archibugi, Daniele and Filippetti, Andrea. *Innovation and Economic Crisis: Lessons and Prospects from the Economic Downturn*, Routledge Studies in Global Competition (London: Routledge, 2011).

Asmussen, Christian Geisler, Pedersen, Torben and Dhanaraj, Charles. "Host-country environment and subsidiary competence: Extending the Diamond Network Model," *Journal of International Business Studies*, vol. 40, no. 1 (2009).

Böhm, Hans and Scholz, Christian. *Human Resource Management in Europe: Comparative analysis and contextual understanding* (London: T & F Books, 2008).

Brennan, Louis. *The Emergence of Southern Multinationals: Their Impact on Europe* (Besingstoke: Palgrave Macmillan 2010).

Brenner, Steffen. 'Self-Disclosure at International Cartels,' *Journal of International Business Studies*, vol. 42, no. 2 (2011).

Colantone, Italo and Sleuwaegen, Leo. "International Trade, Exit and Entry: A Cross-Country and Industry Analysis," *Journal of International Business Studies*, vol. 41 no. 7 (2010).

Dunning, John H. "The Contribution of British Scholarship to International Business Studies," *International Business Review*, vol. 13, no. 2 (April 2004).

Greenaway, David. *The World Economy: Global Trade Policy*, World Economy Special Issues (Oxford: Wiley-Blackwell, 2010).

Johnson, Debra. *European Business*, 2nd Ed. (London: T & F Books 2009).

Kahancová, Marta. "One Company, Four Factories: Coordinating Employment Flexibility Practices with Local Trade Unions," *European Journal of Industrial Relations*, vol. 13, no. 1 (March 2007).

Kidd, John B. and Teramoto, Yoshiya. "The Learning Organization: The Case of the Japanese RHQs in Europe," *Management International Review*, vol. 35, Special Issue (1995).

Lawton, Thomas C. "Evaluating European Competitiveness: Measurements and Models for a Successful Business Environment," *European Business Journal*, vol. 11, no. 4 (1999).

Lowson, Robert. "Analysing the Effectiveness of European Retail Sourcing Strategies," *European Management Journal*, vol. 19, no. 5 (October 2001).

Mayrhofer, Ulrike. "Franco-British Strategic Alliances: A Contribution to the Study of Intra-European Partnerships," *European Management Journal*, vol. 20, no. 1 (February 2002).

Millington, Andrew and Bayliss, Brian T. "The Strategy of Internationalization and the Success of UK Transnational Manufacturing Operations in the European Union,"

Management International Review, vol. 37, no. 3 (Third Quarter 1997).

Nitsch, Detlev, Beamish, Paul and Makino, Shige. "Entry Mode and Performance of Japanese FDI in Western Europe," *Management International Review*, vol. 36, no. 1 (First Quarter 1996).

Papanastassiou, Marina and Pearce, Robert. "Technology Sourcing and the Strategic Roles of Manufacturing Subsidiaries in the UK: Local Competence and Global Competitiveness," *Management International Review*, vol. 37, no. 1 (First Quarter 1997).

Pelkmans, Jacques. "Making EU Network Markets Competitive," *Oxford Review of Economic Policy*, vol. 17, no. 3 (Autumn 2001).

Radosevic, Slavo and Kaderabkova, Anna. *Challenges for European Innovation Policy: Cohesion and Excellence from a Schumpeterian Perspective* (Cheltenham: Edward Elgar, 2011).

Reynaud, Emmanuelle et al. "The Differences in Values Between Managers of the European Founding Countries, the New Members and the Applicant Countries: Societal Orientation or Financial Orientation?" *European Management Journal*, vol. 25, no. 2 (April 2007).

Rugman, Alan M. and Collinson, Simon. "Multinational Enterprises in the New Europe: Are they Really Global?" *Organizational Dynamics*, vol. 34, no. 3 (2005).

Rugman, Alan M. and Verbeke, Alain. "Environmental Change and Global Competitive Strategy in Europe," in Alan M. Rugman and Alain Verbeke (eds.), *Research in Global Strategic Management*, Volume 2: *Global Competition and the European Community* (Greenwich, CT: JAI Press, 1991).

Rugman, Alan M. and Verbeke, Alain (eds.). *Research in Global Strategic Management*, Volume 2: *Global Competition and the European Community* (Greenwich, CT: JAI Press, 1991).

Rugman, Alan M. and Verbeke, Alain (eds.). "Competitive Strategies for Non-European Firms," in B. Burgenmeier and J. L. Mucchielli (eds.), *Multinationals and Europe 1992: Strategies for the Future* (London and New York: Routledge, 1991).

Rugman, Alan M. and Verbeke, Alain. "Europe 1992 and Competitive Strategies for North American Firms," *Business Horizons*, vol. 34, no. 6 (November/December 1991).

Rugman, Alan M., Theil, Rita and Verbeke, Alain. "Entry Barriers and Bank Strategies for the Europe 1992 Financial Directives," *European Management Journal*, vol. 10, no. 3 (September 1992).

Rugman, Alan M., Yip, George and Kudina, Alina. "The International Success of British Companies," *Long Range Planning*, vol. 39, vol. 3 (June 2006).

Rugman, Alan M., Yip, George and Jayaratne, Saliya. "A Note on the Return on Foreign Assets and Foreign Presence for UK Multinationals," *British Journal of Management*, vol. 19, no. 2 (2008).

Rugman, Alan M. and Oh, Chang Hoon. "Regional Integration and the International Strategies of Large European Firms," *International Business Review*, vol. 20 (2011). doi.10.1016/j.ibusrev.2011.05.009.

Taggart, James H. "An Evaluation of the Integration-Responsiveness Framework: MNC Manufacturing Subsidiaries in the UK," *Management International Review*, vol. 37, no. 4 (Fourth Quarter 1997).

Ueltschy, Linda C., Laroche, Michel, Rita, Paulo and Bocaranda, Claudia, "A Pan-European Approach to Customer Satisfaction: An Optimal Strategy?" *Multinational Business Review*, vol. 16, no. 3 (2008), pp. 41–71.

Yip, George, Rugman, Alan M. and Alina Kudina. "International Success of British Companies," *Long Range Planning*, vol. 39, no. 3 (2006).

Chapter 18

JAPAN

Contents

Objectives of the chapter

Japan is arguably the odd one out of the three triad regions of the world. Political, social, cultural, and economic differences underpin its unique business infrastructure and the strengths and weaknesses of its firms, relative to competitors from elsewhere. Historically it has undergone a period of unprecedented growth and internationalization and more recently recession, and this process of change helps explain this uniqueness. To understand what is so unusual about the current period for Japan, and why the ongoing corporate restructuring is so fundamental, we need to understand something of this past.

This chapter has a number of aims. By providing an overview of the key economic, political, social, and cultural characteristics of Japan we can understand more about the Japanese market and the opportunities and constraints it represents for foreign firms. We can also understand more about Japanese corporations: how and why are they different and what are the implications for collaborators and competitors?

Such insights are important for firms defending their own domestic markets against Japanese MNEs, for foreign firms breaking into the Japanese market, and for MNEs acquiring or partnering Japanese firms or recruiting Japanese employees. At a broader level, by making the links between national characteristics and corporate behavior explicit we can improve our understanding of the sources of differences between countries and help managers operate more effectively at the international level. The approach used here for Japan can be applied to other countries whose markets present opportunities or whose firms present competitive threats.[1]

The specific objectives of this chapter are to:

1 *Examine* the underlying factors—economic, political, social, and cultural—that underlie the distinctiveness of Japan, its business practices, and its corporations.

2 *Understand* why Japan is a difficult but rewarding market for foreign firms to enter.

3 *Identify* key strengths and weaknesses of Japanese firms.

4 *Explore* the ongoing changes in Japan and the implications for Japanese firms, their collaborators, and their competitors.

ACTIVE LEARNING CASE

Doing business in Japan

Japan is the third-largest economy in the world after the United States and China. For this and other reasons it is attractive for foreign multinational firms, large and small. It is also very different from other countries—politically, economically, and culturally—and these differences can present major challenges for market entrants.

There are a number of reasons for the imbalance in outward–inward trade and foreign direct investment in Japan. It is a tough, competitive market, characterized until recently by relatively closed interfirm business networks and a unique political, legal, and institutional infrastructure. Surveys and case studies of foreign firms in Japan reveal the difficulties many of them have faced and how they have adapted to succeed. They also reveal how things have changed over the years.

Source: Getty Images/Junko Kimura

Prior to the "lost decade" of the 1990s Japan was lucrative but expensive and relatively attractive but restrictive. The major problem for foreign firms was the high basic costs of operating in Japan, including office rents, a high tax burden, staff costs (for local personnel and expatriates), materials, and other inputs. Firms also reported major recruitment problems and difficulties keeping good Japanese staff, partly because the lack of lifetime employment practices and poor social status meant that many Japanese were reluctant to work for foreign firms. Complex employment legislation and very different human resource management practices also added to the effort required to establish an effective local business.

A variety of market restrictions also faced firms, many stemming from the entrenched *keiretsu* networks, both upstream (between buyers and suppliers) and downstream (between producers, distributors, and retailers). Most Japanese firms had long-term relationships with buyers and suppliers characterized by reciprocal trust rather than short-term contractual or price-based arrangements. Breaking these ties by doing business with outsiders could affect these local relationships, so despite the potential for short-term gains, it tended to be avoided. A wide range of government-related obstacles, including binding red tape and uncertain regulations pertaining to foreigners and foreign companies, also created additional constraints for foreign firms in Japan.

In some cases these barriers to foreign entrants were the result of active protectionism, by colluding firms and their trade associations and various other coordinating agencies, or by the Japanese government itself. In the late 1980s and early 1990s political lobbying over alleged restrictive practices, particularly by the US administration, was at its height. In 1989, for example, the Japanese government bowed to US

pressure and reformed the Large Retail Store Law to allow Toys "Я" Us to open a superstore. This was a high-profile case because of the bilateral negotiations between the United States and Japan that led to the change. Toys "Я" Us went on to open 64 stores. But the Large Retail Store Law still remained to protect small retailers and indirectly supported the tied distribution networks of large *keiretsu*, creating additional barriers for foreign firms. It was again challenged in 1997 as part of another high-profile case by Kodak, against Fuji. This time the case was taken to the World Trade Organization, which ruled in favor of Fuji. Most recently, aided by further reforms to the legislation, Costco and Wal-Mart from the United States (see the Wal-Mart takes Seiyu case study later in this chapter) and Carrefour of France are aggressively challenging traditional network structures and attempting to eliminate costly local wholesalers.

More often than the direct actions of Japanese government agencies or collusion among corporate groupings, the above constraints for foreign firms in Japan simply stemmed from differences in Japanese business infrastructures, legislative mechanisms, management practices, and consumer preferences. As with any overseas market, foreign firms have to adapt or they will fail to succeed. Foreign managers have also cited competition with Japanese companies and the strictness of orders from Japanese customers in terms of quality, delivery, and after-sales service as key constraints in the past. But these are innate characteristics of doing business in Japan and two key reasons why Japanese firms themselves are so innovative. Successfully developing a business in Japan is an excellent test of a firm's competitive advantages.

The extended downturn in Japan's domestic market in the 1990s and early 2000s made it less attractive but easier to enter Japan. Government deregulation, the loosening of *keiretsu* ties, and changing consumer preferences helped foreign investors. Foreign companies also cited falls in land prices, office rent, and utility costs as specific improvements in the Japanese business environment. Similarly, reduced distribution costs and improvements in the availability of qualified personnel were also seen as important factors.

The Japanese government has taken steps to improve access for foreign firms, partly to increase consumer choice and stimulate spending and partly to expose local firms to outside competition. Policies aimed at tax reduction and favorable legal and institutional reforms, such as amendments to the Commercial Code of Japan, alongside improvements in labor market flexibility, have helped to increase FDI into Japan.

There are, however, more fundamental changes taking place that are probably more important for foreign entrants. The changing economic climate of the early and mid-2000s, particularly the high costs of manufacturing and depressed consumer demand, has resulted in a growing preference among consumers to buy cheaper, non-Japanese products and a need for Japanese firms to buy from abroad. Long-term *keiretsu* networks have loosened considerably, opening up supplier, distribution, and retailing opportunities to foreign firms. Social and cultural changes also mean that younger Japanese are much more enthusiastic to work for non-Japanese firms, although senior, experienced managers are still relatively difficult to recruit.

More recent entrants to Japan and established foreign firms expanding their presence are a testimony to these changing conditions and the continued promise of the Japanese market. These include the French firm AXA Non-Life Insurance, Miele, the German household appliances company, and Dyson, the British vacuum cleaner manufacturer. Dyson Japan was established in 1998 and has seen a steady increase in sales, extending its reach to 680 retailers via mass merchandisers and department store networks and achieving a 13 percent market share by 2010.

The British retailer Tesco increased its commitment to the Japanese market by acquiring the neighborhood supermarket business of Fre'c via its wholly owned subsidiary, C Two Network Co. in 2004–5. It had already expanded successfully to control 77 stores since its initial entry in 1994,

partly by buying C Two Network in 2003. Following modest growth in Japan, but on the back of success in other global markets Tesco opened its first "Tesco Express" in Japan in 2007, hoping to succeed by promoting its own brand, where many others had already failed. By 2011 it managed 140 stores, selling via both its Tesco brand and a local brand, Tsurukame. However, despite being the world's third-largest retailer it still struggles to develop its presence and boost sales in Japan.

Although there has been change in Japan, the key lessons from managers who have experienced this change also emphasize the continued importance of traditional Japanese practices. For newcomers they suggest the following:

- Research the culture, the market, the competition, and the relevant network affiliations.

- Understand that in Japan more than any other market "the customer is king," quality is paramount, and a deep-rooted service philosophy is required.

- Be patient ("wait on the stone") and show long-term commitment; personal and corporate reputation is important and takes time to develop.

- Show sensitivity in all interaction: social gatherings are important and rituals and hierarchy have to be respected.

- Invest to adapt products, services, marketing, and management style.

- Continually innovate, stay ahead of the competition.

- Use Japan to learn, to improve, and to access other Asian markets.

Websites: http://www.jetro.go.jp/; http://www.tesco.co.uk; http://www.bccjapan.com/; http://www.meti.go.jp/english/

Sources: Michael Kavanagh, "Australia and Japan sales boost Dyson," *Financial Times*, May 26, 2010; Justin McCurry, "Tesco Hopes for Express Success in Tricky Market: Tesco Opens First Branded Store," www.guardian.co.uk, September 28, 2007; "Tesco Plans to Acquire Japanese Business," Press Release, Tesco PLC, April 27, 2004, at www.tesco.co.uk.; S. C. Collinson, *Small and Successful in Japan: A Study of 30 British Firms in the World's Most Competitive Market* (London: Avebury Press, Ashgate Publishing Group, 1996); JETRO, *The 9th Survey on Attitudes of Foreign-Affiliated Companies toward Direct Investment in Japan* (Tokyo: Japan External Trade Organization, 2004), at http://www.jetro.go.jp/en/stats/survey/; JETRO, *Why Japan? Success Stories* (Tokyo: Japan External Trade Organization, 2004), at http://www.jetro.go.jp/en/invest/whyjapan/success_stories/.

❶ What kinds of challenges are foreign managers likely to meet when trying to set up a subsidiary office in Japan and recruit local employees?

❷ How have keiretsu networks limited foreign firms entering the Japanese market in the past and how is this now changing?

❸ As part of the general growth of foreign direct investment into Japan, why are foreign firms increasingly able and willing to engage in mergers and acquisitions (M&As) with local firms?

❹ Despite widespread changes in Japan and the restructuring of Japanese corporations, why is it still important for foreign managers to understand something of the history and the context in which Japanese businesses have evolved?

INTRODUCTION

Between 1950 and 1973 Japanese GDP grew at an unparalleled average annual rate of 8 percent, over three times the growth rates of the UK and the United States in this period and similar to current growth rates in China. The OECD itself noted this by observing: "by the conventional measures of economic performance (income growth, inflation, unemployment) Japan has out-performed all other OECD economies since entry into the organization in 1964."[2] How did this happen?

Since 1973 until recently Japan's average rate of growth has remained at 3 percent per year. Then, in the last half of the 1990s, the Japanese economy grew at half the OECD average (which was 2.8 percent), and by the end of the 1990s it recorded unprecedented negative growth, shrinking by more than 2 percent. More recently it has shown signs of recovery, but is still undergoing a period of restructuring as it comes to terms with the end of a long era of continued growth and stability.

POLITICAL, SOCIAL, AND CULTURAL CHARACTERISTICS

The 128 million people of Japan are heavily concentrated in the coastal areas and urban regions because of the mountainous nature of the country. Over half of the population lives in and around the three main metropolitan areas of Tokyo, Osaka, and Nagoya, with Greater Tokyo having a population of 30 million.

Up until the end of the 1980s Japan could be characterized politically, socially, and culturally as a highly stable, conservative, and homogeneous country. Economic change since then has been both driven by and a driving force for change across all of these dimensions. To understand the current dynamics affecting the Japanese market, its firms, and its managers we must understand something of its political and social heritage.

A traditionally strong government role in the economy

The branches of the Japanese government are most similar to those in the United States: legislative, executive, and judicial. Legislative power is vested in the Diet, which consists of a popularly elected House of Representatives and House of Councilors. The conservative Liberal-Democratic Party has been in power for most of the postwar period with the support of the powerful business and agriculture lobbies.

Ministry for Economy, Trade, and Industry (METI)
The newer incarnation of MITI which was historically influential at the heart of Japan's postwar economic boom. METI remains a powerful force in the deregulation of the economy

Ministry of Finance (MOF)
Works alongside METI and is similarly influential vis-à-vis regulation and restructuring of Japan's capital markets

Executive power rests with the Cabinet, which is organized and headed by the prime minister, who is elected by the Diet. In addition to the office of the prime minister, there are 17 ministerial divisions in the executive branch. Judicial power is vested in the Supreme Court and there are eight high courts and numerous district courts throughout the country. Overall, Japan is divided into 47 prefectures. Each local political subdivision, including cities, towns, and villages, has its own executive power and operates within the scope of the national law.

Two key ministries were at the heart of Japan's postwar reconstruction, the boom years of rapid growth and, arguably, some elements of its more recent recession. The **Ministry for Economy, Trade, and Industry (METI)**, created in 2001, was previously the Ministry of International Trade and Industry (MITI), which was established in 1951. It was responsible for leading the selective liberalization of the economy and trade particularly in the 1960s and 1970s. It used its strong control to target, promote, and coordinate specific technologies and industry groups to spearhead the national economic development program. The **Ministry of Finance (MOF)** was also highly influential in steering the developing and internationalizing economy via its control over prices and currency exchange in the early days of growth.

One of the more unusual systems that helped coordinate decision making and maintain the consensus among MITI, MOF, and various key flagship firms was the practice of **amakudari**. This involved the regular movement of senior politicians and civil servants from the public sector into private-sector companies, often as highly paid consultants.

These two ministries connected with other ministries and government agencies to influence the evolution of specific forms of business infrastructure, corporate strengths (and weaknesses), and interfirm business practices. The Ministry of Post and Telecommunications (MPT) and MITI, for example, jointly guided the development of NTT, the national telecoms carrier; its supplier group, including NEC, Fujitsu, Hitachi, and Oki; and its de-nationalization and partial break-up during the 1990s.[3]

The early 1990s saw the start of a series of restructurings in Japanese politics, following over a decade when government influence over the economy and, in particular, the strategies of the major firms became increasingly weak. Both the lead political parties and the powerful civil service bureaucracies below them were pushed to justify their roles, responsibilities, and connections with corporate Japan.

However, government in Japan still arguably plays a more important role in the economy and as an influence over corporate strategy than in other OECD countries. Agricultural and foods-related sectors, the construction industry, and financial services, for example, are still very strongly influenced by government via a number of governance mechanisms.

Distinctive cultural characteristics

Although cultural factors are often overemphasized in discussions of Japanese economic strength, there are some distinctive social and cultural elements that underlie the country's success. As described in Chapter 5, the cultural frameworks of Hofstede and Trompenaars indicate a low level of individualism and a high level of uncertainty avoidance compared to Western cultures, reflected in the high priority placed on rituals, routines, and procedures in organizations and society in general. The Japanese are relatively neutral or unemotional in the workplace and prefer more objective rather than subjective forms of decision making. They are also diffuse, in Trompenaars' terminology, with a high correlation between hierarchical relationships in the workplace and social status outside the workplace.

A strong sense of collectivism rather than individualism tends to dominate many aspects of Japanese life. Whether work related or outside work, clubs, groups, and societies exist at all levels and people will tend to belong to several, with a distinct ranking in each according to its focus and their age and experience.

Within companies certain characteristics have strong religious roots, including honor, respect, sincerity, loyalty (**chu**), duty, obligation or responsibility (**giri**), ritual, and hierarchy. These are all central pillars of Japanese society in general and are sometimes referred to as the Japanese Code. At various levels parent–child relationships characterize the hierarchical nature of inter-organizational and interpersonal links, such as government–industry, large firm–small firm, manager–employee, and so on.[4] Respect for elders, ritualistic (and highly complex) language forms and behavior, group activities, and consensus decision making are all important elements. These contrast individualism and meritocratic forms of organization and tend overall to unify the Japanese in their response to **gaijin** or outsiders.

Many of these characteristics are nurtured in the strong Japanese school system. This is characterized by a centrally regulated curriculum (dominated by Monbusho, the Ministry of Education, Science, and Culture): conformist attitudes among pupils, teachers, and

Amakudari
(Literally "descent from heaven") The temporary or permanent movement of public-sector officials in Japan into private corporations as a mechanism for coordinating national policy and company strategy

Chu and giri
Chu, meaning loyalty, and *giri*, meaning duty, obligation, or responsibility, are often used together to denote the traditionally close, trusting relationship between managers and employees; they are also used to describe the ties between older and younger members of a family

Gaijin
A term used for non-Japanese and while not too offensive it is not particularly polite; gai means outside or foreign, jin means person

parents; high standards; and a focus on factual learning and the sciences. As a result of this educational focus Japan has double the number of scientists and engineers per head of population than the UK.

There is a significant amount of competition to get into good schools but a lack of competition between pupils once in school ("the nail that sticks out will be hammered down" is a local saying frequently used to describe this conformity). There is also a strong correlation between the level and place of education and job opportunities for school or university leavers, particularly at the top end of the business and civil service hierarchies: 50 percent of Japanese school leavers attend university or higher education colleges and 75 percent of the 480 Japanese universities are private.[5]

We get a small insight into the difficulties created for non-Japanese by the complexities of Japanese culture if we consider the **hai** dilemma. *Hai* can mean one of at least four levels of yes: recognition, but not necessarily understanding; understanding, but not necessarily acceptance and agreement; responsibility, understanding, but must consult with others and secure their agreement before acceptance; and agreement, which means understanding, agreement, and acceptance. The non-verbal signals from the speaker have to be understood to determine which yes is being meant.

Hai
Yes in Japanese does not necessarily mean "yes I agree," but "yes, I hear what you say"

 Active learning check

Review your answer to Active Learning Case question 1 and make any changes you like. Then compare your answer to the one below.

1 **What kinds of challenges are foreign managers likely to meet when trying to set up a subsidiary office in Japan and recruit local employees?**

One way to answer this question would be to examine the political, economic, and cultural issues in turn. Political challenges include the legislation for registering local companies, licensing, taxation, visas for foreign nationals, and employment regulations. Economic challenges include the costs of premises and business services. But there are other costs, less easy to estimate, that result from the extra time and effort needed to develop customer relationships and adapt to Japanese business practices. All of the above challenges would involve a degree of cultural learning, given that they involve interaction with and an understanding of local people and organizations. Recruiting, managing, and keeping Japanese employees, however, represents one of the biggest challenges for foreign managers. Failure to adapt human resource management practices, incentive schemes, the organizational structure and hierarchy, the definition of roles and responsibilities, and decision-making systems to develop an efficient, motivated local workforce undermines many foreign firms' market-entry strategies in Japan.

ECONOMIC CHARACTERISTICS

Keiretsu
Groupings of Japanese firms with long-term associations and cross-shareholdings; each firm maintains its operational independence but coordinates strategy and often exchanges assets and resources with other firms in its group

Japan is very big and highly competitive. The unusual nature of its rapid growth in the early years stemmed from factors such as the traditional relationship between government and business, its unique capital markets (national finance and investment systems), its traditionally strong **keiretsu** groupings of firms, the role of the corporation in society, and the role of the employee in the firm. These are all linked to its unique social and cultural characteristics, leading many commentators to characterize Japan as having a different form of capitalism.

The size of the Japanese economy, combined with its productivity and the average wealth of its 128 million people, make it the third-largest economy in the world after the United States and China. Other general characteristics include its large (though declining) trade imbalance and even larger imbalance in FDI, compared to its triad counterparts (see Tables 18.1, 18.2, 18.3).

Table 18.1 Economic and trade data for Japan

	2006	2007	2008	2009
GDP per head ($ at purchasing power parity)	31,942.64	33,630.70	33,956.52	32,607.87
GDP (% real change pa)	2.0	2.4	−0.7	−5.0
Government balance (% of GDP)	−4.0	−2.5	−5.8	−10.4
Inflation (%)	0.2	0.1	1.4	−1.3
Public debt (% of GDP)	177.6	170.0	172.1	192.1
Labor costs in manufacturing per hour (US $)	21.31	19.99	19.75	n.a.
Recorded unemployment (%)	4.1	3.9	4.0	5.6

GDP by sector	agriculture: 1.6%; industry: 23.1%; services: 75.4% (2009 est.)
Exports	$516.3 billion (2009 est.); $746.5 billion (2008 est.)
Main exports	transport equipment, motor vehicles, semiconductors, electrical machinery, chemicals
Main export partners	US 17.8%, China 16%, South Korea 7.6%, Taiwan 5.9%, Hong Kong 5.1% (2008)
Imports	$490.6 billion (2009 est.); $708.3 billion (2008 est.)
Main imports	machinery and equipment, fuels, foodstuffs, chemicals, textiles, raw materials
Main import partners	China 18.8%, US 10.4%, Saudi Arabia 6.7%, Australia 6.2%, UAE 6.1%, Indonesia 4.3% (2008)

Sources: http://www.oecd.org/statsportal/; http://www.meti.go.jp/english/statistics/index.html; http://www.jetro.go.jp/; IMF World Economic Outlook and EconStats, May 2010; World Bank, 2010; US Bureau of Labor Statistics, November 2009; US Census Bureau; CIA, *The World Factbook*, 2010; JETRO, *Trade and Investment Statistics, Japan's International Trade in Goods, 2010*.

Table 18.2 Japan's FDI imbalance (millions of US$)

Direct investment flows	2006		2007		2008	
	Inward	Outward	Inward	Outward	Inward	Outward
Japan	−6,506	50,266	22,549	73,549	24,426	128,020
United Kingdom	156,186	86,271	183,386	275,482	96,939	111,411
United States	237,136	224,220	271,176	378,362	316,112	311,796

Source: UNCTAD, *World Investment Report*, Country Fact Sheet, Japan, 2009.

E-resources: http://www.unctad.org.

This imbalance, coupled with the trade dependence on the US market, resulted in the long-running US–Japan trade conflict during the 1980s. Japan's growth period was marked by increased exports (still reflected in its export profile; see Figure 18.1) and outward FDI, but for some time its domestic market remained relatively closed to competitors for a variety of reasons. More recently, linked to the domestic market recession, imports of cheaper products, particularly from China, have created a more balanced trade profile (see Figure 18.2). Trade and FDI trends in the 2000s show that Japan's economy is becoming more integrated within the Asia region and developing particularly strong economic ties with China. Both output (market-oriented) expansion and input (resource or production-oriented) expansion opportunities are being created for Japanese firms by the growth of the Asian economic region.

Table 18.3 Japan's FDI inflows and outflows by source and destination, 2008

Japan's Inward FDI by Country/Region (Balance of Payments basis, net and flow)	Share (%)	Japan's Outward FDI by Country/Region (Balance of Payments basis, net and flow)	Share (%)
Asia	13.77	Asia	17.84
China	0.15	China	4.96
ASEAN4	0.08	ASEAN4	3.09
Asian NIEs	13.51	Thailand	1.54
Singapore	11.06	Indonesia	0.55
Hong Kong SAR (P.R. China)	1.04	Asia NIEs	4.46
North America	48.90	Hong Kong SAR (P.R. China)	0.99
US	48.03	R.Korea	1.81
Canada	0.86	India	4.24
Central and South America	16.37	North America	35.20
Cayman Islands	14.63	US	34.15
Oceania	1.05	Canada	1.04
Western Europe	19.80	Central and South America	22.64
Germany	4.82	Brazil	4.10
Netherlands	10.96	Cayman Islands	17.24
Belgium	−8.30	Oceania	4.63
Luxembourg	1.94	Western Europe	17.13
Switzerland	7.62	Eastern Europe, Russia, etc.	0.49
Eastern Europe, Russia, etc.	0.02	Middle East	0.86
Middle East	−0.007	Africa	1.16
Africa	0.08	World	100.00
World	100.00		
For Reference:		For Reference:	
EU	11.98	EU	17.53

Source: Japan External Trade Organization (JETRO), *Reports and Statistics, Japan's Inward and Outward Foreign Direct Investment*, 2010.

E-resources: http://www.jetro.go.jp/en/reports/statistics/.

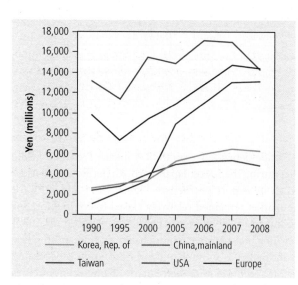

Figure 18.1 Trends in Japan's trade by country/region: exports from Japan

Source: Statistical Handbook of Japan 2009 by the Statistics Bureau of Japan.

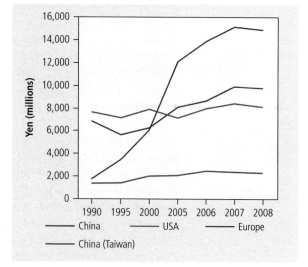

Figure 18.2 Trends in Japan's trade by country/region: imports to Japan

Source: Statistical Handbook of Japan 2009 by the Statistics Bureau of Japan.

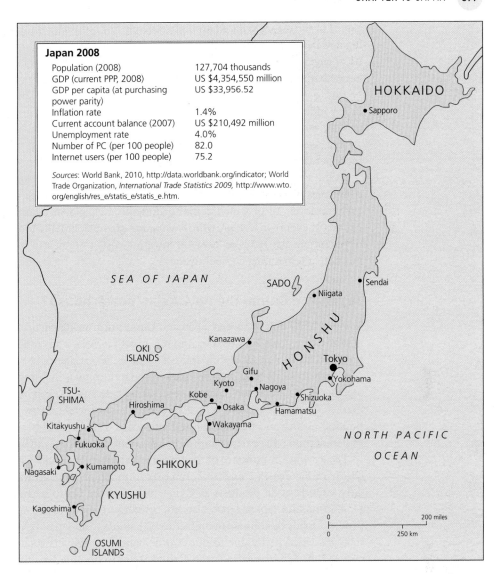

Japan 2008

Population (2008)	127,704 thousands
GDP (current PPP, 2008)	US $4,354,550 million
GDP per capita (at purchasing power parity)	US $33,956.52
Inflation rate	1.4%
Current account balance (2007)	US $210,492 million
Unemployment rate	4.0%
Number of PC (per 100 people)	82.0
Internet users (per 100 people)	75.2

Sources: World Bank, 2010, http://data.worldbank.org/indicator; World Trade Organization, *International Trade Statistics 2009*, http://www.wto.org/english/res_e/statis_e/statis_e.htm.

Japan is home to around a quarter of the top 100 MNEs. The kinds of sectors represented in this list of top firms, together with Japan's trade profile and sources of outward FDI, all point to a surprisingly narrow range of industry strengths. Its competitive superiority has always been limited to relatively few key sectors, as is the case for most other economies.

In the early 1990s just four industries—non-electrical machinery, electrical machinery, transport machinery, and precision machinery—accounted for 75 percent of total Japanese exports. Three product areas—motor vehicles and parts, consumer electronics, and electronic components—were responsible for about one-third of exports. The same industry niches were responsible for the growth of FDI (primarily in production activities) and of foreign sales of Japanese firms.[6] Other data also show how the success of Japanese firms, expressed in terms of the proportion of overseas to total sales, has also been rather limited.[7] Their size, as is the case for many US firms, reflects success in their large domestic and regional markets rather than their global competitiveness.

In his 1990 book *The Competitive Advantage of Nations*, Michael Porter uses Japan to illustrate both the importance of local *rivalry* and *demanding customers* as driving forces behind the evolution of innovative, competitive firms. As shown above, Japan's strong export performance is based around relatively few industries, initially steel and shipbuilding and heavy engineering, then later capital goods production, car manufacturing, electrical engineering, and consumer electronics. In all these sectors very tough competition between many local firms battling for market share (rather than profits) pushed each competitor to develop new products, more rapidly at lower costs. The large number of firms in key industry sectors promoted this rivalry. During its rapid growth phase the country had, for example, 9 indigenous car manufacturers (whereas the United States had only 3), 10 large electronics groups, and over 115 companies producing machine tools, again far more per capita than the United States.

At the same time, tough markets and demanding customers at home pushed Japanese companies to cut costs and emphasize quality, personal service, and buyer-led product customization, all of which came to underlie their global competitiveness during later periods of export-driven growth. Toyota, for example, initially pioneered lean production techniques in the 1950s as a way of lowering costs to undercut local competitors, not to promote international competitiveness.[8]

Japan and China: the new Asian powerhouse?

Trade and FDI flows between Japan and China are growing particularly quickly, raising the potential of a powerful axis of economic growth in Asia. The combination of Japan's technological leadership in specific industry sectors, its excellence in manufacturing and process innovation, its large, wealthy market, and its footholds in Europe and the United States, together with China's low-cost manufacturing base and its evolving, large but low-income market, sets the stage for a very strong regional partnership. However, the turbulent geopolitical history and distinct cultural and social differences between the two nations may well undermine this partnership, or at least limit the pace at which it develops.

The growing importance of the trading relationship between China and Japan is shown clearly in Figures 18.1 and 18.2. Imports from China have grown dramatically, particularly imports of IT products as China surpassed the US to become the major source of IT imports into Japan. Japan also imported more motorcycles and consumer electronic products made by Chinese manufacturers. Exports from Japan to China have also substantially increased partly due to buoyant demand for products such as automobiles. At the end of 2007, China overtook the United States to become Japan's major trading partner, accounting for over 17 percent of exports. The overall trade deficit with China remained at $18 billion. This had lessened by the end of the decade as significant jumps in bilateral trade took place in 2010–2011.

BUSINESS CHARACTERISTICS

Having explored some aspects of the political, social, and economic environment in which Japanese firms have evolved, we now move on to examine some of the factors underlying Japan's economic success. This success in the 1970s and 1980s led to a fear among Western observers that the Japanese had developed an alternative model of market capitalism that would outperform incumbent firms in the United States and Europe. High-profile articles and books on the Japanese threat fed this fear.[9] This also prompted some useful, in-depth research that sought to understand what factors underpinned this success. These include distinctive strengths in manufacturing operations, strong applied research and development (R&D), the *keiretsu* corporate networks, and domestic distribution and retailing systems that connect companies and customers.

Manufacturing strengths

The most detailed comparative studies involving Japanese manufacturers have been carried out in the auto sector looking, for example, at productivity, manufacturing efficiency, continuous process improvement, design quality, return on R&D, and new product development. The success of Japanese firms in this sector is shown by the fact that on average (up until the end of the 1980s) they produced new models of cars with only 55 percent of the engineering hours required by US and European manufacturers, maintaining development lead times that were over 15 months shorter, and sold the cars at a retail price that was, on average, 30 percent lower than competing models from the United States and Europe.[10]

A variety of attributes underlie Japanese manufacturing competitiveness, and while detailed accounts can be found in numerous other sources, some of the main ones are listed here:

- Attention to quality (built in at every stage of development and production processes), often formalized in quality circles (QC) and total quality management (TQM) but related much more to each individual employee's concern for flawless output.

- Strong manufacturer–component supplier linkages (coordinated initial development and subsequent innovation), again formalized within just-in-time (JIT) systems but reliant for their success on the close, informal *keiretsu* relationships between buyers and suppliers.

- Ability to cut production costs (using advanced manufacturing technology, JIT, and flexible and lean manufacturing techniques).

- A high level of automation and use of robotics (increasingly used to control costs as the yen appreciated).

- Higher degree of credibility and responsibility given to engineers and technical expertise.

- *Kaizen*, or continuous improvement, and a focus at all levels on incremental productivity improvement and customer-led product development.

Kaizen
Normally taken to mean "continuous improvement" and is associated with lean or low-cost, high-productivity manufacturing. A more accurate interpretation is "to dismantle and reassemble a process to make it better." As such *kaizen* was an early form of business process re-engineering

Strong applied R&D

Japan has traditionally spent more than most other countries on R&D, consistently investing over 3 percent of the nation's GDP on R&D. This compares to around 2.5 percent in the USA and less than 2 percent on average in the EU27. The recent shift, however, has been the rise of China which overtook Japan in 2010 to become the second-largest R&D investor after the US. In Japan, however, over 75 percent of R&D funding comes from industry, the highest among OECD countries and higher than in China. Contrary to popular myth the Japanese government has always spent relatively smaller amounts on R&D compared to other advanced countries (this is partly related to the low level of defense spending).

At one time Hitachi, Toyota, Matsushita, NEC, and Fujitsu, the top five R&D spenders in Japan, spent as much (in terms of purchasing power parity) as the total R&D expenditure of the entire private sector in the UK.[11] Up until the late 1980s this R&D was predominantly applied or near-market R&D. Japan only started to catch up in terms of more basic blue-sky R&D, moving to the scientific frontiers in some technologies, in the last 15 to 20 years.

Keiretsu

Kinyu
Horizontal conglomerates encompassing a wide range of diversified businesses, centered on a dominant bank and/or trading company

The renowned Japanese corporate groupings, or *keiretsu*, characterized by cross-shareholdings and regular meetings between executives, represent more or less closely tied groups of integrated businesses. There are broadly two types of *keiretsu*, the horizontal (*kinyu*) type and the vertical, manufacturing *keiretsu*. Both are undergoing radical change, as described later in this chapter.[12]

Zaibatsu
The prewar antecedents of
some modern-day *keiretsu*
in Japan; attempts by
the allied forces to break
these up after World War II
largely failed

Many of the former are descended from the prewar ***zaibatsu*** conglomerates, which the allied forces attempted to break up in the late 1940s. Three of the top six are direct descendents of the prewar *zaibatsu*: Mitsui, Mitsubishi, and Sumitomo. The remaining three, Fuyo/Fuji, Sanwa, and Dai-lchi Kangyo, are more like centralized holding companies. These top six alone directly accounted for about 5 percent of the Japanese labor force and 16 percent of total Japanese corporate sales in the early 1980s. But their cross-shareholding networks and their influence across and down the main corporate hierarchies in Japan were far more prevalent than these figures suggest.

The Fuyo *keiretsu* (*Fuyo-kai*) is shown in Figure 18.3, prior to its restructuring. It typifies the horizontal-type *keiretsu*, with a central bank and **sogo shosha**, or international trading company, and a diversified range of interests. These firms played a major role in bringing Japanese products to the world markets in the growth phase and underpin the global FDI network of many Japanese firms today.

Sogo shosha
International trading
companies that help other
Japanese firms import
and export products and
services; they were very
influential in the rapid
growth era in helping local
firms break into overseas
markets

Many of these Japanese banks once dominated the world rankings in asset terms, including Dai-lchi Kangyo Bank, Sumitomo Bank, Fuji Bank, and Sakura Bank. Commercial banks in Japan have always been oriented more toward corporate clients than individual customers compared to Western banks. Unlike arm's-length shareholders in the West, with short-term repayment horizons, Japanese banks and other shareholders (usually affiliated companies, suppliers, distributors, or associated companies) will have built a long-term commitment to supporting *keiretsu* member companies and their employees. As a result capital markets in Japan have not traditionally emphasized return on investment (ROI) and dividends. Corporations have been much freer from the constraints and demands of shareholders and allowed to manage for long-term growth and continue *keiretsu* connections and loyalty to employees. This form of capitalism has significant benefits in a continually growing economy. But it also has weaknesses and can be an inefficient system for resource allocation as has become much more apparent in Japan's recessionary period. Subsequently, there have been fundamental changes to the structure of capital markets in Japan in recent years, as we will see below.

At one time Mitsubishi was said to be the most tightly woven *keiretsu*, based in Tokyo's business district, Marunouchi, which as a result was called Mitsubishi Village. It had over 216,000 employees in businesses ranging throughout the financial, manufacturing, services, and trading sectors from heavy engineering and oil to aerospace and beer. The 29 companies at the heart of the group held an average of 38 percent of each other's shares, a high proportion even for Japanese corporate groups.[13] These companies exchanged directors, cross-financed one another, and engaged in joint investment and cooperative research projects for the benefit of the whole group. Information exchange and interfirm coordination are initiated at the most senior level and the presidents and chairmen of the 29 core firms still meet for lunch in Marunouchi on the second Friday of each month for the **Mitsubishi Kinyokai**, or Friday Club. Within the 29 core companies are an even closer-knit group, the members of which share the Mitsubishi name. The proportion of stable shareholders among this group stood at over 70 percent in 1996 and has since fallen to about 30 percent. The case **International Business Strategy in Action: Kirin Beer goes international** describes one of the companies in the Mitsubishi Group.

Mitsubishi *Kinyokai*
The Friday Club in
Marunouchi, Tokyo, where
the most senior managers
from the 29 core firms
of the Mitsubishi *keiretsu*
gather each month to
discuss business

The newer, vertical *keiretsu* are headed by large manufacturers (Hitachi, Matsushita Electric Industrial, Toyota, and NEC, for example) and tend to belong to a particular manufacturing sector. Here the relationships are between suppliers, a flagship manufacturer and distributors and retailers, in a vertical value chain. Close information exchange, cross-shareholding, personnel exchanges, and joint ventures support excellence in supply-chain management, new product development, standardized IT and logistics, quality and service assurance, and the sharing of management best practices.

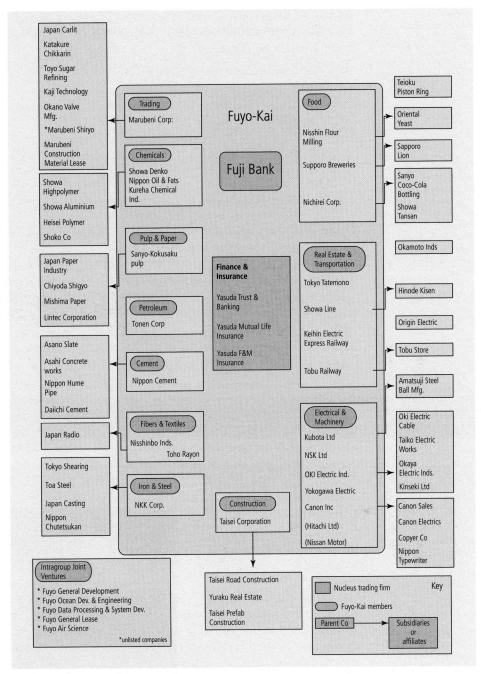

Figure 18.3 The Fuyo *keiretsu* group before restructuring

Source: Sir H. Cortazzi, Modern Japan: A Concise Survey (London: Macmillan, 1993), p. 132.

Co-prosperity pyramid
A supply chain linked to a vertical, manufacturing *keiretsu*. It is hierarchical, with firms in the top tiers engaged in technology sharing, personnel exchanges, cross-shareholding, and long-term trading relationships. The further down the hierarchy a firm sits, the more important price becomes and the less such firms are considered *keiretsu* members

At one time Matsushita, for example, had around 500 prime contractors, or first-level suppliers, and over 6,000 smaller suppliers at lower levels of what is known as a **co-prosperity pyramid** or cooperative manufacturing *keiretsu*. Toyota, by comparison, once had 168 first-tier suppliers, 4,000 second-tier, and around 32,000 third-tier, according to one estimate. Small and medium-sized enterprises (SMEs) at the lower levels may rely on two or three top customers for over 50 percent of their revenue, making them both highly cooperative (that is, willing to change component price or specifications to the buyer's requirements at short notice) and very dependent on the fortunes of manufacturers further up the hierarchy.

✔ Active learning check

Review your answer to Active Learning Case question 2 and make any changes you like. Then compare your answer to the one below.

2 **How have keiretsu networks limited foreign firms entering the Japanese market in the past and how is this now changing?**

The degree to which *keiretsu* networks will affect foreign firms' success in the Japanese market partly depends on which industry or business they are in. In the past, foreign entrants have found it very difficult to find willing suppliers or distributors because many local firms have been tied into long-term relationships with other *keiretsu* members. Traditionally these long-term relationships have meant that foreign firms will be disadvantaged when competing against local firms, regardless of the relative price or benefits of their product or service. Consumers and corporate purchasing departments have tended to show a strong bias toward local brands and local producers. Since the recession, however, price has become more important as a selection criterion and *keiretsu* structures have loosened, providing more opportunities for foreign firms. Imported products, discount stores (bypassing the complex distribution systems), and direct sales have all become acceptable. Japanese firms of all sizes are actively seeking links with firms outside their traditional networks and outside Japan as part of their changing business strategies.

INTERNATIONAL BUSINESS STRATEGY IN ACTION

Kirin Beer goes international

The establishment of the Japan Brewery Company, Ltd. in the late 1880s was a truly international affair. It involved, at various stages and in various roles, a Norwegian, an Englishman, a Scotsman, and a number of Japanese, Americans, and Germans. The symbol of the Kirin, a mythical Eastern cross between a horse and a dragon denoting good fortune, was chosen as its main brand from the start. The firm is the largest beer producer in Japan and one of the four dominant players in the industry alongside Asahi, Sapporo, and Suntory. Its main products are Kirin Lager and Ichiban Shibori, with Kirin Tanrei as Japan's leading *happoshu* (low-malt) beer. Other beverages include canned coffee and tea, fruit juices, and soft drinks. Also active in floriculture and pharmaceuticals, Kirin is part of the Mitsubishi *keiretsu*. In 2010, Kirin revenues was US$24,807 million, of which 79 percent was generated in Japan, 18 percent from Asia and Oceania and 3 percent from other markets.

In recent years the company has been having its share of problems. These all started back in the 1970s when Kirin held 70 percent of the national market. At this time antitrust regulators decided to open the local market to other brewers. As a result, Asahi Beer quickly became

Source: Getty Images/John Chiasson

the country's second-largest brewer, and since then Asahi has continued to erode Kirin's market share with (1) better product development; (2) a successful marketing strategy with commercials aimed at young, active individuals; and (3) a distribution network that introduced what turned out to be a growing trend among beer consumers—canned beer sold in large supermarkets.

In retrospect, one of Kirin's biggest mistakes was that it was too slow in reacting to competition in a market that it long took for granted. For example, despite Asahi's tactics, Kirin continued to rely heavily on its traditional sales approach and its long-established network of "mom-and-pop" stores across the country. In truth, the company was confused regarding how to deal with competition and, as a result, made a number of mistakes. When the giant brewer decided to increase its marketing effort and create television ads directed at young people, the strategy was perceived by many viewers as a poor imitation of Asahi's own advertising strategy and the campaign flopped. As a result of such mistakes by Kirin, Asahi continued to gain market share and moved into top position with a 41.7 percent share of the market for beer and *happo-shu* in 2004. Since then the two firms have continued to battle for the top spot, with the third-placed supplier, Sapporo, well behind. The beer demand in Japan fell for the sixth year in a row. According to Mintel Global Market Navigator, in 2010, Kirin was in the top position of the beer market share by volume, holding 37.7 percent, followed by Asahi 37.5 percent, Suntory 12.3 percent, Sapporo 11.7 percent and finally Orion 0.8 percent. However, in terms of market share by value (US $), Asahi held 40.6 percent, Kirin 35.3 percent, Sapporo 12.0 percent, Suntory 11.2 percent, and Orion 0.8 percent.

Partly in an effort to maintain its position in the Japanese market, Kirin has worked to exploit its traditional image. Kirin Lager, Japan's oldest brew, is now being promoted as the classic Japanese premium beer, the type of beer to enjoy with family and friends. And to promote this image with its other brews as well, Kirin has begun increasing its advertising budget. Unfortunately, this new effort faces a number of challenges. The biggest one may well be that most Japanese beer drinkers admit that all beers taste the same to them—so increased advertising may not generate the desired results.

As well as competing actively for domestic market share, Kirin has expanded abroad. Today its products are available in 40 nations including the United States, the European Union, China, Taiwan, and a host of other Asian countries. In most instances Kirin has teamed up with a local brewer. For example, the company entered into a partnership with Anheuser-Busch that allowed Kirin Beer to be brewed in Los Angeles and then shipped to the rest of the country. The company also holds a 46 percent stake in Lion Nathan Limited, a subsidiary in Australia that has important operations in China. Kirin has also invested a 15 percent stake in San Miguel Corporation, the dominant brewer in the Philippines. So the company is off to a good international start. Competitors, however, are also expanding internationally, creating an ongoing need for product differentiation and good brand marketing. So Kirin still has a long way to go.

One of the things that may help the company is that it is part of Mitsubishi, Japan's largest *keiretsu*. Today the Mitsubishi Group has over 200 operations in 80 countries worldwide. Together with its 500 group companies, Mitsubishi employs a global workforce of over 54,000 people; 29 core members are bound together by cross-ownership and other financial ties. Although the members of this *keiretsu* operate independently, they can call upon one another for help. For example, when Akai Electric had financial problems, Mitsubishi Bank rescued it. When Mitsubishi Heavy Industries' shipbuilding business ran into trouble, it was able to find work at other group companies for those personnel who were laid off. And the cross-holding structure has also come in handy when warding off takeovers. For example, when Texaco bought Getty Oil, it was prepared to sell Getty's 50 percent share of Mitsubishi Oil to Kuwait Petroleum. However, the members of the Mitsubishi Group got together and outbid the Kuwaitis for Getty's shares. The group has also made important acquisitions and struck major deals in a variety of areas. Mitsubishi companies have participated in the $940 million purchase of the Pebble Beach Golf Course in California, won a $400 million power plant deal in Virginia, and launched a $150 million futures trading joint venture in Chicago. Overall, Mitsubishi has hundreds of interdependent companies, and they are building an empire that stretches from Asia to Europe to the United States. With their help, Kirin may be able to become a major international brewer.

Websites: www.kirin.co.jp; www.mitsubishi.com; www.asahibeer.co.jp; http://www.beverageworld.com/beverageworld/headlines/; http://www.kirin.co.jp/english/annual2003/08source.html.

Sources: Naoko Fujimura, "Asahi Tops Kirin in Japan Beer Sales as Demand Falls," January 17, 2011, Bloomberg Businessweek (http://www.businessweek.com/news); "Asahi Surpasses Kirin in Beer Sales," *The Japan Times*, July 12, 2007; Emily Thornton, "Japan's Struggle to Restructure," *Fortune*, June 28, 1993, pp. 84–88; "Japan's Beer Wars," *The Economist*, February 26, 1998; "A Right Old Brewhaha in Japan," *The Economist*, February 22, 2001; Kyodo News, "Japan Brewers' Shipments Rose Slightly in 2004," January 18, 2005, *Kyodo News International*, Tokyo; Kirin Holdings Company Limited, Annual Report, 2010; OneSource, *Thomson Reuters*, 2010; Mintel Global Market Navigator, http://gmn.mintel.com/query/10884473/shares/region.

Distribution, retailing, and customer orientation

Associated with the *keiretsu* industry groupings above are multilayered distribution and retail networks in Japan. At its height it was estimated that there was one retail outlet for every 75 people in Japan (over twice the US ratio) and over 476,000 wholesale stores. These are still organized both by region and by sector and product across Japan and tend to be geared to the large number of small retailers that serve the local markets. This "tied" system of distribution, bound by strong face-to-face ties between sellers and buyers at each level, adds substantial costs to the final product. Again, at its peak, the American Chamber of Commerce in Japan (ACCJ) found that over 48 percent of home electronics products in Japan are sold through exclusively affiliated stores, and about 99 percent of cars are distributed through exclusive dealerships.[14]

Many elements of this complex, high-cost distribution remain in Japan today. Ports in particular are notoriously protected and relatively slower and more expensive than in other OECD countries. The multi-tiered distribution hierarchy has become more simplified, however, driven by the growth in discount stores and cost-reduction measures.[15]

Until recently the strong patriotic preferences of the average Japanese consumer and, perhaps, the average Japanese middle manager responsible for company purchasing policy provided a firm basis for the country's industrial and distribution infrastructure. Outside the luxury or branded consumer goods markets the Japanese have long had a strong preference for Japanese products.

JAPANESE CORPORATIONS

Japan is home to around 25 percent of the top 100 multinational firms. It is not just a large economy and a large market, but a major source of global competitors. Various stereotypes underlie popular beliefs about Japanese firms that are at best inaccurate and sometimes wholly misleading.

At one extreme, during the 1970s and 1980s, Japanese firms were seen to exemplify the best of all management practices. High-profile articles and books on the Japanese threat fed a general fear about the competitive threat they posed and prompted researchers to identify what was different about Japan and its firms and how such differences might convey sustained competitive advantages.[16] At the other end of the extreme, the economic and corporate failures of the period broadly from 1990 to 2003 have prompted wholesale criticism of the Japanese model.

The truth lies somewhere in between. The Japanese economy, culture, and business system underpin both relative strengths and weaknesses in Japanese companies. The former were very evident during the period of social and political stability and economic growth up to the end of the 1980s. The latter have become more apparent since then.

Very broadly speaking, two kinds of Japanese corporations have existed for some time. On the one hand those firms that have escaped the effects of the extended recession, such as Toyota, Honda, Sony, Canon, Sharp, and Toshiba, have been less dependent on the Japanese market (more internationalized) for some time. They increasingly sold products in markets outside Japan, engaged in FDI abroad, and evolved "less Japanese" styles of management well before the recessionary period. They also represent the industries in which Japan achieved its high levels of export competitiveness in the growth years, which is why we know more about them in the West.[17]

On the other hand a large number of firms, the majority of Japanese companies in fact, including firms like Nippon Steel, Sumitomo Chemical, Mitsubishi, Kajima, and Dentsu, are less geographically diversified. They have long remained more dependent on the Japanese market, Japanese suppliers, and Japanese ways of doing things.

Confirmation of this division comes from the McKinsey Global Institute study which shows that although labor productivity in Japan's top firms (such as those above) is 20 percent higher on average than in US firms, they only represent 10 percent of the Japanese economy. The other 90 percent of Japanese firms have an average labor productivity that is 60 percent of US levels.[18]

Table 18.4 shows the top 40 Japanese firms (from a list of the top 500 multinational firms). It also classifies the firms according to their global distribution of sales, showing

Table 18.4 The top 40 Japanese firms

Company	Revenues (billions of US $)	F/T sales	North America (% of total)	Europe (% of total)	Asia–Pacific (% of total)	C
Toyota Motor	146.57	58.6	34.2	11.7	41.4[j]	B
Mitsubishi	128.62	15.3	4.6[z]	na	87.2	D
Mitsui	104.08	41.4	6.8[z]	1.3[u]	58.6[j]	D
Marubeni	85.72	31.5	14.2	3.6	74.1	D
Itochu	80.65	20.9	4	1.8	92.4	D
Sumitomo	77.95	42.3	16.1	13.2	64.6	D
Hitachi	73.16	34.5	10.1	7.6	79.6	D
Honda Motor	69.17	80.1	55.7	9.4	29.8	S
Sony	63.53	70.4	28.3[z]	23.6	29.6[j]	G
Matsushita Electric Industrial	63.39	53.5	17.7	14.4	67.8	D
Nissan Motor	62.96	65.5	44.1	15.7	34.5[j]	B
Sojitz	49.68	20.5	4.9	3.6	91.3	D
Toshiba	47.28	39.1	12.7	9.3	75.8	D
NEC	41.58	20.7	na	na	79.3[j]	D
Tokyo Electric Power	41.13	<10	na	na	>90.0[j]	D
Fujitsu	40.40	24.4	5.3[l]	11.4	75.6[j]	D
Japan Tobacco	39.20	14.8	na	6.7	85.2[j]	D
Nippon Oil	36.27	2.2	0.9	0.3	98.9	D
Sumitomo Mitsui Financial Group	31.10	8.5	3.8[l]	2.1	94.1	D
Ito-Yokado	30.02	36.3	33.1[z]	na	63.8[j]	D
Mizuho Financial Group	28.33	13.8	5.6[l]	5.8	88.7	D
Mitsubishi Electric	28.05	14.1	6.6	6.2	97.7	D
Canon	27.10	74.9	32.7[l]	30.3	26.8[j]	G
Nippon Steel	24.80	<10	na	na	>90.0	D
Mazda Motor	24.71	60.3	31.6	22.3	39.7[j]	G
KDDI	24.12	–	–	–	100	D
Mitsubishi Tokyo Financial Group	23.12	39.5	21.1[z]	10.2	64.3	D
Mitsubishi Heavy Industries	22.57	11.8	6.7	2.9	90.2	D
Denso	21.72	43.7	21.7[l]	13	65.1	D
Fuji Photo Film	21.70	47.8	21.2[l]	14.7	52.2[j]	D
East Japan Railway	21.54	0	0	0	100[j]	D
Mitsubishi Motors	21.35	37.9	23.8	26.1	69.4	D
Sanyo Electric	21.25	49.5	13.4	7.4	77.2	D
JFE Holdings	20.96	<10	na	na	>90.0[j]	D
Bridgestone	19.52	65.1	42.2[l]	12.5	34.9[j]	B
Sharp	19.13	49.3	13.7[l]	14.7	63	D
Suzuki Motor	18.64	52	13.4	17	68.5	D
Daiei	16.89	<10	na	na	>90.0[j]	D
Japan Airlines	16.37	<10	na	na	>90.0[j]	D
Mitsubishi Chemical	16.32	15.2	na	na	93.9	D

Notes: F/T = foreign/total; C = classification (of firm). Data are for 2003. u = United Kingdom; l = Americas; z = United States; j = Japan; D = home-region oriented; S = host-region oriented; B = bi-regional; G = global.

Sources: S. Collinson and A. M. Rugman, "The Regional Nature of Japanese Multinational Business," *Journal of International Business Studies*, vol. 39, no. 2 (2008), pp. 215–230.

their relative dependence on their domestic (Japanese) markets. All but a very few are highly dependent on their domestic market, and only Sony and Canon are global in that they have over 20 percent of their sales in each of the triad regions. Despite the above-mentioned variations in the structures, strategies, and management styles of Japanese firms, there are some common, distinctive characteristics of the stereotypical Japanese firm, relative to its European and American counterparts.

In one of the most extensive studies of the Japanese enterprise system, Fruin highlights high productivity, functional specialization, and manufacturing adaptability as the distinguishing hallmarks of Japanese firms. He identifies these attributes at three connected levels: the factory, the firm, and the interfirm network.[19]

The various social, cultural, and economic characteristics above combine to create certain strengths and weaknesses in Japanese firms. From a wide range of studies[20] we can distill some of the main characteristics of the generic Japanese management style, again traditionally:

Benkyokai
Study associations or work groups for students or colleagues in companies to jointly develop particular areas of knowledge and expertise

- Effective communications internally and with outside firms (decentralized, horizontal information flows) and the use of **benkyokai** or cross-disciplinary, cross-business, and cross-functional workshops.

- Less separation of R&D, design, manufacturing, and marketing functions.

- Lifetime employment, low labor mobility, and substantial investments in training. There is also a strong emphasis on on-the-job training and job rotation within the firm.

- Managers as problem definers, not firefighters, and as educators and mentors, not disciplinarians. This is underpinned by the weak links between performance and pay and the low wage differentials between workers and managers in the age-related hierarchy. Despite the importance of hierarchy and job titles, average CEO incomes in Japan are rarely more than 10 times the salaries of new recruits. In the United States (and increasingly in the UK) there is a much bigger remuneration gap than this.

- Strong group/team ethic, loyalty, and motivation combined with competitiveness between teams.

Nemawashi
Literally means "root tying" and is a process of consultation to get agreement on a particular issue before it becomes explicit policy

- Strict formal hierarchy (based on seniority, rank and title also underpin social status) combined with strong underlying informal networks and a tendency toward consensus-based (**nemawashi** and **ringi**) decision making (horizontal promotion for high fliers and a lack of outsiders entering the firm at senior levels).

Ringi
The formalized consensus process of decision making; the ringisho is a decision proposal circulated around company departments to be revised or approved before implementation

- General "long-termism" with a focus on growth, employment stability, and market share rather than profits and shareholder dividends.

These are obviously generalizations, but are factors that tend to exist more or less in a wide range of Japanese firms. Overall, Japanese firms have a strong focus on human resources. A great deal of their strength (and a source of some weaknesses) lies in the employer–employee relationship and the commitment and loyalty shown by each to the other.

This overview of some of the key characteristics of the Japanese has been highly generalized, aiming to select factors that underpin significant differences in Japan relative to other countries. One of the best early books on Japanese firms and business practices called *Kaisha* ("company") by Abegglen and Stalk[21] sums up some of these distinctive characteristics as the 3Ms:

- *Marketing*: direct links with consumers via retailers and wholesalers and strong customer-led product development.

- *Money*: cross-shareholding and the lack of outside pressure for short-term returns and stock price improvements.

- *Manpower strategy*: worker involvement, loyalty, effective teamworking and devolvement of responsibility combined with hierarchy.

A CHANGING NATION

The recent past decade has seen a number of major changes in Japan's social, economic, and political structure and this change continues. The added difficulties brought about in Japan by the current period of chaotic upheaval is partly related to the unusual degree of stability and consensus that the country has experienced throughout a long high-growth era that is now over.

Starting in the early 1990s Japan has experienced its worst economic recession in the postwar period. Slower growth, reduced investment, declining property prices, and increased unemployment are all secondary effects of earlier declines in profitability, increased domestic costs, and falling domestic demand. These were masked in the late 1980s by rapid growth rates based on strong exports and cheap capital, which ended abruptly when the bubble burst and **endaka** began. The recession is linked to the fast appreciation of the yen, which partly resulted from the 1985 **Plaza Accord** and continued through the mid-1990s, rising 24 percent in value between early 1993 and early 1995.

Between 1990 and 2000, 'the lost decade', unemployment grew from 2.1 to 4.7 percent; GDP growth fell from 5.1 to 1.9 percent; motor vehicle production fell by 25 percent; the sales of large department stores slumped by 13 percent; and residential land prices in Tokyo dropped by 55 percent. The knock-on effects are still being felt.

Alongside this economic slump, significant social and cultural developments have resulted in an unprecedented degree of tension between traditional and modern ways of living and working. Some of the broader elements of social change include the aging population, changing diet and changing health problems, a rising crime rate (though from a very low base rate), new attitudes toward work and leisure and, among some in Japan, a perceived decline in moral values (among others, a new freedom and social openness).

Japan's social homogeneity proved to be a strength in the period of rapid economic development of the past, but may well prove increasingly to be a weakness as it becomes more international. As the country becomes less isolated from the rest of the world the individualistic, Western aspirations of the younger Japanese increasingly clash with the more conservative, group-oriented nature of the older Japanese. The latter are largely responsible for the rapid economic development of Japan in the postwar period through their hard work and their emphasis on building rather than enjoying prosperity.

Shinjinrui ("new human being") is a term that the Japanese have used to describe the younger generation as well as some of the more well-traveled middle-aged citizens who are pushing at the social restrictions that emphasize education, training, and work above personal pleasure, leisure, and family. At the same time a greater degree of interaction with other countries and cultures, plus a growing number of foreigners visiting, working, and living in Japan, are forcing many Japanese to compromise what has been termed their ethnocentric view of the world.

Some of the most obvious changes are seen in the buying patterns of Japanese consumers. Beyond a long-term move to Western foods and clothing styles there has also been a growing preference for "value for money" and an increase in buying from previously frowned-upon foreign firms and discount retail stores. This is partly because of the recessionary pressure on wages but is also an indication that consumers are beginning to realize and object to the fact that Japan's consumer prices were well over the OECD average.

This change in consumer behavior, alongside the increasingly price-oriented, cost-cutting objectives of manufacturers, has challenged the multilayered distribution system that has dominated wholesale and retail networks in Japan. A flatter distribution system has begun to develop, pioneered by discount stores and direct importers, like the Daiei chain, which has experienced a boom in its own-label brands, allowing it to cut prices by using imported products, from Brazilian orange juice to Korean video tapes.

We will now examine some specific aspects of change in Japan: the restructuring of the capital markets, deregulation, and increased inward FDI and the restructuring of Japanese corporations.

Restructuring capital markets

The changing role of banks and the evolution of Japan's financial services industry created persistent instability in the corporate finance system. During the 1980s and 1990s

---

Endaka

Yen appreciation; the growing value of the yen vis-à-vis other currencies which, among other things, made Japan a relatively expensive place to manufacture

Plaza Accord

An agreement signed by the G5 in 1985 in New York, agreeing to devalue the US dollar against the Japanese yen and the deutsche (German) mark; it triggered the bubble economy and eventual economic recession in Japan in the 1990s

Shinjinrui

The new generation of Japanese, with very different values and aspirations than their parents

there was a general move toward using capital markets (bonds and equity) for funding investment, particularly among large manufacturing companies in Japan. Partly as a consequence, banking relationships became less stable with far more companies taking loans from more than one bank and changing their main lender. Loose financial discipline in the high-growth, high-investment years resulted in heavy depreciation charges, often on investments that resulted in overcapacity rather than bringing in extra revenue.

The scale of this instability only became clear after the bubble era when the collapse in property prices, which underpinned much of the private-sector borrowing, left many companies in financial difficulties. In the late 1990s foreign investors took advantage of the depressed prices to buy property in Japan. This triggered a move toward greater transparency of data relating to property values, occupancy rates, and rents, and made it more difficult to use property to hide personal and corporate finances. Credit recovery, loans, and mortgage services, previously restricted to local firms, were also opened up to foreign participants, with tax laws changed to facilitate this.

That conditions were getting tougher for Japanese firms is evident from the data on debt liabilities and bankruptcies. This prompted widespread changes in corporate governance practices in Japan in the mid-2000s.[22] Average return on equity in 1997 was around 4 percent in Japan compared to 20 percent in the United States, a contrast that preceded the recession but had been accepted as part of the financial system. But while US companies achieve returns of around 4.5 percent on average above cost of capital, from 1990 to the mid-2000s Japanese firms (on average) failed to meet the growing costs of capital (that is, they were "value destroyers" rather than "value creators").

As a result of these problems, a process of consolidation, rationalization, and mergers got underway in Japanese capital markets, partly forced on banks from government organizations, as financial deregulation continued (Figure 18.4). Disintermediation has taken place,

Original banks	New bank groups		
IBJ			
Nippon Kangyo Bank	Dai-Ichi Kangyo Bank	IBJ-DKB-Fuji	
Dai-Ichi Bank			
Fuji Bank			
Yasuda Bank	Subsidiary of Fuji Bank		
Taiyo Bank	Taiyo Kobe Bank	Sakura Bank	Sakura-Sumitomo
Kobe Bank			
Mitsui Bank			
Sumitomo Bank			
Mitsui Trust	Mitsui-Chuo Trust		
Chuo Trust			
Hokkaido Takushoku	Acquired by Chuo Trust		
Sumitomo Trust			
Bank of Tokyo	Bank of Tokyo Mitsubishi		
Mitsubishi Bank			
Nippon Trust	Subsidiary of Mitsubishi Bank		
Mitsubishi Trust			
Sanwa Bank			
Toyo Trust	Subsidiary of Sanwa Bank		
Tokai Bank			
Kyowa Bank	Asahi Bank	Tokai-Asahi	
Saitama Bank			
Daiwa Bank	Acquires regional banks		
LTCB	Nationalized		
MCB	Nationalized		

Figure 18.4 Bank group consolidation in Japan

with companies raising finance from capital markets rather than via traditional *keiretsu* cross-shareholding and bank relationships.[23] Private equity and venture capital also played a growing role, as did foreign investors.

Deregulation, increased M&A, and inward FDI

Although external pressure to deregulate the Japanese from European and US corporations and governments has declined, the pressure from inside Japan has grown. Structural reforms, changes to government policy and the legal codes, plus the changing priorities of Japanese firms and customers have led to a significant increase in inward investment. In particular, foreign M&As, largely unheard of before the mid-1990s, have grown substantially, and enjoyed another resurgence in recent years, as shown in Figure 18.5, but these are still relatively less significant than in other advanced economies. The number of foreign takeover bids each year in Japan exceeded 100 for the first time in 2007 and continued to grow until the end of the decade.[24]

European firms have significantly increased their investments in Japan. French firms were early investors in the late 1990s, making large acquisitions in Japan's automobile, auto parts, and finance/insurance industries. Renault's 36.8 percent stake in Nissan in March 1999 contributed to this (see **Real Case: Renault and Nissan: no pain, no gain** at the end of this chapter). Three sectors—finance, transport equipment, and telecommunications—accounted for a significant proportion of M&As. But foreign firms have also made attempts to buy into other sectors, including retailing (see **International Business Strategy in Action: Wal-Mart takes Seiyu**). Between 1996 and 2006 the total value of inward FDI stock had increased four-fold, but then stabilized and still remains relatively low compared to other OECD countries.

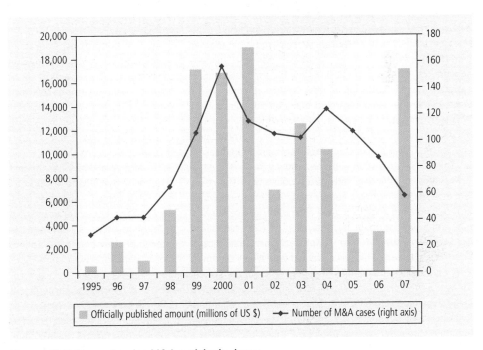

Figure 18.5 Cross-border M&A activity in Japan

Source: JETRO, *White Paper on International Trade and Foreign Direct Investment,* 2007, http://www.jetro.go.jp/en/stats/.

Wal-Mart takes Seiyu

The Japanese landscape is littered with the remains of foreign firms that misjudged the local market. In March 2002, Wal-Mart purchased a 6 percent stake in Seiyu, the fourth-largest supermarket chain in Japan, which has 393 stores selling food, clothing, and general merchandise. The 2001 replacement of Japan's Large-Scale Retail Store Law, which prevented large retail developments, with the more generous Large-Scale Retail Store Location Law has eased Wal-Mart's entry. It retained an option to slowly increase its ownership position in the company to 66.7 percent by 2007. In 2003, after a five-month feasibility study on opportunities in the Japanese market, it took a step in that direction by agreeing to spend $420 million to raise its stake to 34 percent, making Wal-Mart the dominant shareholder. Finally at the end of 2007 it bought out the remaining shares to become sole owner of Seiyu. (This became the subject of an unusual insider-dealing investigation in Japan in 2010.)

To its Japanese operations, Wal-Mart brought a new management style, strategy, supplier networks, and one of the world's most formidable information and distributions systems. With $244 billion in revenues, Wal-Mart also brought the financial power to update Seiyu's ailing 400 stores. However, since 2003 Seiyu has continued to post annual losses.

Success in Japan's retail market remains anything but assured. The Always Low Prices strategy on which Wal-Mart based its North American success must be adapted significantly to cater to the Japanese market. Japanese consumers insist on standards of quality that Wal-Mart is simply not used to offering in other countries. When, in the early 1990s, the Japanese retail giant Ito-Yokado stocked Wal-Mart biscuits in its stores, they were literally shunned because of their sickly taste and poor quality. Some 40 percent of the biscuits in each packet were said to be broken. Ito-Yokado had to discontinue the product.

Further complicating Wal-Mart's strategy is the resilience of Japan's complex supply system. Carrefour, which entered Japan in 2002, is a good example. The French firm has fallen well short of its original plan to persuade all its Japanese suppliers to adopt the Carrefour direct-purchasing system. This has reflected both a lack of familiarity on the part of Japanese suppliers with such a system as well as the vice-like control over suppliers exerted by large Japanese retailers. Wal-Mart's terrifying reputation for squeezing suppliers' margins until the pips squeak— and then some more—may also make it less attractive as a partner for local firms.

Wal-Mart's success in the United States has also been based on low land prices and labor costs. The price of land in the outskirts of North American cities and suburbs has allowed the company to build large warehouse-style retail stores with huge parking lots. Japanese land, however, is significantly more expensive. Despite a recession and the stagnation of the Japanese economy, Japanese labor costs are among the highest in the world. That customers demand personal service does not help either. For similar-sized stores, Wal-Mart will have to hire more retail workers in a Japanese store than in the United States.

Lessons learned by Carrefour show that Wal-Mart will also have to differentiate itself from competitors. Carrefour positioned itself in the Japanese market simply as a discount retailer. With little to distinguish its product mix from those of its local rivals, the firm's stores underperformed, forcing a switch in strategy to emphasize its "Frenchness." It now offers a limited range of French products. After its initial stumble, the company expanded in Japan.

The emphasis on fresh produce in Japanese cuisine means that there is high demand for perishable goods and less for the kind of processed foods that are often the staple of Western discount supermarkets. This was also cited as one reason behind the sluggish sales at the US warehouse retailer, Costco, since it entered Japan in 1999.

Another cultural consideration is that the Japanese are hesitant to purchase bulk quantities even if it would save them money. The reason for this is rather simple. While the Japanese remain among the world's wealthiest consumers with a GDP per head of US $32,000, they have on average only 350 ft^2 (33 m^2) of living space per capita—45 percent less than Americans and 14 percent less than either the British or Germans.

To date, Wal-Mart has been finding ways to tailor its strategy to the Japanese market. The quality of its products has been raised enough to be acceptable. In renovated Seiyu stores, customers can see their sushi order prepared in front of them, as opposed to the prepackaged variety offered in other countries. To lower land costs, Wal-Mart's stores will have two floors instead of the traditional one floor. Labor costs have been reduced by cutting 25 percent of its workforce through voluntary retirement, saving $46 million on annual wages. It is also relying on its China-based suppliers to stock its Japanese shelves.

But other factors have added to the company's problems, particularly from Japan's continuing economic woes and the tough competitive environment. Uniquely in the developed world, consumer prices in Japan have been falling for some time. Growth has remained sluggish. Yet, that in itself might make this the right moment to enter the market. By the time the country starts to grow again, Wal-Mart will have renovated stores, created new relationships with suppliers, linked all Seiyu stores to its computerized logistics system, and learned enough about the Japanese consumer. Its choice of a local partner in the venture should have given it the benefit of local knowledge and a large store base. This is an advantage over other foreign retailers like Carrefour and Costco, which have chosen to build up stores from scratch. But other domestic and foreign competitors are readying up and Seiyu continues to lose Wal-Mart money.

Websites: www.walmart.com; www.seiyu.co.jp; and http://www.jetro.go.jp/en/invest/whyjapan/success_stories/.

Sources: Lindsay Whipp, "Insider trade probe into Walmart-Seiyu deal," *Financial Times*, November 5, 2010; Hiroko Tabuchi and Kazuhiro Shimamura, "Wal-Mart Expects Bigger 2007 Loss in Japan," *Wall Street Journal*—Eastern Edition, February 13, 2008, p. B14; Tak Kumakura, "Wal-Mart Pushes for Full Ownership of Seiyu," *International Herald Tribune*, October 22, 2007; Wal-Mart, *Annual Report*, 2004; "Can Wal-Mart Woo Japan," *Business Week*, May 10, 2004; "Wal-Mart Moves to Control Seiyu," *CNN.com*, December 12, 2002; and "Wal-Mart's Japanese Makeover," *International Herald Tribune*, July 19, 2004.

✔ Active learning check

Review your answer to Active Learning Case question 3 and make any changes you like. Then compare your answer to the one below.

3 **As part of the general growth of foreign direct investment into Japan, why are foreign firms increasingly able and willing to engage in mergers and acquisitions (M&As) with local firms?**

Deregulation by the Japanese government has helped to make it easier in recent years for foreign firms to acquire Japanese firms. Changes in capital markets, some driven by the government, have promoted inflows of foreign capital to reduce the debt burden. Japanese banks are also much more interested in M&A as a means to rescue (or hand over responsibility for) failing local companies. More significant factors are, first, the growing optimism among foreign firms regarding the future prospects of the Japanese market and their confidence in M&A as a means of access. Second, the rise in M&As can be partly attributed to the changing attitudes of senior Japanese managers who see foreign firms as a means to escape their current economic problems. M&As can help drive some of the strategic changes desired by Japanese managers, such as internationalization and diversification. They can also help push through some of the necessary organizational changes, from de-linking from *keiretsu* relationships to changing internal hierarchies and reward systems.

RESTRUCTURING CORPORATIONS

The initial corporate reaction to the recession was to treat falling profits as part of a cyclical trend that companies could weather using their momentum from the previous decade. Japanese managers had little experience on how to handle the radical restructuring and downsizing that became necessary, particularly the problem of labor costs that quickly began to erode domestic manufacturing competitiveness. Labor costs per head in manufacturing were 25 percent higher in 1992 than in 1988, in part because of the rise in white-collar employment, which expanded by a fifth between 1985 and 1992. Managers were particularly slow in reorganizing to overcome their own office and administrative inefficiencies and this, combined with their reticence in cutting employees, resulted in the rapid collapse of corporate earnings at the start of the downturn.[25]

The impact of the corporate restructuring was clear from the series of companies announcing job losses at the start of the 2000's, including Toshiba, Fujitsu, Mitsubishi, and Nissan. Most firms cut their university recruitment programs pushing the unemployment rate for under 24-year- olds to over 10 percent. Some of the largest bankruptcies hit the economy at the start of the decade, including the life insurer Chiyoda Mutual with debts of 2,900 billion yen and the retailer Sogo in with debts of 2,000 billion yen.

Despite rationalization, consolidation, and a significant growth of M&As in key sectors, Japanese companies are still having to restructure their operations substantially in the face of longer-term pressures, including:

- more expensive capital,
- growing competition from low-cost Asian producers,
- declining prices of key manufactures, particularly electronics and autos,
- a slowing domestic economy, and
- growing inroads into the domestic economy by foreign competitors.

These developments had a knock-on effect as Japanese firms responded by restructuring internally and changing their interfirm trading relationships. The main changes are summarized below.

The decline of manufacturing and distribution *keiretsu*

Because a large proportion of Japanese SMEs are subcontractors to larger companies, within the multi-tiered hierarchies, recession and reorganization among the giants have had a direct effect on a large number of SMEs. Restructuring effects, coupled with the appreciation of the yen, have passed on down this hierarchy, from primary (direct) subcontractors through second-, third-, and fourth-level indirect suppliers. Automotive firms, including Mazda and Nissan, attempted to cut their first-line subcontractors (from 62 to 16 in Mazda's case), thereby passing on the responsibility for pushing down input prices to companies further down the chain. Both met with greater success in this slimming down initiative after their respective mergers with Ford and Renault (see **Real Case: Renault and Nissan: no pain, no gain** at the end of this chapter).

The system of cross-shareholding has become increasingly diluted through reductions in mutual equity stakes. In their drive to cut costs large manufacturing firms in Japan now avoid giving their usual suppliers a guaranteed volume of business over the long term but are encouraging them to compete with each other with a new emphasis on price as the deciding factor. More inputs are now bought from abroad so a more price-driven domestic market and freer flows of imports have evolved.

There has also been a decline in the use of exclusive agreements with single distributors or sales organizations. In the past these were the norm and in most sectors it was impossible to have multiple agreements or play distributors and retailers against each other to push up sales. Increasingly now, multiple agreements are accepted and the trader–wholesaler–retailer link need not be tied but competitive, with many players competing at each level in a "less imperfect" market.

The growth of outward FDI and offshore manufacturing

Nearly half of all cars and machines made by Japanese-owned companies are made outside Japan. It has been overtaken by China as the largest producer of automobiles and color televisions (Japan is now a net importer). A telling example of the resultant pressures was Nissan's closure of its 30-year-old Zama car plant near Tokyo in March 1995, the first

Japanese car plant to be closed since World War II. Ironically, part of the plant that made 11.2 million vehicles in its lifetime was turned into a pre-delivery inspection center for Ford vehicles. From 2010-2011 Japan became the leading foreign investor in China, with a particular boost after the March 2011 earthquake. Japanese automotive and machinery firms increased their investments into China and exports from China to Japan increased as a result.

The decline of lifetime employment and changing HRM practices

Many of the changes being forced on Japanese managers are culturally taboo but economically inevitable. One of the most significant is the erosion of the lifetime employment system, which is very unlikely ever to return in its traditional form. Unemployment, traditionally very low and carrying a huge social stigma, officially grew to over 5 percent (unofficial estimates put the peak nearer 8 percent).

Early retirements, horizontal movement of employees, rising use of performance-related pay, and significantly reduced wage increases and bonuses at the annual wage negotiations in Japan also signified the new pressures on companies. The largest companies reduced their usual intake of university graduates and introduced merit-based remuneration schemes. These changes also had significant knock-on effects, not least the rise in the already high rate of suicides. In the long term, Japan will have an increasingly flexible labor market, with implications for all aspects of the traditional employee–employer relationship, in-house training, and company loyalty.[26]

Diversification strategies

Diversification strategies have been the cornerstone of many corporate restructuring plans, some successful, others not.[27] NKK, Japan's second-largest steelmaker, is a good example. Its previously loss-making marine engineering division turned in an operating profit of almost 15 percent on sales of almost $100 million (although NKK overall expects to make a loss of five times this amount). The turnaround in this particular division was due to extensive (and risky) investments into areas outside shipbuilding. These include the leisure industry, manufacturing an indoor ski slope and an artificial surfing beach (Wild Blue), using core technologies from NKK's own test divisions. In addition to diversification within manufacturing, the changing cost structure for industrial production has, in particular, accelerated the shift toward services.

✔ Active learning check

Review your answer to Active Learning Case question 4 and make any changes you like. Then compare your answer to the one below.

4 **Despite widespread changes in Japan and the restructuring of Japanese corporations, why is it still important for foreign managers to understand something of the history and the context in which Japanese businesses have evolved?**

Whether competing with Japanese businesses, collaborating with them, or working for them, their current practices and their distinctive strengths and weaknesses are the result of their historical development in the political, economic, and social context of Japan. Their past is also the clue to their current restructuring, why it is necessary, and why it is not a quick and simple process. Managers in firms looking to enter the Japanese

▶

market need to know about the broader context of Japan because this provides insights into the role of government agencies, the business infrastructure, *keiretsu* networks, business etiquette, the culturally influenced preferences of customers, and the many other differences and difficulties that require adaptation. Japanese firms are a product of this unique environment and relatively few have broken away from their dependence on Japan's domestic market, and most retain elements of traditional Japanese management practices. Foreign managers will better understand the strategic options and organizational challenges they face in alliances, joint ventures, and M&As with Japanese companies if they know something of their home environment.

Several studies, including one by Michael Porter and colleagues, have examined the ongoing changes in Japan and analyzed the challenges facing Japanese managers, to suggest the following guidelines for transforming the Japanese company:[28]

- *Create distinctive, long-term strategies.* Rather than imitating close rivals, break out of the consensus and do something different.

- *Expand the focus of operational effectiveness.* That is, improve office-level productivity as well as plant-level efficiency.

- *Learn the role of industry strategy in structure.* Among a number of strategic changes, firms should avoid getting locked into price-based rivalry.

- *Shift the goal from growth to profitability.* Focusing on market share was only possible with "patient capital" (linked to *keiretsu* and traditional capital markets); shareholder pressure will push for performance-related rewards.

- *Reverse unrelated diversification.* Pare down to your core competencies and let other firms do the rest.

- *Update the Japanese organizational model.* Change internal practices away from hierarchy and consensus toward meritocracy and entrepreneurship.

- *Move away from incremental change.* Become more flexible and responsive to suit the new competitive environment.

The few successful international Japanese firms, including Sony and Toyota, are seen as future models by many because they have adapted successfully to the new realities. In fact, it could be argued that their relatively high level of internationalization prior to the domestic market recession gave them the necessary portfolio of overseas markets and sources of inputs, the global scale and scope advantages needed to weather the local storms. Other firms have failed to adapt, often locked into cultural and institutional routines which were born out of the golden era of economic growth but which are ill-suited to the new realities.[29] Old habits die hard.

CONCLUSIONS

Japan continues in a period of fundamental political, economic, and social transformation. Corporations have been forced by a drawn-out economic recession to alter radically the way they organize and invest. Foreign firms are finding, despite the depressed state of the Japanese market, that there are unprecedented opportunities for alliances and takeovers involving Japanese firms and for introducing new products and services to Japanese customers. There is a new period of internationalization as Japanese firms shift investments out of Japan and attempt to reduce their dependence on local markets, while foreign imports, investment, and M&As are on the increase. Partly because of the significance of the new trading partner and rising power, China, this amounts to processes of regionalization rather than globalization.

Much of this chapter has looked at the traditional way of doing business in Japan, the unique capital markets, *keiretsu*, demanding customers, lifetime employment, and the traditional strengths and weaknesses of Japanese firms. The point of this is that these are enduring facets of Japanese business and they underlie the key distinctiveness that collaborators and competitors need to understand. They also continue to strongly influence the restructuring options open to Japanese firms and the changes in the economy as a whole.

James C. Abegglen, one of the most experienced Western commentators on Japan, sums up this tension between old and new in his book *21st Century Japanese Management: New Systems, Lasting Values.*[30] He describes how success comes from effectively combining the best of old and new. To do this requires some understanding of how adaptability can be promoted in the face of inertia. But it also demonstrates how any in-depth country analysis must take account of the way that distinctive local economic, political, social, and cultural characteristics have evolved in the past and will continue to influence *relative* business practices, markets, and competitiveness in the future.

KEY POINTS

1 The current strengths and weaknesses of Japanese firms result from their evolution in a highly competitive but continually growing domestic economy with unique socio-cultural foundations.

2 The Japanese business environment was traditionally characterized by strong interfirm rivalry; "patient" long-term finance, partly through cross-shareholding arrangements; *keiretsu* relationships, both vertical and horizontal; complex, multi-tiered distribution systems; demanding customers; and strong government intervention in the early years.

3 Socio-cultural factors that supported the Japanese way of doing business include ideals of obligation, loyalty, hierarchy and ritual, and a strong work ethic, linked to mainstream religion; a strong but conformist education system and "groupism" plus consensus-based decision making in general; and complex language and tacit forms of communication.

4 Japanese firms are traditionally loyal to employees, who tend not to move from company to company; hierarchical and bureaucratic but also consensus oriented; good at integrating between functions and teamwork; good at applied R&D and training; long-termist; and close to suppliers and customers.

5 The Japanese market has traditionally been difficult for foreign investors to break into, partly because of the factors listed above and partly because of the system of governance that tends to favor local firms.

6 Japan is changing. Growing social and political heterogeneity alongside a prolonged economic recession is creating unprecedented tensions and forcing drastic corporate restructuring. *Keiretsu* families are loosening or breaking up; firms are diversifying and divesting; lifetime employment is declining; capital markets are heavily restructuring; and deregulation is the norm.

7 Changes in Japan are creating investment, M&A, and market-entry opportunities for foreign firms.

8 The growing regional Asian economy is centered on the major trading partnership between Japan and China.

Key terms

- Ministry for Economy, Trade, and Industry (METI)
- Ministry of Finance (MOF)
- *amakudari*
- *chu and giri*
- *gaijin*

- *hai*
- *keiretsu*
- *kaizen*
- *kinyu*
- *zaibatsu*
- *sogo shosha*
- Mitsubishi *Kinyokai*
- co-prosperity pyramid

- *benkyokai*
- *nemawashi*
- *ringi*
- *endaka*
- Plaza Accord
- *shinjinrui*

REVIEW AND DISCUSSION QUESTIONS

1 List some of the factors underlying the competitive advantages of Japanese firms, developed during the rapid growth era of the 1950s, 1960s, and 1970s.

2 What kinds of social and cultural characteristics of the Japanese underlie their proficiency in manufacturing?

3 How do *keiretsu* structures promote process and product innovation in Japanese firms?

4 Why have inflows of FDI into Japan historically remained lower than FDI outflows?

5 How would a foreign firm wanting to establish a sales and marketing operation in Japan need to adapt to succeed?

6 Why has the economic recession in Japan resulted in outflows of manufacturing investment?

7 What have been the main advantages and disadvantages for many Japanese firms of relying on domestic markets rather than internationalizing?

8 How can we explain Japan's deepening trading relationship with China?

9 What has triggered the restructuring of capital markets in Japan, and what have been the effects on Japanese corporations?

10 How can an economy in recession present new opportunities for foreign investors?

11 What strategic and structural changes are many Japanese firms making in response to the changing economic and competitive environment they face?

12 Why have senior Japanese managers shown a growing admiration for some top foreign CEOs and management gurus?

REAL CASE

Renault and Nissan: no pain, no gain

In March 1999 one of Europe's biggest car makers, Renault, bought a 36.8 percent stake in Nissan, Japan's second-largest vehicle manufacturer. It has since increased its stake to 44.4 percent with Nissan taking a reciprocal 15 percent share in Renault. The alliance has deepened following the far-reaching changes put in place by Carlos Ghosn, installed as President and CEO of Nissan and now revered for having engineered a radical turnaround in the firm's fortunes. Although numerous alliances involving equity participation had taken place before this, notably the

Ford–Mazda alliance, the Renault–Nissan case was seen to be a highly unusual foreign "rescue" of a major Japanese firm in dire straits.

Nissan had made losses in six of the seven years prior to 1999, having been hit hardest of all the major car manufacturers in Japan by the decline in domestic sales and the rise in local manufacturing costs. Factory capacity utilization had fallen to 53 percent, and Carlos Ghosn, the new CEO of Nissan (known as "le cost-killer"), set out to cut 21,000 jobs, close five factories, and cut the number of suppliers in half. Close, *keiretsu* relationships with suppliers and distributors were traditionally seen to be a key strength of Japanese manufacturers (Nissan had formerly been part of the Fuyo *keiretsu*), supporting high-quality products, process innovation, just-in-time supply systems, and rapid, customer-led new product development. In a time of recession they represented an overextended supplier and dealer base, undermining profitability.

Internal restructuring also took place, following Ghosn's plan to introduce stock options and bonuses based on achievement and a performance-based promotions scheme, eventually for both employees and managers.

In the case of both external and internal reorganization there are significant clashes with the traditional Japanese way of doing things. First and foremost, job losses represent an enormous problem for managers and employees alike, almost a personal admission of failure on both sides which has social as well as corporate repercussions. The ties of obligation and loyalty associated with lifetime employment are broken. Indirectly, the breakdown of *keiretsu* links with other firms has a parallel effect, also resulting in job losses and the separation of long-term associations, which include personal friendships between managers and employees in both sets of firms.

Internal changes, particularly the introduction of performance-based remuneration and reward, are also radical in the eyes of the Japanese. Lifetime employment is associated with an age-related hierarchy where salaries only grow toward the end of a manager's tenure in the firm, as a reward for long years of service. To lose this reward, either because the firm no longer needs you or because the basis of remuneration is changed, is a drastic shift in the social contract employees entered into. Moreover, losing out to fast-track younger managers who rise up the hierarchy on the basis of their ability is not expected, particularly as talented managers may themselves have had to wait their turn in the past.

The steps taken by Renault change the rules of the game in Japan. Many would say that a sharp shock to push much needed restructuring was the only way. Renault's rescue was called for partly because of Nissan's accumulated losses, which could no longer be supported in a recession, particularly by investors who could no longer afford to ride

the storm in a time when capital markets were tightening significantly. But it was also needed because of the inherent problems Japanese managers face in trying to drive such radical restructuring themselves. The senior managers responsible for six years of losses are still in charge alongside Ghosn, having "saved face" because an outsider (a *gaijin*) forced the radical steps needed to turn the company around. Without this outside shock many Japanese firms remain locked in to a certain way of doing things because forcing these kinds of changes from the inside on one's work colleagues and friends appears to be too costly. It threatens to destroy the social as well as the business fabric on which the country's impressive historic growth has been founded, and most Japanese do not want to be responsible for this kind of destruction, however creative it might be.

The Renault–Nissan alliance is now heralded as one of the most successful in the business. In the first few years Nissan's $13 billion debt was substantially reduced and it achieved $2.3 billion profits in 2002. The market capitalization of Renault increased three-fold and for Nissan more than four-fold. The combined companies were the third-largest global auto maker in terms of unit sales with a market share of 9 percent since 2009.

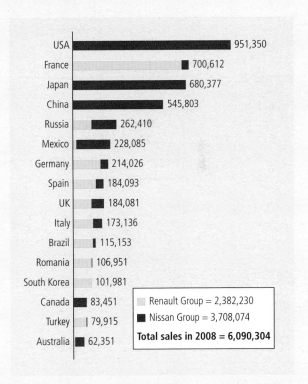

Figure 18.6 The global distribution of Renault and Nissan sales (main markets), 2008

Source: Renault–Nissan alliance facts and figures 2007, www.renault.com/renault_com/en/main.

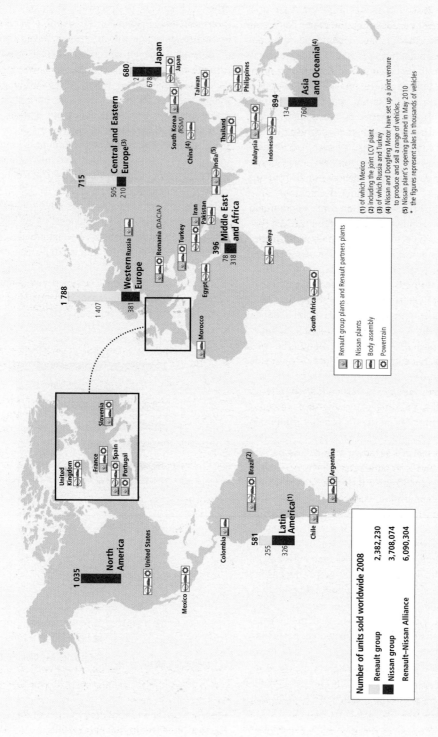

Figure 18.7 Renault–Nissan alliance combined worldwide sales and production sites

Source: Renault–Nissan Alliance Facts and Figures 2008, www.renault.com/renault_com/en/main, www.renault.com/renault_com/en/main/10_GROOPE_RENAULT/_51_Alliance/index.aspx.

On reflection, it represents the combination of two very different organizations, structurally and culturally. Renault was a strongly home-region-oriented firm, heavily dependent on its home economy, France. Alone it was relatively small, holding just 4.2 percent of the global market, but vying with Volkswagen for European market leadership. Nissan was one of the unusual bi-regional auto firms, with strong sales in the United States and a relatively good market position in countries outside the triad regions. The bar chart in Figure 18.6, together with Figure 18.7, shows the individual and combined sales of both firms. These are similar-sized firms with very different geographic footprints that complement each other well. Indeed, for the year ended March 31, 2011, Nissan revenue grew 27 percent compared to 2010 and it achieved a record high of US$102,380 million in the past five years. Renault SA's revenue was US$51,611 million for the year ended December 31, 2010. In contrast to Nissan, Renault SA's revenues have been flat and even declined in the past five years.

A similar pattern of differentiation is true for production. Nissan manufactures just over half of its vehicles in Japan with most of the rest spread fairly evenly among the United States, Mexico, and the UK. It has industrial operations in 19 countries, including manufacturing sites in Taiwan, South Africa, Thailand, the Philippines, and Indonesia. Renault manufactures in 17 countries but makes over 55 percent of its vehicles in France and most of the rest in Europe (see Figure 18.7).

Driven by an alliance board, chaired by the CEO of Renault, the two firms have developed shared production facilities in Mexico, Brazil, and Spain; common engineering platforms for entry-level B segment and mid-level C segment vehicles; common powertrain parts and increased sharing of engines and transmissions; and increasingly integrated IT, information, and communications systems.

Renault's competencies in marketing, design, and financing complement Nissan's capabilities in engineering and manufacturing processes. Synergies are enhanced through the exchange of personnel. About 50 employees from Renault originally joined departments such as supplier relations, product strategy, sales and marketing, and finance in Nissan. Similarly, around 50 Nissan employees began work in the areas of quality control, vehicle engineering, manufacturing, and powertrain in Renault. Beyond this, 250 executives from both firms were assigned to the permanent alliance structures, including cross-company teams and functional task teams, and a further 250 Nissan employees were part of the restructured European sales and marketing divisions of Renault.

Websites: www.nissan.com.jp; www.renault.com.

Sources: "Renault-Nissan Alliance Facts and Figures 2009," www.renault.com/renault_com/en/main; A. M. Rugman, *The Regional Multinationals* (Cambridge: Cambridge University Press, 2005); C. Ghosn and P. Ries, *Shift: Inside Nissan's Historic Revival* (New York: Currency Book/Doubleday 2005); A. M. Rugman and S. Collinson, "The Regional Nature of the World's Automotive Sector," *European Management Journal*, vol. 22, no. 5 (2004), pp. 471–482; R. Kelts, "The Cost Killer Cometh," *Japan Inc*. October 2003, www.japaninc.com; Renault/Nissan, *Annual Report*, 2002; V. Emerson, "An Interview with Carlos Ghosn, President of Nissan Motors, Ltd. and Industry Leader of the Year," *Journal of World Business*, vol. 36 (2001), pp. 3–10; A. Hamey and T. Burt, "'Killer' to Make Unkindest Cut," *Financial Times*, October 18, 1999; Pearson, *Renault Nissan Alliance 2004* booklet; http://www.renault.com/gb/groupe/alliances_p1.htm; Nissan, *Annual Report*, 2007–2011; Renault SA, *Annual Reports*, 2007–2010; OneSource, *Thomson Reuters*, 2011.

1 What broad economic and specific corporate pressures have resulted in the need for a radical shake-up of Nissan?

2 In the context of traditional Japanese employment and working practices and interfirm relationships, why are the changes being pushed by Renault's Ghosn considered radical?

3 What has accounted for Ghosn's success to date with the Nissan restructuring?

4 In what ways are the two companies better together?

REAL CASE

Canon Group

Few companies can claim to be truly global multinationals, but with sales, revenues, production, and employees distributed across the world, the Canon Group of Japan comes as close as any to fitting that title. In 2010, Canon's sales grew 23 percent compared to the previous year 2009 to a record high of US $42.225 billion in the past five years. 77 percent of its sales were generated outside of Japan.

The Americas accounted for 27 percent and Europe for 31 percent, with the remainder elsewhere, including other Asia–Pacific markets.

Canon operates in three business segments. The Office segment provides office network, color network and personal multifunction devices, office, color and personal copy machines, laser printers, large-sized ink-jet printers and digital production printers, among others. The Consumer segment provides digital single-lens reflex cameras, compact digital cameras, interchangeable lens, digital video cameras, ink-jet multifunction devices, single-function ink-jet printers, image scanners, television lens for broadcasting use, among others. The Industrial Equipment and Others segment provides exposure equipment used in semiconductor and liquid crystal displays (LCDs), medical image recording equipment, ophthalmic instruments, magnetic heads, micro motors, computers, handy terminals, document scanners and calculators, among others. Canon is dual listed on Tokyo Stock Exchange and New York Stock Exchange.

The company had its beginnings in 1933, when Precision Optical Instruments Laboratory was established to conduct research into cameras in Roppongi, Minato-ku, Tokyo. In 1947 the company changed its name to Canon Camera Co., and only in 1969 did the company take on the name Canon Inc. In 2010, the company had revenues totalling US $42.225 billion, up from $29 billion in 2003, and 196,074 employees, up from 103,000 in 2003. In contrast to its distribution of sales, 43 percent of its employees are based in Japan and just 7 percent in Europe, 7 percent in North America, and 43 percent elsewhere, predominantly in South-East Asian production centers.

Canon's international expansion started in 1955 with the opening of a New York branch. Initially, the company relied on sole distributors and established some in Europe and Latin America in the late 1950s and early 1960s. The sole distributor system was abolished in 1963 to make way for company-owned subsidiaries under the direct control of the Japanese headquarters.

International expansion goes beyond marketing to include production, research, and development. Taiwan became the site of Canon's first foreign production facility in 1970. Two years later the company opened a manufacturing plant in Germany. By 2001, the company had production facilities in all parts of the triad—Western Europe, the Asia–Pacific region, and North America. Nevertheless, the vast majority of Canon's production facilities remain in Asia, including Japan.

In 1990, R&D centers were opened in the United States, Australia, France, Thailand, and the People's Republic of China. Each R&D facility specializes in a specific product line and is coordinated by a centralized R&D lab in Japan. Together with its R&D strategy, this has made Canon one of the best world innovators and the largest holder of patents after IBM and Samsung.

Canon is organized regionally. Canon USA oversees operations in the Americas. The subsidiary has its own marketing, R&D, and production facilities. Two companies oversee European operations. Together, they have two manufacturing plants in Germany and France, and R&D

centers in the UK and France. Canon's operations in Asia and Oceania, excluding Japan, account for the largest number of employees in foreign countries. Regionwide activities for the Asian market are overseen by the Canon Asia Marketing Group, but marketing operations in this region are fragmented into subregional or national markets. The South-East Asia region is the responsibility of Canon Singapore. Hong Kong has its own subsidiary that is also responsible for Taiwan and part of South Korea. The mainland Chinese market is the responsibility of Canon (China) Co. Japan's home market is still very important. Nearly half of Canon's employees are still working in Japan and companywide R&D is still centralized there. Canon Australia is responsible for operations in the Oceania region.

The firm spends 8 percent of its revenue on R&D. Canon finds not only new technologies, but also new methods of manufacturing products. Canon has been reorganizing its production facilities to take advantage of its global scope, selecting suppliers and production facilities across the world to minimize costs and decrease production time. As a result product design data can now be sent to plants around the world via computer. Information is translated through an automatic translation system allowing faster communication between subsidiaries. The firm is now using simulation technology to minimize the costly process of prototype production.

At a time when other Japanese and many other, large electronic companies are struggling to remain competitive, Canon's profits are soaring. The firm has been able to remain competitive by selecting those business lines in which it can be successful given its strength in R&D and production technology. The firm abandoned the markets for personal computers, typewriters, and liquid crystal displays to concentrate on cameras, printers, and copiers.

Studies suggest that one of Canon's key competencies is its global system for new product development. In particular it has evolved a number of organizational mechanisms for linking R&D and customer requirements globally. This is partly done through alliances and joint ventures in which Canon invests over the long term to derive the benefits of co-learning and joint resource development. Canon contributes its technological capabilities and supplier links and local partners bring expertise relating to local customer preferences, distribution, and marketing.

On the plant floor, Canon's high productivity increases have been based on cell production technology. Here, a small number of workers have responsibility for the final assembly of the product. This type of production not only increases the amount of a product being produced per labor-hour, but also ensures quality as it is easier to backtrack the production process of a single product. It also saves floor space. Since 1998, Canon has decreased the length of its conveyor lines by 12 miles (19 km). However, the productivity increases of applying and perfecting cell technology to its operations are reaching a limit and now Canon is seeking ways of integrating automation technology into its production process.

In 2002, Canon made the unlikely decision to establish a facility in Oita, Kyushu, Japan, to produce digital cameras. CEO Fujio Mitari's explanation is that "If we switch factories each time a place with lower labor costs is found, all investment in equipment is wasted. Instead, we should use our strengths in production, and manufacture products more cheaply than they could be manufactured in locations where the cost of labor is lower." Indeed, nearly 60 percent of Canon products are still manufactured in Japan. The company's long-term plan is to reach a balance between outsourcing and Japanese production. Mitari's position is that anything for which labor costs are more than 5 percent of production costs can be outsourced to low labor-cost areas, such as China, and anything for which labor costs are less than 5 percent of production—typically the more advanced technologically—can be produced domestically.

Website: www.canon.com.

Sources: Canon, *Annual Report*, 2006–2010; "Can Canon Keep Printing Money?" *Business Week*, September 5, 2005; "Hard to Copy," *The Economist*, October 31, 2002; "(Still) Made in Japan," *The Economist*, April 7, 2004; B. Bowonder and T. Miyake, "R&D and Business Strategy: Analysis of Practice at Canon," *International Journal of Technology Management*, vol. 13, nos. 7/8 (1997), pp. 833–853; H. Perks, "Exploring Processes of Resource Exchange and Co-Creation in Strategic Partnering for New Product Development," *International Journal of Innovation Management*, vol. 8, no. 1 (2004), pp. 37–61; OneSource, *Thomson Reuters*, 2011.

1 Explain why, over the course of Canon's internationalization process, certain functions have been moved or expanded to certain global locations.

2 Why has it been important for Canon to internationalize its R&D activities?

3 Speculate as to why Canon is so unusual in its degree of independence from Japan's domestic market, compared to most other Japanese firms.

4 How is Canon still fairly dependent on Japan as a home base?

ENDNOTES

1 This is a recognized approach in management theory. By examining the broader competitive environment within which firms evolve we can identify where specific differences and competitive strengths and weaknesses come from. Evolutionary theories of the firm (Peyton Young), contingency theory (Donaldson), and the theory of nationally bound administrative heritages (Calori et al.) all follow variations of this approach. L. Donaldson, *The Contingency Theory of Organizations* (London: Sage, 2001); R. Calori, M. Lubatkin, P. Very and J. F. Veiga, "Modeling the Origins of Nationally-Bound Administrative Heritages: A Historical Institutional Analysis of French and British Firms," *Organization Science*, vol. 8, no. 6 (1997), pp. 681–696; and H. Peyton Young, *Individual Strategy* and *Social Structure: An Evolutionary Theory of Institutions* (Princeton, NJ: Princeton University Press, 2001). See also Collinson and Rugman, "The Regional Nature of Japanese Multinational Business," in n. 7 below, which applies such theories to explain the limited internationalization of Japanese firms.

2 OECD, *Comparative Economic Performance in OECD Nations* (Paris: OECD, 1989), p. 66, http://www.oecd.org.

3 M. Fransman, *Japan's Computer and Communications Industry* (Oxford: Oxford University Press, 1995).

4 C. Nakane, *Japanese Society* (Tokyo: Charles E. Tuttle, 1973).

5 See http://web-japan.org/factsheet/pdf/EDUCATIO.pdf.

6 R. D. Pearce and M. Papanastassiou, *The Technological Competitiveness of Japanese Multinationals* (Ann Arbor: University of Michigan Press, 1996); J. H. Dunning and J. A. Cantwell, "Japanese Direct Investment in Europe," in

B. Burgenmeier and J. L. Mucchielli (eds.), *Multinationals and Europe 1992* (London: Routledge, 1991).

7 S. Collinson and A. M. Rugman, "The Regional Nature of Japanese Multinational Business," *Journal of International Business Studies*, vol. 39 no. 2 (2008), pp. 215–230; S. Collinson and A. M. Rugman, "The Regional Character of Asian Multinational Enterprises," *Asia Pacific Journal of Management*, vol. 24, no. 4 (2007), pp. 429–446.

8 Sir H. Cortazzi, *Modern Japan: A Concise Survey*, The Japan Times (London: Macmillan, 1993); M. Fruin, *The Japanese Enterprise System* (Oxford: Clarendon Press, 1992); M. Fransman, *The Market and Beyond* (Cambridge: Cambridge University Press, 1990).

9 L. G. Franko, *The Threat of Japanese Multinationals: How the West Can Respond* (Somerset, NY: Wiley, 1983); M. J. Wolf, *The Japanese Conspiracy: Their Plot to Dominate Industry World-wide and How to Deal With It* (New York: Empire Books, 1983); W. G. Ouchi, *Theory Z: How American Business Can Meet the Japanese Challenge* (New York: Horizon Books, 1981); P. F. Drucker, "Behind Japan's Success," *Harvard Business Review*, January/February 1981, pp. 83–90; E. F. Vogel, *Japan as Number One: Lessons for America* (New York: HarperCollins, 1979).

10 M. A. Cusumano and K. Nobeoka, "Structure, Strategy and Performance in Product Development: Observations from the Auto Industry," *Research Policy*, vol. 21 (1992), pp. 265–293; J. P. Womack, D. T. Jones and D. Roos, *The Machine That Changed the World* (New York: Macmillan, 1990).

11 M. Fransman, "The Japanese Innovation System: How It Works," *Science in Parliament*, vol. 49, no. 4 (1992).

12 Sandra Dow and Jean McGuire, "Propping and tunneling: Empirical evidence from Japanese keiretsu," *Journal of Banking & Finance*, vol. 33, no. 10 (2009) pp. 1817–1828; Takehiko Isobe, Shige Makino and Anthony Goerzen, "Japanese Horizontal Keiretsu and the Performance Implications of Membership," *Asia Pacific Journal of Management*, vol. 23, no. 4 (2006), pp. 453–466.

13 W. Dawkins, "Loosening of the Corporate Web," *Financial Times*, November 30, 1994.

14 Ikuo Takahashi and Helge Fluch, "Retailing in Japan: Overview and Key Trends," European Retail Research, vol. 23, no. II (2009); E. Terazono, "Cheap and Cheerful," *Financial Times*, March 15, 1994; "The Emporia Strike Back," *The Economist*, October 29, 1994.

15 JETRO, *Regulations and Domestic Costs Related to the Distribution of Imported Goods* (Tokyo: Japan External Trade Organization, 2005), at http://www.jetro.go.jp/en/stats/survey/.

16 See n. 10.

17 Collinson and Rugman, "The Regional Nature of Japanese Multinational Business," op. cit.

18 "Survey of Japan," *Financial Times*, December 2001.

19 Fruin, op. cit.

20 M. Aoki and R. Dore (eds.), *The Japanese Firm* (Oxford: Oxford University Press, 1994); S. Clegg and T. Kono, *Transformations of Corporate Culture: Experiences of Japanese Enterprises* (New York: Walter de Gruyter, 1998); P. Haghirian, *Understanding Japanese Management Practices* (New York: Business Expert Press, 2010); H. Miyoshi and Y. Nakata, *Have Japanese Firms Changed?: The Lost Decade*, (Basingtoke: Palgrave Macmillan, Palgrave Macmillan Asian Business Series, 2010); M. Sako, *Japanese Labour and Management in Transition: Diversity, Flexibility and Participation* (London: Routledge, 1997); E. Westney, "Japan," in A. M. Rugman and T. Brewer (eds.), *The Oxford Handbook of International Business* (Oxford: Oxford University Press, 2009); R. D. Whitley, "Eastern Asian Enterprise Structures and the Comparative Analysis of Business Organizations," *Organization Studies*, vol. 11, no. 1 (1990), pp. 47–74.

21 J. C. Abegglen and G. Stalk, Jr. *Kaisha: The Japanese Corporation* (Tokyo: Tuttle Publications, 1985).

22 Toru Yoshikawa and Jean McGuire, "Change and Continuity in Japanese Corporate Governance," *Asia Pacific Journal of Management*, vol. 25, no. 1 (2008), pp. 5–24; Toru Yoshikawa, Jean McGuire and Lai Si Tsui-Auch, "Corporate Governance Reform as Institutional Innovation: The Case of Japan," *Organization Science*, vol. 18, no. 6 (2007), pp. 973–988. The monthly report from the Teikoku databank for September 2004 lists a total of 1,119 bankruptcies and

$3,481 million in liabilities, http://www.teikoku.com/bankruptcy/2004/200409.html; M. Abe and T. Hoshi, "Corporate Finance and Human Resource Management: Evidence from Changing Corporate Governance in Japan," Dokkyo University and RIETI presentation, 2003.

23 Nobuyuki Isagawa, "A Theory of Unwinding of Cross-Shareholding Under Managerial Entrenchment," *Journal of Financial Research*, vol. 30, no. 2 (2007), pp. 163–179.

24 U.S. Department of State, 2011 Japan Investment Climate Statement, Bureau of Economic Energy and Business Affairs; http://www.state.gov/e/eeb/rls/othr/ics/2011/157300.htm.

25 B. R. Schlender, "Japan's White-collar Blues," *Fortune*, March 21, 1994.

26 David D. C. Chiavacci, "The Social Basis of Developmental Capitalism in Japan: From Post-war Mobilization to Current Stress Symptoms and Future Disintegration," *Journal of Asian Business & Management*, vol. 6, no. 1 (2007), pp. 35–55; Yoshio Yanadori and Takao Kato, "Average Employee Tenure, Voluntary Turnover Ratio, and Labour Productivity: Evidence from Japanese Firms," *International Journal of Human Resource Management*, vol. 18, no. 10 (2007), pp. 1841–1857.

27 Unsurprisingly, the evidence shows, in keeping with theory, that firms pursuing related diversification strategies are doing better than those involved in unrelated diversification. T. Ushijima and Y. Fukui, "Diversification Patterns and Performance of Large Established Japanese Firms," *Working Paper*, Aoyama Gakuin University Graduate School of International Management, Tokyo, 2004; H. Kim, R. E. Hoskisson and W. P. Wan, "Power Dependence, Diversification Strategy and Performance in *Keiretsu* Affiliated Firms," *Strategic Management Journal*, vol. 25, (2004), pp. 613–636.

28 M. Porter, H. Takeuchi and M. Sakakibara, *Can Japan Compete?* (Basingstoke: Macmillan, 2000); Panos Mourdoukoutas, *New Emerging Japanese Economy: Opportunity and Strategy for World Business* (Mason, OH: Thomson/South-Western Educational Publishers, August 2005); Arnoud DeMeyer, Peter Williamson, Frank-Jürgen Richter and Pamela C. M. Mar, *Global Future: The Next Challenge for Asian Business* (Chichester: Wiley, 2005).

29 Collinson and Rugman, "The Regional Nature of Japanese Multinational Business," op. cit.; See also: A. B. Keizer, *Changes in Japanese Employment Practices: Beyond the Japanese Model*, Routledge International Business in Asia Series (London: Routledge: 2011); P. Haghirian and P. Gagnon *Case Studies in Japanese Management* (New York: Business Expert Press, 2011).

30 James C. Abegglen, *21st Century Japanese Management: New Systems, Lasting Values* (Basingstoke: Palgrave Macmillan, 2006).

ADDITIONAL BIBLIOGRAPHY

Abegglen, James C. *21st Century Japanese Management: New Systems, Lasting Values* (Basingstoke: Palgrave Macmillan, 2006).

Aoki, Masahiko. "The Japanese Firm as a System of Attributes," in M. Aoki and R. Dore (eds.), *The Japanese Firm* (Oxford: Oxford University Press, 1994).

Aoki, Masahiko, Jackson, Gregory and Miyajima, Hideaki (eds.). *Corporate Governance in Japan: Institutional Change and Organizational Diversity* (New York: Oxford University Press, 2007).

Basu, Dipak R. and Miroshnik, Victoria. *Japanese Multinational Companies* (Oxford: Elsevier, 2000).

Beechler, Schon L. and Bird, Alan (eds.). *Japanese Multinationals Abroad* (Oxford: Oxford University Press, 1999).

Chung, C. C., Lee, S-H., Beamish, P. W. and Isobe, T. "Subsidiary Expansion/Contraction During Times of Economic Crisis," *Journal of International Business Studies*, vol. 41, no. 3 (2010), pp. 500–516.

Colcera, E., *The Market for Corporate Control in Japan: M&As, Hostile Takeovers and Regulatory Framework* (New York: Springer, 2010).

Collinson, Simon C. and Rugman, Alan M. "The Regional Nature of Japanese Multinational Business," *Journal of International Business Studies*, vol. 39, no. 2 (2008).

Delios, Andrew and Beamish, Paul W. "Joint Venture Performance Revisited: Japanese Foreign Subsidiaries Worldwide," *Management International Review*, vol. 44, no. 1 (First Quarter 2004).

Dent, C. M. *China, Japan and Regional Leadership in East Asia* (Cheltenham: Edward Elgar, 2010).

Dominici, G. *From Business System to Supply Chain and Production in Japan: Lean production and its roots in Japanese business culture* (VDM Verlag Dr. Muller Aktiengesellschaft & Co., 2010).

Dore, Ronald. *Stock Market Capitalism: Welfare Capitalism: Japan and Germany versus the Anglo-Saxons* (Oxford: Oxford University Press, 2000).

Dore, Ronald and Sako, Mari. *How the Japanese Learn to Work* (London: Routledge, 1998).

Dyer, J. and Chu, W. "The Determinants of Trust in Supplier-Automaker Relations in the US, Japan, and Korea: A Retrospective," *Journal of International Business Studies*, vol. 42, no. 1 (2011), pp. 28–34.

Dyer, Jeffrey H. and Hatch, Nile H. "Using Supplier Networks to Learn Faster," *MIT Sloan Management Review*, vol. 45, no. 3 (Spring 2004).

Furuya, N., Stevens, M. J., Bird, A., Oddou, G. and Mendenhall, M. "Managing the Learning and Transfer of Global Management Competence: Antecedents and Outcomes of Japanese Repatriation Effectiveness," *Journal of International Business Studies*, vol. 40, no. 2 (2009), pp. 200–215.

Goerzen, Anthony and Makino, Shige. "Multinational Corporation Internationalization in the Service Sector: A Study of Japanese Trading Companies," *Journal of International Business Studies*, vol. 38, no. 7 (December 2007).

Hasegawa, Y. and Kimm, A. *Rediscovering Japanese Business Leadership: 15 Japanese Managers and the Companies They're Leading to New Growth* (Chichester: John Wiley & Sons, 2010).

Herstatt, C., Stockstrom, C., Tschirky, H. and Nagahira, A. *Management of Technology and Innovation in Japan* (New York: Springer, 2010).

Ito, K. and Rose, E. L. "The Implicit Return on Domestic and International Sales: An Empirical Analysis of US and Japanese firms," *Journal of International Business Studies*, vol. 41, no. 6 (2010).

Jameson, Mel, Sullivan, Michael J. and Constand, Richard L. "Ownership Structure and Performance of Japanese Firms: Horizontal *Keiretsu*, Vertical *Keiretsu*, and Independents," *Review of Pacific Basin Financial Markets & Policies*, vol. 3, no. 4 (December 2000).

Jung, J. C., Beamish, P. W. and Goerzen, A. "FDI Ownership Strategy: A Japanese–US MNE Comparison," *Management International Review*, vol. 48, no. 5 (2008), pp. 491–524.

Kobayashi, Koji. The Rise of NEC: How the World's Greatest C&C Company is Managed (Oxford: Blackwell, 1991).

Kobayashi, Mami. "Ownership Structure, Shareholder Intervention, and Success in Takeovers," *Japan & the World Economy*, vol. 19, no. 4 (December 2007).

Kotabe, Mike, Martin, Xavier and Domoto, Hiroshi. "Gaining from Vertical Partnerships: Knowledge Transfer, Relationship Duration and Supplier Performance Improvement in the US and Japanese Automotive Industries," *Strategic Management Journal*, vol. 24, no. 4 (April 2003).

Kotabe, M., Mol, M. J. and Ketkar, S. "An Evolutionary Stage Model of Outsourcing and Competence Destruction: A Triad Comparison of the Consumer Electronics Industry," *Management International Review*, vol. 48, no. 1 (2008).

Liker, Jeffrey K., Fruin, W. Mark and Adler, Paul S. (eds.). *Remade in America: Transplanting and Transforming Japanese Management Systems* (New York: Oxford University Press, 1999).

Lincoln, Edward J. *Arthritic Japan: The Slow Pace of Economic Reform* (New York: Brookings Institution Press, 2001).

McGuire, Jean and Dow, Sandra. "The Persistence and Implications of Japanese *Keiretsu* Organization," *Journal of International Business Studies*, vol. 34, no. 4 (July 2003).

Nobeoka, Kentao, Dyer, Jeffrey H. and Anoop, Madhok. "The Influence of Customer Scope on Supplier Learning and Performance in the Japanese Automobile Industry," *Journal of International Business Studies*, vol. 33, no. 4 (Fourth Quarter 2002).

Nonaka, Ikujiro. "Redundant, Overlapping Organization: A Japanese Approach to Managing the Innovation Process," *California Management Review*, vol. 32, no. 3 (Spring 1990).

Nonaka, Ikujiro and Takeuchi, Hirotaka. *The Knowledge-Creating Company: How Japanese Companies Create the Dynamics of Innovation* (Oxford: Oxford University Press, 1995).

Park, P. T. Tae-Hoon. "Hierarchical Structures and Competitive Strategies in Car Development: Inter-Organizational Relationships with Toyota's First-, Second- and Third-Tier Suppliers," *Journal of Asian Business & Management*, vol. 6, no. 2 (June 2007).

Pudelko, Markus and Mendenhall, Mark E. "The Japanese Management Metamorphosis: What Western Executives Need to Know About Current Japanese Management Practices," *Organizational Dynamics*, vol. 36, no. 3 (2007).

Rosenbluth, F. M. and Thies, M. F. *Japan Transformed: Political Change and Economic Restructuring* (Princeton, NJ: Princeton University Press, 2010).

Rugman, Alan M. *Rugman Reviews International Business, Japanese Edition* (Basingstoke: Macmillan, 2009). [Translated and published in Japanese]

Rugman, Alan M. "The Regional Multinationals of Asia," in Y. Kuwana et al. (eds.) *New Frontiers in International Business: Essays in Honour of Kenichi Enatsu*, International Business, vol. 5 (Tokyo, 2008) [pp. 86–108]. [Translated and published in Japanese]

Thomas, L. G. III. "Are We All Global Now? Local vs. Foreign Sources of Corporate Competence: The Case of the Japanese Pharmaceutical Industry," *Strategic Management Journal*, vol. 25, nos. 8/9 (September 2004).

Whitley, Richard, Morgan, Glenn, Kelley, William and Sharpe, Diana. "The Changing Japanese Multinational: Application,

Adaptation and Learning in Car Manufacturing and Financial Services," *Journal of Management Studies*, vol. 40, no. 3 (May 2003).

Witt, M. A. *Changing Japanese Capitalism: Societal Coordination and Institutional Adjustment* (Cambridge: Cambridge University Press, 2008).

Witt, M. A and Redding, G. "Culture, Meaning, and Institutions: Executive Rationale in Germany and Japan," *Journal of International Business Studies*, vol. 40, no. 5 (2009), pp. 859–885.

Zhonghua, W. and Delios, A. "The Emergence of Portfolio Restructuring in Japan," *Management International Review*, vol. 49, no. 3 (2009).

WWW RESOURCES

Japanese Ministry of Economy, Trade, and Industry: http://www.meti.go.jp/english/

Japan External Trade Organization: http://www.jetro.go.jp

Japanese Ministry of Finance: http://www.mof.go.jp/english/

Chapter 19

NORTH AMERICA

Contents

Objectives of the chapter

Within NAFTA, the United States, Canada, and Mexico constitute a thriving economic bloc. More than 32 percent of all US trade is with Canada and Mexico; both those countries conduct well over 75 percent of their international trade with the United States (see Tables 19.1, 19.2, and 19.3 below). Since market access to the United States is fairly open and already well documented, this chapter will focus on the other two members of NAFTA: Canada and Mexico. These countries are very different from the United States and have distinctive business practices. Doing business in these countries requires just as much research and attention to institutional detail as doing business in the EU or Japan.

The specific objectives of this chapter are to:

1 *Examine* the nature of the Canadian and Mexican political and economic systems and their implications for business strategy.

2 *Review* the business environment with primary attention on the industrial, regulatory, banking and finance, and labor relations areas.

3 *Investigate* major economic opportunities that exist in Canada and Mexico and some of the ways of conducting business in these nations.

4 *Consider* specific institutional arrangements, namely, the United States–Canada Free Trade Agreement (FTA) and the North American Free Trade Agreement (NAFTA), which play an important role in shaping opportunities and the business environment in North America.

NAFTA

The North American Free Trade Agreement (NAFTA) came into effect on January 1, 1994. Over the years, it has been the subject of debate and frequent misunderstanding. For example, in the 2008 campaign for the democratic presidential candidate both Senator Hillary Clinton and Senator Barack Obama pledged to renegotiate NAFTA to add environmental policies and to help labor adjustment. Yet, NAFTA was the first international trade agreement to incorporate both of these issues. NAFTA set up an environmental commission to monitor the impact of environmental regulations on trade and investment. NAFTA also incorporated labor adjustment programs in the form of assistance for retraining and upgrading of individual worker skills.

What then is the actual nature of NAFTA and what has been its impact? While NAFTA is a complex international agreement, it only has two basic principles. First, all tariffs on trade in manufactured goods are abolished. Second, the principle of national treatment is applied to foreign direct investment. Together these two basic principles serve to help open the internal markets of all three countries to greater amounts of trade and investment. In other words, regional economic integration is fostered. Indeed, recent data indicate that Canada and Mexico account for about one-third of all US trade (these countries are the largest trading partners for the United States ahead of China, Japan, and the EU, see Table 19.1). Both Canada and Mexico have over three-quarters of their trade with the United States (see Tables 19.2 and 19.3).

NAFTA, however, is not a pure free trade agreement since many sectors are exempted from its provisions. For example, although tariffs have been abolished, the US textile and apparel sector is protected through a system of rules of origin. The latter serve to exclude garments assembled in Mexico from using textile fibers produced in Asia. In a similar manner automobiles cannot be assembled in Mexico and sold in the United States and Canada unless they have most of their components produced in North America. Similarly much of the US agriculture sector is still protected from Mexican competition. In the service sector (which now accounts for about 80 percent of all jobs in the United States and Canada) well over half the sectors were exempted from the principle of national treatment. For example, excluded sectors include all aspects of: health care; education; public administration; transportation; public utilities. This means that each country can enact discriminatory regulations to foster its indigenous firms and exclude foreign nationals from working in these exempted sectors.

In terms of environmental regulations, NAFTA is limited (under multilateral trade rules from the WTO) in its ability

Source: Corbis/Bettmann

to enforce US and Canadian environmental standards upon Mexico. However, NAFTA aims to harmonize environmental standards over time by requiring that Mexico set minimum environmental standards and improve its enforcement to match those of its neighbors within NAFTA. This process is monitored by a trilateral environmental commission headquartered in Montreal, Canada. Research on the environmental aspects of NAFTA by Rugman et al. (1999) showed that as US and Canadian automobile suppliers and specialty chemical firms relocated to Mexico under NAFTA, these firms built new plants which incorporated the high environmental standards (ISO 1400) engineered into their production processes. Thus, environmental standards in Mexico are being improved specifically due to NAFTA. Furthermore, each country retains sovereignty over its environmental laws, although compensation can be sought by a foreign investor if a change in such laws results in unfair economic loss, as assessed by the trilateral environmental commission.

As a result of NAFTA, in the last 15 years there has been a large increase in trade and investment across North America. The region has become even more integrated. Intra-regional exports in NAFTA now stand at 56 percent, up from 33 percent in 1980, see Rugman (2005). Why has NAFTA been so successful?

From the viewpoint of the United States it gains more secure access to the natural resources of Canada and Mexico. In particular, Canada has agreed to continue supplies of oil and gas exports to the United States even in times of economic disruption (in legal terms, existing contractual arrangements will be guaranteed). While Mexico did not incorporate such

Table 19.1 Direction of US trade, 1999–2008

	Exports to				Imports from			
	1999		2008		1999		2008	
Country/region	(billions of US $)	% of total	(billions of US $)	% of total	(billions of US $)	% of total	(billions of US $)	% of total
Canada	162.95	23.59	260.91	20.07	198.82	18.96	339.71	15.68
Mexico	86.38	12.50	151.53	11.65	109.49	10.44	218.08	10.06
Japan	57.73	8.35	66.57	5.12	134.00	12.78	143.35	6.61
China (incl. Hong Kong)	25.71	3.72	93.14	7.16	98.65	9.40	363.22	16.76
EU*	151.86	21.98	275.29	21.17	199.58	19.03	376.98	17.40
All others	206.04	29.83	452.53	34.81	307.86	29.36	724.64	33.45
Total	690.68	100.0	1300.00	100.0	1048.43	100.0	2166.00	100.0

* EU data for 1999 is EU15.

Source: Adapted from IMF, *Direction of Trade Statistics Yearbook*, 2000 and 2009.

Table 19.2 Direction of Canada's trade, 1999–2008

	Exports to				Imports from			
	1999		2008		1999		2008	
Country/region	(billions of US $)	% of total	(billions of US $)	% of total	(billions of US $)	% of total	(billions of US $)	% of total
United States	208.01	87.64	354.67	77.68	143.49	67.00	214.07	52.43
EU*	10.43	4.39	34.23	7.50	21.52	10.05	50.93	12.47
Japan	5.25	2.21	10.42	2.28	10.10	4.71	14.43	3.53
Triad	223.69	94.25	399.33	87.46	175.12	81.77	279.44	68.44
Mexico	1.02	0.43	5.49	1.20	6.26	2.92	16.73	4.09
All others	12.61	5.31	51.71	11.32	32.77	15.30	112.07	27.45
Total	237.33	100.0	456.54	100.0	214.16	100.0	408.25	100.0

* EU data for 1999 is for EU15.

Source: Adapted from IMF, *Direction of Trade Statistics Yearbook*, 2000 and 2009.

Table 19.3 Direction of Mexico's trade, 1999–2008

	Exports to				Imports from			
	1999		2008		1999		2008	
Country/region	(billions of US $)	% of total	(billions of US $)	% of total	(billions of US $)	% of total	(billions of US $)	% of total
United States	120.39	88.27	233.52	80.15	105.26	74.14	151.33	49.03
Canada	2.39	1.75	7.10	2.43	2.94	2.07	9.44	3.05
North America*	122.78	90.02	240.62	82.59	108.21	76.22	160.77	52.09
Western hemisphere†	5.19	3.81	21.86	7.50	3.79	2.67	15.82	5.12
EU‡	5.19	3.81	17.00	5.83	14.00	9.86	38.33	12.42
Japan	0.77	0.56	2.04	0.70	5.08	3.58	16.28	5.27
All others	2.43	1.78	9.80	3.36	10.87	7.65	77.38	25.07
Total	136.39	100.0	291.34	100.0	141.97	100.0	308.60	100.0

* Excluding Mexico.
† Excluding Mexico, Canada, and the US.
‡ EU data for 1999 is EU15

Source: Adapted from IMF, *Direction of Trade Statistics Yearbook*, 2000 and 2009.

energy provisions into its NAFTA agreement, it is clear that the United States now has more secure energy supplies from Mexico than it does from the Persian Gulf. Currently the United States has an option to achieve energy independence within North America if it chooses to increase investments in the Alberta Tar Sands and move away from oil imports from the Persian Gulf. Already the United States imports more oil from Canada and Mexico (27 percent) than it does from Persian Gulf (24 percent), see Rugman (2007).

The big gain for Canada and Mexico from NAFTA is better and more secure long-run access to the US market. What are the implications of this for Canadian and Mexican business? In Canada, a new set of Canadian businesses has emerged. These are successful competitors in the US market. These firms include: Bombardier, BCE, Magna (a major automobile supplier), RIM, Onex, and a set of large financial institutions including the Canadian banks. In Mexico companies such as Cemex and Carso Global Telecom have become major players in the United States.

Perhaps more important is that clusters of world-class businesses have developed in Toronto, Montreal, Calgary, and Vancouver in Canada and in Monterrey in Mexico. In short, the business sectors in both Canada and Mexico are being upgraded and modernized, such that these countries are creating new jobs for skilled and educated workers across the integrated geographic space of North America.

Sources: Alan M. Rugman (ed.), *Foreign Investment and NAFTA* (Columbia, SC: University of South Carolina Press, 1994); Alan M. Rugman, John Kirton and Julie Soloway, *Environmental Regulations and Corporate Strategy A NAFTA Perspective* (Oxford: Oxford University Press, 1999); Alan M. Rugman, "North American Intra-Regional Trade and Foreign Direct Investment," in Alan Rugman (ed.), *Research in Global Strategic Management, Volume 10 of North American Economic and Financial Integration* (Oxford: Elsevier, 2004); Alan M. Rugman, *The End of Globalization* (New York: Amacom, 2000, 2001); Alan M. Rugman, "Continental Integration and Foreign Ownership of Canadian Industry: A Retrospective Analysis," in Lorraine Eden and Wendy Dobson (eds.), *Governance, Multinationals and Growth* (Cheltenham: Edward Elgar, 2005); Alan M. Rugman, "Regional Multinationals and Regional Trade Policy: The End of Multilateralism," in Michele Fratianni, Paolo Savona and John Kirton (eds.), *Corporate, Public and Global Governance* (Aldershot: Ashgate, 2007).

1 How has NAFTA affected Canada?

2 Has NAFTA increased trade between the United States and Canada? Why is this?

3 How has NAFTA affected Mexico?

4 How has NAFTA affected the United States?

5 Does NAFTA include environmental laws?

INTRODUCTION

In Chapter 10 we saw that governments and the various institutions through which they wield their powers are important external factors in the international business environment. This chapter focuses on institutional factors in the North American market that must be considered when looking at the Canadian and Mexican markets. NAFTA has not abolished all trade barriers between the United States, Canada, and Mexico. There are still major impediments to trade and investment. Furthermore, each of the partners retains its own trade laws. A legal mechanism to appeal trade decisions exists, but this is a compromise position. In contrast, EU member states cannot use trade laws against their partners. So although NAFTA is a step toward trade liberalization, business decisions should not assume that "free trade" makes Canada and Mexico identical to the United States.

CANADA

With a land area of almost 3.6 million square miles (9.3 million km²), Canada is second in size only to Russia. Divided into 10 provinces and three territories (see accompanying map), Canada is so large that it encompasses four time zones. The French and British fought over the country, with control passing into British hands in 1763. Canada became a separate nation in 1867, although it did not fully repatriate its Constitution until 1982. Today it remains a leading member of the British Commonwealth.

Canada's economy

Canada's 33 million people enjoy one of the highest standards of living in the world. Consumer tastes and disposable wealth are very similar to those in the United States. Gross domestic product (GDP) in 2010 was about $1.564 trillion (2010 est.) and at current exchange rates. Over the last 16 years, the rate of economic growth has been in the 2 to 4 percent range. Canada has typically had a positive balance of payments, thanks to its food, energy, and motor vehicle exports. Its primary trading partner is the United States, which provided over 52 percent of Canada's imports and accounted for 78 percent of the country's exports in 2008 (see Table 19.2).

Canada's economic growth historically has been based on the export of agricultural staples, especially grains, and on the production and export of natural resource products such as minerals, oil, gas, and forest products. However, major secondary industries have also emerged; Canada now ranks as one of the top 10 manufacturing nations in the world. The service industry is also expanding rapidly, especially financial services in Toronto. However, the country still faces a major productivity challenge. For each hour Canadians work, they produce 5.8 percent less than their US neighbors.[1]

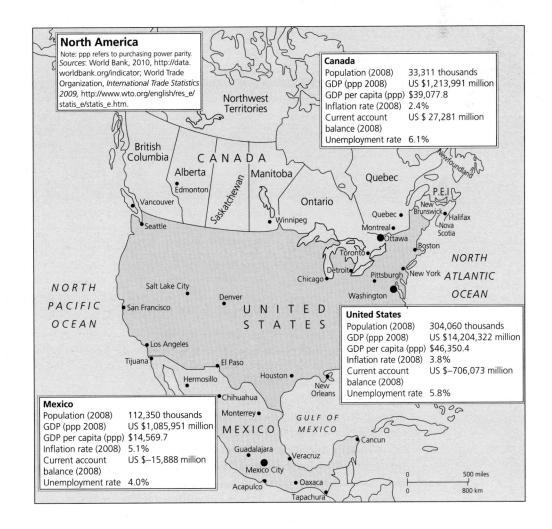

Almost 80 percent of manufacturing activity is located in Ontario and Quebec—including the entire motor vehicle industry, which is Canada's largest segment—while Calgary has become a major high-tech center.[2] Almost one-quarter of all Canada's exports (and imports) are in autos and auto-related products. The Canada–United States Automotive Products Trade Agreement (Autopact) has encouraged this two-way trade over the last 35 years, allowing free trade in autos assembled in either country, provided there was 50 percent value added in Canada. (Under NAFTA, the content provision rose to 62.5 percent.) Financial institutions and other business service industries are also concentrated in central Canada. The eastern and western areas of the country are more dependent on primary industries: fishing, forestry, and mining in the east; agriculture, ore, and mineral fuels in the west. The country's growth was helped by large inflows of FDI; today, 40 percent of the primary and secondary industries are foreign owned. Yet Canada is wealthy enough now, and its economy is sufficiently mature, to have substantial outward FDI, particularly in the United States.

The United States has more FDI in Canada than in any other country, including the UK. Since 1988 this investment has doubled, and in 2009 it stood at about $260 billion. At the same time Canada has invested $250 billion in the United States, more than in any other country.[3] We can see these relationships within individual industries. For example, many US airlines, including American, Delta, and Northwest, fly to Canada, and Air Canada and Canadian Airlines, which was merged in 2001, among others, have US routes. So part of the US international airline strategy involves competing with Canadian carriers that are vying for the US market (see the case **International Business Strategy in Action: Bombardier**). There are many other examples of Canadian investment in the United States. Canadian Pacific has purchased the Delaware & Hudson Railway, and Bombardier Inc. bought the Learjet Corporation of Wichita, Kansas. Many other acquisitions are even larger.

 Active learning check

Review your answer to Active Learning Case question 1 and make any changes you like. Then compare your answer to the one below.

1 **How has NAFTA affected Canada?**

NAFTA eliminates tariffs and makes it easier for efficient Canadian firms to operate competitively in the United States. At the same time, it allows efficient US firms to ship their goods into Canada without paying any tariffs and, in the process, helps drive down prices. So NAFTA helps the Canadian economy by encouraging efficiency, lowering prices, and opening up new markets in the United States.

Differences in the business environment

Despite many similarities between the business environments of the United States and Canada, there are also some important differences.

Canada's industrial climate

The Canadian economy is characterized by private enterprise. However, some industries, such as broadcasting and public utilities, are government owned or subject to substantial government regulation.[4] Over the past decade the trend has been toward privatization and deregulation. In fact, a federal government minister oversees privatization and has been responsible for selling companies that the government feels are no longer essential to meet public policy goals. Firms that have been privatized include Canadair, the deHavilland Aircraft Company, Canadian National Railway's trucking division, Fisheries Products International, and Air Canada.

Bombardier

In 1942 the dreams of a budding young Quebec entrepreneur came true with the incorporation of L'Auto-Neige Bombardier, the world's first snowmobile manufacturer. Although mechanic-turned-industrialist Joseph Armand Bombardier had great plans for his innovative transportation inventions, he could never have foreseen the course his company would take in the next 50 years.

Today, Bombardier is one of the world's top manufacturers of transportation products, with yearly revenues of $9.366 billion and 58,350 employees for the year ended January 31, 2010. Having begun with snowmobile production, Bombardier is now among the world leaders in commuter and general transportation trains, as well as transport vehicles for industrial and military use, sailboats, motorcycles, and, more recently, smaller aircraft. This extension into numerous other industries has transformed Bombardier from a once small-town Quebec company into a global market competitor and leader with over 90 percent of its total business now conducted outside Canada.

The company operates in two segments: aerospace (through Bombardier Aircraft) and rail transportation (through Bombardier Transportation). BA is engaged in the design and manufacture of aviation products and a provider of related services. BT is engaged in the design and manufacture of rail equipment and system and a provider of related services. It also provides bogies, electric propulsion, control equipment and maintenance services, as well as complete rail transportation systems and rail control solutions. BA's aircraft portfolio includes a line of business aircraft, commercial aircraft, including regional jets, turboprops and single-aisle mainline jets and amphibious aircraft.

Bombardier's success is due mostly to the industrious and timely business instincts of company CEO Laurent Beaudoin, who in the past 30 years has followed a strategy of market entry and product improvement through acquisition, instead of relying strictly on R&D. As a result, the company has managed to produce the most technically advanced, innovative, and reliable products on the market and gained substantial market share in many industries, especially with its rubber-wheeled subway car, sold to New York City in the 1980s.

This strategy has been exemplified by Bombardier's entry into the aerospace industry with the acquisition of Canadair in 1986, 12 years after diversifying into the transportation equipment business. The Canadair purchase brought the company a large pool of human resources and technical expertise, which has been applied to develop such "in-house" products as the twin-engine Challenger

Source: Corbis/Keith Dannemiller.

Business Jet. As a result, Bombardier suddenly held lead positions in numerous niche markets, which ensured ongoing relations with such manufacturing giants as Boeing and MacDonnell Douglas. This acquisition quickly resulted in numerous contracts for CF-18 fighters from the Canadian government and contracts for Airbus components from both British Aerospace and France's Aerospatiale.

Further acquisition was a logical step for the company. By acquiring Northern Ireland's Short Brothers, Bombardier extended itself firmly into the European market as a supplier and manufacturer of aerospace technology. At the outset of the 1990s, purchases of both Learjet out of Wichita, Kansas, and Boeing's deHavilland propelled diversification into regional jets and turboprop aircraft. Finally, production of the first-of-its-kind 50-passenger Canadair Regional Jet signified Bombardier's full-fledged entry into the airline industry. With the bulk of its profit already coming from this industry and the shared know-how, technology, resources, and markets of all of these companies pooled under one roof, Bombardier is ripe to become a major player in the aerospace industry through the millennium.

▶

Over the past 10 years, US and Canadian airlines have begun to try to improve their competitive positions through a series of alliances. For example, Air Canada has become part of Star Alliance, a collection of currently 27 international airlines—including United Airlines from the United States—that account for 21 percent of the global market. Similarly, prior to merging with Air Canada in 2000, Canadian Airlines had joined American Airlines and its code-sharing partners around the world in the Oneworld alliance. This is a result of a trend that is grouping the international airline business into several large alliances to compete against each other.

For the North American Airline market, this means an increase in efficiency. In 1993 US carriers were authorized to serve only 44 routes in Canada, and Canadian carriers had a mere 28 routes in the United States. A study at the time revealed that, if the skies between the two countries were allowed to open up, air traffic would double within the next few years. The study also estimated that the resulting increase in tourism and trade would generate $10.3 billion in additional economic activity. These statistics indicate why a new Open Skies agreement between the countries was enacted in 1995 that liberalized the regulatory environment for airlines in both countries. Since the establishment of Open Skies, transborder traffic has increased from 13 million passengers in 1994 to 20 million in 2000. Nonetheless, the 1995 treaty comes short of a full Open Skies agreement because of restrictions on cargo and third-country rights.

Since NAFTA came into effect on January 1, 1994, there was a further incentive to liberalize trade in services such as airline travel. However, under NAFTA's restricted transportation provisions, national treatment does not apply. This means that a US airline can do business across the Canadian borders only on a point-to-point basis, from, say, New York's La Guardia to Toronto. It cannot pick up any passengers within Canada. Similarly, Air Canada can fly from Montreal to New York to Miami, but it cannot compete with US airlines on the internal New York to Miami route.

Despite the lack of national treatment, Air Canada has doubled its flights to the United States and more than tripled its number of routes since the Open Skies agreement. Today, Air Canada handles over 40 percent of the Canada–US traffic and attributes close to 3,000 new jobs to the agreement. Air travel was further eased in 1998 by a bilateral agreement to facilitate pre-clearance of customs and immigration services. This will reduce double inspections by customs and immigration officers in both countries. The large success of these agreements has led both governments to negotiate similar agreements with other countries around the globe.

Website: www.bombardier.com.

Sources: Adapted from Alan M. Rugman, *Foreign Investment and NAFTA* (Columbia, SC: University of South Carolina Press, 1994); www.aircanada.ca; Air Canada, "Air Canada President and CEO Urges U.S. AirLine CEOs Towards Further Liberalization of U.S.–Canada Market," Press Release, December 13, 2001; Canada, Ministry of Transportation, *Canada Transportation Act Review*, July 18, 2001; Bombardier, *Annual Report*, 2010.

Small business is a major part of the economy and accounts for almost 80 percent of all new employment in manufacturing. The service and retail trade industries are characterized by a large number of companies that vary in size; 70 percent of Canadians work in service industries.

Canada's regulatory environment

Commerce and industry in Canada are regulated at every level of government: federal, provincial, and municipal. Many of these regulations are similar to those in the United States.

Competition

Competition Act
A Canadian federal law that regulates anti-competitive practices and prohibits actions that will substantially lessen or prevent competition; it is similar to US antitrust laws

Regulation of competition is under the jurisdiction of the federal Parliament. Legislation in this area was revised in the late 1980s to eliminate restrictive trade policies, stimulate production, and promote the international competitiveness of Canadian business. Although there are no price controls in Canada, there is regulation to review monopolies, acquisitions, and mergers. The regulation of anti-competitive practices is handled under the **Competition Act**, which prohibits individuals and companies from practices that will substantially lessen or prevent competition in the marketplace. The Act outlaws bid rigging, price discrimination, or conspiring to unduly lessen competition, and provides for regulation of acquisitions and mergers. If the purchase price is $400 million or more, the parties must refrain from completing the transaction for a time period ranging from 7 to 21 days. During this time the government reviews the situation and decides whether the purchase will prevent or lessen competition (using international comparisons) and thus be uncompetitive in nature. A ruling is then made.

✔ Active learning check

Review your answer to Active Learning Case question 2 and make any changes you like. Then compare your answer to the one below.

2 **Has NAFTA increased trade between the United States and Canada? Why is this?**

The data show that US–Canada trade has increased as a result of NAFTA. Three reasons can be cited. First, the elimination of all tariffs under NAFTA encouraged exports. Second, both countries are more likely to produce those goods and services for which they have a competitive advantage and to buy the others from their neighbor. Third, as the economies of the two countries grow, so will the amount of trade as each begins to adapt operations to the desires of the other and starts to tap this market further.

Exports and imports

Export permits are required for the shipment of goods having strategic value, such as uranium. They are also required to implement the provisions of various international agreements into which Canada has entered. Import documentation is also required, as well as payment of a goods and sales tax (GST) or the federal part of the harmonized sales tax (HST) except for items specified as non-taxable importations.[5] The GST, which went into effect on January 1, 1991, is a value-added tax. On imports, it is collected by Canadian Customs. GST (5 percent) is payable on most goods at the time of importation. Effective July 1, 2010, the HST applies in the participating provinces at the following rates: 13 percent in Ontario, New Brunswick and Newfoundland and Labrador, 15 percent in Nova Scotia, and 12 percent in British Columbia. The GST applies in the rest of Canada at the rate of 5 percent.[6]

Francization in Quebec

The Canadian federal government has a bilingual policy.[7] But in the province of Quebec, French is the official language for business and education. All firms employing 50 or more people in Quebec must use French at all levels of the organization. Other regulations related to the use of French in Quebec are that: (1) all product labels must be in French, and translations cannot be given greater prominence than the French portion; (2) company names and signs must be in French, but a version of the firm's name in another language may accompany the French version for use outside Quebec; and (3) all signs on the outside of stores must be in French only.[8] Moreover, all education, health services, and other services under provincial jurisdiction are delivered in French. Some exceptions to the French language and sign law policies accommodate the one-fifth of the Quebec population that speaks English. For example, McGill University and Concordia University can operate in English, and English signs can be displayed inside stores, provided they are smaller than French signs.[9]

Banking and finance

Banks in Canada offer a full range of financial services. There are six large Canadian chartered banks with extensive national branch networks that account for 90 percent of the nation's banking industry assets. There are also many smaller (often foreign-owned) banks.[10] All these banks respond to the actions of the central bank, the Bank of Canada, a federal government institution directly responsible for the nation's monetary policy, including (1) regulating credit and currency, (2) controlling and protecting the external value of the Canadian dollar, and (3) regulating the general level of production, trade, prices, and employment, within the scope of monetary policy.

In carrying out its functions, the Bank of Canada buys and sells foreign exchange and sets the interest rate charged to commercial banks. These functions are similar to those carried out by the Federal Reserve in the United States, which helps monitor the US monetary system. The Bank of Canada is also responsible for issuing the country's notes and coins and for managing the federal debt. Canadian interest rates and its exchange rate closely follow those set in the United States, especially in relation to non-North American interest and exchange rates.

Banks operate within the confines of the Bank Act. There are two types: Schedule A and Schedule B. Schedule A banks are Canadian owned and no shareholder has more than 10 percent of the voting stock. Schedule B banks are closely held Canadian-owned or foreign banks. These are allowed to carry on normal banking activities. However, foreign-owned banks cannot, as a group, own more than 16 percent of the total domestic assets of the Canadian banking system. Subsidiaries of US banks are not subject to this restriction because of the US–Canada Free Trade Agreement. In addition, Canadian banks are allowed to operate across the country.

There is also a host of specialized financial institutions that provide limited services throughout the provinces. Examples include savings banks, cooperative credit unions, loan companies, mortgage companies, and insurance companies. Investment bankers provide short-term funds to companies for acquisition or reorganization purposes.

Canada has four major stock exchanges: Toronto, Montreal, Vancouver, and Calgary. Toronto is the major exchange, accounting for approximately 95 percent of dollar trading volume. It is also the financial center of the country.[11]

Labor relations

Canada Labor Code
A federal law that covers areas such as wages, employment practices, work safety, and conciliation of labor disputes

Labor relations are governed by both federal and provincial labor legislation. The **Canada Labor Code** is the federal law that covers such matters as wages, employment practices, work safety, and conciliation in the event of a labor dispute. Provincial governments have similar laws to cover employer–employee relations at the local level.

Unions

With the exception of farmers, domestic help, and white-collar workers, the workforce is heavily unionized. Approximately 30 percent of the total labor force is in unions, compared to approximately 13.5 percent in the United States. Average paid employment (employees) during the first half of 2010 was 14.3 million. However, since union membership rose slightly more rapidly than employment, the unionization rate edged up from 29.5 percent in 2009 to 29.6 percent in 2010. As women experienced disproportionately more gains in unionized jobs, their unionization rate rose to 30.9 percent. The unionization rate for men remained constant at 28.2 percent. As a result, the gap in the rates between men and women widened further in 2010.[12] In some instances the workers are free to choose or reject union membership; in other cases they must become members in order to keep their jobs. The labor–management contract determines these conditions.

As in the United States, once a union has been certified to represent the workers, management must bargain in good faith. The result of such bargaining is a labor–management agreement that determines wage rates, fringe benefits, working conditions, and management rights. Economic nationalism is a strong component of Canadian unionization, and the unions have been major opponents of the FTA, NAFTA, and other economic and political relationships with the United States.

✔ Active learning check

Review your answer to Active Learning Case question 3 and make any changes you like. Then compare your answer to the one below.

3 How has NAFTA affected Mexico?

Mexico's progress under NAFTA will create a market for US goods in that, as the middle and upper classes in the country increase their purchasing power, they will turn more and more to the purchase of US-made goods. From cars to television sets to home appliances, Mexican consumers will be buying products sold by US MNEs. The sale of these goods will create greater interest in Mexico by US multinationals, which will mean even greater opportunities for US firms—and Mexican consumers. The elimination of tariffs under NAFTA ties Mexico into the North American regional triad.

Working conditions

All provinces have legislated minimum wage rates that are periodically adjusted. However, in most sectors wages and salaries are similar to US levels.

A national compulsory contributory pension plan provides retirement benefits to contributors, generally at the age of 65. This age limit varies, however, and there is growing pressure to relax mandatory retirement rules.[13] In addition, many private pension plans are in effect. Other benefits include group life insurance, medical insurance, and subsidized food and housing. Most provincial legislation limits daily or weekly working hours, with mandatory overtime pay for hours worked in excess of these limits. The government also mandates minimum annual paid vacations in almost all industries, which is typically two weeks after a year of employment and up to three or four weeks after longer employment. There are also legislated holidays, which, depending on the city and the province, usually vary between 8 and 12 days.

All provinces prohibit employment discrimination on the basis of race, religion, national origin, color, sex, age, or marital status. There are also provisions for equal pay for equal work, which vary across provinces. They are designed to prevent gender bias in pay levels. For example, Ontario has specific "pay equity" legislation that requires employers to remove gender bias in pay levels; salary adjustments were phased in, starting in 1990. Similar legislation has been enacted in a number of other provinces, including Quebec and Saskatchewan.

Investments

Investment Canada Act (ICA)
An Act designed to create a welcome climate for foreign investment by significantly loosening previous restrictions

The **Investment Canada Act (ICA)** came into effect on June 30, 1985, and is designed to create a welcome climate for foreign investment by significantly loosening previous restrictions. At the same time, however, some regulations still remain in effect. As noted earlier, investments in certain industries are restricted. For example, a license to operate a broadcasting station can be granted only to a Canadian citizen or corporation whose stock is 80 percent owned by Canadian citizens or Canadian-controlled corporations. Generally, non-residents cannot hold more than 25 percent of the issued and outstanding shares of a chartered bank, a life insurance company, a sales finance firm, a loan company, or a trust company. Nor can a single non-resident together with his or her associates hold more than 10 percent of the issued and outstanding shares of these types of companies. Limits are much less stringent in the securities industry, but the government must be kept apprised of such ownership.

Under the ICA, a non-Canadian wishing to acquire a Canadian firm must apply to the ICA for review and approval, if the assets are valued at more than $5 million or the business relates to Canada's cultural heritage or national identity. In the case of US firms buying Canadian operations, under the provisions of the Free Trade Agreement the ICA review takes place at the $150 million level. So the investment climate is much more conducive to US investors than to any others. When the ICA does conduct a review, a number of factors are considered in determining whether the investment will benefit Canada, including employment, technological benefits, and product innovation.

In addition, numerous provincial statutes place restrictions on foreigners seeking to invest in particular industries or activities. For example, in most provinces individuals have to be Canadian residents for at least a year in order to be registered securities dealers. Similarly, foreigners who are registering ownership of land must disclose their citizenship. In Alberta, British Columbia, Manitoba, Ontario, and Saskatchewan, a majority of the board of directors of corporations must be resident Canadians. However, an indirect takeover of a foreign-owned publisher will require that the firm be sold to a Canadian owner, according to the "Baie Comeau Policy."

Canada's multinationals

It is useful to identify Canada's major companies against the background of global competition and triad power. Some larger Canadian firms like Magna International and Bombardier are well known in the United States.

Table 19.4 ranks the 25 largest Canadian-owned companies in decreasing order of size measured by their sales in 2009. The largest firm is Manulife Financial Corp., which had revenues of over CAD $40.107 billion and is widely recognized as being one of Canada's most successful multinationals. With revenues of $24.831 billion, Onex Corporation is a global investment conglomerate that operates in multiple industries, including sugar refining, investment, telecommunications, and automotive parts. Other well-known Canadian industrial multinationals at the top of the list are BCE (Bell Canada Enterprise), Bombardier, Magna International, and Research in Motion (RIM, best known as a developer of smart phone BlackBerry).

Table 19.5 lists the 25 largest foreign-owned firms in Canada. These firms also contribute to the performance of the country, creating jobs and wealth for Canadians. However, all foreign-owned firms must be examined in terms of their relationship to their parent companies. A high degree of autonomy, or development of world-class products in Canada, is necessary for a foreign-owned firm to provide sustained benefits to the country. The Big Three auto companies have not done this. However, some energy firms, such as Imperial Oil (owned by Exxon Mobil), have a history of Canadian development, whereas others such as IBM Canada already operate divisions in Canada on a global basis. Others, such as Asea Brown Boveri (ABB), have a decentralized organizational structure with a large degree of local autonomy. These smaller but more autonomous Canadian firms (ABB is not on the list) have learned to survive within the global networks of their parent organizations, and their managers can help provide leadership to Canadians.

Another indicator of the nature of international expertise among these firms comes from the degree of their exports. Table 19.4 also reports data on the foreign sales of the largest 25 Canadian-owned firms. Exports from Canadian sales of subsidiaries in the United States and others offshore (excluding the United States) are shown. According to the table, these large companies sell approximately 50 percent of their output abroad. The foreign-owned firms in Canada (Table 19.5) also sell abroad, but information on foreign sales is not readily available. Nevertheless, the four companies that do report this information export about 65 percent of their output.

Table 19.4 The largest 25 Canadian-owned companies, by revenues, 2010 ranking

Rank	Company	Industry	Revenues (millions of Canadian $)	F/T* (%) (2009)	Intra-regional sales (%) (2009)
1	Manulife Financial Corp.	Financial	40,107.00	72.93	80.79
2	Royal Bank of Canada	Financial	38,143.00	41.00	86.58
3	Power Corp. of Canada	Financial	33,152.00	50.48	69.76
4	George Weston Ltd.	Food	31,820.00	2.18	100.00
5	Petro Canada, Calgary	Petroleum	27,585.00	19.68	94.95
6	Sun Life Financial	Insurance	27,572.00	58.42	90.28
7	Toronto Dominion Bank	Financial	25,421.00	31.95	89.92
8	Bank of Nova Scotia	Financial	25,064.00	40.00	64.36
9	Suncor Energy	Energy	25,036.00	20.78	94.95
10	Onex Corp	Electronics	24,831.00	37.30	62.70
11	Bombardier	Transport equipment	21,806.11	94.65	27.91
12	Magna International Corp.	Vehicles	19,815.74	77.00	46.91
13	Alimentation Couche Tard Inc.	Merchandiser	18,006.23	79.89	100.00
14	BCE Inc.	Telecommunications	17,735.00	n.a.	n.a.
15	Research in Motion (RIM)	Telecommunications	16,613.00	94.36	63.29
16	Bank of Montreal	Financial	16,067.00	30.00	94.52
17	Empire Co., Ltd	Energy	15,015.00	n.a.	n.a.
18	Thomson Reuters Corp	Information	14,829.57	40.76	59.24
19	Canadian Imperial Bank of Commerce	Financial	13,831.00	19.89	85.67
20	Brookfield Asset Management	Asset management	13,785.00	81.27	66.50
21	Enbridge Inc.	Energy	12,466.00	23.77	100.00
22	Hydro Quebec	Utility	12,344.00	n.a.	n.a.
23	Caisse de depot et placement du Quebec	Financial	12,023.00	n.a.	n.a.
24	Rogers Communications Inc.	Telecommunications	11,731.00	n.a.	n.a.
25	Metro Inc.	Merchandiser	11,196.00	n.a.	n.a.

* F/T refers to foreign sales divided by total sales.

Sources: Authors' calculations, individual company's annual report, and "The Financial Post 500," *National Post*, July 21, 2010. Data are for 2009.

E-resources: http://www.financialpost.com/news/fp500/list.html.

Table 19.6 shows Canadian-based firms ranked according to foreign sales. Manulife Financial Corp., Toronto and Bombardier Inc. have 72.9 percent and 94.65 percent of their sales abroad respectively. In addition, Power Corp's external sales are 50.50 percent. Research in Motion (RIM well known for its smartphone Blackberry) and Magna International have foreign sales of 94.36 percent and 77.00 percent, respectively. For these 25 large firms, the average ratio of foreign sales to total sales is 66 percent for the year 2009.

Table 19.5 The largest foreign-owned companies in Canada, by revenues, 2010 ranking

Rank	Firm	Industry	Revenues (millions of Canadian $)	F/T* (%) (2009)	Intra-regional sales (%) (2009)	Ownership (%)
1	Imperial Oil	Petroleum	21,292.00	16.00	n.a.	US (69.6)
2	Wal-Mart Canada	Merchandiser	17,500.00	20.00	80.00	US (100.0)
3	Husky Energy	Petroleum	15,074.00	41.30	98.50	Barbados (70.6)
4	Encana Corp	Energy	12,681.07	41.00	95.80	Widely held
5	Cenovus Energy Inc.	Energy	11,569.74	33.00	100.00	Widely held (50.0)
6	Novelis Inc.	Metals	11,459.30	98.00	19.00	India (100.0)
7	Costco Wholesale Canada Ltd.	Merchandiser	10,942.00	21.00	93.00	US (100.0)
8	Direct Energy Marketing	Energy	10,890.47	n.a.	n.a.	UK (100.0)
9	Honda Canada Inc.	Vehicles	9,400.00	52.00	32.00	Japan (100.0)
10	Ford Motor of Canada	Vehicles	9,098.00	45.00	60.00	US (100.0)
11	Ultramar Ltd.	Energy	7,317.38	n.a.	n.a.	UK (100.0)
12	Canada Safeway	Food	6,697.40	13.00	100.00	US (100.0)
13	Cargill Ltd.	Agriculture	6,500.00	n.a.	n.a.	US (100.0)
14	Best Buy Canada Ltd.	Merchandiser	5,551.84	11.00	100.00	US (100.0)
15	Home Depot Canada	Merchandiser	5,500.00	7.00	100.00	US (100.0)
16	Sears Canada	Merchandiser	5,200.00	9.00	100.00	US (100.0)
17	Toyota Canada	Vehicles	5,177.00	60.00	46.00	Japan (100.0)
18	ConocoPhillips Canada	Energy	5,018.10	n.a.	n.a.	US (100.0)
19	IBM Canada Ltd	Computer and office	4,877.45	62.00	n.a.	US (100.0)
20	Gerdau Ameristeel Corp	Metals	4,787.32	86.00	100.00	Brazil (72.0)
21	Nova Chemicals Corp.	Chemicals	4,621.05	71.30	78.50	Abu Dhabi (100.0)
22	Hewlett Packard Canada Co.	Computer and office	4,303.93	65.00	n.a.	US (100.0)
23	Aviva Canada Inc.	Insurance	3,473.41	n.a.	n.a.	UK (100.0)
24	Molson Coors Brewing Co.	Beverages	3,466.03	n.a.	n.a.	Widely held
25	Dow Chemical Canada	Chemicals	3,400.00	62.00	n.a.	US (100.0)

* F/T refers to foreign sales divided by total sales.

Sources: Authors' calculations, individual company's annual report, and "The Financial Post 500," *National Post*, July 21, 2010. Data are for 2009.
E-resources: http://www.financialpost.com/news/fp500/list.html.

This demonstrates the tremendous attraction of foreign markets for larger companies in a relatively small market like Canada's, providing further evidence that access to a triad market (in this case, the United States) is critical for success in a global market.

Table 19.7 combines the information in the three previous tables in a new way and reports the sales of the 50 largest firms in North America. There are five non-North American firms in the list in Table 19.7. These are firms from Europe and Asia. The largest foreign-owned firm is Royal Dutch Shell, and in 2009 it had sales of $94 billion in North America which represented 33 percent of its total sales. The other non-North American firms are BP, Toyota Motor, ING Group, and Honda Motor. Table 19.7 is based on the framework from Rugman (2005). It should be noted that all the North American firms in

Table 19.6 The largest Canadian-based firms, by degree of multinationality, 2010 ranking

FP 500 Ranking	Company	Nationality	Revenue (millions of Canadian $)	F/T* (%) (2009)	Intra-regional sales (%) (2009)
30	Novelis Inc.	India	11,459.30	98.00	19.00
41	Barrick Gold Corp.	Canada	9,283.17	97.00	34.20
11	Bombardier Inc.	Canada	21,806.11	94.65	27.91
17	Research In Motion Ltd.	Canada	16,613.03	94.36	63.29
48	Teck Resources Ltd.	Canada	7,674.00	94.00	18.50
52	AbitibiBowater Inc.	Canada	7,224.65	92.00	76.90
82	Nortel Networks Corp.	Canada	4,664.40	92.00	n.a.
36	Agrium Inc.	Canada	10,416.18	88.00	90.10
61	Domtar Corp.	Canada	6,235.56	86.00	90.10
23	Brookfield Asset Management Inc.	Canada	13,785.56	81.30	66.50
14	Alimentation Couche-Tard Inc.	Canada	18,006.23	80.00	100.00
13	Magna International Inc.	Canada	19,815.74	77.00	46.91
49	Fairfax Financial Holdings Ltd.	Canada	7,571.21	75.00	74.70
1	Manulife Financial Corp., Toronto	Canada	40,107.00	72.9	80.79
6	Sun Life Financial Inc.	Canada	27,572.00	58.40	90.28
40	Honda Canada Inc.	Japan	9,400.00	52.00	32.00
3	Power Corp. of Canada	Canada	33,152.00	50.50	69.76
19	Husky Energy Inc.	Barbados	15,074.00	41.30	98.50
2	Royal Bank of Canada	Canada	38,143.00	41.00	86.58
24	Encana Corp.	US	12,681.07	41.00	95.80
8	The Bank of Nova Scotia	Canada	25,064.00	40.00	64.36
7	The Toronto-Dominion Bank	Canada	25,421.00	32.00	89.92
18	Bank of Montreal	Canada	16,067.00	30.00	94.52
5	Petro-Canada	Canada	27,585.00	20.00	94.95

* F/T refers to foreign sales divided by total sales.

Notes: These data were compiled using only the top 100 Canadian companies based on revenues for 2009. The data for foreign sales are limited and some large companies that might otherwise be in the list might be excluded. Intra-regional sales stand for a company's home-region sales.

Source: Authors' calculations, individual companies' annual reports, and "The Financial Post 500," *National Post*, July 21, 2010.

E-resources: http://www.financialpost.com/news/FP500/foreign-sales.html.

Table 19.7 are actually from the United States; there are none from Canada or Mexico. This table illustrates how difficult it is for non-US firms to establish a significant market presence in the United States. However, as we go beyond the 50 largest firms reported in Table 19.7, there are more entries by Canadian, European, and Asian firms. This information can be obtained by examination of the annual reports of companies across the triad.

Multilateral agreement on investment (MAI)

Canada will benefit from any type of multilateral agreement on investment. An attempt to negotiate an MAI was made in Paris at the Organization for Economic Cooperation and Development (OECD) over the 1995 to 1998 period. The draft MAI was based on the lines of NAFTA. United Nations, UNCTAD Ministers may take up the need for an MAI.

An MAI includes the principle of national treatment: equal access for foreign investors to the host country's market (but according to host-country rules). A number of sectors are exempted from the national treatment principle. In the same spirit of the FTA and NAFTA, Canada insists on exemptions on health care, education, social services, cultural industries, and transportation. All regulations on investment are identified, as are all exemptions to the principle of national treatment. Additionally, dispute-settlement mechanisms are put in place to allow individual investors (and companies) to appeal against

Table 19.7 The sales of the 50 largest firms in North America, 2010 ranking

Company name	Country	North America sales revenue (millions of US $)	% of total
Wal-Mart Stores	US	302,599.00	74.13
Berkshire Hathaway	US	112,391.75	99.91
Exxon Mobil	US	110,998.00	36.80
AT&T	US	110,716.20	90.00
ConocoPhillips	US	101,291.00	67.83
McKesson	US	99,387.00	91.40
CVS Caremark	US	98,729.00	100.00
Bank of America Corp.	US	98,278.00	82.14
Cardinal Health	US	97,849.00	98.30
Wells Fargo	US	97,649.64	99.91
Royal Dutch Shell	UK/Netherlands	94,366.00	33.09
Verizon Communications	US	89,504.00	95.80
United Health Group	US	87,138.00	100.00
General Electric	US	85,100.00	54.20
Chevron	US	84,145.00	42.50
BP	UK	83,982.00	35.10
Kroger	US	76,733.00	100.00
Citigroup	US	76,686.00	70.49
J.P. Morgan Chase & Co.	US	75,790.00	65.54
AmerisourceBergen	US	71,789.00	100.00
U.S. Postal Service	US	68,090.00	100.00
Costco Wholesale	US	66,285.00	92.80
Home Depot	US	66,176.00	100.00
Target	US	65,357.00	100.00
WellPoint	US	65,028.00	100.00
Valero Energy	US	64,840.00	95.20
Ford Motor	US	63,687.00	54.10
Walgreen	US	63,335.00	100.00
State Farm Insurance Cos.	US	61,480.00	100.00
Toyota Motor	Japan	60,072.70	29.50
Medco Health Solutions	US	59,804.00	100.00
General Motors	US	57,327.00	54.81
ING Group	Netherlands	51,996.79	31.86
Marathon Oil	US	47,293.00	88.40
Lowe's	US	47,220.00	100.00
Sears Holdings	US	44,043.00	100.00
International Assets Holding	US	43,604.00	100.00
Best Buy	US	42,380.00	86.40
MetLife	US	42,065.00	88.50
Hewlett-Packard	US	41,314.00	36.10
Supervalu	US	40,597.00	100.00
Honda Motor	Japan	40,374.14	43.70
International Business Machines	US	40,184.00	41.50
Boeing	US	39,991.00	58.50
Lockheed Martin	US	39,224.05	86.80
Freddie Mac	US	37,614.00	100.00
Wesfarmers	US	37,466.00	100.00
American International Group (AIG)	US	37,228.00	38.80
Johnson & Johnson	US	36,045.00	58.20
Archer Daniels Midland	US	35,485.00	51.30

Note: Ranking is by sales in North America as measured by revenues. Data are for 2009.

Sources: Adapted from *Fortune*, July 26, 2010 and individual company's annual reports.

E-resources: http://money.cnn.com/magazines/fortune/global500/2010/full_list/.

government regulations and bureaucratic controls. The MAI helps countries harmonize their regulations, although in the areas of competition policy and tax policy not much progress can be expected (no progress was achieved in NAFTA).

The need for an MAI arises because foreign investment has become an important part of the global economy. Today, the majority of international business is not done by traded goods but through services and investments. More than 70 percent of North Americans work in the service sector, with only 30 percent in manufacturing. So the new agenda for international agreements is to negotiate rules for trade in services and investment.

Canada's outward stock of FDI is nearly 75 percent in the United States, with which it already has national treatment through the FTA and NAFTA. Thus, its exporting businesses would prefer an MAI with transparent rules.

Business opportunities in Canada

North American Free Trade Agreement (NAFTA)
A regional free trade agreement between Canada, the United States, and Mexico

United States–Canada Free Trade Agreement (FTA)
A trade agreement that eliminates most trade restrictions (such as tariffs) between these two countries and extends national treatment to foreign investment

Although the Canadian economy began to slow down during the early 1990s, the country still offers excellent investment and trade opportunities for foreign investors. This is particularly true for US firms, thanks to the US–Canada FTA of 1989 and its extension, the **North American Free Trade Agreement (NAFTA)**, which includes Mexico.[14]

The **United States–Canada Free Trade Agreement (FTA)** was designed to eliminate tariffs and most other trade barriers between the two countries.[15] Some of its specific provisions are:

1 All tariffs on US and Canadian goods were to be eliminated by 1998.

2 Most import and export quotas were to be eliminated by 1998.

3 Use of product standards as a trade barrier is prohibited and national treatment of testing labs and certification bodies is established.

4 Many restrictions on agricultural products, wine and distilled spirits, auto parts, and energy goods have been sharply reduced, if not totally eliminated.

5 The size of the government procurement markets that will be open to suppliers from the other country is slightly increased.

6 Travel by business visitors, investors, traders, professionals, and executives transferred within a firm is facilitated.

7 The opportunity to invest in each other's country is facilitated and encouraged through the adoption of national treatment.

8 A binational commission to resolve disagreements that may arise from the enforcement of the FTA has been established; it dealt with some 20 cases in the first three years of the agreement.[16]

Marketing in Canada

Companies doing business in Canada need to know the distribution practices and advertising and promotion channels. In many cases these are similar to those in other countries, but there are some important differences.

Distribution practices

Despite the country's vast size, sales to Canadian industries are characterized by short marketing channels with direct producer-to-user distribution. Many industries are dominated by a few large-scale enterprises that are highly concentrated geographically. It is not unusual for 90 percent of prospective customers of an industrial product to be located in or near two or three cities.

The consumer goods market is more diffused than the industrial market, and the use of marketing intermediaries is often necessary. In many cases complete coverage of the consumer market requires representation in a number of commercial centers across the country. Firms having only one representative or distribution point typically choose Toronto. If the country is divided into two major markets, the other is often Calgary or Vancouver. If the market is divided into three areas, distributors are frequently put in Montreal, Ontario, and Vancouver.[17]

Direct selling is another growing area. This includes the sale of goods from manufacturing premises by mail, home delivery, personal selling, and other non-retail channels. Direct selling now accounts for over $2.18 billion annually in Canada, with 11.2 percent growth in the past five years.[18]

Wholesale and retail trade are also important forms of distribution. Because of the wide dispersion of customers, wholesale trade is critical. However, retail trade is even more important and accounts for more than $393 billion in sales in 2010.[19] Independent stores earn about 88 percent of this, and general merchandisers, including department stores, make up the other 12 percent.[20] Quebec and Ontario account for about 61 percent of all retail sales, and in western Canada, British Columbia and Alberta make up approximately 24 percent of the total.[21] Department stores and supermarkets constitute a large percentage of retail sales. However, as in the United States, they are facing increased competition from discount food stores, showroom retailing, and other forms of self-service retailing. There are also specialized markets for recreation and leisure equipment and associated services, as well as a growing demand for consumer durables. These trends are likely to continue well into the future.

Advertising and promotion

Media used for advertising in Canada include television, radio, newspapers, and magazines. Television and radio advertising are particularly popular because 97 percent of all Canadian households have at least one television, and 99 percent have at least one radio. Hundreds of private firms operate cable television and major broadcasting stations in metropolitan areas, and the country has more than 1,300 television stations and 550 cable television systems, with over 50 percent of the population hooked into a cable system. In addition, the Canadian Broadcasting Corporation (CBC) operates two national television networks, one in English and one in French. There are 1,400 licensed AM and FM radio stations.

More than 100 daily newspapers are published in Canada and are widely used by advertisers, as are trade magazines directed at specific industries such as computers, real estate, banking, and retailing. General interest Canadian magazines such as *Reader's Digest*, *L'actualité*, and *Quest* have raised their share of net advertising expenditures in Canadian periodicals to about 30 percent, approaching the advertising of national newspapers. Two business newspapers, *The National Post* (*Financial Post* section) and *The Globe and Mail* (*Report on Business* section), also are widely read in the business and financial community. More than 450 advertising agencies in Canada can be of assistance in developing advertising and promotion campaigns.

Exporting

One of the most popular ways of doing business in Canada is through exports. As noted earlier, Canada is the United States' largest foreign market. Every year Canadians buy as much US goods as do all the member nations of the EU combined. In fact, over 20 percent of all US exports go to Canada. In recent years the Canadian government has simplified the process for shipping goods into the country. This is particularly true for products coming from the United States, since duties have been eliminated, thanks to the FTA and NAFTA.

✔ Active learning check

Review your answer to Active Learning Case question 4 and make any changes you like. Then compare your answer to the one below.

4 **How has NAFTA affected the United States?**

NAFTA will lead to an increase in trade in the region for three reasons. First, the elimination of all tariffs will encourage exports. Second, all three countries are more likely to specialize in producing those goods and services for which they have a competitive advantage and, in turn, buy the others from their neighbors. Third, as the economies of the member countries grow, so will the amount of trade as each begins to adapt operations to the desires of the other and starts to tap this market. Furthermore, the United States has more secure access to energy and other vital natural resources from Canada and Mexico.

Franchising

Canada is the dominant foreign market for US franchisers. Currently more than 300 US franchise firms operate approximately 10,000 franchise units in Canada. A recent report by *Entrepreneur* magazine rated more than 1,100 US franchises, and of those in the top 10, 8 indicated they were seeking to establish franchises in Canada. Thus, there is a great deal of opportunity for those who want to do business in Canada via the franchise route.

Additionally, in recent years Canadian banks have become more responsive to the needs of franchised operations. Chartered banks now offer various loans and repayment plans for franchises. In some cases they also offer payroll and cash management services. So there is considerable opportunity in international franchise operations in Canada.

MEXICO

With a land area of approximately 760,000 square miles (1.9 million km^2), Mexico is equal in size to almost 25 percent of the contiguous United States. It is the third-largest nation in Latin America and has a population of over 112 million. The country is a federal democratic republic divided into 31 states and the Federal District (Mexico City). Although it endured political turmoil early in the twentieth century and recent drug war in the twenty first century, the government has been stable since World War II. Mexico is a nation where affluence, poverty, natural splendour and urban blight rub shoulders.[22]

Mexico's economy

Mexico's economy is currently in a state of flux, brought on by new economic relations with the United States. Today Mexico has the strongest economy in Latin America. One of the primary reasons has been the economic policies of Carlos Salinas, who, after becoming president in 1988, introduced liberalization rules regarding foreign investment and privatization. These changes have dramatically improved the economy. GDP growth in 1996 was 5.1 percent, but inflation continued to remain in the range of 25 percent. The GDP growth rate was 6.5 percent 5 percent respectively for 2009 and 2010, but inflation had also been reduced to 4.1 percent.[23] The country has also vigorously promoted exports, especially to the United States, which now counts on Mexico for 25 percent of all imported fruit and vegetables. The *maquiladora* industry (see Chapter 10) is another growing source of economic strength for the country.[24] At the same time, Mexico has become a major region for international investment. In the first six months of 2010 Foreign direct investment climbed nearly 30 per cent compared to a year earlier.

MNE investment

The climate for foreign investment in Mexico has grown increasingly favorable in recent years. Although there were strict controls on foreign investment during the 1970s, regulations introduced in 1989 reversed many of these restrictions. As a result, an increasing number of MNEs are investing in Mexico. Nissan invested $1 billion in a new assembly plant to produce cars for export to both the United States and Japan; Volkswagen invested $950 million to expand its plant; Sears Roebuck put $150 million into new stores and malls throughout the country, in addition to renovating older units; Wal-Mart purchased Cifra, a successful Mexican retailer; and PepsiCo expanded its snack business by purchasing a majority stake in Gamesa, Mexico's largest cookie maker.

One of the major reasons for the increase in FDI is the privatization campaign that began in 1982 and that has picked up speed since then. By 2000, the number of state-owned enterprises had decreased to 200 from 1,000 prior to 1982.[25] The government continues to play a major role in the economy, primarily through state-owned entities such as the giant oil firm Pemex, but there has been significant reduction in its ownership. These sales have been made to both foreign companies and Mexican investors.

Another reason for increased FDI has been the changes in investment laws that now permit foreigners to hold major equity positions. In the past, foreign ownership in auto parts companies had been limited to 40 percent of equity, but a new decree now sharply reduces the number of firms subject to this law by creating exemptions based on percentages of export sales and sales to individuals. Today, approximately 80 percent of the economy is open to full foreign ownership.[26]

Labor

Labor is relatively plentiful and inexpensive. However, MNEs report a serious shortage of skilled labor and managerial personnel, particularly at the middle and upper levels of the organization, and despite numerous engineers. Worker absenteeism in recent years has declined, but turnover remains a serious problem, even in the *maquiladora* sector.

Approximately 40 percent of the total workforce is unionized. In industrial operations with more than 25 workers, about 80 percent of the workforce is in unions. Union control over the members has weakened in recent years, and this trend is likely to continue. However, strikes are not uncommon.

There is a three-tier minimum wage structure in Mexico, but increases have not kept up with the cost of living. The minimum wage in Mexican Peso in Mexico City and surrounding towns in 2011 is 59.82 per day (Zone A, including Baja California, Federal District, State of Mexico and large cities), compared to 58.13 Pesos (Zone B, including Sonora, Nuevo Leon, Tamaulipas, Veracruz, and Jalisco) in many other large cities and 56.70 Pesos (Zone C in the rest of the country).[27]

Government regulations require that at least 90 percent of a firm's skilled and unskilled workers be Mexican nationals, and employers must favor Mexicans over foreigners and union personnel over non-union personnel. On the other hand, these regulations are unlikely to limit investment by MNEs since the government permits hiring exceptions.

Mexico and NAFTA

In conjunction with their privatization policies, Mexico sought to motivate business through increased exposure to international competitive forces and access to the dynamic US market.[28] To this end, the government opened negotiations with the US and Canadian governments in Toronto on June 12, 1991, to create NAFTA. This marked the first time that a less developed country had entered into an agreement with two wealthy countries to create a free trade area. NAFTA went into effect on January 1, 1994, and has had a major impact on Mexico's trade and investment.

Trade in several sectors has experienced considerable growth. In the textile and apparel sectors, quotas on Mexican products were phased out and customs duties on all textile and apparel products were eliminated. For automotive products, Mexico immediately reduced its tariffs on cars and light trucks by 50 percent and pledged to eliminate the remaining duties over 10 years. In agriculture, tariff restrictions were lifted on a broad range of goods when NAFTA went into effect.

Mexico's investment climate has also been affected by NAFTA. In the automotive sector, all investment restrictions were eliminated. In transportation, Mexico allowed 49 percent ownership of cars and trucking companies three years after NAFTA went into effect, 51 percent after 10 years, and 100 percent after 10 years. The Mexican finance and insurance sectors have also been liberalized. All these changes have opened up Mexico even more to FDI and, in turn, led to the growth of the Mexican economy and two-way flows of trade and investment with the United States.

As with the US–Canada FTA, binational panels play an important role in resolving trade disputes. Under NAFTA, panels continue to contribute toward trade disputes resolution and now also investment matters. Where investments are concerned, complainants may also take their cases to binding investor–state arbitration.

Regional trade agreements

Latin American Integration Association (LAIA)
A free trade group formed to reduce intra-regional trade barriers and to promote regional economic cooperation; Argentina, Bolivia, Brazil, Chile, Colombia, Ecuador, Mexico, Paraguay, Peru, Uruguay, and Venezuela are all members

Other developments involving Mexico as a leader in the movement toward free trade and privatization have included the efforts to create and sustain regional trade agreements based on NAFTA. One of the major regional integration efforts has been the creation of the **Latin American Integration Association (LAIA)**, a free trade group formed in 1980 to reduce intra-regional trade barriers and promote regional economic cooperation. Argentina, Bolivia, Brazil, Chile, Colombia, Ecuador, Mexico, Paraguay, Peru, Uruguay, and Venezuela are all members. The primary objective of LAIA is to create a Latin American common market. In recent years, its slow process toward economic integration has led some members to create subregional groups. For example, in the southern cone, Argentina, Brazil, Paraguay, and Uruguay have established a common market called **Mercosur**, which was operational by 1996. In the north, Mexico, Colombia, and Venezuela have a similar agreement, and via NAFTA Mexico is likely to be a key bridge between Latin American countries and the United States. NAFTA has a clause permitting accession of other countries. A second major integration effort is the **Andean common market (Ancom)**, a subregional free trade compact designed to promote economic and social integration and cooperation.[29] Bolivia, Colombia, Ecuador, Peru, and Venezuela are all members.

Mercosur
A subregional free trade group formed to promote economic cooperation; the group consists of Argentina, Brazil, Paraguay, and Uruguay

Andean common market (Ancom)
A subregional free trade compact designed to promote economic and social integration and cooperation; Bolivia, Colombia, Ecuador, and Peru are all members

Enterprise for the Americas
An idea launched by President George Bush to create a free trade area from Alaska to Argentine Antarctica

In 1990, US President George Bush launched his **Enterprise for the Americas**, which is aimed at creating an all-American free trade area from Alaska to Argentine Antarctica. The **Free Trade Area of the Americas (FTAA)** that is presently being negotiated by 34 countries would achieve the main objectives of continental integration.[30] If such an idea comes to fruition, it will eliminate the need for LAIA, Ancom, and similar Latin American

Free Trade Area of the Americas (FTAA)
A regional trade agreement that is expected to succeed NAFTA and includes 34 countries across North, Central, and South America

trade agreements. The United States is aware of the need for reducing, and then eliminating, trade barriers in the Americas if it hopes to establish a viable world market that can compete against the European Union and the Asia–Pacific countries. The idea is also appealing to Latin American countries that see the opportunities associated with linking into the North American diamond and profiting from the economic growth it creates. This development will bring about a Western hemisphere trading bloc and may well become a reality in the early twenty-first century.

Doing business in Mexico

A number of strategic approaches are being used to conduct business in Mexico. (See the case **International Business Strategy in Action: Mexico and NAFTA.**) Two primary reasons for the success of these approaches are the high quality of the workforce and the dramatic improvement in the economy over the 1990s. MNEs operating in Mexico report that the quality of the workforce is excellent. For example, senior-level executives at firms such as Caterpillar, Ford, General Electric, IBM, and Procter & Gamble all report that their Mexican workforces produce high-quality output. Moreover, a Massachusetts Institute of Technology study has named Ford's Mercury Tracer plant in Hermosillo the highest-quality assembly plant in the world. The head of IBM Mexico has stated that "for every dollar you pay a Mexican engineer, you get more from him or her than you'd get in other societies around the world."[31]

At the same time, the market for goods and services is growing rapidly. Many MNEs admit that they are not in Mexico because of the low wage rates but because of rapidly growing demand. Despite a high inflation rate and loss of purchasing power, people want to buy consumer goods and live more like their neighbors to the north. Mexicans are also expressing an interest in high-quality merchandise, with the result that companies are now reducing their reliance on agents and dealers and are instead opening sales subsidiaries and warehouses to provide direct technical assistance. A good example is Toyota, which started a plant in 2005 to produce vans for the US market, but later in the year responded to Mexico's growing demand for vans by producing for the domestic market. With a burgeoning population of 106 million and an economy that is growing even faster, Mexico promises to be a major target area for MNEs in the future.[32] At the same time, these developments help Mexico link itself to the triad via the United States.

✔ Active learning check

Review your answer to Active Learning Case question 5 and make any changes you like. Then compare your answer with the one below.

5 Does NAFTA include environmental laws?

There are environmental laws in NAFTA, but these are still up for debate. There are issues of sovereignty. Should an international agreement set the standard for environmental laws or should the individual governments make their own laws to be responsive to their national needs? Although an environmental chapter was included in NAFTA, there is a growing concern among NGOs that environmental laws could be used as a non-tariff barrier to trade, keeping out some goods from the rich US market. Both the US and Canada advocate the use of clean technology in NAFTA and press for higher environmental standards and processes in Mexico.

INTERNATIONAL BUSINESS STRATEGY IN ACTION

Mexico and NAFTA

Many opponents of NAFTA argued that the agreement would lead to the export of US jobs to Mexico, with a resulting decline in gross national product (GNP). Economists, however, reported that the agreement would help save US jobs and that GNP would rise by $30 billion annually once the treaty was fully implemented. Recent research also found that the first five years of NAFTA had improved growth and efficiency in all three of its members. Certainly, MNEs in the motor vehicle and parts industry and the telecommunications industry agreed with the economists and have already formulated strategies to address these impending changes.

The US motor vehicle and parts industry expects to see some jobs go to Mexico. Moreover, the export of vehicles from foreign-owned factories in Mexico doubled in the three years after NAFTA. However, prior to NAFTA, Mexican government regulations forced US auto makers to buy Mexican parts, which in many cases did not meet global standards. This led Mexican subsidiaries of the auto makers to run plants at less than maximum efficiency levels. The government also forced the Big Three car companies to export more than they imported into Mexico. NAFTA has allowed companies to act regionally instead of on a country-by-country basis and to reorganize production more efficiently across North America. In an unexpected surge of events, some of the manufacturing previously assigned to Mexico is being brought back into the United States. For example, Ford relocated its production of Thunderbirds and Mercury Cougars from Cuautitlan to its assembly plant in Lorain, Ohio. At the same time, US auto suppliers are doing better because NAFTA requires 62.5 percent of a vehicle's content to originate in North America. This means that foreign suppliers in Asia and Europe are losing out to regional, high-quality firms such as TRW and Dana. Thus, NAFTA is proving to be a boon to the US motor and auto parts industry.

Telecommunications is another industry in which US firms are doing very well. Annual US telecom exports to Mexico are now in excess of $2.8 billion, and Telmex, the previously state-owned phone company, is 9.1 percent owned by SBC. In 2001, Telmex had 24.2 million phones wired in an all-digital network, up from 12 million in 1993, and US companies have supplied much of this new equipment. At the same time, some business customers in Mexico feel it is taking too long for Telmex to provide the service they need, so they are purchasing private networks that carry voice, data, and images by satellite.

Scientific-Atlanta, a Georgia-based firm, is the market leader in this area and has been able to land a series of large contracts for installing communication systems, including those for Cifra, the country's largest retailer, and for the Mexican Navy. Other companies likely to benefit from the growing market include McCaw, Cantel, and Motorola. As a result, US telecom firms appear to have found a lucrative market just south of the border.

Doing business in Mexico can take a number of different forms. Four strategies have proven particularly profitable. One is to establish a wholly owned subsidiary. This can be an expensive strategy, but it gives the company total control and allows management to make decisions quickly and efficiently. Quite often a local manager runs the subsidiary, and almost always the majority of the management team are locals. However, headquarters exercises key control.

A second approach is to become part of the *maquiladora* program. This strategy works best for firms aiming to export most of their output back to the United States. The *maquiladora* arrangement allows manufacturing, assembly, and processing plants to import materials, components, and equipment duty free, complete the work with Mexican labor, and then ship the finished products back north. Under recent changes in the arrangement, if the company wants, it can sell up to one-third of the output in Mexico and still participate in the program.

A third approach is the so-called shelter program, under which local contractors assume responsibility for all aspects of the manufacturing operation, from site selection to recruitment of personnel to running the factory. After a predetermined time, however, the US company can buy out the shelter operator at a preset price and take over the business.

A fourth approach is a joint venture with a local partner. This combines a foreign company with financial and manufacturing know-how and a local partner that knows how to market the output. A number of US firms have opted for this approach, including Ford, DuPont, and General Electric. In the last case, GE formed a joint venture with MABE, one of Mexico's largest appliance manufacturers. Since then, the two have opened a gas range plant that now produces 800,000 units annually for the US, Canadian, and Mexican markets.

In most cases US MNEs will decide in advance which of these four strategies to implement. However, some firms have discovered that the need for such a decision ▶

is unanticipated. Take the example of Pace Foods, which went to Mexico City to film commercials for its Pace Picante Sauce. The crew did not want to carry back the jars of Pace's hot sauce that they used in the filming, so they told a local store manager to keep the jars and try to sell them. A few weeks later the company got a call from the manager. He had sold all 350 jars and wanted to know what he should do now. Today Pace has a thriving business selling products in Mexico.

Websites: www.ge.com; www.ford.com; www.pacefoods.com; www.dupont.com.

Sources: Alan M. Rugman and John Kirton, "Multinational Enterprise Strategy and the NAFTA Trade and Environment Regime," *Journal of World Business*, vol. 33, no. 4 (December 1998), pp. 438–454; Alan M. Rugman, John Kirton and Julie Soloway, *Environmental Regulations and Corporate Strategy* (Oxford: Oxford University Press, 1999); www.ford.com; www.telmex.com.mx/; Joel Millman, "High-Tech Jobs Transfer to Mexico with Surprising Speed," *Wall Street Journal*, April 9, 1998, p. A18; Laurie P. Cohen, "With Help From INS, US Meatpacker Taps Mexican Work Force," *Wall Street Journal*, October 15, 1998, pp. A1, 8.

Mexico and the double diamond

To maintain its economic growth, Mexico must continue developing international competitive strength.[33] This is currently being done by linking to the US market.[34] In particular, MNEs must view this market not just as a source for export but also as part of the home market (see Figure 10.6). Specifically, this requires:

1 Developing innovative new products and services that simultaneously meet the needs of US and Mexican customers, with the recognition that close relationships with demanding US customers should set the pace and style of product development.

2 Drawing on the support industries and infrastructure of both the US and Mexican diamonds, realizing that the US diamond is more likely to possess deeper and more efficient markets for such industries.

3 Making free and full use of the physical and human resources in both countries.[35]

To do this, Mexico is relying heavily on a series of strategic clusters. The six major ones, in order of importance, are petroleum/chemicals, automotive, housing and household, materials and metals, food and beverage, and semiconductors and computers. The two that are most internationally competitive and provide the best insights into how the Mexican double diamond is used are the petroleum and automotive clusters.

Petroleum cluster

Mexico's petroleum industry accounted for about 8 percent of all exports in 2004. The country has the third-largest proven oil reserves after Venezuela and the United States and is the world's fifth-largest producer. The largest firm is state-owned Petroleos Mexicanos (Pemex), which is the world's largest crude oil producer (does not include refining) and the world's 65th-largest company. In 2009, Pemex had total assets of nearly $103 billion, including pipelines, refineries, tankers, aircraft, and rail cars. This huge asset base helps explain why Mexico is a net exporter of energy, principally oil, natural gas, hydraulic power, nuclear and geothermal power, and coal.

The country also has strong petroleum-related industries and infrastructure. At present, 175 companies are operating about 500 basic and secondary petrochemical plants throughout the country and employing approximately 130,000 people.

Domestic demand of oil-related products in Mexico has been rising sharply, forcing Pemex to become considerably more productive. The export market for this oil is expected to remain at current levels for the foreseeable future. The United States will remain Mexico's largest customer. Moreover, although energy was excluded from NAFTA, ongoing discussions have centered on US access to Mexican oil through imports and increased opportunities for US technologies in the energy sector. For major US companies such as Arco, Chevron, and ConocoPhillips that are selling off some of their domestic properties and looking for exploration opportunities outside the country, Mexico is likely to prove a very attractive location. Turnkey exploration contracts are being used to integrate US expertise and improve Mexican drilling efficiency, thus reducing the cost of oil. This trend will make Mexico one of the lowest-cost producers in the world.

The commodity nature of the energy business provides little opportunity for Mexico to insulate itself from the cyclical changes of both pricing and demand in this cluster. The real opportunities lie in trying to improve efficiencies through various methods: (1) liberalizing exploration programs by allowing more efficient foreign drilling contractors to carry out turnkey operations; (2) reducing the cost base by working with the unions to rationalize jobs that are not required; (3) using foreign technologies in areas where Mexican expertise is lacking; (4) allowing greater participation of foreign firms in producing petrochemicals to expand capacity and competitiveness of commodity products to meet domestic and export demand; (5) using foreign MNEs to bring in technology to produce advanced petrochemicals for use in the US market; and (6) developing alternative, cleaner-burning fuels, such as natural gas and unleaded fuels, to reduce reliance on US imports and comply with international environmental standards.

The potential of this cluster looks promising, even though Mexican proven reserves have recently fallen slightly and the international benchmark price for crude oil has varied from $20 to $150 per barrel. Mexico's vast unexplored areas provide long-term opportunities to continue a strong hydrocarbon-based cluster. Moreover, the proximity of the United States, with its declining proven reserves and growing dependence on imports, will provide Mexico with an export base for improving economies of scale and generating funds for reinvestment in drilling and exploration activities. Thus, Mexico's economic progress will be closely linked to the US diamond.

Automotive cluster

The global auto industry is currently undergoing worldwide restructuring. In the process, Mexico is emerging as a major car and truck producer. Since 1986 the industry has grown rapidly: total unit production in 2002 was 2 million units; however, in 2009, the total unit production was 1,561,052, a drop of 28 percent compared to 2008 due to the world financial crisis leading to fall in exports. Automobile accounts for 15 percent of all exports; 85 percent of all Mexican-built cars are exported to the United States.[36] The Big Three US auto makers have been expanding their capacities in Mexico while closing plants in the United States and Canada. Today, Daimler, Ford, and GM account for about 60 percent of all light-vehicle production. At the same time, European and Japanese firms are investing in Mexico in an effort to tap such benefits as low-cost labor, low capital cost, proximity to the world's largest auto market, growth of domestic demand, and accessibility to related support industries.

Mexico has a strong, rich resource base supporting its automotive cluster as well as an abundance of young, skilled, adaptable labor. Foreign auto firms are finding that these workers are particularly effective after they have been trained in total quality management, just-in-time inventory, and related concepts. In addition, unions in Mexico are much more cooperative with management than their counterparts to the north. As a result, this resource base is now producing some of the highest-quality cars and trucks in North America, and the Hermosillo plant is widely regarded as the number one auto factory on the continent.

There are also strong supporting industries and a well-developed infrastructure in the automotive cluster. The auto parts industry has revenues of $2.93 billion and growing at an annual rate of 10 percent and employs over 500,000 Mexican workers, a five-fold increase since 1990.[37] Parts companies produce for both the domestic and export markets, and many are a result of FDI by US-based auto part firms. For example, GM has component plants in the country as well as financial participation with Mexican auto part companies.

Ford has similar arrangements, as do Volkswagen, Nissan, and a host of other foreign firms. In fact, 30 new auto parts companies settled in Mexico between 1996 and 1998. In one instance, the decision by Volkswagen to produce the VW Beetle fueled foreign investment in auto parts to meet the increasing demand.[38]

While the boom of foreign investment in auto parts initially displaced inefficient local parts producers, a handful of efficiently run local companies have emerged to become multinational producers. For instance, with an initial $30 million investment, Mexico's Nemak has opened a plant in the Czech Republic that employs 200 people.

The primary customers for auto output in Mexico are in the local market. However, the percentage of this output that goes for export is rising every year. In particular, with the signing of NAFTA, Mexico's accessibility to the largest auto market in the world is increasing sharply. This accessibility is especially critical to the country since US protectionism is now threatening to raise import barriers. At the same time, Mexican acceptance of US cars manufactured in Mexico is at an all-time high. The same is true in the United States, where the quality reputation of Mexican assembly plants is being felt at the dealer showroom.

The market potential of the automotive cluster is extremely high. Some problems, however, will have to be dealt with if the country is to continue increasing its competitiveness.[39] Foremost among these is the need for greater technology. One major reason why Mexican autos are cost efficient is the lack of high automation and robotics. It is unlikely that this trend can continue. In addition, the shifting of more and more US and Canadian auto business to Mexico will put major pressure on NAFTA to ensure that these two countries benefit handsomely from this strategy and that other foreign producers, such as the Japanese and Europeans, do not.

Overall, Mexico's economic future is closely linked to that of the United States and Canada. When analyzed in terms of Porter's Diamond, some of the country's strategic clusters have already developed worldwide competitive strength. During the 1990s the petroleum and automotive clusters proved to be highly competitive.

Mexico is likely to begin making major inroads into other areas such as semiconductors and computers. Motorola already has a semiconductor plant in Mexico, and HP, IBM, Toshiba, Samsung, NEC, Philips, and others produce computer hardware components in Mexican facilities. As in its automotive success, this is the result of favorable factor conditions, related and supporting industries, demand conditions, and the structure and rivalry of the firms. As a result, Mexico will find that it can link its diamond framework with that of the United States and become a worldwide competitor in still other areas in the process. Porter's Diamond framework will prove to be a useful paradigm.[40]

KEY POINTS

1 Canada is the single largest trading partner of the United States. There has been a move toward privatization in the past few years as well as toward deregulation. As in the United States, the government attempts to promote competition, and the North American Free Trade Agreement (NAFTA) with Mexico has recognized the high degree of trade between the two countries.

2 Financial institutions are similar to those in the United States, as are labor relations practices. However, a much larger percentage of Canadian employees are unionized, and the unions have been major opponents of the FTA and the subsequent NAFTA.

3 NAFTA will eventually eliminate most trade barriers between the United States and Canada, which should help open up Canada to more economic development. At the same time, the government welcomes foreign investment, and a wide variety of incentive programs are designed to encourage such investments.

4 The approaches to doing business in Canada are similar to those in the United States, with some important regulatory differences. The chapter identified and discussed both.

5 Mexico has the strongest economy in Latin America, and its close business ties to the United States, as reflected by imports, exports, and US FDI, bode well for its future. The potential of the free trade agreement between the two countries and the growth of the *maquiladora* industry are helping Mexico link its economy to that of the United States. Mexico's petrochemical and automotive clusters are key industries in this linkage and are likely to become world-class competitors in their respective areas.

Key terms

- Competition Act
- Canada Labor Code
- Investment Canada Act (ICA)
- North American Free Trade Agreement (NAFTA)
- United States–Canada Free Trade Agreement (FTA)
- Latin American Integration Association (LAIA)
- Mercosur
- Andean common market (Ancom)
- Enterprise for the Americas
- Free Trade Area of the Americas (FTAA)

REVIEW AND DISCUSSION QUESTIONS

1 How high is the Canadian standard of living? Of what value is this information to a company interested in doing business in Canada?

2 Is the Competition Act of any concern to US firms, given that the FTA has eliminated most trade restrictions? Explain.

3 What do companies seeking to set up businesses in Canada need to know about labor relations in that country? Identify and discuss three areas of importance.

4 What are the most important provisions of the Free Trade Agreement and how do they affect US firms doing business in Canada?

5 Are there any restrictions on foreign investments in Canada? Identify and describe two of them.

6 What should a firm seeking to enter the Canadian market know about marketing practices there? Identify and describe three practices.

7 How good are franchise opportunities in Canada? Explain.

8 Why is Mexico doing so well economically? Identify two developments that have been particularly helpful in bringing this about.

9 What is the purpose of the LAIA? Of what value is the organization to its members?

10 How might the creation of an "Enterprise for the Americas" affect the LAIA and Ancom? Give an example.

11 How is Mexico using its petroleum cluster to link itself to the North American triad?

12 How is Mexico using its automotive cluster to link itself to the North American triad?

13 Why are these linkages to the North American triad likely to be economically advantageous to Mexico? Cite two reasons.

REAL CASE

Jumex of Mexico

Founded in 1961, Group Jumex is the largest producer of juices and fruit nectars in Mexico. The country has a population of 106 million people and a hot climate that provides a favorable environment in which Jumex can grow. And grow it has.

Mexico offered other nurturing characteristics to the emerging company in the form of natural resources and market pressures. For one, Jumex has access to an incredible variety of tropical fruits from which it can develop new products. Indeed, the firm offers tamarind, guanabana, and guava nectars as well as the more commonly known mango, peach, pear, and apple.

Tropical fruits are readily available everywhere at a relatively low price, making the blending of juices in customers' homes extremely easy. Juice stands, in which the juice is made on site, are abundant throughout the country. Quality is paramount. Jumex cannot sell products with very little fruit content to Mexicans.

Jumex competes with other domestic producers at home for the juice and nectar market. It also competes with soft drink makers, including Coca-Cola and PepsiCo, for the beverage market. However, Mexican consumers have recently improved the lot of the juice makers, as carbonated drinks are increasingly considered unhealthful.

Competition has made Jumex into an aggressive marketer. The firm uses all types of distribution system to maximize market share. It works with national wholesalers, regional wholesalers, supermarkets, and small convenience stores to establish a price system that allows them to benefit from selling its products.

Mobile communication was provided to the sales team so that orders could be processed immediately no matter how far away the distribution center was. This is very important because of the remoteness of many Mexican communities. Prior to this, a salesperson could take two weeks before returning with paperwork to put in an order. Supermarket computerized distribution systems are now integrated with that of Jumex so that their shelves can be stocked as needed.

While most firms have shifted to aluminum, Jumex has maintained the traditional tin can and created a distinct shape that stands out against the competition. A tin can is alleged to be more biodegradable than an aluminum can. To serve different markets, Jumex also packages in plastic, glass, and juice boxes.

Presently, Jumex exports only about 20 percent of its production but it is highly successful. It has operations in Latin America and the Caribbean, North America, Europe, Asia, and Oceania. Distribution and marketing have been adapted to fit each country. In most of Latin America, because of geographic, market, and cultural similarities, the distribution system that was implemented was very similar to that found in Mexico.

Jumex has been surprisingly successful in the US market, where it is now a leading brand of fruit nectars. Part of this success can be attributed to Mexico's lower production costs and the availability of inexpensive natural resources. Another reason is the predominance of Mexican immigrants across the United States, particularly in large urban areas. Whether these are new immigrants or the children of immigrants who travel frequently to Mexico, they know the product and are familiar with the tropical fruits, creating an initial market for the product. Other Latin Americans or immigrants from tropical areas familiar with the brand or the fruits also push demand.

Another factor that has helped Jumex in developed countries is that its products are considered healthier than carbonated drinks and tend to offer more fruit content than many of its domestic competitors. However, competition in developed countries is likely to heat up in the future as Ceres, a South African juice producer, Jugos del Valle of Mexico, and new entrants from Asia compete in price, quality, and variety of fruit juices. In the health market sector, organic fruit juices from developing and developed countries will also offer competition.

Websites: www.jumex.com.mx.

Sources: "Soft Drinks in Mexico," *Euromonitor*, June 2004; Samuel Bernal, "Jumex le saca jugo al cómputo movil," *Revista Red*, Febrero 2001; www.jumex.com.mx.

1 How has Mexico provided the environment to make Jumex into a competitive fruit and nectar producer in foreign markets?

2 What factors mentioned in this case study have contributed to Jumex's success in the US market?

3 Can you think of any other factors that may have contributed to Jumex's success in the US market?

GlaxoSmithKline in the United States

Among industrialized countries, the US market for pharmaceuticals is the least regulated and thus the largest in the world. Not surprisingly, European companies like AstraZeneca, Aventis, and GlaxoSmithKline (GSK) depend more heavily on the North American market for their revenues than on Europe as a whole. Europe is a more fragmented market, with individual distribution systems and more layers of regulation, and governments are in the habit of imposing price controls. As a result, Europeans spend 60 percent less per capita on pharmaceuticals than their American counterparts.

With $44.240 billion in revenues and 98,854 employees in 2009, GSK is one of the largest pharmaceutical companies in the world. Although incorporated in the United Kingdom, it is not surprising that GSK manages its operations in the United States. Some 30 percent of its sales originate in this host nation, a fact that is consistent with world trends—the United States accounts for nearly 50 percent of the world market for pharmaceuticals. GSK derives 25 percent of its sales from its home-market region. Indeed the European market accounts for 25 percent of the world market for pharmaceuticals. Only 9 percent of its sales come from Asia/Japan, 10 percent from emerging markets and the remainder is derived from ViiV health care (HIV business), other trading and unallocated activities.

Approximately 30 years ago, British Glaxo was a small company in the dried milk, antibiotics, respiratory drugs, and nutritional businesses. The discovery of Zantac, a drug to treat stomach ulcers, catapulted the company into the mainstream pharmaceutical market and financed its expansion into the US market. As the patent for Zantac was about to expire, Glaxo found itself in a sticky situation. Up to that point the company had relied on internal R&D, but this had failed to develop the R&D capabilities for sustainable long-term growth. In 1995, the company merged with Wellcome, a company known for its strength in R&D and its lack of marketing capabilities. The merger was successful in that the new company now had a stream of new drugs that could be marketed using Glaxo's expertise.

By 2000, Glaxo Wellcome was disappointing investors once again. Drug prospects, at least in the short term, were below the industry average and expected revenues from some of its products never materialized. Yet the merger with SmithKline Beecham was not driven by the same urgency as the previous merger. Both companies had a reasonably stable pipeline and a balanced portfolio

of drugs. According to Sir Richard Sykes, then Chairman of Glaxo Wellcome, the deciphering of the human genome would transform the industry and only large companies that could afford to invest in working with this new information would succeed. Together, these two companies are immune to the near-death experience of losing a major blockbuster drug. No one drug accounts for more than 12 percent of the company's revenues.

GSK operates in two product-based industry segments: (1) pharmaceuticals, which include prescription drugs and vaccines; and (2) consumer health care, which includes over-the-counter (OTC) medicines, oral care, and nutritional health care. Prescription drugs are sold mainly to wholesalers, which dispense them to the public through pharmacies. Consumer health-care products are sold through pharmacies, wholesalers, or directly to retail outlets. In July 2009, it acquired Stiefel Laboratories, Inc. In October 2009, it acquired Pfizer Inc.'s HIV business and combined it with its own HIV business to form ViiV Healthcare Limited. In November 2009, it acquired the Algerian pharmaceutical, manufacturing and distribution group, Laboratoire Pharmaceutique Algerien. In December 2009, it acquired NovaMin Technology Inc.

The first step in the development of a drug is R&D. GSK spends $4 billion on R&D and has over 15,000 researchers in 24 R&D sites around the world. Once GSK has developed a new drug, it must obtain government approval in every individual nation where the company markets the product, a process that can differ significantly in each jurisdiction. Production and marketing are the next steps for a new drug. GSK's supply chain is divided into a primary chain and a secondary chain. The primary chain manufactures active ingredients for its products and ships them to the secondary chain, which manufactures the end product. There are 13 primary supply-chain sites based in Australia, India, Ireland, Singapore, the United States, and the UK. In Europe, there are 17 secondary supply-chain sites, while North America houses an additional six. The rest of the world has 32 secondary sites in 19 countries (five in the Middle East and Africa, 22 in Asia–Pacific, and five in Latin America).

Different price regulations at a national level have created some market abnormalities in each region. For instance, Canadian Web-based pharmacies have sprung up to service US consumers seeking cheaper alternatives. GSK sent a heavily worded letter to Canadian wholesalers ▶

that were selling to these pharmacies and threatened to stop supplies. In Spain, GSK developed a two-price system: one lower price for products to be sold in Spain and a higher price for those to be exported to other EU member countries. The EU found this practice illegal.

Websites: www.gsk.com; www.aventis.com; www.astrazeneca.com.

Sources: Alan M. Rugman, *The Regional Multinationals* (Cambridge: Cambridge University Press, 2005); "The Trouble with Cheap Drugs," *The Economist,* January 29, 2004; GSK, *Annual Report,* 2009; OneSource, *Thomson Reuters,* 2011.

1 How is GSK's production organized?

2 Is GSK's secondary supply-chain structure global, regional, or local? Why?

3 What is GSK's basic strategy?

4 Why does GSK spread R&D around the world?

5 What factors have made North America the primary market for GSK? Would the situation be different if we measured units sold? Why?

ENDNOTES

1 John R. Baldwin, Jean-Pierre Maynard and Fanny Wong, "The Output Gap Between Canada and the United States: The Role of Productivity (1994–2002)," *Statistics Canada Analytical Papers,* January 2005.

2 Tamsin Carlisle, "Calgary Becomes Outpost On High-Tech Frontier," *Wall Street Journal,* March 24, 1998, p. A19.

3 OECD, Foreign Direct Investment Statistics, FDI Positions by Partner Country. OECD.StatExtracts Online, http://stats.oecd.org/, 2010.

4 Also, see Rosanna Tamburri, "Canada Considers New Stand Against American Culture," *Wall Street Journal,* February 4, 1998, p. A18; Roger Ricklefs, "Canada Fights to Fend Off American Tastes and Tunes," *Wall Street Journal,* September 24, 1998, pp. B1, 8.

5 Barbara Wickens, "Getting the GST of It," *Maclean's,* September 10, 1990, pp. 40–43.

6 For more information on the GST/HST, see Canada Revenue Agency, http://www.cra-arc.gc.ca/tx/bsnss/tpcs/gst-tps/gnrl/txbl/mprtsxprts/mprtdgds-eng.html, 2010.

7 See Rosanna Tamburri, "Canadians Clash Over Cost of Diversity," *Wall Street Journal,* April 1, 1998, p. A15.

8 For additional insights into the role of Quebec in US–Canadian economic ties, see Thane Peterson and William J. Holstein, "How a Freer Quebec Could Reshape the Continent," *Business Week,* July 9, 1990, pp. 40–43.

9 For a contrast, see Christopher J. Chipello, "Francophones Struggle Outside Quebec," *Wall Street Journal,* February 26, 1998, p. A12; see also Government of Canada, *Canada Business,* http://www.canadabusiness.ca/eng/.

10 Government of Canada, Department of Finance, *Canada's Banks,* August 2002, http://www.fin.gc.ca/toc/2002/bank_-eng.asp.

11 See www.tse.com.

12 Statistics Canada, *Unionization 2010;* http://www.statcan.gc.ca/pub/75-001-x/2010110/article/11358-eng.htm#a2; US Bureau of Labor Statistics, *Union Members Summary,* January 17, 2010.

13 E. Kaye Fulton and Nancy Wood, "A 'Reasonable Limit'," *Maclean's,* December 17, 1990, pp. 20–21.

14 Todd Mason, "Now Tariffs Can't Fall Fast Enough," *Business Week,* October 23, 1989, p. 80.

15 *Summary of the US–Canada Free Trade Agreement* (Washington, DC: US Department of Commerce, International Trade Administration, 1988), p. 12.

16 Ibid., pp. 10–11.

17 *Marketing in Canada* (Washington, DC: US Department of Commerce), International Marketing Information Series, Overseas Business Reports, OBR 88–05, May 1988, p. 8.

18 See http://www.dsa.ca/home.htm.

19 Statistics Canada, *Cansim Database,* Matrix: D657192.

20 Ibid. and Matrix: D657205.

21 Ibid.

22 Also, see Stephen Baker, "Mexico: Can Zedillo Stem the Tide of Crisis?" *Business Week,* April 18, 1994, p. 60; "Mexico Arrests Top Leader of Zetas' Drug Gang," *BBC News Online,* July 4, 2011; and Mexico Country Profile, *BBC News Online,* http://news.bbc.co.uk/1/hi/world/americas/country_profiles/1205074.stm, 2010.

23 CIA World Fact Book, 2010.

24 Also, see Bob Ortega, "Some Mexicans Charge North in NAFTA's Wake," *Wall Street Journal,* February 22, 1994, pp. B1, 5; Mexico Country Profile, *BBC Online,* http://news.bbc.co.uk/1/hi/world/americas/country_profiles/1205074.stm, 2010.

25 "Mexico Proves a Resilient, Robust Market for U.S. Exports," *AgExporter,* January 2002.

26 Ministry of Finance and Public Credit of Mexico, *Mexico's Bimonthly Economic News,* June 13, 2000.

27 See "Labor: Minimum Daily Wages for 2011," http://www.sat.gob.mx/sitio_Internet/asistencia_contribuyente/informacion_frecuente/salarios_minimos/.

28 Len J. Trevino, "Strategic Responses of Mexican Managers to Economic Reform," *Business Horizons,* May/June 1998, pp. 73–80.

29 Some of the material in this section can be found in "Latin American Introduction," *ILT Latin America,* July 1991, pp. 1–13.

30 For more on the FTAA, see www.ftaa-alca.org/.

31 "The Business of the American Hemisphere," *The Economist,* August 24, 1991, pp. 37–38.

32 Also, see Rick Wartzman, "In the Wake of NAFTA, A Family Firm Sees Business Go South," *Wall Street Journal,* February 23, 1999, pp. A1, 10.

33 Jonathan Friedland, "Mexico Is Hit Despite Belt-Tightening," *Wall Street Journal*, September 14, 1998, p. A27.

34 Richard M. Hodgetts, "Porter's Diamond Framework in a Mexican Context," *Management International Review*, vol. 33, Special Issue (1993), pp. 41–54.

35 J. R. D'Cruz and Alan M. Rugman, *New Concepts for Canadian Competitiveness* (Toronto: Kodak Canada, 1992).

36 Susan Carney, "Mexico's Low Labor Costs Tempt Detroit Carmakers," *The Detroit News*, January 7, 2002; International Organization of Motor Vehicle Manufacturers (OICA) http://oica.net/category/production-statistics/, 2009.

37 Geri Smith and Elisabeth Malkin, "Mexico's Makeover," *Business Week*, December 21, 1998; Elisabeth Malkin and Jonathan Wheatley, "Parts Shops Are Tailgating Carmakers to Latin America," *Business Week*, October 23, 2000; US Commerce Service, Buy USA, http://www.buyusa.gov/mexico/en/automotive_manufacturing.html.

38 Malkin and Wheatley, ibid.

39 Elisabeth Malkin, "Holding Off Asia's Assault," *Business Week*, April 13, 1991, pp. 44–45.

40 Alan M. Rugman and Michael Gestrin, "The Strategic Response of Multinational Enterprises to NAFTA," *Columbia Journal of World Business*, vol. 28, no. 4 (1993), pp. 18–29.

ADDITIONAL BIBLIOGRAPHY

Batres, Robertos E. "A Mexican View of the North American Free Trade Agreement," *Columbia Journal of World Business*, vol. 26, no. 2 (Summer 1991).

Birkinshaw, Julian and Hood, Neil. "An Empirical Study of Development Process in Foreign Owned Subsidiaries in Canada and Scotland," *Management International Review*, vol. 37, no. 4 (1997).

Eden, Lorraine (ed.). *Multinationals in North America* (Calgary: University of Calgary Press, 1994).

Feils, Dorothee J. and Rahman, Manzur "Regional Economic Integration and Foreign Direct Investment: The Case of NAFTA," *Management International Review*, vol. 48, no. 2, (2008).

Feinberg, Susan E. "Do World Product Mandates Really Matter?" *Journal of International Business Studies*, vol. 31, no. 1 (Spring 2000).

Feinberg, Susan E. and Keane, Michael P. "US-Canada Trade Liberalization and MNC Production Location," *The Review of Economics and Statistics*, vol. 83, no. 1 (2001).

Globerman, Steven and Shapiro, Daniel M. "The Impact of Government Policies on Foreign Direct Investment: The Canadian Experience," *Journal of International Business Studies*, vol. 30, no. 3 (Fall 1999).

Globerman, Steven and Walker, Michael (eds.). *Assessing NAFTA: A Trinational Analysis* (Vancouver: Fraser Institute, 1993).

Globerman, Steven and Shapiro, Daniel M. "Governance Infrastructure and US Foreign Direct Investment," *Journal of International Business Studies*, vol. 34 (2003).

Gomez, Carolina. "The Influence of Environmental, Organizational, and HRM Factors on Employee Behaviors in Subsidiaries: A Mexican Case Study of Organizational Learning," *Journal of World Business*, vol. 39, no. 1 (February 2004).

Hejazi, Walid and Safarian, A.E. "NAFTA Effects and the Level of Development," *Journal of Business Research*, vol. 58, no. 12 (December 2005).

Hodgetts, Richard. "Porter's Diamond Framework in a Mexican Context," *Management International Review*, vol. 33, no. 2 (Second Quarter 1993).

Hufbauer, Gary C. and Schott, Jeffrey J. *North American Free Trade: Issues and Recommendations* (Washington, DC: Institute for International Economics, 1992).

Hufbauer, Gary C. and Schott, Jeffrey J. *NAFTA Revisited: Achievements and Challenges* (Washington, DC: Institute for International Economics, 2005).

Hufbauer, Gary C., Esty, Daniel C., Orejas, Diana, Rubio, Luis and Schott, Jeffrey J. *NAFTA and the Environment: Seven Years Later* (Washington, DC: Institute for International Economics, 2000).

Keane, Michael P and Feinberg, Susan. "Advances in Logistics and the Growth of Intra-firm Trade: The Case of Canadian Affiliates of U.S. Multinationals. *Journal of Industrial Economics,*" vol. 55, no. 4 (December 2007).

Kirton, John and Maclaren, Virginia (eds.). *Linking Trade, Environment and Social Cohesion* (Aldershot: Ashgate, 2002).

Lovett, Steven R., Coyle, Tom and Adams, Russell. "Job Satisfaction and Technology in Mexico," *Journal of World Business*, vol. 39, no. 3 (August 2004).

Lovett, Steven R., Pérez-Nordtvedt, Liliana, and Rasheed, Abdul A. "Parental Control: A Study of U.S. Subsidiaries in Mexico," *International Business Review*, vol. 18, no. 5 (October 2009).

Rugman, Alan M. *Multinationals in Canada: Theory, Performance and Economic Impact* (Boston, MA: Martinus Nijhoff, 1980).

Rugman, Alan M. "The Role of Multinational Enterprises in US–Canadian Economic Relations," *Columbia Journal of World Business*, vol. 21, no. 2 (Summer 1986).

Rugman, Alan M. *Outward Bound: Canadian Direct Investment in the United States* (Toronto: Canadian–American Committee, and Prentice Hall of Canada, 1987).

Rugman, Alan M. *Multinationals and Canada–United States Free Trade* (Columbia, SC: University of South Carolina Press, 1990).

Rugman, Alan M. (ed.). *Foreign Investment and NAFTA* (Columbia, SC: University of South Carolina Press, 1994).

Rugman, Alan M. (ed.). *North American Economic and Financial Integration* (Oxford: Elsevier, 2004).

Rugman, Alan M. "Thirty Years of International Business Scholarship in Canada," *Canadian Journal of Administrative Sciences*, vol. 25, no. 4 (2008).

Rugman, Alan M. and D'Cruz, Joseph R. "The 'Double Diamond' Model of International Competitiveness: The Canadian Experience," *Management International Review*, vol. 33, no. 2 (Second Quarter 1993).

Rugman, Alan M. and Gestrin, Michael. "The Investment Provisions of NAFTA," in Steven Globerman and Michael Walker (eds.), *Assessing NAFTA: A Trinational Analysis* (Vancouver: Fraser Institute, 1993).

Rugman, Alan M. and Gestrin, Michael. "The Strategic Response of Multinational Enterprises to NAFTA," *Columbia Journal of World Business*, vol. 28, no. 4 (Winter 1993).

Rugman, Alan M. and Verbeke, Alain. "Multinational Corporate Strategy and the Canada–US Free Trade Agreement," *Management International Review*, vol. 30, no. 3 (Third Quarter 1990).

Rugman, Alan M. and Verbeke, Alain (eds.). *Research in Global Strategic Management, Volume 1, International Business Research for the Twenty-First Century: Canada's New Research Agenda* (Greenwich, CT: JAI Press, 1990).

Rugman, Alan M. and Verbeke, Alain. "Foreign Subsidiaries and Multinational Strategic Management: An Extension and Correction of Porter's Single Diamond Framework," *Management International Review*, vol. 33, no. 2 (Second Quarter 1993).

Rugman, Alan M., Kirton, John and Soloway, Julie A. *Environmental Regulations and Corporate Strategy: A NAFTA Perspective* (Oxford: Oxford University Press, 1999).

Sargent, John and Matthews, Linda. "The Drivers of Evolution/ Upgrading in Mexico's Maquiladoras: How Important is Subsidiary Initiative?" *Journal of World Business*, vol. 41, no. 3 (September 2006).

Solocha, Andrew, Soskin, Mark D. and Kasoff, Mark J. "Determinants of Foreign Direct Investment: A Case of Canadian Direct Investment in the United States," *Management International Review*, vol. 30, no. 4 (Fourth Quarter 1990).

Ulgado, Francis M. "Location Characteristics of Manufacturing Investments in the US: A Comparison of American and Foreign-based Firms," *Management International Review*, vol. 36, no. 1 (1996).

Waldkirch, Andreas. "The Effects of Foreign Direct Investment in Mexico since NAFTA," *The World Economy*, vol. 33, no. 5 (May 2010).

Weinstein, Bernard L. and Seman, Michael. "Has the North American Free Trade Agreement Fulfilled Its Promise? An Assessment After 15 Years," *Regional Science Policy & Practice*, vol. 1, no. 2 (November 2009).

Weintraub, Sydney. *NAFTA at Three* (Washington, DC: Center for Strategies on International Studies, 1997).

Weintraub, Sydney. *Unequal Partners: The United States and Mexico,* Pitt Latin American Series (Pittsburg, PA: University of Pittsburgh Press, 2010).

Wisner, Priscilla S. and Epstein, Marc J. "'Push' and 'Pull' Impacts of NAFTA on Environmental Responsiveness and Performance in Mexican Industry," *Management International Review*, vol. 45, no. 3 (2005).

Chapter 20

EMERGING ECONOMIES

Objectives of the chapter

More than 100 nations in the world are not triad members; they lie outside North America, Europe, and Japan. An important subgroup of non-triad countries is the "emerging economies," marked by their rapid economic growth and changing involvement in the global economy. They are increasingly important for MNEs of all sizes: as growing markets whose large populations are starting to have more and more disposable income; as increasingly important sources of inputs, including products, technology, and value-adding capabilities as well as commodities and cheap labor; and as a source of competition, as non-triad firms begin to internationalize into triad markets. These developments represent many new opportunities as well as new risks for MNEs. Increased involvement in emerging market regions for managers means coping with more diversity. This includes the broad cultural, political, and economic diversity resulting from the wide range of countries outside the triad. It also includes diversity of business practices and competitors, which MNEs need to adapt to in order to survive.

The specific objectives of this chapter are to:

1 *Examine* the relative attractions, opportunities, and threats in the triad regions and emerging economies for firms looking to internationalize.

2 *Explain* how many emerging economies are becoming more integrated into the global economy, in terms of trade, FDI, and other forms of interaction and interdependence.

3 *Understand* the nature of the new multinationals from emerging economies, as collaborators and competitors.

4 *Examine* the implications of changes in emerging economies for MNE managers in terms of new strategies and organization structures.

Acer Taiwan goes international

Acer Taiwan ranks as one of the largest PC companies in the world. The overall Acer Group of companies is comprised of 7,757 employees, plus dealers, and distributors in more than 100 countries, earning revenues of US $20.056 billion for the year 2010, of which 6.5 percent was generated from Taiwan, 24 percent from the United States, 46.9 percent from Europe, and 22.6 percent from Asia. In just over five years (2006–2010), sales have almost doubled from $11.814 billion in 2006 to $20.056 billion in 2010. The company is one of the best-known brands in Asia, and a large player in Latin America. In the United States, where HP and Dell dominate, Acer is the third largest competitor in the consumer electronics market. According to Mintel Global Market Navigator, the laptop PCs' market share by volume in the United States in 2009 was that HP held 25.9 percent, Dell 21.5 percent, Acer 15.8 percent, Toshiba 9.7 percent, and Apple 9.4 percent. Not bad for a company no one knew just a few decades ago.

In 1976 CEO Stan Shih and some of his friends managed to pull together $25,000 and start Multitech. With seven employees, the company began developing small electronic products such as pocket calculators and games. Slowly the company began to grow by commercializing microprocessor technology and its applications. Its initial entrance into the PC market was as a supplier. Multitech began producing computers to be sold under other brand names. Then in 1986 the company launched its own brand name computer, Acer, and it began to sell in Europe and in Japan. While the firm still supplies under other brand names, Acer has become one of the best-known PC brands in the world.

How did a small company from Taiwan gain market share in an industry dominated by well-established computer manufacturers? Two key strategies underpinned its rapid international growth. First, it focused on learning: actively developing technological know-how, innovation capabilities, and, later, marketing and branding expertise. It invested in engineering training, initially with the help of the Taiwanese government. In the late 1970s it founded the Microprocessor Training Center where 3,000 engineers were trained for Taiwan's information industry. It also entered into a range of subcontracting relationships and joint ventures with major multinational firms in targeted industries. One of the most prominent was its DRAM semiconductor joint venture with Texas Instruments in 1989. To acquire necessary technologies the company bought a host of firms including Counterpoint Computers, Altos, and Kangaroo Computer. It also entered into cross-licensing agreements with firms like IBM and Intel. Innovation was the constant focus. The rapid development of engineering, design, and R&D capabilities helped Acer improve both its production efficiency and its product development capabilities. In 1986 it came out with a 32-bit PC model before IBM. In 1994 it introduced the world's first dual Intel Pentium PC, in 2001 the first Chinese Palm OS, and in 2004 a 64-bit notebook PC.

Second, Acer followed an incremental, niche strategy in order to expand internationally. Stan Shih explains this decision by noting, "It is better to be a big fish in a small pond than a small fish in a big pond." Small markets, especially in Asia, which were not yet captured by the likes of IBM and Compaq, were a driving force behind Acer's initial international success.

Acer's distribution system was also a novelty. With the product life of computer components at about three months, exporting overseas becomes a problem, but Acer built manufacturing and assembling plants all over the world. The company distributed parts with long product lives by ship, while highly volatile products like processors, PCBs, and memory were shipped by plane. This allowed for just-in-time production that Shih compared to the distribution system of a fast-food chain with perishable and nonperishable ingredients.

The success of the company also owes much to the management structure created by Shih. Unlike traditional Chinese businesses, where management is highly hierarchical and controlled by the owning family, Shih uses decentralized management. Autonomy is important. Managers are encouraged to think like owners, so as to take advantage of all profit opportunities. Additionally, Acer has gone public and employees have the option of buying shares at extremely low prices.

In 2000, Acer spun off its manufacturing operations to focus on globally marketing its brand name products: desktop and mobile PCs, servers and storage, displays, peripherals, and e-business solutions. This began a shift away from production and into design and branding (since 2004 it has produced a "Ferrari" line of notebook PCs), and service-related businesses, partly following the evolution of the industries mapped out by Stan Shih's Smiling Curve in the early 1990s. He predicted that success in the combined computing, IT, consumer electronics, and telecoms industries would increasingly depend on being customer-centric, with customer-driven rather than technology-driven innovation. The firm would need to be committed to providing outstanding service and developing intellectual property such as software, rather than focusing on hardware and production activities.

The retirement of Stan Shih in 2004 led to a significant organizational change at the firm, but it maintained its core strategy under J. T. Wang who has been Chairman of the Board and Chief Executive Officer in Acer Incorporated since April 20, 2011. A more devolved decision-making structure has evolved across a more international group of senior management, a process accelerated by a number of large acquisitions as well as disposals. Acer's buy-out of US-based Gateway in 2007 compares to Lenovo's (successful) takeover of IBM's PC business in 2004 and BenQ's (unsuccessful) takeover of Siemens PC division more recently. This helped Acer move ahead of Chinese rival Lenovo by strengthening its position in the US retail market and giving it control of Packard Bell in Europe.

But the competitive threat posed by mainland Chinese PC and electronics firms remains a key strategic challenge for Acer. In 2010 the firm established its second mainland China manufacturing base in Chongqing and is now calling this its "global IT center".

Websites: www.acer.com; www.ti.com.

Sources: Kathrin Hille and Kevin Allison, "Acer to leapfrog Lenovo with Gateway deal," *Financial Times*, FT.com, August 27, 2007; "Acer Buys Gateway," *Financial Times*, FT.com, August 28, 2007; Willie Chien, Stan Shih and Po-Young Chu, *Business Growth Strategies for Asia Pacific* (New York: Wiley, 2005); Daniel Lyons, "Horse Power," *Forbes*, February 16, 2004, p. 56; Paul Taylor, "In the CEO's Chair: Ky Lee at BenQ," *Financial Times*, March 17, 2004, p. 2; Kathrin Hille, "A Head Start of Being Ethnically Chinese," *Financial Times*, April 7, 2004, p. 10; Stanley Shih, "Talking About Innovation," *Far Eastern Economic Review*, October 17, 2002, p. 44; Stan Shih, *Growing Global* (Taiwan: Acer Corporation Publication, 2001); Stan Shih, *Me-Too Is Not My Style* (Taiwan: Acer Corporation Publication, 1996); Acer, Annual Report, 2006–2010; OneSource, Thomson Reuters, 2011; Mintel Global Market Navigator, 2011, http://gmn.mintel.com.dblibweb.rdg.ac.uk:4000/snapshots/USA/56/shares/single.

1 What was the internationalization strategy of Acer and why was it successful?

2 How are changes in the Asian regional economy, in terms of both growing markets and growing competitors, affecting Acer and should the firm cope?

3 Why did Acer form strategic alliances with IBM and Texas Instruments?

INTRODUCTION

In Chapter 15 we examined some of the country-level risks common in emerging market countries. Although these stand out because of their rapid growth rate, they share many of the same characteristics of non-triad countries in general. Such countries are:

- growing in importance for international managers for both market-seeking investments and resource-seeking investments;

- strongly government controlled, in that government agencies play a central role in negotiating with foreign investors and deciding the local rules of the game;

- less predictable and riskier than triad markets, which investors often underestimate in their pursuit of the high level of rewards on offer;[1] and

- the source of new competitors, as local firms move up the value chain, becoming more sophisticated and more international.

We are concerned with two broad kinds of international expansion in this chapter. First, internationalization from the triad into non-triad regions whereby established MNEs, whose home base is large, mature, and includes expensive markets, expand to sell more outputs in, or buy more inputs from, cheaper emerging economies. Second, the internationalization of newer MNEs from outside the triad which are looking both to complement home-market resources with assets or capabilities from inside the triad and to sell into the much larger triad countries. For each kind of MNE these two forms of internationalization represent some major strategic threats and opportunities.

TRIAD FIRMS AND EMERGING ECONOMY FIRMS: WHY THE MUTUAL INTEREST?

Triad-based and non-triad-based firms will have similar objectives when exploring market-seeking investments. They both want to increase sales in each other's territories and to do this they must customize products and services to suit these markets, establish (or buy) distribution and sales networks, and raise the profiles of their brands. In many cases they may also need to set up manufacturing, assembly, service, or support activities in each other's markets to avoid import duties and/or to support the needs of customers.

When exploring input-seeking investments, triad-based and non-triad-based firms may also have similar strategies, but they tend to be looking for different kinds of inputs. This is because their home regions provide each with a different set of factor endowments, as described by the Porter diamond model in Chapter 10.

Figure 20.1 provides a starting point to understand the attraction for triad firms looking to expand into emerging economies and for firms from emerging economies looking to expand into triad regions. The large markets of North America, Europe, and Japan still dominate the global economy, but they are growing slowly relative to emerging markets both large, like India, China, and Brazil, and small, like Poland or Malaysia. Triad regions also tend to be more expensive, in terms of labor costs, infrastructure, land, materials, and supporting industries, relative to non-triad regions. These represent push factors, accentuating the pull of non-triad locations. Combining these differences means that there are strong incentives for triad-based firms both to sell products, services, and other outputs into these growing markets and to source inputs, such as cheap labor or manufactured components and services, from such places.

For new MNEs evolving in non-triad regions, the main attraction of triad markets is the large, mature markets. But many firms also look to these countries to fill gaps in their assets, resources, and capabilities, from technological know-how or specialist components to brands.

FDI into emerging economies for inputs (**resource-seeking FDI**) and outputs (**market-seeking FDI**) takes a variety of forms. Prudential (UK), along with many other triad firms, cut many of its back-office operations in Reading, England, in 2002 and established a center in Mumbai, India. Although this resulted in around 400 redundancies in the UK, the firm was then able to take advantage of the cheaper (and, in some cases, better) local Indian IT and call-center service workers that have created the local industry reviewed

Resource-seeking FDI
MNEs invest in production-related activities to benefit from cheaper or better sources of inputs in a particular location; these can include raw materials, components, or labor and expertise

Market-seeking FDI
MNEs invest in distribution, sales, or marketing operations in order to sell products or services (outputs) in particular country markets

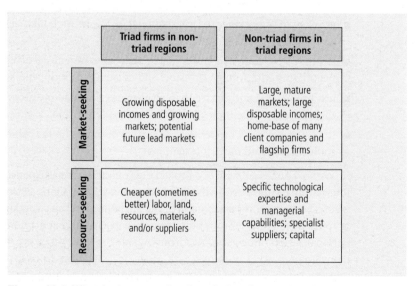

Figure 20.1 What is the attraction for triad and non-triad firms investing in each other's home regions?

in the **Real Case: The Indian IT, software, and services industry** at the end of this chapter. The **Active Learning Case: Kodak in China** in Chapter 15 shows how Kodak created a series of mergers and joint ventures to invest over $1 billion into China, both for producing film products more cheaply (using cheaper labor and raw materials) and for serving the growing Chinese market. Contrasting these, the **Active Learning Case: Acer Taiwan goes international** and the **International Business Strategy in Action: Korean *chaebols*** charting the growth and internationalization of **Korean *chaebols*** Hyundai and Samsung show why and how newer MNEs have broken into triad markets. Yet in many other cases, such as for Tesco in the case **International Business Strategy in Action: From Oserian to Tesco**, firms do not see a need to engage in FDI, because they can get access to the advantages of non-triad locations and maintain control over their supply chains by buying and selling through global markets.

> **Korean *chaebols***
> Traditionally family-dominated, diversified conglomerates. Family ownership has been reduced and many are now focused in particular business sectors, reducing their diversity. There are parallels with Japanese *sogo shosha* in terms of early government support and their relationship with dominant national banks

More generic international business reasons also exist for expanding into these markets, including risk diversification, the opportunity to extend economies of scale and scope, and the opportunity to leverage existing assets or resources for additional revenues. For example, expanding global production by establishing manufacturing plants in non-triad regions serves to diversify risk by reducing dependence on triad locations where input costs and wages are high—but may also rise further. This allows firms to reap economies-of-scale benefits across the overall production function. Similarly, extending established triad brands into new markets helps build the economies of scale needed to pay for media advertising and other brand-building activities. As sports stars and celebrities, such as Tiger Woods (for Nike), develop international reputations, their images can be used to sell products around the world, and companies can earn sufficient revenues to pay for them because they are assets that can be leveraged globally.

✔ Active learning check

Review your answer to Active Learning Case question 1 and make any changes you like. Then compare your answer to the one below.

1 **What was the internationalization strategy of Acer and why was it successful?**

Rather than aiming to break into the triad markets directly, despite the attractions, Acer focused on building a presence in smaller local Asian markets first. In some ways it followed a pattern of gradual, stepwise internationalization. Acer built up from its relatively small home-base diamond in Taiwan and expanded production throughout South-East Asia. It then undertook a double-diamond strategy for accessing the triad markets of North America and Europe. It formed strategic alliances with the US and European MNEs and used these as a stepping stone to FDI in these key triad markets. It also kept its production-based efficiencies of employee involvement in company growth and ongoing R&D to improve the quality of its products.

AN OVERVIEW OF EMERGING ECONOMIES, BY REGION

This growing interest between triad and non-triad regions is apparent in changing patterns of global FDI. As Table 20.1 shows, just under 60 percent of all FDI flows into developed countries, mainly the triad. This compares to 85 percent in 1980. Asia, and particularly South-East Asia, takes the major share of the remaining 37 percent going to developing countries, with 22 percent of the world total, compared to a share of just 1 percent in 1980 and 12 percent in 1990. Africa receives 5 percent. Overall, though, FDI is the largest source of external finance for all developing countries and on average now amounts to over one-third of their GDP, compared to just

Table 20.1 FDI inflows, by host region and economy, 1990–2008 (millions of dollars)

Economy/ Region	1990	1995	2000	2005	2008
World	208,646	335,734	1,387,953	916,277	1,697,353
Developed countries	171,109	204,426	1,107,987	542,312	962,259
Western Europe	103,364	119,148	697,436	433,628	518,339
European Union	96,774	114,560	671,417	421,899	503,453
North America	56,004	68,027	380,798	133,265	360,824
United States	48,422	58,772	314,007	99,443	316,112
Japan	1,753	41	8,323	2,775	24,426
Other developed countries	11,741	17,251	29,752	−27,356	83,095
Developing countries	36,897	115,953	252,459	334,285	620,733
Africa, of which	2,427	5,392	8,728	30,672	87,647
Algeria	40	0	438	1,081	2,647
Egypt	734	595	1,235	5,376	9,495
Morocco	165	332	215	2,933	2,388
Sudan	231	12	392	2,305	2,601
Angola	−335	472	879	−24	15,548
Chad	9	33	116	705	834
Equatorial Guinea	11	65	109	1,860	1,290
Nigeria	588	1,079	930	3,403	20,279
South Africa	−78	1,241	888	6,379	9,009
Latin America and the Caribbean	9,615	30,280	97,537	103,663	144,377
Argentina	1,836	5,609	10,418	4,662	8,853
Brazil	989	4,405	32,779	15,066	45,058
Chile	661	2,956	4,860	6,667	16,787
Colombia	500	968	2,395	10,192	10,564
Ecuador	126	452	720	1,913	974
Peru	41	2,557	810	2,579	4,808
Venezuela	451	985	4,701	2,957	1,716
Bermuda	819	641	10,627	13,615	278
Cayman Islands	49	50	6,922	11,222	10,920
Mexico	2,633	9,655	16,586	18,055	21,950
Asia and the Pacific	24,854	80,281	146,195	199,951	388,709
Saudi Arabia	1,864	21,877	21,884	1,469	38,223
Azerbaijan	0	330	130	1,680	11
Kazakhstan	0	964	1,283	1,738	14,543
China	3,487	37,521	40,715	72,406	108,312
Hong Kong, China	3,275	6,213	61,939	35,897	63,003
India	237	2,151	2,319	6,598	41,554
Indonesia	1,092	4,346	24,550	5,260	7,919
Korea, Republic of	759	1,249	8,572	7,198	7,603
Malaysia	2,611	5,815	3,788	3,967	8,053
Pakistan	250	719	305	2,183	5,438
Singapore	5,575	11,591	17,217	20,083	22,725
Taiwan Province of China	1,330	1,559	4,928	1,625	5,432
Thailand	2,575	2,070	3,350	3,687	10,091
Viet Nam	180	1,780	1,289	2,020	8,050
Central and Eastern Europe	640	15,356	27,508	39,679	114,361
Bulgaria	4	90	1,002	2,223	9,205
Croatia	0	114	1,089	1,695	4,383
Romania	0	419	1,037	6,388	13,305
Russian Federation	0	2,065	2,714	14,600	70,320
Serbia and Montenegro	0	45	25	1,481	3,933

Source: Adapted from United Nations, *World Investment Report*, 2006 and 2009, key data downloads at http://www.unctad.org (Geneva: United Nations Conference on Trade and Development).

10 percent in 1980. As described below, patterns of inward FDI are varied, with some countries or regions showing significant growth while others experience no growth and even decline.[2]

Given the market-seeking and resource-seeking aims of MNE investors, we can see that the varying levels of attractiveness of different non-triad investment destinations are the result of differences in market size and growth rates and the opportunities they present for firms looking for sourcing and production advantages. Opportunities for accessing these kinds of advantages can be enhanced by government **liberalization policies**, which can help to reduce the limitations and constraints on foreign firms' investments and business activities. Liberalization, for many governments in emerging economies, signals a move away from a centrally controlled or coordinated economy, toward a more free market economy. This shift is often accompanied by the widespread privatization of state-owned firms. Again this presents opportunities for MNEs, for example, in telecoms, utilities, or energy industries, to buy into newly privatized firms or establish joint ventures and alliances to access resources or the local market. India provides a clear illustration of this with FDI inflows amounting to over $2 billion between 1991 and 1995, after liberalization, compared to well below $1 billion in the two decades leading up to 1990.

Non-triad countries and regions differ, both in their initial economic attractiveness to MNEs and in the ways that governments are liberalizing parts of the economy; together these explain many of the differences we observe in regional patterns of FDI. Table 20.2 shows that, in the same time period, outflows of FDI from developing countries have grown fairly dramatically. Again South-East Asia is responsible for the dominant share. China's stock of outward FDI has grown from $2.5 billion in 1990 to over $25 billion in 2000, and over $60 billion in 2007. It has since grown at a staggering rate, to over $148 billion in 2008 and over $245 billion in 2009. In addition to this, however, a significant proportion of the much larger outward flows from Hong Kong originally come from mainland China.

We will now briefly review the recent experience of each of the main non-triad regions in terms of inward FDI and look at some examples that provide insights into the drivers of FDI flows. In preparation for the discussion below about MNEs from emerging economies, we will also briefly look at some of the largest firms in these countries that are expanding within and beyond their regions.

Liberalization policies
Government policies that move away from planned economies toward more free market systems; they are marked by the privatization of state-owned businesses, a lowering of tariff and non-tariff barriers, and reductions in the constraints placed on foreign firms' investments and business activities

Table 20.2 FDI from developing countries, 1990–2008 (billions of dollars)

Region/economy	FDI outflows (annual average)			FDI outward stock			
	1995–1999	2000–2004	2005–2008	1995	2000	2005	2008
Developing economies	64.9	70.2	227.0	117.4	862.3	1,273.6	2,356.6
Africa	2.6	0.4	7.5	1.1	44.1	53.9	97.9
South Africa	1.9	16.7	1.5	0.1	32.3	38.5	62.3
Latin America and the Caribbean	18	13.9	53.4	32.8	204.3	345.3	561.4
Brazil	1.3	2.5	14.5	2.5	51.9	71.5	162.2
Chile	1.5	1.5	3.7	4.6	11.2	21.3	31.7
Mexico	0.7	2.4	5.2	6.2	8.3	28.0	45.3
Asia and the Pacific	44.3	55.8	166.0	83.5	613.8	874.3	1,697.2
South, East, and South-East Asia	43.6	51.8	136.5	67.6	597.2	837.6	1,564.4
China	2.2	2.7	27.0	11.3	27.7	46.3	147.9
Hong Kong, China	22.5	27.5	48.3	32.5	388.4	470.4	775.9
India	0.1	1.2	12.6	1.3	1.8	9.5	61.7
Korea, Republic of	4.3	3.6	10.2	4.3	26.8	36.4	95.5
Malaysia	2.2	1.5	8.5	2.9	15.8	44.4	67.5
Memorandum							
World	234.8	645.1	1,552.0	778.1	6,069.8	10,129.7	16,205.6

Source: UNCTAD, *World Investment Report,* 2006 and 2009 (Geneva: UNCTAD, 2006 and 2009), at www.unctad.org.

Asia–Pacific and the Middle East

As shown in Table 20.1, Asia–Pacific and the Middle East receive 23 percent of global FDI flows in 2008, the most of any non-triad region. But FDI is highly concentrated, with 10 out of the 55 economies in the region (for which reliable data are available) accounting for over 90 percent of FDI. China and Hong Kong (China) receive half of the total regional FDI, indicating their growing attractiveness to investors.

We focus on China in the next chapter, but there are examples of events and factors elsewhere in the region that help explain these patterns of investment. Many of the countries in the region continue to liberalize their economies and privatize state-owned assets, both of which are attractive to MNEs. Cross-border M&A has grown steadily, as has the significance of intra-regional M&A, as opposed to investments driven by triad-based firms. But a few large acquisitions and divestments can make a big difference to individual country markets. Following significant growth of FDI into South Korea in the early to mid-2000s, 2006 saw a drop as both Wal-Mart and Carrefour divested from the country to focus on other Asian markets.

FDI into India has grown rapidly, particularly in 2008 when inflows FDI amounted to more than 6 times between 2005 (US$6,598 million) and 2008 (US$41,554 million). A growing economy, continued liberalization, and the attractiveness of evolving IT, software, and services industries (see **Real Case: the Indian IT, software, and services industry**) all provided momentum. GM and IBM increased their presence as did Wal-Mart, Toyota, and Nissan.

The oil-rich countries of Bahrain, Jordan, Kuwait, Oman, and Saudi Arabia also experienced recent upturns in inward FDI, almost exclusively related to their oil industries. Less political turmoil would clearly have resulted in larger inflows to the Middle East region in recent decades.

Intra-regional investments
Investments in the local region rather than in other triad or non-triad regions, such as when Chinese firms invest in other South-East Asian economies

Finally, there are two clear trends that indicate the dynamism of the Asia region. First, the growth of **intra-regional investment** is particularly driven by the regional giants India and China joining countries like Malaysia, South Korea, Taiwan, and Singapore as active investors, but also by the growth of Japanese investment in the region. Second, FDI in services is growing rapidly and now represents over 50 percent of FDI stock in the Asia region. Many of the high-growth economies are becoming increasingly service oriented and have developed efficient institutional and infrastructural conditions for attracting finance, telecoms, and commerce-related activities. In accordance with its commitments to the liberalization of services under its WTO accession agreement, China is opening its service industries to FDI. Restrictions on FDI in industries such as banking and finance, telecoms, logistics and distribution, transportation, and retail and wholesale trade are being removed.

MNEs from Asia–Pacific

The Asia–Pacific region has a large proportion of the 50 largest non-financial MNEs from developing countries listed by UNCTAD (see Table 20.3). The largest number from any country come from Hong Kong (China). Top of the list is Hutchison Whampoa, a diversified conglomerate which focuses on the Asia region. Other major firms from the region include Petronas (oil and petroleum; Malaysia), Singtel (telecoms; Singapore), Samsung Electronics and LG Electronics (South Korea) and Jardine Matheson Holdings (diversified; Hong Kong).

Outward FDI from India has increased significantly in recent years. Indian companies undertake cross-border M&As to gain access to new technologies and expertise, and to build stronger positions in global markets. Steel industry takeovers have been hitting the headlines in recent years, with Mittal Steel's takeover of European firm Arcelor for $32 billion ranking as the world's largest cross-border M&A transaction in 2006. In the same year, the Tata conglomerate acquired the Corus Group for $9.5 billion. It went on to buy Jaguar and Aston Martin from Ford in 2008, to add premium brands to its low-cost automotive portfolio. A further discussion about new multinationals from non-triad regions appears below.

Table 20.3 The top 50 non-financial TNCs from developing economies ranked by foreign assets, 2007ᵃ (millions of dollars, number of employees)

Ranking by foreign assets	TNIᵇ	Corporation	Home economy	Industryᶜ	Assets		Sales		Employment		TNIᵇ
					Foreignᵉ	Total	Foreign	Total	Foreignᵈ	Total	
1	19	Hutchison Whampoa Limited	Hong Kong, China	Diversified	83,411	102,445	33,260	39,579	190,428	230,000	82.7
2	21	Cemex S.A.	Mexico	Non Metalic mineral products	44,269	49,908	18,007	21,780	50,041	66,612	82.2
3	45	LG Group	Republic of Korea	Electrical and electric equipment	30,505	57,772	50,353	81,496	40,688	79,000	55.4
4	60	Samsung Electronics Co., Ltd	Republic of Korea	Electrical and electric equipment	29,173	99,749	82,650	105,232	29,097	84,721	47.4
5	88	Petronas - Petroliam Nasional Bhd	Malaysia	Petroleum expl./ref/distr.	27,431	102,616	27,219	67,473	3,965	36,027	26.0
6	87	Hyundai Motor Company	Republic of Korea	Motor vehicles	25,939	89,571	33,692	74,353	5,178	55,629	27.9
7	92	CITIC Group	China	Diversified	25,514	180,945	3,287	14,970	18,305	107,340	17.7
8	29	Singtel	Singapore	Telecommunications	21,159	24,087	7,102	10,300	8,832	19,500	67.4
9	27	Tata Steel Ltd.	India	Metals and metal products	20,720	31,715	28,254	33,372	23,434	35,870	71.8
10	70	China Ocean Shipping (Group) Company	China	Transport and Storage	20,181	29,194	10,109	21,701	4,135	69,285	40.6
11	69	Formosa Plastic Group	Taiwan Province of China	Chemicals	19,026	86,034	15,898	61,681	70,928	94,815	40.9
12	73	Companhia Vale do Rio Doce	Brazil	Mining and quarrying	18,846	76,717	27,836	33,115	4,568	60,405	38.7
13	90	Oil and Natural Gas Corporation (ONGC)	India	Petroleum expl./ref/distr.	13,331	31,805	4,477	29,526	3,917	32,996	23.0
14	98	Petroleo Brasileiro S.A.-Petrobras	Brazil	Petroleum expl./ref/distr.	11,674	129,715	9,124	87,735	6,783	68,931	9.7
15	84	China State Construction Engineering Corporation	China	Construction and real estate	11,147	24,109	4,954	23,824	30,300	118,000	30.9
16	26	Qatar Telecom	Qatar	Telecommunications	10,909	12,985	1,628	2,850	1,539	1,832	75.0
17	52	America Movil	Mexico	Telecommunications	10,678	32,129	14,105	28,674	34,731	49,091	51.1
18	54	Zain	Kuwait	Telecommunications	10,257	15,758	4,828	6,143	1,151	15,000	50.5
19	93	Petroleos De Venezuela	Bolivia Rep. of Venezuela	Petroleum expl./ref/distr.	10,082	107,672	31,917	96,242	5,140	61,909	16.9
20	39	Capitaland Limited	Singapore	Construction and real estate	9,977	17,930	2,011	2,632	17,732	35,850	60.5
21	38	Hon Hai Precision Industries	Taiwan Province of China	Electrical and electric equipment	9,899	26,733	32,555	52,482	464,148	550,000	61.2

(continues)

Table 20.3 (Continued)

Ranking by foreign assets	TNI[b]	Corporation	Home economy	Industry[c]	Assets		Sales		Employment		TNI[b]
					Foreign[e]	Total	Foreign	Total	Foreign[d]	Total	
22	82	Sasol Limited	South Africa	Chemicals	8,776	20,574	6,546	19,081	6,029	33,928	31.6
23	66	Kia Motors	Republic of Korea	Motor vehicles	8,654	20,789	12,283	21,699	10,368	32,977	43.2
24	34	Flextronics	Singapore	Electrical and electric equipment	8,527	19,524	12,041	27,558	158,227	162,000	61.7
25	72	New World Development Co., Ltd.	Hong Kong, China	Diversified	8,414	21,189	1,728	3,764	17,890	57,000	39.0
26	63	Taiwan Semiconductor Manufacturing Co., Ltd.	Taiwan Province of China	Electrical and electric equipment	8,114	17,596	5,951	9,945	8,485	25,258	46.5
27	67	Quanta Computer Inc.	Taiwan Province of China	Electrical and electric equipment	7,941	10,043	3,043	23,963	22,428	67,291	41.7
28	47	Metalurgica Gerdau S.A.	Brazil	Metals and metal products	7,372	12,974	5,169	8,933	17,913	36,925	54.4
29	78	CLP Holdings	Hong Kong, China	Electricity, gas and water	6,989	17,468	2,676	6,510	1,481	5,695	35.7
30	100	China National Petroleum Corporation	China	Petroleum expl./ref/distr.	6,814	191,185	3,246	122,341	22,000	1,167,129	2.7
31	59	YTL Corp. Berhad	Malaysia	Electricity, gas and water	6,462	10,256	877	1,819	1,931	6,232	47.4
32	28	Orient Overseas International Ltd.	Hong Kong, China	Transport and Storage	6,301	7,214	1,728	5,651	6,130	7,200	67.7
33	22	China Resources Enterprises	Hong Kong, China	Petroleum expl./ref/distr.	6,137	7,779	4,761	6,603	125,550	135,000	81.3
34	4	China Merchants Holdings International	Hong Kong, China	Diversified	6,015	6,254	823	880	5,249	5,448	95.3
35	33	Wilmar International Limited	Singapore	Food, beverages and tobacco	5,765	10,414	8,770	11,425	12,906	23,313	62.5
36	53	Hynix Semiconductor Inc.	Republic of Korea	Electrical and electric equipment	5,765	18,928	8,634	9,234	5,160	18,226	50.8
37	41	Shangri La Asia Limited	Hong Kong, China	Other consumer services	5,716	6,101	988	1,219	1,219	24,000	59.9
38	57	Genting Berhad	Malaysia	Other consumer services	5,490	9,127	741	2,566	16,522	27,117	50.0
39	42	Star Cruises	Hong Kong, China	Transport and Storage	5,157	6,429	2,123	2,576	3,200	20,500	59.4

40	80	Gold Fields Limited	South Africa	Metals and metal products	5,092	9,239	1,284	3,379	2,672	51,192	32.8
41	3	First Pacific Company Limited	Hong Kong, China	Electrical and electric equipment	4,963	5,228	3,075	3,075	51,694	51,722	98.3
42	75	Sinochem Corp.	China	Petroleum expl./ref/distr.	4,812	14,886	24,274	31,412	225	26,632	36.8
43	25	Acer Inc.	Taiwan Province of China	Electrical and electric equipment	4,764	7,499	12,608	14,982	5,293	6,271	77.4
44	81	Naspers Limited	South Africa	Other consumer services	4,730	8,340	683	3,013	2,245	13,812	31.9
45	43	Fraser & Neave Limited	Singapore	Food, beverages and tobacco	4,699	8,927	2,086	3,288	8,949	1,700	56.2
46	64	Sime Darby Berhad	Malaysia	Diversified	4,695	10,879	6,493	10,296	25,432	100,000	43.9
47	46	Steinhoff International Holdings	South Africa	Other consumer services	4,049	5,527	3,629	6,615	16,092	43,364	55.1
48	61	Lenovo Group	China	Electrical and electronic equipment	4,030	7,180	10,226	16,352	5,340	23,111	47.3
49	20	Beijing Enterprises Holdings Ltd.	Hong Kong, China	Diversified	4,027	5,727	1,448	1,448	26,275	34,400	82.2
50	30	Sappi Limited	South Africa	Wood and paper products	4,001	6,344	3,898	5,304	9,802	15,081	67.2

Notes:

a All data are based on the annual reports of TNCs (MNEs) unless otherwise stated.

b TNI, or "Transnationality Index," is calculated as the average of the following three ratios: foreign assets to total sales, foreign sales to total sales, and foreign employment to total employment.

c Industry classifications for companies follows the US Standard Industrial classification as used by the US Securities and Exchange Commission (SEC).

d Foreign employment data are calculated by applying the share of foreign employment in total employment of the previous year to total employment of 2007.

e In a number of cases, companies reported only partial foreign sales. In a number of cases companies reported sales only by destination.

f Foreign sales are based on the origin of the sales. In a number of cases companies reported sales only by destination.

h Foreign assets data are calculated by applying the share of foreign assets in total assets of the previous year to total assets of 2007.

i Foreign sales data are calculated by applying the share of foreign sales in total assets of the previous year to total sales of 2007.

j Data were obtained from the company in response to an UNCTAD survey.

t Data for foreign activities are outside Asia.

m Foreign employment data are calculated by applying the average of the share of foreign employment in total employment of all companies in the same industry (omitting the extremes) to total employment.

Source: United Nations, World Investment Report, 2009 © United Nations 2009 www.unctad.org/wit.

Central and Eastern Europe

Despite years of political and economic change, including liberalization, in the Central and East European (CEE) region, it still attracts a relatively small percentage of global FDI inflows (see Table 20.1). In 2008, FDI inflows to CEE increased to $114,361 million from $39,679 million in 2005.

Poland, the Czech Republic, and Hungary receive larger shares of FDI than other countries in the region but have experienced declines in recent years, as has the Russian Federation. These, plus five other CEE countries (Estonia, Latvia, Lithuania, Slovenia, and Slovakia), joined the EU in May 2004 and saw FDI inflows shrink, but things have improved since then.

Some countries are attracting auto sector FDI, including the Czech Republic, with an investment from Toyota–PSA, and Slovakia, with investments from PSA, Kia, and Hyundai. Volkswagen Slovakia is already that country's largest company and biggest employer by far. Slovakia has a population of just over 5 million people, yet has developed into a leading producer of autos, nearing an output of 180 cars per 1,000 inhabitants, from having no auto industry whatsoever before 1991, when VW took over Skoda's businesses in Bratislava in the Czech Republic. VW has invested around $1.3 billion in Slovakia, and Hyundai's investments are expected to total $1.5 billion eventually. But in all these cases the MNEs were attracted to the region not just because of the combination of cheap labor, good infrastructure, and proximity to Europe's large markets, but also because of the over $1 billion in subsidies and regional development loans they received to sweeten the deal.[3]

In terms of outflows of FDI from the CEE region, the Russian Federation has dominated for some time as the major source. A key question for analysts is whether these capital flows represent genuine strategic investments in other parts of the world or capital flight from a politically tense Russia.

MNEs from Central and Eastern Europe

The largest MNEs in the CEE region are Russian, most of them nationally owned at one time or another and many of them based on the country's abundant natural resources. The Russian oil and gas giants (Gazprom, Rosneft, and Lukoil) have started to expand abroad, including Gazprom's investments in the German energy sector to get direct access to end-users (also see the Real case study in Chapter 15 on Yukos). Telecoms, aluminum, and other industries also feature in the international expansion of CEE firms.

Latin America and the Caribbean

Only 8.5 percent of global FDI went to the Latin America region in 2008, the highest proportion since 1980 and still slightly lower than inflows to China and Hong Kong (China) that year. Inward FDI has grown since then, but the percentage of global FDI going to this region has fallen. The three largest economies of Argentina, Brazil, and Mexico have seen large fluctuations in inflows in the recent past. To various degrees these economies have had a difficult decade in terms of economic growth and recession. A spate of privatizations during the late 1990s gave a temporary boost to inward FDI for these and other regional economies and a number of MNEs increased their involvement in Latin America during this period. An example is Endesa, the Spanish-owned electricity utility, which is the leading supplier in six countries and serves 10.5 million customers (50 percent of its global market) in the region. Through its regional subsidiary Enersis, Endesa bought into or bought out national companies in Argentina, Brazil, Chile, Peru, Colombia, and the Dominican Republic to develop massive economies of scale in energy production, distribution, and services in the region.[4]

Regional-level, as opposed to national-level, competition has evolved in other industries, sometimes pitting home-based MNEs against foreign-owned incomers. In telecoms, for example, Mexico's America Movil and Spain's Telefonica are battling it out for regional domination, both having boosted their holdings when US telecom firms went through a divestment phase. Although the former dominates the Mexican mobile telephony business, it has a long way to go to catch up with Telefonica. Telefonica Moviles, the Spanish firm's regional mobile telecom subsidiary, has a presence in 13 countries in the region, is the market leader in 7 and second in 5, and serves a total of over 40 million customers.[5]

Brazil and Mexico still receive the highest amounts of FDI and, as we would expect, one-third of all FDI into the region came from the United States. Many Latin American countries now face increased competition for US manufacturing investment from China and the Asia region. This is particularly true of Mexico, whose linkage to the North American triad via NAFTA was discussed in Chapter 10, where the Mexico–US double diamond was explained. The mid-2000s saw a decline in the number of *maquiladora* enterprises (which accounted for almost 50 percent of Mexico's merchandise exports) and associated jobs losses. Combined with the decline in inward FDI, this called into question the attractiveness and competitiveness of the region in comparison to a fast-evolving Asia.

MNEs from Latin America

Of the 50 largest non-financial TNCs from developing countries listed by UNCTAD (Table 20.3), a relatively small number are from the Latin American region. As with the Central and East European MNEs (and contrasting those from the Asia–Pacific region) many of the largest are natural resources based. These include the largest of all, Cemex (construction materials; Mexico), Petroleos de Venezuela (Venezuela), Petrobras (Brazil), Companhia Vale do Rio Doce (mining; Brazil), Metalurgica Gerdau (metal products; Brazil), and Perez Companc (oil and petroleum; Argentina).

Africa

As home to most of the world's least developed countries (LDCs), Africa has always recorded low levels of inward FDI because of its relative lack of attractiveness to MNEs. Political instability, weak infrastructure, poor labor skills, and macroeconomic fragility have plagued many parts of the continent for decades. Except for the larger economies of Egypt and South Africa, and the oil producers such as Equatorial Guinea, Angola, Nigeria, and the Sudan, most of the remaining LDCs normally receive less than $200 million FDI per year.

As shown in Table 20.1, only 5 percent of total global FDI normally goes to Africa in 2008, and this tends to be concentrated in resource-rich economies. Oil, diamonds, gold, and platinum in particular have been the main attraction for MNEs. Exxon Mobil, for example, has offshore oil projects in Nigeria, and the French firm Total Oil Nigeria has plans to invest $10 billion in the Nigerian oil industry.[6] For most of Sub-Saharan Africa, however, inflows are limited, although South Africa stands out as a major recipient due to its relatively healthy economy. Chinese investment into Africa, particularly targeting sources of raw materials and resources, is very much in the news. FDI worth an estimated $30–$40 billion, much of it from state-owned enterprises has flowed into Sub-Saharan Africa, but accurate data is not yet available.

FDI in telecoms and services recently overtook investment in mining and extraction in South Africa. At the same time it has extended its investments in other parts of the continent, with firms like BHP Billiton (mining) and Eskom (utilities) expanding into other African markets. Two of South Africa's telecom firms are also majority shareholders in the largest mobile telecom firm in Africa, a joint venture between Telecom SA, VenFin, and Vodafone (35 percent stake) with over 10 million subscribers and almost $2.5 billion in revenues. It competes with MTN Group from South Africa, Orascom (Egypt), Orange (France Telecom), and CelTel International (the Netherlands), all of which are gradually taking market share from the fixed-line industry dominated by national telecom firms. In some industry sectors, despite the lack of inward FDI, there are growing business links between Western firms and local African firms. The Kenya cut flower industry is one example (see **International Business Strategy in Action: From Oserian to Tesco: the Kenyan cut flower industry**).

From Oserian to Tesco: the Kenyan cut flower industry

Kenya is the leading exporter of cut flowers to Europe, with over 30 percent market share. Yet this industry has really grown only over the last 15 years, with export growth accelerating rapidly in the late 1990s and achieving 27 percent growth between 2001 and 2005. How has this new-found global competitive advantage come about in one of the world's least developed countries? The real start of the industry happened in 1994 with the formation of the Kenya Flower Council to support the operations of a number of fast-growing businesses.

Horticultural and cut flower exports provide well over US $1 billion to Kenya's economy and flower exports alone earn over US $600 million. The country has about 7 percent of the global export market. Ecuador and Colombia are key competitors and the Netherlands still dominates with over 50 percent. The major markets are Germany, the UK, and United States, but the major proportion of exports goes to the Dutch auction houses in Holland. Direct sales via supermarket chains, particularly in the UK, have increased dramatically, however.

The country's flower industry employs about 70,000 people, and supports more than half a million people in Kenya. The average basic wage in the flower industry is around US $5,000 compared to Kenya's average GDP per capita of US $800. Most of the flower growing is in the areas of Naivasha, Thika, and Kiambu, where over 2,000 hectares are used for flower production. Although over 30 varieties of flowers are grown in Kenya, roses make up two-thirds of Kenya's flower exports, followed by carnations, statice, and alstromeria.

Local factor conditions

The successful cultivation of flowers requires the following elements:

■ Good physical conditions: high light intensity, abundant water, clean soil, good climate

■ Appropriate seeds and planting material

■ Capital for investment and working capital

■ Productive labor

■ Expertise in growing techniques

■ Good management and organization

■ Pesticides and other chemicals

■ Energy for heating

■ Infrastructure

■ A high level of quality consciousness all along the production and post-harvesting chain

Perhaps more than any other internationally traded good, time-to-market is critical in the cut flower industry. Strict control of humidity, temperature, and air quality is essential for delivering an attractive product to the market. Growers rely heavily on the post-harvest chain of handlers, storage, and transport, and in the absence of a "cold chain" it is not possible for equatorial producers to sell to the main northern markets.

Air freight adds significantly to the total cost and makes up by far the largest component of overall cost to African producers. Air freight, marketing, handling in Europe, and packaging make up 50 percent of all costs for Kenyan growers. In the Netherlands, however, transport accounts for just 14 percent of the costs, but labor makes up 35 percent of costs.

Although cheap labor and a good growing climate are advantageous for growing flowers, some countries have done well for some time without these local factor endowments. The Netherlands does not have climatic, land, or labor advantages but has been a dominant player in the industry for a long time. This is partly due to the power of the Dutch auction houses, which have long overseen the international flower trade.

In Porter's terminology (in the diamond model discussed in Chapter 10) acquired factor conditions, such as the cold-transport infrastructure, plant breeding and greenhouse technologies, and production management capabilities were required before Kenya could leverage its natural endowments and the cheap labor advantage to compete in the open market. It is only in the last 15 to 20 years that these acquired factors have developed.

In 2008 another "Diamond of Advantage" factor, the influence of government, loomed large when the Presidency of Mwai Kibaki faced a vote of no confidence by the people. Political instability took its toll on the flower companies, raising questions about the sustainability of an important industry.

The Oserian Development Company

Oserian ("place of peace" in Maasai), one of the largest privately owned flower farms in the world, was among the first commercial exporters of cut flowers from Kenya. Although it began growing flowers in the early 1980s the company dates from 1967 and was started and is still operated and partly owned by Hans and Peter Zwager. It has over 200 hectares under cultivation next to Lake Naivasha in the Rift Valley and exports over 300 million stems per year. These are mainly sold by East African Flowers (EAF)

BV, through the Teleflower Auction (TFA) in Holland, to other buyers around the world; or by World Flowers in the UK, direct to Tesco. Crops include roses, spray carnations, gypsophila, chrysanthemums, statice, hypericum, euphorbia, delphinium, and perezi. The farm employs about 5,000 people; 85 percent are permanent employees and over 60 percent live on the farm with their families. The facilities include three kindergartens, two primary schools, a secondary school, shopping centers, social halls, and a medical center.

Industry structure: Tesco and the growing power of the supermarkets

Although the Dutch auction houses have traditionally been the focal point of the world flower industry, large retailers are building direct links with growers around the world, using their purchasing power to gain better control over product price, delivery, and quality. African producers appear to be the main beneficiaries of this change in purchasing habits. Supermarkets are interested in African flowers because they are inexpensive and because growers are willing to accept a set price. To the growers this arrangement is attractive because supermarkets buy large quantities at prearranged prices. But in order to live up to their side of the bargain African growers must invest in optimal production methods. Often this includes investments in greenhouses, forced ventilation and heating, and, in all cases, greater attention to quality.

Over the past decade Kenya's direct imports to the UK have grown, partly due to the establishment of direct links with Marks & Spencer and Tesco. The British spend more than $3 billion a year on fresh cut flowers and indoor plants; 85 percent of all flowers sold in the UK are imported, of which about 20 percent come from countries outside the EU.

Around one-quarter of roses sold in the UK are purchased directly from Kenya, mainly by the major supermarkets. Tesco, one of the top three supermarket chains in the world, is the UK's number one food retailer and the largest retailer of flowers and plants. Tesco has been selling houseplants and flowers for the last two decades and sales keep growing, hence the need for reliable ties with suppliers. Tesco became an associate member of the Kenya Flower Council in early 2000 as its direct links with suppliers like Oserian began to grow. By cutting out the Dutch auction houses, Tesco found that it could work directly with growers to reduce prices and improve quality and also pass on customer needs to more directly influence new developments.

Fairtrade

Tesco and Oserian deepened their buyer–supplier alliance by opening a line of Fairtrade roses. These are grown by Oserian and one other farm in Kenya (Finlay Flowers in Kericho), which have been certified to comply with employment, social, and environmental conditions laid down in the Fairtrade agreement.

The agreement was set up in response to concerns among customers and expressed in the media about the conditions under which flowers are grown. This included the employment conditions of workers and the environmental effects on the land and particularly water availability, around, for example, Lake Naivasha. Although Fairtrade roses are slightly more expensive, they represent a differentiated product designed to appeal to ethically minded customers. Tesco does not take an additional profit as 8 percent of the overall export price goes directly to the farms, allocated by joint management and employee committees, to improve employee conditions. This premium is worth up to US $200,000 per year to the two farms involved. This concern for social ethics has strengthened as Oserian became part of the Mavuno Group in 2010 and expanded its direct sales to more global markets.

Sources: http://www.oserian.com/; A. Odhiambo, "Oserian deal with Dutch firm sparks rivalry," *Business Daily*, April 2011, http://www.businessdailyafrica.com/Corporate+News/; "Roses Are Red: Kenya's Flower Industry," *The Economist*, February 7, 2008; Gathoni Muraya, "Local Flower Market Quietly Booming," *Business Day Africa*, March 28, 2007, http://bdafrica.com/index2.php?option=com_content&task=view&id=369&pop=1&page=0&Itemid=255; C. S. Dolan, S. Jafee and R. Thoen, "Equatorial Rose: The Kenyan-European Cut Flower Supply Chain," in R. Kopiki (ed.), *Supply Chain Development in Emerging Markets* (Boston, MA: MIT Press, 2004); Mary Hennock, "Kenya's Flower Farms Flourish," *BBC News Online*, February 14, 2002, at http://news.bbc.co.uk/1/hi/business/1820515.stm; Chris Collinson, *The Business Costs of Ethical Supply Chain Management Report No. 2607*, Natural Resources and Ethical Trade Programme (Chatham: National Resources Institute, 2001), at http://www.nri.org/NRET/2607.pdf; further material from the KFC at http://www.africaonline.co.ke/kfc/index.html; industry data from the Horticultural Crop Development Authority (HCDA), Nairobi; http://www.tesco.com/corporateinfo/.

MNEs from Africa

Just 5 of the 50 largest non-financial TNCs from developing countries listed by UNCTAD (Table 20.3) are from Africa, and they are all South African. Sasol (industrial chemicals), Gold Fields (metal products), Naspers (consumer services), Steinhoff (consumer services) and Sappi (paper products), are major players in their respective sectors throughout the region. At least part of the explanation for the lack of large indigenous firms from other African countries lies in their colonial past and the history of domination by Western multinationals as investors in local mineral or agricultural resources.[7]

SHIFTING PATTERNS OF COMPARATIVE AND COMPETITIVE ADVANTAGE

As we have seen from the breakdown of FDI flows above, FDI into non-triad regions tends to be concentrated in a few countries within each region. Moreover, although FDI still tends to be related to primary resources, such as oil, minerals, and agricultural commodities in many of these countries, there is a growing volume of manufacturing and service-related FDI. This is particularly true for a group of emerging markets or **newly industrialized countries (NICs)**, which have broken the cycle of underdevelopment to achieve economic growth and wealth creation, partly through increased integration with other parts of the global economy. This group includes relatively wealthy countries like South Korea, Singapore, Hong Kong (China), and Taiwan (China), which were together called the "four Asian Tigers" in the 1980s when they began to achieve high rates of economic growth. But there are also other growing economies, particularly in the Asia–Pacific region, that appear to be moving along the same growth path. Why are these economies growing? How are they able to compete with triad firms, export, and sell in triad markets? Why are they attractive as locations for triad FDI? These are important questions as the emergence of these economies, particularly the two giant markets of China and India, is giving rise to some of the most important competitive opportunities and threats for MNEs of all types.

Newly industrialized countries (NICs)
A subgroup of emerging market economies that has experienced rapid economic growth, normally accompanied by political and social change; the forerunners were the four Asian "Tiger" economies: Singapore, South Korea, Taiwan, and Hong Kong. The rapid growth, increased trade and FDI, and integration of China in the global economy show that it is approaching this status

To understand current patterns of growth in many emerging markets we need to briefly review some of the theoretical explanations for the evolving patterns of national-level comparative and competitive advantage (we did this in Chapter 6 and some of the following summarizes our earlier description). In the original landmark study of wealth creation and national competitiveness, the economist Adam Smith stated:

What is prudence in the conduct of every private family, can scarce be folly in that of a great kingdom. If a foreign country can supply us with a commodity cheaper than we ourselves can make it, better buy it of them with some part of the produce of our own industry, employed in a way in which we have some advantage. The general industry of the country, being always in proportion to the capital which employs it, will not thereby be diminished . . . but only left to find out the way in which it can be employed with the greatest advantage.[8]

Theory of absolute advantage
Nations should specialize in particular industries where they have a particular advantage and trade to gain other goods and services; all countries benefit so long as protectionism is minimized

Adam Smith's **theory of absolute advantage** suggested that each nation should *specialize* in producing goods it had a *natural* or *acquired* advantage in producing (and therefore could produce more efficiently than other countries). Exports of these goods would pay for the import of goods that other countries produced more efficiently. There were therefore *net gains from trade* for all countries involved. Smith also became famous for his analysis of specialization and competitive advantage at the firm level.

Over time Smith's views were extended, for example, by David Ricardo's theory of comparative advantage. A notable shift toward looking at sources of competitive advantage and regional variations in these to explain global patterns of competitiveness came in the early 1900s. Two Swedes—Eli Heckscher (in 1919) and Bertil Ohlin (in 1933)—are responsible for developing a basic model that was further refined by the American economist Paul Samuelson. The H–O or HOS model (or theory of factor endowments) takes us beyond the simple assumptions made by Ricardo about labor productivity to look at the *relative availability* of different factors of production (primarily land, labor, and capital) and therefore their *relative price* (rent, wages, and interest) in each country. These will determine the products in which a country has a comparative advantage, and in which it will therefore tend to specialize and trade.[9]

The HOS model maps out the initial conditions for regional specialization in capital-intensive or labor-intensive industries according to local factor advantages but is also a dynamic model, showing how economic conditions change as countries interact through trade. These theories underpin the Porter diamond model (see Chapter 10). They are also incorporated into the interestingly named **Flying Geese model** by Japanese academic Kaname Akamatsu.[10]

Flying Geese model

Flying Geese model
A model suggesting that Asian countries are following Japan's historical economic transition, specializing in particular industries (steel to textiles to clothing to autos to electronics) during particular growth stages. At a particular point in time we should expect to see these industries located in different Asian countries, depending on their resource endowments, labor costs, and capabilities

The Flying Geese model (Figure 20.2) suggests that Asian economies are following similar development paths, but are at different stages along this path, following the lead "goose," Japan. Over time each country, or group, will gain and then subsequently lose specific comparative advantage in a particular industry. Japan has shifted from iron and steel to textiles to clothing to autos to electronics. The four Tiger economies—Hong Kong, South Korea, Singapore, and Taiwan—followed a similar trajectory, although quicker. Other ASEAN (Association of South-East Asian Nations) members such as Indonesia, Malaysia, the Philippines, and Thailand are a little further behind, but the sequence of specialization is similar. In each country the transition is marked by a shift of employment from one sector to another, within the broader move from agriculture to manufacturing and then to services. Overall, rising skills and improved technological capabilities, increased capital investment, and wage inflation (as predicted by the HOS model) drive, and are driven by, the change process.

If we look at a particular industry, the location of production activities and subsequent exports and trade flows change as different economies change their specialization (Figure 20.3). China now dominates as the world's biggest exporter of textiles and

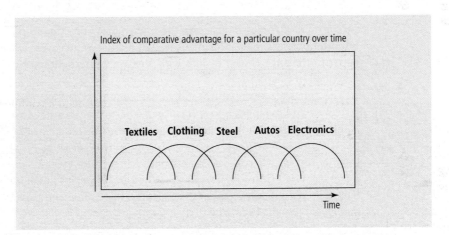

Figure 20.2 "Flying Geese" model: changing national-level specialization

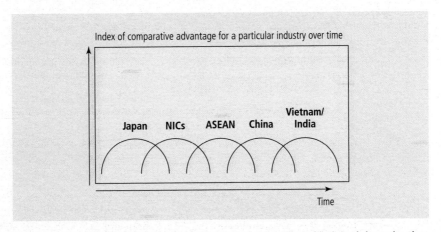

Figure 20.3 "Flying Geese" model: the shifting location of industrial production

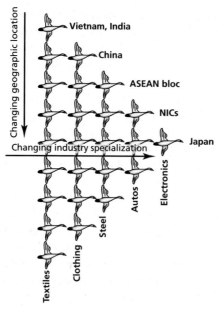

Figure 20.4 "Flying Geese" pattern of shifting comparative advantage

clothing, Korea has a thriving automobile sector, and Singapore and Taiwan have very successful electronics industries. These have grown to the point that Japan, now a net importer of televisions, is losing its lead in many product areas (Figure 20.4). The overall pattern of change is also in line with Vernon's international product life cycle theory described in Chapter 6.[11]

The timescale over which individual countries develop the economic conditions, resources, and capabilities to specialize in a particular industry sector appears to be shortening. Comparative advantage between nations is also therefore shifting faster than in the past (Figure 20.5). It took Toyota and Sony 30 to 35 years to evolve into leading firms in their industries, whereas Samsung (South Korea) and Acer (Taiwan) took 20 to 25 years. Firms like WIPRO, InfoSys, and TCS, which are lead firms in the Indian software industry, have achieved superior competitive positions (albeit in niche areas of customized software and IT services) in 15 to 20 years.

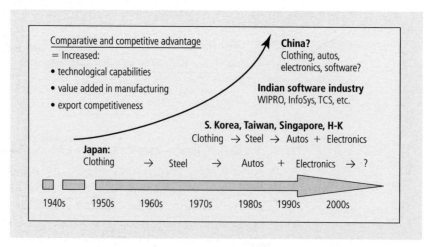

Figure 20.5 Accelerated structural transformation (are the geese flying faster?)

The Flying Geese model is far from perfect and has been widely criticized on a number of counts. Many studies note that the sequential transfer of industrial specialization does not follow the same pattern in each country, or that it tends to be more of a parallel process whereby emerging economies seem to develop capabilities and grow exports across several industries at the same time.[12] The example of the Indian IT and services industry (see Real Case) also demonstrates that leapfrogging is possible. Here an LDC has evolved competitive advantages in an advanced service sector without going through the stages depicted by the model.

For the most critical observers, the model is associated with a desire by Japan to see itself as the lead "goose" in the region from a political and perhaps military perspective (particularly given that its origins date back to the 1930s), as opposed to a useful representation of patterns of economic transformation.

There are, however, some insights we can gain into the processes affecting the changing global locations of different industries and business activities and into the changing relative competitive advantages between countries. With this in mind we need to think about the future for China—the evolving specializations of Chinese firms and the resulting competitive threats for other firms. China represents a powerful combination of cheap and well-educated labor, good infrastructure, a growing domestic market, and massive inflows of capital and technology from abroad. These are driving the rapid development of comparative and competitive advantage in a range of industries, including clothing, autos, white goods, and electronics. What we may be seeing is parallel development across these sectors, rather than sequential, stage-wise development following the lead goose (as shown in Figure 20.5). This theme is taken up in Chapter 20.

✔ Active learning check

Review your answer to Active Learning Case question 2 and make any changes you like. Then compare your answer to the one below.

2 **How are changes in the Asian regional economy, in terms of both growing markets and growing competitors, affecting Acer and should the firm cope?**

Among a range of threats and opportunities China looms large in both respects. Acer has taken a step in the right direction by moving away from manufacturing, where Chinese firms have natural advantages, and into customer-oriented design, development, and services. Acer's advantages also lie in its global distribution and marketing and its brand. These are firm-specific advantages (FSAs), which Lenovo and other Chinese firms will take some time to develop. The evolving political relationship between Taiwan and mainland China or the People's Republic of China is also an important factor, influencing some of the strategic options open to firms like Acer. But other parts of Asia, including Japan, are changing and the firm could do well to develop an international strategy that focused more on the regional than the global.

Emerging economies as sources of innovation

A natural extension to the above theories on comparative and competitive advantage is to examine innovation as a relative (and sustainable) source of advantage at the national, industry, and firm level. Traditional theories about the MNE tended to view the triad as a source of innovation and non-triad regions as recipients in a simple outward diffusion model. But other studies, which go beyond the Flying Geese model, have shown how firms that develop the independent capacity to innovate, continually upgrading their FSAs and

Globalizing...	Assets	Capabilities	Connections	Reputation
Innovation and technology	Patents, licenses, IPR; specialized tools hardware, software, etc.	Low-end (maintenance) to high-end (blue-sky R&D) expertise	Strategic alliances; buyer and supplier links; R&D networks/ global capability inputs	Credibility, trust, track record, recognition
Marketing and brands	Own valued brands, logos, trademarks, awards, etc.	Brand management protection, development expertise	Formal co-branding; supplier or buyer, distribution, and retailing affiliations	Reputation for quality, price, innovation, etc.; market positioning, brand recognition; market presence

Figure 20.6 Firm-specific advantages (FSAs) for the new multinationals

reducing their reliance on location-specific endowments (CSAs), such as cheap labor, can achieve more sustainable competitive advantages.[13]

Specific combinations of country-specific advantages (CSAs) and firm-specific advantages (FSAs) explain Japan's competitive advantage in auto exports, Taiwan's semiconductor industry, and Indian IT and software businesses, for example (see also Figure 20.6). Local conditions (the CSAs) also "breed" certain organizational forms, assets, capabilities, or expertise (FSAs) that turn out to be relative strengths in other markets. Honda's original export success in the United States came from its ability to make smaller, fuel-efficient autos, which it was forced to do to succeed in the domestic Japanese market during the postwar period. Porter cites demanding customers, industry rivalry, and efficient and effective supply chains (the *keiretsu* structures described in Chapter 18) as key local drivers of the innovative capabilities of Japanese auto firms.[14] Both product and process innovation tend to be important. Continuously learning how to produce better (cheaper, more desirable) products and services in better (cheaper, more efficient, faster) ways is the key. But the dual effects of CSAs and FSAs that lead to international competitiveness can arise by chance as well as by design, and usually result from an unanticipated combination of both.

As the Real Case on the Indian software industry below shows, and the Oserian case study looking at the Kenyan cut flower industry also shows above, firms in developing and emerging economies have an increasing range of opportunities to exploit local endowments and develop new competitive advantages. However, the openness of the global economy means that local players have to compete with MNEs which are also looking to exploit specific CSAs and often have equal access.

The Brazilian biofuels industry, for example, has evolved since the 1970s because petroleum has traditionally been expensive and sugar cane cheap and available. Following the government's Proálcool program of incentives, the country gets more than 30 percent of its automobile fuels from sugar cane-based ethanol (mainly from bagasse which is cane waste); 85 percent of new cars there can run on biofuels. In a world where governments, consumers, and companies aim to move toward more environmentally-friendly sources of energy, Brazil has emerged as a leader in agricultural processing and automotive technologies related to ethanol-based fuels. However, in contrast to India's IT sector, or China's white goods industry, the few, small-scale automotive producers in Brazil appear to have lost out to the multinationals, failing to exploit their own country's head-start in ethanol fuel technologies. GM is seizing the opportunity by establishing a number of joint ventures in Brazil to co-develop better automotive technology in this field. It is gaining a lead in duel-fuel systems and all of its cars produced in Brazil are "FlexFuel" vehicles. Rather than attracted by low costs, GM's choice of location for its R&D was driven by the need to access the best capabilities available globally.[15]

International studies, including the World Competitiveness Report, use science and technology indicators, such as patenting output, to assess and compare the growing innovative capacity of different countries in different industries and technologies. In recent years Singapore, Taiwan, Korea, Malaysia, Chile and the Czech Republic have all ranked well as up-and-coming innovators.[16] The development of world-class universities and other attributes of advanced national science and technology infrastructures (or "national innovation systems") has made some emerging economies attractive to R&D FDI from MNEs. China ranks third as a preferred location for foreign R&D investment, after the United States and the UK, while India, Singapore, and Brazil are all in the top 20.[17] Microsoft, Siemens, and Philips have invested heavily into the Republic of Korea, for example, because of the available range of expertise in high-technology fields. Microsoft's Mobile Innovation Lab develops wireless technologies and software for mobile devices. Siemens bought into Dasan Networks and develops communications and information systems technology for its global markets. Following acquisitions of parts of the LG Group, Philips has developed an R&D center focused on TV technology. This influx of high-technology investment further adds to the importance of emerging economies as sources of, rather than passive recipients of, innovation.

MARKET ACCESS TO THE TRIAD

For non-triad firms the triad regions encompass by far the largest, wealthiest, and most sophisticated markets in the world. Access can be subject to complex arrangements with varying degrees of economic trade liberalization and protectionism that are inherent in the institutional and political structures of these regions. The triad represents both globalization and sovereignty dimensions. The EU is the most politically integrated, in terms of institutional structures, and the Japanese-based bloc is the least. NAFTA is a free trade agreement, not a common market, but NAFTA contains provisions for the accession of Latin American and Caribbean and Central American nations, and it may then evolve into stronger political linkages like the EU model.

To develop global industries, non-triad nations need both trade and investment from the triad nations and also access to the markets of at least one of the triads. This implies that the focus of business strategy for firms in a smaller, non-triad nation should be to secure inward triad investment and market access for exports to a triad bloc. This can be done by direct business contact of a double-diamond type, but it is helped and reinforced by formal linkages arranged by the governments. As demonstrated in the previous chapter, both Canada and Mexico have already gone this route.

In Chapter 2 we identified "clusters" of nations that are making such arrangements with triad blocs. In general, NAFTA is the basis for a trading bloc of the Americas; the EU is the locus for East European and African nations; Japan is the hub for many Asian businesses. Some smaller, non-triad nations may attempt to open the doors to two triad markets. For example, both South Korea and Taiwan have equal trade and investment with the United States and Japan. Firms from these countries need two double diamonds. (See **International Business Strategy in Action: Korean *chaebols:* Hyundai and Samsung**). Australia still has a large amount of trade with the UK and the EU, but its trade with Japan and other Asian nations is increasing rapidly. Indeed, the geographical basis of the triad serves to reinforce the dependence of neighboring nations on their dominant regional economic partner.

INTERNATIONAL BUSINESS STRATEGY IN ACTION

Korean *chaebols*: Hyundai and Samsung

Between 1970 and 2000, South Korea's GDP grew by 750 percent. Industrial production increased at an even higher rate and grew to account for over 95 percent of GDP in 2004. GDP per capita grew from $100 in 1963 to $10,000 in 1995 and over $25,000 today. The so-called "Miracle on the Han River" has made the country the 12th largest in the world in terms of GDP, and it continues to grow faster than most advanced economies.

In South Korea's transition to industrialization, a transition that many other poor countries have tried to make with little success, *chaebols* played a major role. South Korea still maintains a healthy rate of growth, although it is not as rapid as in the boom years, particularly since the Asian financial crisis of 1997–1998. This also marked a turning point in the role of the *chaebols*, whose opaque, interdependent structures and cross-shareholdings are increasingly being questioned by South Koreans themselves, as well as by outsiders.

According to Global Fortune 500, 2011 ranking, the five largest *chaebols* are Samsung Electronics, Hyundai Motor, SK Holdings, POSCO, and LG Electronics. Across the world, these companies have become household names producing everything from ships to autos to electronics. During the 1960s, *chaebols* prospered under a government-fostered development plan. When Park Chung Hee became South Korea's president after a military *coup d'état*, he instituted an import-substitution strategy that favored large local producers and provided them with cheap credit, tax breaks, and other benefits. After Park Chung Hee's death, low-interest loans continued to be made available to *chaebols* because of ties with banks. Since banks could not let a borrower the size of *chaebols* fail, credit was made available regardless of profitability, depriving the non-*chaebol* business sector from much needed credit.

In the 1990s, the *chaebols* took on debt to finance large expansion projects. The Asian financial crisis in 1997–1998 reduced their revenues to such an extent that these companies could no longer pay their creditors. For a long time, *chaebols* managed to conceal their troubles by providing member companies with intra-conglomerate loans. In addition, foreign and domestic investors became increasingly aware of murky financial reporting practices. By the end of the crisis, Daewoo had become bankrupt.

In 1997, the IMF was called to bail out the South Korean economy after an unprecedented drop on the Korean won created a debt crisis. As part of the bailout, South Korea was to restructure its *chaebols*. Debt-to-equity ratios had to be reduced. Financial reporting had to become transparent. Most importantly, non-core businesses were to be spun off. To oversee the transformation of the *chaebols* and, in turn, the Korean economy, the Financial Supervisory Commission (FSC) was established in 1998. Although *chaebols* have reduced their debt-to-equity ratios, unreliable financial reporting continues to occur. Most importantly, many *chaebols* continue to resist selling off their non-core businesses.

Hyundai Automotive and Samsung Electronics are two of the most successful and international firms from South Korea, but they have taken different development paths to get where they are.

Chaebols had their origins in the vision of individuals. In 1946 Chung Ju Yung, who worked as a delivery boy for a rice mill in the 1930s, purchased an auto repair shop that was the early foundation of the Hyundai group. In 1947 Hyundai Engineering and Construction was established to take advantage of reconstruction contracts at the end of World War II. By 1976, Hyundai brought its country into the auto business with the introduction of the Pony.

Hyundai Automotive spun off from its conglomerate parent and merged with Kia to form one vehicle company, now the fifth largest in the world in terms of unit sales. In recent years it has experienced significant increases in overseas sales, particularly in the United States and Europe. As an indication of its standing Hyundai won top place as the most reliable car manufacturer in an influential consumer survey in the United States, joining Japanese car manufacturers in the top spots for

Source: Corbis/Reuters

the first time. It has also made significant inroads into the Chinese market, particularly in 2008 with its joint-venture partner Beijing Automotive. In 2010, Hyundai Motor's revenues were US $97 billion, representing an impressive growth of 1.47 times from US $67 billion in 2006. In 2010, Hyundai Automotive generated 49.3 percent of its revenue from Korea, 14.8 percent from Asia, 21.8 percent from North America, and 14.1 percent from Europe. Hyundai Automotive is a home-region MNE.

In 1938, Byung-Chul Lee founded Samsung and began exporting food to China, and not long after that he opened a light manufacturing business. The 1970s saw Samsung enter into the chemical and heavy manufacturing industries. In the 1980s, the company entered the aerospace and telecommunications industry. During this decade, Samsung also became a major world supplier of semiconductors.

Samsung Electronics is one of the largest and most profitable South Korean companies, with sales of $106 billion in 2007 and $134 billion in 2010. Samsung Electronics generates 16.7 percent of its total sales from Korea, 15.7 percent from China, 16.1 percent from Asia (total 48.5 percent from Asia), 28.1 percent from America, and 23.4 percent from Europe. Although it ranks with Panasonic and Hewlett-Packard amongst the top three global firms in electrical appliances and electronics, it is now the largest electronics firm in the world by some accounts. The 1997 Asian crisis forced Samsung to switch its focus from cheap consumer electronics to the top end of the market. The firm sold over 100 non-core businesses and let go 30 percent of its employees, a significant step in a country with traditionally militant trade unions. The refocusing on R&D, design, and marketing has since paid off. Driven by its four design centers in London, Tokyo, San Francisco, and Seoul, Samsung won more prizes from the Industrial Design Society of America in 2005 than any other firm. It was world number two in mobile phones, number one in DRAM memory chips, flash memory chips, hard drives, and TFT-LCDs. Key innovative products include LED-backlit LCD TVs, Galaxy S mobile phones and the Galaxy tablet which rivals the iPad.

Contrasting the route taken by Hyundai Automotive, Samsung Electronics is still part of the Samsung *chaebol*, the largest in South Korea, with businesses ranging from shipbuilding, engineering, and chemicals to financial services, hotels, and a theme park. The conglomerate is nearly four times larger than its nearest rivals LG and SK and accounts for about one-third of the country's stock market capitalization. The group is controlled through a complicated web of shareholdings that bind its 27 subsidiaries, although over 60 percent of Samsung Electronics shares are in the hands of foreign investors.

This opaque structure still worries minority shareholders, who have seen their returns eroded from the widespread *chaebol* practice of using profitable businesses to subsidize weaker affiliates and fund risky expansion. Samsung would arguably be in an even stronger position today had it not been called upon to bail the group out of a failed foray into the auto sector in the late 1990s, among other ill-advised diversifications.

Websites: www.daewoo.com; www.hyundai.com; www.hyundai-motor.com; www.samsung.com; www.samsungelectronics.com; www.seriworld.org/.

Sources: Jason Leow and Gordon Fairclough, "Hyundai Freshens China Effort," *Wall Street Journal*, April 8, 2008; "As Good as It Gets? Special Report on Samsung Electronics," *The Economist*, January 15, 2005; C. Wright, "After the Crisis, the Fight Back," *Financial Times*, March 1, 2005, p. 6; A. Ward, "Hyundai Wins 'Most Reliable' Ranking in US," *Financial Times*, September 6, 2004, p. 15; A. Fifield, "Seoul to Clamp Down on *Chaebol*," *Financial Times*, March 1, 2005, p. 15; A. Fifield and J.-A. Song, "SK Corp Steps Up Its Cautious Courtship," *Financial Times*, December 1, 2004, p. 12; Samsung, *Annual Reports*, 2007–2010; OneSource, Thomson Reuters, 2011; "The Global Fortune 500," 2011 ranking, *Forbes*, July 25, 2011 issue, http://money.cnn.com/magazines/fortune/global500/2011/countries/SouthKorea.html; Hyundai Motor, *Annual Reports*, 2006–2011.

Later in this chapter we take a look at the Indian software and IT services industry. Within this industry there are small but significant examples of how success in one particular niche market can support triad access for firms in unrelated sectors. In March 2000 the UK's Tetley Tea Group was acquired by Tata Tea Limited. Coming more than 50 years after the end of 200 years of British colonial rule that had supported British-owned tea estates in India, this shift of power is an appropriate symbol for the twenty-first century. But the takeover was only made possible because of the financial success of Tata's IT division, Tata Consultancy Services (TCS). Both are part of the Tata Group, one of India's biggest publicly quoted conglomerates. Tata Tea was originally a tea estates company and is now India's second most popular tea brand with a 21 percent share of the Indian branded teas market, 54 tea estates, and 59,000 employees. Senior management at Tata Tea said:

> We wanted to create a global brand, because the marketplace was global and in a global marketplace only global brands survive, local players get marginalized. We did not want to get marginalized, so we had to either build a global brand or acquire one.

TCS is "Asia's largest global software and services company" (according to its own PR), whose revenues have doubled every two years over the past six years. TCS is the "jewel in the crown" of the Tata conglomerate, making net profits of over $489 million in the year of the Tetley acquisition. Over 90 percent of these revenues come from the firm's software exports, which are double those of its nearest domestic rival. TCS has 11,000 professionals in 50 countries and sells customized software, systems, consultancy services, and, increasingly, e-business products and services to a wide range of businesses partly through alliances with Western giants like Microsoft, IBM, and Netscape. The revenues and enhanced market capitalization gained from the software side provided the financial leverage to move up the value chain in the tea industry, taking over a major Western brand to enter into the UK market. This could be described as a case of "reverse colonization" and there are many more like it to come.[18]

✔ Active learning check

Review your answer to Active Learning Case question 3 and make any changes you like. Then compare your answer to the one below.

3 **Why did Acer form strategic alliances with IBM and Texas Instruments?**

Acer was not familiar with the North American market and was a new kid on the computer block. So it formed strategic alliances, whenever possible, with the dominant US MNEs. In doing so, Acer learned about the US triad market and how to distribute its products there. It also gained new technological capabilities for both process (manufacturing) innovation and product design and development. Acer was then able to move ahead of these once-dominant US firms once it combined its efficiency in production with its new market knowledge of the rich North American customers.

KEY POINTS

1 Emerging economies are increasingly important for MNEs: as growing markets; as sources of cheaper or better production inputs; and as a source of competitors in the shape of new MNEs as non-triad firms internationalize.

2 Emerging economies tend to be controlled more strongly by their governments and are less predictable and riskier than triad markets.

3 Emerging market countries need investment from, and access to, a triad bloc in order to develop global industries. Inflows and outflows of global FDI show that there is growing integration between countries inside and outside the triad.

4 Current trends such as privatization, liberalization, and legislative changes that are designed to encourage foreign direct investment (FDI) are helping emerging economies to tap their economic potential. Intra- and inter-regional trade agreements can also be helpful in creating both mini common markets and smoothing international trade.

5 FDI into Asia is concentrated in 10 fast-growing economies. There is strong intra-regional trade and FDI growth and a marked increase in the importance of service industries; 36 out of the 50 largest non-financial TNCs from developing countries are from the Asia–Pacific region.

6 Despite years of liberalization the Central and East European region attracts relatively small amounts of FDI. Better prospects appear to be ahead for countries that have joined the EU.

7 Latin America and the Caribbean region receive a small percentage of global FDI (less than China). Intra-regional competition is strong but manufacturing exporters are losing out to China.

8 Africa receives less than 4 percent of global FDI and remains relatively unattractive and risky for most investors. South African MNEs are expanding across the region in particular industry sectors.

9 The newly industrialized countries (NICs), a subgroup of non-triad economies, have experienced rapid economic growth and increased trade and FDI, partly by specializing in particular industries and developing comparative and competitive advantages.

10 NICs and other emerging markets in Asia are seen by some to be following the Flying Geese model of economic development. The Indian software industry appears to counter this pattern of sequential industry specialization as well as contradicting the main tenets of Porter's Diamond of Competitive Advantage.

11 Emerging economies are growing in importance as sources of innovation and as locations for R&D investment by MNEs.

Key terms

- resource-seeking FDI
- market-seeking FDI
- Korean *chaebols*
- liberalization policies
- intra-regional investments
- newly industrialized countries (NICs)
- theory of absolute advantage
- Flying Geese model

REVIEW AND DISCUSSION QUESTIONS

1 Why do MNE managers need to develop an understanding of changing economic conditions in non-triad regions?

2 What characteristics do we tend to associate with emerging economies that are important considerations for foreign investors?

3 How have emerging economies liberalized to encourage FDI?

4 How does inward FDI help emerging economies and their domestic industries?

5 Which non-triad regions and countries have achieved the most rapid economic growth in the last 10 to 20 years and what factors have helped their development?

6 Why does Africa receive relatively little inward FDI?

7 What insights does the Flying Geese model of economic development provide for understanding current and future trade and investment flows? What are its weaknesses as a model?

8 How did Indian IT, software, and services firms evolve beyond their reliance on cheap labor to develop firm-specific advantages and internationalize?

REAL CASE

The Indian IT, software, and services industry

With an average per capita GDP of $1,200 (around $3,500 (2010 est.) in PPP terms), India is a less developed country (LDC). It has low literacy rates and high infant mortality rates. There are just five phones and two Internet users for every 100 people. Yet it also boasts one of the fastest-growing knowledge-based industries in the world.

▶

The Indian IT software and services industry has outstripped all other industries, becoming the largest industry in India in terms of market capitalization. During the late 1990s it grew by an average of 50 percent year on year. It is increasingly important to overall GDP and, more significantly, as a contributor to India's exports. Almost 1 million software professionals and a further 5 million people directly and indirectly are employed by the Indian software industry. India controls around 20 percent of the global customized software market, specializing in high-quality solutions and IT services for corporate customers in the banking, finance, and insurance sectors. It is not currently a player in the market for off-the-shelf, packaged software, which is dominated by US firms.

As we know, exports provide a clear indicator of global competitive advantage. Indian software industry exports have grown from under $5 million in 1980 to $700 million in 1996, $6 billion in 2000, $12 billion in 2004, over $30 billion in 2007 and over $47 billion in 2010 (see Figure 20.7). The top firm, Tata Consultancy Services (TCS), a division of the Tata conglomerate, exported over $4 billion worth of IT software and services (with 186,914 employees and revenue of $8 billion for the year ended March 31, 2011). The number two firm, InfoSys Technologies, managed 133,560 employees and revenue of US$6 billion for the year ended March 31, 2011.

However, the sources of advantage underpinning the growth rate and success of the Indian IT industry are not explained by many of the standard international business frameworks, such as the Porter diamond model. Few, if any, of the factors that led to the genesis of the industry were initially present in India. There was no local demand; related and supporting industries, such as telecoms and computing, were highly underdeveloped; the national communications infrastructure was among the worst in the world; and the main factor of production, the skills and knowledge of software programmers and IT business managers (an acquired factor endowment), was initially not home-grown.

The industry began with Indians returning from higher education, IT training, and often work experience in the United States and Europe. Many of the industry founders, such as Wipro Chairman Azim Premji, Ramalinga Raju of Satyam, and S. Ramadorai of TCS, were educated at US universities (although others, such as F. C. Kohli of TCS and InfoSys Chairman Narayana Murthy were not). They noticed the rising demand for customized software programmers and IT expertise in the banking, insurance, financial services, and other industries in the West and saw India as a potential low-cost provider of this expertise. They returned to India and built firms to meet the software needs of the triad, primarily the United States.

Factors that were on their side were the English language skills of the Indians, as this is the main software programming language; the time difference that allowed a 24-hour software development project cycle; new global information and communications network infrastructures; fears over the Y2K or year 2000 problem; and the low cost of labor. "Body shopping," the contracting of Indian programmers and their physical relocation to work with clients abroad, accounted for 90 percent of industry revenues in 1989. The average cost of a software programmer in India in the late 1990s was still about one-twelfth the cost of a US or European programmer. But wage rates were

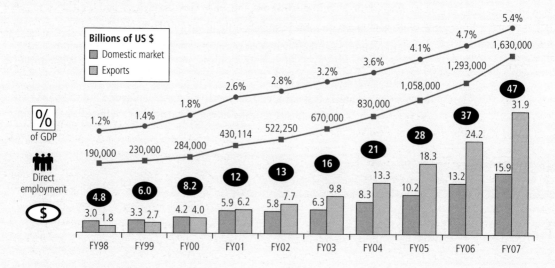

Figure 20.7 The growth of India's IT industry

Source: NASSCOM Report, http://www.nasscom.in/.

relatively much lower in the early stages of the industry's growth cycle and increased at around 25 percent per year from the mid-1990s. The cost of a programmer in China or Russia is now around 20 percent lower than in India, and the same lack of barriers to entry will help firms based in these countries to mount a new competitive threat.

As the industry evolved, government support, particularly the development of software technology parks (the STPI network), the promotion of technical training, and subsidies to ICT infrastructure, became important. Also significant were the activities of US and European multinationals. Initially Western firms subcontracted programming and other tasks to Indian firms to exploit the cheap labor advantage. Many, like Texas Instruments, Microsoft, and Computer Associates, made substantial investments to build local operations to work within the emerging industry clusters in Bangalore and Madras. These global firms promoted innovation both as customers and as suppliers to local firms. They transferred hardware and software technology and assisted in the development of local technological capabilities through technical and management training, investment in R&D, new product and services development, and joint ventures. They also prompted and sometimes assisted in the development of local ICT infrastructure.

Perhaps the most important factor underlying the continued success of the industry is its evolution from an industry based on cheap labor and low costs to one based on value-added expertise, including specialist software and IT systems design and development capabilities. Indian software firms have moved up the value chain, shifting the basis of their competitive advantage from just cost to a combination of cost, quality, and high-end R&D expertise.

Indian firms are also now themselves actively subcontracting to lower-cost providers in China and elsewhere as they move away from contract programming as a major source of their revenues and into e-commerce and Web-related products and services. They are leveraging their advantages in cost and skills through joint ventures with big, established players in the computing, telecom, and consumer electronics industries. The InfoSys–Microsoft joint venture focusing on MS.Net products is an example of this, as is the Mahindra–British Telecom venture. An estimated 300 multinational companies have been engaged in R&D rather than contracting work in India. Intel, Microsoft, Cisco Systems, Samsung Electronics, Oracle, SSA Global, and others have set up R&D activities in Hyderabad, Mumbai, and Bangalore.

As a result of these developments, the industry has divided into a variety of subsectors. The IT software and services sector is still the largest and the key export revenue earner, but growth has slowed. A domestic software and telecom industry, with a thriving venture capital industry, has also emerged in India. This is evidence of a strong and growing industry cluster that has evolved, unusually, *after* the export success of key firms in the industry. IT-enabled services (ITES) and business process outsourcing (BPO) services, including call centers, transcriptions services, and back-office processing such as billing, taxation, and accounting, have been growing rapidly. Hubs of these services are Mumbai, Bangalore, Chennai, Kolkata, Hyderabad, Kochi, Ahmedabad, and Pune. Some of the key players in this market are AMX, Convergys India Services, GE Capital, Standard Chartered, Dell, Healthscribe India, EXL Services, Daksh eServices, Wipro Spectramind, and 24/7 Customer.

The development of the ITES/BPO subsector has brought home some of the threats as well as opportunities of living in a globally connected world for people in Europe and the United States. According to the UK's Communication Workers Union, for example, 33 firms including Barclays, British Airways, Lloyds TSB, Prudential, and Reuters have collectively outsourced 52,000 jobs serving UK customers to India. Norwich Union, the UK's largest insurer, has built up a workforce of 3,700 people in India and plans to double this in the near future. This is a sign of the times, and as global firms discover new ways of accessing cheaper and/or better expertise in other parts of the world, some groups of people will experience new opportunities to join and benefit from the global economy while others will feel increasingly vulnerable to the threat of new competition.

Sources: NASSCOM, *The IT-BPO Sector in India: Strategic Review for 2011*, Executive Summary. NASSCOM, http://www.nasscom.in/upload/Publications/Research/140211/Executive_Summary.pdf; NASSCOM, "Indian IT/ITES Industry: Impacting Economy and Society 2007–08," NASSCOM Foundation Report, 2008; "Soaring Salaries Hit India IT Group Margins," *Financial Times*, September 12, 2007; "Offshoring Pays Off for UK Companies," *Telegraph*, January 25, 2005; "India Makes It to the Global R&D Map," *The Financial Express*, December 6, 2004; D. Gardner, "Bangalore-based Software Company to Use US Web Platform for E-Commerce Solutions," *Financial Times*, September 15, 2000; K. Merchant, "Hidden Gem Seeks Share of Limelight: Information Technology," *Financial Times*, August 9, 2000; K. Merchant and D. Gardener, "New Delhi Woos Silicon Valley Indians: IT Successes Encouraged to Invest," *Financial Times*, September 15, 2000; http://indiainfoline.com/; http://www.nasscom.in/; http://www.indiainvest.com/.

1 How well does the Porter diamond framework explain the beginnings of the Indian IT and software services industry?

2 Why has this kind of industry not developed in other parts of the world, where triad companies also outsource IT activities (such as Barbados)?

3 What are the threats and opportunities for Western software firms arising from this shift in the competitive landscape, and how are they strategically responding to these?

REAL CASE

Bumrungrad International in Thailand

Medical tourism (medical travel, health tourism, or global health care) is not as new as we might think. Spa towns and sanatoriums promoted international travel for health reasons across Europe and beyond, from the eighteenth century onwards. But the industry has entered a new phase as a globally competitive business worth an estimated US $35 billion. Levels of quality, safety, and reliability in locations beyond the triad are now good enough to create choice for patient–customers and for price to become a key factor. As Table 1 shows, there is a clear economic incentive for private and public health care clients to "shop around".

The growing costs of employer health-care schemes in the United States are one reason for the growing popularity of medical tourism. Canada and Mexico have developed thriving businesses based on their proximity to the US market. A few US employers have also begun to build incentives into their benefit packages to encourage employees to travel abroad for health care. This includes paying for travel and subsistence for time away from work in return for cheaper medical bills. The Maine-based retailer Hannaford Brothers, for example, will cover the total costs for employees to travel to Singapore for knee and hip replacements, including travel for a companion accompanying the patient. Cuba attracts 20,000 medical tourists per year, but for obvious reasons these have come from Latin America and Europe rather than the United States.

There are of course added risks for many people in venturing beyond their borders in search of low-cost medical procedures. These can be exacerbated by the legal complexities of extending insurance cover across borders. In an attempt to alleviate some of the risk and uncertainty,

Source: Blend Images/Alamy

international health-care accreditation, offered by organizations like the US-based Joint Commission International (JCI) and the associated Society for International Healthcare Accreditation (SOFIHA), is increasingly important.

There are also ethical issues beyond the economics of supply and demand, not least the problem that wealthy medical tourists divert scarce medical resources and expertise away from the poorest and neediest in developing countries. Massive investments in initiatives like the "MediCity" project in the Guragaon region near New Delhi focus on providing top-class health care for the rich, in the world's poorest areas. Supporters cite the multiplier effect of medical clusters, which include employment and subsequent investment in local people and infrastructure. Critics simply see a further widening of global income and welfare disparities.

Tabel 1 Comparing the international costs of medical procedures

Medical procedure	Cost in the US*	Costs in alternative locations
Heart-valve replacement	$200,000	$10,000 (India) including airfare and vacation
Coronary artery bypass surgery	$100,000	$12,000 (Bumrungrad Hospital, Thailand)
Full facelift	$20,000	$1,250 (South Africa); can be part of a "medical safari"
Knee replacement	$15,000	$5,000 (Colombia); including costs of hospital stay
In vitro fertilization	$12,000	$5,000 (Panama)
Dental bridge	$5,500	$500 (India)
Lasik eye surgery	$3,700	$730 (India and elsewhere)
Colonoscopy	$900	$640 (Bumrungrad Hospital, Thailand)
Root canal	$800	$300 (Panama)

* For most examples these are listed as the minimum cost in US hospitals.

Source: Various.

Bumrungrad International

David Boucher, a 49-year-old American, chose to have a colonoscopy at Bumrungrad International Hospital in Bangkok. His company gladly paid the $640 bill, saving over $250 on the costs of the same procedure in the United States. What is significant is that David Boucher was an assistant vice president of health-care services at Blue Cross & Blue Shield of South Carolina. His firm is part of the largest group provider of health care insurance services in the United States, providing coverage for more than 100 million people. His main reason for undergoing the procedure in Thailand was to advertise the increasingly international options open to his firm's 1.5 million customers. He has been involved in signing a range of alliances with overseas hospitals and in discussions with local corporations and employee groups about this strategic response to the growing costs of health care in the United States. In 2008 Blue Cross took the initiative in medical "offshoring" by creating a partnership with Bumrungrad Hospital through its Companion Global Healthcare subsidiary.

Bumrungrad ("care for the people") International was founded in 1980 and advertises itself as the largest private hospital in South-East Asia. As of December 31, 2010, it has 34 outpatient clinics, which include 250 examination rooms, with the capacity to service of over 4,000 patients per day. It has 554 beds and over 30 specialized treatment centers. With a workforce of 3,259 employees, it achieved a turnover of $317 million in 2010. Of the 1 million plus patients served each year, 430,000 are international and come from 190 different countries. Bumrungrad is a publicly traded company listed on the Thai Stock Exchange. The majority shareholders are Bangkok Bank PCL and the Sophonpanich family.

Several key factors explain Bumrungrad's success. The country has a history of prioritizing health care perhaps dating back to Prince Mahidol of Songla who gained an MD degree from Harvard Medical School in the early twentieth century. Ongoing support from the Thai government and members of the country's ruling elite has made medicine and health care a national priority. The founders of Bumrungrad Hospital have focused on service quality and international credibility partly through their recruitment and incentives practices and by aiming for recognized accreditation. The hospital has more than 200 surgeons who are board-certified in the United States and it was the first hospital in Asia to be accredited by the US-based Joint Commission International (JCI).

To counter any potential criticism over the ethics of diverting medical resources to a top-class, but relatively expensive (for locals) hospital, the Bumrungrad Hospital Foundation was established in 1990. It helps the less privileged in Thailand gain access to free medical treatment and health-care services. The Foundation has provided free medical help to over 100,000 Thais, including 122 pediatric heart operations.

Sources: Laurie McGinley, "Health Matters: The Next Wave of Medical Tourists Might Include You," *Wall Street Journal*, February 16, 2008; Bruce Einhorn, "Outsourcing the Patients," *Business Week*, March 13, 2008; Rory Carroll, "First World Results on a Third World Budget," *Guardian*, September 12, 2007; http://www.bumrungrad.com/ and various websites; OneSource, *Thomson Reuters*, 2011.

1 How is the growing provision of alternative sources of health services around the world likely to affect the triad-based providers, public and private?

2 Explain the rise of Bumrungrad International and the Thai medical tourism industry in terms of country-specific advantages (CSAs) and firm-specific advantages (FSAs).

3 Should health-care "offshoring" be viewed or treated any differently to any other globalizing industry, such as software or BPO services?

ENDNOTES

1 D. W. Conklin, "Analyzing and Managing Country Risks," *Ivey Business Journal*, vol. 66, no. 3 (2002), pp. 360–362; S. E. Feinberg and A. K. Gupta, "MNC Subsidiaries and Country Risk: Internalization as a Safeguard Against Weak External Institutions," *Academy of Management Journal*, vol. 51 (2008).

2 Emerging market and developing country economies overall have grown by an average of over 6.5 percent in recent years, which is much faster than historical trends and much faster than developed economies; "Coming into Flower," *The Economist*, October 16, 2004; For the most recent data see: www.UNCTAD.org and http://www.vcc.columbia.edu/content/emerging-market-global-players.

3 See http://www.slovakembassy-cd-london.co.uk/gfx/documents/Automotive.pdf (2007); Robert Anderson, "Autos: Success from Nowhere at All," *Financial Times*, Special Report Slovakia, May 26, 2004, p. 3; Mark Landler, "Slovakia Vies to Create 'Detroit' of Europe," *International Herald Tribune*, April 14, 2004, p. 11; Chris Wright, "Automakers Jump into Fast Lane of Expansion," *Automotive News* (Detroit), May 3, 2004, p. 26 P.

4 See http://www.endesa.com.

5 See http://www.telefonica.es/accionistaseinversores/.

6 UNCTAD's 2007 World Investment Report focuses on multinational firms, extractive industries and development, and provides an excellent overview of the

extent and impacts of FDI in these sectors worldwide (www.unctad.org).

7 For further discussion see S. C. Collinson, "M&A as Imperialism?" in D. Angwin (ed.), *Images of M&A* (Oxford: Blackwell, 2006).

8 Adam Smith, *The Wealth of Nations*, Book IV:2, Modern Library edition, 1776.

9 Among many introductory sources, see K. Fatemi (ed.), *International Trade in the 21st Century* (Oxford: Pergamon, 1997); C. J. Jepma et al., *Introduction to International Economics* (London and New York: Longman, Heerlen: Open University of the Netherlands, 1997); C. J. Jepma and A. Rhoen (eds.), *International Trade: A Business Perspective* (London and New York: Longman; Heerlen: Open University of the Netherlands, 1996).

10 K. Akamatsu, "Historical Patterns of Economic Growth in Developing Countries," *The Developing Economies*, vol. 1 (1962), pp. 3–25; Kálmán Kalotay, "The European Flying Geese: New FDI Patterns for the Old Continent?" *Research in International Business and Finance*, vol. 18, no. 1 (2004), pp. 27–49. For other analyses, at the industry and firm levels, see L. Kim, "Crisis Construction and Organizational Learning: Capability Building in Catching-up at Hyundai Motor," *Organization Science*, vol. 9 (1998), pp. 506–521; F. J. Contractor (ed.), *Economic Transformation in Emerging Countries: The Role of Investment, Trade and Finance* (Oxford: Elsevier, 1998); Michael Hobday, *Innovation in East Asia: The Challenge to Japan* (Aldershot: Edward Elgar, 1995); Sanjaya Lall, *Learning from the Asian Tigers: Studies in Technology and Industrial Policy* (Basingstoke: Macmillan, 1996); Dosi Giovanni et al., *The Economics of Technical Change and International Trade* (Hemel Hempstead: Harvester Wheatsheaf, 1990); Kim Linsu, *Imitation to Innovation: The Dynamics of Korea's Technological Learning* (Boston, MA: Harvard Business School Press, 1997).

11 Vernon, Raymond, "International Investment and International Trade in the Product Cycle," *Quarterly Journal of Economics*, May 1996, pp. 190–207.

12 Malcolm Dowling and Chia Tien Cheang, "Shifting Comparative Advantage in Asia: New Test of the 'Flying Geese' Model," Journal of Asian Economics, vol. 11, no. 4 (2000), p. 443; Edith Terry, *How Asia Got Rich: Japan, China, and the Asian Miracle* (Armonk, NY: M. E. Sharpe, 2002).

13 See the references in n. 10 above, and Linsu Kim and Richard R. Nelson, *Technology, Learning and Innovation:. Experiences of Newly Industrialising Economies* (Cambridge: Cambridge University Press, 2000).

14 This was one of Porter's original examples from the study of factors underlying export success in particular industries in particular economies which are summarized in the "Diamond of Advantage." Michael E. Porter, *The Competitive Advantage of Nations* (New York: Free Press, 1998). More recent research shows how the overdependence on CSAs by some Japanese firms has led to an inability to adapt and internationalize in response to changing domestic economic conditions; S. Collinson and A. M. Rugman, "The Regional Nature of Japanese Multinational Business," *Journal of International Business Studies*, vol. 39, no. 2 (2008), pp. 215–230.

15 See http://www.gmnext.com/ and John Reed, "GM Chief Hits at UN Data on Biofuel," *Financial Times*, April 20, 2008.

16 See the World Competitiveness Report and discussions about the Innovation Capacity indicators at www.weforum.org/.

17 UNCTAD, *World Investment Report 2005: Transnational Corporations and the Internationalization of R&D*, UNCTAD, Geneva (www.unctad.org).

18 See Collinson, op. cit.; K. Merchant, "Hidden Gem Seeks Share of Limelight: Information Technology," *Financial Times*, August 9, 2000, http://www.ft.com/ftsurvevs/industry/scd2b2.html; http://www.indiainfoline.com/sect/itso/ch01.html; http://www.tata.com/0_people/interviews/20001227_krishna_kumar1; and http://www.tata.com/tcs/index.htm.

ADDITIONAL BIBLIOGRAPHY

Aybar, Bülent and Ficici, Aysun. "Cross-Border Acquisitions and Firm Value: An Analysis of Emerging-Market Multinationals," *Journal of International Business Studies*, vol. 40 (October/November 2009). doi:10.1057/jibs.2009.15.

Backman, Michael and Butler, Charlotte. *Big in Asia: 25 Strategies for Business Success* (New York: Palgrave Macmillan, 2004).

Barclay, Lou Anne. *Foreign Direct Investment in Emerging Economies: The Caribbean* (London: Routledge, 2000).

Bound, Kirsten, Leadbeater, Charles, O'Connor, Simon, Webb, Molly and Wilsdon, James. *The Atlas of Ideas: Europe and Asia in the New Geography of Science* (London: DEMOS, 2007), http://www.demos.co.uk/.

Bresnahan, Timothy and Gambardella, Alfonso (eds.). *Building High-Tech Clusters: Silicon Valley and Beyond* (Cambridge: Cambridge University Press, 2004).

Buck, Trevor. "Modern Russian Corporate Governance: Convergent Forces or Product of Russia's History?" *Journal of World Business*, vol. 38, no. 4 (November 2003).

Casanova, Lourdes. *Global Latinas: Latin America's Emerging Multinationals* (New York: Palgrave Macmillan, 2009).

Chang, Eunmi. "Individual Pay for Performance and Commitment HR Practices in South Korea," *Journal of World Business*, vol. 41, no. 4 (December 2007).

Chang, Sea-Jin. *Financial Crisis and Transformation of Korean Business Groups: The Rise and Fall of Chaebols* (Cambridge: Cambridge University Press, 2003).

Christensen, Clayton M., Chang-Chieh Hang, Kah-Hin Chai and Subramanian, Annapoornima M. "Editorial: Managing Innovation in Emerging Economies: An Introduction to the Special Issue," *IEEE Transactions on Engineering Management*, vol. 57, no.1 (February 2010).

De Mattos, Claudio, Sanderson, Stuart and Ghauri, Pervez. "Negotiating Alliances in Emerging Markets—Do Partners' Contributions Matter?" *Thunderbird International Business Review*, vol. 44, no. 6 (November/December 2002).

De Meyer, Arnoud. *Global Future: The Next Challenge for Asian Business* (Singapore: Wiley, 2005).

Doh, Jonathan P., Rodriguez, Peter, Uhlenbruck, Klaus, Collins, Jamie and Eden, Lorraine. "Coping with Corruption in Foreign Markets," *Academy of Management Executive*, vol. 17, no. 3 (2003).

Doh, Jonathan P., Teegen, Hildy and Mudambi, Ram. "Balancing Private and State Ownership in Emerging Markets' Telecommunications Infrastructure: Country, Industry, and Firm Influences," *Journal of International Business Studies*, vol. 35, no. 3 (May 2004).

Engardio, Peter. *Chindia: How China and India Are Revolutionizing Global Business* (New York: McGraw-Hill, 2006).

Farrell, Diana, Remes, Jaana K. and Schulz, Heiner. "The Truth about Foreign Direct Investment in Emerging Markets," *McKinsey Quarterly*, no. 1 (2004).

Fiegenbaum, Avi, Bavie, Dovev and Shoham, Aviv. "Competitive Positioning of Foreign MNEs in Domestic Markets: Theoretical Extensions and Evidence from the Israeli Market," *Management International Review*, vol. 44, no. 3 (Third Quarter 2004).

Filatotchev, Igor, Strange, Roger, Piesse, Jenifer and Lien, Yung-Chih. "FDI by Firms from Newly Industrialised Economies in Emerging Markets: Corporate Governance, Entry Mode, and Location," *Journal of International Business Studies*, vol. 38, no. 4 (July 2007).

Filatotchev, Igor, Wright, Mike, Uhlenbruck, Klaus, Tihanyi, Laszlo and Hoskisson, Robert E. "Governance, Organizational Capabilities, and Restructuring in Transition Economies," *Journal of World Business*, vol. 38, no. 4 (November 2003).

Friedman, Thomas L. *The World Is Flat: A Brief History of the Twenty-first Century* (New York: Farrar, Straus and Giroux, 2005).

Gill, Indermit Singh and Kharas, Homi J. *An East Asian Renaissance: Ideas for Economic Growth* (Washington, DC: The World Bank, 2007).

Goedhart, Marc H. and Haden, Peter. "Emerging Markets Aren't As Risky as You Think," *McKinsey Quarterly*, Special Edition Issue 4 (2003).

Goldstein, Andrea. *Multinational Companies from Emerging Economies: Composition, Conceptualization and Direction in the Global Economy* (New York: Palgrave Macmillan 2nd ed., 2009).

Gray, Kenneth R. "The Ins and Outs of Doing Business in Europe: Germany, France, Russia, and the Emerging Markets of Eastern Europe," *Thunderbird International Business Review*, vol. 47, no. 1 (January/February 2005).

Grosse, Robert. "International Business in Latin America," in Alan M. Rugman and Thomas L. Brewer (eds.), *The Oxford Handbook of International Business* (New York: Oxford University Press, 2001).

Grosse, Robert and Trevino, Len J. "New Institutional Economics and FDI Location in Central and Eastern Europe," *Management International Review*, vol. 45, no. 2 (Second Quarter 2005).

Hafsi, Taieb, and Farashahi, Mehdi. "Applicability of Management Theories to Developing Countries: A Synthesis," *Management International Review*, vol. 45, no. 4 (Fourth Quarter 2005).

Hamm, Steve, *Bangalore Tiger* (New York: McGraw-Hill, 2006).

Judge, William Q., Naoumova, Irina and Koutzevol, Nadejda. "Corporate Governance and Firm Performance in Russia: An Empirical Study," *Journal of World Business*, vol. 38, no. 4 (November 2003).

Jwa, Sung-Hee and Lee, Kwon (eds.). *Competition and Corporate Governance in Korea: Reforming and restructuring the Chaebol* (Cheltenham: Edward Elgar, 2004).

Krivogorsky, Victoria and Eichenseher, John W. "Effects of Top Management Replacement on Firms' Behavior: Empirical Analysis of Russian Companies," *Management International Review*, vol. 45, no. 4 (Fourth Quarter 2005).

Kumar, Sameer, Jamieson, Jacky and Sweetman, Mathew. "Software Industry in the Fastest Emerging Market: Challenges and Opportunities," *International Journal of Technology Management*, vol. 29, no. 3/4 (2005).

Li, Peter Ping, "Toward a learning-based view of internationalization: The accelerated trajectories of cross-border learning for latecomers," *Journal of International Management*, vol. 16, no. 1 (March 2010).

Lieberthal, K. and Lieberthal, G. "The Great Transition," *Harvard Business Review*, vol. 81, no. 10 (October 2003).

London, Ted and Hart, Stuart L. "Reinventing Strategies for Emerging Markets: Beyond the Transnational Model," *Journal of International Business Studies*, vol. 35, no. 5 (September 2004).

Luo, Yadong. "Market-Seeking MNEs in an Emerging Market: How Parent-Subsidiary Links Shape Overseas Success," *Journal of International Business Studies*, vol. 34, no. 3 (May 2003).

Luo, Yadong. "Building a Strong Foothold in an Emerging Market: A Link between Resource Commitment and Environment Conditions," *Journal of Management Studies*, vol. 41, no. 5 (July 2004).

Luo, Yadong. "Autonomy of Foreign R&D Units in an Emerging Market: An Information Processing Perspective," *Management International Review*, vol. 46, no. 3 (2006).

Manea, Julia and Pearce, Robert. "MNEs' Strategies in Central and Eastern Europe: Key Elements of Subsidiary Behaviour," *Management International Review*, vol. 46, no. 2 (2006).

Mathews, John A., *Dragon Multinational: A New Model for Global Growth* (New York: Oxford University Press, 2002).

McCarthy, Daniel J. and Puffer, Sheila M. "Corporate Governance in Russia: A Framework for Analysis," *Journal of World Business*, vol. 38, no. 4 (November 2003).

McManus, John, Li, Mingzhi and Moitra, Deependra. *China and India: Opportunities and Threats for the Global Software Industry* (Oxford: Chandos Publishing, 2007).

Meyer, Klaus E. "International Research in Transitional Economies," in Alan M. Rugman and Thomas L. Brewer (eds.), *The Oxford Handbook of International Business* (New York: Oxford University Press, 2001).

Meyer, Klaus E. "Perspectives on Multinational Enterprises in Emerging Economies," *Journal of International Business Studies*, vol. 35, no. 4 (2004).

Meyer, Klaus E. and Peng, Mike. "Probing Theoretically into Central and Eastern Europe: Transactions, Resources, and Institutions," *Journal of International Business Studies*, vol. 36, no. 6 (November 2005).

Oh, Chang Hoon and Rugman, Alan M. "Regional Multinationals and the Korean Cosmetics Industry," *Asia Pacific Journal of Management*, vol. 24, no. 1 (2007).

Pak, Yong Suhk and Park, Young-Ryeol. "A Framework of Knowledge Transfer in Cross-Border Joint Ventures: An Empirical Test of the Korean Context," *Management International Review*, vol. 44, no. 4 (Fourth Quarter 2004).

Pangarkar, Nitin and Lim, Hendry. "Performance of Foreign Direct Investment from Singapore," *International Business Review*, vol. 12, no. 5 (October 2003).

Park, Young-Ryeol and Pak, Yong Suhk. "That They Learned from the Crash: A Comparison of Korean Firms FDI Before and After the 1997 Financial Crisis," *Management International Review*, vol. 46, no. 1 (2006).

Prahalad, C. K. *The Fortune at the Bottom of the Pyramid* (Upper Saddle River, NJ: Wharton School/Pearson, 2005).

Prestowitz, Clyde. *Three Billion New Capitalists: The Great Shift of Wealth and Power to the East* (London: Basic Books, 2006).

Puffer, Sheila M. and McCarthy, Daniel J. "The Emergence of Corporate Governance in Russia," *Journal of World Business*, vol. 38, no. 4 (November 2003).

Puffer, Sheila M. and McCarthy, Daniel J. "Can Russia's State Managed, Network Capitalism be Competitive? Institutional Pull versus Institutional Push," *Journal of World Business*, vol. 42, no. 1 (March 2007).

Ramamurti, Ravi. "Developing Countries and MNEs: Extending and Enriching the Research Agenda," *Journal of International Business Studies*, vol. 35, no. 4 (July 2004).

Ramamurti, Ravi and Doh, Jonathan P. "Rethinking Foreign Infrastructure Investment in Developing Countries," *Journal of World Business*, vol. 39, no. 2 (May 2004).

Ramamurti, Ravi and Singh, Jitendra V. (eds.) *Emerging Multinationals in Emerging Markets* (Cambridge: Cambridge University Press, 2010).

Redding, Gordon. "The Smaller Economies of Asia and their Business Systems," in Alan M. Rugman and Thomas L. Brewer (eds.), *The Oxford Handbook of International Business*, (New York: Oxford University Press, 2001).

Redding, Gordon. "The Thick Description and Comparison of Societal Systems of Capitalism," *Journal of International Business Studies*, vol. 36, no. 2 (March 2005).

Roth, Kendall and Kostova, Tatiana. "Organizational Coping with Institutional Upheaval in Transition Economies," *Journal of World Business*, vol. 38, no. 4 (November 2003).

Rugman, Alan M. "How Global Are TNCs from Emerging Markets?" in Karl Sauvant (ed.), *The Rise of Transnational Corporations from Emerging Markets: Threat or Opportunity* (Cheltenham: Edward Elgar, 2008).

Rugman, Alan M. "Globalization, Regional Multinationals and Asian Economic Development," *Asian Business & Management*, vol. 9, no. 3 (September 2010).

Rugman, Alan M. and Collinson, Simon. "The Regional Character of Asian Multinational Enterprises," *Asia Pacific Journal of Management*, vol. 24, no. 4 (2007).

Rugman, Alan M. and Doh, Jonathan P. *Multinationals and Development* (New Haven, CT: Yale University Press, 2008).

Rugman, Alan M. and Lee, In Hyeock (Ian). "Multinationals and Public Policy in Korea," *Asian Business & Management*, vol. 8, no. 1 (March 2009).

Rugman, Alan M. and Oh, Chang Hoon. "Regional Multinationals and the Korean Cosmetics Industry," *Asia Pacific Journal of Management*, vol. 24, no. 1 (March 2007).

Rugman, Alan M. and Oh, Chang Hoon. "Korea's Multinationals in a Regional World," *Journal of World Business*, vol. 43, no. 1 (January 2008).

Rugman, Alan M. and Oh, Chang Hoon. "The International Competitiveness of Asian Firms," *Journal of Strategy and Management*, vol. 1, no. 1 (2008).

Sauvant, Karl P. *The Rise of Transnational Corporations from Emerging Markets: Threat or Opportunity?* (Cheltenham: Edward Elgar, 2009).

Sukpanich, Nessara and Rugman, Alan M. "Multinationals and the International Competitiveness of ASEAN Firms," in Philippe Gugler Julien Chaisse (ed.), *Competitiveness of the ASEAN Countries, Corporate and Regulatory Drivers* (Cheltenham: Edward Elgar, 2010).

Treviño, Len J. and Mixon, Franklin G. "Strategic Factors Affecting Foreign Direct Investment Decisions by Multinational Enterprises in Latin America," *Journal of World Business*, vol. 39, no. 3 (August 2004).

Tsai, Terence and Cheng, Bor-Shiuan. *The Silicon Dragon: High-Tech Industry in Taiwan* (London: Edward Elgar, 2006).

Tsang, Eric W. K. "Influences on Foreign Ownership Level and Entry Mode Choice in Vietnam," *International Business Review*, vol. 14, no. 4 (August 2005).

Wyk, Jay Van. "Doing Business in South Africa," *Thunderbird International Business Review*, vol. 46, no. 4 (July/August 2004).

Yusuf, Shahid and Evenett, Simon J. *Can East Asia Compete? Innovation for Global Markets* (Washington, DC: The World Bank and Oxford University Press, 2002).

WWW RESOURCES

http://globaledge.msu.edu/ibrd/marketpot.asp
http://www.tdctrade.com/
http://asnic.utexas.edu/
http://www.lanic.utexas.edu/
http://reenic.utexas.edu/

http://www.africaguide.com/
http://www.africaonline.com/
http://www.vcc.columbia.edu/content/emerging-market-global-players

Chapter 21

CHINA

Contents

Objectives of the chapter

In the 1950s China's economy was the size of Sudan's. Now, following 30 years of liberalization, it is the second-largest economy in PPP (Purchasing Power Parity) terms. Political change has led to economic and social change which in turn is driving further political change and increasingly turbulent interdependencies with other parts of the globe. Rapid economic growth has led to an expanding domestic consumer market alongside continued poverty and growing disparities in wealth and income across the population of over 1.3 billion people.

The scale, scope, and speed of these changes are unprecedented and the resulting range of commercial and competitive opportunities and threats should be of interest to every manager and every firm worldwide. In this sense China's rise represents a major test of adaptability for firms looking to break into its growing domestic market and for those defending home markets against Chinese imports and FDI. In order to survive many firms need to understand the evolving strengths and weaknesses of Chinese businesses, identify the resulting complementarities and competitive conflicts, and reposition themselves accordingly.

The specific objectives of this chapter are to:

1 *Understand* the nature of the Chinese economy, the role of government, and the characteristics of China's domestic market and its corporations.

2 *Examine* the opportunities and constraints facing Western firms investing in China and the ways in which successful firms have adapted to succeed there.

3 *Analyze* the degree to which Chinese firms are internationalizing, how and where they are selling and/or investing abroad, and what kinds of relative competitive advantages they appear to have.

4 *Reflect* on the implications of China's rise, in "real-world" terms and for academic analysis and understanding of firm performance and business processes.

ACTIVE LEARNING CASE

Oxford Instruments in China

The Oxford of ancient spires and ivory towers is well known among the Chinese. The successful, high-tech spin-off Oxford Instruments (OI) is less well known, but the company has worked to change this. Having sold a range of its products in China for over 10 years and experienced a 30 to 40 percent growth in sales year after year, senior managers at OI decided it was time to invest more heavily. The company opened representative offices in Beijing and Shanghai during the last decade and employed 20 people (including two expatriates). Then, between April 2003 and August 2004, OI registered as a wholly foreign-owned enterprise (**WFOE**) and established a manufacturing facility. This was a major investment for a firm with a turnover of US$336.9 million and 1,341 staff around the world for the financial year ended 31 March 2011. But it was a necessary step given that over 90 percent of OI's sales were from outside the UK, with approximately 10 percent in China. Moreover, its managers learned a number of important lessons along the way.

A key reason for investing directly in the Chinese market, moving to a higher level of both commitment and risk, was to get closer to the growing number of Chinese customers. OI chose to build on the strong platform of representative offices through the establishment of a repair and service center for supporting its microanalysis detector customers in China. It also wanted to provide a platform for the assembly of top-level products. To establish a business entity capable of delivering these kinds of activities it needed some outside help. One way to reduce the risks of FDI is to hire local specialists who know about the local rules of the game and with the relationships and connections to help smooth the way. Another route is to hire experts who understand the international legal and regulatory conditions relating to an FDI project. In fact, when initiating its investment plans in China, OI did both. An international law firm was hired to ensure that global regulatory standards were followed. A local sponsor was also brought in (at a significantly lower cost) to help with the submission of the investment application to government authorities.

The establishment process itself was relatively straightforward. Step 1 was to register the company name. Step 2 was the submission of a feasibility report and articles of association to show the firm would be profitable and (most important) produce good tax returns. The WFOE, Oxford Instruments (Shanghai) Co., Ltd., was then given government approval and granted a trading license around three months after the start of the process. Post-registration procedures,

Source: Simon Collinson

including securing the "red" **company chop** (an official company seal or signature stamp), took a little longer.

Further development of an effective and efficient HQ—subsidiary organization structure and good working relationships between head-office management and local managers in China were seen to be key priorities in the early stages of the China venture. The UK side defined a common internal financial reporting structure and shared the group business strategy, which the senior management in China was then allowed to revise and tailor to the local context and culture. The existing OI China chief representative, a Chinese national employed by OI for five years, was named as the general manager of the new organization. The leadership of this existing member of the OI team, with experience of working both in a related industry and in an English-speaking environment, to head-up the China operation was important for creating the necessary HQ—subsidiary relationships. As with any international expansion, an overarching question for OI was (and continues to be): what business processes and decision-making responsibilities do we move to China and what do we keep in the UK?

Key constraints and challenges cited by OI include time- and resource-consuming Chinese bureaucracy at various levels including central, regional, and local governments, and individual firms (one customer required 11 different VAT invoices for a single sale). It was important for OI to link the new Shanghai facility into its global IT infrastructure but the instability of the local Internet required the company to invest in alternative (and more costly) connection methods. As OI continues to grow in China the task of developing the necessary range of capable, experienced local managers in the sales and marketing functions as well as in operations will continue to be a focus.

Perhaps more significant than these problems have been OI's concerns about protecting its intellectual property rights (IPR) in China. OI's R&D assets and technological capabilities underpin its primary competitive advantage. It has had to take steps to avoid losing these to local Chinese competitors. Some formal protection and registration steps are available, and these have been taken by OI, but this provides limited protection in China. More effective protection of IP is gained through placing an emphasis on the careful recruitment of staff in China and the retention of the development and some manufacturing of key technologies at home in the UK. OI's customers are mainly top universities and organizations with high-level scientific research requirements. These customers are often co-developers of new technologies, so OI has built a range of cooperative alliances in which mutual trust and reciprocity are essential.

Many people talk about the importance of relationships in China. One interpretation is that in the process of developing relationships the Chinese are effectively performing a "credit check." In the absence of stable or reliable formal contracting rules, regulations, processes, and institutions, more emphasis is placed on interpersonal trust as the reliable basis for doing business. What rules there are in China tend not to be applied consistently. This leaves plenty of scope for influencing processes and decisions, which places even more of a premium on having the right connections.

At an early stage in the project the following light-hearted "rules" for doing business in China were presented by a speaker at a "Making it in China" session at the University of Cambridge:

Rule 1: China is a highly regulated country, in which one needs to learn, understand, and follow countless regulations.

Rule 2: China presents a chaotic and unpredictable operating environment in which anything is possible; in fact there are no rules.

Rule 3: Rules 1 and 2 are simultaneously valid.

Understanding these local rules of the game has clearly paid off for OI. In 2008 the company won the UK Exporter of the Year Award "for the company demonstrating the utmost energy, novelty, patience and persistence, in the field of exports from UK to China during the year." It has achieved an average annual growth of 50 percent of export sales to China. From its original Beijing office it has expanded to Shanghai (where it also has a customer support center), Guangzhou, and Chengdu. China has become the fastest-growing market for OI across the world. From annual sales of less than $1 million in 1997, annual sales to China now exceed $34 million.

Website: http://www.oxford-instruments.com/; Oxford Instruments, *Annual Report*, 2010; OneSource, *Thomson Reuters*, 2011.

Sources: This case has been compiled by the authors from a presentation by and discussions with Daniel Ayres, the project manager for the establishment of the manufacturing WFOE in Shanghai. Our sincere thanks to him and Oxford Instruments for allowing us to use the case here.

---

1 Why has OI invested in China? In what ways does its strategy fit with current trends in China?

2 Which "mode of entry" did OI select in China and what kinds of operational and practical challenges did it face?

3 What kinds of threats and opportunities might OI face from new multinational firms from China and what strategic responses should it be considering?

WFOE

A wholly foreign-owned enterprise is a limited liability company under Chinese company law and the preferred mode of investment for foreign MNEs looking to manufacture in China. WFOEs are also known as WOFEs (Wholly Owned Foreign Enterprises)

INTRODUCTION

With over 1.3 billion people, China (see accompanying map) has the largest population in the world, more than Latin America and Sub-Saharan Africa combined. Although it is an ancient civilization the economy was only recently liberalized and opened up to trade and investment following Prime Minister Deng Xiaoping's reforms in 1978. Since then it has been moving from a closed centrally planned communist state toward an open market economy, and is increasingly participating as a major player in the modern world. While the rest of the world increasingly relies on China's economic growth to maintain global economic momentum, China itself is feeling the political and social strains of this

Company chop
An official company seal or signature stamp used to verify company documents, contracts, and often financial transactions

South and East Asia
◉ Capital
• Major city
◯ Newly industrialized economies

unprecedented era of change. Its burgeoning economy attracts growing amounts of FDI as foreign firms take advantage of opportunities to produce products cheaper and sell into its expanding domestic market. Chinese firms are also evolving to compete not just in their own market but also abroad, as a new group of multinationals flexes home-grown advantages beyond the "middle kingdom."

UNPRECEDENTED SCALE, SCOPE, AND SPEED OF GROWTH

Lists of facts and figures that highlight the China phenomenon abound. It is the second-largest economy in PPP GDP, the third-largest trader, the largest producer of rice, wheat, cotton and tobacco, red meat, coal, and aluminum. It has over three trillion dollars in foreign reserves (by far the largest in the world), 170 cities with more than 1 million people, the largest number of atheists of any country, and over 800 million subscribers to wireless phone services. It accounts for over 15 percent of the world's luxury goods and manufactures 70 percent of the world's toys, 60 percent of the world's bicycles, 50 percent of the world's motorcycles, 40 percent of the world's mobile phones, and 35 percent of the world's coal (but reports 80 percent of worldwide deaths related to coal mining).

A particular boost came in 2001 when China joined the World Trade Organization (WTO) and began to attract record levels of FDI. **WTO accession** carried with it the

WTO accession
Admission to the World Trade Organization; in return for the right to access and to engage in fair trade with other national markets, the country must liberalize its own markets

Table 21.1 China: key economic indicators

	2004	2005	2006	2007	2008
GDP per capita ($ at PPP)	3,596.71	4,076.31	4,669.37	5,390.01	5,970.81
GDP (% real change pa)	10.10	10.40	11.60	13.00	9.00
Government consumption (% of GDP)	14.51	14.52	14.21	13.68	13.54
Inflation (%)	3.89	1.82	1.46	4.75	5.86
Official unemployment (%)	4.20	4.20	4.10	4.00	4.20
Current account balance (as % of GDP)	3.55	7.19	9.53	10.99	9.85
Foreign exchange reserves (billions of US $)	609.90	818.90	1,066.93	1,528.20	1,949.25

Sources: Adapted from IMF, World Economic Outlook and Econstats, World Bank and CIA, *The World Fact Book, 2010.*

commitment to phase out non-tariff barriers, provide trading rights to foreign companies, and change conditions on foreign investment, and this has been happening.[1]

The results have been impressive. GDP grew at an average of 8 percent per year, reminiscent of Japan's "catching-up" period in the 1960s and 1970s. Since 2000, when many analysts envisaged a slow down, China has achieved average annual growth rates of over 10 percent (see Table 21.1). Exports and imports, as well as FDI, have surged but with a positive imbalance (exports exceeding imports) resulting in growing foreign reserves and contributing in particular to the massive deficit of the United States. China is now ranked as the fourth-largest economy in nominal GDP terms and second-largest in PPP terms.

The new era of export-led growth has resulted in economic and social development nationally, with a significant overall reduction in poverty across the whole of China (adjusted for purchasing power, China has grown to be 70 percent richer than India). But growth has been concentrated in the industrialized east and in urban areas, where per capita disposable income is more than three times higher than that in the rural areas and growing faster, at almost 13 percent compared to less than 10 percent in rural areas. The country is still classed as "lower-middle income" and 130 million Chinese fall below the international poverty line.[2]

Trade and FDI are major indicators of the level to which an economy is integrated in the global economy and interdependent with other economies. The liberalization process in China centered on opening up the country in terms of inward and outward trade and FDI. In 2009, the global economic downturn reduced foreign demand for Chinese exports for the first time in many years down to $1.204 trillion (2009 est.), but China rebounded quickly, outperforming all other major economies in 2010 with GDP growth around 10 percent. China's external trade recently reached $1.506 trillion (2010 est.). This represents almost 40 percent of GDP. Note, though, that over 50 percent of these exports came from foreign-owned or foreign-invested firms (see Table 21.2). The Chinese government vows

Table 21.2 China: key trade indicators, 2010

Major exports	% of total	Major imports	% of total
Electrical machinery and equipment	10.5	Electrical machinery	22.1
Clothing and garments	9.8	Crude oil and fuels	10.6
Yarn and textiles	5.0	Electrical equipment	3.5
Petroleum products	1.1	Textiles	2.1
Leading markets	% of total economy	**Leading suppliers**	% of total economy
United States	18.4	Japan	13.0
Hong Kong	13.8	South Korea	10.2
Japan	8.2	United States	7.7
South Korea	4.5	Taiwan (Taiwan Province of China)	5.6
Germany	4.2		

Sources: Adapted from CIA, *The World Factbook*; 2010 estimates.

Table 21.3 Direct investment flows, outward and inward (billions of US $)

	Outward FDI flows				Inward FDI flows			
	2005	2006	2007	2008	2005	2006	2007	2008
Brazil	2,517	28,202	7,067	20,457	15,066	18,782	34,585	45,058
Mainland China	12,261	16,130	22,469	52,150	72,406	69,468	83,521	108,312
France	120,971	115,036	224,652	220,046	81,063	81,076	157,973	117,510
Germany	55,515	79,427	179,547	156,457	35,867	42,870	56,407	24,939
Hong Kong	27,201	43,459	61,119	59,920	33,618	42,892	54,365	63,003
India	2,495	9,676	17,281	17,685	6,676	16,881	25,127	41,554
Italy	41,822	42,035	90,775	43,839	19,971	39,159	40,202	17,032
Japan	45,781	50,266	73,549	128,020	2,775	26,506	22,549	24,426
Russia	12,763	17,979	45,916	52,390	12,766	28,732	55,073	70,320
UK	83,708	79,457	275,482	111,411	193,693	139,543	183,386	96,939
US	227,736	216,614	378,362	311,796	101,025	175,394	271,176	316,112

Sources: UNCTAD, *World Investment Report*, 2009 (Geneva, United Nations, 2009).

in the 12th Five-Year Plan adopted in March 2011 to continue reforming the economy and emphasizes the need to increase domestic consumption in order to make the economy less dependent on exports for GDP growth in the future. However, China likely will make only marginal progress toward these rebalancing goals in 2011. Two economic problems China currently faces are inflation—which, late in 2010, surpassed the government's target of 3 percent—and local government debt, which swelled as a result of stimulus policies, and is largely off-the-books and potentially low-quality.[3] China differs considerably from Japan, during its rapid economic growth phase, in this respect. So, while exports are normally seen as an indicator of local competitive advantage, this is not so straightforward in the case of China. Location endowments certainly convey some specific advantages, notably the lower costs of manufacturing that result from the availability of cheap labor. It is clear that the liberalization process has allowed foreign multinationals access to this resource and, certainly in some industries, they are better equipped than local "infant" industry firms to leverage this advantage. So, a significant proportion of China's export boom has been driven by foreign firms "migrating" existing manufacturing facilities from elsewhere into China and gaining the benefits of lower-cost exports to existing markets in the triad regions.

The attractiveness of China to MNEs, and the scale of their involvement, are shown by the sheer volume of FDI inflows over the past 20 years (see Table 21.3). In 2008 China recorded US$108 billion of FDI inflows (many times higher than that of Japan, which has always attracted relatively low amounts of direct investment). China's total stock of FDI is more than four times that for Japan, again despite its relatively recent economic liberalization. The section below will discuss inward investment into China, followed by a review of the constraints facing firms trying to get into its growing domestic market.

Other firms are benefiting, without investing significantly in China, by extending their supply chains to take advantage of low-cost suppliers. At one point in the mid-2000s Wal-Mart imported over $25 billion in one year from China, making it the sixth-largest importer of any "economy," with a larger volume than that of Russia. Wal-Mart's import volume has since decreased and it is beginning to redress the trade imbalance in a small way by expanding its network of retail stores in China. (See the Real Case: Outsourcing and job losses to China in Chapter 6).

Outward FDI from China has grown significantly in recent years (see Table 21.3), partly as a result of the strong government push for international expansion (the "Going Global" strategy pursued by MOFCOM, see below) and the rising use of mergers and acquisitions (M&As) by Chinese firms to access Western markets, technologies, and brands. The final section in this chapter will examine a new breed of Chinese multinational firm.

THE ROLE OF GOVERNMENT

China has evolved from a closed, centrally planned system towards an open, market-oriented economy. Reforms started in the late 1970s with the phasing out of collectivized agriculture, and expanded to include the gradual liberalization of prices, fiscal decentralization, increased autonomy for state enterprises, the foundation of a diversified banking system, the development of stock markets, the rapid growth of the non-state sector, and the opening to foreign trade and investment.

Government reforms and the maintenance of the critical balance between liberalization and continued government control, guiding the development of capitalist enterprises and market incentives, are major factors responsible for the economic success currently experienced by China. They will continue to be critical factors for the sustainability of growth and development, as both the domestic and international contexts become increasingly turbulent. Comparisons between China and Russia are common and can be instructive. One study characterizes the differences as follows:

> China gave priority to administrative reform, aligned bureaucratic incentives at all levels with growth and development objectives, and enhanced enterprise and local autonomy while preserving the capacity of the center to exercise control. This approach transformed government bodies into real owners of the reform process and led to privatization over time that was largely welfare enhancing. Russia, on the contrary, gave priority to economic over state restructuring. Major reforms including mass privatization were implemented in an environment of a weak state, which did not have the capacity to protect its ownership rights and coordinate reforms. As a result, privatization was a wasteful process associated with asset stripping and consequently with lack of legitimacy of newly established property rights.[4]

The Chinese government has emphasized market-led growth by raising personal incomes and consumption while helping newly privatized industries to increase productivity through technology transfer and improved management. These aims, together with a policy of export-led growth, have been supported by the influx of FDI, also driven by the liberalization process. Multinational investors have pushed up exports while creating alliances and joint ventures which have helped local firms develop the necessary assets and skills to become more productive (although some studies argue that the effect has been to limit the competitiveness of local enterprises as they have become subordinate suppliers to Western MNEs).

China's central and provincial governments have worked on a "three-step development strategy," since the 1980s. This has involved regional development initiatives, now focused on controlling growth in the east of the country and subsidizing growth inland. "Key national projects" have supported infrastructure development on a massive scale, and the targeting of strategic industries, assets, and technological capabilities. Over time these kinds of government-directed initiatives have become increasingly international, as part of the "**Going Global**" strategy. Premier Wen Jiabao has strengthened this approach, building on the initial impetus by Premier Zhu Rongji in 2001, as part of the government push for the development of national industry champions and the procurement of natural resources abroad. Both underpin a broader agenda of economic nationalism including energy security, geo-political positioning, and national competitiveness.

Going Global
A key strategy of the Chinese government as part of the 11th Five-Year Plan, to internationalize target industry sectors and companies

Another major policy objective in China is to boost high-technology industry sectors. In 2010 PRC President Hu Jintao stated: "*A nation's technological competitiveness determines its place and future in international competition.*" Efforts are led by the National Development and Reform Commission as part of the country's 12th Five-Year Plan. Key industries, including information technology, biotechnology, aerospace, new materials, high-tech services, new energies, and marine science and technology, are the focus of this initiative. The government is also facilitating both local technology-based start-up firms and encouraging high-tech FDI by upgrading the R&D infrastructure to develop innovative, patentable technologies. There has been a huge expansion in the number of researchers in China since 1999. China now counts more researchers than Japan, and is on its way to potentially overtake the EU in this regard. The country is already second only to the United States in terms of advanced technology exports, and it recently overtook Japan this year to become the second-largest investor in R&D (spending $121 billion in 2010). It spent around half of the UK budget on R&D in 1994 and now spends well over three times as much as the UK each year.

In the coming years China plans to reduce its external imbalances; boost domestic demand, particularly consumer demand, and rebalance investment and consumption; further promote balanced external sector development; speed up financial reform; and further improve the exchange regime "in a gradual and controllable manner." There are, however, a range of ongoing problems, including: large disparities in per capita income between regions; unemployment, particularly affecting previous employees of **state-owned enterprises (SOEs)**, and migrants; corruption and other economic crimes; poor health and safety standards (for employees and consumers); environmental damage and social problems related to the economy's rapid transformation; a rapidly aging population, due to the one-child policy.

State-owned enterprises (SOEs)
Companies that are owned, financed, and controlled by government

The government retains substantial control over some areas of the economy (such as energy and transportation, financial markets, news media, infrastructure, land, and property) and is influential in others (aerospace, telecoms, construction, retailing, and creative media) and less involved in others (automotive and consumer products). This means there are different levels and types of control exerted in different spheres of life. Add to this the variety of levels of government, from central to provincial to city and town, and the fact that these are no longer "harmoniously aligned." Also add the fact that the application or implementation of laws and regulations varies greatly according to the specific location, situation, and people involved and we begin to get an idea of the reasons why China plays by different rules of the game (see **Active Learning Case: Oxford Instruments in China** above).[5]

MNE INVESTMENT INTO CHINA

The massive growth of FDI into China has created the largest array of international mergers and acquisitions, alliances, joint ventures, and partnerships ever witnessed. These are clearly a major source of complementary assets, resources, and capabilities for the Western multinationals and the local companies involved, which engage in a reciprocal give-and-take as part of the process of market entry.

China holds the double attraction for MNEs of a cost-effective source of production inputs, particularly cheap labor, and a growing consumer market. These strategic drivers equate to two simple forms of investment rationale: input-oriented investments and output-oriented investments. The former are designed to gain access to local resources, endowments, and country-specific advantages (CSAs) that will help the firm develop, produce, or deliver a product or service cheaper or better in some way. The latter are designed to expand sales by tapping into new and/or growing markets. Greater profitability should result from either or both, if they prove successful.

First and foremost, China has a reputation as a cheap manufacturing hub so cost advantages are still the primary motivator for many companies. The average factory wage (around $200 per month, but varying by region and type of employment) is far less than in more industrialized Pacific Rim countries such as Taiwan and much lower than anywhere in the triad regions. In addition to low labor costs, other positives of sourcing in China include: lower capital costs and low-cost product design and R&D; large manufacturing capacities; and, for some, improvements in quality. The negatives include: communication problems, low product quality, long initial start-up times, intellectual property theft, increased management complexity, operational and supply-chain challenges (see the section below).

INTERNATIONAL BUSINESS STRATEGY IN ACTION

Airbus in China

Passenger volumes in China's air transportation industry are expected to grow annually by 11 percent over the next 20 years. This will make it the world's second-largest aviation market, requiring an additional 1,790 aircraft to cope with the increased volume. Forty-nine new airports and 701 airport expansion projects are also expected under China's Five-Year Plan. The Chinese government maintains a strong degree of control over the civil aviation industry. Respective agencies aim to improve the reliability and efficiency of the transport infrastructure and promote competitiveness among domestic firms. The General Administration of Civil Aviation of China (CAAC) is the government agency responsible for the non-military aviation industry. It has rationalized the country's airlines, completing mergers with the "Big 3"—Air China, China Eastern, and China Southern—and some of the smaller airlines.

CAAC and other agencies are also central to the expressed aim of the Chinese government to develop an indigenous "Made-in-China" aircraft to rival Boeing and Airbus. There is no doubt this can be done and the economic rationale is less relevant at this stage than the political symbolism. The government has begun funding this as a prestige project and will continue to do so until it succeeds. There are question marks, however, over how long it will take and how reliable, safe, and therefore marketable the final product will be.

The government's determination, coupled with the inherent advantages of low-cost production and the rapid rate of technology transfer and local learning, have impressed one experienced Chinese expatriate in the aerospace industry. He proposed:

> Within the next 15 years there will be three major commercial aerospace corporations; Boeing, Airbus and a Chinese firm. Soon after there may well be two; one of which will be the Chinese firm.[7]

One senior British executive in China described the "Stairway to Heaven." The three stages toward local technological maturity in aerospace manufacturing:

- Stage (1) "Made-to-print": local manufacturers follow simple designs for low-end (and later, high-end) manufacturing.
- Stage (2) Local firms take on responsibility for product modules or "build-kits," including some redesign and process innovation.

Source: Getty Images/Chinafotopress

- Stage (3) Full engineering partnerships with Western firms, with shared design and development, local responsibility for technology, quality, etc., and risk and revenue sharing (suppliers as shareholders in ongoing development processes).

Foreign firms in China, including Airbus and Boeing, Rolls-Royce and General Electric, are part of this plan. In order to gain access to the growing domestic market, estimated to be worth over $300 billion over the next 20 years, they have had to establish partnerships with local Chinese manufacturers. These involve subcontracting, technology transfer, and training with an expressed aim of increasing the local content of aircraft.

AVIC1 (Aviation Industry Corporation of China) and AVIC2 are responsible for all aerospace manufacturing in China. AVIC1 concentrates on large aircraft and is the main organization charged with developing a complete Chinese-made aircraft. However, rather than one unified "China" interest group there are local rivalries and factions competing with each other to become the lead player, not a simple them-and-us situation. As in other industries in China local competition drives learning. There is "collaborative competition" guided, more or less, by the government, depending on the industry. On October 28, 2008, AVIC1 and AVIC2 officially merged because the previous separation resulted in split resources and led to redundant projects. The major focus of AVIC is to efficiently develop indigenous military technologies and to eventually compete with Boeing and Airbus in the civilian airline industry. During the Airshow China 2008, AVIC appeared in public for the first time. In the Singapore Air Show in February 2010, AVIC introduced the Comac 919 aircraft for the first time outside

▶

the mainland. The aircraft is designed and built entirely in China will compete directly against industry stalwarts A320 and Boeing 737 after completing flight trials in four years. It should be available commercially by 2016.

Airbus subcontracts around $60 million per year to five Chinese firms and this is expected to double over the next five years. Components made in China include A320 wing parts, passenger doors, and landing gear bay. Two major joint ventures are at the center of Airbus operations in China, in the towns of Xian (Xian Aircraft Corporation with 28,000 employees) and Shenyang (Shenyang Aircraft Corporation with 20,000 employees). Both the local firms are state-owned enterprises (SOEs) operating under the AVIC1 umbrella organization. The head of the Xian plant is also the local town mayor.

The company has transferred manufacturing technology and put in place a range of training programs to develop the local capabilities at these plants, and among local component suppliers. While improved productivity is important, the quality and reliability of the components produced here are far more important, given the safety-critical nature of the final product.

Process improvement and innovation at the plant level are monitored or measured by a number of indicators. These include output and productivity measures, such as improvements in scrap yield and customer reject rates. The increased use of quality circles, "lean" management systems, and techniques such as the use of "visibility boards" which map out operations on the plant floor and monitor process changes, all indicate improvements in managerial and process-related capabilities. Other advances, such as a move from the use of 2-D to 3-D design drawings, demonstrate engineering, design, and product development innovations—all of which show how local Chinese managers, engineers, and plant-level personnel are learning through their interaction with Western counterparts.

Sources: S. C. Collinson, B. Sullivan-Taylor and J. L. Wang, "Adapting to the China Challenge: Lessons from Experienced Multinationals," Advanced Institute of Management (AIM) Research Executive Briefing, London (2007), http://www.aimresearch.org/publications/adaptingtochina. pdf; Aude Lagorce, "China's Next Bid for Glory: Aviation Supremacy," *Wall Street Journal*, April 14, 2007, http://www.marketwatch.com/news/story/ story.aspx?guid=%7B9DBEEE55-F714-48EE-A77F-2F49C7202FDF%7D; http://www.buyusa.gov/china/en/aerospace.html; http://www.airbus.com/ en/; AVIC, http://www.avic.com.cn/; Juliana Liu, "Chinese planes challenge Boeing and Airbus," *BBC News*, February 2, 2010.

At the same time the rapid growth of the economy and the country's growing purchasing power are increasing consumer purchasing power as well as channeling investment into transportation, energy, utilities, communication systems, and other parts of its infrastructure. In response to these attractions, MNEs have made a large number of investments in China and the country now hosts the largest number of MNE affiliates of any economy, employing around 24 million people.[6]

Most investments have been in the form of equity joint ventures or WFOEs. However, because of the evolving legislation governing foreign investment into China, there has been a noticeable shift in the mode of market entry by foreign firms toward M&As and WFOEs. Ten Asian locations (Hong Kong, Macau, Taiwan province, Japan, the Philippines, Thailand, Malaysia, Singapore, Indonesia, and South Korea), account for around 60 percent of FDI inflows. This shows a strong regional effect, with Japan, China, and the larger satellite Asian economies evolving a strong, mutually beneficial growth cycle of trade and FDI. The United States, Japan, and the EU account for roughly similar proportions of FDI in China. Around 70 percent of FDI each year is in manufacturing industries and cumulative FDI in China's high-tech industry is over $120 billion, with more than 700 foreign-affiliated high-tech companies operating R&D facilities in China. But service-related FDI is also growing. Investment in China's burgeoning retail industry, for example, is very healthy. Based on a first-mover strategy, Carrefour (France) has become the fifth-largest retailer in China, while Wal-Mart (United States), which ranked the 14th largest, recently expanded its presence in China through the acquisition of Trust-Mart.

But the major distinguishing feature of China's inward FDI is the wide range of firms and industries involved. The top MNEs from all industries have a presence, including Occidental Petroleum (coal mining), Motorola (producing semiconductors and mobile phones), General Motors and VW (joint ventures with a Shanghai automotive company), Dow Chemical (a polyurethane production joint venture), Heinz (a baby-food plant), Procter & Gamble (a joint venture producing laundry and personal care products), Hewlett-Packard (electronics joint ventures), RJR Nabisco (manufacturing Ritz crackers, among other food products), Airbus and Boeing (a series of joint ventures), Rolls-Royce (aero engines), Seagram (whiskey and wine), Babcock and Wilcox (a joint venture making boilers), Mitsubishi (a venture to build elevators). Other firms on this growing list include Bell Telephone, DaimlerChrysler, General Bearing, Gillette, Lockheed, Pabst Brewing, Peugeot, Squibb, VW, and Xerox. P&G even spent $300 million in one year just marketing one product: Oil of Olay!

A regional investment pattern is also increasingly strong. For example, in terms of sales, Taiwanese firm Hongfujin Precision Industry (Shenzhen), a subsidiary of Hon Hai Precision Industry (also known as the Foxconn Group), has surpassed Motorola (China) in size, becoming the largest foreign affiliate in China. Overall, the firm employs close to 1 million Chinese, mainly in the coastal region of Shenzen. But it has plans to move manufacturing into cheaper regions away from the east coast, including Chengdu and Wuhan. However, Foxconn has been involved in several controversies—most relating to how it manages employees in China, where it is the largest private employer. The decision to increase staff numbers and to move inland followed the suicides of 13 Chinese employees in 2010. On May 20, 2011, an explosion and fire broke out at one of the factories in Chengdu. The incident affected the iPad 2 assembly line and caused 3 deaths and 15 injured workers. The incidents threatened to tarnish the image of top global brands, such as Apple, Dell and Nokia, for which Foxconn produces laptops and smartphones. However, despite all these unfavorable news headlines, China still attracts electronics manufacturing companies, such as Taiwanese firms Quanta Computer and Inventec which are prominent in the list of top foreign affiliates in China. An increasing number of transnational corporations (TNCs) have established regional headquarters in Chinese cities such as Beijing and Shanghai. IBM relocated its global procurement headquarters to Shenzhen some time ago and is unlikely to move this inland.

Some firms have been successful in China. Although it is not doing so well elsewhere in the world, GM has generated profits for some time from its China operations. It accounts for an estimated 80 percent of the group's Asia–Pacific operations, which make about a fifth of the firm's net profits. Sales in China, driven by the Buick Saloon and Excelle Sedan, gave GM a market share approaching 10 percent to challenge Volkswagen, the long-time market leader (although most analysts predict overcapacity problems, reducing profits for all car firms in China in the coming years).[8]

As described in Chapter 15, Kodak has also done well in China, on the back of a $2 billion investment program that began in 1997. By working with the higher echelons of the central government in Beijing, Kodak managed to change the rules of the game in many ways, to gain exclusive rights to produce and sell photographic film in China. Its market share grew significantly as a result, compared to archrival Fuji, which has seen its share slip as Kodak has grown.

Other firms investing in China believe, despite losing money, that they have invested in "a foot in the door" to the most important growing region in the world. But there is a third group of firms that have failed either to break into the market or to gain any return on their investments in China. Many following something of a "herd mentality" to get into China have failed to do their homework and been surprised to find how different, difficult, and risky the country is for inward investors (see the section below). Among those firms which failed miserably in China was New Zealand's Fonterra. Fonterra used to own 43% in the joint venture with SanLu Group. SanLu was a state-owned Chinese dairy products company based in Shijiazhuang, the capital city of Hebei Province. It was one of the oldest and most popular brands of infant formula in China before it went bankrupt. In September 2008, SanLu was involved in an adulterated milk powder scandal, affecting some 294,000 Chinese infants and killing six. Their baby milk powder had been tainted with melamine, which can cause kidney stones and other complications. It received a bankruptcy order from Shijiazhuang Court on 24 December 2008 and several of its top managers were sentenced to long prison terms. As a direct consequence of the criminal contamination of milk in China, Fonterra recognised an impairment charge of $139 million against the carrying value of its investment in SanLu. Following this impairment charge, Fonterra's best estimate at that point of time, of the book value of its investment in SanLu was approximately $62 million, which was 69 per cent below its previous carrying value. In the process, Fonterra has learnt a painful lesson in international business.

A spate of acquisitions and investments in the beer industry in the mid-2000s bears a strong resemblance to a period in the mid-1990s when foreign firms rushed to enter the Chinese market and lost out. Between 1993 and 1996 international beer firms invested over $1 billion in the Chinese market and found that capacity far outstripped demand, prices were unsustainably low, and production plants were small scale and inefficient. Although the local breweries were virtually bankrupt, local governments, concerned about rising unemployment, were pumping money into them, making it impossible for foreign firms to compete. Fosters, Carlsberg, Bass, and Asahi all bailed out at a loss, leaving the two largest local players, Tsingtao and Yanjing, to increase their dominance. Carlsberg alone lost $2 million between 1998 and 2000 before selling out.[9]

In 2002 China overtook the United States as the largest beer market in the world and foreign firms rushed to invest once again. In 2004 Anheuser-Busch acquired the Harbin Brewery Group Ltd., Heineken NV bought 21 percent of Guangdong Brewery Holdings Ltd., Scottish & Newcastle plc acquired a minority stake in Chongqing Beer Group, and Interbrew SA acquired a majority stake in Zhejiang Shiliang Brewery Co. Ltd. More recently, in 2011 Anheuser-Busch InBev announced a deal to acquire 100% of Liaoning Dalian Daxue Brewery Co., Ltd. of China to expand its market share there. Most are doing much better in the Chinese market this time around, but local players are strong and beginning to look at market opportunities abroad.

Foreign R&D investment

MNEs, particularly those in IT hardware, the automotive industry, and pharmaceuticals and biotechnology, invest massively in R&D. Some of the largest investors, such as Ford Motor, Pfizer, DaimlerChrysler, Siemens, Toyota Motor, and GM, spend more on R&D than the vast majority of developing countries. Only China, Taiwan, South Korea, and Brazil come close to these individual firms in terms of total, national-level R&D expenditure. So the recent shift of R&D investment from the triad to emerging market economies and especially to China is significant. The share of foreign affiliates in R&D in the developing world increased from 2 percent to 18 percent between 1996 and 2002 and has continued to grow.[10] China is the most favored destination for MNEs looking to invest in R&D abroad.

There are now over 300 foreign R&D centers in the country. In many cases inward investors are competing for privileged access to the Chinese market and will offer high-technology investments to gain government support for projects. GM's automotive R&D center, for example, was established in the late 1990s when global car companies were fighting to get the best joint ventures with a few, government-supported local firms. Boeing (United States) and Airbus (a European consortium) were also under pressure to transfer technologies and established local training in return for access.

Electronics and ICT (Information and Communication Technology) firms were among the earliest entrants. Motorola established the first China-based R&D center of any MNE in 1990 and now has 15 centers there, employing over 1,500 engineers. Microsoft has five centers with Microsoft Research Asia (MRA), one of the largest R&D centers in the world, responsible for the firm's basic R&D for the Asian region. Nokia also has five centers in China, making its initial investment in 1998. General Electric located one of only three of its global R&D centers in Shanghai in 2003.

Pharmaceutical firms have followed suit, including $100 million research centers for both Novartis and GSK in the late-2000's. The former, based in Shanghai, focuses on the infectious causes of specific types of cancer endemic in China and Asia. It also works to combine Western technology and drug-discovery approaches with the traditional methods of Chinese medicine.[11] For pharmaceutical firms the relatively low costs of field trials in China is one reason to invest.

More generally the shortage of science, technology, and engineering expertise in the West is a major driver. While the EU is said to have a shortfall of around 700,000 science and engineering personnel, China hosts around 750,000 (second only to the United States) who are also cheaper to employ. Alongside this input-oriented or resource-oriented rationale for FDI in R&D, there are output-oriented or market-oriented reasons for R&D investments. These include the fact that industrial partners have moved to China. So, for example, much of the R&D conducted by Motorola's semiconductor and component divisions requires close collaboration with customers. Existing, Western-based customers have moved manufacturing activities to China and new customers are also emerging in China and the Asian region. These trends combine to create a strong incentive for Motorola to move its R&D "center of gravity" away from the West. China is also becoming a lead market for some technologies. Again, taking the Motorola example, advanced consumer use of mobile phone services in China makes it a lead market for user-led innovation, prompting firms to locate R&D activities there to keep up with adoption trends.

Over the longer term we can expect benefits for research institutes, universities, and local firms as MNE R&D networks supplement and support China's national system of innovation. The Chinese government has identified foreign R&D investments as a critical part of China's technology development strategy, originally outlined in the 10th Five-Year Plan (2001–2005), now a core part of subsequent Five-Year Plans. China overall spends more than double the UK on R&D, and this has been growing at around 9 percent per year in recent years, in line with GDP growth. The country has 17 million people in higher education and has established more than 60 industrial parks dedicated to Chinese graduates returning from overseas to set up businesses. Well-educated graduates and a very good science and technology infrastructure, relative to other developing and emerging countries, are important national assets for China. These are now underpinning the growth of high-tech firms, such as Beijing Yuande Bio-Medical, from Beijing Medical University; Datang Microelectronics, from Beijing's Telecoms Research Institute; and Innova Superconductor and Tsinghua Solar, both from Tsinghua University.[12]

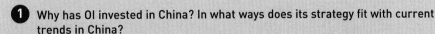
✔ Active learning check

Review your answer to Active Learning Case question 1 and make any changes you like. Then compare your answer to the one below.

❶ Why has OI invested in China? In what ways does its strategy fit with current trends in China?

OI's investment in China was mainly "market-seeking" in that the firm had experienced growing sales through exports to China in the past and expected to further increase sales by establishing a presence in the market, alongside its customers. This investment has paid off well, with both exports and locally manufactured product sales growing well. FDI to establish local customer services and representative sales offices has supported this success. OI is benefiting from cheaper local assembly costs for some products and has recently developed some R&D partnerships. These count as "resource-seeking" investments. Its strategy has continued to fit well with current trends in China. The growth in local demand for its products comes from both Chinese firms and foreign MNEs, including OI's customers in the United States and Europe, that have moved operations to China. China may also evolve into an important source of inputs for its worldwide product development and R&D efforts in the future.

GETTING INTO CHINA

According to folklore in China, "the mightiest dragon cannot crush the local snake";[13] in other words, local advantage can help a great deal in fending off larger and wealthier "predators." In response to the very different market conditions and complex local rules of the game in China it is more common for multinationals to use intermediaries in the process of establishing a local presence here than elsewhere in the Pacific Rim. Government agencies such as those connected to the Ministry of Foreign Trade and Economic Cooperation offer such assistance, as do banks, law firms, and a vast range of consultancies.

As discussed above, the Chinese economy is centrally planned to some degree and the rights of all firms and individuals are strongly influenced by central, regional, and local government agencies. The government has a priority list of desired investments: ventures involving advanced technology, exports, or the generation of foreign exchange are given the highest priority. Understanding the policy agenda and the people responsible for formulating, revising, and implementing it is critical for market-entry strategies and continued survival in China. Local policy is also connected to high-level political forces that are important to understand. For example, at the international level, China has been running a large trade surplus with the United States in recent years, and there is every reason to believe that, unless this situation is corrected, the US government will limit Chinese imports. The European Union has also been talking about limiting clothing imports from China because of the threat to local manufacturers (effectively because they are "too competitive"). These political reactions could result in a backlash against triad MNEs in China. These and other sources of country risk that can affect the success of an overseas investment should also be taken into account when considering the mode of entry adopted by MNEs.

In terms of mode of entry, firms can invest via a range of FDI mechanisms, including Sino-foreign joint ventures, joint exploitation, and exclusively foreign-owned enterprises (or WFOEs), foreign-funded shareholding companies, and joint development companies:

1 Sino-foreign joint ventures, also known as joint shareholding corporations, generally require the capital from the foreign party to be at least equal to a 25 percent share in the enterprise, according to Chinese regulations.

2 Cooperative businesses, also called contractual cooperation businesses, have the rights and obligations of different parties embedded in the contract. The foreign partner generally supplies all or most of the capital while the Chinese party supplies land, factory buildings, and other facilities.

3 Exclusively foreign-owned enterprises take the form of limited liability companies and regulations formally call for these to "adopt international advanced technology and facilities" or "all or most of the products must be export-oriented."

4 Joint exploitation, development, and production enterprises relate to maritime and overland oil exploitation.

5 Foreign-funded shareholding companies involve Chinese and foreign shareholders holding the shares of the company and accepting liability according to proportional ownership. The shares held by foreign investors must account for more than 25 percent of the total registered capital.

Lessons from foreign firms that established operations in China some time ago and have developed some experience adapting to the local business environment illustrate some of the key difficulties. A survey by the US Embassy in Beijing and Gallup received 286 responses from American investors in China.[14] About half said they were profitable and a further half of the remaining firms were investing more in anticipation of future profits. They reported a number of difficulties that created additional risks or costs or required adaptation. The biggest problems were said to be, in order of importance:

■ Transparency of laws and regulations

■ Cost of doing business

■ Customs procedures/export procedures

■ Foreign exchange regulations/exchange rate risk.

Drawing on a number of surveys some key issues for foreign entrants are as follows:

■ Market-access rights from equity holdings to taxation levels vary by industry and are changing rapidly. At least three, often more, levels of government, including local, regional, and central government agencies, have a direct and strong influence over the local rules of the game and give preferential treatment to local firms and to particular kinds of foreign investors.

■ Chinese tax laws and other regulations governing business practices are complex. Despite the expense it is necessary to use attorneys, accountants, and consultants familiar with Chinese requirements.

Guanxi
Denotes personalized or informal networks of relationships in China. They can be important preconditions for smoothing the way or gaining favors or advantages, particularly when both society and the economy are dominated by central government. There are parallels with the concept of social capital

■ Contracting tends to be based around relationships and connections (***guanxi***) rather than formal, legal documents. These are the basis of mutual trust, with due diligence on potential business partners performed by checking their network connections, as opposed to formal market mechanisms. Relationships with the right connections are critical. Developing *guanxi* connections with the wrong partners creates obligations that may act as a trap. Contracts are just a starting point for doing business, not the end goal.

■ Intellectual property rights (IPR) are not well protected, legally or via any local business ethics. Investors need to carefully consider the implications of this, including the possibility of local firms getting and using key assets such as brands, patents, and business systems. One example of technology theft is in the high speed bullet train project. Foreign companies were apparently lured in and encouraged to hand over their technology with promises of a share of China's domestic market. One of the bullet trains was subsequently involved in a serious accident leaving 40 dead and more than 200 people injured in Zhejiang, Eastern China on July 23, 2011. Having built by a joint venture between Chinese firm CSR Corp. and Canadian firm Bombardier, the accident led to a revealing series of accusations. This included allegations of mass corruption that went all the way to top of the railway ministry, then later technical problems. The Japanese firm Kawasaki and Germany's Siemens were involved and they had warned the Chinese companies for years about the dangers of scaling up this kind of technology on this rapid pace. The underlying aim of Chinese companies is to combine foreign technology with native low cost labour and capital to undercut foreign firms in international markets. In this case, the domestic market was used as a testing ground and the Chinese firms became involved in high-speed projects in Venezuela and Turkey. Exports were meant to provide the payback. The accident, however, is a blow to China's marketing efforts. Foreign train manufacturers were already challenging the legality of Chinese exports which included their technology. Now potential purchasers in the U.S., Thailand and Russia may be even harder to convince.

■ Keeping face and being respectful are important. Group orientation and steeper hierarchies characterize Chinese organizations.[15]

- Learning the language may be important in order to provide insights into the local business culture. But too much of a willingness to do things the local way can be seen as a sign of compromise and ultimately weakness. Respect and credibility often come from asserting one's own practices and rules of the game.

- The role of the Chinese partner in the success or failure of a joint venture or alliance cannot be overemphasized. Good partners will have the connections to overcome obstructive red tape and enable success; bad partners may have no power or knowledge to deal with obstructive bureaucrats, may violate confidentialities, and/or establish competing businesses.

- Although there is a large, cheap general labor pool, skilled managers, particularly those with marketing expertise, are difficult to find and keep. Engineers and technicians are similarly difficult to hold onto.[16]

In some business sectors joint ventures are required, or were required until recently, by the Chinese government. In a joint venture the local partner is typically responsible for providing the land and buildings and for carrying out local marketing. The MNE is expected to contribute the equipment, technology, and capital and to be responsible for export marketing. In those cases where the multinational is manufacturing for sales in China, high-quality products, excellent service, and good promotional efforts are critical to success. Researchers have found that outstanding service and effective promotion can often make up for some lack of quality. However, price reductions and special sales terms are unlikely to offset poor quality. Similarly, while customer relations are important, they are often not enough to make up for poor quality or poor service. The Chinese want to buy the best quality available.

In light of these challenges joint ventures have a number of both benefits and problems. Majority-owned joint ventures give foreign firms an element of control combined with the benefits of gaining immediate access to experienced managers and their local relationship networks. Experienced managers report on the benefits of being able to access local business knowledge, including customer and supplier connections and getting assistance with local officials and regulations. Local firms and/or experienced local experts are normally important for helping customize and adapt existing products and services for local markets and for developing new ones targeted at the Chinese market. Table 21.4 outlines some of these synergies between foreign and local firms.

Table 21.4 Common examples of synergies between foreign multinationals and local Chinese firms

Type of partnership	Foreign multinational firm provides . . .	Local Chinese firm provides . . .
Manufacturing joint venture or subsidiary– local supplier alliance	Finance. Technology, production systems, management systems (control, coordination best practices, performance measurement, IT, etc.). Management expertise, engineering, and plant-level training	Land, labour, facilities, finance. Links to/knowledge of suppliers, buyers, contractors, distributors. Access to local resources, materials. HRM expertise, recruitment capabilities. Local government connections, knowledge of local regulations
Product development joint venture	Finance. Technology and product development tools, processes, best practices, and expertise. Links to other sources of expertise inside and outside the firm	Facilities. Finance. Some engineering, technical expertise. Knowledge of regulations, IPR protection strategies, and relevant connections. Links to/knowledge of customer preferences and distribution channels

✔ Active learning check

Review your answer to Active Learning Case question 2 and make any changes you like. Then compare your answer to the one below.

2 **Which "mode of entry" did OI select in China and what kinds of operational and practical challenges did it face?**

OI registered as a wholly foreign-owned enterprise (WFOE) and established a manufacturing facility through this route rather than via a joint venture. Its major challenges, like many foreign firms in China, included the need to: understand and comply with local regulatory and legal conditions and deal with Chinese central and local authority bureaucracies; develop relationships with local customers and adapt to their contracting behaviors; recruit and train (and retain) local experts; develop an effective working relationship between the local offices and the UK-based divisions; and protect its intellectual property rights.

Studies show that recruiting, managing, and motivating personnel rank very high among key difficulties faced by foreign managers, even when working with local partners. Skill shortages and weaknesses in Chinese management, and the resulting low levels of labor productivity, also presented significant problems. But this can also reflect a failure on the part of foreign managers to (1) differentiate between labor costs and productivity in preparation for investing in China,[17] and (2) sufficiently adapt management and working practices to get the best out of a Chinese workforce.

According to experienced expatriates one of the most remarkable aspects of China is the sheer drive and motivation of its people. In general they are very hard-working and ambitious. Local cultural values and China's past history do have a strong influence on workplace behavior, underlying a reluctance to take the initiative and the need for detailed instructions, for example. But a massive appetite for learning, advancement, and the rewards of capitalism among the people are central to China's growth drive. Cheap labor is one of China's major attractions, but experienced labor is increasingly scarce and there is a talent war for particular kinds of employees. As a result labor rates are increasing and firms are putting in place a range of strategies to retain good employees. Rises in wage costs may well outpace improvements in the productivity of the country's workforce, which could result in lower export competitiveness.[18]

OUTWARD INVESTMENT AND THE NEW MULTINATIONALS FROM CHINA

As mentioned above (see Table 21.3) outflows of FDI from China have grown rapidly over the last decade, albeit from small beginnings. For some observers growing outward FDI is a sign of the impending competition from emerging Chinese MNEs set to dominate particular global industries in the near future. For others this "infant stage" of international expansion is set to continue for some time with Chinese firms still ill-equipped to significantly expand overseas operations.

Private Chinese companies are stepping up their outward investment, but large SOEs account for the bulk of FDI outflows from China. The government is pushing for internationalization under its current "Going Global" campaign which is central to the current Five-Year Plan set by the CPC Central Committee. As a result much outward FDI (over 70 percent in most years) comes from large Chinese companies under the state-owned

Asset Supervision and Administration Commission of the State Council. Total amounts are still, however, a small proportion of global FDI and dwarfed by the stock of inward FDI in China.[19] One study suggests that China's outward FDI tends to come from "state-controlled enterprises with government sanctioned monopoly status" and is biased toward tax havens and neighboring economies.[20] The existing capital markets and corporate ownership structures tend to promote international expansion among larger firms championed by the government, particularly in the areas of energy and raw materials (which China is short of), rather than firms that may have particular strategic advantages.

Chinese firms are certainly appearing increasingly prominently in lists of corporate rankings. Table 21.5 shows the top 25 Chinese firms in the *Forbes* ranking of the global 2000 corporations. It also compares across years, showing how certain firms have moved

Table 21.5 Top 25 Chinese (mainland) firms in the *Forbes 2000* list, 2010 ranking

Forbes 2010 rank, 2010 (2009)	Name	Category	Sales (millions of US $)	Profits (millions of US $)	Assets (millions of US $)	Stock holders' equity (millions of US $)
1	7 (9)	Sinopec	Oil and gas operations	187,517.7	5,755.6	188,793.1	63,506.9
2	8 (15)	State Grid	Utilities	184,495.8	343.0	269,801.7	90,088.8
3	10 (13)	China National Petroleum	Oil and gas operations	165,496.5	10,272.5	325,384.1	185,946.0
4	77 (99)	China Mobile Communications	Telecommunications	71,748.6	11,656.3	138,243.2	81,171.5
5	87 (92)	Industrial & Commercial Bank of China	Financial	69,295.1	18,832.2	1,726,241.9	98,710.0
6	116 (125)	China Construction Bank	Financial	58,361.2	15,627.9	1,409,602.4	81,364.4
7	118 (133)	China Life Insurance	Financial	57,019.1	3,124.8	227,720.2	9,689.0
8	133 (242)	China Railway Construction	Construction	52,044.3	960.2	41,451.6	7,802.2
9	137 (252)	China Railway Group	Diversified	50,704.4	1,008.2	45,668.8	8,926.3
10	141 (155)	Agricultural Bank of China	Financial	49,741.5	9,514.1	1,300,887	49,985.2
11	143 (145)	Bank of China	Financial	49,681.5	11,867.5	1,281,408.7	74,883.0
12	156 (185)	China Southern Power Grid	Utilities	45,735.3	250.5	64,514.3	21,577.0
13	182 (n.a.)	Dongfeng Motor	Motor vehicles	39,402.0	719.7	25,711.5	3,558.6
14	187 (292)	China State Construction Engineering	Construction	38,116.7	838.8	42,856.9	10,166.5
15	203 (170)	Sinochem Group	Petrochemical	35,576.7	659.3	25,135.9	6,722.2
16	204 (419)	China Telecommunications	Telecommunications	35,557.3	581.1	96,735.2	50,549.5
17	223 (359)	Shanghai Automotive	Motor vehicles	33,628.9	1,070.2	29,766.3	7,449.8
18	224 (341)	China Communications Construction	Construction	33,465.4	703.6	39,897.0	6,618.0
19	242 (218)	Noble Group	Diversified	31,183.1	556.0	10,655.0	2,955.4
20	252 (318)	China National Offshore Oil	Oil and gas operations	30,679.9	3,633.5	75,926.3	33,984.2
21	254 (415)	Citic Group	Diversified	30,604.8	2,765.6	315,488.0	19,806.5
22	258 (385)	China FAW Group	Motor vehicles	30,236.8	1,382.5	19,260.4	4,831.2
23	275 (428)	China South Industries Group	Motor vehicles	28,756.7	273.6	27,813.1	3,856.6
24	276 (220)	Baosteel Group	Materials	28,590.9	1,448.5	58,883.3	30,109.7
25	302 (281)	Hutchison Whampoa	Diversified	26,937.9	1,827.8	89,168.8	36,566.7

Data are for 2009. *Forbes* uses a composite ranking incorporating sales, profits, assets, and stock holders' equity.

Source: "Fortune Global 500", *Fortune*, July 26, 2010.

E-resources: http://money.cnn.com/magazines/fortune/global500/2010.

up the list and certain industry sectors have become more prominent. Utilities sector firms, banks, energy, and infrastructure companies dominate, and these are all sectors with strong government involvement.

But the *Forbes 2000* list and many other rankings which show a growing presence of Chinese firms simply measure size and/or profitability, not the degree of internationalization. Larger Chinese firms are arguably the result of the growing domestic market, not international expansion. When we examine the distribution of assets and sales of these large Chinese firms we see that they do remain highly dependent on their domestic and regional markets. All of China Telecom's sales are intra-regional, as are 98 percent of the Bank of China's sales, and 86 percent of PetroChina's (China National Petroleum) sales.[21]

Studies that examine the degree to which Chinese firms have internationalized do suggest that they are still heavily reliant on country-specific advantages (CSAs) and have yet to develop the requisite firm-specific advantages (FSAs) to break into overseas markets to any great extent. More significantly, the rationale for focusing on domestic and regional (Asian) market opportunities appears to be a significant influence shaping outward FDI.[22]

When they do venture abroad, Chinese firms follow the same logic as other MNEs. They are driven by the two main reasons, input-oriented investment (for resources) and output-oriented investment (for market access). As regards the former, a notable increase in Chinese investments in Africa has been driven by the growing demand for energy resources and raw materials in China. In recent years up to 40 percent of the global growth in oil demand has come from China, hence large-scale investments in Nigeria and other African countries with oil reserves. In 2008 a reciprocal deal worth a massive $9 billion was designed to give the Democratic Republic of Congo badly needed infrastructure in return for access to its raw materials. It involves the building of around 2,400 miles (4,000 km) of road, 2,000 miles (3,000 km) of railway, plus 32 hospitals, 145 health centers, and two universities. China will get access to an estimated 10 million tons of copper and 400,000 tons of cobalt in return.[23]

When we examine output-oriented or market-facing investment it is interesting to note the changes in the kinds of exports and FDI coming out of China, as indicators of its changing competitive advantage. In 1985 just 2.6 percent of Chinese exports were categorized as high technology, whereas almost 50 percent of exports were based on primary products or manufactured products based on natural resources. Twenty years later 25 percent of exports are high technology and less than 10 percent are from the latter category above. The initial boost in higher-value exports came from MNEs using China as an export base for their products. But high-technology, high-value products are increasingly exported by local Chinese firms that are moving up the learning curve.

Local Chinese firms and other firms based outside the triad are able to learn via subcontracting relationships and joint ventures with larger multinational firms. In this sense MNEs are, to a certain extent, "breeding" their future competitors through technology and capability transfer that takes place within these interfirm relationships. This may be an unintended consequence of an alliance, or it may be made explicit, through the transfer of equipment, know-how, and training; the licensing of patents or brands; and other activities that are part of the negotiated contract. Western MNEs often trade their own knowledge, technology, assets, resources, and networks in order to get access to local knowledge, technology, assets, resources, and networks as part of a market-entry or expansion strategy.

In the 6 months to the end of March 2011, Chinese businesses invested $64.3bn in Europe in acquisitions, trade deals and loan agreements; more than double the amount over the previous 11 quarters. This marked the start of a period of growing investment into Europe and other parts of the Triad, with the dual aim of accessing large (though mature) consumer markets and buying assets, technology and expertise to complement the cheap labour and other CSA endowments.

Overall, this means that China is evolving beyond its dominance as a global exporter of textiles, clothing, and toys and into areas such as autos (see the Real Case on Nanjing Auto below), white goods (see the case **International Business Strategy in Action: Haier abroad** below), consumer electronics, and mobile phones. In telecoms, for example, Chinese firms Huawei Technologies, Zhongxing Telecom, and Datang Telecom are but three government-backed, high-tech competitors which are quickly gaining ground against foreign equipment manufactures, including Ericsson, Lucent, Nortel, and Cisco Systems. Huawei commands the greatest market share in China for optical systems equipment, outselling all foreign competitors.[24] Although Motorola and Nokia still dominate China's mobile handset manufactures, domestic enterprises such as Bird, TCL, and Konka are chipping away the leaders' market share. In the semiconductor sector, US government analysts judge China now to be only two years or less behind US manufacturing technology and only one generation behind the commercial state of the art.[25] Huge Dragon, and China's largest manufacturer of high-definition televisions, Konka, are other examples of up-and-coming local firms. Similarly in computer software, local firms Founder, Red Flag, UFSoft, Neusoft, Kingdee, and Top Group are both partnering and competing with Microsoft, Oracle, IBM, and Sun Microsystems in niche areas.[26]

Lenovo, a high-profile Chinese firm, made the news in December 2004 when it bought IBM's PC business for $1.75 billion. This was a landmark deal for China, not least because of IBM's status as the archetypal US computer firm. Lenovo, originally called Legend when it was spun off from the Chinese Academy of Sciences in the mid-1980s, makes about 30 percent of PCs in China and is number two in laser printers. The sale gave IBM $650 million in cash, along with an 18.9 percent stake in Lenovo worth $600 million. The merged firm had sales of about $12 billion a year, as well as a five-year license for IBM's PC brands. Lenovo's PC operations were then moved to be headquartered in upstate New York, rather than Beijing, and the company opened an R&D center in California's Silicon Valley, as a "listening post."[27] Lenovo is now listed amongst China's leading "power brands," many of which are in the white goods and consumer electronics sectors, such as Galanz, Changhong, SVA, TCL, and Haier.[28]

As Chinese firms do aim to move higher up the value chain, design and R&D activities will become increasingly important, as well as access to advanced market economies abroad. For some fledgling MNEs this means investing overseas to acquire technologies, build or buy distribution networks and brands, and develop a wider portfolio of expertise, in keeping with the framework described in Chapter 20 (Figure 20.6: Firm-specific advantages for the new multinationals).

For some observers the growth of a new breed of multinationals from emerging economies warrants a new theoretical approach or set of explanatory frameworks. This is necessary, say some, because the current frameworks have developed out of the experience of Western-based MNEs and their international operations in other mature economies of the triad and expansion into emerging and developing economies. Although the two main types of FDI, input-oriented (resource-seeking) and output-oriented (market-seeking) FDI, are still relevant, the motivations of MNEs from emerging economies are significantly different. Studies indicate that they are internationalizing to fill current competitive disadvantages, such as technological capabilities and brands, rather than exploiting existing

INTERNATIONAL BUSINESS STRATEGY IN ACTION

Haier abroad

Haier is arguably one of the fastest-growing consumer products multinationals ever. It began life in 1984 as a government-owned refrigerator manufacturer and grew 68 percent per year on average between 1984 and 2005 to become one of the world's largest white goods manufacturers alongside Whirlpool, AB Electrolux (Sweden), BSH Bosch und Siemens Hausgeräte GmbH (Germany), GE Consumer (US), and GD Midea Holding Co., Ltd. (China). With a workforce of 53,412 employees, it has established 15 manufacturing complexes and 30 overseas plants, 8 design centers, and a network of 58,800 sales agents worldwide. It has also become one of the most successful brands China has so far produced and controls more than 30 percent of China's refrigerator, washing machine, and freezer markets. In 2010, Haier sales were US $8,839.6 million, of which over 90 percent was generated in China and less than 10 percent was foreign sales.

Haier began exporting products to overseas markets in 1990. Six years later it started to internationalize through FDI in South-East Asia before moving further abroad to the larger triad markets (see the milestones in Table 1). It

Table 1 Haier goes global

Date	Haier's internationalization milestones
1990	Exports first batch of refrigerators to Europe, focusing on Germany
1993	Haier refrigerators and other products enter the Middle East market
1995	Begins exports to the US, first in OEM form, later under the Haier brand. Also establishes a local assembly plant in South-East Asia
1996	Enters the Indonesian market through a joint venture (its first outside China)
1997	Enters Malaysia and the Philippines with greenfield investments
1999	Greenfield investment worth $30 million in Camden, South Carolina, signals the start of Haier America Refrigerator Corp. Ltd. and Haier's first overseas factory
2000	The first "Made in America" refrigerators come off the production lines in the US
2001	A second overseas factory is established in Pakistan
	Acquires a refrigerator plant in Italy and sets up a joint venture in Nigeria
2002	Haier products enter the Australian and New Zealand markets
	Establishes trading companies in Malaysia and Thailand
	A joint venture between Haier and Japan's Sanyo is established in Japan
2003	Manufacturing operations in Jordan produce washing machines for the Middle East markets
	Haier enters the home computer market
2004	Haier home computers are sold into the French market
	An electronics manufacturing operation is established in Dubai
2005	Wholly owned subsidiary set up in Australia
2007	Buys an Indian refrigerator factory and begins manufacturing in India
2008	Haier (Thailand) buys Sanyo's refrigerator factory in Thailand
2009	25 Year anniversary celebrated in Qingdao, China and European HQ in Varese, Italy
2010	Distribution, sales and service centres established in the UK and other triad countries

Source: Lou Linwei/Alamy

▶

deliberately followed a step-by-step international expansion strategy aimed at "building volume and gaining international experience" in Asia, starting with a joint venture in Indonesia in 1996.

A major step was taken in 1999, with a greenfield investment in South Carolina, making Haier the largest Chinese-invested company in the United States, a decision made at a time when the US home appliance industry was in a downturn and most appliance manufacturers there were moving their manufacturing bases to other low-cost countries, including China. More recently Haier has established manufacturing operations in India. This allowed it to save up to 30 percent of the cost of locally sold refrigerators by avoiding import duties, as well as service its growing Indian customer base more efficiently.

Haier products are now available in 12 of the leading 15 chain stores in Europe and in the top 10 chain stores in the United States. Its product range extends from refrigerators and freezers to commercial air-conditioners, microwave ovens, washing machines, dishwashers, televisions, mobile phones, and computers. As well as manufacturing in the United States, Italy, Pakistan, Jordan, India, and Nigeria, it has localized aspects of product design, distribution, and sales processes to suit its international markets. The company also set itself a target of doubling foreign sales in subsequent years.

Learning to internationalize

Haier has successfully managed to overcome some of the key challenges for Chinese firms looking to go global. Key to this has been the strong emphasis on quality, technological innovation, and brand building. Foreign alliances and partnerships have also been an important factor, supporting access to, or the internal development of, the relevant assets and capabilities underlying these strengths.

The strong emphasis on quality dates back to a famous incident involving the CEO of the Haier Group, Zhang Ruimin, in the mid-1980s. At what was the Qingdao Refrigerator Factory he used a hammer to smash up a number of defective refrigerators in front of managers and workers to drive home the importance of zero-defect manufacturing. Technological innovation, both process related and product related, has also been a cornerstone

of senior managements' philosophy and the firm reinvests a growing proportion of sales revenue into R&D. The company has worked with over 200 foreign manufacturing firms in the home appliance design sector. It has also led over 60 national R&D and technology development projects as part of the Chinese government's push for local capability development in target industries.

In addition to a highly active brand-building strategy for the domestic China market, Haier has actively promoted its corporate and product brands overseas. In the US market, for example, it gained recognition through a high-profile sponsorship deal with the National Basketball Association (NBA) and for a period was the sole sponsor for the televised NBA competition.

One senior manager describes Haier's internationalization strategy as a three-stage process:

> First, we should set up a large overseas production and sales network. Second, all Haier's products that meet the local market demand should move into the major sales channels. And last, the company should produce mainstream products in local markets.

Haier is clearly advancing down the route to becoming more global in terms of sales and FDI. However, it is difficult to assess whether profits have flowed from this expansion process. We need to ask how much the firm still depends on the two key country-specific advantages (CSAs) that all Chinese firms need to break away from: (1) the cheap-labor advantage, and (2) the home-market advantage, which provides profits from consumers, retailers, and distribution networks which the firm knows well.

Sources: Giulia Segreti, "Purchase opens doors and minds," *Financial Times*, April 25, 2011, http://www.ft.com/; Jeannie Jinsheng Yi and Shawn Xian Ye, *The Haier Way: The Making of a Chinese Business Leader and a Global Brand* (Paramus, NJ: Homa & Sekey Books, 2003); H. Liu and K. Li, "Strategic Implications of Emerging Chinese Multinationals: The Haier Case Study," *European Management Journal*, vol. 20, no. 6 (2002) pp. 699–706; Florence Chong, "Why China Must Have World-Class Brands? It is not a question for debate. It is a must!?" *Asia Today International*, April 4, 2006, http://www.asiatoday.com.au/feature_reports.php?id=208; Ying Fan, "The Globalisation of Chinese Brands," *Marketing Intelligence & Planning*, vol. 24, no. 4 (2006), pp. 365–379. http://www.haier.com/; Haier, *Annual Report*, 2010; OneSource, *Thomson Reuters*, 2011; Euromonitor International, 2011, http://www.portal.euromonitor.com/Portal/Pages/Magazine/IndustryPage.aspx; Mintel Global Market Navigator, 2011, http://gmn.mintel.com/query/10928149/shares/region.

advantages to expand abroad. (The case of Nanjing Auto's takeover of MG supports this view, see Real Case below).[29]

This view is opposed by others who see existing frameworks as sufficient, perhaps with minor adaptations, to explain and predict the behavior of Chinese firms. Despite differences in underlying culture, capital markets, economic history, and the context from which these firms have emerged, the existing explanations for internationalization are still perfectly adequate.[30]

✔ Active learning check

Review your answer to Active Learning Case question 3 and make any changes you like. Then compare your answer to the one below.

3 **What kinds of threats and opportunities might OI face from new multinational firms from China and what strategic responses should it be considering?**

OI is arguably already in a good competitive position in that its profitability stems mainly from its technological capabilities and investments in R&D, rather than low costs. Most large Chinese firms are building from an initial low-cost advantage, so whilst OI might experience some competition in its low-end businesses, it seems secure for now in the more technologically sophisticated business lines. IPR theft is a continuing threat and may help newcomers catch up rapidly in some key niche areas. But, while any high-technology start-ups or established instrumentation firms in China might eventually be able to compete on the basis of new technology developments, they are weak in terms of customer relationships and brand recognition and therefore have limited access to markets outside China. There may be opportunities for OI to partner with smaller start-ups to develop new products, or build relationships with larger customers to provide products, technical services, and support as they internationalize.

KEY POINTS

1 One of the most important trends of our time is the economic development of China and its growing importance in terms of trade and FDI, as a cheap manufacturing base, as a growing market, and as a source of competitive opportunities and threats for all MNEs. Its economic growth and rising influence in the global economy may, however, be slowed or halted by social and political forces, domestic or international.

2 In terms of the scale, scope, and speed of economic growth, China is unprecedented. It is larger and growing faster, across a broader range of industries, than Japan during its rapid development phase.

3 The Chinese government at various levels has a strong influence over the economy, business practices, and the opportunities open to MNEs. The "Going Global" policy and initiatives to develop target industries and indigenous innovation capabilities are central to the plans of central government.

4 Inward and outward FDI have grown. MNEs are attracted to the growing domestic market and opportunities for cheaper manufacturing. MNEs are also establishing R&D activities in China.

5 MNEs looking to get into the Chinese market need to be aware of its particular differences and difficulties, including changing regulations governing foreign investors; customs, tax, and foreign exchange procedures; specific cultural traits and the importance of *guanxi*; the problems with intellectual property rights; and the need to secure good partnerships and local expertise.

6 The current concern is that China and other emerging economies are increasingly competitive in manufacturing, taking investment and jobs from the triad regions. The key concern in the near future will be with their competitiveness in high-technology and knowledge-based businesses.

7 Some Chinese firms are expanding abroad. The extent and impacts of this internationalization of a "new breed" of MNEs are hotly debated.

Key terms

- wholly foreign-owned enterprise (WFOE)
- company chop
- WTO accession
- Going Global
- state-owned enterprises (SOEs)
- *guanxi*

REVIEW AND DISCUSSION QUESTIONS

1 What indicators point to the increasing importance of China and Chinese firms in the global economy? Describe two factors that have helped China's recent economic growth.

2 What makes China an attractive location for inward FDI by MNEs?

3 Give some examples of the national development policies pursued by the Chinese government. Explain how these affect the options open to foreign firms investing in China.

4 What makes China an attractive location for foreign R&D activities?

5 What modes of market entry are open to foreign firms investing in China?

6 What guidelines must MNEs follow when doing business in China? Identify and briefly describe three specific difficulties for foreign firms breaking into the Chinese market.

7 What are the main pros and cons of establishing a joint venture with a local firm for an MNE looking to sell products to the growing consumer market in China?

8 Do you think China will remain a manufacturing hub? How might Chinese firms develop competitive advantages in high-technology and service industries, and what are the implications for triad-based MNEs?

9 What kinds of Chinese firms account for most outward FDI from China?

10 Explain why Chinese firms are investing in Africa.

11 Do you think Chinese MNEs warrant a new theoretical approach to understanding multinational firms and their reasons for internationalizing?

REAL CASE

Citigroup in China

The banking industry faces many barriers to globalization. Overcoming cultural differences and dealing with varying regulations and financial systems make it very difficult to establish a truly global bank. Citigroup (or Citi), formed in 1998 by the merger of Citicorp and Travelers Group, is a leader in international banking and one of the largest companies in the world, in terms of assets. In 2010 it had $65 billion in revenues and 263,000 staff around the world (compared to 358,000 at its peak in 2008) and served over 200 million customer accounts in more than 100 countries. 40 percent of its income originates in the United States, 18 percent from Europe and Middle East, 19 percent from Latin America, and 23 percent from Asia.

Citigroup enters a developing country via mergers and acquisitions where possible, and implements its own marketing strategy. In the first stage of development, it caters to the global customer (usually a large corporation) by providing short-term loans, cash management, and foreign exchange services. During a country's second stage of development, as demand grows in the face of a burgeoning middle class, Citigroup begins to offer personal financial products.

In China, the political climate has limited Citigroup expansion plans in the Asia region. Citigroup opened its first office in China in 1902 but was thrown out by the new communist government of Chairman Mao in 1949. Even after it was allowed back into the country, its business was restricted mainly to foreign currency. China's market potential, however, always attracted the bank, and when the country began to show interest in opening its borders and joining the World Trade Organization, Citigroup stepped in as a key broker in negotiations with the US government. The bank's efforts are paying off. In the 1990s, the Chinese began to open their economy and make commitments for further reforms. By 2001, import tariffs had been lowered to an average of 15 percent from 44 percent in 1992, and continued to decrease, averaging 9 percent by 2006 and less in subsequent years.

Deregulation is allowing Citigroup to implement its emerging market strategy in China. In the initial phase, the bank marketed only to large foreign corporate clients. By 2004, it had expanded its customer base to include travellers, business people, wealthy Chinese with foreign exchange needs, and local businesses. Citigroup's international network has also made it attractive to Chinese MNEs operating in other markets. Among these is Lenovo, a Chinese PC manufacturer that today controls over 25 percent of the domestic market and has begun to expand abroad. Other examples include Konka (electronics), Haier (consumer appliances), and China Telecom. Local banks do not have the same level of international service.

Deregulation not only allows Citigroup to open fully functional branches to cater to the wealthy and, increasingly, to the middle class, but also attracts more foreign clients. UPS and FedEx, for instance, both seek to open 100 percent-owned delivery systems in China. Home to the largest number of mobile phone subscribers in the world and nowhere near saturation, China also expects to attract telecom service providers and product manufacturers. In short, opportunities for foreign investment in China are creating a large number of MNE subsidiaries from which Citigroup can draw its client pool.

Citigroup's second marketing stage for emerging markets is expanding into personal banking. To some degree, Citigroup now offers consumer banking, corporate and investment banking, and insurance in the Chinese market. The bank does not yet provide a full range of consumer services to the entire population. Indeed, its banking fees are kept high for all but very large deposits to attract only the wealthier segments of the population. In 2010 it launched its 'Citigold Private Client' services into China, Singapore and Hong Kong targeted at high net-worth individuals. It also developed its online banking services.

In 2002, the firm was first allowed to offer foreign exchange services to Chinese nationals but is not yet allowed to offer consumer banking in yuan. In 2004, it partnered with the Shanghai Pudong Development Bank to offer a dual-currency credit card that could be used in yuan and US dollar transactions, the first of its kind in China. The credit card business is tricky in China because there is no credit rating agency, but by moving forward with this service, Citigroup's goal is to create brand awareness that will allow it to dominate the market once it matures. The bank is likely to move consumers into mortgages, personal loans, pension funds, and other financial products in the final stage of its market-entry strategy.

Although Citigroup has a definite first-mover advantage in the Chinese market, it still faces competition from domestic banks. These include the Industrial and Commercial Bank of China and other large foreign competitors such as HSBC, which also has extensive experience in the region. The Pudong deal was relatively small compared to rivals' acquisitions and it has continued to look for bigger opportunities. Mainland China recently generated only 2 percent of Citigroup's Asian revenues, as against higher percentages from smaller economies, including Hong Kong (12 percent), South Korea (14 percent), and India (10 percent). It clearly has much work to do to build a position in China commensurate with its global standing.

Websites: www.citigroup.com; www.fedex.com; www.ups.com; www.legend.com.cn; www.konka.com; www.haier.com; www.chinatelecom.com.cn; www.icbc.com.cn; www.hsbc.com.

Sources: *Citi Annual Report 2010*; "ICBC Tops Citigroup as World's Biggest," *China Daily*, July 23, 2007; "Year of the Citi in China?" *Business Week*, January 23, 2006; Anthony Spaeth, "China's Legend in the Making," *Time.com*, May 8, 2000; "Citigroup Allowed to Build Mansion in Shanghai," *People's Daily*, December 4, 2000; Michael Shari, Brian Bremner, Heather Timmons and Becky Gaylord, "Citibank Conquers Asia," *Business Week* (online edition), February 26, 2001, p. 44, "Foreign Bank Integration Accelerates in China," *The Banker*, May 3, 2004; "Citibank Business in Beijing," *China Daily*, March 26, 2004; "Another First: Citibank Wins Foreign Exchange Approval," *China Daily*, March 20, 2002; CitiGroup, *Annual Report*, 2010; OneSource, *Thomson Reuters*, 2011.

1 How can a foreign organization such as Citigroup make an initial assessment of a host-country market (such as China) in deciding how to do business there? What is involved in this process?

2 What kinds of opportunities and constraints does Citigroup face in China? Despite its early-mover advantages why does it appear to have limited presence there?

3 Why is the Chinese government an important influence in banking and the financial services industry? How has it tended to intervene in the market to assert its influence?

Nanjing Auto makes the MG

China became a net exporter of cars for the first time in 2005, due in part to the large-scale inward investment from non-Chinese car manufacturers, channelled into joint ventures with local firms in this industry. But exports account for a small proportion of total sales. As annual production in China reaches 20 million, demand from the domestic automotive market has grown fast enough to make China the largest automotive market in the World.

VW entered China well ahead of the competition through a joint venture with government-owned Shanghai Automotive Industry Corporation (SAIC) in 1984. A second joint venture with the First Automotive Works (FAW) in 1991 helped it reach a dominant position (56 percent market share) in the growing Chinese car market before other foreign competitors were even allowed to enter. GM was a later entrant and had been involved in a range of technology transfer initiatives before being allowed to establish manufacturing operations in 1997 through a $1.6 billion joint venture with SAIC. GM reached a 10 percent market share to challenge VW. But both GM and VW faced growing competition from new foreign entrants after the 2001 WTO deregulation rulings began to take effect. Ford, Honda, Toyota, Hyundai, and Suzuki all entered the market in the early to mid-2000s. More significantly, local car-makers also started to come into their own around this time.

SAIC, which merged with Nanjing Automotive Corporation (NAC) in 2008, Chery Automobile, and FAW are the largest local producers. SAIC has a string of joint ventures, including with VW and GM, while FAW has partnerships with Mazda and Toyota, in addition to its main ally, VW. In contrast, Chery is one of the more independent local players as is Geely Automotive Holdings. Initially established as a fridge maker, Geely has steadily accelerated sales and expanded its manufacturing operations to reach a 5 percent share of the mainland market.

Low cost is the one key advantage at this stage for indigenous car firms, gained through cheap labor, available land, and capital (in China much of it initially from the government). This only temporarily makes up for weaknesses in most other areas, from manufacturing technology, process innovation, product design, to sales and branding. But the industry has moved up the value chain in its short history. Low-cost advantages are increasingly complemented by capabilities in design, engineering, manufacturing, marketing, and management which are driving process and product innovation. Most firms have partly developed and partly bought into these assets and capabilities through joint ventures with Western carmakers. More unusually NAC accessed them directly by acquiring one of the oldest and best-known car firms in the UK, MG.

Based in Longbridge in the heart of the West Midlands manufacturing region, MG was part of MG-Rover, a corporation that combined two famous British car brands that dated back to the early 1900s. A turbulent history of take-overs and management failures had brought the firm to collapse in the early 2000s, despite the strength of its design, engineering, and technology divisions and the loyalty of customers. In May 2005 NAC bought the MG brand name, physical assets including the powertrain technology, and the manufacturing rights to the MG range of cars in a deal worth over $80 million. In parallel NAC's then competitor SAIC announced it would build the Rover 75 (relaunched as the Roewe) in China using the rights it bought from MG-Rover in 2004.

NAC shipped the MG assets to China and, in the space of a year, by March 2007 the firm had set up production in the Pukou High-Tech Development Zone in Nanjing and locally made cars were rolling off the plant line. The aim was to develop the plant to eventually produce 200,000 autos, 250,000 engines, and 100,000 gear boxes, with an explicit strategy to keep costs low by expanding and improving the local Chinese supply chain. To do this it has embarked on a wide range of recruitment and training programs, which involve ex-MG-Rover plant managers, engineers, designers, and other employees from the UK operation and from suppliers. These are providing the Chinese with the capabilities not just to operate the plant, but to improve the product design, manufacturing quality, and cost and to conduct R&D and engineering development to create future automotive products.

The acquisition provides an interesting illustration of how far the kinds of advanced assets and capabilities required to produce and sell complex products can be bought and transferred across continents. It begs the question: how far can changes in ownership drive geographic shifts in competitive advantage? What it shows is that knowledge, expertise, and skills have to be transferred alongside hardware and technology for the full set of manufacturing process and product competencies to be developed by the recipient firm. This takes a long time, during

Source: Getty Images/Matthew Lewis

Nanjing Automobile Corporation (UK) Ltd

Engines
Although development is still ongoing, the 450 is likely to eventually be offered with a 1.8-litre turbocharged petrol engine as well as a 2.0-litre diesel motor.

Styling
Seen on the Roewe 750, the Audi-style four-sided chrome grille will feature on the new Focus rival. Chunky looks and a rising waistline will give the four-door a distinctive look.

Chassis
The new model is set to be based on a cut-down version of the original Rover 75 platform, which includes a development of German firm BMW's hi-tech Z-axle system.

Suspension
It's in the development of the suspension that Brit expert Ricardo has played the biggest role. It is hoped the 450 will have handling to take on mainstream rivals.

Source: Rex Features/Auto Express

markets, taking on competitors in both regions. With one acquisition a new MNE is born.

Sources: This case was partly developed on the basis of interviews conducted as part of a larger study of MNEs in China. See S. C. Collinson, B. Sullivan-Taylor, and J. L. Wang, "Adapting to the China Challenge: Lessons from Experienced Multinationals," Advanced Institute of Management (AIM) Research, Executive Briefing, London, 2007, http://www.aimresearch.org/publications/adaptingtochina.pdf; http://www.mg-uk.co.uk/; Jason Subler and Shen Yan, "Chinese Carmakers Merge to Take on Multinationals," *Guardian*, December 27, 2007; "The World's Big Carmakers Have Unwittingly Created a New Chinese Rival," *The Economist*, February 22, 2007; Yu Qiao, "Global, Local Firms Jostle for Position," *China Daily*, April 21, 2007.

which the recipient remains dependent on knowledge and expertise from the firm and/or regional "cluster" of firms in which the original capabilities evolved.

Some of these capabilities will be transferred via training programs and by recruiting some of the MG-Rover managers, designers, and engineers directly to work in China. Others will be accessed by redeveloping some functions at the original Longbridge plant in the UK, linked to the main manufacturing plant in China. Subsequent plans by NAC for Longbridge have included an R&D, engineering, and test center for MG models; HR recruitment and purchasing and logistics centers to serve China and Longbridge; a sales and marketing base for the UK and Europe; and eventually a local assembly plant for European markets. NAC is effectively developing a new multinational network to leverage the location-specific complementarities between the Midlands and Nanjing. It hopes to produce cars for both

1 How have foreign car firms historically established themselves in the Chinese market (what form of FDI?), and why is this mode of market entry normally used?

2 List some examples of firm-specific advantages (FSAs) that are held by foreign car manufacturers and some examples of country-specific advantages (CSAs) in China relevant to this industry.

3 What are the relative costs and benefits of acquiring particular kinds of FSAs, in the way that NAC has done, compared to establishing a joint venture?

ENDNOTES

1 The WTO Agreement on Trade-Related Investment Measures (TRIMs) is still being implemented. It should eventually lead to the end of Chinese requirements on trade and foreign exchange balance, local content, and export performance for foreign investors. The Chinese government is also committed to relaxing foreign investment restrictions in many important service industries, including distribution services, telecommunications, financial services, and professional services; http://www.wto.org.

2 "The Great Divide," *The Economist*, March 5, 2005.

3 See http://www.tdctrade.com/main/china.htm; CIA World Fact Book, China, https://www.cia.gov/library/publications/the-world-factbook/geos/ch.html.

4 Jeffrey B. Miller and Stoyan Tenev, "On the Role of Government in Transition: The Experiences of China and Russia Compared," *Comparative Economic Studies*, vol. 49 (2007), pp. 543–571.

5 A range of texts listed in the further bibliography can provide background on the evolving role of government in China. There are many online sources of information as well, including the official central government website: http://english.gov.cn/ and other semi-official or at least non-controversial sites, including http://www.chinatoday.com/gov/a.htm and http://www.china.org.cn/. There are many other sites, that are more critical of the regime in China.

6 UNCTAD, *World Investment Report*, 2007, at www.unctad.org.

7 This was a respondent in an extensive survey of multinational firms in China across a variety of industries; S. C. Collinson, B. Sullivan-Taylor and J. L. Wang, "Adapting to the China Challenge: Lessons from Experienced Multinationals," Advanced Institute of Management (AIM) Research, Executive Briefing, London, 2007 http://www.aimresearch.org/publications/adaptingtochina.pdf.

8 Jason Dean and Peter Stein, "Inland China Beckons as Hon Hai Seeks Fresh, Cheaper Labor Force," *Wall Street Journal*, September 4, 2010, http://online.wsj.com/article/; "China Surprise," *The Economist*, April 2, 2005; also see Kim Woodard and Anita Qingli Wang, "Acquisitions in China: A View of the Field," 2004, at http://www.chinabusinessreview.com/public/0411/woodward.html.

9 Tim Clissold gives an extensive and amusing account of the local rules of the game in his book *Mr. China*, (London: Constable and Robinson, 2004). It is based around his experience as a British investor who teamed up with a Wall St. banker in China in the early 1990s. Together they invested over $400 million in a range of industries (including auto components and beer) in China and lost most of it because of the lack of legal and institutional infrastructure, fraud, and their own naivety regarding Chinese business practices; Fonterra, www.fonterra.com; "Fonterra Takes 69pc Sanlu Writedown," *Business Day*, 24 September, 2008; http://www.stuff.co.nz/business/industries/642763.

10 UNCTAD, *World Investment Report – Transnational Corporations and the Internationalization of R&D*, 2005, UNCTAD, *Globalization of R&D and Developing countries*, *Proceedings of the Expert Meeting Geneva*, January 24–26, 2005.

11 Kerry Capell, "Novartis in China: East Meets West in R&D," *Business Week*, November 6, 2006.

12 Ming Zeng and Peter J. Williamson, "The Hidden Dragons," *Harvard Business Review*, October 2003, pp. 92–99.

13 This is a quote from Tim Clissold's book, op. cit., taken from "The Battle of Ningshan" in *Journey to the West*, an unattributed sixteenth-century Ming dynasty novel.

14 The US Commercial Service based in China, part of the US Department of Commerce, provides a Country Commercial Guide. This is continually revised and updated, informed by ongoing studies and surveys. See http://www.usembassy-china.org.cn/fcs/ccg_2008_secured.pdf.

15 Among numerous how-to texts on coping with Chinese culture to "make it big" in the Chinese market, see, for example, John L. Graham and Mark N. Lam, "The Chinese Negotiation," *Harvard Business Review*, October 2003, pp. 82–91; Tom Orlik, "China's Runaway Investment Train," *Wall Street Journal*, July 26, 2011; Saira Syed, "The Price of High-Speed Ambitions," *BBC Business Online*, July 28, 2011.

16 This list partly comes from interviews and discussions, including several with Alice Huang, Managing Director of Enter Consulting, a firm based in Shanghai that supports inward investors. See Collinson et al., op. cit.

17 This is a common theme in studies, stemming from the tendency for firms to focus due-diligence efforts on cost cutting and "sell" investment propositions internally and externally on the basis of simple financial metrics. Comparative data on labor costs per hour are relatively easy to gather. Productivity is context specific and influenced by multiple factors and much more difficult to anticipate.

18 See, "How Rising Wages Are Changing the Game In China," *Business Week*, March 27, 2006. This pattern, of rising costs of particular kinds of labor, was predicted by Eli Hecksher (in 1919) and Bertil Ohlin (in 1933) in an economic model that was further refined by the American economist Paul Samuelson. The H-O or HOS model (or theory of factor endowments) took trade theory beyond the simple assumptions made by Ricardo about labor productivity to look at the relative availability of different factors of production (primarily land, labor, and capital) and therefore their relative price (rent, wages, and interest) in each country. These will determine the products in which a country has a comparative advantage, and in which it will therefore tend to specialize and trade. See, for example, J. R. Markusen, *Multinational Firms and the Theory of International Trade* (Boston, MA: MIT Press, 2004).

19 Chen Hua, "China's FDI Meets Challenges," *China Business Weekly*, April 21, 2005, http://www.chinadaily.com.cn/english/doc/2005-04/21/content_436121.htm; "Chinese Exporters Seek New Openings," *BBC.co.uk*, March 1, 2001.

20 Randall Morck, Bernard Yeung and Minyuan Zhao, "Perspectives on China's Outward Foreign Direct Investment," *Journal of International Business Studies*, vol. 39, (2008) pp. 337–350.

21 These data come from Alan M. Rugman, "Do We Need a New Theory to Explain Emerging Market Multinationals?" Paper prepared for the Columbia University "Five Diamond

International Conference: Thinking Outward: Global Players from Emerging Markets," April 2008, pp. 28–29, New York.

22 Ibid.

23 For a lively overview of this unusual partnership see BBC's *Newsnight* reports on China in Africa at http://news.bbc.co.uk/2/hi/programmes/newsnight/7343060.stm. The debate regarding the net effects of China's investment continues and parallels with long-running discussions regarding the developmental costs and benefits of previous periods of colonialism.

24 Peter Marsh, "Chinese Investment in Europe: Focus on Deals High Up Value Chain," *Financial Times*, April 26, 2011; Hong Liu and Kequan Li, "Strategic Implications of Emerging Chinese Multinationals: The Haier Case Study," *European Management Journal*, vol. 24, no. 6 (2002), p. 699; Yubing Wu, "China's Refrigerator Magnate," *The McKinsey Quarterly*, no. 3 (2003), http://www.mckinseyquarterly.com/.

25 OECD, *Science, Technology and Industry Outlook, 2004: China*; http://www.oecd.org; Kathleen Walsh, *Foreign High-Tech R&D in China: Risks, Rewards and Implications for US–China Relations* (Washington, DC: Henry L. Stimson Center, 2004), at http://www.stimson.org. See also a special issue of

R&D Management on "Managing R&D in China," vol. 33, no. 4 (September 2004).

26 In fact China's software industry is comparable in size to India's but is not export oriented. All the major firms are focused on serving local customers and foreign firms based in China.

27 Jerry Biediger et al., "Strategic Action at Lenovo," *Organizational Dynamics*, vol. 34, no. 1 (2005) pp. 89–102.

28 Ying Fan, "The Globalization of Chinese Brands," *Marketing Intelligence & Planning*, vol. 24, no. 4 (2006) pp. 365–379.

29 One study that supports this view is John Child and Suzana B. Rodrigues, "The Internationalization of Chinese Firms: A Case for Theoretical Extension?" *Management and Organization Review*, vol. 1, no. 3 (2005), pp. 381–410. Another that takes a slightly different perspective, but still sees emerging economy MNEs as "special cases," is John A. Mathews, "Dragon Multinationals: New Players in 21st Century Globalization," *Asia Pacific Journal of Management*, vol. 23 (March 2006), pp. 5–27.

30 See Rugman, op. cit. and Rajneesh Narula, "Globalization, New Ecologies, New Zoologies, and the Purported Death of the Eclectic Paradigm," *Asia Pacific Journal of Management*, vol. 23 (June 2006), pp. 143–151.

ADDITIONAL BIBLIOGRAPHY

Anderson, Jonathan and Hu, Fred. *The Five Myths about China and the World* (Hong Kong: Goldman Sachs, 2003).

Buckley, Peter, Clegg, Jeremy and Tan, Hui. "The Art of Knowledge Transfer: Secondary and Reverse Transfer in China's Telecommunications Manufacturing Industry," *Management International Review*, vol. 43, no. 2 (2003).

Buckley, Peter, Clegg, Jeremy L., Cross, Adam R., Liu, Xin, Voss, Hinrich and Zheng, Ping. "The Determinants of Chinese Outward Foreign Direct Investment," *Journal of International Business Studies*, vol. 38, no. 4 (2007).

Breslin, Shaun. *China and the Global Political Economy* (Basingstoke: Palgrave-Macmillan, 2007).

Breslin, Shaun. "The Political Economy of Development in China: Political Agendas and Economic Realities," *Development*, vol. 50, no. 3 (2007).

Chen, Kun and Kenney, Martin. "Universities/Research Institutes and Regional Innovation Systems: The Cases of Beijing and Shenzhen," *World Development*, vol. 35, no. 6 (2007), pp. 1056–1074.

Chen, Roger. "Corporate Reputation: Pricing and Competing in Chinese Markets–Strategies for Multinationals," *Journal of Business Strategy*, vol. 25, no. 6 (2004).

Cheong, Young R. and Xiao, Geng. "Global Capital Flows and the Position of China: Structural and Institutional Factors and Their Implications," in J. J. Teunissen (ed.), *China's Role in Asia and the World Economy: Fostering Stability and Growth* (The Hague: Forum on Debt and Development (FONDAD)), pp. 113–175.

Child, John. "China and International Business," in Alan M. Rugman and Thomas L. Brewer (eds.), *The Oxford Handbook of International Business* (Oxford: Oxford University Press, 2009).

Child, John and Tse, David K. "China's Transition and Its Implications for International Business," *Journal of International Business Studies*, vol. 32, no. 1 (Spring 2001).

Clissold, Tim. *Mr. China: A memoir* (London: Collins Publishing, 2006).

Coase, Ronald and Wang, Ning. *How China Became Capitalist* (Basingstoke: Palgrave Macmillan, 2011).

De Mattos, Claudio, Sanderson, Stuart and Ghauri, Pervez. "Negotiating Alliances in Emerging Markets–Do Partners' Contributions Matter?" *Thunderbird International Business Review*, vol. 44, no. 6 (November/December 2002).

De Meyer, Arnoud. "Technology Transfer into China: Preparing for a New Era," *European Management Journal*, vol. 19, no. 2 (April 2001).

Deng, Ping, "Why do Chinese firms tend to acquire strategic assets in international expansion," *Journal of World Business*, vol. 44, no. 1, (2009).

Doh, Jonathan P., Rodriguez, Peter, Uhlenbruck, Klaus, Collins, Jamie and Eden, Lorraine. "Coping with Corruption in Foreign Markets," *Academy of Management Executive*, vol. 17, no. 3 (2003).

Doh, Jonathan P., Teegen, Hildy and Mudambi, Ram. "Balancing Private and State Ownership in Emerging Markets' Telecommunications Infrastructure: Country, Industry, and Firm Influences," *Journal of International Business Studies*, vol. 35, no. 3 (May 2004).

Dunning, John. "Comment on Dragon Multinationals: New Players in 21st Century Globalization," *Asia Pacific Journal of Management*, vol. 23 (June 2006).

Eberhardt, Markus, McLaren, Julie, Millington, Andrew and Wilkinson, Barry. "Multiple Forces in Component Localization in China," *European Management Journal*, vol. 22, no. 3 (June 2004).

Engardio, Peter. *Chindia: How China and India Are Revolutionizing Global Business* (New York: McGraw-Hill 2006).

Enright, Michael J., Scott, Edith E. and Chang, Ka-mun. *Regional Powerhouse: The Greater Pearl River Delta and the Rise of China* (Singapore: Wiley, 2005).

Farrell, Diana, Remes, Jaana K. and Schulz, Heiner. "The Truth about Foreign Direct Investment in Emerging Markets," *McKinsey Quarterly*, no. 1 (2004).

Fernandez, Juan Antonio and Underwood, Laurie, *China CEO: Voices of Experience from 20 International Business Leaders* (Singapore: Wiley, 2006).

Fishman, Ted C. *China Inc.: How the Rise of the Next Superpower Challenges America and the World* (New York: Scribner, 2006).

Goedhart, Marc H. and Haden, Peter. "Emerging Markets Aren't as Risky as You Think," *McKinsey Quarterly*, Special Edition Issue 4 (2003).

Gray, Kenneth R. "The Ins and Outs of Doing Business in Europe: Germany, France, Russia, and the Emerging Markets of Eastern Europe," *Thunderbird International Business Review*, vol. 47, no. 1 (January/February 2005).

Grosse, Robert. "International Business in Latin America," in Alan M. Rugman and Thomas L. Brewer (eds.), *The Oxford Handbook of International Business* (New York: Oxford University Press, 2001).

Hamilton, Stewart and Zhang, Jinxuan. *Doing Business With China: Avoiding the Pitfalls* (Basingstoke: Palgrave Macmillan, 2011).

Hu, Mei-Chih and Matthew, John A. "National Innovation Capacity in East Asia," *Research Policy* vol. 34 (2005), pp. 1322–1349.

Isobe, Takehiko, Makino, Shige and Montgomery, David B. "Resource Commitment, Entry Timing and Market Performance of FDI in Emerging Economies: The Case of Japanese Joint Ventures in China," *Academy of Management Journal*, vol. 43, no. 3 (June 2000).

Jefferson, Gary, Bai, Huamao, Guan, Xiaojing and Yu, Xiaoyun. "R&D Performance in Chinese Industry," *Economics of Innovation and New Technology*, vol. 15(4/5) (2006).

Jing Li and Yong Li, "Flexibility versus commitment: MNEs' ownership strategy in China," *Journal of International Business Studies*, vol. 41, no. 9 (2010).

Kai Li, Griffin, Dale, Heng Yue and Longkai Zhao. "National culture and capital structure decisions: Evidence from foreign joint ventures in China," *Journal of International Business Studies*, vol. 42, no. 4 (2011).

Keeley, James and Wilsdon, James. *China: The next science superpower?* Demos Reports (2007), http://www.demos.co.uk/files/China_Final.pdf.

Kumar, Sameer, Jamieson, Jacky and Sweetman, Mathew. "Software Industry in the Fastest Emerging Market: Challenges and Opportunities," *International Journal of Technology Management*, vol. 29, nos. 3/4 (2005).

Kynge, James. *China Shakes the World: A Titan's Rise and Troubled Future—and the Challenge for America* (New York: Houghton Mifflin, 2006).

Lai Si Tsui-Auch and Möllering, Guido, "Wary managers: Unfavorable environments, perceived vulnerability, and the development of trust in foreign enterprises in China," *Journal of International Business Studies*, vol. 41, no. 6 (2010).

Lieberthal, Kenneth and Lieberthal, Geoffrey. "The Great Transition," *Harvard Business Review*, vol. 81, no. 10 (October 2003).

Lin, Hao-Chieh and Hou, Sheng-Tsung. "Managerial Lessons From the East: An Interview With Acer's Stan Shih," *Academy of Management Perspectives*, vol. 24, no. 4 (2010).

Ling, Zhijun and Avery, Martha. *The Lenovo Affair: The Growth of China's Computer Giant and Its Takeover of IBM-PC* (Singapore: Wiley, 2006).

London, Ted and Hart, Stuart L. "Reinventing Strategies for Emerging Markets: Beyond the Transnational Model," *Journal of International Business Studies*, vol. 35, no. 5 (September 2004).

Liu, Xiaohui, Lu, Jiangyong, Filatotchev, Igor, Buck, Trevor and Wright, Mike. "Returnee Entrepreneurs, Knowledge Spillovers and Innovation in High-tech Firms in Emerging Economies," *Journal of International Business Studies*, vol. 41, no. 7 (2010).

Luo, Yadong. "Industrial Dynamics and Managerial Networking in an Emerging Market: The Case of China," *Strategic Management Journal*, vol. 24, no. 13 (December 2003).

Luo, Yadong. "Building a Strong Foothold in an Emerging Market: A Link between Resource Commitment and Environment Conditions," *Journal of Management Studies*, vol. 41, no. 5 (July 2004).

Luo, Yadong and Tung, Rosalie. "International Expansion of Emerging Market Enterprises: A Springboard Perspective," *Journal of International Business Studies*, vol. 38, no. 4 (2007).

Mathews, John A. *Dragon Multinational: A New Model for Global Growth* (New York: Oxford University Press, 2002).

McManus, John, Li, Mingzhi and Moitra, Deependra. *China and India: Opportunities and threats for the Global Software Industry* (Oxford: Chandos Publishing, 2007).

Meyer, Klaus E. "International Research in Transitional Economies," in Alan M. Rugman and Thomas L. Brewer (eds.), *The Oxford Handbook of International Business* (Oxford: Oxford University Press, 2009).

Meyer, Klaus E. "Perspectives on Multinational Enterprises in Emerging Economies," *Journal of International Business Studies*, vol. 35, no. 4 (2004).

Navarro, Peter and Autry, Greg. *Death by China: Confronting the Dragon and a Global Call to Action* (Upper Saddle River, NJ: Prentice Hall, 2011).

Nolan, Peter. *Transforming China: Globalization, Transition and Development* (London: Anthem, 2004).

OECD. *OECD Reviews of Innovation Policy: China Synthesis Report* (Paris: OECD, 2007).

Ping Li, Peter, *Disruptive Innovation in Chinese and Indian Businesses: The Strategic Implications for Local Entrepreneurs and Global Incumbents* (London: Routledge, 2012).

Prestowitz, Clyde. *Three Billion New Capitalists* (New York: Basic Books, 2006).

Pun, Ngai. *Made in China: Women Factory Workers in a Global Workplace* (Durham, NC: Duke University Press, 2005).

Quer, Diego, Claver, Enrique and Rienda, Laura. "Business and Management in China: A Review of Empirical Research in Leading International Journals," *Asia Pacific Journal of Management*, vol. 24 (2007).

Redding, Gordon. "The Smaller Economies of Asia and their Business Systems," in Alan M. Rugman (ed.), *The Oxford Handbook of International Business* (Oxford: Oxford University Press, 2009).

Rugman, Alan M. and Doh, Jonathan. *Multinationals and Development* (New Haven, CT: Yale University Press, 2008).

Rugman, Alan M. and Li, Jing. "Will China's Multinationals Succeed Globally or Regionally?" *European Management Journal*, vol. 25, no. 5 (2007).

Story, Jonathan. *China Uncovered: What You Need to Know to Do Business in China* (London: Financial Times, Pearson, 2010).

Sull, Donald N. *Made In China: What Western Managers Can Learn from Trailblazing Chinese Entrepreneurs* (Boston, MA: Harvard Business School Press, 2005).

Sun, Pei, Mellahi, Kamel and Thun, Eric. "The dynamic value of MNE political embeddedness: The case of the Chinese automobile industry," *Journal of International Business Studies*, vol. 41, no. 7 (2010).

Taylor, Robert (ed.). *International Business in China: Understanding the Global Economic Crisis* (London: Routledge, 2011).

Williamson, Peter. J. and Zeng, Ming. "Strategies for Competing in a Changed China," *MIT Sloan Management Review*, vol. 45, no. 4 (Summer 2004).

Wyk, Jay Van. "Doing Business in South Africa," *Thunderbird International Business Review*, vol. 46, no. 4 (July/August 2004).

Yizheng, Shi. "Technological Capabilities and International Production Strategy of Firms: The Case of FDI in China," *Journal of World Business*, vol. 36, no. 2 (2001).

Yong Gao, Gerald and Yigang Pan. "The Pace of MNEs' Sequential Entries: Cumulative Entry Experience and the Dynamic Process," *Journal of International Business Studies*, vol. 41, no. 9 (2010).

Yusuf, Shahid and Evenett, Simon J. *Can East Asia Compete? Innovation for Global Markets* (Washington, DC: The World Bank and Oxford University Press, 2002).

Zeng, Ming and Williamson, Peter J. *Dragons at Your Door: How Chinese Cost Innovation Is Disrupting Global Competition* (Boston, MA: Harvard Business School Press, 2007).

Zheng Zhao, Anand, Jaideep and Mitchell, Will. "A Dual Networks Perspective on Inter-Organizational Transfer of R&D Capabilities: International Joint Ventures in the Chinese Automotive Industry," *Journal of Management Studies*, vol. 42, no. 1 (2005).

Zhibin Gu, George. *China's Global Reach: Markets, Multinationals, and Globalization* (Palo Alto, CA: Fultus Corporation, 2006).

WWW RESOURCES

http://globaledge.msu.edu/ibrd/marketpot.asp
http://www.stats.gov.cn/english/index.html
http://english.gov.cn/
http://www.chinatoday.com/
http://www.china.org.cn/

http://www.usembassy-china.org.cn
http://www.tdctrade.com/main/china.htm
http://asnic.utexas.edu/
http://www.aimresearch.org/publications/adaptingtochina.pdf
http://news.bbc.co.uk/

Chapter 22

CORPORATE ETHICS AND THE NATURAL ENVIRONMENT

Contents

Objectives of the chapter

Over the course of this text we have seen how much the world of international business has changed in the last decade. In the next decade, there will be even more changes to the field of international business. This will affect both the country and firm factors and the strategies of multinational firms. One of the most prominent changes is the increased attention paid to corporate social responsibility—essentially the ethical behavior of the firm. In this chapter we explore two useful frameworks to help analyze the future of international business. First, we consider how multinational enterprises (MNEs) often serve as "flagship" firms at the hubs of business networks. We relate this to country-level (environmental) and firm-level strategies and future trends. Second, we develop a framework to analyze the impact of civil society on trade and investment agreements. This will incorporate a discussion of corporate ethics and the role of **non-governmental organizations (NGOs)** as they can affect such agreements.

The specific objectives of this chapter are to:

1 *Examine* how these changing developments will create both challenges and opportunities for MNEs over the next decade.

2 *Explain* why research will continue to be of critical importance to the field of international business.

3 *Examine* three frameworks in which MNEs can cope with their changing political and economic environments.

4 *Relate* the importance of the NGOs and ethical issues to the strategies of multinational enterprises.

The environment, NGOs and MNEs

What do Apple, Google, Microsoft, Coca-Cola, Procter & Gamble and Amazon.com have in common? In 2011, they were among the world's most admired companies in the Fortune annual ranking. The nine key attributes of reputation are innovation, people management, use of corporate assets, social responsibility, quality of management, financial soundness, long-term investment, quality of products and services, and global competitiveness. These rankings are calculated based on a survey of business people's perceptions. The top 20 firms according to business people are shown in Table 1.

Of course, non-governmental organizations (NGOs) may not like these companies and today in a world of corporate social responsibility, the viewpoints of NGOs and other stakeholders are important. In particular, NGOs are often critical of the poor environmental performance of MNEs. Partly in response to this, the survey also highlights eight companies which are devising innovative ways to make their firms greener, including Coca-Cola, Southwest Airlines, Procter & Gamble, Google, Microsoft, Fedex, Amazon.com, and McDonald.

Coca-Cola has developed technology to produce fully recyclable plastic bottles which are 30 percent composed of plastic made from sugar cane. This reduces the amount of petroleum byproducts used to make the plastic. Coke wants to share the technology. The company has partnered with Heinz so the ketchup maker can use partially plant-based bottles for 120 million ketchup containers.

Southwest Airlines is one of the few airlines which wash the plane engines at night so that they burn fuel more efficiently during flights the next day. Southwest is also investing in the Federal Aviation Administration's updated navigation system, which help planes fly the best routes, save excess fuel costs. The next initiative is to lighten the cabins of the planes. So, Southwest is adding lighter weight carpeting, seat covers and life vests. The company is running its new cabin design by regulators and hopes to make an official announcement about it later this year. The end result will be even more fuel-efficient flights, which translate to an even greater profit margin for Southwest.

IT companies like Google and Microsoft are trying to focus on data center efficiency, which requires lots of power. Furthermore, Microsoft has formed partnerships with industry rivals to promote green technology. Along with AMD, Intel, Oracle and other technology giants, Microsoft is on the board of a project called the Green Grid, which is designed to use IT to promote sustainability.

Table 1 The world's most admired companies, 2011

Rank 2011	Name	Country	Sector
1	Apple	United States	Computers
2	Google	United States	IT/ Search engine
3	Berkshire Hathaway	United States	Investment
4	South West Airlines	United States	Airlines
5	Procter & Gamble	United States	FMCG
6	Coca-Cola	United States	FMCG
7	Amazon.com	United States	Online retail
8	Fedex	United States	Express courier
9	Microsoft	United States	IT
10	McDonald	United States	Food/beverage
11	Wal-Mart Stores	United States	Retail
12	IBM	United States	Software
13	General Electric	United States	Diversified
14	Walt Disney	United States	Media/leisure
15	3M	United States	Diversified
16	Starbucks	United States	Beverage
17	Johnson & Johnson	United States	Pharmaceuticals
18	Singapore Airlines	Singapore	Airlines
19	BMW	Germany	Automotive
20	American Express	United States	Credit card

Source: Adapted from "Survey of the World's Most Admired Companies," *Fortune*, March 21, 2011 issue; http://money.cnn.com/magazines/fortune/mostadmired/2011/full_list/.

▶

Amazon.com doesn't make many tangible things, but it ships large quantities of books every day. And when the online store asked customers how it could improve the shopping experience, buyers said they wanted less packaging. Amazon has worked with suppliers such as Philips to cut out the clamshells and stick with boxes that are easy to open and made from recyclable materials. By cutting wasteful packaging, the company has also reduced its carbon footprint.

In general, the managers of both large MNEs and smaller firms are extremely aware of their wider social and ethical responsibilities. Most of these firms have developed explicit environmental programmes and have appointed senior managers responsible for corporate social responsibility activities. Some firms have even hired former NGO activists and environmental politicians to help improve the firms' environmental policy and social programmes. However, the success of these managerial initiatives remains open to question, as discussed in this chapter.

Websites: www.coca-cola.com, www.amazon.com, www.google.com, www.microsoft.com, www.fedex.com, www.pg.com, www.fedex.com, www.southwest.com,

Source: "Survey of the World's Most Admired Companies," *Fortune*, March 21, 2011 issue, http://money.cnn.com/magazines/fortune/mostadmired/2011/full_list/; "Eight Green Stars at Most Admired Companies", *Fortune*, http://money.cnn.com/galleries/2011/fortune/1103/gallery.most_admired_green_leaders.fortune/7.html.

---

1 How have NGOs changed the external environment in which MNEs operate? Why is Apple the world's most admired firm by business people? Why is a firm like Google likely to be more admired by NGOs?

2 As MNEs operate across the world, why are there no "global" or "international" environmental agreements to set rules for sustainable development?

3 Where would a company like Coca-Cola, or others in Table 1, be positioned in Figure 22.7? Why?

INTRODUCTION

Non-governmental organizations (NGOs)
Private-sector groups that act to advance diverse social interests (see also civil society)

MNEs are finding that one of the major challenges they face is to develop effective strategies for coping with changing environments. There is an ongoing process of triad-based attack and counterattack, and today's success could be dislodged by the competition tomorrow. The international microcomputer chip industry is a good example. During the 1980s the Japanese dominated this industry, pushing out many US and European competitors to gain the majority of the world market. In the early 1990s US firms (most notably Intel) counterattacked and regained the lead.[1] This process explains development in many industries, from autos to computers to real estate.[2] It also helps to explain why continual innovation and strategy modification are necessary for MNEs to retain their competitive advantage. In doing so, multinationals will be focusing increased attention on strategies that are designed to cope with changing environments.

Perhaps the most important change in the external environment affecting firms doing international business has been the development of stakeholder theory and the increased attention paid to corporate social responsibility. In the second part of this chapter we will focus upon such issues of corporate ethics and the need for MNEs, and other firms, to develop strategies that exhibit FSAs in corporate social responsibility. In other words, a firm does not need merely to react to external government controls and regulations, or to new social pressures, but it can proactively develop a first-mover response, such that it gains an FSA in ethical behavior. The main examples we use deal with issues of concern in the sphere of the natural environment. Thus, we conclude this book with a focus on the issue of corporate strategy and environmental regulations, especially as these are relevant to international trade and investment agreements.

It is important to link the two new frameworks developed here back to the familiar firm and country factors in the FSA–CSA matrix of Chapter 2. Essentially environmental regulations, and other societal pressures on the firm, can be regarded as CSAs. Whether they are positive or negative CSAs can be shown on the vertical axis of the FSA–CSA matrix.

The novel thinking developed in this chapter is that the firm can turn such regulations into an FSA. Of course, this FSA would be shown in quadrant or cell 3 of the FSA–CSA matrix. Thus this chapter is an extension of the thinking first developed in Chapter 2 and then related to strategic management (in Chapter 8), organization structure (in Chapter 9), and the integration/responsiveness framework (in Chapters 10 and 17). Another way of looking at environmental regulations is as part of the home-country diamond (in Porter's single-diamond model). They can also be part of the host-country CSAs in terms of the double-diamond framework, as discussed in Chapter 10.

We conclude that the two frameworks developed in this final chapter serve to summarize many of the conceptual themes developed throughout this book. Finally, in keeping with our practice throughout the book, we give real-world examples in this chapter of the nature of corporate social responsibility and ethical behavior by MNEs and other firms doing international business.

DEVELOPING EFFECTIVE STRATEGIES

MNEs are supplementing or supplanting their old strategies in a number of ways in order to compete more effectively worldwide.[3] Two of the most recent developments include going where the action is and developing new business networks with governments, suppliers, customers, and competitors.

Going where the action is

One strategy that is proving increasingly important is the need to go international in order to keep up with the competition.[4] Successful multinationals have operations in the home countries of their major triad competitors. For example, IBM's strongest competitors are located in the United States, Europe, and Japan. In turn the company has facilities in all three places, to monitor the competition as well as to conduct research. Moreover, the communication network among the company's facilities allows each one to share information with the others and to provide assistance. This also helps the company to maintain a strong competitive posture.[5]

Another reason for locating near major competitors is that some markets develop faster than others and the experience and knowledge that is learned here can help in other markets. For example, in the US market IBM is now trying to develop a strategy of providing the best service in the industry. In the past the company had often referred service problems to its dealers. However, now the firm is attempting to address these issues directly, ensuring a higher level of service and taking back customers who were lured away by smaller firms with better service, support, and prices. If this strategy works well, the company is likely to use it in other worldwide locations where small firms have been gaining market share. Today, IBM makes very sizeable profits from software and services. Now IBM is customer-led, it is asked by its clients for what they want from IBM, and IBM is producing solutions rather than specific products to link together the complicated global infrastructure. IBM is also making a big push into cloud computing, developing software to move big corporate clients into the cloud and building vast data centres to host them. It is also looking at ways in which technology can make an impact in the healthcare sector, with sensors to monitor patients remotely. But these are competitive sectors where IBM may struggle to achieve the kind of market dominance it once achieved in mainframe computers.[6]

Another important aspect of a location-focused strategy is that MNEs often establish a home base for each major product line, and a multiproduct-line company will have "centers for excellence" all over the world. These centers are responsible for providing global leadership for their respective product lines. For example, Asea Brown Boveri, a Swiss firm, uses Sweden as the home base for transmission equipment. Research, development, and production are centralized in that country. Nestlé, the giant food company, has the world headquarters for its confectionery business in the UK because this home base is more dynamic in terms of the marketing environment and the high per capita consumption of confectionery products. At the same time Nestlé has made its Italian company, Buitoni, the world center for pasta operations. Meanwhile, Siemens has designated the United States as the world home base for medical electronics because this is where the market is most dynamic and will provide the company with the best chance of developing and maintaining state-of-the-art products.

It is also important to realize that the product line will dictate the degree of globalization. For example, food companies in Europe tend to be less international and more regional in focus. Local tastes vary widely and there are only modest gains to be achieved through large-scale operations, so European food companies tend to have an extensive local presence. The same is true for home appliances, which are often produced for regional markets. On the other hand, when European companies have become truly global, they have tended to focus on products that do not require high levels of integration on a worldwide basis.

So some companies have a need for global centers throughout the world, whereas others tend to stay in closer geographic proximity because of the nature of their product lines. Still others combine both of these approaches, as seen in the case **International Business Strategy in Action: 3M.**

 Active learning check

Review your answer to Active Learning Case question 1 and make any changes you like. Then compare your answer to the one below.

1 **How have NGOs changed the external environment in which MNEs operate? Why is Apple the world's most admired firm by business people? Why is a firm like Google likely to be more admired by NGOs?**

NGOs have captured public attention and won a lot of support in North America and Western Europe for their "green" and anti-globalization agendas. MNEs cannot afford to ignore NGOs, especially US and EU MNEs whose home base "diamond" is threatened by NGOs which can influence government policy and regulation. Apple has gained recognition as the most successful MNE because it has an innovative approach to consumer electronics such as the iPhone and iPad, which are very successful with consumers around the world. In contrast, Google while still being consumer friendly has also developed an explicit environmental energy saving strategy, making it more popular with green environmentalists.

INTERNATIONAL BUSINESS STRATEGY IN ACTION

3M

The 3M company is a major MNE that has over 50,000 products comprising everything from office supplies to construction and building maintenance to chemicals. It employs over 80,000 people and has operations in 60 countries. How does the firm manage such a large international operation? One way is by matching its global strategies with the needs of the local market. Some goods such as home video cassettes are standardized and are sold on the basis of price and quality. Culture and local usage are not important considerations. Other products are greatly influenced by local preferences or regulations; telecommunications is an example. Each country or region of the world has its own modifications for local application.

The company balances its global strategies and national responses on a region-by-region basis. For example, in Europe the company has set up a series of business centers to address local differences. The company also uses European management action teams (EMATs) to balance the needs of subsidiaries in responding to local expectations with the corporation's need for global direction. Today, 3M has 50 EMATs in Europe, each consisting of from 8 to 14 people, most of whom are marketing personnel. These groups are charged with bringing the firm's global plans to life by helping their execution at the local level. EMAT meetings, which usually occur quarterly, are designed to create action plans for the European subsidiaries. When the meetings are over, the members then return to their respective subsidiaries and begin executing the plans. In Asia the company uses a different approach, relying heavily on its Japanese operation to provide much of the needed direction to the subsidiaries. At the same time there are regional centers in Singapore and South Korea that help subsidiaries to address their local markets. In Latin America, meanwhile, 3M uses a macro approach, conducting business on a national rather than regional basis.

The company also carefully identifies those products that it will sell in each geographic area while following two basic strategies: (1) try to be the first in the market with new offerings because this strategy puts the competition at a disadvantage; and (2) grow new markets gradually by picking out those products that address the country's most pressing needs and focus exclusively on them. Commenting on its worldwide strategy, a company executive said:

> We don't believe in formulating a single global strategy for selling video cassettes in India and laser imagers in France and Post-it brand notes in Brazil. For each of 3M's 23 strategic business centers in each region the company's strategy is a blend of global, regional, and local companies and that will continue.

Website: www.3m.com.

Sources: Adapted from Harry Mammerly, "Matching Global Strategies with National Responses," *Journal of Business Strategy*, March/April 1992, pp. 8–13; www.3m.com; 3M, *Annual Report*, 2009.

INTERNATIONAL BUSINESS RESEARCH FRAMEWORKS

No study of international business would be complete without paying attention to the role and importance of theoretical frameworks. In Chapter 2 we introduced the firm (FSA) and country (CSA) matrix while in Chapters 10 and 17 we used the integration and national responsiveness matrix. Much of what has been discussed in this book is based on the research findings leading to such basic frameworks. In many cases the data were drawn from government statistics, company records, and business reports on recent developments and strategies. In other cases the information was garnered from formal studies that examined managerial behaviors among senior managers. Collectively, research provides important input for building international business theories and for formulating and implementing future strategies. As a result, it is useful to both academicians and practitioners.

Unfortunately, research findings can be confusing and contradictory. For example, many studies are extremely limited in focus and thus cannot be generalized to a universal setting. Similarly, when research is broadly based, it is likely that the findings cannot be generalized to specific situations. Porter's Diamond, for example, helps to explain how triad nations develop competitive advantage. However, its value to non-triad nations, as explained in Chapter 10, is limited and the findings must be revised and modified in order to apply them. Despite such shortcomings, however, international business research will continue to be of critical importance to the field. Such research will allow us to test theories and to refine their practical applications.

Theories of international business

A great many theories have relevance to the study of international business. In some cases these are first constructed and then tested. A good example is Adam Smith's theory of labor specialization. Smith presented this concept over 200 years ago in his *Wealth of Nations*, and in recent years learning curve analysts have confirmed these findings. Of course, not all theories have had to wait centuries before being proven. However, this example does illustrate that international business research can be advanced through the formulation of useful theories.[7]

In other cases theories are being tested for the purpose of reconfirming earlier findings. This is particularly important in learning how well a theory stands the test of time. A good example is the theory of lifetime employment in Japan. For many years theorists have argued that lifetime employment creates a highly motivated workforce and Western organizations would be wise to copy this approach. More recent research, however, reveals that lifetime employment is less useful as a motivator than as a control tool for ensuring worker loyalty and performance. In return for guaranteed employment, workers stay with the firm for their entire career, work hard, and are compliant with management's wishes. Sometimes unions are employer dominated and then they serve more to maintain harmony within the employee ranks than to represent the workers.

Based on an analysis of empirical data collected on this topic, two researchers recently concluded, "Lifetime employment is offered within a context of loyalty and benevolence based on cultural values. Its impact, however, is to increase the control of Japanese employees by managers."[8] Moreover, these researchers found that lifetime employment was not widely used by firms in tight labor markets because it was not possible to control the workers, who could easily find jobs with other companies and who derived little motivation from such guarantees.

This type of research is also important because it generates new hypotheses for testing. For example, as workers in large companies with guaranteed lifetime employment near retirement (55 to 60 years of age), will management replace them with younger people who are not given such guarantees? As the competitive environment increases, will companies stop offering these guarantees because they reduce the firms' flexibility in responding to changing conditions? Will young workers entering the Japanese workforce during this decade be motivated by such guarantees, or will they turn them down because they are unwilling to commit their career to one firm in return for job security? These types of questions will be focal points for future international business research efforts, since changing economic, cultural, and social environments are creating new conditions in which MNEs must compete. Research can help to shed light on the effect of these changes.

Practical applications of the theory

Research is also going to play an increasing role in helping to uncover how and why multinationals succeed. In particular, greater attention will be given to strategy research that is designed to explain why some firms do better than others and how these strategies are changing. For example, during the 1970s traditional international business strategy gave strong support to **strategic fit**, the notion that an organization must align its resources in such a way as to mesh with the environment. Auto firms had to design and build cars that were in demand, and this might mean a variety of models and accessories, depending on the number of markets being served. Similarly, electronics firms had to maintain state-of-the-art technology so as to meet consumer demand for new, high-quality, high-performance products. Today, however, successful multinationals realize that they must do much more than attempt to attain a strategic fit. The rapid pace of competitive change is requiring linkages between all segments of the business from manufacturing down to point-of-purchase selling, and in every phase of operation there must be attention to value-added concepts.[9] So the basic strategic concepts of the past, once widely accepted, must be reconsidered and sometimes reformulated.

Other research areas likely to receive future attention will be cross-national collaborative research by individuals from two or more countries and joint efforts by international and non-international researchers. The world of international business is getting larger every day, and it is critical that research be designed not only to help explain what is happening and why it is occurring, but also to help predict future developments and thus better prepare students and practitioners for the international challenges of the twenty-first century.

Strategic fit
A strategic management concept which holds that an organization must align its resources in such a way as to mesh effectively with the environment

THE FIVE PARTNERS BUSINESS NETWORK FRAMEWORK

In the future governments will become more selective in their approach to industrial policy, aware that in the past billions of dollars have been wasted by bureaucratic efforts to stream-line and refocus economic efforts. This recent trend is likely to result in more government–business efforts. However, the success of international business firms will depend more heavily on the companies themselves than on the government. Some of these developments will include the forging of new business networks for competitive advantage and the development of new relationships with non-business sector groups.[10]

Forging new business networks

Increasingly, the relationship of successful MNEs with their suppliers, customers, and competitors is changing. New strategies based on trust and reciprocal support are replacing the old business–client relationship in which companies sought to dictate the terms and conditions of sales and services.

In the case of suppliers, the current trend is toward reducing this number to a small group of reliable, efficient, and highly responsive firms. These suppliers are then brought into a close working relationship with the MNE so that both sides understand the other's strategy and plans can be formulated for minimizing working problems. The multinational will detail its needs and the supplier will draw up plans that ensure timely, accurate delivery. Another trend is the increase in the amount of responsibility being given to suppliers. Previously they were charged only with manufacturing, assembly, and delivery. Now many MNEs use their network partners to develop new materials and components, to perform industrial engineering functions, and to assume liability for warranties.

In the case of customers, network linkages now involve changing the focus of the relationship from one in which sales representatives would work directly with MNE purchasing agents to one in which sellers interact more directly with their customers. D'Cruz and Rugman have explained this idea in the case of **flagship firms**, characterized by global competitiveness and international benchmarks.[11] In the conventional system the flagship firm and its customers maintain an arm's-length relationship. However, new relationships are now being forged in which there is a direct link between the flagship firm and its most important customers (see Figure 22.1, segments 1 and 2), whereas traditional relations are maintained with some distributors to serve the firm's less important customers. At the same time, network linkages are being developed with key distributors to serve other customers better. (Again see Figure 22.1, segments 3 and 4, etc.)

Network arrangements are also being created between international competitors in the form of joint ventures, technology transfers, and market-sharing agreements such as a Japanese firm selling the product of a US firm in the Japanese market in return for a similar concession in the United States. Mazda and Ford Motor are excellent examples.

These strategic relationships among suppliers, customers, and competitors are becoming integral parts of MNE strategies, as are linkages to non-business organizations such as unions with which multinationals are now sharing their strategies in the hope of creating a working relationship that will save jobs and ensure company profitability. Partnerships are also being fostered with universities that can help to educate and train human resources, and research institutions that can provide scientific knowledge that is useful for helping organizations to develop and maintain worldwide competitiveness. Another group that is getting increased attention is government, since this institution can be particularly helpful in supporting legislation that will encourage the upgrading of the workforce, development of state-of-the-art technology and products, exports, and the building of world-class competitors. Figure 22.2

Flagship firms
Multinational firms characterized by global competitiveness and international benchmarks

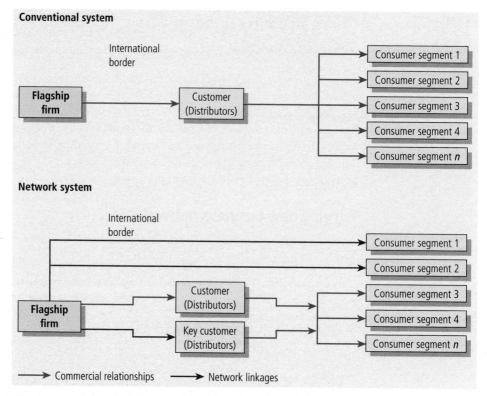

Figure 22.1 Network linkage and the changing shape of international distribution systems

Source: © Alan Rugman and Joseph R. D'Cruz, 2000. Reprinted from *Multinationals as Flagship Firms: Regional Business Networks* by Alan M. Rugman and Joseph R. D'Cruz (2000).

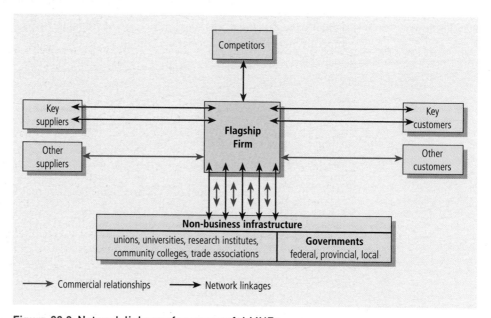

Figure 22.2 Network linkages for successful MNEs

Source: © Alan Rugman and Joseph R. D'Cruz, 2000. Reprinted from *Multinationals as Flagship Firms: Regional Business Networks* by Alan M. Rugman and Joseph R. D'Cruz (2000).

Five partners
A business network consisting of five partner organizations: the flagship firm (a multinational enterprise), key suppliers, key customers, key competitors, and the non-business infrastructure

provides an illustration of the basic structure of the **five partners** in an effective network. Notice how these relationships go beyond commercial transactions and involve network linkages to a wide variety of other groups. This is one of the waves of the future in international business.

COPING WITH CHANGING ENVIRONMENTS

The international environment of the future will continue to be one of rapid change, and MNEs will have to stay abreast of a number of developments. The political and economic environments will present the greatest challenges.

Political environment

As already seen, the political environment affects MNE activities in many ways. For example, all major triad groups have trade barriers that are designed to limit the sale of foreign goods in their countries. This in turn typically results in trade negotiations that are designed to open up these markets and/or to reduce trade deficits. Protectionism trends are particularly treacherous because they are psychological as well as legislative.[12] That is, even when trade barriers are lowered, there is a tendency for people to be protectionist and to "buy local."

Many managers say that they favor open markets, but, when questioned closely, they state strong support for protectionist strategies such as government assistance to domestic businesses and help for home-based firms that are seeking to go international.[13] In short, many business people speak out for free trade but advocate policies that put foreign firms at a distinct disadvantage. The Japanese are some of the strongest supporters of free trade. However, according to the US trade representative these opinions are not translated into action. For example, Japanese telecom fees make it difficult for foreign companies to compete effectively.[14]

The ability of US firms to penetrate foreign markets will also be influenced by US government policies. The Clinton administration was initially more vigorous than its predecessor in pushing for open markets in Asia.[15] US government trade policy toward Japan and South-East Asia generally aims to open markets in the region. The objective was to increase the market share of US firms in this geographic triad region as well as to reduce the large trade deficit that the United States is running, most noticeably with China. The latter is likely to receive particular attention, given that in recent years China has sold far more to the United States than it has purchased from it.[16] The Bush administration reacted to the failure of the WTO Doha Round of multilateral trade negotiations by working out sets of bilateral free trade agreements, such as one with South Korea, although this was stalled by the Congress and still not approved by Spring 2008. In December 2010, both the United States and South Korea have hailed their long-awaited free trade agreement negotiated as a "win–win" deal. President Barack Obama said the deal was "essential" in boosting US exports.

At the same time overseas companies are lobbying their governments to negotiate greater access to the US market. For example, the governments of less industrialized countries are putting pressure on triad countries to liberalize agricultural trade. International institutions like the IMF, as well as non-governmental organizations (NGOs) like Oxfam, criticize the United States, the EU, and Japan, some of the more vocal supporters of free trade, for subsidizing their agricultural and manufacturing industries to the detriment of less developed countries.

A related issue is political risk. For example, in Latin America, Venezuela and Brazil have left-leaning populist governments. Venezuela is a large exporter of oil and Brazil is the manufacturing hub for Latin America, a host country for VW and Mercedes-Benz, among others.[17] The financial crisis in Argentina led to some factories being abandoned, followed by worker occupation of these factories. These workers started producing again and sought to be legitimized by the government as owners of the factory.[18]

Hong Kong, the former British colony, was returned to China in 1997. The Chinese government agreed to allow the region to maintain relative autonomy and to continue functioning under its own economic and political systems for 50 years after the takeover.[19] China is now heavily investing in Hong Kong and has more total direct investment there than in any other country. At the same time two-thirds of foreign investment in China comes from Hong Kong Chinese. Many Hong Kong business people believe that relations with China have worked out for the betterment of both sides.

Another country where political risk is being re-evaluated is Vietnam.[20] Relations between the United States and Vietnam are now normalized, and the country has business ties with US multinationals that can provide assistance in helping to rebuild the economy. The IMF and the World Bank provided funds for critical highway and seaport projects. At the same time, Vietnam has been attracting billions of dollars in manufacturing investment from European and Asian companies. Now that the US trade embargo has ended, Vietnam has attracted US banks, aircraft, and power plant manufacturers to help in the rebuilding effort. One major reason that Vietnam is interested in rapprochement with the United States is that it sees it as a counterbalance to Japan and the growing military might of China. As relations between the two countries continue to thaw, political risk will decline and Vietnam will become an increasingly popular area for investment opportunities.

The continuing development of free trade agreements will also work to lessen political risk. For example, the North American Free Trade Agreement (NAFTA) binds Canada, the United States, and Mexico together into an interdependent market in which each nation profits by working harmoniously with the others.[21] The same is true for members of the EU as well as for other economic unions, from those being fostered in Latin America to those in Africa and the former Soviet Union. Firms doing business in these geographic areas will find that the greatest ongoing challenge is more likely to be economic than political. There will also be further consolidation of the world's trade agreements into a triad-based system (see Table 22.1).

Economic environment

The economic environment will be replete with opportunities for MNEs. US multinationals, for example, will continue to be a dominant force in the export market, as seen by the fact that the United States has consistently ranked as the world's largest exporter over the last decade. Meanwhile Asia–Pacific MNEs, except for those of Japan and Australia, will benefit from the comparatively lower cost of the labor in their home countries.

New economic opportunities will also be provided by the rise of non-triad-based firms that become successful MNEs. In Mexico, for example, Anheuser-Busch before being acquired by InBev, used to own approximately 50 percent of Grupo Modelo, maker of Corona and the country's largest brewer. In July 2008, Belgian brewing company InBev completed the acquisition of Anheuser-Busch for US $52 billion dollar in equity, creating the world's largest beer company, Anheuser-Busch InBev. After years of unsuccessfully vying to be the market leader in Peru and losing to local Inka Cola, Coca-Cola's Peruvian bottling and distribution was transferred to its competitor. In turn, Inka Cola products are now sold in North America, mostly to immigrant South Americans, through the Coca-Cola company. As non-triad countries develop, new opportunities for telecommunication and other infrastructure companies will materialize.

New goods and services will help to create new markets. An example is Apple's iPod, an MP3 player that can store a large quantity of music. Firms are competing to provide ever better MP3 players to gain a share of this growing market. New PC technology is also decreasing the weight of laptops while improving their processing speed, their graphics, and their

Table 22.1 The world's major trade agreements

| EU (27) | | EFTA (4) | NAFTA (3) | ASEAN (10) | Mercosur (4) | Andean Group (4) | OPEC (12) | Council of Arab Economic Unity (12) | CARICOM (15) | LAIA (12) | ECOWAS (15) | SADC (14) |
EU (15)	+EU (12)											
Austria	Bulgaria	Iceland	Canada	Brunei Darussalam	Argentina	Bolivia	Algeria	Egypt	Antigua and Barbuda	Argentina	Benin	Angola
Belgium	Cyprus	Liechtenstein	Mexico	Cambodia	Brazil	Colombia	Angola	Iraq	Bahamas	Bolivia	Burkina Faso	Botswana
Denmark	Czech Rep.	Norway	United States	Indonesia	Paraguay	Ecuador	Indonesia	Jordan	Barbados	Brazil	Cape Verde	Dem. Rep. of Congo
Finland	Estonia	Switzerland		Laos	Uruguay	Peru	Iran	Libya	Belize	Chile	Côte d'Ivoire	Lesotho
France	Hungary			Malaysia			Iraq	Mauritania	Dominica	Colombia	Gambia	Madagascar
Germany	Latvia			Myanmar			Kuwait	Syria	Grenada	Cuba	Ghana	Malawi
Greece	Lithuania			Philippines			Libya	Yemen	Guyana	Ecuador	Guinea	Mauritius
Ireland	Malta			Singapore			Nigeria	United Arab Emirates	Haiti	Mexico	Guinea-Bissau	Mozambique
Italy	Poland			Thailand			Qatar	Kuwait	Jamaica	Paraguay	Liberia	Namibia
Luxembourg	Romania			Vietnam			Saudi Arabia	Palestine	Montserrat	Peru	Mali	South Africa
Netherlands	Slovakia						United Arab Emirates	Somalia	Saint Lucia	Uruguay	Niger	Swaziland
Portugal	Slovenia						Venezuela	Sudan	St. Kitts and Nevis	Venezuela	Nigeria	Tanzania
Spain									St. Vincent and the Grenadines		Senegal	Zambia
Sweden									Suriname		Sierra Leone	Zimbabwe
UK									Trinidad and Tobago		Togo	

Key: EU—European Union; EFTA—European Free Trade Agreement; OPEC—Organization of Petroleum Exporting Countries; NAFTA—North American Free Trade Agreement; CARICOM—Caribbean Community and Common Market; ASEAN—Association of South-East Asian Nations; Mercosur—Mercado Comun del Sur; LAIA—Latin American Integration Association; ECOWAS—Economic Community of West African States; SADC—Southern African Development Community.

Sources: Adapted from http://europa.eu.int/abc-en.htm; www.opec.org; www.efta.int; www.caricom.org/; http://wellsfargo.com/inatl/wrldalm/intro/other/; www.sice.oas.org/; and www.aladi.org/.

multimedia capabilities. These products lend themselves to a globalization strategy since purchasers buy them based primarily on performance characteristics and not on cultural requirements. As a result, computer industry MNEs are likely to find this century offering both new opportunities and new challenges. The opportunities will come in the form of emerging markets since sharp declines in PC prices tend to increase demand sharply. The major challenge will come in the form of increased competition since PC technology tends to be easy to emulate, and so the barriers to entry for new firms are often quickly surmounted.

An accompanying development is the rise of the Internet as a source of competition. Today a growing number of MNEs are becoming electronic companies, or e-corporations for short.[22] The Internet is driving down costs and helping companies reach thousands of new potential customers worldwide.[23] As a result, MNEs are now throwing out their old business models and creating new ones that will help them do business electronically with customers who in the past were not accessible to them.[24] One of the keys to this new development is the rapid rise of both businesses and households with Internet access. As recently as 2010 approximately 58.4 percent of the European population and 77.4 percent of that in North America used the Internet.[25] As a result, e-commerce is now accounting for a growing percentage of GDP in these economies.[26]

Major MNEs that are finding themselves unable to compete in the ever-changing international arena are restructuring[27] and realigning markets. Examples include (1) aircraft manufacturing, where Boeing is having to scurry to meet competition from Airbus; (2) autos, where General Motors, Ford, and Chrysler are trying to stave off the onslaught of Japanese competition in their home market; and (3) household electronics, where such well-known manufacturers as Sony, Panasonic, and LG are finding that the markets for products such as DVDs are becoming saturated and that Chinese manufacturers are proving themselves to be excellent competitors.

New strategies, carefully crafted to the specific market, will offer increased opportunities for MNEs. In Japan, for example, the success of firms such as Toys "Я" Us and Spiegel is a result of learning how to work within the system. As discussed in the Real Case in Chapter 3, Toys "Я" Us set up its own retail stores by teaming up with the former director of McDonald's Japan for local knowledge and investment capital. It relentlessly pursued its objective of its discounted "category killer" toys despite vigorous opposition from small, local merchants who opposed letting Toys "Я" Us into the Japanese market. Thanks to its dogged determination, the company was eventually given permission to open a large retail store and by 2000 it had over 100 stores. As of 2009, it had 167 stores in Japan.[28] Spiegel, famous for its mail-order business, formed a joint venture with Sumitomo Trading Company and introduced an upscale fashion catalogue in Japan. The company directed its efforts at women from 20 to 40 years of age. Catalogue selling proved so successful that by the mid-1990s the joint venture was generating annual sales of over $160 million. These efforts, which are characterized by strategies that are designed to circumvent problems in the distribution system rather than trying to meet them head on, are typical of those strategies that will be used in Japan and other foreign locations during the years ahead.

Business-to-business (B2B)

An example of an ethnocentric MNE is Air Liquide, the French manufacturer of industrial and medical gases. At its Paris headquarters, the vice presidents for each geographic region are all French. All regional managers in foreign offices are French and have previously worked in Paris. This allows Air Liquide to have a standardized, "global" strategy that treats the world as one integrated market. This works as the nature of the industry is B2B. The main customers of Air Liquide are other large industrial manufacturers in oil, iron and steel, and other types of chemicals. These companies depend on the gases supplied by Air Liquide. It has flagship relationships with many of those manufacturers.

The main competitors of Air Liquide are the UK-based BOC Group and Linde AG. While Air Liquide is more concentrated in the core gas business, its competitors are more diversified into the gases needed for consumers, transportation, etc.

In general, the largest number of B2B relationships would be between ethnocentric partners. Then there are clear rules of the game—both partners are in mature, standardized industries with easy-to-maintain, long-term relationships. So, B2B occurs in chemicals, autos and auto parts, oil, and other "commoditized" sectors.

THE TRADE AND INVESTMENT FRAMEWORK

The tendency toward international trade liberalization has been exemplified by two recent developments, namely the North American Free Trade Agreement (NAFTA) of 1993 and the deeper integration of the European Union (EU). Both these regional triad agreements have developed from previous agreements. The principles of the 1989 United States–Canada Free Trade Agreement (FTA) are also the basis for NAFTA. Similarly, before 1995, the European Union was the European Community (EC). Albeit very different, in terms of goals and content, these two examples of trade and investment liberalization create a protected business environment for member countries, while in turn discriminating against third-country businesses.[29]

From the Canadian and Mexican perspective, the main rationale for negotiating the FTA, and subsequently NAFTA, was to secure access to the US market for both exports and FDI. Mexico also sought to create a secure economy for inward flows of FDI. In contrast, the EU's predecessor, the EC, was considered by many observers to create a "Fortress Europe" at the expense of third-country firms.[30]

Figure 22.3 classifies the different industries in the countries affected by trade liberalization in NAFTA. (It will also provide an initial framework for the EU.) The vertical axis denominates economic integration and the horizontal axis reflects the political sovereignty of nation states. The left side column therefore shows low political sovereignty in the form of national treatment. With national treatment, discrimination against foreign investors is not permitted; they are to be treated equally with domestic investors in the application of host-country laws and regulations.

Quadrant 1 refers to business sectors where there is high economic integration and low political sovereignty. But not all aspects of "free trade" agreements are here. Quadrant 2 refers to business sectors with low economic integration and low political sovereignty.

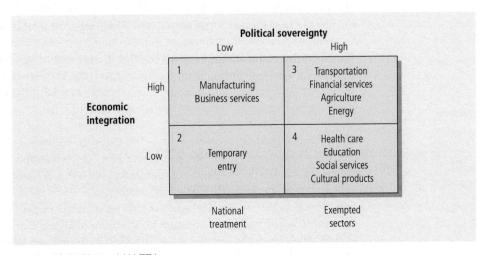

Figure 22.3 FDI and NAFTA

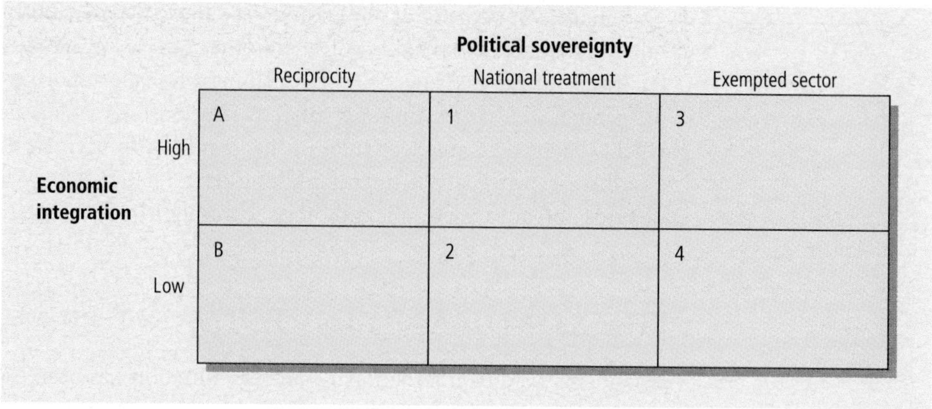

Political sovereignty

		Reciprocity	National treatment	Exempted sector
Economic integration	High	A	1	3
	Low	B	2	4

Figure 22.4 NAFTA and the EU

These are sectors that tend to be naturally local, such as labor. Quadrant 3 refers to business sectors with combined high levels of economic integration and political sovereignty. While national treatment refers to the obligation of member states to treat all businesses from other member countries as if they were domestic businesses, this does not always apply; there are exempted sectors. Sectors in quadrant 3 are exempted from national treatment despite the efficiencies that would result from the application of national treatment. The last matrix section, quadrant 4, refers to sectors that are typically local and are exempted from national treatment.

According to the NAFTA document, national treatment in quadrant 1 applies to sectors such as manufacturing and business service. In quadrant 2 are the temporary entry permits for business service professionals (such as consultants and engineers). Exempted sectors are in quadrants 3 and 4. Those with a high level of economic integration in quadrant 3 include transportation, financial services, energy, and agriculture. Those with low levels of economic integration in quadrant 4 are health care, education, social services, and cultural products.

This framework was also a model for the Free Trade Area of the Americas (FTAA), agreed to at Quebec City in 2001. Unfortunately it was not implemented, due to opposition by Brazil. NAFTA was also the model for the Asia–Pacific Economic Cooperation (APEC), although this will not be fully effective until 2015 and 2020.

Figure 22.4 shows the more complex EU matrix. The two extra quadrants in the extreme left column capture the concept of an even lower level of political sovereignty, reciprocity. The EU 1992 measures and subsequent "deepening" programs of political, social, and economic integration aim at quadrant A in everything but select sectors, such as culture. The manufacturing sector and business services are in quadrant A, which also includes banking and mutual funds, securities, insurance, transportation, broadcasting, tourism, and information services. In addition, there are harmonization laws regulating company behavior, including mergers and acquisitions, trademarks and copyrights, cross-border mergers, and accounting operations across borders. Another important objective of harmonization is the opening of public procurement. It is clear that such harmonization efforts place almost all economic sectors in quadrant A of Figure 22.4.[31] In conclusion, in contrast to NAFTA, the EU has a much deeper degree of economic, political, and social integration and a consequent loss of sovereignty for its member states.

Although both NAFTA and the EU can be analyzed in this way, many groups are opposed to such trade and investment liberalization. When they are opposed, they frequently cloak themselves in the guise of ethics, as we will see in the case **International Business Strategy in Action: Is The Body Shop an ethical business?**

✔ **Active learning check**

Review your answer to Active Learning Case question 2 and make any changes you like. Then compare your answer to the one below.

 As MNEs operate across the world and NGOs operate globally, why are there no "global" or "international" environmental agreements to set rules for sustainable development?

The reason that there is no effective international environmental agreement is that there is no single international institution that can enforce one. The WTO deals with trade matters, not environmental issues. The United Nations deals with human rights in a political but not economic context. Further, the MNEs really do not operate globally, but are mainly "triad" based. And here, the US and EU triad blocs are often at odds on environmental, trade, and investment policies. Paradoxically, the NGOs are criticizing MNEs for something that they do not do: operate globally. The more responsible NGOs, which believe in sustainable development, should lobby the respective home-based triad authorities. This is where the power is—not with "global" governance. To ensure a safe environment, NGOs need to learn the realities of triad power.

ENVIRONMENT AND MNEs

Civil society
A group of individuals, organizations, and institutions that act outside the government and the market to advance a diverse set of interests

The issue of globalization has opened up a gulf between representatives of **civil society** such as NGOs on the one hand and international business such as MNEs on the other. Unfortunately these oppositions of opinion have become entrenched. In this section we will categorize perceptions regarding the role of international institutions and future alternatives for trade liberalization and indicate a range of more constructive responses for both MNEs and NGOs.

"Mobilizer" NGOs criticize the global trade and investment regime and believe that the major international institutions promoting free trade, such as the WTO, IMF, and World Bank, should be eliminated or fundamentally overhauled. "Technical" NGOs are relative insiders, willing to work with the mainstream international institutions in order to reduce perceived ineffectiveness or inequity in policy making. However, technical NGOs are now perceived by many national governments and business lobbies as having a common agenda with the mobilizers. This widespread perception has seriously affected the technical NGOs' capacity to achieve important objectives on their usually benevolent agendas.

In addition it is difficult to see how the WTO can address the multitude of goals prescribed by the anti-global mobilizers. The WTO is an understaffed bureaucracy with little political impact. The secretariat to the General Agreement on Tariffs and Trade (GATT) has successfully acted on behalf of national governments to cut tariffs, mainly on manufactured goods. Its value lies in the improved market access it opens to previously protected markets, thereby increasing overall economic efficiency; it functions by implementing rules of fairness agreed upon by sovereign states.

Unfortunately the WTO also embodies several asymmetric elements: on the one hand, it is consistently moving toward trade liberalization, but on the other, it is unable to eliminate the protectionist policies in some sectors put in place by many of its members.

Furthermore, a major structural change at the new WTO, as compared to GATT, is the increased use of trade law and litigation for dispute settlement. As the stream of disputes swell the WTO is taking on a different shape. Instead of devoting most of its resources to promoting multinational trade liberalization and non-discrimination, the WTO is forced to focus much energy and expertise on resolving bilateral trade disputes.

INTERNATIONAL BUSINESS STRATEGY IN ACTION

Is The Body Shop an ethical business?

When it comes to the ethical company, The Body Shop is hailed as the prototype of the responsible firm. The company's website not only states the company's values but urges visitors to become active in the fight to end animal cruelty, to protect human rights, and to implement fair trade practices. Its founder, Anita Roddick, started the company in 1976 by opening a small store in Brighton, England, to support her family. In 1978, the opening of a small store in Brussels became its first overseas expansion. By the 1980s, the company was opening two stores per month. Today, The Body Shop has grown into an MNE with 1,900 stores in 50 countries around the world.

The company has a lengthy résumé of its social achievements. In the animal rights arena, The Body Shop joined the campaign for a ban on animal testing for cosmetic products. This was a major factor in the 1998 decision of the UK government to ban animal testing in the industry. On the environmental front, the company has publicly joined NGO causes. For example, in the 1980s, the company sponsored Greenpeace posters, joined the "Save the Whales Campaign," and started a signature petition to ask the Brazilian government to halt the burning of the Amazon forest. The company also brought attention to Shell's involvement in Nigeria. Shell's operations were blamed for severe environmental deterioration, prosecution of protestors, and bribery of state officials. The Body Shop has converted many of its operations into Ecotricity, or energy from renewable resources, and helped create an academy of business with an ethical curriculum in the University of Bath.

The Body Shop's image is tied to that of its founder. Anita Roddick was an active participant on environmental rallies, fair trade missions, and in lobbying governments. She also defied the cosmetics industry's portrayal of women and urged women to accept cellulite and wrinkles as a natural part of their bodies. She stated publicly that cosmetics claiming to solve these problems do not really work, an assertion that has created a backlash from competitors. Since the company went public in 1985, she often found herself at odds with shareholders. In fact, in 1998 shareholders pressured her to step down from the CEO chair in favor of Patrick Gournay, who oversaw a major restructuring that saw 300 job cuts, the company's withdrawal from manufacturing, and a management hiring spree to revitalize the company. In 2000, Roddick announced that she would slowly retire from managing The Body Shop to concentrate on her

Source: Getty/Forrest Anderson

activism. She died in 2009. The Body Shop became part of the French company L'Oreal Group in 2006, but is run independently and now has more than 2,100 stores in 55 countries.

Another signature of The Body Shop is the "Trade not Aid" slogan. Under it, the company has sought to advance the plight of indigenous communities in Third World countries by promoting "Fair Trade." The goal is to support marginalized sectors of society to develop a livelihood within the context of sustainable development. Today, the company sources cocoa butter, babassu oil, and massagers, among other ingredients and products, from Community Trade suppliers in 26 countries, including India, Honduras, Nepal, and Mexico. In 2002–2003, the company purchased £5 million in natural products through its Community Trade program.

In the 1990s, the company suffered a severe blow to its reputation when *Business Ethics* published an article by Jon Entine claiming that the company was the opposite of what it represented itself to be. Entine accused the company of selling drugstore quality products at a large premium by marketing cosmetics with petrochemical ingredients as natural products. In addition, the author claimed the company misrepresented the amount of its donations to charity, did not adhere to its own principles of "Fair Trade," and had itself committed unnecessary environmental damage. For instance, Entine mentions an incident in which The Body Shop went back on a contract to purchase large amounts of shea butter from suppliers in Ghana. This left the suppliers with a lot of useless stock that they could not sell anywhere else. There are also alleged incidents of the company forcing low margins on suppliers in Third World countries. And, a franchisee in France claimed that The Body Shop dumped a load of plastic containers in a landfill site.

A number of consumer groups, NGOs, and Internet websites have all jumped on the wagon. The website mcspotlight.com claims that The Body Shop sells products with ingredients that have been tested on animals, as long as the testing was not done for cosmetics, and that some of its products contain gelatin, an animal product. The same website claims that, in industrialized countries, The Body Shop pays its employees near minimum wages and is unwilling to recognize unions. The company is also accused of exaggerating the importance of its Community Trade program and of using the Kayapo Indians of Brazil for promotions without compensating them.

The Body Shop has denied most allegations and threatened a number of news media with legal action but has only taken action against a few, including Channel 4 of England. For the company, which was built on the confidence of the "conscious customer," the consequences of this bad publicity could be devastating. Premium prices are, after all, what customers are willing to pay for that extra social responsibility.

Whether the allegations are true or not, The Body Shop can still claim to be a pioneer of corporate responsibility because it brought the issues to the table. Many companies have emulated its principles, including Boots of the UK, which has developed its own brand of environmentally-friendly cosmetics to compete with The Body Shop.

Websites: www.the-body-shop.com; www.greenpeace.org.

Sources: Sharlene Buszka, "A Case of Greenwashing: The Body Shop," in *Proceedings of the Association of Management and the International Association of Management 15th Annual Conference, Organizational Management Division*, vol. 15, no. 1 (1997), pp. 199–294; www.mcspotlight.org/; "Passion or Profit," *FT.com*, February 13, 2002; "Body Swap," *FT.com*, February 13, 2002; Alison Smith, "US Team Hopeful of Reviving Flagging Fortune," *Financial Times*, February 13, 2002, p. 20.

While the WTO has been successful for 54 years in dealing with the technical tariff cuts, it is not very well equipped to deal with the new agenda of international trade and investment liberalization. Tariff cuts have allowed shallow integration across many manufacturing sectors. Today's agenda, with major implications for MNEs engaged in FDI, is one of deep integration.

Figure 22.5 contrasts the various perceived roles and outcomes of the WTO. The institutional reality is largely that of quadrant 1, while the anti-global movement has been successful in creating an image of the WTO as in quadrant 4.

The technical NGOs' perspective is usually positioned in quadrant 2. Here, an assessment of the efficiency outcomes of improved market access is often combined with a belief in the power of the WTO to actually dictate fundamental national policy choices that could favor the redistribution of wealth. The dominant picture suggested by the stakeholders

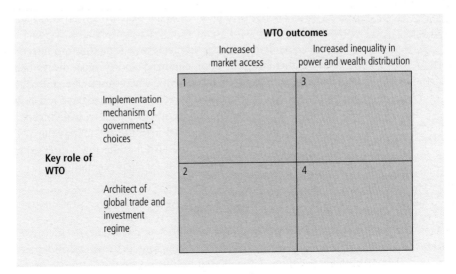

Figure 22.5 Different perceptions of the WTO

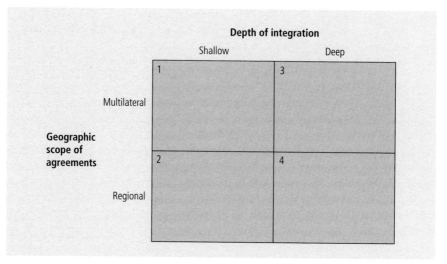

Figure 22.6 Institutional alternatives for trade and investment

hurt by free trade and investment is positioned in quadrant 3. These stakeholders typically include labor, management, and owners of non-competitive firms in import-competing sectors, which lack exports or outward FDI. Their view is that the WTO may indeed be an implementation mechanism of sovereign governments' choices, but it results in increased inequality in the international distribution of economic power and wealth.

Two parameters critically determine the future options for further trade and investment liberalization: the choice between bilateral or regional and multilateral negotiations and between shallow or deeper integration. These choices are represented in Figure 22.6.

Quadrant 1 represents the old, highly successful GATT process of tariffs cuts and shallow integration. Quadrant 3 represents the new agenda of the WTO in terms of deep integration, including investment liberalization. Quadrant 2 represents the old regional trade agreements with tariff cuts (the Andean pact, the Caribbean initiative, ASEAN, etc.). Quadrant 4 represents the new type of regional trade agreements, such as NAFTA. These include national treatment for FDI and also enhanced market access for services and intellectual property. Quadrant 3, with deep multilateral integration, undoubtedly constitutes an optimal situation for all nations concerned in terms of long-term wealth creation, but is at present not feasible because of constraints such as the structure of the WTO and US policy preferences. Quadrant 2 represents the worst-case scenario of shallow, regional integration.

This analysis demonstrates the perverse effects that mobilizers can have on trade and investment liberalization. Poor countries and groups always benefit more from multilateral than from regional agreements. They cannot be shut out from the former, and individual nations such as the United States always have less power in multilateral than in regional cases because of the number of countries involved. The strengthening, not the weakening, of mainstream global institutions such as the WTO—so despised by the mobilizers—may well represent the fastest route for poorer countries toward achieving fundamentally higher living standards for their population.

The pattern of MNE responses

Figure 22.7 categorizes MNE responses to civil society criticisms. The vertical axis distinguishes between a strategy that differentiates between stakeholders with whom a dialogue is possible and those with whom it is not, and, on the bottom, a strategy of uniform response. The horizontal axis makes a distinction between a broad stakeholder perspective on the

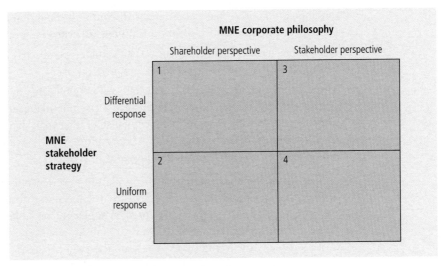

Figure 22.7 MNE strategies and civil society

right, whereby goals other than shareholder wealth maximization are considered relevant, and, on the left, a narrower shareholder, profit-maximizing perspective.

Quadrant 2 reflects the outdated perspective on MNEs, paradoxically adopted by most mobilizers. They view MNEs as profit maximizers, who will systematically refuse a constructive dialogue with any stakeholder representing civil society. Quadrant 1 represents an equally outdated response that is now being rejected by most large MNEs. Management has a shareholder perspective and its differential response is usually a PR exercise whereby an MNE provides lip service to the goals of friendly stakeholders but in fact is not serious about stakeholder management.

In fact, many MNEs are now positioned in quadrant 3. They pursue a stakeholder management model, perhaps driven by sustainable development environmental considerations. Here MNEs try to identify those salient stakeholders that can contribute to a win–win situation for the firm and society at large. These firms face the challenge of distinguishing between destructive mobilizers and benevolent, technical NGOs.

The main danger is for MNEs to fall in the quadrant 4 trap, whereby their stakeholder management approach can be abused by mobilizers, because the firm has not set up proper screening mechanisms to establish which stakeholder demands are legitimate and which are not. This problem is faced by many companies operating in both developing and advanced countries that are unfairly accused of unethical behavior (for example, Shell in the disposal of a North Sea oil rig where Greenpeace misrepresented the position in order to win publicity).

A useful alliance could take place between MNEs with a quadrant 1 viewpoint in Figure 22.7 and the technical NGOs of quadrant 2. An example of this is the idea of sustainable development, whereby MNEs are the actors making new and environmentally sensitive investments. In contrast, alliances between the protected and inefficient firms in quadrant 3 and mobilizer NGOs in quadrant 4 are not useful. Yet this was exactly the type of coalition put together in Seattle in 1999 to disrupt the WTO meetings. There, labor, mobilizer NGOs, and even technical NGOs made common cause against business and governments.

Three suggestions are offered as to how MNEs should proceed:

1 The activities of external stakeholders should be discussed at the board and top management level, and an overall strategy should be developed to deal with them. It is important to make a distinction between technical NGOs and anti-global mobilizers. Initiatives should be developed to work with the former. Clear arguments should be

developed to appropriately counter the discourse of the mobilizers, and this should be combined with an effective communication strategy to reach relevant audiences.

2 Sustainable development and ethical stakeholder perspectives should be embedded within the organization and its culture.

3 The firm should not engage in a debate with mobilizers (or even technical NGOs) through a small set of PR people; instead all senior managers should be trained to articulate the concept of stakeholder capitalism, rather than shareholder capitalism, and the contribution of the organization to the resulting wealth creation. In other words, all senior managers in the firm should engage with NGOs.

As a result of the above initiatives firms should experience a dramatic improvement in both profile and performance. The firms that will do best in future will be those that take leadership positions with respect to stakeholder management, capture the concept of values-driven rather than profit-driven capitalism, and respect their most important resource—namely, their employees. These policies will be the most effective tools at the microeconomic level against ideology-driven mobilizers.

For their part, NGOs, especially the technical ones, need to understand that anti-global rhetoric is leading to regional integration and bilateral agreements, as a politically more feasible—but ultimately less efficient—alternative to global integration. This does not benefit the objectives of civil society. Free trade and investment liberalization have not yet been achieved due to the vested interests and misperceptions of some components of civil society and affected stakeholders. We now need to recognize and correct these misperceptions as a precondition to achieving an overarching increase in world welfare and incomes.

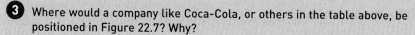

✔ Active learning check

Review your answer to the Active Learning Case question 3 and make any changes you like. Then compare your answer to the one below.

3 **Where would a company like Coca-Cola, or others in the table above, be positioned in Figure 22.7? Why?**

Coca Cola is probably positioned in quadrant 3 of Figure 22.7. In order to protect its worldwide brand, which has to be delivered locally through host country partners and bottling subsidiaries, it is highly responsive to different stakeholder groups with whom it engages in a dialogue to pursue a differential response. Such local responsiveness is particularly important to an MNE dealing with local host government regulations and NGOs. As a result, Coca-Cola is highly ranked as one of the more environmentally responsive and socially aware companies.

KEY POINTS

1 There will be an increase in the amount of international business research that is being conducted. This will come in the form of both theory testing and the practical application of information. Both academicians and practitioners will find this development helpful.

2 Multinationals, as flagship firms, are beginning to develop new business network relationships with suppliers, competitors, governments, unions, universities, and a host of other external groups. This networking relationship is proving particularly helpful in increasing productivity, profitability, and overall competitiveness.

3 The two environments that will present the greatest challenges for MNEs in the future are the political and the economic. The rising tide of protectionism will require that multinationals deal astutely with foreign governments. They will also have to weigh carefully the political risk associated with investing in countries that are now beginning to shed their central planning systems and to move toward free enterprise economies.

4 The principle of national treatment reduces political sovereignty, although some sectors are exempted in NAFTA, the FTAA, and APEC. In contrast, the EU has deep integration across political and social areas, as well as economic.

5 The interaction between MNEs and NGOs is complex but can be better understood by constructing an analytical framework.

Key terms

- non-governmental organizations (NGOs)
- strategic fit
- flagship firms
- five partners
- civil society

REVIEW AND DISCUSSION QUESTIONS

1 Why is theory testing of value to the field of international business research? What can be learned from such information?

2 In addition to theory testing, how is international business research of value to both scholars and practitioners? In your answer, give an example of how each group can benefit from such research.

3 In what ways are MNEs developing new business networks? Give two examples and then explain why these developments are likely to help the companies maintain their competitive strengths.

4 How is the political environment likely to change during the future? Give one example and relate its significance for multinationals.

5 How is the economic environment likely to change in the future? Give one example and relate its significance for multinationals.

6 How does NAFTA differ from the EU?

7 Why are NGOs opposed to MNEs? What should MNEs do?

REAL CASE

Dell: B2C

Dell is a leader in personal computers. It competes with Toshiba, HP, Acer, Samsung, Sony, Lenovo, Asustek, etc. Dell is based in Austin, Texas, and has production factories in Tennessee. It also produces in Ireland, Malaysia, Brazil, and China. Dell operates in four business segments: large enterprise, public, small and medium business, and consumer. It designs, develops, manufactures, markets, sells, and supports a range of products and services that can be customized to individual customer requirements. In February 2011, it acquired Compellent Technologies, Inc. During the fiscal year ended January 28, 2011, it completed five acquisitions Kace Networks, Inc., Ocarina Networks Inc., Scalent Systems Inc., Boomi, Inc., and InSite One, Inc. For the fiscal year ended 28 January 2011, Dell's revenues increased 16 percent to $61.49 billion compared to the previous year. Net income increased 84 percent to

$2.64 billion. Revenues reflect an increase in income from large enterprise segment, higher income from public segment, an increase in income from small and medium business segment and higher income from consumer segment. Dell generated 52 percent of its sales in the United States and 48 percent from foreign sales.

But its success lies in marketing directly to consumers rather than in any technological or cost advantages associated with production. Dell introduced the Dell Direct model, a business-to-consumer (B2C) concept, which has now been copied by major competitors. By eliminating retailers, Dell can deal directly with individual customers, offering detailed and richly configured systems. There is consumer customization, plus services and support. This method saves on inventory and introduces new technology quickly. Dell became a market leader with the first B2C direct business model.

The computer industry is at a mature stage of manufacturing. This means that there is pressure either to be extremely cost competitive or to develop value-added services that build on the computer itself. The five major computer manufacturers have responded to these market changes in different ways. IBM invented the personal computer and was perhaps the first to move strongly toward customer service. But eventually in 2004 it got out of personal computers altogether, selling the business to China's Lenovo as PC become commoditized. In late 2002, Hewlett-Packard and Compaq merged to try to consolidate production but also to develop the service end. This left Apple and Dell as the firms driven by low cost and technology.

In China, Dell has developed an innovative B2C concept that is allowing it to quickly increase its market share. PC manufacturers have been flocking to China because of high expected growth. Dell entered the Chinese market in the 1990s, trailing behind IBM and Compaq. Soon Dell became the second largest foreign PC market player, after three local Chinese manufacturers. One way in which Dell was able to achieve this was by introducing the affordable Smart PC. Another has been to offer tailor-made PCs over the Internet. A Chinese customer virtually builds his or her desired computer and then Dell assembles and delivers it. Implementing B2C retailing has not been easy because Chinese people are not used to credit cards. To overcome this obstacle, the company has made deals with major banks to allow customers to go to a branch and make a payment that is then reported to Dell. More recently, the largest Chinese computer manufacturers started to compete aggressively in the lower end of the market, forcing Dell to move upmarket where it expects to reap the benefits of a growing number of luxury-minded individuals. As of 2009, China's laptop PC market share by volume and value of the top five market leaders are as follows: Lenovo China Co., Ltd. 29.5 percent, HP Development Company 16.2 percent, Asustek Computer Corporation 10.2 percent, Dell Group 9.2 percent, Hasee Computer Co., Ltd. 6.5 percent.

Source: Getty Images/Business Wire

Throughout the world, Dell has tried to add service value in its B2C process. It has 80 Internet sites on which more than 65,000 institutional customers do business with Dell. Through www.dell.com customers can order, price, and configure products. Dell maintains after-sales service with customers. It also brings new technology quickly to the customer. In short, Dell's B2C system allows the MNE to engage in mass customization.

Websites: www.dell.com; www.dell.com.cn; www.hp.com; www.hp.com. cn; www.compaq.com; www.compaq.com.cn; www.ibm.com; www.ibm. com.cn; and www.acer.com.

Sources: www.dell.com; Dell, *Annual report*, 2009; OneSource Global Business Browse database, *Thomson Reuters*, 2011; "IBM at 100: From Typewriters to the Cloud," *BBC News Online*, June 14, 2011; Mintel Global Market Navigator database, China—Laptop PCs: Company market share by volume and by value, 2009, http://gmn.mintel.com/query/10146777/shares/region; "Dell CTO Paul Prince: Applications are the Key," *BBC News Online*, January 20, 2011.

1 What is meant by B2C? How does Dell achieve B2C?

2 Why is Dell so successful in China?

3 Is B2C a viable strategy in the mature, competitive computer industry of today?

REAL CASE

Maersk Group

An example of the business-to-business (B2B) relational contracts found in the flagship model can be found in some of the operations of Maersk. This is the world's largest container-based shipping group. It has B2B relationships with companies that use its containers, with port authorities, and with supplies of its energy resources.

A.P. Moller-Maersk (APM) is a Denmark-based shipping group with sales of $56.1 billion and assets of $66.76 billion in 2010. The group owns and operates container carriers, bulk carriers, supply and specialty ships, and tankers. The group also provides various services in the areas of energy, shipping and offshore, and retail. The A.P. Moller-Maersk Group comprises approximately 1,100 companies. The group owns and operates more than 500 container vessels with a total capacity of around 3 million TEU (Twenty-foot Equivalent Units).

The main competitors to Maersk are shown in Table 1.

The Maersk Group divides its business into six segments: container shipping and related, tankers, offshore and related, terminals, oil and gas, retail and other, and technology. These are shown in Figure 22.8.

1 Container and related activities:
   – Maersk Line
   – Damco
   – Maersk Container Industry
   – Safmarine
   – MCC Transport

2 Energy:
   – Maersk Oil

3 Tankers and offshore-related activities:
   – Maersk Tankers
   – Maersk Drilling
   – Maersk FPSO
   – Maersk Supply Service

4 Terminal activities
   – APM Terminals

5 Retail and related business (not discussed here):
   – Dansk Supermarked
   – Switzer

6 Technology
   – Maersk Fluid Technology
   – Maersk Maritime Technology

Maersk Line is one of the leading liner shipping companies in the world, serving customers all over the globe. The company also has nearly 3,000,000 containers and operates across 130 countries. The Maersk Group provides similar container services across north/south trade lanes under the Safmarine name.

Maersk Logistics was combined with Damco in 2007 and no longer exists.

Damco offers services such as inland haulage, customs house brokerage, and refrigerated services. The company

Table 1 Top six container shipping companies in order of TEU capacity, February 25, 2011

Company	TEU capacity*	Market share	Number of ships
A.P. Moller-Maersk Group	2,176,416	14.6%	586
Mediterranean Shipping Company SA	1,923,790	12.9%	460
CMA CGM Group	1,231,245	8.2%	399
Evergreen Marine Corporation	606,090	4.1%	160
Hapag-Lloyd	593,798	4.0%	132
CSAV Group	591,710	4.0%	160

* TEU capacity and market-share figures from February 25, 2011, from Alphaliner Report, February 25, 2011. http://www.alphaliner.com/top100/index.php.

Source: John Gapper, "Bye-bye, American Shipping Lines," *Financial Times*, February 23, 2011. http://www.ft.com.

Container shipping and related	Tankers, offshore and related
Maersk Line	Maersk Tankers
Damco	Maersk Drilling
Maersk Container Industry	Maersk FPSOs
Safmarine	Maersk Supply Service
MCC Transport	Maersk LNG

Terminal activities
APM Terminals

Oil and gas activities
Maersk Oil

Retail and other
Dansk Supermarked
Odense Steel Shipyard
Svitzer

Technology
Maersk Fluid Technology
Maersk Maritime Technology

Figure 22.8 Segmentation of the Maersk Group activities

Sources: Adapted from Maersk website, Business Areas, http://www.maersk.com/AboutMaersk/Pages/BusinessAreas.aspx.

also offers customized and integrated solutions for operations such as supply-chain management; warehousing and distribution; and ocean freight. The company primarily provides its services to the retail, electronics, fast-moving consumer goods, and chemical industries.

APM Terminals is one of the world's largest operators of container terminals with over 50 container terminals spanning 34 countries and five continents. The company primarily engages in the development of port infrastructure necessary to meet the future demands of the global container trade. APM Terminals works closely with governments, country leaders, customers, truckers, and the entire shipping community to ensure supply-chain efficiency and world-class service.

Maersk Container Industry produces various types of reefer containers for the transportation of goods through ship, rail, or truck.

Maersk Oil operates the oil production of more than 700,000 barrels per day and more than 1,000 million cubic feet (28 million m^3) of gas production per day in the Danish and British parts of the North Sea, offshore Qatar, in Algeria, and in Kazakhstan. It conducts exploration activities in those areas as well as offshore Norway, the US Gulf of Mexico, Brazil, Angola and Oman.

Through **Maersk Tankers, Maersk Contractors, and Maersk Supply Services** the company offers solutions for the transport of crude oil, refined products, and gas; various supply vessel activities (including anchor handling, platform supply, and cable laying); drilling activities with mobile production units, and drilling rigs and ships, including advanced jack-up rigs, salvage and towage activities, as well as door-to-door transport and inter-European freight and passenger transport.

Maersk Tankers owns and operates one of the world's largest and most modern fleets of crude, product and gas tankers. The fleet consists of more than 230 vessels.

Maersk Drilling (formerly known as Maersk Contractors) provides drilling and production services to oil companies. The company commands an extensive and technologically advanced fleet of some of the world's most advanced harsh environment jack-up rigs, 375 ft and 350 ft jack-up rigs, deepwater semi-submersibles, drilling barges and workover barges.

Maersk Supply Services is primarily engaged in the field of tow-out and installation of large offshore installations, and other chartering services. The company maintains more than 50 offshore support vessels.

Examples of flagship partnerships

Maersk Line has flagship relationships. As explained above, it is one of the leading liner shipping companies. It operates over 580 container vessels and more than 3,000,000 containers. This amounts to 11,363.63 miles (18,288 km) of containers. Although the Maersk organization is extensively vertically integrated and produces vessels, containers, and oil through subsidiaries, Maersk Line is highly dependent on their business networks. Mr. Søren Skou, the Partner Chief Executive Officer of Maersk Liner Business, recognizes the importance of partnerships, stating that *"communication and partnerships are as important as the physical movement of goods."*

Maersk Line maintains a strategically critical relationship with its competitors. In the midst of flattening sales, the beginning of 2008 saw agreements between the top three largest container ship lines of Maersk Line, Mediterranean Shipping Co., and CMA CGM sharing vessel space on the trans-Pacific trade. Government relations are also of high importance. In 2007, the Maersk Group spent $950,000 lobbying the federal government on issues such as port safety, railroad regulations, and ballast water legislation. The group is also a member of

C–TPAT (Customs–Trade Partnership Against Terrorism), headed by the Department of Homeland Security. Maersk Line Limited, another Maersk Group subsidiary, transports more US government cargo related to military and humanitarian missions than any other company. In 2007, this amounted to 140,000 TEU of US military cargo alone. The Maersk organization also maintains ties with research and educational institutions. In Denmark, Maersk is engaged in a corporate partnership with the Copenhagen Business School designed to provide real-world business applications and attract talent. Additionally, Maersk Line is also engaged in development projects such as that of an energy-saving cooling system involving Wageningen University, sponsored by the Dutch government. Other flagship relationships include:

IBM: In 2005, IBM and Maersk Logistics joined forces to bring real-time, enhanced visibility to global supply-chain operations by improving the quality of container tracking and enabling increased security of transported goods. The solution includes highly intelligent wireless tracking

devices and an advanced technology network for use by manufacturers, retailers, logistics providers, carriers, and governments to share real-time cargo information.

NVOCCs: As Non-Vessel Operating Common Carriers, larger freight forwarders compete directly with Maersk Logistics but also have attractive contracts with Maersk Line and Safmarine. In fact, it is possible that leading forwarders such as Kuehne & Nagel and ABX logistics have more attractive contracts than Maersk Logistics.

Source: www.maersk.com/en. Maersk, *Annual report*, 2009. *Hellenic Shipping News*, 29 February 2008, www.shipid.com/news/4324/Maersk_spends_950_000_on.html. Analysis by authors of this book.

1 Who are the major competitors of Maersk?

2 To what extent and to whom does Maersk act as a key supplier?

3 What is the key competitive advantage (firm-specific advantage) of Maersk?

ENDNOTES

1 See, for example, Dean Takahashi, "How the Competition Got Ahead of Intel in Making Cheap Chips," *Wall Street Journal*, February 12, 1998, pp. A1, 11; see also "Intel Unveils 22nm 3D Ivy Bridge Processor," *BBC News Online*, May 4, 2011, http://www.bbc.co.uk/news/technology-13283882.

2 Jeanne B. Pinder, "Japan's New York Realty Investing Plunges," *New York Times*, March 19, 1993, p. C10.

3 Shaker A. Zahra, "The Changing Rules of Global Competitiveness in the 21st Century," *Academy of Management Executive*, vol. 13, no. 1 (February 1999), pp. 36–42.

4 Also see James B. Treece et al., "New Worlds to Conquer," *Business Week*, February 28, 1994, pp. 50–52; and "HTC Profits Double as Smartphone Demand Grows. BBC News Online, June 6, 2011, http://www.bbc.co.uk/news/business-14041085"

5 Also see Howard Thomas, Timothy Pollock and Philip Gorman, "Global Strategic Analyses: Frameworks and Approaches," *Academy of Management Executive*, February 1999, pp. 70–82; and Alan M. Rugman, *Regional Multinationals* (Cambridge: Cambridge University Press, 2005).

6 Also see David Kirkpatrick, "Why the Internet Is Boosting IBM's Mainframe Sales," *Fortune*, January 11, 1999, pp. 148–149; and "IBM at 100: From Typewriters to the Cloud," *BBC News Online*, 14 June 2011, http://www.bbc.co.uk/news/business-13726776.

7 Otto Andersen, "On the Internationalization Process of Firms: A Critical Analysis," *Journal of International Business Studies*, vol. 24, no. 2 (Second Quarter 1993), pp. 209–231; Sumantra Ghoshal and Nitin Nohria, "Horses for Courses: Organizational Forms for Multinational Corporations," *Sloan Management Review*, Winter 1993, pp. 23–35; see also John H. Dunning, "The Key Literature on International Business Activities:

1960–2006" in Alan M. Rugman (ed.), *The Oxford Handbook of International Business*, 2nd edn. (Oxford: Oxford University Press, 2009).

8 Jeremiah J. Sullivan and Richard B. Peterson, "A Test of Theories Underlying the Japanese Lifetime Employment System," *Journal of International Business Studies*, vol. 22, no. 1 (First Quarter 1991), p. 79.

9 Richard M. Hodgetts, "A Conversation with Michael E. Porter," *Organizational Dynamics*, Summer 1999, pp. 25–26.

10 Joseph R. D'Cruz and Alan M. Rugman, *Multinationals as Flagship Firms: Regional Business Networks* (Oxford: Oxford University Press, 2000). This book is based on earlier work such as: Alan M. Rugman and Joseph R. D'Cruz, *New Compacts for Canadian Competitiveness* (Toronto: Kodak Canada, 1992), p. 31; and Joseph R. D'Cruz and Alan M. Rugman, "Business Networks for International Competitiveness," *Business Quarterly*, vol. 56, no. 4 (Spring 1992), pp. 101–107.

11 D'Cruz and Rugman. *Multinationals as Flagship Firms*, op. cit.

12 For an example of this psychological reaction, see David E. Sanger, "64 percent of Japanese Say US Relations Are 'Unfriendly'," *New York Times*, July 6, 1993, pp. A1, 6.

13 For more on this, see Rosabeth Moss Kanter, "Transcending Business Boundaries: 12,000 World Managers View Change," *Harvard Business Review*, vol. 69, no. 3 (May/June 1991), pp. 151–164.

14 "US Targets Trade Partners" *BBC.co.uk*, April 3, 2002.

15 See, for example, Keith Bradsher, "US Upset with Japan on Chip Pact," *New York Times*, March 4, 1993, pp. C1, 2.

16 "China 'Too Slow' to Open Markets," *BBC.co.uk*, December 19, 2003; "US Tells China to Look to its Own Consumers," *BBC News Online*, May 9, 2011; and "US to Meet China in

Washington to Tackle Thorny Issues," *BBC News Online*, May 8, 2011; "US China Trade Imbalance," *BBC News Online*, May 10, 2011.

17 Rob Hugh-Jones, "Analysis: Rice's Latin American Tour," *BBC.co.uk*, April 20, 2005.

18 Alicia Jrapko, "Workers Seize Control of 150 Plants," *Worker's World*, May 8, 2003.

19 "Country Profiles: Regions and Territories: Hong Kong," *BBC.co.uk*, May 25, 2005.

20 Mark Landler, "Back to Vietnam, This Time to Build," *New York Times*, September 13, 1998, Section 3, pp. 1, 11.

21 See "Mexico: A Market that Is Ready for Services," *New York Times*, July 21, 1993, pp. C10–15; Bob Graham, "Free Trade Means Fair Trade," *Miami Herald*, July 22, 1993, p. 21A; and Andreas Waldkirch. "The Effects of Foreign Direct Investment in Mexico since NAFTA," *The World Economy*, vol. 33, no. 5 (May 2010).

22 Gary Hamel and Jeff Sampler, "The E-Corporation," *Fortune*, December 7, 1998, pp. 80–92.

23 R. Duane Ireland and Michael A. Hitt, "Achieving and Maintaining Strategic Competitiveness in the 21st Century: The Role of Strategic Leadership," *Academy of Management Executive*, February 1999, pp. 43–57.

24 Heather Green and Linda Himelstein, "Throw Out Your Old Business Model," *Business Week E-Biz*, March 22, 1999, pp. EB22–23.

25 See www.internetworldstats.com; Eurostat, 2010, http://epp.eurostat.ec.europa.eu/portal/page/portal/statistics/search_database.

26 Robert D. Hof, Gary McWilliams and Gabrielle Savers, "The 'Click Here' Economy," *Business Week*, June 22, 1998, pp. 122–128.

27 Claude H. Deutsch, "Digital Polish for Factory Floors," *New York Times*, March 22, 1999, pp. C1, 7.

28 Debora L. Spar, *Ruling the Waves: Cycles of Discovery, Chaos and Wealth* (New York: Harcourt, 2001); and www.toyrus.com.

29 Alan M. Rugman and Alain Verbeke, "Corporate Strategy after the Free Trade Agreement and Europe 1992," in John Longair (ed.), *Proceedings: Regional Integration in the World Economy: Europe and North America* (Ottawa: Conference Board of Canada, March 1990).

30 See Gerard Curzon, "Ten Reasons to Fear Fortress Europe," Mimeo, Graduate Institute of International Studies, Geneva, 1989; and B. Burgenmeir and J. L. Mucchielli, *Multinational and Europe 1992* (London: Routledge, 1990) for an overview.

31 Rugman and Verbeke, op. cit.

ADDITIONAL BIBLIOGRAPHY

Bhagwati, Jagdish. *In Defense of Globalization* (Oxford: Oxford University Press, 2004).

Brewer, Thomas L. and Young, Stephen. *The Multilateral Investment System and Multinational Enterprise* (Oxford: Oxford University Press, 1998).

Clarkson, Max B. E. "A Stakeholder Framework for Analyzing and Evaluating Corporate Social Performance," *Academy of Management Review*, vol. 20, no. 1 (January 1995).

Darnall, Nicole, Henriques, Irene and Sadorsky, Perry. "Adopting Proactive Environmental Strategy: The Influence of Stakeholders and Firm Size," *Journal of Management Studies*, vol. 47, no. 6 (September 2010).

D'Cruz, Joseph R. and Rugman, Alan M. "Developing International Competitiveness: The Five Partners Model," *Business Quarterly* (Winter 1993).

D'Cruz, Joseph R. and Rugman, Alan M. "Business Network Theory and the Canadian Telecommunications Industry," *International Business Review*, vol. 3, no. 3 (1994).

Devinney, Timothy M. "Is the Socially Responsible Corporation a Myth? The Good, Bad and Ugly of Corporate Social Responsibility," *Academy of Management Perspectives*, vol. 23, no. 2 (2009).

Dunning, John H. *Multinational Enterprises and the Global Economy* (Reading: Addison-Wesley, 1993).

Dunning, John H. *The Globalization of Business: The Challenge of the 1990s* (London and New York: Routledge, 1993).

Dyer Jeff and Chu, Wujin. "The Determinants of Trust in Supplier–Automaker Relations in the US, Japan, and Korea: A Retrospective," *Journal of International Business Studies*, vol. 42. doi:10.1057/jibs.2010.48 (2011).

Egelhoff, William G. "Information-Processing Theory and the Multinational Enterprise," *Journal of International Business*, vol. 22, no. 3 (Third Quarter 1991).

Ghoshal, Sumantra and Bartlett, Christopher A. "The Multinational Corporation as an Interorganizational Network," *Academy of Management Review*, vol. 15, no. 4 (October 1990).

Giddens, Anthony. *Runaway World: How Globalization is Reshaping Our Lives* (London: Profile Books, 1998).

Gray, John. *False Dawn: The Delusions of Global Capitalism* (London: Granta Books, 1998).

Guntz, Hugh P. and Jalland, R. Michael. "Managerial Careers and Business Strategies," *Academy of Management Review*, vol. 21, no. 3 (July 1996).

Husted, Bryan W. and Allen, David B. "Corproate Social Responsibility in the Multinational Enterprise: Strategic and Institutional Approaches," *Journal of International Business Studies*, vol. 37 (2006).

Husted, Bryan W. and Allen, David B. "Strategic Corporate Social Responsibility and Value Creation," *Management International Reivew*, vol. 49, no. 6 (December 2009).

Jain, Subhash C. and Vachani, Sushil (eds.) *Multinational Corporations and Global Poverty Reduction* (Cheltenham: Edward Elgar, 2006).

Jean, Ruey-Jer (Bryan), Sinkovics, Rudolf R. and Cavusgil, S. Tamer. "Enhancing International Customer–Supplier Relationships through IT Resources: A Study of Taiwanese Electronics Suppliers," *Journal of International Business Studies*, vol. 41. doi:10.1057/jibs.2010.4 (2010).

Kim, W. Chan and Mauborgne, Renée A. "Effectively Conceiving and Executing Multinationals' Worldwide Strategies," *Journal of International Business Studies*, vol. 24, no. 3 (Third Quarter 1993).

Kirton, John J., Daniels, Joseph P. and Freytag, Andreas (eds.). *Guiding Global Order: G8 Governance in the 21st Century* (Aldershot: Ashgate, 2001).

Kogut, Bruce. "Methodological Contributions in International Business Research and the Direction of Academic Research Activity," in Alan M. Rugman and Thomas Brewer (eds.), *The Oxford Handbook of International Business* (Oxford: Oxford University Press, 2001).

Kolk, Ans. "Trends in Sustainability Reporting by the Fortune Global 500," *Business Strategy and the Environment*, vol. 12, no. 5 (September/October 2003).

Kolk, Ans. "Corporate Social Responsibility in the Coffee Sector: The Dynamics of MNC Responses and Code Development," *European Management Journal*, vol. 23, no. 2 (April 2005).

Kolk, Ans. "Environmental Reporting by Multinationals from the Triad: Convergence or Divergence?" *Management International Review*, vol. 45, Special Issue 1 (2005).

Kolk, Ans. "Sustainability, Accountability and Corporate Governance: Exploring Multinationals' Reporting Practices," *Business Strategy and the Environment*, vol. 17, no. 1 (January 2008).

Kolk, Ans. "Trajectories of Sustainability Reporting by MNCs," *Journal of World Business*, vol. 45, no. 4 (October 2010).

Kolk, Ans and Pinkse, Jonatan. "Stakeholder Mismanagement and Corporate Social Responsibility Crises," *European Management Journal*, vol. 24, no. 1 (February 2006).

Kolk, Ans and van Tulder, Rob. "International Business, Corporate Social Responsibility and Sustainable Development," *International Business Review*, vol. 19, no. 2 (April 2010).

Fortanier, F., Kolk, Ans and Pinkse, Jonatan. "MNEs, Global CSR Standards and Domestic Institutions: Harmonization and Country-of-origin Effects in CSR Reporting," *Management International Review* (forthcoming 2011).

Li, Shaomin, Fetscherin, Marc, Alon, Ilan, Lattemann, Christoph and Yeh, Kuang. "Corporate Social Responsibility in Emerging Markets," *Management International Review*, vol. 50, no. 5 (October 2010).

Martinez, Jon I. and Jarillo, J. Carlos. "Coordination Demands of International Strategies," *Journal of International Business Studies*, vol. 22, no. 3 (Third Quarter 1991).

McDermott, Gerald A. and Corredoira, Rafael A. "Network Composition, Collaborative Ties, and Upgrading in Emerging-Market Firms: Lessons from the Argentine Autoparts Sector," *Journal of International Business Studies*, vol. 41, 308–329. doi:10.1057/jibs.2009.7 (2010).

Morrison, Allen J. and Inkpen, Andrew C. "An Analysis of Significant Contributions to the International Business Literature," *Journal of International Business Studies*, vol. 22, no. 1 (First Quarter 1991).

Nehrt, Chad. "Maintaining a First Mover Advantage When Environmental Regulations Differ Between Countries," *Academy of Management Review*, vol. 23, no. 1 (January 1998).

Nebus, James and Rufin, Carlos. "Extending the Bargaining Power Model: Explaining Bargaining Outcomes Among Nations, MNEs, and NGOs," *Journal of International Business Studies* vol. 41 (August 2010). doi:10.1057/jibs.2009.43.

Ohmae, Kenichi. "Managing in a Borderless World," *Harvard Business Review*, vol. 67, no. 3 (May/June 1989).

Rosenzweig, Philip M. and Singh, Jitendra V. "Organizational Environments and the Multinational Enterprise," *Academy of Management Review*, vol. 16, no. 2 (April 1991).

Rugman, Alan M. "Multinationals and Trade in Services: A Transaction Cost Approach," *Weltwirtschaftliches Archiv*, vol. 123, no. 4 (December 1987).

Rugman, Alan M. *The End of Globalization* (London: Random House, 2000). (Also published in 2001 by AMACOM/ McGraw-Hill.)

Rugman, Alan M. and D'Cruz, Joseph R. "A Theory of Business Networks," in Lorraine Eden (ed.), *Multinationals in North America* (Alberta: University of Calgary Press, 1993).

Rugman, Alan M. and D'Cruz, Joseph R. *Multinationals as Flagship Firms: Regional Business Networks* (Oxford: Oxford University Press, 2000, paperback, 2002).

Rugman, Alan M. and Verbeke, Alain. *Corporate Response to Global Change*, Research in Global Strategic Management, vol. 3 (Greenwich, CT: JAI Press, 1992).

Rugman, Alan M. and Verbeke, Alain. *Beyond the Three Generics*, Research in Global Strategic Management, vol. 4 (Greenwich, CT: JAI Press, 1993).

Rugman, Alan M. and Verbeke, Alain. "Corporate Strategies and Environmental Regulations: An Organizing Framework," *Strategic Management Journal*, vol. 19, Special Issue (April 1998).

Rugman, Alan M. and Verbeke, Alain. "Six Cases of Corporate Strategic Response to Environmental Regulations," *European Management Journal*, vol. 18, no. 4 (August 2000).

Rugman, Alan M. and Verbeke, Alain. "Towards a Theory of Multinational Enterprises and the Civil Society," in A. Ghobadian et al. (eds.), *Strategy and Performance, Achieving Competitive Advantage in the Global Marketplace* (Basingstoke: Palgrave Macmillan, 2004).

Rugman, Alan M., Kirton, John and Soloway, Julie. *Environmental Regulations and Corporate Strategy* (Oxford: Oxford University Press, 1999).

Rugman, Alan M. and Doh. Jonathan. *Multinationals and Development* (New Haven, CT: Yale University Press, 2008).

Scherer, Andreas Georg and Palazzo, Guido. "The New Political Role of Business in a Globalized World: A Review of a New Perspective on CSR and its Implications for the Firm, Governance, and Democracy," *Journal of Management Studies*, vol. 48, no. 4 (June 2011).

Stiglitz, Joseph E. *Globalization and its Discontents* (New York: Norton, 2002).

Tulder, Rob van and Kolk, Ans. "Multinationality and Corporate Ethics: Codes of Conduct in the Sporting Goods Industry," *Journal of International Business Studies*, vol. 32, no. 2 (June 2001).

Wright, Richard W. *International Entrepreneurship: Globalization of Emerging Business*, Research in Global Strategic Management, Vol. 7 (Oxford: Elsevier/JAI Press, 1999).

Vachani, Sushil, Doh, Jonathan P. and Teegen, Hildy. "NGOs' Influence on MNEs' Social Development Strategies in Varying Institutional Contexts: A Transaction Cost Perspective," *International Business Review*, vol. 18, no. 5 (October 2009).

Yip, George S. "Global Strategy in a World of Nations?" *Sloan Management Review*, vol. 31, no. 1 (Fall 1989).

Yaziji, Michael and Doh, Jonathan. *NGOs and Corporations: Conflict and Collaboration* (Cambridge: Cambridge University Press, 2009).

Zahra, Shaker A. "The Changing Rules of Global Competitiveness in the 21st Century," *Academy of Management Executive*, vol. 13, no. 1 (February 1999).

GLOSSARY

Acceptance zone. An area within which a party is willing to negotiate.

Achievement oriented. Where status is earned rather than a right. Recruitment and promotion opportunities tend to be more dependent on performance, as in a meritocracy.

Ad valorem duty. A tax that is based on a percentage of the value of imported goods.

Adjusted present value (APV). An NPV that takes into account sources of country risk that might impact a project's expected future cash flows.

Advertising. A non-personal form of promotion in which a firm attempts to persuade consumers of a particular point of view.

Amakudari. (Literally "descent from heaven.") The temporary or permanent movement of public-sector officials in Japan into private corporations as a mechanism for coordinating national policy and company strategy.

Ambidexterity. The ability of a firm 'to be aligned and efficient in its management of today's business demands while simultaneously being adaptive to changes in the environment.

Andean common market (Ancom). A sub-regional free trade compact designed to promote economic and social integration and cooperation; Bolivia, Colombia, Ecuador, and Peru are all members.

Andean Community. An economic union consisting of Bolivia, Colombia, Ecuador, and Peru.

Antidumping duties (AD). Import tariffs intended to protect domestic producers from foreign products sold at less than their cost of production or at lower prices than in their home market.

Arbitrageur. A person or firm that deals in foreign exchange, buying or selling foreign currency with simultaneous contracting to exchange back to the original currency. Arbitrageurs thus do not undertake exchange risk.

Arm's length price. The price that exists or would exist on a sale of a given product or service between two unrelated companies—as contrasted with an intra-company transfer price.

Ascription oriented. Where status is more of a right than earned. Recruitment and promotion opportunities tend to be more dependent on seniority, ethnicity, gender, religion, or birth.

Association of South-East Asian Nations (ASEAN). An economic union founded in 1967 that includes Brunei Darussalam, Cambodia, Indonesia Laos, Malaysia, Myanmar, the Philippines, Singapore, Thailand, and Vietnam; this economic bloc focuses not on reducing trade barriers among members but, rather, on promoting exports to other nations.

Autonomous infrastructure. An infrastructure used by multinationals that compete in dissimilar national markets and do not share resources.

Backward integration. The ownership of equity assets used earlier in the production cycle, such as an auto firm that acquires a steel company.

Balance sheet hedging. The use of financial instruments denominated in foreign currency to eliminate exchange rate (translation) risk from the balance sheet of a company.

Basic mission. The reason that a firm is in existence.

Benkyokai. Study associations or work groups for students or colleagues in companies to jointly develop particular areas of knowledge and expertise.

Born global firms. Business organizations that, from inception, seek to derive significant competitive advantage from the use of resources and the sale of outputs in multiple countries.

Born regional firms. Tend to locate their overseas businesses in their home region of the triad to escape the liability of inter-regional foreignness.

Business managers. Managers responsible for coordinating the efforts of people in a corporate organization; for example, in a matrix structure.

Canada Labor Code. A federal law that covers areas such as wages, employment practices, work safety, and conciliation of labor disputes.

Caribbean Basin Initiative. A trade agreement that eliminates tariffs on many imports to the United States from the Caribbean and Central American regions.

Cartel. A group of firms that collectively agree to fix prices or quantities sold in an effort to control price.

Centrally-determined economy. An economy in which goods and services are allocated based on a plan formulated by a committee that decides what is to be offered.

Center-for-local, local-for-local, local-for-global and global-for-global. Structural archetypes for the location of three innovation-related activities; sensing, responding and implementing. These result from the need for some innovation activities to be centralized and/or standardized and others to be de-centralized and/or customized (or 'localized').

Chu, meaning loyalty and **giri,** meaning duty, obligation, or responsibility. These terms are often used together to denote the traditionally close, trusting relationship between managers and employees. They are also used to describe the ties between older and younger members of a family.

Civil society. A group of individuals, organizations, and institutions that act outside the government and the market to advance a diverse set of interests.

Clearing account. A centralized cash management bank account in which one MNE affiliate reviews payment needs among various MNE affiliates and arranges to make payments of net funds due from each affiliate to others through the clearing account.

Cluster analysis. A marketing approach to forecasting customer demand that involves grouping data based on market area, customer, or similar variables.

Codetermination. A legal system that requires workers and their managers to discuss major strategic decisions before companies implement the decisions.

Collaboratories. Refers to 'agile, in-market research activities which connect with Universities and science and technology institutes in different countries.' While the term is used by IBM, the approach is used by many R&D-intensive firms.

Collectivism. The tendency of people to belong to groups who look after each other in exchange for loyalty.

Common market. A form of economic integration characterized by the elimination of trade barriers among member nations, a common external trade policy, and mobility of factors of production among member countries.

Communication. The process of transferring meanings from sender to receiver.

Communism. A political system in which the government owns all property and makes all decisions regarding production and distribution of goods and services.

Comparative advertising. The comparing of similar products for the purpose of persuading customers to buy a particular one.

Competition Act. A Canadian federal law that regulates anticompetitive practices and prohibits actions that will substantially lessen or prevent competition; it is similar to US antitrust laws.

Competitive intelligence. The gathering of external information on competitors and the competitive environment as part of the decision-making process.

Competitive scope. The breadth of a firm's target market within an industry.

Compound duty. A tariff consisting of both a specific and an ad valorem duty.

Concurrent engineering. The process of having design, engineering, and manufacturing people working together to create a product, in contrast to working in a sequential manner.

Consolidation. The translation of foreign affiliate accounts and addition to home-country accounts for the purpose of reporting complete (global) condition of a company. Consolidation of foreign affiliate accounts that are denominated in other currencies necessarily produces translation risk.

Container ships. Vessels used to carry standardized containers that can be simply loaded onto a carrier and then unloaded at their destination without any repackaging of the contents of the containers.

Contract management. A process by which an organization (such as the government) transfers operating responsibility of an industry without transferring the legal title and ownership.

Control. The fundamental function of management that involves developing profit plans for the firm and its divisions and then deciding what to do when actual operating results differ from those planned.

Controlling. The process of determining that everything goes according to plan.

Coordinated infrastructure. An infrastructure used when there is a high degree of similarity among national markets and business units share resources in an effort to help each other raise overall sales.

Co-prosperity pyramid. A supply chain linked to a vertical, manufacturing *keiretsu*. It is hierarchical, with firms in the top tiers engaged in technology sharing, personnel exchanges, cross-shareholding, and long-term trading relationships. The further down the hierarchy a firm sits the more important price becomes and the less they are considered *keiretsu* members.

Corporate culture. The shared values, traditions, customs, philosophy, and policies of a corporation; also, the professional atmosphere that grows from this and affects behavior and performance.

Corruption. The misuse of public power for private benefit.

Cost strategy. A strategy that relies on low price and is achieved through approaches such as vigorous pursuit of cost reductions and overhead control, avoidance of marginal customer accounts, and cost minimization in areas such as sales and advertising.

Cost-of-living allowance. A payment to compensate for differences in expenditures between the home country and the foreign location.

Council of Ministers. The major policy decision-making body of the EU and one of its major institutions, consisting of one minister from each of the 27 member states.

Council of the European Union. The major policy decision-making body of the EU; it consists of one minister from each of the 27 member states and is one of four major institutions of the EU.

Countertrade. Barter trade in which the exporting firm receives payment in products from the importing country.

Countervailing duties (CVD). Import tariffs intended to protect domestic producers from harmful subsidization by foreign governments.

Country risk analysis. Examines the chances of non-market events (political, social, and economic) causing financial, strategic, or personnel losses to a firm following FDI in a specific country market.

Country-specific advantages (CSAs). Strengths or benefits specific to a country that result from its competitive environment, labor force, geographic location, government policies, industrial clusters, etc.

Court of Auditors. A court that has one judge appointed from each EU member country; this court monitors the financial aspects of the union.

Court of Justice. A court that has one judge appointed from each EU member country; this court serves as the official interpreter of EU law.

Cultural assimilator. A programmed learning technique designed to expose members of one culture to some of the basic concepts, attitudes, role perceptions, customs, and values of another culture.

Cultural convergence. The growing similarity between national cultures, including the beliefs, values, aspirations, and the preferences of consumers, partly driven by global brands, media, and common global icons.

Culture. The acquired knowledge that people use to interpret experience and to generate social behavior.

Culture clash. When two cultural groups (national or corporate) meet, interact, or work together and differences in their values, beliefs, rules of behavior, or styles of communication create misunderstandings, antagonism, or other problems.

Currency diversification. An exchange risk management technique through which the firm places activities or assets and liabilities into multiple currencies, thus reducing the impact of exchange rate change for any one of them.

Currency inconvertibility. The inability of a firm to transfer profit from a subsidiary in a host country to other areas of the organization or to shareholders because of host government restrictions on profit remittances.

Currency option. A derivative financial instrument where the owner has the right but not the obligation to exchange money denominated in one currency into another currency at a pre-agreed exchange rate on a specified date. The right to buy is the call option and the right to sell is the put option. It allows the company to take advantage of favorable movements in exchange rates. Options are the only form of hedging that does this.

Customs union. A form of economic integration in which all tariffs between member countries are eliminated and a common trade policy toward non-member countries is established.

Debt–equity ratio. The value of a firm's total debt divided by the value of its total equity. A higher ratio implies greater leverage, and potentially greater risk.

Decision making. The process of choosing from among alternatives.

Delayed differentiation. A strategy in which all products are manufactured in the same way for all countries or regions until as late in the assembly process as possible, at which time differentiation is used to introduce particular features or special components.

Demand-Flow™ Technology (DFT). A production process that is flexible to demand changes.

Democracy. A system of government in which the people, either directly or through their elected officials, decide what is to be done.

Differentiation strategy. A strategy directed toward creating something that is perceived as being unique.

Diffuse. A tendency for workplace relationships and obligations, including relative status and hierarchical position, to extend into social situations and activities outside of work.

Distribution. The course that goods take between production and the final consumer.

Divestiture. (Also see *Privatization.*) A process by which a government or business sells assets.

Dumping. The selling of imported goods at a price below cost or below that in the home country.

Dynamic capability. The firm's ability to integrate, build, and reconfigure internal and external competences to address rapidly changing environments.

Economic integration. The establishment of transnational rules and regulations that enhance economic trade and cooperation among countries.

Economic risk. The risk of financial loss or gain to an MNE due to the effects of unanticipated exchange rate changes on future cash flows that are denominated in foreign currencies.

Economic union. A form of economic integration characterized by free movement of goods, services, and factors of production among member countries and full integration of economic policies.

Embargo. A quota set at zero, thus preventing the importation of those products that are involved.

Emotional. An acceptance of emotion and subjectivity as the bases for some decision making and a preference for explicit displays of emotions and feelings in the workplace.

Empowerment. The process of giving employees increased control over their work.

Endaka. Yen-appreciation; the growing value of the yen vis-à-vis other currencies which, among other things, made Japan a relatively expensive place to manufacture.

Enterprise for the Americas. An idea launched by President George Bush to create a free trade area from Alaska to Argentine Antarctica.

Esprit de corps. The spirit of a group that makes the members want the group to succeed.

Estimation by analogy. A method of forecasting market demand or market growth based on information generated in other countries, such as determining the number of refrigerators sold in the United States as a percentage of new housing starts and using this statistic in planning for the manufacture of these products in other world markets.

Ethnocentric. A belief in the superiority of one's own ethnic group. The dominance of the home-country culture in decision making, human resource management, and overall corporate culture in a multinational firm.

Ethnocentric predisposition. The tendency of a manager or multinational company to rely on the values and interests of the parent company in formulating and implementing the strategic plan.

Ethnocentric solution. A centralized decision-making framework in which financial decisions and control for foreign affiliates are largely integrated into home-office management.

Ethnocentrism. The belief that one's way of doing things is superior to that of others.

Eurobond. A bond denominated in foreign currency issued in any country's financial market. Most eurobonds are issued in London or in Luxembourg (for tax reasons).

Eurocurrency. A bank deposit in any country, which is denominated in a foreign currency. A yen-denominated bank deposit in Germany is a euro-yen deposit, a form of eurocurrency.

Eurodollar. A dollar-denominated bank deposit outside of the United States.

European Coal and Steel Community (ECSC). A community formed in 1952 by Belgium, France, Italy, Luxembourg, the Netherlands, and West Germany for the purpose of creating a common market that would revitalize the efficiency and competitiveness of the coal and steel industries in those countries.

European Commission. A 27-member group chosen by agreement of member governments of the EU; the Commission is the executive branch of the EU.

European Council. Composed of the heads of state of each EU member country as well as the president of the European Commission. Meetings of the Council take place at least twice a year and their purpose is to resolve major policy issues and to set policy direction.

European Free Trade Association (EFTA). A free trade area currently consisting of Iceland, Liechtenstein, Norway, and Switzerland; past members included the UK (before it joined the EU).

European Monetary Union (EMU). The agreement among, initially, 11 of the European Union countries to eliminate their currencies and create the euro. European Union countries do not necessarily have to join the EMU.

European Parliament. A group of 785 representatives elected directly by voters in each member country of the EU; the Parliament serves as a watchdog on EU expenditures.

European Research Cooperation Agency. A research and development alliance that emphasizes projects in the fields of energy, medicine, biotechnology, communications, information technology, transport, new materials, robotics, production automation, lasers, and the environment.

European Union (EU). A treaty-based institutional framework that manages economic and political cooperation among its 27 member states: Austria, Belgium, Bulgaria, Cyprus, Czech Republic, Denmark, Estonia, Finland, France, Germany, Greece, Hungary, Ireland, Italy, Latvia, Lithuania, Luxembourg, Malta, the Netherlands, Poland, Portugal, Romania, Slovakia, Slovenia, Spain, Sweden, and the United Kingdom.

Exchange controls. Controls that restrict the flow of currency.

Exchange rate. The value of one currency in terms of another. For example, $US 2.00 /€1.

Exchange risk. The risk of financial loss or gain due to an unexpected change in a currency's value.

Exchange risk adaptation. An exchange risk management technique through which a company adjusts its business activities to try to balance foreign-currency assets and liabilities, and inflows and outflows.

Exchange risk avoidance. An exchange risk management technique through which the firm tries to avoid operating in more than one currency.

Exchange risk transfer. An exchange risk management technique through which the firm contracts with a third party to pass exchange risk onto that party, via such instruments as forward contracts, futures, and options.

Expatriates. Individuals who reside abroad but are citizens of the multinational's parent country; they are citizens of the home, not the host country.

Export tariff. A tax levied on goods sent out of a country.

Exports. Goods and services produced by a firm in one country and then sent to another country.

Expropriation. The governmental seizure of private businesses coupled with little, if any, compensation to their owners.

External economies of scale. Efficiencies brought about by access to cheaper capital, highly skilled labor, and superior technology.

Factor conditions. Land, labor, and capital.

Factor endowment theory. A trade theory which holds that nations will produce and export products that use large amounts of production factors that they have in abundance and will import products requiring a large amount of production factors that they lack.

FDI cluster. A group of developing countries usually located in the same geographic region as a triad member and having some form of economic link to this member.

Firm-specific advantages (FSAs). Strengths or benefits specific to a firm and a result of contributions that can be made by its personnel, technology, and/or equipment.

Five partners. A business network consisting of five partner organizations: the flagship firm (a multinational enterprise), key suppliers, key customers, key competitors, and the non-business infrastructure.

Flagship firms. Multinational firms characterized by global competitiveness and international benchmarks.

Flying Geese model. A model suggesting that Asian countries are following Japan's historical economic transition, specializing in particular industries (steel to textiles to clothing to autos to electronics) during particular growth stages. At a particular point in time we should expect to see these industries located in different Asian countries, depending on their resource endowments, labor costs, and capabilities.

Focus strategy. A strategy that concentrates on a particular buyer group and segments that niche based on product line or geographic market.

Foreign bond. A bond issued by a foreign company in another country's financial market. In Japan, these are called "Samurai bonds."

Foreign direct investment (FDI). Equity funds invested in other nations.

Foreign exchange. Foreign-currency-denominated financial instruments, ranging from cash to bank deposits to other financial contracts payable or receivable in foreign currency.

Foreign exchange broker. A company that provides specialized services to commercial banks in the interbank foreign exchange market, essentially functioning to unite interested buyers and sellers of foreign-currency-denominated bank deposits. Brokers intermediate about half of all wholesale foreign exchange transactions in New York and London.

Foreign exchange traders. Bankers who deal in foreign exchange, buying and selling foreign currencies on behalf of clients and/or for the bank itself. Typically they deal in foreign-currency-denominated bank deposits.

Foreign investment controls. Limits on foreign direct investment or the transfer or remittance of funds.

Foreign investment review agency. A government agency that reviews applications for foreign direct investment projects and approves or disapproves the projects, according to standards established by the government.

Foreign Sales Corporation Act. Legislation designed to allow US exporters to establish overseas affiliates and not pay taxes on the affiliates' income until the earnings are remitted to the parent company.

Foreign trade zones. Areas where foreign goods may be held and processed and then re-exported without incurring customs duties (same as a free trade zone).

Forward integration. The purchase of assets or facilities that move the company closer to the customer, such as a computer manufacturer that acquires a retail chain which specializes in computer products.

Forward rate. An exchange rate contracted today for some future date of actual currency exchange. Banks offer forward rates to clients to buy or sell foreign currency in the future, guaranteeing the rate at the time of the agreement.

Free trade area. An economic integration arrangement in which barriers to trade (such as tariffs) among member countries are removed.

Free Trade Area of the Americas (FTAA). A regional trade agreement that is expected to succeed NAFTA and include 34 countries across North, Central, and South America.

Free trade zone. A designated area where importers can defer payment of customs duty while further processing of products takes place (same as a foreign trade zone).

Fronting loan. A third-party loan in which an MNE home office deposits funds with a financial institution, which then lends to the MNE's affiliate in a country where the MNE faces political risk or currency transfer restrictions.

Funds positioning techniques. Mechanisms such as transfer pricing, intercompany loans, and timing of payments that are used to move funds from one affiliate to another in a multinational firm.

Gaijin. A term used for non-Japanese and while not too offensive is not particularly polite. *Gai* means outside or foreign, *jin* means person.

General Agreement on Tariffs and Trade (GATT). A major trade organization that has been established to negotiate trade concessions among member countries.

Geocentric. Neither home nor host country culture dominates decision making, human resource management, and overall corporate culture in a multinational firm.

Geocentric predisposition. The tendency of a multinational to construct its strategic plan with a global view of operations.

Geocentric solution. A decision-making framework in which financial decisions and evaluation related to foreign affiliates are integrated for the firm on a global basis.

Gestion. The skill or practice of controlling, directing, or planning something, especially a commercial enterprise or activity.

Global area structure. An organizational arrangement in which primary operational responsibility is delegated to area managers, each of whom is responsible for a specific geographic region.

Global functional structure. An organizational arrangement in which all areas of activity are built around the basic tasks of the enterprise.

Global product structure. An organizational arrangement in which domestic divisions are given worldwide responsibility for product groups.

Global sourcing. The use of suppliers anywhere in the world, chosen on the basis of their efficiency.

Globalization. The production and distribution of products and services of a homogeneous type and quality on a worldwide basis.

Grande Ecole. One of the "grand" or great schools considered to be the pinnacle of French higher education, highly selective and prestigious and the main source of the country's business and political leaders.

Guanxi. Personalized or informal networks of relationships in China. They can be important preconditions for smoothing the way or gaining favors or advantages, particularly when both society and the economy are dominated by central government. There are parallels with the concept of social capital.

Hai. "Yes" in Japanese does not necessarily mean "yes I agree," but "yes, I hear what you say."

Hardship allowance. A special payment made to individuals posted to geographic areas regarded as less desirable.

Heckscher–Ohlin theory. A trade theory that extends the concept of comparative advantage by bringing into consideration the endowment and cost of factors of production and helps to explain why nations with relatively large labor forces will concentrate on producing labor-intensive goods, whereas countries with relatively more capital than labor will specialize in capital-intensive goods.

Hedge. A strategy to protect the firm against risk, in this case against exchange rate risk.

Home-country nationals. Citizens of the country where the multinational resides.

Horizontal integration. The purchase of firms in the same line of business, such as a computer chip firm that acquires a competitor.

Host-country nationals. Local people hired by a multinational.

Humane orientation. Cultures that emphasize helping others, charity, and people's wider social obligations.

Ideology. A set of integrated beliefs, theories, and doctrines that helps to direct the actions of a society.

Import tariff. A tax levied on goods shipped into a country.

Imports. Goods and services produced in one country and brought in by another country.

Indigenization laws. Laws which require that nationals hold a majority interest in all enterprises.

Individualism. The tendency of people to look after themselves and their immediate family only.

Industrial democracy. The legally mandated right of employees to participate in significant management decisions.

Industry clusters, or "agglomeration economies". Geographic concentrations of interconnected businesses, including suppliers, specialist contractors and associated institutions.

Initial screening. The process of determining the basic need potential of the multinational's goods and services in foreign markets.

Innovation. The renewal and enlargement of the range of products and services and the associated markets; the establishment of new methods of production, supply and distribution; the introduction of changes in management, work organization, and the working conditions and skills of the workforce.

Integrative techniques. Strategies designed to help a multinational become a part of the host country's infrastructure.

Intermodal containers. Large metal boxes that fit on trucks, railroads, and airplanes and help reduce handling costs and theft losses by placing the merchandise in a tightly sealed, easy-to-move unit.

Internal economies of scale. Efficiencies brought about by lower production costs and other savings within a firm.

International business. The study of transactions taking place across national borders for the purpose of satisfying the needs of individuals and organizations.

International division structure. An organizational arrangement in which all international operations are centralized in one division.

International Fisher effect. Theory of exchange rate determination that states that differences in nominal interest rates on similar-risk deposits will be eliminated by changes in the exchange rate.

International human resource management (IHRM). The process of selecting, training, developing, and compensating personnel in overseas positions.

International joint venture (IJV). An agreement between two or more partners to own and control an overseas business.

International logistics. The designing and managing of a system to control the flow of materials and products throughout the organization.

International market assessment. An evaluation of the goods and services that the multinational can sell in the global marketplace.

International marketing. The process of identifying the goods and services that customers outside the home country want and then providing them at the right price and place.

International Monetary Fund (IMF). The international organization founded at Bretton Woods, New Hampshire, in 1994 that includes most countries of the world and offers balance of payments support to countries in crisis along with financial advising to Central Banks.

International monetary system. The arrangement between national governments/central banks that oversees the operation of official foreign exchange dealings between countries. The central organization in the system today is the International Monetary Fund.

International product life cycle (IPLC) theory. A theory of the stages of production of a product with new "know-how"; it is first produced by the parent firm, then by its foreign subsidiaries, and finally anywhere in the world where costs are the lowest; it helps explain why a product that begins as a nation's export often ends up as an import.

International screening criteria. Factors used to identify individuals regarded as most suitable for overseas assignments.

International trade. The exchange of goods and services across international borders.

Internationalization. The process by which a company enters a foreign market.

Intra-regional investments. Investments in the local region rather than in other triad or non-triad regions, such as when Chinese firms invest in other Southeast Asian economies.

Investment Canada Act (ICA). An act designed to create a welcome climate for foreign investment by significantly loosening previous restrictions.

Just-in-time (JIT) inventory. The delivery of parts and supplies just as they are needed.

Kaizen. Normally taken to mean "continuous improvement" and is associated with lean or low-cost, high-productivity manufacturing. A more accurate interpretation is "to dismantle and re-assemble a process to make it better." As such *kaizen* was an early form of business process reengineering.

Keiretsu. Groupings of Japanese firms with long-term associations and cross-shareholdings. Each firm maintains its operational independence but coordinates strategy and often exchanges assets and resources with other firms in its group.

Kinesics. A form of non-verbal communication that deals with conveying information through the use of body movement and facial expression.

Kinyu keiretsu. Horizontal conglomerates encompassing a wide range of diversified businesses, centered on a dominant bank and/or trading company.

Korean *chaebols*. Traditionally family-dominated, diversified conglomerates. Family ownership has been reduced and many are now focused in particular business sectors, reducing their diversity. There are parallels with Japanese *sogo shosha* in terms of early government support and their relationship with dominant national banks.

Latin American Integration Association (LAIA). A free trade group formed to reduce intra-regional trade barriers and to promote regional economic cooperation. Argentina, Bolivia, Brazil, Chile, Colombia, Ecuador, Mexico, Paraguay, Peru, Uruguay, and Venezuela are all members.

Leontief paradox. A finding by Wassily Leontief, a Nobel prize economist, which shows that the United States, surprisingly, exports relatively more labor-intensive goods and imports capital-intensive goods.

Liberalization policies. Government policies that move away from planned economies toward more free-market systems. They are marked by the privatization of state-owned businesses, a lowering of tariff and non-tariff barriers, and reductions in the constraints placed on foreign firms' investments and business activities.

LIBOR. The London Inter-Bank Offered Rate is the interest rate on large-scale foreign-currency-denominated deposits offered from one bank to another in London.

License. A contractual arrangement in which one firm (the licensor) provides access to some of its patents, trademarks, or technology to another firm in exchange for a fee or royalty.

Licensee. A firm given access to some of the patents, trademarks, or technology of another firm in exchange for a fee or royalty.

Licensor. A company that provides access to some of its patents, trademarks, or technology to another firm in exchange for a fee or royalty.

Lighter aboard ship (LASH) vessel. Barges stored on a ship and lowered at the point of destination.

Localization of production. The manufacturing of goods in the host market.

Localization of profits. The reinvestment of earnings in the local market.

Macro political risk. A risk that affects all foreign enterprises in the same way.

Managerial development. The process by which managers obtain the necessary skills, experiences, and attitudes that they need to become or remain successful leaders.

Maquiladora industry. A free trade zone that has sprung up along the US–Mexican border for the purpose of producing goods and then shipping them between the two countries.

Maquiladoras. (Also see *Twin factories*.) Production operations set up on both sides of the US–Mexican border in a free trade zone for the purpose of shipping goods between the two countries.

Market coordination infrastructure. An infrastructure used by firms that compete in similar national markets but do little resource sharing among their businesses.

Market growth. The annual increase in sales in a particular market.

Market indicators. Indicators used for measuring the relative market strengths of various geographic areas.

Market intensity. The richness of a market or the degree of purchasing power in one country as compared to others.

Market size. An economic screening consideration used in international marketing; it is the relative size of each market as a percentage of the total world market.

Market-driven economy. An economy in which goods and services are allocated on the basis of consumer demand.

Market-seeking FDI. MNEs invest in distribution, sales, or marketing operations in order to sell products or services (outputs) in particular country markets.

Masculinity. The degree to which the dominant values of a society are success, money, and material things.

Material handling. The careful planning of when, where, and how much inventory will be available to ensure maximum production efficiency.

Matrix structure. An organizational arrangement that blends two organizational responsibilities such as functional and product structures or regional and product structures.

Mercantilism. A trade theory which holds that a government can improve the economic well-being of the country by encouraging exports and stifling imports to accumulate wealth in the form of precious metals.

Mercosur. A subregional free trade group formed to promote economic cooperation; the group consists of Argentina, Brazil, Paraguay, and Uruguay.

Micro political risk. A risk that affects selected sectors of the economy or specific foreign businesses.

Ministry for Economy, Trade and Industry (METI). Superseded MITI, which was at the heart of Japan's post-war economic boom.

Ministry of Finance (MOF). A historically influential Japanese ministry that remains a powerful force in the deregulation of the economy.

Ministry of International Trade and Industry (MITI). A Japanese ministry charged with providing information about foreign markets and with encouraging investment in select industries and, in the process, helping to direct the economy.

Mitsubishi *Kinyokai*. The Friday Club in Marunouchi, Tokyo, where the most senior managers from the 29 core firms of the Mitsubishi *keiretsu* gather each month to discuss business.

Mittelstand. About 3.4 million small- and medium-sized firms defined as having less than 50 million euros turnover that make up the heart of the German economy.

Mixed economies. Economic systems characterized by a combination of market and centrally driven planning.

Mixed structure. A hybrid organization design that combines structural arrangements in a way that best meets the needs of the enterprise.

Modular integrated robotized system (MIRS). A software-based production process that relies entirely on robots.

Modular manufacturing. A manufacturing process that consists of modules that can be easily adapted to fit changing demand.

Monetary exchange rate. The price of one currency stated in terms of another currency.

Multilateral netting. Payment of net amounts due only between affiliates of a MNE that have multiple transactions among the group, which can be partially netted out among them, so then only the net funds need to be transferred.

Multinational enterprises (MNEs). A company headquartered in one country but having operations in other countries.

National Innovation Systems (NIS). Characterized by the quality of local scientific, technological, design-related and creative expertise, combined with institutional relationships between enterprises, universities and government research organisations. Regional variations in these components partly account for firm-level differences in innovation-related capabilities and competitiveness.

National responsiveness. The ability of MNEs to understand different consumer tastes in segmented regional markets and to respond to different national standards and regulations imposed by autonomous governments and agencies.

Nationalization. A process by which the government takes control of business assets, sometimes with remuneration of the owners and other times without such remuneration.

Nemawashi. Literally means "root-tying" and is a process of consultation to get agreement on a particular issue before it becomes explicit policy.

Neo mercantilism. A trade theory which holds that a government can improve the economic well-being of the country by encouraging exports and stifling imports.

Neutral. A preference for unemotional, objective analysis of a situation or a decision and for limited displays of emotions and feelings in the workplace.

Newly industrialized countries (NICs). A sub-group of emerging market economies that has experienced rapid economic growth, normally accompanied by political and social change. The forerunners were the four Asian "Tiger" economies: Singapore, South Korea, Taiwan, and Hong-Kong. The rapid growth, increased trade and FDI, and integration of China in the global economy suggest it is approaching this status.

Nominal interest rate. The actual rate of interest offered by a bank, typically given as an annual percentage rate.

Non-governmental organizations (NGOs). (Also see *Civil society*.) Private-sector groups that act to advance diverse social interests.

Non-tariff barriers. Rules, regulations, and bureaucratic red tape that delay or preclude the purchase of foreign goods.

North American Free Trade Agreement (NAFTA). A regional free trade agreement between Canada, the United States, and Mexico.

Organization for Economic Cooperation and Development (OECD). A group of 30 relatively wealthy member countries that facilitates a forum for the discussion of economic, social, and governance issues across the world.

Particularism. Judging a situation and adjusting rules and procedures according to the specific of the situation or individuals involved.

Personal selling. A direct form of promotion used to persuade customers of a particular point of view.

PEST framework. Examines the political, economic, socio-cultural, and technological conditions in particular country markets.

Plaza Accord. An agreement signed by the G5 in 1985 in New York agreeing to devalue the US dollar against the Japanese yen and the Deutsche (German) mark. It triggered the bubble economy and eventual economic recession in Japan in the 1990s.

Political risk. The probability that political forces will negatively affect a multinational's profit or impede the attainment of other critical business objectives.

Political union. An economic union in which there is full economic integration, unification of economic policies, and a single government.

Polycentric. Each subsidiary, division, or function reflects the culture of its host country. Local managers' cultural predispositions and decision making dominate over those of home-country managers in a multinational firm.

Polycentric predisposition. The tendency of a multinational to tailor its strategic plan to meet the needs of the local culture.

Polycentric solution. A decentralized decision-making framework in which financial decisions are largely allocated to foreign affiliates, and financial evaluation of affiliates is done in comparison with other firms in that context.

Portfolio investment. The purchase of financial securities in other firms for the purpose of realizing a financial gain when these marketable assets are sold.

Power distance. A cultural dimension that measures the degree to which less powerful members of organizations and institutions accept the fact that power is not distributed equally.

Privatization. The process of selling government assets to private buyers.

Process mapping. A flow charting of every step that goes into producing a product.

Product managers. Managers responsible for coordinating the efforts of their people in such a way as to ensure the profitability of a particular business or product line.

Production system. A group of related activities designed to create value.

Promotion. The process of stimulating demand for a company's goods and services.

Protective and defensive techniques. Strategies designed to discourage a host country from interfering in multinational operations.

Proxemics. A form of non-verbal communication that deals with how people use physical space to convey messages.

Psychic distance. A measure of the similarity or difference between two cultures. Also commonly defined as the measurable distance between the home market and a foreign market resulting from the perception of cultural and business differences.

Purchasing power parity. The theory of exchange rate determination that states that differences in prices of the same goods between countries will be eliminated by exchange rate changes.

Quota. A quantity limit on imported goods.

Real interest rate. The nominal interest rate adjusted for price changes. Domestically, this means adjusting for inflation. Internationally, this means adjusting for exchange rate (currency price) changes.

Regiocentric predisposition. The tendency of a multinational to use a strategy that addresses both local and regional needs.

Regional managers. In a geocentric matrix, managers charged with selling products in their geographic locale.

Regression analysis. A mathematical approach to forecasting that attempts to test the explanatory power of a set of independent variables.

Repatriation. The process of returning home at the end of an overseas assignment.

Repatriation agreement. An agreement that spells out how long a person will be posted overseas and sets forth the type of job that will be given to the person upon returning.

Resource managers. In a matrix structure, managers charged with providing people for operations.

Resource-seeking FDI. MNEs invest in production-related activities to benefit from cheaper or better sources of inputs in a particular location; these can include raw materials, components, or labor and expertise.

Resource-sharing infrastructure. An infrastructure used by firms that compete in dissimilar national markets but share resources such as R&D efforts and manufacturing information.

Return on investment (ROI). A percentage determined by dividing net income before taxes by total assets.

Ringi. The formalized consensus process of decision making. The *ringisho* is a decision proposal that is circulated around company departments to be revised or approved before implementation.

Roll-on-roll-off (RORO) vessels. Ocean-going ferries that can carry trucks that drive onto built-in ramps and roll off at the point of debarkation.

Secular totalitarianism. A system of government in which the military controls everything and makes decisions that it deems to be in the best interests of the country.

Sequential. Cultures that view time in a sequential or linear fashion. Order comes from separating activities and commitments.

Shinjinrui. The new generation Japanese, with very different values and aspirations than their parents.

Single European Act (SEA). An Act passed by the EU that contains many measures to further integrate the member states, along economic and political dimensions, and that allows the Council of Ministers to pass most proposals by a majority vote, in contrast to the unanimous vote needed previously.

Single European market (SEM). A market consisting of all members of the EU, bound together by a single currency, a special charter, complete harmonization of social and economic policies, and a common defense policy.

SMEs or small-and-medium-sized enterprises (SMEs). Defined by Governments using different criteria for policy purposes. SMEs are firms with less than 250 employees in Europe, but less than 500 in the United States. Indian manufacturing firms qualify as SMEs if they invest less than US$2 million in plant and equipment.

Socialization. The process of enculturation, or the adoption of the behavior patterns of the surrounding culture.

Sogo shosha. International trading companies that help other Japanese firms import and export products and services. They were very influential in the rapid growth era in helping local firms break into overseas markets.

Special drawing right (SDR). The currency of the IMF. Accounts at the IMF are denominated in SDRs, and the IMF has issued about $US 30 billion of SDRs as currency since its inception in 1969.

Specific. A tendency to limit workplace relationships and obligations, including relative status and hierarchical position, to the workplace.

Specific duty. A tariff based on the number of items being shipped into a country.

Speculator. A person or firm that takes a position in foreign exchange with no hedging or protection mechanism. The person would take this action to try to gain from expected exchange rate changes.

Spot rate. The exchange rate offered on the same day as the request to buy or sell foreign currency. Actual settlement (payment) may occur one or two days later.

Standardized training programs. Generic programs that can be used with managers anywhere in the world.

State-owned enterprises (SOEs). Companies that are owned, financed, and controlled by government.

Strategic alliance. A business relationship in which two or more companies work together to achieve a collective advantage.

Strategic business units (SBUs). Operating units with their own strategic space; they produce and sell goods and services to a market segment and have a well-defined set of competitors.

Strategic cluster. A network of businesses and supporting activities located in a specific region, where flagship firms compete globally and supporting activities are home based.

Strategic fit. A strategic management concept which holds that an organization must align its resources in such a way as to mesh effectively with the environment.

Strategic management. Managerial actions that include strategy formulation, strategy implementation, evaluation, and control and encompass a wide range of activities, including environmental analysis of external and internal conditions and evaluation of organizational strengths and weaknesses.

Strategic planning. The process of evaluating the enterprise's environment and its internal strengths and then identifying long- and short-range activities.

Strategy formulation. The process of evaluating the enterprise's environment and its internal strengths.

Strategy implementation. The process of attaining goals by using the organizational structure to execute the formulated strategy properly.

Synchronic. Cultures that view events in parallel over time. Order comes from coordinating multiple activities and commitments.

Tailor-made training programs. Programs designed to meet the specific needs of the participants, typically including a large amount of culturally based input.

Tariff. A tax on goods shipped internationally.

Tax havens. Jurisdictions that offers the MNE a lower tax rate (or no tax) than in other places, so that MNEs can locate some of their business activities there and thus reduce overall tax payments.

Theocratic totalitarianism. A system of government in which a religious group exercises total power and represses or persecutes non-orthodox factions.

Theory of absolute advantage. A trade theory which holds that nations can increase their economic well-being by specializing in goods that they can produce more efficiently than anyone else.

Theory of comparative advantage. A trade theory which holds that nations should produce those goods for which they have the greatest relative advantage.

Third-country nationals. Citizens of countries other than the one in which the multinational is headquartered or the one in which they are assigned to work by the multinational.

Time-to-market accelerators. Factors that help reduce bottlenecks and errors and ensure product quality and performance.

Totalitarianism. A system of government in which one individual or party maintains complete control and either refuses to recognize other parties or suppresses them.

Trade adjustment assistance. Assistance offered by the US government to US businesses and individuals harmed by competition from imports.

Trade creation. A process in which members of an economic integration group begin to focus their efforts on those goods and services for which they have a comparative advantage and start trading more extensively with each other.

Trade diversion. Occurs when members of an economic integration group decrease their trade with non-member countries in favor of trade with each other.

Training. The process of altering employee behavior and attitudes in a way that increases the probability of goal attainment.

Transaction risk. The risk of financial loss or gain to an MNE due to unanticipated exchange rate changes affecting future cash flows from transactions that are denominated in foreign exchange.

Transfer price. The price used for an intra-company payment for shipment of products or services from one affiliate to another in an MNE. These prices can be used to reduce taxes, move funds to desired locations, etc.

Transit tariff. A tax levied on goods passing through a country.

Transition strategies. Strategies designed to help smooth the move from foreign to domestic assignments.

Translation risk. The risk of losses or gains on the MNE's balance sheet, due to unhedged exchange rate changes during an accounting period.

Transnational network structure. An organization design that helps MNEs take advantage of global economies of scale while also being responsive to local customer demands.

Transparency. The *clarity* and *consistency* of policies and legislation applied in the governance of businesses.

Trend analysis. The estimation of future demand by either extrapolating the growth over the last three to five years and assuming that this trend will continue or by using some form of average growth rate over the recent past.

Triad. The three major trading and investment blocs in the international arena: the United States, the EU, and Japan.

Twin factories. (Also see *Maquiladoras.*) Production operations set up on both sides of the US–Mexican border for the purpose of shipping goods between the two countries.

Uncertainty avoidance. The extent to which people feel threatened by ambiguous situations and have created institutions and beliefs for minimizing or avoiding those uncertainties.

Unconventional cargo vessels. Vessels used for shipping oversized and unusual cargoes.

United States–Canada Free Trade Agreement (FTA). A trade agreement that eliminates most trade restrictions (such as tariffs) between these two countries and extends national treatment to foreign investment.

Universalism. The uniform application of rules and procedures, regardless of situation, context, or individuals involved.

Value chain. The way in which primary and support activities are combined in providing goods and services and increasing profit margins.

Vertical integration. The ownership of assets involved in producing a good or service and delivering it to the final customer.

Virtual integration. A networking strategy based on cooperation within and across company boundaries.

Weighted Country Risk Assessment Model. Combines an investment project appraisal with country risk analysis.

Weighted-average cost of capital (WACC). The firm's cost of obtaining funds from the various sources available. Each source of funds is weighted (multiplied) by the percentage of total capital it provides. Thus, the WACC is W_1 (cost of using retained earnings) + W_2 (cost of bank borrowing) + W_3 (cost of other source of funds), where each cost is stated as an annual percentage rate and each W is the percentage of total capital from that source.

Work councils. Groups that consist of both worker and manager representatives and are charged with dealing with matters such as improving company performance, working conditions, and job security.

Working capital. Short-term financial instruments such as bank deposits and marketable securities that can be optimized by the MNE on a global basis.

World Bank. The world's largest development bank, formed along with the IMF at Bretton Woods in 1944. Its original name was the International Bank for Reconstruction and Development (IBRD). The World Bank assists developing countries with loans and economic advising for economic development.

World Trade Organization (WTO). An international organization that deals with the rules of trade among member countries. One of its most important functions is to act as a dispute-settlement mechanism.

WTO accession. Admission to the World Trade Organization; in return for the right to access and to engage in fair trade with other national markets, the country must liberalize its own markets.

Zaibatsu. The pre-war antecedents of some modern-day *keiretsu* in Japan. Attempts by the allied forces to break these up after World War II largely failed.

INDEX

Headings in **bold** are also listed in the Glossary